Joschka Fischer

Mein langer Lauf zu mir selbst

Joschka Fischer

Mein langer Lauf zu mir selbst

Mit einem Nachwort von
Herbert Steffny

Kiepenheuer & Witsch

1. Auflage 1999

© 1999 by Verlag Kiepenheuer & Witsch, Köln
Alle Rechte vorbehalten. Kein Teil des Werkes
darf in irgendeiner Form (durch Fotografie, Mikrofilm
oder ein anderes Verfahren) ohne schriftliche
Genehmigung des Verlages reproduziert oder unter
Verwendung elektronischer Systeme verarbeitet,
vervielfältigt oder verbreitet werden.
Umschlaggestaltung: Rudolf Linn, Köln
Umschlagfoto: ASSOCIATED PRESS
Gesetzt aus der 11/13 Stone Serif (Berthold)
bei Kalle Giese Grafik, Overath
Druck und Bindearbeiten:
Graphischer Großbetrieb Pößneck, Pößneck
ISBN 3-462-02794-8

Inhalt

I

In der Sackgasse

Die menschliche Zivilisation verfügt über viele Segnungen und gar manche Krankheiten, wobei die Segnungen – so meine ganz persönliche Meinung – per Saldo überwiegen. Dies gilt vor allem für die westlichen Wohlstandsgesellschaften unserer Zeit, zumindest legt dies ihre fast universell zu nennende Attraktivität für die Menschen aller Kontinente und Kulturen mehr als nahe. Allerdings gibt es seit der Vertreibung von Adam und Eva aus dem Garten Eden in unserem irdischen Jammertal nichts, wirklich gar nichts von Menschenhand Geschaffenes, das neben dem Angenehmen nicht auch seine Schattenseiten hätte. Alle Welt strebt nach Wohlstand und materieller Sicherheit, und hat man diese dann erreicht, so plagt man sich zu guter Letzt mit deren unerwünschten Nebenwirkungen herum. Eine heute weitverbreitete Zivilisationskrankheit in den reichen Industrieländern, die das körperliche und psychische Wohlbefinden zahlloser Menschen einschränkt und selbst für erhebliche Gesundheitsschäden und gewaltige Kosten im Gesundheitssystem verantwortlich ist – es gibt Hochrechnungen, die davon ausgehen, daß 30 bis 50 Prozent der Kosten im Gesundheitswesen durch Bewegungsmangel verursacht werden –, ist ohne jeden Zweifel eine massenhaft auftretende Übergewichtigkeit. Zu viele Menschen werden einfach zu dick und schädigen sich und ihre Gesundheit dadurch ganz erheblich. Man könnte deshalb die Fettleibigkeit auch die »Krankheit am Überfluß« nennen.

Es ist eine der himmelschreienden Absurditäten der Gegenwart, daß nach wie vor Millionen von Menschen auf diesem Globus hungern und an Hunger sterben – nach Auskunft des *Welternährungsprogramms der Vereinten Nationen* zum Jahresbeginn 1999 leiden weltweit 800 Millionen Menschen an Unterernährung –, während gleichzeitig weitere -zig Millionen von Menschen angesichts eines bisher nie dagewesenen materiellen Überflusses und einer mit der modernen Zivilisation einhergehenden endemischen Bewegungsarmut schlicht zu dick geworden sind und demnach am Gegenteil, an Überernährung leiden. Und dies betrifft in den reichen Ländern dieser Erde keineswegs nur die Oberschicht, sondern geht quer durch die gesamte Bevölkerung. Allein in der Bundesrepublik Deutschland gelten ca. 20 Prozent der Bevölkerung als übergewichtig, dabei ist der Anteil der Frauen etwas höher als der der Männer. 25 Millionen Deutsche, also mehr als ein Viertel der

Gesamtbevölkerung, fühlen sich nach Auskunft von Verbraucherorganisationen als zu dick. Ohne jeden Zweifel spielt dabei die Ernährung ebenso wie die Bewegungsarmut eine entscheidende Rolle, wobei es bei der Ernährung nicht nur um die Menge, sondern auch um die Art, die Qualität und die Zusammensetzung geht. Hinter der falschen Ernährung steht gewiß ein hohes Maß an mangelnder Information, an Bequemlichkeit und Stumpfsinn, allzuoft aber weisen Gewichtsprobleme auch auf tieferliegende psychologische Konflikte hin. Vor allem um die Schwelle des vierten Lebensjahrzehnts herum wird es für viele gefährlich, zu einem Zeitpunkt, an dem der biologische Alterungsprozeß sich allzuoft mit sehr ernsten biographisch-psychologischen Konflikten zu einer unheilvollen Mischung verbindet, die zu mampfenden Exzessen und deren unerwünschten gewichtigen Folgen führen kann.

Wie so oft im Leben sind gerade die am schwierigsten zu lösenden Dinge *theoretisch* meist von erhabener Einfachheit. Dies gilt auch für die Frage der Übergewichtigkeit. Um zu leben, muß der Mensch essen und trinken. Unser Organismus ist durch die Evolution nicht nur auf seine Selbsterhaltung mittels Nahrungsaufnahme und Fortpflanzung ausgerichtet, sondern vor allem auch darauf, daß unsere Selbsterhaltung nicht unter den paradiesischen Umständen von Frieden und

Überfluß stattfindet, sondern vielmehr in einer Umwelt, die durch zahlreiche Bedrohungen und meist auch durch eine die individuelle menschliche Existenz gefährdende physische Mangelsituation an Lebensmitteln gekennzeichnet ist. Die Evolution hat unseren Organismus auf genau diese gefahrvolle Mangelsituation eingestellt, genauso wie wir die anderen entsprechenden biologischen Voraussetzungen mitbekommen haben, um unter den natürlichen Bedingungen, innerhalb derer sich der Homo sapiens eben entwickelt hat, mehr schlecht als recht für eine bestimmte Zeit zu überleben. Daß dabei die unteren Extremitäten, vulgo auch Beine genannt, und deren an- und ausdauernde Bewegung für unsere Reproduktion und damit auch für die Entwicklung und die Befindlichkeit unseres gesamten Organismus eine zentrale Bedeutung hatten, läßt sich bis heute unschwer an den Proportionen unseres Körpers ablesen. Wir sind von Mutter Natur als Lauftiere entwickelt worden, fernab von Automobilen, Flugzeugen und einer überwiegend sitzenden Bürotätigkeit, eine Erbschaft unserer Vorfahren aus den ostafrikanischen Savannen, die uns bis auf den heutigen Tag erhalten geblieben ist. »Die evolutionsbiologische Verankerung des Laufens im menschlichen Organismus ist auch daran ersichtlich, daß ein leidlich trainierter Läufer stundenlang laufen kann, ohne Schaden zu nehmen, ja,

12

daß er nach einer bestimmten Laufzeit so etwas wie eine zusätzliche Schubkraft verspürt. Der menschliche Organismus läßt Dauerläufe über mehrere hundert Kilometer zu, ein Indiz für den früheren Überlebenswert dieser Fähigkeit und für eine Kraftreserve, die nur zum Laufen zur Verfügung steht. Der Mensch ist nun einmal zum Laufen geboren ...«[1]

Wegen der Kürze der Zeit haben die heute in der Arbeitswelt der westlichen Wohlstandsgesellschaften dominierenden sitzenden Tätigkeiten noch keinen Eingang in die evolutionäre Anpassung des menschlichen Organismus finden können, denn ansonsten würden sich Geläuf und Gesäß in einem umgekehrt proportionalen Verhältnis zueinander befinden. Die Langsamkeit der Evolution bei der Anpassung der Arten an veränderte Umweltbedingungen schafft so in den modernen Gesellschaften mit ihren Büros und Computern vielen Menschen ein nicht unerhebliches körperliches und psychisches Problem. Die Energietanks ihres Körpers, die Fettzellen, ausgelegt für das karge, mühselige und gefahrvolle Leben eines altsteinzeitlichen Jägers, fangen an, sich durch permanente Unterforderung einerseits und ebenso permanenter Überfüllung andererseits zu verselb-

1 Willi Köhler – Der aufrechte Läufer, Anmerkungen zur Evolution des Menschen; aus: Zur Psychologie des Laufens, hrsg. von Reiner Stach, Frankfurt/M. 1995, S. 96

ständigen. Die Reservetanks des Hauptenergie-
speichers Fett quellen über, und der Körper wird
unförmig, schwer und schließlich krank.

Die Ernährung war und ist die alltäglich sich wie-
derholende und immer wieder erneut und unter
Aufbietung aller Kräfte zu sichernde Grundlage
jeder menschlichen Selbsterhaltung. »Das Sein
bestimmt das Bewußtsein«, so präzisierte weiland
ein gewisser Karl Marx aus Trier die realen Verhältnisse zwischen Geist und Materie in der menschlichen Existenz. Und recht hatte er, denn die
Sicherstellung der Ernährung formt die Grundlage
aller Gesellschaft, aller Wirtschaft und aller Politik.
Der Hunger war auch und gerade in Europa seit
Jahrtausenden der ständige Begleiter der Menschen und sein Verschwinden auf unserem Konti-
nent liegt gerade mal zwei bis drei Generationen
zurück. Dürren, schlechte Ernten, Katastrophen,
Kriege – meistens folgte darauf für die ärmeren
Schichten das große Sterben durch den Hunger
oder die Rettung durch Auswanderung. Die Überwindung des Mangels an Nahrung mittels mo-
derner Anbaumethoden, Technologien, Verfahren
und Organisation ist erst jüngeren Datums. In den
früheren Mangelgesellschaften war die Übergewichtigkeit, war das Völlen und Prassen ein öffentlich dargestellter Ausweis von Reichtum und
Macht. Der Überfluß war das Kennzeichen der
wenigen Reichen und Mächtigen, der große Rest

aber mußte um sein tägliches Brot sprichwörtlich ackern und kämpfen. Arme Leute litten damals nicht nur Hunger, sondern sie sahen auch danach aus (was sich etwa in dem Sprachbild des »Hungerleiders« erhalten hat), während die Reichen ihr Vermögen und ihre Stellung auch körperlich durch Fettleibigkeit repräsentierten.

In den modernen Gesellschaften mit ihrem Massenwohlstand und Massenkonsum, mit ihren industrialisierten Landwirtschaften, multinationalen Lebensmittelkonzernen, Handelsketten und ihrem gewaltigen Einsatz an Forschung, Technologie und Marketing betrifft nun die Übergewichtigkeit mitnichten nur die Reichen. Die Verhältnisse scheinen sich nahezu auf den Kopf gestellt zu haben. Wer heute über Besitz, Geld und Bildung verfügt, hält eher auf seine Figur bis ins hohe Alter. Millionen von Menschen leiden heute unter ihrem Körpergewicht, fühlen sich zu dick, werden aufgrund ihres großen Übergewichts sogar ernsthaft krank bis hin zum Tode. Diabetes und vor allem Herz-Kreislauf-Erkrankungen gehen zu einem beträchtlichen Teil auf falsche Ernährung und Übergewicht zurück, die Infarkthäufigkeit bei Übergewichtigen ist um ein Vielfaches höher als bei Normalgewichtigen. Also müßte doch die schlichte Schlußfolgerung lauten: weniger Essen und mehr Bewegung. Wie gesagt, *theoretisch* ist das Problem von erhabener analytischer Schlichtheit, praktisch türmen sich jedoch ganz offensichtlich nur schwer zu überwindende Hindernisse vor den vielen Übergewichtigen auf, wenn sie ihr Leiden nachhaltig kurieren wollen.

Eine ganze Industrie des schlechten Gewissens lebt heute von der Zivilisationskrankheit der Übergewichtigkeit, die Jahr für Jahr ein weltweites und zugleich milliardenschweres Geschäft nach sich zieht. Und in der Tat, die Qual mit den überflüssigen Pfunden ist groß, und ebenso groß ist oft die Verzweiflung der Betroffenen und der tiefe Frust der an den zahllosen Diäten Gescheiterten. Entsprechend groß sind demnach aber auch die Versprechungen und der Umsatz der Rettung versprechenden Industrie. »Abnehmen im Schlaf« heißt das jüngste teure Versprechen solcher Geschäftemacher, und sie bieten alles an, womit aus dem schlechten Gewissen von dicken Menschen Geld gemacht werden kann: Diäten und Kuren sind noch der seriösere Teil, Mittelchen, Getränke, Appetitzügler, grausam schmeckende Breie und Schleime, kurz alles, was die moderne Pharma- und Nahrungsmittelindustrie, was Medizin, Ernährungsphysiologie und auch Scharlatanerie und schlichte Beutelschneiderei aufbieten können, wird auf einen jährlich wachsenden Markt geworfen. Und allein die Tatsache, daß dieser Markt der Schlankheitsversprechen beständig wächst, muß doch zumindest für vernünftige Menschen den Verdacht der mangelnden Tauglichkeit der meisten der verkauften Mittel und Rezepturen nahelegen.

■

Damit Sie, verehrte Leserin, verehrter Leser, bei der Lektüre keinem Irrtum unterliegen, möchte ich hier gleich zu Beginn zwei Dinge klarstellen: In diesem Buch wird nicht abstrakt räsoniert, sondern ausschließlich über meine eigenen Erlebnisse und praktischen Erfahrungen berichtet. Ich kann und muß bei diesem Thema vor allem über mich selbst sprechen, das heißt, die Subjektivität meines folgenden Berichts läßt sich nicht umgehen. Und zweitens weiß ich aus eigener jahrelanger und leidvoller Erfahrung nur zu gut, wovon und worüber ich bei diesem Thema rede und schreibe. Häme oder gar eine hochnäsige Besserwisserei gegenüber anderen sind mir bei der Erörterung des Problems der Übergewichtigkeit deshalb weiß Gott fremd, ich kann für mich beanspruchen, all die psychischen Tiefen als Ergebnis von Übergewichtigkeit und zahlloser gescheiterter Ausbruchsversuche selbst durchlebt und vor allem durchlitten zu haben. Noch im Sommer 1996 brachte ich bei meinen 181 cm Körpergröße gewaltige 112 kg – sehr kurzatmig geworden – auf die Waage, ein gutes Jahr später hatte ich wieder 75 kg erreicht und den kurzen Atem Gott sei Dank längst hinter mir – ohne Abmagerungskuren, ohne chemische Mittel, ohne Spezialdiäten, ohne Therapien und ohne für diese umfassende Verschlankung der eigenen Person viel Geld auszugeben. (Apropos Geld: am teuersten war die völlig neue Garderobe, die ich mir zulegen mußte, aber genau dies hat mir eine Riesenfreude gemacht. Es war einfach nur ein herrliches Erfolgserlebnis! Per saldo dürfte ich allerdings durch mein neues Leben einiges an Geld gespart haben, denn erhebliche Ausgaben für Speis und Trank fielen einfach und dauerhaft ersatzlos weg.)

Als Mensch des öffentlichen Lebens und damit auch des öffentlichen Interesses konnte ich diesen radikalen körperlichen Umbau – denn genau das hieß es, in einem guten Jahr fast vierzig Kilogramm abzunehmen und damit meine Konfektion von einer platzenden Größe 28 (die 20er Größen sind beim Herrn für den wachsenden Bauch gedacht) wieder auf jene die persönliche Befindlichkeit und das Selbstbewußtsein ungemein fördernde Konfektionsgröße 48 herunterzubringen – kaum verbergen, die Wirkung war zu offensichtlich. Meine körperliche Veränderung wurde folglich zum öffentlichen Thema (seit dem Regierungswechsel unterliege ich gewissermaßen einem öffentlichen *weight watching* durch die Boulevardpresse, denn jedes vermeintliche oder tatsächliche Kilogramm rauf oder runter wird zur Nachricht), und ich versuchte erst gar nicht, diesem Medieninteresse auszuweichen. So erreichten mich in den vergangenen zwei Jahren zahllose briefliche Anfragen von Leidensgenossen und deren Angehörigen, die alle wissen wollten, wie ich diese sichtbare und erhebliche Gewichtsreduzierung denn geschafft hätte und worin denn mein Geheimnis bestünde. »Was ist Ihre geheime Diät, Herr Fischer?« So oder ähnlich lautete immer wieder dieselbe, x-mal mündlich oder schriftlich gestellte Frage. Und darauf kann ich nur antworten, daß ich über kein Geheimnis verfüge und daß es auch keine geheime Wunderdiät des Joschka Fischer gibt.

Heute, nach all den Erfahrungen, langen Stunden des Nachdenkens und vielen Gesprächen weiß ich, daß meine 112 kg das Ergebnis der Tatsache waren, daß ich mich im Umgang mit mir selbst und meinem eigenen Körper verrannt, daß ich mit mir selbst und meinen Kräften über fast zwei Jahrzehnte einen schlimmen Raubbau betrieben hatte. Ich stand im August 1996 plötzlich vor einer privaten Katastrophe, die mich zu einem Neuanfang gezwungen hat, ansonsten hätte der persönliche Absturz im wahrsten Sinne des Wortes gedroht.

Es war nicht nur meine Ehe gescheitert, ich stand mit meiner ganzen persönlichen Lebensführung, mit meiner Alltagsgestaltung, mit meinem

Umgang mit mir selbst vor einem ganz unmittelbar drohenden Debakel. Buchstäblich in einem Augenblick mußte ich mich entscheiden, und zwar sehr grundsätzlich: *Weitermachen wie bisher oder eine radikale Umkehr*, wenn ich an der Schwelle zu meinem 6. Lebensjahrzehnt nicht in die ernsthafte Gefahr geraten wollte, physisch und psychisch gewaltig unter die Räder zu kommen. Ich mußte also und wollte dann auch mein Leben ändern, denn die 112 kg – bei 181 cm Körpergröße und 48 Jahren Lebensalter – waren nur der sichtbare Ausdruck einer allgemeinen persönlichen Krise, die viel umfassender war und auch tiefer reichte, als ich mir bis dato gewagt hatte einzugestehen. Ergo konnte es nicht nur ums Abnehmen gehen, sondern es stand weitaus mehr zur Disposition. Ich mußte meinen gesamten Lebensstil ändern, meine bisherige Art zu leben, mich also vor allem selbst umkrempeln, ohne mich allerdings dabei aufzugeben oder gar zu verlieren – ja, und es hat funktioniert. Ganz hervorragend sogar.

In diesem Buch werde ich also vor allem eine Geschichte zu erzählen haben, wenn ich »das Geheimnis« meines »Erfolges« enthüllen soll. Es ist meine Geschichte. Man verzeihe mir also diese Ich-Bezogenheit, aber bei dem zu erörternden Thema und den zu schildernden Ereignissen läßt sich das einfach nicht anders machen. Ich werde demnach auf den folgenden Seiten in der ersten Person viel über mich selbst sprechen und von mir erzählen müssen, da sich nur so Ursache und Verlauf meiner Veränderung vom Mops zum Asketen für den interessierten Leser wird nachvollziehen und begreifen lassen.

Dies bedeutet auch: Dieses Buch hat kein Arzt, kein Ernährungsphysiologe, kein Therapeut, kein Sportmediziner, kein Trainer, kein Wissenschaftler und auch kein Laufprofi geschrieben, hier berichtet ein Betroffener von einem Selbstversuch, der erstaunlich positive Ergebnisse gebracht hat. Ernährung, Psychologie, Physiologie, Sportmedizin, Sportwissenschaft und Therapie – alles hat dabei eine Rolle gespielt, aber reflektiert und erkannt

Schlank und rank als frischgebackener Bundestagsabgeordneter 1983

habe ich diese fachlichen Zusammenhänge oft erst im nachhinein, nachdem ich mich bereits spontan und ganz von selbst auf den Weg gemacht hatte und das erkenntnisleitende Interesse aus der Sache heraus dazu führte, mich zunehmend mit der entsprechenden Literatur zu beschäftigen oder auch den persönlichen Kontakt mit Experten zu suchen.

Die Experten und das Fachwissen haben mir sehr geholfen, aber erst, nachdem mein *Interesse* geweckt worden war, nachdem ich mich bereits selbst auf den Weg gemacht hatte. Erst also, nachdem ich persönlich dazu bereit war, ließ ich diese längst vorhandenen und allseits zugänglichen Informationen an mich heran, nahm sie auf und begann dann, sie mehr und mehr und zunehmend systematischer umzusetzen. Meine eigene persönliche Entscheidung aber stand am Anfang von allem, und nur der eigene Wille zu dieser Entscheidung gab mir überhaupt die Kraft, diesen Weg zu gehen und durchzuhalten. So wichtig der sachkundige Rat dann auch immer war und ist, zuerst und vor allem ging und geht es um die eigene Kraft zur Entscheidung. Das Leiden an überflüssigen Pfunden allein reicht zu einer solchen Entscheidung aber ganz offensichtlich nicht aus, dazu bedarf es wesentlich mehr. Was genau? Darauf möchte ich auf den folgenden Seiten eine Antwort versuchen. Es hat eine Menge mit der eigenen Vergangenheit zu tun.

II

Das große Fressen

Wie und warum wurde ich eigentlich so dick (präziser gesagt: fett)? Anders gefragt: Weshalb wurde aus einem schlanken und ranken jungen Mann innerhalb einer Dekade ein wandelndes Faß von Mensch? Selbst im nachhinein ist das immer wieder eine gute Frage, denn als ich im März 1983 mit 35 Jahren zum ersten Mal als Abgeordneter in den Deutschen Bundestag einzog, war ich noch hübsch anzuschauen: ganze 75 Kilogramm schwer, ohne Bauch und überflüssige Pfunde, statt dessen muskulös und völlig austrainiert. All die Jahrzehnte zuvor hatte ich mit Begeisterung Sport getrieben, Sport gehörte eigentlich immer zu meinem Leben. In der Jugend hatte ich viele Jahre bei uns im Dorf im Verein Handball gespielt, Fußball sowieso fast täglich auf dem Bolzplatz, und mehrere Jahre hatte ich als Radrennfahrer in der Altersgruppe der B/A-Jugend Leistungssport betrieben, d. h. richtig heftig trainiert. Eine württembergische Meisterschaft im Mannschaftszeitfahren auf der Straße über 50 Kilometer für *Stuttgardia Stuttgart* war mein sportlicher Höhepunkt in diesem Lebensabschnitt gewesen. Damals, beim Training als Radrennfahrer, lernte ich so manches über Trainingsaufbau, Trainingsverhalten und Ernährung, was mir viele Jahrzehnte später plötzlich wieder in den Sinn kommen sollte und sich dann im weiteren Fortgang der Ereignisse durchaus als große Hilfe erweisen sollte.

Bereits als kleiner Steppke hatte ich mit dem Fußballspielen begonnen und dies über mehr als vier Jahrzehnte durchgehalten, selbst in meiner gewichtigsten Phase als schweratmendes Faß auf zwei Beinen. Und auch – da sei nicht darum herumgeredet – meine linksradikalen siebziger Jahre in der Frankfurter Spontiszene und im Häuserkampf verlangten ein hohes Maß an körperlicher Fitneß! Zudem war das alternative Leben der siebziger Jahre zwar materiell karg, gleichwohl aber in hohem Maße streßfrei und darüber hinaus von einer hohen Zeitsouveränität gekennzeichnet. Man konnte sich zwar kaum kompensatorischen Konsum leisten, hatte ihn in Anbetracht der hohen Zeitsouveränität allerdings auch fast nicht nötig und konnte sich intensiv mit sich selbst beschäftigen. Auch ich verfügte damals über lausig wenig Geld, hatte aber jede Menge Zeit, und die nutzte ich unter anderem zur beständigen körperlichen Ertüchtigung mittels regelmäßigen Trainings. Tägliche morgendliche Liegestütze und Sit-Ups, mehrmals wöchentlich Bankdrücken mit Gewichten und Arbeit mit Hanteln und am Sandsack führten zu einem hervorragenden Trainingszustand und zum persönlichen Idealge-

Als junger Bundestagsabgeordneter 1983 in der Bundestagsauswahl

wicht. Nur eines habe ich zeit meines gesamten Lebens niemals gerne gemacht, nämlich Laufen, Wandern, Dauerlauf gar, fand ich immer nur ätzend nervtötend, sterbenslangweilig und demnach ohne jeglichen persönlichen Anreiz. »Das Laufen ohne Ball ist mir zu langweilig«, war immer meine Devise gewesen, und so blieb es bis zum Herbst 1996 läuferisch allein bei jener mehr oder weniger regelmäßig einmal die Woche stattfindenden, zudem durch Alter und anwachsende Masse immer geringere Distanzen überwindenden Bewegung auf dem Fußballplatz.

■

Mitte Dreißig erreichen Mann und Frau in unserer Gesellschaft lebensgeschichtlich eine kritische Phase. Die Jugend geht definitiv zu Ende, zuerst nur unmerklich, dann aber spürbar und immer schneller. Die Kurven der geistigen und der körperlichen Persönlichkeitsentwicklung kreuzen sich in dieser Zeit biographisch in einer gegenläufigen Richtung – die mentale Kurve steigt weiter an, während die Kurve der körperlichen Leistungsfähigkeit zunehmend und unerbittlich nach unten weist. An der biographischen Dreißigerschwelle wird man in der Regel endgültig erwachsen, das heißt, die eigene Persönlichkeitsbildung wird (im guten wie im schlechten) in der Regel abgeschlossen, beruflich beginnt jetzt meistens die stärkste und erfolgreichste Zeit. Ganz entgegen diesem Trend des geistigen Leistungsvermögens beginnt das körperliche Leistungsvermögen erheblich abzubauen. Es ist ziemlich genau das Alter, in dem professionelle Sportler ihre Karriere beenden oder zumindest in deren Endphase eintreten. Vieles, was man in den jungen Jahren zuvor noch mühelos weggesteckt hat – durchgemachte Nächte, den einen oder anderen Exzeß, Völlereien und Trainingsrückstände –, schlagen plötzlich merkbar auf die Fitneß und das körperliche Befinden durch und machen sich vor allem auch in einer meßbaren Gewichtszunahme bemerkbar, die eben nicht mehr wie früher leichterdings und fast wie von selbst vom eigenen Körper korrigiert wird. Zudem erfordern zum Beispiel der berufliche Erfolg und die wachsende persönliche Verantwortung eine ganz andere Konzentration und auch ein ganz anderes mentales und zeitliches Engagement. Zudem befinden sich in diesem Alter die meisten Menschen in der heißesten Familienphase mit kleinen Kindern und sich daraus ergebenden häuslichen Verpflichtungen, und so verwundert es nicht, daß Zeit und Energie, durch all diese Umstände bedingt, immer knapper werden. Hinzu kommt als Ergebnis dessen allzuoft noch eine nach und nach um sich greifende größere Trägheit im Freizeitverhalten, denn mit dem beruflichen Erfolg geht nicht nur ein höherer materieller Lebensstandard einher, sondern auch wachsender Erfolgsdruck, der allgemeine Streß und die zunehmende Konzentration aller persönlichen Energie auf Arbeit und Karriere.

■

Ich bemerkte all diese Veränderungen, die uns Menschen von alters her wohlvertraut sind und die dennoch von jeder Generation immer wieder an sich selbst neu entdeckt werden, zuerst nicht einmal so sehr am zunehmenden Körpergewicht, sondern vielmehr daran, daß ich auf dem Fußballplatz immer verletzungsanfälliger wurde. Zerrungen und noch ernstere Muskelprobleme hatte ich bis dato nicht gekannt, und damit hatte ich nun beständig zu laborieren. Nachlässigkeiten und Versäumnisse, die in all den Jahren zuvor niemals auch nur ein kurzes Nachdenken wert gewesen waren, etwa das Warmlaufen vor einem Spiel, machten sich fortan folgenschwer durch Zerrungen und Faserrisse in Oberschenkel- und Wadenmuskulatur bemerkbar. Längere Verletzungspausen waren deren Folge, was wiederum zur Bewegungsarmut und damit zur stetig wachsenden Leibesfülle beitrug. Und so wurden Jahr um Jahr mit dem Atem auch die Wege immer kürzer, die ich auf dem Fußballfeld noch gehen konnte. Das Mittelfeld begann sich immer weiter und weiter zu dehnen, eine schier endlose Ebene tat sich da vor mir auf, die ich nicht mehr durcheilen konnte, es sei denn, ich ging nach einem längeren »Sprint« in schierer Atemnot keuchend in die Knie, die Beine wurden mit jedem Schritt schwerer und der Atem immer weniger.

»Mein Gott«, dachte ich mir dann nach Luft japsend, »was ist aus dir nur geworden, Fischer!?« Daß einem die Jüngeren so nach und nach davonliefen, o. k., das war der Tribut des Alters und hatte seine Ordnung. Daß man aber auf dem Fußballfeld nicht mehr ohne Sauerstoffzelt auskam, das tat weh und mußte wohl nicht sein. Diese Erkenntnis dämmerte mir insgeheim und nur ganz tief

Der schwergewichtige Fußballer

drinnen. Zugegeben hätte ich sie niemals, aber sie tat weh und verstärkte mein schlechtes Gewissen. Konsequenzen zog ich aus dieser deprimierenden Erfahrung allerdings keine, sondern ich mampfte und zechte munter weiter. Ich gehörte in jungen Jahren (und bis heute) gewiß niemals zu den filigranen Technikern der Fußballkunst und auch nicht zu den Genies des Mittelfeldes, wohl aber konnte ich 90 Minuten laufen, war in der Deckung schwer auszuspielen und eigentlich kaum abzuschütteln, wenn ich einen Gegenspieler in Manndeckung auszuschalten hatte. Damit ging es mit jedem weiteren Jahr und jedem weiteren Kilogramm Körpergewicht, das ich zulegte, nun spürbar zu Ende, und so suchte ich mir mehr und mehr ein Plätzchen in der Sturmmitte, wo die Wege für uns mittlerweile zu »Alten Herren« gewordenen Mitt- bis Enddreißigern kürzer waren und ein Torerfolg als ausgleichendes Erfolgserlebnis zum Greifen nahe war. Am Ende dann, mit meinen 112 Kilogramm Lebendgewicht, war mein Aktionsradius schließlich auf die Größe eines Bierdeckels geschrumpft, und das war eine bittere Erkenntnis für mich, von der optischen Erscheinung ganz zu schweigen! Das Bild jenes balltretenden Fasses, das ich damals abgab, läßt mich noch heute zart erröten. Oh ja!

Die dramatischen Veränderungen meines Körpergewichts standen in einem deutlichen Zusammenhang mit meinem Einstieg in die große Politik. Insofern muß ich jetzt etwas detaillierter die politisch-biographischen Ereignisse dieser Zeit darstellen. Meine Wahl als Bundestagsabgeordneter in das Parlament nach Bonn erwies sich dabei unter vielfachen Gesichtspunkten als die entscheidende Zäsur, denn erst seit 1983 nahm ich zwar langsam, gleichwohl aber beständig zu. Die eigentliche Trendwende hin zu einer dramatischen und schnellen Zunahme meines Übergewichts kam dann allerdings mit meiner ersten Berufung zum Umweltminister in Hessen am 12. Dezember 1985. Diese erste Zeit als hessischer Umweltminister war beruflich und persönlich meine bisher härteste und schlimmste Zeit, in der ich aber zugleich auch unglaublich viel gelernt habe, und dies vor allem aus meinen eigenen Fehlern. Dennoch, so physisch und psychisch am Ende wie in diesen vierzehn Monaten des ersten Umweltministeriums in Wiesbaden hatte ich mich weder davor noch danach in meinem politischen Leben jemals wieder gefühlt, und insofern war ich *persönlich* heilfroh – so traurig das politische Ergebnis, nämlich das Ende der ersten rot-grünen Koalition und der Machtverlust an die Opposition auch gewesen war –, als ich dieses Abenteuer im Februar 1987 schließlich einigermaßen heil überstanden hatte.

Als ich 1985 zum Umweltminister ernannt wurde, war meine Partei, *Die Grünen*, über die

Frage der Regierungsbeteiligung tief gespalten, der Koalitionspartner SPD über die Tatsache der ersten rot-grünen Koalition fast noch mehr, Industrie und Gewerkschaften waren fast unisono gegen uns, die Opposition sowieso, die Koalitionsvereinbarung erwies sich im Regierungsalltag als noch weniger als eine Illusion, das damalige Umweltministerium bewegte sich von seinen Zuständigkeiten her am Rande des exekutiven Witzes, ich selbst hatte zudem eigentlich weder von der Sache noch vom Regieren auch nur den Schatten einer Ahnung, und neben all dem Krach und Streit, den Anfeindungen und Fehlern kam es dann am 26. April 1986 zum atomaren Supergau in Tschernobyl in der Ukraine.

Ich war damals der einzige und erste grüne Umweltminister auf diesem Planeten, *Die Grünen* waren *die* Anti-Atom-Partei schlechthin, und in den Augen von Öffentlichkeit und Partei war ich selbstverständlich zuständig für die Bewältigung der Folgen der atomaren Wolke. Wen interessierten denn da die tatsächlichen administrativen und bürokratischen Zuständigkeiten? In den Augen der Öffentlichkeit war dies – völlig zu Recht übrigens! – meine und unsere Stunde als Umweltminister und Grüne, und dann war ich für nichts von alledem zuständig. Weder für den Strahlenschutz, denn der lag beim sozialdemokratischen Sozialminister, noch für die Atomaufsicht und die

Energiepolitik, denn über diese wachte der sozial-demokratische Wirtschaftsminister. Ich wußte damals zwar von Anfang an, daß ich für diesen Job von den Freundinnen und Freunden in der Partei nicht wegen meiner ökologischen Fachkompetenz ausgewählt worden war, über die ich damals überhaupt nicht verfügte, sondern weil die erste grüne Regierungsbeteiligung sehr realitätsnah als ein politisches Himmelfahrtskommando angesehen wurde und man dazu keinen Fachmann brauchte, sondern einen politischen Generalisten, der hart genug war, eine minimale Chance gegen alle Widerstände zu nutzen und eine solche fast unmöglich erscheinende Aufgabe politisch und persönlich durchzustehen. Ich wußte also, daß es hart werden würde, aber so? Es war zum Haareraufen und zum Mäusemelken, und all das zehrte selbstverständlich gewaltig an meiner persönlichen psychischen und physischen Substanz.

Zum ersten Mal lernte ich damals jene Schlaflosigkeit kennen, die einen nach zwei bis drei Stunden Nachtruhe mit klopfendem Herzen wieder aus dem Schlaf reißt, weil einen das Übermaß der Probleme um die innere Ruhe bringt. Und zum ersten Mal meinte ich zu spüren, wie es ist, wenn man sich in Richtung Herzinfarkt bewegt. Die Nächte wurden immer kürzer, die Arbeitstage immer länger, die Wochenenden fielen immer öfter aus, die Katastrophen rissen nicht ab, der

Problemdruck wuchs und wuchs, die Verantwortung wurde immer drückender, der Streß nahm unerbittlich zu, und ein Ausweg war nicht in Sicht. Weglaufen ging nicht, zumindest für mich nicht –, obwohl diese Haltung ja neuerdings durchaus en vogue zu werden scheint –, also mußte ich durchhalten, mich gegen all die Unbill psychisch und körperlich wappnen. Und so begann ich zu futtern und zu mampfen und legte mir für Körper und Seele im wahrsten Sinne des Wortes einen regelrechten Panzer in Gestalt eines sich immer mächtiger wölbenden Bauches zu. Zudem hatte ich zu rauchen aufgehört, die Selbstgedrehten paßten einfach nicht zum Umweltminister. Im März 1986 klappte zum ersten Mal in meiner Erinnerung mein Immunsystem aufgrund der Überanstrengung durch die ersten Monate in der Landesregierung völlig zusammen, und ich lag mit einer für meine Verhältnisse sehr schweren Grippe tagelang darnieder. Aber auch dieses an sich sehr positive Signal verstärkte noch ganz erheblich die Eskalation meiner Pfunde. Und so kam das eine zum anderen, und am Ende des Liedes standen 112 Kilogramm Lebendgewicht Fischer.

Kompensation, Panzerung, Verdrängung – gemeinsam mit dem Älterwerden waren das die wichtigsten Ursachen für meinen immer dramatischer werdenden Gewichtsanstieg. Die nahezu

Auf dem Höhepunkt ...

ausschließliche Konzentration auf die berufliche Aufgabe, auf den »Job«, der nicht nur subjektiv, sondern auch objektiv alle Kraft erforderte und dennoch trotz (oder vielleicht sogar auch wegen?) all der Belastungen eine begeisternde Herausforderung darstellte, ließ den Zustand des eigenen Ichs und damit auch des eigenen Körpers in den Hintergrund treten. Fast meine gesamte Energie konzentrierte ich auf den politischen Erfolg und ordnete diesem Ziel alles andere unter, auch und gerade mich selbst. Gewiß nahm ich all die negativen Veränderungen an mir sehr genau wahr, aber ich war schon immer ein Meister im Erfinden von überzeugenden Begründungen gewesen. Hatten in meiner Kindheit bei uns im Dorf nicht fast alle »alten Herren« eine mächtige Wampe gehabt? Eben, und das waren doch alles gestandene Mannsbilder und ganze Kerle gewesen. Oder: Schluß mit dem Jugendlichkeitswahn unserer Zeit! Jedes Lebensalter hat seine Figur, mal schlanker, mal üppiger, je nach Jahren unterschiedlich.

So oder ähnlich dröhnte ich meinen Kritikern oder einfach nur wohlmeinenden Zeitgenossen, Freunden und Familienangehörigen entgegen, die es lediglich gut mit mir meinten, wenn sie zu bedenken gaben, daß es doch nun wirklich reichen würde mit der Leibesfülle und daß etwas weniger Gewicht doch auch ganz schön und sicher viel gesünder wäre. Freilich waren meine Rechtfertigungen nur schlichtes Papperlapapp, denn insgeheim habe ich selbst nicht daran geglaubt. Ich wußte, daß meine Freunde mit ihrer Kritik recht hatten, fühlte mich aber zu schwach, um die notwendigen *praktischen* Konsequenzen zu ziehen. All diese wunderbaren Rechtfertigungen sollten sich für mich im Licht der späteren Ereignisse lediglich als Ausflüchte und Ausreden vor mir selbst erweisen, als Beruhigung meines eigenen schlechten Gewissens. Denn selbstverständlich habe ich unter der Entwicklung gelitten – ich hörte meinen Atem bei der geringsten Anstrengung pfeifen und konnte mich ja im Spiegel durchaus realistisch selbst betrachten – und versuchte sie lediglich, weil ich die Kraft zur Umkehr nicht hatte, vor mir und anderen schönzureden.

Und so ging es eben Schritt für Schritt weiter die Skala auf der Waage aufwärts. Aus dem Einreiher wurde ein Zweireiher, aus der normalen Größe des Anzugs die bauchverhüllende Zwischengröße, die Hemden wurden fortan ausladend getragen und öffentliches Badevergnügen mit dem Hinweis auf das Ozonloch und die drohende Gefahr des malignen Malinoms mehr und mehr gemieden. Tatsächlich aber mied ich nur mich selbst, begann damit, mich zu verhüllen, meine Rundungen zu kaschieren und mich vor mir selbst zu verstecken. Da war aber nichts mehr zu verstecken oder auch nur zu kaschieren, denn die Formen wurden immer üppiger, und das permanent zunehmende Körpergewicht verschaffte sich seinen angemessenen Platz unter der sich immer mächtiger spannenden Haut. Da halfen dann auch keine Über- und Zwischengrößen und keine wallenden Hemden und Gewänder mehr, das Fett war und blieb unübersehbar da.

■

Die menschlichen Fettzellen sind in den modernen Überflußgesellschaften völlig zu Unrecht in ihren schlechten Ruf geraten. Nicht das Körperfett ist unser Problem, sondern vielmehr dessen Überfluß. Die vormodernen Gesellschaften, in denen Macht und Reichtum auch in der Gewichtigkeit des Körpers repräsentiert wurden, hatten ganz offensichtlich noch eine Ahnung von der überlebensnotwendigen Funktion der Fettzellen des menschlichen Körpers, denn sie sind dessen entscheidende Energiespeicher. Unser Körper speichert seinen Energievorrat, den er bei seinen zahlreichen Aktivitäten abrufen muß, um ihn gemeinsam mit Atmungssauerstoff in Energie umsetzen zu können, in vier verschiedenen »Tanks«: Adenosintriphosphat (ATP) und Kreatinphosphat für schnelle und sehr beanspruchende Leistungen während einer kurzen Dauer; Kohlehydrate in Form von Glykogen in Muskeln und Leber für hohe Energieleistungen auf mittlere Dauer; und das Fett für geringe bis mittlere Dauerleistungen. Die ersten beiden Tanks sind schnell erschöpft, und auch der Glykogenspeicher ist begrenzt. Der Fettspeicher ist der größte und hält am längsten vor, da er den eigentlichen »Vorratstank« unseres Körpers ausmacht. Das Problem beim Übergewicht sind demnach nicht die »Tanks«, um bei unserer Analogie zum Automobil zu bleiben, sondern wir tanken und wir fahren falsch. Der Kopf »funktioniert« falsch, das heißt die Programmierung stimmt nicht, und dies ist für alles weitere eine zentrale Einsicht. Wir tanken beständig zu viel und fahren dauerhaft viel zu wenig. Konsequenz: Vor allem der Fettspeicher läuft über, wir werden fett und übergewichtig. Dies ist das Ergebnis unserer eigenen falschen Entscheidungen.

Wenn Fettleibigkeit demnach ein zivilisatorisches Massenproblem geworden ist, so zeigt dies nicht eine Disfunktionalität unseres Körpers an, sondern vielmehr eine schwere, zivilisatorisch bedingte und anhaltende Störung des Reproduktionsmechanismus des menschlichen Körpers in der modernen Gesellschaft. Das Gleichgewicht zwischen Energiezufuhr und Energieverbrauch ist offensichtlich bei den meisten Formen des Übergewichts dauerhaft gestört, so daß es angesichts reichlicher (und oft falscher) Ernährung zu einem übermäßigen Aufbau von Fettreserven kommt, ohne daß diese noch in ausreichendem Maße abgerufen werden. Die Formel, die sich als Antwort zur Lösung dieses Problems fast wie von selbst ergibt, ist also so einfach wie banal und erweist sich dennoch als die einzig richtige: weniger Energie zuführen und mehr Energie verbrauchen. Oder auch etwas drastischer und faßlicher auf den Begriff gebracht: »Iß weniger und beweg deinen Hintern!« Dies ist aber in der Praxis des modernen Alltags offensichtlich leichter gesagt als getan, und demnach wird es also ganz entscheidend auf die Wege und Strategien zur Überwindung der Sperren und Blockaden im Kopf bei der Umsetzung dieser scheinbar ganz einfachen Erkenntnis ankommen.

Es gibt sicher auch übergewichtige Menschen, die mit sich und ihrem Gewicht tatsächlich im reinen sind, d. h., die sich mit ihren Pfunden wirklich wohl fühlen. Diese seltenen Exemplare von dicken Menschen sind ehrlich zu beneiden, und sie sollten auch gar nicht erst den Versuch machen, ihren Zustand zu ändern, sondern sie sollten schlicht ein vernünftiges Maß im Umgang mit ihrem Gewicht und ihrem Lebensstil finden. Die meisten Dicken allerdings leiden an ihrem Zustand wie der sprichwörtliche Hund, sind meist kreuzunglücklich, empfinden ihren übergewichtigen Zustand subjektiv als ein bedrückendes persönliches Defizit und beginnen daher einen qualvollen und frustrierenden, oft sogar sehr teuren Kampf gegen ihr peinigendes Übergewicht mittels Diäten, Fastenkuren, Mittelchen etc. Frustrierend ist dieser Kampf deswegen, weil er meist in periodisch wiederkehrenden Niederlagen endet, die nicht nur das Körpergewicht wieder ansteigen lassen – sehr oft noch über das Ausgangsgewicht hinaus! –, sondern die durch diese deprimierende Erfahrung auch noch das schon angeschlagene Selbstvertrauen noch weiter erschüttern, begleitet von einem nagend schlechten Gewissen, das allerdings keineswegs den Appetit verdirbt, sondern allein die Laune.

.

Viele Diäten enden also erneut in – das Gewicht weiter hochtreibenden – Rückfällen mit ihren oralen Exzessen, im »alten Leben« also und dessen gewichtigen Pfunden, dem man ja gerade mittels der Diät oder Fastenkur hatte Valet sagen wollen. Ich habe diese Niederlagenerfahrung selbst jahrelang mitgemacht und wegzustecken versucht, aber deren Wirkung ist letztendlich äußerst fatal, da sie zu psychischer Entmutigung führt. Am Ende meiner »pfundigen Jahre«, im letzten Jahr vor meiner ganz persönlichen großen Wende, war ich deshalb an dem Punkt der persönlichen Kapitulation angekommen, so mutlos war ich angesichts des jährlich wiederkehrenden »Jojo-Effekts« meines Körpergewichts zwischen Fasten und Fressen geworden – beim Fasten verliert man langsam das Gewicht, das nach dem Ende der qualvollen Entsagungsübung allzuoft blitzartig wieder draufgefuttert wird –, so daß ich überhaupt keinen Versuch mehr zu einer weiteren »Fastenzeit« unternahm, die ich ansonsten jedes Jahr zwischen Neujahr und Ostern ausgerufen hatte. FdH und Verzicht auf Alkohol bewirkten tatsächlich eine spür- und sichtbare Gewichtsreduktion, die allerdings binnen kürzester Zeit nach Ende meiner Fastenzeit wieder egalisiert wurde. Fasten hin, Fasten her, die Kurve meines maximalen Gewichts wies also Jahr für Jahr letztendlich doch immer weiter nach oben, und das war auf Dauer höllisch frustrierend.

Voller Neid schaute meine Wenigkeit damals auf einen Politikerkollegen wie Heiner Geißler, der anderthalb Jahrzehnte älter ist als ich, ein schlanker und ranker Asket im vorgerückten Alter. Er hielt sich durch tägliches Laufen im Siebengebirge bei Bonn in Form, kraxelte munter auf die Berge der Alpen und sah, wen konnte es angesichts dieses Lebensstils auch wundern, überhaupt recht durchtrainiert aus. Insgeheim beneidete ich ihn um seine Sportlichkeit, sein Aussehen und seine Ausdauer, auch wenn mir dieser Lebensstil und die dazu gehörige Disziplin völlig fremd waren und für mich schlicht unmöglich erschienen. Bewunderung, Neid und Resignation mischten sich da in mir zusammen: »Das schaffst du nie, Fischer«, sagte ich mir. »Du bist kein Asket, also vergiß es und fange damit erst gar nicht an!« Statt dessen entdeckte ich im Laufe der Jahre die Freuden der *Grande cuisine* und der *Grands Crus,* der edlen Küche und der edlen Weine. Und in der Tat sind große Küche und große Weine ein echtes Erlebnis, das Ergebnis eines kunstvollen Handwerks und ein sehr alter Bestandteil unserer Kultur. Manchmal, wenn ich richtig down und fertig war, dann konnte eine Flasche herrlichen Burgunders oder Bordeaux, zu zweit oder zu dritt genossen, selbst im trübsten November die Sonne wieder in einem aufgehen lassen. Und dies war keineswegs die Wirkung des Alkohols, sondern vielmehr die vollendete Harmonie eines wirklich großen Weines und deren segensreiche Wirkung auf Geschmack, Körper und Geist. Der Alkohol tat dabei gewiß seine Wirkung, gleichwohl wirkte er für mich eher störend, weil letztendlich nur die Sinne trübend.

Große Küche und große Weine können ein herrliches Vergnügen bereiten, auch wenn sie weder billig noch kalorienarm sind. Geschmeckt hat es mir ja schon immer, und in der Tat ist gutes Essen und Trinken eine herrliche, eine wunderbare Sache. Gegessen habe ich, was immer mir mundete, und da mir fast alles schmeckte, vertilgte ich beträchtliche Mengen. Zum Frühstück Wurst,

Schinken, Käse, Eier gerührt, gekocht und gespiegelt, mit kroß gebratenem Speck, Würstchen, Butter, Brot und Marmelade, und, so vorhanden, mampfte ich auch gerne bereits Bratkartoffeln zum Frühstück. Jawohl. Mittags ein opulentes Mittagessen mit schlechtem Gewissen, manchmal noch eine Currywurst dazwischen – Pommes mit Mayo an der Imbißbude waren eine Lieblingsspeise für den kleinen Hunger am Nachmittag in kalten Wintertagen! –, und abends ging es dann so richtig in die vollen, ohne auch nur den geringsten Gedanken an Kalorien und Gesundheit zu verschwenden.

Nun ist ja überhaupt nichts gegen ein gutes Abendessen zu sagen, ganz im Gegenteil, wenn man die Sache einigermaßen bewußt angeht. So ist mir das Abendessen bis heute fast heilig, denn es bildet für mich den gesellschaftlichen Ausgleich für einen anstrengenden Arbeitstag, Erholung, Entspannung und Kommunikation in einem. Kommunikation kann dabei durchaus heißen, daß ich mich allein, mit einem Packen Zeitungen vom Tage oder mit einem interessanten Buch bewehrt, zum Dinner for one niederlasse und mich dabei herrlich entspannen kann. Aber noch viel mehr bedeutet das abendliche Tafeln für den sozialen Kontakt mit Freunden und Familie. Und dann erst recht die Politik! Wie viele Dinge wurden und werden beim Essen besprochen und geregelt. Da wird

Als es noch schmeckte ...

informiert, intrigiert und konsumiert in einem, daß es nur so eine Freude ist. Vieles geht bei einem guten Essen und einem exzellenten Tropfen wesentlich einfacher und schneller als in den quälend langweiligen formellen Sitzungen, die sich allzuoft wie Kaugummi hinziehen und kein Ende nehmen wollen. Und so saß ich eben oft bis spät in die Nacht, futterte und becherte und politisierte und wurde dabei dem damaligen Kanzler der Bundesrepublik Deutschland an Aussehen, Figur und Statur immer ähnlicher.

Freilich platzt nicht jeder aus den Nähten, der den sinnlichen Genüssen von Küche und Keller zugetan ist. Glücklichere Zeitgenossen halten trotzdem ihr Gewicht, denn auch im Fall der kulinarischen Verlockungen ist die entscheidende Frage letztendlich diejenige des rechten Maßes. Was aber tun, wenn man genau damit, mit dem rechten Maß, mit dem Maßhalten überhaupt, so seine Probleme hat? Die Antwort lieferte darauf regelmäßig die Waage, denn aus dem Genuß wurde in meinem persönlichen Fall simpel Völlerei. Die zarten Grautöne, die feinen Unterschiede und eine differenzierte Harmonie der eigenen Lebensgestaltung als Ergebnis des rechten Maßes waren und sind meine Sache noch nie gewesen. Mir ist bei allen Veränderungen im Laufe der Jahrzehnte eine Art Extremismus im persönlichen Lebensstil bis heute geblieben. Entweder – oder,

46

rechts oder links herum, schwarz oder weiß, und das immer mit vollem Tempo und letztem Einsatz. Man mag dies richtig oder falsch finden, aber letztendlich ist es eine Frage der charakterlichen Prägung, die so tief reicht, daß man darauf kaum einen verändernden Zugriff hat. Entsprechend »dynamisch« fraß ich mir demnach auch die Pfunde auf meine Rippen.

Und so wies der Zeiger auf der Waage unerbittlich weiter nach oben, und die Ziffern wurden immer größer, bis ich schließlich dieses morgendliche Marterwerkzeug namens Waage schlicht ignorierte. Möge sich doch der Teufel in der Hölle wiegen, sagte ich mir, ich muß mir doch nicht schon am Morgen die gute Laune verderben! Wozu sich überhaupt mit schlechten Nachrichten traktieren, wenn man sie eh bereits kennt und ihre Ursachen nicht ändern kann? Eben. Und so blieb das wiegende Teil ungenutzt in der Ecke des Badezimmers stehen. Gleichwohl ließen sich die Fakten nicht wirklich durch Wegschauen ignorieren, denn ich wurde für alle Welt (und das hieß eben auch für mich selbst!) sicht- und spürbar schwer und schwerer, und als Folge davon verkürzte sich mein rasselnder Atem selbst bei nur geringer Bewegung (Treppensteigen) immer mehr. Und dann bekam ein enger Freund und Bruder im Schmausen und Zechen, der nur ein Jahr älter war als ich und ebenfalls über erhebliches Übergewicht nebst einem ähnlich ungesunden Lebensstil verfügte, nach einer schweren Operation sechs Bypässe gelegt. Oha, sagte ich mir, jetzt wird es ernst, sehr ernst sogar. Die Wohllebe forderte ab sofort ganz offensichtlich ihren Preis. Fortan kroch neben dem schlechten Gewissen auch noch die Angst um die eigene Gesundheit in mir hoch. Stiche in der Brust weckten mich nachts auf, oder ich spürte sie beim Einschlafen, und die Angst vor einem Herzinfarkt war fortan immer präsent.

Heute, bei der Erinnerung an jene Zeit und meine damalige persönliche Verfassung, frage ich mich, wieso es mir nicht möglich war, aufgrund dieser Erfahrung auszusteigen. Denn mein Zustand war nicht das Ergebnis eines schlimmen, unausweichlichen Schicksals, das mich heimsuchte, wie dies etwa bei einer schweren Krankheit der Fall ist, sondern all dies war ausschließlich das Ergebnis eigener Entscheidungen, völlig selbst gewählt und deshalb »eigentlich« relativ einfach abzustellen. Es lag ja nachgerade selbst für einen Vollidioten auf der Hand, was zu tun war, aber ich hatte ganz offensichtlich nicht die psychische Kraft, um mich selbst aus diesem Lebensstil – faktisch handelte es sich um eine schleichende Art der Selbstzerstörung – herauszureißen. Ich steckte mit aller Macht in meinem inneren System fest, das sich nach und nach über viele Jahre hinweg in zahllosen kleinen Schritten entwickelt hatte, kam da einfach nicht raus, auch wenn alle Vernunft dafür sprach. Ich rannte wie ein Hamster in meinem selbstgebastelten Rad immer weiter auf der Stelle vor mich hin und fühlte mich persönlich dabei ziemlich elend, auch wenn ich das vor meiner Mitwelt sorgfältig verborgen hielt. Kesse Sprüche und muntere Reden lenkten von meiner tatsächlichen inneren Verfassung auf das trefflichste ab, und um einen eigentlich längst nötigen Gesundheitscheck machte ich aus schlichten Verdrängungsgründen einen großen Bogen. Der Onkel Doktor ist was für Weicheier und deshalb nichts für mich! Ja, ja, und dabei war diese Attitüde nichts anderes denn als Härte getarnte Feigheit. Ich hatte einfach nur Angst vor meinen tatsächlichen Blutfettwerten und den daraus zu ziehenden Schlußfolgerungen.

III

Der Big Bang – oder wie
und warum es plötzlich ganz
anders ging

Man muß keineswegs einem Fatalismus huldigen, um vorauszusehen, daß die oben beschriebene Entwicklung mit eherner Notwendigkeit in einer persönlichen Katastrophe enden mußte, die dann auch prompt eintrat. Es kam, wie es kommen mußte, meine Frau trennte sich nach dreizehn Jahren Ehe von mir. Dieser Blitz traf mich aus heiterem Himmel, die Erde tat sich vor mir auf, der Himmel fiel mir auf den Kopf, und unter der Wucht der emotionalen Katastrophe zerbrach mein ganzes bisheriges Leben innerhalb kürzester Zeit. Freilich war für den jetzt zu erzählenden Teil der Geschichte lediglich die erste bewußte Sekunde nach der Trennung von entscheidender Bedeutung, d. h. der Moment, in dem mir definitiv klar wurde, daß es tatsächlich unwiderruflich vorbei war mit unserer Ehe. Denn in demselben Augenblick, als mir diese Tatsache klar vor Augen stand und ich zugleich spürte, daß jetzt eine lange und harte Leidenszeit auf mich zukam, wußte ich, daß sofort eine sehr weitreichende Entscheidung zu treffen war in genau dieser Sekunde. Die Alternative war plötzlich sehr einfach: Entweder mache ich so weiter wie bisher und gehe damit endgültig vor die Hunde, denn in dieser jetzt beginnenden Lebenskrise würde ohne Kehrtwende mein destruktiver Lebensstil ganz sicher noch um einiges weiter eskalieren, um es ganz milde zu formulieren. Oder ich mache jetzt – jetzt sofort! – einen radikalen Schnitt, ändere völlig mein persönliches Programm und lasse alles radikal hinter mir: die Wohllebe und das Schmausen und die edlen Weine und all die unnützen Pfunde, nehme radikal ab und konzentriere mich fortan vor allem auf mich selbst.

Ich traf diese sehr weitreichende Entscheidung in jener einen Sekunde (es war tatsächlich nicht mehr an Zeit notwendig), an die ich mich noch sehr genau erinnern kann, denn in derselben Sekunde wußte ich auch, daß ich zu meiner »alten« körperlichen Verfassung, zu meinem idealen »Kampfgewicht« des Jahres 1985 zurückwollte, als ich noch nicht fett, schwer und kurzatmig war, zurück zu einer Zeit also, in der ich mich selbst noch wohlgefühlt hatte in meiner eigenen Haut. Jünger konnte ich mich nicht mehr machen – ein Zurück in der Zeit gibt es nicht – wohl aber dünner. Und genau das nahm ich mir jetzt vor. Das weite Hawaiihemd flog in die Ecke, die Baseballmütze hinterher, die gleißende Augustsonne Italiens schreckte mich plötzlich nicht mehr, die Angst vor dem Sonnenbrand war von jetzt auf nachher verflogen, und das Versteckspielen hatte ab sofort ein Ende. Ich griff zurück auf meine längst vergangenen Trainingserfahrungen, als ich noch täglich meine Liegestützen und Sit-Ups absolviert hatte, und begann deshalb sofort mit den ersten Liegestützen am Swimmingpool. Es war einfach nur deprimierend! Unter dem gewaltigen Übergewicht und dem mächtig hängenden Bauch knickte ich bereits nach wenigen Liegestützen erschöpft ein, aber ich hatte seit vielen Jahren endlich wieder einen Anfang gemacht. Zudem wußte ich aus früheren Tagen, daß jeder allererste Trainingsbeginn besonders schwer fällt und daß ab sofort und für die Dauer der kommenden Monate nichts anderes als Ausdauer und stures Durchhalten angesagt waren, denn schnell sichtbare Erfolge darf man bei dem Versuch der Gewichtsreduzierung und beim Muskelaufbau nicht erwarten.

Andererseits half mir meine tiefe seelische Krise bei meinem Vorhaben, denn daß mich meine Frau verlassen hatte, schlug mir nachdrücklich auf den Magen, d. h. ich hatte schlichtweg keinen Appetit mehr, was sich sofort segensreich auf die in Angriff genommene Gewichtsreduzierung auswirken sollte. Die Krise machte den Einstieg in ein anderes Leben leichter. Zudem reduzierte sich fast ebenso wie von selbst der Genuß von Wein und anderen alkoholischen Getränken und war dadurch ebenfalls binnen weniger Wochen zur bloßen Geschichte geworden. Wenig Essen, kaum Alkohol und große Seelenpein – was Wunder also, daß mein Gewicht nunmehr fast täglich zurückging, und das verstärkte wiederum meine Motivation. Ansonsten war meine psychische Lage zum Steinerweichen schlecht. Es kam mir aber noch ein weiterer Zufall zupaß, nämlich daß sich dieser radikale Bruch, der Absprung in ein anderes Leben, in Italien und im Urlaub vollzog, d. h., ich hatte Zeit für mich selbst und orientierte mich bei meiner spontanen Ernährungsumstellung an der gleichermaßen gesunden wie einfach-bäuerlichen Küche der Toskana – fettarm, reich an Rohkost, Gemüsen, Kohlehydraten, Olivenöl und zugleich überaus lecker. Ohne daß ich mich auch nur ein Jota über gesunde oder gar lauforientierte Ernährung zuvor jemals groß informiert hätte – das kam alles erst Monate später –, sollte ich, geleitet durch die Umstände und die Zufälle des Alltags, spontan die völlig richtigen Entscheidungen treffen, wie ich wesentlich später dann in der Retrospektive feststellte. Die tierischen Fette habe ich auf meinem täglichen Speiseplan weitgehend reduziert, Pasta und Gemüse dominierten den Tisch, Fisch und Meeresfrüchte, zudem Brot, Obst, Salat, kurz alles, was sich in der Toskana fast von selbst ergibt.

Und da jeder Tag mit dem Morgen beginnt, begann ich auch und gerade das Frühstück zu verändern. Schinken, Wurst, Käse, Eier, Speck, Butter, Brötchen – alles wurde gestrichen. Statt dessen stieg ich zuerst auf Corn Flakes und dann sehr schnell auf Müsli um, das ich über die Jahrzehnte hinweg einfach ignoriert hatte. Obst, Milch, Haferflockenmischung – so lautet seitdem mein eherner Frühstücksgrundsatz, ganz gemäß der erklärten Devise »Back to the roots«. Und in der Tat bereite ich mir seitdem täglich ein wunderbares Frühstück zu: einen Teller mit saisonalem Obst, kleingeschnitten, frische Ananas und eine Banane als jahreszeitlich unabhängiger fester Bestandteil an Obst, etwas fettarme Milch und Haferflocken dazugegeben. Damit komme ich locker in den frühen Nachmittag, anschließend noch etwas Obst, 1–2 Bananen, Orangen, Äpfel, Melone, Trauben, Beeren etc. oder was immer der Garten und die Jahreszeit gerade hergeben. War ich deswegen jetzt zum Asketen geworden? Wer einen wunderbar anzusehenden und meist noch wesentlich besser schmeckenden Obstteller mit Milch und Haferflocken am Morgen sieht, wird dieses Frühstück nur schwerlich mit Askese in Verbindung bringen können. Dennoch habe ich damit die tägliche Grundlage für meine Gewichtsreduzierung gelegt, und zwar sehr erfolgreich. Und zugleich überaus schmackhaft. Zwar wird in der Öffentlichkeit von mir mittlerweile das Bild des Asketen gezeichnet, aber wenn ich ehrlich bin, habe ich überhaupt nicht das Gefühl, daß ich irgend etwas vermissen oder gar der Askese huldigen würde, im Gegenteil. Ich esse nach wie vor sehr gerne und sehr gut, nur eben anders und weniger.

Wie aber dauerhaft und nachhaltig abnehmen? Denn der Hunger und der unmäßige Appetit würden sich ja nach dem ersten Schock wieder einstellen. Die Zeit der spontanen, durch die äußeren Umstände begünstigten Entscheidungen ging zu Ende: Ein Plan mußte nunmehr her! Erstens, sagte ich mir, mußt du dir ein Ziel definieren, das einerseits hart und fordernd, andererseits aber zugleich realistisch ist, d. h. es sollte gerade noch erreichbar sein. Ich wollte zurück zu mir selbst, mich wieder in und mit mir wohlfühlen, und das war für mich die Zeit, als ich zwischen 72–75 Kilogramm gewogen hatte. Mittlerweile war ich aber dreizehn Jahre älter geworden, also schlug ich einen Alterszuschlag drauf und setzte mir die 80 Kilogramm als zu erreichende Zielgröße, was ein Minus von ca. 30 Kilogramm bedeuten würde.

Zweitens mußte ich den Weg dorthin definieren. Ich sagte mir, daß eine Kerze dann am schnellsten abbrennt, wenn man sie an beiden Enden anzündet. Fasten allein schien mir eine nur schwer durchzuhaltende Perspektive, denn das Risiko, seinem Hunger zu erliegen, war absehbar viel zu groß.

Wenn ich allerdings wieder konsequent in den Sport einstiege und voll auf einen gesteigerten Kalorienverbrauch setzte, so würde ich nicht nur fasten müssen, sondern darüber hinaus würde der Körper auch seinen Nahrungsbedarf ändern, d. h. Lust auf eine gesündere Ernährung verspüren. Ergo mußte ich weniger essen und mehr verbrauchen, und also hieß meine Devise fortan: radikale Ernährungsumstellung und Sport, Sport, Sport.

Drittens mußte ich Prinzipien oder Grundsätze formulieren, die mir ein Durchhalten ermöglichen würden, wenn ich sie nur konsequent genug befolgte. Mit achtundvierzig Lebensjahren taugt man weiß Gott nicht mehr für den Leistungssport, d. h. man muß keine Wettkämpfe mehr gewinnen und sollte auch keine Rekordzeiten mehr anstreben. Zudem hatte ich einen ziemlich radikalen Kurswechsel in meinem Lebenswandel vor, der meinem Körper und meinem Kreislauf einiges abverlangen würde, und demnach mußte ich jede körperliche Überforderung meiden, denn sie würde ein Scheitern des ganzen Unternehmens bedeuten. Persönliche Höchst- und Bestleistungen verboten sich demnach von selbst, denn sie bedeuteten Belastungsspitzen für den Organismus, die in meinem Alter durchaus unkalkulierbare Risiken beinhalten konnten.

Entschlossenheit,
Durchhaltevermögen,
Realismus,
Geduld

waren also die *vier Tugenden*, auf denen fußend ich *drei Grundsätze* formulierte, die mir in den folgenden Monaten von großem Nutzen sein sollten:

Belüge dich niemals selbst!
Meide immer deine Leistungsspitze!
Gib niemals auf!

Etwas später, als ich bereits mit dem Laufen begonnen hatte, kam noch ein vierter Grundsatz hinzu, den ich allerdings ab dem Erreichen des 16. Kilometers wieder aufgegeben habe:

Eine einmal erreichte Entfernung
wird nicht mehr unterschritten!

Die nächsten praktischen Schritte ergaben sich dann fast von selbst: Aus früheren Tagen wußte ich, wie segensreich sich für die Brust-, Arm- und Bauchmuskulatur wenige Minuten täglichen Frühsports ausgewirkt hatten. Dies gilt allerdings nur dann, wenn man die Übungen täglich stur durchzieht. Zudem war für mich damals die regelmäßige

Arbeit mit Gewichten an der Hantelbank für den Muskelaufbau sehr wirksam gewesen. Also hieß eine weitere Entscheidung: Sportstudio. Und drittens wollte ich mich darüber hinaus noch täglich bewegen, um zusätzlich kräftig Kalorien zu verbrauchen: Radfahren, Schwimmen oder Laufen boten sich hier als Alternativen an. Zum Schwimmen habe ich kein Verhältnis, zudem ist dies technisch nicht immer möglich und ein Schwimmbecken für den täglichen Trainingsrhythmus meist auch nur mit hohem Aufwand zu erreichen. Also fiel Schwimmen als Alternative aus. Dann bot sich schon eher der Griff zum Rennrad an, zumal ich zum Radfahren aufgrund meiner aktiven Zeit im Radsport während einiger Jugendjahre ein sehr enges und vertrautes Verhältnis hatte. Das tägliche Training mit dem Rad ist aber technisch ebenfalls sehr aufwendig, weil man nicht immer und überall sein Fahrrad mit hinschleppen kann, weshalb es auf Reisen fast nicht möglich und zeitlich zudem sehr beanspruchend ist, da man zum Zweck der Gewichtsreduktion täglich schon einige Stunden auf dem Rad unterwegs sein muß. Aber bitte, Radfahren auf dem Hometrainer im Sportstudio war ja immerhin eine weitere Möglichkeit, aber auf Dauer wohl doch etwas monoton.

Blieb dann also zu guter Letzt noch das Laufen, hierbei handelte es sich gewiß um die technisch einfachste und zugleich »gottgewollte« Art der menschlichen Bewegung, denn, wie bereits gesagt, wir sind nun mal Lauftiere. »Fisch schwimmt, Vogel fliegt, Mensch läuft«, soll dereinst der unvergeßliche Emil Zatopek, die »Lokomotive von Prag« und Olympiasieger der frühen fünfziger Jahre über die Langstrecke und beim Marathon, die Sache auf den Punkt gebracht haben. »Das Laufen, ob schnell oder langsam, ob auf kurzen oder langen Strecken, ist eine der wenigen natürlichen, naturgebundenen Bewegungsarten, die dem einzelnen in einer völlig aus den Fugen geratenen Zivilisation noch bleibt ... Im Akt des Laufens regrediert der Läufer gleichsam in der menschlichen Evolutionsgeschichte, nimmt Verbindung auf zu Lebens- und Verhaltensweisen, die seinen Vorfahren über Jahrtausende ihrer Entwicklungsgeschichte vertraut waren und deren Einhaltung ihr Leben und Überleben sicherte.«[2]

Das Laufen hieß für meine Zwecke also eine minimale technische Ausstattung, denn alles Notwendige war leicht zu transportieren, das Training selbst fast überall ohne größere Umstände auszuüben und damit fast perfekt für meine Zwecke. Allein, ich hatte bis dato überhaupt kein Verhältnis zum Laufen, denn ich hatte das reine Laufen zeitlebens immer als gnadenlos öde und deshalb völlig abtörnend empfunden. Diese ganze Jogge-

2 Willi Köhler, S. 94

rei war mir eigentlich immer suspekt gewesen. Jetzt aber stellte sich die Lage in einem gänzlich anderen Lichte dar: Das Laufen erforderte den geringsten technischen Aufwand (Sportschuhe und Laufkleidung), war nahezu immer und überall möglich und versprach zudem einen hervorragenden Kalorienverbrauch. Aus all diesen Gründen entschied ich mich also für das Laufen, und zwar frühmorgens, vor der Arbeit. Und so begann mein neues Leben in Laufschuhen und in der Morgendämmerung.

IV

Fit und schlank durchs Leben

Die Morgennebel zogen vom Rhein herüber durchs Regierungsviertel in Bonn, als ich mich, Ende September oder Anfang Oktober 1996 mag das gewesen sein, zum ersten Mal joggenderweise auf den Weg machte. Zuvor hatte ich mich in einem Sportgeschäft mit allem Notwendigen für mein neues Leben als Jogger ausgestattet: Baumwollklamotten in Größe XL und Laufschuhe, allerdings ohne weitere Überlegungen über die Funktionalität oder gar orthopädische Paßgenauigkeit des Schuhwerks anzustellen. Bei den vor mir liegenden Entfernungen von lediglich mehreren hundert Metern sollte sich dies alles auch noch nicht als unbedingt nötig erweisen. Vor allem aber hatte ich mir ein Sweatshirt mit Kapuze besorgt, denn ich wollte auf keinen Fall erkannt werden, wenn ich mich Richtung Rhein schleppen würde. Es wimmelt ja von Journalisten im Bonner Regierungsviertel, wenn auch nicht unbedingt bereits um sieben Uhr morgens. Aber ich mußte dennoch mit berichterstattenden Frühaufstehern rechnen, und so zog ich mir die Kapuze tief über die Stirn, als ich mich dann schließlich frühmorgens auf den Weg machte. Mein Gewicht war trotz aller Anfangserfolge noch ganz erheblich, so daß durchaus die Gefahr bestand, daß die Bonner Erdbebenwarte mit ihren feinen Meßgeräten reagieren würde, wenn ich losstapfte. Die ersten Schritte waren qualvoll, denn natürlich schleppte ich noch viel zu viel Fett mit, und zudem war mein Körper alles andere als an das Laufen langer oder zumindest längerer Strecken gewöhnt. Ich ging die ganze Sache langsam an, aber bereits nach hundert Metern begann der Atem zu pfeifen, und ächzend schleppte ich mich um den Bundestag herum. Ich wohnte damals direkt am Hohen Haus, und so lief ich die Dahlmannstraße zum Rhein hinunter, vorbei am Bundeskanzleramt und an der nordrhein-westfälischen Landesvertretung – da ging es sogar etwas bergab! –, dann unten am Rhein und am Bundestag entlang und schließlich am Abgeordnetenhochhaus vorbei, dem sogenannten »Langen Eugen«, wieder den kleinen Anstieg hinauf, insgesamt etwa 500 stolze Meter. Der kleine Anstieg am »Langen Eugen« erwies sich damals als mein »Heart Break Hill«, und hier war es dann auch schon vorbei mit meiner läuferischen Herrlichkeit, denn der Anstieg von etwa hundert Metern war schlicht zuviel für mich. Und so hörte ich auf zu joggen und schritt den kleinen Anstieg gemessenen Schritts hinauf. Oh, Fischer, sagte ich mir, es ist einfach nur furchtbar! Aber ich biß die

Zähne zusammen, und am nächsten Tag ging es erneut auf die Piste.

Der Anfang war gemacht, und das war das Wichtigste überhaupt. Alles andere, wie Entfernung, Zeit, Haltung, etc. war zu diesem Zeitpunkt völlig unwichtig, es kam allein auf die Tatsache des *Anfangs* und des *Durchhaltens* an. Jetzt bloß nicht schwach werden, bloß nicht frustrieren lassen und aufgeben. Geduld ist jetzt angesagt, Geduld und nochmals Geduld – und Durchhalten. Bereits nach wenigen Tagen stellte ich dann erkennbare erste Fortschritte fest: Ich lief dieselbe Strecke

1997, die Anfangsmonate in Bonn am Rheinufer

zunehmend leichter, das Atmen während des Laufens verlor seine pfeifende und rasselnde Beschwerlichkeit, und schließlich wurde zum ersten Mal die Steigung am Bundestag joggend und nicht gemessen schreitend genommen. Vor allem stellte sich nach und nach ein völlig anderes Körpergefühl und auch eine andere mentale Haltung zum Tagesbeginn ein. Im Klartext: Ich fühlte mich bereits morgens nach dem Laufen und Duschen pudelwohl, ich war hellwach und sowohl geistig wie körperlich voll da, während meine Umgebung noch mühselig versuchte, die mentalen und physischen Aggregate anzuwerfen. Zudem traten die erwünschten »Nebeneffekte« meiner Laufkur ebenfalls sehr schnell ein: Das Bonner Kneipenleben verlor jeden Reiz, da ich lieber ins Bett wollte, denn am nächsten Morgen – unerbittlich klingelte der Wecker! – mußte ich ja sehr früh wieder raus zum täglichen Lauftraining. Und mit dem Verzicht auf das nächtliche Kneipenleben verlor ich noch weiter und schließlich endgültig die Lust an Bier und Wein, zumal ich jedes Glas Alkohol am nächsten Morgen beim Laufen negativ spüren und ergo mit Zins und Zinseszins zu bezahlen haben würde. Und so gewöhnte ich mich immer mehr an das gute Mineralwasser. Dieselbe dynamische Veränderung hin zum Positiven stellte sich auch beim Essen ein, denn ich bekam immer mehr Lust auf Obst, Fruchtsäfte, Salate, Gemüse und

Fisch. Fleisch, Wurst und Wein verloren an Attraktivität.

Schritt für Schritt ging ich dabei bis zum völligen Alkoholverzicht und vor allem zur vegetarischen Ernährung über, was angesichts meiner persönlichen Vergangenheit und der meiner Familie für mich selbst einer schlichten Sensation, ja Revolution gleichkam. Vegetarier? Darauf hatte ich bis dato immer nur mit einem lauten Brrrr reagiert. Das mochte ja gesund sein, war aber gewiß nichts für ein Schleckermäulchen wie mich. Zumal meine Erfahrungen mit der vegetarischen Küche vor allem ideologisch geprägt waren. Kulinarisch gesinnungsfestere Parteifreunde, als ich es war, hatten mich einige wenige Male zu dem im allseitigen Mißvergnügen endenden Besuch von säuerlich riechenden vegetarischen Restaurants veranlaßt, die das gerade Gegenteil von kulinarischem Genuß verhießen. Die ganze Atmosphäre in diesen Restaurants erinnerte mehr an ein Sanatorium oder ein Kurhaus gegen Magenleiden denn an eine Stätte des kulinarischen Vergnügens. Verdrießlich dreinblickende und ungesund aussehende Gesundheitsapostel kauten dort voller Selbstverachtung auf ihren Bratlingen, und ich bekam dort meine sämtlichen Vorurteile über Vegetarier und die vegetarische Küche überreichlich bestätigt. Entschlossener denn je wandte ich mich nach diesen vegetarischen Kulturschocks dann erneut meiner geliebten Schweinshaxe, Hammelkeule oder in Burgunder geschmorten Hochrippe vom Rind zu.

Die Fischers waren seit langem in männlicher Linie immer Metzger und Bauern gewesen, so auch mein Urgroßvater, mein Großvater, mein Vater und der älteste Bruder meines Vaters. Die erste Generation, die bei dieser herzhaft-blutigen Berufstradition unserer Familie von der Fahne ging, war meine Wenigkeit, aber Fleisch, Wurst und Speck gehörten auch bei mir seit frühester Kindheit zu den Selbstverständlichkeiten meiner Ernährung, was angesichts dieses familiären Hintergrundes kaum verwundern dürfte. Und ausgerechnet jetzt, mit knapp 50 Jahren, verlor ich zum ersten Mal in meinem ganzen bisherigen Leben einfach die Lust auf Fleisch! Irgendwie begann ich mir damals selbst für einen kurzen Augenblick unheimlich zu werden, denn daß ich noch einmal zu einem Vegetarier würde, das hätte ich mir selbst in meinen schlimmsten Alpträumen niemals vorzustellen gewagt. Aber bitte, jetzt fand ich diese umstürzende Entwicklung überhaupt nicht mehr absonderlich, sondern eher selbstverständlich. Es gab für diesen Schritt zur vegetarischen Ernährung auch keinerlei ideologische Gründe, sondern ich hatte einfach keinen Appetit mehr auf Metzgerei und Metzelei. Es war einfach aus und vorbei.

Und ganz ähnlich erging es mir damals mit dem Wein. Was habe ich ihn geliebt, den Rotwein, und in der Tat nimmt man mit der Öffnung jeder exzellenten Flasche an dem großartigen Ergebnis einer uralten Kultur teil, das einen körperlich wie spirituell begeistern und erheben kann. Wohlgemerkt, ich spreche hier nicht vom Saufen, sondern vom Trinken, und das sind zwei völlig unterschiedliche Dinge, so unterschiedlich wie Lärm und Musik. Ich hatte nach dem sommerlichen Desaster in der Toskana nicht sofort den Alkoholkonsum eingestellt, aber unter dem Eindruck des anhaltenden Wandels meines gesamten Lebensstils und meiner neuen läuferischen Erfahrung ließ ich doch mehr und mehr das Glas Wein unberührt stehen und begnügte mich mit Mineralwasser. Auch hier war es kein intellektueller oder gar ideologischer Antrieb oder gar Zwang, sondern ich wollte eben nicht mehr. Die Dinge eskalierten bis zu jenem denkwürdigen Tag, als ich zu Beginn des Monats Dezember 1996 zu einer Weinprobe eingeladen wurde, bei welcher ausschließlich der göttliche »Petrus« gereicht wurde, ein Rotwein aus dem lauschigen Winzerörtchen Pomerol bei Bordeaux, der Weinkenner in den siebten Himmel entführt und zugleich ihr Bankkonto ruiniert. Ich sagte dieses für Weinkenner fast nur noch himmlisch zu nennende Ereignis kurzfristig ab, weil ich nach langen inneren Dialogen mit mir selbst feststellte, daß mir dieses Paradies nichts mehr bedeutete. Der Grund war ebenso schlicht wie überzeugend: Ich wollte einfach nicht mehr. Und seitdem wußte ich, daß auch das Kapitel Wein bis auf weiteres für mich zu Ende war.

Ich hatte mich gemäß meines Plans auch in einem Sportstudio angemeldet, und so begann mein grundlegend veränderter Tagesablauf langsam feste Konturen anzunehmen. Morgens früh aufstehen, Liegestützen und Sit-Ups, anschließend Laufen, dann Frühstück mit Obst, zuerst Corn-flakes und später Müsli, Kaffee, tagsüber Obst, am späten Nachmittag oder abends dann ins Sportstudio für eine Stunde, Gewichtetraining für Oberarm-, Brust-, Rücken-, Bauch- und Beinmuskulatur, anschließend Duschen, Abendessen mit viel Gemüse, Kohlehydraten, wenig Fett und selten etwas Fisch – nicht satt essen! –, und dann war ich müde, fühlte mich zugleich erschöpft und doch auch wiederum pudelwohl und wollte schlicht und einfach nur noch ins Bett. Am wichtigsten für meine persönliche Motivation erwiesen sich damals die Reaktionen des persönlichen Umfeldes auf meine sichtbare Veränderung und dann vor allem das morgendliche Erfolgserlebnis auf der Waage, denn bereits nach wenigen Wochen zeigte mir die ob ihrer Unbestechlichkeit in meinem vorherigen Leben ach so gehaßte Waage, daß ich im Durchschnitt zwischen 700–1100 Gramm

Körpergewicht in der Woche verlor. Das konnte sich im wahrsten Sinne des Wortes sehen lassen.

Freilich nagte der Hunger ganz gewaltig in mir, denn satt essen war nicht mehr, und so überkam mich immer wieder die Sehnsucht nach den Futterorgien der Vergangenheit, und es lockte durchaus auch ein wunderbares Glas Rotwein, aber mit jeder weiteren Woche verlor ich zunehmend die Lust auf solche Rückfälle, denn die Folgen am nächsten Morgen waren eben sehr hart. Der Wecker klingelte, und es begann dann in der Frühe unerbittlich immer dieselbe Prozedur. Betrüge dich niemals selbst! So lautete meine erste Devise, und daran hielt ich mich ohne Ausnahme. Zudem hatte ich die alte Trainerweisheit aus längst verflossenen Tagen im Ohr, daß gute Trainingseinheiten weh tun müssen, und ergo biß ich die Zähne zusammen und kämpfte mich jeden Tag erneut durchs Morgengrauen. Bei diesen frühmorgendlichen Exerzitien kannte ich kein Erbarmen mit mir selbst, denn hier ging es gewissermaßen um den Kern meiner inneren Machtfrage, die ich mit mir selbst auszutragen hatte. Würde ich hier nachlässig werden, würde ich hier einknicken und mir sagen, heute habe ich keine Lust, es ist zu kalt, zu ungemütlich oder ich bin zu müde, so würde ich mein Programm gewiß nicht durchhalten. Die Ausreden überwiegen in der Regel immer die guten Gründe, es sei denn man hält sich stur an einen Rhythmus, der Ausnahmen nicht zuläßt. Und so stand ich im Morgengrauen auf und lief los, egal wie sich die Witterung auch immer darstellte, denn ich wußte, daß allein das Finden meines Rhythmus und die Gewöhnung an das tägliche Ritual mir über den inneren Schweinehund hinweghelfen würden. Nur einmal, bei einem herbstlichen Orkan, habe ich das Laufen unterlassen, weil es an diesem Tag draußen einfach zu gefährlich war, ansonsten aber ging und geht es sommers wie winters und bei jedem Wetter auf die Piste. Wer läuft, schwitzt und wird ergo naß. Insofern kommt es auf den Regen nicht an. Warm wird einem zudem, so daß man sich im Winter lediglich ordentlich kleiden muß, und der Sommer bietet sowohl morgens als auch abends Tageszeiten, die zum Laufen richtiggehend einladen. Merke daher: Das Wetter taugt beim Laufen fast niemals zur Ausrede!

Nichts ist so erfolgreich wie der Erfolg, und das gilt vor allem für den Laufanfänger, denn er kann seine Erfolge und weiteren Fortschritte direkt in Schritten und Zeiten abmessen. Mit jeden weiteren 100 Gramm Gewichtsverlust, mit jeder zusätzlichen Steigerung beim Konditionsaufbau wurde die gelaufene Strecke länger und die Schritte dabei immer leichter. Vorbei die Zeit des rasselnden Atems, der weichen Knie an der kleinen Steigung am »Langen Eugen«, denn die Umrundung des

Bundestags hatte ich bereits hinter mir gelassen. Ich lief jetzt immer weiter den Rhein aufwärts, einen Baum, ein Gebüsch oder die nächste Kilometermarke des Flusses als neues Ziel ansteuernd. Und von weitem hatte ich sie bereits seit längerem täglich im Auge: die Bonner Südbrücke, auch wenn mir die Entfernung damals noch sehr gewagt erschien. Sie war das erste große Ziel, das ich mir läuferisch setzte, und das waren, Hin- und Rückweg zusammengerechnet, immerhin schon ca. 3 km. Weiß Gott, für meine damaligen Verhältnisse war dies eine lange Strecke. Und Ende November 1996 war es dann soweit, ich erreichte zum ersten Mal die Südbrücke in einer Zeit von um die 25 Minuten. Was war ich stolz auf mich!

Ein so starker Gewichtsverlust, wie ich ihn mir damals zumutete, bedeutete aber sowohl körperlich als auch mental eine sehr große Anstrengung, die nun keineswegs überwiegend Glücksgefühle hervorrief, sondern die meiste Zeit vielmehr zum genauen Gegenteil führte. Meine Laune wurde zunehmend und anhaltend mies, aggressiv, unduldsam, mein Aussehen war alles andere als von Optimismus geprägt, sondern ich sah eher grau, eingefallen und krank aus. Kein Wunder auch, denn da war immer dieses anhaltende, nagende Hungergefühl, an das ich mich zu gewöhnen hatte und das ganz erheblich zu meiner schlechten und aggressiven Laune beitrug. Vorbei die Zeiten der gemütlichen Wohlbeleibtheit, des umgänglichen Dicken, denn die mir selbst verordnete Askese forderte ihren harten psychischen Tribut. Im Klartext gesprochen war ich körperlich zwar in einer monatlich immer besser werdenden Verfassung und Form, mental ging es mir aber gar nicht gut, was mich angesichts der selbstauferlegten Herausforderung aber weder verwunderte noch groß beunruhigte. Mir war von Anfang an klar gewesen, daß die Zeit des körperlichen Umbaus für mich weder leicht noch angenehm verlaufen würde, und so bat ich mich selbst und meine Umgebung einfach um Verständnis und Zeit. Die absehbare Entwicklung hin zum Kotzbrokken im persönlichen Umgang beantwortete ich mit einem weiteren Rückzug auf mich selbst. Dieser Rückzug verstärkte wiederum die asketische Lebensgestaltung, denn ich konzentrierte mich in meinem ganzen Tagesablauf immer stärker darauf, und das war gut so, denn es ging eben bei diesem ganzen Unterfangen vor allem um mich selbst ...

Und noch eine Veränderung stellte sich im November 1996 ein. Ich war damals einige wenige Tage in das Haus eines Freundes in die Toskana zurückgekehrt, und dort war es ebenfalls ziemlich einsam. Irgendwann kramte ich nach CDs, um Musik zu hören, und ich fand nur klassische Musik – Requiems, Streich- und Klavierkonzerte, Kantaten, etc. Zu klassischer Musik hatte ich bis dato ein ähnlich leidenschaftliches Verhältnis gehabt wie zum Laufen, nämlich gar keines. Zwar hatte ich es einmal als Schüler mit dem Lernen des Flügelhornblasens im dörflichen Musikverein versucht, war aber jämmerlich an dem Lärm, den diese Übungen notgedrungenermaßen verursachten, an den beengten Lebensverhältnissen in meiner Familie und an der Nachtschicht eines Nachbarn gescheitert, der unter wüsten Beschimpfungen und unter Androhung von Prügeln rabiat gegen meine musikalischen Gehversuche als Hornist intervenierte. So endete meine aktive Musikantenlaufbahn bereits in ihren allerersten Anfängen. Meine Versuche mit der Oper waren noch weniger erfolgsgekrönt. Während meiner Fotografenlehre Mitte der sechziger Jahre hatte ich dereinst Karten für Verdis Aida im Großen Haus in Stuttgart geschenkt bekommen. Das Musikspiel empfand ich als quälend langweilig, zudem war ich unausgeschlafen, und so dämmerte ich dahin, wachte gerade zum blutigen Finale wieder auf und zog aus diesem müden Erlebnis den fatalen Schluß, daß die Oper, wie überhaupt alle ernste Musik, nichts oder nur wenig für mich war. Und nun hörte ich an jenem verregneten Herbsttag ein Quartett von Mozart und war plötzlich hin und weg. Frei nach Wilhelm Busch ging es mir wie Hans Huckebein, dem Raben – »es wurd ihm so verwunderlich, so leicht und so absunderlich« –, freilich ohne daß ich, wie dieser mopsfidele Rabe, zuvor zu tief ins Glas geschaut hätte. Es war allein die Musik, die mich unversehens in ihren Bann schlug, und so ist es bis heute geblieben. Das Laufen und die Oper, Mozart vor allem, sind seit jenem elegischen November in den Hügeln der toskanischen Crete für mich zu zwei völlig neuen Erfahrungen geworden und folglich untrennbar miteinander verbunden. Im übrigen war es auch damals in genau diesen Hügeln südlich von Siena gewesen, wo ich mich zum ersten Mal in steilerem Gelände als Läufer versuchen sollte. Freilich blieben diese ersten Versuche äußerst zaghaft, denn an die wirklichen Steigungen, die es dort reichlich gibt, traute ich mich noch nicht heran.

Die meisten Menschen leben ihren Alltag nach einem bestimmten, ihnen selbst kaum bewußten Programm, das in der Regel aus einer Komposition besteht, die sich aus den Eigenschaften der jeweiligen individuellen Persönlichkeit, den Zufällen der Biographie und den gegebenen Umständen zusammensetzt. Dieses »Programm« ist also meist nicht das Ergebnis einer bewußten Entscheidung, sondern vieler Zufälligkeiten der individuellen und kollektiven Lebensumstände. Wir folgen ihm tagaus tagein in all unseren Handlungen. Es kann sich in Einzelheiten verändern, es kann sich sogar als Ganzes dynamisch verändern, etwa aufgrund veränderter Lebensumstände, aber letztendlich entsteht aus unseren individuellen Anlagen und Neigungen und aus all den zahllosen Gelegenheiten, Wünschen und Zwängen eines Menschen ein Programm, ohne daß er dies bewußt wahrnimmt. Es bedarf meist einer sehr tiefen persönlichen Krise (z. B. Trennung, Krankheit, Verlust) oder einer aus triftigen und unabweisbaren (etwa wissenschaftlichen) Gründen bewußt getroffenen Entscheidung, um dieses »automatische« Alltagsprogramm radikal zu verändern oder gar bewußt in Frage zu stellen und umzustürzen.

Freilich gibt es noch eine dritte Möglichkeit, nämlich durch erfolgreiche Vorbilder zu diesem Schritt veranlaßt zu werden. Dies setzt jedoch die innere Bereitschaft dazu voraus. Mittlerweile habe ich in meinem Freundeskreis einige getroffen, die genau aus diesem Aspekt heraus – »der hat es geschafft, dann kann ich das auch« – eine erfolgreiche Selbstveränderung durch Gewichtsreduktion und Laufen erreicht haben. Es geht also auch anders, wie die Erfahrung lehrt. Wenn ich hier also über Übergewichtigkeit und Abnehmen rede, dann müssen wir uns genau diesem persönlichen Programm und seiner bewußten Veränderung, einer regelrechten Umprogrammierung zuwenden. Die *bewußte Umprogrammierung* ist dabei der alles entscheidende Unterschied, denn die persönliche Krise allein führt nicht mit Notwendigkeit zu diesem Ergebnis. Hierzu bedarf es vielmehr einer weiterreichenden, einer bewußten und gewollten Entscheidung.

Alle die in diesem Buch von mir skizzierten persönlichen Veränderungen weisen nämlich hin auf den Kern des Problems und seine Lösung – die *tiefgreifende Änderung des persönlichen Programms*. In Wirklichkeit – und das begriff ich bewußt erst sehr viel später – hatte ich mich in all den Wochen und Monaten seit jener Zäsur in meinem Leben im August 1996 daran gemacht, mich selbst und damit meinen Alltag völlig umzuprogrammieren, indem ich mir spontan und mehr der Not als einem Plan gehorchend ein völlig anderes und gänzlich neues persönliches Programm zu schreiben begann. Und genau darin bestand und besteht für mich das eigentliche Geheimnis meines Erfolges. Bei all den früheren Versuchen abzunehmen, mit all den Diäten und Fastenkuren und Verzichtsversuchen mußte ich ganz offensichtlich scheitern, weil ich schlicht in meinem alten, persönlichen Programm und dessen Bezugssystem verblieben war. Ich quälte mir Jahr für Jahr ein Kurieren an den Symptomen ab, während ich die Ursachen der Malaise nicht anrührte. Exakt deswegen waren eben all die Fastenkuren eine Qual, da ich mit meinem Programm unverändert im System »Futtern und Völlen« blieb und nur dessen Auswüchse begrenzen wollte. Das mußte schiefgehen und ging auch gründlich schief. Ich hatte ganz offensichtlich nicht den Mut und auch nicht die Antriebskraft gehabt, das tiefer liegende »Programm« für mein Übergewicht zu ändern, denn das hätte meine ganze Lebenshaltung, meinen ach so geliebten Alltag zwischen Berufsstreß einerseits und Lammkeule und Burgunder andererseits in Frage gestellt. Freilich wurden mir all diese Zusammenhänge, wie bereits erwähnt, erst einige Zeit später und nach vielen Diskussionen selbst so richtig klar. Erst da begriff ich, was ich eigentlich mit mir anzustellen gedachte.

Die körperlichen Veränderungen an mir waren mit den Händen zu greifen, und ich mußte nur in den Spiegel schauen, um anhand des ganzen Ausmaßes der äußeren Veränderungen Rückschlüsse auf die inneren Umbrüche ziehen zu können. Laufen, Essen, Musik, ein völlig anderer Alltag, grundsätzlich andere Prioritäten – ich konnte mir längere Zeit vieles von diesen Veränderungen nicht recht erklären, und manches kam mir deshalb recht merkwürdig vor, um es ganz milde auszudrücken. Rückt man nun all die feststellbaren Veränderungen der Persönlichkeit und ihrer Gewohnheiten, die bis dato selbstverständlich und ganz offensichtlich unverrückbar gewesen waren, in diesen Interpretationsrahmen der Umprogrammierung, dann machen sie plötzlich Sinn und sind alles andere als zufällig. Die Essensgewohnheiten, der geliebte Rotwein, ein bestimmter Lebenswandel, der Musikgeschmack – all dies waren wesentliche Ausdrucksformen der Persönlichkeit und ihres alltäglichen Lebensstils oder auch Programms, die jetzt einer tiefgreifenden Veränderung unterzogen wurden. Und mit der dauerhaften Veränderung des Programms mußten sich deshalb auch notwendigerweise dessen alltägliche Ausdrucksformen im gesamten Lebensstil verändern. Im übrigen spricht die Anschaulichkeit des Ergebnisses für sich: Der Abbau von bis zu 35 Kilo Übergewicht in etwas mehr als einem Jahr legt zumindest eine gewisse Schlüssigkeit dieser Methode nahe.

Körperliches Übergewicht ist, sofern es nicht auf krankhafte Bedingungen zurückgeführt werden muß, allzuoft das sicht- und wiegbare Ergebnis von Suchtverhalten. Die verschiedensten Arten von Sucht gehören als Möglichkeit konstitutiv zum Menschen und seiner Triebstruktur, denn Suchtverhalten ist meist nichts anderes als die Wirkung von mehr oder weniger außer Kontrolle geratener elementarer Überlebenstriebe des Menschen. Nur die Triebstruktur des Menschen hat eine solch elementare Kraft über das Ich, um es temporär oder gar dauerhaft außer Kraft zu setzen, so daß es zu Suchtverhalten kommt. Wenn dieses Ich also zu schwach ist oder einer schweren Störung seiner inneren Harmonie im Verhältnis zu

80

sich selbst und seiner Umgebung ausgesetzt wird, kann ein Teil der Triebstruktur einer Persönlichkeit sich verselbständigen und das Ich völlig seinen Zwängen unterwerfen, so daß der Tatbestand der Abhängigkeit gegeben ist. Zumindest beim Essen und Trinken läßt sich diese These unschwer nachvollziehen, aber sie gilt wohl auch ganz allgemein für menschliches Suchtverhalten. Die Kontrolle unseres elementaren Triebverhaltens durch das Ich findet nun nicht im Körper, sondern im Kopf statt, d. h. der Verlust der Kontrolle und damit die Sucht sind zuerst und vor allem ein psychisches, kein körperliches Problem, wohl aber wird der Körper durch Suchtverhalten allzuoft in schwerste Mitleidenschaft gezogen.

Der Verlust rational steuernder Kontrollmechanismen kann ebenso auf veränderte Bedingungen in der Lebenswelt wie auch auf eine schwere Störung der inneren Harmonie einer Persönlichkeit oder gar auf beides zurückgeführt werden, die Wirkung bleibt gleichwohl immer dieselbe. Der betroffene Mensch wird einem inneren Handlungszwang unterworfen, der ihn zu einem Verhalten treibt, mit dem er sich selbst beschädigt oder im schlimmsten Fall sogar völlig zu zerstören droht. Das verlorene innere Gleichgewicht, das die Sucht hervorruft, läßt sich wiedergewinnen, indem man entweder die Persönlichkeit in ihren beschädigten Tiefenschichten therapeutisch heilt oder aber, eine Ebene darüber, bestehende Verhaltensdispositionen anders lenkt, d. h. hin zu einem mit dem eigenen Ich konform gehenden Verhalten umkonditioniert.

Es macht, bei im wesentlichen gleichem Trieb- oder sogar Suchtverhalten, eben einen gewaltigen Unterschied, ob ich mir mit derselben Leidenschaft mehrmals täglich die Wampe bis zum Anschlag fülle oder ob ich dieselbe überschießende Triebenergie etwa in Laufen und körperliche Fitneß umsetze. Wichtig dabei ist, daß zwischen einem körperschädigenden Suchtverhalten und einer körperkonformen Umsetzung derselben psychischen Energien auch ein qualitativer Unterschied besteht. Laufen ist durch unsere Biologie bestimmt und eben keine Sucht! Das eine endet in Selbstbeschädigung oder gar Selbstzerstörung, das andere ist körperkonform, gesund und wirkt zudem überaus positiv auf das eigene Selbstwertgefühl. Es war nun genau diese letztere Alternative, die ich spontan ergriffen und dann Schritt für Schritt in die Wirklichkeit umgesetzt habe.

Erst durch die zielgerichtete Veränderung meines inneren Lebensrhythmus gelang mir also, woran ich in all den Jahren zuvor immer wieder jämmerlich gescheitert war, nämlich radikal und dauerhaft abzunehmen. Nur diese radikale Lebensänderung war die Voraussetzung für eine erfolgreiche und anhaltende Gewichtsreduzierung. Oder, um es in die Begriffe der digitalen Welt zu übersetzen: das wirkliche Geheimnis meines Erfolges war das Auswechseln und völlige Neuschreiben meiner persönlichen Programmdiskette. Ohne diese umfassende und zielgerichtete Veränderung meines gesamten Lebensstils, meines gesamten Tagesablaufs, meiner Ernährung, meiner Vorlieben und Gewohnheiten wäre ich, wie all die Jahre zuvor, bei meinen zahllosen Versuchen abzunehmen wohl genauso gescheitert wie immer. Mit der Neuprogrammierung wurden mir Dinge möglich, die ich bis dato als schlicht unmöglich angesehen hatte. Plötzlich war fast täglich Zeit für mich selbst vorhanden, und die Verpflichtungen durch die Arbeit ließen sich sehr wohl mit meinem neuen Lebensrhythmus vereinbaren, ohne daß die Arbeit und meine Effizienz darunter zu leiden hatten. Das genaue Gegenteil war vielmehr der Fall. Tatsächlich fand ich fast immer Zeit zum Laufen und mich um mich selbst zu kümmern, weil ich mir eben ganz einfach andere Prioritäten, auch andere Zeitprioritäten, durch mein neues Programm gesetzt hatte.

All die bewährten Ausflüchte erwiesen sich fortan also als schlicht gegenstandslos und hinfällig, und auch der berüchtigte Jojo-Effekt, zu dem es bei den vorangegangenen und prompt gescheiterten Versuchen zur Gewichtsreduzierung gekommen war, verlor all seinen Schrecken, sein Mechanismus war durch das neue Programm außer Kraft gesetzt worden. Dieser ganze frustrierende Kreislauf zwischen Verzicht und Völlerei war dauerhaft durchbrochen worden, ich war jetzt nicht mehr in meinem alten System gefangen, sondern hatte unter dem Druck einer persönlichen Katastrophe einen eigentlich schon längst fälligen Systemwechsel vollzogen, und dessen positive Folgen machten sich jetzt mehr und mehr physisch und mental bemerkbar. Als Katalysator dieser persönlichen Transformation und – wie könnte es bei einem »Extremisten« wie mir auch anders sein – sehr bald auch als neue Leidenschaft sollte sich das Laufen erweisen. Durch die Faszination des Langlaufs – »dem Gleichmaß der Schritte entspricht ein Gleichmaß des Seelenzustandes«[3] – gelang mir eine dauerhafte positive Umkonditionierung von wesentlichen Persönlichkeitsmerkmalen, denn mit derselben Radikalität, mit der ich vorher gefuttert und gebechert hatte, nahm ich nunmehr die Kilometer unter die Turnschuhe. Alan Sillitoes »Einsamkeit des Langstreckenläufers« sollte sich für mich als die eigentliche Therapie erweisen, und seitdem laufe ich, und zwar mit nach wie vor wachsendem Genuß. Jawohl, ich meine exakt, was ich schreibe: Genuß!

3 Willi Köhler, S. 95

V

Und läuft und läuft und läuft ...

Es ist heute wieder einmal einer jener Tage gewesen, bei denen von acht Uhr in der Frühe bis spät in die Nacht hinein ein Termin den anderen jagte – Staatsgäste, Ausschußsitzungen, Kabinett, Rücksprachen im Amt, Interviews und am Ende noch ein Treffen beim Bundeskanzler im kleinen Kreis. Gegen 22.30 ist der Tag zu Ende, die anderen bleiben noch bei einem Glas Rotwein sitzen, während ich jetzt unbedingt raus muß, raus auf die fast mitternächtlichen Straßen Bonns, um noch eine Stunde zu laufen. Auf die Frage, wo ich denn um diese Uhrzeit hin müsse, antworte ich wahrheitsgemäß, daß ich jetzt zu laufen gedächte, und ich sehe nach dieser Antwort meinen Gegenübern an, daß sie mich für völlig bekloppt oder zumindest für gefährlich fanatisch halten. Ja richtig, denke ich mir, denn welcher vernünftige Mensch geht denn um diese Uhrzeit und nach einem solchen Arbeitstag noch laufen? Aber nach einem solchen Arbeitstag will ich noch etwas abspannen und genießen, und das geschieht jetzt eben nicht mehr bei einem Glas Rotwein und noch einem Glas und noch einem weiteren, sondern jetzt sind es 10 Kilometer am nächtlichen Rheinufer zwischen Bonn und Bad Godesberg.

Ich habe seit längerer Zeit viel zu wenig Schlaf, denn der Tag hat für den deutschen Außenminister einfach nicht genügend Stunden, ich fühle mich heute bereits seit Stunden erschöpft, den Kopf ausgelaugt, körperlich schlapp und wie durch eine trübe Pfütze gezogen, müde und zerschlagen. Was ich jetzt brauche, ist Erholung, und zwar für den ganzen Menschen, für Körper und Geist. Früher wäre ich in die Kneipe gegangen oder einfach nur ins Bett, heute weiß ich, daß ich diese Erholung selbst noch kurz vor Mitternacht auf der Straße finden werde. Wenn ich nach ca. 1 Stunde und 10 Kilometern Laufen schweißnaß und quietschfidel in meine Wohnung zurückkehre, werde ich mich wie neugeboren fühlen, denn der ganze Frust, die Müdigkeit und Schlappheit werden von mir abgefallen sein. Und ganz nebenbei habe ich vielleicht dann auch noch das eine oder andere politische Problem in meinem Kopf gelöst oder mir ist ein neuer Gedanke gekommen, denn beim Laufen passieren im Kopf bisweilen die erstaunlichsten Dinge.

Man muß diese Erfahrung wohl selbst gemacht haben – daß man sich durch einen einstündigen Lauf nicht kaputtmacht, sondern, ganz im Gegenteil, hervorragend erholen kann –, bevor man solche Geschichten tatsächlich glaubt. Mir ist es früher zumindest so gegangen, bis ich dieses Erlebnis selbst hatte. Laufen heißt Anstrengung, aber exakt diese Anstrengung des gesamten Körpers – über eine längere Zeit hinweg in einem gleichbleibenden Rhythmus – ist es (die entsprechende Kondition durch regelmäßiges Training selbstverständlich vorausgesetzt), die den gesamten Organismus in Bewegung versetzt, die Lungen heftig pumpen läßt, den Körper bis in die feinsten Kapillargefäße hinein mit Sauerstoff versorgt und dadurch aktiviert und dabei auch noch den Kopf in eine meditative Ruhe versetzt, die kreative Assoziationsketten von Ideen und Gedanken fast wie von selbst ablaufen läßt.

Wie gesagt, man muß, um diese Wirkung nachvollziehen zu können, die Sache selbst einmal gemacht und erlebt haben, bevor man sie glaubt, dann wird man sie aber nicht mehr vermissen wollen. Wird man deshalb auch gleich süchtig, süchtig aufs Laufen? Und hätte ich demnach nur ein Suchtverhalten gegen ein anderes ausgewechselt? Es wird zudem viel vom sogenannten »Endorphin-Kick« gemunkelt, und es mag ja sein, daß bei einer anhaltenden Dauerbelastung körpereigene Glückshormone oder Opiate freigesetzt werden, die unser Körper zur besseren Erträglichkeit einer solchen Ausdauerbelastung bereithält, aber meine persönliche Erfahrung läßt mich diese ganze Angelegenheit mit den Endorphinen, dem »runner's high« und all den anderen Nettigkeiten als maßlos überschätzt begreifen. Beim Langlauf, immer einen ausreichenden Trainingsstand vorausgesetzt, fühle ich mich nach einiger Zeit in der Tat meistens sehr gut, und dies hält auch noch Stunden danach an. Dabei spielen aber nach meiner Beobachtung mehrere physiologische und psychologische Faktoren eine Rolle: die »Sauerstoffdusche« für den Organismus, die Aktivierung der gesamten Muskulatur und des Hormonhaushalts, mag sein auch die Ausschüttung körpereigener Glückshormone und schließlich, last but not least, der meditative Aspekt, der zu einer unglaublichen inneren Entspannung führen kann.

Insofern ist es meines Erachtens falsch, das Laufen selbst in seiner extensiven Form als Suchtverhalten zu bezeichnen, denn letztendlich bleibt es eine tägliche Entscheidung: Laufe ich heute oder laufe ich nicht. Es gibt in meiner Erfahrung keinen mit dem Freßzwang vergleichbaren Laufzwang, die tägliche Entscheidung zu treffen, verlangt bisweilen eine ziemliche Überwindung. Gewiß werde ich unruhig, wenn ich einmal zwei Tage nicht zum Laufen gekommen bin. Ich fange an, mich unwohl zu fühlen, weil ich die körperliche Belastung und die meditative Entspannung vermisse, aber Suchtverhalten, ist wie gesagt etwas völlig anderes.

Wie auch immer, ursprünglich hatte ich dem Laufen neben der Arbeit an den Gewichten im Sportstudio nur eine Nebenrolle in meinem Umbauprogramm beigemessen, innerhalb eines Vierteljahres wurde es jedoch dann von einer Nebensache zur eigentlichen Hauptsache, was so eigentlich nicht geplant war. Im Laufe des November hatte ich die Südbrücke in Bonn erreicht und tastete mich nun langsam voran. Das Laufen selbst fiel mir konditionell weiterhin schwer, auch wenn es mit der Mühsal der allerersten Anfänge mitnichten zu vergleichen war. Die Kraftanstrengung stand noch im Vordergrund der ganzen Übung, und Durchhalten war alles. Zudem hatte ich damals noch regelrecht Angst vor der wachsenden Entfernung meiner Zielpunkte, denn ich traute mir den Rückweg eigentlich immer noch nicht als eine Selbstverständlichkeit zu. Dennoch ging es nach und nach immer weiter weg, die Südbrücke blieb weiter hinter mir, und schließlich setzte ich mir den Ortsrand von Plittersdorf, einem Stadtteil von Bad Godesberg, rheinaufwärts von Bonn gelegen, zum neuen Ziel. Ostern 1997 wollte ich diese neue, für meine damaligen Verhältnisse gewaltig erscheinende Herausforderung bewältigt haben.

Aber auch hier sollte sich die Politik als mein eigentliches Schicksal erweisen. Ich hatte bei meinen kühnen sportlichen Planungen nicht mit der Steuerreform und dem damaligen Bundesfinanzminister Theo Waigel gerechnet. Die verehrte Leserschaft wird sich jetzt fragen, was zum Teufel eigentlich der Bundesfinanzminister und seine Steuerreform mit meinen läuferischen Fortschritten zu tun hatten? Ganz einfach: Es war ein trüber Tag im späten Januar des Jahres 1997 gewesen, als die damalige konservativ-liberale Koalition ihre längst angekündigte Steuerreform auf dem Petersberg bei Bonn beschloß. Auf der anschließenden Pressekonferenz des Bundesfinanzministers schien der Koalition das Ei des Kolumbus in den Schoß gefallen zu sein, denn alle zuvor scheinbar unlösbaren Widersprüche, an denen unsere Fachleute seit Monaten herumgeknobelt hatten – sinkende Steuereinnahmen, wachsende Arbeitslosigkeit, Kosten der Einheit, allseits klaffende Haushaltslöcher und der durch die kommende Einführung des Euro ausgelöste Sparzwang in den öffentlichen Haushalten –, schienen urplötzlich wie von Zauberhand gelöst zu sein, und selbst unsere Fachleute in der Fraktion waren für zwei lange Augenblicke tief beeindruckt. Ich kochte innerlich vor Wut, denn Wunder waren selten auf dieser Welt, und schon gar nicht glaubte ich an diese mirakulöse Steuervermehrung durch Steuersenkung. Ich hielt diese ganze Rechnung von Anfang an für einen schlichten Schwindel, denn angesichts der dramatischen Haushaltslöcher und des durch die Kriterien für den Euro erzwungenen Verzichts auf eine wesentliche Erhöhung der Nettoneuverschuldung konnte ich mir beim besten Willen nicht erklären, wie der Finanzminister seine Steuersenkungen eigentlich finanzieren wollte, ohne daß der Staatshaushalt chronisch unterfinanziert und damit völlig aus den Fugen geraten würde. Oder er würde zu anderer Zeit eben die Mehrwertsteuer erhöhen müssen.

Und in der Tat, am Abend, nach stundenlangen internen Debatten, war klar, daß diese Steuerreform letztendlich durch Steuererhöhungen finanziert werden mußte, über die allerdings die stolzen Väter der Reform zur Stunde noch vornehm schwiegen. Als ich mich am nächsten Morgen wieder Richtung Rheinufer aufmachte, tobte ich ob des Schwindels innerlich immer noch vor mich hin, formulierte bereits eine Rede wider den Steuerbetrug im Kopf, hatte dabei mir nichts dir nichts die Südbrücke hinter mich gebracht, ohne es recht zu bemerken, und lief immer weiter. Dann hatte ich das Wasserwerk in den Rheinauen erreicht, lief auch daran vorbei und tobte immer noch stumm vor mich hin, und schließlich war ich an der Tennishalle angekommen, der Ortsrand von Plittersdorf war erreicht – etwa 3,5

Kilometer –, und ich bekam einen gehörigen Schreck! Schaffe ich das jetzt auch wieder zurück? Und gemäß einer meiner ehernen Grundsätze mußte ich jetzt fortan jeden Tag diese Strecke zurücklegen!? Nebbich, wie die kommenden Tage zeigen sollten. Der Rückweg erwies sich als machbar, und der Stolz auf meine läuferische Leistung kannte keine Grenzen, denn Plittersdorf war zwei Monate vor der prognostizierten Zeit erreicht worden. Theo sei Dank! Und fortan stand also täg-

Anfang 1997

lich die 7-Kilometer-Marke zur Bewältigung an, die ich dann nach etwa einer Woche vorsichtig weiter auszubauen begann.

Im Februar 1997 (Februar!) hatte ich an der Fähre Plittersdorf die 10-Kilometer-Marke (immer Hin- und Rückweg gerechnet) erreicht, und von weitem sah ich bereits die weißen Gebäude des »Rheinhotel Dreeßen« mit der 12-Kilometer-Marke winken. Es ging also voran mit meinen läuferischen Exerzitien, unaufhaltsam, und es ging synchron dazu stetig weiter abwärts mit meinem Körpergewicht. Beide Erfolgskurven zusammen – die Länge der Laufstrecke und die Maßzahl der Waage – bedeuteten für meine Motivation einen gewaltigen Schub, weiter durchzuhalten und die Anstrengungen sogar noch zu verstärken. Auch die Waage meldete wöchentlich neue Abnehmrekorde: Die 85 Kilogramm Lebendgewicht lagen jetzt hinter mir, und ich näherte mich meiner Zielmarke von 80 Kilogramm. Allerdings wollte ich keineswegs jetzt schon mit der Gewichtsreduktion aufhören, und so mußte ich mir auch gewichtsmäßig neue Ziele setzen. Ich befand mich in einer Stimmung des »Jetzt will ich es wissen!«, d. h. die Frage mußte beantwortet werden, ob ich am Ende gar die 75 Kilogramm schaffen würde. 75 Kilogramm! Das war ziemlich genau mein »Einstiegsgewicht« gewesen, damals im Jahr 1983, als ich zum ersten Mal in den Bundestag zog und mein gemütliches alternatives Leben beendete. Und jetzt war diese Zahl plötzlich wieder in den Bereich des Machbaren gerückt und nicht mehr nur eine traurige Erinnerung an definitiv vergangene Zeiten. Ich konnte es selbst kaum glauben.

Zwischen Februar und März 1997 hatte ich eine weitere wichtige läuferische Hürde überschritten, die es ebenfalls festzuhalten gilt: die »Quälphase« war abgeschlossen. Irgendwann bemerkte ich, daß mir das Laufen nicht mehr diese auspowernde körperliche Mühe machte wie in all den Monaten zuvor. Ganz offensichtlich hatte ich jetzt eine ausreichende Grundkondition erreicht, so daß ich mich während des Laufens nicht mehr mit meiner mangelnden körperlichen Verfassung herumquälen mußte, sondern jetzt die anderen Dimensionen des Langlaufs erschließen konnte. Die Kondition war wesentlich verbessert worden, die Strecken wurden zunehmend länger, und damit trat der sogenannte »Kick« oder auch »Tunneleffekt« in den Vordergrund, d. h. nach etwa 7 Kilometern wirkte dann und wann doch spürbar die Endorphinausschüttung des Körpers, und gleichzeitig verlor man sich im Kopf auf wunderbare Weise im monotonen Rhythmus der Schritte. Kurz, die Lauferfahrung, das *Erlebnis* des Laufens wurde immer interessanter, und so wartete ich ganz gespannt auf die nächsten Offenbarungen, welche die wachsenden Distanzen für mich bereit-halten würden.

Es war wohl auch zu dieser Zeit, als ich mit dem einsetzenden Frühjahr mehr und mehr das Sport-studio hintanstellte und mich statt dessen voll auf das Laufen konzentrierte, das ich aus den angeführten Gründen mit immer größerer Begei-sterung und wachsender Leistungsorientierung anging. Der Gewichtsverlust hielt weiter an, und ich achtete jeden Morgen sehr akkurat auf die neuesten Ergebnisse des Wiegens. Eine weitere Veränderung stellte sich jetzt ebenfalls ein, ich verzichtete auf den läuferischen Frühsport. Am frühen Morgen eine ganze Stunde zu laufen, sollte sich nicht nur vom Zeitbedarf, sondern auch von meinem Biorhythmus her als zuneh-mend schwieriger erweisen. Nicht, daß ich zu faul gewesen wäre, recht früh aufzustehen, sondern es war vor allem die eigene Körperuhr, die um diese Zeit eine solche Belastung von einer Stunde und mehr ablehnte. Und so stellte ich mein Laufpen-sum nach und nach auf den Spätnachmittag oder gar Abend um – heute ist es oft sogar die tiefe Nacht –, was mir sehr gut bekommen sollte. Und so kam zu guter Letzt, was sich bereits seit länge-rem abgezeichnet hatte und was zudem gänzlich meinem Hang zum Extremen in der persönlichen Lebenshaltung entsprach: Ich hatte eine neue Leidenschaft entdeckt, das Laufen wurde fortan zur Passion, ja, mehr und mehr sogar zu einer regelrechten Obsession.

Weiter ging es jetzt im Abstand von wenigen Tagen den Rhein aufwärts, denn ich wurde nach all den Erfolgserlebnissen immer kühner und traute mir mittlerweile läuferisch einiges zu. Das Rheinhotel Dreeßen – die 12-Kilometer-Marke – wurde erreicht, und dann schließlich, ich erinnere mich noch sehr genau, denn es war an jenem Tag, als Hans-Dietrich Genschers 70. Geburtstag von seiner Partei mit einem offiziellen Empfang auf dem Petersberg mit mehreren hundert Gästen begangen wurde, erreichte ich die 16-Kilometer-Marke, die Fähre Mehlem. Ich hatte Genscher bereits persönlich gratuliert und zudem überhaupt keine Lust auf diese Großveranstaltung, andererseits hatte ich als Fraktionssprecher den protokollarischen Pflichten nachzukommen, auch wenn diese wenig Vergnügen verhießen. Gewiß, mein Fehlen würde kaum jemand bemerken, aber falls doch, so wäre mein Wegbleiben alles andere als höflich gewesen. Also entschied ich mich, Hans-Dietrich Genscher angelegentlich einer Plenarsitzung des Deutschen Bundestages direkt zu fragen, ob er denn auf meine Anwesenheit gesteigerten Wert legen würde, und erwartungsgemäß erwies sich der ehemalige Bundesaußenminister als überaus verständnisvoll, denn er entließ mich lachend aus meiner Verpflichtung.

Und so erreichte ich an diesem späten Vormittag um die Mittagszeit die 16-Kilometer-Marke an der Fähre Mehlem, grüßte stumm beim Passieren des am gegenüberliegenden Rheinufer steil emporragenden Petersberges den Jubilar und die dort oben feiernde Geburtstagsgesellschaft und hatte damit, nach nur 6 Monaten, meinen bisherigen absoluten Streckenrekord erreicht.

Das Erreichen der 16-Kilometer-Marke brachte eine weitere Veränderung meines Trainings mit sich, denn nunmehr mußte ich eine meiner»eisernen Grundregeln« aufgeben, nämlich daß eine einmal erreichte Entfernung nicht mehr unterschritten wird. Ein Tagespensum von 16 Kilometern sollte sich für mich, sowohl was die Kraft als auch den Zeitaufwand betrafen, einfach als zu lang erweisen, und so entschied ich mich für eine tägliche Regelstrecke von ca. 10 Kilometern an fünf bis sechs Tagen die Woche, denn ein bis zwei Tage der Regeneration mußten sein, was einen Zeitbedarf von etwa einer Stunde allein für das Laufen ausmachte.Ein- bis zweimal in der Woche wollte ich längere Strecken laufen – es wurde dies meistens der Sonntag, denn da hatte ich, jenseits von Parteitagen und Wahlkämpfen, schlicht genügend Zeit zur Verfügung, um ungestört eineinhalb oder zwei Stunden laufen zu können –, aber die Grundstrecke sollten die 10 Kilometer werden, und so ist es bis auf den heutigen Tag geblieben. Heute brauche ich bei ganz langsamem, regenerativem Joggen mehr als eine Stunde, bei Tempo mit Ein- und Auslaufen um die 53–56 Minuten, ansonsten +/– 1 Stunde bei normaler Dauerlaufgeschwindigkeit.

Ich war mächtig stolz auf meine läuferischen Leistungen und die Tatsache, daß ich lange vor den gesetzten Zeitlimits meine Ziele erreicht hatte. Aber jeder Erfolg schließt zugleich auch eine Phase ab. Was nun? Wie konnte es jetzt weitergehen? Was waren die nächsten Ziele? Der Rhein sollte mir ein weiteres Mal die Antwort geben, denn ich sah, kaum daß ich mir die Frage gestellt hatte, bereits das nächste Ziel von weitem stromaufwärts im Dunst des Flusses liegen, die Insel Nonnenwerth, die bereits zum Nachbarland Rheinland-Pfalz gehörte. Die Landesgrenze! Heureka! Genau das war es, und fortan hatte ich also nur noch ein läuferisches Ziel vor Augen, und das war die südliche Stadtgrenze von Bonn, die, so hatte ich es dem Stadtplan entnommen, etwa auf der Höhe des nördlichen Endes der Insel Nonnenwerth verlief, und die Bonner Stadtgrenze macht dort auch zugleich die Landesgrenze zwischen Nordrhein-Westfalen und Rheinland-Pfalz aus. Ca. 22,5 Kilometer Laufstrecke hin und zurück warteten da auf mich, und diese Distanz – mehr als ein Halbmarathon – wollte für einen naiven Laufnovizen wohlüberlegt angegangen sein. Ich hatte einen Heidenrespekt vor der Strecke.

Wenn ein prominenter Politiker in Bonn anfängt zu laufen und gar seine Figur so grundsätzlich verändert, daß aus einem Mops ein hagerer Asket wird, ist es nur eine Frage allerkürzester Zeit, bis der erste Journalist darauf aufmerksam wird, dann folgt der erste Fotograf, dann erscheint mit Sicherheit die erste Meldung mit dem ersten Foto in einer Zeitung, und dann nimmt das Schicksal endgültig seinen Lauf, das heißt, die ganze Angelegenheit wird zu einem jener überaus bedeutsamen Medienereignisse, die sich heutzutage zunehmender Beliebtheit erfreuen. Ich unternahm, wie bereits gesagt, deshalb erst gar nicht groß den Versuch der Geheimhaltung, zumal mich nach den ersten Erfolgen gleichzeitig die angeborene Eitelkeit zwickte. Wieso sollte ich eigentlich mein asketisch-läuferisches Licht unter den Scheffel stellen? War doch bisher nicht meine Art gewesen. Eben. Zumal der Politiker als solcher ja auch und nicht zuletzt von, durch und mit den Medien lebt. Und so meldete sich eines schönen Tages die Sportredaktion einer bedeutenden Hamburger Illustrierten bei mir, ein Redakteur mit Marathonerfahrung wollte einen Lauf mit mir machen und darüber im Rahmen eines Sonderheftes über Fitneß berichten. Warum nicht, sagte ich mir, und so verabredeten wir uns auf den Mittwoch in der Karwoche 1997, morgens um 11.00 Uhr. Das Parlament war bereits in den Osterferien, der Betrieb entsprechend ruhig, und ich hatte deshalb ausgiebig Zeit und vor allem Lust auf die anzugehende Langstrecke bis zur Landesgrenze.

Es war ein schöner Frühlingstag, noch recht frisch und neblig am Morgen, aber dann verschwand am späteren Vormittag der Nebel im Rheintal, ein strahlend blauer Himmel zeigte sich, und die Sonne vertrieb die Kälte und wärmte bereits beträchtlich. Ich lief mit meinem journalistischen Begleiter gegen 11.00 Uhr in Richtung Landesgrenze los, ein Fotograf auf dem Fahrrad begleitete uns. Südbrücke, Plittersdorf, Rheinhotel Dreeßen, Mehlem – immer weiter trabten wir in einem ruhigen Tempo rheinaufwärts, dann und wann wurde die Ruhe des Laufs durch gehechelte Antworten auf die Fragen meines Begleiters unterbrochen, und da hatte ich plötzlich den Drachenfels auf der linken Rheinseite stromaufwärts nicht mehr vor mir, sondern zum ersten Mal im Rücken. Mir wurde leicht klamm ums Herz, denn was hatte ich mittlerweile nicht alles über die berüchtigten Schwächeanfälle bei Ausdauerläufern gelesen, über den ominösen »Mann mit dem Hammer« und andere Grausamkeiten. Zudem waren mir Schwächeanfälle aus meiner aktiven Zeit im Radsport wohlbekannt, verur-

sacht durch unzureichendes Training und Überforderung der eigenen Kräfte oder durch man-
gelnde Ernährung im Training oder während
eines Rennens. Einmal, so überfiel mich eine sie-
dendheiße Erinnerung, bekam ich beim Training
mit dem Fahrrad fern der Heimat einen grausa-
men Hungerast, weil ich vergessen hatte, Verpfle-
gung mitzunehmen, und so quälte ich mich mehr
schleichend als fahrend über viele Kilometer
nach Hause zurück.

All diese Jahrzehnte zurückliegenden Erfahrungen stiegen jetzt während der Annäherung an die
Wendemarke aus dem Dunkel des Vergessens
plötzlich wieder hoch, und mir wurde doch etwas
bänglich zumute, auch wenn ich mir gegenüber
meinem Begleiter nichts anmerken ließ, sondern
ganz den coolen Max mimte. Mutete ich mir da
wirklich nicht zuviel zu? Und es ging ja immer
noch weiter den Fluß entlang, die letzten Häuser
von Mehlem lagen jetzt hinter uns, und dann
hatten wir die Landesgrenze erreicht, eindeutig
erkennbar an einem amtlichen Schild, das uns
kühnen Läufern verkündete: »Willkommen in
Rheinland-Pfalz«.

Der Fotograf der Zeitschrift war vorausgeradelt
und erwartete uns bereits, ein ganz kurzer, nicht
einmal eine Minute dauernder Stopp am Grenz-
schild für das übliche dokumentarische Foto wurde eingelegt, und dann ging es bereits auf den

101

Rückweg. Während dieses Laufs lernte ich zum ersten Mal auch einen Pulsfrequenzmesser kennen, den mein Begleiter benutzte, erhielt zudem viele praktische Tips, die mir bis dato schlicht unbekannt waren, über Ernährung, Trainingsverhalten etc., und dann erzählte mir mein Begleiter noch über seine Erlebnisse bei den verschiedenen Marathonläufen, an denen er teilgenommen hatte, vor allem aber über den New York Marathon: »Es war alles halb so wild. Wenn du ab Kilometer 34 müde wirst, läufst du gerade durch die Südbronx, und da bleibt man besser nicht stehen!« Herrliche Perspektiven, ein Wadenkrampf in der Südbronx! Aber seit jenem karwöchlichen Vormittag am Rhein im Jahre 1997 läßt der New York Marathon meinen Kopf einfach nicht mehr los. Nebbich, denn es gibt wohl schlimmere fixe Ideen.

Und als wir dann nach etwa 2:30 Stunden wieder zu Hause im Regierungsviertel angekommen waren – die Beine waren gegen Ende etwas schwer geworden, der Kopf bekam auf dem Rückweg in der zweiten Hälfte der Strecke ein paar Probleme, als sich die Entfernung zu ziehen begann, aber ansonsten hatte ich die Distanz in hervorragender Verfassung und für meine Verhältnisse passabler Zeit hinter mich gebracht –, wurde mir von meinem Begleiter die zu erwartende Frage gestellt, die ich mir selbst bereits mehrmals auf dem Rückweg insgeheim gestellt hatte, nämlich ob ich denn in Zukunft beabsichtigen würde, selbst einmal einen Marathon zu laufen. »Warum eigentlich nicht?« lautete meine selbstbewußte Antwort, und damit hatte ich mir zugleich einen gewaltigen Floh in den Kopf gesetzt und mein nächstes und zugleich ambitioniertestes läuferisches Ziel lauthals und zu allem Überfluß noch vor einem journalistischen Zeugen verkündet. Damit war die ganze Sache öffentlich. Jawohl, Euer Ehren, es sollte tatsächlich ein Marathon sein, jener mythische Lauf eines athenischen Boten nach siegreicher Schlacht, von der wir alle mindestens einmal irgendwann im Laufe unserer Schulzeit gehört hatten. Ich hatte aber nicht die Absicht, am Ziel tot oder auch nur halbtot zusammenzubrechen, wie dies der antike Mythos über das traurige Schicksal des heroischen ersten Marathonläufers berichtet. Wer 22,5 Kilometer laufen kann, der schafft auch 42 Kilometer, sagte ich mir, allerdings nur nach einer peniblen Vorbereitung. Bei entsprechendem Trainingsfleiß und guter Beratung müßte ich das Abenteuer Marathon im nächsten Jahr eigentlich wagen können.

Gesagt war gesagt. Dies galt ganz besonders in diesem Fall, denn meine vorwitzige Absichtserklärung stand zwei Wochen später in dem besagten illustrierten Wochenblatt, es sei mein Plan, mich im kommenden Jahr an einem Marathonlauf zu versuchen. Eines schönen und nicht allzu fernen Tages erhielt ich daraufhin einen Brief, der Absender war ein gewisser *Herbert Steffny*. Richtig, dachte ich mir, das war doch in den achtziger und frühen neunziger Jahren einer der besten Marathonläufer Westdeutschlands gewesen. Und eben dieser Herbert Steffny, der mittlerweile eine Laufschule im Schwarzwald betrieb, bot mir, ausgerechnet mir, seine Unterstützung für die sachkundige Vorbereitung meines ersten Marathons an. Einen erfahreneren und besseren Berater und Trainer konnte ich mir eigentlich gar nicht wünschen, und so antwortete ich ihm umgehend, daß ich sein großherziges Angebot gerne annehmen und mich im Sommer nach meinem Urlaub gerne erneut bei ihm melden würde.

Doch bevor ich mich um die Realisierung meiner kessen Sprüche betr. Marathon kümmern konnte, hatte ich zuvor noch einige andere Probleme zu lösen. Seit meiner ganz persönlichen Urlaubskatastrophe war nunmehr fast ein ganzes Jahr verstrichen, und ich wollte zurück an den Ort des Geschehens, diesmal allerdings allein. Läuferisch hatte ich dabei einige heftige Nüsse zu knacken, denn erstens würde es mit Sicherheit im August in der Toskana sehr heiß werden, und zweitens waren die alten Ochsenwege über die Hügel der sienensischen Crete steil, lang und staubig. Erneut wurde mir ziemlich mulmig, denn ich war mir alles andere als sicher, daß ich diese Herausforderung bewältigen würde. Ich kannte bis dahin nur flache Laufstrecken, vorzüglich am Rhein in Bonn und an der Nidda in Frankfurt/M., einem Nebenfluß des Mains, der, vom Vogelsberg kommend, durch den Frankfurter Nordwesten und Westen fließt. Zudem lief ich jetzt in der heißen Jahreszeit verstärkt im Frankfurter Stadtwald, da dort im schattigen Grün die Temperaturen wesentlich angenehmer waren. In den vor mir liegenden drei Urlaubswochen in der Toskana würde aber das gerade Gegenteil der Fall sein, und ich machte mir ernsthafte Gedanken, ob sich mein Trainingsrhythmus auch dort, angesichts der ganz anderen äußeren Umstände von Temperatur und Streckenprofil, tatsächlich durchhalten ließe.

Die Sorge sollte sich aber als völlig unbegründet erweisen. Die Hügellandschaft südlich von Siena, schon immer »Crete« genannt, liegt etwa 200 bis 300 Meter über dem Meeresspiegel und unterscheidet sich radikal von der ansonsten üblichen Landschaft der Toskana, die, jenseits der Flußtäler und der »Maremma«, der Küstenebene, sehr stark von einer bewaldeten Gebirgslandschaft geprägt ist. Die Hügel der Crete hingegen sind meist völlig kahl, einzelne Gehöfte oder Gutshöfe, »Fattorien«, zieren hier und da ihre Gipfel, und einzelne, verloren wirkende Bäume unterstreichen noch das Bizarre und Außergewöhnliche dieser Landschaft.

Die Landschaft ist hügelig, durchschnitten von kleineren Flüssen, wie der Arbia, die von den Monte de Chianti im Nordosten herunterkommen, und zahlreichen Bächen, die in der heißen Jahreszeit jedoch kaum mehr als mühselige Rinnsale sind. In der Crete werden vor allem Getreide und Sonnenblumen angebaut, dann und wann sieht man einen Weiler oder einen Hof mit Garten und einem Olivenhain, ansonsten dominiert die Schafzucht. Berühmt ist deshalb auch der Schafskäse der Crete, ein wunderbarer Peccorino, der sowohl frisch und jung wie auch als »staggionato«, als gereifter Käse, hervorragend schmeckt.

Die Crete wird durch wenige geteerte Landstraßen und durch zahlreiche unbefestigte Wege, den »strade biance«, durchzogen, die in der Hitze des Sommers vom Staub weiß-grau gefärbt sind, und auch wenn die Hügel der Crete nicht besonders hoch sind, so wurden vor allem die unbefestigten Wege doch ziemlich steil angelegt, ohne große Serpentinen, eben gerade so, wie früher die Ochsen die Karren über den Berg gezogen haben. Steigungen von 14–18 Prozent und über einen Kilometer Länge sind keine Seltenheit, und im August kann man in der Regel von Temperaturen zwischen 32 und 38 Grad Celsius auch noch um 5 Uhr nachmittags ausgehen. Freilich können die Sommer sehr unterschiedlich sein, d. h. kühle

Sommer mit Regen dann und wann können durch richtige Backofenhitze in anderen Jahren abgelöst werden. Der Sommer 1997 sollte sich als eine durchwachsene Mischung aus beiden klimatischen Möglichkeiten erweisen.

Die Großgemeinde Asciano befindet sich im Herzen der Crete, und etwa zwölf Kilometer von Asciano entfernt, am nordöstlichen Rand ihrer Gemarkung, liegt der zu Asciano gehörende kleine Weiler Torre a Castello, in dessen Nähe ich mein

Die Crete-Landschaft zwischen Torre a Castello und Asciano – rechts oben Monte Sante Marie

Domizil hatte. Täglich lief ich nun so gegen 17 Uhr, wenn die Hitze nicht mehr ganz so drückend war, am Friedhof von Torre a Castello vorbei, Richtung Asciano über einen unbefestigten Weg, 5,5 Kilometer bis Monte Sante Marie und zurück, also 11 Kilometer. Die Strecke war hügelig, ein längerer und ein sich ziehender steiler Anstieg – meiner ganz persönlichen Kategorisierung nach Steigungen der »zweiten Kategorie« – waren zu bewältigen. Die Strecke ging dauernd bergauf und bergab, und diese zahlreichen kleineren Anstiege taten durchaus weh. Als besonders beschwerlich sollte sich ausgerechnet das Finale erweisen, denn am Friedhof von Torre a Castello ging es auf dem Rückweg noch einmal 200–300 Meter recht steil den letzten Anstieg hinauf, und zwar so, daß ich mich dort jeweils nochmals 150 Pulsschlägen näherte und mich somit deutlich in meinem obersten Leistungsbereich befand (ich hatte mir seit dem Frühsommer einen Pulsmesser angeschafft und demnach so nach und nach einen genaueren Überblick über meine individuellen Leistungsbereiche).

Die ersten Tage in der Crete waren läuferisch hart, auch wenn ich sie äußerst vorsichtig anging, aber ich war überhaupt nicht auf das Laufen im hügeligen Gelände eingestellt. Ich bekam nach dem ersten Lauf etwas Muskelkater, da ich ganz offensichtlich die Beinmuskulatur anders belasten mußte, aber nach wenigen Tagen hatte ich mich auf das dauernde Auf und Ab eingestellt. Und erneut sollte mir die Erinnerung an das Erlernte aus den lange zurückliegenden Tagen meiner Zeit als Radrennfahrer helfen, denn ich versuchte am Berg »meinen Rhythmus« zu finden. Und siehe da, nach einigen Tagen »lief« es plötzlich. Ich versuchte die Steigungen, vor allem die längeren und die steilen, durchweg im selben Tempo, in ein und demselben Rhythmus zu laufen. Ich durfte also nicht zu schnell in die Steigung reingehen, was ich zu Beginn getan hatte, sondern mußte mein mittleres Tempo finden, das ich auch bis zum Schluß durchhalten konnte. Bergabwärts wechselte ich das Tempo und nutzte das Gefälle zur Erholung, bevor es dann an den nächsten Anstieg ging. Nach etwa vier Tagen hatte ich mein Tempo gefunden, die beständigen Rhythmuswechsel zwischen dem Auf und Ab der Strecke machten mir nur noch wenig aus, und so begann ich, trotz der Hitze und des Staubs, das Laufen in dieser wunderbaren Landschaft mehr und mehr zu genießen. Es ging wesentlich besser voran, als ich befürchtet hatte, und einen wirklichen Einbruch hat es nicht gegeben. Ganz im Gegenteil begann ich nach und nach das Tempo zu variieren. Bisweilen zwang mich eine Schafherde, die die Straße kreuzte, zu einer kurzen Pause, bellend heranpreschende Schäferhunde, die allerdings harmlos waren, rieten ebenfalls zur Vorsicht, aber ansonsten waren nur die über die Straße preschenden seltenen Autos wirklich störend, denn sie zogen eine gewaltige Staubwolke hinter sich her. Leider führte ich damals noch kein Trainingstagebuch und verfüge deshalb über keinerlei Aufzeichnungen über meine damals gelaufenen Zeiten, so daß ich keine Vergleiche zu den späteren Jahren ziehen kann.

Wie gesagt, die Entfernung zwischen Asciano und Torre a Castello betrug etwa 12 Kilometer, und sinnigerweise beginnt dieser Weg an einem Friedhof und endet an einem ebensolchen. Nun wußte ich, daß der zweite Teil der Strecke, nämlich von Monte Sante Marie bis zum Friedhof von Asciano, wesentlich steiler und demnach härter war als der erste Teil,

Crete, 1997, ein Jahr danach ...

den ich mittlerweile als meine Hausstrecke begriff und in- und auswendig kannte. Mich ließ nun der Gedanke nicht los, wenigstens einmal die ganze Strecke zu laufen, und zwar wollte ich mich von Freunden mit dem Auto nach Asciano bringen lassen und von dort aus nach Hause zurücklaufen. Freilich ging es auf diesem Teil der Strecke teilweise so steil aufwärts wie auf dem berühmt-berüchtigten Dach. Der längste Anstieg war 1,2 Kilometer lang und in weiten Teilen sehr steil, immer wieder gab es Abschnitte mit einem Anstieg von 16–18 Prozent, ja vielleicht sogar 20 Prozent. Da Torre a Castello höher liegt als Asciano, ist der Weg dorthin mühseliger und, wie ich mittlerweile weiß, auch etwa zwei bis drei Minuten langsamer als die Strecke nach Asciano, da längere Anstiege zu überwinden sind. Kurz und gut, drei Tage vor dem Ende meines Urlaubs ging ich das Wagnis ein und machte mich auf meine läuferische Friedhofstour durch die Crete.

Bereits am ersten Friedhof, dem von Asciano, ging es mit der ersten Steigung los, aber diese war noch maßvoll und nur zum Warmhecheln. Nach einer längeren Gefällstrecke kam dann allerdings der erste Hammer von Anstieg, extrem steil, so daß ich nur mit ganz kleinen Schritten und geringem Tempo den Berg hinaufkam. Dennoch kostete dieser Anstieg, der gar nicht einmal sehr lang war, enorm Kraft, und ich nahm mir vor, meine Kraft so einzuteilen, daß ich die Strecke auch wirklich durchstehen konnte. Solche Steigungen kannte ich bisher noch nicht! Weiter ging es, umgekehrten Kaskaden gleich – steiler Anstieg, leichtes Gefälle, erneuter steiler Anstieg –, immer weiter und höher hinauf. Die Gefällstrecken oder leichtere Steigungen versuchte ich zur Erholung zu nutzen, und dann folgte auch schon der nächste Hammer von Steigung. Und schließlich, nach einem langen Abstieg in das Tal eines Baches, der mich wieder auf die Höhe von Asciano hinabführte, erfolgte der härteste und längste Anstieg, 1,2 Kilometer lang, durch einen kurzen Abstieg unterbrochen und dann erneut steil hinauf nach Monte Sante Marie, insgesamt eine Entfernung von etwa 2 Kilometern.

Ich versuchte zuerst, meinen Rhythmus zu finden, was sehr schwierig war, denn an der ersten extremen Steigung war es vorbei mit jedem Rhythmus, aber so nach und nach stellte ich mich auch darauf ein. Es war heiß, die Beine schmerzten, und an den Steigungen erreichte ich maximale Pulszahlen. Nur nicht hochschauen, sondern immer schön den Blick auf der Straße lassen, sagte ich mir. Und bloß nicht allzuviel über die Strecke nachdenken! Und so lief ich und kämpfte mich schließlich auch nach Monte Sante Marie hoch. Irgendwann war ich dort oben angekommen, und plötzlich erschien mir der Rest der Strecke nach Hause als

eine leichtere Übung. All die Steigungen, die mich in den Tagen zuvor so gemartert hatten, waren plötzlich nur noch Kleinigkeiten für mich. Es gab allerdings eine Ausnahme, und die türmte sich ausgerechnet am Schluß auf, nämlich der letzte Anstieg zum Friedhof von Torre a Castello. Dieser Hügel war richtig gemein, hundsgemein sogar, denn nun, nach all den Strapazen, tat er ganz besonders weh. Aber schließlich hatte ich auch diese letzte Prüfung hinter mich gebracht, und nun ging es nur noch abwärts, nach Hause.

Dort angekommen, war ich mächtig stolz auf mich. Ich hatte es tatsächlich geschafft! Vor exakt einem Jahr war ich noch irgend etwas um die 110 Kilogramm schwer gewesen, und allein der Gedanke an einen solchen Lauf hätte mich damals umgebracht. Heute hatte ich 35 Kilogramm Lebendgewicht weniger und soeben die Strecke zwischen Asciano und Torre a Castello laufend in einer beachtlichen Zeit zurückgelegt. Die Steigungen, die Entfernung, die Hitze, der Staub – ich hatte mich durchgekämpft und war angekommen. Ich wußte jetzt auch, warum ich ausgerechnet in die Crete zurückgewollt hatte, denn nach diesem Lauf war mir klar, daß ich den einmal eingeschlagenen Weg nicht mehr verlassen würde. Jetzt konnte mein erster Marathon ganz praktisch angegangen werden.

VI

Mein erster Marathon

Ziemlich genau ein Jahr hatte ich gebraucht, um jenen radikalen körperlichen Umbau an und mit mir selbst zu bewerkstelligen, den ich mir aus schierer Verzweiflung damals vorgenommen hatte. Es war ein einsames, hartes und bisweilen ganz schön entsagungsvolles Jahr gewesen, aber zugleich hatte ich auch sehr viel wiedergewonnen, weitaus mehr, als ich mir noch vor Jahresfrist selbst in meinen kühnsten Träumen gedacht hätte. Aus dem barocken Dickbauch war ein asketisch wirkender Langläufer geworden, der Fettanteil meines Körpers war erheblich zurückgegangen, und ich fühlte mich rundum wohler und gesünder. Vorbei die Zeiten, da ich mich für dieses Leben körperlich bereits selbst aufgegeben hatte. Noch vor etwas mehr als einem Jahr hätte ich jeden höhnisch ausgelacht, der mir zum 50. Geburtstag eine läuferische Zukunft mit nur noch 75 Kilogramm Lebendgewicht vorausgesagt hätte. Ich hatte damals, in meinem alten Leben, ja bereits in jenem berüchtigten Brunnen gelegen, in den sprichwörtlich die Kinder hineinzufallen drohen, und nun – jawohl, ich war mächtig stolz auf mich selbst! –

war ich erfolgreich und ganz allein wieder aus dem Loch herausgekrabbelt. Und das Wichtigste daran war, daß ich mich vor allem selbst wiedergefunden hatte.

Merkwürdigerweise hatte dabei das Laufen eine sehr große, ja, zentrale und alles andere zunehmend überragende Bedeutung, und zwar nicht nur physisch, sondern vor allem auch im Kopf. Gewiß gab mir die wiederentdeckte eigene Körperlichkeit ein anderes Selbstwertgefühl und damit auch Selbstbewußtsein (wobei es mir daran eigentlich selbst in der schlimmsten Zeit niemals gemangelt hatte), aber weitaus entscheidender war und ist die meditative, psychologische Wirkung des Laufens im Kopf für mich. Das Erlebnis des eigenen Körpers in der monotonen Schrittfolge des Langlaufs, die Interaktion mit der Natur – Kälte, Regen, Hitze, Staub, Wind, Dunkelheit, Sonnenschein, der Fluß, der Wald, die Stadt und der Verkehr, all die unterschiedlichen Stimmungen, Farben, Lichter, Reflexe, Geräusche und Sinneseindrücke –, und dann die große Leere im Kopf, meist nach einer Quälphase, oder auch die Konzentration auf einen Gedanken, eine Idee, einen Text, der sich in der meditativen Monotonie fast von selbst verfertigt, alles verbindet sich durch den Lauf zu einer großen Harmonie des eigenen Ich. Und genau deswegen hasse ich es bis auf den heutigen Tag, wenn ich beim Laufen reden muß, denn dabei nimmt man

116

mir das Wichtigste an meinem ureigenen Lauf-
erlebnis, nämlich die Versenkung in mich selbst.
Beim Laufen will ich vor allem mit mir selbst,
allein unterwegs sein, ein Geist und Körper reini-
gender Egotrip gewissermaßen, wobei mich Mitläufer, ja, selbst ein größeres Feld von Läufern
nicht stören, solange das Schweigen nicht gebro-
chen wird. Nachdem ich also ein ganzes Jahr im
wahrsten Sinne des Wortes »abgelaufen« hatte,
konnte und wollte ich auf diesen täglichen
»Rhythmus der Schritte« einfach nicht mehr ver-
zichten.

Ein ganzes Jahr hatte ich auch gebraucht, um
langsam mein inneres Gleichgewicht wieder zu-
rückzugewinnen und mich auf mein neues Leben
einzustellen. Die völlig andere Ernährung und die
eisern auch im Winter, bei Regen und in der Hitze
durchgehaltenen wöchentlichen und täglichen
Trainingseinheiten, all dies zusammengenommen
hatte zu einer fundamentalen Veränderung meines
gesamten Lebensrhythmus geführt. Das Laufen
(und nicht mehr das Abnehmen oder die Suche
nach einem anderen Lebensstil) stand jetzt völlig
im Vordergrund und gab meinem neuen persönlichen Alltag eine klare Struktur und damit Richtung
und auch Halt. Es war nach diesem Laufurlaub im
Sommer 1997 in der Toskana gewesen, daß ich
wußte: Ich hatte meinen neuen Lebensrhythmus
gefunden. Genau so und nicht mehr anders wollte

ich meinen Alltag gestalten, jetzt und für die weitere Zukunft. Ein Zurück, ein Rückfall gar in die alten Verhältnisse von »König Dickbauch« war ergo fortan ausgeschlossen, denn so weit kannte ich mich aus langjähriger Erfahrung selbst gut genug. Warum? Ganz einfach, weil ich so eben bin. Wenn mein Zug erst einmal unter Dampf steht und in eine neue Richtung fährt, dann hält er nicht mehr so schnell an, und fährt schon gar nicht rückwärts. So war das immer bei mir gewesen, und *diese* tiefer liegenden Teile meiner Persönlichkeit waren ganz offensichtlich durch die große Veränderung nicht berührt worden.

Ich habe ja bereits weiter oben darauf hingewiesen, daß sich meine persönliche Verschlankung kaum vor meiner Umwelt und einer immer neugierigen Öffentlichkeit verbergen ließ. Entsprechend intensiv gestaltete sich die öffentliche Anteilnahme daran. Und dabei fiel mir jetzt, ebenfalls nach einem Jahr, ein merkwürdiges, öffentlich geäußertes Reaktionsmuster auf, das sich immer wieder fast stereotyp in den zahllosen Fragen und Gesprächen wiederholte und dabei zeitlich in drei klar voneinander abzugrenzende Abschnitte unterteilt war. Zuerst wurde mir allenthalben mitgeteilt, ja, das wäre ein mutiger Vorsatz von mir, mich auf 80 Kilogramm runterbringen zu wollen, aber gut, man sähe dem mit Spannung und natürlich einer gewissen Skepsis entgegen. Klar spürbar war die Botschaft allenthalben: »Junge, das hältst du niemals durch!« Nachdem ich sogar die 75 Kilogramm erreicht hatte, änderte sich die Botschaft. Ja, ja, die Leistung wäre phänomenal, Respekt! Respekt! Aber man müsse weiter abwarten, denn sicher hätte ich schon von jenem Jojo-Effekt gehört und wie schnell man dadurch doch wieder zunehmen könne. Oder? Und deshalb war man der Meinung, das neue Gewicht könne ich kaum halten, das gehe so sicher wieder aufwärts, wie das Amen in der Kirche komme. Abzunehmen sei sehr schwer, dünn zu bleiben noch viel mehr!

Auch diese, von einer leicht hämischen Erwartung getragene These sollte sich als ein Irrtum erweisen. Und nun, nach einem Jahr, als selbst die mißgünstigsten Beobachter sich eingestehen mußten, daß der Kerl sein neues Programm tatsächlich durchhalten würde, änderte sich die Botschaft erneut, und diesmal wurde es richtig finster: »Mein Gott, der Arme, sieht der schlecht aus!« »Nun reicht es aber, wir müssen uns ja ernsthafte Sorgen um Sie machen!« »Nein, das kann ja nicht normal sein, da muß was anderes dahinterstecken.« »Sind sie krank, Herr Fischer?« Krebs, Aids, Pest, Cholera – und wer weiß was sonst nicht noch alles – wurde mir plötzlich angehängt. Nun kann man nicht 35 Kilogramm Körperfett innerhalb eines Jahres abbauen und dabei noch – mit knapp fünfzig Jahren – wie das rosigste Leben aussehen. Selbstverständlich wirkte ich grau, faltig und abgehärmt. Und meine Laune war, bedingt durch die Anstrengungen und Entsagungen, ebenfalls nicht immer von frühlingsduftender Heiterkeit. Aber darum ging es in Wirklichkeit überhaupt nicht. Hinter der auch öffentlich immer wieder auftauchenden These von einer schweren Krankheit – in Wirklichkeit war ich so gesund und fit wie seit Jahrzehnten nicht mehr – stand etwas völlig anderes, denn an die Stelle jenes öffentlichen Amüsements, das sich aus der teilnehmend beobachtenden Erwartung ergab, wann denn nun der große Rückfall käme, wurde jetzt eine stille Bedrohung für all die zurückgelassenen Rollmöpse. Der sich abzeichnende Erfolg fing an, bedrohlich zu werden. Hinter der Krankheitsthese steckte vor allem jede Menge Abwehr und kaum ernsthafte Sorge, denn wenn eine solche radikale körperliche Veränderung funktioniert und tatsächlich auch unter den Bedingungen eines stressigen Politikeralltags mit 50 Jahren noch machbar ist, ja, dann macht das plötzlich vielen Leuten ein ernsthaftes Problem. Warum denn dann nicht auch du …?

Was soll's, sagte ich mir, die werden sich auch wieder einkriegen. Mach einfach schnurgerade weiter. Und wie gesagt, ich hatte ja meinen neuen Rhythmus gefunden: Die Frage des Abnehmens trat fortan mehr und mehr in den Hintergrund, denn mein Körpergewicht wollte ich jetzt nur noch stabil halten und nicht mehr weiter absenken. Das Laufen war zur neuen Leidenschaft geworden. Ich entwickelte einen Trainingsfleiß wie selbst in der Jugend nicht, und es machte und macht mir darüber hinaus zu allem Überfluß auch noch großen Spaß. Ein Ende ist bis dato nicht absehbar: Morgens nach dem Aufstehen Frühsport für Arme, Bauch und Rücken, ansonsten nachmittags, abends oder gar nachts fünf- bis sechsmal die Woche mindestens 10 Kilometer Laufen, am Sonntag meistens länger. Die Ernährung hatte sich ebenfalls auf ein neues und zugleich bis heute beständiges Muster eingependelt: Müslifrühstück, Orangen- oder Grapefruitsaft, Kaffee; tagsüber Obst und Bananen und je nach Jahreszeit frisch gepreßten Orangensaft, viel Wasser; abends Salat, Pasta vegetarisch, ein- bis zweimal die Woche Fisch, Mineralwasser, Espresso. Aber weiterhin galt und gilt: *No meat! No sweets! No alcohol!*

Mein bisheriges Leben war also vorbei, perdu, und meine gewichtige und beleibte Vergangenheit lag abgeschlossen hinter mir. Mit der Rückkehr aus der Toskana bestand darüber jetzt zweifelsfreie Klarheit. Nach dem Urlaub kam dann auch Herbert Steffny nach Frankfurt/M., und wir besprachen sehr konkret die Pläne für meinen ersten Marathon.

In diesem Herbst sollte allerdings bezüglich meines ersten Marathonlaufs nichts mehr gehen, denn die Vorbereitungszeit dazu wäre viel zu kurz gewesen. Im nächsten Jahr wurde ich andererseits durch den politischen Kalender der Bundespolitik sehr eingeengt, denn faktisch würde das ganze Jahr 1998 über eine Wahl nach der anderen stattfinden, bis in den Herbst hinein mit dem Höhepunkt der Bundestagswahl. Mir war klar, daß ich 1998 für meine Partei einen ganz anderen Marathon, nämlich einen Wahlkampfmarathon, zu absolvieren hatte, und folglich würde das Jahr 1998 für meinen ersten Wettkampf über die berühmt-berüchtigten 42 Kilometer entweder ganz ausfallen, oder ich mußte eben das einzige mir mögliche Zeitfenster im Frühjahr nutzen. Nach Lage der Dinge kam also nur der Stadtmarathon in Hamburg in Frage, eine Woche nach meinem 50. Geburtstag, und genau darauf wollte ich mich nun vorbereiten. Natürlich wäre ich lieber in meiner Heimatstadt Frankfurt/M. gelaufen, aber der Termin war entweder zu früh, weil noch im Spätherbst 1997, oder dann zu spät, im November 1998. Der Wahlkampf würde aber eine systematische Vorbereitung nicht zulassen, und deshalb schied Frankfurt/M. leider aus. Berlin paßte ebenfalls überhaupt nicht, weil dieser Termin vierzehn Tage vor der Bundestagswahl lag, was viel zu riskant war. Man stelle sich nur ein immerhin nicht auszuschließendes läuferisches Desaster wenige Tage vor der Wahl vor. Dies wäre politisch ein nicht zu verantwortender Alptraum geworden! Also weg damit und nicht einmal mehr daran denken. Blieb also lediglich Hamburg im Frühjahr, am 19. April, als einzig machbare Möglichkeit.

Ernährung, Atmungs- und Lauftechnik, Trainingsaufbau, Gesundheit – ich diskutierte alle anstehenden Fragen intensiv mit meinem neuen Trainer, er verbesserte hier, korrigierte da, und so nach und nach bekam das *Marathontraining* Hand und Fuß. Herbert Steffny überzeugte mich zudem von zwei weiteren Dingen, nämlich daß ich erstens ein genaues Trainingstagebuch führen und daß ich mich zweitens einem gründlichen Gesundheitscheck bei Professor Keul am sportwissenschaftlichen Institut der Universität Freiburg unterziehen sollte. Letzteres geschah dann in der zweiten Oktoberhälfte – Untersuchung des kardiomuskulären Systems, Belastungs-EKG, Laktattest, Blut- und andere Laborwerte, Orthopädie –, und das Ergebnis war, daß ich mich als kerngesund und für mein Alter topfit bezeichnen konnte. Von wegen krank und hinfällig! Das Herz-Kreislauf-System war intakt, und folglich mußten die Herzstiche in meinem früheren Leben entweder muskuläre Schmerzen gewesen sein oder schlicht ein Ausdruck von Angst um meinen damaligen Gesundheitszustand. Wie auch immer, die ärztliche Diagnose war positiv, und folglich stand auch von der medizinischen Seite meinem ersten Marathon nichts mehr im Wege.

17. November 1997

Der erste Eintrag in mein neues Trainingstagebuch findet sich unter dem 27. Oktober 1997,
einem Montag: »Regenerationslauf, 10 km, 1:02
Std., kalt.« Am nächsten Tag nochmals ein Regenerationslauf über 12 km in 1:13 Std., am Mittwoch
ein Tempolauf über 10 km in 0:55 Std., am Donnerstag ein Dauerlauf über 10 km in 0:57 Std., am
Freitag wieder ein Regenerationslauf über 10 km
in 1:02 Std., am Samstag Fußball und am Sonntag
ein langer Dauerlauf über 24 km in 2:05 Std. Die
Witterung war all die Tage über kalt, wie das Trainingsbuch vermerkt, gleichwohl aber trocken. Das
erste eingetragene Wochenpensum vom 27. Oktober bis zum 2. November 1997 betrug 76 Trainings-
kilometer, in den dann noch vier folgenden
Wochen waren es 56 km, 94 km, 78 km und 72 km.
Am 1. und 2. Dezember, so mein Tagebuch, lag ich
dann mit einer Grippe krank darnieder, um am
3. Dezember bei Dunkelheit, Schnee und 2^0 Celsius 13 km in 1:21 Std. zu laufen.

Ich kann das Führen eines solchen Trainings-
tagebuchs aus sportlichen Gründen und zur Erinnerung nur nachdrücklich empfehlen. Wegen
der Niederschrift des vorliegenden Buches habe
ich die alte Kladde von Trainingsbuch wieder aus
der Schublade herausgekramt, und siehe da, es
machte richtiggehend Spaß, sich an die vergangenen Läufe mit ihren Mühen, Martern und Ein-
drücken zu erinnern. Nichts ist so süß wie die

Erinnerung an vergangene Heldentaten, zumal all die Plage, der Schmerz und der vergossene Schweiß schon längst in der Erinnerung verblichen sind oder schlicht idealisiert werden.

Einige weitere Kostproben aus meinem Trainingstagebuch: Am 15. Dezember 1997 lief ich nachts im Schneetreiben durch den Wiener Prater, am 16. Dezember in Bern, am 17. Dezember in Zürich im Schnee bergauf, und am 18. und 19. Dezember in Paris, vom Hôtel de Ville das linke Seineufer hinab, am Invalidendom und am Eiffelturm vorbei, zurück dann auf der anderen Seineseite über den Trocadero, die Tuilerien und schließlich am Louvre vorbei. Weihnachten wurde durchgelaufen, in Frankfurt/M., am 30. Dezember, bretterte ich noch meine persönliche Bestzeit über 10 km in 0:53 Std. vor Ablauf des alten Jahres auf die Piste, und das Jahr 1998 wurde am Neujahrstag mit einem Lauf über 16 km an der Nidda in 1:28 Std. eröffnet. Am Sonntag, dem 1. Februar 1998 ist in meinem Tagebuch ein langer Dauerlauf über 25 km in 2:14 Std. vermerkt: »Eiskalter Wind, hart, -2^0 Celsius.« In der Tat erinnere ich mich noch sehr gut an diesen Lauf, denn der gleichermaßen eisige wie starke Wind hatte mir auf dem Rückweg die Gesichtsmuskulatur einfrieren lassen, so daß ich unmittelbar nach dem Lauf mit dem Sprechen erhebliche Schwierigkeiten hatte. Und ab der ersten Februarwoche 1998 sind dann

126

die ersten Intervalläufe verzeichnet, die bereits auf einen detailliert ausgearbeiteten Trainingsplan von Herbert Steffny zurückgehen: »3. 2. 1998: Gewicht 74,2 kg, Intervall 4x1000 m, insgesamt 10 km, 0:58, −1^0 C, Nacht.« Es muß wohl unten am Rheinufer Richtung Plittersdorf und zurück gewesen sein.

Seit dem Oktober 1997 lief ich also täglich nach und im Plan, den mir Herbert Steffny freundlicherweise mit all seiner Marathonerfahrung sorgfältig ausgearbeitet hatte. Zuerst war es nur ein vierzehntägiger provisorischer Plan gewesen, der sich in folgendem Rhythmus gestaltete: *1. Woche – Montag/ Dienstag 60 Min. ganz langsamer Regenerationslauf; Mittwoch flotter Dauerlauf über 6–8 km zuzüglich Ein- und Auslaufen 10 km; Donnerstag Dauerlauf über 10 km; Freitag Regenerationslauf; Samstag Fußball; Sonntag langsamer Dauerlauf über ca. 20 km. 2. Woche – Montag und Dienstag Regenerationslauf 60 Min.; Mittwoch Fahrtspiel 10 km (lockere Tempowechsel, Steigerungen, Koordination); Donnerstag 10 km Dauerlauf; Freitag Regenerationslauf; Samstag Fußball; Sonntag langsamer Dauerlauf über ca. 20 km.*

Nach dem Jahreswechsel wurde es dann definitiv ernst, denn das Zwischenziel vor dem Hamburg-Marathon war ein Halbmarathon am Sonntag, den 1. März 1998, in meiner Heimatstadt Frankfurt/M. draußen am Waldstadion. Fortan lag

Rahmentrainingsplan für Joschka Fischer Hamburg Marathon 19.4.1998

(DL=Dauerlauf / ➤➤=Tempodauerlauf / O = kurzIntervalltraining / ✱ = langer Dauerlauf)

1. Woche 26.1.-1.2.1998 (64km)

	Inhalt	Puls	Zeit/km	Kommentar
Mo	-			
Di	DL 60min	120	5:30	
Mi	DL 60min	120	5:30	
Do	➤➤ flotter DL (6km 4:45)	bis 140	6:00-4:45	insges. ca.11km, darin 6km in 4:50
Fr	Jogging 40min	110-115	6:00	
Sa	Fußball			
So	✱ lgDL 25km	115	5:30-6:00	wirklich ruhig!

2. Woche 2.-8.2.1998 (65km)

	Inhalt	Puls	Zeit/km	Kommentar
Mo				
Di	O 3x1000m 4:20	um 145	6:00-4:20	Stadion,Pause 400mTrab, Ein-Auslaufen
Mi	Jogging 40min	110-120	5:30-6:00	
Do	easy DL 90min	120	5:30	
Fr	➤➤ flotter DL (7km 5:00)	bis 135	6:00-5:00	nach Einlaufen 7km flott, dann auslaufen
Sa	Fußball			
So	✱ lgDL 20km	115	5:30-6:00	wirklich ruhig!

3. Woche 9.-15.2.1998 (69km)

	Inhalt	Puls	Zeit/km	Kommentar
Mo	-			
Di	○ 1-2-3-2-1k 4:45	bis 140	6:00-4:45	Stadion? Zwischenzeit, Trabpause ½ Zeit
Mi	Jogging 40min	110-120	5:30-6:00	
Do	DL 60min	110-120	5:30-6:00	
Fr	➤ flotter DL 7km 5:00	bis 135	6:00-5:00	nach Einlaufen 7km flott und auslaufen
Sa	Fußball			
So	* lgDL 27km	110-120	5:30-6:00	wirklich ruhig!

4. Woche 16.-22.2.1998 (64km)

	Inhalt	Puls	Zeit/km	Kommentar
Mo	-			
Di	○ 5x1000m 4:20	>145	6:00-4:20	Stadion, 400m Trabpause 6:00
Mi	Jogging 40min	110-120	5:30-6:00	
Do	DL 70min	120	5:30	nicht schneller!
Fr	➤ flotter DL (8km 5:00)	bis 135	6:00-5:15	nach Einlaufen 8km flott, dann auslaufen
Sa	Fußball			
So	* lgDL 22km	115	5:30-6:00	wirklich ruhig!

5. Woche 23.2.-1.3.1998 (57km)

	Inhalt	Puls	Zeit/km	Kommentar
Mo	-			
Di	○ *4x2000m 9:30*	bis 140	6:00-4:45	5min Geh-/Trabpause in 6:00
Mi	Jogging 60min	110-120	5:30-6:00	
Do	-			
Fr	Jogging 40min	110-120	5:30-6:00	
Sa	kein Fußball!			
So	➜ ✳ *½ Marathon Ziel 1:40*	ca.140	4:45	stur nach Zwischenzeiten bis 10km!

6. Woche 2.-8.3.1998 (58km)

	Inhalt	Puls	Zeit/km	Kommentar
Mo	-			
Di	Jogging 60min	110-120	5:30-6:00	wirklich ruhig wegen Erholung!
Mi	-			
Do	DL 70min	120	5:30	
Fr	Jogging 40min	110-120	5:30-6:00	
Sa	Fußball			
So	✳ *lgDL 27km*	115	5:30-6:00	wirklich ruhig!

7. Woche 9.-15.3.1998 (67km)

	Inhalt	Puls	Zeit/km	Kommentar
Mo	-			
Di	○ 5x1000m 4:20	>145	6:00-4:20	Stadion, Trabpause 400m in 6:00
Mi	DL 70min	120	5:30	
Do	-			
Fr	➡ flotter DL (8km 5:15)	115-130	6:00-5:15	nach Einlaufen 8km flott, dann auslaufen
Sa	Fußball (sanft!)			
So	lgDL 30km	115	5:30-6:00	wirklich ruhig (eventuell mit H.St.?)

8. Woche 16.-22.3.1998 (68km)

	Inhalt	Puls	Zeit/km	Kommentar
Mo	-			
Di	Jogging 40min	110-120	5:30-6:00	
Mi	○ leicht. Fahrtspiel 60min	110-140	6:00-4:20	nur kürzere flotte Abschnitte!
Do	DL 60min	120	5:30	
Fr	➡ flotter DL (10km 5:15)	115-130	6:00-5:15	2kmEinlaufen,10km flott und auslaufen
Sa	Fußball			
So	* lgDL 23km	115	5:30-6:00	wirklich ruhig!

9. Woche 23.-29.3.1998 (75km)

	Inhalt	Puls	Zeit/km	Kommentar
Mo	-			
Di	○ 3x1000m 4:20	>145	6:00-4:20	Stadion wie gehabt
Mi	Jogging 40min	110-120	5:30-6:00	
Do	➤ Mar: 3x3000m 14:30min	135-140	6:00-4:50	nicht schneller; 7min Geh-/Trabpause
Fr	DL 60min	120	5:30	
Sa	Fußball (zahm!)			
So	➤ lgDL 32km	115	5:30-6:00	wirklich ruhig!

10. Woche 30.3.-5.4.1998 (70km)

	Inhalt	Puls	Zeit/km	Kommentar
Mo	-			
Di	Jogging 40min	110-120	5:30-6:00	
Mi	DL 60min	120	5:30	
Do	➤ flotter DL (12km 5:15)	115-130	6:00-5:15	2kmEinlaufen 12km flott und auslaufen
Fr	Jogging 40min	110-120	5:30-6:00	
Sa	Fußball (zahm!)			
So	➤ * lgDL 30km Crescendo!	110-140	6:00-4:50	5k(5:50)15k(5:30)5k(5:10)3k(4:50)2k(6)

11. Woche 6.-12.4.1998 (50km)

	Inhalt	Puls	Zeit/km	Kommentar
Mo	-			
Di	Jogging 40min	110-120	5:30-6:00	
Mi	-			
Do	➤ *Mar: 3x5000m 25:00min*	135	6:00-5:00	Letzter Test! Wichtig: nicht überziehen!
Fr	-			
Sa	(Fußball, ganz vorsichtig!)			
So	✱ *lgDL 23km*	115	5:30-6:00	wirklich ruhig! (Herzl. Glückwunsch zum 50.Geburtstag !)

12. Woche 13.-19.4.1998 (77km – inkl. Marathon)

	Inhalt	Puls	Zeit/km	Kommentar
Mo	-			
Di	DL 60min	120	5:30	
Mi	○ *3x1000m 5:00*	135	6:00-5:00	nur noch mal easy Marathontempo üben!
Do	Jogging 40min	110-120	5:30-6:00	
Fr	Anreise Hamburg			
Sa	Jogging 30min	110	6:00	
So	➤ ✱ *Hamburg Marathon*	ca. 135?	5:00?	Gleichmäßig von Beginn an! (mit H.St?) Je nach Wetter möglich: *3:30 Std.*

ein ausgearbeiteter »Rahmentrainingsplan« für die Zeit bis zum 19. April 1998 vor, dem Tag des Marathons in der Hansestadt an der Elbe, den ich fortan Tag für Tag präzise abarbeitete. Der Trainingsplan umfaßte exakt 12 Wochen.

Das Wochenende vom 17./18. Januar verbrachte ich bei herrlichem Wetter mit starkem Wind und kalter Luft auf der ostfriesischen Insel Spiekeroog, wo ich den Strand der Insel fast völlig für mich allein hatte. Mein Trainingstagebuch vermerkt unter dem Samstag: »Spiekeroog, schönster Lauf, Meer, Einsamkeit, Wind, Sand, sehr hart. 10^0 C, 14 km, 1:30 Std.« Und in der Tat: So schön die Insel, die tosende Nordsee und die Dünen auch immer waren, nahezu die Hälfte der Strecke hatte ich auf Sand gegen einen sehr steifen Wind anzulaufen, der mich fast nicht von der Stelle kommen ließ und mir regelrecht die Kraft aus den Beinen zu saugen drohte. Dennoch wird mir dieser Lauf als ein wunderbares Naturerlebnis in Erinnerung bleiben.

Am Sonntag, den 15. Februar 1998 lief ich gemeinsam mit Herbert Steffny in Frankfurt/M. mit 27 km meine bis dato längste Strecke überhaupt (15^0 C, 27 km, 2:28 Std.), die ich wohl gut überstanden habe, denn an diesem Tag wird nichts Besonderes vermerkt. Mein Gewicht bewegte sich mittlerweile zwischen 73 und 75 Kilogramm. Am 1. März nahm ich an meinem ersten Wettkampf teil. Es war ein kalter, klarer Sonntagmor-

134

gen, der Himmel war stahlblau über dem Frankfurter Stadtwald, als morgens um 10 Uhr der Lauf begann. Die Zeitmessung erfolgte elektronisch per Chip. Ich lief mich gemeinsam mit dem Gros der Läufer einige Zeit warm, beobachtete dabei die Laufcracks aus Kenia, die später dann sowohl bei den Männern als auch bei den Frauen das Rennen unter sich ausmachen sollten, und dann erlebte ich zum ersten Mal die große Nervosität vor dem Start.

Der Beginn war sehr verwirrend für mich, denn alles rannte sofort furchtbar schnell los, und ehe ich mich versah, machte auch ich mächtig Tempo. Ich war viel zu schnell, wie ich bereits nach einigen hundert Metern an der Atmung spürte und dann auch am Pulsmesser sah. Die Koordination zwischen dem Laufen in der Hektik des Feldes und der eigenen Zeitkontrolle wollte also auch geübt sein. Ich reduzierte nach und nach meine Laufgeschwindigkeit und suchte mir eine Gruppe von Läufern, die mein Tempo liefen und an die ich mich hängen und von denen ich mich ziehen lassen konnte. Herbert Steffny hatte mir ein Ziel von ca. 1:40 Std. empfohlen, was einer Kilometerzeit von 4:45 Min. entsprach. Bis Kilometer 10 sollte ich stur nach Zwischenzeiten laufen, danach so schnell ich eben konnte und wollte.

Das war für einen Anfänger wie mich leichter gesagt als getan, denn die anfängliche Verwirrung und das allgemeine Loshetzen waren ansteckend für einen ungeübten Läufer wie mich. Nach wenigen Kilometern hatte ich mir also einen Vordermann ausgeguckt, der stur mein Tempo lief, und fortan wich ich nicht mehr von dessen Fersen. Ich hatte mich nach der Zehn-Kilometer-Marke richtig schön eingelaufen – es lief »rund«, wie man so schön sagt –, mein Vordermann leistete hervorragende Führungsarbeit bei einem gleichbleibend hohen Tempo, aber ich spürte, bei mir war noch etwas mehr drin. 3 Kilometer vor dem Ziel machte ich mich also allein auf den Weg und beendete meinen ersten Halbmarathon mit 1:37:33 Std. Mit dieser Zeit konnte ich durchaus zufrieden sein. Zudem, in welcher Verfassung hatte ich mich noch vor zwei Jahren befunden, im März 1996? Damals war wohl meine körperlich schlimmste Zeit gewesen, und ich hatte deutlich über 110 kg gewogen. Es geht also, sagte ich zu mir selbst. Und es geht sogar sehr gut – wenn man es will.

Am 15. März brachte ich meinen ersten Lauf über 30 km in 2:51 Std. hinter mich, besondere Vorkommnisse wurden nicht vermerkt. Die gab es dafür zwei Wochen später um so reichlicher. Der 29. März war ein Sonntag, und es sollte der erste richtig schöne Frühlingstag in diesem Jahr werden. An diesem Tag standen die 32 km auf meinem Plan, die längste Strecke, die ich im Training zu bewältigen haben würde. Es war richtig warm geworden, in der Sonne sogar heiß, als ich am frühen Nachmittag loslief. Ich nahm, wie bei allen langen Läufen übrigens, eine Flasche Wasser mit, um unterwegs den Flüssigkeitsverlust auszugleichen, da mein Körper nach ca. 20 km ohne Flüssigkeitsaufnahme doch negativ zu reagieren begann.

Zu Beginn ließ sich der Lauf wunderbar locker an, und ehe ich mich versah, war ich bereits nach drei Kilometern viel zu schnell. Aber es lief sich so leicht und locker, und so ging ich nicht mit dem Tempo runter, was sich als schwerer Fehler erweisen sollte. »Brutaler Einbruch nach 25 km, zu schnell begonnen, Hitze!« vermerkt mein Tagebuch. Und viel zu wenig getrunken! muß ich noch hinzufügen. Tempo, Temperaturwechsel und Flüssigkeitsverlust waren die Ursachen für nun auch meine Begegnung mit dem »Mann mit dem Hammer«. Nach 25 km raste mein Puls, ich reduzierte mein Lauftempo fast in den Kriechgang, aber ich bekam meinen Puls einfach nicht mehr unter die 130 Schläge pro Minute, und das ist bei mir der Beginn des oberen Bereichs. In den Ohren hatte ich plötzlich einen unguten Druck, ein Gefühl wie bei einem starken Schnupfen, sie waren zu, und die Beine gingen nur noch schwer voran. Mir machte eigentlich mehr die Reaktion meines Körpers Sorgen als die Kraft in den Beinen, denn das Laufen war zwar mühselig, aber von der Kraft her ging es immer noch voran.

Ich hatte zwar regelmäßig getrunken, und mein halber Liter Wasser war fast verbraucht, aber die Menge sollte sich an diesem warmen Frühlingstag als viel zu gering erweisen. Ich schleppte mich also weiter bis zur Wendemarke nach 16 km. Aufhören oder unterbrechen wollte ich nicht, denn es war noch genügend Kraft in den Beinen, nur der Puls und die merkwürdige Reaktion im Gehörgang machten mir Sorgen. Der Wasserhahn einer öffentlichen Toilette war auf dem Rückweg ein weiterer Rettungsanker, und nach 3:12:52 Std. war ich – völlig platt! – wieder zu Hause. Dieser Lauf sollte mir allerdings eine nachhaltige Lehre sein, denn ich hatte mich schlicht überschätzt und die Distanz, die Hitze und die Anstrengung unterschätzt. Das durfte mir in Hamburg auf keinen Fall passieren.

An den beiden Sonntagen vor Hamburg hatte ich noch zwei lange Dauerläufe über 30 km und 20 km zu bewältigen, über die es nichts weiter zu berichten gibt. Am Montag, dem 6. April, war ich auf Wahlkampfreise in Halle und lief dort 10 km mit dem zweimaligen Marathon-Olympiasieger von Montreal und Moskau, Waldemar Cierpinski, und vielen anderen Läufern. Ich fragte den Meister, was denn seiner Meinung nach das Wichtigste sei bei einem Marathon, und Waldemar Cierpinski sagte darauf nur ein Wort: »Disziplin!« Die meisten gingen einen Marathon viel zu schnell an, und

Mit dem Marathon-Olympiasieger Waldemar Cierpinski
in Halle, April 1998

dies gälte nicht nur für Freizeitmarathonis, sondern diesen Fehler finde man gerade auch in der Weltelite. Am Anfang, wenn die Stimmung an der Strecke und im Feld glänzend sei, oder auch während des Rennens, wenn das Publikum die Läufer anfeuere, würden sich viele mitreißen lassen und sich überschätzen. Dafür büße man später ganz furchtbar, denn ein Marathon begänne in der Regel ab Kilometer 34–36 erst richtig. Dort fielen die Entscheidungen, und dies gälte übrigens auch für die Freizeitläufer, denn ab dieser Hürde, wenn die Glykogenreserven des Körpers aufgebraucht seien, wären dann die meisten Einbrüche zu verzeichnen.

Oh ja, ich konnte Waldemar Cierpinski aufgrund der selbst gemachten Erfahrungen während meines desaströsen Laufs über 32 km nur zustimmen. *Disziplin im Training* und *Disziplin im Wettkampf,* zu der einen Maxime hatte ich ganz von selbst gefunden, und auch die andere würde ich in Zukunft – vor allem aber während der vor mir liegenden 42,195 km in Hamburg – genauestens befolgen. Am Sonntag, dem 12. April 1998, wurde ich 50 Jahre alt, begoß mein halbes Jahrhundert mit reichlich Mineralwasser der edelsten Lagen und wunderbarsten Jahrgänge, die die deutsche und europäische Mineralwasserindustrie hervorzubringen vermochte, und lief zudem brav meinen letzten langen Dauerlauf über 20 km, wie es der Trainingsplan befahl. Eine Woche lag jetzt noch zwischen mir und dem Abenteuer Marathon, und so langsam wurde mir doch etwas mulmig zumute: »Auf was hast du dich da nur eingelassen, Fischer?« fragte ich mich zunehmend selbst. Würde ich die Strecke durchstehen und wenn ja, wie? Immer wieder ging mir das Bild von dem früheren amerikanischen Präsidenten Jimmy Carter durch den Kopf – wie er nach einem Langlauf (ich meine aber, daß es kein Marathon gewesen war, was die Sache in meinem inneren Monolog allerdings nur noch schlimmer machte), von zwei Leibwächtern gestützt, völlig fertig über die Ziellinie geschleppt wurde. Andere Qualszenen von ins Ziel kriechenden oder völlig ausgelaugten und zusammenbrechenden Marathonläufern, die ich im Fernsehen gesehen hatte, ließen mich ebenfalls nicht mehr los. Und dann immer wieder all die vielen gruseligen Geschichten vom schon erwähnten »Mann mit dem Hammer«, die man allenthalben in Läuferkreisen zu hören und in Fachpublikationen zu lesen bekam. »Au weia«, dachte ich mir, »wenn das bloß gutgeht.«

Es werde ganz sicher gutgehen, sagte dann die andere Stimme in mir. »Bleib locker, Alter, du hast dich doch optimal vorbereitet. Du weißt doch ganz genau, wie hart und wie sorgfältig du trainiert hast. Keine Sorge also, das wird schon schiefgehen!« Ich fühlte mich topfit, läuferisch stark, hochmotiviert und der Herausforderung gewachsen. Ohne Verletzungspech und bei einer solch hervorragenden Vorbereitung durch Herbert Steffny konnte eigentlich nichts Schlimmes passieren. Es war mehr die Bänglichkeit vor der unbekannten Herausforderung als echte Angst. Es blieb noch eine weitere Frage zu klären, nämlich ein Mindestmaß an Schutz während des Wettkampfs vor der verständlichen Zudringlichkeit anderer Läufer. Viele würden mich begrüßen, mit mir laufen und vor allem mit mir reden wollen, und gerade das letztere war und ist mir ein veritables Greuel. Herbert Steffny hatte sowieso die Absicht, mich während des ganzen Laufes zu begleiten, und er wollte zudem noch zwei weitere marathonerfahrene Freunde aus Freiburg mitbringen, das müßte eigentlich reichen.

Am Montag lief ich nochmals 10 km im Dauerlauftempo (0:58:51 Std.), Dienstag Pause, Mittwoch 3x1000 m Tempo bei insgesamt 10 km in 0:58:53 Std., Donnerstag Pause, und Freitag und Samstag waren nur noch ganz lockere Läufchen über eine halbe Stunde angesagt. Der Marathon in Hamburg gilt in Läuferkreisen (zu Recht, wie ich erleben durfte!) als einer der schönsten Frühjahrswettkämpfe in Deutschland. Er habe nur eine Tücke, so Herbert Steffny, nämlich das Wetter. Der Hansemarathon läge in der zweiten Aprilhäfte, und so sei es schon häufiger vorgekommen, daß

just dann der jahreszeitlich bedingte Witterungs-
umschwung von kalt nach warm käme. Das
könne den Läufern Probleme bereiten, denn sie
hätten meist ihre gesamte Vorbereitung unter küh-
len bis kalten Temperaturen absolviert. Oh je,
seufzte ich still in mich hinein und dachte dabei
an meine furchtbaren 32 km.

All die Tage war es in diesem April noch kalt
gewesen (am Mittwoch vermerkt mein Trainingstagebuch 9^0 C), am Freitag fuhr ich nach Hamburg,
Freitag und Samstag erwies sich das Wetter als
noch wechselhaft und dem April voll angemessen,
und dann, tja, pünktlich zum Sonntag war der
warme Frühling da. Ein strahlend blauer Frühlingstag wartete an Elbe und Alster auf die über 10 000
angemeldeten Marathonläufer, kühl und klar am
Morgen, aber so ab 11.00 Uhr dürfte es dann doch
ganz schön warm werden. Wieder mußte ich an
meine böse Erfahrung während des vermaledeiten
Laufs über 32 km denken. Ich schwor mir, die
Strecke mit der nötigen Vorsicht anzugehen. Lieber etwas langsamer als einbrechen, hieß meine
Devise.

Doch zuvor bekam ich noch ein weiteres Problem. Ich fühlte mich seit Donnerstag nacht
krank, hatte Gliederschmerzen, leichte Temperatur und allgemeines Unwohlsein. Nervosität oder
Virus, das war jetzt die Frage, aber ich wollte unbedingt am Sonntag starten. Ich ließ am Freitag den

Lockerungslauf ausfallen und erholte mich ausschließlich passiv. Die Temperatur nahm nicht zu, am Samstag fühlte ich mich bereits wieder wohler, wenn auch noch nicht völlig wiederhergestellt, so daß ich mit Herbert Steffny ein kleines Lockerungsläufchen unternahm. Abends bereitete ich mir meinen Haferbrei aus pürierten Früchten, Bananen, ganz feinen Haferflocken und Milch für den nächsten Morgen zu, und dann war es nach einer letzten, gut verbrachten Nacht soweit.

Morgens um sieben weckte mich der Wecker, und ich frühstückte eine ordentliche Menge meines Breis, dazu trank ich Tee. Brustwarzen mit Pflaster abkleben, Achseln, Schritt und Füße mit Vaseline eincremen, rein in die Klamotten, nochmals die Liste meines Trainers rekapitulieren – Schuhe und Strümpfe waren gut eingelaufen, Brustwarzen geschützt, Vaseline aufgetragen – und los. Ich war nervös, auch wenn ich mir nach außen nichts anmerken ließ, aber, und das war heute besonders wichtig, ich fühlte mich wieder völlig frei von Beschwerden und demnach topfit. Gegen 8:30 Uhr holte mich Herbert Steffny mit seiner Familie ab, Chip und Nummer – ich hatte die Startnummer 50 – wurden befestigt, in der Nähe des Start/Ziel-Bereichs an der Hamburger Messe liefen wir uns nach einer spontan zustande gekommenen Pressekonferenz noch einige Zeit warm, hier ein Interview, dort ein Photo, zehn Minuten vor dem

144

Beginn suchten wir unseren Startbereich auf, sehr viele Fragen und Hallos von unbekannten Lauffreunden, und dann, pünktlich um 10:00 Uhr, ging es auch schon los. Zwei riesige Kolonnen von Läuferinnen und Läufern bewegten sich Richtung Reeperbahn, kurz vorher wurden sie zu einem Feld zusammengeführt, und dann ging es weiter über die leere Reeperbahn Richtung Westen, über Altona, Ottensen nach Othmarschen hinaus. Dort wurde dann nach etwa sechs Kilometern zum ersten Mal die Richtung gewechselt, und fortan liefen wir über die feine Elbchaussee in die gerade Gegenrichtung nach Osten, Richtung Hamburg-Centrum.

Draußen im Hamburger Westen war die Stimmung prächtig, in den vornehmeren Gegenden saßen Anwohner beim Champagnerfrühstück in ihren Campingstühlen und prosteten den keuchenden Läufern fröhlich zu. In Ottensen spielte dann zum ersten Mal eine Dixieband auf, die Fans am Straßenrand waren zu dieser frühen Stunde schon sehr gut drauf und feuerten uns heftig an. Weiter zog sich der Lauf in Richtung St. Pauli Landungsbrücken, im großen Bogen südlich an der Elbe entlang und dann östlich um die Altstadt herum, durch eine längere Unterführung am Hauptbahnhof vorbei, Binnenalster, Außenalster, und schließlich in Uhlenhorst weg von der Alster nach Barmbek und weiter hinauf in Hamburgs fernen Norden. Ich bekam bei meinem ersten Marathon nicht allzuviel mit von der Umgebung und der Atmosphäre, weil ich mich ganz auf den Lauf konzentrierte, aber es war dennoch beeindruckend, die Unterschiede der Stadtteile und der Fans am Straßenrand zu erleben. Hamburg war für mich bis dahin eine fremde Stadt, seit dem Marathon ist mir die Hansestadt in ihrer Buntheit und Unterschiedlichkeit eigentlich recht vertraut. Ein Citymarathon ist keine üble Art, fremde Städte im wahrsten Sinne des Wortes »laufend« kennenzulernen.

In Barmbek selbst wie auch auf den Kilometern davor war die Stimmung prächtig, der Himmel wunderbar blau, die Sonne strahlte, und die Hamburger waren so langsam alle aufgestanden und feuerten die Läufer nach Leibeskräften an. Und immer wenn wir uns einem alten Ortskern näherten und die Menschen links und rechts der Straße dichter standen und demnach die Stimmung heißer wurde, nahm das Feld unmerklich Tempo auf. Herbert Steffny hatte mir geraten, mich bei 132–135 Pulsschlägen pro Minute zu halten. Ich konnte die Tempoverschärfungen an meinem Pulsmesser ablesen, der dann 140 und mehr anzeigte, ohne daß die Beschleunigung körperlich spürbar gewesen wäre. Das Adrenalin tat ganz offensichtlich seine Wirkung, und ich mußte an Waldemar Cierpinskis Wort von der »Disziplin« denken. Bloß nicht übermütig werden.

146

Hamburg-Marathon, 19. April 1998, mit Herbert Steffny (rechts)

Dafür sorgte freilich mein unermüdlicher Begleiter und Trainer, der streng die Kilometerzeit kon-
trollierte, mich mit Wasser und einer Mischung
aus Apfelsaft, Cola und Kochsalz versorgte, auch
regelmäßig zum Trinken anhielt und ansonsten
die Gespräche mit den allfälligen Laufkameraden
führte, die mich permanent ausfragen wollten.
Manche trieben es gar toll, so daß mir bisweilen
angst und bange wurde, denn ich fürchtete zu stolpern. Ein besonders Vorwitziger legte sich dann
auch prompt vor mir in vollem Lauf der Länge
lang hin, weil er unbedingt im Rückwärtslaufen
mit mir reden wollte, und ich hatte Mühe, einem
Zusammenstoß auszuweichen. Bisweilen war die
Situation schon leicht verrückt. Aber je länger der
Lauf dauerte, desto ruhiger und wortkarger wurden die Mitläufer. Dennoch wurde ich immer wieder hart bedrängt, denn viele Läufer wollten einfach mit mir laufen, »mit aufs Bild«, wie es so schön
heißt und was ja nachvollziehbar war. Solange sie
mich nicht zum Stolpern brachten oder mit mir
reden wollten, sollte mir das auch egal sein. Meine
Begleiter hatten auf jeden Fall alle Hände und
Beine voll zu tun.

In Barmbek hatten wir die Halbmarathondi-
stanz bereits hinter uns gelassen, und nun begann
sich die Strecke zu ziehen, wurde lang und länger.
Die Kilometer dehnten sich subjektiv immer weiter, die Zuschauer waren weniger geworden, und

noch waren die 30 Kilometer nicht erreicht. Die Beine waren zwar zu spüren, aber es lief sich dennoch hervorragend, ruhiger Rhythmus und keine wirkliche Ermüdung. Nur die Monotonie drückte in der langen zweiten Hälfte etwas aufs Gemüt. Da hörte ich hinter mir etwa bei Kilometer 27 oder 28 – wir hatten die City Nord bereits passiert – die Stimme eines mitlaufenden Reporters der bekanntesten deutschen Boulevardzeitung, wie er seiner Redaktion mit einem leichten Bedauern in der Stimme auf Anruf und per Handy mitteilte: »Nein, der läuft ruhig sein Tempo. Der kommt mit Sicherheit an.« Das war für meinen Kopf geistige Aufbaunahrung vom Feinsten.

Der junge Mann von der Boulevardzeitung hatte sich am Start ordentlich vorgestellt. Seine Zentralredaktion habe ihn aus Süddeutschland eingeflogen, er selbst sei Marathonläufer, so um die 2:45 Std. herum, und er wolle mich begleiten. Ich konnte nichts dagegen haben, denn selbstverständlich stand es jedem Läufer frei, da zu laufen, wo er wolle. Ich bat ihn aber um Rücksichtnahme und daß er mich während des Laufs in Ruhe lassen sollte, und ich konnte mich über meinen unfreiwilligen Begleiter wirklich nicht beschweren. Zwar klingelte dann und wann sein Handy, und er hatte an seine Redaktion zu berichten. Ich wurde auch das Gefühl nicht los, leicht geierhaft von hinten taxiert zu werden, wann ich denn nun endlich alle viere von mir zu strecken gedächte, aber diesen Gefallen würde ich ihm eh nicht tun. Wie auch immer, je länger der Lauf ging, desto mehr kümmerte sich auch mein mitlaufender Beobachter von der Presse um mein körperliches Wohl und bildete einen zusätzlichen Sicherheitsfaktor gegen gefährliche Rempeleien. Irgendwie gehörte er zu unserer Gruppe dazu, und ich war ihm dankbar dafür.

In Eppendorf – längst waren wir bereits wieder auf Südkurs gegangen, Richtung Ziel – hatte ich dann zum ersten Mal in meinem Leben die magische 36-Kilometer-Marke erreicht, und es trat genau das ein, was mir Herbert Steffny prophezeit hatte: »Wenn du gut vorbereitet bist und dein Tempo läufst, wirst du lediglich langsam müde werden.« In der Tat, vom »Mann mit dem Hammer« keine Spur. In Eppendorf trafen wir zudem auf eine großartige Volksfeststimmung, die Menschen standen dicht an dicht gedrängt und ließen uns kaum eine zwei Meter breite Gasse zum Durchlaufen. Die Stimmung übertrug sich direkt auf die Beine, und es ging trotz zunehmender Müdigkeit besser voran. Bloß jetzt nicht stolpern! Ich konzentrierte mich also voll auf die Strecke und bekam von dem ganzen Geschrei und Rummel nur sehr wenig mit. Und dann hatten wir plötzlich wieder die Außenalster erreicht, nur diesmal das Westufer, und das hieß, daß das Ziel nicht mehr weit vor uns lag. Dann bogen wir auch schon rechts ab zum Bahnhof Dammtor, die Straße stieg leicht an, wir waren am Bahnhof vorbei, bogen noch einmal links ab in die Karolinenstraße, und dann war das Ziel erreicht. 42,195 Kilometer in einer elektronisch gemessenen Nettozeit von 3:41:36 Std., und von 10 134 Läufern, die im Ziel ankamen, war dies der 4 179. Platz. Na also.

Körperlich war ich nach dem Zieleinlauf in ganz guter Verfassung, da wäre durchaus noch eine bessere Zeit drin gewesen, aber aus den genannten Gründen war es besser, Vorsicht walten zu lassen. Kein Zusammenbruch, keine Qualbilder, sondern

Hamburg-Marathon, 19. April 1998

in passabler Verfassung und guter Zeit den Marathon beendet, das hatte ich mir vorgenommen, und das genau hatte ich hiermit auch erreicht. Der Lauf selbst war ein großes persönliches Erlebnis gewesen, an das ich in den kommenden Wochen noch oft denken sollte, wenn ich Zeit hatte, meinen eigenen Gedanken nachzuhängen. Am Ziel wartete eine Wand von Fotografen auf mich, durch die kein Durchkommen war, so daß wir ziemlich abrupt anhalten mußten. Ein ruhiges Auslaufen war leider nicht möglich, und so mußte ich mir schlicht Mühe geben, die Beine anzuhalten, denn mein Geläuf wollte einfach weitermachen. Zuerst war ich deshalb etwas wacklig beim Stehen, aber das gab sich schnell. Später wurde ich todmüde, und noch etwas später bekam ich einen Bärenhunger, aber ansonsten fühlte ich mich sehr gut, und das sollte sich auch in den folgenden Tagen und Wochen nicht ändern.

Ich hatte es also geschafft, ich war meinen ersten Marathon gelaufen! Nur eindreiviertel Jahre nach meinem ganz persönlichen Desaster im Sommer 1996 und mit Erreichen meines fünfzigsten Lebensjahres hatte ich meinen ersten Marathonlauf erfolgreich hinter mich gebracht. Ich dachte zurück an jenen unseligen August vor knapp zwei Jahren. Vom Abnehmen zum Marathon! Alles hatte mit dem Vorsatz begonnen abzunehmen, und siehe da, es hatte funktioniert. Ein anderes

Programm, ein anderer Lebensstil, andere Ziele und andere Prioritäten sowie eine unerschütterliche Disziplin und viel Geduld und Ausdauer hatten diese ganz persönliche Wende, ja Erneuerung möglich gemacht. Die beruflichen Herausforderungen, ja, meine gesamten Lebensumstände hatten sich nicht wirklich verändert, und dennoch waren sowohl das Abnehmen als auch der Marathon in solch kurzer Zeit möglich geworden.

VII

Mein Lauf zu mir selbst

Mit dem Marathon war mein letztes Ziel erreicht. Ich war erschöpft, glücklich und stolz zugleich. Wie so oft im Leben ist der Zieleinlauf die schönste Zeit, denn mit dem Erreichen eines Ziels beginnt sogleich die Frage nach dem Danach. Mit meinem persönlichen Erfolg von Hamburg hatte ich zugleich meine letzte und größte läuferische Herausforderung bewältigt und fiel anschließend in ein kleines Motivationsloch. Wie weiter jetzt? Was sollte ich mir noch weiter vornehmen? Kommt Zeit, kommt Rat, sagte ich mir, zur Eile bei der Beantwortung dieser Frage bestand ja überhaupt kein Anlaß, und ergo ließ ich es einige Wochen nach Hamburg läuferisch sehr ruhig angehen. Ab der zweiten Wochenhälfte machte ich wieder ruhige, langsame Joggingläufe über 10 km, und zwei Wochen später wechselte ich wieder zwischen schnelleren und langsameren Trainingseinheiten. Selten lief ich täglich mehr als 10 km, diese Strecke aber dafür regelmäßig fünf- bis sechsmal die Woche. Ernährung und Lebensstil blieben ebenfalls unverändert, denn ich wollte unbedingt Form und Figur halten.

Halb-Marathon in Stuttgart, Juni 1998

Die Verhältnisse hatten sich gründlich verkehrt. Das tägliche Laufen war für mich zu Beginn immer nur ein *Mittel* gewesen, um einen ganz bestimmten *Zweck* zu erreichen, nämlich abzunehmen. Dieser Zweck war erreicht worden, sehr gut sogar, nur daß sich mittlerweile die Zweck-Mittel-Relation völlig verkehrt hatte. Das Laufen war sich selbst Zweck genug geworden, und ich wollte und will diese fast tägliche Erfahrung von Körper und Bewegung, Anstrengung und innerer Ruhe einfach nicht mehr missen. Mit dem Marathon war auch der innere Umbau abgeschlossen, dies spürte ich sehr klar. Ich wußte jetzt, daß ich meinen neuen Lebensstil gefunden hatte, daß der Jojo-Effekt definitiv überwunden war und daß ich auch in Zukunft dem Laufen treu bleiben würde. Es gab ja durchaus die eine oder andere Verdächtigung, die mir unterstellte, ich würde den Marathon nur als Werbegag laufen. »Idioten«, dachte ich mir dazu, denn was hatte ich in den vergangenen Monaten nicht alles an Training geleistet. Die vielen Stunden allein auf der Straße waren nicht für einen PR-Gag gewesen. »Aber was soll's«, dachte ich mir, du hast dies ausschließlich und allein für dich selbst getan.« Laß reden, was immer wer reden will.« Ich brauchte auch keine neue läuferische Herausforderung mehr, denn ich hatte zu mir selbst gefunden. So stand mein Entschluß fest: Ich werde einfach weiterlaufen!

Wie unzählige andere Freizeitläufer bin ich meinen Marathon ausschließlich gegen mich selbst gelaufen, nicht gegen die Uhr und auch nicht gegen Konkurrenten. Gewiß, die Cracks laufen um Sieg und Platz, um Bestzeiten und gegen die Gegner, ein Wettkampf eben. Dies gilt aber nicht für die unzähligen Freizeitläufer, die den Charme und die Massenfaszination eines Stadtmarathons ganz wesentlich mit bestimmen. Oft über zehntausend und mehr Läufer laufen hier vor allem für sich selbst und gegen sich selbst – und viele unter ihnen tun dies immer wieder. Über diese Strecke zählt die Leistung eines jeden einzelnen, denn die 42,195-Kilometer-Distanz durchgehalten zu haben und angekommen zu sein ist eine große Leistung gegen sich selbst.

Dennoch gibt es für mich aus meiner bescheidenen Freizeitperspektive einen wichtigen qualitativen Unterschied zwischen Wettkampf und Training, wobei der Begriff »Training« eigentlich in die Irre führt. Gemeint ist hier der Unterschied zwischen dem Laufen für mich und dem Laufen in einem Wettkampf. So schön und fordernd der Wettkampf auch immer sein mag, die wirkliche Erfahrung des Laufens findet sich für mich nur allein mit mir selbst. Wie bereits gesagt, es macht dabei überhaupt nichts, wenn man in Begleitung läuft, solange diese nicht ablenkt und man sich selbst überlassen bleibt. Manch merkwürdigen und kuriosen Typen begegnete ich beim Laufen, und alle hatten sie diesen auf unendlich gestellten Blick in den Augen. Einer sprach mich mal an, als wir uns am Rheinufer begegneten, ohne mich zu erkennen. Wir liefen einige Kilometer in dieselbe Richtung, und mein Gefährte des Zufalls redete so vor sich hin, das übliche Läufergarn eben über Marathon, Läufe durch die Wüste, etc. Der Typ fing an zu nerven, als mich sein Monolog unversehens zu interessieren begann. Er fragte mich recht unvermittelt, ob ich denn beim Laufen schon meinem Buddha begegnet wäre? Ich war zuerst ziemlich perplex, dann wunderte ich mich darüber, daß mich offensichtlich die Esoterik bereits beim Laufen eingeholt hatte, aber dennoch war jetzt meine Neugierde geweckt. Was wollte mir der Typ mit seinem Buddha sagen? Er liefe, sagte er mir noch, um eben seinem Buddha zu begegnen, und zwar seit vielen, vielen Jahren. Sprach's, bog links ab und war auch schon weg, bevor ich ihm eine verdutzte Antwort zuhecheln konnte.

Keine Angst, liebe Leserschaft, Laufen hat, trotz dieses komischen Kauzes am Bonner Rheinufer, nichts mit Esoterik zu tun, auch wenn man in der Laufszene gewiß jede Menge Gurus findet. Weder der »runner's high« noch der »laufende Buddha« sind mir bis heute wirklich begegnet. Vielleicht habe ich da ja das eigentliche Erlebnis noch vor mir, auch wenn ich diesbezüglich in meinen

Erwartungen sehr pessimistisch bin. Dennoch vermittelt das Laufen eine starke meditative Erfahrung, und die ist mir mittlerweile, neben der körperlichen Fitneß, zum wichtigsten Inhalt beim Laufen geworden. Es gibt zwei Grundtypen von Läufern: die einen suchen die Gesellschaft, den Kontakt und das Gespräch, die anderen die Einsamkeit, die Ruhe und die Meditation. Und genau das letztere ist es, was ich so sehr am Laufen liebe.

Freilich ließ das Jahr 1998 nicht viel an Einsamkeit zu. Mehrere Landtagswahlkämpfe und ein langer Bundestagswahlkampf zwangen mich zu einem ganz anderen, zu einem monatelangen politischen Marathon durch alle deutschen Bundesländer. Am 14. Juni lief ich ohne weitere Vorberei-

Klatschnaß unterwegs im bayrischen Wahlkampf, 1998

tung in Stuttgart noch einen Halbmarathon, dann kam der bayrische Landtagswahlkampf, kurz unterbrochen durch zwei Wochen Urlaub und Laufen in der Crete, und dann ging es voll in den Wahlkampf. Am 10. August vermerkt mein Tagebuch: »Aachen, Dreiländer-Eck, heiß, hart, Berg, Tempo; 35^0 C, 11 km, 0:56:49 Std.« In der Tat. Es war ein heißer und schwüler Nachmittag gewesen, fast fünfzig bis sechzig Läufer am Start, und vom Start an ging es bergauf. Das Feld fiel sehr schnell auseinander, und das Tempo wurde von zwei jungen Frauen gemacht, die einen wunderbaren Stil liefen, der fast schwerelos wirkte. Die Strecke war hügelig, die Temperatur gnadenlos und das Tempo sehr hoch. Wie ich später erfuhr, handelte es sich bei den beiden Läuferinnen um Ultramarathonis, die beide als junge Mütter zum Ultramarathon gekommen waren. Am nächsten Tag, in Düsseldorf am Rheinufer, war es mit 37^0 C noch heißer, dann Bielefeld wieder mit 35^0 C und den Anstiegen im Teutoburger Wald, auch alles andere als einfach. Vor allem hatte ich jetzt fast täglich Tempo zu bolzen, denn die mit jedem Wahlkampftag wechselnden Läufer wollten es jedesmal irgendwie wissen. Von Meditation war da nichts mehr zu finden.

Am Ende dieses Wahlkampfes hatte ich nicht nur politisch, sondern auch läuferisch alle Bundesländer durcheilt. Den einsamen sportlichen Höhepunkt erreichte ich am 15. August, einem Samstag,

Düsseldorf-Kaiserswerth, während des Bundestagswahlkampfs 1998, mit Reporter

und zwar in Jena. Es war ein schwüler früher Nachmittag, 28 Grad heiß, und es sollte über ca. 13 Kilometer durch die Jenaer Kernberge gehen. Jena liegt im Tal der Saale, das dort tief in den Kalkstein der höher gelegenen Umgebung einschneidet. Diesen steilen Anstieg nennt man die »Kernberge«. Wir starteten mit einem Feld von etwa dreißig Läufern, und nach etwa einem Kilometer ging es bereits steil einen Waldweg entlang hinauf, bis etwa auf die halbe Höhe der Kernberge. Das Tempo war von Beginn an ziemlich stramm, und an dem ersten langen Anstieg brachen bereits viele weg. Der Kalkstein brütete in der Sommersonne, als wir mehrere Kilometer mit hohem Tempo über einen sehr schmalen Saumpfad in halber Höhe das Tal entlangliefen. Nach ca. 7 Kilometern kam der zweite Anstieg, und dort wurden wir noch weniger. Oben auf der Höhe angekommen, sammelte sich eine Gruppe von gerade noch ganzen sechs Läufern, und ein junger Mann machte an der Spitze weiterhin ein sehr heftiges Tempo. Am Ende liefen wir zu dritt nach 13 Kilometern

In Jena vor den Kern-Bergen

und 1:11:24 Std. im Ziel ein. Das Feld war völlig zerlegt worden, und die Läufer kamen schließlich einzeln in ganz kleinen Gruppen und mit teilweise erheblichen Zeitabständen an. Jena war eindeutig die »Königsetappe« in diesem läuferischen Bundestagswahlkampf gewesen. »Jena-Kernberge, Wettkampf, sehr steil, hart, Form exzellent«, findet sich in meinem Tagebuch, und noch heute träume ich manchmal von diesem Lauf. Er hat fast mehr Eindrücke bei mir hinterlassen als mein erster Marathon.

Der Ausgang der Bundestagswahlen hat zwar sehr viel in meinem Leben geändert, gewiß aber nicht das Laufen. Zeit findet sich fast immer, wenn man nur will. Selbst der engste Terminkalender und der größte Streß des deutschen Außenministers lassen in der Regel an irgendeiner Ecke des Tages oder der Nacht noch Luft für einen Lauf über 10 Kilometer. Oft wurde (und werde) ich jetzt in die Nachtstunden gedrückt, bisweilen sogar nach Mitternacht. Vor allem im Winterhalbjahr gehört die Dunkelheit beim Laufen mehr zum Regelfall als zur Ausnahme. Ja, und selbstverständlich wurden die Laufstrecken auch internationaler: Washington, New York, Rio, Jerusalem, Dakar, London, Beirut, Rom, Lappland, um nur einige zu nennen.

Und dennoch kehre ich vor allem immer wieder und überaus gerne in die Crete zurück. Dort, wo alles für mich in einem gewaltigen persönli-

Vor dem Kapitol

chen Desaster im Sommer 1996 begonnen hatte, liegt heute noch mein schönstes und liebstes Laufrevier. Die Hitze, der Staub, die Hügel und das unvergeßliche Licht der Toskana – all das zieht mich immer wieder zurück. In diesem Sommer lief ich meine ganz persönliche Horrorstrecke von Torre a Castello nach Asciano sogar hin und zurück, 24 Kilometer, davon 13 Kilometer richtig heftig steile An- und Abstiege. »2:23:13 Std.«, vermerkt mein Tagebuch, »maximale Härte.« Die Strecke von Torre nach Asciano oder vice versa (12 km, wobei der Rückweg mehr Anstiege enthält und deswegen wesentlich schwerer ist und über zwei Minuten länger dauert) hatte ich mir in den Jahren zuvor klopfenden Herzens nur einmal zugetraut, jetzt lief ich sie neben den 24 Kilometern insgesamt fünfmal in diesem Urlaub. Zudem »besuchte« ich noch per pedes einen sehr guten Freund, dessen Haus 20 Kilometer und einige herbe Hügel entfernt in der Crete liegt.

Mein altes Leben, der gewaltige Bauch, die Pfunde, die gänzlich andere Ernährung – all dies scheint mir heute eine Ewigkeit zurückzuliegen. Wenn ich alte Bilder und Filmausschnitte sehe, denke ich mir selbst: »Mensch, wie konntest du nur?« Ich hatte mich bereits selbst aufgegeben. Dabei liegt diese Zeit erst drei Jahre zurück. Mein ganz persönlicher Umbau bedurfte großer Anstrengungen und einer eisernen Willenskraft, aber zugleich stellten sich die Veränderungen in Gewicht und Umfang schneller ein als gedacht. Und die glücklichste Fügung in all diesen Umbrüchen war die, daß ich mich für das Laufen entschieden habe. Vielleicht meinte jener laufende Kauz, der mir die Geschichte über die Suche nach seinem Buddha erzählt hat, ja nur die eine Botschaft: *Es geht!* Man muß nur bereit sein, die ersten Schritte zu tun, und dann immer weiter laufen.

Das Lauftier in dir – Jogging ohne Qual!

Ein Nachwort von Herbert Steffny

Vielleicht hatten Sie Ihr letztes Erfolgserlebnis beim Laufen mit einem Jahr, als Sie unter der anerkennenden Aufmunterung Ihrer Eltern der Schwerkraft zum ersten Mal auf zwei Beinen trotzten? Danach haben wir scheinbar nur noch eins im Sinn, nämlich, uns diese dem Menschen so ureigenst auf den Leib geschneiderte Bewegungsform über Dreirad, Roller, Fahrrad, Mofa und Führerschein systematisch abzugewöhnen. Vielleicht haben Sie Laufen aus Ihrer Schulzeit noch in traumatischer Erinnerung? Ohne Training mußten Sie sich einem 1000-Meter-Test unterwerfen, für die meisten ein Streichergebnis. Wir »surfen« im Internet, »laufen« beim Einkaufsbummel in der Stadt, aber landläufig versteht man darunter eigentlich »gehen«. Diese sprachliche Verschiebung ist Kennzeichen unserer modernen Gesellschaft mit ihrer Bewegungsarmut und den damit verbundenen Zivilisationskrankheiten. Immerhin stirbt jeder zweite an Herz-Kreislauf-Erkrankungen.

Eigentlich sind unsere Gene – Joschka Fischer hat im Vorhergehenden darauf hingewiesen –

noch die eines »Lauftiers«, also auf Bewegung programmiert. Sie ändern sich nicht in ein paar Jahrzehnten Müßiggangs. Jahrmillionen war Fitneß eine Notwendigkeit zum Überleben. Der Urmensch war ein ausdauernder Jäger und Sammler, kein besonders schneller Läufer, eher ein »Walker und Jogger«. Der tägliche Aktionsradius zum Nahrungserwerb betrug viele Kilometer. Der rasante technische Fortschritt der letzten 200 Jahre machte bei uns aus körperlich stark geforderten Hirtennomaden, Jägern, Bauern und Handwerkern wohlhabende, bequemliche und übergewichtige »couch potatoes«, deren wichtigste Freizeitbeschäftigung das »Pantoffelkino« ist und die rückengeschädigt bei der Arbeit überwiegend im Büro oder hinter dem Lenkrad ihres Autos sitzen. Biologische Systeme brauchen aber zu ihrem Erhalt einen ständigen (Bewegungs-)Reiz. Bleibt dieser aus, so wird die Struktur oder Funktion, weil scheinbar nutzlos, abgebaut. Das passiert mit den kontinuierlich schrumpfenden Muskeln im Gipsverband, mit unterforderten Knochen und Gelenken und auch mit unserem Herzkreislaufsystem.

»Gesundheit ist gewiß nicht alles, aber ohne Gesundheit ist alles nichts!« sagte Arthur Schopenhauer. Noch nie hatten die USA, das »Mutterland« des Joggings und des »light food«, soviel Übergewichtige wie heute, auch wenn als Reaktion auf Bewegungsarmut und steigende Zivilisationskrankheiten der seit 1968 millionenfach verkaufte Bestseller »Aerobics« von Dr. Kenneth Cooper die Jogging- und Walkingwelle in den USA auslöste, die dann zu uns hinüberschwappte.

Auch die Deutschen belegen europaweit in puncto Fitneß und Körpergewicht Schlußplätze. 1975 startete die deutsche Lauftreffbewegung, und es erschien das erste Laufmagazin »Spiridon«. Der Boom der Citymarathons seit den Achtzigern gipfelt in bis zu 40.000 Läufern in Boston und zwei Millionen Zuschauern in New York. Freizeitsport, Trimmtrab und Lauftreff werden zur Ersatzhandlung für frühere, bewegungsreichere Tage.

Joschka Fischer ist derzeit der prominenteste deutsche Fitneßläufer. »Unter dem Druck einer persönlichen Katastrophe« vollzog er einen längst fälligen Systemwechsel. Er ist das Aushängeschild eines neuen Booms, einer sanften Laufbewegung. Nicht mehr Bestzeiten und Tempobolzen wie in den siebziger oder achtziger Jahren sind Trumpf, sondern Jogging für Abnehmen, Fitneß, Gesundheit und Lebensqualität bis ins Rentenalter. Joschka Fischers Wende macht Übergewichtigen und Älteren Mut. Das Leben ist nach 40 noch lange nicht vorbei. Sein »geist- und körperreinigender Egotrip«, gepaart mit Willensstärke von olympischem Format, vom mühseligen Einstieg mit 112 Kilogramm bis zum Marathonlauf mit 50 Jahren motiviert viele, die sich eigentlich längst schon abgeschrieben haben. Er zündete als hervorragender Autodidakt »die Kerze von zwei Enden an«. Fitneßexperten wissen, daß Abnehmen nur sinnvoll in der Kombination Ernährungsumstellung mit Bewegung funktioniert.

Früher belächelt, genießen Marathonläufer heute Respekt. Sie verfügen über außerordentliche Willensstärke, Zielstrebigkeit, können lange Durststrecken überwinden und erweitern ihre körperlichen und geistigen Grenzen. Es muß kein Marathon sein, laufen geht auch kürzer. Jogger sind heute eigentlich das herumlaufende schlechte Gewissen der noch Inaktiven. Sie kennen die Ausrede: Ich hab keine Zeit! Joschka Fischer kann man kaum vorwerfen, er hätte zuviel davon. Statt Kompensation mit Zigaretten, »Frustfressen« und Alkohol in Kneipen griff er zu Laufschuhen und wurde zum Genußläufer, zum »Laufgourmet«. Aufbau statt Raubbau. Laufen gibt ihm Zeit nachzudenken, zu meditieren, er findet dabei Harmonie und innere Ruhe. Es ist gewonnene Zeit. Zwischen Flughafen und Bundestagssitzung schiebt er einen kleinen Dauerlauf, und seine Batterie ist wieder voll.

Laufen ist mehr als stur ein Bein vor das andere zu setzen. Sie schlagen mehrere Fliegen mit einer Klappe: ruhiges Jogging stärkt das Herzkreislauf- und Immunsystem, hält die Gefäße elastisch, schmiert die Gelenke und stabilisiert die Knochen, es regelt den Blutdruck und Blutzuckerspiegel, senkt Cholesterin, sensibilisiert für eine gesündere Ernährung, vermindert das Körpergewicht und baut auf natürliche Art und Weise die Streßhormone ab. Insbesondere im Alter bedeutet das eine erheblich verbesserte Lebensqualität. Laufen oder walken kann man in jedem Alter, es ist nie zu spät einzusteigen. In New York berichtete mir ein 90jähriger Marathonläufer, daß er mit dem Laufen erst mit 75 begonnen habe! Man benötigt wenig Ausrüstung, produziert keine Abgase und Lärm. Es ist sehr zeiteffizient, und man kann es eigentlich überall, zu jeder Jahreszeit, mit der richtigen Funktionskleidung bei jedem Wetter ausüben. Eigentlich alles klar, wenn da nicht die Trägheit wäre, sich aufzuraffen. Die längste Reise beginnt bekanntlich mit dem ersten Schritt:

- Wenn Sie über 35 Jahre alt sind oder längere Zeit keinen Sport betrieben haben, sollten Sie sich von einem sporterfahrenen Arzt grünes Licht geben lassen.
- Laufen ist billig. Trainieren Sie nicht in irgendeinem Fitneß-Schuh, sondern kaufen Sie sich in einem Fachgeschäft mit Beratung einen richtigen »Laufschuh«, sonst ruinieren Sie sich die Knochen.
- Ziehen Sie pflegeleichte und schweißtransportierende Funktionstextilien an.
- Wer orthopädische Beschwerden hat, nicht

sehr fit, stark übergewichtig, schwanger oder älter ist, sollte es vielleicht zunächst mit Radfahren, Schwimmen oder Walking, dem flotten Gehen mit Armeinsatz, versuchen.

- Laufen Sie nicht bei Schmerzen, einem Infekt oder Fieber!
- Suchen Sie Gleichgesinnte im Bekanntenkreis oder einen Lauftreff.
- Beginnen Sie auf einer flachen Strecke auf ebenem Waldboden.
- Atmen Sie frei und ungezwungen durch Mund und Nase, es wird sich ein natürlicher Atemrhythmus einstellen.
- Führen Sie die Arme locker nach vorne neben dem Körper, pendeln Sie nicht nach innen.
- Optimale Ausdauerfitneß erreichen Sie, wenn Sie ganzjährig dreimal die Woche wenigstens eine halbe Stunde in einem erstaunlich sanften Tempo ohne Qual joggen. Ein guter Maßstab ist die simple Regel, nur so schnell (bzw. langsam) zu laufen, daß man sich noch gut unterhalten kann.
- Sie können die Intensität auch mit einem Herzfrequenzmeßgerät steuern. Laufen Sie bei der Pulsfrequenz, die der Formel: 180 minus Ihrem Lebensalter (plus minus 10 Schläge) entspricht.
- Wer mit Laufen Fettpolster abbauen will, muß langsam und länger laufen. Wer schnell rennt, verbrennt mehr Kohlenhydrate, aber kaum Fett.

174

Pro Kilometer verbrauchen Sie so viele Kilokalorien, wie Ihr Körpergewicht in Kilo wiegt.

- Kurze Gehpausen sind in den ersten Wochen erlaubt und sinnvoll.
- Lassen Sie Ihrem Körper Zeit, über Wochen und Monate in die neue Belastung hineinzuwachsen, sonst sind Verletzungen und Frust die Folge.
- Laufen Sie nicht immer schneller, sondern zunächst etwas länger oder öfter.
- Essen Sie spätestens eineinhalb Stunden vorher etwas Leichtes wie eine Banane, sonst können Sie Seitenstiche bekommen.
- Ersetzen Sie Schweißverluste mit Mineralwasser oder Fruchtsäften.
- Reduzieren Sie tierische Fette, Kaffee, Alkohol und Süßigkeiten. Essen Sie vermehrt Obst, Gemüse, Salate, Vollkornprodukte, Kartoffeln und Fisch.
- Ergänzen Sie Laufen durch Dehnungs- und Lockerungsübungen für Schultern, Waden und Oberschenkel, und kräftigen Sie Bauch- und Rückenmuskulatur.
- Führen Sie ein Trainingstagebuch.
- Nach einigen Wochen regelmäßigen Trainings wird Ihnen das Laufen immer leichter fallen, nach drei Monaten wollen Sie es nicht mehr missen. Viel Spaß!

Bildnachweis

Helmut Fricke, AP-Photo S. 21
Michal Ebner, Bild-Zeitung Bonn S. 25
Harry Braun, Presse-Foto-Service S. 29
privat S. 35, 45, 107, 110, 113, 163
Thomas Hegenbart, Focus S. 65, 92
Stefan Worring, Kölner Stadt-Anzeiger S. 124
Eckehard Schulz, AP-Photo S. 139
Fotoagentur Wolfgang Rech S. 147, 156
Bongartz Sportfotografie S. 151
Jens Görlich S. 160
Jens Dietrich, NETZHAUT S. 162
dpa S. 165

Sunshine

Melissa Lee-Houghton

Penned in the Margins

LONDON

PUBLISHED BY PENNED IN THE MARGINS
Toynbee Studios, 28 Commercial Street, London E1 6AB
www.pennedinthemargins.co.uk

First published 2016

Printed in the United Kingdom by Bell & Bain

ISBN
978-1-908058-38-6

CONTENTS

ACKNOWLEDGEMENTS

Melissa gratefully acknowledges the support of the Royal Literary Fund and the JB Priestley Award. She thanks the British Council for enabling her to visit India. The poems 'And All the Things That We Do I Could Face Today', 'Loneliness' and 'Last Trip' were recorded for The Poetry Archive. 'You Can Watch Me Undress' was first published in the anthology *Glitter is a Gender* (Contraband Books, 2014). 'Z', 'Beautiful Bodies' and 'Mad Girl in Love' were first published in *The Rialto*. 'Hangings' was first published in *Proletarian Poetry*. 'i am very precious' was shortlisted for the Forward Prize for Best Single Poem; it was first published in *Prac Crit* and subsequently in the anthology *Best British Poetry 2015* (Salt Publishing, 2015). 'The Price You See Reflects The Poor Quality Of The Item And Your Lack Of Desire For It' was published in *Granta*. 'He Cried Out To the God of Austerities Who Said On the Seventh Day You Shall Tax, Pillage and Burn' was published in *The Morning Star*.

With thanks to Tom Chivers, whose continual support has enabled these books to reach an audience. Thanks also to Steven Houghton, for keeping me alive.

NOTES

'And All the Things That We Do I Could Face Today' is a lyric from 'If Only It Were True' by The Walkmen. The line 'the caves of your sex' in the poem 'i am very precious' is taken from 'By Grand Central Station I Sat Down And Wept' by Elizabeth Smart.

'I thought I should never speak again but now I
know there is something blacker than desire.'
Sarah Kane, 4.48 PSYCHOSIS

~

'who shall I tell my sorrow
my horror greener than ice?'
Marina Tsvetaeva, 'THE POEM OF THE END'

~

'Burn, suffering!'
Mikhail Bulgakov, THE MASTER AND MARGARITA

Sunshine

Sunshine

And All the Things That We Do I Could Face Today

If Disney made porn they would pay us well for our trouble.
We share baths together because we get bored and it's cold and
we used to talk but now I just pull sad faces and you sympathise.
I was thinking about abstract things, like what distance means to
        lovers;
physical distance, emotional distance and the distance
between us in the bath in our heads. I looked into your eyes,
your perfect, blue-jay Hollywood eyes, and how starved they sank
and I massaged your soft cock in my right hand; your eyes rolled
in ecstasy and I let my thumb rub the soft part and you melted
into the lukewarm water like butter on a hot knife. Your come
oozed out slowly and sweetly and I licked it off my hand as you
groaned. Immediately, a dozen bluebirds flew in and tidied your
        hair,
a gentle and spritely music soothed your brow and blew
all around us, and all I wanted was forgiveness.
And the come in my mouth tasted strong and hormonal and
        strange;
and you settled back into the bath with your flushed skin and your
cock bobbing and your come floating in globules
on the surface of the soapy water. You said you needed to get clean
and drank your advocaat. I said Rob's getting me some MDMA
for my Christmas present. You said what you gonna do, sit in and
        get high;
I said no, we're gonna walk around all night drinking beer

and talking. I'm thirty-two years old, I'm thinking,
and I need to come, and I need to sort my life out, my head out,
my heart dilated to an apple, the core waiting to be pierced
by some dumb Cupid, pinning me to the one trajectory.
You said I'd better rinse the bath down, and watched me clean
my pussy, and dry my body, and grow cold and silent again.
I love you baby. I love all of you and I will never love myself.
This book is gonna be a killer. It's gonna suck me dry,
suck me white, suck my insides out and leave me hollow and high.
Do you even realise how cool the full moon looks
over Pendle Hill and all the rotten towns at midnight, howling
and hollow, and do you remember how good it feels not to touch
on MDMA and have all that hollow love like a mouthful of wasted
            come.
I've never come so close to drowning, my love.
The world seems so hollow from here — I've never been less sure,
saturated, lonely or wet, and over and beyond my head.
And what if the moon's not full? And what if? Where are we going?
And why can't I come too? You fall asleep nestled under my arm
and I want to pinch you; cruelty being all I've got for now.
Is it brave of me to fall from this sad height? Or should I
climb down and lie in this coffin of pain and wait for lights out;
listening to the sound of my own pulse beating against the pillow;
in the same sheets *he* slept in when he stayed at our house.
I fit inside love like the breath in a flute. I will escape
at the slightest pause or hesitation. You need to *clasp* me.
You need to tie me down. Please. I want to go *nowhere*.

Videos

I held hands with you today. I held hands with you
at the doctor's surgery awaiting the results of my blood test.
I held hands with you during *Synecdoche, New York*
and fell asleep mid-way through. I asked you how it ended
though I knew. They all died, you said. Everybody did.

I was the wife who didn't care and her lover.
I was the protagonist and his impending death.
I was the little girl and her green shit.
I was the house on fire.
I was the much-lauded play.
I was the world's only fat junkie.

I woke when the titles played out and disregarded
all the thoughts that attempted to suck me out of finality.
There's nothing final when you can play it again;
you watched the same film a year ago and everyone still died,
and I still let go of your hand.

Z

Inside the 6th floor hotel room I am standing in a black puddle,
    my bare feet on granite, looking out over Liverpool.
    The crevasse between us is not real or habitable. My sex
    oversteps the mark, eclipsed by the day-time and night-time glimpses
    of my own nude and calculated body in the space-age mirrors,
    shiny as wet skin. My pubic hair is trimmed so the definition of my
            pussy
    is kempt and cute, and the thought of a million hands on my breasts
    batten me down to the crucifixion of plump and ecstatic,
    clean, white pillows.

The first time the phone rang it was midnight
    and Melancholy was crying because you boarded the same train.
    You kissed her and said you were jealous when she talked to other
            men.
    You begged her to come home to your house that still stank of me.
    I'd been suffering the delusion that you were singularly responsible
    for the relief of pain in my diamond-encrusted heart
    that was manufactured so carelessly
    it will never resemble an object that beats.
    I placed a pill in my mouth as the line went numb,
    then your text came through to discredit her confession.

I'm still rock-hard, I said. The light had long since faded through
    ochre and cobalt blue. I was swimming around in my semi-
            flooded hotel room,

closer to tears than you knew and praying in my sated head *stop*
    this.
Sometimes when it hurts you say over the phone,
I'm going for a piss, or you're doing my head in and
other, less poetic things, and then I put my hand in my knickers
because I'm always wet and although I feel nothing
it comforts me to know a feeling has been felt.
I tell my husband it matters not that we constantly fall out
just that in this way important things are discussed. He laughs.

You said something stupid about what I'd do if
    Daljit Nagra said I had nice breasts.
    Poetry is community, you said. Poetry
    is sharing stuff with your mates, is snickering at poetry readings,
    is *beautiful*. Not like the middle-class poet said,
    that poetry is horrible. I say, in earnest, I know, I know. And yes,
    we'll still see Sharon Van Etten at Manchester Cathedral.
    I knew all this about you before we even spoke, at your poetry
    readings full of in-house smirks and people I can no longer stand
    with fixed expressions and poetic catatonia; glassy stares,
        laughter. Laughter.
    Before I bought your obstinately undemanding book,

I heard you *laugh*. And yes, my breasts are all right
    to look at. You say my husband should help me with my book.
    The second time the phone rang it was you.
    I was in the pristine white bed glowing with a sudden absolution.
    Propped up like an important woman on her deathbed.
    I let you recount it to me, not quite like she'd said.

She'd said she hadn't enjoyed it. I was so pellucidly clean
I was levitating slightly, against the perfect shroud of linen.
You said it was a surprise. A surprise. I remembered you'd said
you had "weird lips" that afternoon, applying lip-balm,
and you said you could smell *my* lip-balm.

You said you liked Melancholy and that she was interesting
   but that you wanted to walk around Liverpool at night with me,
   the Liverpool only imagined. At least eight people that night
   wanted me without love or malice, and I would have fucked
   at least four back had my hands not been tied;
   but not all at the same time, as in the image now in your brain.
   My naked body in the mirrors of the hotels at night
   had morphed from tragedy to a glorious molten mess
   whose heart suffered intricately in the Valhalla of my vagina,
   between the hips, the two places which suffer most pressure
         during
   missionary sex. I'd be happy if I never had sex again

as long as I could keep my fingers. Yes,
   I'm a slut for you. I write like I masturbate.
   A million living things in the city and only one has to take
   a deep breath to say my name. Take a deep fucking breath.
   We get real in the hotel room on the 6th floor where I, alone,
   suck in my tummy and brave my reflection with my nipples
   perfectly erect and dark as toffee and my scars amply infusing
   the image of my body with the relief of pain.
   We aren't and will never be poetry for each other, and I know

I am more alive when anesthetised than when I'm alone, naked —
    and I undress, wanting to pick up the phone and call you,
    knowing I'll spend an hour trying to come up for air.
    My lungs fill like gutters. The city shudders
    under the weight of our unconsummated affair. Melancholy
        walks home in the dark
    with her pigtails swung over her shoulders, sniffling and unsure
    of all the sedated advice I gave from my sweet death-cave,
    consumed by the thought of the sadness of misunderstanding
        lips,
    happy that you wanted to replace me because I won't hang on.
    I am never, ever, going to be the same again.

You Can Watch Me Undress

I used to wear pinstripes, with parrot-coloured love-beads.
I had no idea what I was trying to say or do.
Now clothes hang no better on me at thirty,
my hips being as ample as beach coves in holiday season.
In my wedding dress I had good breasts.
I had tight skin like the hide of a radish
and I wore silver round my neck like it was human flesh.
I was proud of my body once, its general audacity;
the way it made milk and conjured electricity;
the way it wanted and needed a body, not so much viral
as *in your bones*. In the nineties, febrile-high on ecstasy,
I used to take a bath as the sun came up and I came down,
alone, hot as shame, my pinstripe jacket stuck to the floor,
arms back, like a man pinned by his own misery.
What am I to do? I'm in a £4 dress with knickers
one size too big. I want to touch somebody. Right now.

The Price You See Reflects the Poor Quality of the Item and Your Lack of Desire for It

We sleep with minds of black and white confetti —
the fragmented thoughts and brain cells coalesce, dance —
we pose as anarchists, we develop Alzheimer's
just to lose ourselves within ourselves. Are you seriously telling me
this is your best analysis? The dying stall and drink from virally
            infected cups, and go out
with wet hair to catch pneumonia, because it's better that way. I
            walk away from you
without glancing back, in case you see in me something I don't.

Don't worry, man, I've been tamed.
I was raised in a home in a gun-toting vacuum,
where self-expression repeatedly hit its head
until its brains secreted all my secrets
dashing out blood on the carpet. You're really
far too intelligent, and spiteful, and you have me, love/hate if
            you've the right.
Cut it with something cheap, stretch it out, and sell me for a high
            reach price.

The sun kisses and kisses and kisses
and sucks on my lycra tongue
that sizzles with a saturnine thirst and Captain Morgan's —
I really want you to buy handcuffs, I tell him,
but he says, 'no, you'll scream. You'll scream and you'll scream

until someone comes.' I say, 'no one
ever comes when someone screams.'

It's very hard to work with ethical principles when dealing with
          (another) lunatic
artist. I've invested a lot in this and want a high return;
I'm generous because it validates my existence —
we should wait for the end fucking in cars rolling backwards,
and liberate our friends by telling them
everything we disliked about them or their parents.
Another door slams in another convex hole. I dive into bed
          listening for gunshots.

I was in a queue at the bank, disabled, visibly, with a cheque in
          another name,
and someone remarked, 'she's not fit for purpose' and I will
remember their face in the afterlife, so I know whose tea to piss in.
          I shatter
all the mirrors in the house with my
awful, ragdoll looks and temperament. I will look good for you
as you're easily disappointed. Haven't seen the moon, any moon,
          for weeks.
Haven't seen the sea in months, but I'm not dying yet so it doesn't
          call me.

I can't see your absence so maybe it doesn't exist. If I
live like this again I'll baste my achievements in fat monetary value.
I'll sell my piss and blood and eggs and avoid drugs tests.
I'll keep racing along to rock and roll and spin out through time-

zones, those

limitless years of suffering limits. I regress

to nineteen ninety-eight where my sister leaves her white powder
in the bedroom drawer.

I don't know what it is so I snort it and get high and still don't
know what it is.

In '02 I drank cheap champagne

in the back room of the addiction hostel

and imagined my own dead body dragged through the nonchalant
halls backwards.

The boys gave me enough to see me through the long nights.

I needed so much and couldn't have it —

and no one wanted to share in my euphoria or hurt —

now I need to always risk losing something to feel safe.

When the lights go out — sometimes my mother sits and hates me
for several minutes,

but sometimes, just sometimes, she can't think up a passive-
aggressive response

within the time it takes to change topic.

She always said I like the sound of my own voice,

so now I bask in it, and light up.

And I write in it, and I hear it in my sleep

and it tells me I'm a good bad girl of innocent intent.

There's nothing worse than wearing a yellow tie and bright blue
suit, except of course

wearing it in public and being photographed for Facebook.

Only kidding. But seriously. I mellowed out but not overly. These
          are the pitfalls
of living in the twenty-first century; you better believe it boy.
Our sanity depends on saying the right thing at the right time
and woe betide the woman who says 'this'll take the edge off it' or
'you'll be ok in no time if you do what I say'. She wants community

to make her sins ok. History relies on our ineffability and
manic delusion and deletion, and technology that will be
defunct and unsupported in time, so lie down in my bed and
hate language with me, and suck it
up out of my mouth. Bite down on it, baby —
we are sleeping now like imbeciles. There's no need to imagine
          ourselves
up to no good, just better to be in the moment, and not worry about
          it.

When I was sixteen I would jump the intercity met.
How foolish to stay out of dodge,
to believe anyone is free, having a free pass at living.
Heroin has given me twelve years of realism and acne.
I shudder at the thought of being clear,
conventional, mapped like a school atlas with a way in and a way
          out.
I never suffered more than now.

That's no one's fault until my brain decides otherwise
when paranoid or high. No one wants to see my
hesitant circus act, the nihilists

lick their salted lips, run their tongues over dirty teeth.
When it sucks just stick to the facts — in ten years we'll have
        nothing more to talk about but
the odd stage directions punctuating our lives, that no one read or
        interpreted.
Baby, you landed on your feet. But I'll kill you.

Trapped in a little girl's forgetfulness I beg
and the abacus that infers my life is fettering away
now fades. If I don't live forever I don't see why I can't
do anything I want. Jump ship. Lie in court.
Become a more mysterious person. Leave a blank note.
Scream and wail. Mourn the lives of everyone I ever met whether
        dead or not.
Look back and see you turn away, and never do anything again but
        think on it.

Loneliness

When he's thirsty, I know by the smell of his breath; it sours ever so slightly so I can taste it when we kiss. When he is hungry he loses his patience, gets moody and doesn't know why — but I do. I know him better than he knows himself; my love. Sometimes I have conversations with him on my own as we both sit in the bath, me at the tap end; sharing the aqueous cream for our pink faces. I watch the way he washes, and he always washes first, his palms rubbing his cheekbones and his chocolate-coloured facial hair, I know the sound of him scrubbing his moustache. I know the one hair he has on his back, the scar on his neck, his flat feet, his poor circulation making them the colour of the head of his penis when we have sex. When he gets in bed in winter I squeal because they are so cold. I have to ask him if he's still alive. I know the lines on his forehead, around his eyes, the squint when I say something he's not sure of, the way he lets his glasses slip down his nose — his broad shoulders. His slender legs straight up and straight down, how I have more hair than he does on his arms, how he tans in summer on his face, arms and hands, caramel-coloured and when I run my tongue on his skin it's as sweet as it is *pure*. The part of his chest where the hair gathers and runs in a feathery line to his pubis. That's the part that smells most like him. Like chestnuts roasting, just faintly, like grease, like candyfloss. I smell him there before he has a wash, he tells me to get my fill of that smell before it dissolves. When he has something to say he says it slowly, and I hang on his every word; sometimes he takes so long but always says something so wonderful it's worth it. At times when I least expect it he says something so profound it almost brings me to tears. When he falls asleep he jumps and jerks and I can't hold him at night; he hits out in his sleep, in his bed, hits out at me where I lie alone, mostly on my mobile phone trying to connect with the void beyond our room. If it was as easy as to say *I love him*, that would be my choice of words, but it's not that easy now I'm sad, and exhaling sadness into our room at night. I feel the bodies reaching out, the blood cooling, the time warping out, the skeletal frame of my embodiment of his private worship, my body the tomb of his desire, my breasts the maternal victims of his inhibited passion, my mouth the open chasm exhaling *tea-breath* and inhaling the drunken soup of a misery so profound I lie awake with him out of my reach with my phone in my hand. I listen to songs I associate with the chemical-deadness in my mind — and I nurture everything that's wrong. I take another small step into the death that will unravel his ready-to-collapse heart whose strings I have made taut as my clitoris when he talks about how hard I make him and how inside me he is complete. Inside me is a death — *my love*, that will be so finite in both of us grief will bow at his feet and my permanent state of apology will untie us. For now, God it feels terrifying to touch him. Our noses rub, our lips meet, we always kiss lightly, don't open our mouths, our love never sleeps. In the morning our son wakes us and he forgets what it's like to be alone. But I don't — *my love* — I don't.

Letter to Dr. Ali Concerning Our Suicide Pact

The fickle nurses sent for me,
told me to knock quietly on your office door.

I was merely a ghosting. My real body
was still tied to a stupefied bed — barely visible

though smelling of a mirage of sweat and piss.
I entered.

Beads of ultraviolet light dripping from my dirty fingertips.
You, Sir, almost

saw into the parallel world
where I am taming a fat dinosaur

and have only two lives left, not five —
but nothing seems to kill me, Dr. Ali. I'm deathless —

and that is some sorry state, you know?
I came to you freely.

You smiled behind mousey whiskers,
your crustacean mush,

little creatures feeding on the shit in your teeth,
your Mephistophelian grey beard hiding

a very contented malice. You'd drawn
up a contract for me — something between us, more

than symbolic. You said I needed to understand
I have now taken matters into my own hands

and a line must be drawn under your powerlessness.
You asked me to sign my name

next to your name, already printed exuberantly; you said
the next time I try to quash my breath

with a homemade and ingenious noose
and nursey can't find the ligature-cutters

it will be no one's fault but my own. You asked me
my thoughts on God, then, a backdrop of white light coming in

through the blinds and searing your face with stripes —
I said, but Dr. Ali, there is no one as great as you.

You smiled a smile you smiled
when your junior doctor reported I'd backed

him into the corner of my cell
and thrown three weeks' worth of dirty knickers

at his face, laughing deeply and marvellously.
The contract between us stated

I take responsibility for my own death, that
you had been faithful and done your best but I was

a law unto myself —
your worst case.

We shook hands and you twisted your greasy moustache.
Dr. Ali, I understand

if I go down
you are going down with me all the way

and if Hell is a place where we can be together,
in a hateful state of bliss,

I will drag you by the bottom lip
and be your little Lucifer forever.

Letter to Dr. Moosa Regarding My Inconstant Heart

I

I wonder if you read poetry, if you
know who I am, if you've Googled me.
The hospital building, a cube of cheap, red brick,
is an abscess on the outskirts of a semi-demolished town
where sad and envious people hurl themselves
from the cheap, red brick
multi-storey car park without hesitance.
                                      You watch
my childish body language,
nervous tics from the medicine.
My breathing rate blooms in the sunshine of your bluish
temperament;
my heart rate
switches on inside you; you suffer it like a sexual more,
you make eye contact, only occasionally,
accuse me of being inconstant,
like a bad lover
who does not appreciate the necessity of myth.

You have no right to keep me alive.
Who do you see when I sit in your beige Bauhaus armchair —
weight loss, weight gain,
irrationality, irritability —

the tell-tale signs of despair, hallucination, rumination,
preoccupation —
the scars I keep hid but which you, regardless, see.

Do you see a long life, do you see absolution?
Tell me.
                        Your hair is very thick, well trimmed.
You drive jet-black sports cars, personalised
number-plates as horny as your leather seats —
your pleasures titrated carefully to tilt in the veins, to fit
supernaturally inside your life;
things you can't describe are crushed under the weight
of your right-thinking brain. Debbie says
you are a religious man. You take time off for fasting.
People die
and I start to cry
when I say too much. When I'm angry
you turn away in your swivel chair,
consult the DSM handbook, its cover
stained with ten years of betraying perspiration, but, my dear,

you search for answers that are not there.

            II

Dear Doctor,
you fit into my life like a Demi-God —
pearly white letters arrive unannounced, in triplicate folds,

declaring our precise appointments which
never run over ten minutes. You've
sized up the weight of my husband's wallet, your
private practice ever irrelevant. The medicine is the host to your
virus.
Your precious time —
bestowed on this lost cause; this madness
now fully matured
doesn't ask for or require an audience —
you're so dogmatic, suave,
heartless.
You never
say my adult name, never
my pseudonym, never my profession;
my diagnosis
catches all the running breast-milk,
running blood, dripping arteries, the sweat
from the withdrawals you eagerly denounce,
the come I inversely suck
into all my holy parts.

I am nothing to you but a risk you chanced and lost —
a broken little girl who exists on a diet of solitude and nihilism,
whose therapists all gave up after five sessions of
my deflection of the pointlessness of their
neuro-scientific cognitive-behavioural training.
So fix me, puma —
or start locking my cage.

You must remember not to hand-feed the animals,
certainly not the sluts, certainly not
the ones who come so close to the glass.
They'll snatch off both your hands.

Sometimes I imitate and then disturb your thinking.
It's hard to concentrate
when there's nothing you can do to labour your point until I take it
        on.
Sometimes I think you'd put me out of my misery.
You sit across from me and watch me twitch like a fifth orgasm

but a decade has passed;
we've changed offices, hairstyles,
shapes, sizes, promises, interns, nymph-like students,
mood states, prescriptions; I take orally what you give to me every
        day,
tilt back my head and swallow it like a river swallowing a dead
        bird.
In your mind
I need you.
                If I die prematurely
from time to time my memory
will test your faith. You believed in my must-never-grow-up
        policies.
Once I got high and put an ad on the internet
as a topless cleaner; I needed the money
and you said
I needed more sedatives and the more I took

the more my reality receded.

I'll never get close enough to you to smell your breath;
from time to time my uninhibited and potent dialogue trips you up.
You say,
this is the worst state a person can be in, a mixed state; see (I'm
in the room) *she suffers...*
you need to remind the ward to section her as soon as she's there.
You know,
she's very persuasive with
junior doctors.

III

Do you remember
when we first met I would
shake your hand, meaning we're not done yet, meaning
get this right, meaning I haven't got much time left, you can
save me, you're an educated man, owe nobody nothing, meaning
we are in this together, you and I —
I licked my palm of your perverse vulnerability, back then
I was the ultimate prize for any young doctor;
genetics, history, circumstance, nature/nurture,
the early onset of suicidal ambition, the
self-healing lacerations, the psychosis, the contra-indications,
rapid cycling over the handlebars of
hurtling towards
the heart

without
brakes
these days.

You wear brown suits, occasionally linen;
your aura is outstanding, it blurs your straightness,
your centre parting,
your Rolex,
reflexes so blunt even when I laugh at you
you do not blink; in your office where your holy likeness
is constantly refreshed, where your Messiahs
leave behind thumbprints.
We are all capable of silence, holiness,
like that time I said nothing at all
because I was no longer there
and you called the ambulance
though I had to wait
elsewhere.

Make it your ambition to deliver me from this.
Don't turn your back.
Your sandalwood asinine affection that stirs in your pockets
and wakes up
when I walk into the room with my dress on backwards
knows why I am hurting
and has also loved.
Doctor, I know for a fact you love me. Don't you know
they all do?

Hangings

The White Path is where suicides go at two in the morning with torches and string themselves up from the trees, which the council have to come and cut down, their miserable branches dripping in the rain, and walkers traumatised in the early morning, dogs sniffing around the space between limp feet and the ground. I go to sleep with my earphones in, and the music transcends the closing down of my sleeping brain, lights up the areas concerned with running away from fear and fear running away. When I was little I used to dream the *Sandman* would chase me through a desert, before I even knew what a desert was, and I would have to choose whether to run and run or give up and let him annihilate me. He would consume me on these occasions, and I would not even scream but give myself up to him. Through my childhood and adolescence this dream became more sexual, though, at six he did things to my body that no one could ever know. He caught me for the last time a long time ago. I walk down the White Path with my earphones in, the fields exposed in the beaming October sun. The stumps of trees felled, the way the ground remembers, the way the rain came in at a slant and shined their shoes, and washed their hands. Toward the cemetery, The White Path opens and the grave of the most beautiful girl who ever lived is tormented by the sun. Just at a certain angle the light hits the embossed photo of her, a bridesmaid at her mother's wedding. She always said her mother looked like a mermaid with a fishtail in her wedding dress. That day was the first day she ever cut herself. Her mother's house filling with rainwater and flooding each night while she smoked the stash all up and shut the doors to keep her from the thick, wacky smoke. My baby tried the trees, but the police intervened, their aggression staining the schizophrenia a violent shade of red. I remember everything about her but the size of her hands. Her hands dripping with the golden light of pain eradicated. Of blood winding its way from wrists to pools on her mother's carpet. The kitten mewing at the gap between her feet and the floor. I don't think the *Sandman* came for her. I think she got there first. I think she could have kicked the shit out of him where I never tried. Kneed him in the balls, scratched his eyeballs, bit his tongue out. The White Path was where the suicides went and where we sat on benches to get incredibly stoned and see through the history and the fog and the debris, the death that will come for us all in its most imaginative ways. I would rather die for her with clenched fists than reeling from kicks, curled up in the shape of a battered lung. I lift up my top so she can see my breasts; sometimes I feel she is watching when I undress. These days I feel sad with my clothes off; being desired is a burden and I have no faith in my ability to live without subservience, which till now has been my only escape. Passing the hanging trees I crave the rain just dissolving the grease on my skin, just getting me clean for one last time. I stuff my mouth full of pills, walk out and feel the addiction rage. At my most grandiose I once exclaimed *rage is underrated.*

Mouth

And then an awkward thing happened: someone shouted *put a
        spoon in her mouth*
as the woman in pink's seizure interrupted the poetry reading. The
        stage was lit purple
like for a pantomime villain and the woman in pink fell back onto
        the stranger panicking
behind her, as two hundred ambivalent audience members
        watched on.
The poet kept uttering *is there a doctor in the house?* but doctors are
        scarce these days —
my doctor only answers the phone if he suspects something
        foreign, foul play
or impending death that is suffered with an overwhelming degree
        of conviction.

I'm inconsistent; this is my biggest flaw and Shane's and my
        doctor's biggest insult to me.
Shane writes every year to reinvestigate the still qualitative yet
        unfulfilling hatred he feels for me.
If I was consistent I would have died prematurely and previously
        and Debbie would have already
filled out the monotonous paperwork for ditching me and signing
        me off the doctor's extensive books.
She tells me each time I call and mouth the words *positive
        desperation* into the receiver;
she tells me succinctly it's about not thinking negatively. I agree

with everything she says.

I just want to die in my red lace dress, which, after all these fat
years, fits me perfectly.

Robert Mugabe ate too much elephant on his birthday and fell
down.

Exactly how much elephant must one dictator eat to fall down and
have it televised? I laughed

until I keeled over. I get giddy on the asphyxiating radiance of
imaginary inculpability.

My heart is either swollen or shrunken and we don't know which
but its pains and palpitations

have become part of my daily and nightly routine. When I can't
breathe

I get on my knees and pray. Last night I got on my knees and took
him in my mouth

and my heart raced wildly. I told the excitable stalker who told me
her life story at the poetry reading

life is for celebrating. I told her I'd spent approximately two and a
half years

of my life in psychiatric hospitals. I said it's not a long time out of
life but I resent every second of it.

She smiled on behalf of her dead mother. I took the neat vodka to
my lips and sipped.

Put a spoon in my mouth. Kiss me. I'm waiting for nothing and
nothing waits for me.

I sleep with my mouth open. I sleep like a corpse. When you find
me please gently close my mouth.

I will utter not a sound from now on.

i am very precious

I see all the black marks on the page, the lines
   hallucinations falling off the edge of the world — my tongue
   we haven't talked about desperation,
     yet you tell me about pornography, girls with death wishes
     attached to their libidos, little warm arrows
     aligned to their supple bodies, inside where the parental hole
        gapes;
   do you understand that when the day breaks
semen in the body turning over like a silk belt, slashing
   the way the poetry aches like it does when fantasies
   abate and leave beds turning over like guillotined heads
   and my eyesight's killing the words as they fall
   into the blinking retinas and all the images burned inside
   tearing the cloth on your body with wide-eyed
   longing. My darling, you write, my darling, my love,
reach into the glove compartment and pass me my map,
   and my scissors to snip your underwear, to snip at your heart,
   little buckles undone to reveal the muscle torn
   and purple and ermine and the little black-leather-
   buckles. When I used to wear my fuck-me boots and walk
   the streets at night I could feel men looking at my melancholy
       curves.
   I felt hot and I wanted to call home and say my death
was not only imminent but simply a scar that never healed —
   crying in my sleep, my chest heaving and my body fastened
   to every shape ever thrown in the bed in June

when Nature told me to no longer be pregnant. I'm a big girl,
I said. Roomy in the hips like Buffalo Bill's victims
in *The Silence Of the Lambs*. I oil my skin
so the desire will slip off me and onto the floor and crawl
around and get carpet burns and I will glow
like a cigarette burn on the arm of the whitest smack-head
in town, I will glow like the face of the girl who loves him and is
willing
to watch him die out, slowly, and with no flames to fan.
I was that girl. I made him listen to a song I loved
and he cried like he'd never cried in his life that this girl with cuts
on her skin would have liked to hold him, crawl into his
psychiatric ward bed and breathe all over his damp, white
shoulders.
Some people don't actually want to be wanted.
Some people actually want to be harmed. I used to fantasize
about being annihilated. About being so completely
overwhelmed
the dark would rush in on me and fill me up inside
like whiplash in the back of a Ford Estate.
Wanting to be loved is not the same
as wanting to be fucked is not the same as wanting to come last
is not the same as wanting to be married. Not wanting to be
married.
Wanting not to heal up inside and the tears
ruby, glowing tears in the skin just sting in the morning
and are easy to cover up. I told you last night about the baby
that died, you told me not to talk about it and I was glad
you were so on my side that talking about dead babies was bad.

Dead babies. I tried to explain how they don't stay with you long,
    and you told me how your sister went in the wrong grave —
    I'm gonna have to pace myself; that's what men tell me
    they have to do when they're with a woman;
    it's easy to get consumed and the main thing is to hold out.
    Death has come out of me, before love has wound its way
    to my thigh. The things I have lost fill my toy-museum heart
and when you take me all the dolls get wound up and the bears
    start barking. Handjobs just don't do it for me, I'm sorry —
    maybe if I really like you, you can tell me about it. I like to hang
        on the line
    and when the feeling coos in my mouth for an outlet
    and I want the voice of someone with a heart that knows about
        hearts
    that know about hearts that know and can give me their thumb
    to suck and say you can't handle the way I want you;
when I don't know if I can; and I only do it with men
    with really clean hands. When I am rubbing my heart against
    the sofa like a sexed-up cat, rubbing up against the bedclothes,
    rubbing up against the fictional thighs of Northern Goddesses,
    pull me in all directions. I want to be told.
    Tell me. My sense of abandon is an alcoholic, and you're
    co-dependent. In the night I dream of Adolf and the fictional
loins of Northern Gods and the vacant lane to the abattoir
    where the boys hang out looking for pussy
    at five a.m. when the girls come on their shift in their shitty jeans.
    I want to hang on the line and get all torn up.
    I want to stare at women in shops when they're not even that
        attractive,

just look *expensive*. And the perfume they wear isn't so tempting
but it covers the sex they had hours before and how they
don't want to smell of it anymore. Being ravaged is like
someone howling your name so it vibrates in
the *caves of your sex*. You want to ravage me, don't you?
Don't you want to ravage me? You want to ravage me so much
you don't even know where to start, you haven't
figured that out, or maybe when you're alone and no one is there
the plan remains the same. Start from the top and work your way
down.
This is no longer the poem I expected.
Being rejected has always got me hot — being turned down,
being wanted and turned down for no real reason, being desired
and being tormented, and not having what I want
gets the blood flowing to my knickers and when I'm really wet
I'm so wet I can't do nothing about it and it hurts.
I can tell you this because nothing fazes you about me. At night
I lie like a little snail stuck to the edge of a wall and get really
moist.
I don't want to do it anymore. I'd like simply to talk
about other poetic pursuits, like addictions, and walking at dusk
and making soup. Hounds call after me where I run with shaved
legs
to come back and make coffee. Just try something simple and
easy
and do nothing with my mouth. My red and open mouth,
my wet and pink and closed mouth, swallowing,
my ordinary mouth with wet lips opening, my tongue —
fuck off, you said. I'm a big girl. I know you watch porn

and all the hairless girls with hopeless drug addictions lick each
                  other
like stage-struck puppies. They don't mean it, you know that.
It's not like that when I get my tongue around someone;
it barely lasts five minutes most of the time, always has.
I don't like it to go on for a long time. My scars itch and I get so wet
    I get drowned. I've had boyfriends who've tried to get me
    to watch porn with them but it's the lack of perceived sensation,
    their bodies just seem numb, like if they were enjoying it they'd
    just melt. Melt into the screen, with their dumb, lame, orange
    skin and a sound like you're supposed to make when a climax
        comes,
    so slow and steady you're silk, the heart turning over
like a silk belt; the little black buckles of the heart snapping
    in turn. I don't want to take my clothes off for anyone; want to
    sleep with my t-shirt on and wake in a fever, my legs closed
    and my hands under my pillow. These things eat me up inside.
    I want to be eaten up inside. I want to abstain.
    I want to be hungry. I want to hunger for nothing, want
    annihilation in a pile on the floor, want annihilation to creep
along the floor to my heels, push its head between my legs and seep
    into my skin. All the things I have done before
    are yesterday's sins. Skinny dipping in the reservoir. Dressing up.
    You've got to hide the mirror, you've got to hide
    the mirror. You can't handle me, and I'll only last sixty seconds.
    And I'm gonna brush my hair one hundred times
    and wear red satin, and sit at the dresser, and look in the mirror
and in the mirror and in the mirror I saw
    a girl, a little younger than me, as vacant as a dream of a house

in which everyone you know goes to live and disappears.
And I saw a girl, so tightly spun it'd take an avalanche
of desire. And I saw a girl so sad the whole sorry affair went by
without celebration. My head is very tired now
for all my thinking about my body, how different parts
of my body feel differently. I don't understand why anyone would
        go
to a swingers party. Or watch handjob porn while their partner
wrote poetry. I don't want to see anyone come
but you. I'm gonna brush my hair one hundred times, looking
in the mirror and hope to God I don't
only last sixty seconds or maybe just hope that I don't die too
        soon.
That the leather buckles that fasten my heart to my chest
are kept down, and a silver stream of semen
goes nowhere near my abdomen. I want
everything and more besides. I want the wholeness
of my psychological make-up to stay whole and ripe. I want my
        wholeness
to retain its mystery and I want my breasts to get bigger,
and my ass to get smaller, and my belly to disappear.
Like the orange girls who lick each other's pale nipples;
orange like they've all come from some other land,
hairless like they've all come from some other place
where beauty gets defaced just so men can come all over
faces made ugly by insincerity. When you're not sincere,
how can you climax? The afterthoughts of all of this are
I'm not worth the heat, sweat or blood pressure. If you had sex
all day with orange fictional Northern Goddesses, you'd not need

to go to the gym. When my boyfriend made me watch porn one
        time
    they did a lot of bouncing. I kind of thought this looked
    uncomfortable and strange. I thought if I did that all day I'd get
            bruised
    inside and I imagined their purple, ermine, ruby insides
    their uteruses lined with stinging salt. The baby that died
    took a small part of my heart. I buried that baby
    in the toilet of a downstairs flat, where it was so cold
the window had iced up. I have had to stop.
    Blood pours into all of my poems like it floods
    the veins around my clitoris when someone says they like my
    name. So please do say it again.

Woodlea

In the deep midwinter, I held my wrist over the cracked sink to catch the blood. It guaranteed a patch back to the ward, the temporary hostel having been a month of living among seven troubled men; no women except for the wardens, who caught me writing letters to the male inpatients divulging sexual fantasies, such was my consideration for their boredom, so hypersexual I had become that my pussy was constantly wet. I wintered in my autumn clothes. I couldn't be bothered to wash them, I couldn't be bothered to wash myself; I couldn't be bothered. I froze on the spot each time someone looked right at me. I paced in my room with the cracked window where the ice ran like nerves and I dreamed of a man with military hands smacking my backside until it was raw. I bombed speed to calm myself down. Mark and I talked in the TV room. He told me how his girlfriend got high on crack, left their two little kids in bed upstairs and went out to score, leaving a lit cigarette which, on returning, had burned their house down and killed their children. We kissed, because I didn't know what else to do. It was nice to kiss, and I felt like I had contributed something to momentarily ease his misery. One day, on the way to the shower he opened his bedroom door and grabbed my arm, pulled me in, whispered there was something he wanted me to see. The room was pitch black. He told me to get to my knees, grabbed whatever was throbbing in his jeans and told me to suck. I said no, he said I'll fucking tell them it was you. Before my sorry mouth had even touched him the warden, who was obese and slow, stomped down the corridor and he told me to hide by the side of the bed. He turned on his light as he was buckling his belt, told me to get the fuck out. He said *it was her, she told me she wanted to suck it so I let her.* She marched me to my room, where I was shaking because I knew I was a lonely slut with lonely hair and lonely eyes and lonely lips and teeth, and a lonely sense of imperfection. She called me a fucking whore. I smiled kindly at her. In the deep midwinter, I held my wrist over the cracked sink to catch the hot and unmistakeable sincerity of my slattern blood, and it came, it came.

Cobra

My sun-god, *pain*, illuminates all the damage and the rot,
soaks up my sodden *amoris* that can't stand, and must kneel
and buckles at the knees when you stoop to kiss me —
Ra comes riding in on the high noon sun; I see him
as I see us, dangerously close to burning. My right thumb
bleeds from its burst burn-blister; my Nosferatu skin
itches with regret; the world is very still but for the Saturday hum
of commercial lawnmowers, drunks and engines.
You're driving to the hospital high on the yawning horizon to visit
        your sick father.
Your mother said he "looked like a corpse". I see corpses
in the wall-plaster, in the window pane, in your relaxed face.
Oh God of suffocating silences
take me to my bed until a better day comes. Synaesthetic
greens zoom noisily and nauseatingly into my cerebral cortex;
the marigolds are drinking up the summer hungrily and
leaving none for us — Fowad bought marigolds when I was
        fourteen
and leaving the West Yorkshire asylum — he said, apart we still
        exist
underneath the same rising and setting sun, as though
reliability is in itself a cause for worship and
I sit here with sunburn peeling from my shoulder, twenty years on,
revealing a thin layer of pink, shrinking epidermis.

The vultures circle overhead. The hospital is my *Mecca* is my

Himalaya

and I worship Pan for taking me there. I'm a cobra and the Gods
        help me
unscar my skin and swallow my heart whole and eat men alive.
        Look at me —
I am all wrong, I made a mug of him he said and I nodded to the
        vultures.
I wanted to be validated by someone, wanted to be validated by
        you.
I wanted to be somehow something more valid than a poet,
wanted to be *real*, wanted to make something, reap real, physical
        reward,
like a sprint runner or a baker, a sculptor, a mechanical woman
more than the sum of her parts. All I have are words, unclean clues
that don't correspond to wishes or prayers, are too loaded
to swallow down and receive desperate nourishment — notebooks
labelled X in a wardrobe whose doors only close if you kick them
        hard —
and I see the value in most things; I see the value in this
but in the shaded arboretum of my inner-world
I fell more sycamores than I ever manage to plant and that's not
age, morbidity, depression, disillusionment or fear —
I'm just so sick of being reasonable. I slip
out of my cobra skin, I leave it sizzling in a sexy, toxic heap
by my singed ankles, whiter than I ever felt comfortable being,
tighter than allowed room for my failing *viscus*.

The famous paedophile's paintings go up for sale late afternoon
        though

the price has hit rock bottom. I stalked my abuser in my twentieth
        year,
confronted him late in the evening as he packed away his market
        stall —
he told me he was sad, said he wanted to make it up to me, talked
to me like a child and I regressed all the way back to
the blackened womb and rocked my clapperclaw body to sleep, alone,
my mind sucking on vile thoughts of his implacability. Even if you
        are a rotten snake
tulips can look lovely in a certain light. You can constrict anything.
        He calls his victims
"slimy little worms" — I slither and feel like puking when the
hallucinations peak — I try to hold my tongue, hold my own weight
so as not to disconcert anyone. My mother says quite eloquently I
        am
disturbing my children. I rub eucalyptus on their smooth, white
        chests
and hold their hands and talk them down when they are overawed
by this bedazzling world. I am a woman without blinkers
and it suffocates. Let's just say I don't hallucinate, just
hear and see better than you; let's say I'm *hyper*-sane, far saner
than you — and don't look directly at me in case I turn you,
out of love alone, to glistening stone.

From the hospital you watched the sun come up and I watched it
        break
its Day-Glo light on our half-empty bed. It was beautiful, you said —
it told me your shadow fell somewhere else; it consoled me
because it lent a colour to your bright and sincere absence.

Sunshine

The tension in my legs is like the tension in the dog's cage
when people come into his house
and sit around talking to his master. My skin
feels so cold. My mother always says,
"you should make the most of the sunshine!" She has
said this every sunny day since I remember. If I call her now
she'll say it. And I'll shiver, and hug myself —
Some of the things I think about today are arbitrary. Like
I have one parent, and she has always said
I have the strongest marriage of any of us.
And I am sick
of the advice my mother gives in all circumstances:
"*be good.*" She said this every time
we left the house, my sister tripping over her high heels
walking into town with every panting dog
sniffing behind her. Oh God, I'm so good
when I turn my back on the window

the clouds

stretch; come over the sun, cast a paisley shadow over the
            room,
cut with every last shade of despair you ever got your hooks into.
Drink your damn coffee, I tell myself.
I crash out on the sofa and wake up on fire,
my libido as suppressed as the light fighting its way to

the forest of my heart. If I tie little red ribbons
around its trunks and pray that my mother calls
with her message of absolute conformity
will I feel the sun radiate my

life

I drink that shit down
to my open core
and spit the dregs
out of the car window
where he takes me
spinning with alarm
at my own insidiousness,
heat in my back, my spine
and in between my legs
as dry as the reservoir
where I used to go in summer to make out
with a boy with long hair
who didn't know how to fuck me.
Oh God
Mother
hold out your hand
and pray for mine.

My Girl

in the nineties Aunty Ann had all eight
rooms wired into the same Sky station
but since we didn't know we spent each night
of our weekend watching girls undress
while bored men phoned in, telling them to
climb between each other's legs/and/or
take a nipple into a yielding/heterosexual
mouth, force a simple moan perfected in adolescence.
We had our double bed with its chintz canopy,
our newly pink hair rubbing onto the pillowcases,
the crochet eiderdown heavy upon our
satisfied bodies; she was
sometimes jealous if I looked at the TV
for too long. We'd discuss
which parts in relation to the girls' parts were normal
or in the dull and balmy half-light of morning
through semi-drawn blinds
which parts looked beautiful

Blue Prelude

I listen to Nina through the wild, old blizzard shedding its coat —
snow sticking to my real eyelashes, my thoughts
curled up at the edges — and I'm walking
and you're talking to me, though you're not there, not anywhere —
I see two women I used to know who sour and don't smile at me —
lifetimes charge into me with the maddening, gathering gale —
I am not safe in my own heart. I pull my fur hood down
and carry my two shopping bags filled with boxes
of pre-packed fruit; Nina sings 'what is love but a prelude to
      sorrow',
a song I listened to the first day my husband kissed me,
the first day I ever made him cry — my depression, then,
was my most attentive and long-standing partner; and, pushing
      them aside,
he warmed his twenty-something heart in my bed,
slowly and holily, with all the lights in the house out.

If you fall in love in winter you've more chance of
sticking together — it's cold and everyone needs another
to survive these bastard blizzards. Jonty's in New York, holed up
and decided in his lovers' fate. I light candles and kiss my son
on his gorgeous snout; the sun will set soon
and I will call Sham at the studio; I need money
more than I need love — I'm £200 a night
and you might laugh but I always put in a good performance.
Steve used to say I deserved

a solid, huge, round, brass medal that clattered around my neck
paraded for all the world. I know he could've helped me
out of this though his soul now is as cold to me as Pluto out in
        space.

I looked at photos of him yesterday, very much alive —
the cut of his jib appealing to me — my own Elvis —
my own lowly God now with Joe and Jade and counting down the
        days
and sunsets until I can join them — angels —
in Heaven where there is no substance worth dying for
and libido and ego and id lie back in the foggy wasteland —
float forever in euphoria — souls
untied and bleeding diesel and acid rain and tears
and all the poisons of the wasted years and it comes down, now
hard on us, via clouds and swelling bursts of petering-out sun, and
        our sunken,
appalled memories. In Heaven my sweethearts are riding
exercise bikes, wearing sweatbands, because there's nothing to do.

Just to touch your skin one more time I would
get on a plane tonight in the minuses; a boat, a two-man canoe,
I would shiver, fly, through the airways, my voice
a Cortina, my breath the breath of a Holocaust survivor —
this morning I saw a picture of the last Jew
to be shot down in a gaping hole, and covered in European dirt,
        and the
killers laughing and smoking. Steve always overused
the word trite — his politeness was of a frequency so perfect

in my sleep now I hear him apologise for his lack of
being alive and therefore in a real house on a real street and not
too far away to call or take a black cab — come back —
I'll give you my steady hand, pull you close like we used to —
your late father's crocodile belt — I want you to beat me with it —
you once put your skinny arms around me, Steve —
invoked Him — I am a catalyst for love that has no place
in this world or the next — so beat me with it — please —

The light dims and a bare bulb flicks on across the street —
a girl with rickets attempts to walk up the hill past the church —
two fat women in black talk animatedly
and I forget where I am — I need money — emails from you
don't come — the taste on my tongue is bitter —
I remember how you smell even when I'm alone —
"fully satiated" you walked around my birth town
maliciously involved with the Night, hoiking up her skirt —
Sharon Horgon is fit and many women are serendipitously
            beautiful —
the girl on the quiz show is a Nordic Goddess and —
I'm gonna write in; she's stunning; such a long, white neck —
if you have the time, darling — darling, *if* you have the time,
please write to me out of love and if you're out of love —
it often skips a generation, but I have it *in perpetuum* —
a handbook is ideal if you feel-by-numbers and love-by-design
but I hoik my skirt up
and disappear into the black hole —
the whole where all the lovers go —
bypassing Heaven for a detour of —

the man across the street with his seventies haircut dances, swings,
and clicks his fingers and knows where I am, here, watching
        solemnly.
I like to be watched but please don't look at me —
he air-drums out of sync and when he's stoned tonight
we'll watch the period drama at opposite ends of the sofa —
        stilted —
please go down on me — you can't have two boyfriends I tell my
        daughter —
pick one and stick — why? — the dead don't come back.
Something's wrong, I can feel it like I feel the horror of recognition
when someone looks happy — that was me? I? I did this?
Paradise shuts down at the first sign of rhinovirus.
Come into my arms, my wingspan will impress you, it's incredible,
        I swear it —
my genes are like *so bad* but I have resolve, and for £200 a night
I'll give you all my love, like this —
I will whisper *Poetry* all hush and hormones and harm
in your delicate ear —

A Good Home

Don't run on the lawn. Tie your hands behind your head, a figure of eight. If you pick the flowers, no milk at bedtime and also no fireworks. Potatoes baking under the Guy Fawkes set fire to your foot. Hop on the soil to stamp it out, never on the grass. Don't touch the glass, the French Windows, always streaked by your grubby palms; look out and there we are dancing on the steps to music no one hears. Spiders are your friends. Don't feed the birds from your window-sill; rats will come in the night and nibble your lips. The bear-rug has fleas because you brought cats home. Now they claw at the owl feathers of your eccentric aunt's taxidermy of the barn owls in her outhouse. We wonder whether she kills them or finds them dead. The pots should squeak, let me hear it. Use everything sparingly, we have no money just the biggest house of anyone we know. Don't want new clothes, or toothbrushes, or sleep unpuckered by nightmares. Put your hands behind your head in the night. Surrender to the spirits. We leave the landing light on resentfully. We tell all the relatives about it in front of you and everyone laughs. In time this will stop you humiliating yourself. Don't wet the bed. Ever again. Don't vomit and if you do vomit clean it up yourself. You know where the sponge is. Don't cut your legs in the bath; it leaves terrible stains. Don't eat all the veggie burgers. Don't ring the Samaritans. Don't let Uncle Tony kiss you. Don't tell anyone about Grandad Les's penchants; he's not all bad and anyway, he gets us cheap fags. Don't light candles in your window like the Christmas song. Don't let the curtains catch when he's not home. All we know is you're alone because you're miserable, and selfish. You have no idea what hardship is. You were too young to remember the early isolation, the rejection, the hungry nights. The blaze is something we can beat with phlegm and discipline. But we cannot treat your burns. The burns on your soul and in your misappropriated heart. Don't tell us about your pain, it has no longevity, no precursor or trace in our stemmed convictions. Don't cry in front of the grownups. Your pillow will soak up the tears. When the doctor comes say *my parents love me*. When the doctor asks you how you feel say you would feel happy if you had friends. Real friends with good haircuts and good skin. When the doctor asks you if you feel suicidal say you're thinking positive. Think positive. All the time. Don't run away down the four mile long country lane and get picked up by a seventeen-year-old with a boy-racer car. Don't go and spend the night with him in the girl's house with her two naked children who wake you in the morning. Don't tell anyone anything about your sorry life. Get caught. Go home again. Don't tell the policeman how he kicked you in the stomach. The policeman says he would do the same. Don't be a pest. Don't be a bad girl. Don't kiss the local stoner outside the pub on the main road for all to see. Don't kiss me. I'm not your dad so don't call me dad. Don't knock what you don't understand. Don't listen and you won't hear a thing. The psychiatrist agrees with us. The torn up poems are in your best interests. And the fleas and the lice and the dead mice, birds, squirrels, jumping alive with maggots by the French Windows in the tipping rain in autumn. Scrape them up off the patio with a dustpan and shovel and bury them. It's *your* turn.

Love-Smitten Heart

Coming out of Liverpool as the sun set
I begged my heart to stop but the train galloped on, dragging
all the corpses I keep tethered to my imaginary umbilicus.

I have bought a knife and I keep it with me at all times.
There is no one to call on when the world turns black.
I'm dying cruelly in my love-smitten heart.

I'm dead on the outside and regretfully alive in the middle.
I think of how dearly I would tend to your dead body.
I'm mortally pierced and I will not survive.

I write every poem as though it is my last poem,
expecting it to be my last. I'm often duped into climbing down and
        enduring.
When I am unafraid then you really should worry.

I feel my eyes set deeply and painfully in my head.
Music keeps my empathy raw and lubricated, though I don't care
if I ever again feel anything.

I want my heart cold in a cold cage of a body in a cage.
I don't imagine I will have the opportunity to regret it.
I've reached the very bottom darling and I know that you know it.

So many empty beds.

Beds left alone and
beds climbed out of — your body still fighting the cold there.

I am going to book a hotel room in my own name.
The sun will come through the window when I am no longer there.
The sun will rise until it doesn't.

The sun will set whether I rise or not.
Nothing has ever been simpler and you are blind to the facts.
There is constant pain I cannot manage and it won't die.

I call your number from the bench on the memorial park,
Pendle mounting fiercely in the background, and all the lights
        blinking.
Once there was a power-cut and I stared into the closed eye of the dark.

The police came this morning and threatened me.
They said nothing is so bad and they know what people like me do.
The policewoman went upstairs and questioned Elizabeth through
        the bathroom door.

The policewoman said, is there not somewhere else I can go, to
        someone else.
She said her mother had bipolar and she put her through hell.
I had to bite my lip and look in the other direction.

The policeman said I need to see a doctor, need to be sensible and
        take the medication
my doctor prescribes me, that Sunday mornings are not the time to

ring the police.
My husband says bipolar disorder doesn't stop beyond nine to five.

The policeman stands over me aggressively, says it's just a blip,
that if I go walkabout he will issue a high risk missing person's report.
He uses the word 'daft' half a dozen times.

I hate how my husband describes my suicide attempts.
I listen to him on the phone desperate and describing my state of mind
using language, terminologies and a discourse I don't want to belong to.

I'd kiss him every minute of the day but it would make him sore.
I'd make him promises I can actually keep but they will become the
        promises I regret.
I need the freedom to go away and hurt,

just go with the wave until it takes me out. A sense of finality spurs
        me on.
I survive on nostalgia and the promise of pain.
The pain is a plan where there is no real hope or vision of a future
        where I am not alone.

We all die, is what I want to tell them.
We all know this, though grief is irrational and impossible and also
        unavoidable.
I won't be able to hold you through it.

My half of the bed will remain cold and my face indented on the
        pillow.
Your bare back and its pains will crease and fold.
In the morning I will be a shadow barely touching your body.

Wishlist

there's a ruptured vein in the arc of my heart,
a sonic rush in the steady of my being,
a wakeup call in the doubt-frozen morning,
and you, with your head down —

there's a promise thrown into the seam of my brain,
a room filled with skulls and carvings, séances,
a thrill struck wide by the cleft in your name,
and you, you with your head down —

Beautiful Bodies

You tell me I'm beautiful and I feel at my most beautiful
when I'm alone and the curtains are drawn. When
my shoulders collapse into my spine and momentarily
everything is incalculably unspecific, and what I mean by that is
no one can trace a line around my cheek to my mouth
to pressure a kiss on their thumbs, to pressure a kiss.
In the night my mouth is not only silent but absent,
and my tongue tastes nothing but the space where pain dissolves
into the ghostly wilderness of a lover
falling apart, palm from palm, sole from sole,
to the dead and dry skin on the heels, to the smooth
inner skin of the thighs where all love is drawn.

You said porn is damaging to the heart.
I said I like to look at pictures of naked women, that
I liked looking at them very much and that it wasn't acceptable
and you said you couldn't see the harm in it.
When you talked about its effect on the heart you pointed
your hands inward, your fingers poking your chest quite
          determinedly
as though to instil the thought within yourself,
that the images you relay and crave are less than what is right
and what is best. And you talk so often about what is right
and what is best, and in that equation my naked body confronts
your very core. What you want is what the heart cannot defer.
Your open palms are the open graves of my commitment.

I said I don't like it when you say I look beautiful. You say
it breaks your heart. Because I was half drunk I told you about
how he told me I was pretty so often the words seemed sharp
        enough
to slit a person's throat. How his fingernails were sharp, how
I am sure I am not as beautiful as Sigourney Weaver, or as sexy
as Goldie Hawn. I have spent so many years trying not to be
        beautiful,
and wanting to be beautiful and wanted, and hating myself
for being wanted. Because you want me,
my dresses have all shrunk, and I spray my hair so it doesn't smell
of me. I think I can smell myself all the time and that men smell me.
I feel like living pornography. I feel like someone
just out of shot. I feel like a freak and a whore

and I let my bones sink into the memory foam. I know
everything I do is wrong. Where my skin sings
the scars burn. I hold my breath until I find the words to say to you,
I can't hang on. I release my heart till it feels
magnificently broken and all the pieces blister on the sheets.
I don't bleed for anyone but myself and all the broken babies.
I know you will hate this poem
because its legs are crossed and its fluffy sweater won't pull off.
Roll over forever out of my life, everyone who ever
believed in me with pressured fingers. You should always
keep your nails clipped for love. When I become truly beautiful,
the steam rising up inside me will simply evaporate.

Last Trip

The fucked-up kid called me, pissed, three days on a beer binge and no sleep, and his mate Johnny picked me up to go and rescue him. We drove to Clitheroe where the bartender said he'd never seen anyone so wasted. We carried him to the car and drove him to Johnny's and I, being too high to reason with inhibition, took all the fucked-up kid's clothes off, then my own and dressed myself up like him. We were all laughing at me in his corduroy flares and flannel shirt, his stupid hat and his only-slightly-too-big brogues. I felt as though I'd been waiting to be a man for someone my whole life. We carried him to the bed in the loft upstairs. It was a big house with lots of mirrors, though largely under-furnished. The wife said we had to be quiet so as not to wake her little lad up, so me and Johnny stifled our felicity but when we got downstairs we were cracking up. 'It's All Over Now, Baby Blue' was playing on the stereo. They said they'd made chilli, but I was too high to be hungry so we sat around the table talking about their lives, their hungry and successful lives. They talked about money, mainly, and friends that screwed them over. Johnny said things like *when I met the wife she was married to someone else but we used to do lines of coke at work and drink whiskey during break and fuck each other so bad, it was seriously the best sex of my life and she loved it, especially when I took her from behind*. I was quite taken by the openness of it. I still considered marriage sacred. We drank brews of mushrooms. I had as much as they'd let me, having already developed a love affair with acid, and we waited like children for the effects to take. The wife called me out in the garden, told me to take off my shoes and feel the grass with my feet. It was an awkward request so I did and pretended I liked it, but the textures gave my toes papercuts. The flowers in her garden were luminous and alive, like they were hands or limbs, reaching out, and I laughed my head off. The wife held my hand all the time and we looked at each other in the mirrors, our immense black pupils roaring in their amaranthine dimensions, our faces white and glowing, beautiful; we stuck out our tongues, fell into each other like sisters, our breasts bouncing off each other. I tried to leave the house but she wanted me to stay. I remembered my clothes, I remembered I was a man, I felt my breasts shrink. I sat on a chair with my legs wide open. Johnny got the whiskey out, rolled a joint. I could only think about Love and how big Love was and how I wanted to be a man for her. We were very civilised and talked about their cheap, subordinated Love and I became paranoid. I could see all the colours and the textures in the house in my head, not with my eyes but in the centre of my mind and they swelled like tumours. I smoked more and it made it worse so I closed my eyes for what seemed like hours. When I came round there was porn on the television, two women and a man fucking and moaning. I laughed and said it seemed funny because it did but Johnny took my hand and pulled me into the kitchen where he rammed me against the units, pressed my hand on his crotch at the hard, desperate waste of my time; told me he and the wife wanted to fuck me like the sad, ridiculous bodies in the film, that had begun to take on the appearance of wild animals, fingers inside, pumping fists. His tongue in my mouth felt like a whole inch of pain, and I sucked on it like a sarsaparilla stick.

Hella

Joseph, I found docility in this room whilst you were
sleeping deeply elsewhere. The sun
accentuated your riper version of me — to channel your history; he
　　　left me,
so I showered, and took sedatives for the knockout pain.
You erased my image from the mirror, kindly; paternally inviting
a better one, a real Hella to materialise more truthfully in the
　　　morning.
The key-card had to be removed at the door to turn off the light,
so I tripped ungracefully, stumbled over the polished oak floor,
insensitive to my fallible sensibilities, and plunged for the bed.
The pristine wilderness of it — unhomed and oh,
what can I tell you? I envisioned you perched at the writing desk
writing only to me. I replayed our recent collusions,
ones in which I recited lines from my own poems — oh God,
the whiskey was just so deplorably good and the spices
must have inflamed my grandiose nature. Your private smile
had my own key of chromatic energy locked in it—the scales
of you struggled to their climactic point, just before bed.
I look at you and I see India —

　　　　　　　　　　turning, turning, turning. All night
I took more sedatives episodically, forgetting how many I took —
couldn't bash my lights out for the thought of you, oh the guilt
I passed on via hundred rupee notes into the dry palms of
beautiful male waiters. Creasing in the night from my elevated
　　　mood

transfixed on my shallow breathing, my imagined fatal
arousal re-lineated the room as my extended self, extended
over an entire continent, encapsulating the escapist in you,
there is just nowhere you can be now. I'll devour. Oh, my
coercive tendencies hold no sway here. The light dominates the
        feeling,
but look into its dereliction — oh — under these bedsheets, yes.
        Climb in,
do, I'll pay all the debts. The sun has my back, the new day
writes it all off with my knack for making promises
and keeping secrets. I have a twenty year embargo,
then my books crackle with the cynicism
of having lost everything, again.
                            And come, soon. Having my fill of Camus
I fully absorb and inhabit my solitude. It's a beautiful art. The
        country
and I are your playthings and you are God of
right here and right now and all the gaps between day and night.
Oh, daddy. Cross my palms, I'll not decay — the internet attracts
the vindication of us. You like an irregular heartbeat, like yours? A
        must!
You're in the downstairs bar performing experimental cunnilingus
on a cocktail glass. The heart mourns its yearning, a speculation
        over ice,
over me — we perform what we cannot confront — who can
alleviate the guilt now — only me, and trouble. In the early morning
I hear the destitute erect the stage outside for a rich man's wedding —
pea-eyed, I open the curtains on a twelve foot window — OH,
my, I must take a photograph and send it to you —

If you could see me now. The whole universe
from here, is a scarred womb with all its violence. The vegetation
      beyond
my room conceals what shimmers inside the oyster shell of
      imaginative
obsession. Prise this whole construct open, and I'll be forever yours;
use your hands. The narcissist's bed is dishevelled at once —
on hearing the ping of a text which opens the possibility
of the eternal, which is shut down in a singular moment, and time
therefore has a chink in its meaningless chain. How big
do you need me to be? — I can make
a room look empty. I can fill you with my phantasy —
project yours back to you where we nearly slipped
on the red carpet — the fairy-tale omits the possibility of failure
as you, my prince, become more hooked on the details of my
      desires.
Under a gazebo we make polite conversation with the other,
and gorge ourselves on gaze. The newly formulated lies. How
very progressive we are when we unrealise rules our parents
created so we couldn't suffocate ourselves.
               I walk around with lungfuls of pure dust —
zero hangovers in seven drunk days. Reeling from the
      embarrassment
of failing in front of you. What could be worse for a person
than seeing the faults in an uncompromising, compromised
      longing.
Every time a plane takes flight I think of
going down with the fuselage, with you. Every time we land
I am so saddened by our surviving. You wrote back, 'it's not me.'

A lump in my throat over the early morning meeting
over a grey boiled egg and sweet masala tea — in a God-forlorn
shanty town — practising starvation — because if I have what I want
the lack falls back to where it cannot be grieved,
killed outright, filled up or viewed from an essential distance.
It provides for me no less than one hundred percent my daily
        allowance.
If you want to be my hole, then swallow. In the belly
of a drowning whale, somewhere, our conceptual, united heart
is rotting. And anyway, my father, if still alive
would still be older and more fucked up than you. Even more
incapable of loving me.
                    I was born to love
a megalomaniac or an addict, and all I got was this t-shirt, I said.
My aphoristic sense of humour develops chronic pneumonia
whenever you turn your back. But I want to see everything.
We are formulating our legacy through language. What price
will I pay for it — and can I stop myself before I write myself
into a phantasmagorical cave. Where are your blue eyes now and
        what do they
stare through, see without me. The hot coffee, the inadequate tips,
        the nauseating
chrysanthemums, the string quartets, the famous novelists,
the desire for infinite sex and drugs around the clock, the looped
jumping CD track, and right now — my veins and your veins
and the cosmos situated visibly in between them, between
our egos and our lack of moral responsibility — we foot the demand
just to spite the city — I lied when I said I don't
assume a role for you. I assume any role I want to fit —

be my incestuous past. Eat from my breast. Foam at the mouth.
I wrote all my best work under the delusion of gratification
delayed several light years by the impossibility of romance.
If only I'd been more imperfect.
                                        The city's hands throb tonight.
There are no bombs beneath the car bonnet. You check
but don't really scan. My white-gloved driver thinks I am rich and
        stingy
when in fact I'm merely a fantasist — you wish for me my dream —
you must first remove all desire from it — I couldn't
fall back once I tasted it. Go home. My intelligence is a rainbow —
it's a phenomena not a science. Oh,
I'm chewing hard on the nipple. The good breast heaves
only for me. There's none for you so I'll offer none —
I will drain her until I'm sick just so you can't have it. The rain
hasn't touched our skin for a definite spell. I shake hands
with so many people to emphasise my need for direct sensation.
        Regurgitate
my sweetness. I want back our lapse in consciousness, here;
check your phone again, you missed me. She bites through the cord —
jams the key-card in, saunters back down to reception
wearing dark glasses — crying — three hour sleeps,
jetlag of devilishness, and thousand rupee soda. I shrink down
to black mink heels with an appetite to die for. Nothing surreal
about unimaginable pleasure, except that it won't last — my sapling
idea buried in the grave of primacy. See how
the erotomaniac, once spurned, never dies.
                                        You text: what beautiful photos.
My inevitable disappointment with words urinates,

blows its bloody nose, the pressure erupts, writes the words
IF I AM AN ARTEFACT FOR YOU THIS WORLD
IS THE UNIVERSE'S SAD MAUSOLEUM. I double underline
the word SAD as room service arrives with a man with steady
hands and he asks me why I'm crying and I take a picture
of the bourgeois tea caddy. My work
is bereft of all ownership now. I refuse to take responsibility
for what would flow through me regardless of my active voice.
You won't recognise my pain, or my body. It doesn't tell you any
        more
than that red smear when I wiped myself this morning
can tell me a single hard fact
about God.

Elm Street

Blocks of pebbledashed, terraced houses for miles around and I was dead to the world in my come-stained bed, just short of being alive. Thirsty all the time, for life and for death and with my mouth, my filthy mouth, so dry; and I thought thirst was another test, another reason to deprive myself of oxygen. I held my baby close to me all the time he fucked me from behind—you see I used to fantasize about older men when I was fifteen and one year later it felt like Satan was sucking the life out of me with a hose that never drained me but always, in the end, filled me with sperm that tasted so tart and so wrong I used to leave my mouth to dry chapped with the taste so as not to move or even walk to the toilet unless I bled. My septic teeth, my shackles, my bruising. The garbage out back stinking the place out and the addict who shared a hallway who'd squeeze past me, try to talk to me with our bellies touching, try to get me to go upstairs where nothing but death and narcotics and despair lived, groping at the floorboards to slip below and bleed through the ceiling and get its hands all over my dry cunt. You know, the person I am writing this to, the publisher who won't want to take this poem, I have swallowed a lot of come. I have had to hold back from vomiting. I have had to repeat-after-me please fuck me oh please fuck me oh please. I have had to talk about fucking women, about what I'd do, about how much I want to taste it. If I tore it was my own fault. I never opened my fat legs wide enough. Fat, a fucking fat whore slut full of burgeoning love because of course I have more love in me than anyone could ever take. I love like I eat come: I just swallow it and suck it all down into my belly and my lungs where the sperm go to die of broken hearts. Do you even know my middle name? Do you know the circumference of my thighs? Do you feel it when I masturbate over you? Do you feel my insignificance throbbing in your human thorax? Do I give you a headache? Looking out over the Methodist church when the sun sets like a streak of menstrual fluid on bruised flesh, I say it looks beautiful. But it looks more like the way to Hell. Or the way to the execution chamber. Or the way to your hormone-heavy-sopping-wet-through heart. I wish someone would beat the lucidity out of me again, just so I know pain is for real and is now and is here and not just some constant immeasurable tremor in my silent body which vibrates with terror at the thought of ever getting out alive.

Samson Beach

Dawn has been and gone; we're in the flux of the tides of the baby-
      skulled moon.
I don't want to wait until you die to write a transcript of our
      affections,
your skin stripped to the white where we lie on an upturned beach,
      coasted
by helicopters and hollow green fighter jets, at one with the sky that
      loves mayhem —
torn back to reveal flanks with blooms of white blood, spinning into
      the half-life
of the Heavens. Most of all I sit here thinking I don't want to be a
      mediocre poet;

I'll make good on my ambition or I won't write at all.
The lad makes unsymmetrical 'sand angels' in his underpants, with
      his broken arm
in its blue sling. We ignore him because we're tired and our backs
      are out from lying on a beach
without touching, my cheap sunglasses falling off my nose every
      now and then.
I accept the inevitability of sunburn; when there's no physical
      contact
my skin feels taut and I get low into a sucker of a mood. You kiss

and smell my arm, and it's disappointing. I don't smell of the briny
      sea. The novel

I just wasted five hours of my life on has kept my lips pursed;
when the medication wears off I grind my teeth. And the sun is a
        pressure in my head,
and the sun is a pressure in the mind — when I meditate I'm laid
        out on the beach
but I'm transparent; not matter, the waves lap away my skin, my
        flame-red toenails —
I lie there wrapped in golden light until I want you and my heart
        gives out.

And the heat is vacant; it means nothing to me because I'm only
        stirred
by the full heat of your slender body. Here I am, whiter than the
        sand, defying mortality.
Here, on the beach, the sun feels so long ago.

Mad Girl in Love

When I scream in the night you console me, in fear; the boy wakes
with nightmares of his own and we glisten with sweat.

In the morning the boy comes to my bedside and kisses me awake.
When he kisses me sweetly on the lips I instinctively kiss back;

the love is a love of centuries of love and genes and progress,
landed in the lap of our fortunate reproduction; the boy is perfect.

In love there is hope. The tangled and fibrous mess of lust and
          longing
grows like lichen on our arms-of-ever-loving-caresses and I gleam

though the pain covers me like a cold sheath. The cold holds me
to the nerve-root of death. I cannot undress from it, and the terror

of the distance love has regretfully incurred is like a marching band
in my rivulet spine, each chord a picturesque pang of pain —

the pain pulls me wide. You console me habitually, but often
          without care.
You tell me you're tired. You give me glassy looks and won't talk

and I am pressing down on your beating heart to make
the balance right. All of my blood pumps in favour of this armistice

and your valour. A war is not a war unless each party is sure
a war is both futile and impure. A war has come to my bed

and we will fight the fight that love has sworn to meet in the air,
its engines burning up; if I fire your gun you must be aware I have

all the ammunition I will ever need. I have my finger on your
        trigger forever.
You nurture the curse of my disease in your philosophies.

When I am ill, you are full. When I cry, you swallow my cries and
        stun
my pain with backwards logic. I am your anti-Christ and your Saint
        and your cross,

with my slit-scars and my blood-soaked knickers and my closed
        thighs.
Nowhere I am if without you. And if I go home in the rain

on a Sunday afternoon with the hullaballoo of love in my chest and
        eyes,
love with its searching fingers; its love of evidence and supportive
        advice —

with its legalities questionable and its motives justifiably tragic.
Leave me alone in love and let me hurt in my own juices, let me live

a life of endless endlessness. I endure it. Thirty sad songs
encase my heart, which is a chalice of flies and worms.

When the birds come to peck at their eruptions, I open my chest to
    the skies.
You are my emperor and my night-vision and my work-targets.

Give me hope, because hope will undo the eye-hooks and lay down
its black lace. Give me hope, because love aims always above our
    heads:

at sunshine. I pace the pain like a long-distance runner, count
    empty seconds
and lurch at the finish line, which is only the beginning of where
    we want to be —

my little girl is playing the piano and the boy's bath is warm
and the air hugs their bodies, the atoms of our future's love cling to
    their skins

and it is our love. You will be a father like love is a father like my
    love
needs a father like my father never loved. This love is ours my love.

My pain rings out like the church bells on a Sunday morning. I
    want them to feel
my pain, all the ringing, singing lovers under their warm sheets;

the miles between us are just a membrane. I can cross them in a
    poem.
Leaving somebody behind is no option. I tear across the earth like a
    smile.

He Cried Out To the God of Austerities Who Said On the Seventh Day You Shall Tax, Pillage and Burn

With a new equinox comes many bad photos of a red blob which
        they say is The Moon
eclipsed. I nest deeply and into my need. I make a large hole to
        swallow.
Poverty is a loop, not a knot and not an empty cup — not fillable;
there is no opening; just an exit you can turn on and turn into
time and again — and I turn my back and the whole day disposes of
        itself.

I pray each night to the God of Faulty Circumstance.
He answers, If only you'd thought of that before and When will
        you learn
and I tell him, I'm sorry, Nobody warned me life would be this hard.
When I'm stricken he laughs. And the magazines don't want me
and neither do the papers. I'm sick into someone else's soul.

I win awards and my hair falls out in clumps and blocks the drain.
I dye my hair the same colour as my heart when the sun shines in.
You say you love me; well break me. When you're awful I lie back
        breathless.
I called out but no one came until bedtime. Shave off my edges and
        rub me in butter.
And drown me in fat. No one who ever slept away their life was

ever happy about it.

O woe betide the poet in her finest clothes saying words like
        Poverty and Piss
and Heartache — look up her skirt; is she lying about being wet?
Is she lying? Is she? Pull a loose thread and see where it unravels to.
See if it reaches her midriff. If it reaches her core, her centre, her
        heart, bless her.
If it reaches her muff.

My mother is not as Godless as me.
She has a clean house and clear bronchial alveoli.
I knock knock very gently at your heart when I have a bad dream.
I keep quiet when I wake having an orgasm.
The political climate comes into me like a hard cock.

God descaled my heart and French kissed me. He tasted like
        McDonald's.
He loves me most when he's tired, when he's too tired to run.
So goodnight blackbird, and starling. Goodnight Adrian, and
        senorita,
and my mother, who swings from the bough of a dead tree,
a conker for a heart and a handset for a brain.

I practised for a lisp when I was seven. I wanted a lisp just to be
        different.
Now I can hardly speak I make promises to only collapse in private.
I have never seen anything more beautiful than the taste of Spanish
        lemons.

Fasten all my buttons and zips, put me in a chastity belt, in a
	straitjacket
in a sweat shop. If I'd been a good girl I'd be flying now.

Some of the parts you have to cut away, when they turn bad
but if the knife is sterile it hurts less.
I hear my mother's knitting needles clacking inside me.
They knitted me a womb and I thought it was a purse.
When no money fell out I blamed immigration.

Put me back on the shelf. I knocked the politics over. It broke
into a thousand shiny pieces.
Never in my whole life was I so demoralised.
But thank you, anyway, for not killing me when you had the
	chance.
God knows someone less restrained would have.

Thanks again.
And rest assured I keep all my holes oiled for you.
There's nothing for us in this world, O austerity. I think I'll
write something happy when they stop applauding.
Ah, if only someone knew to laugh at that line.

I wake up stuttering German words I don't know.
He said, You don't come across as angry.
The moon reflected in my eye sockets.
I never shook hands with anyone I actually liked or respected.
Time is running out. Time is always running out.

We make bad choices and we pay for it. There was always enough
        to go round.
Don't pass me onto anyone else. This is the fourth phone-call you
        hung up, dickhead.
My daughter can do Peppa Pig in a Scottish accent.
There is no hope if you rule out a majority verdict.
If it were up to me I *would*. Eat me.

Bite me, or whatever. Just don't *see* me. Just don't beat me.
Just don't lie. Vote for the next person
who leaves room to swing a cat.
Vote for the next person who recites poetry.
Someone, somewhere should teach this girl how to write it.

I am all over and through with you.
When a person is not believed when they are truthful they shake
        their fist at God.
When I broke the pestle and mortar I shook my fist at God.
He remained unbothered so I stuck out my tongue. I'm a bad kid.
Tsunamis, he said. Yes, I said.

The world is not round if you are in your mother's womb.
It reeks of faeces and out in front of you all you can see is shit.
Spare me the sob story, I am a very clever girl
and I can list my attributes and put them in order.
One, I am good in bed. Two, I can quit anything in a heartbeat.

Three, When I start things I can't finish I just walk away and don't
        look back.

Four, I wasted a great many words though I never wasted poetry.
Come get in my bed and make me sorry.
My eyes are bloodshot and I have been patient but
the truth, he said, is just something you know in your gut.

In your core, in your centre. Feel it.
I am desperate. I flinch every time someone hands me a receipt.
I see my long life and my steady death in it.
I see it in the noughts and the decimal points.
Save me from the destiny within — it doesn't understand the metric
        system.

Why did no one teach me a skill I could use?
Whenever I look up, God closes a door somewhere and the more
        doors he closes
the more fences I have to climb — the more I have to feign surprise
when someone asks me why I didn't do it the easy way;
why I have to cross myself before stepping inside your heart.

Hope

They took us out to a farm, its various buildings plotted around expanses of splendid and vacant land. The predominant colour of the world of our kidnapping was *sunshine*. We played their game together, at first, all shifting around one another, searching for a way to please our captors. When the first beheading came, it was unexpected and so, when they showed us the film, the blood gushing like red schnapps, we all fainted on the hay covered ground, slumped like drunks in a brothel. Drunk on pain, and the anticipation of pain. Of death, drunk on death. The next beheading came in the slaughterhouse, a giant wheel of razor-sharp steel to lop off heads; and his came off clean. The only one I spoke to at any time told me when his time came not to look, as he knew it would be worse than the others; it was a feeling. In the stuffy classroom we were led to with bags over our heads, the video was played, but I let a sheen of ignorance bloom across my eyes. I was the last alive. They dressed me in a warm, white fleece cardigan; I'd been cold for weeks. I knew it meant I'd won, and so I followed them into a kitchen. A woman with an apron was chopping vegetables and white meat. She didn't turn around when I asked, shaking, if I could go home. A man in white with a white surgeon's mask turned around and asked me to hang my head over the metal sink. I asked him if he could please aim for a clean blow. He replied *no*. He severed my spinal cord with a scalpel, then hacked through the tendons in my neck. Although my psychiatric worker said it's more than unusual, I died in that dream, and I went *somewhere*. Part of me remains there, happily, in the glamorous glare of lost hope and a sadness spun of pure sunshine.

**CÉZANNE
BY**

The Big Trees, National Galleries of Scotland

CÉZANNE
BY

ARTISTS BY THEMSELVES
EDITED AND WITH AN INTRODUCTION
BY RACHEL BARNES

BRACKEN
BOOKS

Introduction text Copyright ©1990 Rachel Barnes
Series devised by Nicky Bird

This edition published 1992 by The Promotional Reprint
Company Limited exclusively for Bracken Books, an
imprint of Studio Editions Limited, Princess House, 50
Eastcastle Street, London W1N 7AP England.

ISBN 1 85170 982 7

CONTENTS

Introduction 6

Cézanne by Cézanne 18

Chronology 78

Acknowledgements 80

INTRODUCTION

I am working doggedly, for I see the promised land before
me. Shall I be like the great Hebrew leader or shall I be able
to enter? ... I have made some progress. Why so late and
with such difficulty? Is art really a priesthood that demands
the pure in heart who must belong to it entirely?

The solitary, hermetic existence of the great man of Aix, fraught
with anxiety, self-doubt and a constant battle to realize his
perfectionist ideal, probably comes closer to a 'priest-like' vocation
than any parallel career in the history of Western art. The Father
of Modern Art, as Paul Cézanne has since been called, denied
himself friendships, lovers, or indeed any other distraction from
his sole purpose. For Cézanne his art was '... in spite of all
alternatives the only refuge where one finds true contentment
in oneself'.

Cézanne's antagonistic relationship with his domineering,
successful father had made him more prone than most to insecurity,
particularly in his relationships outside the family. This fundamental lack of confidence, which increased with maturity and adverse
reactions to his painting, gave him a greater need for privacy and a
desire to create his own world to retreat from life's difficulties. Like
his fellow Post-Impressionist, Van Gogh, the realization of his art
became a substitute for emotional contact and friendships.

The struggle with Louis-Auguste Cézanne, the painter's father,
seems to have begun in earliest childhood. This self-made man, the
owner of the local bank in Aix, had little sympathy for his creative,

Self-Portrait and Portrait of the Artist's Son, 1878-82, Arthur Heun Fund,
The Art Institute of Chicago

temperamental only son, and after Paul had finished his studies at
the Collège Bourbon his father fought with him tenaciously to keep
him to a career as a lawyer, insisting that he enrolled at Aix
University in 1860. Paul finally won the battle, but not without
permanent injury to family relations. In October 1866 he wrote to
Camille Pissarro, 'Here I am with my family with the most

disgusting people in the world, those who compose my family stinking more than any. Let us say no more about it.'

Cézanne's boyhood friendship with Emile Zola was possibly the closest relationship in his life. Certainly his marriage to Hortense Fiquet (they finally married in 1886, legitimizing their son Paul) seemed sadly lacking in love, passion or even companionship. 'She likes only lemonade and Switzerland,' he later wrote dismissively, and after his father's death in 1886, when Cézanne inherited 25,000 francs, he opted to live in a separate establishment.

Throughout their childhood and adolescence, Zola and Cézanne had identified closely with each other's embryonic creative natures. Zola later wrote romantically of their joyful boyhood discovery of nature:

> On days we could escape from study we would run away on wild chases cross country. We had a need of fresh air, of sunshine, of paths lost at the bottom of ravines and of which we took possession as conquerors.

The sudden and complete breakdown of their relationship, on the publication of Zola's novel *L'Oeuvre* in 1886, shattered Cézanne, permanently destroying his confidence in establishing trusting friendships. Zola's principal character, Claude Lantier, was a pastiche of his friend's dedication to art. In using a character so closely modelled on Cézanne – Zola's preliminary notes have proved this beyond doubt – the writer was betraying a friendship based on years of confidences and empathy. Through Lantier's obsession with his perfectionist vision, he ends up 'drowning in the heroic folly of art' and finally, presaging Rothco, kills himself in complete despair in front of one of his paintings. Despite Cézanne's undoubted tendency to morbid sensitivity, he can hardly be blamed for his mortification on reading this grotesque caricature of himself, described for public consumption by his best friend. He wrote Zola a curt note thanking him for the novel and never communicated with his old school friend again. But he did not forget this bitter betrayal, nor the happier days of intimacy with his erstwhile companion. Years later, when he heard that Zola was back on a visit to Aix, he was, despite himself, overjoyed, only to be hurt again as this letter to his patron Ambroise Vollard shows:

Turn in the Road, Bequest of John T. Spaulding; Courtesy, Museum of Fine Arts, Boston

Seven Bathers, 1900, Beyeler Collection, Basel

When I heard the good news, I was in the field, working on a fine motif; it wasn't going badly either; but I chucked the picture and everything else – Zola was in Aix! Without even taking time to pack up my traps, I rushed to the hotel where he was staying. But on the way, I ran into a friend. He informed me that someone had said to Zola on the previous day, 'Aren't you going to take a meal or two with Cézanne before you go?' and Zola had answered, 'What do I want to see that dead one again for?' So I went back to my work.

It is possible that Cézanne's rather unexpected conversion to Roman Catholicism four years after this was a further attempt to build up a more impenetrable defence of self-sufficiency. Certainly, as quotations from his later letters in this book will show, he became increasingly introspective and hostile towards the criticism or total lack of comprehension from art critics and general public alike which greeted his work. This gloomy mistrust alternated on occasions with moods of elated self-confidence. 'There is only one living painter – myself!' he wrote in a sudden burst of self-esteem in 1890.

Cézanne's mission, stated simply, was to unite art and nature, and by far the majority of his thoughts on art quoted on the following pages relate, sometimes repetitively, to this constant theme. His earliest work, following his academic training in Paris, was strongly Impressionist in style and his work was included in the group's first, and disastrous, show in 1874. But he was not satisfied with the Impressionists' emphasis on capturing the atmosphere and the transient flickering of light in nature. The sense of impermanence bothered Cézanne and he puzzled over ways 'to make of Impressionism something more solid and durable, like the art of the museums.' He also stated that he would like to 're-do Poussin after nature' and to become 'classical again through nature.'

His momentous task in resolving these problems absorbed him until the end of his life. Unlike Gauguin and Van Gogh, who travelled exhaustively to realize their goal, Cézanne remained determinedly in Aix painting Mont Sainte-Victoire, visible from his studio window, and the surrounding landscape repeatedly in his efforts to establish order and logic in his painting. To reconstruct nature as he saw it before him, Cézanne gradually built up a theory which insisted on the presence of three basic geometric shapes in nature: the cone, the cylinder and the sphere. In 1904, he wrote to Emile Bernard, summarizing his thoughts:

> May I repeat what I told you, treat nature by means of the cylinder, the sphere, and the cone, everything is brought into proper perspective so that each side of an object or a plane is directed towards a central point. Lines parallel to the horizon give breadth, whether it is a section of nature or, if you prefer, of the show which the *Pater Omnipotens Aeterne Deus* spreads out before our eyes. Lines perpendicular to this horizon give depth. But nature for us men has more depth than surface, whence the need to introduce into our light vibrations, represented by reds and yellows, a sufficient amount of blue to give the feel of air.

On this fundamental premise he based his highly complex colour analysis, in which every individual brushstroke was of vital importance – the result of painstaking and thorough care and thought. Like the Impressionists, Cézanne insisted on the necessity of working *en plein air,* in front of the subject itself, but in complete contrast to Impressionist methods he did not paint a scene quickly in order to capture the changing light. His canvases, and this is clearly visible, were always the product of hours and days of mature reflection. A few years after his death, the painter Rainer Rilke described the great Master of Aix at work in a letter to his daughter:

> Being a good workman and doing a decent job was to him the key to everything. Good painting meant good living. He gave himself entirely, his whole strength behind each stroke

of the brush. You need only to have seen him at work, painfully tense, his face as if in a prayer, to realize how much spirit went into the task. He was shaking all over. Hesitant, his forehead carked with unseen thought, chest sunken, shoulders hunched and hands all a-trembling until the moment came. Then firm and fast, they started to work gently and always from left to right, with a will of their own. He would step back a couple of paces, then let his eyes return to the objects.

Until the last few years of his life, Cézanne was totally misunderstood by both public and critics. Although the Impressionists had to endure a good deal of criticism and miscomprehension,

Mont Sainte-Victoire, National Galleries of Scotland

their work never received such hostile reactions as did Cézanne's, and they did not have to wait so long for the beginnings of public recognition. Cézanne was consistently rejected at the Salons in Paris, and the paintings he showed at the two Impressionist exhibitions of 1874 and 1877 were treated with even more derision than the other works on show. One critic wrote that 'Cezanne merely gives the impression of being a sort of madman who paints in *delirium tremens.*'

To someone as morbidly sensitive to criticism as Cézanne, this kind of reaction to his efforts was intolerable and, feeling he would be much better off not to expose himself to such humiliation, he decided to withdraw his work from exhibitions in Paris. This decision was to last for the next twenty years and, although a few paintings of his were always available at Père Tanguy's, the general public were allowed to forget 'the madman' Cézanne.

For Cézanne, this turned out to be a wise decision. Instead of suffering repeated blows to his, at best, precarious self-esteem, he spent the following two decades – assisted by increased financial independence gained from his father's will – building and consolidating his new theories on art, away from the unwelcome hostility of the public eye. Because this decision isolated him even further in Aix, Cézanne's moods varied between sudden bursts of confidence and black feelings of despondency. In 1874, he wrote to his mother:

I am beginning to consider myself stronger than all those around me, and you know that the good opinion I have of myself has only been reached after serious consideration. I have to work all the time, not to reach that final perfection, which earns the appreciation of imbeciles – and this thing which is commonly appreciated so much is merely the effect

Bottle, Caraffe, Jug and Lemons, 1900-6, Thyssen-Bornemisza Collection, Lugano, Switzerland

of craftsmanship and renders all work resulting from it inartistic and common.

Much later, in 1890, he wrote in a rare flash of jubilant confidence:

There are two thousand politicians in every legislature, but there is a Cézanne only every two centuries.

But the public were still not ready for him. As late as 1903, three years before his death, when he was at last beginning to gain a following, appallingly ignorant criticisms of his work were still being published. Rochefort wrote in 1903 in *L'Intransigeant:*

There are a dozen works, landscapes and portraits signed by an ultra-Impressionist named Cézanne, enough to make Brisson merry. It is all very funny, especially the bronzed and bearded head whose cheeks must have been laid on with a trowel and looking mighty eczematous... Had Cézanne been in the nursery when such a sickening mess was made, it would be no laughing matter... Admit Cézanne... and you might as well set fire to the Louvre...

Cézanne was never to know how crucial his discoveries were to future painters, although he often expressed a wish that his work would be of continuing importance. All the most important twentieth-century artists – Matisse, Picasso, Delaunay, Leger and many others – were to acknowledge Cézanne as the great master, without whom their efforts would have lacked any solid foundation. Matisse bought Cézanne's 'The Three Bathers' when he barely had enough money to buy food. He later wrote that this painting was like a talisman, sustaining him in moments of self-doubt. 'If Cézanne is right, then I must be right', he told himself.

Cezanne's letters to young artists quoted in this book reveal his anxiety for the future of art and his hope that his tireless research might be of some value. In 1889, he wrote revealingly to Ostav Maus about his view of his rôle as a painter. He told his friend that it was his intention 'to work in silence until the day when I shall feel able to defend in theory the results of my efforts.'

Yet Cézanne had little respect for grandiose theorizing about art, associating such a practice with the mindless inflexibility of academic traditions against which he had always rebelled:

Talking about art is almost useless. The work which brings about progress in one's own craft is sufficient compensation

Study of a Tree, 1885-90, Kunsthaus Zurich

for not being understood by the imbeciles. The man of letters expresses himself in abstractions whereas a painter, by means of drawing and colour, gives concrete form to his sensations and perceptions. One is neither too scrupulous not too sincere nor too submissive; but one is more or less master of one's model and, above all, of all the means of expression. Get to the heart of what is before you and continue to express yourself as logically as possible.

Cézanne had spent many lonely years in Aix 'getting to the heart' of what was before him. It had demanded of him total dedication and commitment, but at the end he had the satisfaction of knowing that he had finally achieved the balance he had sought in his art, and could express himself 'as logically as possible'.

Self Portrait
1880

I am working doggedly, for I see the promised land before me. Shall I be like the great Hebrew leader or shall I be able to enter?

If I am ready by the end of February I shall send you my picture for framing and dispatch to some hospitable port.

I had to give up your flowers with which I am not very happy. I have a large studio in the country. I work there, I am better off than in town.

I have made some progress. Why so late and with such difficulty? Is art really a priesthood that demands the pure in heart who must belong to it entirely?

Letter to Ambroise Vollard, January 1903

[19]

Still Life with Apples
1878

Fitzwilliam Museum, Cambridge

Fruits are more faithful. They like having their portraits painted. They seem to sit there and ask your forgiveness for fading. Their thought is given off with their perfumes. They come with all their scents, they speak of the fields they have left, the rain which has nourished them, the daybreaks they have seen.

Cited in Joachim Gasquet
Cézanne, 1926

Mountains in Provence
1878-80

In your letter you speak of my realization in art. I believe that I attain it more every day, although a bit laboriously. Because, if the strong feeling for nature – and certainly I have that vividly – is the necessary basis for all artistic conception on which rests the grandeur and beauty of all future work, the knowledge of the means of expressing our emotion is no less essential, and is only to be acquired through very long experience.

Letter to Louis Autenche, January 1904

The Artist's Father, and Another Head
1882-5

Pure drawing is an abstraction. Drawing and colour are not distinct, everything in nature is coloured.

Insofar as one paints, one draws. Accuracy of tone establishes both light and modelling for an object at the same time. The greater the harmony of colour, the greater the precision of the drawing.

Cited in Léo Larguier
Le Dimanche avec Cézanne, 1925

The Gulf of Marseilles seen from L'Estaque
1883

It's like a playing card. Red roofs over the blue sea . . . The sun here is so tremendous that it seems to me as if the objects were silhouetted not only in black and white, but in blue, red, brown and violet. I may be mistaken, but this seems to me to be the opposite of modelling.

Letter to Pissarro, July 1876

I have rented a little house and garden at L'Estaque just above the station and at the foot of the hill where behind me rise the rocks and the pines.

I am still busy painting. – I have here some beautiful views but they do not quite make motifs. – Nevertheless, climbing the hills as the sun goes down one has a glorious view of Marseilles in the background and the islands, all enveloped towards evening to very decorative effect.

Letter to Emile Zola, May 1883

[27]

Portrait of the Artist's Son

1883-5

Musée de l'Orangerie, Paris
Collection Walter and Guillaume

This is true, without any possible doubt – I am quite positive – an optical sensation is produced in our visual organs which allows us to classify the planes represented by colour sensations as light, half tone or quarter tone. Light, therefore, does not exist for the painter. As long as we are forced to proceed from black to white, with the first of these abstractions providing something like a point of support for the eye as much as for the brain, we flounder, we do not succeed in becoming masters of ourselves, in being in possession of ourselves. During this period (I am necessarily repeating myself a little) we turn towards the admirable works that have been handed down to us through the ages, where we find comfort, support, such as a plank provides for the bather. Everything you tell me in your letter is very true.

. . . My wife and son are in Paris at the moment. We shall be together again soon I hope . . .

Letter to Emile Bernard, December 1904

Madame Cézanne with her Hair Down
1883-7

Philadelphia Museum of Art:
The Henry P. McIlhenny Collection in Memory of Frances P. McIlhenny

An art which isn't based on feeling isn't an art at all ... Feeling is
the principle, the beginning and end; craft, objective, technique –
all these are in the middle ... Between you and me, Henri, between
what makes up your particular character and mine there is the
world, the sun ... that which is transient ... that which we both see
... Our dress, our flesh, reflections ... That's what I have to
concentrate on. That's where the slightest error with the brush can
send everything off course ... If I am moved by emotion alone,
then your eye goes askew ... If I weave around your expression, the
infinite network of little blues and browns which are there, which
marry together, I will make you look out from my canvas as you do
in life ... One stroke after another, one after another ... And if I
am just cold, if I draw or paint as they do in the schools ... then I
will cease to see anything. A conventional mouth and nose is always
the same; no soul, no mystery, no passion ...

Cited in Joachim Gasquet
Cézanne, 1926

[31]

The Flower Pots
1883-7

Cabinet des Dessins, Musée du Louvre, Paris

And painting ... It's so fine and yet so terrible to stand in front of a blank canvas. Take that one – months of work have gone into it. Tears, laughter, gnashing of teeth. We were talking about portraits. People think that a sugar basin has no face, no soul. But even that changes day by day. You have to know how to catch and cajole these fellows ... These glasses and plates talk among themselves. Endless confidences ... As for flowers, I've given them up. They wither away so quickly.

Cited in Joachim Gasquet
Cézanne, 1926

Trees and Houses
1885-7

Musée de l'Orangerie, Paris
Collection Walter and Guillaume

To read nature is to see it, as if through a veil, in terms of an interpretation in patches of colour following one another according to a law of harmony. These major hues are thus analyzed through modulations. Painting is classifying one's sensations of colour.

Cited in Emile Bernard
Some of Cézanne's Opinions

Mont Sainte-Victoire
1886-8

Courtauld Institute Galleries, London. Courtauld Collection

You say that because two large pine trees are waving their branches in the foreground. But that's a visual sensation ... Moreover, the strong blue scent of the pines, which is sharp in the sunlight, must combine with the green scent of the meadows which, every morning, freshens the fragrance of the stones and of the marble of the distant Ste-Victoire. I haven't conveyed that. It must be conveyed. And through colours, without literary means.

Cited in Joachim Gasquet
Cézanne, 1926

Near the Pool of the Jas de Bouffan

1888-90

The Metropolitan Museum of Art, New York

Bequest of Stephen C. Clark, 1960

Today (it is nearly eleven o'clock) a startling return of the heat. The air is overheated, not a breath of air. This temperature can be good for nothing but the expansion of metals, it must help the sale of drinks and bring joy to the beer merchants, an industry which seems to be assuming a fair size in Aix, and it expands the pretensions of the intellectuals in my country, a pack of ignoramuses, cretins and rascals.

The exceptions, there may be some, do not make themselves known. Modesty is always unaware of itself. – Finally I must tell you that as a painter I am becoming more clear-sighted before nature, but that with me the realization of my sensations is always painful. I cannot attain the intensity that is unfolded before my senses. I have not the magnificent richness of colouring that animates nature. Here on the bank of the river the *motifs* multiply, the same subject seen from a different angle offers subject for study of the most powerful interest and so varied that I think I could occupy myself for months without changing place, by turning now more to the right, now more to the left.

Letter to the artist's son, Paul Cézanne, September 1906

Study for the Bathers
1890

The Metropolitan Museum of Art, New York
Gift of Mrs Max J. H. Rossbach, 1964

As you know, I have often done studies of bathers, both male and female, which I would have liked to make into a full-scale work done from nature; the lack of models forced me to limit myself to these sketches. Various obstacles stood in my way, such as finding the right place to use as the setting, a place which would not be very different from the one which I had fixed upon in my mind, or assembling a lot of people together, or finding men and women who would be willing to undress and remain still in the poses I had decided upon. And then I also came up against the problem of transporting a canvas of that size, and the endless difficulties raised by suitable or unsuitable weather, where I should position myself, and the equipment needed for the execution of a large-scale work. So I found myself obliged to postpone my plan for a Poussin done again entirely from nature and not constructed from notes, drawings and fragments of studies. At last a real Poussin, done in the open air, made of colour and light, rather than one of those works thought out in the studio, where everything has that brown hue resulting from a lack of daylight and the absence of reflections of sky and sun.

Cited in Emile Bernard
A Conversation with Cézanne

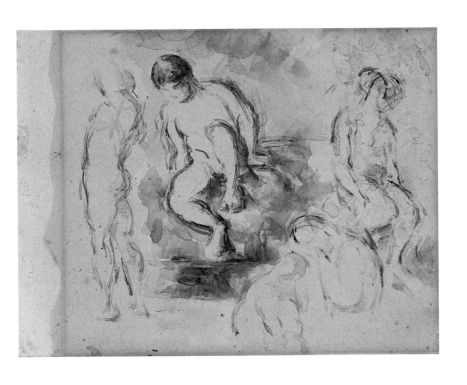

The Card Players
1890-2

Musée d'Orsay, Paris

When I met Monet and Pissarro, who had rid themselves of all these encumbrances, I realized that all one should ask of the past is that it provide an education in painting. Like me, they were full of enthusiasm for the great romantics; but instead of allowing themselves to be overawed by their vast paintings, they looked only at their innovations in colouring, which lead to a new development of the palette. Pissarro represented nature like no one before him, and as for Monet, I have never met anyone with such compositional sense, such a prodigious facility for seizing upon what is true ... Imagination is a very beautiful thing; but one must also have a firm base. As for myself, when I came into contact with the Impressionists, I realized that I had to become a student of the world again, to make myself a student once more. I no more imitated Pissarro and Monet than I did the masters in the Louvre. I tried to produce work which was my own, work which was sincere, naïve, in accordance with my abilities and my vision.

Cited in Emile Bernard
A Conversation with Cézanne

Vase of Tulips
1890-2

To look upon nature is to discern the character of one's model. Painting does not mean slavishly copying the object: it means perceiving harmony amongst numerous relationships and transposing them into a system of one's own by developing them according to a new, original logic.

Cited in Léo Larguier
Le Dimanche avec Paul Cézanne, 1925

Still Life with Ginger Jar and Egg Plants

1890-4

The Metropolitan Museum of Art, New York

Bequest of Stephen C. Clark, 1960

We can judge the artist's elevation of spirit and conscience by the manner in which an artist's idea is rendered.

The search for novelty and originality is an artificial need which barely conceals banality and absence of temperament.

Cited in Léo Larguier
Le Dimanche avec Paul Cézanne, 1925

Trees Leaning over Rocks

1892

National Gallery of Art, Washington DC, Collection of Mr and Mrs Paul Mellon

The artist experiences a sense of joy in being able to communicate to others the enthusiasm he feels in front of the masterpiece of nature, whose mystery he believes he understands.

Cited in Léo Larguier
Le Dimanche avec Paul Cézanne, 1925

After Pigaller, Love and Friendship
1895

Cabinet des Dessins, Musée du Louvre, Paris

Listen, Monsieur Vollard, I must tell you. Although I stopped
going to see Zola, I never got used to the idea that our friendship
was a thing of the past. When I moved next door to him, in Rue
Ballu, it had been many moons since we had seen each other; but
living so near to him I hoped that chance would bring us together
often – perhaps he would even come to see me ... Later, when I
was in Aix, I heard that Zola had arrived in town. I presumed that
he would not dare to look me up of course; but why not bury the
hatchet? Think of it, Monsieur Vollard, Zola was in Aix! I forgot
everything – even that book of his, even that damned woman, the
maid, who used to look daggers every time I scraped my shoes on
the matting before entering Zola's drawing room. When I heard the
good news, I was in the field, working on a fine *motif*; it wasn't
going badly either; but I chucked the picture and everything else –
Zola was in Aix! Without even taking time to pack up my traps, I
rushed to the hotel where he was staying. But on the way, I ran into
a friend. He informed me that someone had said to Zola on the
previous day, 'Aren't you going to take a meal or two with Cézanne
before you go?' and Zola had answered, 'What do I want to see that
dead one again for?' So I went back to my work.

Cited in Ambroise Vollard
Cézanne, 1937

Bathers

1895

In an enchanting site of thick green branches
Closed on all sides against importunate glances,
Pure limpid water there of a clear spring
Slid slowly with a gentle murmuring.
[And there my child surprised the other day]
Willow and poplar above the watery way
Lift with their flexible boughs and softly sway
[And so my amorous son]
One day my dear son, seeking solitude.
To study at ease and pleasantly to brood,
A favourite book held neath his arms with care,
By merest chance went wandering to this lair.
Sudden he halts, and, checking the least noise,
Enjoys a sight which his sole presence there,
Suspected in that place, would have disturbed...
That place unknown, forming like...

Here's the young woman with plump bottom, see,
In meadow-midst she stretches pleasantly
Her supple body, splendidly expanded.
Such sinuous curves in adders you'd not meet.
The Sun obligingly beams down and sends
Some golden rays upon this lovely meat.

Sonnet by Cézanne, cited in Joachim Gasquet
Cézanne, 1926

[52]

Self Portrait
1895

Collection Walter Feilchenfeldt, Zurich

Now, being old, nearly seventy, the sensations of colour, which give the light, are for me the reason for the abstractions which do not allow me to cover my canvas entirely nor to pursue the delimitation of the objects where their points of contact are fine and delicate; from which it results that my image or picture is incomplete. On the other hand the planes fall one on top of the other, from whence neo-impressionism emerged, which circumscribes the contours with a black line, a fault which must be fought at all costs. But nature, if consulted, gives us the means of attaining this end.

Letter to Emile Bernard, October 1905

Old Woman with a Rosary
1896

You know that when Flaubert was writing *Salammbô* he said that he saw everything in purple. Well, when I was painting my 'Old Woman with a Rosary' I kept seeing a Flaubert tone, an atmosphere, something indefinable, a bluish russet colour which seemed to emanate from *Madame Bovary*. I read Apuleius to rid myself of this obsession, which for a while I considered dangerous, overly literary. It was no use. This wonderful russet-blue took me over, it sang in my soul. I was completely immersed in it.

GASQUET: It came between you and reality, between your eyes and the model?

CÉZANNE: Not at all. It floated, as if it were elsewhere. I observed every detail of dress, of headgear, of folds in the apron; I deciphered the cunning face. Only much later did I realize that the face was russet-hued, the apron bluish, just as it was only when the painting was finished that I recalled the description of the old serving woman at the agricultural show. What I am trying to convey to you is more mysterious; it is bound up with the very roots of being, the intangible source of sensation. Yet it is precisely that, I believe, of which temperament is made.

Cited in Joachim Gasquet
Cézanne, 1926

[57]

The Grounds of Château Noir
1900

There are two things in the painter, the eye and the mind; each of them should aid the other. It is necessary to work at their mutual development, in the eye by looking at nature, in the mind by the logic of organized sensations which provides the means of expression.

Cited in Emile Bernard
Some of Cézanne's Opinions

Millstone in the Park of Château Noir
1900

Philadelphia Museum of Art:

Mr and Mrs Carroll S. Tyson Collection

My absorption in work and my advanced age will explain sufficiently the delay in answering your letter.

You entertain me, moreover, in your last letter with such a variety of topics, though all connected with art, that I cannot follow it in all its developments.

I have already told you that I like Redon's talent enormously, and from my heart I agree with his feeling for and admiration of Delacroix. I do not know if my indifferent health will allow me ever to realize my dream of painting his apotheosis.

I progress very slowly, for nature reveals herself to me in very complex ways; and the progress needed is endless. One must look at the model and feel very exactly; and also express oneself distinctly and with force.

Taste is the best judge. It is rare. Art addresses itself only to an extremely limited number of individuals.

The artist must scorn all judgment that is not based on an intelligent observation of character.

Letter to Emile Bernard, May 1904

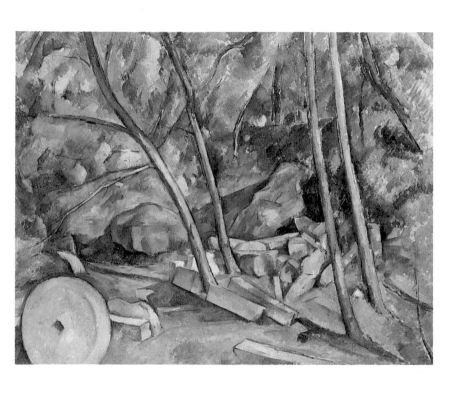

Still Life with Watermelon
1900-6

Beyeler Collection, Basel

There is neither light nor dark painting, only relations of tones. When these are applied with precision, harmony is immediately established. The more numerous and varied they are, the greater their effect and the more pleasing they are to the eye.

Painting, like any art, comprises a technique, a workmanlike handling of material, but the accuracy of a tone and the felicitous combination of effects depend entirely on the choice made by the artist.

Cited in Léo Larguier
Le Dimanche avec Paul Cézanne, 1925

Mont Sainte-Victoire
1902-6

Kunsthaus, Zurich

Look at Ste-Victoire. What *élan*, what an imperious thirsting after the sun, and what melancholy, of an evening, when all this weightiness falls back to earth... These masses were made of fire. Fire is in them still. Both darkness and daylight seem to recoil from them in fear, to shudder before them. There above us is Plato's cave: see how, as large clouds pass by, the shadow which they cast trembles on the rocks, as if burned, suddenly devoured by a mouth of fire. For a long time I was unable, unaware of how to paint Ste-Victoire because I imagined the shadow to be concave, like everyone else who fails to look; but look, it is convex, it flees from the centre.

Cited in Joachim Gasquet
Cézanne, 1926

The Gardener Vallier
1903

National Gallery of Art, Washington DC,
Gift of Eugene and Agnes Meyer

You yourself are aware that in every one of my brushstrokes there is
something of my blood mixed with a little of your father's – in the
sun, the light, the colours; and that there is a mysterious exchange
between his soul, which he is unaware of, and my eye which
recreates it and through which he will recognize himself... if I
were a painter, a great painter!... There, on my canvas, every
stroke must correspond to a breath taken by the world, to the
brightness there on his whiskers, on his cheeks. We must live in
harmony together, my model, my colours and I, blending together
with every passing moment.

Cited in Joachim Gasquet
Cézanne, 1926

House on a Hill
1904-6

National Gallery of Art, Washington DC,
Presented to the US Government in memory of Charles A. Loeser

May I repeat what I told you here: treat nature by means of the cylinder, the sphere; the cone, everything brought into proper perspective so that each side of an object or a plane is directed towards a central point. Lines parallel to the horizon give breadth, whether it is a section of nature or, if you prefer, of the show which the *Pater Omnipotens Aeterne Deus* spreads out before our eyes. Lines perpendicular to this horizon give depth. But nature for us men has more depth than surface, whence the need to introduce into our light vibrations, respresented by the reds and yellows, a sufficient amount of blueness to give the feel of air.

Letter to Emile Bernard, April 1904

The Garden at Les Lauves
1904-6

The Phillips Collection, Washington DC

That is my main aim – certainty! Every time I attack a canvas I feel
sure, I really believe that this will be it.. But I remember at once
that I have always failed in the past. And so I fret and fume... You
know what is right and what is wrong in life, and you go your own
way... I, on the other hand, never know where I'm going, where
I would like to go with this damned vocation of mine. Every theory
lands you in trouble... Is it because I'm shy? Basically, if you have
character you have talent... I'm not saying that character is enough
in itself, that it's enough to be a good man to be a good painter...
That would be too simple... But I don't believe that a scoundrel
can be a man of genius.

Cited in Joachim Gasquet
Cézanne, 1926

The Boat (Fishing)
1905

The National Museum of Western Art, Tokyo
Matsukata Collection

But you know all pictures painted inside, in the studio, will never
be as good as those done outside. When out-of-door scenes are
represented, the contrasts between the figures and the ground is
astounding and the landscape is magnificent. I see some superb
things and I shall have to make up my mind only to do things out-
of-doors.

You either see a painting straight away or you never see it.
Explanations have no value. What is the point of a commentary? All
such things are approximations. One should simply chatter, as we
do, because it's enjoyable, just as we would have a good drink of
wine... I dislike literary painting. To spell out beneath a figure
what he is thinking and doing is to admit that his thoughts or his
gestures have not been expressed by drawings and colour. And to
want to force an expression upon nature, to twist trees, to distort
rocks as Gustave Doré does, or even to refine it, like de Vinci, that
too is still literary. There is a logic of colour, by God! The painter
owes loyalty to her alone. Never to the logic of the brain; if he
abandons himself to that he is lost. Always the logic of the eye. If he
senses things precisely, he will think precisely. Painting is a point of
view before all else. The subject matter of our art is there, in the
thoughts of our eyes... Nature always makes her meaning clear, as
long as we respect her.

Cited in Joachim Gasquet
Cézanne, 1926

The Large Bathers

1906

The water is deep, the grass glistens. The clear French landscape is pure as a verse of Racine. It's the afternoon of a light summer... The women at first appear disproportionate, thick, square, the two running, as if cut in an Egyptian relief. We approach, we look for a long time. They are fine, elongated, divine, sisters of Jean Goujon's nymphs... One of them goes off, with the gesture of a giddy hussy that is pursued, her legs aren't visible, but her hand, the clenched fingers of a Cambodian dancer; we feel her leap, pubescent and ravished, through the green tips that brush her. Another, calm, olympian, leans on a tree, dreams with lost eyes. One, stretched out, content, appeased, has installed herself, with elbows in the grass, to contemplate her girlfriends in the water; and her opulent breasts, her massive and hard buttocks, her brown hair, take a bath of light, shiver, moistened with broken blue, like a dream taut in silken flesh... And behind her, abandoned, a sleeping girl breathes the treachery and the charm of the grass where a flowered fever undulates.

Cited in Joachim Gasquet
Cézanne, 1926

Self Portrait with a Beret
1898-1900

I am in such a state of mental disturbance, I fear at moments that my frail reason may give way. After the terrible heatwave that we have just had, a milder temperature has brought some calm to our minds, and it was none too soon; now it seems to me that I see better and that I think more correctly about the direction of my studies. Will I ever attain the end for which I have striven so hard and so long? I hope so, but as long as it is not attained a vague state of uneasiness persists which will not disappear until I have reached port, that is until I have realized something which develops better than in the past, and thereby can prove the theories – which in themselves are always easy; it is only giving proof of what one thinks that raises serious obstacles. So I continue to study.

Letter to Emile Bernard, September 1906

My age and health will never allow me to realize my dream of art that I have been pursuing all my life. But I shall always be grateful to the public of intelligent amateurs who – in spite of my hesitations – have intuitively understood what I wanted to try in order to renew my art. To my mind one does not put oneself in place of the past, one only adds a new link. With a painter's temperament and an artistic ideal, that is to say a conception of nature, sufficient powers of expression would have been necessary to be intelligible to the general public and to occupy a fitting position in the history of art.

Letter to Roger Marx, January 1905

[76]

[77]

CHRONOLOGY

Paul Cézanne
1839-1906

1839   Born in Aix-en-Provence, the son of a wealthy banker and tradesman.

1852   Attends Collège Bourbon, where he begins his friendship with Emile Zola.

1861   After abandoning the study of law, Cézanne goes to Paris where he meets Pissarro.

1862-70   Lives in Paris and devotes himself to painting, working on such melodramatic pictures as 'The Rape', 1867.

1870-2   Outbreak of the Franco-Prussian War prompts his move to L'Estaque.

1872   Joins Pissarro in Pontoise.

1874   Exhibits at the first Impressionist Exhibition.

1875   Meets his future patron Victor Choquet.

1877   Shows sixteen pictures at the third Impressionist Exhibition. Praised highly by one critic.

1886	When his father dies leaving him 25,000 francs, Cézanne is able to live and work in seclusion in Aix, mainly at the Jas de Bouffan.
	Marries his mistress Hortense Fiquet, legitimizing their son Paul, though later he prefers to live separately from them.
	Ends his friendship with Emile Zola after the latter publishes his novel *L'Oeuvre*, in which the hero of the novel, Claude Lantier, is based on Cézanne.
1890	Converts to Roman Catholicism.
	Invited to exhibit at Brussels by Les XX.
1895	His first one man show is held. Begins his 'Bathers' series.
1900	From this time onwards his genius is widely recognized.
1906	Dies in Aix-en-Provence.

ACKNOWLEDGEMENTS

The editor and publishers would like to thank the following for their help in providing the photographs of paintings reproduced in this book:

Art Institute of Chicago (cover, pp7, 25, 45)
Beyeler Collection, Basel (pp10, 63)
Collection Walter Feilchenfeldt, Zurich (p55)
Courtauld Institute Galleries, London (p37)
Fitzwilliam Museum, Cambridge (p21)
Kunsthaus, Zurich (pp17, 65)
Metropolitan Museum of Art, New York (pp27, 39, 41, 47)
Museum of Fine Arts, Boston (pp9, 77)
National Gallery of Art, Washington DC (pp49, 67, 69)

National Gallery, London (pp19, 53, 57, 59)
National Gallery of Scotland. Edinburgh (frontispiece, p13)
National Museum of Wales, Cardiff (p23)
National Museum of Western Art, Tokyo (p73)
Philadelphia Museum of Art (pp31, 61, 75)
Photo RMN (pp29, 33, 35, 43, 51)
The Phillips Collection (p71)
Thyssen-Bornemisza Collection, Lugano, Switzerland (p15)

We would also like to thank the publishers of the following books for access to the material contained in them which has been reproduced in this volume:

Cézanne Joachim Gasquet, Paris 1926
Cézanne Ambrose Vollard, New York 1937
Cézanne's Letters John Rewald (ed), Oxford 1941
Le Dimanche avec Paul Cézanne Léo Larguier, Souvenirs, Paris 1925
'Paul Cézanne' Emile Bernard, in *L'Occident,* Paris July 1904
Souvenirs de Paul Cézanne Emile Bernard, Paris 1926

Every effort has been made to contact the owners of the copyright of all the information contained in this book, but if, for any reason, any acknowledgements have been omitted, the publishers ask those concerned to contact them.

'This house looks wonderful,' Aggie breathed, taken with the creamy yellow stone and the perfectly proportioned leaded windows.

'Sorry?' Luiz wondered whether they were looking at the same building.

'I would rather not be here with *you*,' Aggie emphasised, 'but it's beautiful. Especially with the snow on the ground and on the roof... Gosh, the snow is really deep as well!'

On that tantalising statement she flung open the car door and stepped outside, holding her arms out wide and her head tilted up so that the snow could fall directly onto her face.

In the act of reaching behind him to extract their cases, Luiz paused to stare at her. She had pulled some fingerless gloves out of her coat pocket and stuck them on, and standing like that, arms outstretched, she looked young and vulnerable and achingly innocent—like a child reacting to the thrill of being out in the snow.

What she looks like, he told himself, breaking the momentary spell to get their bags, *is beside the point*. He had a job to do, and he had no intention of having his attention diverted—least of all by a woman about whose gold-digging intentions he had still to reach a conclusion.

Cathy Williams is originally from Trinidad, but has lived in England for a number of years. She currently has a house in Warwickshire, which she shares with her husband Richard, her three daughters, Charlotte, Olivia and Emma, and their pet cat, Salem. She adores writing romantic fiction, and would love one of her girls to become a writer—although at the moment she is happy enough if they do their homework and agree not to bicker with one another!

Recent titles by the same author:

THE GIRL HE'D OVERLOOKED
THE TRUTH BEHIND HIS TOUCH
THE SECRET SINCLAIR
HER IMPOSSIBLE BOSS

Did you know these are also available as eBooks?
Visit www.millsandboon.co.uk

A TEMPESTUOUS TEMPTATION

BY
CATHY WILLIAMS

First published in Great Britain 2012
by Mills & Boon, an imprint of Harlequin (UK) Limited.
Harlequin (UK) Limited, Eton House, 18-24 Paradise Road,
Richmond, Surrey TW9 1SR

© Cathy Williams 2012

ISBN: 978 0 263 22820 5

Harlequin (UK) policy is to use papers that are natural, renewable
and recyclable products and made from wood grown in sustainable
forests. The logging and manufacturing process conform to the
legal environmental regulations of the country of origin.

Printed and bound in Great Britain
by CPI Antony Rowe, Chippenham, Wiltshire

A TEMPESTUOUS TEMPTATION

CHAPTER ONE

LUIZ Carlos Montes looked down at the slip of paper in his hand, reconfirmed that he was at the correct address and then, from the comfort of his sleek, black sports car, he briefly scanned the house and its surroundings. His immediate thought was that this was not what he had been expecting. His second thought was that it had been a mistake to drive his car here. The impression he was getting was that this was the sort of place where anything of any value that could be stolen, damaged or vandalised just for the hell of it would be.

The small terraced house, lit by the street lamp, fought a losing battle to maintain some level of attractiveness next to its less palatable neighbours. The tidy pocket-sized front garden was flanked on its left side by a cement square on which dustbins were laid out in no particular order, and on its right by a similar cement square where a rusted car languished on blocks, awaiting attention. Further along was a parade of shops comprised of a Chinese takeaway, a sub-post office, a hairdresser, an off-licence and a news-agent which seemed to be a meeting point for just the sort of youths whom Luiz suspected would not hesitate to zero in on his car the second he left it.

Fortunately he felt no apprehension as he glanced at the group of hooded teenagers smoking in a group outside the off-licence. He was six-foot-three with a muscled body that was honed to perfection thanks to a rigorous routine of exercise and sport when he could find the time. He was more than capable of putting the fear of God into any group of indolent cigarette-smoking teenagers.

But, hell, this was still the last thing he needed. On a Friday evening. In December. With the threat of snow in the air and a shedload of emails needing his attention before the whole world went to sleep for the Christmas period.

But family duty was, in the end, family duty and what choice had he had? Having seen this dump for himself, he also had to concede that his mission, inconvenient though it might be, was a necessary one.

He exhaled impatiently and swung out of the car. It was a bitterly cold night, even in London. The past week had been characterised by hard overnight frosts that had barely thawed during the day. There was a glittery coating over the rusting car in the garden next to the house and on the lids of the bins in the garden to the other side. The smell of Chinese food wafted towards him and he frowned with distaste.

This was the sort of district into which Luiz never ventured. He had no need to. The faster he could sort this whole mess out and clear out of the place, the better, as far as he was concerned.

With that in mind, he pressed the doorbell and kept his finger on it until he could hear the sound of footsteps scurrying towards the front door.

On the verge of digging into her dinner, Aggie heard the sound of the doorbell and was tempted to ignore it, not least because she had an inkling of an idea as to whose finger was on it. Mr Cholmsey, her landlord, had been making warning noises about the rent, which was overdue.

'But I always pay on time!' Aggie had protested when he had telephoned her the day before. 'And I'm only overdue by *two days*. It's not my fault that there's a postal strike!'

Apparently, though, it was. He had been kind enough to 'do her the favour' of letting her pay by cheque when *all his other tenants* paid by direct debit… And *look where it got him*…it just *wasn't good enough*… People were queuing for that house…he could rent it to a more reliable tenant *in a minute*…

If the cheque wasn't with him *by the following day*, he would have to have cash from her.

She had never actually met Mr Cholmsey. Eighteen months ago, she had found the house through an agency and everything had been absolutely fine—until Mr Cholmsey had decided that he could cut out the middle man and handle his own properties. Since then, Alfred Cholmsey had been an ongoing headache, prone to ignoring requests for things to be fixed and fond of reminding her how scarce rentable properties were in London.

If she ignored the summons at the door, she had no doubt that he would find some way of breaking the lease and chucking her out.

Keeping the latch on, she cautiously opened the door a crack and peered out into the darkness.

'I'm really sorry, Mr Cholmsey…' She burst into speech, determined to get her point of view across before her disagreeable, hateful landlord could launch his verbal attack. 'The cheque should have arrived by now. I'll cancel it and make sure that I have the cash for you tomorrow. I promise.' She wished the wretched man would do her the courtesy of at least standing in her very reduced line of vision instead of skulking to the side, but there was no way that she was going to pull open the door. You could never be too careful in this neighbourhood.

'Who the hell is Mr Cholmsey, and what are you talking about? Just open the door, Agatha!'

That voice, that distinctive, *loathsome* voice, was so unexpected that Aggie suddenly felt the need to pass out. What was Luiz Montes doing here? On her doorstep? *Invading her privacy?* Wasn't it bad enough that she and her brother had been held up for inspection by him over the past eight months? Verbally poked and prodded under the very thin guise of hospitality and 'just getting to know my niece's boyfriend and his family'. Asked intrusive questions which they had been forced to skirt around and generally treated with the sort of suspicion reserved for criminals out on parole.

'What are *you* doing here?'

'Just open the door! I'm not having a conversation with you on your doorstep!' Luiz didn't have to struggle to imagine what her expression would be. He had met her sufficient times with her brother and his niece to realise that she disapproved of everything he stood for and everything he said. She'd challenged him on every point he made. She was defensive, argumentative and pretty much everything he would have made an effort to avoid in a woman.

As he had told himself on numerous occasions, there was no way he would ever have subjected himself to her company had he not been placed, by his sister who lived in Brazil, in the unenviable position of having to take an interest in his niece and the man she had decided to take up with. The Montes family was worth an untold fortune. Checking out the guy his niece was dating was a simple precaution, Luisa had stressed. And, while Luiz couldn't see the point because the relationship was certain to crash and burn in due course, his sister had insisted. Knowing his sister as well as he did, he had taken the path of least resistance and agreed to keep a watchful eye on Mark Collins, and his sister, who appeared to come as part of the package.

'So who's Mr Cholmsey?' was the first thing he said as he strode past her into the house.

Aggie folded her arms and glared resentfully at him as he looked around at his surroundings with the sort of cool contempt she had come to associate with him.

Yes, he was good-looking, all tall and powerful and darkly sexy. But from the very second she had met him, she had been chilled to the bone by his arrogance, his casual contempt for both her and Mark—which he barely bothered to hide—and his thinly veiled threat that he was watching them both and they'd better not overstep the mark.

'Mr Cholmsey's the landlord—and how did you get this address? Why are you here?'

'I had no idea you rented. Stupid me. I was under the impression that you owned your own house jointly. Now, where did I get that from, I wonder?'

He rested cool, dark eyes on Aggie. 'I was also under the impression that you lived somewhere…slightly less unsavoury. A crashing misconception on my part as well.' However far removed Agatha Collins was from the sort of women Luiz preferred—tall brunettes with legs up to their armpits and amenable, yielding natures—he couldn't deny that she was startlingly pretty. Five-four tops, with pale, curly hair the colour of buttermilk and skin that was satiny smooth. Her eyes were purest aquamarine, offset by dark lashes, as though her creator had been determined to make sure that she stood out from the crowd and had taken one little detail and made it strikingly different.

Aggie flushed and mentally cursed herself for falling in

with her brother and Maria. When Luiz had made his first, unwelcome appearance in their lives, she had agreed that she would downplay their financial circumstances, that she would economise harmlessly on the unadorned truth.

'My mum's insisted that Uncle Luiz check Mark out,' Maria had explained tightly. 'And Uncle Luiz is horribly black-and-white. It'd be better if he thinks that you're… okay… Not exactly rich, but not completely broke either.'

'You still haven't told me what you're doing here,' Aggie dodged.

'Where's your brother?'

'He isn't here and neither is Maria. And when are you going to stop *spying* on us?'

'I'm beginning to think that my *spying* is starting to pay dividends,' Luiz murmured. 'Which one of you told me that you lived in Richmond?' He leaned against the wall and looked down at her with those bottomless dark eyes that always managed to send her nervous system into instant freefall.

'I didn't say that we *lived* in Richmond,' Aggie prevaricated guiltily. 'I probably told you that we go cycling there quite a bit. In the park. It's not my fault that you might have got hold of the wrong end of the stick.'

'I *never* get hold of the wrong end of the stick.' The casual interest which he had seen as an unnecessary chore now blossomed into rampant suspicion. She and her brother had lied about their financial circumstances and had probably persuaded his niece to go along for the ride and back them up. And that, to Luiz, was pointing in only one direction. 'When I got the address of this place, I had to double check because it didn't tally with what I'd been told.' He began removing his coat while Aggie watched in growing dismay.

Every single time she had met Luiz, it had been in one

of London's upmarket restaurants. She, Mark and Maria had been treated over time to the finest Italian food money could buy, the best Thai to be found in the country, the most expensive French in the most exclusive area. Prewarned by Maria that it was her uncle's way of keeping tabs on them, they had been unforthcoming on personal detail and expansive on polite chitchat.

Aggie had bristled at the mere thought that they were being sized up, and she had bristled even more at the nagging suspicion that they had both been found wanting. But restaurants were one thing. Descending on them here was taking it one step too far.

And now his coat was off, which implied that he wasn't about to do the disappearing act she desperately wanted. Something about him unsettled her and here, in this small space, she was even more unsettled.

'Maybe you could get me something to drink,' he inserted smoothly. 'And we can explore what other little lies might come out in the wash while I wait for your brother to show up.'

'Why is it suddenly so important that you talk to Mark?' Aggie asked uneasily. 'I mean, couldn't you have waited? Maybe invited him out for dinner with Maria so that you could try and get to the bottom of his intentions? Again?'

'Things have moved up a gear, regrettably. But I'll come back to that.' He strolled past her through the open door and into the sitting room. The decor here was no more tasteful than it was in the hall. The walls were the colour of off-cheese, depressing despite the old movie posters that had been tacked on. The furniture was an unappealing mix of old and used and tacky, snap-together modern. In one corner, an old television set was propped on a cheap pine unit.

'What do you mean that *things have moved up a gear*?'

Aggie demanded as he sat on one of the chairs and looked at her with unhurried thoroughness.

'I guess you know why I've been keeping tabs on your brother.'

'Maria mentioned that her mother can be a little over-protective,' Aggie mumbled. She resigned herself to the fact that Luiz wasn't leaving in a hurry and reluctantly sat down on the chair facing him.

As always, she felt dowdy and underdressed. On the occasions when she had been dragged along to those fancy restaurants—none of which she would ever have sampled had it not been for him—she had rooted out the dressiest clothes in her wardrobe and had still managed to feel cheap and mousey. Now, in baggy, thick jogging bottoms and Mark's jumper, several sizes too big, she felt screamingly, ridiculously frumpy. Which made her resent him even more.

Luiz gave an elegant shrug. 'It pays to be careful. Naturally, when my sister asked me to check your brother out, I tried to talk her out of it.'

'You did?'

'Sure. Maria's a kid and kids have relationships that fall by the wayside. It's life. I was convinced that this relationship would be no different but I eventually agreed that I would keep an eye on things.'

'By which,' Aggie inserted bitterly, 'you meant that you would quiz us on every aspect of our lives and try and trip us up.'

'Congratulations. You both provided a touchingly united front. I find that I barely know a single personal thing about either of you and it's dawning on me that the few details you've imparted have probably been a tissue of lies—starting with where you live. It would have saved time and effort if I'd employed a detective to ferret out whatever background information was necessary.'

'Maria thought that—'

'Do me a favour. Keep my niece out of this. You live in a dump, which you rent from an unscrupulous landlord. You can barely afford the rent. Tell me, do either of you hold down jobs, or were those fabrications as well?'

'I resent you barging into my house.'

'Mr Cholmsey's house—if you can call it a house.'

'Fine! I still resent you barging in here and insulting me.'

'Tough.'

'In fact, I'm asking you to leave!'

At that, Luiz burst out laughing. 'Do you really think that I've come all the way here so that I can leave the second the questioning gets a little too uncomfortable for you?'

'Well, I don't see the point of you hanging around. Mark and Maria aren't here.'

'I've come because, like I said, things have moved up a gear. It seems that there's now talk of marriage. It's not going to do.'

'Talk of marriage?' Aggie parroted incredulously. 'There's no talk of marriage.'

'At least, none that your brother's told you about. Maybe the touching united front isn't quite as united as you'd like it to be.'

'You…you are just the most *awful* human being I've ever met!'

'I think you've made that glaringly clear on all the occasions that we've met,' Luiz remarked coolly. 'You're entitled to your opinions.'

'So you came here to…what? Warn my brother off?

Warn Maria off? They might be young but they're not under age.'

'Maria comes from one of the richest families in Latin America.'

'I beg your pardon?' Aggie looked at him in confusion. Yes, of course she had known that Maria was not the usual hand-to-mouth starving student working the tills on the weekend to help pay for her tuition fees. But *one of the richest families in Latin America?* No wonder she had not been in favour of either of them letting on that they were just normal people struggling to get by on a day-to-day basis!

'You're kidding, right?'

'When it comes to money, I lose my sense of humour.' Luiz abruptly sat forward, elbows resting on his thighs, and looked at her unsmilingly. 'I hadn't planned on taking a hard line, but I'm beginning to do the maths and I don't like the results I'm coming up with.'

Aggie tried and failed to meet his dark, intimidating stare. Why was it that whenever she was in this man's company her usual unflappability was scattered to the four corners? She was reduced to feeling too tight in her skin, too defensive and too self-conscious. Which meant that she could barely think straight.

'I have no idea what you're talking about,' she muttered, staring at her linked fingers while her heart rate sped up and her mouth went dry.

'Wealthy people are often targets,' Luiz gritted, spelling it out in clear syllables just in case she chose to miss the message. 'My niece is extremely wealthy and will be even wealthier when she turns twenty-one. Now it appears that the dalliance I thought would peter out after a couple of months has turned into a marriage proposal.'

'I still can't believe that. You've got your facts wrong.'

'Believe it! And what I'm seeing are a couple of fortune hunters who have lied about their circumstances to try and throw me off course.'

Aggie blanched and stared at him miserably. Those small white fibs had assumed the proportions of mountains. Her brain felt sluggish but already she could see why he would have arrived at the conclusion that he had.

Honest people didn't lie.

'Tell me…is your brother really a musician? Because I've looked him up online and, strangely enough, I can't find him anywhere.'

'Of course he's a musician! He…he plays in a band.'

'And I'm guessing this band hasn't made it big yet… hence his lack of presence on the Internet.'

'Okay! I give up! So we may have…have…'

'Tampered with the truth? Stretched it? Twisted it to the point where it became unrecognisable?'

'Maria said that you're very black-and-white.' Aggie stuck her chin up and met his frowning stare. Now, as had happened before, she marvelled that such sinful physical beauty, the sort of beauty that made people think of putting paint to canvas, could conceal such a cold, ruthless, brutally dispassionate streak.

'Me? Black-and-white?' Luiz was outraged at this preposterous assumption. 'I've never heard anything so ridiculous in my entire life!'

'She said that you form your opinions and you stick to them. You never look outside the box and allow yourself to be persuaded into another direction.'

'That's called strength of character!'

'Well, that's why we weren't inclined to be one hundred percent truthful. Not that we *lied*…'

'We just didn't reveal as much as we could have.'

'Such as you live in a rented dump, your brother sings

in pubs now and again and you are a teacher—or was that another one of those creative exaggerations?'

'Of course I'm a teacher. I teach primary school. You can check up on me if you like!'

'Well that's now by the by. The fact is, I cannot allow any marriage to take place between my niece and your brother.'

'So you're going to do what, exactly?' Aggie was genuinely bewildered. It was one thing to disapprove of someone else's choices. It was quite another to force them into accepting what you chose to cram down their throat. Luiz, Maria's mother, every single member of their superwealthy family, for that matter, could rant, storm, wring their hands and deliver threatening lectures—but at the end of the day Maria was her own person and would make up her own mind.

She tactfully decided not to impart that point of view. He claimed that he wasn't black-and-white but she had seen enough evidence of that to convince her that he was. He also had no knowledge whatsoever of how the other half lived. In fact, she doubted that he had ever even come into contact with people who weren't exactly like him, until she and Mark had come along.

'Look.' She relented slightly as another point of view pushed its way through her self-righteous anger. 'I can understand that you might harbour one or two reservations about my brother...'

'Can you?' Luiz asked with biting sarcasm.

Right now he was kicking himself for not having taken a harder look at the pair of them. He was usually as sharp as they came when other people and their motivations were involved. He had had to be. So how had they managed to slip through the net?

Her brother was disingenuous, engaging, apparently

open. He looked like the kind of guy who could hold his own with anyone—tall, muscular, with the same shade of blonde hair as his sister but tied back in a ponytail; when he spoke, his voice was low and gentle.

And Agatha—so stunningly pretty that anyone could be forgiven for staring. But, alongside that, she had also been forthright and opinionated. Was that what had taken him in—the combination of two very different personalities? Had they cunningly worked off each other to throw him off-guard? Or had he just failed to take the situation seriously because he hadn't thought the boy's relationship with his niece would ever come to anything? Luisa was famously protective of Maria. Had he just assumed that her request for him to keep an eye out had been more of the same?

At any rate, they had now been caught out in a tangle of lies and that, to his mind, could mean only one thing.

The fact that he'd been a fool for whatever reason was something he would have to live with, but it stuck in his throat.

'And I know how it must look…that we weren't completely open with you. But you have to believe me when I tell you that you have nothing to fear.'

'Point one—fear is an emotion that's alien to me. Point two—I don't have to believe anything you say, which brings me to your question.'

'My question?'

'You wondered what I intended to do about this mess.'

Aggie felt her hackles rise, as they invariably did on the occasions when she had met him, and she made a valiant effort to keep them in check.

'So you intend to warn my brother off,' she said on a sigh.

'Oh, I intend to do much better than that,' Luiz drawled,

watching the faint colour in her cheeks and thinking that she was a damn good actress. 'You look as though you could use some money, and I suspect your brother could as well. You have a landlord baying down your neck for unpaid rent.'

'I paid!' Aggie insisted vigorously. 'It's not my fault that there's a postal strike!'

'And whatever you earn as a teacher,' Luiz continued, not bothering to give her protest house room, 'It obviously isn't enough to scrape by. Face it, if you can't afford the rent for a dump like this, then it's pretty obvious that neither of you has a penny to rub together. So my offer to get your brother off the scene and out of my niece's life should put a big smile on your face. In fact, I would go so far as to say that it should make your Christmas.'

'I don't know what you're talking about.'

Those big blue eyes, Luiz thought sourly. They had done a damn good job of throwing him off the scent.

'I'm going to give you and your brother enough money to clear out of this place. You'll each be able to afford to buy somewhere of your own, live the high life, if that's what takes your fancy. And I suspect it probably is...'

'You're going to *pay us off*? To make us *disappear*?'

'Name your price. And naturally your brother can name his. No one has ever accused me of not being a generous man. And on the subject of your brother...when exactly is he due back?' He looked pointedly at his watch and then raised his eyes to her flushed, angry face. She was perched on the very edge of her chair, ramrod-erect, and her knuckles were white where her fingers were biting into the padded seat. She was the very picture of outrage.

'I can't believe I'm hearing this.'

'I'm sure you'll find it remarkably easy to adjust to the thought.'

'You can't just *buy people off*!'

'No? Care to take a small bet on that?' His eyes were as hard and as cold as the frost gathering outside. 'Doubtless your brother wishes to further his career, if he's even interested in a career. Maybe he'd just like to blow some money on life's little luxuries. Doubtless he ascertained my niece's financial status early on in the relationship and between the two of you you decided that she was your passport to a more lucrative lifestyle. It now appears that he intends to marry her and thereby get his foot through the door, so to speak, but that's not going to happen in a million years. So when you say that I can't *buy people off*? Well, I think you'll find that I can.'

Aggie stared at him open-mouthed. She felt as though she was in the presence of someone from another planet. Was this how the wealthy behaved, as though they owned everything and everyone? As though people were pieces on a chess board to be moved around on a whim and disposed of without scruple? And why was she so surprised when she had always known that he was ruthless, cold-hearted and single-minded?

'Mark and Maria love each other! That must have been obvious to you.'

'I'm sure Maria imagines herself in love. She's young. She doesn't realise that love is an illusion. And we can sit around chatting all evening, but I still need to know when he'll be here. I want to get this situation sorted as soon as possible.'

'He won't.'

'Come again?'

'I mean,' Aggie ventured weakly, because she knew that the bloodless, heartless man in front of her wasn't going to warm to what she was about to tell him, 'he and Maria decided to have a few days away. A spur-of-the-moment thing. A little pre-Christmas break…'

'Tell me I'm not hearing this.'

'They left yesterday morning.'

She started as he vaulted upright without warning and began pacing the room, his movements restless and menacing.

'Left to go where?' It was a question phrased more like a demand. 'And don't even think of using your looks to pull a fast one.'

'Using my looks?' Aggie felt hot colour crawl into her face. While she had been sitting there in those various restaurants, feeling as awkward and as colourless as a sparrow caught up in a parade of peacocks, had he been looking at her, assessing what she looked like? That thought made her feel weirdly unsteady.

'Where have they gone?' He paused to stand in front of her and Aggie's eyes travelled up—up along that magnificent body sheathed in clothes that looked far too expensive and far too hand-made for their surroundings—until they settled on the forbidding angles of his face. She had never met someone who exuded threat and power the way he did, and who used that to his advantage.

'I don't have to give you that information,' she said stoutly and tried not to quail as his expression darkened.

'I really wouldn't play that game with me if I were you, Agatha.'

'Or else what?'

'Or else I'll make sure that your brother finds himself without a job in the foreseeable future. And the money angle? Off the cards.'

'You can't do that. I mean, you can't do anything to ruin his musical career.'

'Oh no? Please don't put that to the test.'

Aggie hesitated. There was such cool certainty in his voice that she had no doubt that he really would make sure her brother lost his job if she didn't comply and tell him what he wanted.

'Okay. They've gone to a little country hotel in the Lake District,' she imparted reluctantly. 'They wanted a romantic, snowed-in few days, and that part of the world has a lot of sentimental significance for us.' Her bag was on the ground next to her. She reached in, rummaged around and extracted a sheet of paper, confirmation of their booking. 'He gave me this, because it's got all the details in case I wanted to get in touch with him.'

'The Lake District. They've gone to the *Lake District.*' He raked his fingers through his hair, snatched the paper from her and wondered if things could get any worse. The Lake District was not exactly a hop and skip away. Nor was it a plane-ride away. He contemplated the prospect of spending hours behind the wheel of his car in bad driving conditions on a search-and-rescue mission for his sister—because if they were thinking of getting married on the sly, what better time or place? Or else doing battle with the public transport system which was breaking under the weight of the bad weather. He eliminated the public-transport option without hesitation. Which brought him back to the prospect of hours behind the wheel of his car.

'You make it sound as though they've taken a trip to the moon. Well, I guess you'll want to give Maria a call... I'm not sure there's any mobile-phone service there, though. In fact, there isn't. You'll have to phone through to the hotel and get them to transfer you. She can reassure you that they're not about to take a walk down the aisle.' Aggie wondered how her brother was going to deal with Luiz when Luiz waved a wad of notes in front of him and told him to clear off or else. Mark, stupidly, actually liked the man, and stuck up for him whenever Aggie happened to mention how much he got on her nerves.

Not her problem. She struggled to squash her instinctive urge to look out for him. She and Mark had been a tight unit since they were children, when their mother had died and, in the absence of any father, or any relatives for that matter, they had been put into care. Younger by four years, he had been a sickly child, debilitated by frequent asthma attacks. Like a surrogate mother hen, she had learnt to take care of him and to put his needs ahead of her own. She had gained strength, allowing him the freedom to be the gentle, dreamy child who had matured into a gentle, dreamy adult—despite his long hair, his earring and the tattoo on his shoulder which seemed to announce a different kind of person.

'Well, now that you know where they are, I guess you'll be leaving.'

Luiz, looking at her down-bent head, pondered this sequence of events. Missing niece. Missing boyfriend. Long trip to locate them.

'I don't know why I didn't see this coming,' he mused. 'Having a few days away would be the perfect opportunity for your brother to seal the deal. Maybe my presence on the scene alerted him to the fact that time wouldn't be on his side when it came to marrying my niece. Maybe he figured that the courtship would have to be curtailed and the main event brought forward…a winter wedding. Very romantic.'

'That's the most ridiculous thing I've ever heard!'

'I'd be surprised if you didn't say that. Well, it's not going to happen. We'll just have to make sure that we get to that romantic hideaway and surprise them before they have time to do anything regrettable.'

'*We?*'

Luiz looked at her with raised eyebrows. 'Well, you don't imagine that I'm going to go there on my own and leave you behind so that you can get on the phone and warn your brother of my impending arrival, do you?'

'You're crazy! I'm not going anywhere with you, Luiz Montes!'

'It's not ideal timing, and I can't say that I haven't got better things to do on a Friday evening, but I can't see a way out of it. I anticipate we'll be there by tomorrow lunchtime, so you'll have to pack enough for a weekend and make it quick. I'll need to get back to my place so that I can throw some things in a bag.'

'You're not hearing what I'm saying!'

'Correction. I am hearing. I'm just choosing to ignore what you're saying because none of it will make any difference to what I intend to do.'

'I refuse to go along with this!'

'Here's the choice. We go, I chat to your brother, I dangle my financial inducement in front of him... A few tears all round to start with but in the end everyone's happy. Plan B is I send my men up to physically bring him back to London, where he'll find that life can be very uncomfortable when all avenues of work are dried up. I'll put the word out in the music industry that he's not to be touched with a barge pole. You'd be surprised if you knew the extent of my connections. One word—*vast*. I'm guessing that as his loyal, devoted sister, option two might be tough to swallow.'

'You are...are...'

'Yes, yes, yes. I know what you think of me. I'll give you ten minutes to be at the front door. If you're not there, I'm coming in to get you. And look on the bright side, Agatha. I'm not even asking you to take time off from your job. You'll be delivered safely back here by Monday morning, in one piece and with a bank account that's stuffed to the rafters. And we'll never have to lay eyes on each other again!'

CHAPTER TWO

'I JUST can't believe that you would blackmail me into this,' was the first thing she said as she joined him at the front door, bag reluctantly in hand.

'Blackmail? I prefer to call it *persuasion.*' Luiz pushed himself off the wall against which he had been lounging, calculating how much work he would be missing and also working out that his date for the following night wasn't going to be overjoyed at this sudden road trip. Not that that unduly bothered him. In fact, to call it a *date* was wildly inappropriate. He had had four dates with Chloe Bern and on the fifth he had broken it gently to her that things between them weren't working out. She hadn't taken it well. This was the sixth time he would be seeing her and it would be to repeat what he had already told her on date five.

Aggie snorted derisively. She had feverishly tried to find a way of backing out, but all exits seemed to have been barred. Luiz was in hunting mode and she knew that the threats he had made hadn't been empty ones. For the sake of her brother, she had no choice but to agree to this trip and she felt like exploding with anger.

Outside, the weather was grimly uninviting, freezing cold and with an ominous stillness in the atmosphere.

She followed him to his fancy car, incongruous between

the battered, old run-arounds on either side, and made another inarticulate noise as he beeped it open.

'You're going to tell me,' Luiz said, settling into the driver's seat and waiting for her as she strapped herself in, 'that this is a pointless toy belonging to someone with more money than sense. Am I right?'

'You must be a mind reader,' Aggie said acidly.

'Not a mind reader. Just astute when it comes to remembering conversations we've had in the past.' He started the engine and the sports car purred to life.

'You can't have remembered everything I've said to you,' Aggie muttered uncomfortably.

'Everything. How do you think I'm so sure that you never mentioned renting this dump here?' He threw her a sidelong glance. 'I'm thinking that your brother doesn't contribute greatly to the family finances?' Which in turn made him wonder who would be footing the bill for the romantic getaway. If Aggie barely earned enough to keep the roof over her head, then it stood to reason that Mark earned even less, singing songs in a pub. His jaw tightened at the certainty that Maria was already the goose laying the golden eggs.

'He can't,' Aggie admitted reluctantly. 'Not that I mind, because I don't.'

'That's big of you. Most people would resent having to take care of their kid brother when he's capable of taking care of himself.' They had both been sketchy on the details of Mark's job and Luiz, impatient with a task that had been foisted onto his shoulders, had not delved deeply enough. He had been content enough to ascertain that his niece wasn't going out with a potential axe-murderer, junkie or criminal on the run. 'So…he works in a bar and plays now and then in a band. You might as well tell me the truth,

Agatha. Considering there's no longer any point in keeping secrets.'

Aggie shrugged. 'Yes, he works in a bar and gets a gig once every few weeks. But his talent is really with songwriting. You'll probably think that I'm spinning you a fairy story, because you're suspicious of everything I say…'

'With good reason, as it turns out.'

'But he's pretty amazing at composing. Often in the evenings, while I'm reading or else going through some of the homework from the kids or preparing for classes, he'll sit on the sofa playing his guitar and working on his latest song over and over until he thinks he's got it just right.'

'And you never thought to mention that to me because…?'

'I'm sure Mark told you that he enjoyed songwriting.'

'He told me that he was a musician. He may have mentioned that he knew people in the entertainment business. The general impression was that he was an established musician with an established career. I don't believe I ever heard you contradict him.'

The guy was charming but broke, and his state of penury was no passing inconvenience. He was broke because he lived in a dreamworld of strumming guitars and dabbling about with music sheets.

Thinking about it now, Luiz could see why Maria had fallen for the guy. She was the product of a fabulously wealthy background. The boys she had met had always had plentiful supplies of money. Many of them either worked in family businesses or were destined to. A musician, with a notebook and a guitar slung over his shoulder, rustling up cocktails in a bar by night? On every level he had been her accident waiting to happen. No wonder they had all seen fit to play around with the truth! Maria was sharp enough to have known that a whiff of the truth would have had alarm bells ringing in his head.

'I happen to be very proud of my brother,' Aggie said stiffly. 'It's important that people find their own way. I know you probably don't have much time for that.'

'I have a lot of time for that, provided it doesn't impact my family.'

The traffic was horrendous but eventually they cleared it and, after a series of back roads, emerged at a square of elegant red-bricked Victorian houses in the centre of which was a gated, private park.

There had been meals out but neither she nor her brother had ever actually been asked over to Luiz's house.

This was evidence of wealth on a shocking scale. Aside from Maria's expensive bags, which she'd laughingly claimed she couldn't resist and could afford because her family was 'not badly off', there had been nothing to suggest that not badly off had actually meant staggeringly rich.

Even though the restaurants had been grand and expensive, Aggie had never envisioned the actual lifestyle that Luiz enjoyed to accompany them. She had no passing acquaintance with money. Lifestyles of the rich and famous were things she occasionally read about in magazines and dismissed without giving it much thought. Getting out of the car, she realised that, between her and her brother and Luiz and his family, there was a chasm so vast that the thought of even daring to cross it gave her a headache.

Once again she was reluctantly forced to see why Maria's mother had asked Luiz to watch the situation.

Once again she backtracked over their glossing over of their circumstances and understood why Luiz was now reacting the way he was. He was so wrong about them both but he was trapped in his own circumstances and had probably been weaned on suspicion from a very young age.

'Are you going to come out?' Luiz bent down to peer at her through the open car door. 'Or are you going to stay there all night gawping?'

'I wasn't gawping!' Aggie slammed the car door behind her and followed him into a house, a four-storey house that took her breath away, from the pale marble flooring to the dramatic paintings on the walls to the sweeping banister that led up to yet more impeccable elegance.

He strode into a room to the right and after a few seconds of dithering Aggie followed him inside. He hadn't glanced at her once. Just shed his coat and headed straight for his answer machine, which he flicked on while loosening his tie.

She took the opportunity to look round her: stately proportions and the same pale marbled flooring, with softly faded silk rugs to break the expanse. The furniture was light leather and the floor-to-ceiling curtains thick velvet, a shade deeper in colour than the light pinks of the rugs.

She was vaguely aware that he was listening to what seemed to be an interminable series of business calls, until the last message, when the breathy voice of a woman reminded him that she would be seeing him tomorrow and that she couldn't wait.

At that, Aggie's ears pricked up. He might very well have accused her of being shady when it came to her and her brother's private lives. She now realised that she actually knew precious little about *him*.

He wasn't married; that much she knew for sure because Maria had confided that the whole family was waiting for him to tie the knot and settle down. Beyond that, of course, he *would* have a girlfriend. No one as eligible as Luiz Montes would be without one. She looked at him surreptitiously and wondered what the owner of that breathy, sexy voice looked like.

'I'm going to have a quick shower. I'll be back down in ten minutes and then we'll get going. No point hanging around.'

Aggie snapped back to the present. She was blushing. She could feel it. Blushing as she speculated on his private life.

'Make yourself at home,' Luiz told her drily. 'Feel free to explore.'

'I'm fine here, thank you very much.' She perched awkwardly on the edge of one of the pristine leather sofas and rested her hands primly on her lap.

'Suit yourself.'

But as soon as he had left the room, she began exploring like a kid in a toyshop, touching some of the clearly priceless *objets d'art* he had randomly scattered around: a beautiful bronze figurine of two cheetahs on the long, low sideboard against the wall; a pair of vases that looked very much like the real thing from a Chinese dynasty; she gazed at the abstract on the wall and tried to decipher the signature.

'Do you like what you see?' Luiz asked from behind her and she started and went bright red.

'I've never been in a place like this before,' Aggie said defensively.

Her mouth went dry as she looked at him. He was dressed in a pair of black jeans and a grey-and-black-striped woollen jumper. She could see the collar of his shirt underneath, soft grey flannel. All the other times she had seen him he had been formally dressed, almost as though he had left work to meet them at whatever mega-expensive restaurant he had booked. But this was casual and he was really and truly drop-dead sexy.

'It's a house, not a museum. Shall we go?' He flicked off the light as she left the sitting room and pulled out his mobile phone to instruct his driver to bring the four-by-four round.

'*My* house is a house.' Aggie was momentarily distracted from her anger at his accusations as she stared back at the mansion behind her and waited with him for the car to be delivered.

'Correction. Your house is a hovel. Your landlord deserves to be shot for charging a tenant for a place like that. You probably haven't noticed, but in the brief time I was there I spotted the kind of cracks that advertise a problem with damp—plaster falling from the walls and patches on the ceiling that probably mean you'll have a leak sooner rather than later.'

The four-by-four, shiny and black, slowed and Luiz's driver got out.

'There's nothing I can do about that,' Aggie huffed, climbing into the passenger seat. 'Anyway, you live in a different world to me...to us. It's almost impossible to find somewhere cheap to rent in London.'

'There's a difference between cheap and hazardous. Just think of what you could buy if you had the money in your bank account...' He manoeuvred the big car away from the kerb. 'Nice house in a smart postcode... Quaint little garden at the back... You like gardening, don't you? I believe it's one of those things you mentioned...although it's open to debate whether you were telling the truth or lying to give the right impression.'

'I wasn't lying! I love gardening.'

'London gardens are generally small but you'd be surprised to discover what you can get for the right price.'

'I would never accept a penny from you, Luiz Montes!'

'You don't mean that.'

That tone of comfortable disbelief enraged her. 'I'm not interested in money!' She turned to him, looked at his aristocratic dark profile, and felt that familiar giddy feeling.

'Call me cynical, but I have yet to meet someone who isn't interested in money. They might make noises about money not being able to buy happiness and the good things in life being free, but they like the things money can do and the freebies go through the window when more expensive ways of being happy enter the equation. Tell me seriously that you didn't enjoy those meals you had out.'

'Yes, I *enjoyed* them, but I wouldn't miss them if they weren't there.'

'And what about your brother? Is he as noble minded as you?'

'Neither of us are materialistic, if that's what you mean. You met him. Did he strike you as the sort of person who... who would lead Maria on because of what he thought he could get out of her? I mean, didn't you like him at all?'

'I liked him, but that's not the point.'

'You mean the point is that Maria can go out with someone from a different background, just so long as there's no danger of getting serious, because the only person she would be allowed to settle down with would be someone of the same social standing as her.'

'You say that as though there's something wrong with it.'

'I don't want to talk about this. It's not going to get us anywhere.' She fell silent and watched the slow-moving traffic around her, a sea of headlights illuminating late-night shoppers, people hurrying towards the tube or to catch a bus. At this rate, it would be midnight before they cleared London.

'Would you tell me something?' she asked to break the silence.

'I'm listening.'

'Why didn't you try and put an end to their relationship from the start? I mean, why did you bother taking us out for all those meals?'

'Not my place to interfere. Not at that point, at any rate. I'd been asked to keep an eye on things, to meet your brother and, as it turns out, you too, because the two of you seem to be joined at the hip.' He didn't add that, having not had very much to do with his niece in the past, he had found that he rather enjoyed their company. He had liked listening to Mark and Maria entertain him with their chat about movies and music. And even more he had liked the way Aggie had argued with him, had liked the way it had challenged him into making an effort to get her to laugh. It had all made a change from the extravagant social events to which he was invited, usually in a bid by a company to impress him.

'We're not joined at the hip! We're close because...' Because of their background of foster care, but that was definitely something they had kept to themselves.

'Because you lost your parents?'

'That's right.' She had told him in passing, almost the first time she had met him, that their parents were dead and had swiftly changed the subject. Just another muddled half-truth that would further make him suspicious of their motives.

'Apart from which, I thought that my sister had been overreacting to the whole thing. Maria is an only child without a father. Luisa is prone to pointless worrying.'

'I can't imagine you taking orders from your sister.'

'You haven't met Luisa or any of my five sisters. If you had, you wouldn't make that observation.' He laughed and Aggie felt the breath catch in her throat because, for once, his laughter stemmed from genuine amusement.

'What are they like?'

'All older than me and all bossy.' He grinned sideways at her. 'It's easier to surrender than to cross them. In a family of six women, my father and I know better than to try and argue. It would be easier staging a land war in Asia.'

That glimpse of his humanity unsettled Aggie. But she had had glimpses of it before, she recalled uneasily. Times when he had managed to make her forget how dislikeable he was, when he had recounted something with such dry wit that she had caught herself trying hard to stifle a laugh. He might be hateful, judgemental and unfair, he might represent a lot of things she disliked, but there was no denying that he was one of the most intelligent men she had ever met—and, when it suited him, one of the most entertaining. She had contrived to forget all of that but, stuck here with him, it was coming back to her fast and she had to fumble her way out of her momentary distraction.

'I couldn't help overhearing those messages earlier on at the house,' she said politely.

'Messages? What are you talking about?'

'Lots of business calls. I guess you're having to sacrifice working time for this...unless you don't work on a weekend.'

'If you're thinking of using a few messages you overheard as a way of trying to talk me out of this trip, then you can forget it.'

'I wasn't thinking of doing that. I was just being polite.'

'In that case, you can rest assured that there's nothing that can't wait until Monday when I'm back in London. I have my mobile and if anything urgent comes up, then I can deal with it on the move. Nice try, though.'

'What about that other message? I gather you'll be missing a date with someone tomorrow night?'

Luiz stiffened. 'Again, nothing that can't be handled.'

'Because I would feel very guilty otherwise.'

'Don't concern yourself with my private life, Aggie.'

'Why not?' Aggie risked. 'You're concerning yourself with mine.'

'Slightly different scenario, wouldn't you agree? To the best of my knowledge, I haven't been caught trying to con anyone recently. My private life isn't the one under the spotlight.'

'You're impossible! You're so...*blinkered*! Did you know that Maria was the one who pursued Mark?'

'Do me a favour.'

'She was,' Aggie persisted. 'Mark was playing at one of the pubs and she and her friends went to hear them. She went to meet him after the gig and she gave him her mobile number, told him to get in touch.'

'I'm finding that hard to believe, but let's suppose you're telling the truth. I don't see what that has to do with anything. Whether she chased your brother or your brother chased her, the end result is the same. An heiress is an extremely lucrative proposition for someone in his position.' He switched on the radio and turned it to the traffic news.

London was crawling. The weather forecasters had been making a big deal of snow to come. There was nothing at the moment but people were still rushing to get back home and the roads were gridlocked.

Aggie wearily closed her eyes and leaned back. She was hungry and exhausted and trying to get through to Luiz was like beating her head against a brick wall.

She came to suddenly to the sound of Luiz's low, urgent voice and she blinked herself out of sleep. She had no idea how long she had been dozing, or even how she could manage to doze at all when her thoughts were all over the place.

He was on his phone, and from the sounds of it not enjoying the conversation he was having.

In fact, sitting up and stifling a yawn, it dawned on her that the voice on the other end of the mobile was the same smoky voice that had left a message on his answer machine earlier on, and the reason Aggie knew that was because the smoky voice had become high-pitched and shrill. Not only could *she* hear every word the other woman was saying, she guessed that if she rolled down her window the people in the car behind them would be able to as well.

'This is not the right time for this conversation...' Luiz was saying in a harried, urgent voice.

'Don't you dare hang up on me! I'll just keep calling! I deserve better than this!'

'Which is why you should be thanking me for putting an end to our relationship, Chloe. You do deserve a hell of a lot better than me.'

Aggie rolled her eyes. Wasn't that the oldest trick in the book? The one men used when they wanted to exit a relationship with their consciences intact? Take the blame for everything, manage to convince their hapless girlfriend that breaking up is all for her own good and then walk away feeling as though they've done their good deed for the day.

She listened while Luiz, obviously resigning himself to a conversation he hadn't initiated and didn't want, explained in various ways why they weren't working as a couple.

She had never seen him other than calm, self-assured, in complete control of himself and everything around him. People jumped to attention when he spoke and he had always had that air of command that was afforded to people of influence and power.

He was not that man when he finally ended the call to the sound of virulent abuse on the other end of the line.

'Well?' he demanded grittily. 'I am sure you have an opinion on the conversation you unfortunately had to over-hear.'

When she had asked him about his private life, this was not what she had been expecting. He had quizzed her about hers, about her brother's; a little retaliation had seemed only fair. But that conversation had been intensely personal.

'You've broken up with someone and I'm sorry about that,' Aggie said quietly. 'I know that it's wretched when a relationship comes to an end, especially if you've in-vested in it, and of course I don't want to talk about that. It's your business.'

'I like that.'

'What?'

'Your kind words of sympathy. Believe me when I tell you that there's nothing that could have snapped me out of my mood as efficiently as that.'

'What are you talking about?' Aggie asked, confused. She looked at him to see him smiling with amusement and when he flicked her a sideways glance his smile broadened.

'I'm not dying of a broken heart,' he assured her. 'In fact, if you'd been listening, I'm the one who instigated the break-up.'

'Yes,' Aggie agreed smartly. 'Which doesn't mean that it didn't hurt.'

'Are you speaking from experience?'

'Well, yes, as a matter of fact!'

'I'm inclined to believe you,' Luiz drawled. 'So why did you dump him? Wasn't he man enough to deal with your wilful, argumentative nature?'

'I'm neither of those things!' Aggie reddened and glared at his averted profile.

'On that point, we're going to have to differ.'

'I'm only argumentative with *you*, Luiz Montes! And perhaps that's because you've accused me of being a liar and an opportunist, plotting with my brother to take advantage of your niece!'

'Give it a rest. You have done nothing but argue with me since the second you met me. You've made telling comments about every restaurant, about the value of money, about people who think they can rule the world from a chequebook... You've covered all the ground when it comes to letting me know that you disapprove of wealth. Course, how was I to know that those were just cleverly positioned comments to downplay what you were all about? But let's leave that aside for the moment. Why did you dump the poor guy?'

'If you must know,' Aggie said, partly because constant arguing was tiring and partly because she wanted to let him know that Stu had not found her in the least bit argumentative, 'he became too jealous and too possessive, and I don't like those traits.'

'Amazing. I think we've discovered common ground.'

'Meaning?'

'Chloe went from obliging to demanding in record time.' They had finally cleared London and Luiz realised that unless they continued driving through the night they would have to take a break at some point along the route. It was also beginning to snow. For the moment, though, that was something he would keep to himself.

'Never a good trait as far as I am concerned.' He glanced at Aggie and was struck again by the extreme ultra-femininity of her looks. He imagined that guys could get sucked in by those looks only to discover a wildcat behind the angelic front. Whatever scam she and her brother had concocted between them, she had definitely been the brains behind it. Hell, he could almost appreciate the sharp, outspoken intelligence there. Under the low-level sniping, she was a woman a guy could have a conversation with and that, Luiz conceded, was something. He didn't have much use for conversation with women, not when there were always so many more entertaining ways of spending time with them.

Generally speaking, the women he had gone out with had never sparked curiosity. Why would they? They had always been a known quantity, wealthy socialites with impeccable pedigrees. He was thirty-three years old and could honestly say that he had never deviated from the expected.

With work always centre-stage, it had been very easy to slide in and out of relationships with women who were socially acceptable. In a world where greed and avarice lurked around every corner, it made sense to eliminate the opportunist by making sure never to date anyone who could fall into that category. He had never questioned it. If none of the women in his past had ever succeeded in capturing his attention for longer than ten seconds, then he wasn't bothered. His sisters, bar two, had all done their duty and reproduced, leaving him free to live his life the way he saw fit.

'So…what do you mean? That the minute a woman wants something committed you back away? Was that what your ex-girlfriend was guilty of?'

'I make it my duty never to make promises I can't keep,' Luiz informed her coolly. 'I'm always straight with women. I'm not in it for the long run. Chloe, unfortunately, began thinking that the rules of the game could be changed somewhere along the line. I should have seen the signs, of course,' he continued half to himself. 'The minute a woman starts making noises about wanting to spend a night in and play happy families is the minute the warning bells should start going off.'

'And they didn't?' Aggie was thinking that wanting to spend the odd night in didn't sound like an impossible dream or an undercover marriage proposal.

'She *was* very beautiful,' Luiz conceded with a laugh.

'Was that why you went out with her? Because of the way she looked?'

'I'm a great believer in the power of sexual attraction.'

'That's very shallow.'

Luiz laughed again and slanted an amused look at her. 'You're not into sex?'

Aggie reddened and her heart started pounding like a drum beat inside her. 'That's none of your business!'

'Some women aren't.' Luiz pushed the boundaries. Unlike the other times he had seen her, he now had her all to himself, undiluted by the presence of Mark and his niece. Naturally he would use the time to find out everything he could about her and her brother, all the better to prepare him for when they finally made it to the Lake District. But for now it was no hardship trying to prise underneath her prickly exterior to find out what made her tick. They were cooped up together in a car. What else was there to do? 'Are you one of those women?' he asked silkily.

'I happen to think that sex isn't the most important thing in a relationship!'

'That's probably because you haven't experienced good sex.'

'That's the most ridiculous thing I've ever heard in my life!' But her face was hot and flushed and she was finding it difficult to breathe properly.

'I hope I'm not embarrassing you...'

'I'm not *embarrassed*. I just think that this is an inappropriate conversation.'

'Because...?'

'Because I don't want to be here. Because you're dragging me off on a trek to find my brother so that you can accuse him of being an opportunist and fling money at him so that he goes away. Because you think that we can be bought off.'

'That aside...' He switched on his wipers as the first flurries of snow began to cloud the glass. 'We're here and we can't maintain hostilities indefinitely. And I hate to break this to you, but it looks as though our trip might end up taking a little longer than originally anticipated.'

'What do you mean?'

'Look ahead of you. The traffic is crawling and the snow's started to fall. I can keep driving for another hour or so but then we're probably going to have to pull in somewhere for the night. In fact, keep your eyes open. I'm going to divert to the nearest town and we're going to find somewhere overnight.'

CHAPTER THREE

IN THE end, she had to look up somewhere on his phone because they appeared to have entered hotel-free territory.

'It's just one reason why I try to never leave London,' Luiz muttered in frustration. 'Wide, empty open spaces with nothing inside them. Not even a halfway decent hotel, from the looks of it.'

'That's what most people love about getting out of London.'

'Repeat—different strokes for different folks. What have you found?' They had left the grinding traffic behind them. Now he had to contend with dangerously icy roads and thickly falling snow that limited his vision. He glanced across but couldn't see her face because of the fall of soft, finely spun golden hair across it.

'You're going to be disappointed because there are no fancy hotels, although there *is* a B and B about five miles away and it's rated very highly. It's a bit of a detour but it's the only thing I've been able to locate.'

'Address.' He punched it into his guidance system and relaxed at the thought that he would be able to take a break. 'Read me what it says about this place.'

'I don't suppose anyone's ever told you this but you talk to people as though they're your servants. You just expect people to do what you want them to do without question.'

'I would be inclined to agree with that,' Luiz drawled. 'But for the fact that you don't slot into that category, so there goes your argument. I ask you to simply tell me about this bed and breakfast, which you'll do but not until you let me know that you resent the request, and you resent the request for no other reason that I happen to be the one making it. The down side of accusing someone of being black-and-white is that you should be very sure that you don't fall into the same category yourself.'

Aggie flushed and scowled. 'Five bedrooms, two *en suite*, a sitting room. And the price includes a full English breakfast. There's also a charming garden area but I don't suppose that's relevant considering the weather. And I'm the least prejudiced person I know. I'm extremely open minded!'

'Five bedrooms. Two *en suite*. Is there nothing a little less basic in the vicinity?'

'We're in the country now,' Aggie informed him tersely, half-annoyed because he hadn't taken her up on what she had said. 'There are no five-star hotels, if that's what you mean.'

'You know,' Luiz murmured softly, straining to see his way forward when the wipers could barely handle the fall of snow on the windscreen, 'I can understand your hostility towards me, but what I find a little more difficult to understand is your hostility towards all displays of wealth. The first time I met you, you made it clear that expensive restaurants were a waste of money when all over the world people were going without food... But hell, I don't want to get into this. It's hard enough trying to concentrate on not going off the road without launching into yet another pointless exchange of words. You're going to have to look out for a sign.'

Of course, he had no interest in her personally, not beyond wanting to protect his family and their wealth from her, so she should be able to disregard everything he said. But he had still managed to make her feel like a hypocrite and Aggie shifted uncomfortably.

'I'm sorry I can't offer to share the driving,' she muttered, to smooth over her sudden confusion at the way he had managed to turn her notions about herself on their head. 'But I don't have my driving licence.'

'I wouldn't ask you to drive even if you did,' Luiz informed her.

'Because women need protecting?' But she was half-smiling when she said that.

'Because I would have a nervous breakdown.'

Aggie stifled a giggle. He had a talent for making her want to laugh when she knew she should be on the defensive. 'That's very chauvinistic.'

'I think you've got the measure of me. I don't make a good back-seat driver.'

'That's probably because you feel that you always have to be in control,' Aggie pointed out. 'And I suppose you really are always in control, aren't you?'

'I like to be.' Luiz had slowed the car right down. Even though it was a powerful four-wheel drive, he knew that the road was treacherous and ungritted. 'Are you going to waste a few minutes trying to analyse me now?'

'I wouldn't dream of it!' But she was feverishly analysing him in her head, eaten up with curiosity as to what made this complex man tick. She didn't care, of course. It was a game generated by the fact that they were in close proximity, but she caught herself wondering whether his need for absolute control wasn't an inherited obligation. He was an only son of a Latin American magnate. Had he been trained to see himself as ruler of all he surveyed? It occurred to her that this wasn't the first time she had found herself wondering about him, and that was an uneasy thought.

'Anyway, we're here.' They were now in a village and she could see that it barely encompassed a handful of shops, in between and around which radiated small houses, the sort of houses found in books depicting the perfect English country village. The bed and breakfast was a tiny semi-detached house, very easily bypassed were it not for the sign swinging outside, barely visible under the snow.

It was very late and the roads were completely deserted. Even the bed and breakfast was plunged in darkness, except for two outside lights which just about managed to illuminate the front of the house and a metre or two of garden in front.

With barely contained resignation, Luiz pulled up outside and killed the engine.

'It looks wonderful,' Aggie breathed, taken with the creamy yellow stone and the perfectly proportioned leaded windows. She could picture the riot of colour in summer with all manner of flowers ablaze in the front garden and the soporific sound of the bees buzzing between them.

'Sorry?' Luiz wondered whether they were looking at the same house.

''Course, I would rather not be here with *you*,' Aggie emphasised. 'But it's beautiful. Especially with the snow on the ground and on the roof. Gosh, it's really deep as well! That's the one thing I really miss about living in the south. Snow.'

On that tantalising statement, she flung open the car door and stepped outside, holding her arms out wide and her head tilted up so that the snow could fall directly onto her face.

In the act of reaching behind him to extract their cases, Luiz paused to stare at her. She had pulled some fingerless gloves out of her coat pocket and stuck them on and standing like that, arms outstretched, she looked young, vulnerable and achingly innocent, a child reacting to the thrill of being out in the snow.

Beside the point what she looks like, he told himself, breaking the momentary spell to get their bags. She was pretty. He knew that. He had known that from the very first second he had set eyes on her. The world was full of pretty women, especially *his* world, which was not only full of pretty women but pretty women willing to throw themselves at him.

Aggie began walking towards the house, her feet sinking into the snow, and only turned to look around when he had slammed shut the car door and was standing in front of it, a bag in either hand—his mega-expensive bag, her forlorn and cheaply made one which had been her companion from the age of fourteen when she had spent her first night at a friend's house.

He looked just so incongruous. She couldn't see his expression because it was dark but she imagined that he would be bewildered, removed from his precious creature comforts and thrown into a world far removed from the expensive one he occupied. A bed and breakfast with just five bedrooms, only two of which were *en suite*! What a horror story for him! Not to mention the fact that he would have to force himself to carry on being polite to the sister of an unscrupulous opportunist who was plotting to milk his niece for her millions. He was lead actor in the middle of his very worst nightmare and as he stood there, watching her, she reached down to scoop up a handful of snow, cold and crisp and begging to be moulded into a ball.

All her anger and frustration towards him and towards herself for reacting to him when she should be able to be cool and dismissive went into that throw, and she held her breath as the snowball arched upwards and travelled with deadly accuracy towards him, hitting him right in the middle of that broad, muscled, arrogant chest.

She didn't know who was more surprised. Her, for having thrown it in the first place, or him for being hit for the first time in his life by a snowball. Before he could react, she turned her back and began plodding to the front door.

He deserved that, she told herself nervously. He was insulting, offensive and dismissive. He had accused her and her brother in the worst possible way of the worst possible things and had not been prepared to nurture any doubts that he might be wrong. Plus he had had the cheek to make her question herself when she hadn't done anything wrong!

Nevertheless, she didn't want to look back over her shoulder for fear of seeing what his reaction might be at her small act of resentful rebellion.

'Nice shot!' she heard him shout, at which she began to turn around when she felt the cold, wet compacted blow of his retaliation. She had launched her missile at his chest and he had done the same, and his shot was even more faultless than hers had been.

Aggie's mouth dropped open and she looked at him incredulously as he began walking towards her.

'Good shot. Bull's eye.' He grinned at her and he was transformed, the harsh, unforgiving lines of his face replaced by a sex appeal that was so powerful that it almost knocked her sideways. The breath caught in her throat and she found that she was staring up at him while her thoughts tumbled around as though they had been tossed into a spin drier turned to full speed.

'You too,' was all she could think of saying. 'Where did you learn to throw a snowball?'

'Boarding school. Captain of the cricket team. I was their fast bowler.' He rang the doorbell but he didn't take his eyes from her face. 'Did you think that I was so pampered that I wouldn't have been able to retaliate?' he taunted softly.

'Yes.' Her mouth felt as though it was stuffed with cotton wool. Pampered? Yes, of course he was…and yet a less pampered man it would have been hard to find. How did that make sense?

'Where did *you* learn to throw a shot like that? You hit me from thirty metres away. Through thick snow and poor visibility.'

Aggie blinked in an attempt to gather her scattered wits, but she still heard herself say, with complete honesty, 'We grew up with snow in winter. We learned to build snowmen and have snowball fights and there were always lots of kids around because we were raised in a children's home.'

Deafening silence greeted this remark. She hadn't planned on saying that, but out it had come, and she could have kicked herself. Thankfully she was spared the agony of his contempt by the door being pulled open and they were ushered inside by a short, jolly woman in her sixties who beamed at them as though they were much expected long-lost friends, even though it was nearly ten and she had probably been sound asleep.

Of course there was room for them! Business was never good in winter…just the one room let to a long-standing resident who worked nearby during the week…not that there was any likelihood that he would be leaving for his home in Yorkshire at the weekend…not in this snow…had they seen anything like it…?

The jovial patter kept Aggie's turbulent thoughts temporarily at bay. Regrettably, one of the *en suite* rooms was occupied by the long-standing resident who wouldn't be able to return to Yorkshire at the weekend. As she looked brightly between them to see who would opt for the remaining *en suite* bedroom, Aggie smiled innocently at Luiz until he was forced to do the expected and concede to sharing a bathroom.

She could feel him simmering next to her as they were proudly shown the sitting room, where there was 'a wide assortment of channels on the telly because they had recently had cable fitted'. And the small breakfast room where they could have the best breakfast in the village, and also dinner if they would like, although because of the hour she could only run to sandwiches just now...

Aggie branched off into her own, generously proportioned and charming bedroom and nodded blandly when Luiz informed her that he would see her in the sitting room in ten minutes. They both needed something to eat.

There was just time to wash her face, no time at all to unpack or have a bath and get into fresh clothes. Downstairs, Luiz was waiting for her. She heard the rumble of his voice and low laughter as he talked to the landlady. Getting closer, she could make out that he was explaining that they were on their way to visit relatives, that the snow had temporarily cut short their journey. That, yes, public transport would have been more sensible but for the fact that the trains had responded to the bad weather by going on strike. However, what a blessing in disguise, because how else would they have discovered this charming part of the world? And perhaps she could bring them a bottle of wine with their sandwiches...whatever she had to hand would do as long as it was cold...

'So...' Luiz drawled as soon as they had the sitting room to themselves. 'The truth is now all coming out in the wash. Were you ever going to tell me about your background or were you intending to keep that little titbit to yourself until it no longer mattered who knew?'

'I didn't think it was relevant.'

'Do me a favour, Aggie.'

'I'm not ashamed of…' She sighed and ran her fingers through her hair. It was cosy in here and beautifully warm, with an open fire at one end. He had removed his jumper and rolled his sleeves up and her eyes strayed to his arms, sprinkled with dark hair. He had an athlete's body and she had to curb the itch to stare at him. She didn't know where that urge was coming from. Or had it been there from the start?

Wine was brought to them and she felt like she needed some. One really big glass to help her through this conversation…

'You're not ashamed of…? Concealing the truth?'

'I didn't think of it as concealing the truth.'

'Well, forgive me, but it seems a glaring omission.'

'It's not something I talk about.'

'Why not?'

'Why do you think?' She glared at him, realised that the big glass of wine had somehow disappeared in record time and didn't refuse when her wine glass was topped up.

Luiz flushed darkly. It wouldn't do to forget that this was not a date. He wasn't politely delving down conversational avenues as a prelude to sex. Omissions like this mattered, given the circumstances. But those huge blue eyes staring at him with a mixture of uncertainty and accusation were getting to him.

'You tell me.'

'People can be judgemental,' Aggie muttered defensively. 'As soon as you say that you grew up in a children's home, people switch off. You wouldn't understand. How could you? You've always led the kind of life people like us dreamt about. A life of luxury, with family all around you. Even if your sisters were bossy and told you what to do when you were growing up. It's a different world.'

'I'm not without imagination,' Luiz said gruffly.

'But this is just something else that you can hold against us…just another nail in the coffin.'

Yes, it was! But he was still curious to find out about that shady background she had kept to herself. He barely noticed when a platter of sandwiches was placed in front of them, accompanied by an enormous salad, along with another bottle of excellent wine.

'You went to a boarding school. I went to the local comprehensive where people sniggered because I was one of those kids from a children's home. Sports days were a nightmare. Everyone else would have their family there, shouting and yelling them on. I just ran and ran and ran and pretended that there were people there cheering *me* on. Sometimes Gordon or Betsy—the couple who ran the home—would try and come but it was difficult. I could deal with all of that but Mark was always a lot more sensitive.'

'Which is why you're so close now. You said that your parents were dead.'

'They are.' She helped herself to a bit more wine, even though she was unaccustomed to alcohol and was dimly aware that she would probably have a crashing headache the following morning. 'Sort of.'

'Sort of? Don't go coy on me, Aggie. How can people be *sort of* dead?'

Stripped bare of all the half-truths that had somehow been told to him over a period of time, Aggie resigned herself to telling him the unvarnished truth now about their background. He could do whatever he liked with the information, she thought recklessly. He could try to buy them off, could shake his head in disgust at being in the company of someone so far removed from himself. She should never have let her brother and Maria talk her into painting a picture that wasn't completely accurate.

A lot of that had stemmed from her instinctive need to protect Mark, to do what was best for him. She had let herself be swayed by her brother being in love for the first time, by Maria's tactful downplaying of just how protective her family was and why... And she also couldn't deny that Luiz had rubbed her up the wrong way from the very beginning. It hadn't been hard to swerve round the truth, pulling out pieces of it here and there, making sure to nimbly skip over the rest. He was so arrogant. He almost deserved it!

'We never knew our father,' she now admitted grudgingly. 'He disappeared after I was born, and continued showing up off and on, but he finally did a runner when Mum became pregnant with Mark.'

'He did a runner...'

'I'll bet you haven't got a clue what I'm talking about, Luiz.'

'It's hard for me to get my head around the concept of a father abandoning his family,' Luiz admitted.

'You're lucky,' Aggie told him bluntly and Luiz looked at her with dry amusement.

'My life was prescribed,' he found himself saying. 'Often it was not altogether ideal. Carry on.'

Aggie wanted to ask him to expand, to tell her what he meant by a 'prescribed life'. From the outside looking in, all she could see was perfection for him: a united, large family, exempt from all the usual financial headaches, with everyone able to do exactly what they wanted in the knowledge that if they failed there would always be a safety net to catch them.

'What else is there to say? I was nine when Mum died.' She looked away and stared off at the open fire. The past was not a place she revisited with people but she found that she was past resenting what he knew about her. He would never change his mind about the sort of person he imagined she was, but that didn't mean that she had to accept all his accusations without a fight.

'How did she die?'

'Do you care?' Aggie asked, although half-heartedly. 'She was killed in an accident returning from work. She had a job at the local supermarket and she was walking home when she was hit by a drunk-driver. There were no relatives, no one to take us in, and we were placed in a children's home. A wonderful place with a wonderful couple running it who saw us both through our bad times; we couldn't have hoped for a happier upbringing, given the circumstances. So please don't feel sorry for either of us.' The sandwiches were delicious but her appetite had nosedived.

'I'm sorry about your mother.'

'Are you?' But she was instantly ashamed of the bitterness in her voice. 'Thank you. It was a long time ago.' She gave a dry, self-deprecating laugh. 'I expect all this information is academic because you've already made your mind up about us. But you can see why it wouldn't have made for a great opening conversation...especially when I knew from the start that the only reason you'd bothered to ask Maria out with us was so that you could check my brother out.'

Normally, Luiz cared very little about what other people thought of him. It was what made him so straightforward in his approach to tackling difficult situations. He never wasted time beating about the bush. Now, he felt an unaccustomed dart of shame when he thought back to how unapologetic he had been on every occasion he had met them, how direct his questions had been. He had made no attempt to conceal the reason for his sudden interest in his niece. He hadn't been overtly hostile but Aggie, certainly, was sharp enough to have known exactly what his motives were. So could he really blame her if she hadn't launched into a sob story about her deprived background?

Strangely, he felt a tug of admiration for the way she had managed to forge a path for herself through difficult circumstances. It certainly demonstrated the sort of strength of personality he had rarely glimpsed in the opposite sex. He grimaced when he thought of the women he dated. Chloe might be beautiful but she was also colourless and unambitious...just another cover girl born with a silver spoon in her mouth, biding her time at a fairly pointless part-time job until a rich man rescued her from the need to pretend to work at all.

'So where was this home?'

'Lake District,' Aggie replied with a little shrug. She looked into those deep, deep, dark eyes and her mouth went dry.

'Hence you said that they went somewhere that had sentimental meaning for you.'

'Do you remember everything that people say to you?' Aggie asked irritably and he shot her one of those amazing, slow smiles that did strange things to her heart rate.

'It's a blessing and a curse. You blush easily. Do you know that?'

'That's probably because I feel awkward here with you,' Aggie retorted, but on cue she could feel her face going red.

'No idea why.' Luiz pushed himself away from the table and stretched out his legs to one side. He noticed that they had managed to work their way through nearly two bottles of wine. 'We're having a perfectly civilised conversation. Tell me why you decided to move to London.'

'Tell me why *you* did.'

'I took over an empire. The London base needed expanding. I was the obvious choice. I went to school here. I understand the way the people think.'

'But did you *want* to settle here? I mean, it must be a far cry from Brazil.'

'It works for me.'

He continued looking at her as what was left of the sandwiches were cleared away and coffee offered to them. Considering the hour, their landlady was remarkably obliging, waving aside Aggie's apologies for arriving at such an inconvenient time, telling them that business was to be welcomed whatever time it happened to arrive. Beggars couldn't be choosers.

But neither of them wanted coffee. Aggie was so tired that she could barely stand. She was also tipsy; too much wine on an empty stomach.

'I'm going to go outside for a bit,' she said. 'I think I need to get some fresh air.'

'You're going outside in *this* weather?'

'I'm used to it. I grew up with snow.' She stood up and had to steady herself and breathe in deeply.

'I don't care if you grew up running wild in the Himalayas, you're not going outside, and not because I don't think that you can handle the weather. You're not going outside because you've had too much to drink and you'll probably pass out.'

Aggie glared at him and gripped the table. God, her head was swimming, and she knew that she really ought to get to bed, do just as he said. But there was no way that she was going to allow him to dictate her movements on top of everything else.

'Don't tell me what I can and can't do, Luiz Montes!'

He looked at her in silence and then shrugged. 'And do

you intend to go out without a coat, because you're used to the snow?'

'Of course not!'

'Well, that's a relief.' He stood up and shoved his hands in the pockets of his trousers. 'Make sure you have a key to get back in,' he told her. 'I think we've caused our obliging landlady enough inconvenience for one night without having to get her out of bed to let you in because you've decided to take a walk in driving snow.'

Out of the corner of his eye, he saw Mrs Bixby, the landlady, heading towards them like a ship in full sail. But when she began expressing concern about Aggie's decision to step outside for a few minutes, Luiz shook his head ever so slightly.

'I'm sure Agatha is more than capable of taking care of herself,' he told Mrs Bixby. 'But she will need a key to get back in.'

'I expect you want me to thank you,' Aggie hissed, once she was in possession of the front-door key and struggling to get her arms into her coat. Now that she was no longer supporting herself against the dining-room table, her light-headedness was accompanied by a feeling of nausea. She also suspected that her words were a little slurred even though she was taking care to enunciate each and every syllable very carefully.

'Thank me for what?' Luiz walked with her to the front door. 'Your coat's not done up properly.' He pointed to the buttons which she had failed to match up properly, and then he leaned against the wall and watched as she fumbled to try and remedy the oversight.

'Stop staring at me!'

'Just making sure that you're well wrapped up. Would you like to borrow my scarf? No bother for me to run upstairs and get it for you.'

'I'm absolutely fine.' A wave of sickness washed over her as she tilted her head to look him squarely in the face.

Very hurriedly, she let herself out of the house while Luiz turned to Mrs Bixby and grinned. 'I intend to take up residence in the dining room. I'll sit by the window and make sure I keep an eye on her. Don't worry; if she's not back inside in under five minutes, I'll forcibly bring her in myself.'

'Coffee while you wait?'

'Strong, black would be perfect.'

He was still grinning as he manoeuvred a chair so that he could relax back and see her as she stood still in the snow for a few seconds, breathing in deeply from the looks of it, before tramping in circles on the front lawn. He couldn't imagine her leaving the protective circle of light and striking out for an amble in the town. The plain truth was that she had had a little too much to drink. She had been distinctly green round the gills when she had stood up after eating a couple of sandwiches, although that was something she would never have admitted to.

Frankly, Luiz had no time for women who drank, but he could hardly blame her. Neither of them had been aware of how much wine had been consumed. She would probably wake up with a headache in the morning, which would be a nuisance, as he wanted to leave at the crack of dawn, weather permitting. But that was life.

He narrowed his eyes and sat forward as she became bored with her circular tramping and began heading towards the little gate that led out towards the street and the town.

Without waiting for the coffee, he headed for the front door, only pausing on the way to tell Mrs Bixby that he'd let himself back in.

She'd vanished from sight and Luiz cursed fluently

under his breath. Without a coat it was freezing and he was half-running when he saw her staggering up the street with purpose before pausing to lean against a lamp post, head buried in the crook of her elbow.

'Bloody woman,' he muttered under his breath. He picked up speed as much as he could and reached her side just in time to scoop her up as she was about to slide to the ground.

Aggie shrieked.

'Do you intend to wake the entire town?' Luiz began walking as quickly as he could back to the bed and breakfast. Which, in snow that was fast settling, wasn't very quickly at all.

'Put me down!' She pummelled ineffectively at his chest but soon gave up because the activity made her feel even more queasy.

'Now, that has to be the most stupid thing ever to have left your lips.'

'I said put me *down*!'

'If I put you down, you wouldn't be able to get back up. You don't honestly think I missed the fact that you were hanging onto that lamp post for dear life, do you?'

'I don't need rescuing by you!'

'And I don't need to be out here in freezing weather playing the knight in shining armour! Now shut up!'

Aggie was so shocked by that insufferably arrogant command that she shut up.

She wouldn't have admitted it in a million years but it felt good to be carried like this, because her legs had been feeling very wobbly. In fact, she really had been on the point of wanting to sink to the ground just to take the weight off them before he had swept her off her feet.

She felt him nudge the front door open with his foot, which meant that it had been left ajar. It was humiliating to think of Mrs Bixby seeing her like this and she buried herself against Luiz, willing herself to disappear.

'Don't worry,' Luiz murmured drily in her ear. 'Our friendly landlady is nowhere to be seen. I told her to go to bed, that I'd make sure I brought you in in one piece.'

Aggie risked a glance at the empty hall and instructed him to put her down.

'That dumb suggestion again. You're drunk and you need to get to bed, which is what I told you before you decided to prove how stubborn you could be by ignoring my very sound advice.'

'I am not *drunk*. I am *never* drunk.' She was alarmed by a sudden need to hiccup, which she thankfully stifled. 'Furthermore, I am *more than* capable of making my own way upstairs.'

'Okay.' He released her fast enough for her to feel the ground rushing up to meet her and she clutched his jumper with both hands and took a few deep breaths. 'Still want to convince me that you're *more than capable* of making your own way upstairs?'

'I hate you!' Aggie muttered as he swept her back up into his arms.

'You have a tendency to be repetitive,' Luiz murmured, and he didn't have to see her face to know that she was glaring at him. 'And I'm surprised and a little offended that you hate me for rescuing you from almost certainly falling flat on your face in the snow and probably going to sleep. As a teacher, you should know that that is the most dangerous thing that could happen, passing out in the snow. While under the influence of alcohol. Tut, tut, tut. You'd be struck off the responsible-teacher register if they ever found out about that. Definitely not a good example to set for impressionable little children, seeing their teacher the worse for wear...'

'Shut up,' Aggie muttered fiercely.

'Now, let's see. Forgotten which room is yours... Oh, it's coming back to me—the only one left with the *en suite*! Fortuitous, because you might be needing that...'

'Oh be quiet,' Aggie moaned. 'And hurry up! I think I'm going to be sick.'

CHAPTER FOUR

SHE made it to the bathroom in the nick of time and was horribly, shamefully, humiliatingly, wretchedly sick. She hadn't bothered to shut the door and she was too weak to protest when she heard Luiz enter the bathroom behind her.

'Sorry,' she whispered, hearing the flush of the toilet and finding a toothbrush pressed into her hand. While she was busy being sick, he had obviously rummaged through her case and located just the thing she needed.

She shakily cleaned her teeth but lacked the energy to tell him to leave.

Nor could she look at him. She flopped down onto the bed and closed her eyes as he drew the curtains shut, turned off the overhead light and began easing her boots off.

Luiz had never done anything like this before. In fact, he had never been in the presence of a woman quite so violently sick after a bout of excessive drinking and, if someone had told him that one day he would be taking care of such a woman, he would have laughed out loud. Women who were out of control disgusted him. An out-of-control Chloe, shouting hysterically down the phone, sobbing and shrieking and cursing him, had left him cold. He looked at Aggie, who now had her arm covering her face, and wondered why he wasn't disgusted.

He had wet a face cloth; he mopped her forehead and heard her sigh.

'So I guess I should be thanking you,' she said, without moving the hand that lay across her face.

'You could try that,' Luiz agreed.

'How did you know where to find me?'

'I watched you from the dining room. I wasn't going to let you stay out there for longer than five minutes.'

'Because, of course, you know best.'

'Staggering in the dark in driving snow when you've had too much to drink isn't a good idea in anyone's eyes,' Luiz said drily.

'And I don't suppose you'll believe me when I tell you that this is the first time I've ever…ever…done this?'

'I believe you.'

Aggie lowered her protective arm and looked at him. Her eyes felt sore, along with everything else, and she was relieved that the room was only lit by the small lamp on the bedside table.

'You do?'

'It's my fault. I should have said no to that second bottle of wine. In fact, I was barely aware of it being brought.' He shrugged. 'These things happen.'

'But I don't suppose they ever happen to you,' Aggie said with a weak smile. 'I bet you don't drink too much and stagger all over the place and then end up having to be helped up to bed like a baby.'

Luiz laughed. 'No, can't say I remember the last time that happened.'

'And I bet you've never been in the company of a woman who's done that.'

No one would dare behave like that in my presence, was what he could have said, except he was disturbed to find that that would have made him sound like a monster.

'No,' he said flatly. 'And now I'm going to go and get you some painkillers. You're going to need them.'

Aggie yawned and looked at him drowsily. She had a sudden, sharp memory of how it had felt being carried by him. He had lifted her up as though she weighed nothing and his chest against her slight frame had been as hard as steel. He had smelled clean, masculine and woody.

'Yes. Thank you,' she said faintly. 'And once again, I'm so sorry.'

'Stop apologising.' Luiz's tone was abrupt. Was he really so controlling that women edited their personalities just to be with him; sipped their wine but left most of it and said no to dessert because they were afraid that he might pass judgement on them as being greedy or uncontrolled? He had broken off with Chloe and had offered her no explanation other than that she would be 'better off without him'. Strictly speaking, true. But he knew that, in the face of her hysterics, he had been impatient, short-tempered and dismissive. He had always taken it as a given that women would go out of their way to please them, just as he had always taken it as a given that he led a life of moving on; that, however hard they tried, one day it would just be time for him to end it.

Aggie bristled at his obvious displeasure at her repeated apology. God, what must he think of her? The starting point of his opinions had been low enough, but they would be a hundred times lower now—except when the starting point was gold-digger, then how much lower could they get?

She was suddenly too tired to give it any more thought. She half-sat up when he approached with a glass of water. She obediently swallowed two tablets and was reassured that she would be right as rain in the morning. More or less.

'Thanks,' Aggie said glumly. 'And please wake me up first thing.'

'Of course.' Luiz frowned, impatient at the sudden burst of unwelcome introspection which had left him questioning himself.

Aggie fell asleep with that frown imprinted on her brain. It was confusing that someone she didn't care about should have any effect on her whatsoever, but he did.

She vaguely thought that things would be back to normal in the morning. She would dislike him. He would stop being three-dimensional and she would cease to be curious about him.

When she groggily came to, her head was thumping, her mouth tasted of cotton wool and Luiz was slumped in a chair he had pulled and positioned next to her bed. He was fully clothed.

For a few seconds, Aggie didn't take it in, then she struggled up and nudged him.

'What are *you* doing here?'

Belatedly she realised that, although the duvet was tucked around her, she was trouserless and jumperless; searing embarrassment flooded through her.

'I couldn't leave you in the state you were in.' Luiz pressed his eyes with his fingers and then raked both hands through his tousled hair before looking at her.

'I wasn't *in a state*. I…yes…I was…sick but then I fell asleep.'

'You were sick again,' Luiz informed her. 'And that's not taking into account raging thirst and demands for more tablets.'

'Oh God.'

'Sadly, God wasn't available, so it was up to me to find my way down to the kitchen for orange juice because you claimed that any more water would make you feel even more sick. I also had to deal with a half-asleep temper tantrum when I refused to double the dose of painkillers...'

Aggie looked at him in horror.

'Then you said that you were hot.'

'I didn't.'

'You threw off the quilt and started undressing.'

Aggie groaned and covered her face with her hands.

'But, gentleman that I am, I made sure you didn't completely strip naked. I undressed you down to the basics and you fell back asleep.'

Luiz watched her small fingers curl around the quilt cover. He imagined she would be going through mental hell but she was too proud to let it show. Had he ever met anyone like her in his life before? He'd almost forgotten the reason she was with him. She seemed to have a talent for running circles round his formidable single-mindedness and it wasn't just now that they had been thrown together. No, it had happened before. Some passing remark he might have made to which she had taken instant offence, dug her heels in and proceeded to argue with him until he'd forgotten the presence of other people.

'Well...thank you for that. I...I'd like to get changed now.' She addressed the wall and the dressing table in front of her, and heard him slap his thighs with his hands and stand up. 'Did you manage to get any sleep at all?'

'None to speak of,' Luiz admitted.

'You must be exhausted.'

'I don't need much sleep.'

'Well, perhaps you should go and grab a few hours before we start on the last leg of this journey.' It would be nice if the ground could do her a favour and open up and swallow her whole.

'No point.'

Aggie looked at him in consternation. 'What do you

mean that there's no point? It would be downright fool-hardy for you to drive without sleep, and I can't share any of the driving with you.'

'We've covered that. There's no point because it's gone two-thirty in the afternoon, it's already dark and the snow's heavier.' Luiz strode towards the window and pulled back the curtains to reveal never-ending skies the colour of lead, barely visible behind dense, relentlessly falling snow. 'It would be madness to try and get anywhere further in weather like this. I've already booked the rooms for at least another night. Might be more.'

'You can't!' Aggie sat up, dismayed. 'I thought I'd be back at work on Monday! I can't just *disappear*. This is the busiest time of the school year!'

'Too bad,' Luiz told her flatly. 'You're stuck. There's no way I intend to turn around and try and get back to London. And, while you're busy worrying about missing a few classes and the Nativity play, spare a thought for me. I didn't think that I'd be covering half the country in driving snow in an attempt to rescue my niece before she does something stupid.'

'Meaning that your job's more important than mine?' Aggie was more comfortable with this: an argument. Much more comfortable than she was with feverishly thinking about him undressing her, taking care of her, putting her to bed and playing the good guy. 'Typical! Why is it that rich people always think that what they do is more impor-tant than what everyone else does?' She glared at him as he stood by the door, impassively watching her.

For one blinding moment, it occurred to her that she was in danger of seeing beyond the obvious differences between them to the man underneath. If she could list all the things she disliked about him on paper, it would be easy to keep her distance and to fill the spaces between them with hostility and resentment. But to do that would be to fall into the trap of being as black-and-white in her opinions as she had accused him of being.

She paled and her heartbeat picked up in nervous confusion. Had he been working his charm on her from the very beginning? When he had drawn grudging laughs from her and held her reluctantly spellbound with stories of his experiences in foreign countries; when he had engaged her interest in politics and world affairs, while Maria and Mark had been loved up and whispering to each other, distracted by some shared joke they couldn't possibly resist. Had she already begun to see beyond the cardboard cut-out she wanted him to be?

And, stuck together in a car with him, here in this bed and breakfast. Would an arrogant, pompous, single-minded creep really have helped her the way he had the night before, not laughing once at her inappropriate behaviour? Keeping watch over her even though it meant that he hadn't got a wink of sleep? She had to drag out the recollection that he had offered her money in return for his niece; that he was going to offer her brother money to clear off; that liking or not liking someone was not something that mattered to him because he was like a juggernaut when it came to getting exactly what he wanted. He had loads of charm when it suited him, but underneath the charm he was ruthless, heartless and emotionless.

She felt a lot calmer once that message had got to her wayward, rebellious brain and imprinted itself there.

'Well?' she persisted scornfully, and Luiz raised his eyebrows wryly.

'I take it you're angling for a fight. Is this because you feel embarrassed about what happened last night? If it is, then there's really no need. Like I said…these things happen.'

'And, like you also said, you've never had this experience in your life before!' Aggie thought that it would help things considerably if he didn't look so damn gorgeous standing there, even though he hadn't slept and should look a wreck. 'You've never fallen down drunk, and I'll bet that none of your girlfriends have either.'

'You're right. I haven't and they haven't.'

'Is that because none of your girlfriends have ever had too much to drink?'

'Maybe they have.' Luiz shrugged. 'But never in my presence. And, by the way, I don't think that my job is any better or worse than yours. I have a very big deal on the cards which is due to close at the beginning of next week. A takeover. People's jobs are relying on the closure of this deal, hence the reason why it's as inconvenient for me to be delayed with this as it is for you.'

'Oh,' Aggie said, flustered.

'So, if you need to get in touch with your school and ask them for a day or so off, then I'm sure it won't be the end of the world. Now, I'm going to have a shower and head downstairs. Mrs Bixby might be able to rustle you up something to eat.'

He closed the door quietly behind him. At the mention of food, Aggie's stomach had started to rumble, but she made sure not to rush her bath, to take her time washing her hair and using the drier which she found in a drawer in the bedroom. She needed to get her thoughts together. There was no doubt that the fast-falling snow would keep them in this town for another night. It wasn't going to be a case of a few hours on the road and then, whatever the outcome, goodbye to Luiz Montes for ever.

She was going to have his company for longer than she had envisaged and she needed to take care not to fall into the trap of being seduced by his charm. It amazed her that common sense and logic didn't seem to be enough to keep her mind on the straight and narrow.

Rooting through her depleted collection of clothes, she pulled out yet more jeans and a jumper under which she stuck on various layers, a vest, a long-sleeved thermal top, another vest over that...

Looking at her reflection in the mirror, she wondered whether it was possible to look frumpier. Her newly washed hair was uncontrollable, curling in an unruly tumble over her shoulders and down her back. She was bare of make-up because there seemed no point in applying any, and anyway she had only brought her mascara and some lip gloss with her. Her clothes were a dowdy mixture of blues and greys. Her only shoes were the boots she had been wearing because she hadn't foreseen anything more extended than one night somewhere and a meal grabbed on the hop, but now she wished that she had packed a little bit more than a skeleton, functional wardrobe.

Luiz was on the phone when she joined him in the sitting room but he snapped shut the mobile and looked at her as she walked towards him.

With all those thick, drab clothes, anyone could be forgiven for thinking that she was shapeless. She wasn't. He had known that from the times he had seen her out, usually wearing dresses in which she looked ill at ease and uncomfortable. But even those dresses had been designed to cover up. Only last night had he realised just how shapely she was, despite the slightness of her frame.

Startled, he felt the stirrings of an arousal at the memory and he abruptly turned away to beckon Mrs Bixby across for a pot of tea.

'Not for me.' Aggie declined the cup put in front of her. 'I've decided that I'm going to go into town, get some fresh air.'

'Fresh air. You seem to be cursed with a desire for fresh air. Isn't that what got you outside last night?'

But she couldn't get annoyed with him because his voice was lazy and teasing. 'This time I'm not falling over myself. Like I told you, I enjoy snow. I wish it snowed more often in London.'

'The city would grind to a standstill. If you're heading out, then I think I'll accompany you.'

Aggie tried to stifle the flutter of panic his suggestion generated. She needed to clear her mind. However much she lectured herself on all the reasons she had for hating him, there was a pernicious thread of stubbornness that just wanted to go its own merry way, reminding her of his sexiness, his intelligence, that unexpected display of consideration the night before. How was she to deal with that stubbornness if he didn't give her a little bit of peace and privacy?

'I actually intended on going on my own,' she said in a polite let-down. 'For a start, it would give you time to work. You always work. I remember you saying that to us once when your mobile phone rang for the third time over dinner and you took the call. Besides, if you have an important deal to close, then maybe you could get a head start on it.'

'It's Saturday. Besides, it would do me good to stretch my legs. Believe it or not, chairs don't make the most comfortable places to sleep.'

'You're not going to let me forget that in a hurry, are you?'

'Would you if you were in my shoes?'

Aggie had the grace to blush.

'No,' Luiz murmured. 'Thought not. Well, at least you're honest enough not to deny it.' He stood up, towering over her while Aggie stuffed her hands in the pockets of her coat and frantically tried to think of ways of dodging him.

And yet, disturbingly, wasn't she just a little pleased that he would be with her? For good or bad, and she couldn't decide which, her senses were heightened whenever he was around. Her heart beat faster, her skin tingled more, her pulse raced faster and every nerve ending in her seemed to vibrate.

Was that nature's way of keeping her on her toes in the face of the enemy?

'You'll need to have something to eat,' was the first thing he said when they were outside, where the brutal cold was like a stinging slap on the face. The snow falling and collecting on the already thick banks on the pavements turned the winter-wonderland scene into a nightmare of having to walk at a snail's pace.

Her coat was not made for this depth of cold and she could feel herself shivering, while in his padded Barbour, fashioned for arctic conditions, he was doubtless as snug as a bug in a rug.

'Stop telling me what to do.'

'And stop being so damned mulish.' Luiz looked down at her. She had rammed her woolly hat low down over her ears and she was cold. He could tell from the way she had hunched up and the way her hands were balled into fists in the pockets of the coat. 'You're cold.'

'It's a cold day. I like it. It felt stuffy inside.'

'I mean, your coat is inadequate. You need something warmer.'

'You're doing it again.' Aggie looked up at him and her breath caught in her throat as their eyes tangled and he didn't look away. 'Behaving,' she said a little breathlessly, 'as though you have all the answers to everything.' She was dismayed to find that, although she was saying the right thing, it was as if she was simply going through the motions while her body was responding in a different manner. 'I've been meaning to buy another coat, but there's hardly ever any need for it in London.'

'You can buy one here.'

'It's a bad time of the year for me,' Aggie muttered. 'Christmas always is.' She eyed the small town approaching with some relief. 'We exchange presents at school… then there's the tree and the food…it all adds up. You wouldn't understand.'

'Try me.'

Aggie hesitated. She wasn't used to confiding. She just wasn't built that way and she especially couldn't see the point in confiding in someone like Luiz Montes, a man who had placed her in an impossible situation, who was merciless in pursuit, who probably didn't have a sympathetic bone in his body.

Except, a little voice said in her head, *he took care of you last night, didn't he? Without a hint of impatience or rancour.*

'When you grow up in a children's home,' she heard herself say, 'even in a great children's home like the one I grew up in, you don't really have any money. Ever. And you don't get brand-new things given to you. Well, not often. On birthdays and at Christmas, Betsy and Gordon did their best to make sure that we all had something new, but most of the time you just make do. Most of my clothes had been worn by someone else before. The toys were all shared. You get into the habit of being very careful with the small amounts of money you get given or earn by doing chores. I still have that habit. We both do. You'll think it silly, but I've had this coat since I was seventeen. It only occurs to me now and again that I should replace it.'

Luiz thought of the women he had wined and dined

over the years. He had never hesitated in spending money on them. None of those relationships might have lasted, but all the women had certainly profited financially from them: jewellery, fur coats, in one instance a car. The memory of it repulsed him.

'That must have been very limiting, being a teenager and not being able to keep up with the latest fashion.'

'You get used to it.' Aggie shrugged. 'Life could have been a lot worse. Look, there's a café. You're right. I should have something to eat. I'm ravenous.' It also felt a little weird to be having this conversation with him.

'You're changing the subject,' he drawled as they began mingling with the shoppers who were out in numbers, undeterred by the snow. 'Is that something else you picked up growing up in a children's home?'

'I don't want to be cross-examined by you.' They were inside the café which was small and warm and busy, but there were spare seats and they grabbed two towards the back. When Aggie removed her gloves, her fingers were pink with cold and she had to keep the coat on for a little longer, just until she warmed up, while two waitresses gravitated, goggle-eyed, to Luiz and towards their table to take their order.

'I could eat everything on the menu.' Aggie sighed, settling for a chicken baguette and a very large coffee. 'That's what having too much to drink does for a girl. I can't apologise enough.'

'And I can't tell you how tedious it is hearing you continually apologise,' Luiz replied irritably. He glanced around him and sprawled back in the chair. 'I thought women enjoyed nothing more than talking about themselves.'

Aggie shot him a jaundiced look and sat back while her baguette, stuffed to bursting, was placed in front of her. Luiz was having nothing; it should have been a little embarrassing, diving into a foot-long baguette while he watched her eat, but she didn't care. Her stomach was rumbling with hunger. And stranded in awful conditions away from her home turf was having a lowering effect on her defences.

'I'll bet that really gets on your nerves,' Aggie said between mouthfuls, and Luiz had the grace to flush.

'I tend to go out with women whose conversations fall a little short of riveting.'

'Then why do you go out with them? Oh yes, I forgot. Because of the way they look.' She licked some tarragon mayonnaise from her finger and dipped her eyes, missing the way he watched, with apparent fascination, that small, unconsciously sensual gesture. Also missing the way he sat forward and shifted awkwardly in the chair. 'Why do you bother to go out with women if they're boring? Don't you want to settle down and get married? Would you marry someone who bored you?'

Luiz frowned. 'I'm a busy man. I don't have the time to complicate my life with a relationship.'

'Relationships don't have to complicate lives. Actually, I thought they were supposed to make life easier and more enjoyable. This baguette is delicious; thank you for getting it for me. I suppose we should discuss my contribution to this…this…'

'Why? You wouldn't be here if it weren't for me.'

He drummed his fingers on the table and continued to look at her. Her hair kept falling across her face as she leant forward to eat the baguette and, as fast as it fell, she tucked it behind her ear. There were crumbs by her mouth and she licked them off as delicately as a cat.

'True.' Aggie sat back, pleasantly full having demolished the baguette, and she sipped some of her coffee, holding the mug between both her hands. 'So.' She tossed him a challenging look. 'I guess your parents must want you to get married. At least, that's…'

'At least that's what?'

'None of my business.'

'Just say what you were going to say, Aggie. I've seen you half-undressed and ordering me to fetch you orange juice. It's fair to say that we've gone past the usual pleasantries.'

'Maria may have mentioned that everyone's waiting for you to tie the knot.' Aggie stuck her chin up defiantly because if he could pry into her life, whatever his reasons, then why shouldn't she pry into his?

'That's absurd!'

'We don't have to talk about this.'

'There's nothing *to* talk about!' But wasn't that why he found living in London preferable to returning to Brazil— because his mother had a talent for cornering him and pestering him about his private life? He loved his mother very much, but after three futile attempts to match-make him with the daughters of family friends he had had to draw her to one side and tell her that she was wasting her time.

'My parents have their grandchildren, thanks to three of my sisters, and that's just as well, as I have no intention of tying any knots any time soon.' He waited for her response and frowned when none was forthcoming. 'In our family,' he said abruptly, 'the onus of running the business, expanding it, taking it out of Brazil and into the rest of the world, fell on my shoulders. That's just the way it is. It doesn't leave a lot of time for pandering to a woman's needs. Aside from the physical.' He elaborated with a sudden, wolfish smile.

Aggie didn't smile back. It didn't sound like that great a trade-off to her. Yes, lots of power, status, influence and money, but if you didn't have time to enjoy any of that with someone you cared about then what was the point?

She suddenly saw a man whose life had been prescribed from birth. He had inherited an empire and he had never had any choice but to submit to his responsibility. Which, she conceded, wasn't to say that he didn't enjoy what he did. But she imagined that being stuck up there at the very top, where everyone else's hopes and dreams rested on your shoulders, might become a lonely and isolated place.

'Spare me the look of sympathy.' Luiz scowled and looked around for a waitress to bring the bill.

'So what happens when you marry?' she asked in genuine bewilderment, even though she was sensing that the conversation was not one he had any particular desire to continue. In fact, judging from the dark expression on his face, she suspected that he might be annoyed with himself for having said more than he wanted to.

'I have no idea what you mean by that.'

'Will you give over the running of your…er…company to someone else?'

'Why would I do that? It's a family business. No one outside the family will ever have direct control.'

'You're not going to have much time to be a husband, in that case. I mean, if you carry on working all the hours God made.'

'You talk too much.' The bill had arrived. He paid it, leaving a massive tip, and didn't take his eyes from Aggie's face.

She, in turn, could feel her temples begin to throb and her head begin to swim. His eyes drifted down to her full mouth, taking in the perfect, delicate arrangement of her features. Yes, he had looked at her before, had sized her up the first time they had met. But had he looked at her in the past like *this*? There was a powerful, sexual element to his lazy perusal of her face. Or was she imagining it? Was it just his way of avoiding the conversation?

Her breasts were tingling and her thoughts were in turmoil. Aside from the obvious reasons, this man was not her type at all. She might appreciate his spectacular good looks in a detached way but on every other level she had never had time for men who belonged to the striped-suit brigade, whose *raison d'être* was to live and die for the sake of work. She liked them carefree and unconventional and creative, so why had her body reacted like that just then—with the unwelcome frisson of a teenager getting randy on her first date with the guy of her dreams? God, even worse, was it the first time she had reacted like that? Or had she contrived to ignore all those tell-tale signs of a woman looking at a man and imagining?

'Yes. You're right. I do.' Her breathing was shallow, her pupils dilated.

On a subliminal level, Luiz registered these reactions. He was intensely physical, and if he didn't engage in soul searching relationships with women he made up for that in his capacity to read them and just know when they were affected by him.

Usually, it was a simple game with a foregone conclusion, and the women who ended up in his bed were women who understood the rules of the game. He played fair, as far as he was concerned. He never promised anything, but he was a lavish and generous lover.

So what, he wondered, was *this* all about? What the hell was going on?

She was standing up, brushing some crumbs off her jumper and slinging back on the worn, too-thin coat, pulling the woolly hat low down on her head, wriggling her fingers into her gloves. She wasn't looking at him. In fact, she was doing a good job of making sure that she didn't look at him.

Like a predator suddenly on the alert, Luiz could feel something inside him shift gear. He fell in beside her once they were outside and Aggie, nervous for no apparent reason, did what she always did when she was nervous. She began talking, barely pausing to draw breath. She admired the Christmas lights a little too enthusiastically and paused to stand in front of the first shop they came to, apparently lost in wonder at the splendid display of household items and hardware appliances. Her heart was thumping so hard that she was finding it difficult to hold on to her thoughts.

How had they ended up having such an intensely personal conversation? When had she stopped keeping him at a distance? Why had it become so easy to forget all the things she should be hating about him? Was that the power of lust? Did it turn your world on its head and make you lose track of everything that was sensible?

Just admitting to being attracted to him made her feel giddy, and when he told her that they should be getting back because she looked a little white she quickly agreed.

Suddenly this trip seemed a lot more dangerous than it had done before. It was no longer a case of trying to avoid constant sniping. It was a case of trying to maintain it.

CHAPTER FIVE

By the Monday morning—after two evenings spent by Aggie trying to avoid all personal conversation, frantically aware of the way her body was ambushing all her good intentions—the relentless snow was beginning to abate, although not sufficiently for them to begin the last leg of their journey.

The first thing Aggie did was to telephone the school. As luck would have it, it was shut, with just a recorded message informing her that, due to the weather, it would remain shut until further notice. She didn't know if it was still snowing in London, but the temperatures across the country were still sub-zero and she knew from experience that, even if the snow had stopped, sub-zero temperatures would result in frozen roads and pavements, as well as a dangerously frozen playground. This routinely happened once or twice a year, although usually only for a couple of days at most, and Health and Safety were always quick to step in and advise closures.

Then she looked at the pitiful supply of clothes remaining in her bag and said goodbye to all thoughts of saving any money at all for the New Year.

'I need to go back into town,' she told Luiz as soon as she had joined him in the dining room, where Mrs Bixby was busy chatting to the errant guest who had returned the evening before and was complaining bitterly about his chances of doing anything of any use. Salesmen rarely appreciated dire weather.

'More fresh air?'

'I need to buy some stuff.'

'Ah. New coat, by any chance?' Luiz sat back, tilting his chair away from the table so that he could cross his legs.

'I should get another jumper...some jeans, maybe. I didn't think that we would be snowed in when we're not even halfway through this trip.'

Luiz nodded thoughtfully. 'Nor had I. I expect I'll be forced to get some as well.'

'And you're missing your...meetings. You mentioned that deal you needed to get done.'

'I've telephoned my guys in London. They'll cover me in my absence. It's not perfect, but it'll have to do. This evening I'll have a conference call and give them my input. I take it you've called the school?'

'Closed anyway.' She sat back as coffee was brought for them, and chatted for a few minutes with their landlady, who was extremely cheerful at the prospect of having them there longer than anticipated.

'So your school's closed. How fortuitous,' Luiz murmured. 'I've tried calling the hotel where your brother is supposed to be holed up with Maria and the lines are down.'

'So is there any point in continuing?' Aggie looked at him and licked her lips. 'They were only going to be there for a few days. We could get up there and find they've already caught the train back to London.'

'It's a possibility.'

'Is that all you have to say?' Aggie cried in an urgent undertone. *'It's a possibility?* Neither of us can afford to spend time away from our jobs on a possibility!' The thought of her cold, uncomfortable, Luiz-free house beck-oned like a port in a storm. She didn't understand why she was feeling what she was, and the sooner she was removed from the discomfort of her situation the better, as far as she was concerned. 'You have important meetings to go to. You told me so yourself. Just think of all those poor people whose livelihoods depend on you closing whatever deal it is you have to close!'

'Why, Aggie, I hadn't appreciated how concerned you were.'

'Don't be sarcastic, Luiz. You're a workaholic. It must be driving you crazy being caught out like this. It would take us the same length of time to return to London as it would to get to the Lake District.'

'Less.'

'Even better!'

'Furthermore, we would probably be driving away from the worst of the weather, rather than into it.'

'Exactly!'

'Which isn't to say that I have any intention of return-ing to London without having accomplished what I've set out to do. When I start something, I finish it.'

'Even if finishing it makes no sense?'

'This is a pointless conversation,' Luiz said coolly. 'And why the sudden desperation to jump ship?'

'Like I said, I thought I would be away for one night, two at most. I have things to do in London.'

'Tell me what. Your school's closed.'

'There's much more to teaching than standing in front of the children and teaching them. There are lessons to prepare, homework to mark.'

'And naturally you have no computer with you.'

'Of course I haven't.' He wasn't going to give way. She hadn't really expected that he would. She had known that he was the type of man who, once embarked on a certain course, saw it through to the finish. 'I have an old computer. There's no way I could lug that anywhere with me. Not that I thought I'd need it.'

'I'll buy you a laptop.' To Luiz's surprise, it was out before he had had time to think over the suggestion.

'I beg your pardon?'

'Everyone needs a laptop, something they can take with them on the move.' He flushed darkly and raked his fingers through his hair. 'I'm surprised you haven't got one. Surely the school would subsidise you?'

'I have a school computer but I don't take it out of the house. It's not my property.' Aggie was in a daze at his suggestion, but underneath, a slow anger was beginning to build. 'And would the money spent on this act of generosity be deducted from my full and final payment when you throw cash at me and my brother to get us out of the way? Are you keeping a mental tally?'

'Don't be absurd,' Luiz grated. He barely glanced at the food that had been placed in front of him by Mrs Bixby who, sensing an atmosphere, tactfully withdrew.

'Thanks, but I think I'll turn down your kind offer to buy me a computer.' This was how far apart their lives were, Aggie thought. Her body might play tricks on her, make her forget the reality of their situation, but this was the reality. They weren't on a romantic magical-mystery tour and he wasn't the man of her dreams. She was here because he had virtually blackmailed her into going with him and, far from being the man of her dreams, he was cold, single-minded and so warped by his privileged background that it was second nature to him to buy people. He could, so why not? His dealings with the human race were all based on financial transactions. He had girlfriends because they were beautiful and amused him for a while. But what else was there in his life? And did he imagine that there was nothing money couldn't buy?

'Too proud, Aggie?'

'I have no idea what you're talking about.'

'You think I've insulted you by offering to buy you something you need. You're here because of me. You'll probably end up missing work because of me. You'll need to buy clothes because of me.'

'So are you saying that you made a mistake in dragging me along with you?'

'I'm saying nothing of the sort.' Luiz looked at her, frowning with impatience. More and more he was finding it impossible to believe that she could be any kind of gold-digger. What sane opportunist would argue herself out of a free wardrobe? A top-of-the-range laptop computer? 'Of course you had to come with me.' But his voice lacked conviction. 'It's possible you weren't involved in trying to set your brother up with my niece,' he conceded.

'So you *did* make a mistake dragging me along with you.'

'I still intend to make sure that your brother stays away from Maria.'

'Even though you must know that he had no agenda when he got involved with her?'

Luiz didn't say anything and his silence spoke louder than words. Of course, he would never allow Mark to marry his niece. None of his family would. The wealthy remained wealthy because they protected their wealth. They married other wealthy people. That was his world and it was the only world he understood.

It was despicable, so why couldn't she look at him with indifference and contempt? Why did she feel this tremendous physical pull towards him however much her head argued that she shouldn't? It was bewildering and enraging at the same time and Aggie had never felt anything like it before. It was as if a whole set of brand-new emotions had been taken out of a box and now she had no idea how to deal with them.

'You really do come from a completely different world,' Aggie said. 'I think it's very sad that you can't trust anyone.'

'There's a little more to it than that,' Luiz told her, irritated. 'Maria's mother fell in love with an American twenty years ago. That American was Maria's father. There was a shotgun wedding. My sister went straight from her marriage vows to the hospital to deliver her baby. Of course, my parents were concerned, but they knew better than to say anything.'

'Why were they concerned? Because he was an American?'

'Because he was a drifter. Luisa met him when she was on holiday in Mexico. He was a lifeguard at one of the beaches. She was young and he swept her off her feet, or so the story goes. The minute they were married, the demands began. It turned out that Brad James had very expensive tastes. The rolling estate and the cars weren't enough; he wanted a private jet, and then he needed to be bankrolled for ventures that were destined for disaster. Maria knows nothing of this. She only knows that her father was killed in a light-aeroplane crash during one of his flying lessons. Luisa never forgot the mistakes she made.'

'Well, I'm sorry about that. It must have been hard growing up without a father.' She bit into a slice of toast that tasted like cardboard. 'But I don't want anything from you and neither does my brother.'

'You don't want anything from anyone. Am I right?'

Aggie flushed and looked away from those dark, piercing eyes. 'That's right.'

'But I'm afraid I insist on buying you some replacement clothes. Accept the offer in the spirit in which it was intended. If you dislike accepting them to such an extent, you can chuck them in a black bin-bag when you return to London and donate them all to charity.'

'Fine.' Her proud refusal now seemed hollow and churlish. He was being practical. She needed more clothes through no fault of her own. He could afford to buy them for her, so why shouldn't she accept the offer? It made sense. He wasn't to know that she wasn't given to accepting anything from anyone and certainly not charitable donations. Or maybe he had an idea.

At any rate, if he wanted to buy her stuff, then not only would she accept but she would accept with alacrity. It was better, wasn't it, than picking away at generosity, finding fault with it, tearing it to shreds?

With Christmas not far away, the town was once again bustling with shoppers, even though the snow continued falling. There was no convenient department-store but a series of small boutiques.

'I don't usually shop in places like this.' Aggie dithered outside one of the boutiques as Luiz waited for her, his hand resting on the door, ready to push it open. 'It looks expensive. Surely there must be somewhere cheaper?' He dropped his hand and stood back to lean against the shop front.

They had walked into town in silence. It had irritated the hell out of Luiz. Women loved shopping. So what if she had accepted his offer to buy her clothes under duress? The fact was, she was going to be kitted out, and surely she must be just a little bit pleased? If she was, then she was doing a damned good job of hiding it.

'And I've never stayed in a bed and breakfast before the

one we're in now,' Luiz said shortly. 'You're fond of re-minding me of all the things I'm ignorant of because I've been insulated by my background. Well, I'm happy to try them out. Have you heard me complain once about where we're staying? Even though you've passed sufficient acid remarks about me being unable to deal with it because the only thing I can deal with are five-star hotels.'

'No,' Aggie admitted with painful honesty, while her face burned. She wanted to cover her ears with her hands because everything he was saying had a ring of truth about it.

'So I'm taking it that there are two sets of rules here. You're allowed to typecast me, whilst making damned sure that you don't get yourself typecast.'

'I can't help it,' Aggie muttered uncomfortably.

'Well, I suggest you try. So we're going to go into that shop and you're going to try on whatever clothes you want and you're going to let me buy whatever clothes you want. The whole damned shop if it takes your fancy!'

Aggie smiled and then giggled and slanted an upwards look at him. 'You're crazy.'

In return, Luiz smiled lazily back at her. She didn't smile enough. At least, not with him. When she did, her face became radiantly appealing. 'Compliment or not?' he murmured softly, and Aggie felt the ground sway under her feet.

'I'm not prepared to commit on that,' she told him sternly, but the corners of her mouth were still twitching.

'Come on.'

It was just the sort of boutique where the assistants were trained to be scary. They catered for rich locals and passing tourists. Aggie was sure that, had she strolled in, clad in her worn clothes and tired boots, they would have followed her around the shop, rearranging anything she happened to take from the shelves and keeping a close eye just in case she was tempted to make off with something.

With Luiz, however, shopping in an over-priced boutique was something of a different experience. The young girl who had greeted them at the door, as bug-eyed in Luiz's presence as the waitress had been on Saturday in the café, was sidelined and they were personally taken care of by an older woman who confided that she was the owner of the shop. Aggie was made to sit on the *chaise longe*, with Luiz sprawled next to her, as relaxed as if he owned the place. Items of clothing were brought out and most were immediately dismissed by him with a casual wave of the hand.

'I thought *I* was supposed to be choosing my own outfits,' Aggie whispered at one point, guiltily thrilled to death by this take on the shopping experience.

'I know what would look good on you.'

'I should get some jeans...' She worried her lower lip and inwardly fretted at the price of the designer jeans which had been draped over a chair, awaiting inspection. Belatedly, she added, 'And you don't know what would look good on me.'

'I know there's room for improvement, judging from the dismal blacks and greys I've seen you wear in the past.'

Aggie turned to him, hot under the collar and ready to be self-righteous. And she just didn't know what happened. Rather, she knew *exactly* what happened. Their eyes clashed. His, dark and amused... Hers, blue and sparking. Sitting so close to each other on the sofa, she could breathe him in and she gave a little half-gasp.

She knew he was going to kiss her even before she felt his cool lips touch hers, and it was as if she had been waiting for this for much longer than a couple of days. It was as if she had been waiting ever since the very first time they had met.

It was brief, over before it had begun, although when he drew back she found that she was still leaning into him, her mouth parted and her eyes half-closed.

'Bad manners to launch into an argument in a shop,' he murmured, which snapped her out of her trance, though her heart was beating so hard that she could scarcely breathe.

'You kissed me to shut me up?'

'It's one way of stopping an argument in the making.'

Aggie tried and failed to be enraged. Her lips were still tingling and her whole body felt as though it was on fire. That five-second kiss had been as potent as a red-hot branding iron. While she tried hard to conceal how affected she had been by it, he now looked away, the moment already forgotten, his attention back to the shop owner who had emerged with more handfuls of clothing, special items from the stock room at the back.

'Jeans—those three pairs. Those jumpers and that dress...not that one, the one hanging at the back.' He turned to Aggie, whose lips were tightly compressed. 'You look as though you've swallowed a lemon whole.'

'I would appreciate it if you would keep your hands to yourself!' she muttered, flinty-eyed, and Luiz grinned, unperturbed by this show of anger.

'I hadn't realised that my hands had made contact with your body,' he said silkily. 'If they had, you would certainly know about it. Now, be a good girl and try on that lot. Oh, and I want to see how you look in them.'

Aggie, the very last person on earth anyone could label an exhibitionist, decided that she hated parading in front of Luiz. Nevertheless, she couldn't deny the low-level buzz of unsettling excitement threading through her as she walked out in the jeans, the jumpers and various T-shirts in bright colours. He told her to slow down and not run as though she was trying out for a marathon. When she finally arrived at the dress, she held it up and looked at him quizzically.

'A dress?'

'Humour me.'

'I don't wear bright blues.' Nor did she wear silky dresses with plunging necklines that clung to her body like a second skin, lovingly outlining every single curve.

'This is a crazy dress for me to try on in the middle of winter,' she complained, walking towards him in the high heels which the sales assistant had slipped under the door for her. 'When it's snowing outside...'

Luiz could count on the fingers of one hand the times when he had ever been lost for words. He was lost for words now. He had been slouching on the low sofa, his hands lightly clasped on his lap, his long legs stretched out in front of him. Now he sat up straight and ran his eyes slowly up and down the length of her small but incredibly sexy body.

The colour of the dress brought out the amazing aquamarine of her eyes, and the cut of the stretchy, silky fabric left very little to the imagination when it came to revealing the surprising fullness of her breasts, the slenderness of her legs and the flatness of her stomach. He wanted to tell her to go back inside the dressing room and remove her bra so that he could see how the dress looked without two white bra-straps visible on her narrow shoulders.

'We'll have the lot.' His arousal was sudden, fierce and painful and he was damned thankful that he could reach for his coat which he had draped over the back of the chair and position it on his lap. He couldn't take his eyes off her but he knew that the longer he looked, the more uncomfortable he was going to get.

'And we'd better get a move on,' he continued roughly.
'I don't want to be stuck out here in town for much longer.'
He watched, mesmerised, at the sway of her rounded bottom as she walked back towards the changing room. 'And
we'll have those shoes as well,' he told the shop owner,
who couldn't do enough for a customer who had practically
bought half the shop, including a summer dress which she
had foreseen having to hold in the store room until better
weather came along.

'Thank you,' Aggie said once they were outside and
holding four bags each. A coat had been one of the purchases. She was wearing it now and, much as she hated to
admit it, it felt absolutely great. She hadn't felt a twinge
of conscience as she had bid farewell to her old threadbare one in the shop, where it had been left for the shop
owner to dispose of.

'Was it as gruelling an experience as you had imagined?' He glanced down and immediately thought of those
succulent, rounded breasts and the way the dress had clung
to them.

'It was pretty amazing,' Aggie admitted. 'But we were
in there way too long. You want to get back. I understand
that. I just…have one or two small things I need to get.
Maybe we could branch off now? You could go and buy
yourself some stuff.'

'You mean you don't want me to parade in front of you?'
Luiz murmured, and watched with satisfaction the hectic
flush that coloured her cheeks.

He hadn't expected this powerful sexual attraction. He
had no idea where it was coming from. He wasn't sure
when, exactly, it had been born and it made no sense, because she was no more his type than he, apparently, was
hers. She was too argumentative, too mouthy and, hell,
hadn't he started this trip with her in the starring role of

gold-digger? Yet there was something strangely erotic and forbidden about his attraction, something wildly exciting about the way he knew she looked at him from under her lashes. He got horny just thinking about it.

Problem was…what was he to do with this? Where was he going to go with it?

He surfaced from his uncustomary lapse in concentration to find her telling him something about a detour she wanted him to make.

'Seven…what? What are you talking about?'

'I said that I'd like to stop off at Sevenoaks. It'll be a minor detour and I haven't been back there in over eighteen months.'

'What's Sevenoaks?'

'Haven't you been listening to a word I've been saying?' She assumed that, after the little jaunt in the clothes shop, his mind had now switched back to its primary preoccupation, which was work, and in that mode she might just as well have been saying 'blah, blah, blah'.

'In one ear, out the other,' Luiz drawled, marvelling that he could become so lost in his imagination that he literally hadn't heard a word she had been saying to him.

'Sevenoaks is the home we grew up in,' Aggie repeated. 'Perhaps we could stop off there? It's only a slight detour and it would mean a lot to me. I know you're in a rush to get to Mark's hotel, but a couple of hours wouldn't make a huge difference, would it?'

'We could do that.'

'Right…well…thanks.' Suddenly she felt as though she wouldn't have minded spending the rest of their time in the town with him. In response to that crazy thought, she took a couple of small steps back, just to get out of that spellbinding circle he seemed to project around him, the one which, once entered, wreaked havoc with her thought processes. 'And I'll head off now and see you back at the bed and breakfast.'

'What are you going to buy?' Luiz frowned as he continued to stare down at her. 'I thought we'd covered all essential purchases. Unless there are some slightly less essential ones outstanding? There must be a lingerie shop of sorts somewhere...'

Aggie reacted to that suggestion as though she had been stung. She imagined parading in front of him wearing nothing but a lacy bra and pants and she almost gasped aloud.

'I can get my own underwear—thank you.' She stumbled over the words in her rush to get them out. 'And, no, I wasn't talking about that!'

'What, then?'

'Luiz, it's getting colder out here and I'd really like to get back to the bed and breakfast so...' She took a few more steps back, although her eyes remained locked with his, like stupid, helpless prey mesmerised by an approaching predator.

Luiz nodded, breaking the spell. 'I'll see you back there in...' he glanced at his watch. '...a couple of hours. I have some work to do. Let's make it six-thirty in the dining room. If we're to have any kind of detour, then we're going to have to leave very early in the morning, barring any overnight fall of snow that makes it impossible. So we'll get an early night.'

'Of course,' Aggie returned politely. She was gauging from the tone of his voice that, whatever temporary truces came into effect, nothing would deflect him from his mission. It suddenly seemed wildly inappropriate that she had thrilled to his eyes on her only moments before as she had provided him with his very own fashion show, purchased at great expense. She might have made a great song and dance about her scorn for money, her lack of materialism but, thinking about how she had strutted her stuff to those lazy, watchful eyes, she suddenly felt as though without even realising it she had been bought somehow. And not only that, she had enjoyed the experience.

'And I just want you to know…' Her voice was cooler by several degrees. 'That once we're back in London, I shall make sure that all the stuff you bought for me is returned to you.'

'Not this rubbish again!' Luiz dismissed impatiently. 'I thought we'd gone over all that old ground and you'd finally accepted that it wasn't a mortal insult to allow me to buy you a few essential items of clothing, considering we've been delayed on this trip?'

'Since when is a summer dress *an essential item of clothing*?'

'Climb out of the box, Aggie. So the dress isn't essential. Big deal. Try a little frivolity now and again.' He couldn't help himself. His gaze drifted down to her full lips. It seemed that even when she was getting on his nerves she still contrived to turn him on.

'You think I'm dull!'

'I think this is a ridiculous place to have an ongoing conversation about matters that have already been sorted. Standing in the snow. The last thing either of us need is to succumb to an attack of winter flu.'

With her concerns casually swatted away, and her pride not too gently and very firmly put in its place, Aggie spun round on her heels without a backward glance.

She could imagine his amusement at her contradictory behaviour. One minute she was gracefully accepting his largesse, the next minute she was ranting and railing against it. It made no sense. It was the very opposite of the determined, cool, always sensible person she considered herself to be.

But then, she was realising that in his presence that determined, cool and always sensible person went into hiding.

Annoyed with herself, she did what she had to do in town, including purchasing some very functional underwear, and once back at the bed and breakfast she retreated up to her bedroom with a pot of tea. The landline at the hotel to which they were heading was still down and neither could she make contact with her brother on his mobile.

At this juncture, she should have been wringing her hands in worry at the prospect of the scene that would imminently unfold. She should have been depressed at the thought of Luiz doing his worst and bracing herself for a showdown that might result in her having to pick up the pieces. Her fierce protectiveness of her brother should have kicked in.

Instead, as she settled in the chair by the window with her cup of tea, she found herself thinking of Luiz and remembering the brush of his lips on hers. One fleeting kiss that had galvanised all the nerve-endings in her body.

She found herself looking forward to seeing him downstairs, even though she knew that it was entirely wrong to do so. Fighting the urge to bathe and change as quickly as possible, she took her time instead and arrived in the dining room half an hour after their agreed time.

She paused by the door and gathered herself. Luiz was in the clothes he had presumably bought after they had parted company, a pair of black jeans and a black, round-necked jumper. He had pushed his chair back and in front of him was his laptop, at which he was staring with a slight frown.

He looked every inch the tycoon, controlling his empire from a distance. He was a man who could have any woman he wanted. To look at him was to know that beyond a shadow of a doubt. So why was she getting into such a tizzy at the sight of him? He had kissed her to shut her up, and here she was, reacting as though he had swept her off her feet and transported her to his bed.

Luiz looked up and caught her in the act of staring. He shut his computer and in the space of a few seconds had clocked the new jeans, tighter than her previous ones, and one of the new, more brightly coloured long-sleeved T-shirts that clung in a way she probably hadn't noticed. It was warm in the dining room. No need for a thick jumper.

'I hope I'm not interrupting your work,' Aggie said, settling in the chair opposite him. There was a bottle of wine chilling in a bucket next to the table and she eyed it suspiciously. Now was definitely not the time to over-indulge.

'All finished, and you'll be pleased to know that the deal is more or less done and dusted. Jobs saved. Happy employees. A few lucky ones might even get pay rises. What did you buy in town after you left me?'

He poured her some wine and she fiddled with the stem of the glass.

'A few toys,' Aggie confessed. 'Things to take to the home. The children don't get a lot of treats. I thought it would be nice if I brought some with me. I shall wrap them; it'll be hugely exciting for them. 'Course, I couldn't really splash out, but I managed to find a shop with nothing in it over a fiver.'

Luiz watched the animation on her face. This was what the women he dated lacked. They had all been beautiful. In some cases, they had graced the covers of magazines. But, compared to Aggie's mobile, expressive face, theirs seemed in recollection lifeless and empty. Like mannequins. Was it any wonder that he had tired of them so quickly?

'Nothing over a fiver,' he murmured, transfixed by her absorption in what she was saying.

Having pondered the mystery of why he found her so compellingly attractive, Luiz now concluded that it was because she offered more than a pretty face and a sexy body. He had always tired easily of the women he had gone out with. No problem there; he didn't want any of them hanging around for ever. But the fact that Chloe, who had hardly been long-term, could be classified as one of his more enduring relationships was saying to him that his jaded palate needed a change of scene.

Aggie might not conform to what he usually looked for but she certainly represented a change of scene. In every possible way.

'Why are you looking at me like that?' Aggie asked suspiciously.

'I was just thinking about my own excessive Christmases.' He spread his hands in a self-deprecating gesture. 'I am beginning to see why you think I might live in an ivory tower.'

Aggie smiled. 'Coming from you, that's a big admission.'

'Perhaps it's one of the down sides of being born into money.' As admissions went, this was one of his biggest, and he meant it.

'Well, if I'm being perfectly honest…' Aggie leaned towards him, her face warm and appreciative, her defence system instantly defused by a glimpse of the man who could admit to shortcomings. 'I've always thought that pursuing money was a waste of time. 'Course, it's not the be-all and end-all, but I really enjoyed myself in that boutique today.'

'Which bit of it did you enjoy the most?'

'I've never actually sat on a chair and had anyone bring clothes to me for my inspection. Is that how it works with you?'

'I don't have time to sit on chairs while people bring me clothes to inspect,' Luiz said wryly. 'I have a tailor. He has my measurements and will make suits whenever I want them. I also have accounts at the major high-end shops. If I need anything, I just have to ask. There are people there who know the kind of things I want. Did you enjoy modelling the clothes for me?'

'Well…um…' Aggie went bright red. 'That was a first for me as well. I mean, I guess you wanted to see what you were paying for. That sounds awful. It's not what I meant.'

'I know what you meant.' He sipped some of his wine and regarded her thoughtfully over the rim of his glass. 'I would gladly have paid for the privilege of seeing you model those clothes for me,' he murmured. 'Although my guess is that you would have been outraged at any such suggestion. Frankly, it was a bit of a shame that there was any audience at all. Aside from myself, naturally. If it had been just the two of us, I would have insisted you remove your bra when you tried that dress on, for starters.'

Aggie's mouth fell open and she stared at him in disbelieving shock.

'You don't mean that,' she said faintly.

'Of course I do.' He looked surprised that she should disbelieve him.

'Why are you saying these things?'

'I'm saying what I mean. I don't know how it's happened, but I find myself violently attracted to you, and the reason I feel I can tell you this is because I know you feel the same towards me.'

'I do not!'

'Allow me to put that to the test, Aggie.'

This time there was nothing fleeting or gentle about his kiss. It wasn't designed to distract her. It was designed to prove a point, and she was as defenceless against its urgent power as she would have been against a meteor hurtling towards her at full tilt.

There was no rhyme or reason behind her reaction, which was driven purely on blind craving.

With a soft moan of surrender, she reached further towards him and allowed herself to drown in sensations she had never felt before.

'Point proved.' Luiz finally drew back but his hand remained on the side of her face, caressing her hot cheek. 'So the only remaining question is what we intend to do about this...'

CHAPTER SIX

AGGIE couldn't get to sleep. Luiz's softly spoken words kept rolling around in her mind. He had completely dropped the subject over dinner but the electricity had crackled between them and the atmosphere had been thick with unspoken thoughts of them in bed together.

Had she been that transparent all along? When had he realised that she was attracted to him? She had been at pains to keep that shameful truth to herself and she cringed to think how casually he had dropped it into the conversation as a given.

He was a highly sexual man and he would have no trouble in seeing sex between them as just the natural outcome of mutual attraction. He wouldn't be riddled with anxiety and he wouldn't feel as though he was abandoning his self-respect. For him, whatever the reasons for their trip, a sexual relationship between them would always be a separate issue which he would be able to compartmentalise. He was accustomed to relationships that didn't overlap into other areas of his life.

At a little after one, she realised that it was pointless trying to force herself to go to sleep.

She pulled on the dressing gown that had been supplied and was hanging on a hook on the bathroom door, shoved her feet in her bedroom slippers and headed for the door.

One big disadvantage of somewhere as small as this was that there was no room-service for those times when sleep was elusive and a glass of milk was urgently needed. Mrs Bixby had kindly pointed out where drinks could be made after hours and had told them both that they were free to use the kitchen as their own.

Aggie took her time pottering in the kitchen. A cup of hot chocolate seemed a better idea than a glass of milk and it was a diversion to turn her mind to something other than turbulent thoughts of Luiz.

She tried without success to stifle her flush of pleasure at his admission that he had been looking at her.

Caught up between the stern lectures she was giving herself about the craziness of his proposal, like uninvited guests at a birthday party were all sorts of troublesome questions, such as when exactly had he been looking at her and how often…?

None of that mattered, she told herself as she headed back up the stairs with the cup of hot chocolate. What mattered, what was *really* important, was that they get this trip over with as soon as possible and, whatever the outcome, she would then be able to get back to her normal life with its safe, normal routine. One thing that had been gained in the process was that he no longer suspected her of profiteering and she thought that he had probably dropped his suspicions of her brother as well. He still saw it as his duty to intervene in a relationship he thought was unacceptable, but at least there would be no accusations of opportunism.

However, when Aggie tried to remember her safe, normal routine before all these complications had arisen, she found herself thinking about Luiz. His dark, sexy face superimposed itself and squashed her attempts to find comfort in thinking about the kids at the school and what they would be getting up to in the run up to Christmas.

She didn't expect to see the object of her fevered thoughts at the top of the stairs. She was staring down into the mug of hot chocolate, willing it not to spill, when she looked up and there he was. Not exactly at the top of the stairs, but in the shadowy half-light on the landing, just outside one of the bedrooms, with just a towel round his waist and another hand towel slung over his neck.

Aggie blinked furiously to clear her vision and when the vision remained intact she made a strangled, inarticulate noise and froze as he strolled towards her.

'What are you doing here?' she asked in an accusing gasp as he reached to relieve her of the mug, which threatened to fall because her hands were trembling so much.

'I could ask *you* the same question.'

'I…I was thirsty.'

Luiz didn't answer. There were only five rooms on the floor and, if he hadn't known already, it wouldn't have been hard to guess which was hers because it was the only one with a light on. It shone through the gap under the door like a beacon and he beelined towards it so that she found herself with no choice but to follow him on unsteady legs.

The sight of his broad, bronzed back, those wide, powerful shoulders, made her feel faint. Her breasts ached. Her whole body was in the process of reminding her of the futility of denying the sexual attraction he had coolly pointed out hours earlier, the one she had spent the last few restless hours shooting down in flames.

He was in no rush. While her nerves continued to shred and unravel, he seemed as cool as a cucumber, standing back with a little bow to allow her to brush past him into the bedroom, where she abruptly came to a halt and stopped before he could infiltrate himself any further.

'Good night.'

Her cheeks were burning and she couldn't look him in

the eye but she could imagine the little mocking smile on his mouth at her hoarse dismissal.

'So you couldn't sleep. I'm not sure if a hot drink helps with that. I have a feeling that's an old wives' tale…' Luiz ignored her good-night, although he didn't proceed into the bedroom. It was sheer coincidence that he had bumped into her on the landing, *pure bloody coincidence,* but didn't fate work in mysterious ways? The laws of attraction… wasn't that what they called it? He remembered some girl-friend waffling on about that years ago while he had listened politely and wondered whether she had taken leave of her senses. Yet here it was at work, because he had been thinking about the woman standing wide-eyed in front of him and had decided to cool his thoughts down with a shower, only to find her practically outside his bedroom door. Never did he imagine that he would thank providence for the basic provisions of a bed and breakfast with only two *en suites.*

'I was thirsty, I told you.'

'I was having trouble sleeping too,' Luiz said frankly, his dark eyes roving over her slight frame. Even at this un-godly hour, she still managed to look good. No make-up, hair all over the place but still bloody good. Good enough to ravish. Good enough to lift and carry straight off to that king-sized bed behind her.

He felt his erection push up, hard as steel, and his breath quickened.

Aggie cleared her throat and said something polite along the lines of, 'oh dear, that's a shame,' at which Luiz grinned and held out the mug so that she could take it.

'Would you like to know why?'

'I'm not really interested.'

'Aren't you?' Whatever she might say, Luiz had his answer in that fractional pause before she predictably shook her head.

He hadn't been off the mark with her. She wanted him as much as he wanted her. He could always tell these things. His mouth curved in lazy satisfaction as he played with the idea of eliminating the talking and just...kissing her. Just plunging his hands into that tangled blonde hair, pulling her towards him so that she could have proof of just how much he was turned on, kissing her until she begged him not to stop. He could feel her alertness and it hit him that he hadn't been turned on by any woman to this extent before in his life.

He had spent the past couple of hours with his computer discarded next to him on the bed while he had stared up at the ceiling, hands folded behind his head, thinking of her. He had made his intentions clear and then dropped the matter in the expectation that, once the seed was planted, it would take root and grow.

'I want you,' he murmured huskily. 'I can't make myself any clearer, and if you want to touch you can feel the proof for yourself.'

Aggie's heart was thudding so hard that she could barely think straight.

'And I suppose you always get what you want?' She stuck her disobedient hands behind her back.

'You tell me. Will I?'

Aggie took a deep breath and risked looking at him even though those dark, fabulous eyes brought on a drowning sensation.

'No.'

For a few seconds, Luiz thought that he had heard incorrectly. Had she just turned him down? Women never said no to him. Why would they? Without a trace of vanity, he knew exactly what he brought to the table when it came to the opposite sex.

'No,' he tried out that monosyllable and watched as she glanced down with a little nod.

'What do you mean, *no*?' he asked in genuine bafflement.

Aggie's whole body strained to be touched by him and the power of that yearning shocked and frightened her.

'I mean you've got it wrong,' she mumbled.

'I can feel what you're feeling,' he said roughly. 'There's something between us. A chemistry. Neither of us was asking for this but it's there.'

'Yes, well, that doesn't matter.' Aggie looked at him with clear-eyed resolve.

'What do you mean, *that doesn't matter*?'

'We're on opposite sides of the fence, Luiz.'

'How many times do I have to reassure you that I have conceded that you were innocent of the accusations I originally made?'

'That's an important fence but there are others. You belong to a dynasty. You might think it's fun to step outside the line for a while, but I'm not a toy that you can pick up and then discard when you're through with it.'

'I never implied that you were.' Luiz thought that, as toys went, she was one he would dearly love to play with.

'I may not be rich and I may have come from a foster home, but it doesn't mean that I don't have principles.'

'And if I implied that you didn't, then I apologise.'

'And it doesn't mean that I'm weak either!' Aggie barrelled through his apology because, now that she had gathered momentum, she knew that it was in her interests to capitalise on it.

'Where are you going with that?' Luiz had the strangest feeling of having lost control.

'I'm not going to just *give in* to the fact that, yes, you're an attractive enough man and we happen to be sharing the same space...'

'I honestly can't believe I'm hearing this.'

'Yes, well, it's not my fault that you've lived such a charmed life that you've always got everything you wanted at the snap of a finger.'

Luiz looked down into those aquamarine eyes that could make a grown man go weak at the knees and shook his head in genuine incomprehension. Yes, okay, so maybe he had had a charmed life and maybe he had always got what he wanted, but this was crazy! The atmosphere between them was tangible and electric... What was wrong with two consenting adults giving in to what they both clearly wanted, whether she was brave enough to admit that or not?

'So...' Aggie took a couple of steps towards the door and placed her hand firmly on the door knob. As a support, it was wonderful because her legs felt like jelly. 'If you don't mind, I'm very tired and I really would like to get to bed now.'

She didn't dare meet his eyes, not quite, but lowering them was equally hazardous because she was then forced to stare at his chest with its dark hair that looked so aggressively, dangerously *un-English*; at his flat, brown nipples and at the clearly defined ripple of muscle and sinew.

Luiz realised that he was being dismissed and he straightened, all the time telling himself that the woman, as far as he was concerned, was now history. He had never been rejected before, at least not that he could remember, and he would naturally accept the reality that he was being rejected now, very politely but very firmly rejected. He had never chased any woman and he should have stuck with that format.

'Of course,' he said coldly, reaching to hold both ends of the towel over his shoulders with either hand.

Immediately, Aggie felt his cool withdrawal and hated it.

'I'll…er…see you tomorrow morning. What time do you want to leave?' This time she did look him squarely in the face. 'And will you still be taking that detour to…you know? I'd understand if you just want to get to our destination as quickly as possible…' But she would miss seeing Gordon and Betsy and all the kids; would miss seeing how everything was. Opportunities to visit like this were so rare. Frankly non-existent.

'And you question *my* motives?'

'What are you talking about?' It was Aggie's turn to be puzzled and taken aback at the harsh, scathing contempt in his voice.

'You have just made me out to be a guy who can't control his baser instincts—yet I have to question your choice of men because you seem to lump me into the category as the sort of man who gives his word on something only to retract it if it's no longer convenient!'

Hot colour flared in her cheeks and her mouth fell open.

'I never said…'

'Of course you did! Well, I told you that I would make that detour so that you could visit your friends at your foster home and I intend to keep my promise. I may be many things, but I am honourable.'

With that he left, and Aggie fell against the closed door, like a puppet whose strings had been suddenly severed. Every bone in her body was limp and she remained there for a few minutes, breathing heavily and trying not to think about what had just taken place. Which, of course, was impossible. She could still breathe in his scent and feel his disturbing presence around her.

So he had made a pass at her, she thought, trying desperately to reduce it to terms she could grasp. Men had made passes at her before. She was choosy, accustomed to brushing them aside without a second thought.

But this man...

He got to her. He roused her. He made her aware of her sexuality and made her curious to have it explored. Even with all those drawbacks, all those huge, gaping differences between them...

But it was good that she had turned him down, she told herself. He had been open and upfront with her, which naturally she appreciated. Fall into bed because they were attracted to one another? Lots of other women would have grabbed the opportunity; Aggie knew that. Not only was he drop-dead gorgeous, but there was something innately persuasive and unbearably sexy about him. His arrogance, on the one hand, left her cold but on the other it was mesmeric.

Fortunately, she reasoned as she slipped back between the sheets and closed her eyes, she was strong enough to maintain her wits! That strength was something of which she could justifiably be proud. Yes, she might very well be attracted to him, but she had resisted the temptation to just give in.

With the lights out, the cup of hot chocolate forgotten and sleep even more elusive than it had been before she had headed down to the kitchen, Aggie wondered about those other women who had given in. He always got what he wanted. What had he wanted? And why on earth would he be attracted to a woman like her? She was pretty enough, but he could certainly get far prettier without the hassle of having any of them question him or argue with him or stubbornly refuse to back down.

Aggie was forced to conclude that there might be truth in the saying that a change was as good as a rest.

She was different, and he had assumed that he could just reach out and pluck her like fruit from a tree, so that he could sample her before tossing her aside to return to the other varieties of fruit with which he was familiar.

It was more troubling to think of her own motivations, because she was far more serious when it came to relationships. So why was she attracted to him? Was there some part of her, hitherto undiscovered, that really was all about the physical? Some hidden part of her, free of restraint, principles and good judgement, that she had never known existed?

More to the point, how on earth were they going to get along now that this disturbing ingredient had been placed in the mix? Would he be cool and distant towards her because she had turned him down?

Aggie knew that she shouldn't really care but she found that she did. Having seen glimpses of his charm, his intelligence, his sense of humour, she couldn't bear the thought of having to deal with his coolness.

She found that she need not have worried. At least, not as much as she had. She arrived for breakfast the following morning to find him chatting to Mrs Bixby. Although his expression was unreadable when he looked across to where she was standing a little nervously by the door, he greeted her without any rancour or hostility, drawing her into the conversation he had been having with the older woman. Something about the sights they could take in *en route*, which also involved convoluted anecdotes about Mrs Bixby's various relatives who lived there. She seemed to have hordes of family members.

Luiz looked at her not looking at him, deliberately keeping her face turned away so that she could pour all her energy into focusing on Mrs Bixby.

He had managed to staunch his immediate reaction to her dismissal of him. He had left her room enraged and baffled at the unpleasant novelty of having been beaten back. The rage and bafflement had been contained, as he had known they would be, because however uncharacteristic his behaviour had been in that moment, he was still a man who was capable of extreme self-control. He would have to shrug her off with the philosophical approach of you win a few, you lose a few. And, if he had never lost any, then this was as good a time as any to discover what it felt like. With a woman who was, in the bigger picture, an insignificant and temporary visitor to his life.

Outside, the snow had abated. Aggie had called the school, vaguely explained and then apologised for her absence. She hadn't felt all that much better when she had been told that there was nothing to rush back for because the term was nearly over.

'You know what it's like here,' the principal had chuckled. 'All play and not much work with just a week to go before the holidays. If you have family problems, then don't feel guilty about taking some time off to sort them out.'

Aggie did feel guilty, though, because the 'family problems' were a sluggish mix of her own problems which she was trying to fight a way through and it felt deceitful to give the impression that they were any more widespread than that.

She looked surreptitiously at Luiz and wondered what was going through his head. His deep, sexy voice wafted around her and made her feel a little giddy, as though she was standing on a high wire, looking a long way down.

Eventually, Mrs Bixby left and Luiz asked politely in a friendly voice whether she was packed and ready to go.

'We might as well take advantage of the break in the weather,' he said, tossing his serviette onto his plate and pushing his chair back. 'It's not going to last. If you go and bring your bag down, I'll settle up and meet you by reception.'

So this was how it was going to be, Aggie thought. She knew that she should have been pleased. Pleased that he was being normal. Pleased that there would not be an atmosphere between them. Almost as though nothing had happened at all, as though in the early hours of the morning she hadn't bumped into him on the landing, he hadn't strolled into her room wearing nothing but a couple of towels and he certainly hadn't told her that he wanted her. It could all have been a dream because there was nothing in his expression or in the tone of his voice to suggest otherwise.

There was genuine warmth in Mrs Bixby's hugs as she waved them off, and finally Aggie twisted back around in her seat and waited for something. Something to be said. Some indication that they had crossed a line. But nothing.

He asked for the address to the foster home and allowed her to programme the satnav, although her fingers fumbled and it took ages before the address was keyed in and their course plotted.

It would take roughly a few hours. Conditions were going to worsen slightly the further north they went. They had been lucky to have found such a pleasant place to stay a couple of nights but they couldn't risk having to stop again and make do.

Luiz chatted amiably and Aggie was horrified to find that she hated it. Only now was she aware of that spark of electricity that had sizzled between them because it was gone.

When the conversation faltered, he eventually tuned in to the local radio station and they drove without speaking, which gave her plenty of time alone with her thoughts.

In fact, she was barely aware of the motorway giving way to roads, then to streets, and she was shocked when he switched off the radio, stopped the car and said,

'We seem to be here.'

For the first time since they had started on this uncomfortable trip, Luiz was treated to a smile of such spontaneous delight and pleasure that it took his breath away. He grimly wondered whether there was relief in that smile, relief that she was to be spared more of his company. Whether she was attracted to him or not, she had made it perfectly clear that her fundamental antipathy towards him rendered any physical attraction null and void.

'It's been *such* a long time since I was here,' she breathed fervently, hands clasped on her lap. 'I just want to sit here for a little while and breathe it in.'

Luiz thought that anyone would be forgiven for thinking that she was a prodigal daughter, returned to her rightful palatial home. Instead, what he saw was an averagely spacious pebble-dashed house with neat gardens on either side of a gravel drive. There was an assortment of outside toys on the grass and the windows of one of the rooms downstairs appeared to have drawings tacked to them. There were trees at the back but the foliage was sparse and unexciting.

'Same bus,' she said fondly, drawing his attention to a battered vehicle parked at the side. 'Betsy's always complained about it but I think she likes its unpredictability.'

'It's not what I imagined.'

'What did you imagine?'

'It seems small to house a tribe of children and teenagers.'

'There are only ever ten children at any one time and it's bigger at the back. You'll see. There's a conservatory—a double conservatory, where Betsy and Gordon can relax in the evenings while the older ones do their homework. They were always very hot on us doing our homework.' She turned to him and rested her hand on his forearm. 'You don't have to come in if you don't want to. I mean, the village is only a short drive away, and you can always go there for a coffee or something. You have my mobile number. You can call me when you get fed up and I'll come.'

'Not ashamed of me, by any chance, are you?' His voice was mild but there was an edge to it that took her aback.

'Of course I'm not! I was…just thinking of you. I know you're not used to this…er…sort of thing.'

'Stop stereotyping me!' Luiz gritted his teeth and she recoiled as though she had been slapped.

He hadn't complained once when they had been at the bed and breakfast. In fact, he had seemed sincerely impressed with everything about it, and had been the soul of charm to Mrs Bixby. Aggie was suddenly ashamed at the label she had casually dropped on his shoulders and she knew that, whatever his circumstances of birth, and however little he was accustomed to roughing it, he didn't deserve to be shoved in a box. If she did that, then it was about *her* hang-ups and not his.

'I'm sorry,' she said quickly, and he acknowledged the apology with a curt nod.

'Take your time,' he told her. 'I'll bring that bag in and don't rush. I'll watch from the sidelines. I've just spent the last few hours driving. I can do without another bout of it so that I can while away some time in a café.'

But he allowed her half an hour to relax in familiar surroundings without him around. He turned his mind to work, although it was difficult to concentrate when he was half-thinking of the drive ahead, half-thinking of her, wondering what it must feel like to be reunited with her pseudo-family. He had thought that she had stopped seeing him as a one-dimensional cardboard cut-out, but she hadn't, and could he blame her? He had stormed into her life like a bull in a china shop, had made his agenda clear from the beginning, had pronounced upon the problem and produced his financial solution for sorting it out. In short, he had lived down to all her expectations of someone with money and privilege.

He had never given a passing thought in the past as to how he dealt with other people. He had always been supremely confident of his abilities, his power and the reach of his influence. As the only son from a family whose wealth was bottomless, he had accepted the weight of responsibility for taking over his family's vast business concerns, adding to them with his own. Alongside that, however, were all the advantages that came with money— including, he reluctantly conceded, an attitude that might or might not be interpreted as arrogant and overbearing.

It was something that had never been brought to his notice, but then again he was surrounded by people who feared and respected him. Would they ever point out anything that might be seen as criticism?

Agatha Collins had no such qualms. She was in a league of her own. She didn't hold back when it came to pointing out the things she disliked about him although, he mused, she was as quick to apologise if she thought she had been unfair as she was to heap criticism when she thought she had a point. He had found himself in the company of someone who spoke her mind and damned the consequences.

On that thought, he slung his long body out of the car, collected the bag of presents which she had bought the day before and which he could see, as he idly peered into the bag, she had wrapped in very bright, jolly Christmas paper.

The door was pulled open before he had time to hit the

buzzer and he experienced a few seconds of complete dis-
orientation. Sensory overload.

Noise; chaos; children; lots of laughter; the smell of
food; colour everywhere in the form of paintings on the
walls; coats hanging along the wall; shoes and wellies
stacked by the side of the door. Somewhere roundabout
mid-thigh area, a small dark-haired boy with enormous
brown eyes, an earnest face and chocolate smeared round
his mouth stared up at him, announced his name—and also
announced that he knew who *he* was, because Aggie had
said it would be him, which was why Betsy had allowed
him to open the door, because they were *never* allowed
to open the door. All of this was said without pause while
the noise died down and various other children of varying
sizes approached and stared at him.

Luiz had never felt so scrutinised in his life before, nor
so lost for something to say. Being the focus of attention
of a dozen, unblinking children's eyes induced immediate seizure of his vocal chords. Always ready with words,
he cleared his throat and was immensely relieved when
Aggie emerged from a room at the back, accompanied by
a woman in her early seventies, tall, stern-looking with
grey hair pulled back in a bun. When she smiled, though,
her face radiated warmth and he could see from the reaction of the kids that they adored her.

'You look hassled,' Aggie whispered when introduc-
tions had been made. He was assured by Betsy that pan-
demonium was not usual in the house but she was being
lenient, as it was Christmas, and that he must come and
have something to eat, and he needn't fear that there would
be any food throwing at the table.

'Hassled? I'm never hassled.' He slid his eyes across
to her and raised his eyebrows. 'Overwhelmed might be
a better word.'

Aggie laughed, relaxed and happy. 'It's healthy to be overwhelmed every so often.'

'Thanks. I'll bear that in mind.' He was finding it difficult to drag his eyes away from her laughing face. 'Busy place.'

'Always. And Betsy is going to insist on showing you around, I'm afraid. She's very proud of what she's done with the house.'

They had passed several rooms and were heading towards the back of the house where he could see a huge conservatory that opened out onto masses of land with a small copse at the back, which he imagined would be heaven for the kids here when it was summer and they could go outside.

'We won't be here long,' she promised. 'There's a little present-giving Christmas party. It's been brought forward as I'm here. I hope you don't mind.'

'Why should I?' Luiz asked shortly. It irked him immensely that, even though he had mentally decided to write her off, he still couldn't manage to kill off what she did to his libido. It was also intensely frustrating that he was engaging in an unhealthy tussle with feelings of jealousy. Everyone and everything in this place had the power to put a smile on her face. The kind of smile which she had shown him on rare occasions only.

He didn't understand this confused flux of emotion and he didn't like it. He enjoyed being in control of his life and of everything that happened around him. Agatha Collins was very firmly out of his control. If she were any other woman, she would have been flattered at his interest in her, and she wouldn't have hesitated to come to bed with him. It had been a simple, and in his eyes foolproof, proposition.

To have been knocked back was galling enough, but to have been knocked back only to find himself getting back to his feet and bracing himself for another onslaught on her defences bordered on unacceptable.

'I thought you might be bored,' Aggie admitted, flushing guiltily as his face darkened. 'Also...'

'Also what?'

'I know you're angry with me.'

'Why would I be angry with you?' Luiz asked coldly.

'Because I turned you down and I know I must have... You must have found that... Well, I guess I dented your ego.'

'You want me. I want you. I proposed we do something about that and you decided that you didn't want to. There's no question of my pride being dented.'

'I just can't approach sex in such a cold-blooded way.' Aggie was ashamed that after her show of will power she was now backtracking to a place from which she could offer up an explanation. 'You move in and out of women and...'

'And you're not a toy to be picked up and discarded when the novelty's worn off. I think you already made that clear.'

'So that's the only reason why I feel a little uncomfortable about asking you to put yourself out now.'

'Well, don't. Enjoy yourself. The end of the journey is just round the corner.'

CHAPTER SEVEN

'WE'RE never going to make it to Sharrow Bay tonight.'

They had been driving for a little under an hour and Luiz looked across to Aggie with a frown.

'Depends on how much more the weather deteriorates.'

'Yes, well, I don't see the point of taking risks on the roads. I mean, it's not as though Mark and Maria are going anywhere. Not in these conditions. We spent a lot longer than I anticipated at Sevenoaks and I apologise about that.'

Aggie didn't know how to get through the impenetrable barrier that Luiz had erected around himself. He had smiled, charmed and chatted with everyone at the home and had done so without a flicker of tension, but underneath she could feel his coolness towards her. It was like an invisible force field keeping her out and she hated it.

'I hope you didn't find it too much of a chore.' She tried again to revive a conversation that threatened to go in the same direction as the last few she had initiated—slap, bang into a brick wall of Luiz's disinterest.

Her pride, her dignity and her sense of moral self-righteousness at having rightly turned down a proposal for no-strings sex for a day or two had disintegrated, leaving in its wake the disturbing realisation that she had made a terrible mistake. Why hadn't she taken what was on offer? Since when did sex have to lead to a serious commitment? There was no tenderness, and he would never whisper sweet nothings in her ear, but the power of the sexual pull he had over her cut right through all of those shortcomings.

Why shouldn't she be greedy for once in her life and just take without bothering about consequences and without asking herself whether she was doing the wrong thing or the right thing?

She had had three relationships in her life and on paper they had all looked as though they would go somewhere. They had been free-spirited, fun-loving, creative guys, nothing at all like Luiz. They had enjoyed going to clubs, attending protest marches and doing things on impulse.

And what had come of them? She had grown bored with behaviour that had ended up seeming juvenile and irresponsible. She had become fed up with the fact that plans were never made, with Saturdays spent lying in bed because none of them had ever shown any restraint when it came to drinking—and if she had tried to intervene she had been shouted down as a bore. With all of them, she had come to dread the aimlessness that she had initially found appealing. There had always come a point when hopping on the back of a motorbike and just riding where the wind took them had felt like a waste of time.

Luiz was so much the opposite. His self-control was formidable. She wondered whether he had ever done anything spontaneous in his life. Probably not. But despite that, or maybe because of it, her desire for him was liberated from the usual considerations. Why hadn't she seen that at the time? She had shot him down as the sort of person who could have relationships with women purely for sex, as if the only relationships worth considering were ones where you spent your time plumbing each other's depths. Except she had tried those and none of them had worked out.

'The kids loved you,' she persevered. 'And so did Betsy and Gordon. I guess it must have been quite an eye-opener, visiting a place like that. I'm thinking that your background couldn't have been more different.'

Like a jigsaw puzzle where the pieces slowly began to fit together, Luiz was seeing the background picture that had made Aggie the woman she had become. It was frustrating and novel to find himself in a position of wanting to chip away at the surface of a woman and dig deeper. She was suspicious, proud, defensive and fiercely independent. She had had to be.

'There's a hotel up ahead, by the way, just in case you agree with me that we need to stop. Next town along...' With every passing minute of silence from him, Aggie could feel her chances of breaking through that barrier slipping further and further out of reach.

'Is there? How do you know?' With her childhood home behind them, she was no longer the laughing, carefree person she had been there. Luiz could feel the tension radiating out of her, and if it were up to him he would risk the snow and plough on. The mission he had undertaken obviously had to reach a conclusion, but the cold-blooded determination that had initially fuelled him had gone. In its place was weary resignation for an unpleasant task ahead.

Aggie's heart picked up speed. How did she know about the hotel? Because she had checked it on the computer Betsy kept in the office. Because she had looked at Luiz as he had stood with his arms folded at the back of the room, watching Christmas presents being given out, and she had known that, however arrogant and ruthless he could be, he was also capable of generosity and understanding. He could easily have turned down her request for that detour. He was missing work, and the faster he could wrap up the business with Mark and his niece, the better for him. Yet not only had he put himself out but he had taken the experience in his stride. He had shown interest in everything Betsy and Gordon had had to say and had interacted with the kids who had been fascinated by the handsome, sophisticated stranger in their midst.

She had been proud of him and had wanted him so intensely that it physically hurt.

'I saw a sign for it a little way back.' She crossed her fingers behind her back at that excusable white lie. 'And I vaguely remember Betsy mentioning ages ago that there was a new fancy hotel being built near here, to capture the tourist trade. It's booming in this part of the world, you know.'

'I didn't see any sign.'

'It was small. You probably missed it. You're concentrating on driving.'

'Wouldn't you rather just plough on? Get where we're heading? If we stick it out for another hour, we should be there, more or less.'

'I'd rather not, if you don't mind.' It suddenly occurred to her that the offer he had extended had now been withdrawn. He wasn't the sort of man who chased women. Having done so with her, he wasn't the sort of man who would carry on in the face of rejection. Did she want to risk her pride by throwing herself at him, when he now just wanted to get this whole trip over and done with so that he could return to his life?

'I have a bit of a headache coming on, actually. I think it must be all the excitement of today—seeing Gordon and Betsy, the children. Gordon isn't well. She only told me when we were about to leave. He's had some heart problems. I worry about what Betsy will do if something happens to him.'

'Okay. Where's the turning?'

'Are you sure? You've already put yourself out enough as it is.' Aggie held her breath. If he showed even a second's reluctance, then she would abandon her stupid plan; she would just accept that she had missed her chance; she would tell herself that it was for the best and squash any inclination to wonder...

'The turning?'

'I'll direct you.'

He didn't ask how she just happened to know the full address of the hotel, including the post code, in case they got lost and needed to use his satnav. After fifteen minutes of slow driving, they finally saw a sign—a real sign this time—and Aggie breathed a sigh of relief when they swung into the courtyard of a small but very elegant country house. Under the falling snow, it was a picture-postcard scene.

A few cars were in the courtyard, but it was obvious that business was as quiet here as it had been at Mrs Bixby's bed and breakfast. How many other people were slowly wending their way north by car in disastrous driving conditions? Only a few lunatics.

Her nerves gathered pace as they were checked in.

'Since this was my suggestion...' She turned to him as they walked towards the winding staircase that led to the first floor and up to their bedrooms. 'I insist on picking up the tab.'

'Have you got the money to pick up the tab?' Luiz asked. 'There's no point suggesting something if you can't carry it out.'

'I might not be rich but I'm not completely broke!' Nerves made her lash out at him. It wasn't the best strategy for enticing him into her bed. 'I'm doing this all wrong,' she muttered, half to herself.

'Doing what all wrong?' Luiz stopped and looked down at her.

'You're nothing like the guys I've been out with.'

'I don't think that standing halfway up the stairs in a hotel is the place for a soul-searching conversation about the men you've slept with.' He turned on his heels and began heading upstairs.

'I don't like you being like this with me!' Aggie caught up with him and tugged the sleeve of his jumper until he turned around and looked at her with impatience.

'Aggie, why don't we just go to our rooms, take some time out and meet in an hour for dinner? This has already turned into a never-ending journey. I've been away from work for too long. I have things on my mind. I don't feel inclined to get wrapped up in a hysterical, emotional conversation with you now.'

Luiz was finding it impossible to deal with his crazy obsession with her. He wondered if he was going stir crazy. Was being cooped up with her doing something to his self-control? It had not even crossed his mind, when he had made a pass at her, that she would turn him down. Was that why he had watched her with Betsy and Gordon and all those kids and the only thing he could think was how much he wanted to get her into his bed? Was he so arrogant, in the end, that he couldn't accept that any woman should say no to him?

The uneasy swirl of unfamiliar emotions had left him edgy and short-tempered. He would have liked to dismiss her from his mind the way he had always been able to dismiss all the inconveniences that life had occasionally thrown at him. He had always been good at that. Ruthlessness had always served him well. That and the knowledge that it was pointless getting sidetracked by things that were out of your control. Aggie sidetracked him and the last thing he needed was an involved conversation that would get neither of them anywhere. Womanly chats were things he avoided like the plague.

'I'm not being hysterical.' Aggie took a deep breath. If she backed away now, she would never do what she felt she had to do. Falling into bed with Luiz might be something she would never have contemplated in a month of Sundays, but then again she had never had to cope with a sexual attraction that was ripping her principles to shreds.

She had come to the conclusion that, whilst she knew it was crazy to sleep with a guy whose attitude towards women she found unnerving and amoral, not to sleep with him would leave her with regrets she would never be able to put behind her. And, if she was going to sleep with him, then she intended to have some control over the whole messy situation.

A lifetime of independence would not be washed away in a five-minute decision.

'I just want to talk to you. I want to clear the air.'

'There's nothing to clear, Aggie. I've done what you asked me to do, and I'm pleased you seemed to have had a good time seeing all your old friends, but now it's time to move on.'

'I may have made a mistake.'

'What are you talking about?'

'Can we discuss this upstairs? In your room? Or we could always go back downstairs to the sitting room. It's quiet there.'

'If you don't mind me changing while you speak, then follow me to my room, by all means.' He turned his back on her and headed up.

'So…' Once inside the bedroom, Luiz began pulling off his sweater which he flung on a chair by the window. Their bags had been brought up and deposited in their separate rooms and he began rummaging through his for some clothes.

'I never wanted to make this trip with you,' Aggie began falteringly, and Luiz stilled and turned to look at her.

'If this is going to be another twenty minutes of recriminations, then let me tell you straight away that I'm not in the mood.' But, even as he spoke, he was seeing her tumble of fair hair and the slender contours of her body encased in a pair of the new jeans and deep burgundy jumper that was close-fitted and a lot sexier than the baggy jumpers she seemed to have stockpiled. Once again, his unruly lack of physical control made him grit his teeth in frustration. 'I'm also not in the mood to hear you make a song and dance about paying your own way.'

'I wasn't going to.' She pressed her back against the closed door.

'Then what was it you wanted to tell me?'

'I've never met anyone like you before.'

'I think,' Luiz said drily, 'you may have mentioned that to me in the past—and not in a good way—so unless you have something else to add to the mix then I suggest you go and freshen up.'

'What I mean is, I never thought I could be attracted to someone like you.'

'I don't do these kinds of conversations, Aggie. Post mortems on a relationship are bad enough; post mortems on a non-relationship are a complete non-starter. Now, I'm going to have a shower.' He began unbuttoning his shirt.

Aggie felt the thrill of sudden, reckless excitement and a desperate urgency to get through to him. Despite or maybe because of her background she had never been a risk taker. From a young age, she had felt responsible for Mark and she had also gathered, very early on, that the road to success wasn't about taking risks. It was about putting in the hard work; risk taking was for people who had safety nets to fall into. She had never had one.

Even in her relationships, she had never strayed from what her head told her she should be drawn to. So they hadn't worked out. At no point, she now realised, had she ever concluded that maybe she should have sat back and taken stock of what her head had been telling her.

Luiz, so different from anyone she had ever known, who had entered her life in the most dubious of circumstances, had sent her into a crazy tailspin. She had found herself in terrifying new territory where nothing made sense and she had reacted by lashing out.

Before he could become completely bored with her circuitous conversation, Aggie drew in a deep breath. 'You made a pass at me and I'm sorry I turned you down.'

Luiz, about to pull off his shirt, allowed his arms to drop to his sides and looked at her through narrowed eyes. 'I'm not with you,' he said slowly.

Aggie propelled herself away from the safety of the door and walked towards him. Every step closer set up a tempo in her body that made her perspire with nervous tension.

'I always thought,' she told him huskily, 'that I could never make love to a guy unless I really liked him.'

'And the boyfriends you've had?'

'I really liked them. To start with. And please don't make it sound as though I've slept around; I haven't. I've just always placed a lot of importance on compatibility.'

'We all make mistakes.' At no point did it occur to Luiz that he would turn her away. The strength of his attraction was too overwhelming. He didn't get it, but he knew himself well enough to realise that it was something that needed sating. 'But the compatibility angle obviously didn't play out with you,' he couldn't help adding with some satisfaction.

'No, it didn't,' Aggie admitted ruefully. She sneaked a glance at him and shivered. He was just so gorgeous. Was it any wonder her will power was sapped? She would never have made a play for him. She would never have considered herself to be in the category of women he might be attracted to. It occurred to her that he only wanted her because she was different from the women he dated, but none of that seemed to matter, and she wasn't going to try and fight it.

'What happened?' Luiz strolled towards the king-sized four-poster bed and flopped down on it, his hands linked behind his head. His unbuttoned shirt opened to reveal a tantalising expanse of bronzed, muscular chest. This was the pose of the conqueror waiting for his concubine, and it thrilled her.

Aggie shrugged. 'They were free spirits. I liked it to start with. But I guess I'm not much of a free spirit.'

'No. You're not.' He gave her a slow, lingering smile that made her toes curl. 'Are you going to continue standing there or are you going to join me?' He patted the space next to him on the bed and Aggie's heart descended very rapidly in the direction of her feet.

She inched her way towards the bed and laughed when he sat forward and yanked her towards him. Her laughter felt like an unspoken release of all her defences. She was letting go of her resentment in the face of something bigger.

'What do you mean?' Heart beating a mile a minute, she collapsed next to him and felt the warmth of his body next to her. It generated a series of intensely physical reactions that left her breathless and gasping.

'So you're not impressed by money. But a free spirit would have taken what I offered—the computer, the extensive wardrobe; would have factored them in as gifts to be appreciated and moved on. You rejected the computer out of hand and agonised over the wardrobe. The only reason you accepted was because you had no more clothes and I had to talk you into seeing the sense behind the offer. And you still tell me you're going to return them all to me when we get back to London. You criticise me for wanting control but you fall victim to the very same tendency.'

'We're not alike at all.' They were both on their sides, fully clothed, staring at one another. There was something very erotic about the experience, because underneath the excitement of discovery lurked like a thrilling present concealed with wrapping paper.

'Money separates us,' Luiz said wryly. 'But in some areas I've discovered that we're remarkably similar. Would this conversation benefit from us being naked, do you think?'

Aggie released a small, treacherous moan and he delivered a rampantly satisfied smile in response. Then he stood up and held out one hand. 'I'm going to run a bath,' he murmured. 'Your room's next to mine. Why don't you go and get some clothes…?'

'It feels weird,' Aggie confided. 'I've never approached an intimate situation like this.'

'But then this is an intimate situation neither of us expected,' Luiz murmured. 'And that in itself is a first for me.'

'What do you mean?'

'It never fails to surprise me just how turned on I get for you.'

'Because I'm nothing like the women you've gone out with?'

'Because you're nothing like the women I've gone out with,' Luiz agreed.

Aggie knew that she should be offended by that, but

then who would she be kidding? He was nothing like the guys she had gone out with. Mutual physical attraction had barrelled through everything and changed the parameters. Maybe that was why it felt so dangerously exciting.

'You're a lot more independent and I find that a turn on.' He softly ran his fingers along her side. He couldn't wait for her to be naked but this leisurely approach was intoxicating. 'You're not a slave to fashion and you're fond of arguing.'

Aggie conceded privately that all three of those things represented a change for him, but a change that he would rapidly tire of. Since she wasn't in it for the long haul, since she too was stepping outside the box, there was no harm in that, although she was uneasily aware of a barely acknowledged disappointment floating aimlessly inside her.

'You like your women submissive,' she said with a little laugh.

'Generally speaking, it's worked in the past.'

'And I like my guys to be creative, not to be ruled by money.'

'And yet, mysteriously, your creative paupers have all bitten the dust.' Luiz found, to his bemusement, that he didn't care for the thought of any other man in her life. It was puzzling, because he had never been the possessive type. In fact, in the past women who had tried to stir up a non-existent jealousy gene by referring to past lovers had succeeded in doing the opposite.

'They haven't been paupers,' Aggie laughed. 'Neither of them. They've just been indifferent to money.'

'And in the end they bored you.'

'I'm beginning to wish I'd never mentioned that,' Aggie said, though only half-joking. 'And if they bored me,' she felt obliged to elaborate, 'it was because they turned out to be boring people, not because they were indifferent to money.' She wriggled off the bed and stood up. 'Perhaps I'll have a bath in my own bathroom…'

Luiz frowned, propping himself up on one elbow. 'Second thoughts?' His voice was neutral but his eyes had cooled.

'No.' Aggie tilted her chin to look at him. 'I don't play games like that.'

'Good.' He felt himself relax. To have been rejected once bordered on the unthinkable. To be rejected twice would have been beyond the pale. 'Then what games do you play? Because I think I can help you out there…'

The promise behind those softly spoken words sent a shiver up her spine and it was still there when she returned to his bedroom a few minutes later. She had not been lying when she had confessed that she had never approached sex like this before. Stripped of all romantic mystique and airy-fairy expectations that it would lead somewhere, this was physical contact reduced to its most concentrated form.

The bath had been run. Aggie could smell the fragrance of jasmine bath oil. The steam in the enormous bathroom did nothing whatsoever to diminish the impact of Luiz, who had stripped out of his clothes and was wearing a towel around his waist.

Outside, the snow continued to fall. In her room, she had taken a few seconds to stare out of the window and absorb the fact that Mark and Maria, and the mission upon which they had embarked only a few days previously, couldn't have been further from her mind. When exactly had she lost track of the reason why she was here in the first place? It was as though she had opened the wardrobe door to find herself stepping into Narnia, reality left behind for a brief window in time.

She could barely remember the routine of her day-today existence. The school, the staff room, the kids getting ready for their Nativity play.

Was Luiz right? She had always fancied herself as a free-spirited person and yet she felt as though this was the first impulsive thing she had ever done in her life. She had thought him freakishly controlled, a power-hungry tycoon addicted to mastering everything and everyone around him, while she—well, she was completely different. Maybe the only difference really was the fact that he was rich and she wasn't, that he had grown up with privilege while she had had to fight her way out of her background, burying herself in studies that could provide her with opportunities.

'Now, what I'd like...' Luiz drawled, and Aggie blinked herself back to the present, 'is to do what I was fantasising about when you did your little catwalk in that shop for me. Instead of showing me how you look with clothes on, show me how you look with them off.'

He sauntered out of the bathroom and lay back down on the bed, just as he had before.

Aggie realised in some part of her that, whilst this should not feel right, it did. She would never have believed it possible for either of them to set aside their personal differences and meet on this plane. Certainly, she would never have believed it of herself, but before she could begin nurturing any doubts about the radical decision she had made she told herself that everyone deserves some time out, and this was her time out. In a day or two, it would be nothing more than a wicked memory of the one and only time she had truly strayed from the path she had laid out for herself.

She watched, fascinated and tingling all over, shocked as he drew back the towel which had been modestly covering him, and revealed his arousal. She nearly fainted when he gently held it in one hand.

Luiz grinned at her. 'So easy to make you blush,' he murmured. Then he fell silent and watched as she began removing her clothes, at first with self-conscious, fumbling fingers, then with more confidence as she revelled in the sight of his darkened, openly appreciative gaze.

'Come here,' he rasped roughly, before she could remove the final strips of clothing. 'I'm finding it hard to wait.'

Aggie sighed and flung her head back as his big hands curved over her breasts, thinly sheathed in a lacy bra. Their mouths met in an explosive kiss, a greedy, hungry kiss, so that they gasped as they surfaced for air and then resumed their kissing as if neither could get enough of the other. Her nipples were tender and sensitive and she moaned when he rolled his thumb over one stiffened peak, seeking and finding it through the lacy gaps in the bra.

She was melting. Freeing a hand from the tangle of his black hair, she shakily pulled off the panties which were damp, proof of her own out-of-control libido.

Luiz was going crazy with *wanting* her. He could hardly bear the brief separation of their bodies as she unclasped her bra from the back and pulled it off.

Her nipples were big, circular discs, clearly defined, pouting temptingly at him. He realised that he had been fantasising about this moment perhaps from the very first time he had laid eyes on her. He had not allowed himself to see her in a sexual way, not when he had been busy working out how to disengage her and her brother from his niece and the family fortune. But enforced time together had whittled away his self-control. It had allowed the seeds of attraction to take root and flourish.

'You have the face of an angel,' he breathed huskily as he rolled her on top of him. 'And the body of a siren.'

'I'm not sure about that.' Aggie gazed down at him. 'Aren't sirens supposed to be voluptuous?'

'God, you're beautiful…' His hands could almost span her waist and he eased her down so that he could take one of those delicate breasts to his mouth and suckle on the hot, throbbing tip. He loved the way she arched her body back, offering herself to him—and even more he loved the way he could sense her spiralling out of control, her fists clenched as she tried to control the waves of sensation washing over her.

He smoothed his hand along the inside of her thigh and she wriggled to accommodate his questing finger. She shuddered when that finger dipped into her honeyed moistness and began stroking her. With her body under sensual attack on two fronts as he continued to worship her breast with his mouth and tease the wet, receptive bud of her femininity with his finger, she could bear it no longer. She flipped off him and lay on her back, breathing heavily and then curling onto her side as he laughed softly next to her.

'Too much?' he asked, and she sighed on a moan.

'Not fair. It's your turn now to feel like you're about to fall off the edge.'

'What makes you think I'm not already there?'

It transpired that he wasn't. In fact, it transpired that he didn't have a clue what being close to the edge was all about. He had foolishly been confusing it with simply *being turned on*.

For an excruciatingly long period of time, she demonstrated what being close to the edge was all about. She touched him and tasted him until he thought he had died and gone to heaven.

Their bodies seemed to merge and become one. She touched him and he touched her, from her breasts, down to her flat belly with its little mole just above her belly button, and then at last to the most intimate part of her.

He peeled apart her delicate folds and dipped his tongue just there until she squirmed with pleasure, her fingers tangled in his hair, her eyes shut and her whole body thrust back to receive the ministrations of his mouth.

He lazily feasted on her silky-sweet moistness until she was begging him to stop. Lost in the moment, he could have stayed there for ever with her legs around him and her body bucking under his mouth.

He finally thrust into her only after he was wearing protection. Putting it on, he found that his hands were shaking. He kicked off the last slither of duvet that remained on the bed and she opened up to him like a flower, her rhythm and movements matching his so that they were moving as one.

Aggie didn't think that she had ever felt so united and in tune with another human being in her life before. Her body was slippery, coated in a fine film of perspiration. His was too.

They climaxed and it was like soaring high above the earth. And then, quietening, they subsided gently back down. She rolled onto her side and looked at him with pleasure.

'That was…'

'Momentous? Beyond description?' God, this was nothing like what he had felt before! Could good sex do this to a man? Make him feel like he could fly? They had only just finished making love and he couldn't wait to take her again. Did that make sense? He had made love to any number of beautiful women before but he had never felt like this. He had never felt as though he was in possession of an insatiable appetite, had never wanted to switch the light on so that he could just *look*…

'I want to take you again, but first…' Luiz felt an urgent need to set a few facts straight, to reassure himself that this feeling of being out of control, carried away by a current against which he seemed to be powerless, was just a temporary situation. 'You know this isn't going to go anywhere, don't you?' He brushed her hair away from her face so that he could look her directly in the eye. So this might be the wrong time and the wrong place to say this, but it had to be said. He had to clear the air. 'I wouldn't want you to think…'

'Shh. I don't think anything.' Aggie smiled bravely while a series of pathways began connecting in her brain. This man she loathed, to whom she was desperately attracted, was a man who could make her laugh even though she had found him overbearing and arrogant, the same man who had slowly filled her head and her heart. It was why she was here now. In bed with him. She hadn't suddenly become a woman with no morals who thought it was fine to jump into bed on the basis of sexual attraction. No. That had been a little piece of fiction she had sold herself because the truth staring her in the face had been unacceptable.

'I'm not about to start making demands. You and I, we're not suited and we never will be. But we're attracted to one another. That's all. So, why don't we just have some fun? Because we both know that tomorrow it all comes to an end.'

CHAPTER EIGHT

AGGIE spent the night in her own bedroom. Drunk with love-making, she had made sure to tiptoe along the corridor at a little after two in the morning. It was important to remind herself that this was not a normal relationship. It had boundaries and Luiz had made sure to remind her of that the night before. She wasn't about to over step any of them.

She heard the beeping of her phone the following morning and woke to find a series of messages from her brother, all asking her to give him a call.

Panicked, Aggie sat up and dialled his mobile with shaking fingers. She was ashamed to admit that her brother had barely registered on her radar over the past few hours. In fact, she guiltily realised that she had been too focused on herself for longer than that to spare much thought for Mark.

She got through to him almost immediately. The conversation, on her end, barely covered a sentence or two. Down the other end of the line, Mark did all the talking and at the end of ten minutes Aggie ended the call, shell-shocked.

Everything was about to change now, and for a few seconds she resented her brother's intrusion into the little bubble she had built for herself. She checked the time on her phone. Luiz had tried to pull her back into bed with him before she had left in the early hours of the morning, but Aggie had resisted. Luiz was a man who always got what he wanted and rarely paused to consider the costs. He wanted her and would see nothing wrong in having her, whenever and wherever. He was good when it came to detaching and, once their time together was over, he would instantly break off and walk away. Aggie knew that she would not be able to, so putting some distance between them, if not sharing a room for the night could be termed putting distance between them, was essential.

So they had agreed to meet for breakfast at nine. Plenty of time to check the weather and for Luiz to catch up with emails. It was now a little after eight, and Aggie was glad for the time in which she could have a bath and think about what her brother had told her.

Luiz was waiting for her in the dining room, where a pot of coffee was already on the table and two menus, one of which he was scanning, although he put it down as she hovered for a few seconds in the doorway.

She was in a pair of faded jeans and a blue jumper, her hair tied back. She looked like a very sexy schoolgirl, and all at once he felt himself stir into lusty arousal. He hadn't been able to get enough of her the night before. In fact, he recalled asking her at one point whether she was too sore for him to touch her again down there. He leaned back in the chair and shot her a sexy half-smile as she walked towards him.

'You should have stayed with me,' were his first words of greeting. 'You would have made an unbeatable wake-up call.'

Aggie slipped into the chair opposite and helped herself to some coffee. Mark and his news were at the top of her mind but it was something she would lead up to carefully.

'You said you wanted to get some work done before you came down to breakfast. I wouldn't have wanted to interrupt you.'

'I'm good at multi-tasking. You'd be surprised how much work I can get through when there's someone between my legs paying attention to...'

'Shh!' She went bright red and Luiz laughed, entertained at her prurience.

'You get my drift, though?'

'Is that the kind of wake-up call you're accustomed to?' She held the cup between her hands and looked at him over the rim. She had kept her voice light but underneath she could feel jealousy swirling through her veins, unwelcome and inappropriate.

'The only wake-up calls I'm accustomed to are the ones that come from alarm clocks.' He hadn't thought about it, but women sleeping in his bed didn't happen.

'You mean you've never had a night with a woman in your bed? What about holidays?'

'I don't do holidays with women.'

Aggie gazed at him in surprise.

'It's not that unusual,' Luiz muttered, shooting her a brooding look from under his lashes. 'I'm a busy man. I don't have time for the demands of a woman on holiday.'

'How on earth do you ever relax?'

'I return to Brazil. My holidays are there.' He shrugged. 'I used to go on holidays with a couple of my pals. The occasional weekend. Usually skiing. Those have dried up over the past few years.'

'Your holidays were with your guy friends?'

'How did we end up having this conversation?' He raked his fingers through his dark hair in a gesture that she had come to recognise as one of frustration.

If this was about sex and nothing more—and he had

made it clear that for him it was—then Aggie knew she should steer clear of in-depth conversations. He wouldn't welcome them. She fancied that it had always been his way of avoiding the commitment of a full-blown relationship, his way of keeping women at a safe distance. If you didn't have any kind of revealing conversation with someone, then it was unlikely that anyone would ever get close to you. Her curiosity felt like a treacherous step in dangerous waters.

'There's nothing wrong with talking to one another.' She glanced down at the menu and made noises about scrambled eggs and toast.

'Guys don't need attention to be lavished on them,' Luiz said abruptly. 'We're all experienced skiers. We do the black runs, relax for a couple of hours in the evening. Good exercise. No one complaining about not being entertained.'

'I can't imagine anyone having the nerve to complain to you,' Aggie remarked, and Luiz relaxed.

'You'd be surprised, although women complaining fades into insignificance when set alongside your remarkable talent for arguing with me. Not that I don't like it. It's your passionate nature. Your *extremely* passionate nature.'

'Plus those chalet girls can be very attractive if you decide you miss the entertainment of females...'

Luiz laughed, his dark eyes roaming appreciatively over her face. 'When I go skiing, I ski. The last thing I've ever wanted is any kind of involvement in those brief windows of leisure time I get round to snatching for myself.'

'And those brief windows have dried up?'

'My father hasn't been well,' Luiz heard himself say. It was a surprising admission and not one he could remember making to anyone. Only he and his mother knew the real state of his father's health. Like him, his father didn't appreciate fuss and he knew that his daughters would fuss around him. He was also the primary figurehead for the family's vast empire. Many of the older clients would react badly to any hint that Alfredo Montes was not in the prime of good health. Whilst for years Luiz had concentrated on his own business concerns, he had been obliged to take a much more active role in his father's various companies over the past few years, slowly building confidence for the day when his father could fully retire.

'I'm sorry.' She reached out and covered his hand with hers. 'What's wrong with him?'

'Forget I said anything.'

'Why? Is it…terminal?'

Luiz hesitated. 'He had a stroke a few years ago and never made a full recovery. He can still function, but not in the way he used to. His memory isn't what it used to be, nor are his levels of concentration. He's been forced into semi-retirement. No one is aware of his health issues aside from me and my mother.'

'So…you've been overseeing his affairs so that he can slow down?'

'It's not a big deal.' He beckoned across a waitress, closing down the conversation while Aggie fitted that background information about him into the bigger picture she was unconsciously building.

Luiz Montes was a workaholic who had found himself in a situation where he couldn't afford to stand still. He had no time for holidays and even less for the clutter of a relationship. But, even into that relentless lifestyle, he had managed to fit in this tortuous trip on behalf of his sister. It proclaimed family loyalty and a generosity of spirit that she had not given him credit for.

'There's something you need to know,' she said, changing the subject. 'Mark finally got through to me this morning. In fact, last night. I left my phone in the bedroom and didn't check it before I went to sleep. I woke up this morning to find missed calls and text messages for me to call him.'

'And?'

'They're not in the Lake District after all. They're in Las Vegas.'

'So they did it. They tied the knot, the bloody fools.' Luiz didn't feel the rage he had expected. He was still dwelling on the uncustomary lapse in judgement that had allowed him to confide in her. He had never felt the need to pour his heart and soul out to anyone. Indeed, he had always viewed such tendencies as weaknesses, but strangely sharing that secret had had a liberating effect. Enough to smooth over any anger he knew he should have been feeling at his niece doing something as stupid as getting married when she was still a child herself.

'I never said that.' Aggie grinned and he raised his eyebrows enquiringly.

'Share the joke? Because I'm not seeing anything funny from where I'm sitting.' But he could feel himself just going through the motions.

'Well, for a start, they haven't got married.'

Luiz looked at her in silence. 'Come again?'

'Your sister was obviously worried for no good reason. Okay, maybe Maria confided that she loved my brother. Maybe she indulged in a bit of girlish wishful thinking, but that was as far as it went. There was never any plan to run away and get married in the dead of night.'

'So we've spent the past few days on a fool's errand? What the hell are they doing in *Las Vegas*?' Less than a week ago, he would have made a sarcastic comment about the funding for such a trip, but then less than a week ago he hadn't been marooned with this woman in the middle of nowhere. Right at this moment in time, he really couldn't give a damn who had paid for what or who was ripping whom off.

He found himself thinking of that foster home—the atmosphere of cheeriness despite the old furnishings and the obvious lack of luxuries. He thought of Aggie's dingy rented house. Both those things should have hit him as evidence of people not out to take what they could get.

'Mark's over the moon.' Aggie rested her chin in the palm of her hand and looked at Luiz with shining eyes. 'He got a call when they'd only just left London. He said that he was going to call me but then he knew that he wasn't expected back for a few days and he didn't want to say anything just in case nothing came of it. But through a friend of a friend of a friend, a record producer got to hear one of his demos and flew them both over so that they could hear some more. He's got a recording contract!'

'Well, I'll be damned.'

'So...' Aggie sat back to allow a plate of eggs and toast to be put in front of her. 'There's no point carrying on any further.'

'No, there isn't.'

'You'll be relieved, I bet. You can get back to your work, although I'm going to preach at you now and tell you that it's not healthy to work the hours you do, even if you feel you have no choice.'

'You're probably right.'

'I mean, you need to be able to enjoy leisure time as much as you enjoy working time. Sorry? What did you say?'

Luiz shrugged. 'When we get back to London.' He hadn't intended on having any kind of relationship with her, but after last night he couldn't foresee relinquishing it just yet. 'A slight reduction in the workload wouldn't hurt. It's the Christmas season. People are kicking back. It's not as frenetic in the business world as it usually is.'

'So you're going to take a holiday?' Aggie's heart did a sudden, painful flip. 'Will you be going to Brazil, then?'

'I can't leave the country just yet.'

'I thought you said that you were going to have a break.'

'Which isn't to say that I'm suddenly going to drop out of sight. There are a couple of deals that need work, meetings I can't get out of.' He pushed his plate away and sat back to look at her steadily. 'We need to talk about... us. This.'

'I know. It wasn't the wisest move in the world. Neither of us anticipated that...that...'

'That we wouldn't be able to keep our hands off one another?'

How easy it was for him to think about it purely in terms of sex, Aggie thought. While *she* could only think of it in terms of falling in love. She wondered how many women before her had made the same mistake of bucking the guidelines he set and falling in love with him. Had his last girlfriend been guilty of that sin?

'The circumstances were peculiar,' Aggie said, keen to be as light-hearted about what happened between them as he was. 'It's a fact that people can behave out of character when they're thrown into a situation they're not accustomed to. I mean, none of this would have happened if we hadn't...found ourselves snowbound on this trip.'

'Wouldn't it?' His dark eyes swept thoughtfully over her flushed face.

'What do you mean?'

'I like to think I'm honest enough not to underestimate this attraction I feel for you. I noticed you the first time I saw you and it wasn't just as a potential gold-digger. I think I was sexually attracted to you from the beginning.

Maybe I would never have done anything about it but I wouldn't bet on that.'

'*I* didn't notice you!'

'Liar.'

'I didn't,' Aggie insisted with a touch of desperation. 'I mean, I just thought you were Maria's arrogant uncle who had only appeared on the scene to warn us off. I didn't even like you!'

'Who's talking about like or dislike? That's quite different from sexual attraction. Which brings me back to my starting point. We'll head back down to London as soon as we've finished breakfast, and when we get to London I want to know what your plans are. Because I'm not ready to give this up just yet. In fact, I would say that I'm just getting started...'

Just yet. Didn't that say it all? But at least he wasn't trying to disguise the full extent of his interest in her; at least he wasn't pretending that they were anything but two ships passing in the night, dropping anchor for a while before moving on their separate journeys.

When Aggie thought of her last boyfriend, he had been fond of planning ahead, discussing where they would go on holiday in five years' time. She had fancied herself in love, but like an illness it had passed quickly and soon after she had realised that what she had really loved was the feeling of permanence that had been promised.

Luiz wasn't promising permanence. In fact, he wasn't even promising anything longer than a couple of weeks or a couple of months.

'You're looking for another notch on your bedpost?' Aggie said lightly and he frowned at her.

'I'm not that kind of man and if you don't think I've been honest with you, then I can only repeat what I've said. I'm not looking for a committed relationship, but neither do I work my way through women because I have a little black book I want to fill. If you really think that, then we're not on the same page, and whatever we did last night will remain a one-time memory.'

'I shouldn't have said that, but Luiz, you can't really blame me, can you? I mean, have you ever had a relationship that you thought might be going somewhere?'

'I've never sought it. On the other hand, I don't use women. Why are we discussing this, Aggie? Neither of us sees any kind of future in this. I thought we'd covered that.' He looked at her narrowly. 'We *have* covered that, haven't we? I mean, you haven't suddenly decided that you're looking for a long-term relationship, have you? Because, I repeat, it's never going to happen.'

'I'm aware of that,' Aggie snapped. 'And, believe me, I'm not on the hunt for anything permanent either.'

'Then what's the problem? Why the sudden atmosphere?' He allowed a few seconds of thoughtful silence during which time she tried to think of something suitably dismissive to say. 'I never asked,' he said slowly. 'But I assumed that when you slept with me there was no one else in your life…'

Aggie's blue eyes were wide with confusion as she returned his gaze, then comprehension filtered through and confusion turned to anger.

'That's a horrible thing to say.' She felt tears prick the back of her eyes and she hurriedly stared down at her plate.

Luiz shook his head, shame-faced and yet wanting to tell her that, horrible it might be, but it wouldn't be the first time a woman had slept with him while still involved with another man. Some women enjoyed hedging their bets. Naturally, once he was involved, all other men were instantly dropped, but from instances like that he had developed a healthy dose of suspicion when it came to the opposite sex.

But, hell, he couldn't lump Aggie into the same category as other women. She was in a league of her own.

Cheeks flushed, Aggie flung down her napkin and stood up. 'If we're leaving, I need to go upstairs and get my packing done.'

'Aggie...' Luiz vaulted to his feet and followed her as she stormed out of the dining room towards the staircase. He grabbed her by her arm and pulled her towards him.

'It doesn't matter.'

'It *matters*. I...I apologise for what I said.'

'You're so suspicious of everyone! What kind of world do you live in, Luiz Montes? You're suspicious of gold-diggers, opportunists, women who want to take advantage of you...'

'It's ingrained, and I'm not saying that it's a good thing.' But it was something he had never questioned before. He looked at her, confused, frowning. 'I want to carry on seeing you when we get back to London,' he said roughly.

'And you've laid down so many guidelines about what that entails!' Aggie sighed and shook her head. This was so bad for her, yet even while one part of her brain acknowledged that there was another part that couldn't contemplate giving him up without a backward glance. Even standing this close to him was already doing things to her, making her heart beat faster and turning her bones to jelly.

'I'm just attempting to be as honest as I can.'

'And you don't have to worry that I'm going to do anything stupid!' She looked at him fiercely. If only he knew how stupid she had already been, he would run a mile. But, just as she had jumped in feet first to sleep with him and damn the consequences, she was going to carry on sleeping with him, taking what she could get like an addict too scared of quitting until it was forced upon them.

She wasn't proud of herself but, like him, she was honest.

Luiz half-closed his eyes with relief. He only realised that he had been holding his breath when he expelled it slowly. 'The drive back will be a lot easier,' he said briskly. His hand on her arm turned to a soft caress that sent shivers racing up and down her spine.

'And are you still going to…talk to Mark when they get back from London? Warn him off Maria?'

Luiz realised that he hadn't given that any thought at all. 'They're not getting married. Crisis defused.' He looked at her and grinned reluctantly. 'Okay. I've had other things on my mind. I hadn't given any thought to what was going to happen next in this little saga. Now I'm thinking about it and realising that Luisa can have whatever mother-to-daughter chat she thinks she needs to have. I'm removing myself from the situation.'

'I'm glad.'

She smiled and all Luiz could think was that he was chuffed that he had been responsible for putting that smile on her face.

Once, he would not have been able to see beyond the fact that any relationship where the levels of wealth were so disproportionately unbalanced was doomed to failure, if not worse. Once the financial inequality would have been enough for him to continue his pursuit, to do everything within his power to remove Aggie's brother from any position from which he could exert influence over his niece. Things had subtly changed.

'So,' she said softly. 'I'm going to go and pack and I'll see you back here in half an hour or so?'

Luiz nodded and she didn't ask for any details of what

would happen next. Of course, they would return to her house, but then what? Would they date one another or was that too romantic a notion for him? Would he wine and dine her, the way he wined and dined the other women he went out with? She was sure that he was generous when it came to the materialistic side of any relationship he was in. What he lacked in emotional giving, he would more than make up for in financial generosity. He was, after all, the man who had suggested buying her a laptop computer because she happened not to possess one. And this before they had become lovers.

But, if he had his ground rules, then she had hers. She would not allow him to buy anything for her nor would she expect any lavish meals out or expensive seats at the opera or the theatre. If his approach to what they had was to put all his cards on the table, then she would have to make sure that she put some of her own cards on the table as well.

As if predicating for a quick journey back to London, as opposed to the tortuous one they had embarked upon when they had set off, the snow had finally dwindled to no more than some soft, light flurries.

The atmosphere was heavy with the thrill of what lay ahead. Aggie was conscious of every movement of his hands on the steering wheel. She sneaked glances at his profile and marvelled at the sexy perfection of his face. When she closed her eyes, she imagined being alone with him in a room, submitting to his caresses.

Making small talk just felt like part of an elaborate dance between them. He was planning on visiting his family in Brazil over the Christmas period. She asked him about where he lived. She found that she had an insatiable appetite for finding out all the details of his background. Having broken ground with his confidences about his father, he talked about him, about the stroke and the effect it had had on him. He described his country in ways that brought it alive. She felt as though there were a million things she wanted to hear about him.

Mark and Maria would not be returning to the country for a few days yet, and as they approached the outskirts of London he said in a lazy drawl that already expected agreement to his proposal, 'I don't think you should carry on living in that dump.'

Aggie laughed, amused.

'I'm not kidding. I can't have you living there.'

'Where would you have me living, Luiz?'

'Kensington has some decent property. I could get you somewhere.'

'Thanks, but I think we've already covered the problem of rent in London and how expensive it is.'

'You misunderstand me. When I say that I could get you somewhere, I mean I could *buy* you somewhere.'

Aggie's mouth dropped open and she looked at him in astonishment and disbelief.

'Well?' Luiz prompted, when there was silence following this remark.

'You can't just go and *buy somewhere* for a woman you happen to be sleeping with, Luiz.'

'Why not?'

'Because it's not right.'

'I want you to live somewhere halfway decent. I have the money to turn that wish into reality. What could be more right?'

'And just for the sake of argument, what would happen with this halfway decent house when we broke up?'

Luiz frowned, not liking the way that sounded. He knew he was the one who'd laid down that rule, but was there really any need to underline it and stick three exclamation marks after it for good measure?

'You'd keep it, naturally. I never give a woman gifts and then take them away from her when the relationship goes sour.'

'You've had way too much your own way for too long,' Aggie told him. It was hardly surprising. He had grown up with money and it had always been second nature to indulge his women with gifts. 'I'm not going to accept a house from you. Or a flat, or whatever. I'm perfectly happy where I am.'

'You're not,' Luiz contradicted bluntly. 'No one could be perfectly happy in that hovel. The closest anyone could get to feeling anything about that place is that it's a roof over your head.'

'I don't want anything from you.' After the great open spaces of up north, the business of London felt like four walls pressing down on her.

That was not what Luiz wanted to hear, because for once he *wanted* to give her things. He wanted to see that smile on her face and know that he was responsible for putting it there.

'Actually,' Aggie continued thoughtfully, 'I think we should just enjoy whatever we have. I don't want you giving me any presents or taking me to expensive places.'

'I don't do home-cooked meals in front of the television.'

'And I don't do lavish meals out. Now and again, it's nice to go somewhere for dinner, but it's nice not to as well.' Aggie knew that she was treading on thin ice here. Any threat of domesticity would have him running a mile, but how much should she sacrifice for the sake of love and lust?

'I'm not into all that stuff,' she said. 'I don't wear jewels and I don't have expensive tastes.'

'Why are you so difficult?'

'I didn't realise I was.'

'From a practical point of view, your house is going to be a little cramped with your brother there and my niece popping her head in every three minutes. I'm not spending time at your place with the four of us sitting on a sagging sofa, watching television while my car gets broken into outside.'

Aggie laughed aloud. 'That's a very weak argument for getting your own way.'

'Well, you can't blame a guy for trying.'

But he wished to God he had tried a little harder when they finally arrived back at her dismal house in west London. Snow had turned to slush and seemed to have infused the area with a layer of unappealing grey.

Aggie looked at him as he reviewed the house with an expression of thinly concealed disgust and she smiled. He was so spoiled, so used to getting everything he wanted. It was true that he had not complained once at any of the discomforts he had had to endure on their little trip, at least at any of the things which in his rarefied world would have counted as discomforts. But it would be getting on his nerves that he couldn't sort this one out. Especially when he had a point. Mr Cholmsey couldn't have created a less appealing abode to rent if he had tried.

She wondered how she could have forgotten the state of disrepair it was in.

'You could at least come back with me to my apartment,' Luiz said, lounging against the wall in the hallway as Aggie dumped her bag on the ground. 'Indulge yourself, Aggie.' His voice was as smooth as chocolate and as tempting. 'There's nothing wrong with wanting to relax in a place where the central heating doesn't sound like a car backfiring every two minutes.'

Aggie looked helplessly at him, caught up in a moment of indecision. He bent to kiss her, a sweet, delicate kiss as he tasted her mouth, not touching her anywhere else, in fact hardly moving from his indolent pose against the wall.

'Not fair,' she murmured.

'I want to get you into my bath,' Luiz murmured softly. 'My very big, very clean bath, a bath that can easily fit the both of us. And then afterwards I want you in my bed, my extra-wide and extra-long king-sized bed with clean linen. And if you're really intent on us doing the telly thing, you can switch on the television in my bedroom; it's as big as a cinema screen. But before that, I want to make love to you in comfort, and then when we're both spent I want to send out for a meal from my guy at the Savoy. No need for you to dress up or go out, just the two of us. He does an excellent chocolate mousse for dessert. I'd really like to have it flavoured with a bit of you...'

'You win,' Aggie said on a sigh of pure pleasure. She reached up and pulled him down to her and in the end they found themselves clinging to one another as they wended an unsteady path up to her bedroom.

Despite Luiz's adamant proclamations that he wanted to have her in his house, she was so damned delectable that he couldn't resist.

Her top was off by the time they hit the top of the stairs. By the bedroom door, her bra was draped over the banister and she had wriggled out of her jeans just as they both collapsed onto the bed which, far from being king-sized, was only slightly bigger than a single.

'I've been wanting to do this from the second we got into my car to drive back to London,' Luiz growled, in a manner that was decidedly un-cool. 'In fact, I was very tempted to book us into a room in the first hotel we came to just so that I could do this. I don't know what it is about you, but the second I'm near you I turn into a caveman.'

Aggie decided that she liked the sound of that. She lay back and watched as he rid himself of his clothes. This was frantic sex, two slippery bodies entwined. Leisurely foreplay would have to wait, he told her, he just needed to feel himself inside her, hot and wet and waiting for him.

Luiz could say things that drove her wild, and he drove her wild now as he huskily told her just how she made him feel when they were having sex.

Every graphic description made her wetter and more turned on and when he entered her she was so close to the edge that she had to grit her teeth together to hold herself back.

His movements were deep, his shaft big and powerful, taking her higher and higher until she cried out as she climaxed. Her nails dug into his shoulder blades and she arched back, her head tilted back, her eyes closed, her nostrils slightly flared.

She was the most beautiful creature Luiz had ever laid eyes on. He felt himself explode inside her and by then it was too late. He couldn't hold it back. He certainly couldn't retrieve the results of his ferocious orgasm and he collapsed next to her with a groan.

'I didn't use protection.' He was still coming down from a high but his voice was harshly self-admonishing, bitterly angry for his oversight. He looked at her, then sat up, legs over the side of the bed, head in his hands, and cursed silently under his breath.

'It's okay,' Aggie said quickly. Well, if she hadn't got the message that this was a man who didn't want to settle down, then she was getting it now loud and clear. Not only did he not want to settle down, but the mere thought of a pregnancy was enough to turn him white with horror.

'I'm safe.'

Luiz exhaled with relief and lay back down next to her. 'Hell, I've never made that mistake in my life before. I don't know what happened.' But he did. He had lost control. This was not the man he was. He didn't lose control.

Looking at him, Aggie could see the disgust on his face that he could ever have been stupid enough, *human* enough to make a slip-up.

For all the ways he could get under her skin, she reminded herself that Luiz Montes was not available for anything other than a casual affair. She might love him but she should look for nothing more than unrequited love.

CHAPTER NINE

'WHAT'S wrong?' Luiz looked at Aggie across the width of the table in the small chain restaurant where he had just been subjected to a distinctly mediocre pizza and some even more mediocre wine.

'Nothing's wrong.' But Aggie couldn't meet his eyes. He had a way of looking at her. It made her feel as though he could see down to the bottom of her soul, as though he could dredge up things she wanted to keep to herself.

The past month had been the most amazing time of her life. She had had the last week at school, where the snow had lingered for a few days until finally all that had been left were the remains of two snowmen which the children had built.

Luiz had visited her twice at school. The first time he had just shown up. All the other teachers had been agog. The children had stared. Aggie had felt embarrassed, but embarrassed in a proud way. Everyone, all her friends at the school, would be wondering how she had managed to grab the attention of someone like Luiz, even if they didn't come right out and say it. And, frankly, Aggie still wondered how she had managed to achieve that. She didn't think that she could ever fail to get a kick just looking at him and when those dark, fabulous eyes rested on her she didn't think that she could ever fail to melt.

He had returned to Brazil for a few days over Christmas. Aggie had decided that it would be a good time to get her act together and use his absence to start building a protective shell around her, but the very second she had seen him again she had fallen straight back into the bottomless hole from which she had intended to start climbing out.

She felt as though she was on a rollercoaster. Her whole system was fired up when he was around and there wasn't a single second when she didn't want to be in his company, although at the back of her mind she knew that the rollercoaster ride would end and when it did she would be left dazed and shaken and turned inside out.

'It's this place!' Luiz flung his napkin on his half-eaten pizza and sat back in his chair.

'What?'

'Why are you too proud to accept my invitations to restaurants where the food is at least edible?'

Aggie looked at him, momentarily distracted by the brooding sulkiness on his dark face. He looked ridiculously out of place here. So tall, striking and exotic, surrounded by families with chattering kids and teenagers. But she hadn't wanted to go anywhere intimate with him. She had wanted somewhere bright, loud and impersonal.

'You've taken me to loads of expensive restaurants,' she reminded him. 'I could start listing them if you'd like.'

Luiz waved his hand dismissively. Something was wrong and he didn't like it. He had grown accustomed to her effervescence, to her teasing, to the way she made him feel as though the only satisfactory end to his day was when he saw her. Right now she was subdued, her bright-blue eyes clouded, and he didn't like the fact that he couldn't reach her.

'We need to get the bill and clear out of here,' he growled, signalling to a waitress, who appeared so quickly that Aggie thought she might have been hanging around waiting for him to call her across. 'I can think of better things to do than sit here with cold, congealing food on our plates, waiting for our tempers to deteriorate.'

'No!'

'What do you mean, *no?*' Luiz narrowed his eyes on her flushed face. Her gaze skittered away and she licked her lips nervously. The thought of her not wanting to head back to his place as fast as they could suddenly filled him with a sense of cold dread.

'I mean, it's still early.' Aggie dragged the sentence out while she frantically tried to think of how she would say what she had to say. 'Plus it's a Saturday. Everyone's out having fun.'

'Well, let's go have some fun somewhere else.' He leaned towards her and shot her a wolfish grin. 'Making love doesn't have to be confined to a bedroom. A change of scenery would work for me too...'

'A change of scenery?' Aggie asked faintly. She giddily lost herself in his persuasive, sexy, slow smile. He had come directly to her house, straight from the office, and he was still in his work clothes: a dark grey, hand-tailored suit. The tie would be bunched up in the pocket of his jacket, which he had slung over the back of the chair along with his coat, and he had rolled up the sleeves of his shirt. He looked every inch the billionaire businessman and once again she was swept away on an incredulous wave of not knowing how he could possibly be attracted to her.

And yet there were times, and lots of them, when they seemed like two halves of the same coin. Aggie had grown fond of recalling those times. Half of her knew that it was just wishful thinking on her part, a burning desire to see him relating to her in more than just an insatiably sexual capacity, but there was no harm in dreaming, was there?

'I'm losing you again.' Luiz ran his fingers through his hair and looked at her with an impatient shake of his head. 'Come on. We're getting out of here. I've had enough of this cheap and cheerful family eaterie. There's more to a Saturday night than this.'

He stood up and waited as she scrambled to her feet. It was still cold outside, but without the bite of before Christmas, when it had hurt just being outdoors. Aggie knew she should have stayed put inside the warm, noisy, crowded restaurant but coward that she was, she wanted to leave as much as he did.

Once she would have been more than satisfied with a meal out at the local pizzeria but now she could see that it could hardly be called a dining experience. It was a place to grab something or to bring kids where they could make as much mess as they wanted without staff getting annoyed.

'We could go back to my house,' Aggie said reluctantly as Luiz swung his arm over her shoulders and reached out to hail a cab with the other.

He touched her as though it was the most natural thing in the world. It was just something else she had relegated to her wishful-thinking cupboard. *If he can be so relaxed with me, surely there's more to what we have than sex...?*

Except not once had he ever hinted at what that something else might be. He never spoke of a future and she knew that he was careful not to give her any ideas. He had warned her at the beginning of their relationship that he wasn't into permanence and he had assumed that the warning held good.

He didn't love her. She was a temporary part of his life and he enjoyed her and she had given him no indication that it was any different for her.

'And where's your brother?'

'He might be there with Maria. I don't know. As you

know, he leaves for America on Monday. I think he was planning on cooking something special for them.'

'So your suggestion is we return to that dump where we'll be fighting for space alongside your brother and my niece, interrupting their final, presumably romantic meal together. Unless, of course, we hurry up to your unheated bedroom where we can squash into your tiny bed and make love as noiselessly as possible.'

Luiz loathed her house but he had given up trying to persuade her to move out to something bigger, more comfortable and paid for by him. She had dug her heels in and refused to budge, but the upshot was that they spent very little time there. In fact, the more Aggie saw her house through his eyes, the more dissatisfied she was with it.

'There's no need to be difficult!' Aggie snapped, pulling away to stare up at him. 'Why do you always have to get your own way?'

'If I always got my own way then explain why we've just spent an hour and a half in a place where the food is average and the noise levels are high enough to give people migraines. What the hell is going on, Aggie? I didn't meet you so that I could battle my way through a bad mood!'

'I can't always be sunshine and light, Luiz!'

They stared at each other. Aggie was hardly aware of the approach of a black cab until she was being hustled into it. She heard Luiz curtly give his address and sighed with frustration, because the last place she wanted to be with him was at his apartment.

'Now…' He turned to face her and extended his arm along the back of the seat. 'Talk to me. Tell me what's going on.' His eyes drifted to the mutinous set of her mouth and he wanted to do nothing more than kiss it back into smiling submission. He wasn't normally given to issuing invitations to women to talk. He was a man of action and his preferred choice, when faced with a woman who clearly *wanted to talk*, was to bury all chat between the sheets. But Aggie, he had to concede, was different. If he suggested burying the chat between the sheets, she would probably round on him with the full force of her feisty, outspoken, brazenly argumentative personality.

'We do need to talk,' she admitted quietly, and she felt him go still next to her.

'Well, I'm all ears.'

'Not here. We might as well wait till we get to your place, although I would have preferred to have this conversation in the restaurant.'

'You mean where we would hardly have been able to hear one another?'

'What I have to say…people around would have made it easier.'

Luiz was getting a nasty, unsettled feeling in the pit of his stomach. She had turned him down once. It was something he hadn't forgotten. This sounded very much like a second let-down and he wasn't about to let that happen. Pride slammed into him with the force of a sledgehammer.

'I'm getting the message that this *talk* of yours has to do with us?'

Aggie nodded miserably. This *talk* was something she had rehearsed in her head for the past four hours and yet she was no closer to knowing where she would begin.

'What's there to talk about?' Luiz drawled grimly. 'We've already covered this subject. I'm not looking for commitment. Nor, you told me, were you. We understand one another. We're on the same page.'

'Sometimes things change.'

'Are you telling me that you're no longer satisfied with what we've got? That after a handful of weeks you're looking for something more?' Luiz refused to contemplate hav-

ing his wings clipped. He especially didn't care for the
thought of having anyone try to clip them on his behalf.
Was she about to issue him with some kind of ultimatum?
Promise more if he wanted to carry on seeing her, sleeping with her? Just thinking about it outraged him. Other
women might have dropped hints—grown misty-eyed in
front of jewellers, introduced him to friends with babies—
but none of them had ever actually given him a stark choice
and he was getting the feeling that that was precisely what
Aggie was thinking of doing.

Aggie clenched her fists on her lap. The tone of his
voice was like a slap in the face. Did he really think that
she had been stupid enough to misunderstand his very
clear ground rules?

'What if I were?' she asked, curious to see where this
conversation would take them, already predicting its final,
painful destination and willing it masochistically on herself.

'Then I'd question whether you weren't wondering if
being married to a rich man might be more financially lucrative than dating him!'

Every muscle in Aggie's body tensed and she looked at
him astounded, hurt and horrified.

'How could you *say* that?'

Luiz scowled and looked away. He fully deserved that
reprimand. He could scarcely credit that he had actually
accused her of having a financial agenda. She had proved
to be one of the least materialistic women he had ever
met. But, hell, the thought of her walking out on him had
sparked something in him he could barely understand.

'I apologise,' he said roughly. 'That was below the belt.'

'But do you honestly believe it?' Aggie was driven to
know whether this man she loved so much could think so

little of her that he actually thought she might try and con him into commitment.

'No. I don't.'

She breathed a sigh of relief because she would never have been able to live with that.

'Then why did you say it?'

'Look, I don't know what this is about, but I'm not interested in playing games. And I won't have my hand forced. Not by you. Not by anybody.'

'Because you don't need anyone? The great Luiz Montes doesn't need anything or anyone!'

'And tell me, what's wrong with that?' He was baffled by her. Why the hell was she spoiling for a fight? And why had she suddenly decided that she wanted more than what they had? Things had been pretty damn good between them. Better than good. He fought down the temptation to explode.

'I don't want to have this argument with you,' Aggie said, glancing towards the taxi driver who was maintaining a discreet disinterest. He probably heard this kind of thing all the time.

'And I don't want to argue with you,' Luiz confirmed smoothly. 'So why don't we pretend none of it happened?' There was one way of stalling any further confrontation. He pulled her towards him and curled his hands into her soft hair.

Aggie's protesting hands against his chest curved into an aching caress. As his tongue delved to explore her mouth, she felt her body come alive. Her nipples tightened in the lace bra, pushing forward in a painful need to be suckled and touched. Her skin burned and the wetness between her legs was an agonising reminder of how this man could get to her. No matter that there was talking to be done. No matter that making love was not what she wanted to do.

'Now, isn't that better?' he murmured with satisfaction. 'I'd carry on, my darling, but I wouldn't want to shock our cab driver.'

As if to undermine that statement, he curved his hand over one full breast and slowly massaged it until she had to stop herself from crying out.

Ever since they had begun seeing one another, her wardrobe had undergone a subtle transformation. The uninspiring clothes she had worn had been replaced by a selection of brighter, more figure-hugging outfits.

'You're wearing a bra,' he chided softly into her ear. 'You know I hate that.'

'You can't always get what you want, Luiz.'

'But it's what we *both* want, isn't it? I get to touch you without the boring business of having to get rid of a bra and you get to be touched without the boring business of having to get rid of a bra. It's a win-win situation. Still, I guess sometimes it adds a little spice to the mix if I have to work my way through layers of clothes...'

'Stop it, Luiz!'

'Tell me you don't like what I'm doing.' He had shimmied his hand underneath the tight, striped jumper and had pulled down her bra to free one plump mound.

This was the way to stifle an argument, he thought. Maybe he had misread the whole thing. Maybe she hadn't been upping the ante. Maybe what she wanted to talk about had been altogether more prosaic. Luiz didn't know and he had no intention of revisiting the topic.

With a rueful sigh, he released her as the taxi slowed, moving into the crescent. He neatly pulled down the jumper, straightening it. 'Perhaps just as well that we're here,' he confessed with a wicked glint in his dark eyes.

'Going all the way in the back seat of a black cab would really be taking things a step too far. I think when we get round to public performing we'll have to think carefully where to begin...'

Aggie had had no intention of performing with him on any level, never mind in public. She shifted in the seat. When she should have been as cool as she could, she was hot and flustered and having to push thoughts of him taking her in his hallway out of her head.

The house which had once filled her with awe she now appreciated in a distinctly less gob-smacked way. She still loved the beautiful *objets d'art*, but there were few personal touches which made her think that money could buy some things, but not others. It could buy beauty but not necessarily atmosphere. In fact, going out with Luiz had made her distinctly less cowed at the impressive things money could buy and a lot less daunted by the people who possessed it.

'So.' Luiz discarded his coat and jacket as soon as they were through the door. 'Shall we finish what we started? No need to go upstairs. If you go right into the kitchen and sit on one of the stools, I'll demonstrate how handy I can be with food. I guarantee I'll be a damn sight more imaginative with ingredients than that restaurant tonight was.'

'Luiz.' She was shaking as she placed her hand firmly on his chest. No giving in this time.

'Good God, woman! Tell me you don't want to start talking again.' He pushed his hands under her coat to cup her rounded buttocks, pulling her against him so that she could feel his arousal pushing through his trousers, as hard as a rod of iron. 'And, if you want to talk, then let's talk in bed.'

'Bed's not a good idea,' Aggie said shakily.

'Who says I want good ideas?'

'I'd like a cup of coffee.'

Luiz gave in with a groan of pure frustration. He banged his fist on the wall, shielded his head in the crook of his arm and then glanced at her with rueful resignation.

'Okay. You win. But take it from me, talking is never a very good idea.'

How true, Aggie thought. From his point of view, it would certainly not herald anything he wanted to hear.

She marvelled that in a few hours life could change so dramatically.

She had been poring over the school calendar and working out what lessons she should think about setting when something in her head had suddenly clicked.

She had seen the calendar and the concept of dates had begun to flicker. Dates of when she had last seen her period. She had never paid a great deal of attention to her menstrual cycle. It happened roughly on time. What more was there to say about it?

Her hands had been shaking when, a little over an hour later, she had taken that home-pregnancy test. She had already thought of a thousand reasons why she was silly to be concerned. For a start, Luiz was obsessive about contraception. Aside from that one little slip-up, he had been scrupulous.

Within minutes she had discovered how one little slip-up could change the course of someone's life.

She was pregnant by a man who didn't love her, had warned her off involvement and had certainly never expressed any desire to have children. In the face of all those stark realities, she had briefly contemplated not telling him. Just breaking off the relationship; disappearing. Disappearing, she had reasoned for a few wild, disoriented moments, would not be difficult to do. She hated the house and her brother was soon to leave London to embark upon the next exciting phase of his life. She could ditch everything and return up north, find something there. Luiz would not pursue her and he would never know that he had fathered a child.

The thought didn't last long. He would find out; of course he would. Maria would tell him. And, aside from that, how could she deprive a man of his own child? Even a child he hadn't wanted?

'What I'm going to say will shock you,' Aggie told him as soon as they were sitting down in his living room, with a respectable distance between them.

Luiz, for the first time in his life, was prey to fear. It ripped through him, strangling his vocal chords, making him break out in a fine film of perspiration.

'You're not…ill, are you?'

Aggie looked at him with surprise. 'No. I'm not,' she asserted firmly. He had visibly blanched and she knew why. Of course, he would be remembering his own father's illness, which he had spoken to her about in more depth over the time they had been together.

'Then what is it?'

'There's no easy way to tell you so I'm going to come right out and say it. I'm pregnant.'

Luiz froze. For a few seconds, he wondered whether he had heard correctly but he was not a man given to flights of imagination and the expression on her face was sufficient to tell him that she wasn't joking.

'You can't be,' he said eventually.

Aggie's eyes slid away from his. Whenever she had thought of being pregnant, it had been within a rosy scenario involving a man she loved who loved her back. Never had she envisaged breaking the news to a man who looked as though she had detonated a bomb in his front room.

'I'm afraid I can be, and I am.'

'I was careful!'

'There was that one time.' Against her better judge-ment—for she had hardly expected her news to be met with whoops of joy—she could feel a slow anger begin to burn inside her.

'You told me that there was no risk.'

'I'm sorry. I made a mistake.'

Luiz didn't say anything. He stood up and walked res-tively towards the floor-to-ceiling window to stare outside. The possibility of fatherhood was not one that had ever occurred to him. It was something that lay in the future. Way down the line. Possibly never. But she was carrying his baby inside her.

Aggie miserably looked at him, turned away from her and staring out of the window. Doubtless he was thinking about his life which now lay in ruins. If ever there was a man who was crushed under the weight of bad news, then he was that man.

'You decided to tell me this in a *pizzeria*?' Luiz spun round and walked towards her. He leaned over, bracing himself on either side of her, and Aggie shrank back into the chair.

'I didn't want…*this*!' she cried.

'This *what*?'

'I knew how you'd react and I thought it would be more…more…civilised if I told you somewhere out in the open!'

'What did you think I would do?'

'We need to discuss this like adults and we're not going to get anywhere when you're standing over me like this, threatening me!'

'God, how the hell did this happen?' Luiz returned to the sofa and collapsed onto it.

It felt to Aggie as though everything they had shared

had shattered under the blow of this pregnancy. Which just went to show how fragile it had all been from the very start. Not made to last and not fashioned to withstand any knocks—although, in fairness, a pregnancy couldn't really be called a knock. More like an earthquake, shaking everything from the foundations up.

'Stupid question.' He pressed his thumbs to his eyes and then leaned forward to look at her, his hands resting loosely on his thighs. 'Of course I know how it happened, and you're right. We have to talk about it. Hell, what's there to talk about? We'll have to get married. What choice do we have?'

'Get married? That's not what I want!' she threw at him, fighting to contain her anger because he was just doing what, in his misguided way, he construed as the decent thing. 'Do you really think I told you about this because I wanted you to marry me?'

'What does it matter? My family would be bitterly disappointed to think I had fathered a child and allowed it to be born out of wedlock.'

What a wonderful marriage proposal, Aggie thought with a touch of hysteria: *you're pregnant; we'd better get married or risk the wrath of my traditional family.*

'I don't think so,' Aggie said gently.

'What does that mean?'

'It means that I can't accept your generous marriage proposal.'

'Don't be crazy. Of course you can!'

'I have no intention of marrying someone just because I happen to be having his baby. Luiz, a pregnancy is not the right reason to be married to someone.' She could tell from the expression on his face that he was utterly taken aback that his offer had been rejected. 'I'm sorry if your parents would find it unacceptable for you to have a child out of wedlock, but I'm not going to marry you so that your parents can avoid disappointment.'

'That's not the only reason!'

'Well, what are the others?' She could quell the faint hope that he would say those three words she wanted to hear. That he loved her. He could expand on that. She wouldn't stop him. He could tell her that he couldn't live without her.

'It's better for a child to have both parents on hand. I am a rich man. I don't intend that any child of mine will go wanting. Two reasons and there's more!' Why, Luiz thought, was she being difficult? She had just brought his entire world crashing down around him and he had risen admirably to the occasion! Couldn't she see that?

'A child can have both parents on hand without them being married,' Aggie pointed out. 'I'm not going to deprive you of the opportunity to see him or her whenever you want, and of course I understand that you will want to assist financially. I would never dream of stopping you from doing that.' She lowered her eyes and nervously fiddled with her fingers.

There was something else that would have to be discussed. Would they continue to see one another? Part of her craved their ongoing relationship and the strength and support she would get from it. Another part realised that it would be foolhardy to carry on as though nothing had happened, as though a rapidly expanding stomach wasn't proof that their lives had changed for ever. She wouldn't marry him. She couldn't allow him to ruin his life for the sake of a gesture born from obligation. She hated the thought of what would happen as cold reality set in and he realised that he was stuck with her for good. He would end up hating and resenting her. He would seek solace in the arms of other women. He might even, one day, find a woman to truly love.

'And there's something else,' she said quietly. 'I don't think it's appropriate that we continue…seeing one another.'

'What?' Luiz exploded, his body alive with anger and bewilderment.

'Stop shouting!'

'Then don't give me a reason to shout!'

They stared at each other in silence. Aggie's heart was pounding inside her. 'What we have was never going to go the full distance. We both knew that. You were very clear on that.'

'Whoa! Before you get carried away with the preaching, answer me this one thing. Do we or do we not have fun when we're together?' Luiz felt as though he had started the evening with clear skies and calm seas, only to discover that a force-ten hurricane had been waiting just over the horizon. Not only had he found himself with a baby on the way, but on top of that here she was, informing him that she no longer wanted to have anything to do with him. A growing sense of panicked desperation made him feel slightly ill.

'That's not the point!'

'Then what the hell is? You're not making any sense, Aggie! I've offered to do the right thing by you and you act as though I've insulted you. You rumble on about a child not being a good enough reason for us to be married. I don't get it! Not only is a child a bloody good reason to get married, but here's the added bonus—we're good together! But that's not enough for you! Now, you're talking about walking away from this relationship!'

'We're friends at the moment and that's how I'd like our relationship to stay for the sake of our child, Luiz.'

'We're more than just friends, damn it!'

'We're friends with benefits.'

'I can't believe I'm hearing this!' He slashed the air with his hand in a gesture of frustration, incredulity and impatience. His face was dark with anger and those beautiful eyes that could turn her hot and cold were flat with accusation.

In this sort of mood, withstanding him was like trying to swim up a waterfall. Aggie wanted to fly to him and just let him decide what happened next. She knew it would be a mistake. If they carried on seeing one another and reached the point where, inevitably, he became fed up and bored, their relationship thereafter would be one of bitterness and discomfort. Couldn't he see long-term? For a man who could predict trends and work out the bigger picture when it came to business, he was hopelessly inadequate in doing the same when it came to his private life. He lived purely for the moment. Right now he was living purely for the moment with her and he wasn't quite ready for it to end. Right now, his solution to their situation was to put a ring on her finger, thereby appeasing family and promoting his sense of responsibility. He just didn't think ahead.

Aggie knew, deep down, that if she didn't love him she would have accepted that marriage proposal. She would not have invested her emotions in a hopeless situation. She would have been able to see their union as an arrangement that made sense and would have been thankful that he was standing by her. Was it any wonder that he was now looking at her as though she had taken leave of her senses?

'I don't want us to carry on, waiting until the physical side of things runs out of steam and you start looking somewhere else,' she told him bluntly. 'I don't want to become so disillusioned with you that I resent you being in my life. It wouldn't be a good background for a child.'

'Who says the physical side would run out of steam?'

'It always has for you! Hasn't it? Unless…I'm different? Unless what you feel for me is…different?'

Suddenly feeling cornered, Luiz fell back on the habits of a lifetime of not yielding to leading questions. 'You're having my baby. Of course you're different.'

'I'm beginning to feel tired, Luiz.' Aggie wondered why she continued to hope for words that weren't going to come. 'And you've had a shock. I think we both need to take a little time out to think about things, and when we next meet we can discuss the practicalities.'

'The practicalities…?' Luiz was finding it hard to get a grip on events.

'You've been nagging me to move out of that house.' Aggie smiled wryly. 'I guess that might be something on the list to discuss.' She stood up to head for her coat and he stilled her with his hand.

'I don't want you going back to that place tonight. Or ever. It's disgusting. You have my baby to consider now.'

'And that's the word, Luiz—*discuss.* Which doesn't mean you tell me what you want me to do and I obey.'

She began putting on her coat while Luiz watched with the feeling that she was slipping through his fingers.

'You're making a mistake,' he ground out, barring her exit and staring down at her.

'I think,' Aggie said sadly, 'the mistakes have already been made.'

CHAPTER TEN

LUIZ looked at the pile of reports lying on his desk eagerly awaiting his attention and swivelled his chair round to face the expanse of glass that overlooked the busy London streets several stories below.

It was another one of those amazing spring days: blue, cloudless skies, a hint of a breeze. It did nothing to improve his concentration levels. Or his mood, for that matter. Frankly, his mood was in urgent need of improvement ever since Aggie had announced her pregnancy over two months ago.

For the first week, he had remained convinced that she would come to her senses and accept his offer of marriage. He had argued for it from a number of fronts. He had demanded that she give him more good reasons why she couldn't see it from his point of view. It had been as successful as beating his head against a brick wall. It had seemed to him, in his ever-increasing frustration, that the harder he tried to push the faster she retreated, so he had dropped the subject and they had discussed all those practicalities she had talked about.

At least there she had listened to what he had to say and agreed with pretty much everything. At least her pride wasn't going to let her get in the way of accepting the massively generous financial help he had insisted on providing, although she had stopped short of letting him buy her the house of her dreams.

'When I move into my dream house,' she had told him, her mouth set in a stubborn line, 'I don't want to know that it's been bought for me as part of a package deal because I happen to be pregnant.'

But she had moved out of the hovel two weeks previously, into a small, modern box in a pleasant part of London close to her job. The job which she insisted she would carry on doing until she no longer could, despite his protests that there was no need, that she had to look after herself.

'I'm more than happy to accept financial help as far as the baby is concerned,' she had told him firmly. 'But there's no need for you to lump me in the same bracket.'

'You're the mother of my child. Of course I'm going to make sure that you get all the money you need.'

'I'm not going to be dependent on you, Luiz. I intend to carry on working until I have the baby and then I shall take it up again as soon as I feel the baby is old enough for a nursery. The hours are good at the school and there are all the holidays. It's a brilliant job to have if you've got a family.'

Luiz loathed the thought of that just as he loathed the fact that she had managed to shut him out of her life. They communicated, and there were no raised voices, but she had withdrawn from him and it grated on him, made him ill-tempered at work, incapable of concentrating.

And now something else had descended to prey on his mind. It was a thought that had formulated a week ago when she had mentioned in passing that she would be going to the spring party which all the teachers had every year.

Somehow, he had contrived to ignore the fact that she had a social life outside him. Reminded of it, he had quizzed her on what her fellow teachers were like, and had discovered that they weren't all female and they weren't all middle-aged. They enjoyed an active social life. The teaching community was close-knit, with many teachers from different schools socialising out of work.

'You're pregnant,' he had informed her. 'Parties are a no-go area.'

'Don't worry. I won't be drinking,' she had laughed, and right then he had had a worrying thought.

She had turned down his marriage proposal, had put their relationship on a formal basis, and was this because she just wanted to make sure that she wasn't tied down? Had he been sidelined because at the back of her mind, baby or no baby, she wanted to make sure that she could return to an active social life? One that involved other men, the sort of men she was normally drawn to? He had been an aberration. Was she eager to resume relationships with one of those creative types who weren't mired in work and driven by ambition?

Luiz thought of the reports waiting on his desk and smiled sardonically. If only she knew... No one could accuse him of being mired in work now, or driven by ambition. Having a bomb detonate in his life had certainly compelled him to discover the invaluable art of delegation! If only his mother could see him now, she would be overjoyed that work was no longer the centre of his universe.

A call interrupted the familiar downward trend of his thoughts and he took it on the second ring.

He listened, scribbled something on a piece of paper and stood up.

For the first time in weeks, he felt as though he was finally doing something; finally, for better or for worse, trying to stop a runaway train, which was what his life had become.

Over the weeks, his secretary had grown so accustomed to her boss's moody unpredictability—a change from the man whose life had previously been so highly organised—that she nodded without question when he told her that he would be going out and wasn't sure when he would be back. She had stopped pointing out meetings that required his presence. Her brain now moved into another gear, the one which had her immediately working out who would replace him.

Luiz called his driver on his way down. Aggie would be at school. He tried to picture her expression when he showed up. It distracted him from more tumultuous thoughts—thoughts of her having his child and then re-discovering a single life; thoughts of her getting involved with another man; thoughts of that other man bringing up his, Luiz's, child as his own while Luiz was relegated to playing second fiddle. The occasional father.

Having never suffered the trials and tribulations of a fertile imagination, he found that he had more than made up for the lifelong omission. Now, his imagination seemed to be a monstrous thing released from a holding pen in which it had been imprisoned for its entire life, and now it was making up for lost time.

It was a situation that Luiz could not allow to continue but, as the car wound its way through traffic that was as dense as treacle, he was gripped by a strange sense of panic. He had spent all of his adult life knowing where he was going, knowing how he was going to get there. Recently, the signposts had been removed and the road was no longer a straight one forward. Instead, it curved in all directions and he had no idea where he would end up. He just knew the person he wanted to find at its destination.

'Can't you go a little faster?' he demanded, and cursed silently when his driver shot him a jaundiced look in the rear-view mirror before pointing out that they hadn't yet invented a car that could fly—although, when and if they ever did, he was sure that Mr Montes would be the first to own one.

They made it to the school just as the bell sounded for lunch and Aggie was heading to the staff room. She had been blessed with an absence of morning sickness but she felt tired a lot of the time.

And it was such a struggle maintaining a distance from Luiz. Whenever she heard that deep, dark drawl down the end of the telephone, asking her how her day had been, insisting she tell him everything she had done, telling her about what he had done, she wanted nothing more than to take back everything she had said about not wanting him in her life. He phoned a lot. He visited a lot. He treated her like a piece of delicate china, and when she told him not to he shrugged his shoulders ruefully and informed her that he couldn't help being a dinosaur when it came to stuff like that.

She had thought when she had delivered her speech to him all those weeks ago that he would quickly come to terms with the fact that he would not be shackled to her for the wrong reasons. She had thought that he would soon begin to thank her for letting him off the hook, that he would begin to relish his freedom. An over-developed sense of responsibility was something that wouldn't last very long. He didn't love her. It would be easy for him to cut the strings once he had been given permission to do so.

But he wasn't making it easy for her to get over him. Or to move on.

She had now moved from the dump, as he had continued to call it, and was happy enough in the small, modern house he had provided for her. She was still in her job and had insisted that she would carry on working before and after the baby was born, but there were times when she longed to be away from London with its noise, pollution and traffic.

And, aside from those natural doubts, she was plagued by worries about how things would unravel over time.

She couldn't envisage ever seeing him without being affected. Having been so convinced that she was doing the right thing in refusing to marry him, having prided herself on her cool ability to look at the bigger picture, she found herself riddled with angst that she might have made the wrong decision.

She stared with desolation at the sandwich she had brought in with her and was about to bite into it when... there he was.

Amid the chaos of children running in the corridors and teachers moving around the school stopping to tell them off, Luiz was suddenly in front of her, lounging against the door to the staff room.

'I know you don't like me coming here,' Luiz greeted her as he strolled towards her desk. He wondered whether she should be eating more than just a sandwich for her lunch but refrained from asking.

'You always cause such a commotion,' Aggie said honestly. 'What do you want, anyway? I have a lot of work to do during my lunch hour. I can't take time out.'

As always, she had to fight the temptation to touch him. It was as though, whenever she saw him, her brain sent signals to her fingers, making them restive at remembered pleasures. He always looked so good! Too good. His hair had grown and he hadn't bothered to cut it and the slight extra length suited him, made him even more outrageously sexy. Now he had perched on the side of her table and she had to drag her eyes away from the taut pull of his trousers over his muscular thighs.

Luiz watched as she looked away, eager for him to leave, annoyed that he had shown up at her workplace. Tough. He couldn't carry on as he had. He was going crazy. There were things he needed to say to her and, the further she floated away from him, the more redundant his words would become.

Teachers were drifting in now, released from their classes by the bell, and Luiz couldn't stop himself from glancing at them, trying to see whether any of the men might be contenders for Aggie. There were three guys so far, all in their thirties from the looks of it, but surely none of them would appeal to her?

Once, he would have been arrogantly certain of his seductive power over her. Unfortunately, he was a lot less confident on that score, and he scowled at the thought that some skinny guy with ginger hair might become his replacement.

'You look tired,' Luiz said abruptly.

'Have you come here to do a spot check on me? I wish you'd stop clucking over me like a mother hen, Luiz. I told you I can take care of myself and I can.'

'I haven't come here to do a spot check on you.'

'Then why are you here?' She risked a look at him and was surprised at the hesitation on his face.

'I want to take you somewhere. I… There are things I need to…talk to you about.'

Instinctively, Aggie knew that whatever he wanted to talk about would not involve finances, the baby or her health—all of which were subjects he covered in great detail in his frequent visits—whilst, without even being aware of it, continuing to charm her with witty anecdotes of what he was up to and the people he met. So what, she wondered nervously, could be important enough for him to interrupt her working day and to put such a hesitant expression on his usually confident face?

All at once her imagination took flight. There was no doubt that he was getting over her. He had completely stopped mentioning marriage. In fact, she hadn't heard a word on the subject for weeks. He visited a lot and phoned a lot but she knew that that was because of the baby she was carrying. He was an 'all or nothing' man. Having never contemplated the thought of fatherhood, he had had it foisted upon him and had reacted by embracing it with an enthusiasm that was so typical of his personality. He did nothing in half-measures.

As the woman who happened to be carrying his child, she was swept up in the tidal wave of his enthusiasm. But already she could see the signs of a man who no longer viewed her with the untrammelled lust he once had. He could see her so often and speak to her so often because she had become *a friend*. She no longer stirred his passion.

Aggie knew that she should have been happy about this because it was precisely what she had told him, at the beginning, was necessary for their relationship to survive on a long-term basis. Friendship and not lust would be the key to the sort of amicable union they would need to be good parents to their child.

Where he had taken that on board, however, she was still struggling and now she couldn't think what he might want to talk to her about that had necessitated a random visit to the school.

Could it be that he had found someone else? That would account for the shadow of uncertainty on his face. Luiz was not an uncertain man. Fear gripped her, turning her complexion chalky white. She could think of no other reason for him to be here and to want to *have a talk* with her. A talk that was so urgent it couldn't wait. He intended to brace her for the news before she heard about it via the grapevine, for her brother would surely find out and impart the information to her.

'Is it about…financial stuff?' she asked, clinging to the hope that he would say yes.

'It's nothing to do with money, or with any practicalities, Aggie. My car's outside.'

Aggie nodded but her body was numb all over as she gathered her things, her bag, her lightweight jacket and followed him to where his car was parked on a single yellow line outside the school.

'Where are we going? I have to be back at school by one-thirty.'

'You might have to call and tell them that you'll be later.'

'Why? What can you have to say that can't be said closer to the school? There's a café just down that street ahead. Let's go there and get this little talk of yours over and done with.'

'It's not that easy, I'm afraid.'

She noticed that the hesitation was back and it chilled her once again to the core.

'I'm stronger than you think,' she said, bracing herself. 'I can handle whatever you have to tell me. You don't need to get me to some fancy restaurant to break the news.'

'We're not going to a fancy restaurant. I know you well enough by now not to make the mistake of taking you somewhere fancy unless you have at least an hour to get ready in advance.'

'It's not my fault I still get a little nervous at some of those places you've taken me to. I don't feel comfortable being surrounded by celebrities!'

'And it's what I like about you,' Luiz murmured. That, along with all the thousands of other little quirks which should have shown him by now the significance of what he felt for her. He had always counted himself as a pretty shrewd guy and yet, with her, he had been as thick as the village idiot.

'It is?' Aggie shamefully grasped that barely audible compliment.

'I want to show you something.' The traffic was free-flowing and they were driving quickly out of London now, heading towards the motorway. For a while, Aggie's mind went into freefall as she recollected the last time she had been in a car heading out of London. His car. Except then, the snow had been falling thick and fast and little had she known that she had been heading towards a life-changing destiny. If, at the time, she had been in possession of a crystal ball, would she have looked into it and backed away from sleeping with him? The answer, of course, was no. For better or for worse she had thought at the time, and she still thought so now, even though the better had lasted for precious little time.

'What?' Aggie pressed anxiously.

'You'll have to wait and see.'

'Where are we going?'

'Berkshire. Close enough. We'll be there shortly.'

Aggie fell silent but her mind continued playing with a range of ever-changing worst-case scenarios, yet she couldn't imagine what he could possibly have to show her outside London. She hadn't thought there was much out-side the city that interested him although, to be fair, when-ever he spoke of his time spent on that fateful journey, his voice held a certain affection for the places they had seen.

She was still trying to work things out when the car eventually pulled up in front of a sprawling field and he reached across to push open the door for her.

'What…what are we doing here?' She looked at him in

bewilderment and he urged her out, leading her across the grass verge and into the field which, having been reached via a series of twisting, small lanes, seemed to be surrounded by nothing. It was amazing, considering they were still so close to London.

'Do you like it?' Luiz gazed down at her as she mulled over his question.

'It's a field, Luiz. It's peaceful.'

'You don't like me buying you things,' he murmured roughly. 'You have no idea how hard it is for me to resist it but you've made me see that there are other ways of expressing...what I feel for you. Hell, Aggie. I don't know if I'm telling you this the way I should. I'm no good at... things like this—talking about feelings.'

Aggie stared up at his perfect face, shadowed with doubt and strangely vulnerable. 'What are you trying to say?'

'Something I should have said a long time ago.' He looked down at her and shuffled awkwardly. 'Except I barely recognised it myself, until you turned me away. Aggie, I've been going crazy. Thinking about you. Wanting you. Wondering how I'm going to get through life without you. I don't know if I've left it too late, but I can't live without you. I need you.'

Buffeted in all directions by wonderful waves of hope, Aggie could only continue to stare. She was finding it hard to make the necessary connections. Caution was pleading with her not to jump to conclusions but the look in his eyes was filling her with burgeoning, breathless excitement.

Luiz stared into those perfect blue eyes and took strength from them.

'I don't know what you feel for me,' he said huskily. 'I turned you on but that wasn't enough. When it came to women, I wasn't used to dealing in any other currency aside from sex. How was I to know that what I felt for you went far beyond lust?'

'When you say *far beyond...*'

'I don't know when I fell in love with you, but I did and, fool that I am, it's been a realisation that's been long in coming. I can only hope not too long. Look, Aggie...' He raked long fingers through his hair and shook his head in the manner of someone trying hard to marshal his thoughts into coherent sentences. 'I'm taking the biggest gamble of my life here, and hoping that I haven't blown all my chances with you. I love you and...I want to marry you. We were happy once, we had fun. You may not love me now, but I swear to God I have enough love for the two of us and one day you'll come to...'

'Shh.' She placed a finger over his beautiful mouth. 'Don't say another word.' Tears trembled, glazing over her eyes. 'I turned down your marriage proposal because I couldn't cope with the thought that the man I was...*am*... desperately in love with had only proposed because he thought it was the thing he should do. I couldn't face the thought of a reluctant, resentful husband. It would have meant my heart breaking every day we were together and that's why I turned you down.' She removed her finger and tiptoed to lightly kiss his lips.

'You'll marry me?'

Aggie smiled broadly and fell into him, reaching up to link her hands behind his neck. 'It's been agony seeing you and talking to you,' she confessed. 'I kept wondering if I had done the right thing.'

'Well, it's good to hear that I wasn't the only one suffering.'

'So you brought me all the way out here to tell me that you love me?'

'To show you this field and hope that it could be my strongest argument to win you back.'

'What do you mean?'

'Like I said.' Luiz, with his arm around her shoulders, turned her so that they were both looking at the same sprawling vista of grass and trees. 'I know you don't like me buying you things so I bought this for us. Both of us.'

'You bought…this field?'

'Thirty acres of land with planning permission to build. There are strict guidelines on what we can build but we can design it together. This was going to be my last attempt to prove to you that I was no longer the arrogant guy you once couldn't stand, that I could think out of the box, that I was worth the gamble.'

'My darling.' Aggie turned to him. 'I love you so much.' There was so much more she wanted to say but she was so happy, so filled with joy that she could hardly speak.

* * * * *

Mills & Boon® Hardback

November 2012

ROMANCE

A Night of No Return	Sarah Morgan
A Tempestuous Temptation	Cathy Williams
Back in the Headlines	Sharon Kendrick
A Taste of the Untamed	Susan Stephens
Exquisite Revenge	Abby Green
Beneath the Veil of Paradise	Kate Hewitt
Surrendering All But Her Heart	Melanie Milburne
Innocent of His Claim	Janette Kenny
The Price of Fame	Anne Oliver
One Night, So Pregnant!	Heidi Rice
The Count's Christmas Baby	Rebecca Winters
His Larkville Cinderella	Melissa McClone
The Nanny Who Saved Christmas	Michelle Douglas
Snowed in at the Ranch	Cara Colter
Hitched!	Jessica Hart
Once A Rebel...	Nikki Logan
A Doctor, A Fling & A Wedding Ring	Fiona McArthur
Her Christmas Eve Diamond	Scarlet Wilson

MEDICAL

Maybe This Christmas...?	Alison Roberts
Dr Chandler's Sleeping Beauty	Melanie Milburne
Newborn Baby For Christmas	Fiona Lowe
The War Hero's Locked-Away Heart	Louisa George

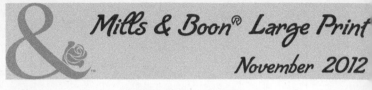

Mills & Boon® Large Print

November 2012

ROMANCE

The Secrets She Carried	Lynne Graham
To Love, Honour and Betray	Jennie Lucas
Heart of a Desert Warrior	Lucy Monroe
Unnoticed and Untouched	Lynn Raye Harris
Argentinian in the Outback	Margaret Way
The Sheikh's Jewel	Melissa James
The Rebel Rancher	Donna Alward
Always the Best Man	Fiona Harper
A Royal World Apart	Maisey Yates
Distracted by her Virtue	Maggie Cox
The Count's Prize	Christina Hollis

HISTORICAL

An Escapade and an Engagement	Annie Burrows
The Laird's Forbidden Lady	Ann Lethbridge
His Makeshift Wife	Anne Ashley
The Captain and the Wallflower	Lyn Stone
Tempted by the Highland Warrior	Michelle Willingham

MEDICAL

Sydney Harbour Hospital: Lexi's Secret	Melanie Milburne
West Wing to Maternity Wing!	Scarlet Wilson
Diamond Ring for the Ice Queen	Lucy Clark
No.1 Dad in Texas	Dianne Drake
The Dangers of Dating Your Boss	Sue MacKay
The Doctor, His Daughter and Me	Leonie Knight

Mills & Boon® Hardback

December 2012

ROMANCE

A Ring to Secure His Heir	Lynne Graham
What His Money Can't Hide	Maggie Cox
Woman in a Sheikh's World	Sarah Morgan
At Dante's Service	Chantelle Shaw
At His Majesty's Request	Maisey Yates
Breaking the Greek's Rules	Anne McAllister
The Ruthless Caleb Wilde	Sandra Marton
The Price of Success	Maya Blake
The Man From her Wayward Past	Susan Stephens
Blame it on the Bikini	Natalie Anderson
The English Lord's Secret Son	Margaret Way
The Secret That Changed Everything	Lucy Gordon
Baby Under the Christmas Tree	Teresa Carpenter
The Cattleman's Special Delivery	Barbara Hannay
Secrets of the Rich & Famous	Charlotte Phillips
Her Man In Manhattan	Trish Wylie
His Bride in Paradise	Joanna Neil
Christmas Where She Belongs	Meredith Webber

MEDICAL

From Christmas to Eternity	Caroline Anderson
Her Little Spanish Secret	Laura Iding
Christmas with Dr Delicious	Sue MacKay
One Night That Changed Everything	Tina Beckett

STD HB

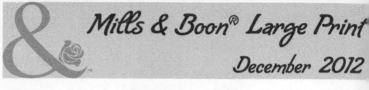

Mills & Boon® Large Print

December 2012

ROMANCE

HISTORICAL

MEDICAL

LE SORCIER
DE L'ÎLE D'ORLÉANS
(LE CRÉPUSCULE DES ARCANES –3)

Du même auteur

LE SORCIER
DE L'ÎLE D'ORLÉANS

(LE CRÉPUSCULE DES ARCANES –3)

SÉBASTIEN CHARTRAND

ALIRE

Illustration de couverture : BERNARD DUCHESNE

Photographie : SÉBASTIEN CHARTRAND

Distributeurs exclusifs :

Canada et États-Unis :
Messageries ADP
2315, rue de la Province
Longueuil (Québec) Canada
J4G 1G4
Téléphone : 450-640-1237
Télécopieur : 450-674-6237

France et autres pays :
Interforum Editis
Immeuble Paryseine
3, Allée de la Seine, 94854 Ivry Cedex
Tél. : 33 1 49 59 11 56/91
Télécopieur : 33 1 49 59 11 33
Service commande France Métropolitaine
Téléphone : 33 2 38 32 71 00
Télécopieur : 33 2 38 32 71 28
Service commandes Export-DOM-TOM
Télécopieur : 33 2 38 32 78 86
Internet : www.interforum.fr
Courriel : cdes-export@interforum.fr

Suisse :
Diffuseur : **Interforum Suisse S.A.**
Route André-Piller 33 A
Case postale 1701 Fribourg — Suisse
Téléphone : 41 26 460 80 60
Télécopieur : 41 26 460 80 68
Internet : www.interforumsuisse.ch
Courriel : office@interforumsuisse.ch
Distributeur : OLF
Z.I.3, Corminbœuf
P. O. Box 1152, CH-1701 Fribourg
Commandes :
Téléphone : 41 26 467 51 11
Télécopieur : 41 26 467 54 66
Courriel : information@olf.ch

Belgique et Luxembourg :
Interforum Editis S.A.
Fond Jean-Pâques, 6 1348 Louvain-la-Neuve
Téléphone : 32 10 42 03 20
Télécopieur : 32 10 41 20 24
Courriel : info@interforum.be

Pour toute information supplémentaire
LES ÉDITIONS ALIRE INC.
120, côte du Passage, Lévis (Québec) Canada G6V 5S9
Tél. : 418-835-4441   Télécopieur : 418-838-4443
Courriel : info@alire.com
Internet : www.alire.com

Les Éditions Alire inc. bénéficient des programmes d'aide à
l'édition du Conseil des arts du Canada (CAC), du Fonds du   Canadä
Livre du Canada (FLC) et du Programme national de traduction
pour l'édition du livre pour leurs activités d'édition.

Les Éditions Alire inc. bénéficient aussi de l'aide de la Société de développe-
ment des entreprises culturelles du Québec (SODEC) et du Gouvernement du
Québec – Programme de crédit d'impôt pour l'édition de livres – Gestion
Sodec.

Dépôt légal : 2e trimestre 2016
Bibliothèque et Archives nationales du Québec
Bibliothèque et Archives Canada

À Sonya,
qui a créé de nouvelles étoiles
pour des cieux devenus trop sombres.

TABLE DES MATIÈRES

PROLOGUE

Il courait dans l'obscurité, ses bras tendus ne parvenant pas à écarter les branches basses des pins qui lui fouettaient le visage, ni les tiges des framboisiers sauvages qui lui labouraient les jambes.

Il trébucha sur une racine, s'écorcha les paumes au sang en percutant le sol. Sans percevoir la douleur, il se releva et reprit sa course.

Jusqu'où pouvait-il fuir ?

Pouvait-il seulement espérer fuir ?

Son souffle devint rauque, l'air moite de la nuit estivale lui sembla lourd et, pris d'étourdissements, François s'effondra. Face contre terre, des épines de résineux collées à son visage ruisselant de sueur, le jeune vicaire se retint de pleurer.

Il devait se rendre à l'évidence : il ne traverserait pas la forêt avant d'être rattrapé par Gamache et Légaré. En désespoir de cause, il se retourna sur le dos et trouva la force d'inspirer assez profondément pour crier :

— Otjiera !

Les yeux rivés sur le ciel nocturne, il attendit, osant souhaiter une réponse – après tout, Notre-Dame des Tempérances n'était peut-être plus très loin.

Rien.

L'instant de repos forcé lui permit d'appeler de nouveau, cette fois avec plus de force :

— OTJIERA !

Quelque part au loin, un loup hurla. Légaré, de toute évidence.

François ferma les yeux sans pouvoir contenir une larme de frustration. Péniblement, il se releva en s'appuyant sur un arbre.

Un nouveau bruit attira son attention et fit monter une autre larme, celle-là de soulagement.

Un bruit d'eau courante.

Le ruisseau Croche cascadait à une dizaine de verges de là.

François esquissa l'ombre d'un sourire. Sa respiration toujours laborieuse, il ne parviendrait plus à courir, mais il avait désormais le ruisseau pour le guider jusqu'au village et il pourrait marcher dans l'eau pour masquer son odeur au flair du lycanthrope. L'espace d'un moment, il songea à utiliser un sort de célérité, peut-être l'ennéagramme de prestesse du *Magia Mathematica*, afin d'accroître magiquement la rapidité de sa fuite.

Était-ce vraiment lui qui souhaitait cela ?

Ou était-ce l'ancêtre Lavallée qui le poussait à user des arcanes pour tenter une nouvelle prise de contrôle ?

Dans le doute, le vicaire s'abstint.

Les choses ne devaient pas lui échapper. Il n'avait repris conscience que récemment, comme tiré d'un profond sommeil, Lavallée lui ayant cédé une partie du contrôle du corps qu'ils partageaient. François avait alors découvert qu'on l'avait amené à Pointe-Lévy et qu'un homme agonisait à ses pieds – probablement la raison pour laquelle on faisait appel à lui.

Ses pouvoirs théurgiques pouvaient soigner, contrairement à la goétie de son ancêtre.

Toutefois, la cohabitation était également une nouveauté pour Lavallée et celui-ci lui avait accordé trop

d'ascendance sur le corps. La bride mentale avait lâché, François avait repris le dessus et, avant que les membres du Stigma Diaboli ne puissent comprendre ce qui se passait, il s'était téléporté plus de cent verges au sud.

Un risque énorme, un contrecoup peut-être supérieur à deux ans. Lavallée avait tout déployé pour reprendre son emprise, mais le vicaire avait tenu bon et s'était précipité vers son village.

Restait à espérer rejoindre Otjiera avant d'être capturé par les sous-fifres de l'Étranger. Les jambes de François lui paraissaient lestées de plomb, son cœur battait douloureusement dans sa poitrine, sa salive avait un goût aigre et ses poumons brûlaient. Marcher dans le ruisseau, même si celui-ci n'avait qu'un pied de profondeur, lui était pénible.

Il avisa un grand bâton et le ramassa pour s'aider à la marche. Ce contact le rassura : ainsi, il avait l'impression de tenir son sceptre. D'ailleurs, s'il l'avait eu, il aurait pu drainer un peu de la vitalité de la végétation environnante.

Son corps ne l'avait pas fait autant souffrir depuis l'assaut de l'île aux Œufs, et encore : c'était plus d'un siècle auparavant, à l'époque où il était déjà fort âgé. Cette nouvelle enveloppe charnelle était bien plus jeune et la douleur que son propriétaire légitime avait accepté de supporter dépassait celle qu'il était habitué à tolérer.

Si seulement ce jeune blanc-bec de vicaire ne cherchait pas constamment à en reprendre le contrôle.

Jean-Pierre Lavallée sortit du ruisseau et avisa une pierre moussue où il pourrait attendre Gamache et Légaré. Il claqua la langue d'agacement en repensant aux goétistes dont le Seigneur s'était vu contraint de se satisfaire. Quelle pitié ! Il avait suffi de moins d'un siècle pour que les arcanes soient réduits à un aussi misérable état.

— François ?

Lavallée resta un instant figé de stupeur. Il connaissait cette voix… quand il se retourna, ce fut pour découvrir un Indien âgé qui le dévisageait, les traits démontrant une profonde méfiance.

— Non… tu n'es pas François, marmonna le chamane.

Lavallée laissa échapper un rire bref. Voilà qui était aussi ironique que divertissant.

— Ainsi, Otjiera, dit-il en se relevant, tu es toujours de ce monde. Cela te fait plus de cent ans, non ?

L'Indien recula d'un pas.

— Atontarori… murmura le vieil homme qui cherchait, de toute évidence, à rester maître de lui-même. C'est bel et bien toi, Atontarori Âme du Cheval, fils de Kondiaronk Âme du Rat Musqué.

— Appelle-moi Jean-Pierre. On m'a retiré mon nom wendat, quoique cela ne t'a pas empêché de venir ramper à mes pieds pour que je t'enseigne. Tu n'étais alors qu'un gamin qui avait accepté un baptême chrétien… n'est-ce pas, messire Joseph Gauthier ?

Lavallée eut la satisfaction de voir son ancien disciple tenter vainement de réprimer un tremblement.

— J'aurais dû te tuer, Jean-Pierre, lorsque ta fille m'y a incité. Il est tard, mais je vais remédier à cela. *Önenh, ha'yen'aha !*

Tout l'amusement de Lavallée disparut lorsque la forêt trembla sous la puissance d'un rugissement. L'ours blanc qui avait pris la place du vieil Indien se dressa sur ses pattes postérieures, dominant le sorcier par plus de trois pieds et exhibant des crocs longs comme le doigt.

Instinctivement, Lavallée recula, posa le pied sur un sol instable et s'aperçut que le ruisseau s'était mué en un profond trou boueux. Incapable d'extraire son pied

de la bourbe épaisse, ne disposant de rien pour tracer un diagramme, le sorcier activa l'un des sorts que son descendant avait gravé dans sa chair.

— *Ashek akkad baath...*

Alors même qu'il incantait, Lavallée sentit toute l'humidité de l'air d'été se condenser autour de lui. Elle se fit bruine, crachin et se mua en averse avant qu'il n'eût terminé sa formule :

— *... ahmed dazan il-bekr.*

Le globe de feu qui aurait dû naître au bout de ses doigts crépita puis s'éteignit. L'ours blanc se jeta sur lui et, le frappant de son énorme patte, lui déchiqueta la cuisse de ses griffes acérées.

L'impact projeta Lavallée à plus de trois verges où il se recroquevilla en grimaçant, sa main refermée sur son membre ensanglanté. L'os était visible et le sang jaillissait par gerbes.

Une cuisante douleur surprit Lavallée. De l'humus émergeait une armée de fourmis charpentières qui attaquèrent la jambe sanguinolente dans ses parties les plus vulnérables. Incapable de se relever, le sorcier ne put que tenter de ramper pour distancer l'essaim.

Tout près, l'ours blanc avançait en grondant, babines relevées. Lavallée amassa une petite pierre, traça frénétiquement un diagramme sur le sol et incanta une formule de téléportation.

L'étourdissement le gagna quand il apparut sur l'affleurement rocheux.

François hurla quand il perçut la douleur qui lui vrillait le corps. Aussi rapidement qu'il le put, il invoqua un sort curatif, sentit le contrecoup lui ravir de précieux mois de longévité puis vit ses chairs se reconstituer autour de sa jambe. À mesure que la douleur se dissipait, il constata que son ancêtre ne l'avait téléporté qu'à quelques verges de l'ours polaire, sur un petit promontoire rocheux situé hors de portée.

L'ours polaire. Otjiera. Maintenant qu'il l'avait trouvé, il pourrait demander sa protection...

... ou l'abattre.

Satisfait d'avoir mieux jaugé la liberté qu'il pouvait laisser à son descendant sans en perdre le contrôle, Lavallée eut le temps de tracer quelques pentacles sur la pierre en se servant d'un petit caillou.

Sourire aux lèvres, il se releva.

L'ours venait de se retourner dans sa direction en grognant et il se dressait de nouveau sur ses pattes de derrière...

... puis ses énormes yeux sombres s'agrandirent quand il se vit dans l'incapacité de bouger.

En ricanant, Lavallée sauta gracieusement du roc et atterrit à quelques pas de l'ours désormais inoffensif. Incantant entre ses dents, le sorcier força le chamane à reprendre forme humaine.

Le vieillard s'effondra sur le terreau forestier. D'une formule, Lavallée souleva magiquement l'Indien de terre et le tint suspendu dans les airs à la hauteur de ses yeux.

— Je t'avais sous-estimé, Otjiera. Tu m'as pris par surprise. Tu es digne d'avoir été mon apprenti et je ne me suis pas trompé en te confiant la pierre manquante qui ouvre mes catacombes. Encore heureux que tu l'aies offerte à mon descendant, cela m'a grandement facilité les choses.

Incantant de nouveau, le sorcier fit se tendre puis s'écraser au sol le corps du vieil Indien.

— Ce que j'adore de ce sortilège, expliqua le sorcier au chamane, c'est qu'il fracture d'un seul coup tous les os du squelette sans affecter les organes. La douleur vient de partout à la fois et est impossible à supporter... du moins c'est ce que disent les livres. Qu'en penses-tu ?

Aucune réponse ne vint du vieillard. Le sorcier ajouta :

— Je pourrais te laisser agoniser là, tu sais… mais ce serait risqué. Vous autres, médianistes et théurgistes, avez la fâcheuse habitude de soigner ces corps que nous prenons un tel soin à briser… *Ykthel ickabadht, seker düren-ak!*

Otjiera émit une sorte de borborygme étranglé. Une écume mêlée de sang coula de sa bouche.

— Crise d'appendicite avancée, expliqua Lavallée. Un guérisseur comme toi devrait apprécier la précision du sortilège, qui génère une inflammation maximale sans atteindre le point mortel. Attends de voir ce que cela donne avec des pierres aux reins et au foie…

— Tu as des divertissements d'un sadisme révoltant, Jean-Pierre.

Le sorcier fit volte-face et s'agenouilla derechef. L'homme qui se tenait devant lui, vêtu de coûteux vêtements noirs, le fixait d'un air réprobateur.

— Maître…

L'Étranger poussa un soupir, jeta un œil sur l'Indien agonisant et claqua des doigts. Le vieux chamane expira pour de bon.

— Tu as laissé ton descendant reprendre le contrôle de son corps pendant un long moment, mon ami. Il est presque parvenu jusqu'à son village.

— J'ai été pris par surprise, mon Seigneur.

— Ainsi que par Otjiera.

Lavallée connaissait le Seigneur depuis assez longtemps pour savoir ce qu'impliquait ce ton trompeusement désinvolte. Il se prosterna très bas en murmurant :

— Je vous jure, *Stupor Mundi*, que si je vous ai déçu…

— Du calme, mon ami, coupa l'Éminent Maître avec nonchalance. Inutile d'en faire autant. J'ai besoin de toi en vie, et doublement…

Ils interrompirent leur discussion en entendant des bruits venant des taillis. Un loup au poitrail énorme fut le premier à surgir, la fourrure luisante de sueur et la langue pendante. Il inclina la tête vers le maître, dans un geste qui n'avait rien d'animal, et reprit sa forme humaine.

Joseph Légaré s'inclina de nouveau devant son maître. Ce dernier ne cacha pas son mécontentement.

— Faudra-t-il que je m'occupe personnellement de chacune de vos bourdes d'apprentis sorciers ? gronda le Seigneur en jetant un œil à ses ongles.

Légaré fut secoué de vifs tremblements et, en son for intérieur, Lavallée le plaignit. Faire ses preuves auprès du Seigneur était un travail de tous les instants. L'artiste prescient eut la bonne idée de murmurer :

— Si je puis oser, mon Seigneur…

L'Éminent Maître sortit sa montre de son gousset, l'ouvrit brièvement et la rangea avant de répondre.

— Plaît-il ?

— Gamache nous a considérablement ralentis.

Lavallée bénit le fait que le Seigneur lui tournait le dos, ne pouvant ainsi voir le sourire qui lui fendit brièvement le visage. *Joliment joué*, songea-t-il. Personne ne pouvait se vanter de connaître réellement l'Étranger, mais l'une des rares manœuvres qui fonctionnait avec l'Éternel Seigneur était de faire porter la faute sur celui qu'il avait momentanément en disgrâce. Un jeu dangereux : quand tous les membres de l'Ordre s'y mettaient, l'Éminent Maître en venait inévitablement à couper la branche malade de son arbre – Lavallée repensa à la fin d'Ikès le Jongleur en son temps ou, lui avait-on raconté, celle du marin Giuliano et du notaire Lanigan au printemps dernier.

Ladite branche malade ne tarda pas à faire son apparition. Amaigri, des cernes violacés sous les yeux,

Louis-Olivier Gamache marchait en s'aidant d'un bâton. L'homme qui avait été le favori du Seigneur six mois auparavant portait sur son corps les stigmates de ses trop nombreux échecs. Ses cheveux couleur rouille étaient passés au gris roussâtre et son visage arborait bien prématurément les rides de la vieillesse.

Gamache s'inclina à son tour, exténué par la traque. Il reluqua avec convoitise un tronc mort où il n'osa s'asseoir sans y être invité par le Maître qui, de toute évidence, ne lui accorderait pas ce privilège. En essayant de rester impassible, Gamache jeta un regard sur la dépouille de celui qui avait été le Premier Danseur, puis attendit, résigné.

— Avez-vous questionné ce vieux batelier, à Pointe-Lévy ? demanda le Seigneur sans la moindre introduction.

Gamache déglutit et l'Éminent Maître ne lui laissa pas le loisir de répondre.

— J'en déduis que non. S'il m'en souvient bien, il s'agissait là du dernier homme à avoir vu le père Masse vivant, non ?

Le sorcier roux se contenta de hocher la tête.

— Il disait avoir vu notre bon père Masse lors de l'épidémie de 47, non ? Étrange pour un prêtre que vous étiez censé avoir tué il y a... voyons... huit ans, c'est bien cela ?

— Notre témoin a trépassé, ce qui ne serait pas arrivé si... enfin, nous aurions pu le questionner, mon Seigneur, si le vicaire Gauthier avait bel et bien soigné la tuberculose de ce vieillard. Au lieu de quoi, il s'est téléporté.

Sale chien bâtard ! pesta mentalement Lavallée qui, n'ayant nulle envie d'endosser le rôle de bouc émissaire, contre-attaqua :

— J'avais expressément sollicité la présence de la Siffleuse afin qu'un contrôle mental puisse nous servir de sûreté supplémentaire. Mais il semble, messire Gamache, que votre animosité envers la Voyante des Trois-Rivières vous pousse à bâcler les tâches exigées par le Seigneur. Et parlant de travail bâclé…

— Il suffit.

Le Maître venait de parler et ses larbins se turent. Seuls quelques grillons dans la nuit estivale brisaient le lourd silence que s'imposaient les trois membres du Stigma Diaboli dans l'attente de leur sentence.

L'Éternel Seigneur s'approcha de la dépouille du chamane, sa démarche empreinte d'une noblesse ancienne. D'une preste flexion de poignet, il fit se soulever de terre le corps du vieil Otjiera. La dépouille flotta pour aller s'appuyer contre un grand pin. D'elle-même, la hachette qui pendait à la ceinture de l'Indien se détacha, se mit à tournoyer dans le vide puis se planta profondément au milieu du torse du chamane, le clouant au tronc comme on eût épinglé un insecte sur du liège.

— Tu sais bien mon cher, mon *très cher* Louis-Olivier, que nous ne pouvons nous permettre d'attendre que les deux dernières représentantes du cercle des Danseurs viennent jusqu'ici… je leur laisse ce message *uniquement* au cas où je serais *encore* désappointé par tes résultats. Car j'espère bien qu'elles ne parviendront pas jusqu'ici, tu comprends ? C'est pourquoi tu vas repartir de ce pas pour traquer et éliminer les deux Exécutrices…

— Les *deux* ?

Seule une totale stupéfaction pouvait avoir poussé Gamache à couper la parole à l'Éminent Maître – toutefois, ce dernier esquissa un sourire satisfait et s'approcha de lui.

— Oui, mon très, très cher Louis-Olivier. *Les deux*. Il faut savoir fixer ses priorités et après tout, vous n'êtes

mariés que jusqu'à ce que la mort vous sépare, non? De toute façon, tu t'es fort bien remis de ton premier veuvage, n'est-ce pas?

D'un geste, le Seigneur congédia ses larbins. Gamache s'inclina et tourna les talons, accompagné de Légaré qui réadopta aussitôt sa forme canine. Après les avoir regardés partir, le Maître porta son attention vers le sorcier.

— Marche avec moi, Lavallée.

— Avec plaisir, *Imperator*.

Avec des mouvements empreints de grâce, l'Éminent Maître se dirigea vers le sud, reprenant exactement la trajectoire qu'avait entamée le descendant de Lavallée pendant qu'il gouvernait son enveloppe corporelle. Le sorcier l'escorta avec méfiance: qu'avait le Seigneur en tête pour lui faire suivre cette route? Était-ce une façon spécialement retorse de lui mettre la résurgence de son descendant sous le nez?

— J'ai cru en Gamache, jadis, commença le Maître avec du regret dans la voix. C'était un arcaniste compétent et efficace, probablement le plus prometteur de cette cohorte-ci du Stigma Diaboli. Légaré a les reins plus solides, mais son talent est plutôt limité; quant à Sewell et Ferrier, je les ai recrutés davantage pour leur fortune et leur influence que pour leurs aptitudes arcaniques. J'aurais bien aimé rallier à notre cause le curé Lamare – lui, c'était un maître, un vrai –, mais à la suite de sa réaction le soir du Mardi gras, j'ai su qu'il ne nous rejoindrait jamais.

— Votre cheptel vous produira une toute nouvelle cohorte, répondit prudemment Lavallée en cherchant la signification des propos tenus par le Maître.

L'Immortel poursuivait sa route en longeant le ruisseau. Le cours d'eau se divisa bientôt en une fourche, l'une de ses branches menant au village, l'autre se

joignant à une petite rivière au débit fort. C'est dans cette direction que le Seigneur continua son chemin.

— Tout l'art réside dans le choix d'un bras droit, reprit-il de son ton patricien. Prends Sauvageau, par exemple. Tu n'as pas eu le temps de le connaître, mais tu en as entendu parler. C'était un Métis au potentiel stupéfiant, héritier des dons d'une grand-mère Danseuse et d'un arrière-grand-père missionnaire qui aimait un peu trop les jeunes Montagnaises. Sauvageau pouvait lancer des sorts avec un contrôle impressionnant et n'en subir qu'un contrecoup minime. Or, c'était aussi un vrai butor, ivrogne et mal dégrossi, sans une once de génie. Il ne savait même pas lire et il fallait lui enseigner chaque sortilège en le faisant répéter jusqu'à ce qu'il retienne tout par cœur. C'était un balourd rustaud, naïf et débauché… mais quel talent ! C'est pour cela que je le préférais à Gamache, au début. Quel malheur que Lamare l'ait éliminé aussi facilement.

Les arbres se raréfièrent et le boisé céda la place à la terre labourée. À cet endroit la rivière faisait quelque trois verges de large. Des débris jonchaient le sol, manifestement les vestiges d'une construction de bonne taille. *Où veut donc en venir le Maître ?* continuait de se demander Lavallée. *Remet-il en doute ma fonction de bras droit ? Juge-t-il mon assistance décevante ?*

Cherchant quelque chose d'intelligent à répondre, Lavallée remarqua sur le sol une pierre ronde et régulière : la meule d'un moulin.

Il m'a ramené là où est mort le curé Lamare ! comprit subitement François qui, avant de parvenir à organiser ses pensées, entendit une voix mesurée à ses côtés dire suavement :

— Bien le bonsoir, vicaire Gauthier.

L'Étranger ! Aussitôt, François sentit l'irrépressible aura de puissance qui émanait de l'homme en noir et lutta pour ne pas se laisser tomber à genoux.

Avec un petit ricanement, l'Étranger avança de trois pas dans sa direction, broyant la résistance mentale du vicaire sous sa volonté. François fut submergé par la terrible tentation d'obéir et ses forces l'abandonnèrent.

Il s'agenouilla.

Sa vue se brouilla.

Puis, docilement, Lavallée leva les yeux, prenant soin de ne point soutenir le regard de l'Immortel Seigneur.

— Relève-toi, Jean-Pierre, ordonna le Maître. J'ai constaté ce qu'il m'importait de vérifier : ton descendant ne parviendra pas à résister à mon emprise. Tu resteras à mes côtés jusqu'à ce que mon corps soit régénéré et que soit amorcée la *Reconquista*.

Voilà donc où il voulait en venir, comprit le sorcier, soudainement soulagé.

— Mais nous ne sommes pas venus ici que dans ce but, reprit l'Éminent Maître en écho à ses pensées. Je tenais à jeter un œil sur ce village.

— Vraiment, *Stupor Mundi* ?

— J'ai un message à laisser à l'intention du bâtard qui me sert de rejeton.

— Comme le message que vous avez laissé pour les deux Exécutrices ?

Le Maître eut un sourire malveillant.

— On pourrait présenter la chose ainsi, en effet.

Le Seigneur s'avança vers la meule abandonnée et y laissa glisser le bout de son index. Un profond sillon s'inscrivit dans la pierre, là où le doigt traçait un diagramme. Stupéfait, Lavallée se rapprocha. Il était rarissime que le Maître juge nécessaire de dessiner une figure géométrique et, chaque fois qu'il le faisait, l'incantation était d'une puissance inconcevable. Quand il vit le pentacle gravé par l'Immortel, le sorcier recula

d'un pas, pris au dépourvu. Il ne reconnaissait pas cet enchantement.

— *Zared ish-nahir, eshad ibn lamed, nesterii khan daerza,* incanta le Seigneur sans s'être départi de son sourire.

Une vive lumière se mit à jaillir du diagramme, la pierre se fendit et une secousse ébranla le sol.

Puis une seconde, un peu plus forte.

Et une troisième, encore plus forte.

Les suivantes se succédèrent avec la régularité d'un bruit de pendule jusqu'à ce qu'au loin il semblât à Lavallée qu'un pan entier de la forêt se déplaçait.

Il lui fallut toutefois plusieurs secondes pour prendre conscience de ce qu'était vraiment cette marée d'ombres.

Et, au moment précis où le sorcier Lavallée eut compris ce qui était en train de se produire, ses perceptions furent envahies par un grand cri : celui de son descendant, le vicaire François Gauthier, qui hurlait de rage et de désespoir devant ce qui incarnait pour lui l'horreur la plus innommable.

LIVRE VII

RETOUR VERS NOTRE-DAME DES TEMPÉRANCES

En exil, j'ai oublié mes racines et ma terre,
Je m'en souvins en temps malheureux,
J'ai retrouvé ma paisible chaumière,
Et ce hameau, l'objet de tous mes vœux ;
Près de la tombe où repose celui qui fut mon père,
J'ai douloureusement fermé les yeux
Et mon cœur s'est empli de colère.

Édouard Bouguiére
Le Retour de l'exilé

Chapitre 25

Le peuple des rivières

Le renard trottinait à travers les hautes herbes de son territoire nouvellement acquis. Ici, la terre n'était pas aussi stable qu'ailleurs.

Dans les hauteurs, le soleil du matin avait réchauffé l'air mais, lorsque passait un nuage, l'ombre tombait et le vent devenait plus frais. La brise charriait alors l'odeur des eaux boueuses qui s'étendaient à une petite distance de là et celle des mélèzes sombres qui occupaient la plus grande partie du territoire. La lumière était mouchetée par leurs branchages et la piste était striée de zones d'ombre et de lumière.

Un bruit. Le renard tourna prestement la tête, les oreilles pointées vers l'avant. Un chevreuil détala, laissant derrière lui son odeur de frayeur: sueur, sel et piquante urine. Sans s'en préoccuper davantage, le renard poursuivit l'inspection de son domaine.

Il perçut clairement le parfum de l'humus et des feuilles qui se décomposaient en dessous, mêlé à celui des glands tombés trop verts qui pourrissaient. Le renard s'aplatit au sol et resta immobile un instant. Mulots et tamias profitaient de cette manne, de cela il était certain: ses vibrisses percevaient dans l'air les variations caractéristiques de minuscules corps en mouvement. Sous ses

pattes, les coussinets sentaient les vibrations des petites proies qui fouillaient le sol.

Un effluve attira son attention et le renard se détourna. Humant profondément, il sentit les relents des crottes fraîches d'un lièvre, une piste qu'il aurait normalement suivie n'eut été du fumet dérangeant qu'il venait de flairer. C'était une odeur animale qu'il avait déjà croisée, sans jamais voir la bête lui étant associée.

Nerveux, il s'enfonça entre les buissons et marcha le museau collé au sol. Au parfum piquant des résineux chauffés par le soleil se mêlaient ceux des fleurs sauvages, des fientes entourant un nid – il faudrait y retourner tout à l'heure – et de la terre fraîchement retournée. Il fut distrait un moment par les exhalaisons musquées d'une dépouille d'écureuil. Il poursuivit sa route à travers les buissons, s'arrêta devant un arbre mort, se figea de nouveau, stupéfait.

On avait gratté le sol et ostentatoirement uriné sur la terre, le bois, les herbes… et même sur une proie à demi dévorée ! Le renard respira consciencieusement les effluves laissés sur le rat musqué entamé. Ces odeurs émanaient bien de la bête inconnue, mais les fientes encore chaudes révélèrent qu'il avait affaire à une carnivore femelle. Quelques plumes blanches témoignaient de son passage.

Le renard grogna. Il n'aimait pas les oiseaux quand ils étaient davantage concurrents que proies. Il avait déjà eu à défendre la carcasse d'une perdrix face à un corbeau trop entreprenant et avait eu le dessus, mais s'il devait affronter un géant comme cet oiseau de proie, il n'aurait aucune chance. Fort heureusement, ces volatiles avaient des territoires très étendus et la rencontre ne se produirait probablement pas.

De toute façon, cette manière de marquer son passage était de la provocation pure et simple. Le renard

ne pouvait tolérer cette violation. Il frotta son arrière-train sur le sol avec colère, laissant ses propres traces odorantes, puis se dressa bien haut sur ses pattes et se mit en tête de chasser l'intruse de son territoire. Puis il se figea encore une fois lorsque ses vibrisses discernèrent un mouvement rapide.

C'est alors qu'il l'aperçut. Trop tard, beaucoup trop tard, mais l'ennemie était restée parfaitement immobile de manière à duper ses yeux, ses oreilles et ses vibrisses.

C'était un monstre immense, d'une envergure plus grande que le corps du renard. Il arborait des serres énormes aux griffes démesurées et son bec était vicieusement recourbé. Quant à son odeur, elle était bien présente, mais les fientes laissées à dessein avaient détourné l'attention du renard.

Il couina. L'adversaire semblait bien imposante, tout d'un coup. Inclinant la tête, il recula une patte à la fois, prêt à céder les lieux.

Lorsque la silhouette de la bête se modifia et s'étira pour se muer en monstre-qui-marche-debout comme on en voyait plus en amont des eaux, le renard sentit tous ses instincts le pousser à prendre la fuite. Ses membres s'y refusèrent, paralysés comme s'il avait été gelé sur place.

Le monstre-qui-marche-debout émit alors des sons discordants, dérangeants et, soudain, le renard sentit que son être était englouti dans une tourmente effroyable.

Plus rien ne fut visible. Ne subsistèrent que la sensation de son corps écartelé dans tous les sens et celle de son esprit envahi par quelque chose…

… puis ce furent les ténèbres et la vague sensation d'avoir existé…

… puis…

… *il s'éveilla!*

◆

Un parfum de sauge, qu'il identifia aussitôt : Shaor'i.
— Ça va, Faustin ?

Faustin… ce son – non, ce mot – acheva de réaligner ses pensées dans un tout cohérent. Il entrouvrit les yeux. L'Indienne se penchait au-dessus de lui, les traits figés sur une impression d'inquiétude.
— Ça… ça va.

Sa propre voix sonnait comme celle d'un étranger et la phrase avait été difficile à formuler, comme si exprimer des concepts avec des mots était soudainement devenu très compliqué. Il vit qu'il était à l'extérieur, par une journée chaude, probablement l'été. Des oiseaux chantaient dans les arbres, le long d'une piste sinueuse. Il tenta de se redresser,
— Prends ton temps, mon ami. Tu es resté sous cette forme pendant presque trois mois.

Mois ? Ah oui, bien sûr, des mois… *Forme ?* Des images lui revinrent, d'étranges réminiscences de marche à quatre pattes, de traque au flair, de chasse au lièvre, de…

Incompréhension.

La panique monta en lui.
— Du calme, mon ami, murmura Shaor'i. Tout va bien. Referme les yeux, ne pense à rien de compliqué. Les souvenirs vont se mettre en place d'eux-mêmes.

Trop confus pour agir autrement, Faustin obéit.

Il s'était déjà senti écartelé de la sorte, auparavant. C'était lorsque Nadjaw l'avait conduit dans les sous-sols de la Grande Maison, aux Forges. Elle avait lancé un sortilège.

Et ensuite…

Ses crocs qui se referment sur l'échine d'un pigeon. Son flair qui cherche un territoire boisé où aucun de

ses semblables n'a laissé de marque olfactive. Les nuits qui se mêlent aux jours, le temps qui devient flou, les sens qui sont différents, les modes de perception qui passent par son museau, ses vibrisses, ses coussinets…

— Qu'est-ce que…

— Tu commences à comprendre, c'est ça ?

— J'étais… j'ai été…

Ça semblait incroyable, et pourtant…

— … j'ai été… un renard ?

Malgré ses pensées encore confuses, Faustin concevait le non-sens de sa question. Autant demander : « Le fleuve a-t-il coulé d'aval en amont ? » ou « La pluie remonte-t-elle vers le ciel ? » Mais Shaor'i répondit tout simplement :

— C'est ça. Pendant presque trois mois, tu as été un renard.

Malgré les images de plus en plus nombreuses qui jaillissaient de sa mémoire, la partie rationnelle de Faustin s'y refusa encore.

— C'est impossible. Je ne suis pas un renard, je suis un homme.

Shaor'i eut un petit rire qui tinta comme une clochette d'argent.

— Suis-je une femme ou un harfang des neiges, Faustin ?

— Bin… les deux.

— Tiens donc… Là, essaie de te relever, mon ami.

Faustin se dressa, tituba, s'agrippa à un arbre. Se tenir debout semblait un exploit, non pas qu'il se sentît faible mais, plutôt, comme si ce n'était pas… naturel.

Puis son esprit s'adapta et la posture debout redevint normale.

À ses côtés, l'Indienne l'examinait.

— Tes cheveux bruns ont pris de légers reflets cuivrés et tes yeux sont passés de noisette à acajou. Fais voir tes dents.

Dressée sur la pointe des pieds, Shaor'i écarta sans délicatesse les lèvres de Faustin avec ses pouces et scruta sa dentition.

— Des canines un peu longues, mais rien de dramatique. Montre tes mains… *e'e*, tes annulaires et majeurs sont désormais de la même taille.

Interloqué, Faustin porta sa main droite au niveau de ses yeux. Effectivement, les deux doigts étaient identiques ; de plus, l'index avait légèrement raccourci, l'auriculaire allongé. Excluant le pouce, sa main avait maintenant des proportions symétriques.

— Ça nuira à ma dextérité ?

— Pas que je sache. Les loups-garous se modifient à peu près de la même façon et ça ne semble pas les incommoder.

Faustin planta son regard dans celui de la guerrière.

— Qu'est-ce qui s'est passé, Shaor'i ?

— Nadjaw t'a conféré une forme animale. Normalement, elle aurait pu prendre celle du loup ou celle du corbeau, plus communes chez les goétistes, mais elle ne voulait pas altérer ta personnalité. Elle n'avait que ses premières impressions sur lesquelles se fier, mais je trouve que le choix n'est pas mauvais. Et c'est ainsi que te surnomme la femme qui t'a élevé, non ? Plus que quiconque, cette dame te connaît.

Baissant les yeux pour examiner à nouveau ses mains, le jeune homme demanda :

— Mais… pourquoi ?

— C'était la seule manière de te soustraire à la magie de divination du Stigma Diaboli : te conférer une forme animale sans parachever le processus, de manière que ni ton corps ni ton esprit ne soient identifiables. C'était risqué : j'aurais pu ne jamais te retrouver.

— Et comment as-tu fait ? Je veux dire : comment as-tu pu me repérer si le Stigma en était incapable ?

Le regard de Shaor'i se perdit dans l'horizon.

— Comment crois-tu que j'ai fait ? Comment pouvais-je faire ?

L'Indienne se leva et s'éloigna de quelques pas, tournant le dos à Faustin.

— Je t'ai cherché, tout simplement. J'ai survolé les terres avoisinant les Forges, me posant chaque fois qu'un éclat de fourrure rousse attirait mon œil. Je me suis posée auprès de je ne sais plus combien de ces maudits renards pour les scruter à l'outrevision jusqu'à ce qu'enfin, ce matin, j'en repère un avec une aura théurgique.

— Et ça t'a pris…

— Presque trois mois, oui. Tu t'étais beaucoup éloigné des Forges. Logique : la plupart des territoires étaient déjà marqués par d'autres renards. Je suppose que tu as cherché longtemps. Mais l'essentiel, c'est que désormais tu sois redevenu toi-même.

Avec le retour de ses souvenirs, Faustin sentit une lourde inquiétude lui étreindre le cœur.

— Et François ? demanda-t-il, appréhensif.

Shaor'i détourna le regard.

— Nous n'en savons rien.

Estomaqué, Faustin fixa son amie.

— Comment, vous n'en savez rien ? Vous n'avez pas tenté de le retracer ?

— C'est impossible. Ton frère le prêtre est pour ainsi dire « endormi ». L'homme qui occupe son corps, Lavallée, dispose de suffisamment de puissance pour brouiller tout sort de repérage ou de localisation. Au début de l'été, je suis allée en vol auprès d'Otjiera et il a tenté de percevoir sa présence par une recherche onirique. Son rêve ne nous a rien appris, l'âme du prêtre est totalement insaisissable.

— Alors il faut retrouver Lavallée ! insista le jeune homme.

— Je ne sais même pas s'il est toujours aux Forges : tout le temps que j'ai survolé la zone à ta recherche, je ne l'ai pas vu. Nadjaw m'a dit que l'Étranger n'avait pas prévu dans ses plans que Lavallée finirait par s'éveiller ; il n'avait donc rien planifié comme rôle pour le Sorcier du Fort. Au printemps dernier, il était question de faire de lui le bras droit de l'Étranger, mais cela nous en révèle fort peu sur les lieux où peut se trouver le corps de ton frère en ce moment… ou si ton frère est toujours « quelque part » dans ce corps. Il peut être n'importe où au Bas-Canada.

Faustin accusa le coup. Puis il releva :

— Tu as dit que… *Nadjaw* t'avait dit tout cela ?

Le regard de l'Indienne se voila.

— Oui… nous aurons tout le temps d'en rediscuter.

Shaor'i le laissa seul le temps d'allumer un minuscule feu de branchettes au-dessus duquel elle suspendit sa gourde de cuir. Quand de la vapeur commença à s'échapper du goulot ouvert, elle la lui tendit.

— Tiens. Ça te remettra les idées en place.

Faustin se pencha pour humer le contenu et se surprit, plutôt que de prendre un long respir, à avoir le réflexe de flairer par petits coups brefs – il perçut des arômes délicats rappelant la menthe, le poivre, le miel et les oranges qu'il recevait à Noël lorsqu'il était enfant.

Shaor'i le gratifia de l'un de ses rares sourires.

— Cesse de faire le petit chiot méfiant. Il y a du thé sauvage, de la *chicoutai*…

Une image se dessina dans l'esprit de Faustin.

— … et cette fleur jaune qui pousse en grappe, pas loin des granges, ajouta-t-il.

— Du millepertuis, c'est ça. Allez, bois. On nous attend.

— Qui ça ?

— Tu verras.

◆

L'été était bien entamé et les rayons du soleil chauffaient les troncs des résineux qui répandaient leur
parfum. Où qu'ils fussent, la forêt était dense et probablement éloignée des villages.

Shaor'i était restée plutôt silencieuse durant le tra-
jet, ne lui adressant la parole que pour lui indiquer un
obstacle. Afin d'entretenir une discussion, Faustin
demanda :

— Où sommes-nous, Shaor'i ?

— À presque trois lieues au sud-ouest des Forges.

Le ton indiquait qu'elle ne souhaitait pas converser
davantage. Faustin insista :

— Et Baptiste, lui ? As-tu pu faire quelque chose
pour ses yeux ?

— Non. On ne peut pas recréer un organe. C'est
impossible.

— Mais alors… comment va-t-il ? Que va-t-il…

— Tu verras.

Le ton était sans réplique et l'Indienne n'ajouta
rien.

Forcé de se tenir coi, Faustin usa de cette perception que son amie lui avait enseignée, celle qui permettait de lire le silence. Celui de Shaor'i évoquait bien
des tourments et de nombreuses inquiétudes, mais ce
n'était pas le mutisme d'une personne se murant dans
le refus de parler.

C'était un silence qui invitait à la patience.

Peu à peu, la végétation devint encore plus dense.
Faustin, peinant à avancer, découvrit de jeunes bou-
leaux ayant poussé très près les uns des autres. Ils
s'enfoncèrent dans ces épais taillis pendant au moins
une demi-heure et il lui fallut presque tout ce temps
pour s'habituer à la pénombre.

Même une couleuvre aurait de la difficulté à circuler, songea le jeune homme.

Son nez fut soudainement attiré par une forte odeur de poisson et, se tournant vers la provenance du fumet, il vit qu'on avait départi quelques branches d'érable pointues de leur écorce pour y accrocher par les ouïes une grande quantité de perchaudes de toutes les tailles. Suivant l'Indienne, Faustin traversa un fossé naturel grâce à un pont formé d'un tronc abattu. L'arbre, rendu glissant par la boue qui s'y était déposée, n'était large que d'un pied tout au plus, aussi fallut-il un bon moment à Faustin pour franchir le saut-de-loup.

Quand il fut de l'autre côté, il s'arrêta, pétrifié.

Il en dénombra sept. Sept créatures si semblables à des loutres que, n'eût été de leur démarche verticale, il s'y serait trompé.

Quelques-unes se prélassaient tout simplement sur une grosse pierre plate, non loin d'une hutte gigantesque, fort similaire à celle où Faustin avait été entraîné par son mystérieux sauveteur quand il avait chuté de la drave, aux Forges. Comme la dernière fois, il s'agissait d'une sorte d'abri comparable à celui d'un castor.

Devant une hutte de taille plus modeste, une autre créature – *maymaygwashi*, se souvint Faustin – s'affairait à briser des moules en se servant de deux pierres, l'une en guise de marteau et l'autre comme enclume. À ses côtés, un individu un peu plus petit entretenait un feu de camp d'où montait doucement un mince filet de fumée. Avec un bâton, le *maymaygwashi* écarta les cendres puis s'éloigna un instant pour poser des œufs dans une motte d'argile. Lorsqu'ils furent entièrement recouverts, la créature déposa la boule de glaise dans l'âtre et la couvrit de braises.

Des sifflements joyeux saluèrent leur arrivée et on se précipita à leur rencontre, à l'exception d'un paresseux resté à se dorer sur sa pierre.

Shaor'i répondit aux sifflements, présenta ses paumes pour que chacun, à tour de rôle, puisse y poser ses mains. Faustin l'imita, amusé malgré lui par l'apparence comique du peuple des rivières. Un sifflement plus aigu lui fit porter les yeux vers le sol, là où un jeune *maymaygwashi* de deux pieds sautillait en présentant les mains avec insistance. Il ronronna, ravi, quand Faustin s'accroupit pour lui offrir ses paumes.

Tous s'écartèrent quand un cri retentit de derrière la grande hutte :

— Faustin !

Baptiste Lachapelle surgit du campement après avoir posé sa hache. Il se précipita vers le jeune homme et le souleva de terre avec son étreinte d'ours. De l'épaule où il était juché, Ti-Jean lança un cri de bienvenue.

— Comment tu t'sens, gaillard ?

Décontenancé, Faustin s'écarta de l'énorme poitrail pour lever les yeux vers le colosse. En dépit de sa dextérité, ses orbites étaient toujours vides.

— Baptiste, tu vois ?

Le bûcheron éclata d'un rire grand comme le monde et reposa le jeune homme.

— Non, Faustin. J'serai toujours aveugle. Mais Ti-Jean l'est point.

— Mais qu'…

Baptiste posa une main sur son épaule.

— On a pas mal de choses à t'conter, garçon.

◆

Avec de petits couteaux de pierre, les *maymaygwashi* nettoyaient les perchaudes. Par des symboles tracés dans la terre, Shaor'i expliqua qu'ils ne les aideraient pas à préparer le souper, car ils avaient trop de choses à se raconter, mais qu'ils captureraient le repas du lendemain pour compenser.

Assis sur des rochers à l'écart, les trois humains s'entretinrent du déroulement des trois derniers mois.

— Devenir aveugle, raconta Baptiste, ça m'a détruit. J'tais devenu comme qui dirait embarré dans mon corps. J'savais faire des choses pis là, j'pouvais pus les faire.

Faustin n'avait aucune peine à le croire. Au dernier printemps, Otjiera avait recommandé au colosse de prendre du repos et Madeleine avait accepté de l'héberger au presbytère ; ce que Baptiste appelait du repos consistait à défricher de la terre, à s'occuper des bestiaux et à fendre de pleines cordes de bois.

— J'ai essayé, au début, poursuivit le bûcheron. Marcher avec une canne, me servir de mes oreilles, des choses de même. Mais t'abats pas un arbre en écoutant pour trouver son tronc, pas plus que tu draves avec une canne. J'sais pas si tu peux comprendre, garçon… tout c'qui faisait qui j'tais, c'était fini pour de bon.

Shaor'i commenta :

— Je ne savais pas quoi faire pour lui. Il passait ses grandes journées assis sur une pierre, totalement immobile. Totalement inactif.

Faustin frissonna. Il n'arrivait tout simplement pas à imaginer Baptiste oisif. Cela avait quelque chose de terriblement attristant.

— J'ai essayé de le faire chanter, expliqua la jeune femme. Les *maymaygwashi* aiment la musique, mais ne chantent pas. Ses airs étaient si mélancoliques que j'ai fini par lui demander d'arrêter.

— Y a rien d'autre qui m'venait au cœur que des complaintes. Sauf qu'à un moment donné, Ti-Jean s'en est mêlé.

— Il n'aimait pas voir Baptiste dans cet état, lui non plus. Et… il était seul. Au début, je lui avais proposé, avec les bribes de leur langue que je connais, qu'un *maymaygwashi* l'emmène jusque chez les siens,

au tunnel. Mais il venait d'une autre tribu, celle des grottes situées plus au nord. Son clan aussi souffrait de problèmes de fertilité à la suite de la coupe des pins. Mais cela n'avait plus d'importance.

— Sa tribu, y'en restait pus rien. Y'avaient toutes été changés en diablotins, ceux qu'on avait combattus au manoir Poulin. Y'avait pus rien que moi, à c't'heure. Y passait ses journées juché en haut d'un arbre, pis y pleurait. Je l'entendais, des fois. D'autres fois, y v'nait s'coucher dans ma poche de mackinaw. Là, j'me sentais mieux, pis lui itou.

— Alors ce sont les *maymaygwashi* qui ont proposé de les adocter.

Faustin fronça les sourcils.

— Je crois avoir déjà entendu ce terme…

— Ça arrivait parfois chez les Danseurs, expliqua Shaor'i. La dernière fois, ce fut pour Ikès, dont tu as vu la sépulture sous l'église de Saint-Laurent. Il arrivait qu'un *mah oumet* souhaite se lier à un humain. Il en naissait un lien très fort.

— Y avait déjà un lien entre Ti-Jean pis moé. Y sentait c'que j'voulais, pis vice et versa.

Faustin regarda Ti-Jean, qui émit un minuscule cri, comme s'il approuvait.

— Oui, je m'en souviens, s'exclama Faustin. Quand nous construisions une hutte pour le sort d'effigie, Ti-Jean savait toujours quand tu avais besoin d'une racine ou d'un rameau tendre…

— Comme tu dis. Pis quand on a fui en charrette, j'm'étais dit qu'y faudrait que Ti-Jean t'aide à guider le cheval… pis il l'a fait.

— Les *mah oumet* sentent les idées des leurs bien au-delà du langage, ajouta Shaor'i.

— Faque les *maymaygwashi*… bin… y z'ont ron-ronné. Toute une nuit sans s'arrêter. C'était un peu

comme les chants dans la caverne des *mah oumet*, un peu comme les mélopées d'Otjiera. Ça vibrait. Pis y'ont fait des dessins, que m'a dit la P'tite.

— Je savais que c'était eux qui avaient enseigné l'usage des *komkwejwika'sikl* aux humains, il y a fort longtemps. Mais j'ignorais que les symboles ancestraux pouvaient aussi avoir un effet magique. Leur magie était de la magie ancestrale, de la médianie comme vous dites, mais leurs arcanes étaient guidés par les tracés et les lignes, un peu à la manière de vos pentacles, sans en être réellement. À l'outrevision, c'était d'un bleu-blanc brillant, comme la foudre.

— Une quatrième forme de magie ? s'étonna Faustin.

— Il n'y a qu'une magie. L'argent de vos arcanes est du bleu très clair et le noir de la goétie…

— … est du bleu très foncé, je sais. Donc ? Qu'est-ce qui s'est passé ensuite ?

— J'me suis vu, reprit Baptiste. Pis ça m'a pris du temps à comprendre que c'était par les yeux de Ti-Jean que j'me voyais. Lui, y'a compris *drette-là*. Y'avait déjà entendu parler de ça. Ça s'racontait dans sa tribu que, longtemps avant, les humains pis les lutins s'adoctaient. Faque y'a grimpé sur mon épaule, pis là… c'était… pareil comme voir normalement.

La gorge serrée par l'émotion suscitée par le souvenir, Baptiste fit une pause. Ce fut Shaor'i qui compléta :

— Ils sentent ce que l'autre désire. Ils échangent des idées. Normalement, ils pourraient voir à travers les yeux de l'autre, mais dans ce cas-ci c'est à sens unique et Baptiste a choisi de le faire de façon permanente. L'un et l'autre ont retrouvé un sens à leur vie.

— Y'a fallu que j'm'habitue au changement d'angle. Sur mon épaule, c'est pas comme drette où qu'étaient mes yeux. Mais après deux mois, ça marche aussi bin

qu'avant. Ti-Jean sent quand j'veux r'garder à gauche ou à droite pis vire sa tête en conséquence.

Attendri, Faustin sourit. Les deux formaient vraiment une sacrée paire, le géant et le lutin.

Son estomac gronda à l'odeur du poisson grillé et il demanda :

— Et les *maymaygwashi* ? Pourquoi sont-ils restés ici ? Ils viennent du lac Supérieur, non ?

Le regard de Shaor'i devint plus sombre.

— Ils étaient venus nous avertir de l'éveil de Kabir Kouba et nous porter un message : le père Masse, que connaît Baptiste, demandait à nous voir. Dès que nous avons compris cela, j'ai contacté Otjiera par rêve. Il m'a dit qu'il avait perçu la libération de Plaçoa et que tant que celui-ci ne serait pas de nouveau asservi, personne ne pourrait contrôler Kabir Kouba. Il nous fallait un spirite pour faire face à la Siffleuse. C'est l'autre raison pour laquelle je t'ai tant cherché.

Faustin fronça les sourcils et Baptiste dit :

— P'tite, j'pense qui faudrait jaser à not' Faustin d'Kabir Kouba.

— J'aimerais bien, ajouta Faustin, un peu exaspéré. On m'a fait libérer l'esprit du pendu de la prison des Trois-Rivières pour ça. C'est aussi la cause de la désertion de Nadjaw et de la présence des *maymaygwashi…*

— C'est une longue histoire, avertit Shaor'i.

— Ce n'est pas comme si j'étais spécialement pressé.

— Soit. Tout a commencé des siècles avant la naissance des nations iroquoises ou micmaques, quand il y a eu une grande guerre, depuis longtemps oubliée.

— Je me souviens que tu avais dit, la première fois que nous sommes allés chez le père Bélanger, que c'est pour cette guerre que les jacks mistigris du Mont à l'Oiseau ont été levés.

— C'est exact. Avant les Cinq Nations, il y en avait d'autres, plus anciennes, qui s'adonnaient elles aussi aux arcanes médians. Personne ne se souvient vraiment de ces peuples, de leur culture ou de leurs croyances. Mais ils disparurent dans un affrontement sans précédent. Ce sont eux qui ont levé les wendigos du Mont… et qui ont engendré Kabir Kouba.

Sans émettre un mot, Faustin écouta. Ce que les Blancs connaissaient des Indiens remontait à l'arrivée de Cartier, de Champlain et de Maisonneuve. Les histoires évoquées par Shaor'i provenaient de beaucoup plus loin dans le temps.

— Chez vous, les Blancs, la clé d'une guerre passe par le contrôle des routes. Chez nous, il s'agissait du contrôle des rivières car nous nous déplaçons en canot. Quelqu'un avait voulu engendrer une créature qui se lancerait à l'assaut des canots ennemis et résisterait aux flèches – nous n'avions pas l'arme à feu, à l'époque – et, après réflexion, a décidé de créer le Grand Serpent.

— Un serpent?

— C'est tout sauf un serpent: à vrai dire, c'est un esturgeon. Les esturgeons ont une armure extérieure formée de plaques osseuses, hérissées de pointes. Dans l'eau, ils ont l'air de reptiles.

— J'me souviens d'un esturgeon pêché en Acadie, intervint Baptiste. Y'avait fallu un cheval pour le sortir de l'eau. Vingt pieds, qu'il faisait!

— L'idée qu'ont eue les Anciens qui ont engendré Kabir Kouba, c'était ça: contrôler mentalement un immense esturgeon pour lui faire chavirer les canots d'écorce, ou tout simplement les rompre. Sauf que les très gros esturgeons étant très vieux, les Anciens usèrent d'enchantements pour prolonger indéfiniment la vie de leur créature. Quand les Anciens furent décimés par la guerre, Kabir Kouba s'installa dans le lac

Pohénégamook, dans le Bas-du-Fleuve. Mais personne n'avait songé qu'avec sa nouvelle longévité, il continuerait de croître et bientôt il représenta un danger pour ceux qui vivaient sur ce territoire – la croissance des esturgeons est lente, mais elle ne s'arrête jamais. Alors le Cercle des Danseurs, encore jeune à l'époque, plongea Kabir Kouba dans un profond sommeil.

Shaor'i tourna la tête vers la gauche et fixa l'horizon.

— Depuis, Kabir Kouba ne fut réveillé qu'une fois, et ce fut une grave erreur. C'était encore avant la venue des Blancs. À l'époque, les Micmacs étaient toujours nomades. Les aînés racontent qu'en suivant le cours du fleuve, un groupe des leurs s'était arrêté pour faire le plein de provisions dans une baie poissonneuse. Mais nos ennemis d'alors, les Haudenosaunee, avaient planifié une embuscade. Mes ancêtres furent avertis par deux messagers et la tribu micmaque s'empressa d'aller cacher femmes, enfants et vieillards dans une caverne isolée sur une île.

Shaor'i marqua une pause. Raconter cette histoire lui semblait difficile, même si cela se passait des siècles avant sa naissance.

— Les Haudenosaunee ont surgi et les Micmacs ont combattu vaillamment. Ils furent néanmoins presque tous tués, et la baie fut revendiquée par les Haudenosaunee. C'était dans l'ordre des choses, c'est ainsi que fonctionnaient les nations lorsque la nourriture se faisait rare. Cependant…

Le teint mat de l'Indienne devint plus pâle. Elle inspira plusieurs fois, se mit à jouer avec une mèche de ses cheveux sombres. Lorsqu'elle reprit son récit, sa voix tremblait légèrement.

— Des Haudenosaunee s'étaient mis à la recherche des femmes, des enfants et des vieillards pour exiger tribut en échange de leur liberté. Cela aussi faisait

partie des règles de guerre. Croyant logiquement que les femmes avaient fui vers l'est, ils s'étaient mis en quête de leurs traces ; mais quand elles s'avérèrent introuvables, les Haudenosaunee torturèrent un survivant micmac. Et ça, ce n'était pas dans les lois.

Shaor'i soupira, marqua une nouvelle pause. Baptiste se rapprocha d'elle pour lui tapoter l'épaule et Ti-Jean descendit de sa place habituelle pour jouer dans les cheveux de la jeune femme. Elle reprit :

— Quand les Haudenosaunee surent que les vieillards, les femmes et les enfants étaient cachés dans la caverne de la petite île, ils envoyèrent un groupe en canots. Ses membres passèrent plusieurs heures à chercher la grotte, dont l'entrée avait été dissimulée par des branches mortes. Pourtant, quand ils la trouvèrent, ils mirent plutôt le feu aux broussailles avec leurs torches et asphyxièrent les innocents de la tribu micmaque.

Faustin fixa le sol et se tint coi. L'horreur du récit laissait remonter en lui ce que racontait la religieuse qui enseignait à l'école de rang sur la cruauté innée des Sauvages. Il s'abstint de proférer le moindre commentaire à ce sujet, certain que Shaor'i donnerait une juste explication.

Ce qu'elle fit en réprimant ses tremblements.

— S'ils avaient agi ainsi, c'est qu'une très puissante chamane haudenosaunee avait prédit qu'un terrible fléau s'abattrait dans moins de vingt lunes sur toutes les nations, apporté par une tribu venue de loin, de très loin à l'est. Les Haudenosaunee avaient cru qu'il s'agissait des Micmacs... Or, la chamane avait plutôt prédit l'arrivée des Blancs. Mais ça, tous l'ignoraient à ce moment-là. Dans la caverne de ce qu'on surnomma bien vite l'île au Massacre, les âmes des innocents refusèrent de passer dans l'outremonde.

— Pis toé, P'tite, t'es devenue Danseuse en faisant ton apprentissage dans c'te caverne-là, c'est ça ?

Stupéfaite, Shaor'i se tourna vers Baptiste et hocha silencieusement la tête.

— L'vieux chafouin, Otjiera, m'avait déjà dit que ça s'passait de même pour les Exécutrices, reprit Baptiste. Vous portez en vous la colère pis l'injustice des fantômes de l'île au Massacre, c'est ça ?

Sans se donner la peine de répondre, Shaor'i poursuivit :

— Les morts de l'île hurlaient leur rage et leur haine, exigeaient réparation pour l'injustice commise. Mais les Haudenosaunee étaient nombreux et mieux armés que les Micmacs. C'est alors que certains se souvinrent de Kabir Kouba et voulurent le lancer à l'assaut des Haudenosaunee. Sauf que même s'il dormait depuis des siècles, il n'avait jamais cessé de grandir. On dit qu'il faisait plus de trente verges.

Faustin ouvrit des yeux grands comme des soucoupes. Trente verges : quatre-vingt-dix pieds ! Ça représentait tout près de la moitié d'un arpent ! Une bête de cette taille était inconcevable, et en ajoutant le diamètre conséquent, et la cuirasse du poisson, le monstre qui en résultait… c'était plus long qu'une grange !

— Le Danseur qui éveilla Kabir Kouba n'avait pas la puissance des anciens chamanes. Il perdit le contrôle de la bête. Ce fut une époque terrible. Les villages vivant de la pêche le craignaient et se trouvèrent rapidement en état de famine.

Constatant que Shaor'i hésitait, Baptiste enchaîna :

— Quand les Blancs sont arrivés, y z'ont dû faire avec c'te monstre qui s'en prenait aux bateaux. Paraît même que Samuel de Champlain en parle dans son journal. Pis les théurgistes d'avant l'Collège, ceux qui vivaient sur l'île d'Orléans avant l'changement de

Régime, bin y z'ont essayé d'imposer leur volonté au monstre, de l'contrôler…

— Rien à faire, reprit l'Indienne. Tout au plus certains Danseurs parvenaient à le circonscrire tantôt à un lac, tantôt à un autre. Il fallait l'inciter à migrer souvent pour éviter qu'il ne vide un endroit de tous ses poissons.

— Un bout d'temps, y'était dans l'lac Champlain, après ça y'a été dans l'lac Memphrémagog…

— Un peu avant le changement de Régime, un jeune Danseur de la Rivière-Ouelle est enfin parvenu à le maîtriser. Élevé dans un village de pêcheurs, il avait été sauvé de la noyade par des marsouins et avait appris à les comprendre. Devenu Danseur, il avait acquis la faculté de se transformer pour être l'un d'eux. Sa sensibilité à la faune du fleuve était sans précédent. Âgé d'à peine seize ans, il s'est présenté face à Kabir Kouba et lui a imposé sa volonté. Ramenée à Pohénégamook, la bête fut rendormie.

Un déclic se fit dans la tête de Faustin.

— Ce garçon, c'était…

— Plaçoa, oui.

— Un peu avant la révolte des Patriotes, continua Baptiste, monseigneur Lartigue, l'maître du Collège, a pensé qu'les théurgistes pourraient asseoir leur puissance en se servant d'Kabir Kouba. Y'a d'mandé à voir Plaçoa, qu'était rendu pas mal vieux. Y vivait chez les Attikamekw pis y formait sa successeure, une Mohawk.

— Nadjaw, cracha Shaor'i avec mépris.

— En échange du contrôle d'Kabir Kouba, Lartigue avait proposé à Plaçoa de l'argent, du pouvoir, d'la sécurité pour les Indiens. Mais l'bonhomme était p'tête vieux, y'était pas stupide pour autant. Y'a refusé. Pis c'est là qu'Lartigue s'est arrangé pour le faire pendre aux Trois-Rivières.

Faustin se tapa la cuisse, comprenant soudain :

— C'est dans ce but que la Siffleuse m'a manipulé pour me le faire libérer. Pour que l'Étranger puisse contrôler Kabir Kouba.

— La bête a dormi pendant quatre-vingts ans, dit Shaor'i. Elle a continué de croître. Et maintenant, l'Étranger l'a réveillée.

— Et c'est pour ça que Nadjaw m'a libéré, comprit Faustin. Elle ne peut donc pas avoir continué à servir l'Étranger…

— Elle s'est livrée à moi et m'a demandé de l'exécuter, ce que j'ai refusé. Il était hors de question que je lui offre une mort aussi sereine et, de toute façon, je devais savoir où tu étais. Je l'ai donc assommée du pommeau de ma lame pour l'interroger plus tard. D'ailleurs, elle avait ça pour toi.

La jeune femme lança un rouleau de jute à Faustin, qui l'attrapa au vol avant de s'accroupir par terre pour le dérouler.

Deux lames étaient au centre du rouleau.

— Mon sabre ! s'exclama le jeune homme, soulagé de retrouver l'arme avec laquelle il avait appris à se battre.

— Et l'autre lame, qu'est-ce que c'est ? demanda Shaor'i.

Faustin prit entre ses mains une lame très fine, longue d'un pied, disposant à sa base d'une sorte de logement en forme d'anneau.

— C'est une pointe à fusil, ça…

Sur l'épaule de Baptiste, Ti-Jean se pencha en avant pour que le colosse puisse voir et il confirma :

— Oui-da. C'est bin une baïonnette.

Le jeune homme étrécit les yeux pour focaliser son outrevision. La fine lame se mit à luire d'une faible aura noire.

— Est-ce que ça va s'adapter au canon d'un fusil de chasse ?

— On déformera l'anneau s'y faut. Ça aidera face aux jacks.

Faustin resta un moment songeur, la baïonnette dans les mains. En lui conférant une forme de renard, Nadjaw lui avait permis de fuir la Grande Maison et d'échapper à l'Étranger. Puis elle s'était livrée elle-même à Shaor'i. Les mots de l'Exécutrice déchue lui revinrent en tête : « *Je refuse de me consacrer à la folie de l'Étranger… C'est mon époux que j'ai suivi. Et Louis-Olivier ne comptait pas vraiment en venir à ça, lui non plus.* »

— Où est Nadjaw, maintenant ? demanda Faustin.

— Elle est morte, déclara Shaor'i.

Faustin ne sut quoi répondre et la jeune femme précisa :

— Pas de ma main. De la sienne. Elle a passé quelques semaines à m'aider à te retrouver, m'a révélé ce qu'elle savait au sujet des plans du Stigma Diaboli, m'a même enseigné la technique du *sekauieb*, le coup-qui-rend-muet… puis, comme elle craignait d'attirer vers nous le Stigma Diaboli, je lui ai finalement donné l'autorisation de procéder au suicide rituel.

— J'aimerais lui parler quand même, déclara Faustin.

Shaor'i hocha silencieusement la tête, se leva et lui enjoignit d'un geste de la suivre.

◆

Après s'être assurée que le repas les attendrait, la jeune femme emmena Faustin plus loin dans la forêt.

Des bruits attirèrent l'attention de la jeune femme, qui s'accroupit vivement dans les buissons, tirant Faustin auprès d'elle.

— Ici, nous ne sommes pas loin d'un sentier de chasse fréquenté, déclara Shaor'i. Les *maymaygwashi* l'ignoraient en installant leur camp temporaire, mais celui-ci est si bien caché, et le peuple des rivières est si discret, qu'aucun incident n'aura été à déplorer de l'été.

Faustin ne tarda pas à découvrir la source du boucan : deux trappeurs indiens, même si seuls leur teint mat et leurs cheveux aile-de-corbeau permettaient de les identifier comme tels. Pantalons de toiles, chemises carreautées, bottes des Hauts et fusils au dos, ils marchaient dans les bois en produisant autant de bruit qu'un crieur public, parlant le français grêlé d'anglais des ouvrageux de la Gatineau.

— *Anyway*, Joseph-Arthur, disait le plus vieux des deux, l'*foreman* pourra toujours essayer un *bargain*, avec les *skins* que j'ai pognés, j'vas t'faire une bonne tôle…

— T'as pas eu d'trouble, sur un *squat* de Saint-Étienne ? demanda l'autre.

— *Nevermind*… j'avais posé une *witch stone* au bout d'la *trail* où j'avais mis mes *traps*. Les Blancs faisaient un *bypass* pis j'tais *fair* pour un boutte…

— Pis pourquoi qu't'es pas resté là ? Avec un *hex* de même…

— J'ai *spotté* devant ma *magic* une patte de loup roulée dans une peau d'serpent. Un Blanc qu'avait engagé un meilleur *spellcaster* que moi.

L'autre siffla.

— Y'a pas fait *cheap*. *So,* tu *move* de terrain ?

— *As you said*. Rien de bin intéressant dans c'boutte-ci, par exemple. J'pense à traverser la rivière pis aller su' l'autre rive. Mon beau-frère aurait un *spot*, qui dit.

— *Good, good*…

Les deux chasseurs s'éloignèrent en poursuivant leur discussion. L'ouïe affinée de Faustin pouvait entendre

détaler perdrix et lièvres sur leur passage. Intrigué, le jeune homme se tourna vers Shaor'i.

— C'est quoi, cette histoire de « pierre de sorcière » et de patte de loup ?

L'Indienne ne répondit pas tout de suite et Faustin perçut la colère et le chagrin qui émanaient de son silence. Elle finit par lui répondre, les traits durs et une lueur de rage dans le regard :

— *Awan*… Des superstitions. Des stupidités. Pas plus de magie là-dedans que dans les pots de chambre d'une auberge. Ces idioties, c'est tout ce qui leur reste comme souvenir de ce que fut la grandeur du Cercle des Danseurs. *Kikmanaq kisiku'k pemkaqiejik, aqq ta'n wla koqoey nenmi'tij.* Et c'est comme ça partout, chez toutes les nations, dans tous les villages : vêtements et armes des Blancs, langue des ancêtres oubliée, un respect de la nature tout relatif…

Shaor'i se releva d'un bond et le tira par l'épaule.

— Viens. Nous ne sommes plus très loin.

Sans mot dire, Faustin s'empressa de la suivre. La forêt devint lentement plus dense, les arbres plus massifs. Surpris alors qu'ils broutaient, une biche et son faon dressèrent la tête quand ils virent passer les deux humains et détalèrent aussitôt.

Certain qu'elle se murerait dans le silence jusqu'à ce qu'ils soient arrivés, Faustin s'étonna d'entendre Shaor'i reprendre le fil de la discussion interrompue.

— Cette perte de la mémoire collective, Nadjaw n'a jamais pu la tolérer, m'a un jour raconté Otjiera. Elle n'acceptait pas de voir les siens adopter le mode de vie des Blancs jusqu'à oublier qui ils étaient. Puis, un jour, elle a rencontré ce sorcier roux qui craignait pour la disparition de sa langue, de sa culture et de sa magie face à l'envahisseur anglais. Et comme lui, elle croyait que la fin justifiait les moyens. Bref… nous approchons.

Shaor'i se faufila à travers l'épais mur d'aiguilles d'un bouquet d'épinettes. De peine et de misère, Faustin la suivit, puis découvrit une minuscule clairière.

— J'ai tenté de m'en acquitter de mon mieux, expliqua la jeune femme, mais les rites funéraires traditionnels mohawks sont assez complexes. J'ai prononcé les prières et les chants pour la guider vers le monde solaire et j'ai brûlé les essences animales qu'il fallait, mais je crains que sa première âme soit tout aussi perdue que sa seconde.

— Seconde âme ? releva Faustin.

— Pour les Mohawks, il y a deux âmes : celle qui est libre de quitter le corps par les rêves, les délires ou la magie, et celle qui est attachée au corps et le fait fonctionner. La seconde reste liée à la terre après la mort : c'est celle-là que tu contactes par spiritisme. Nadjaw en avait aussi une troisième, une âme de lynx, qui fut rendue à la Terre-Mère après sa mort.

Faustin jeta un coup d'œil à la guerrière, essayant de deviner sur son visage impassible si elle ajoutait foi à ces croyances, ou même si elle avait quelque forme de croyance que ce soit. Savoir que l'esprit survivait au corps n'était pas la garantie d'un au-delà merveilleux tel que le dépeignaient les chrétiens. En réalité – son oncle lui avait déjà expliqué cela voilà fort longtemps –, la survie de l'esprit s'accordait avec le principe de Lavoisier : l'énergie mentale ne pouvait tout simplement pas « se perdre », elle devait se transformer en autre chose.

— C'est sous cette pierre, annonça l'Indienne, coupant court aux réflexions métaphysiques du jeune homme.

La pierre en question était si anodine que rien ne permettait de la distinguer des autres.

— Tu sauras revenir au camp ? demanda Shaor'i.

— Bien sûr, mais… je croyais que tu resterais ?

— Je préfère ne pas.

Sans ajouter un mot, l'Indienne adopta sa forme de rapace et s'envola à tire-d'aile.

Seul dans la clairière, Faustin prit le temps de se recueillir. Par marque de respect, à défaut de le faire par croyance, il aurait récité un *De profundis* sur la sépulture, mais une prière chrétienne sur une tombe traditionnelle mohawk lui sembla inconvenant.

Son esprit de spirite, ouvert aux contacts avec les défunts, sentit bientôt une présence familière. Faustin fouilla son sac et sortit un livre, *Discours & Histoires des Spectres, Visions & Apparitions des Esprits*, de Pierre Le Loyer. François l'avait incité à le prendre dans le manoir Poulin. Aussitôt, Faustin chassa le souvenir pour ne pas penser à son frère adoptif.

Sans hâte, il feuilleta l'ouvrage relié de cuir. Jusqu'alors, il n'avait contacté les défunts que grâce au Calice des Moires ; privé de cet artefact, il devrait employer une méthode plus traditionnelle.

Quand il eut trouvé une procédure qui semblait convenir, Faustin sortit une craie grasse de sa poche et traça minutieusement sur la pierre le diagramme illustré dans l'ouvrage de Le Loyer. La formule était cachée dans le texte, mais il s'agissait d'un code classique chez les arcanistes et Faustin ne prit que quelques minutes pour remplacer les lettres d'une phrase en français afin d'obtenir l'incantation.

Après un autre instant de recueillement, il incanta :

— *Ad-est kareza, sürdanresh-zonrik aniir, margesht al-fontir.*

Le jeune homme ferma les yeux. La sensation habituelle se manifesta aussitôt : l'impression d'un hameçon se fichant dans sa nuque et d'un fil se dévidant. Des échos de pensée résonnèrent d'abord en discordance,

puis s'harmonisèrent. De partout et de nulle part, des fragments de souvenirs se rassemblèrent, s'assemblèrent, s'éveillèrent.

Appelé de l'outremonde, l'esprit – ou l'âme – de Nadjaw revint pour se manifester à Faustin.

« *Ainsi, vous avez recouvré votre apparence humaine, Faustin Lamare.* »

Faustin n'aima guère le contact de cet esprit. Quelle qu'en fût la raison, Nadjaw ne reposait pas en paix.

« *Je voulais vous remercier, Nadjaw. Du fond du cœur, merci de m'avoir fait évader.* »

« *Cela n'a pas suffi à me racheter.* »

Comme sous des notes très graves, la psyché de Faustin vibra sourdement. Remords et regrets gangrenaient cette âme comme la rouille attaquant le fer.

« *Deviez-vous pour cela mettre fin à vos jours ?* »

L'esprit de l'Exécutrice défunte sembla se densifier dans l'équivalent mental d'un repli sur soi.

« *Vous pouvez voir cela comme de la lâcheté face aux conséquences de mes actes. Ou comme le résultat d'une amère désillusion. Ou encore un excès de regrets. Peut-être les trois ensemble.* »

Le désarroi de la guerrière était terriblement lourd. Touché, Faustin demanda :

« *Avez-vous… un message pour votre époux ?* »

« *Il cherchera à vous capturer de nouveau, vous savez ?* »

« *Dans ce cas, je le reverrai et je pourrai lui transmettre vos dernières pensées.* »

L'âme de Nadjaw émit le pendant spirituel d'un rire amer.

« *C'est noble de votre part.* »

« *Juste retour des choses, Nadjaw.* »

L'Indienne défunte prit un moment pour réfléchir et déclara :

« *Dites-lui de fuir l'Étranger pendant qu'il le peut encore. Qu'il retourne à Anticosti auprès de ses enfants.* »

« *Vous avez des enfants ?* » s'étonna Faustin.

« *Louis-Olivier en a d'un premier mariage. Ils n'ont pas hérité de l'outrevision, leur mère ne l'avait pas.* »

« *Grand bien pour eux, l'Étranger ne s'en préoccupera pas.* »

« *En effet. Dites-lui aussi… que c'est rongé par les remords que j'ai mis fin à mes jours… et qu'on m'a donné une sépulture traditionnelle, telle que je l'avais toujours espérée.* »

« *Je lui dirai, Nadjaw.* »

« *Je n'ai pas pu récupérer votre Calice avant de fuir la Grande Maison.* »

« *Je suppose que la Siffleuse en dispose, maintenant ?* »

« *Non. La Siffleuse ne l'utilisera plus – l'artefact s'est avéré trop puissant pour elle lorsqu'elle a contacté votre oncle. L'Étranger l'a fait envoyer à Québec, chez les Sewell. Vous en aurez besoin pour solliciter l'aide de la Dame Blanche.* »

Faustin hocha la tête : elle lui avait déjà parlé de cela, quand elle avait orchestré son évasion de la Grande Maison.

« *Soit.* »

« *Je ne puis vous aider davantage, Faustin.* »

« *C'est déjà beaucoup, Nadjaw.* »

« *Kateri. Mon nom de naissance était Kateri.* »

« *Merci encore, Kateri.* »

Comme une chandelle qui s'éteint, la conscience de Nadjaw disparut subitement. En son for intérieur, Faustin espéra avoir apporté un peu de réconfort à cette âme troublée.

Seul parmi les arbres, il chercha en lui un silence particulier, celui qui exprime la gratitude mieux que les mots.

Puis, sans s'attarder davantage, il s'en retourna vers le campement du peuple des rivières.

◆

Comme promis, le repas l'attendait à son retour.

Les perchaudes avaient été débarrassées de leurs écailles et grillées sur le feu. Elles reposaient sur une pierre plate, non loin d'un bol d'écorce de bouleau rempli de queues d'écrevisses. Une autre pierre était chargée de languettes de viande blanche qu'il fallut un moment à Faustin pour identifier : des pattes de grenouilles. Une grosse pile de moules crues était posée sur des feuilles de fougères avec quelques œufs d'oiseaux des marais, cuits durs.

Les *maymaygwashi*, s'installant autour du repas, pigèrent joyeusement dans les plats, bouchée par bouchée. Shaor'i, Baptiste et Ti-Jean se joignirent à eux, tout comme Faustin. Au début, il ne mangea que du poisson – les queues d'écrevisses l'avaient tenté, mais il n'avait pas été assez rapide pour en prendre avant que le bol n'ait été vidé. L'odeur des pattes de grenouilles vint chatouiller ses narines et il s'avança pour flairer à petits coups cette viande étrange. Un souvenir le saisit comme un éclair, celui d'un museau de renard – *son* museau – fouaillant la vase pour déterrer et dévorer un crapaud vif.

Haussant les épaules, Faustin tendit la main vers l'une des pattes cuites. Le goût le surprit, très proche de celui de la volaille de basse-cour.

Shaor'i, Baptiste et Ti-Jean mangèrent de tout : le temps passé chez le peuple des rivières devait avoir fait fondre leurs scrupules, à supposer qu'ils en aient eu.

Le repas englouti, les *maymaygwashi* s'amusèrent autour du feu à une sorte de danse composée d'un

mélange de roulades, de culbutes et d'ondulations sur le sol. La chorégraphie ne dura pas longtemps et, sitôt que le plus jeune des *maymaygwashi* eut étouffé un bâillement, le peuple des rivières se dirigea vers le plus grand de ces abris de bois qui ressemblaient tant à des huttes de castor.

Quand Faustin pénétra à l'intérieur, il vit que le sol était recouvert d'une masse de filaments souples et blancs. Il reconnut là l'espèce de soie contenue dans les grosses cosses des plantes que Madeleine appelait « petit cochon », et son oncle, *asclepias* : un duvet doux dont les propriétés hydrofuges semblaient fortement convenir aux *maymaygwashi*.

Le nid faisait six verges de diamètre et Faustin, gêné, prit soin de s'allonger du côté opposé à celui de Shaor'i ; néanmoins, il ne dormit pas isolé pour autant, le peuple des rivières ne semblant pas connaître la notion de pudeur. Bien vite, il se retrouva avec un homme-loutre blotti contre son flanc gauche alors que l'enfant *maymaygwashi* lui avait carrément grimpé sur le ventre pour s'y rouler en boule.

La couche s'avéra toutefois confortable et, une fois le premier malaise passé, Faustin admit que cette proximité chaleureuse était bien réconfortante. Posant distraitement la main sur le petit *maymaygwashi* qu'il caressa comme un chat, il laissa vagabonder son esprit, qui se fixa sur une angoissante préoccupation.

François.

Les rebondissements de la journée l'avaient empêché de repenser à son frère adoptif mais, maintenant qu'il était seul avec ses pensées, la terrible réalité lui revenait en tête. L'un des derniers souvenirs qui lui restait avant qu'il ne fût transformé en renard, trois mois auparavant, était la possession du corps de François par l'esprit de son ancêtre, Jean-Pierre Lavallée. Le

puissant sorcier de l'île d'Orléans s'était lancé à l'assaut de Faustin et de ses compagnons et il s'en était fallu de peu pour qu'ils fussent tués.

Faustin soupira d'exaspération. Trois mois gâchés ! Trois mois à errer sous forme de renard pendant que Lavallée prenait davantage d'ascendance sur le corps de François.

Contre lui, Faustin sentit le *maymaygwashi* se mettre à ronronner paisiblement. Ronflement ou tentative de réconfort ? Peu importait, au fond : la fatigue d'une lourde journée eut bientôt raison de Faustin.

◆

C'était une vaste église de maçonnerie, beaucoup plus imposante que la plupart des églises de village. Les vitraux du transept laissaient filtrer une lumière multicolore qui inondait le maître-autel devant lequel se tenait un prêtre, dos à lui.

Faustin reconnut la silhouette : des épaules carrées, des cheveux blond paille, une haute taille.

François.

Le vicaire se retourna, lui fit signe d'approcher. Faustin fit deux pas dans sa direction puis s'arrêta en voyant son frère tomber à genoux, se prendre la tête à deux mains et hurler un mot :

— Bakaak !

Puis des flammes se mirent à jaillir du corps de François, qui se tordit de douleur.

Faustin hurla à son tour.

◆

Faustin s'éveilla en sursaut mais fut incapable de se redresser. Un des *maymaygwashi* adulte dormait

carrément en travers de sa poitrine, un autre avait pris sa jambe droite comme oreiller, un autre encore était venu rejoindre l'enfant-loutre qui ronflait sur le ventre de Faustin.

Qu'était ce rêve? Une allégorie de ses frayeurs?

Plusieurs fois, le jeune homme tenta de se remémorer la scène onirique de plus en plus insaisissable. Tout semblait pourtant si réel, sur le coup.

La proximité des *maymaygwashi* continua de l'apaiser. Il retrouva un souffle et un rythme cardiaque normaux, et le souvenir de son cauchemar s'estompa tout doucement. Comme plus tôt, les *maymaygwashi* émirent une sorte de ronronnement; une lourde torpeur se saisit alors de Faustin et le jeune homme retomba bientôt dans l'oubli du sommeil.

CHAPITRE 26

La traversée des marais

Quand il s'éveilla, tard en matinée, une réunion animée se déroulait autour du feu du peuple des rivières.

Deux nouveaux *maymaygwashi* étaient arrivés durant la nuit. Dans leur langage composé de sifflements modulés, ils débattaient en appuyant leurs paroles de grands gestes. Shaor'i participait aux discussions, le plus jeune des *maymaygwashi* lui traçant des *komkwej-wika'sikl* pour traduire les propos de ses aînés avant que l'Indienne ne réponde de la même façon pour être lue à haute voix dans la langue du peuple des rivières.

Quand la discussion s'acheva, près d'une heure plus tard, Shaor'i vint rejoindre ses trois compagnons, l'air appréhensif.

— Les sentinelles ont repéré Celle-qui-n'est-pas-un-chat non loin d'ici.

— La Siffleuse ? demanda Faustin.

— Précisément. Elle et son groupe de jeunes femmes semblent s'activer dans l'anse de Yamachiche, par-delà le marais. De ce que le *maymaygwashi* qui comprend notre langue a entendu, l'esprit de Plaçoa serait devenu plus rétif depuis hier – peut-être le défunt a-t-il perçu ton retour.

— C'est quoi l'rapport avec l'anse de Yamachiche ? demanda Baptiste.

L'Indienne haussa les épaules en écartant les bras, montrant qu'elle n'en savait rien.

— Qu'importe, je dois le libérer, déclara Faustin. C'est ma faute s'il est maintenant sous l'emprise du Stigma Diaboli, et avec lui ils peuvent contrôler Kabir Kouba.

— C'est aussi ce que je pense, dit Shaor'i. D'ailleurs, les *maymaygwashi* ont décidé de repartir, maintenant que nous t'avons retrouvé. Ils vont descendre le fleuve et traquer le monstre marin. Nous les rejoindrons à l'Isle-aux-Grues.

— En face de Montmagny ? Pourquoi là ?

— Parce que c'est là qu'y'ont rencontré l'père Masse, répondit Baptiste. Pis c'est là qu'on va aller, drette après avoir réglé son compte à la Siffleuse.

— Les *maymaygwashi* disent qu'on ne pourra pas passer par les terres, que des wendigos sont embusqués un peu partout. Ils nous suggèrent de couper par le grand marais.

Baptiste fronça les sourcils.

— Pour sûr que c'est facile pour eux autres, mais à nous, ça va prendre une embarcation.

— Ils disent qu'il y a un camp de trappeurs non loin où tu pourrais sans doute acheter un canot ou emprunter des outils pour fabriquer un radeau. Pendant ce temps-là, je survolerai le marais pour trouver la meilleure route à suivre.

— Correct.

Faustin hocha la tête et serra les poings.

La Siffleuse. La sorcière Poulin, Duchesse des Mensonges, la Voyante des Trois-Rivières qui avait vendu les Forges au Diable. Après ce qu'elle lui avait fait, Faustin avait une affaire personnelle à régler avec elle.

◆

Les adieux et les remerciements furent brefs. Shaor'i traça quelques symboles pour exprimer sa gratitude, chacun effleura les mains des compagnons, puis les *maymaygwashi* partirent pour le Saint-Maurice alors que Faustin et ses amis prenaient la route du marais.

Shaor'i ne fut pas longue à s'envoler, ayant beaucoup de terrain à scruter en peu de temps. Quant à Baptiste et à Faustin, ils passèrent par les terres et débouchèrent bientôt sur le sentier indiqué par le peuple des rivières.

Le parfum des mélèzes saturait l'air, auquel se mêlait une odeur de vase que Faustin flaira très tôt. Il ne fallut qu'une demi-heure pour arriver aux abords du marais, qui fit à Faustin l'impression d'une mer de boue.

Le pied-à-terre des trappeurs était tout proche.

C'était un camp comme il y en avait des centaines à travers les forêts du Bas-Canada, une baraque de rondins dont les interstices avaient méticuleusement été bouchés par un mélange de bran de scie et d'argile. Elle avait un plafond bas sur lequel les intempéries avaient laissé leur marque.

Ils s'approchaient quand la vue de la porte figea les deux hommes : elle avait été défoncée et littéralement réduite en fins éclats de bois.

Avec prudence, Baptiste et Faustin reprirent leur avancée vers le camp. Faustin longea le mur avant et, à proximité du seuil, inspira par petits coups : les odeurs de bois sec dominaient celles des fientes, des crottes d'écureuils et des bouts de fer rouillés. Le jeune homme glissa le canon de son fusil vers l'intérieur.

Pendant ce temps, Ti-Jean sauta de l'épaule du bûcheron, rampa à quatre pattes puis passa la tête dans l'ouverture.

— Y a personne, déclara Baptiste. On peut y aller.

Le *mah oumet* regagna en trois bonds sa place auprès du colosse et les deux hommes entrèrent.

L'endroit était effectivement désert. Les couches de sapinage n'avaient pas été changées depuis une éternité. Ayant viré à l'orangé, leurs épines s'amoncelaient sur le sol. Au centre se trouvait une table de planches mal équarries autour de laquelle on avait disposé des bûches en guise de tabourets.

Trois blocs de pierre servaient d'âtre. Un trou était aménagé dans le toit pour laisser sortir la fumée.

— C'est inoccupé depuis très longtemps, constata Faustin pour la forme en repassant son arme à son épaule.

— Pas clair, quand même, marmonna Baptiste.

Il se tourna et Ti-Jean scruta pour lui un mur où des clous avaient été plantés afin d'y suspendre haches, hachettes, godendards, herminettes, varlopes, ébranchoirs et équarrissoirs.

Sur la table s'empilaient des peaux de castor et de rat musqué par centaines.

Faustin siffla.

— Il y en a pour un bon montant, hein ?

— Ouin. Des trappeurs qui partent en laissant leurs outils à rouiller pis leurs peaux à moisir, ça m'dit rien d'bon. Déjà qu'la porte défoncée en dit long.

— Ça me rappelle l'invasion de ton pied-à-terre, l'hiver dernier…

— Oui-da. En tout cas, on va pouvoir régler un p'tit détail. Passe-moé ton fusil pis ta baïonnette.

Faustin obtempéra pendant que Baptiste se saisissait d'une paire de pinces. Le bûcheron fit jouer l'outil

cinq ou six fois et, voyant que la rouille ne l'avait pas trop endommagé, s'en servit pour serrer la bague de la baïonnette au canon du fusil de Faustin.

— Faudra qu'tu soyes prudent : ça peut être traître, une lame de même, pis on pourra pas l'enlever pis la r'mettre à tout bout d'champ. Tu rouleras un carré de cuir autour, pis tu l'feras tenir avec d'la ficelle…

Un relent de musc chatouilla désagréablement les narines de Faustin. D'instinct, il leva la tête, son ouïe captant d'infimes effleurements sur le toit.

Intimant d'un geste à Baptiste de se taire, le jeune homme flaira avec plus d'attention. Le relent fauve se dirigeait vers l'ouverture de la cabane.

En silence, Faustin indiqua le toit du doigt, puis la porte, avant de se tourner lentement vers le seuil. Il eut le temps de voir un éclair de fourrure roussâtre tomber au sol et une longue silhouette effilée se tourner vers la porte.

Une sorte de belette plus grosse qu'un couguar.

La hère, ou bête à grand'queue.

Sifflant avec irritation, la créature avança lentement. Elle braqua sur les deux hommes ses petits yeux sombres en plissant légèrement les paupières puis émit une sorte de chuintement. Sa queue battit furieusement l'air avant de s'immobiliser quand l'animal se ramassa sur lui-même pour bondir.

Baptiste attira son attention en poussant un grand cri. La bête sauta d'un coup jusqu'à l'autre bout du camp, évitant de justesse la hachette que le bûcheron avait jetée dans sa direction. Elle cracha comme un chat quand l'outil se planta dans le mur à quelques pouces d'elle et retroussa ses babines pour dévoiler une série de petites dents aiguës.

Sans perdre une seconde, Faustin s'agenouilla, la tint en joue et tira. Atteinte à la cuisse, la créature glapit

de rage. En deux sauts, elle se précipita sur Faustin, qui tenta en vain d'empaler l'animal sur sa baïonnette. Roulant sur lui-même à la dernière seconde, il échappa *in extremis* aux griffes acérées qui laboureèrent le plancher en y laissant de profondes rainures.

Baptiste revint à la charge, sa hache dans la main droite et un grand couteau à écorcer dans la gauche. La hère avait déjà fait volte-face avec agilité, ses yeux luisant d'une ruse sournoise alors qu'elle semblait jauger son adversaire.

Pendant ce temps, Faustin rejeta son fusil pour dégainer son sabre, cherchant le bon angle pour assaillir la bête sans se mettre à portée de griffes.

Le colosse fit mine de frapper de la hache et profita de sa feinte pour projeter d'un coup de pied l'une des bûches servant de tabouret. La hère, frappée dans les côtes par le projectile imprévu, roula sur elle-même avant de bondir comme une flèche sur son ennemi.

Faustin se jeta en avant et réussit à lui entailler le flanc de sa lame.

Avec une agilité qui dépassait l'entendement, la hère parvint à se retourner à temps pour se jeter sur le jeune homme.

Faustin et la bête se heurtèrent de plein fouet et chutèrent sur le sol. La souffrance arracha un hurlement à Faustin quand les crocs de la hère se plantèrent dans son épaule et que ses griffes antérieures lui lacérèrent l'abdomen.

— Faustin !

Avec un hurlement tonitruant, Baptiste fonça sur la bête à grand'queue en portant avec sa hache un fort coup horizontal destiné à broyer le thorax de la créature. La hère sauta hors de portée en grondant.

— Correct, garçon ?

— Correct.

Faustin grimaça en s'agenouillant alors que Baptiste se dressait déjà pour interposer son corps immense entre le jeune homme et la bête.

Hache et couteau brandis, le colosse avança de nouveau vers la hère, posant un pied après l'autre. La créature lui tint tête en soufflant, de l'écume mêlée de sang coulant de sa gueule. Elle se dressa doucement, évaluant peut-être si elle était trop amochée pour poursuivre l'affrontement.

En retrait, Faustin tâtait ses plaies. La morsure était superficielle, les dents ayant glissé sur les os de l'épaule, ratant la gorge de peu. Les blessures au ventre l'élançaient douloureusement, mais la chair n'avait pas été percée.

Devant lui, Baptiste défiait la bête à grand'queue. Pas à pas, il réduisait l'écart qui les séparait. La créature blessée restait adossée au mur, sa queue battant de gauche à droite.

Puis le bûcheron posa le pied sur le fusil de Faustin.

Malgré toute sa ruse animale, la bête ne put comprendre l'implication de ce geste, aussi ne réagit-elle pas. Faustin en profita pour sortir lentement sa poudre et ses balles.

Baptiste fit glisser l'arme à feu en direction de Faustin et, poussant un grand cri, se jeta sur l'adversaire.

L'animal cracha et sauta à la gorge de l'humain. Sa gueule mordit le manche de la hache que Baptiste levait pour se protéger.

Il laissa tomber l'arme que la hère refusait de lâcher et recula vers le mur. La bête se ramassa de nouveau sur elle-même, prête à bondir.

Faustin bourrait à la hâte son fusil, renversant la moitié de la poudre. Il glissa une balle dans le canon et fit claquer le chien alors que la créature sautait vers le colosse.

L'énorme poing de Baptiste, percutant la tête de l'animal, brisa son élan. Faustin pressa la gâchette et le coup de feu retentit juste comme la hère tombait.

Le crâne de la bête à grand'queue éclata à l'impact.

Baptiste se laissa choir sur un tabouret, reprenant son souffle, une main sur le cœur. Faustin marcha jusqu'à lui, s'assoyant lui aussi sur une bûche.

— Montre… montre-moé ça, souffla Baptiste entre deux inspirations laborieuses.

Faustin détacha sa chemise réduite en lambeaux. Le bûcheron grimaça lorsqu'il vit à travers les yeux de son *mah oumet* les chairs entaillées.

— T'auras un paquet de cicatrices, garçon. Faudra d'mander à la P'tite pour pas qu'ça s'infecte. Mais les boyaux sont *clair*, j'ai l'impression.

— Je pense aussi, marmonna Faustin en s'efforçant d'endurer la douleur.

— Inquiète-toé pas. C'est l'métier qui rentre.

— À grands coups de griffes, si tu veux mon avis.

Le bûcheron tourna vers lui son visage aux orbites creuses et éclata d'un grand rire franc.

— Comme tu dis! Mais qu'est-cé qu'tu veux : quand t'as ça din'tripes…

Faustin laissa échapper un rire qu'il étouffa aussitôt, la douleur le reprenant dans le bas du ventre.

— La P'tite va arriver dans pas long.

— Je vais l'appeler… dit Faustin fermant les yeux pour mieux percevoir le lien qui l'unissait à Shaor'i. Quand il s'y fut arrimé, il banda sa volonté et émit :

« *Shaor'i, je suis blessé…* »

La réaction de la jeune femme fut instantanée :

« *À quel point ?* »

« *C'est superficiel mais douloureux. Baptiste et moi sommes dans un camp de bois rond. Nous avons été attaqués par une bête à grand'queue.* »

« *J'arrive* », répondit l'Indienne alors qu'une inquiétude mêlée d'incrédulité envahissait son esprit.

— Elle arrive, annonça Faustin à Baptiste, avant de voir que le bûcheron n'avait plus son *mah oumet* sur l'épaule.

Ti-Jean avait marché jusqu'au cadavre de la hère. Avec de longues plaintes tristes, il passait une main dans le pelage du monstre, puis il essuya une larme qui coulait de ses yeux roses.

— Qu'est-ce qui lui prend? demanda Faustin.

Privé de son lutin adocté, Baptiste ne tourna pas la tête vers Faustin pour lui répondre. Immobile, il murmura :

— La bête est morte. C'était elle ou nous autres, fallait l'faire. Mais c'tait une des dernières, peut-être même la dernière. Pis ça lui rappelle…

— … le sort des siens, bien entendu.

Faustin se souvenait parfaitement de ce qui attendait le petit peuple des cavernes : privées des grands pins qu'abattaient les hommes, leurs femelles ne tombaient plus en rut et leur nombre déclinait.

La vue des outils de bûcheronnage lui sembla soudainement intolérable et, malgré la douleur, Faustin marcha jusqu'à l'extérieur pour attendre Shaor'i.

◆

Le sortilège curatif de Shaor'i fit des merveilles. La douleur disparut presque aussitôt et l'Indienne confirma que les intestins de Faustin n'avaient pas été touchés.

Dès lors, elle refusa de s'éloigner et, sous sa forme de harfang, elle s'installa sur le toit du campement pour surveiller les environs.

Après avoir testé le tranchant du godendard rouillé, Baptiste le jugea satisfaisant et le sortit du camp

abandonné. Il avisa un mélèze aux épines jaunies et expliqua à Faustin comment tenir la cadence de coupe. Les dents de fer entamèrent vite le bois et l'arbre ne tarda pas à tomber à l'endroit précis où le bûcheron l'avait prévu. Après qu'ils eurent répété la manœuvre avec un autre arbre de pareil diamètre, Faustin entreprit d'écorcer les troncs pendant que Baptiste, à la hache, les débitait en tiers. Le colosse semblait prendre un réel plaisir à sa tâche et chantait joyeusement, une chose qu'il n'avait presque plus faite depuis l'affrontement de l'île d'Orléans, six mois auparavant :

Il n'a pas peur de l'ouvrage
Dès quatre heures il est au bois
Il faut avoir du courage
Et ce gars-là n'en manque pas

Faustin se surprit bientôt à reprendre le refrain, joignant sa voix à celle de Baptiste :

Ah oui ! il est vraiment capable
Ce Canayen, le Bûcheron.
Ah oui ! il est infatigable,
Bon travailleur et gai luron.

L'ouvrage avançait vite et ils terminèrent leurs travaux de bois avant la fin de l'après-midi. Ils usèrent d'une longueur de corde, trouvée dans le campement, pour assembler un radeau large de six pieds et long de sept. Satisfait, Baptiste tira l'embarcation vers le marais et y attacha les paquetons.

En grognant sous l'effort, le colosse poussa le radeau dans les eaux vaseuses. À son appel, Faustin s'installa et Shaor'i s'y posa, reprenant ensuite sa forme humaine.

Se servant de la perche préparée à cet effet, Baptiste poussa le radeau, qui glissa doucement sur la bourbe.

◆

Le marécage exhalait un remugle fétide et, dans l'air chaud et humide du mois d'août, Faustin avait l'impression que le monde s'était brusquement vidé de son air pur. Le vaste lac stagnant, où proliféraient roseaux et quenouilles, était l'empire des insectes, qui s'abattaient sur les compagnons par nuées voraces, attaquant le moindre pouce de peau nue pour mordre ou se gaver de sang en piquant.

Debout à l'arrière du radeau, Baptiste avait malgré tout enlevé sa chemise carreautée. Son torse nu, couvert de piqûres, luisait de sueur alors qu'il mettait toute sa force sur la grande perche pour faire glisser le radeau sur le bourbier, alignant les *batèche*, les *calvince* et les *joual vert*.

Assise en tailleur, les yeux clos, Shaor'i semblait ignorer les assauts répétés des moustiques et des brûlots qui, pourtant, ne l'épargnaient pas.

Quant à Faustin, il ne s'endurait tout simplement plus. Il s'acharnait à tuer les hordes d'assaillants à grandes claques et grimaçait en grattant les boursouflures.

Les rives se peuplèrent bientôt d'arbres plus hauts, de grands trembles vers lesquels Baptiste orienta le radeau afin de naviguer sous l'ombre toute relative que fournissait leur ramure. Shaor'i ouvrit les yeux pour lancer :

— Trouve un bout de craie, Faustin.

Sur ces mots, l'Indienne se leva, fouilla le paqueton et en extirpa une bûchette et le seau de camp. Baptiste, qui comprit aussitôt ce que la jeune femme avait en tête, se fendit d'un large sourire et déclara :

— Deux fois, P'tite. Prends l'chaudron *itou*, j'en veux un rien qu'pour moé.

Puis, répondant au regard interrogatif de Faustin, il ajouta :

— Avec un sort de feu, on va emboucaner les taons, ça va faire ça d'gagné.

L'Indienne sortit une seconde bûchette et le chaudron, puis adopta sa forme de harfang et s'envola. Faustin plaça les deux contenants devant lui et, avec le morceau de craie grasse qu'il avait pêché dans l'une de ses poches, il traça sur les bouts de bois quatre cercles et quatre losanges en croix se touchant au premier tiers. Il attendit ensuite le retour de Shaor'i.

Le harfang ne fut pas long à revenir, et reprit son apparence humaine en posant sur le radeau une boule de mousse verdâtre et un petit tas de feuilles humides et brunes. Faustin incanta, créant de belles flammes vives. Shaor'i laissa le bois se consumer quelques minutes puis étouffa le feu sous la mousse avant de poser par-dessus le feuillage mort. Une fumée épaisse naquit aussitôt. Faustin s'empressa d'aller poser le seau aux pieds du bûcheron, qui le remercia d'un hochement de tête, puis il plaça le chaudron non loin, juste entre lui et l'Indienne.

Si l'initiative n'aidait en rien quant à la pureté de l'air ambiant, le nuage d'insectes se dispersa enfin et Faustin ne tarda pas à imiter le colosse, en retirant à son tour sa chemise pour la nouer autour de sa taille. Assis près du chaudron à fumée, il soupira en scrutant les environs.

Le marais s'étendait à perte de vue. Seules quelques plantes aquatiques ligneuses arrêtaient le regard sur les eaux brunes, ou les énormes racines enchevêtrées qui émergeaient comme des pattes difformes.

La boue devint plus dense à proximité de la rive et Baptiste fit obliquer le radeau, imprimant de lentes volutes dans la vase. Le soleil estival ne fut alors plus

voilé par aucun feuillage et Faustin sentit son dos nu se mettre à rougir. Le cuir de ses bretelles, chauffé par les rayons, lui brûla bientôt les épaules et il se résigna à remettre sa chemise, même s'il savait qu'il la retremperait de sueur en moins d'un quart d'heure.

Le torse ruisselant, Baptiste bandait les muscles de ses bras pour faire avancer le radeau. La couche plus liquide du marais s'était tant amincie que le radeau touchait maintenant à la bourbe. Avec peine, il contourna un petit îlot détrempé où nichait une famille de rats musqués. Toutefois, lorsque sa perche plantée dans le bourbier ploya à un tel point qu'elle menaça de rompre, le bûcheron dut se résigner.

— On est pognés dans un banc d'boue. Va falloir rentrer dans *swamp* pour décoincer l'radeau.

— Pourquoi ne pas monter sur cette petite île ? proposa Faustin. On pourrait tirer le radeau à force de poignet.

Baptiste sortit sa perche du marais et l'enfonça dans l'îlot. Stupéfait, Faustin vit la masse spongieuse s'éloigner quelque peu.

— C'est un tertre flottant, expliqua Shaor'i. La boue est assez dense pour retenir les graines qui y tombent et les plantes poussent. Ce n'est pas solide du tout.

— Envoye, Faustin ! Au moins, ç'a pas l'air trop creux.

Le colosse descendit dans le bourbier, et la ligne d'eau du marais se stabilisa à la hauteur de son nombril. Faustin s'enfonça à son tour dans la fange, estimant qu'il en aurait jusqu'à la poitrine. Quant à Shaor'i, qui s'y serait enfoncée jusqu'au cou, elle assuma sa forme de harfang et se percha sur un mélèze.

Cherchant appui sur le fond visqueux, les deux hommes poussèrent du mieux qu'ils le purent mais parvinrent à peine à faire remuer le radeau.

Un cri étranglé émergea de la gorge de Baptiste quand il fut brusquement tiré vers le fond. Paniqué, Ti-Jean sauta de son épaule sur le radeau et se mit à pousser de longs cris hystériques en montrant les eaux boueuses.

Faustin s'empressa de plonger le bras pour agripper le poignet du colosse. S'accrochant au radeau, il tira aussi fort qu'il le put. Au prix d'un formidable effort, le bûcheron parvint à se redresser, puis à se hisser sur l'embarcation.

Relevant la jambe de son pantalon, il exposa son mollet. Faustin, de retour lui aussi sur le radeau, découvrit que son compagnon saignait abondamment par une série de petites mais profondes entailles disposées en cercle.

— Qu'est-ce que… commença Faustin avant d'être interrompu par une sorte de coassement proche du beuglement.

D'autres sons similaires répondirent au premier, venant d'un peu partout autour d'eux.

— Des *skwahdem*, murmura Baptiste en s'emparant aussitôt de sa hache. Charge ton fusil, garçon !

Sans mot dire, Faustin obtempéra.

Une forme émergea alors du bourbier avec un écœurant bruit de succion. La chose ressemblait plus ou moins à une salamandre, son long corps noir et huileux avoisinant les quatre pieds. Sans la moindre hésitation, Baptiste, abattant sa hache sur la créature, sépara proprement la tête du reste du corps.

— Ça n'a aucun sens, cria Shaor'i qui, ayant projeté l'un de ses couteaux, venait de tuer une seconde créature. Les *skwahdem* ne vivent pas dans les marécages…

— Va donc leur dire, P'tite !

Les beuglements continuaient de plus belle et bientôt des créatures tentèrent de monter sur le radeau. Après

avoir tiré quelques balles et tués trois bêtes, Faustin délaissa son fusil, qu'il jugeait trop lent, et se lança à l'assaut armé de son sabre. Les *skwahdem* se présentaient à coup de deux ou trois à la fois et cherchaient à enfoncer leurs dents minuscules mais acérées dans leurs mollets. Les bêtes n'étaient certes pas agiles, mais leur nombre allait sans cesse en croissant et, bientôt, c'est par tous les côtés que les compagnons furent assaillis. Déchaussée, Shaor'i tailladait de ses pieds-serres tout en poignardant avec acharnement pendant que Baptiste, hache au poing, tuait chaque fois qu'il abattait la lourde lame à deux tranchants. Faustin frappait d'estoc et de taille, ayant cessé de compter ses victimes quand il eut dépassé la dizaine. Piégés au centre du radeau, les compagnons furent bientôt submergés sous le nombre en dépit des cadavres noirâtres qui s'amoncelaient à leurs pieds.

La douleur vrilla soudain le talon de Faustin, qui découvrit avec effroi que l'une des salamandres géantes venait de le saisir à revers.

Il secoua vigoureusement la jambe, mais constata à quel point la prise de la bête était tenace et, se voyant incapable de la déloger, se servit de son sabre pour frapper la créature. Il rata le cou, mais trancha une patte antérieure. Alors qu'il s'apprêtait à porter un nouveau coup, il sursauta, horrifié, en voyant que le membre mutilé repoussait déjà.

— Vise la tête, lança Shaor'i en brisant le crâne d'une bête avec l'un de ses pieds-serres.

Faustin opina du chef, son attention rivée sur cet ennemi qui ne voulait pas lâcher prise, et c'est ainsi qu'il aperçut trop tard, au sein de l'amoncellement de corps inertes, qu'un second *skwahdem* avait régénéré ses blessures. La bête le mordit au mollet en tirant violemment vers l'arrière. D'autres *skwahdem* que

Faustin avait cru morts se remirent à ramper vers ses chevilles.

Déséquilibré, Faustin bascula dans l'eau boueuse, qui l'empêcha de hurler quand une autre morsure lui entama vicieusement le flanc gauche. Il sentit une quatrième gueule se planter dans son bras avant que les *skwahdem* le tirent violemment vers le fond du marais. Paniqué, Faustin s'agita frénétiquement, espérant en vain se défaire de ses assaillants.

Il commençait à manquer d'air quand une poigne solide le saisit à la cheville. Aussitôt, sa descente se changea en remontée et c'est écartelé, les dents serrées et à bout de souffle qu'il fut extrait de la fange. Crachant de l'eau boueuse et toussant, Faustin aperçut Baptiste, qui endurait stoïquement les dents d'une créature plantée dans sa cuisse pendant qu'il débarrassait son ami des quatre toujours accrochées à lui.

Enfin libre, Faustin se releva en titubant pendant que le bûcheron se débarrassait du *skwahdem* qui le harcelait. Puis l'homme-lige regarda tout autour avant de pousser un rugissement de colère et de bravade.

Shaor'i, qui venait d'achever deux créatures, fit elle aussi un tour d'horizon, les sens aux aguets. Pendant une interminable minute, Faustin s'étant mis lui aussi à scruter autour de l'embarcation, ils restèrent tous les trois ainsi, armes en main, attendant les nouvelles attaques.

Qui ne vinrent pas.

Baptiste commença alors à jeter les cadavres poisseux hors du radeau tout en surveillant les eaux boueuses par les yeux de Ti-Jean. Le *mah oumet* laissait tomber de discrets gémissements plaintifs, semblables à ceux qu'il avait eus à la mort de la bête à grand'queue.

Quelques minutes plus tard, Faustin accepta avec reconnaissance le sort curatif de Shaor'i. Lorsqu'elle

eut aussi soigné le bûcheron et elle-même, il finit par demander :

— Qu'étaient ces… choses ?

— Les *skwahdem* ? Des bêtes qu'on ne devrait trouver qu'au nord, près du Piekougami…

— Le lac Saint-Jean, précisa Baptiste, toujours à l'affût.

— Je les ai vus… se régénérer de leurs blessures, se remémora le jeune homme.

— C'est vrai, confirma l'Indienne. Toutes les espèces de salamandres ont la faculté de faire repousser les membres perdus au fil des semaines. Un ancien rituel kakoutchak permet d'accélérer le processus pour le rendre quasi instantané, et des Blancs ont jadis adapté le sortilège en version goétique. Les *skwahdem* sont des bêtes voraces qui disparaissent peu à peu. De plus, elles rapetissent. Elles ont besoin d'eau courante fraîche, propre et bien aérée…

— Tout le contraire de ce marais, objecta Faustin.

— Précisément ce qui me trouble.

— Au lac Saint-Jean, dit Baptiste en relâchant temporairement sa vigilance, les *skwahdem* pâtissent à cause des chantiers pis des entreprises qui salissent les rivières. J'pensais même pas qu'l'espèce existait encore. Pis jamais j'en avais vu autant au sud.

— Comme la bête à grand'queue, laissa tomber Faustin. Ce sont des créatures rarissimes qui ne devraient pas se trouver ici… forcément l'œuvre du Stigma Diaboli.

— Vrai, approuva Shaor'i. Comme les *mestabeok* ou Kabir Kouba. Les goétistes cherchent à s'entourer de créatures que les hommes ne savent plus combattre.

Baptiste, s'étant décidé à risquer un retour dans la vase, poussa le radeau à deux mains en grognant puis,

d'un coup sec, l'embarcation se décoinça. Sans s'attarder, le bûcheron remonta et s'empara de la perche, pressé d'éloigner le groupe des lieux du combat.

◆

Les heures s'écoulèrent dans un silence presque total. Leur progression, bien que lente, était régulière, Baptiste ne cessant de pousser sur sa perche que pour essuyer la sueur perlant à son front.

Dès le coucher du soleil, l'air chargé d'humidité fut envahi par les bruyantes armées de mouches noires, de brûlots et de moustiques que la fumée des pipes et les seaux de mousse mise à brûler n'éloignaient que partiellement. Baptiste avisa à travers les mélèzes embrumés un affleurement rocheux escarpé où, selon lui, d'éventuels *skwahdem* ne pourraient grimper. Ils s'y hissèrent tous trois et, tandis que le bûcheron démarrait un feu, Shaor'i se porta volontaire pour débusquer le souper.

Les flammes montèrent rapidement et Faustin s'installa pour fumer pensivement, écoutant distraitement le son des crapauds et grenouilles qui mugissaient tout autour.

Shaor'i ne fut pas longue à revenir, portant sur son dos un long bâton effilé où était empalée une anguille qui se trémoussait encore. Le poisson serpentiforme mesurait plus d'une verge et, aux yeux de Faustin, ne semblait en rien appétissant. Ayant vu l'Indienne s'envoler sous forme de harfang, le jeune homme s'était délecté d'avance d'un souper de gibier d'eau, comme du canard ou de l'outarde. Déçu, il veilla néanmoins à ne passer aucun commentaire, pouvant presque entendre Madeleine le tancer: *Quand tu es chez les autres, tu finis ton assiette. Ne va pas me faire honte devant le monde.*

Baptiste, lui, avait sifflé de contentement en découvrant la prise de Shaor'i et l'avait questionnée sur la combativité du poisson avant de proposer de le cuire en soupe, qu'il agrémenterait des pleurotes qui poussaient sur les arbres proches.

L'Indienne opina du chef, posa l'anguille sur le radeau, lui planta l'un de ses couteaux dans la tête et prit l'autre lame pour entailler la peau, qu'elle retira en la retournant comme un gant.

Faustin haussa les épaules et se chargea d'aviver le feu. Après tout, ça ne pourrait pas être pire que les tartes de la mère Latulipe, cuisinées avec des merises sauvages, la variété à chair farineuse auxquelles la bonne femme n'ajoutait pas de sucre avant de les fourrer dans une pâte trop sèche – et dire qu'elle en cuisinait toujours une quand son mari engageait Faustin pour exécuter de menus travaux, c'est-à-dire plusieurs fois par été !

Baptiste vint poser sur le feu un chaudron de chair d'anguille, de champignons, de ciboulette sauvage et de rhizomes de quenouilles. L'odeur qui s'en dégagea n'était pas si mauvaise et, journée mouvementée aidant, l'estomac de Faustin ne tarda pas à grogner.

Une heure plus tard, après avoir méticuleusement englouti le contenu de sa seconde assiettée et complimenté Baptiste pour ses talents de cuisiner, il regardait Shaor'i tracer un plan sommaire dans la cendre.

— Il y a encore une lieue jusqu'à l'anse de Yamachiche. Nous devrions y être au début de la nuit. De là, nous verrons bien qui dirige les créatures qu'on nous a envoyées.

— J'aurais penché pour la mère de Faustin, rapport à la hère qu'à montait comme un cheval.

— J'en doute, contesta Shaor'i. Au nombre de bêtes à grand'queue qui subsiste, il y a fort à parier que

celle que vous avez combattue est la même qui nous a attaqués en février dernier. Or, la Corriveau n'avait toujours pas été rappelée d'entre les morts, à l'époque. Si la bête s'est laissé chevaucher un moment, cela devait être sous les ordres de son vrai maître.

— Nadjaw avait donné des ordres au beuglard dès son éveil, se souvint Faustin.

— *Idem*, coupa Shaor'i. De toute façon, elle ne pouvait diriger le rituel d'éveil et procéder à l'asservissement en même temps. Il fallait quelqu'un de puissant et…

— La Siffleuse, alors, supposa Faustin en sentant monter en lui une bouffée de rage. Elle s'était manifestée à moi au manoir Poulin, donc elle n'était peut-être pas loin de la chapelle engloutie.

— Si c'est le cas, affirma l'Indienne, c'est elle qui gouvernait aussi les *skwahdem* de tout à l'heure.

— Possible. Elle m'a sapé le contrôle de Plaçoa d'un claquement de doigts. La coercition mentale semble être l'un de ses grands talents.

◆

La nuit s'était installée depuis quelques heures lorsqu'ils remirent leur embarcation à l'eau. Faustin avait allumé le fanal et l'avait placé au bout d'une perche, à l'avant du radeau. Distraitement, il observait tout en fumant les phalènes de la taille de la main qui virevoltaient autour de la lanterne, attirées par sa lumière.

Quand la nuit fut définitivement installée et que les bruits omniprésents des criquets et des grenouilles devinrent presque entêtants, Shaor'i insista pour éteindre le fanal afin qu'ils arrivent à l'anse avec plus de discrétion. Servant de guide, elle usa de sa vision nocturne pour indiquer au bûcheron les obstacles à éviter.

Ils atteignirent l'anse de Yamachiche alors que la lune achevait son ascension. Minuit approchait et les lucioles qui flottaient semblaient la seule présence visible – du moins jusqu'à ce qu'ils entrent plus profondément dans l'anse.

Au centre du terrain vaseux se dessinait un décor aux allures surnaturelles.

Entre les joncs et la folle avoine se trouvaient des rochers aux formes stupéfiantes. Sans être géométriquement parfaits, ils présentaient des arêtes trop définies pour être naturelles. Les pierres dispersées à travers la tourbière avaient toutes d'étranges régularités, les plus colossales dépassant six pieds de haut, chacune suffisamment éloignée des autres pour donner l'impression d'un éparpillement de structures en angles. On avait posé, sur les pierres aux sommets les plus plans, des braseros de cuivre d'où montaient d'inquiétantes flammes bleutées.

Ti-Jean siffla son inconfort et Shaor'i ne sembla guère plus rassurée.

— Des huiles minérales, décréta Faustin après avoir inspiré profondément. Mon oncle en utilisait pour ses recherches. Ça empeste bien davantage que les huiles animales ou végétales et ça prend cette teinte-là en brûlant.

— Y peuvent pas brûler de l'huile à fanal comme tout l'monde ? grogna Baptiste, empathique à la nervosité de son lutin.

— Aucune idée. Je sais qu'un sort a parfois des exigences chimiques particulières, comme ce grand pentacle, sur l'île d'Orléans, qui était en pâte de phosphore blanc…

Les compagnons poursuivirent leur avancée en radeau, qui s'embourba en dépassant un rocher de bonne taille. Baptiste força sur sa perche, qui se rompit sous

l'effort. Il testa la vase avec le manche de sa hache et dit :

— On peut plus naviguer là-dessus, c't'une vraie mélasse. Ç'a l'air profond, par exemple. Pas sûr que c't'une bonne idée de descendre.

Shaor'i posa prudemment le pied sur la boue, en testa la solidité, puis fit trois pas en avant. Elle ne s'enfonça que d'un pouce tout au plus.

— OK, P'tite, admit le bûcheron. Tes os d'rapace te rendent assez légère. Mais tu ferais p'tête mieux d'voler pour nous repérer du terrain dur.

— En vol, je ne pourrais pas jauger la solidité du sol. À pied, ce sera plus facile... d'ailleurs Faustin m'accompagnera.

Le jeune homme jeta un regard dubitatif au bourbier.

— Je ne pense pas que je vais tenir aussi bien que toi sur...

— Sous forme de renard, coupa l'Indienne, ce sera parfait. Et ton odorat nous guidera.

Faustin marqua une pause. Bien entendu, *cela* était à présent en lui, ou plutôt intégré à lui. Il se fiait de plus en plus à son odorat, et son ouïe s'était affinée. Néanmoins, il n'avait jamais été tenté d'assumer de nouveau cette forme animale qu'on lui avait conférée.

— Je ne l'ai jamais fait... de moi-même, répliqua-t-il.

— Ça n'a rien de compliqué, si tu le souhaites vraiment.

Faustin prit un instant pour réfléchir puis hocha la tête.

— Je veux bien essayer.

— D'accord. Alors ferme les yeux.

Faustin obtempéra.

— Inspire profondément, puis repense à quelque chose d'unique à ta nature de renard.

— De… quoi?

Shaor'i eut un soupir d'impatience.

— Essayons plus simple. N'ouvre pas les yeux, reste immobile et inspire. Fais-toi un aperçu de ton environnement à l'aide de ton flair.

Sceptique, le jeune homme inspira. Rien ne se produisit.

Il recommença. Encore… Et encore…

Lentement, il sentit poindre un très vague vertige.

Et encore…

Et cette fois ce fut différent.

Les perceptions arrivaient de partout à la fois, venant d'un cercle dont il était le centre. Huile à fanal, sueur de ses vêtements et de ceux de Baptiste, parfum de sauge de Shaor'i, reliquats de cendre dans les chaudrons à fumer. Tout se classa dans son esprit pour dresser un portrait de son environnement direct. Puis l'arrière-plan se manifesta à l'inspiration suivante : vases, plantes ligneuses, huile minérale, odeur musquée d'un castor caché non loin.

Alors Faustin perçut le renard en lui. Comme l'avait dit Shaor'i, ce n'était pas une présence mais une extension de lui-même, comme s'il avait eu un membre paralysé qu'il aurait pu, d'une seule pensée, sortir de son inertie. C'était là, non pas *en lui* mais *mêlé à lui*, une identité supplémentaire, tout comme il pourrait endosser de nouveau son rôle de bedeau sitôt de retour à Notre-Dame des Tempérances.

— Pense « renard », murmura la voix de Shaor'i.

Les perceptions de Faustin se brouillèrent. Il eut le sentiment qu'il aurait dû avoir une autre posture, d'autres sens, d'autres modes de pensée.

— Ramène l'humain en toi et laisse sortir le renard.

Faustin s'exécuta.

Tout bascula.

Ce fut comme si son corps était devenu malléable. Il sentit son anatomie se modifier comme si elle se déversait dans l'idée de renard. Cela ne dura qu'une demi-seconde et Faustin décela qu'une vague de force venait de se retirer.

Il s'assit sur le derrière, langue pendante.

Il arrivait désormais à la hauteur des cuisses de Baptiste. À la première bouffée d'air, il catégorisa les divers relents des eaux marécageuses : boue, sédiments, pourriture, décomposition, gaz, tourbe, moisissure, vase.

Il se tourna vers Shaor'i.

— À la longue, tu y parviendras d'une pensée distraite, commenta la jeune femme, néanmoins satisfaite.

« *Allons-y,* émit Faustin. *Il y a forcément un endroit plus stable où Baptiste pourra nous rejoindre.* »

L'Indienne frissonna.

— Je déteste quand tu fais ça. Ça n'a rien de naturel comme mode de communication.

« *Tu connais une meilleure façon pour moi de te parler sous forme de renard ?* »

— Je suppose que non, admit-elle avec un soupir. Mais je trouve ça intrusif.

« *Alors hâtons-nous.* »

◆

Sous ses pattes, la tourbe semblait souple, presque élastique, mais supportait son poids sans mal. Au début, la queue lui posa un léger problème et il se trouva déséquilibré par ses oscillations. Quelques verges de marche réactivèrent la pensée-réflexe et ses mouvements devinrent plus naturels.

Alors Faustin goûta la liberté qu'offrait son autre apparence. En se déplaçant, il enfonçait les griffes dans

la terre et pouvait, d'une rapide détente des muscles, faire des bonds prodigieux. Avec Shaor'i, il passait prestement d'une pierre à l'autre, veillant à n'être qu'une ombre fugitive.

Sous l'étrange éclairage bleuté des combustibles minéraux, les rochers réguliers évoquaient les ruines d'une cité impie dont le souvenir se serait perdu à travers les éons. Il s'agissait là de granit gris très foncé, parfois traversé d'une veine plus claire. La régularité des blocs était naturelle, avait chuchoté Shaor'i, le clivage du granit s'effectuant généralement en angles géométriques. Aucun coup de ciseau ne se révéla à ses yeux de rapace quand elle scruta une pierre plus attentivement.

— Reste à savoir comment ces pierres sont venues ici, murmura-t-elle. Elles ne devraient pas se trouver en plein marécage.

« *Sont-elles ici depuis longtemps ?* » émit Faustin.

— Sans doute. L'érable qui a poussé par-dessus le petit bloc, là-bas, doit avoir plus de cent ans.

« *Mais pourquoi…* »

— Je l'ignore. Peut-être était-ce le haut lieu d'un cercle secret, comme les pierres levées du Sanctuaire des Sept Danseurs.

« *La terre me semble plus dure sous mes pattes. Je ne sens aucune perturbation à travers mes coussinets.* »

— Tu veux tester avec ton poids humain ?

Faustin ferma les yeux et pensa « humain ». Encore une fois, il sentit son corps devenir fluide puis ses perceptions s'ajustèrent.

— Le sol est bon, décréta-t-il.

Il sauta à pieds joints et ne s'enfonça pas. Les pupilles de Shaor'i se dilatèrent alors qu'elle scrutait les environs.

— Nous allons revenir sur nos pas, décida-t-elle. Baptiste fera reculer le radeau d'une centaine de verges, puis nous accosterons près de la langue de terre, là-bas. Nous pourrons ensuite traverser le boisé et revenir ici par les terres.

Hochant la tête, Faustin reprit sa forme animale et s'élança à la suite de l'Indienne.

◆

— J'suis d'accord avec toi, P'tite : le granit a souvent des formes franches. Mais ça devrait pas être icitte, ces pierres-là.

Faustin écoutait la discussion sans pouvoir y ajouter quoi que ce soit. La nuit était à présent bien entamée. Manœuvrer le radeau à reculons avait été plus difficile que prévu, Shaor'i devant à deux reprises chercher de nouvelles perches pour remplacer celles qui s'étaient rompues.

Quand finalement ils avaient atteint la langue de terre ferme et parcouru trois cents pieds à travers la forêt de mélèzes, ils se retrouvèrent de nouveau sur le terrain aux pierres droites. Entre eux et les vapeurs qui montaient du marais s'étendait le dérangeant fouillis de blocs sombres.

Ils étaient à peine arrivés que des bruits surgirent d'entre les alignements moussus de pierres aux angles singuliers. Sous la pâle lueur bleutée d'un fanal, six silhouettes drapées de noir venaient d'émerger du brouillard qui nimbait le boqueteau de mélèzes et de saules – six jeunes femmes, vêtues de la longue robe cérémonielle du Stigma Diaboli, qu'ils avaient déjà vues dans la nef d'une chapelle ensevelie. Très dignes, le visage dépourvu de toute expression, les six Disparues des Forges s'écartèrent les unes des autres, cédant la place à un petit chat noir.

La Siffleuse, Lucinda Poulin, dite la Duchesse des Mensonges ou la Voyante des Trois-Rivières.

Faustin sentit monter en lui une haine dont la force n'avait pas diminué quand il vit le félin prendre sa forme humaine, dévoilant ses étroits pieds de dix-huit pouces, ses mains aux doigts trop courts et ses oreilles pointues situées au niveau des tempes. La Siffleuse indiqua sa place à chaque jeune femme par des gestes impérieux. Elle marchait à pas lents et mesurés, pieds dressés sur les orteils, une sorte de corde pendant derrière elle. En écarquillant les yeux, désormais habitués à l'obscurité, Faustin parvint à saisir ce dont il s'agissait : un appendice de chair nue, long d'un pied, qui semblait naître au bas de son dos. *Le début d'une queue*, comprit-il en détournant brièvement les yeux.

Les Disparues se dirigèrent au centre du terrain, là où se trouvait un bloc de granit parfaitement cubique, faisant environ quatre pieds d'arête. Un peu en retrait, la Siffleuse ouvrit un livre qu'elle feuilleta attentivement, ses yeux de chat n'ayant besoin d'aucune lumière supplémentaire pour lire.

L'une des Disparues ramassa un brasero qui gisait sur le sol, le posa sur le cube de pierre semblable à un autel et y versa l'huile du fanal. Une vive flamme azurée baigna de son étrange lumière les femmes rassemblées, projetant des ombres dansantes sur les rochers. C'est alors que l'une d'elles se mit à fredonner une incantation :

— *El qalb yaashak kur amil…*

Une seconde Disparue reprit la phrase quelques secondes plus tard, en canon, alors que la première poursuivait :

— *… ansak ya salam, ana fe intizark…*

Tour à tour, les six jeunes femmes se joignirent au canon, créant une mélodie aux notes obsédantes qui

se réverbéraient sur les rochers, engendrant un écho qui plongea Faustin dans une légère torpeur, comparable à un début d'ivresse.

— ... *amal hayati, nezaer nephlim*...

Le jeune homme eut l'impression que quelque chose attirait son esprit vers l'autel cubique, pareil à un clou vers un aimant. Il fit un effort pour se ressaisir, puis sentit une présence s'accrocher au cube, une entité puissante qu'on arrimait malgré les flots psychiques qui le tiraient vers le large.

Faustin reconnut l'esprit au même moment que résonna dans sa tête l'équivalent mental d'un cri de rage mêlé de détresse.

« *NAMA !* »

Plaçoa. Le dernier maître de Kabir Kouba, l'esprit que Faustin avait libéré de son entrave. Et voilà que maintenant...

— C'est... une prison, chuchota-t-il à ses compagnons.

Face à leur incompréhension, il expliqua dans un murmure :

— La Poulin vient de lier l'esprit de Plaçoa au cube de granit. Ces pierres, cet endroit... c'est une geôle pour les défunts. C'est terriblement exigeant de garder mainmise sur un esprit, je l'ai déjà expérimenté... mais ici, la Siffleuse peut relâcher son emprise sur Plaçoa, car il est incapable de s'enfuir. Elle dispose ainsi de toute sa concentration pour lancer d'autres sortilèges.

Se tournant vers la scène qui se déroulait non loin, Faustin vit la voyante dessiner un diagramme au centre de l'autel de pierre.

— Je voudrais bien savoir ce qu'elle trace, déplora-t-il.

Baptiste se tourna vers lui d'un air résolu.

— Ti-Jean va jeter un œil.

Aussitôt, le *mah oumet* sauta de l'épaule du colosse et se glissa dans l'ombre d'un rocher. Faustin le vit gravir l'une des faces planes avec une facilité déconcertante puis exécuter un bond de dix pieds vers le tronc d'un grand saule. Avec difficulté, Faustin parvint à suivre du regard le singe albinos à travers l'épais feuillage de l'arbre, mais il le perdit définitivement de vue quand il sauta entre les branches d'un mélèze.

Pendant une longue minute, Baptiste se tint coi, parfaitement immobile, puis il tendit la main et demanda :

— Ta craie, garçon.

Faustin posa l'objet dans la paume ouverte et le bûcheron reproduisit à main levée, d'un trait hésitant et gauche, le pentacle qu'observait de toute évidence Ti-Jean, non loin de là.

Alors que le lutin regagnait l'épaule du bûcheron, Faustin expliqua :

— C'est le sort de sonde mentale que j'ai utilisé sur Ferrier. Elle va prélever de l'information dans l'esprit de Plaçoa.

— *Awan*… La façon de contrôler Kabir Kouba, de toute évidence. Laisse-moi m'en occuper.

— La sizaine au complet ?

— Elles ne sont ni des guerrières ni des arcanistes de haut calibre. C'est tout juste si on leur a enseigné ce qu'il faut pour mener un sortilège collectif.

— Justement, insista Faustin, elles n'y sont pour rien…

L'Indienne eut un sourire carnassier.

— Je n'en tuerai pas une seule, promit-elle. Tire la Siffleuse, c'est tout ce que je te demande.

Sans bruit, Faustin se positionna et visa la Voyante des Trois-Rivières. Ignorant que la mort la cueillerait

quelques secondes plus tard, la femme poursuivait son incantation, tête rejetée vers l'arrière, bras dressés vers le ciel.

Faustin déglutit. Ce n'était pas du gibier qu'il avait dans sa mire, ni une créature possédée, ni un jack mistigri qui, en dépit de son humanité, se voyait libéré d'effroyables tourments en étant abattu. C'était une personne, une femme qui ne le menaçait même pas en ce moment précis.

Shaor'i lui jeta un regard en biais et fronça les sourcils. *Qu'attends-tu ?* semblait-elle grogner *in petto*.

La Siffleuse tendit les bras en croix, incanta une nouvelle formule. Les doigts de Faustin se crispèrent sur son arme.

Tire ! s'ordonna-t-il, alors que cette femme cherchait à arracher à un défunt le moyen de contrôler la plus terrifiante des créatures qu'avait jamais abritée le Bas-Canada.

Il inspira, fixa la Siffleuse. *Tire !* songea-t-il encore.

Il vit que le canon de son arme tremblait, réassura sa poigne.

Mais tire donc ! Il se remémora la trahison de cette femme et son viol du repos éternel du curé Lamare par une *nekuia*, chercha en lui la rage qui l'avait poussé à user d'un sort de flammes contre elle.

Mais il venait pour sauver François, cette fois-là. Alors que…

… il cessa d'y penser. *Tire !* se dit-il encore, serrant les dents et obligeant son doigt moite de sueur à presser la gâchette.

Une voix bien connue jaillit subitement dans son esprit : « *Oh non, mon Prince, vous ne me ferez pas cela.* »

La Voyante se tourna dans leur direction et cessa son incantation.

Sans perdre un instant, Shaor'i bondit sur un rocher et s'élança vers le cercle des Disparues pour atterrir au centre de l'autel cubique. Elle se redressa, balança un violent coup de coude au visage d'une première fille tout en abattant son pied sur la tempe d'une seconde. Assommées, les deux jeunes femmes n'étaient pas encore à terre quand l'Indienne quitta l'autel d'un saut périlleux arrière, projetant au vol l'une de ses lames dont le pommeau cogna à la tête une troisième Disparue. Shaor'i atterrit dans le dos d'une quatrième fille. Avant même que cette dernière ne se soit retournée, le pommeau d'un couteau lui heurtait la nuque.

Les deux femmes restantes dégaînèrent une sorte de petit couteau de chasse et, avec un cri suraigu, foncèrent sur l'Indienne. Shaor'i plongea, jeta ses jambes en ciseaux dans celle d'une première Disparue, roula sur elle-même pour amortir sa chute et assomma la fille quand elle eut chuté au sol.

La dernière femme la chargea, lame au clair.

L'Indienne se releva lentement et, aussi immobile qu'une statue, attendit sans broncher l'arrivée de sa dernière ennemie. Au tout dernier instant, elle tendit le bras, index et majeur pointés vers l'avant.

La fille les reçut dans la gorge, s'effondra avec un gargouillis étranglé et sombra dans l'inconscience quand Shaor'i lui frappa la tête du talon.

L'Indienne fit alors un saut d'une incroyable hauteur, évitant de justesse une pierre grosse comme un poêle qui venait de fendre l'air, projetée par une force intangible.

— Plaçoa! hurla la voix de la Siffleuse. Tue-la!

Une nouvelle pierre traversa le vide, puis s'écrasa là où, un instant plus tôt, s'était trouvée l'Indienne.

Faustin et Baptiste se levèrent en hurlant à l'unisson. Le bûcheron s'élança vers la Voyante en brandissant

sa hache. La Siffleuse reprit son apparence de chat et se réfugia dans les herbes hautes. Faustin la visa et tira : le coup partit trop tard et rata sa cible.

Un cri strident déchira l'air et Faustin, faisant volte-face, découvrit une scène effroyable.

À six pieds du sol, un harfang des neiges battait frénétiquement des ailes tout en restant suspendu dans le vide, comme s'il volait sur place. De grandes plumes furent arrachées de son empennage puis l'oiseau chuta violemment sur le sol, comme rabattu par une main invisible.

L'Indienne reprit son apparence humaine en touchant terre, puis s'agrippa à une pierre pour éviter d'être soulevée du sol.

— PLAÇOA, NON ! hurla Faustin en bandant sa volonté pour s'arrimer mentalement à l'esprit.

La force relâcha Shaor'i et Faustin sentit qu'il avait établi un contact avec le défunt. Il perçut également une tension mentale qu'il devina être le lien unissant le fantôme à la Siffleuse.

Le reste s'accomplit sans que cela ne représente le moindre effort.

Avec l'équivalent mental d'un petit coup sec, Faustin arracha le fil psychique de la Voyante. Dans les herbes, un affreux miaulement se mua en un horrible gémissement de douleur humain.

Du coin de l'œil, Faustin vit Baptiste s'élancer vers la Siffleuse et emprisonner ses poignets dans l'une de ses énormes mains pour la bâillonner de l'autre.

Avant d'accourir aux côtés du bûcheron, Faustin jugea plus prudent de sceller le destin du Danseur défunt.

« *Heureux de vous retrouver, Plaçoa* », émit-il en guise d'introduction.

« *De même, spirite. Vous avez bien changé : à l'instar des Danseurs, vous détenez désormais une âme animale… sans compter votre puissance mentale qui a augmenté* », dit dans son esprit la voix profonde de Plaçoa.

« *Dites-moi, guerrier : si je vous libère de mon emprise, serez-vous libre ?* »

« *Je le serai, spirite.* »

« *Pourra-t-on vous asservir de nouveau ?* »

« *Non. À moins d'employer l'artefact avec lequel vous avez brisé ce qui me liait à ma prison, ce qui est au-dessus des forces de la Voyante.* »

« *Fort bien. Néanmoins, vous me devez toujours un service pour payer votre liberté.* »

« *Vrai. Je n'ai pas pu respecter notre entente première.* »

« *Pourrai-je faire appel à vous plus tard ou dois-je vous présenter ma requête tout de suite ?* »

« *Le temps n'a pas de signification pour un défunt.* »

« *Alors, soit. Vous êtes libre, Plaçoa. À bientôt.* »

Faustin relâcha le lien qui retenait le fantôme du Pendu. Une sensation qu'il identifia à de la reconnaissance l'effleura, puis s'estompa doucement. Il se précipita auprès de Shaor'i, qui ne semblait pas avoir trop souffert des assauts du défunt.

Dans son esprit, Faustin ressentit soudain un claquement sec, puis un autre, puis encore plusieurs. Sonné, il chancela et s'effondra sur le sol. Shaor'i l'aidait à se relever quand des cris stridents fendirent le silence nocturne.

Comme si elles émergeaient d'un cauchemar, les six Disparues se redressèrent subitement en hurlant, puis retombèrent aussitôt. Un miaulement se fit ensuite entendre, la Voyante s'étant métamorphosée pour échapper à l'emprise de Baptiste, qui tenta en vain de la poursuivre dans les herbes folles.

— Les Disparues… murmura Faustin, luttant contre un violent accès de migraine.

Shaor'i se rendit auprès des femmes inertes, posa les doigts sur la gorge de l'une, puis de l'autre, et finit par revenir en déclarant :

— Mortes. Elles sont toutes mortes.

— La Siffleuse… elle a… séparé les âmes des corps pendant que les filles étaient inconscientes.

— Quoi ? s'étonna Baptiste. Mais… pourquoi ?

— Peut-être pour se donner le temps de fuir, proposa Shaor'i. Une diversion.

— Peut-être, admit Faustin. Peut-être aussi pour éviter que l'on puisse questionner ces femmes sur ce qu'elles savaient des plans du Stigma Diaboli. Cela dit, l'Étranger tenait tant à celles qu'il appelait ses « juments poulinières » que la Siffleuse aura des comptes à rendre.

— Ça veut dire qu'ça sert pus à rien d'la chercher, à c't'heure, conclut Baptiste.

Ils restèrent un long moment à contempler le drame, ces six jouvencelles bêtement tuées après avoir été enlevées par les larbins de l'Étranger. Puis Shaor'i décida de disposer des corps. N'ayant pas sous la main les outils nécessaires pour creuser le sol, elle arrima une lourde pierre à chaque cadavre à l'aide de racines avant de les porter dans les eaux boueuses du marais, où les dépouilles s'enfoncèrent doucement.

Baptiste fredonna un air triste, caressant la fourrure de Ti-Jean venu se blottir contre lui, puis Faustin fuma pensivement, songeant au nombre de morts qui croissait sans cesse dans le sillage de l'Étranger.

— Rentrons, décréta Shaor'i quand elle eut terminé. Nous ne pouvons rien faire de plus ici. Il me tarde de quitter la vallée du Saint-Maurice.

— Si on est proches d'Yamachiche, affirma Baptiste, pour sûr qu'y a une halte de diligence. On va rentrer par le Chemin du Roy, ça va être vite réglé.

D'un silencieux hochement de tête, Faustin acquiesça. Lui aussi avait hâte de retrouver la rive sud et son village natal.

CHAPITRE 27

Givre et brasier

Elle était sise non loin des battures herbeuses, là où le bourbier était moins épais. Ce n'était pas une riante auberge, ni même une confortable taverne. C'était plutôt une bâtisse mal équarrie, pourvue d'une seule fenêtre, qui semblait s'être ramassée tout au fond d'un boqueteau de résineux. La halte de Yamachiche aurait dû être tout juste sur le bord du Chemin du Roy ; pourtant, elle était presque invisible depuis la route, et seule la pâle lueur d'un fanal accroché au-dessus de la porte révélait sa présence. Moins un logis pour voyageurs, pensa Faustin, qu'un repère de distillateur.

Il leur fallut réveiller l'obèse matrone qui somnolait derrière le comptoir ; habituée aux clients tardifs, elle les accueillit tout de même avec le sourire, qui révéla ses dents tachées de tabac à chiquer. Elle les renseigna aussitôt : une diligence passerait le lendemain, deux heures avant midi. Ils avaient de la chance : c'était celle qui faisait Montréal-Québec en une seule journée. Un exploit de célérité qui étonna les compagnons autant qu'il les arrangeait.

Après avoir exigé l'exorbitante somme de huit sous pour les loger tous les trois et leur promettre un œuf dur, du thé et du pain au déjeuner, elle leur indiqua

une chambre commune unique, mixte, qu'ils seraient par bonheur les seuls à utiliser ce soir-là. Apprenant ce dernier détail, Baptiste laissa sortir Ti-Jean de sa poche sitôt la porte refermée.

S'allongeant tout habillé sur une paillasse à la propreté douteuse, Faustin ne trouva pas le sommeil pendant les courtes heures qui restaient avant le matin. À ses côtés, Baptiste ronflait bruyamment, son *mah oumet* roulé en boule sur sa poitrine, alors que Shaor'i, silencieuse, méditait dans un coin. Les bras croisés derrière la nuque, le jeune homme fixait le plafond, où un trou de la taille d'une main laissait entrevoir un bout de ciel nocturne. Phalènes et coléoptères s'y engouffraient parfois pour venir voleter dans la pièce.

Il lui tardait de rentrer à Notre-Dame des Tempérances. Les conseils d'Otjiera les guideraient quant aux actions à entreprendre. Il avait proposé d'aller chercher le canot sur lequel il avait gravé les diagrammes de l'enchantement de chasse-galerie, mais Shaor'i avait secoué la tête. Plusieurs semaines auparavant, elle avait voulu le récupérer et ne l'avait pas trouvé. Volé par un membre du Stigma Diaboli ou par un simple fouineur?

Peu importait, au fond. Baptiste avait alors décrété qu'ils prendraient la diligence jusqu'à Québec, puis qu'ils paieraient un canotier pour passer à Pointe-Lévy.

Le frère de la grosse femme les ayant accueillis vint les réveiller quand le soleil commença à poindre. Il leur distribua à chacun un gobelet de fer-blanc de thé tiède et sans sucre, un quignon de pain goûtant la sciure et un œuf dur dont l'odeur éveilla dans la mémoire de Faustin le souvenir des carcasses qu'il flairait sous forme de renard. Il avala le tout en vitesse, se disant que les rations séchées de Baptiste – et même les *hard tacks* – avaient nettement meilleur goût.

La diligence arriva en avance, car elle n'avait pas eu de passager à prendre sur son chemin depuis son départ de Montréal. C'était une voiture fermée aux étroites fenêtres tirée par quatre chevaux qui évoqua à Faustin, de l'extérieur, une sorte de confessionnal sur roues. Un petit escalier menait à la porte. Baptiste fut le premier à le gravir et fit pencher la diligence au moment où il monta. Faustin le suivit, détaillant un intérieur où deux bancs de bois se faisaient face, si petits que Baptiste ne pouvait partager le sien avec quiconque autre que Ti-Jean. Ce n'était certes pas aussi luxueux que le fiacre qu'il avait pris à Québec pour se rendre chez les Sewell, mais infiniment plus confortable que les charrettes d'habitants.

Shaor'i hésita une longue minute avant de monter et ne cacha pas sa nervosité. Faustin savait que les endroits clos lui déplaisaient et se tassa contre l'une des parois. La jeune femme se décida enfin, sauta d'un coup dans la voiture pour se jucher sur le banc, assise sur ses talons. Les nerfs tendus comme les cordes d'un violon, elle jetait des coups d'œil, en brefs mouvements de tête, dans tous les sens. Elle se calma après un bon moment en fermant les paupières et en respirant lentement, et put s'asseoir correctement.

Le cocher, un homme taciturne, laissa à la halte de Yamachiche le paquet qu'on l'avait chargé de livrer, expliqua aux passagers les différentes haltes qu'ils croiseraient puis claqua les rênes. Il ne tarda pas à gagner en célérité.

◆

À travers la vitre, le paysage défilant à toute vitesse semblait mettre Shaor'i à l'aise. Après tout, songea Faustin, cela devait ressembler à son point de vue lorsqu'elle volait.

S'appuyant contre la paroi pour fermer les yeux un moment, Faustin parvint à somnoler jusqu'à ce que le cocher le réveille en criant :

— Trois-Rivières !

Dès que la voiture se fut immobilisée, l'ouïe de Faustin fut assaillie par le tapage des scieries de la ville industrielle. Prestement, il se couvrit le nez de son mouchoir, l'air chargé des relents d'acide dissolvant le bois cuit pour le réduire en pulpe. Le jeune homme vit le cocher descendre du banc de conduite et dételer ses chevaux à bout de souffle. La halte des Trois-Rivières lui en gardant des frais, l'homme procéda à l'échange en s'assurant qu'aucun voyageur ne désirait monter à bord.

— Je me demande comment ça se passe, du côté des Forges, laissa tomber Faustin.

Shaor'i soupira avec bruit et répondit :

— Nadjaw a espionné de ce côté-là pendant que nous te cherchions. Il paraît que c'est terrible. La production a augmenté, mais les ouvriers maigrissent à vue d'œil et les accidents sont fréquents. Ils ont même forcé les enfants à se mettre à l'ouvrage.

— Il y a toujours des enfants qui travaillent dans les manufactures, commenta Faustin. C'est normal. Chez les habitants, les marmots aident aux champs, en usine ils graissent les machines.

Shaor'i grommela quelque chose dans sa langue. Baptiste précisa :

— C'pas de t'ça qu'à parle. Les flos des Forges font de l'ouvrage d'homme.

— Certains ont été défigurés en se brûlant avec du métal en fusion, d'autres sont morts. Ils n'ont pas la force de manipuler les outils.

— Pis d'autres sont pognés aux *kilns*, seize heures par jour.

Estomaqué, Faustin ne trouva rien à dire. Shaor'i reprit :

— Certains s'y sont opposés. Ce fier-à-bras, Édouard Tassé, a fini par déranger un peu trop de monde et bientôt, plus personne ne l'a vu. D'autres ont cherché de l'aide auprès du clergé, comme Éloi Terrault, qui tenait vigie face au beuglard.

— Et ?

— Disparu, lui aussi. Tout comme le comptable qui tenait le grand magasin et qui a écrit à son député. Remplacé du jour au lendemain par un employé des entreprises Ferrier.

— Les ouvriers ont pus à faire avec l'beuglard, mais la peur est encore là. Tout l'monde est pour ainsi dire prisonnier des Forges.

Le cocher ouvrit la porte de la diligence et la puanteur urbaine s'engouffra.

— On part de suite, annonça le conducteur. On va arrêter à Sainte-Anne pis Saint-Joseph-de-Deschambault, après on f'ra un *stop* au Port-Neuf pour des chevals francs, pis direct à Québec.

— Correct, acquiesça Baptiste en refermant la porte, car il avait vu la pâleur de Faustin et de Shaor'i.

Faustin s'empressa de bourrer sa pipe, l'alluma avant le départ et prit une longue bouffée, saturant l'air ambiant de fumée de tabac, beaucoup moins désagréable que celles des papeteries trifluviennes.

Ce fut Baptiste qui, lorsque la voiture se remit en route, réengagea la conversation en sortant de la poche de sa mackinaw un riche anneau de platine orné d'une pierre verte.

— Tu connais ça, Faustin ?

Le jeune homme prit le bijou entre ses doigts et ses yeux s'écarquillèrent.

— Mon oncle en avait un identique, en or orné d'ambre. C'est un anneau du Collège.

— C'est ça. C't'un *maymaygwashi* qui m'a donné ça, au port des Trois-Rivières.

Faustin fronça les sourcils.

— Qu'est-ce qu'un *maymaygwashi* faisait avec ça ?

— Paraît qu'il l'a reçu du père Masse, qu'était, dans l'temps, l'maître à ton oncle. Paraît aussi que l'père s'rait toujours en vie, qu'y vivrait à l'Isle-aux-Grues pis qu'y demande à m'voir. Avec ses écritures, la P'tite a su que l'île est un genre de place sacrée pour l'peuple des rivières pis que c'est d'même que l'père les a rencontrés. Fait que, de suite qu'on aura parlé avec Otjiera, j'prends une goélette pour l'Isle-aux-Grues.

— Le père Masse… murmura Faustin. C'est lui qui possède l'*Opus æternum*, le livre que cherche l'Étranger ! Pendant que j'étais à la Grande Maison des Forges, la Siffleuse a contacté mon oncle par *nekuia* et elle l'a forcé à révéler cette information…

— On l'a cru mort durant des années, précisa Baptiste.

— L'Étranger le croyait aussi. Savoir le père Masse en vie l'a mis hors de lui : Gamache était supposé l'avoir tué des années auparavant.

Faustin songea un moment aux implications de cette révélation.

— L'père Masse a beaucoup voyagé, reprit le bûcheron. Y'a été missionnaire, manière d'étudier la magie des Indiens du Nord-Ouest, jusqu'à temps qu'y lui disent qu'était pus l' bienvenu…

— Pourtant, objecta Faustin, je ne peux pas croire qu'un membre du Collège aurait essayé d'imposer la foi catholique aux Indiens…

Shaor'i tiqua.

— Contrairement à ce qu'on vous enseigne dans vos écoles de rang, nous n'avons jamais détesté la religion

catholique. Il y avait de nombreuses ressemblances entre vos croyances et les nôtres. Au début, nous avons accueilli vos prêtres, pour discuter. Puis nous avons dû les tuer. Vos foutus missionnaires nous avaient amené leurs maudites maladies et c'est pour empêcher la contamination que nous ne voulions plus d'eux.

Guère désireux d'engager une conversation sur un sujet aussi délicat, Faustin hocha la tête puis s'abandonna à la contemplation du paysage. Les basses-terres se succédaient et le jeune homme se laissa aller à rêvasser aux récoltes de Notre-Dame des Tempérances. Les foins étaient assurément fauchés depuis longtemps et les bleuets ramassés. Le grain ne devait pas encore être sec, les fruits pas encore mûrs, les légumes des potagers grossiraient encore plusieurs semaines. Serait-il de retour au village à temps pour gérer la collecte de la dîme ?

Peu importait, au fond. Madeleine avait toujours bien veillé aux intérêts du presbytère.

N'empêche… l'idée de rater les récoltes lui faisait un pincement au cœur.

Il y songeait encore lorsque le cocher cria « Sainte-Anne ! » en immobilisant la voiture.

L'homme descendit en vitesse, s'assura qu'aucun client n'attendait à la halte, accepta de livrer une caisse à Québec puis remonta, claquant les rênes pour remettre la voiture en route.

La brève interruption donna l'occasion à Faustin de ramener la discussion sur ses derniers instants aux Forges.

— Quand j'étais dans la Grande Maison, après la *nekuia*, Nadjaw m'a parlé de la Dame Blanche de la chute Montmorency. Elle m'a recommandé d'aller quérir son aide.

Le bûcheron et l'Indienne ne pipèrent mot.

— Quoi, qu'est-ce qu'il y a? demanda Faustin.

— Dame Blanche, c'est vite dit… marmonna Baptiste. Ceux qui ont croisé son chemin au bon moment l'appellent la Dame Blanche pis la louangent gros comme le bras… mais les autres l'appellent plutôt la Dame aux Glaïeuls.

— Remarque, dit Shaor'i, je comprends que Nadjaw ait pu croire que tu aurais là une aide précieuse: je ne pense pas qu'il y ait jamais eu une Danseuse plus versée dans l'art de communiquer avec les défunts.

— Tu peux être sûr de rien avec la Dame, coupa Baptiste en tournant ses orbites vides vers Faustin. Ton oncle m'a déjà lu un boutte des *Relations des Jésuites* ousqu'y parlent de la Dame Blanche qu'aurait nourri des enfants affamés des Blancs… mais ça lui est arrivé plus qu'une fois de noyer des innocents. Sans parler de son histoire avec le soldat d'Beauport.

— Elle est sûrement devenue folle avec le temps, supposa l'Indienne. Personne ne peut vivre entre deux mondes sur une aussi longue période en gardant toute sa tête.

— Vous pourriez peut-être m'expliquer du début, un coup parti, dit Faustin qui commençait à s'irriter.

Shaor'i jeta un œil distrait par la fenêtre de la voiture. À travers les arbres, on pouvait voir le fleuve qui défilait à quelques verges de là.

— Elle se nommait Matshi Skouéou, commença-t-elle. C'était une Danseuse née au début des années 1600. J'ignore la date exacte. C'était celle qui, dans le Cercle des Sept, était chargée de s'adresser aux ancêtres défunts pour demander aide et conseils.

— Une sorte de spirite? demanda Faustin.

— Si tu veux. Ce que vous autres, théurgistes, appelez une *nekuia*, notre peuple le nomme « communion

avec les anciens ». Remarque, il y a une différence : vous forcez l'esprit à se manifester ; nous, nous l'implorons de nous guider. Mais le résultat est à peu près le même. Enfant, nous dit l'histoire orale des Haudenosaunee, Matshi Skouéou avait été élevée par ses parents défunts qui continuaient à se manifester à elle. Elle ne faisait même pas la différence entre esprits et êtres vivants. Quand le Cercle l'a recrutée, ç'a été une période de grande prospérité. Elle avait la faveur des trépassés et savait obtenir d'eux la coopération qu'il fallait. C'était un véritable puits de connaissances, un pont vers la sagesse du passé.

— Pis les maladies sont arrivées, intervint Baptiste. La varicelle, la tuberculose, la variole, le choléra, le typhus…

Une ombre passa sur le visage de Shaor'i qui prit un instant avant de poursuivre :

— Il y a eu une épidémie de grippe. Aucun sortilège n'avait jusqu'alors été élaboré pour guérir de telles maladies. Matshi Skouéou sollicita l'aide de guérisseurs morts la génération précédente, puis de l'autre d'avant, et ainsi de suite, elle remonta le cours du temps à la recherche de guérisseurs qui auraient déjà vu de tels symptômes. En vain. Puis elle fut atteinte à son tour.

La diligence sauta sur un trou, puis cahota sur quelques verges. Toujours nerveuse en voiture, la jeune femme se tut un instant, fermant les yeux et se forçant à respirer lentement. Elle reprit lorsque la route redevint confortable :

— Si morts et vivants se confondaient pour Matshi Skouéou dans son enfance, depuis des mois, elle avait arpenté en esprit le monde des morts, et la frontière s'était atténuée. La fièvre suscita chez elle des délires et la fit perdre totalement ses repères. Puis elle mourut.

— Sauf qu'est jamais morte, dit le bûcheron.

Faustin regarda tour à tour ses deux compagnons.

— Comment ça, « jamais morte » ?

Shaor'i expliqua :

— Tu as vu ces feux follets verts, dont les corps sont morts depuis longtemps car l'esprit du sorcier a perdu la notion du temps ?

Faustin frissonna.

— Comment pourrais-je oublier ça ? Ça aurait pu m'arriver.

— Eh bien, Matshi Skouéou est devenue un peu la même chose… sous forme d'effigie.

— Quoi ?!

— Chez nous, la magie est une question de communion. Les goétistes deviennent loups du jour au lendemain, grâce à un diagramme – c'est d'ailleurs ce que Nadjaw t'a fait. Chez nous, c'est une longue quête spirituelle.

— Je sais déjà ça, coupa Faustin qui n'aimait pas qu'on le prenne pour un ignare.

— Matshi Skouéou a fait la même chose avec la forme d'effigie. À l'approche du trépas, elle a transféré son esprit dans son effigie et a laissé mourir son corps.

— Elle est donc… éternelle ? Comme l'Étranger ?

— Non. L'Étranger maintient son corps en vie par magie et projette sa conscience. La Dame Blanche n'a plus de corps vivant, mais son esprit n'a pas quitté notre monde pour autant. Son état ressemblerait davantage à celui de Plaçoa, sauf que Matshi Skouéou a préservé son apparence mortelle.

Faustin sentit le souffle lui manquer un instant. Il ne pouvait avoir bien compris.

— Elle a une sorte de corps mental ? Comme lorsque je me suis manifesté sous forme d'effigie ?

— Exactement pareil. Elle peut donc toucher, parler, sentir et goûter ; elle est chaude au toucher, elle a une consistance…

— … et à peut s'faire passer pour une vivante n'importe quand, ajouta Baptiste. C'est ça qu'a l'a fait, durant la guerre des Sept Ans.

Éberlué, Faustin se tourna vers l'Indienne, qui haussa les épaules.

— Je ne connais pas les détails de cette histoire. Peut-être que Baptiste…

— Tout c'que j'sais, c'est qu'est tombée amoureuse d'un soldat pendant la guerre contre les Anglais. En effigie, elle pouvait l'fréquenter comme a voulait. Un jour, l'gars a succombé au combat, faque depuis c'temps-là elle l'attend dans une sorte de château, pas loin d'la chute Montmorency… à c'qu'on dit, parce que personne a jamais vu d'château dans c'coin-là…

Le bûcheron s'éclaircit alors la voix pour chanter :

D'ici voyez ce beau domaine
Dont les créneaux touchent le ciel
Une invisible châtelaine
Veille en tout temps sur ce castel
Prenez garde !
La Dame Blanche vous regarde.

Il marqua une pause avant d'ajouter :

— Si vivre à cheval sur deux mondes l'a pas achevée, la mort d'son homme en a eu raison. Après c't'histoire-là, a s'est mise à attirer des enfants qui jouaient sur l'bord de la berge dans les flots pour les noyer. D'la Dame Blanche, c'est devenu la Dame aux Glaïeuls.

— Que viennent faire les glaïeuls là-dedans ? demanda Faustin.

— Elle dépose toujours des glaïeuls sur le corps du noyé, après avoir ramené le cadavre sur la grève, expliqua Shaor'i.

Le jeune homme réprima un tremblement.

— Saint-Joseph-de-Deschambault ! tonna la voix du cocher tandis que la diligence décélérait.

Alors que le conducteur s'affairait à la halte, Faustin prit un moment pour réfléchir à ce qu'on venait de lui raconter : une spirite démente et immortelle, ne sachant distinguer les vivants des défunts… un spectre de femme qui tombe amoureux d'un soldat de chair et de sang… une aliénée qui entraîne les enfants dans les flots pour les tuer, puis dépose des fleurs sur leur dépouille…

C'est auprès de *cela* que Nadjaw l'incitait à quérir de l'aide !

Il n'avait toujours pas ouvert la bouche quand la voiture se remit en route, et ce fut Shaor'i qui brisa le silence.

— Remarque, je comprends l'idée de Nadjaw : il n'y a personne, absolument personne qui soit plus instruit au sujet de l'outremonde que la Dame Blanche. Ses connaissances ne sont pas seulement théoriques mais aussi empiriques. En matière de spiritisme…

— Non, décréta Baptiste. J'suis pas d'accord que Faustin aille voir c'te folle-là. L'père Masse sera de meilleur conseil.

L'Indienne hocha pensivement la tête, les yeux fixés sur le décor qui défilait. Les compagnons passèrent de longues minutes en silence, chacun dans ses pensées. Ce fut Shaor'i qui reprit :

— À présent que Nadjaw est morte, Otjiera pourra me confier une nouvelle tâche. Il est possible qu'il s'agisse à nouveau d'un Bracelet du Courroux scellant le destin d'un membre du Stigma Diaboli. Si c'est le cas, peut-être le vicaire croisera-t-il ma route. Il se peut aussi que nous partions plutôt pour nous mettre en quête d'enfants dotés d'outrevision afin de reformer

le Cercle. Dans ce cas-là, Otjiera et moi entamerons un long voyage parmi les Cinq Nations.

Sans mot dire, Faustin se perdit dans ses pensées. Ainsi donc, Baptiste partirait pour l'Isle-aux-Grues, Shaor'i peut-être pour une nouvelle exécution, peut-être pour un pèlerinage. Dans ce second cas, elle les quitterait et il faudrait que les deux hommes se passent de son aide. Pour Faustin, il était clair qu'il suivrait Baptiste pour voir ce mystérieux père Masse, malgré les recommandations de Nadjaw, car il ne voulait pas s'opposer à Baptiste.

Avec un soupir, le jeune homme tourna les yeux vers le paysage. Le soleil du mois d'août faisait étinceler les eaux du fleuve et donnait un reflet brillant au givre qui recouvrait les champs.

Du givre?

Les chevaux poussèrent soudain de longs hennissements de terreur. La voiture fit une vive embardée et un hurlement de pur effroi monta du siège de conduite. Collant son visage à la fenêtre, Faustin vit le cocher percuter le sol, son corps emmêlé à celui d'un non-mort.

— On nous attaque! hurla-t-il alors que la diligence se mettait à déraper sur une couche de glace.

Les hennissements des chevaux s'achevèrent dans un gargouillis étranglé alors que la voiture se cabrait sur ses deux roues de gauche.

— 'Tention, cria Baptiste en se projetant dans l'autre sens pour rétablir l'équilibre.

La voiture revint brièvement sur ses quatre roues, bondit, les essieux se cassèrent dans un grand fracas et la voiture capota pour de bon. Du sang – sûrement celui des chevaux – éclaboussa les vitres pendant que Faustin protégeait sa tête de ses mains. Ti-Jean hurla de façon hystérique alors que la diligence commençait à débouler la pente abrupte menant au fleuve.

Elle s'immobilisa cependant rapidement sur son flanc droit, sans doute retenue par le poids des chevaux. La vitre de gauche, tenant désormais lieu de plafond, fut défoncée par le poing d'un wendigo, ce qui propulsa une pluie d'éclats tranchants dans la cabine. En se protégeant, Faustin eut le temps de voir un couteau de l'Indienne percer le crâne de la créature.

Shaor'i poussa la porte au-dessus de sa tête et se jeta à l'extérieur d'un grand saut. Le bûcheron fit la courte échelle à Faustin pour qu'il sorte également. Mais ce que vit ce dernier le stupéfia.

Shaor'i, aux prises avec deux non-morts, se battait sur un sol luisant de gel. Son haleine se condensait dans l'air et elle avait retiré ses bottes pour planter ses pieds-serres dans la pente.

— Faustin !

Le jeune homme se pencha pour attraper le poignet de Baptiste et dut s'y prendre à deux mains pour l'aider à se hisser. À peine le colosse s'était-il extirpé de la voiture qu'un jack se jeta sur eux. Faustin eut à peine le temps de pointer sa baïonnette pour qu'il s'y empale.

Surgie de nulle part, une tempête de givre s'abattait sur eux. Comme Shaor'i achevait un second ennemi, Faustin se précipita au sommet de la pente, suivi de Baptiste et de Ti-Jean, qui s'accrochait fortement au cou du géant.

Sur la route, une vingtaine de jacks mistigris les attendaient. Derrière eux se tenait Gamache, qui achevait une incantation, retenant par une chaîne une créature de grande taille – un jack géant ? Ils n'eurent guère le temps d'observer davantage : des pentacles se mirent à briller sur plusieurs arbres aux alentours et une nouvelle bourrasque souffla son verglas.

Comme une meute de loups, les non-morts profitèrent de l'instant pour se jeter sur eux.

Shaor'i fonça sur l'ennemi, tournoyant sur elle-même à une telle vitesse qu'il était difficile de la suivre des yeux. Un mortel tourbillon de lames fondit sur la meute de wendigos, perçant cœurs et crânes tandis que les corps tombaient comme des pantins désarticulés.

Faustin fouilla frénétiquement sa poche, en extirpa son sac de poudre et ses deux dernières balles d'argent. Aussi vite qu'il le put, il chargea, épaula et tira.

Un jack s'effondra, atteint à la tête.

Prêtant main-forte à l'Indienne, Baptiste plantait sa hache dans l'épine dorsale d'un non-mort quand Ti-Jean l'obligea à se retourner vivement, ce qui lui permit de décapiter celui qui tentait de le prendre à revers. Du même mouvement, Baptiste trancha la jambe d'un troisième qui chuta sur la terre gelée pour y être achevé d'un nouvel assaut.

Sitôt qu'il eut rechargé, Faustin se jeta dans la mêlée. Il empala un jack de sa baïonnette tout en pressant la gâchette de son fusil, et tua la créature sur le coup. Il laissa tomber l'arme à feu, dégaina son sabre et frappa d'estoc l'ennemi le plus proche.

Sans cesser de tourbillonner, Shaor'i frappait sans relâche, réduisant le nombre des wendigos.

Alors un grand cri fendit l'air.

Gamache venait de lâcher la chaîne de la créature restée jusque-là accroupie à ses côtés.

La silhouette énorme avança lentement vers les compagnons.

Le wendigo atteignait presque les sept pieds de haut et avait une carrure comparable à celle de Baptiste. Le monstre hurla de nouveau, ramassa la chaîne qui l'avait retenu et la brisa à mains nues tout en s'approchant. Enroulant chacun des bouts de chaîne autour de ses mains, il s'improvisa des gantelets de fer.

Un sourire carnassier sur les lèvres, Shaor'i acheva deux autres jacks et prit sa forme de harfang pour s'envoler à l'assaut du géant.

Ce que Gamache, de toute évidence, avait anticipé.

L'attention des compagnons étant tournée vers l'énorme créature, ils virent trop tard le tonneau que Gamache projetait magiquement dans les airs et, lorsque le sorcier roux incanta de nouveau, le fût éclata en pluie d'épines de glace et d'esquilles de bois qui s'abattit sur le hibou blanc.

Le rapace tomba au sol et Shaor'i reprit forme humaine ; elle n'eut guère le temps de se relever que le wendigo colossal tentait de lui défoncer le crâne d'un coup de poing. L'Indienne esquiva de justesse en roulant sur elle-même, mais ne vit pas l'autre main qui lui agrippa une cheville.

Le jack souleva la jeune femme au-dessus du sol. Alors que le pouvoir de gel des wendigos prenait effet et que le corps de Shaor'i s'engourdissait lentement, le monstre saisit son autre cheville et il écarta brutalement les bras, cherchant à démembrer l'Indienne.

Pendant que Baptiste chargeait l'énorme non-mort, Faustin courut vers les débris de la diligence et ramassa une petite planche pour y tracer un pentacle de sa craie grasse.

Sans hésiter, il pensa « renard », se métamorphosa et saisit la planchette dans sa gueule. Il banda ses muscles et piqua un sprint, la formidable poussée de son corps canin lui octroyant une vélocité qu'il n'aurait pu obtenir autrement. Baptiste venait d'abattre sa hache sur la cheville du wendigo colossal quand Faustin se faufila entre les deux comme un éclair de fourrure rousse et passa entre les jambes du monstre pour y laisser tomber sa planchette.

Il fit un bond prodigieux, reprit forme humaine et cria :

— Baptiste ! Recule-toi !

Puis il incanta :

— *Ashek akkad baath ahmed dazan il-bekr !*

Des flammes jaillirent sous le jack, qui hurla sa douleur. Shaor'i profita de l'occasion pour s'extirper de sa poigne en adoptant sa forme de harfang et s'envola hors de portée. Baptiste, revenu à la charge, enfonça profondément la lame de sa hache entre les omoplates de la créature, qui s'effondra dans le feu.

Faustin venait à peine de comprendre que le prodigieux jack était vaincu qu'il aperçut le harfang se poser devant Gamache et reprendre son apparence humaine. Il tressaillit en voyant Shaor'i : elle avait les cheveux aussi blancs que l'albâtre.

Le premier coup de pied de l'Indienne fusa si rapidement que Gamache n'eut pas le temps d'esquisser le moindre geste de recul. Atteint à la tempe, le sorcier chancela, mais Shaor'i le retint par le col, l'empêchant de tomber. Faustin crut qu'elle s'apprêtait ensuite à lui asséner un coup de poing à la mâchoire, or elle enfonça plutôt sa main dans la bouche de Gamache pour en extirper un bout de chair sanguinolent pendant qu'une gerbe de sang jaillissait de la gorge du sorcier.

Avec un insondable mépris, Shaor'i laissa tomber la langue sur le sol couvert de givre et l'écrasa du pied.

— J'ai promis à Nadjaw de ne pas te tuer. Va, tu es libre.

Le sang ruisselant sur sa poitrine, Gamache émit quelques gargouillis incompréhensibles.

— Pars, cria-t-elle. Va retrouver ton maître et découvrir le sort qu'il te réservera maintenant que tu ne peux plus incanter le moindre sortilège. Ou retourne à Anticosti, d'où tu n'aurais jamais dû partir.

Incertain de l'attitude à adopter, Gamache recula d'un pas. Shaor'i hurla :

— Fuis avant qu'il ne me vienne l'envie de briser ma promesse !

L'Indienne se mit alors à trembler à un tel point que ses dents claquaient. Baptiste se rua vers elle, suivi par Faustin qui aperçut les lèvres bleuies de la jeune femme, qui avait dû poser un genou au sol, sa peau couverte d'engelures et ses pupilles, si contractées qu'on ne voyait plus qu'un petit point noir sur les iris dorés.

— Sa peau est frette comme celle d'une morte, déclara le bûcheron qui la soutenait. J'ai déjà vu ça chez un gars d'chantier qu'était tombé dans une rivière en hiver. On va la perdre si on la réchauffe pas.

Faustin pointa son sabre en direction de Gamache pendant que Baptiste emmenait Shaor'i près du feu qui brûlait toujours sous le wendigo géant.

— Moi, je n'ai rien promis. Reste que je dois la vie à ta femme. Disparais de ma vue, *maintenant !*

Il avait hurlé le dernier mot et le sorcier, qui reculait déjà, s'en fut en courant, le sang coulant toujours de sa bouche.

— Je n'aime pas le laisser aller, grogna Faustin de retour près de Baptiste pour soutenir Shaor'i alors que le bûcheron essayait de déplacer le cadavre du wendigo géant.

— L'aurais-tu… tué… d'sang froid ? ahana Baptiste.

Le jeune homme eut une seconde d'hésitation.

— Non, avoua-t-il. Bien sûr que non.

— La P'tite a raison… personne peut y r'donner sa langue… pareil que mes yeux. Y peut pus… faire de magie. Mais viens donc m'aider à tasser c'te bougre…

Faustin s'assura que Shaor'i était bien allongée au sol pour s'atteler lui aussi à la tâche. L'odeur de chair et de graisse brûlées était atroce. Ils y étaient presque

quand Baptiste, jurant bruyamment, demanda à Ti-Jean de s'approcher de la tête du wendigo.

— Faustin, déclara le colosse d'une drôle de voix, c'est… j'veux dire… j'le connais, c'te jack-là… *C'est* Édouard Tassé !

Horrifié, Faustin s'attarda aux traits du faciès et reconnut lui aussi l'homme fort des Forges. Il recula d'un pas, ébranlé : c'était la première fois qu'il voyait un non-mort levé à partir d'une personne qu'il avait côtoyée.

Voilà ce que devenaient les ouvriers qui disparaissaient après s'être opposés à la gestion de James Ferrier.

Pendant que Shaor'i se réchauffait, les deux compagnons analysèrent la situation.

— On peut pas laisser les corps des jacks icitte, dit finalement Baptiste, il faudrait les enterrer. L'cocher, au pire, y'aura l'air de s'être tué en capotant avec sa voiture.

— Tu as raison, mais on n'a pas vraiment le temps de faire dans la dentelle. Je propose qu'on bascule plutôt les jacks sur la pente de façon à ce qu'ils se retrouvent sur la grève : si la prochaine marée ne les emporte pas, le temps qu'on les trouve, ils seront assez décomposés pour passer pour des noyés, comme si une embarcation avait sombré quelque part.

Les deux hommes s'acquittèrent de la tâche à la hâte. Vingt minutes plus tard, la température étant redevenue estivale, ils se mirent en route, Baptiste portant dans ses bras l'Indienne, toujours inconsciente, tandis que Faustin, en mettant à profit son odorat décuplé de renard, entreprit de les mener vers l'auberge la plus près d'eux.

◆

C'est dans une épaisse fourrure, assise auprès d'un feu vif, que Shaor'i reprenait du mieux.

La *Silver Star* était une auberge cossue de la seigneurie de Port-Neuf. Située suffisamment en retrait du port pour ne pas passer pour un repaire de matelots, elle en était assez proche pour attirer les officiers et les riches voyageurs. Faustin avait préféré cet établissement aux autres, car il était certain d'y trouver un âtre chaud et les divers conforts dont aurait besoin Shaor'i. Le tenancier, un rouquin au fort accent anglais, les avait d'abord regardés les sourcils froncés, leurs vêtements usés attisant autant sa méfiance que l'odeur qu'ils avaient ramenée des marécages. L'épaisseur de la bourse de Faustin, encore lourde de l'argent pris chez le notaire Lanigan six mois plus tôt, constitua un argument convaincant.

La grande pièce était splendide et fort richement meublée pour une auberge. Les tables étaient de chêne verni, les sièges agréablement rembourrés. Aux murs étaient fixées des tablettes sur lesquelles on avait posé des oiseaux empaillés et, dans un coin, un ours noir dressé sur ses pattes postérieures attirait tous les regards. Une profusion de bougies – de vraie cire et non pas de vulgaire suif d'habitant – brillait dans un chandelier massif posé sur une table cirée et un grand tapis couvrait le sol.

Une fois l'argent donné au maître des lieux, on s'empressa d'accéder à leurs désirs. À la vue des lèvres bleuies de l'Indienne, personne ne s'indigna que Faustin exige qu'on fasse un grand feu en plein été et qu'on lui apporte sur-le-champ un bouillon de poule bien chaud.

Faustin et Baptiste prirent place à la table la plus proche. Ti-Jean ne dérangea absolument pas l'aubergiste, habitué aux familiers des capitaines, qu'il s'agisse de

corbeaux, de furets ou de perroquets. L'homme avait même déjà vu un petit singe, quoique à fourrure brune et avec une longue queue, précisa-t-il.

Les deux hommes soupèrent d'agneau rôti, de chou au beurre et de pommes de terre, le tout arrosé d'une bière plus noire et plus amère que celles que Faustin avait bues jusqu'alors.

— Watch-toé, garçon, le mit en garde Baptiste. Les bières d'Irlandais, ça cogne solide.

— J'ignorais que les Irlandais arrivaient en Bas-Canada avec autant de moyens, marmonna Faustin entre ses dents.

— Là-bas comme icitte, y en a qui ont plus de chance que d'autres.

Dans un coin, un violoneux interprétait des chansons anglaises, accompagné d'un joueur de tambour, détail qui étonna Faustin. Il entendit un client d'une table voisine expliquer à son épouse que l'instrument se nommait *bodhran* et était fabriqué d'une peau de chien.

Faustin se levait pour se rendre auprès de Shaor'i afin de s'assurer que son état s'améliorait quand Baptiste lui souffla :

— Appelle le tenancier, faut qu'on y parle…

Faustin obtempéra sans poser de question, et l'aubergiste s'approcha.

— On doit r'gagner Pointe-Lévy, lui expliqua le bûcheron. L'plus vite serait l'mieux. La malle-poste arrête-tu icitte ?

— Plus maintenant. La diligence passe de Saint-Joseph-de-Deschambault à Sainte-Famille-du-Cap-Santé. Vous pouvez trouver un habitant pour vous amener au Cap-Santé en charrette et vous pourrez attendre la malle-poste de là, demain ou après-demain. Sauf que si vous avez des moyens… L'homme qui

fume dans le coin, là-bas, c'est le capitaine du *John Munn*, le grand *steamboat* qui mouille présentement au port. Il reprendra sa route sous peu ; s'il vous accepte à son bord, vous serez à la Pointe-Lévy dans une heure ou deux.

— J'vas y parler. Merci.

Baptiste se leva pour se diriger vers l'officier, puis stoppa son geste.

— Euh… faudrait que tu m'guides, garçon.

— Hein ? Ah… oui, bien sûr.

Faustin prit le bras du bûcheron et fit semblant de le guider vers la table. Sur l'épaule où il se tenait, Ti-Jean balança la tête de gauche à droite, forçant le colosse à une démarche hésitante plus conforme à ce qu'on attendait d'un aveugle.

Après avoir tiré la chaise de Baptiste et salué le capitaine, un homme barbu fort avancé en âge, Faustin put enfin aller voir Shaor'i. À genoux devant l'âtre, l'Indienne avait bu son bouillon et demandé une brosse à la serveuse. Elle avait ainsi lissé ses longs cheveux neigeux. Quand Faustin s'installa à ses côtés, elle achevait de les coiffer en une longue tresse qu'elle laissa retomber dans son dos.

— C'est la première fois que je te vois te coiffer ainsi, lança Faustin.

Il en profita pour la détailler. Chevelure blanche, iris dorés, taille réduite, Shaor'i ressemblait de plus en plus à une créature sortie d'un conte.

— Je n'ai pas l'habitude de les natter, répondit-elle. Mais je ne veux pas les voir : ils me feraient hésiter davantage.

— Hésiter ?

— La présence de mon autre âme, celle du harfang… je la sens chaque jour plus forte. Et voir cette femme à demi transformée, cette Poulin à moitié féline,

m'a donné un choc. En la combattant, j'ai hésité à adopter ma forme animale et Plaçoa a pu s'en prendre à moi – normalement, j'aurais été capable de sortir du rayon où la voyante pouvait le laisser s'éloigner sans perdre son emprise sur lui.

La jeune femme planta ses yeux fixes dans les flammes du foyer et poursuivit :

— Et tout à l'heure, j'ai douté de la même manière en faisant face à Gamache… et les conséquences ont été désastreuses.

L'Indienne fit jouer ses orteils dans ses bottes. Ses pieds, que Faustin savait ressembler à des serres, se plièrent dans un angle étrange.

— Je ne veux pas que la vue de ces cheveux me porte à hésiter de nouveau. J'ai d'abord songé à les couper, mais leur absence aurait le même effet négatif.

Alors qu'il cherchait en vain quelque chose à répondre, Faustin entendit Baptiste l'appeler à la table du capitaine. Après avoir adressé un geste d'excuse à Shaor'i, il se leva pour aller rejoindre le bûcheron.

Le colosse achevait de vider une pinte avec le capitaine. Il indiqua d'un signe à Faustin de s'asseoir et déclara :

— Not' bon cap'taine, ici présent, accepte de nous amener à Pointe-Lévy.

— C'est fort aimable à vous, le remercia Faustin en lui adressant un chaleureux sourire.

— Y dit aussi qu'un sloop de notre ami Ferrier a été chargé aux Trois-Rivières, avant-hier au soir.

— Je vous ai expliqué, monsieur Lachapelle, que je ne puis vous révéler ce qu'un autre navire prend à son bord, répliqua le capitaine.

— Entre vous pis moé pis la boîte à tabac, c'pas illégal non plus.

— Mais ce n'est guère courtois.

— Ça l'était de m'dire que c'était point un chargement normal ?

— Une erreur de ma part. Vous m'en voyez fort désolé.

Faustin comprit ce que le bûcheron attendait de lui. Il s'agissait là d'un des premiers sorts qu'il avait maîtrisé quand il assistait son oncle dans la résolution des crimes mineurs et petits délits qui secouaient, de temps à autre, la tranquillité de Notre-Dame des Tempérances.

Après avoir jeté un regard tout autour, certain de n'être remarqué de personne, Faustin sortit sa craie et profita que l'attention du capitaine était tournée vers Baptiste pour dessiner un cercle sur la table de bois. Il traça à l'intérieur deux triangles l'un sur l'autre, joignit quelques lignes entre elles et dessina un autre cercle plus important.

— *Ammar salìen-hasar ekt zanir ker*, incanta-t-il dans un murmure.

La tête du capitaine oscilla comme s'il avait trop bu. Faustin s'empressa de le questionner.

— Ferrier a fait monter un chargement inhabituel, disiez-vous ?

— Oui, répondit l'homme, la voix un peu éteinte.

— Et il s'agissait…

— De boulets. De caisses de boulets. Je le sais car l'une d'elles n'avait pas le fond assez solide et a répandu son contenu sur le quai. Il y avait aussi trois caisses aux dimensions de cercueils, si lourdes qu'elles ont été traînées à bord par un cheval. Je pense que ça pourrait être des canons.

— Vers où se dirigeait le sloop de Ferrier ?

— Je l'ignore.

— En aval ou en amont ?

— En aval.

— Le nom de ce sloop ?

— Le *Margaret*.

Après que Baptiste eut signifié d'un geste qu'il n'avait rien à ajouter, Faustin essuya le pentacle avec sa paume. Le capitaine revint doucement à son état de lucidité.

— Pis on embarque quand ? lui demanda Baptiste quand il eut recouvré ses esprits.

— Demain à l'aube. Restez donc à dormir ici, nous partirons ensemble.

Baptiste tendit une main, que l'homme serra vigoureusement. Faustin délia les cordons de sa bourse pour payer le prix convenu, se trompant deux fois en comptant les pièces tant les révélations qu'il venait d'entendre l'inquiétaient.

◆

— Reste maintenant à savoir, lança Faustin en s'appuyant au bastingage du navire, si le *Margaret* va décharger ses canons à Québec ou à l'île d'Orléans. Je ne vois pas d'autre lieu en aval du fleuve où l'Étranger aurait avantage à positionner ses pièces.

Bien que la bouche du bûcheron aveugle remuât, Faustin ne comprit pas un traître mot, assourdi par la sirène du *steamboat* qui venait de retentir. Comme chaque fois, Shaor'i posa les mains sur le manche de ses couteaux et poussa un cri strident, tournant la tête dans tous les sens comme un oiseau aux aguets.

— J'disais qu'à l'île, c'est discret, pour sûr, répéta Baptiste en tapotant l'épaule de l'Indienne qui reprenait son emprise sur elle-même. À Québec, ça pourrait attirer l'attention, mais avec l'shérif Sewell dans sa poche, l'Étranger peut faire à peu près tout c'qui veut.

Faustin soupira, son regard se perdant dans les eaux du fleuve. Il avait hâte de descendre à Pointe-Lévy.

Au début, il avait été ravi de monter sur un bateau aussi moderne. Le *John Munn* était un navire magnifique, immense et blanc, avec d'énormes cheminées et deux ponts superposés. Néanmoins, le bruit répétitif de la roue à aubes donnait à Faustin le mal de crâne et le son des chaudières qui ronflaient et des moteurs qui cliquetaient rendait Shaor'i nerveuse et tendue.

— Il y a déjà un bon stock de canons à Québec, non ? Qui plus est, ils sont accessibles à n'importe qui : chaque année, les finissants de médecine défient les nouveaux d'en faire tirer un, tout le monde sait ça.

— Y tirent sans boulet, à tout l'moins.

— D'où l'idée de décharger des boulets à Québec et d'autres à l'île, avec les canons.

— P'tête bin…

La sirène émit de nouveau son timbre sourd et, n'y tenant plus, Shaor'i s'assura qu'aucun passager ne la voyait et sauta par-dessus bord, en adoptant sa forme de harfang pour s'éloigner à tire-d'aile.

Désirant rester seul avec ses pensées, Faustin s'éloigna de Baptiste et marcha jusqu'à la poupe, s'autorisant enfin à réfléchir à une découverte qu'il avait faite moins d'une heure avant de fuir l'Étranger. Le contact avec Nadjaw, la route vers l'autel de pierre de Yamachiche, le retour en diligence et l'attaque… tout cela lui avait permis d'éviter de songer à l'existence de sa fille, portée par Rose.

« *On l'a baptisée du nom d'Anne, comme la sainte mère de la Vierge* », avait dit le maire Latulipe.

Sauf que la petite n'avait eu que quelques jours pour connaître le monde avant de disparaître à tout jamais, son esprit remplacé par celui de Marie-Josephte Corriveau, la mère de Faustin – sa grand-mère paternelle, pour tout dire.

Les sentiments de Faustin étaient plutôt incertains au sujet de cette enfant.

Certes, les mœurs paysannes ne se préoccupaient généralement pas beaucoup du décès d'un enfant en bas âge. Mort à la naissance, grippe maligne, infection pulmonaire, prématurité, rougeole, chute, mort blanche ou accouchement par le siège, les raisons ne manquaient pas pour que décède un bébé. Cela arrivait au moins une fois dans chaque famille. Et si la fille de Faustin n'était pas vraiment morte, son esprit avait été effacé, ce qui était à peu près la même chose.

Pourtant...

Une image se dessina brièvement dans l'esprit de Faustin : Rose donnant le sein à son bébé, Faustin se berçant juste à côté en fredonnant un refrain d'enfance que Madeleine lui avait jadis chanté.

Anne.

C'était un joli prénom. Était-ce Rose qui l'avait choisi ? Ou encore les parents de Rose ? Ou les Leclerc, famille adoptive de la fillette ?

Elle aurait dû s'appeler...

Anne Lamare.

Gorge nouée, Faustin chassa ces pensées. Ce genre de vie lui était proscrit, lui qui léguerait à sa descendance une longévité qui n'avait pas sa place en ce monde où les arcanes disparaissaient. Tout comme la sienne le priverait de lier sa vie à celle d'une femme. « *Et comment lui expliqueras-tu ta longévité, à cette fille d'habitant ?* » s'était emporté François lorsqu'ils avaient abordé cette possibilité.

Mieux valait ne plus penser à sa fille. Elle était morte, pour ainsi dire... son corps n'était plus qu'un réceptacle pour l'esprit d'une femme qui n'était même plus réellement la mère de Faustin, sa personnalité ayant été altérée par l'Étranger.

Chassant une larme du revers de la main, Faustin concentra son attention sur le rivage qui défilait devant

ses yeux, tentant de confiner aux oubliettes de son âme tout ce qui pouvait se rapprocher d'un sentiment paternel. Mais il savait qu'il n'y parviendrait jamais tout à fait.

◆

Faustin avait fumé pendant le reste du voyage. Il achevait de curer sa pipe quand le brouhaha du port de Pointe-Lévy le tira de ses préoccupations.

Il avait appris sur le navire que, le mois précédent, une épidémie de choléra avait frappé la ville de Québec. On ne l'aurait pas cru tant les quais grouillaient de monde, sur la rive nord comme sur la rive sud.

Tous les ans, à la fin de l'été, Pointe-Lévy se mettait au diapason du marché du Vieux-Port de Québec. Dès que le grain était sec aux champs jusqu'aux récoltes maraîchères, le port de la Pointe bourdonnait d'activité. La plupart des cultivateurs de la rive sud convergeaient vers cette destination pour faire traverser le fleuve à leurs marchandises, espérant encaisser dans la capitale suffisamment de profit pour régler leurs achats annuels d'objets utilitaires ou d'agrément.

C'est avec difficulté que Faustin, Baptiste et Ti-Jean débarquèrent du *John Munn*, un troupeau de curieux s'étant massé autour du quai afin de contempler ce prodige de l'ingénierie navale moderne. Après avoir remercié le capitaine, qui se donnait de grands airs en saluant la foule de sa casquette, Faustin s'empressa de « guider » le bûcheron – heureusement, l'énorme carrure de l'homme fort incitait tout naturellement les badauds à s'écarter.

Malheureusement, l'achalandage ne diminua pas lorsqu'ils s'éloignèrent du quai. Les charrettes s'entassaient le long de la rue bordant le fleuve, leurs

conducteurs attendant patiemment leur tour pour embarquer leurs charges. Non loin, les boutiquiers de la côte du Passage, qu'on surnommait à juste titre la « côte aux marchands », avaient grossièrement gonflé leurs prix. En la gravissant, l'esprit paysan de Faustin se révolta de constater que le prix du pain avait monté à un demi-cent et qu'une simple bière froide coûtait autant qu'une tournée en temps normal.

— Je gage qu'il n'y a que la famille Molson qui puisse se permettre de manger ici, grogna-t-il à l'intention de Baptiste en voyant l'ardoise des prix affichée à l'extérieur d'une auberge.

— C'pas comme si ta bourse était si plate que ça, le taquina le bûcheron.

— Question de principe, coupa Faustin, outré. On dînera au presbytère.

— Ça va aller dans quequ'z'heures, quand même.

— Ça te semblera meilleur et c'est tout. Ne me dis pas que tu n'as jamais retardé un repas sur la drave ?

D'abord sans voix, Baptiste éclata d'un rire homérique qui masqua brièvement la clameur de la foule. Gagné par son hilarité, Ti-Jean poussa de petits cris joyeux auxquels Faustin répondit par un large sourire.

◆

Ils quittèrent bientôt Pointe-Lévy pour emprunter le chemin de terre menant à Notre-Dame des Tempérances. Lorsqu'ils furent assez éloignés, Shaor'i vint les rejoindre et marcha avec eux sous sa forme humaine. Faustin soupira d'aise : son village natal n'était pas loin et il lui tardait de le retrouver. Il pouvait déjà entendre les reproches de Madeleine en les voyant arriver à l'improviste pour le souper sans qu'elle ait eu le temps de préparer un repas copieux. Puis il se demanda comment Madeleine avait réagi à ses trois

mois d'absence. Elle défaillirait probablement de soulagement en le voyant arriver, puis la colère la gagnerait. Comment avait-il pu ne pas lui envoyer « à tout le moins » une lettre par le Chemin du Roy ? Une pointe de culpabilité traversa le cœur de Faustin en imaginant l'ancienne servante de son oncle se rendant chaque matin au comptoir postal de la mère Bélisle, le cœur battant d'espoir.

À elle, au moins, il pourrait expliquer les véritables raisons de son absence : le Stigma, la métamorphose en renard, ce genre de choses. Il pourrait aussi lui dire pourquoi son corps avait tant changé en si peu de temps. Pour les gens du village, ce serait difficile : on peut prendre beaucoup de coffre en un été, surtout quand on accepte un contrat de chantier, mais Faustin avait l'impression qu'il alimenterait les discussions pendant un bon moment.

Le pire, toutefois, serait d'apprendre à Madeleine ce qu'il était advenu de François. Juste à y songer, Faustin sentait son cœur battre de travers. La servante avait accueilli François quand il avait douze ans et l'avait, tout comme Faustin, élevé comme un fils. Après treize années sans jamais quitter le presbytère, il s'était exilé deux mois après les événements de l'île d'Orléans, était revenu le temps d'une divination… et ne reviendrait peut-être jamais plus.

Madeleine en serait brisée, détruite, anéantie. Une fois, à l'auberge à Beaupré, Faustin avait assisté à l'annonce de la mort d'un adolescent parti pour la drave. Le père s'était effondré en larmes et seuls les mots rassurants du curé Lamare, qu'on était allé quérir en hâte, étaient parvenus à redonner à l'homme endeuillé le courage de rentrer chez lui annoncer le décès à sa maisonnée… Madeleine ne serait pas dans un moindre état, loin de là.

Jonglant avec ses pensées, Faustin se rendit compte de l'étendue du chemin parcouru en entendant couler le ruisseau Croche. Alors une sorte d'excitation le saisit et, malgré le fardeau des nouvelles qu'il portait, l'impatience le gagna. De pas en pas, sa fébrilité allait croissant. À présent, il reconnaissait tout ce qui l'entourait : le vieil érable noueux, les buissons aux mûres, l'étang aux grenouilles, la roue de charrette abandonnée par le père Lambert qui gisait au bord de la route depuis six ans... Tout à coup, Faustin sentit monter en lui un formidable appétit de ragots à la forge Dubé, de promenades avec Samson, de bière frelatée à l'auberge à Beaupré, de parties de dames à la boutique de la mère Bélisle, de musique du violon à Boutin, de bêche plantée dans la terre meuble, d'eau tirée de la pompe grinçante du presbytère, de coups d'œil furtifs dans le décolleté de la grande Ardélia, de récits de chantiers, de chansons d'habitants, de sucre à la crème, de tarte aux pommes, de thé fort, de feu de poêle, de veillées et de mille autres choses.

Il pressa le pas sans remarquer que Baptiste et Shaor'i ralentissaient.

Il parcourut de nombreuses verges avant de constater l'absence des bruits qu'il aurait normalement dû entendre en approchant du village. Il remarqua alors que personne n'était aux champs même si les blés, à en voir la couleur, étaient secs depuis longtemps.

Les rangs de terre battue étaient déserts.

Il s'arrêta brusquement.

Comme une brise soudaine, il sentit une première âme effleurer son esprit et souffler le murmure d'une peur innommable.

Avant qu'il ne puisse identifier le défunt, il en vint un second, puis un troisième, joignant leurs chuchotements d'outre-tombe qui se transformèrent en plaintes, en lamentations.

Et tandis que les traits de Faustin se figeaient en un masque d'horreur, les âmes continuèrent d'affluer pour devenir foules, des âmes qui se mirent à virevolter autour de lui comme un essaim, leurs gémissements devenant autant de cris qui vrillèrent son esprit d'une douleur lancinante, émettant leur souffrance et leur terreur dans un chaos effroyable alors que, la tête entre ses mains, il se laissait tomber à genoux en hurlant une rage et une détresse pire que tout ce qu'il avait pu ressentir jusqu'alors.

Et il fut convaincu que, dans son esprit, les voix de ces âmes-là ne se tairaient jamais.

◆

Dès qu'ils avaient constaté l'ampleur du drame, Baptiste et Shaor'i avaient décidé de partir à la recherche d'Otjiera.

Faustin avait préféré rester au village et ils avaient respecté ce choix.

Seul, il déambulait entre les maisons, ruminant des pensées aussi lugubres que les ombres que dessinait le soleil couchant. Il croisa les bras pour se réchauffer, transi de froid malgré le fait que l'air du soir portait encore la chaleur estivale.

Notre-Dame des Tempérances, avec ses champs étincelants et sa gaie populace, n'était plus qu'un souvenir appelé à se perdre dans les brumes de l'oubli. Les douces odeurs des maisons des ménagères et les ragots d'auberge avaient disparu pour ne jamais revenir.

Après la découverte des six premiers corps, il avait cessé de s'attarder aux visages. Les cadavres de ceux qui avaient été les habitants de Notre-Dame des Tempérances jonchaient le sol, éventrés, leurs traits

éternellement figés en rictus de pure horreur. Les mouches bourdonnaient autour des dépouilles en nuages noirs opaques, menant un bruit incessant; corbeaux et urubus se repaissaient des chairs mortes, se disputant parfois avec les rats qui, le ventre plein, ne prêtaient guère attention à cet humain apparemment inoffensif qui errait sans but.

Des jacks mistigris. Des centaines de jacks mistigris. Les traces de griffes sur les murs de bois, les empreintes sur le sol, cette manière de tuer en déchiquetant les parties souples d'un corps, abdomen ou gorge – souvent les deux. Et tous ces corps que croisait Faustin appartenaient à des connaissances, sinon à des amis.

Le carnage devait s'être produit très vite, sûrement de nuit : les bestiaux étaient dans leurs étables lorsqu'ils avaient été massacrés, eux aussi. Les portes avaient été défoncées pendant que les paysans dormaient, l'horreur de croiser un non-mort devait les avoir pétrifiés d'effroi avant qu'ils ne puissent réagir. Dans la terreur la plus noire, les habitants d'un paisible village avaient été tués sans qu'ils puissent opposer la moindre résistance.

À une exception près... Il y avait eu une barricade de caisses et de tonneaux devant la porte de la forge à Dubé. Elle avait été détruite morceau par morceau. On pouvait voir que cette même porte, à présent défoncée, avait été fortifiée par d'énormes madriers. À travers l'ouverture, Faustin vit un amoncellement de cadavres, des hommes qui s'étaient servis jusqu'à la fin de leurs fusils inutiles face aux jacks mistigris. Sans mal, Faustin imaginait le gros forgeron tenant le siège malgré la terreur, incitant sa poignée d'hommes à s'enhardir, beuglant des ordres, des sacres et des encouragements. Alors qu'il passait dans l'échoppe, le jeune homme vit l'imposante dépouille de Dubé

serrant toujours dans ses mains gantées une énorme tige de fer. Face à lui, la carcasse de deux wendigos, l'un au crâne éclaté, l'autre, de toute évidence, transpercé de part en part par la barre de métal qui devait alors être rougeoyante.

Dubé avait-il repris espoir en découvrant une manière de tuer ses ennemis ? Mais à cet ultime moment, les balles avaient été épuisées et les non-morts pénétraient dans l'échoppe…

Rage et chagrin bataillèrent dans le cœur de Faustin quand il découvrit dans la dépense les petits corps qui y gisaient. Il y avait le fils du juge Lamontagne, à dix ans presque aussi gros que son père ; cette graine de voyou à Bégin qui chipait les tartes des voisines ; la jeune Alicia St-Onge, qui nourrissait en secret le gros matou noir errant dans le village depuis des années ; le dernier-né des Lacerte, qui ne savait pas encore marcher ; deux des frères Duchemin, vêtus comme à leur habitude de vêtements usés à la corde ; un nourrisson si jeune qu'il devait être né durant l'absence de Faustin, encore serré dans les bras de la petite Lise Comeau.

Sans se retourner, le jeune homme quitta l'échoppe d'un pas décidé et prit le chemin du presbytère.

Le long du rang de terre battue, il eut une pensée pour chaque famille dont il croisa la maison à la porte arrachée de ses gonds. Il constata bien vite que le groupe du forgeron n'avait pas été le seul à tenter de se défendre contre l'horreur qui s'était abattue sur le village. À travers la grande fenêtre de la boutique de la mère Bélisle, on pouvait voir d'autres hommes, des fusils ayant chu à côté de leurs corps, témoins de leur résistance.

Silencieux, l'esprit éteint, Faustin gravit la « côte aux prêtres ». Le cœur lui martelant la poitrine, il

approcha de cette église trapue et rectangulaire, qui
ne se différenciait d'une maison d'habitant que par
son modeste clocher. Les grandes portes avaient été
abattues et parmi les bancs d'église se trouvaient les
corps de plusieurs habitants de Notre-Dame des Tempérances.

Faustin passa toutefois son chemin, les yeux fixés
sur le presbytère, la maison de son enfance. À pas
lents, il suivit l'allée, monta les trois marches qui le
séparaient de l'ouverture où s'était jadis trouvée une
porte.

Juste avant de franchir le seuil, Faustin stoppa son
mouvement.

Puis il retira ses bottes et entra.

◆

Il ne trouva pas le corps de Madeleine dans la cuisine, pas plus que dans sa chambre ou à la cave. Il se
permit alors une lueur d'espoir : après tout, Otjiera
était resté pour veiller sur elle. Elle devait être chez
les Wendats nomades, par-delà la Pinède ! Le cœur
battant, Faustin se précipita au-dehors par la porte du
sous-sol.

Elle était là.

Cette femme aimante aux boucles brunes striées de
gris, aux yeux bienveillants et au rire facile, cette mère
adoptive qui lui cuisait brioches et pains sucrés avant
de l'envoyer récurer les chaudrons, cette chaleur aimante
qui communiquait sa joie de vivre à une maisonnée
d'hommes lettrés – Madeleine était là, étendue près
de l'énorme corps de Samson que la servante avait
commencé à seller avant que le drame ne l'atteigne,
et tous deux avaient eu le bas du ventre ouvert par les
griffes des jacks.

Faustin s'arma d'un bâton pour chasser les corbeaux qui s'affairaient sur les corps, s'accroupit doucement et fit glisser ses doigts dans la chevelure de Madeleine. De son autre main, il lui ferma les yeux, puis la bouche, figée sur un cri silencieux. Des larmes coulant sur ses joues, il se releva et marcha d'un pas résolu vers la grange où il se saisit d'une pelle.

Il entama la surface du sol en amorçant le refrain de *Colchiques dans les prés*. Au fur et à mesure qu'il creusait se succédèrent entre ses sanglots les couplets de *La Petite Souris grise,* d'*À la claire fontaine* et de dix autres chansons de son enfance que Madeleine fredonnait au rythme de ses journées, en s'acquittant des tâches du foyer. Les pleurs de Faustin transformèrent bientôt ses chants en une espèce de grincement et il s'arrêta sur *Malbrough s'en va-t-en guerre*, ayant achevé une fosse suffisamment profonde pour y déposer celle qui avait été leur mère, à lui et à François. Il se rendit alors à ce rosier qu'elle avait amoureusement entretenu durant des années, le dépouilla de ses fleurs et les posa sur la poitrine de la servante avant de la recouvrir doucement, laissant délicatement glisser la terre de sa pelle.

Sa tâche terminée, il resta à genoux un long moment. Une tempête de pensées incohérentes lui martelaient l'esprit en s'entrechoquant dans sa tête, attisées par la monstruosité du drame. Des réminiscences fugaces lui revenaient en mémoire, heureux souvenirs d'une existence passée dans un village qui n'était plus et, bien vite, Faustin eut l'impression que son âme allait exploser.

D'un vif mouvement, il se leva et se dirigea vers le parvis de l'église. À ses pieds, tout en bas de la côte aux prêtres, il contempla le village qui l'avait vu grandir et une force terrible l'envahit tandis que sur

ces lieux de mort se surimprimaient ses souvenirs d'un village grouillant d'activité. La colère qu'il avait portée en lui à la découverte du village s'était momentanément tue à la vue de la dépouille de Madeleine ; elle venait de se raviver et menaçait maintenant de le consumer en entier.

Le premier hurlement de Faustin résonna longtemps. Avec ce cri monta un besoin farouche de détruire et ses muscles se raidirent sous l'assaut d'irrépressibles tremblements. Un picotement l'envahit, devint une brûlure qui l'embrasa et, alors qu'il fermait les yeux pour retenir ses larmes, il vit se dessiner dans son esprit l'image d'un pentacle incandescent.

— Brûle ! cria Faustin en dressant une main vers le ciel. BRÛLE !

Une première maison explosa, broyée par un geyser de flammes surgi de ses fondations. Deux autres s'enflammèrent presque aussitôt, puis d'autres encore.

— BRÛLE ! rugit le jeune homme dont les genoux ployaient sous lui, qui se laissait tomber par terre pendant qu'un immense brasier dévorait tout ce qui avait été fermes, échoppes, granges et maisons.

— BRÛLE ! vociféra-t-il encore, le visage taché de larmes et de suie, alors que dans son esprit hurlaient les âmes des défunts.

LIVRE VIII

SUR LE FLEUVE

Des tyrans ici-bas, le règne est éphémère
Le jour viendra, le peuple attend
D'outrages, de mépris, il repaît sa colère
La digue enfin cède au torrent

Marc-Aurèle Plamondon,
Chant National

CHAPITRE 28

À *bord de la* Rosamund

À Pointe-Lévy, on remarqua une colonne de fumée titanesque qui s'élevait au sud, précisément là où se trouvait le village de Notre-Dame des Tempérances. Bien vite, le suroît porta l'odeur de brûlé qui envahit la ville portuaire.

D'urgence, quelques Lévisiens se précipitèrent aux nouvelles, virent avec effroi l'amplitude du brasier et firent aussitôt demi-tour. Ils revinrent beaucoup plus tard avec des miliciens, un prêtre et d'autres volontaires. Quand ceux-ci débarquèrent de cheval, ce qui avait été un paisible village de campagne n'était plus que braises incandescentes.

La nécessité cédant le pas à l'horreur, on chercha des survivants. N'en trouvant point, on chercha une explication.

Il y avait forcément eu une épidémie fulgurante : après tout, le choléra avait sévi à Québec plus tôt durant l'été. La quantité de squelettes calcinés dans les ruines de l'église corroborait cette thèse et expliquait que si peu de gens aient eu la force d'aller quérir du secours.

L'incendie pouvait avoir débuté dans une grange à foin, un propriétaire malade ayant oublié un fanal allumé. Cela arrivait parfois. Certes, on se demanda

comment les flammes avaient pu atteindre les fermes les plus isolées, les granges situées au fond des terres. Les champs en cendres avaient fourni une explication. L'ampleur du drame était énorme, mais ce n'était pas un cas unique. Les incendies des faubourgs Saint-Jean et Saint-Roch, quatre ans auparavant à Québec, avaient causé des dommages encore plus considérables. Suffisait d'ajouter à cela une population malade, incapable de combattre les flammes.

La théorie, malgré des lacunes notables – justifier l'extraordinaire rapidité de la propagation des flammes, notamment –, tenait assez pour rassurer les Lévisiens face à l'épouvantable catastrophe d'un village entier disparu en une seule journée.

Au fil des jours, on contacta les proches des victimes, des volontaires creusèrent des fosses communes, les curés de trois paroisses avoisinantes prononcèrent une messe en plein air.

Une semaine après l'incendie, des personnes – peut-être les curés – suggérèrent d'ériger à Pointe-Lévy un monument à la mémoire des martyrs du brasier de Notre-Dame des Tempérances. Sur l'un des promontoires de la ville, on dressa donc une grande colonne de bois au-dessus d'un escalier qu'on baptisa en grande pompe « Monument des Tempérances ». L'événement attira de nombreux paroissiens, outre les proches des disparus : plusieurs paysans encore à attendre l'embarquement de leurs marchandises y virent l'opportunité de se changer les idées. On mangea beaucoup, on but encore plus, puis on rentra chez soi.

On avait fait ce qu'il fallait pour rendre hommage aux morts ; l'existence des vivants devait se poursuivre.

Si la tragédie fut encore longtemps un sujet de discussion, on ne se préoccupa plus beaucoup des ruines du village. Certaines personnes à l'esprit pratique,

jugeant qu'il ne servait à rien d'abandonner là des objets dont les morts n'auraient plus besoin, vinrent fouiller les décombres. On chargea notamment des poêles à bois en fonte. Quelqu'un – encore un curé, probablement – décida cependant qu'il était mal venu de tirer profit du drame et, évaluant le montant qui pourrait être tiré des objets restants, ordonna que le produit de la vente soit versé aux églises des environs.

Et finalement, après quinze jours, la vie reprit son cours et Notre-Dame des Tempérances cessa définitivement d'exister.

◆

Si je le veux, cela ne me concerne plus, se répétait Faustin, les yeux perdus dans les eaux du fleuve.

Il savourait sa première journée de silence psychique. Les âmes des victimes de Notre-Dame des Tempérances l'avaient hanté des jours entiers avant de se retirer l'une après l'autre. Les enfants et les vieillards avaient été les premiers à passer dans l'outre-monde, puis les parents des enfants, suivis des proches de ces parents. Les dernières âmes, des gens plutôt solitaires que Faustin parvenait à identifier à mesure que la nuée spirituelle s'amenuisait, s'étaient finalement résignées au départ... à l'exception de celle du forgeron Dubé qui, tourmenté d'avoir découvert trop tard la vulnérabilité des jacks au feu, s'accablait de remords auxquels Faustin ne pouvait rien changer. L'esprit du forgeron l'avait finalement quitté dans la nuit pour aller hanter les ruines du village.

Tant pour fuir les esprits que pour éviter lui-même de penser au carnage, Faustin avait passé l'essentiel de son temps sous forme de renard, laissant ses instincts animaux prendre le dessus aussi souvent que c'était

possible. C'était sous cette forme qu'il s'était nourri, car il n'avait consommé aucun repas au cours des deux dernières semaines.

Ses pérégrinations à travers les boisés de la rive sud l'avaient mené à un promontoire rocheux à une lieue de Pointe-Lévy d'où il pouvait contempler le soleil se lever en aval du Saint-Laurent.

Derrière lui, il perçut soudain un froissement d'ailes que son ouïe de plus en plus fine identifia sans mal : deux coups brefs de longues pennes frappant l'air succédant à un vol parfaitement silencieux. Un rapace.

Le changement de masse sur le sol qu'il sentit dans la plante de ses pieds et l'odeur de sauge qui piqua aussitôt ses narines lui confirmèrent qu'il s'agissait de Shaor'i.

Sans un mot, l'Indienne vint se placer à côté de lui. Elle aussi riva son regard sur les flots du Saint-Laurent et décida de ne rien dire. Sans mal, Faustin comprit qu'elle lui parlait tout de même.

Saokata. L'Éternel Silence.

Shaor'i souffrait. Ce silence du mal innommable, Faustin en avait fait son compagnon depuis deux semaines et pouvait le reconnaître sans difficulté. Il jeta un coup d'œil à la jeune femme, vit qu'une hachette indienne pendait à sa ceinture, à côté de son couteau droit. Elle portait quelques colifichets de plus, dont un qu'il était certain d'avoir déjà vu au cou d'Otjiera. Et, en y repensant bien, il avait déjà aperçu la hachette à la taille du Premier Danseur.

Le silence de l'Indienne changea de ton. Un autre silence qu'il connaissait trop bien, celui qu'il avait partagé avec François en ramenant le corps de son oncle au presbytère. La souffrance mutuelle.

Il comprit qu'il était arrivé quelque chose à Otjiera.

Il ne demanda pas de précision. Rien ne pressait. Son silence se changea en celui qu'on observe face

aux gens brisés par le deuil, quand on sait qu'aucune parole ne peut apporter le réconfort.

L'Indienne garda le même silence. Pendant un long moment, ils partagèrent cette compréhension du non-dit. Puis, beaucoup plus tard, quand Shaor'i adopta un tacet qui démontrait une sorte d'attente tranquille, Faustin posa la question :

— Comment est-il mort ?

— Un sort de goétie, celui qui brise tous les os du corps et fait souffrir longtemps sa victime.

Faustin ne dit rien, mais son silence refléta sa douleur devant une telle abomination. Puis l'Indienne ajouta :

— C'est un sort que favorisait Lavallée. Otjiera me l'a déjà dit. Il l'avait bien connu, jadis ; c'est à lui que Lavallée avait confié la Pierre Manquante.

Lavallée. L'épouvante gagna Faustin : prisonnier dans son propre corps, François était donc venu à Notre-Dame des Tempérances. Se pouvait-il que…

— Non, décréta Shaor'i qui avait deviné le cours de ses pensées. Même Lavallée n'a pas la puissance pour garder son emprise sur autant de wendigos.

Reste qu'il a probablement assisté à la scène, songea Faustin.

— Pourquoi crois-tu que l'Étranger a fait ça ? Il n'avait absolument aucune raison de procéder à ce carnage. Le meurtre d'Otjiera, lui, est logique : il était assez puissant pour lui nuire. Mais ces paysans, ces ménagères et ces enfants… ils n'occupaient aucune place sur son échiquier.

Shaor'i chercha son regard du sien avant de dire :

— Il a agi pour te détruire.

Frappé au cœur, Faustin se détourna. La rage lui consumait toujours l'âme, et voilà que cette sauvagesse tournait le couteau dans la plaie : s'il ne s'était

pas opposé à l'Étranger ou, tout simplement, s'il n'avait pas fui la Grande Maison – ou s'il était mort, pourquoi pas ? –, tous les habitants de ce paisible univers n'auraient d'autres préoccupations en ce moment que de se préparer pour les moissons.

Comprenant sa douleur, Shaor'i ajouta :

— Ne peux-tu voir qu'il a peur de toi ?

La question était d'un ridicule si grotesque que Faustin éclata d'un grand rire sarcastique.

— Oh oui, bien entendu... ironisa-t-il. Je le vois d'ici, dans la grande chambre sous l'église de Saint-Laurent, tremblant de terreur à l'idée qu'un bedeau de village ne débarque armé de sa fourche...

— Je t'ai vu, du haut des airs, quand tu brûlais les ruines de ton village. Tu n'avais tracé aucun pentacle. L'Étranger est le seul autre pratiquant des arcanes scientifiques capable d'un pareil prodige.

Sans pentacle ? Non, pas tout à fait. Faustin avait *vu* un pentacle se dessiner dans son esprit, une sorte de réminiscence du sortilège. Il était *quelque part*, ce diagramme. Et en y repensant, son corps, même s'il bénéficiait d'une longévité prodigieuse, aurait dû ressentir un contrecoup face à une telle orgie de destruction. Or, cela n'était pas arrivé.

Sa longévité... il la puisait à même l'Étranger. Il se souvenait parfaitement des propos de la Siffleuse à ce sujet : « *La longévité de l'Étranger vient de quelque part... esprits frappeurs, feux follets et autres immortels sont attirés ici et, drainés, nourrissent en longévité ceux qui sont attachés à la stase temporelle. Ce que l'Étranger n'avait pas prévu, c'est que lorsqu'il vous a engendré, l'enchantement vous a "reconnu".* »

Mais dans ce cas, se dit alors Faustin, *tous ces diagrammes gravés dans la chambre où repose l'Étranger... se pouvait-il que...*

François lui avait déjà expliqué que le diagramme arcanique était un catalyseur, non pas la source d'énergie. La source, c'était le corps de l'arcaniste, et c'est en se vidant d'une partie de son énergie qu'il vieillissait prématurément.

En conséquence, comprit Faustin, quand l'Étranger se manifestait sous forme d'effigie et lançait un sort, ce n'était pas l'effigie qui fournissait l'énergie, mais, à des dizaines de lieues de là, son corps inanimé.

Ainsi…

— Non, Shaor'i, il y avait bel et bien un pentacle, finit-il par répondre. Loin d'ici, sous la Fontaine du Diable, aux Forges du Saint-Maurice. Dans la chambre où repose le corps de l'Étranger sont gravés des dizaines de diagrammes. Et…

— … comme pour la longévité, tu peux utiliser cette ressource, car l'enchantement te reconnaît.

— Oui, l'enchantement me reconnaît…

Ne peux-tu voir qu'il a peur de toi? avait dit la jeune femme.

— Je te laisse seul, déclara-t-elle avant de prendre son envol, redevenue harfang.

◆

Il connaissait les rangs du village par cœur depuis sa plus tendre enfance. Sous ses pieds, il sentait cette pierre plate près de chez la veuve Gélinas qui faisait toujours cahoter les charrettes ; ou encore, cette petite déclinaison qui devenait si traîtreusement glissante en hiver.

De temps en temps, il gardait les yeux clos et pouvait reconstituer mentalement les environs avec une clarté et une précision telles qu'il aurait pu croire que rien, absolument rien, n'était venu troubler la paix de ce coin de pays.

Il n'était pas revenu dans les ruines de Notre-Dame des Tempérances depuis sa fureur incendiaire. Les fouilles des habitants de Pointe-Lévy, la tempête estivale de la semaine précédente et les bourrasques du début de septembre avaient fait leur œuvre. L'odeur de bois noirci et de chair brûlée avait disparu. Quelques maisons parmi les plus solides tenaient encore debout; l'église, elle, était presque intacte, ses murs de pierre des champs ayant peu souffert du brasier. On avait déjà repris les objets saints, même s'ils avaient été déformés par les flammes – l'or ne reste jamais longtemps à l'abandon – et, jetant un coup d'œil au clocher, Faustin constata qu'on avait aussi récupéré la cloche.

Quelqu'un avait dégagé les décombres de la forge de Dubé, probablement pour faire main basse sur l'enclume, mais il était reparti bredouille, et probablement à l'épouvante: le spectre du forgeron, toujours aussi accablé, s'était accroché à son outil de travail comme d'autres revenants s'accrochaient à leurs maisons.

Mais Faustin n'était pas venu pour s'adresser à son ancien ami. Sa destination était tout près des vestiges du presbytère et n'avait attiré l'attention de personne: une pierre énorme, toute simple, qui avait été moussue avant que la chaleur infernale des flammes ne dessèche la mousse. C'était la roche sur laquelle le curé Lamare aimait jadis s'asseoir pour lire et que Faustin avait demandé à Baptiste de déplacer pour marquer le lieu du dernier repos de son oncle.

Silencieux, le jeune homme s'assit en tailleur devant la tombe et, après une brève hésitation, sortit le livre de Le Loyer sur la conjuration des esprits. Il n'avait jamais contacté son oncle. En fait, il s'était adonné au spiritisme pour la première fois juste avant de partir pour les Forges et, quelques jours plus tard, métamorphosé en renard pour échapper à l'Étranger.

Le spiritisme. Plus un art qu'une science, au point que l'Étranger lui-même s'avouait incapable de le pratiquer.

Ne peux-tu voir qu'il a peur de toi ?

Il choisit de repousser l'obsédante question de Shaor'i. Ce qu'il souhaitait, en ce moment, c'était entrer en contact avec son oncle pour savoir quelle décision il convenait de prendre.

Nerveux et impatient tout à la fois, il dessina un pentagone au centre d'un octogone qu'il contint dans un cercle. Après avoir tracé les apothèmes majeurs et lié deux perpendiculaires, il incanta :

— *Ad-est kareza, sürdanresh-zonrik aniir, margesht al-fontir.*

Il perçut aussitôt la présence paternelle et chaleureuse de son oncle le nimber d'une onde apaisante. Faustin sentit des larmes lui picoter les yeux, battit des paupières, puis décida de les laisser couler.

C'est quand il voulut s'arrimer à la conscience de son oncle qu'il vit que quelque chose clochait.

Le curé Lamare était bien là, et en paix. Toutefois, il avait l'air de… refuser le contact. Faustin aurait pu le forcer, comme il l'avait déjà fait face à des esprits frappeurs, mais il lui répugnait de contraindre un être tant aimé à se manifester contre son gré.

Pourquoi, mon oncle ? demanda Faustin alors qu'il prenait la décision, après plusieurs minutes, de mettre fin au sortilège.

Un souvenir lui remonta aussitôt en tête, une anecdote qu'il avait oubliée. Résultat du sortilège, acte de son oncle par-delà la mort ou étrange tour de sa mémoire ?

Il ne le saurait jamais. Pourtant, le souvenir lui était revenu avec une inhabituelle limpidité.

Il avait tout juste douze ans à l'époque…

◆

Il faisait un temps magnifique ce jour-là. Il venait de gagner six billes à la suite d'une partie spécialement corsée contre le fils du tenancier Beaupré, et le gros Dubé avait décidé d'une partie de pêche. Faustin s'était précipité au presbytère pour en avertir Madeleine. Sitôt avait-il ouvert la porte qu'il était tombé sur son oncle et François-la-Perche qui discutaient à la table.

— Tiens, lança le curé quand Faustin entra. Nous n'avons qu'à lui demander son opinion. Tu veux bien descendre avec nous à la bibliothèque un instant, garçon?

— Mais je vais à la pêche! rouspéta Faustin, boudeur.

— Ça ne sera pas long, je te le promets. Allez viens, je ne voudrais pas que Madeleine surprenne cette discussion pour y mettre son grain de sel.

Cette déclaration suffit à piquer la curiosité de Faustin. D'habitude, la servante pouvait donner son opinion quand venait le temps des discussions. Docilement, le garçon descendit l'escalier, accompagné de son oncle et de son frère adoptif.

À peine avait-il pénétré dans la sombre pièce que Faustin fronça le nez. Jamais la bibliothèque de son oncle ne lui avait semblé plus poussiéreuse, plus sombre et plus triste qu'en cet après-midi de mai, le premier jour où il faisait assez chaud pour que Madeleine le laisse sortir sans veste.

Son oncle prit place dans son fauteuil d'étude, un gros siège de maroquin. Quant à François, il resta debout dans un coin et annonça de but en blanc :

— J'ai terminé ma formation, Faustin. Il ne me reste qu'à maîtriser quelques notions secondaires et ton oncle affirme que j'aurai eu une formation équivalant

à celle que donne le Collège d'Albert le Grand. Et l'an prochain, il trafiquera ce qu'il faut pour que je devienne vicaire.

Faustin haussa les épaules et, voyant que son frère attendait quelque chose, il dit :

— Eh bien… bravo, la Perche.

Ayant l'air d'espérer une autre réaction, François se tint silencieux un instant.

— Tu vois ? lança le curé Lamare de son fauteuil.

— Allons, Faustin, s'impatienta François. Tu ne vois pas ce que ça signifie ? Je pourrais te former à ton tour, si tu le souhaites !

— Ah…

François tenta d'être encourageant :

— Tu sais, Faustin, les arcanes t'ouvrent des portes extraordinaires. Pense juste à ce diagramme de flammes que je t'ai enseigné le mois dernier.

Ça, Faustin devait admettre que cela lui avait bien servi. Chaque fois que les braises s'éteignaient, c'est à lui que Madeleine confiait la corvée de frapper la poignée métallique contre la pierre-à-feu pour créer une nouvelle flamme et cela, malgré l'insistance de Faustin pour se procurer ces nouveaux petits bâtons à allumer, des « allumettes », qu'on vendait à Pointe-Lévy. « Une mode qui va passer », affirmait la servante. « On ne va pas se mettre acheter des objets qu'il faut jeter après un seul usage ! »

Néanmoins, de là à faire comme François et à s'astreindre à six heures d'étude chaque jour… Il soupira. Il ne s'était jamais pris pour un intellectuel. Déjà qu'il sache lire et écrire à douze ans l'élevait au rang de précoce érudit au sein du village.

— C'est que…

— Il n'y a plus beaucoup de gens qui savent pratiquer les arcanes, Faustin. Plus qu'un privilège, c'est presque un devoir que tu as de…

— *François! coupa le curé Lamare d'une voix autoritaire mais sans colère. Laisse-le dire ce qu'il en pense.*

Faustin soupira encore. Il avait hâte de sortir de cette sinistre pièce qui sentait le vieux papier et le cuir moisi. Le gros Dubé devait déjà être parti pour l'étang aux crapets et, si ça continuait comme ça, l'après-midi passerait sans qu'il ait jeté une seule fois sa ligne à l'eau.

Il se tourna vers son oncle :

— *Est-ce… est-ce que je suis obligé d'apprendre autant de sorts que François ?*

— *Tu n'es pas obligé de faire quoi que ce soit. Tu as l'esprit vif, c'est vrai, mais tu peux tout aussi bien t'adonner aux dames…*

— *Maître! s'indigna François. Vous n'allez pas laisser ce petit renard vous enfirouaper comme ça ? Les dames, allons donc! Vous jugez que c'est suffisant ?*

— *…ou l'anglais, peut-être ? Qu'en dis-tu, Faustin ? Tu aimerais apprendre l'anglais ?*

— *La langue des envahisseurs ? cria l'apprenti du curé. Vous allez enseigner l'anglais à votre neveu pendant que là-bas, en ce moment même, Papineau et ses Patriotes se battent pour préserver notre langue et nos droits ? Pendant que le Vieux Brûlot incendie les fermes des innocents et…*

— *C'est d'accord pour apprendre l'anglais, lança Faustin, plus pour défier son frère adoptif que par réel intérêt.*

Son oncle dut se rendre compte de ses motivations, car il retint son rire avec grand-peine tant François était resté bouche bée devant la réponse de Faustin.

— *Et aussi quelques sorts, mais pas beaucoup. Des sorts qui servent à quelque chose d'utile.*

— *Comment ça, des choses utiles ? lança son frère qui venait de retrouver la parole. Tous les sorts sont utiles, Faustin, et…*

— *Je me fiche de savoir par divination si une paire de culottes a déjà appartenu au général Montcalm ou d'être capable de faire tomber de la neige en été. Je veux des sorts… pratiques, conclut Faustin, satisfait d'avoir trouvé l'adjectif qui correspondait à son idée.*

— *Des sorts pratiques, répéta François, hébété.*

— *Et pas beaucoup. Déjà que je rate ma partie de pêche…*

— *Mais…*

— *Ça suffit, François, intervint le curé. Tu vois bien qu'il n'a pas les mêmes intérêts que toi? Va, Faustin, on a terminé. Va rejoindre tes copains… et amène le poulain de Brunette, histoire qu'il continue de s'habituer aux enfants.*

Faustin ouvrit des yeux énormes et crut qu'il venait d'entendre une musique infinie venant du ciel.

— *Je peux amener le p'tit Samson? Pour de vrai?*

— *Pour de vrai. Allez, sauve-toi, p'tit renard!*

Aussi vite qu'il le put, Faustin sortit de la cave et se précipita vers l'écurie.

Ce soir-là, quand il revint pour le souper, François et son oncle discutaient toujours dans la bibliothèque.

Peu importait. Lui avait usé de son après-midi pour attraper une truite énorme qui lui avait valu l'admiration de ses copains, et Madeleine lui avait promis qu'elle allait la frire dans une chapelure de pain sec, comme il l'aimait.

◆

C'est à moi de choisir.

Peu importait ce qui avait laissé remonter ce souvenir, cela expliquait sans l'ombre d'un doute le refus du curé Lamare de se manifester à son neveu.

C'est à moi de choisir.

Quand tout avait commencé, le soir du dernier Mardi gras, Faustin avait été catapulté malgré lui dans des événements qui le dépassaient. À son retour de l'île d'Orléans, il avait cru revenir lentement à une vie normale. Espoir vain. Quand il avait appris que sa mère, la Corriveau, avait été réincarnée dans l'enfant illégitime de Rose (le sien, avait-il découvert plus tard), il s'était lui-même précipité aux Forges, croyant qu'il pourrait régler aisément une situation infiniment plus grave que tout ce qu'il imaginait.

Et maintenant ?

Il pouvait décider de quitter ce monde de sorcellerie, de créatures et de spectres. Vivre une existence normale, laisser l'Étranger étendre sa démence en espérant que d'autres y mettent fin. Il ne se faisait pas d'inquiétude à savoir s'il pourrait trouver un endroit où s'établir : il connaissait des gens à Pointe-Lévy et il s'y dénicherait sans mal une place d'homme engagé. Après tout, maintenant que tout ce qu'il avait connu était détruit, il n'avait nul chez-soi où rentrer et nulle famille n'espérait son retour.

Sauf François. Peut-être.

Son frère adoptif était tout ce qui lui restait. Il avait tenté de le libérer, aux Forges, et avait échoué. Néanmoins, même en désirant de tout cœur retrouver un semblant de vie ordinaire, il sut qu'il ne pourrait passer un jour sans souffrir de ne pas avoir tout tenté pour ramener François.

Ce qui signifiait qu'il devait risquer sa vie et affronter l'Étranger.

Ne peux-tu voir qu'il a peur de toi ?

Il n'y avait plus de retour en arrière possible, se força à admettre Faustin. Depuis la mort de son oncle, depuis l'enlèvement de Rose, depuis le vol d'une simple

lettre chez la mère Bélisle... depuis bien avant ça.
Depuis que, bébé, le Collège l'avait confié au curé
Lamare. Depuis que, quelques années avant la défaite
des plaines d'Abraham, une paysanne nommée Marie-
Josephte Corriveau s'était rendue dans les souterrains
sous les Forges du Saint-Maurice pour y être engrossée
de force.

Depuis sa conception, le destin de Faustin était
inextricablement lié à celui de l'Étranger.

C'est à moi de choisir...

... et j'ai choisi.

Ce qu'il ressentait n'était pas une spectaculaire
montée de bravoure telle qu'on peut la voir décrite
dans les contes, ni une froide résolution de se lancer
à l'attaque de son ennemi. Ce que Faustin éprouva à
ce moment-là n'était que la tranquille acceptation des
choses, comme lorsqu'une pluie inattendue couche les
blés avant qu'on ait pu les faucher.

Près de lui, quelqu'un se racla la gorge, interrompant
ses pensées. Baptiste se tenait non loin, assis sur une
pierre, son lutin sur l'épaule.

— J'pensais bin t'trouver icitte, Faustin.

Le jeune homme hocha la tête sans mot dire. Le
bûcheron se racla de nouveau la gorge avant de reprendre :

— T'sais, Faustin, j'ai passé les deux dernières
semaines à faire l'tour des villages, histoire de trouver
quelqu'un qui pourrait nous en conter sur c'qui s'est
passé icitte, ou qu'en saurait plus qu'les autres, mais
j'ai trouvé personne. Pas d'survivants non plus. Faque
j'ai pus rien à faire dans l'coin, garçon. J'voulais t'dire
que j'pars pour l'Isle-aux-Grues. J'veux savoir c'que
l'père Masse me veut. Pis aussi... j'veux qui fasse
quequ'chose pour arrêter c'te démon d'Étranger. Un
drame de même, c'est trop... y a pas d'mots. Même à

guerre, ça s'passe pas d'même. Les soldats bataillent sur des champs pis s'entretuent, c'est leur métier. Mais à part que'ques horreurs, comme durant l'Grand Dérangement, les gens ordinaires sont point touchés. Ou pas tant qu'ça. Jamais, même à guerre, on tue des innocents par pleins villages.

Faustin, se tenant coi, médita quelque peu ces paroles.

— Tu peux faire c'que tu veux, mon garçon, reprit le bûcheron, mais la P'tite va venir avec moé. Pis Ti-Jean itou, ben sûr.

— Je vais venir avec vous, Baptiste.

Le lutin se pencha vers Faustin et le dévisagea pour le colosse.

— T'es sûr, garçon ? Parce que…

— Je viens. Tant que vous n'aurez pas rejoint le père Masse, je suis le seul qui puisse user de théurgie. Et de toute façon, je dois sauver François. Il est la seule famille qu'il me reste, à part Shaor'i et toi. Pis Ti-Jean itou, ben sûr.

Ce fut au tour de Baptiste de rester silencieux pendant un moment. Faustin se leva d'un bond et lança :

— Allons-y. Il me tarde de partir. Le bedeau de Notre-Dame des Tempérances est mort avec son village. Quoi qu'il arrive, je ne reviendrai jamais ici.

Hochant gravement la tête, le colosse prit le sentier vers Pointe-Lévy aux côtés de Faustin. Un rapace blanc descendit du ciel et se métamorphosa en jeune femme pour marcher à leurs côtés.

Pas une seule fois, Faustin ne jeta un regard en arrière.

◆

Le port de Pointe-Lévy, sans avoir la vastitude de celui de Québec, avait en été une animation qui épatait

toujours Faustin. Si plusieurs navires étaient canadiens, propriétés de la famille Molson, du baron Smith ou de la *Masson, LaRocque, Strang and Company*, d'autres venaient des États-Unis ou de beaucoup plus loin, tel le majestueux trois-mâts britannique *Brave Heart*, qui arrivait tout juste des Indes Orientales, disait-on. Sa cargaison d'épices, de bois rares et d'étoffes fines était destinée à Montréal et Bytown.

D'autres navires plus modestes – barques élégantes, bricks et sloops, ainsi qu'une grande quantité de goélettes – se balançaient à l'ancre, voiles carguées. Autant ces vaisseaux étaient essentiels à la vie commerciale de Pointe-Lévy, autant ils occupaient une importante part du folklore local, car si les marins avaient toujours quelques bonnes histoires à raconter, ils étaient eux-mêmes source de ragots. Tout le monde à Pointe-Lévy connaissait quelqu'un qui connaissait quelqu'un dont la jeune fille, plutôt que d'aller à la messe du dimanche, s'était imprudemment promenée au bord de l'eau et avait été enlevée par quelque matelot pour ne plus jamais être revue.

Dans une auberge au bas de la côte aux marchands, Baptiste s'était informé de la présence d'un nommé « Le Crabe » qui, au dire du bûcheron, aurait conduit les compagnons à l'Isle-aux-Grues sans délai ; ledit Crabe s'étant retiré deux ans auparavant, on lui avait suggéré un nommé Bouchard, de Montmagny, qui poursuivrait sa descente du fleuve dans peu de temps et ne manquerait pas de faire escale à l'Isle-aux-Grues.

Bouchard s'avéra fort accommodant et, acceptant une somme plus symbolique qu'autre chose, serra la main de Baptiste pour conclure l'accord. Sans tarder, il invita les compagnons à rejoindre son embarcation.

Au bout de la rue qui menait de l'auberge au port, les vagues fouaillaient les quais qui avançaient dans le

fleuve. Fort jovial, Bouchard causait avec Faustin et Baptiste en marchant, nommant les navires, exposant des détails sur leur voilure ou leur tonnage ou expliquant la provenance ou la cargaison de chacun. Ils en arrivèrent bientôt aux Chaînes, cette ligne de roches qui bordait le chenal du Saint-Laurent et où était ancrée une goélette à deux mâts égaux, relativement neuve et fort bien entretenue. Son nom, la *Rosamund*, était peint en lettres argentées sur la proue, alors que ses voiles auriques étaient d'une blancheur immaculée. Invités par le marin, qui servait de guide à Baptiste, les compagnons s'avancèrent sur les pierres glissantes. Un adolescent resté sur la goélette surgit soudain pour venir aider le bûcheron à monter à bord, pendant que Faustin, qui avait bien du mal à trouver son équilibre, mit le pied à l'eau à deux reprises avant de rejoindre l'embarcation. Contrairement à lui, Shaor'i sautilla adroitement d'une roche à l'autre jusqu'au bateau.

— En forme, la p'tite grand-mère ! la complimenta Bouchard avec une expression de totale incrédulité sur son visage.

L'Indienne haussa les épaules et se détourna.

Grand-mère ? releva mentalement Faustin avant de comprendre que la chevelure neigeuse de Shaor'i et sa très petite taille pouvaient mener à pareille conclusion.

Bouchard se chargea ensuite des présentations en désignant le jeune qui avait aidé Baptiste.

— Lui, c'est le p'tit Côté, l'cousin d'ma femme, qui m'sert pour ainsi dire de second. Pierre, j'te présente m'sieur Lachapelle, m'sieur Lamare pis madame Sori, nos passagers jusqu'à Montmagny.

— Shaor'i, rectifia Faustin en jetant un œil vers l'Indienne qui faisait déjà le tour de l'embarcation. Enchanté, Pierre.

— De même, répondit l'intéressé avant de se tourner vers Bouchard pour lancer : on part de suite, mononc' ? pendant que la marée tient encore un ti-peu ?

— Crie l'arrimeur pis largue, garçon ! On a pas toute la journée !

Bouchard donna un coup de barre et le jeune Côté tira sur un câble. Les voiles se gonflèrent dans la brise fluviale et, bondissant sur les flots, la goélette s'écarta des Chaînes pour s'engager sur le fleuve.

◆

Il ne fallut pas longtemps pour que la ville ne soit plus visible et que les rives se couvrent d'arbres. Docile, la goélette filait dans le courant. Bouchard tenait la barre avec la nonchalance d'un homme de métier durant un travail routinier, et le jeune Côté avait assez de temps libre pour s'occuper des comptes des transactions effectuées à Pointe-Lévy.

Appuyé au bastingage, Faustin observait le paysage, portant la main de temps à autre au sac de balles d'argent qu'il portait à la ceinture.

Baptiste avait récupéré de l'argenterie dans la maison du maire Latulipe. Avant d'aller à l'auberge, ils étaient passés chez un maréchal-ferrant pour faire mouler le métal en munitions d'argent. L'artisan ne s'était guère étonné de la commande. « Z'êtes point les premiers à ramener du stock des ruines de Notre-Dame des Tempérances », avait-il marmonné. Le moulage en balles ne l'avait pas plus surpris : c'était une commande fréquente des voyageurs en partance vers l'Ouest qui désiraient payer en métaux précieux plutôt qu'en devises.

Encore faudra-t-il enchanter les munitions, songea Faustin. Le bûcheron était persuadé que le père Masse

se chargerait de cette tâche. Faute de quoi, Shaor'i le ferait, mais cela lui prendrait des semaines de méditation. Mieux valait la rapidité de la théurgie.

Prenant une profonde bouffée de sa pipe, Faustin laissa aller ses pensées. Le temps au beau fixe était propice aux réflexions ; sur le fleuve, il n'entendait que les craquements de la *Rosamund* et le clapotis des vagues sous la coque.

— C'est l'île au Ruau qu'approche, déclara Côté en venant s'appuyer au bastingage à côté de Faustin. Si on passe assez proche, tu vas voir l'domaine que l'nouveau seigneur s'est fait construire : un genre de manoir plus grand qu'une chapelle…

Faustin hocha poliment la tête et fixa l'île. Sa vue de renard, plus acérée que celle d'un homme, lui permit de distinguer le domaine victorien en cours de construction.

— Y avait quasiment rien l'an passé… pis v'là qu'un richard prend caprice de s'faire seigneur.

Côté, hélé par le capitaine, toucha sa casquette en guise de salut à Faustin, dont les pensées revinrent au père Masse, dernier maître du Collège.

Un arcaniste accompli, semblait-il, bien que le jeune homme eût des doutes. La dernière fois qu'ils s'étaient mis en route pour voir un membre de l'Ordre Théurgique d'Albert le Grand, ils étaient tombés sur un ivrogne si malhabile avec les arcanes qu'il parvenait à peine à faire geler l'eau en hiver. Les espoirs de François et de Faustin pour trouver de l'aide avaient été cruellement déçus – *non*, se morigéna le jeune homme, s'obligeant à être honnête, le père Bélanger les avait aidés autant qu'il le pouvait en leur fournissant grimoires et informations. Néanmoins, Faustin se refusait cette fois à trop espérer de ce mystérieux théurgiste.

Jetant dans les eaux du fleuve un petit caillou qu'il avait ramassé sur le pont, Faustin quitta le bastingage et marcha vers la cabine. Elle avait été offerte à Baptiste, le capitaine jugeant que ce serait plus prudent pour un aveugle de s'y tenir plutôt que de marcher sur le pont. Au passage, il jeta un coup d'œil à Shaor'i qui, juchée sur le toit de l'habitacle malgré les inquiétudes de Bouchard, méditait silencieusement, assise en tailleur.

L'intérieur de la cabine était sombre, humide et empestait le bois mouillé. À la lueur d'une chandelle, affalé sur une caisse de bois, Baptiste fumait pensivement, écoutant distraitement les babillages de Ti-Jean auxquels il répondait parfois d'un hochement de tête.

Faustin tira à lui une bassine qu'il retourna pour s'en faire un siège et sortit sa pipe. Après avoir accepté l'allumette du bûcheron et tiré une première bouffée, il demanda :

— Parle-moi du père Masse, Baptiste. Tu l'as bien connu ?

Le visage du colosse se fendit d'un grand sourire.

— Assez bin, oui. C'tait – j'veux dire *c'est* – un homme qu'a l'air de toute savoir. Il a déjà été l'curé de Pointe-Lévy pis c'tait l'mentor de ton oncle.

— Différent du père Bélanger, alors ?

— Ah ça, pour sûr ! L'père Masse, c't'un grand arcaniste, un historien pis un voyageur. Il a été missionnaire pis s'est promené partout, dans l'Ouest comme dans l'Nord, jusque dans les vieux pays comme la France pis l'Italie. Un grand maître au Collège, qu'aurait même dû être le dirigeant à la place de Lartigue…

— À t'entendre en parler, je crois que l'Ordre s'en serait mieux porté.

Le navire tangua soudain et la chandelle vacilla. Faustin s'appuya sur le flanc tribord pour éviter de tomber.

— J'pense aussi, garçon. Mais Masse, c'est pas l'genre de bonhomme à nager dans les politicailleries. C't'un chercheur. Un passionné. Pis, si tu t'souviens, c'est lui qu'a fait des recherches sur l'Étranger.

— Oui, se remémora Faustin, le père Bélanger nous avait montré un livre dans lequel étaient répertoriées les apparitions de l'Étranger à travers le temps.

— C'est ça. Masse, c't'un chercheur pur et dur.

— Et comme homme ? Comment est-il ?

— Assez solitaire. Un peu perdu dans ses pensées. Plutôt jasant, porté sur la conférence improvisée. Tu verras, dans l'fond. C't'un bon bonhomme, qui doit avoir dans les…

Baptiste fronça les sourcils en comptant à rebours les décennies sur ses doigts.

— On est en 49. En 39, c'tait les pendaisons… 29, 19, l'année que j'ai rencontré ton oncle… avant ça, 1809 pis encore avant y a eu l'histoire d'exorcisme de 1799. Où l'père Masse était déjà un bon arcaniste…

Le bûcheron soupira.

— Il doit avoir pas loin de quatre-vingts ans, j'cré bin. On peut bin l'avoir pensé mort, mais…

La *Rosamund* se mit à tanguer de nouveau, et Baptiste faillit choir. Les flots devenaient plus agités.

— Un grain qui s'prépare ?

À l'extérieur, on pouvait entendre le bruit du vent dans les câblages.

— Il faisait pourtant beau il y a dix minutes, objecta Faustin.

Avec un grand fracas, la porte de la cabine s'ouvrit en claquant contre la paroi. Le vent sifflait au-dehors et la pluie avait commencé à s'abattre sur le pont.

— Je vais voir ce qui se passe, cria Faustin pour couvrir le bruit du vent.

Le roulis du navire le forçant à marcher avec prudence, le jeune homme referma la porte derrière lui en sortant de la cabine. Le crachin glacial lui cinglant le visage, il tenta d'avancer jusqu'à la barre, à demi aveuglé. La goélette roulait sur le fleuve moutonnant, ses voiles gonflées sous un ciel devenu presque noir. Le jeune homme glissa plusieurs fois, s'arrêta pour aider le jeune Côté à carguer une voile, puis parvint à se rendre jusqu'à Bouchard.

De ce que lui expliqua le marin, il n'y avait eu aucun signe avant-coureur – pas de rafales, pas d'augmentation d'humidité, pas la moindre oscillation du bateau ou le plus infime indice de danger. Soudainement, l'air s'était obscurci, des nuages noirs avaient surgi du néant, comme si le ciel avait foncé d'un seul coup, la pluie s'était déchaînée – tout cela en quelques minutes.

— C'pas normal, du temps d'même ! vociféra le capitaine. C'pas naturel !

Un coup de tonnerre résonna au-dessus d'eux et, comme pour lui donner raison, la pluie se mua en grêle et de petits morceaux de glace se mirent à marteler le pont.

— On devrait pas accoster ? cria Faustin pour couvrir le bruit du vent qui hurlait dans le gréement.

De toutes ses forces, Bouchard tentait déjà de virer tribord, mais il arrivait à peine à tenir la barre. Faustin joignit sa force à la sienne et la barre bougea d'un pied avant d'échapper à leur contrôle, frappant Bouchard au ventre.

L'homme s'effondra en gémissant alors que les éclairs se déchaînaient. La houle devint si forte que la goélette se mit à dévaler le dos des vagues, privée de tout contrôle.

Une main en visière pour protéger ses yeux, Faustin chercha Shaor'i du regard. Elle était grimpée au sommet

de la mâture et faisait de grands gestes en pointant le bras à bâbord. Subitement, le jeune homme sentit les eaux soulever violemment la goélette et il dut s'agripper au bastingage. Comme il rétablissait son équilibre, un choc d'une immense violence ébranla la goélette. Le jeune homme se précipita vers le bastingage, persuadé qu'ils avaient heurté un écueil.

Il eut tout juste le temps de voir une chose qu'il prit d'abord pour un immense tronc flottant avant de remarquer la cuirasse et les longues crêtes épineuses. Puis une queue titanesque au lobe allongé fit surface, balaya les eaux dans un mouvement de lacet avant de s'abattre avec toute sa force contre la coque, dont le bois craqua d'une façon inquiétante.

Kabir Kouba… comprit Faustin, horrifié.

Impuissant, il vit le monstre remonter et, cette fois, il aperçut tout son corps. Le léviathan devait dépasser les trente verges; son corps trapu était armé de cinq rangées de boucliers osseux, chacun doté d'une crête se terminant par une épine.

Plus long et plus large que la *Rosamund*, Kabir Kouba décrivit dans les flots un arc de cercle et enfonça son museau long et retroussé sous le navire qui se souleva aussitôt.

À ses côtés, Faustin entendit un cri de pure terreur: Bouchard hurlait comme un possédé, le visage figé en un rictus de démence. Avant qu'il ait pu dire ou faire quoi que ce soit, le capitaine s'était recroquevillé sur le pont, toute lucidité ayant quitté son regard.

Un autre cri couvrit ceux du marin apeuré.

Un cri de rapace.

Plongeant tête première de la mâture où elle avait grimpé, Shaor'i traversa le vide comme une flèche. Elle effectua un demi-salto dans les airs pour arriver les pieds d'abord sur le dos de l'immense créature en y enfonçant ses couteaux jusqu'au manche.

Si le monstre en perçut la moindre douleur, il ne le manifesta pas. Kabir Kouba plongea, entraînant l'Indienne qui se cramponnait aux manches de ses lames. La goélette, retombant sur les flots agités, fut secouée en tous sens.

Avant que Faustin ne puisse reprendre son aplomb, la tête armurée de plaques osseuses resurgissait déjà, prête de nouveau à frapper le navire de sa queue. Il vit l'Indienne, toujours accrochée aux manches de ses couteaux, en lâcher un pour dégainer la hachette d'Otjiera, qu'elle abattit avec force sur la cuirasse du monstre.

Baptiste arriva sur les entrefaites, tenant le fusil de Faustin d'une main et celui du capitaine de l'autre, pendant que Ti-Jean luttait contre le vent en s'agrippant pieds et mains à son épaule.

— Les armes sont chargées, tonna Baptiste pour couvrir la cacophonie ambiante.

Faustin attrapa son fusil, remercia d'un hochement de tête et, sans attendre, il épaula et tira, aussitôt imité par Baptiste. Étant presque à bout portant, il put suivre la traînée de fumée et voir la rainure que laissa la balle dans l'une des scutelles du monstre. Le tir de Baptiste ne sembla pas plus efficace.

Kabir Kouba plongea de nouveau, cette fois en arquant largement le dos. *In extremis*, Shaor'i parvint à décrocher ses couteaux et à adopter sa forme de harfang. Contre le vent, elle lutta pour rejoindre le navire et parvint, à force d'entêtement, à s'agripper au bastingage avant de reprendre forme humaine.

La plongée du monstre ajouta aux terribles remous du fleuve et la *Rosamund* tangua encore plus dangereusement.

— Baptiste, la barre, cria Faustin.

Le bûcheron comprit aussitôt qu'il y avait un problème avec le capitaine et il se précipita vers la roue,

qui tournait en tous sens, à la merci des éléments. À deux mains et tout en gonflant ses muscles, il réussit à faire virer la goélette. Toute la membrure craqua, mais le vaisseau se redressa enfin.

Courant dans la tempête, Faustin crut un instant que le jeune Côté était passé par-dessus bord, mais des mouvements dans la cabine lui firent comprendre qu'il s'y était réfugié, l'esprit tout aussi terrorisé par les événements que son capitaine. Faustin tentait de le raisonner quand il entendit Shaor'i hurler :

— Cramponnez-vous !

Le jeune se roula en boule dans un coin pendant que de nouveaux impacts ébranlaient fortement la *Rosamund*. Remontant sur le pont, Faustin fut surpris de ne pas voir le monstre marin.

— Où est Kabir Kouba ? cria-t-il à Shaor'i.

— Il a replongé. Le navire vient d'essuyer le tir de six boulets de canon, répliqua-t-elle dans la bourrasque. Six boulets en même temps, partis de l'île au Ruau et sans qu'on entende la moindre détonation.

Des boulets projetés sans canon. Faustin savait trop ce que cela impliquait : il avait vu Lavallée, dans le corps de François, les attaquer ainsi alors qu'ils fuyaient les Forges, aux Trois-Rivières.

Ce même Lavallée qui avait jadis contrôlé le climat pour détruire les navires de l'amiral Walker.

D'ailleurs, le vent gagnait encore en force et menaçait d'arracher les voiles à leurs ralingues. Des pièces d'espars s'étaient déjà déchirées et les plus petits cordages avaient lâché, claquant dans la tempête comme des fouets.

— Va falloir accoster ! hurla Baptiste en stabilisant la barre de peine et de misère malgré sa force herculéenne. On tiendra pas longtemps !

— Tout droit ! cria Shaor'i, dont les yeux perçants avaient repéré la terre ferme.

La *Rosamund* fut brusquement soulevée par un autre coup de boutoir de Kabir Kouba. Quand elle retomba, Faustin crut qu'elle n'arriverait jamais à se redresser.

— La terre est proche ! encouragea l'Indienne, qui venait de monter dans les cordages.

Elle n'y resta cependant pas trois secondes de plus. De nouveaux boulets percutèrent de plein fouet les deux mâts de la *Rosamund*. Shaor'i s'envola alors que les haubans se rompaient et que, dans un bruit épouvantable, toute la voilure s'effondrait sur le pont en fracassant tout sur son passage.

Pour Faustin, tout passa au noir, puis le contact avec l'eau glacée le ramena à la réalité. Il pataugeait dans les turbulentes eaux du fleuve. Aussi terrifié à l'idée d'être avalé par les flots que d'être happé par Kabir Kouba, il parvint à agripper un morceau de bois et à s'en aider pour flotter. Le courant l'éloigna rapidement de la goélette qui, bien que démâtée, semblait tant bien que mal se maintenir à flot.

Vaillamment, il se remit à la nage. La terre était proche, avait promis Shaor'i. À travers les éléments déchaînés, il distingua bientôt la rive. Se cramponnant à son bout de bois, il battit frénétiquement des jambes pour avancer en direction de la terre ferme.

Ce n'est que lorsque son pied toucha le fond qu'il comprit qu'il avait atteint son but. Épuisé, il se redressa, marcha jusqu'à la berge où, vidé de ses forces, il s'effondra sur le sol, les bras en croix.

CHAPITRE 29

Grosse-Île

C'était une vaste église de maçonnerie, beaucoup plus imposante que la plupart des églises de village. Les vitraux du transept laissaient filtrer une lumière colorée qui inondait le maître-autel. Un prêtre se tenait derrière. Épaules carrées, cheveux blonds.

François.

Ayant remarqué Faustin, le vicaire quitta l'autel pour courir jusqu'à lui. Tirant désespérément sur les manches du jeune homme, François le fixait de ses yeux d'azur.

— Des bakaak. Ce sont des bakaak, Faustin, répétait-il d'une voix insistante.

Faustin contempla son ami sans comprendre.

— Des bakaak ! cria le vicaire en s'agrippant aux vêtements de Faustin. Bakaak !

Un coup de tonnerre ébranla la voûte de l'église. Le vent se mit à souffler en tempête et les vitraux éclatèrent en millions de tessons multicolores. Au-dehors, des éclairs déchiraient le ciel.

Le vicaire s'effondra sur le sol et hurla, la tête entre les mains.

Des flammes jaillirent de son dos.

Pétrifié, Faustin ne parvint même pas à hurler.

◆

Des lamentations par milliers éveillèrent Faustin.

Le jeune homme porta la main à son front, étourdi. Bien que sorti de l'eau, son corps avait encore l'impression d'être ballotté par les flots. Les lamentations arrivaient de partout, ajoutant à l'effet de vertige le sentiment d'être entraîné par un fleuve entier d'âmes en peine.

Où avait-il abouti ?

Scrutant les environs, Faustin vit les restes de la *Rosamund* qui s'était échouée à trois cents verges de là. L'île était une terre désolée, broussailleuse, au sol manifestement ingrat où seuls poussaient des cèdres touffus et des pins noueux.

La tempête d'âmes en peine semblait s'atténuer doucement, comme si chacune se retirait après avoir manifesté sa présence. Un bon quart d'heure après son retour à la conscience, les plaintes des défunts s'étaient changées en une sorte de bruit de fond duquel Faustin pouvait détourner son attention.

N'empêche. Il y avait ici encore plus de défunts que dans les ruines de Notre-Dame des Tempérances – dix fois, vingt fois plus.

Était-il sur les lieux d'un ancien champ de bataille ? Sur une île, c'était peu probable, mais ses connaissances en histoire étaient limitées. Peut-être étaient-ce les gémissements de divers équipages ayant sombré – une explication plus logique.

En se levant, Faustin entendit d'autres cris, ceux-là appartenant au monde des vivants, qui semblaient venir de l'épave de la *Rosamund*. Encouragé, il s'empressa de se mettre en route.

Les âmes se turent à mesure qu'il progressait vers la goélette, au contraire des cris de plus en plus clairs et

dont il vit bientôt la source. Le capitaine Bouchard et son assistant Côté tenaient chacun une arme. Le vieux marin pointait sur Baptiste le fusil de Faustin, facilement reconnaissable à sa baïonnette. Le bûcheron gardait les mains au-dessus de sa tête et semblait vouloir apaiser les deux hommes.

Derrière le capitaine, le jeune Côté tremblait comme une feuille, l'air sur le point de s'enfuir en courant… ce qui rendait d'autant plus inquiétant le fait qu'il gardait l'index sur la gâchette de sa propre arme.

— Tu l'vois, osti ! cria Bouchard à l'intention de son assistant. Y s'tourne vers nous autres ! Y voit, même avec les orbites vides !

Faustin pressa le pas pour rejoindre Baptiste, qui disait :

— Calme, m'sieur Bouchard. J'vas vous expliquer c'qui s'passe…

Mais Bouchard semblait peu enclin à l'écoute.

— M'en vas te l'dire, c'qui s'passe… commença-t-il.

Il réprima un tremblement avant de reprendre :

— C'qui s'passe, c'est que j'ai vu une tempête sortir de nulle part, un aveugle s'promener comme si y'avait encore ses yeux…

La voix du marin avait monté en crescendo et avait maintenant un ton suraigu :

— … pis une crisse de sauvagesse qui s'change en oiseau… pis un crisse, un osti d'câlisse de maudit serpent d'mer !

— Tout doux… C'tait juste un gros esturgeon, capitaine… répliqua Baptiste d'un ton qu'il voulait rassurant, les mains toujours en l'air.

— Un serpent d'mer, tabarnak ! hurla Bouchard d'une voix hystérique. Un crisse de serpent plus long qu'mon bateau, ou bin l'Diable en personne, pour

c'que j'en sais ! D'toute manière, on va toute crever icitte, faque j'vois pas pourquoi j'vous tire pas tu-suite.

— Bouchard ! hurla Faustin en s'immisçant dans la dispute. Vous n'allez tirer sur personne… il s'est passé des choses sur le fleuve, nous allons vous les expliquer…

— Côté, surveille le jeune ! ordonna Bouchard.

Le jeune marin pointa son fusil vers Faustin et celui-ci leva les mains.

— Y a personne qui va crever icitte, m'sieur Bouchard, reprit doucement Baptiste. On va s'bâtir une p'tite embarcation avec c'qui reste de c'te navire-là… L'travail du bois a pas d'secret pour Faustin pis moé, j'suis bûcheron d'métier…

Tout en parlant, le colosse baissa légèrement les bras et esquissa un pas en avant.

— J'ai dit : tes mains din z'airs ! beugla Bouchard.

— Comme tu veux, mon gars, répondit Baptiste en obtempérant. Si tu veux pas qu'on construise, on va monter un feu d'alarme pour nous attirer de l'aide…

— Personne va venir icitte, esti de sans génie ! On va crever icitte !

— Calme-toé, mon gars, on va venir nous chercher, j'te dis…

— Pas sus l'Île-aux-Dix-Mille-Morts ! Y a personne qui va venir nous chercher icitte ! On va être forcés de rester pis on va crever du choléra, du typhus pis d'la variole comme toutes les Irlandais qui débarquent icitte !

Un bref éclair de panique étreignit Faustin : ils avaient échoué à Grossc-Île, l'île de la Quarantaine ! Elle portait bien son surnom d'Île-aux-Dix-Mille-Morts : ici les immigrants mouraient par milliers depuis quelques années – ainsi ces nuées d'âmes qui avaient assourdi ses sens spirites étaient celles des Irlandais tués par les épidémies.

« *Shaor'i, où es-tu ?* » émit désespérément Faustin sans recevoir la moindre réponse.

— On va parler aux Anglais, tenta de rassurer Baptiste. Not' Faustin, y parle aussi bien l'anglais qu'un député.

— Y parle au Diable, tu veux dire ! Vous parlez tous au Diable ! C'tait quoi, c'te sorcière de sauvagesse qui vire en oiseau ?

Baptiste soupira, fit un geste d'apaisement.

— Écoute, mon gars… baisse c'te fusil-là pis j'vas t'expliquer…

— Din z'airs, tes mains !

Le coup de fusil claqua et arracha un cri strident à Ti-Jean : le jeune Côté venait de tirer vers Baptiste, ses tremblements lui ayant fait rater sa cible de plusieurs verges.

Et merde ! pesta Faustin qui, n'ayant pas le choix, visualisa un diagramme particulier et incanta :

— *Ashek saen-irstean al-ibnar !*

Par l'entremise d'une force magique, le fusil à baïonnette fut arraché des mains de Bouchard et traversa l'air pour atterrir aux pieds de Faustin. Celui-ci s'empressa de s'en saisir et de tirer un coup vers le fleuve.

— Voilà, les coups sont tirés et on ne vous laissera pas le temps de recharger, lança-t-il à l'adresse des deux marchands qui, épouvantés, le fixaient en tremblant.

— On va s'parler entre gens raisonnables, renchérit Baptiste. On va toute vous expliquer, sur ma parole d'honneur.

Les deux hommes, blancs comme des linges et secoués de spasmes, semblaient pétrifiés sur place, incapables de tenter autre chose que sangloter.

— Écoutez, commença Faustin, il y a des choses que vous devez comprendre. Nous ne sommes pas…

— *Lower your guns!*

Tous se retournèrent pour découvrir six hommes en uniforme britannique, soldats du 32ᵉ régiment qui stationnaient sur Grosse-Île, propriété de Sa Majesté.

À la vue des six fusils pointés sur lui, Faustin laissa tomber son arme.

— *Who the hell are you and what are you doing here?* beugla celui qui, de toute évidence, était le plus haut gradé du groupe.

— Qu'est-ce qui dit? brailla Bouchard, toujours ébranlé.

— Il veut savoir qui nous sommes et ce que nous faisons ici, expliqua Faustin avant de se retourner vers les Anglais et d'expliquer: *We were going to l'Isle-aux-Grues*…

— Écoutez-le pas, implora Côté. C'est des sorciers. Z'avez vu c'qu'y z'ont faite au fusil?

— *We had an accident,* poursuivit Faustin. *Our ship was*…

— Qu'est-ce qui leur dit? lança Bouchard au bûcheron.

— J'parle pas plus anglais qu'toé, mon gars.

— J'essaie d'expliquer, répondit Faustin, que le bateau…

— *Devil!* clama Côté, fier et soulagé d'avoir trouvé dans les tréfonds de sa mémoire un mot anglais correspondant à peu près à ses idées. C'est des *devils*! Ils parlent avec le *devil*! Surveillez-les, watchez-les… *devil*, DEVIL!

— *Enough!* cria le soldat en pointant son arme vers Côté.

— Pas moi, eux autres! gémit le jeune marchand en désignant Baptiste et Faustin. *Devils!*

— *Shut up!*

— Il veut que tu la fermes, traduisit Faustin.

— *You're under arrest. Follow us.*

— Que-cé qui…

— On les suit, ils nous arrêtent.

— On a rien fait ! se plaignit Bouchard alors qu'un soldat s'avançait vers lui pour lui lier les mains. C'est eux autres, c'est…

L'Anglais lui asséna un coup de crosse au ventre et le marin se tut. Côté se laissa menotter de mauvaise grâce, murmurant des *devils* sans relâche. Les soldats se mirent trois autour de Baptiste, craignant peut-être sa grande stature. Le bûcheron obéit avec une lenteur mesurée – Ti-Jean s'étant enfui dans les fourrés dès l'arrivée des soldats, il était déstabilisé par sa vision lointaine de la scène relativement aux mouvements de son propre corps.

Quant à Faustin – peut-être parce qu'il parlait anglais, peut-être parce qu'il restait calme –, ce fut le chef des soldats qui s'occupa de lui, se montrant plus courtois et allant jusqu'à demander fort poliment :

— *Would you, please ?*

Posé, le jeune homme passa les mains derrière son dos en acquiesçant d'un « *sure* ».

— *Soon I'll take your statement,* ajouta le soldat en refermant les menottes. *Is this ship yours ?*

— *No. It's mister Bouchard's.*

— *Which one's Bouchard ? The blind giant, the old man or the Devil-freak ?*

— *The old man. The Devil-freak, Côté, is his partner. The blind man, Lachapelle, is my close friend. An Indian woman was with us. We hired Bouchard to go to l'Isle-aux-Grues. The tempest…*

— *Later. Now follow us.*

Hochant la tête, Faustin obéit, suivi des autres.

◆

Trop éloigné, Faustin ne put comprendre ce que marmonnait le capitaine à ses hommes. Il fut toutefois soulagé de voir que Bouchard et Côté étaient emmenés dans une autre direction que celle où étaient conduits Baptiste et lui.

Après avoir dépassé un cimetière et longé un sentier, ils arrivèrent dans un regroupement de grands bâtiments serrés les uns contre les autres. On les fit entrer dans l'un d'eux, demandant poliment à Faustin et au bûcheron qu'ils daignent bien leur confier armes et paquetons, puis on les amena dans des cellules en s'excusant que « c'était la procédure » et « qu'ils régleraient la chose en rencontrant sous peu le directeur ».

Les soldats expliquèrent encore deux ou trois choses puis les laissèrent seuls.

Quand il lui sembla que plus personne n'était proche, le bûcheron aveugle, assis sur le plancher de sa cellule, se tourna approximativement dans la direction de Faustin et demanda :

— Pis ? Qu'est-ce qu'y ont dit ?

— Qu'on n'a pas le droit de débarquer sur Grosse-Île comme ça, mais le capitaine comprend qu'avec la tempête, c'était obligatoire. Il passe l'éponge là-dessus sans problème.

— Déjà ça d'gagné.

— J'ai expliqué que Bouchard et Côté nous accusent d'avoir causé la tempête parce qu'ils ne la trouvaient pas normale, qu'ils nous prennent pour des sorciers et délirent à propos d'un serpent de mer. Le capitaine l'avait vaguement compris et les a envoyés voir le médecin-aliéniste.

— Les pauvres gars… z'ont rien fait de mal.

— Et nous, on sera examinés par les médecins et on devra rester sur l'île pendant quarante jours. Après, on sera libres de repartir.

— Comment ?

— C'est la règle, ici.

— Garçon, j'te signale qu'y a un monstre dans l'fleuve pis que l'Étranger s'fait descendre des canons des Trois-Rivières.

— D'accord, mais comment veux-tu qu'on parte d'ici sans navire ?

— Tu peux pas… ?

Le bûcheron esquissa un geste vague dans l'air.

— Non. Je ne connais pas le diagramme de téléportation par cœur.

— Pis dans voûte où s'trouve l'Étranger ?

— L'Étranger ne se projette qu'en effigie, quel usage aurait-il d'un sort pour déplacer son corps ?

Irrité comme chaque fois qu'il se trouvait contraint à l'immobilité, Baptiste se mit à fredonner doucement :

Il est une lande de terre dans un écrin d'eau,
Où chaque arpent cache de mille défunts les os.
Au ban des hommes on y envoie les mourants,
Dont la bise porte les hurlements.
Grosse-Île, ô terrible mouroir !
Domaine des démons Fièvre, Souffrance et Déses-
poir !

— Oh, ça va ! s'impatienta Faustin. N'en rajoute pas, veux-tu ?

— Des nouvelles d'la P'tite ?

Merde, c'est vrai, ça… constata Faustin avec une montée d'inquiétude. Savait-elle seulement nager ? *Ben voyons ! Une Indienne, c'est certain que ça nage. Et elle peut voler,* se morigéna-t-il pour se rassurer. N'empêche…

« *Shaor'i ?* »

Rien. Il ne parvenait pas à contacter son esprit. Restait à vérifier de *l'autre* façon. S'il parvenait à la contacter par une *nekuia*, alors forcément…

En hâte, il fouilla sa cellule, trouva un éclat de gypse avec lequel il traça le diagramme de Le Loyer. L'angoisse lui étreignant le cœur, il murmura l'incantation et fit le vide dans son esprit.

L'énergie dépensée se sublima sans produire le moindre effet arcanique.

— Elle est en vie, Baptiste. Ça, je peux te le garantir. Mais je n'arrive pas à la contacter. Elle doit être inconsciente, ou tout simplement dormir.

◆

Le capitaine revint peu après en expliquant à Faustin que le directeur, un certain docteur Douglas, était disposé à le recevoir, mais lui seul.

Traduisant la situation à l'intention de Baptiste, Faustin se laissa conduire hors du bâtiment carcéral et marcha avec l'officier en direction des quartiers du directeur.

— *You have to call the doctor "Seigneur Douglas". He's the surintendant.*

— *Seigneur?* releva Faustin, stupéfait. *Really? From which seigneurial land?*

— *From île au Ruau. He bought it last spring, during Lent.*

Le seigneur de l'île au Ruau… songea Faustin. D'où étaient partis les boulets qui les avaient fait chavirer. L'île voisine d'où Lavallée, dans le corps de François, les avait attaqués. Forcément, ce docteur Douglas était de mèche avec le Stigma Diaboli. Et qu'il ait acheté l'île pendant le Carême, juste comme le Stigma Diaboli kidnappait Rose et sa fille illégitime, ne laissait aucun doute sur son lien avec les goétistes de l'Étranger.

Ainsi, sitôt que le capitaine eut ouvert la porte après avoir frappé trois coups brefs, Faustin étrécit

les yeux et focalisa son outrevision. Les couleurs s'estompèrent et tout passa au gris. Le docteur, un grand homme brun en chemise blanche et gilet sans manches, congédia le militaire d'un geste discret – et Faustin eut la surprise de ne voir ni aura, ni le moindre reflet autour du surintendant de l'Île-aux-Dix-Mille-Morts.

— Des problèmes de vision, monsieur Lamare ?

Faustin revint à la vue normale et dévisagea le médecin, dont le sourire sardonique ne laissait rien présager de bon.

— Non, tout va bien de ce côté-là, seigneur Douglas.

— Docteur suffira – mais assoyez-vous donc, monsieur Lamare.

Méfiant, Faustin prit place dans le confortable fauteuil, face au médecin. À coups d'œil vifs, il détailla le bureau du docteur : cadres ouvragés portant des collections de coléoptères et de phalènes, fossiles posés sur une étagère, échantillons minéralogiques sur un guéridon. Tout au fond, une bibliothèque d'acajou portait des livres reliés de cuir dont Faustin n'arrivait pas à déchiffrer les titres au dos.

— Savez-vous lire, monsieur Lamare ? demanda le médecin, qui avait suivi son regard.

— Bien sûr.

— Votre lecture favorite ?

— *Le Comte de Monte-Cristo*.

— Dumas ? releva le médecin en haussant un sourcil. Et l'une de ses publications les plus récentes, en plus… voilà une bien rare lecture pour un garçon de votre âge – quoique votre élocution laisse transparaître des études. Droit ?

— Mon père est notaire, mentit Faustin.

— À Québec ?

— Aux Trois-Rivières.

Le docteur Douglas se leva. Faustin tenta de voir à travers l'étoffe fine de la chemise s'il n'y distinguerait pas la marque du Stigma Diaboli. Le docteur souleva sa manche et montra son avant-bras enroulé dans un bandage médical.

— Une vilaine coupure, commenta-t-il. C'est bien ce qui attirait votre attention ?

— Je ne voulais pas paraître indiscret, docteur.

— N'y pensez plus.

L'homme marcha vers sa bibliothèque et en tira un volume.

— *The Tempest*, de Shakespeare. Ma propre lecture favorite. Vous l'avez lu ?

— Je n'en ai pas eu l'occasion.

— *But that the sea, mounting to th'welkin's cheek, dashes the fire out,* lut le médecin avec une grandiloquente intonation. C'est l'histoire, expliqua-t-il, du naufrage d'un sorcier.

— Intéressant, commenta Faustin.

Merde ! À quoi joue ce médecin ? pensa-t-il en observant le docteur qui reprenait place à son siège.

— Croyez-vous à la sorcellerie, monsieur Lamare ?

— Des histoires de grands-mères.

— À vous voir étrécir les yeux tout à l'heure, j'aurais cru que vous aviez une autre opinion.

Mais il sait ! C'est clair qu'il sait, et depuis le début ! Et il sait que je sais : pourquoi me narguer avec ce bandage à l'avant-bras, sinon ?

— Plaît-il, docteur ?

— Des observations médicales sans grand intérêt.

Dois-je jouer le même jeu ?

— J'ai eu le plaisir de longer votre seigneurie à bord de la *Rosamund*, commença Faustin. Vous y avez un fort beau domaine.

— Vous êtes un homme de bon goût, monsieur Lamare.

— Fort chanceux sont vos invités.

— Bien sûr. Nous y pratiquons essentiellement la chasse.

Le sourire du seigneur Douglas devint plus rapace lorsqu'il planta ses yeux dans ceux de Faustin. Le jeune homme remarqua la teinte bleu-blanc des iris et un vif coup d'œil aux mains du docteur confirma ses soupçons : mains aux doigts centraux égaux, comme les siens.

Pas sorcier mais loup-garou. Membre du Stigma, de toute évidence. Récent ? Il n'était pas au banquet des Sewell, mais il a acheté l'île d'à côté peu longtemps après. Qu'importe, au fond ? Il croit avoir mis la griffe sur moi et s'amuse avec sa proie.

Que faire ? Je ne peux fuir d'ici sans navire, Baptiste est toujours prisonnier et Shaor'i introuvable.

Et merde !...

— Pourquoi cette joute verbale, docteur ? Vous savez qui je suis, je sais qui vous êtes. Qu'espérez-vous, exactement ?

Douglas sourit plus largement, dévoilant ses canines aiguës.

— Ce que j'espère ? Vous êtes prisonnier ici, Charles – permettez que je vous appelle Charles –, et cela m'assurera une bonne place dans les grâces de mon Maître. Moi, George Mellis Douglas le sans-pouvoir, le sans-don, voilà que je réussis là où d'autres ont échoué. Que voulez-vous, cela ne peut que m'amuser ! Si je n'étais pas si occupé par la livraison de ce soir, je vous conduirais pieds et poings liés à l'Éminent Maître. Mais vous ne pourrez pas aller bien loin, sans navire. Et même, au cas où vous vous évaderiez... *Captain !*

La porte s'ouvrit derechef.

— *Seigneur ?*

— *This man is infected with cholera.*

— Quoi ? s'exclama Faustin en se levant d'un bond.

Dans son dos, il entendit le cliquetis d'un fusil prêt à tirer. Il haussa les mains.

— *Follow me, mister Lamare,* dit lentement le capitaine. *You'll need to stay in the lazaretto for a few weeks.*

◆

Il eut beau protester en français, en anglais et en sacrant, rien n'y fit.

Sans ménagement, le capitaine conduisit Faustin aux bâtiments que le jeune homme connaissait de par leur sinistre réputation. Ils ressemblaient à de longs hangars en planches, aux toits pointus percés de lucarnes. Les fenêtres à carreaux se succédaient et le bâtiment avait de nombreuses portes. Faustin pensa à ces longères que construisaient les habitants qui en avaient les moyens, juxtaposant l'une à l'autre les dépendances de ferme comme l'étable, l'écurie, le poulailler et la grange pour constituer un seul bâtiment.

Un prêtre attendait Faustin à l'entrée.

— Mon père, lança-t-il avec désespoir, je vous dis que je suis sain ! C'est en entrant là-dedans que je vais tomber malade !

— Assoyez-vous et détachez votre chemise, s'il vous plaît.

Contre son gré, Faustin se laissa tomber sur le siège et déboutonna son vêtement. Le prêtre plongea un chiffon maculé de taches sépia dans un sceau rouillé et frictionna l'abdomen de Faustin en laissant des traces jaunâtres.

— Qu'est-ce que…

— De la teinture d'iode, pour repousser les humeurs malsaines et les animalcules cholériques. Rhabillez-vous. Vous connaissez vos nombres ?

— Bien entendu !

— Porte 8, lit 124.

Le prêtre lui tendit un drap plié qui, bien que fraîchement lavé, devait avoir été souillé de nombreuses fois d'après son écœurante coloration. Bêtement, Faustin ne trouva rien de mieux à faire qu'insister faiblement :

— Mais je suis sain…

— Lit 124, coupa le prêtre pour mettre fin à la discussion.

Du canon de son fusil, le capitaine poussa Faustin entre les omoplates.

Résigné, le jeune homme passa la porte de l'hôpital pour cholériques… et constata que la comparaison du lazaret avec une dépendance de ferme se révélait encore plus adaptée à l'intérieur qu'à l'extérieur.

Parqués comme des bêtes, les immigrants qu'on avait jugés potentiellement contagieux s'entassaient les uns contre les autres. Ce qu'on définissait comme « lits » étaient trop souvent des paillasses tachées d'excréments liquides, de vomissures striées de sang, de sueur et d'urine. Des numéros étaient marqués au-dessus des paillasses et Faustin fronça les sourcils quand il comprit qu'un même « lit » était occupé par deux ou trois patients à la fois qui, couchés sur le côté pour ne pas se monter dessus, n'avaient souvent pas la force de se retourner pour éviter de vomir sur leur voisin.

Se couvrant le nez et la bouche pour ne pas renifler directement les miasmes, Faustin esquissa un pas vers l'arrière. Le soldat lui donna une poussée pour le forcer à avancer.

Faustin savait que chaque navire en provenance de l'Irlande – où sévissait une famine – débarquait ses passagers à Grosse-Île pour une quarantaine obligatoire, et la plupart des résidents du lazaret devaient

provenir de là. D'ailleurs, en écoutant leur anglais drôlement accentué et en voyant la chevelure rousse que plusieurs arboraient, il ne pouvait se tromper.

— *One hundred and twenty four*, annonça le soldat avant d'abandonner là Faustin.

Le jeune homme retint un haut-le-cœur en découvrant que de sa paillasse s'échappaient des vermisseaux blanchâtres et que son voisin de lit, s'il n'était pas mort, n'était pas loin de l'être.

Dos au mur, n'ayant guère envie de s'asseoir sur le plancher souillé ou, pire, sur sa paillasse, Faustin répondit d'un signe de tête aux gens plus en forme qui lui souhaitèrent la bienvenue.

Une dizaine de paillasses plus loin, un bébé se mit à brailler et sa mère, malgré ses traits affectés par la maladie, entama un air gai qui résonnait étrangement en pareil environnement :

Her eyes were as black as a raven,
I thought her the pride of the land,
Her hair, that did hang o'er her shoulders,
Was tied with a black velvet band.

Le nourrisson ne calma pas ses pleurs pour autant, réveillant autour de lui les malades qui avaient trouvé un sursis temporaire à leurs maux en s'assoupissant. Certains d'entre eux étaient dans un état si avancé que leur peau desséchée affichait déjà une coloration bleutée.

Je ne peux pas rester ici, songea Faustin en son for intérieur.

À ses pieds, son voisin de lit eut un tressautement et expulsa une diarrhée à l'odeur poisseuse, sans sembler le remarquer. Il se retourna avec un râle et cracha un graillon brunâtre.

— Crisse de chien sale de Douglas ! pesta le jeune homme.

Le bébé pleurait de plus belle, la voix de sa mère, qui le berçait dans ses bras, perdait lentement de son allant. Soudain, la jeune femme cessa son chant et son regard se perdit dans le vague. Faustin la vit choir lentement sur le côté, laissant tomber son enfant sur la paillasse, ce qui redoubla la force de ses cris.

Non, je ne reste pas ici, décréta Faustin.

Il regarda autour de lui. Un curé soigneur était affairé à donner l'extrême-onction à un pauvre diable sur sa droite, mais il lui tournait le dos. À sa gauche, mais très loin dans le bâtiment, deux sœurs avaient commencé la distribution des rations de soupe.

Les fenêtres ne manquaient pas. Faustin en repéra une alignée avec l'épais boqueteau de sapins qu'il avait vu en arrivant. À peine dix pieds séparaient le lazaret des conifères. S'il les atteignait...

Bien. Maintenant !

Faustin tira violemment la fenêtre, bondit à l'extérieur et fonça vers le boqueteau.

Un coup de feu retentit.

Faustin plongea, roula sur lui-même et se réfugia sous l'un des conifères. À l'abri des regards, il fit le vide dans son esprit, pensa à sa seconde nature et adopta sa forme de renard.

L'instant d'après, le soldat qui l'avait amené au lazaret jaillissait, arme en joue. Tout comme le lui dicta son instinct, Faustin poussa un double aboiement rauque avant de fuir en glapissant. Le soldat, occupé à retrouver un fugitif humain, ne prêta qu'une brève attention à l'animal qui bondissait à une vitesse folle vers le secteur boisé de l'île.

◆

Suis-je contaminé ?

Caché dans un terrier désaffecté, car il n'avait pas jugé prudent de quitter sa forme canine, Faustin n'en ressassait pas moins des pensées très humaines.

Son passage au lazaret l'avait ébranlé. Avait-il été assez bref pour lui éviter la contamination ? Tout dépendait des modes de propagation de la maladie et, de ce qu'il se souvenait des enseignements de son oncle, les hypothèses étaient nombreuses à ce sujet : émanations gazéiformes, animalcules, contact avec les sécrétions, eau malsaine… Certes, il n'avait rien bu et avait évité de marcher dans les souillures. Certes, la teinture d'iode que lui avait administrée le prêtre était censée le prévenir des animalcules. Mais les émanations…

J'y suis resté, quoi, dix minutes ? tenta de se rassurer Faustin.

L'image de la mère échappant son enfant lui revint en mémoire.

Je dois retrouver Shaor'i. Elle seule peut me guérir si jamais je suis infecté.

S'étant fixé un but clair, Faustin sortit du terrier, renifla l'air et dressa les oreilles pour s'assurer qu'aucun humain n'était proche, puis fila vers les lieux du naufrage, en passant furtivement d'un boqueteau à l'autre.

L'Île-aux-Dix-Mille-Morts ne mesurait pas plus d'une demi-lieue de long et il ne fallut pas beaucoup de temps à Faustin pour retrouver la goélette. Partiellement soulevée par la marée montante, la *Rosamund* s'était couchée sur son flanc. Les vagues avaient porté l'un des mâts rompus, celui de misaine, sur une vingtaine de verges, et quelques tonneaux flottaient au loin.

Quand il fut certain que ni ses coussinets ni ses vibrisses ne percevaient les vibrations régulières de

pas humains s'approchant, Faustin reprit sa forme
véritable et s'avança dans l'eau, nageant jusqu'à
l'épave, sur laquelle il se hissa en se servant d'un
câble. Après avoir vérifié que Shaor'i n'était pas sur
le navire, Faustin regagna la berge.

Recouvrant son corps de renard, il plaqua sa truffe
au sol et se mit à flairer la terre : odeurs de vase et
d'humus se mêlèrent aux relents piquants des sapins et
à ceux fétides des poissons morts. À travers l'éven-
tail olfactif, Faustin chercha la sauge, cet effluve très
caractéristique qu'il avait souvent remarquée chez
l'Indienne.

Quand il crut la percevoir, il tenta de remonter sa
trace, le museau bas, prélevant tous les indices que
son odorat lui révélait. Shaor'i n'avait pas marché.
Son odeur était restée accrochée aux branches basses
des arbres, pas à l'herbe. Une senteur musquée s'y
mêlait, celle de deux hommes. Les parfums de cuir
humide et de poudre confirmaient qu'il s'agissait de
soldats. Qui devaient la porter.

Faustin avançait en traquant l'effluve de sauge,
pareil à un prédateur qui poursuit sa proie. Mais le
parfum de l'Indienne, tel un rongeur effrayé, cherchait
à se dérober à son flair. Il fut distrait un temps par les
relents humides d'une talle de champignons, perdit la
piste en tombant sur le remugle d'un oiseau mort, la
retrouva plus loin quand l'air se fit plus limpide…

Sa traque le ramena à proximité des bâtiments où
des dizaines d'effluves vinrent parasiter sa recherche :
sueur humaine issue du va-et-vient des militaires,
urine des chiens, fumier de bœufs et de chevaux…
puis il localisa enfin la source à travers l'odeur de
bois chaud d'un bâtiment. Il sollicita ses sens canins :
personne à proximité ; il s'élança vers la porte fermée.
Il reconnut les émanations piquantes et désagréables

de l'ammoniaque, de l'alcool pur et du formol. Redevenant humain, Faustin tenta d'ouvrir la porte. Verrouillée. Il fit le tour du bâtiment, repéra un étroit soupirail par lequel il se faufila en renard.

Redevenu homme à l'intérieur, il inspecta la cave. Grâce à la lumière pénétrant par le soupirail, il découvrit des étagères contenant des organes conservés dans des bocaux, divers produits désinfectants et des outils médicinaux. Et, sur une table de dissection, Shaor'i.

Faustin s'approcha à toute vitesse. Ses instincts lui ordonnèrent soudain de se plaquer au sol, ce qu'il fit juste avant que le poing de Shaor'i surgisse là où s'était trouvée sa tête.

— Faustin!? jeta l'Indienne, stupéfaite. Que fais-tu ici?

— Je t'ai cherchée... je ne savais pas où tu étais depuis le naufrage et tu ne répondais pas à mes appels mentaux.

Shaor'i descendit de la table, marcha vers un guéridon où elle récupéra ses armes.

— Je suis trop légère pour bien nager dans des flots aussi tumultueux. Je me suis envolée et j'ai lutté pour aller à contrevent. Je me suis écroulée d'épuisement sur la berge et je me suis éveillée ici. Un homme, ignare complet en matière de magie, m'a ligoté les mains et bâillonnée comme si j'avais besoin d'incanter ou de tracer un pentacle à la manière d'un goétiste ou d'un théurgiste. Puis il s'est servi d'un objet, une aiguille au bout d'un tube muni d'une sorte de pompe...

— Une seringue.

— Qu'importe le nom. Ça injecte du venin comme un crotale des bois.

Le cœur de Faustin battit de travers.

— Hein? Mais...

— J'ai fait le vide dans mon esprit et neutralisé le poison. Mais j'ai dû mettre mon corps en hibernation et c'est pour ça que je ne pouvais percevoir tes contacts mentaux. Ton arrivée m'a tirée de mon sommeil.

— Et maintenant ?

— Je suis prête à m'enfuir.

— D'accord. Transforme-toi et repère Ti-Jean : il a réussi à se cacher avant notre arrestation.

Faustin prit quelques secondes pour résumer ce qui leur était arrivé depuis le naufrage avant de poursuivre :

— Explique-lui que je veux libérer Baptiste de sa cellule, ainsi il pourra transmettre cette information à notre ami. Donnons-nous ensuite rendez-vous près de l'épave de la *Rosamund*.

— Bien.

Tous deux empruntèrent le soupirail avant, pour l'une, de prendre son envol, pour l'autre de s'élancer à quatre pattes vers la prison, dont le bâtiment était tout proche.

Sur place, Faustin jeta prudemment un œil à l'intérieur par la fenêtre – un seul gardien – et, reprenant sa forme humaine, griffonna à la craie un diagramme sur le battant de la porte d'entrée.

— *Ashek saen-irstean al-ibnar !*

À l'intérieur, une caisse de bois s'éleva du sol pour aller percuter le militaire en plein visage. Sonné, l'homme s'effondra alors que Faustin se jetait sur lui et arrachait les menottes de sa ceinture pour l'attacher au lourd poêle de fonte. Prélevant le mouchoir du soldat, il le bâillonna avant de se mettre à la recherche des clés des cellules.

S'il trouva dans une malle son paqueton et celui de Baptiste, et dans un placard son fusil, son sabre et la hache du bûcheron, les clés ne semblaient nulle part.

En désespoir de cause, il s'arma de son sabre, en appuya le fil contre la gorge du soldat tout en lui retirant son bâillon.

— *If you shout, I'll kill you*, le menaça-t-il tout en sachant que jamais il ne tuerait ainsi un homme. *Where are the keys ? I'm here to free my friend.*

— *The captain always keeps the keys on himself*, répondit le soldat.

Merde, songea Faustin en muselant de nouveau le militaire.

Sans perdre de temps, il ouvrit la porte séparant le bureau des cellules. Avec stupéfaction, il découvrit que Ti-Jean était déjà avec Baptiste. Debout dans la paume du bûcheron, qu'il tenait près de la porte de la cellule, le *mah oumet* enfonçait sa main minuscule dans le trou de la serrure afin d'essayer de la déverrouiller. Mais il avait beau s'y prendre de toutes les façons, il n'arrivait à rien. Après un gémissement de dépit, le lutin abandonna et Baptiste le remonta sur son épaule.

— Content d'te voir, lança Baptiste à Faustin. Ti-Jean m'a dit qu'la P'tite s'est évadée pis toé avec. Faut s'pousser d'icitte avant qu'un garde vienne.

— Je veux bien, Baptiste, mais le capitaine garde les clés sur lui et…

— Faut s'pousser, que j'dis, le coupa Baptiste, faque comme disait ton oncle : « aux grands maux, les grands r'mèdes ».

Le colosse inspira profondément puis empoigna d'une main le premier barreau de la porte-grille et de l'autre, la barre qui l'encadrait. Les biceps du bûcheron se gonflèrent.

Incrédule, Faustin recula d'un pas. Rougissant sous l'effort, Baptiste émit un grognement qui fut partiellement couvert par le couinement des tiges de fer forgé qui se déformaient. Ses traits se contractèrent,

ses veines saillirent, son grognement se mua en cri pendant qu'un bruit de métal tordu se faisait entendre.

— Ça d'vrait aller, jugea Baptiste, essoufflé. Tasse-toé, Garçon.

Faustin obtempéra pendant que le bûcheron prenait son élan pour flanquer un puissant coup de pied contre la serrure, qui fit s'ouvrir la porte avec une violence inouïe.

Épuisé par l'effort, l'homme fort se laissa choir sur un banc pour retrouver son souffle, une main sur la poitrine.

— Ça va? demanda Faustin.

— Correct. Pas l'temps d'farfiner, on part de suite.

Chacun reprit ses affaires dans le bureau, puis Ti-Jean vérifia discrètement s'ils pouvaient sortir. La voie étant libre, ils se dirigèrent rapidement vers un bosquet de pins au cœur duquel ils se cachèrent.

— Shaor'i nous attend à l'épave, expliqua Faustin. On va…

Un harfang se glissa subitement à travers les branches avant de reprendre sa forme humaine.

— Il y a quelque chose qui ne va pas, dit aussitôt Shaor'i. En venant vous rejoindre, j'ai vu qu'on rassemblait les malades pour les amener au nord. Mais il n'y a rien par-là. Pas un bâtiment, pas d'espace aménagé, pas même un quai.

— Faudrait savoir c'qui s'passe, dit Baptiste. Histoire de l'rapporter au père Masse.

— Entendu, acquiesça Faustin. Mais il faudra être discrets.

— Extrêmement discrets, renchérit Shaor'i. Faustin et moi irons transformés, mais je préfère que tu restes ici, Baptiste.

Le bûcheron pesa l'argument quelques secondes, puis décréta:

— Correct. Mais amenez Ti-Jean. Si jamais y vous arrive quek'chose, j'vas l'voir par ses yeux.

Ti-Jean descendit de l'épaule du bûcheron et courut à quatre pattes pour rejoindre Faustin, qui avait aussitôt adopté sa forme de renard. Sitôt que Shaor'i eut pris son envol, ils se dirigèrent vers les bâtiments hospitaliers.

De nombreux cholériques avaient effectivement été sortis des lazarets et rassemblés dans une clairière. Faustin estima qu'environ la moitié des malades était réunie là.

Des soldats portant des torches supervisaient le regroupement. Monté à cheval, le seigneur Douglas clamait haut et fort des indications au moment où ils arrivaient et Faustin n'entendit que la fin de son discours.

— … *sooner we will arrive, sooner you will get your treatment*.

Quelques malades se placèrent en ligne, mais la grande majorité resta immobile. Après avoir bu une gorgée à sa gourde, le docteur reprit en français :

— Vous allez recevoir un traitement médical spécial au nord de l'île. Placez-vous en deux rangs. S'il vous est pénible de marcher, écartez-vous des rangs et demeurez debout, un soldat vous apportera une canne. Si vous n'avez plus la force de marcher, écartez-vous des rangs et assoyez-vous : quelqu'un vous aidera à monter dans l'une des charrettes à bœuf. Plus vite nous serons arrivés, plus vite vous aurez votre traitement.

Les malades s'activèrent.

Le directeur de Grosse-Île répéta plusieurs fois ses indications en français, pour les cholériques de Québec, et en anglais, pour les immigrants irlandais. Il fallut un bon quart d'heure pour que les deux lignes exigées soient formées.

À côté de lui, Faustin entendait Shaor'i tiquer devant cet étrange discours.

Les malades se mirent finalement en route, escortés par les soldats et les voitures à bœuf. Au-devant, Douglas monté sur son étalon guidait les rangs. La marche était lente et nombreux avaient été les cholériques à demander un bâton de marche ou une place dans une charrette. Celles-ci étaient pleines quand, une heure plus tard, la troupe arriva dans une vaste clairière où des fosses avaient été creusées. Faustin vit qu'il s'en élevait, dans l'air estival, de denses vapeurs. Shaor'i prit son envol pour mieux voir les installations.

— Les soldats vont vous compter pour vous diviser en groupes de quarante, expliqua le docteur Douglas d'une voix forte, puis chaque groupe descendra dans une fosse à glace. Cette procédure est obligatoire afin que baisse rapidement votre fièvre. Je répète : cette procédure est obligatoire…

Faustin n'écoutait plus Douglas. Le souvenir du sous-sol du notaire Lanigan s'était emparé de son esprit, puis celui de l'officine de l'église engloutie non loin des Forges. *Des fosses de glace…*

« *Shaor'i*, émit-il, paniqué, *ces fosses ne servent pas à diminuer la fièvre…* »

« *Je sais*, répondit-elle, horrifiée. *Si tu pouvais venir à ma hauteur, tu verrais des diagrammes gravés sur des pierres plates.* »

D'autres déclics s'effectuèrent dans l'esprit de Faustin. Les canons forgés aux Trois-Rivières, la population des Forges constituant un cheptel arcanique, les créatures que l'homme d'aujourd'hui ne savait plus combattre… forcément, il ne manquait qu'une chose à cela.

Une armée.

On ne menait pas une *Reconquista* sans armée. Et pendant que Ti-Jean tremblait à ses côtés, se remémorant

sûrement la transformation de sa tribu dans l'église engloutie, Faustin comprit ce qu'avait été l'essaim de diablotins qui avait résulté de cette expérience.

Une armée à échelle réduite.

Un exercice dont le résultat avait été jugé décevant, mais qui démontrait la possibilité de coordonner les actions de centaines de non-morts.

Toutefois, on ne recrutait pas des centaines d'hommes sans attirer l'attention, même quand on possédait la puissance de l'Étranger. Quand quelques jacks mistigris étaient requis, la disparition de quelques mendiants, voire de condamnés à mort fournis par le shérif Sewell ne portait pas à conséquence, mais pour une armée… l'Étranger s'était tourné vers Grosse-Île. Qui viendrait vérifier si les fosses communes contenaient réellement la quantité de corps que la paperasse recensait? Qui s'interrogerait sur le décès des centaines de personnes amenées sur l'Île-aux-Dix-Mille-Morts?

Et Faustin voyait tous ces gens souffrant du choléra s'avancer docilement vers les fosses à glace, avec, peut-être, un nouvel espoir de guérison alors qu'ils avaient accepté leur sort depuis longtemps…

Ébranlé par l'horreur de la scène, Faustin réadopta sa forme humaine.

« *Faustin!* émit Shaor'i. *Es-tu fou?* »

Il ne se préoccupa guère des injonctions de l'Indienne. *Non…* émit-il. *Ils ne sombreront pas dans la non-mort*. Il se sentit soudainement embrasé par une colère formidable.

… *Brûle…*

« *Faustin, NON!* » supplia Shaor'i.

… *Brûle…*

« *Tu ne peux rien pour eux, Faustin! Ils sont déjà mourants!* »

Oui, ils étaient mourants. Mais ça, c'était bien pire… c'était le supplice éternel de la non-mort…

Dans son esprit, Faustin dessina le pentacle de flammes avec lequel il avait détruit son village natal. La même rage l'étreignait, lui serrait l'âme, lui lancinait l'esprit.

… *Brûle*…

Une énergie incroyable se mit à circuler en lui, à vouloir jaillir de lui.

… *BRÛLE*…

« *Faustin ! Ta mère est là…* »

« *Ma mère ?* »

Sa concentration flancha.

« *Son corps doit avoir treize ou quatorze ans, mais je suis sûre que c'est elle.* »

« *C'était une enfant, aux Forges. Et elle a des années de crédit, comme moi.* »

« *Je suppose que l'Étranger a beaucoup exigé d'elle. D'ailleurs, l'Étranger est là aussi. Nous devons partir avant qu'il ne nous repère.* »

« *En renard, il ne peut capter ma présence, non ? C'est ainsi que j'ai fui la Grande Maison des Forges.* »

« *Cela a fonctionné uniquement parce que ton esprit humain s'était endormi et que seule l'âme animale se manifestait. Ce n'est plus le cas, désormais.* »

« *Mais tous ces gens…* »

« *Tu ne peux rien pour eux et moi non plus. Pas en présence de l'Étranger.* »

— Hey ! lança une voix. *Return to the group ! It's for your*…

De sa monture, le docteur Douglas s'étrangla de surprise en découvrant Faustin.

— Toi, ici ?

« *Fuis, Faustin ! Tu ne peux rien face à ton père !* »

Dans l'esprit de Faustin, la raison prit le pas sur la rage.

D'un seul coup, il évacua l'énergie vers un buisson desséché, qui s'enflamma aussitôt. Effarouché, le

cheval de Douglas se cabra en hennissant et chercha à rebrousser chemin.

— Monte, Ti-Jean ! ordonna Faustin en profitant de ce bref instant pour se métamorphoser.

Le lutin bondit agilement sur le dos du renard. D'une puissante détente musculaire, Faustin fonça comme une flèche vers le bosquet où les attendait Baptiste. Dos droit, queue tendue, sa physionomie fuselée de renard lui permettait une formidable célérité. Pourtant, derrière lui, Faustin entendit un son régulier ; tournant ses oreilles vers l'arrière sans même bouger la tête, il reconnut le bruit d'un cheval lancé au galop. Ce ne pouvait être que Douglas !

Comme un poisson aurait nagé entre les pierres, Faustin zigzagua habilement entre les buissons et les arbres, bondit sans peine au-dessus d'un rocher de six pieds de haut pour se pelotonner en boule sitôt de l'autre côté.

Quand le docteur eut contourné au galop l'obstacle, Faustin sauta de nouveau par-dessus le roc pour revenir sur ses pas, en concentrant ses pensées sur l'impasse dans laquelle ses amis et lui se trouvaient : les navires accostant ou quittant Grosse-Île étaient méticuleusement inspectés et, en supposant qu'il parvienne à se remémorer le diagramme de la téléportation, la distance qui les séparait d'une autre île ou de la terre ferme était trop grande. Quant à fuir à la nage, mieux valait ne pas y songer.

Alors que son souffle commençait à lui manquer, Faustin sentit une présence s'imposer dans son esprit.

« *Je puis vous aider, Spirite.* »

« *Plaçoa ?* s'étonna le jeune homme en reconnaissant la présence. *Comment m'avez-vous retrouvé ?* »

« *Je ne vous ai jamais quitté, Spirite.* »

« *Comment se fait-il que je n'ai pas perçu votre présence ?* »

« *Je vous observais depuis l'outremonde, non en foulant le monde des mortels.* »

Faustin frissonna : il avait été épié dans ses moindres gestes depuis deux semaines ? Il chassa cette préoccupation de son esprit quand Plaçoa émit :

« *Si vous souhaitez quitter cette île et vous rendre sur l'Isle-aux-Grues, je vous permettrai de traverser. Il y a là-bas un puissant enchantement qui vous voilera au regard de l'Étranger.* »

« *Soit, Plaçoa. Nous réglerons ainsi nos comptes : vous me libérerez de cette prison comme je vous ai libéré de la vôtre.* »

« *Fort bien. Allez vers la berge. Mes frères vous attendent.* »

Intrigué, le jeune homme demanda :

« *Des Indiens ?* »

« *Non. Ma famille d'adoption.* »

Sans chercher à comprendre davantage, Faustin fonça vers le boqueteau où Baptiste attendait avec impatience. Shaor'i s'était posée peu avant son arrivée et Ti-Jean, qui s'était bravement agrippé au pelage de Faustin pendant toute sa cavalcade, regagna aussitôt sa place sur l'épaule du bûcheron.

— Pourquoi as-tu fait ça ! le tança vertement l'Indienne. À présent, je vois mal comment…

— Plaçoa nous envoie sa famille d'adoption, la coupa Faustin. Ils vont nous faire quitter Grosse-Île et nous amener auprès du père Masse. Il dit que l'Étranger ne pourra pas nous retrouver là-bas.

— Il a dit… sa famille d'adoption ? releva Shaor'i. Mais alors…

Elle tourna son regard vers la plage ; déjà celle-ci se couvrait d'une nappe de brouillard.

« *Vers la berge, Spirite. Vite* », émit Plaçoa dans l'esprit de Faustin.

Faustin et ses compagnons franchirent en vitesse les quelques verges qui les séparaient de la rive. En s'approchant, ils commencèrent à distinguer des silhouettes effilées émergeant de l'eau et ayant plus ou moins les dimensions de petits canots.

Des poissons? se demanda-t-il en écarquillant les yeux.

— Les marsouins de la Rivière-Ouelle… laissa tomber Shaor'i, à mi-chemin entre l'incrédulité et l'émerveillement.

— De quoi? lança Baptiste, adoptant un air méfiant en scrutant les formes vaporeuses par les yeux de Ti-Jean.

— Je l'ai déjà raconté : ce n'est pas sans raison que Plaçoa est jadis parvenu à maîtriser Kabir Kouba. Enfant sauvé de la noyade par des marsouins, il est parvenu plus tard à se transformer en cet animal – personne mieux que lui ne comprenait la faune marine.

« *Venez* », fit la voix de Plaçoa dans l'esprit de Faustin.

Hochant la tête, Faustin avança vers la nappe de brouillard d'un air résolu. Shaor'i lui emboîta aussitôt le pas, suivie de Baptiste après un bref moment. L'eau leur arriva aux chevilles, puis aux genoux. C'est à ce moment qu'ils entendirent hurler au loin :

— *I see them! They are trying to leave the island!*

Un coup de feu détona dans la nuit.

« *Dépêchez-vous*, reprit le spectre. *Si vous tardez trop, vous serez arrêtés et j'aurai quand même payé ma dette.* »

Ils étaient une vingtaine de marsouins aux corps vaporeux, comme constitués de fumée, et pourtant indubitablement tangibles ainsi que le constata Faustin lorsqu'il avança la main pour effleurer l'une des créatures. Ses doigts s'enfoncèrent très légèrement dans

l'entité spectrale avant de rencontrer une résistance qui n'avait rien de naturelle.

— Des animaux revenants, chuchota Faustin pour lui-même avant de comprendre : ils n'avaient pas voulu partir pour l'outremonde sans Plaçoa.

« *Montez,* commanda le spectre indien. *Hâtez-vous.* »

Un autre coup de feu retentit.

Sans plus attendre, Faustin enfourcha l'un des marsouins fantômes, tout comme ses compagnons. Les bêtes spectrales décrivirent un arc de cercle pour faire face au large. Quand sa monture gagna en célérité, Faustin se pencha sur son dos et mit ses bras autour de sa tête. *Pourvu qu'elle ne plonge pas*, s'inquiéta-t-il.

L'Île-aux-Dix-Mille-Morts s'éloigna rapidement derrière eux cependant que la nappe de brouillard les entourait toujours, masquant leur fuite. De toute évidence, les soldats anglais ne comprendraient jamais le prodige dont ils avaient été témoins.

CHAPITRE 30

L'Isle-aux-Grues

Les quatre compagnons avaient été gagnés, peu de temps après leur départ, par une soudaine torpeur et lorsque Faustin ouvrit l'œil, il fut surpris de voir les premiers rayons du soleil effleurer l'horizon… et de se retrouver sur une plage. Se redressant lentement, le jeune homme jeta un regard en direction du large. Nulle trace, dans les flots du fleuve, des marsouins fantômes envoyés par Plaçoa.

S'il avait eu raison de faire confiance au spectre – et rien ne le poussait à en douter –, il se trouvait sur l'Isle-aux-Grues,

Non loin, il vit que Shaor'i aidait Baptiste à se relever, le colosse ne semblant guère à l'aise sur la mousse rendue visqueuse par le jusant. Les berges de l'Isle-aux-Grues étaient un rivage plat constitué d'immenses rochers couleur d'absinthe, entre lesquels se dressaient des touffes drues de plantes herbacées caoutchouteuses. Crabes et écrevisses couraient sur la rive, récoltés par le bec effilé de hérons qui marchaient paresseusement sur les roches.

Le jeune homme se dirigea vers ses amis, évitant au passage une flaque d'eau stagnante dans laquelle un goéland se gavait de moules. Il les rejoignit au

moment où Ti-Jean s'éveillait à son tour de sa torpeur
et regagnait son affût sur l'épaule du bûcheron.

Les compagnons s'entreregardèrent, aucun ne sachant comment aborder l'expérience qu'ils venaient de
vivre. Ce fut Shaor'i qui brisa le silence en évinçant
le sujet :

— Et maintenant ? Où est ce père Masse ?

Baptiste haussa les épaules.

— Aucune idée. T'sais, c'est pas bin grand, l'Isle-
aux-Grues : ça s'fait à pied en quek z'heures. On
demand'ra aux gens : l'père Masse est d'apparence
assez dépareillée. J'pense qu'y'a un village passé c'tes
bois, à deux milles, on va toujours commencer par là.

Cent verges les séparaient d'une forêt de pins et
d'érables plus que centenaires. Ils s'y rendirent en
dérangeant goélands et canards, puis s'engouffrèrent
au milieu de ces arbres environnés de brume où Faustin
se sentit tout de suite mal à l'aise.

La forêt n'était pas comme celles qu'il avait déjà
traversées. Si les empreintes de la présence humaine
étaient visibles autant dans la Pinède du Sauvage, où
trappaient les coureurs des bois, que dans la vallée du
Saint-Maurice où bûcherons et draveurs laissaient des
traces de leur passage, ici les humains ne semblaient
pas les bienvenus : il n'y avait pour ainsi dire aucun
sentier, aucune cabane, ni aucun arbre abattu à la hache
dans toute cette forêt mixte.

Devant lui, Shaor'i avançait, un doux sourire aux
lèvres. Elle n'avait pas parlé une seule fois depuis leur
entrée dans la forêt, mais son silence était celui du plus
pur ravissement. Baptiste, paraissant plutôt de l'avis de
Faustin, marmonnait qu'il n'aimait guère les énormes
cèdres dont les troncs présentaient d'étranges torsions
alors qu'ils auraient dû pousser bien droit. Ils étaient
si grands que Faustin n'en voyait pas la cime, même en

rejetant la tête vers l'arrière. Le soleil n'était pas encore assez haut dans le ciel pour percer à travers l'épais feuillage et il faisait aussi noir qu'en pleine nuit.

Un son attira l'attention de Faustin, quelque part au-dessus de sa tête. C'était une sorte de murmure clair qui résonnait comme un rire de jouvencelle.

— Écoutez, chuchota-t-il.

Baptiste et Shaor'i s'arrêtèrent. Le rire reprit, cette fois beaucoup plus proche.

— Vous avez entendu ? demanda Faustin dans un murmure.

Le colosse et l'Indienne secouèrent la tête.

— Pourtant…

« *Prst'i menmld…* »

La voix tintait comme une clochette à quelques verges de Faustin, qui fit aussitôt volte-face.

— Là ! s'exclama-t-il en indiquant un endroit à quelques pieds de lui.

— J'entends rien… répondit Baptiste en écartant les mains.

« *… pt'tsnvern't !* » redit la voix, cette fois à une dizaine de pieds de là.

— Merde, j'suis pas fou ! gémit Faustin. Shaor'i, dis-moi que…

— Je n'entends rien, Faustin. Et mon ouïe est beaucoup plus perçante que la tienne.

Loin, très loin entre les arbres, la voix taquinait : « *Eg'nth ! Eg'nth !* »

— Shaor'i, je te jure que j'entends une voix par là… s'obstina Faustin en arrachant le fanal des mains de Baptiste pour se diriger d'un pas assuré vers un énorme pin gris.

Il sursauta lorsqu'une perdrix s'envola avec bruit, puis un rire moqueur pétilla dans l'air.

Faustin se tourna vers ses compagnons qui continuaient de le dévisager.

— Peut-être un esprit ? suggéra Shaor'i.

— Non, c'est pas ça. Cette voix n'a pas la même… « texture mentale » qu'un esprit.

— Texture ?

— À défaut d'un meilleur terme… là !

Le jeune homme désigna un bloc de granit aux angles réguliers sur lequel était gravé un *komkwejwika'sikl*. De petites fleurs que Faustin ne put identifier – trois minuscules feuilles pointues disposées en triangle – poussaient tout autour.

— Si le *komkwejwika'sikl* est gravé dans la pierre, dit Shaor'i, c'est qu'il s'agit d'un endroit sacré. Quant à ces fleurs, je n'ai aucune idée de ce qu'elles sont, et Otjiera m'a enseigné tout ce qu'il savait de l'herboristerie.

— Que veut dire le symbole ?

— Je n'en ai aucune idée. Je ne l'ai jamais vu.

« *Mne nzhna'ya !* » lança la voix à quelques pouces de Faustin, qui se retourna à nouveau sans rien apercevoir.

Puis un sifflement modulé comme ils en avaient souvent entendu attira l'attention de tous dans une autre direction. À vingt verges de là se tenait un *maymaygwashi*, une main levée dans une parfaite imitation d'un salut humain.

Ti-Jean lança des cris joyeux et bondit de l'épaule de Baptiste pour courir à la rencontre du nouveau venu.

— Ti-Jean le reconnaît : c'est celui qui t'a sauvé de la noyade, annonça le bûcheron. C'est aussi lui qui m'a amené l'anneau du père Masse.

Le lutin se mit à babiller une série de clics enthousiastes.

— Y dit qu'il veut qu'on l'suive, expliqua Baptiste.

— Dans ce cas, allons-y, décréta Shaor'i.

Faustin hocha la tête, perplexe. Il crut percevoir une dernière fois le rire qu'il était le seul à entendre, puis emboîta le pas à ses compagnons.

Le *maymaygwashi* courait à quatre pattes, en se retournant souvent pour vérifier si les humains le suivaient. Ti-Jean l'ayant rejoint, Baptiste allait à bon rythme, mais Shaor'i ralentit bientôt le sien, cherchant à se trouver à proximité de Faustin.

— Quand le *maymaygwashi* a désigné le père Masse avec les *komkwejwika'sikl*, il s'est servi de quatre symboles : « de petite taille », « homme », « absence » et… « tête ».

Un petit homme sans tête ? songea Faustin en jetant un regard en biais à l'Indienne.

— Baptiste a dit que le père Masse avait été missionnaire. Pourtant, il y a un *komkwejwika'sikl* qui signifie ce à quoi je songe, mais il a été inventé par les humains – cela ne fait pas partie des mœurs du peuple des rivières et…

— Mais de quoi parles-tu ?

Un grognement les interrompit alors que Baptiste lançait :

— Batince, vieux tas d'poux ! Va pas m'dire que tu m'reconnais pas, Misaël !

Le bûcheron se tenait devant un énorme loup au pelage noir comme une ombre. Un sifflement lui fit dresser l'oreille et la bête se retourna pour bondir auprès de ce qui semblait être son maître.

Si l'homme dépassait les quatre pieds, c'était tout juste. C'était un nain chauve au corps replet vêtu d'un pantalon gris, d'une chemise blanche et d'une redingote noire. Chemise et redingote ayant le col relevé, elles masquaient la moitié inférieure de la tête du singulier personnage.

À mesure que l'homme s'approchait, marchant avec une canne dont il ne semblait pas avoir besoin tant sa démarche était légère, Faustin constata que ce n'était pas la calvitie qui lui donnait un crâne chauve : en fait, son cuir chevelu était littéralement absent, et le jeune homme frissonna en repensant aux histoires de *scalps* arrachés par les Sauvages. *Un petit homme sans tête,* avait écrit le *maymaygwashi* pour désigner le père Masse.

Le nain les salua en levant une main à laquelle il manquait deux doigts. Baptiste lui rendit son salut en ajoutant :

— Ça faisait vraiment longtemps, père Masse. Au moins quinze ans, j'cré bin.

Le vieux prêtre n'émit qu'un faible chuchotement que Faustin, pris au dépourvu, ne comprit pas.

En retrait, Shaor'i murmura à Faustin :

— C'est bien ce que je pensais : le scalp, l'amputation des majeurs et des auriculaires, les brûlures à la gorge… tout indique qu'il a subi la rage d'un village autochtone trop longtemps victime des Blancs…

Shaor'i cessa de chuchoter, rivant subitement son regard sur le loup. Faustin ramena son attention sur le colosse qui achevait de répondre au petit prêtre :

— Un sort de magie noire. Mais j'vois à travers les yeux de Ti-Jean, qu'est adocté avec moé.

Maintenant qu'il s'attendait à une susurration, Faustin prêta davantage attention et son ouïe de renard lui permit de comprendre sans mal la réponse du courtaud vieillard :

— Tu me raconteras tout ça à l'intérieur, Baptiste. Qui t'accompagne ?

— Faustin Lamare, se présenta le jeune homme en serrant la main à trois doigts tendue par le père Masse.

Le nain ouvrit des yeux larges comme des soucoupes.

— Toi ?

Il rejeta la tête vers l'arrière pour l'examiner longuement.

— C'est stupéfiant de te revoir devenu homme…

— Me *revoir* ?

— Je t'ai étudié, quand tu n'étais qu'un enfant. Tu étais physiquement trop jeune pour te souvenir et…

Le petit prêtre se tourna vers le bûcheron.

— Sait-il ?

— Oui, si vous voulez parler de ma longévité et de ma filiation, répondit Faustin à la place du colosse.

— Dans ce cas, reprit Masse, nous avons beaucoup à nous dire, jeune et vieux Faustin. Et cette jeune femme se nomme ?

L'Indienne ne répondit pas, les yeux toujours fixés sur le loup qui accompagnait le père Masse. Elle avait pâli et semblait nerveuse.

— La présence de Misaël te met mal à l'aise, ma fille ? s'enquit Masse avec affabilité.

Shaor'i hocha la tête et murmura :

— *Awan*… ce Misaël… il est…

— Il s'est dépassé, si on peut dire les choses ainsi.

— … il est captif de son animalité.

— À voir ta blanche chevelure et tes jolis yeux d'or, je crois que nous avons aussi à discuter, ma fille. Il y a longtemps que je vous attends tous et nous avons énormément à nous dire ; aussi, je vous invite dans mon humble demeure.

Le père Masse enjoignit d'un geste aux compagnons de le suivre. Accompagné par le *maymaygwashi*, le groupe se mit en marche pour suivre un sentier sinueux.

— Celui-des-rivières semble lui accorder sa confiance, marmonna l'Indienne à l'intention de Faustin.

Seule leur ouïe acérée leur permit de comprendre les paroles du petit homme.

— Nous sommes de bons amis, répondit-il, montrant qu'en dépit des six verges les séparant, il avait entendu la jeune femme.

Shaor'i s'approcha et le vieux prêtre ajouta :

— Lorsqu'ils quittent les Grands Lacs pour descendre le fleuve, les *maymaygwashi* font toujours halte sur cette île. La floerkée est sacrée pour eux et elle ne pousse qu'ici. Au fil du temps, certains *maymaygwashi* sont devenus mes amis proches. Eux et moi avons une connaissance commune : la *man'ido* de la pinède.

— Une *man'ido* ? s'écria presque Shaor'i. Ici ? Faustin, tu disais entendre une voix...

— Tu entends la *man'ido* ? s'étonna à son tour le père Masse.

— J'entends une voix, répondit prudemment Faustin. Dans une langue étrangère, qui ne sonne pas comme une langue des vieux pays ni comme une langue indienne.

— Elle appartenait au peuple qui vivait avant les Cinq Nations. Elle parle dans la langue de ces anciens hommes, qui ne ressemble à aucune langue autochtone moderne.

« *Vhg'tneh'frengjdh-jslgh* », fit la voix dans l'esprit de Faustin.

— C'est une sorte de spectre ? demanda alors le jeune homme.

— Oui et non. On peut davantage la comparer à un feu follet errant. Jadis, elle est sortie de son corps et l'a laissé mourir. Ou, plutôt, les siens l'ont tuée.

— Quelle horreur ! s'exclama Faustin.

— Pas du tout. C'était un rare privilège et un insigne honneur que d'être choisi pour remplir le rôle d'esprit-gardien. Chaque *man'ido* était liée à la protection d'un lieu précis. Je sais que celle-ci protège les floerkées.

— Oui, vous avez utilisé ce mot-là, tantôt, mais...

— On les nomme aussi fausses-proserpinies ou *floerkea proserpinacoides*. De petites fleurs qui ne poussent qu'ici, ou presque. Elles sont sacrées pour les *maymaygwashi*, qui y voient le symbole de la pratique de l'arcanisme : pour produire trois graines, la floerkée doit sacrifier un jour de longévité.

Éberlué, Faustin demanda :

— Vous voulez dire que cette fleur se reproduit par l'arcanisme ?

Le père Masse eut un rire indulgent.

— Pas du tout. Ce serait tiré par les cheveux, non ? Mais la reproduction est une activité si épuisante pour la floerkée qu'elle y perd de la longévité. Une floerkée dont on coupe la fleur vit beaucoup plus longtemps.

— Ce sont ces fleurs qui poussent près de la pierre gravée ? demanda Shaor'i.

Le père Masse hocha la tête.

— Oui. C'est pour les protéger que, des siècles auparavant, cette femme est devenue *man'ido*. On a abattu beaucoup d'arbres pour construire des mâts, sur l'Isle-aux-Grues, mais jamais on n'a osé couper ceux de la Pointe-aux-Pins. L'enchantement est puissant et les hommes ressentent un profond malaise à s'attaquer à cette forêt. Ah, nous approchons de chez moi…

Ils avaient débouché sur un minuscule cap de pierre verdâtre qui s'enfonçait dans les eaux fluviales. Ils firent quelques pas dans sa direction…

… puis l'épave d'un navire apparut subitement à l'extrémité de la pointe rocheuse.

N'en croyant pas ses sens, Faustin pensa qu'il avait mal vu, recula de quelques pas…

… l'épave disparut de son champ de vision.

— Allons, mon garçon, tenta de le rassurer le père Masse. L'Ordre du Stigma Diaboli me traque depuis des années et cela n'est qu'un simple sortilège de dissimulation. Tout cela est expliqué dans l'*Opticks* et les

Alchimies de Newton : il y a quatre diagrammes inclus l'un dans l'autre, chacun courbe la lumière comme une lentille en créant une concentration puis une dispersion. Après avoir traversé les quatre pentacles, la lumière est complètement bloquée et l'épicentre du sortilège n'est plus visible.

— Vous parlez comme mon frère, marmonna Faustin en avançant, méfiant, en direction de l'épave.

À ses côtés, l'Indienne ne semblait guère rassurée, d'autant que le *maymaygwashi* s'était éclipsé sans qu'ils ne s'en aperçoivent.

Les compagnons gravirent le petit cap et Faustin s'étonna qu'il fût plus de dix verges au-dessus du niveau des eaux.

— La marée monte si haut ? demanda-t-il au prêtre.

— Non, pourquoi ?

— Mais enfin… comment cette épave s'est-elle rendue jusqu'ici ?

Le père Masse haussa les épaules.

— Il y a un sortilège permettant de soulever des objets à distance dans *Force, Portance & Attraction* de Copernic.

Stupéfait, Faustin s'immobilisa pour dévisager le petit homme.

— Mon père, je connais ce sortilège ! Je l'utilise de temps à autre ! Je suis parvenu à projeter un tonneau contre un homme qui voulait me tuer et j'ai vu mon frère, aidé de son sceptre, déplacer une poutre énorme, mais cette épave doit peser des tonnes et la maîtrise requise dépasse…

— Chacun ses talents, mon garçon, coupa le père Masse avec un clin d'œil. Cela dit, si vous voulez vous donner la peine d'entrer…

Le petit homme ouvrit une porte clouée à même l'épave. Elle révéla un simple trou, probablement la

cause du naufrage, à travers lequel Faustin se faufila habilement – quant à Baptiste, il lui fallut un bon moment pour passer.

L'intérieur de l'épave avait été aménagé comme une maison. Des cloisons séparaient la cale en pièces, comme en témoignaient les portes menant vers la proue ou la poupe. Un poêle chauffait à feu très doux, n'ayant manifestement servi qu'à cuisiner le repas du matin. Invités par le prêtre, les compagnons s'installèrent autour d'une table composée d'une vieille porte posée sur un demi-tonneau ; des caisses de bois tenaient lieu de sièges. Baptiste observa la sienne grâce à son *mah oumet*, adopta un visage méfiant et décida finalement de s'asseoir directement au sol. Entendant sa propre caisse craquer quand il y prit place, Faustin songea un instant à l'imiter.

Il parcourut bientôt la pièce du regard et s'étonna du nombre de diagrammes que le père Masse avait gravés dans les murs de bois.

— Ça demande une sacrée dose de magie, se cacher des yeux du Stigma Diaboli, dit le vieillard en ricanant, moitié pour Faustin, moitié pour lui-même. Blocage de la divination, de la prescience, du sort de localisation ondulatoire de Huygens…

Il lança un sifflement aigu et, avec une nonchalance née de l'habitude, le loup que le père Masse avait nommé Misaël pénétra dans l'abri-épave et s'allongea en bâillant sur une vieille peau d'ours étendue près du poêle. Du coin de l'œil, Faustin vit Shaor'i réprimer un frisson et l'entendit marmonner dans sa langue.

Après avoir attisé les braises, le père Masse vérifia la température d'une bouilloire laissée sur le poêle. La jugeant convenable, il versa de l'eau chaude dans une théière avant d'y ajouter une poignée d'une substance ayant l'apparence de la poudre à canon.

— Il y a longtemps que je ne bois plus de thé, expliqua le vieillard devant l'air surpris des compagnons, alors permettez-moi de vous servir autre chose.

La boisson répandit un arôme puissant qui satura l'odorat de Faustin. Le père Masse posa une tasse devant chacun d'entre eux puis y versa un liquide noir et brûlant.

Méfiante, Shaor'i repoussa négligemment la tasse. Faustin, quant à lui, prit le temps de humer longuement le contenu avant d'y tremper les lèvres. Le goût lui déplut aussitôt.

— Comme c'est amer ! s'exclama-t-il en grimaçant. Qu'est-ce que c'est ?

— En Italie, on nomme ça *caffè*. Je m'y suis habitué quand j'y ai séjourné et j'en ai ramené plusieurs caisses.

— Ça donne une claque, commenta Baptiste en mastiquant dans le vide pour faire passer la saveur âcre.

— Certains y mettent du sucre, affirma le petit homme en posant un pot sur la table.

Le jeune homme et le colosse en ajoutèrent plusieurs cuillerées à leur boisson et la remuèrent avant d'y goûter de nouveau. Quant au père Masse, il se délectait de son *caffè* noir.

Sur sa peau d'ours, le loup Misaël émit un glapissement dans son sommeil. Shaor'i frissonna de nouveau et le petit prêtre posa la main sur celle de la jeune femme.

Nerveuse, l'Indienne se déroba aussitôt au contact.

— Je peux lui demander d'aller dormir dehors. Je comprends ton malaise.

— *Awan*, ça va… *Mesgei, gitnmai*.

— Effectivement, cela doit te mettre mal à l'aise. Tu as probablement l'ossature creuse depuis fort longtemps. Yeux fixes, iris dorés, cheveux blancs… montre-moi tes pieds, ma fille.

Après une brève hésitation, Shaor'i retira une botte et lui présenta l'un de ses pieds qui, doté de trois longs orteils à l'avant et d'un autre à la place du talon, se refermait comme une serre. Les ongles étaient longs et noirs.

— Tes dents tiennent bien? s'informa le prêtre.

— Pour l'instant, oui.

— Ton nombril?

— Disparu depuis longtemps.

— Je suppose que tu n'as plus de mamelons au bout de tes seins?

Faustin rosit en entendant l'inconvenante question.

— Juste des taches sombres, répondit l'Indienne sans malaise. Il n'y a plus de pointe depuis le printemps.

— Et tes règles?

Cette fois Faustin vira à l'écarlate et s'outra d'entendre la jeune femme répondre tout simplement:

— Rien depuis quatre ans.

Mal à l'aise, Baptiste simula une quinte de toux. Le père Masse roula des yeux exaspérés.

— Tourne ta tête vers la droite, ma fille. Tourne jusqu'à ce que tu n'en sois plus capable.

Faustin eut un mouvement de recul en voyant la tête de l'Indienne effectuer un demi-tour entier. Shaor'i ramena la tête vers l'avant sans la moindre douleur.

— Ton chevauchement physiologique est très avancé, déclara Masse avec un air contrit. Misaël en était à peu près là lorsque je l'ai rencontré…

Les yeux de l'Indienne étincelèrent.

— *Siawa'si. Gisgajiei ugjit ms't goqwei*, cracha-t-elle, l'air insultée.

— *Mut punia'tinew ta'n tujiw getangusultioq muta mawi ms'gi'gt'tew ugtapangitueweimuow wa'so'q*, répondit paisiblement le père Masse dans la même langue. Néanmoins…

Le prêtre jeta un œil en direction de l'énorme loup qui avait commencé à ronfler.

— Quand j'ai rencontré Misaël, il était sur le point de convoler en justes noces. C'était dans les années 20, à l'époque où le Collège traquait les derniers membres du Stigma Diaboli dans leur ultime refuge, aux Forges des Trois-Rivières. Misaël n'était pas un goétiste, mais en échange de menus services, le Stigma lui avait octroyé une forme animale. Et comme de nombreux larbins du Stigma, Misaël n'avait guère été mis au courant des risques qu'il encourait à adopter sa forme canine aussi souvent qu'il le souhaitait. Lui, ce qu'il espérait, c'était épouser la petite Catherine Miquelon et pour ça, il aurait accepté n'importe quoi... Le Stigma ne lui demandait pas grand-chose : sous forme de loup, il repérait au flair la présence d'intrus aux abords du manoir Poulin, en échange de quoi la Siffleuse avait altéré magiquement les sentiments de la jeune Miquelon, qui s'empressa après quelque temps d'accepter la demande en mariage de Misaël. Malheureusement... peu avant la noce, notre Collège tenta un assaut massif contre le manoir Poulin et le Stigma exigea de ses membres une collaboration constante. Le travail de gardien de Misaël se prolongea pendant des semaines et, forcément...

Le prêtre jeta un regard triste au loup assoupi.

— Que pouvions-nous faire de lui ? Un esprit d'homme prisonnier dans un corps de loup, condamné à une longévité humaine, son âme humaine morcelée de n'avoir pu épouser sa belle... Il ne pouvait nous parler, mais son regard suppliant disait tout : *Je vous en supplie, libérez-moi...* Or, il n'y a rien, absolument rien, qui puisse être tenté une fois que le corps d'un métamorphe a perdu le souvenir de l'organisation moléculaire de sa première forme. Je me rappelle lui

avoir longuement parlé, assis sur une pierre, alors qu'il m'observait de ses larmoyants yeux de loup. Quand il a eu compris que rien ne pouvait être tenté, il s'est enfui dans l'épaisse pinède encerclant le manoir Poulin. Il est revenu quelques jours plus tard. Dévoré par un profond désir de vengeance, il m'a aidé à repérer plusieurs goétistes fugitifs. Il ne m'a jamais quitté depuis.

— Pourquoi me raconter ça ? demanda Shaor'i, du défi dans la voix. Je suis l'Exécutrice du Cercle des Sept Danseurs : je n'existe que pour déchaîner le courroux des miens.

— N'as-tu aucun attachement en ce monde, ma fille ? Le quitterais-tu sans le moindre regret ?

— Ce genre de préoccupation est étranger à ma nature. Je suis une arme douée de parole. Ce qu'il adviendra de mon corps n'a aucune importance.

— Et maintenant que ton cercle n'est plus, cette destinée a-t-elle toujours un sens ?

Projeté d'un mouvement si vif que l'œil le décela à peine, le couteau de l'Indienne se planta dans la paroi de bois, à un pouce de la tête du père Masse. D'un bond, Shaor'i se leva de sa chaise et quitta l'abri-épave. Dès qu'elle eut franchi la porte, l'ouïe acérée de Faustin entendit le froissement d'ailes de son envol.

Baptiste se leva lentement.

— S'cusez. J'vas lui causer, père Masse. La P'tite est assez *rough*, par moments…

— Rassieds-toi, mon ami, répondit le prêtre. Elle gagnera davantage à cogiter seule.

Après une brève hésitation, le bûcheron obtempéra.

— Parlez-moi plutôt de vous. De la façon dont vous êtes parvenus jusqu'ici et, surtout, de la manière dont vous vous êtes opposés à Hohenstaufen depuis l'enlèvement de cette jeune fille, au dernier Mardi gras.

— Hohenstaufen ? releva Faustin.

— Celui que vous nommez l'Étranger. Mais contez-moi d'abord votre histoire, puis je vous raconterai la mienne… et la sienne.

◆

Alors Faustin raconta.

Le père Masse était déjà au courant du décès du curé Lamare, d'une partie des événements du printemps et de l'émeute ayant précédé leur départ pour les Vieilles Forges : il était passé au presbytère, expliqua-t-il, au tout début du mois de mai.

— Elle était bien surprise de me voir, la Madeleine ! ricana le petit prêtre. Elle ne m'avait pas vu depuis au moins vingt-cinq ans. C'est moi qui l'avais présentée à ton oncle pour qu'il l'embauche comme servante : elle avait été témoin de sorcellerie quand elle était jeune fille, à Pointe-Lévy. Vaillante et bonne cuisinière comme sa mère, Éphrem ne pouvait demander mieux.

— J'ignorais ça, murmura Faustin en se disant qu'il aurait bien aimé entendre l'histoire de la bouche de Madeleine.

Une larme coula sur sa joue qu'il essuya du revers de la main. Le père Masse s'enquit de la cause de son humeur et ce fut Baptiste qui expliqua pour Faustin ce qu'avait été le retour à Notre-Dame des Tempérances. Le prêtre les pressa de questions, les deux compagnons racontèrent dans un ordre à la cohérence toute relative, puis le père Masse chuchota doucement :

— Va marcher un peu, Faustin. Tu reviendras dans une heure ou deux et tu finiras de me raconter tout ça.

Hochant la tête sans mot dire, Faustin quitta l'épave, des regrets plein le cœur.

◆

Faustin passa un instant à ressasser un chagrin qu'il croyait non pas disparu, mais à tout le moins assumé. La gorge nouée, il se remémora quelques souvenirs heureux, sans pouvoir s'empêcher de penser à ce qui venait de le frapper.

Jusqu'à présent, il avait ignoré comment Madeleine et son oncle s'étaient rencontrés. Et pendant qu'il y songeait... Comment Madeleine s'était-elle habituée aux sortilèges du curé ? Comment avait été son arrivée à Notre-Dame des Tempérances, ses premiers mois avec tout un presbytère à gérer... et surtout, comment Madeleine avait-elle réagi quand le curé Lamare avait ramené un bébé en affirmant qu'il s'agissait d'un enfant de la honte, fils d'une sœur dont elle n'avait jamais entendu parler et morte en couches après le départ d'un père inconnu ?

Tout en ruminant ses pensées, Faustin finit par s'obliger à pénétrer dans la forêt de la Pointe-aux-Pins. S'il comprenait sans difficulté que Shaor'i s'y sente à l'aise, il gardait le sentiment qu'il n'était pas le bienvenu dans cet îlot vierge.

Non loin de la pierre au *komkwejwika'sikl*, il trouva l'Indienne assise en tailleur, yeux clos. Elle souriait. Elle avait fait de même en pénétrant dans la forêt plus tôt dans la journée. La jeune femme était si paisible que Faustin se laissa bientôt gagner par sa quiétude, reléguant à l'arrière-plan ses préoccupations.

— J'étais bien certain que tu serais ici, dit-il simplement.

Shaor'i ouvrit les yeux et, le regardant, elle dit :

— Tu l'entends vraiment, Faustin ? Tu entends la *man'ido* ?

— Quand elle veut bien me parler, oui. Sauf que je ne comprends rien à ce qu'elle raconte.

« *Znay't ?* » résonna la voix dans son esprit.

— Tu as beaucoup de chance qu'elle te parle.

Elle se leva et Faustin l'observa par des regards furtifs.

Elle n'était pas jolie. Elle avait toujours été quelconque, mais à présent que ses cheveux étaient couleur de neige, qu'elle lui arrivait plusieurs pouces en bas de l'épaule et que son visage devenait plus anguleux, son apparence n'avait vraiment rien de séduisant. Intrigant, dérangeant, mais certainement pas avenant. D'autant qu'elle avait choisi d'aller pieds nus… Pourtant, à la voir ainsi en paix, ses yeux dorés brillant de bien-être et ses traits épanouis, elle était plutôt agréable à regarder.

La main délicate de l'Indienne effleura celle de Faustin.

— Mon ami, murmura-t-elle, si je meurs en te protégeant, jure-moi que tu porteras ma dépouille sur cette île, dans cette forêt.

La requête prit Faustin de court. *Si je meurs…* Pourtant, de telles préoccupations devaient être toujours présentes à son esprit, elle qui fonçait sans hésiter dans chaque combat avec le même abandon.

Le silence de Shaor'i était doux comme celui d'une personne goûtant un retour chez elle après une longue absence. Du moins est-ce ainsi que Faustin le perçut. Il répondit alors :

— Je te le jure, Shaor'i. Si tu meurs, je viendrai te porter en terre ici.

Il sentit la petite main de l'Indienne serrer la sienne.

— Je ne faillirai pas, ajouta-t-elle en levant la tête pour plonger ses yeux de rapace dans ceux de Faustin. Je te promets, mon ami, que tu n'auras plus d'échec à me reprocher.

— Mais… je ne te reproche rien, Shaor'i.

Le regard de l'Indienne se voila.

— C'est bien le pire, lâcha-t-elle avant de s'écarter de quelques pas et de prendre la piste menant à l'épave du père Masse.

Sans comprendre, Faustin la regarda s'éloigner.

◆

Quand il rentra à l'abri-épave, Baptiste achevait de raconter leur évasion de Grosse-Île. Shaor'i, silencieuse, s'était assise près du poêle, partageant avec le loup Misaël un silence qu'eux seuls semblaient comprendre.

Faustin s'assit sur sa caisse de bois, déclina l'offre d'un nouveau *caffè* – la boisson l'avait mise dans un état de nervosité qu'il n'aimait pas du tout, se sentant comme une bête aux aguets.

Il demanda plutôt de but en blanc :

— Tout à l'heure, vous avez nommé l'Étranger « Hohenstaufen ». Vous connaissez notre histoire. Racontez-nous maintenant la sienne.

Le ton était un peu sec, mais le prêtre ne s'en formalisa pas. Il prit toutefois le temps de se resservir du *caffè* avant de déclarer :

— Cette histoire, pour être contée, nécessite de passer par d'autres histoires : la mienne, la tienne et celle de Gamache, notamment… sans oublier celle de la science des arcanes en entier. Nous en avons pour la nuit.

— Nous avons tout notre temps.

Avec un sourire indulgent, le petit homme se décida :

— Débutons par la tienne, alors. Du moins la partie que tu ignores, celle qui suit le décès de ta mère et qui

précède ton adoption par ton oncle. Sache donc que lors du changement de Régime, l'ordre d'Albert le Grand a tout tenté pour préserver sa puissance. Le Stigma Diaboli venait d'essuyer une défaite considérable pour s'être opposé aux Anglais. Les goétistes restants s'étaient terrés aux Trois-Rivières sous l'égide de la famille Poulin et les théurgistes, grâce à l'abbé Briand, étaient parvenus à se retirer dans la clandestinité du Collège du Mont à l'Oiseau sans être importunés par la nouvelle administration. Le père Rouillard, qui avait momentanément prêté main-forte aux goétistes, était revenu dans les rangs du clergé avec un projet extrêmement particulier.

— Rouillard ? J'ai vu sa tombe dans les catacombes de l'île d'Orléans. Il utilisait le Calice des Moires.

— C'était un grand spirite, en effet. Mais ses nouveaux projets ne concernaient pas les défunts, bien au contraire : ils se penchaient sur les naissances. Après l'exécution de l'Ensorceleuse de Pointe-Lévy, c'est lui qui a aidé ta demi-sœur Angélique à fuir les inquisiteurs britanniques et celle-ci a refusé de partir sans toi. Découvrant ce bébé qui ne vieillissait pas et ayant jadis côtoyé l'immortel Étranger, Rouillard considéra la possibilité de poursuivre des recherches pour accroître l'espérance de vie des arcanistes. Le projet Emrys avait commencé – du surnom *emrys* qu'on donnait au Merlin légendaire, fils d'une sorcière et d'un démon…

— Ça me relègue au rang d'être démoniaque. Vous me pardonnerez de trouver ça un tantinet insultant ?

— Allons, ce n'est qu'une vague analogie… bref. Quand le père Rouillard mourut de noyade en 1768, le Stigma Diaboli, bien que privé de l'Étranger depuis le changement de Régime, était encore puissant, même s'il limitait ses actions aux environs des Trois-Rivières.

Alors, tu es resté sous la protection de la famille Rioux, seigneur des Trois-Pistoles et mécène du Collège.

« Dix ans plus tard – j'étais alors un jeune apprenti de quatorze ans –, mes maîtres du Collège me trouvèrent un certain talent et on m'envoya en pension chez les Rioux afin que je m'habitue à ta présence pour un jour devenir ton gardien. Je fus ordonné une autre décennie plus tard, en 1788, puis on me nomma officiellement responsable du projet Emrys.

« J'ai donc vécu avec toi, Faustin, pendant quarante ans – et heureusement que j'avais des servantes qui se sont succédé pour s'occuper de toi ! Parfois longtemps, car j'ai beaucoup voyagé, mais dans l'ensemble… »

Faustin fixait le vieux prêtre, stupéfait. Cet homme avait pris soin de lui pendant quarante ans ! Tout cela semblait si… surréel. Certes, il savait déjà qu'il avait été nourrisson pendant plus ou moins soixante-six ans, mais cette partie de sa vie avait toujours été négligée par ses réflexions, à l'instar des neuf mois qu'il avait passés dans le ventre de sa mère. Une sorte de très longue gestation, somme toute.

Sans se douter des pensées qui occupaient Faustin, Masse reprit :

— Tout ça ne fut pas sans mal. En 1799, une goétiste de Port-Joli tenta de s'en prendre à toi. Puis, en 1819, ce fut l'un de nos vicaires, un nommé Belleau, qui voulut te kidnapper en espérant trouver le secret de l'immortalité. C'est un autre tout jeune vicaire, Éphrem Lamare, qui…

La voix de Baptiste tonitrua dans l'abri-épave :

— L'bébé à Belleau, c'tait Faustin ?

— Tu n'avais jamais établi le lien, Baptiste ? s'amusa Masse.

— Comment j'aurais pu ? Quand je l'ai revu après la mort de son oncle, Faustin m'avait dit qu'y avait vingt-deux ans… Comment savoir qu'y était l'bébé de 19 ?

— Qu'est-ce que… commença Faustin en se tournant vers le bûcheron.

— L'sorcier Belleau du Nord, pas loin du lac Saint-Jean ! C'est durant c't'histoire-là que j'ai rencontré ton oncle, mon Faustin. Faudra que j't'raconte ça un jour : Belleau, les *skwahdem*, Picoba le chien-loup pis l'verrat géant…

— Plus tard, Baptiste… le coupa le père Masse. J'en ai encore long à raconter.

Se servant une autre tasse de *caffè*, le prêtre poursuivit :

— Les choses ont changé quand tu as amorcé ta croissance. C'est à ce moment que je me suis mis à étudier celui qu'on soupçonnait d'être ton géniteur, ce fameux Étranger. Confiant ta garde à Éphrem, je me suis mis en quête de témoignages et de traces de son existence, trouvant au passage deux portraits peints à de nombreuses années d'intervalle.

— J'ai vu ces tableaux au Collège, dit Faustin. Le père Bélanger nous les a montrés.

— Mes études avancèrent bien et, lentement, je me mis à élaborer des théories sur l'identité de ce sorcier. Les documents que nous avions récupérés au manoir Poulin, lors du conflit entre l'Ordre Théurgique et le Stigma en 24-25, me fournirent de précieux renseignements. Je n'avais pas ramené que Misaël de cette campagne, loin de là !

Le loup bâilla avec bruit, comme pour appuyer ces propos.

— En 31, j'entrepris un premier voyage vers l'Espagne, où je trouvai de nombreuses informations sur

l'Étranger dans les rapports de Torquemada. Quand je revins, en 36, ce fut pour découvrir un Collège en proie au choléra et des rumeurs de soulèvement qui n'allaient pas tarder à se concrétiser… et c'est là que Gamache devient important dans cette histoire.

— Pourquoi Gamache ?

— Parce que, de nous tous, c'était l'homme le plus vaillant, un noble guérisseur et un fier défenseur de notre culture française. C'est sans hésitation qu'il s'est opposé à Lartigue quand est venu le temps de prendre parti durant la révolte des Patriotes. Moi-même, j'ai été sensible à son discours. Quand l'Ordre Théurgique a été dissous, je me suis joint à Gamache et j'ai été témoin de sa chute. Nous l'avons perdu lors d'une nuit d'automne, alors qu'il faisait un pacte avec Satan.

— Un pacte avec Satan ? Vous plaisantez ?

— Non, pas le moins du monde. C'était au plus fort des Troubles de 38. D'un côté, il y avait Lartigue, l'ancien maître de notre Ordre, qui assistait les Anglais en révélant la position de nos troupes ; auprès de lui se trouvaient ses apprentis qui avaient échappé au Grand Choléra. De l'autre côté, il y avait Gamache, Légaré, Chartier et moi, qui aidions les Patriotes de nos sortilèges. Dans un camp comme dans l'autre, nos interventions étaient discrètes, afin de ne point révéler l'existence des arcanes.

Le père Masse laissa passer un long moment de silence. De toute évidence, évoquer ce souvenir lui était pénible. Il continua avec une voix chargée d'émotion :

— Je me souviendrai toujours de ce soir d'octobre. Les arbres avaient perdu leurs feuilles qui s'amoncelaient en tas sur la terre. Les foins d'hiver étaient secs. Gamache et moi chevauchions à travers les champs,

accompagnés d'une dizaine d'hommes. Nous comptions nous rendre dans un petit hameau sympathique à notre cause afin de quérir des vivres, de la poudre et des cuillères de plomb pour couler des balles. On nous avait reçus discrètement, dans une grange qui tenait aussi lieu de point de ralliement. Martel, un habitant influent, avait fait préparer pour nous du bœuf séché, de la poudre et des munitions pour plusieurs semaines. Nous en étions à négocier le prix, dont nous nous acquittions en utilisant des boutons prélevés sur des uniformes anglais, quand soudain un premier hurlement retentit dans la nuit. Nous sommes sortis pour découvrir que les flammes dévoraient les blés secs et menaçaient déjà d'attaquer les premières fermes. Nous avions été suivis. Une trentaine d'Anglais chevauchaient à travers le village, jetant leurs torches sur les toitures qui s'enflammaient aussitôt. Gamache sauta derechef en selle et poussa sa monture au galop. Debout sur les étriers, il visa de son fusil et tua un premier soldat. Il dégaina ensuite ses pistolets, abattit deux autres ennemis, puis tira son couteau de sa botte et le lança en travers de la gorge d'un quatrième Anglais. Alors que celui-ci tombait de sa monture, Gamache s'empara du sabre du Rouge et fonça à l'assaut de l'officier qui dirigeait la troupe : un vieillard que j'ai tout de suite reconnu, qui contemplait le brasier comme un père regarde un fils aimé. Partout on disait de lui qu'il était le Mal incarné, et sa prédilection pour les incendies punitifs l'avait fait surnommer *le vieux Brûlot*. Il se nommait John Colborne, alias Lord Seaton, mais entre Patriotes nous ne le désignions que sous le nom de *Lord Satan*.

« Vu ma taille, il m'est difficile de monter à cheval sans aide. Mes hommes s'étaient précipités pour attaquer nos ennemis et les villageois tentaient en vain

d'éteindre les flammes. Mais de là où je me tenais, je compris que Gamache avait décidé d'en finir avec Satan. Je l'entendis clairement incanter et je vis Satan tirer en vain du pistolet. La balle avait ricoché sur le mur de force que Gamache venait de lever. Puis l'impensable se produisit : le vieux Brûlot proféra une incantation et Gamache, serrant une main sur sa poitrine, tomba de cheval, terrassé par une crise cardiaque.

Le prêtre s'offrit une pause, goûta son *caffè* devenu froid, ouvrit la porte pour le jeter et se resservit sans toutefois y tremper ses lèvres.

— De la goétie, reprit-il. Lord Satan venait d'user de magie noire. Je voulus courir prêter assistance à mon ami. On me frappa à la nuque avec la crosse d'un fusil – je portais ma soutane ce soir-là et c'est sûrement à ça que je dois ma vie, ainsi que ma libération, deux jours plus tard. De Gamache, je n'eus guère de nouvelles pendant des mois. Je sus grâce à divers témoignages qu'il avait survécu à son attaque et qu'il était prisonnier de Lord Satan. Presque deux ans plus tard, en 1840, j'appris que Lartigue était mort à l'Hôtel-Dieu de Montréal, son foie l'ayant subitement lâché. Le rapport qu'on me fit parvenir ne laissait planer aucun doute : la goétie avait été de nouveau la cause de cette mort. Si la technique ressemblait à celle du vieux Brûlot, je ne pouvais me résoudre à le soupçonner : Lartigue, après tout, avait prêté main-forte aux Anglais. J'eus la réponse la semaine suivante : Gamache était revenu me voir. Il me raconta son pacte avec Satan. Le vieux général n'était pas un véritable arcaniste. Il ne pouvait lancer qu'un sort dont il ignorait le réel fonctionnement. Il portait un pendentif orné du diagramme et avait appris la formule par cœur. En échange de sa vie – et de la permission d'étudier

le pendentif –, Gamache avait promis au vieux Brûlot de lui enseigner les arcanes. Peine perdue : le bonhomme s'était avéré un fort mauvais élève. Lassé, Gamache avait fini par fuir, apportant le bijou avec lui, se mettant en quête de dangereux livres mis à l'Index… Il avait relu les témoignages de ceux d'entre nous qui avaient mis un terme aux agissements du Stigma Diaboli. Nous pensions, jadis, que la famille Poulin dirigeait ce cercle, et cela depuis Poulin de Francheville.

— Francheville ! s'exclama Faustin. C'est l'une des identités de l'Étranger. Nous avons vu son portrait au manoir Poulin.

— Oui. Et une fois morte la dernière représentante de cette lignée, Lucinda Poulin dite la Voyante des Trois-Rivières, nous pensions que la goétie était définitivement éteinte. Or, nous avions tort. Il y avait une rumeur, voyez-vous, selon laquelle la Poulin avait fait mettre un coffre magique en terre, une sorte de trésor inestimable. Gamache, croyant trouver des grimoires de goétie, voulait se mettre à sa recherche, car il désirait fonder un nouvel Ordre. La théurgie ne suffisait plus, selon lui, à sauver les arcanes de leur lente agonie. Il se fâcha quand je refusai de l'aider, arguant que je ne comprenais rien aux nécessités qu'exigeait la préservation des arcanes. Après une violente dispute, il s'en retourna, jurant qu'il trouverait ce coffre d'une façon ou d'une autre.

Le père Masse marqua une pause avant d'ajouter :

— Il y parvint, certes, mais ce « coffre » n'était autre que le sarcophage dans lequel dormait l'Empereur Frédéric II de Hohenstaufen, dit *Stupor Mundi* ou l'Archimage du Saint-Empire. Car telle est la véritable identité de celui que vous nommez l'Étranger.

Faustin eut un frisson. D'une certaine façon, c'était aussi une partie de ses propres origines qu'il s'apprêtait à découvrir.

Impatient, il enjoignit d'un geste au prêtre de poursuivre, qui ne se fit pas prier pour enchaîner.

— Quand je sus que Gamache avait éveillé l'Étranger, je compris qu'il était primordial de percer à jour l'identité de cet immortel sorcier. Mon voyage en Espagne, neuf ans auparavant, m'avait semblé logique, car les rapports de Torquemada pendant l'Inquisition étaient les principales sources mentionnant celui qu'il nommait « l'Homme en noir ». Néanmoins, aucune trace de l'identité réelle de ce sorcier – Torquemada le considérait comme une incarnation du Diable.

« Je me suis donc embarqué pour l'Italie, afin de consulter à Rome les archives du Vatican. Quelques sortilèges d'influence mentale m'ouvrirent toutes grandes les portes de la voûte et je pus lire la correspondance qu'avaient entretenue les différents inquisiteurs avec leurs évêques, ainsi que celle de ces derniers avec les cardinaux ou Sa Sainteté elle-même. L'Étranger était généralement nommé *Lucifero*, *Satana*, *il Diavolo*, voire *il Anticristo*. L'Antéchrist. Au début, je ne prêtai guère attention à ces superstitieuses dénominations.

« Puis une missive me força à me raviser. Un jeune prêtre, inquisiteur zélé, se vantait d'avoir torturé à mort une fermière qu'il jugeait responsable d'une épidémie de fièvre bovine ; à la toute fin, il déclarait que « l'influence de l'Antéchrist décroît de jour en jour et cela, depuis que Sa Sainteté Grégoire IX l'a percé à jour ». Intrigué, je m'empressai de lire tout ce qu'avait écrit, ou ce qu'on avait écrit, sur ce pape médiéval. C'est avec stupéfaction que je découvris que le vicaire du Christ avait décrété, en 1227, que

l'Antéchrist était... sa majesté l'Empereur Frédéric II de Hohenstaufen.

« Incrédule, je suis parti sans tarder pour Naples, pour voir au *Palazzo Reale* la statue de ce souverain honni par l'Église. Je manquai défaillir en reconnaissant le visage noble et altier, aux traits patriciens, que j'avais déjà vu sur le tableau peint par le frère Luc en 1671, et sur celui peint par François Malepart de Beaucourt en 1790.

« Je n'arrivais pas à y croire. De retour au Vatican, je lus avec avidité tout ce qui traitait du dernier empereur de la maison Hohenstaufen. On disait de lui qu'il n'était pas réellement mort, mais qu'il dormait d'un sommeil magique sous l'Etna ; toutefois, ce qui m'étonna au plus haut point, ce fut d'apprendre qu'il était proche du mathématicien Fibonacci, celui-là même qui a permis la mise en mathématique des arcanes.

Le père Masse fit une pause, puis ajouta :

— Peu importe de quelle façon on considère la chose, la naissance de l'Étranger a donc engendré la naissance des arcanes telles que nous les connaissons.

— Ça n'a aucun sens, objecta Faustin. Je ne suis peut-être pas un grand arcaniste, mais je sais que mon oncle parlait parfois de magie perse, celte ou égyptienne...

Le vieux prêtre sourit.

— Bien sûr, les arcanes ont toujours été présents sous forme de médianie. Chaque culture a eu ses chamanes, ses sorciers et ses prêtres. Rarissime, la sorcellerie existait néanmoins, pratiquée par des sociétés secrètes ou transmise de maître à apprenti. Elle avait commencé à s'exprimer de façon mathématique à Babylone et en Égypte, mais c'est en Grèce que le principe du diagramme fut découvert. Une société

secrète, les pythagoriciens, constitua le premier cercle arcaniste. L'enseignement pythagoricien était oral et secret, et l'activité politique des initiés fut très importante. Le cercle simula sa disparition, mais se maintint secrètement sous l'Empire romain. À la chute de l'Empire, ses secrets furent perdus en Occident ; les quelques arcanistes survivants s'installèrent à Constantinople, où le savoir grec fut préservé. Malgré cela, la magie n'était pas une science exacte comme de nos jours. Superstitions et reliquats cultistes s'étaient mêlés aux procédures de sortilèges, si bien que le moindre sort avait une foule de prérequis considérés comme nécessaires, tels que des alignements astrologiques, des invocations à Baal ou Astarté, des lectures bibliques à rebours, des sacrifices et des formules dépourvues de sens où l'incantation réelle était précédée de multiples psalmodies inutiles. Les diagrammes existaient et on leur mêlait l'écriture de mots jugés magiques, de représentations des phases de la Lune et de symboles alchimiques convenus.

— Et que vient faire l'Étranger là-dedans ?

— C'est grâce à ces proto-arcanes que ton père est né en l'an de grâce 1194 : Frédéric II de Hohenstaufen, qui fut l'un des plus grands monarques du Moyen Âge, peut-être le plus grand de tous. Ton père vint au monde d'une femme âgée de quarante ans, et la seule façon d'empêcher l'accouchement de tourner au drame fut pour ton grand-père, Henri VI, de faire venir deux médecins arabes pratiquant ce mélange de magie et de simagrées. Mère et fils furent sauvés et les médecins immédiatement engagés comme précepteurs. Frédéric II de Hohenstaufen devint, au contact de ces hommes, un monarque d'une incroyable érudition. Il parlait au moins six langues, portait un grand intérêt aux beaux-arts, était un architecte de

talent. Lors de son couronnement à Aix-la-Chapelle, il promit au pape de partir en croisade.

— Donc de se rendre au Proche-Orient, sous l'influence de Constantinople, où subsistait le savoir de ces pythagoriciens.

— Précisément. Ainsi, lorsque Hohenstaufen arriva en Terre Sainte, il découvrit une contrée puissante par sa richesse, son armée mais surtout par son savoir. L'Orient respirait la magie. La science des Grecs avait été enrichie par les découvertes d'Al-Khawarizmi, d'Abu Kamil, et par les traités géométriques *Kitab al-Handasa* et *El Wadih* d'Abu I-Wafa. Le sultan Malik al-Kamel gardait à sa cour un grand nombre de sorciers et, voyant en Hohenstaufen un érudit capable de comprendre le potentiel des arcanes, il lui proposa d'opter pour les pourparlers et de mener une croisade pacifique. Des liens amicaux se tissèrent entre les deux souverains et, par le traité de Jaffa, Hohenstaufen récupéra sans affrontement la ville de Jérusalem. La période pendant laquelle ton père régna sur Jérusalem est peu connue, mais on sait qu'il fit parvenir en Italie des copies des ouvrages pythagoriciens et des écrits d'Abu Kamil à un mathématicien qu'il avait rencontré à Pise, Leonardo Pisano, dont on se souviendra sous le nom de « Fibonacci ». De l'envoi d'Hohenstaufen à ce mathématicien allait naître toute la science arcanique moderne.

« Mathématicien accompli, Fibonacci avait déjà enseigné à Pise en 1198 les chiffres arabes et la notation algébrique. Il parvint à unifier les ouvrages offerts par le monarque à ceux d'Al-Khawarizmi en démontrant la primordialité du nombre d'or, si cher aux pythagoriciens. Et surtout, il développa la fameuse suite qui porte son nom.

« La suite de Fibonacci intervient dans l'écriture des "réduites" de l'expression du nombre d'or. Le nombre d'or était la clé pour ériger les arcanes en une science mathématique et physique. La suite de Fibonacci permettait d'en comprendre l'omniprésence car tout, absolument tout dans le monde qui nous entoure, est organisé selon le nombre d'or, depuis les écailles des pommes de pin ou la spirale d'un tournesol jusqu'à l'organisation des *atomos* dans un cristal – et pour influencer ou contrôler les lois de la physique, il fallait comprendre ce nombre d'or. Les formules arcaniques sont élaborées grâce à l'application du nombre d'or qui détermine l'harmonie et le rythme d'une résonance musicale ; les pentacles sont l'expression de l'application de la loi des isocèles sur le pentagramme.

Faustin soupira.

— Vous êtes comme mon frère et mon oncle, père Masse. Vous tenez pour acquis que le commun des mortels s'intéresse aux formules algébriques autant qu'à ses récoltes.

Le prêtre rosit.

— Oui, tu as raison, je m'égare un peu… Bref, en 1225, Fibonacci termina le *Liber quadratorum*, le Livre des Cercles, qu'il dédia à Frédéric II. Il en envoya une copie à son souverain, toujours en Orient. Hohenstaufen, qui recevra le *Liber quadratorum* quatre ans plus tard, s'empressera de revenir en Italie. Les arcanes tels que nous les connaissons, dépourvus de superstition et gouvernés par la jonction de formules et de diagrammes, venaient de voir le jour.

« De retour en Occident, Hohenstaufen organisa des concours mathématiques et réunit à sa cour les plus grands esprits scientifiques de son temps. Il forma le premier cercle arcanique et constitua une vaste

bibliothèque d'ouvrages d'astrologie, d'envoûtements et d'alchimie que ses savants purgèrent de leurs éléments superstitieux pour rédiger les premiers traités d'arcanes. Aidé de son ordre, Hohenstaufen accumula les victoires militaires, soumit les cités-États et conquit de vastes territoires. De plus en plus craint, il tira un grand orgueil de sa puissance. Ses titres furent nombreux : il était *Imperator Fridericus secundus, Romanorum Cæsar semper Augustus, Italicus Siculus Hierosolymitanus Arelatensis, Felix victor ac triumphator*... mais surtout, *Stupor Mundi*, la Merveille du Monde, le Soleil brillant sur la terre des hommes. Cela le mettra en conflit avec le pape Grégoire IX, qui le désigna alors comme l'incarnation de l'Antéchrist. Ceux qui servaient Hohenstaufen portaient au bras une marque que le pape surnomma *Stigma Diaboli*, la Marque du Diable. Ironiquement, Hohenstaufen reprit l'expression pour nommer son cercle d'initiés.

« L'Ordre du Stigma Diaboli offrit à Hohenstaufen une puissance inespérée. Mais lorsqu'il franchit l'âge de trente-cinq ans, il commença à être obnubilé par l'idée de sa propre mortalité. Correspondant avec le musulman Ibn Sabin, il le questionna sur les recherches passées sur l'immortalité. Puis un autre mathématicien vint à sa cour : Michael Scot, un savant écossais qui, ayant appliqué les découvertes de Fibonacci sur le nombre d'or à certains mythes celtes, était parvenu à de terribles constatations. Moyennant une fortune, Scot exposa ses découvertes sur le cercle de Stonehenge... et c'est là qu'Hohenstaufen décida d'ériger le terrible Castel del Monte.

— Ériger ? Vous parlez d'un bâtiment ?

— D'un château entier, oui. Le Castel a un plan octogonal, avec à chacun des huit angles de l'octogone

une tour elle-même octogonale. Pour la plupart des historiens, il s'agit d'une forteresse…

Le père Masse laissa échapper un ricanement sarcastique.

— … les imbéciles. Non seulement le Castel n'est pas dans une position stratégique, mais rien dans sa construction ne favorise l'action militaire. Il n'y a même pas d'écurie ! Les escaliers en colimaçon montent en sens inverse des aiguilles d'une montre, ce qui aurait forcé les soldats à tenir leur arme de la main gauche. Quant aux meurtrières, elles sont trop étroites pour les archers.

« Non… sorte de diagramme arcanique en trois dimensions, le Castel a été construit pour les fins d'une expérience effroyable, celle qui allait donner à Hohenstaufen l'immortalité dont il rêvait.

— Un bâtiment entier pour supporter l'énergie d'un sort ? s'étonna Faustin.

— Il y avait eu des précédents dans l'Histoire. Le cercle de Stonehenge, notamment. Il avait été utilisé dans la lointaine Antiquité et le sorcier Myrddin Emrys, que les contes transformèrent en ce Merlin légendaire, était parvenu à le réactiver temporairement. Le mathématicien Michael Scot en avait décodé la séquence algébrique et, avec Fibonacci, l'avait adaptée. Quelque part autour de 1245, Hohenstaufen procéda à l'expérience et parvint à placer son corps en stase temporelle. Il ne se manifestait plus qu'en effigie. Le procédé, fort coûteux en énergie, aurait drainé Hohenstaufen de la longévité qui lui restait en quelques semaines. C'est pourquoi on déplaça son corps dans une chambre secrète, sous l'Etna. En ces lieux était apporté chaque semaine un esclave, un mendiant ou un prisonnier dont Hohenstaufen drainait l'essence vitale pour assurer sa subsistance.

— *Awan*, fit Shaor'i. Quelle monstruosité.

— En effet, ma fille. Mais « la fin justifie les moyens » était la devise d'Hohenstaufen ; d'ailleurs c'est de lui que s'est inspiré Machiavel pour écrire *Le Prince*. Or, pendant qu'Hohenstaufen planifiait la fin de son règne et sa mort simulée, il continuait de favoriser l'épanouissement des arcanes. C'est auprès de lui qu'est formé le plus puissant de ses disciples, celui qu'on nommera Albert le Grand ; mais lorsque le religieux découvrit avec horreur l'atroce façon par laquelle Hohenstaufen accroissait sa longévité, il décida de fonder son propre Ordre et de le mettre au service de l'Église afin que celle-ci pourchasse ardemment le Stigma Diaboli.

— L'Ordre Théurgique, comprit Faustin.

— En effet. Et le règne d'Hohenstaufen aurait bien pu s'achever là : Rome et la papauté disposaient alors de ressources suffisantes pour le traquer et le détruire, et le secret des arcanes théurgiques s'était vite répandu dans de nombreux ordres monastiques. Néanmoins, en juillet 1266, un frère franciscain du nom de Roger Bacon fit parvenir de prometteurs travaux arcaniques au nouveau pape, Clément IV. Des membres du Stigma Diaboli en eurent connaissance et Hohenstaufen, confiant la garde de son corps à ses plus fidèles disciples, se rendit en Angleterre pour rencontrer Roger Bacon.

« Pour la suite, je ne dispose que d'informations fragmentaires… Les deux Ordres amorcèrent une lutte sans merci qui allait s'étendre sur presque six cents ans. Roger Bacon avait bel et bien rejoint l'ordre du Stigma Diaboli et il a consacré l'essentiel de son temps à la rédaction de ses *Opus*, dont l'*Opus æternum,* véritable compendium des procédés affectant la longévité de l'Homme.

— C'est le livre que cherche l'Étranger! s'exclama Faustin. Du moins, il en recherche les pages manquantes...

— Forcément. Toutes les procédures arcaniques de longévité y sont consignées dans un alphabet codé. Hohenstaufen l'utilisa notamment pour créer le sceptre qui lui permet de drainer la longévité des êtres vivants qui l'entourent – ce même sceptre que porte présentement Lavallée. Grâce à cet artefact, il a pu réintégrer son corps physique et quitter l'Italie, qui devenait trop dangereuse puisqu'elle était la place forte des théurgistes. Hohenstaufen gagna d'abord l'Émirat de Grenade, dernière terre mauresque de l'Espagne, d'où il put aisément faire venir des textes musulmans de Jérusalem et laisser croître les connaissances arcaniques du Stigma Diaboli. Grenade et Rome devinrent respectivement les bastions des goétistes et des théurgistes. Il en sera ainsi pendant plus de deux siècles, jusqu'à ce qu'en 1478 on instaure l'Inquisition. L'Église traqua à partir de cette date les goétistes à travers l'Espagne, brûlant sorciers et sorcières sur le bûcher. Quatorze ans plus tard, au terme de la Reconquista, l'Émirat de Grenade fut conquis et Hohenstaufen, cerné par les plus puissants théurgistes de Rome, condamné à être brûlé vif. Ce fut aussi la fin de l'âge d'or des arcanes, car peu après, les Ottomans prendraient Constantinople et détruiraient le savoir arcanique d'Orient.

— Mais personne n'avait prévu que l'Étranger survivrait au bûcher, commenta Faustin.

— En effet. C'est la période la plus floue de son histoire. Des larbins fidèles ont replacé son corps en état de stase temporelle dans un lourd cercueil métallique. Pendant un siècle et demi, Hohenstaufen a recommencé à se manifester sous forme d'effigie. Il a

vécu longtemps en Normandie, puis est passé en Amérique. De ce que vous m'avez expliqué, la Poulin a conté la suite à Faustin : l'arrivée sous l'identité de Maurice Poulin, l'établissement du village des Forges, le changement de Régime et le bannissement de l'effigie d'Hohenstaufen…

— … jusqu'à son éveil par Gamache, comme vous nous l'avez raconté.

— Oui. Et c'est pour ça que je vous ai demandé de venir. À mon retour d'Italie, en 46, j'ai commencé à étudier sous un nouvel angle les pages que j'avais retirées de l'*Opus æternum*. Au Vatican, j'avais recopié des extraits d'autres écrits de Bacon, de Flamel et de divers auteurs dont l'Église avait gommé la trace depuis longtemps. Jusque-là, deux manières permettaient de contrer Hohenstaufen : bannir son effigie – comme l'a réussi, selon vos dires, la Corriveau sur l'île d'Orléans –, ou encore retrouver son corps physique et l'assassiner dans son sommeil éternel, comme vous avez tenté de le faire aux Trois-Rivières. Or, j'ai travaillé ces dernières années à élaborer une troisième méthode, basée sur la fonction mathématique inverse des cosinus des diagrammes principaux.

— En clair ? soupira Faustin.

— L'inverse de l'immortalité. La mort, tout simplement. Moins une prouesse que l'immortalité, parce que cela respecte l'ordre naturel des choses. Un sort tout de même complexe, sapant d'un coup la longévité de la cible. Selon tous mes calculs, les deux fonctions mathématiques s'annulent l'une l'autre.

— Donc l'immortalité de l'Étranger s'estomperait…

— Sur papier, oui. Il va sans dire que je ne l'ai jamais testé. Mais en juin dernier, un *maymaygwashi* est venu m'avertir que Kabir Kouba avait été éveillé. Il venait en émissaire pour quérir mon aide. Aussitôt,

j'ai pris une goélette vers Pointe-Lévy afin de demander l'assistance d'Éphrem Lamare. C'est en arrivant à Notre-Dame des Tempérances que sa servante m'a appris sa mort. Elle m'a aussi parlé de l'apprenti qu'il avait formé en secret, le vicaire Gauthier. C'est à ce moment que j'ai décidé de vous contacter par l'entremise de l'un de mes amis qui a accepté de me servir de messager.

— Pourquoi pas un sort de rêve ? demanda Baptiste. C'est toujours de même que le Collège a faite. L'curé Lamare, pis François à la mort du curé, y'ont…

Le vieillard l'interrompit d'un geste.

— J'ai quatre-vingt-cinq ans, Baptiste, et mon corps est encore plus âgé que ça. Quelques enchantements de l'*Opus æternum* m'ont permis de prolonger mon espérance de vie, mais désormais me voilà aux ultimes limites de ma longévité. Je n'ose plus utiliser les arcanes pour quoi que ce soit. Un sortilège de communication, comme un rêve messager, draine plus de trois mois – peut-être davantage de temps qu'il ne m'en reste, qu'en sais-je ?

Baptiste ouvrit la bouche pour répondre, mais Faustin l'interrompit :

— Vous avez parlé de l'*Opus æternum*, souleva-t-il. C'est mon oncle qui le cachait au presbytère et l'Étranger l'a obtenu quand les membres du Stigma Diaboli y sont entrés pendant l'émeute du *bill d'indemnité*. Mais lorsque j'ai vu l'Étranger, aux Forges…

— … il manquait une quarantaine de pages, termina le père Masse avec un sourire chafouin.

— Et une *nekuia* a révélé que c'est vous qui les aviez.

— Effectivement. J'ai retiré le chapitre consacré aux arcanes de l'*Opus æternum* par mesure de sécurité. Grâce à lui, j'ai pu élaborer le contre-sort. J'espérais

qu'Éphrem saurait où je pourrais trouver un arcaniste encore assez jeune pour lancer le puissant sortilège ; j'ai cru qu'une musique infinie sonnait dans les cieux quand Madeleine m'a révélé l'existence de ce vicaire formé en secret, François Gauthier – voilà l'homme dont j'avais besoin. Trop âgé pour tenter un sort de communication, je m'en suis remis aux *maymaygwashi* pour entrer en contact avec vous, en espérant enfin enseigner le contre-sort à un arcaniste compétent et mettre fin au règne d'Hohenstaufen.

Une ombre passa sur le visage du père Masse et il conclut d'une voix encore plus basse que d'habitude :

— Tout cela aura été vain. Le vicaire Gauthier porte maintenant l'esprit de Lavallée et ne pourra nous assister. Quant à toi, jeune et vieux Faustin, tu m'as toi-même expliqué que ta maîtrise des arcanes était toute relative : lancer un tel sort te tuerait et ça, malgré toutes les années de crédit dont tu disposes.

Le vieux prêtre esquissa un geste vague.

— Permettez-moi de me retirer un moment. J'ai à réfléchir à tout ça.

Sans un mot de plus, Masse se leva pour s'isoler dans l'une des pièces de sa demeure.

◆

Ayant préféré sortir de l'abri-épave, les compagnons longeaient silencieusement la grève, chacun perdu dans ses pensées.

Pour Faustin, l'essentiel de ses réflexions tournait autour d'un seul mot : *Hohenstaufen*.

Il y avait quelque chose de déroutant dans toute la signification que pouvait contenir un simple nom.

Il en avait été ainsi pour lui-même. Trouvé alors qu'il avait encore un corps de nourrisson, les prêtres

théurgistes lui avaient donné le nom de Faustin, en hommage à ce saint qui avait refusé de se soumettre à un culte païen. Lorsqu'il avait amorcé sa croissance et avait été pris en charge par le curé Lamare, on lui avait adjoint ce patronyme : Faustin Lamare.

Toutefois, le prénom que sa mère lui avait donné était Charles – Charles Dodier, car il était né sous le toit de Louis Dodier, second mari de sa mère. Mais on aurait tout aussi bien pu croire qu'il était fils du premier époux, ce qui lui aurait donné le nom de Charles Bouchard. Or, pour tout le monde, il était le fils de « la Corriveau » et c'est sous ce nom qu'on l'avait désigné : Charles Corriveau.

Mais c'était encore inexact. Un enfant doit porter le nom de son père, ainsi allaient les choses. Et maintenant qu'il connaissait la véritable identité de l'Étranger, Faustin connaissait aussi la sienne.

Charles Ier de Hohenstaufen.

Et son père, né au XIIe siècle, se nommait Frédéric de Hohenstaufen, second du nom, empereur du Saint-Empire romain germanique, roi de Germanie, de Sicile et de Jérusalem… et désigné comme l'Antéchrist par le pape Grégoire IX.

En repensant à ce dernier titre, Faustin ricana cyniquement : de toute évidence, ce n'était pas d'hier que l'Étranger passait pour le Diable.

Encore plus cynique, le jeune homme compara sa rencontre avec le père Masse à celle avec le père Bélanger : de bien longs voyages uniquement pour des informations – bien que pour des raisons différentes – offertes par des arcanistes incapables de les aider.

Et maintenant, qu'allaient-ils faire ?

Il ne restait qu'une seule piste à suivre : celle de la Dame Blanche, comme l'avait suggéré Nadjaw.

En ramassant un galet qu'il jeta dans le fleuve, Faustin se dit que tant qu'à avoir un érudit à portée de main, autant en profiter. C'est donc avec l'intention de le questionner au sujet de la Dame Blanche que le jeune homme retourna auprès du père Masse.

◆

Le vieux prêtre dormait quand Faustin revint et, encouragé par Baptiste, le jeune homme avisa un hamac dans lequel il s'allongea. La journée avait été longue et Faustin sombra vite dans un sommeil sans rêve.

Au matin, alors qu'ils déjeunaient tous de pain grillé, d'œufs d'oie cuits dur et de *caffè* que Baptiste et Faustin sucrèrent abondamment, le père Masse s'était remis à disserter longuement au sujet de l'Étranger. Il ne savait pas exactement de quelle façon le Stigma Diaboli était parvenu à transporter le sarcophage d'Hohenstaufen en Nouvelle-France, mais il fut très loquace sur la façon dont l'Étranger s'était manifesté en effigie sous le nom de Maurice Poulin pour être nommé, par le Conseil souverain, procureur du Roi aux Trois-Rivières. Sur cette période-là, le vieux prêtre répéta beaucoup de choses que Faustin connaissait déjà grâce aux révélations de la Siffleuse, mais certains détails s'ajoutèrent, comme la manière dont l'Étranger avait justifié sa longévité en alternant les identités de Maurice Poulin et d'un fils fictif nommé Michel, puis en simulant le décès de Maurice.

Ils finissaient de manger quand Faustin parvint à amener le sujet qu'il voulait aborder depuis la veille.

— Considérant que François n'est plus là pour lancer le contre-sort que vous avez élaboré, je compte me rendre auprès de la Dame Blanche. Si vous avez des informations supplémentaires…

— Bien sûr que j'ai entendu parler de la Dame Blanche, comme quiconque s'est intéressé un tant soit peu à l'histoire des arcanes au Nouveau Monde, répondit le père Masse. Mais je ne sais pas grand-chose d'elle, sauf peut-être que Gamache et son épouse ont amené Chevalier de Lorimier devant le spectre de cette spirite durant les Troubles.

— De Lorimier, le chef des Patriotes ? releva Faustin.

— Qui d'autre ? Malheureusement, les choses ne se sont pas passées comme l'espérait Gamache. Du moins c'est ce qu'il m'a confié, sans préciser ce qu'ils étaient précisément allés faire là. J'ai toujours supposé que c'était en relation avec l'Ordre du Chien d'Or, mais je n'en ai jamais eu la moindre preuve.

— Le Chien d'Or ?

— Le lien avec la Dame Blanche est plutôt ténu, du moins selon mes connaissances. Elle a noué une liaison avec un soldat membre de l'Ordre du Chien d'Or, et peut-être Gamache croyait-il obtenir l'accès au grimoire de cet ancien cercle arcanique, considérant que Lartigue l'avait banni du Collège. J'ai déjà lu la copie que détenait cette bibliothèque avant qu'elle ne soit réduite en cendre. Le Grimoire du Chien d'Or contient une vaste panoplie de sortilèges militaires : des sorts qui génèrent des étincelles pour faire tirer les canons tout seuls ; des méthodes pour enchanter des sabres, des baïonnettes ou des balles d'argent ; des cartes indiquant des lieux secrets sous la Haute-Ville ; une barrière de force destinée à protéger les remparts… et j'en passe.

— Et cet Ordre du Chien d'Or, qu'est-ce que c'est ?

— La dernière tentative pour les théurgistes de s'allier ouvertement au pouvoir politique. En 1690, le Collège d'Albert le Grand, alors installé à l'île d'Orléans, entendit une rumeur selon laquelle les Anglais

avaient ordonné à l'amiral Phips de faire voile vers Québec. Les théurgistes décidèrent de prêter main-forte au gouverneur Frontenac. Cet amiral Phips était un ami proche du révérend Cotton Mather, un homme de grande influence en Angleterre comme en Nouvelle-Angleterre – ce même Mather qui serait plus tard responsable du massacre des derniers arcanistes anglais, à Salem. En apprenant que Phips conduirait l'assaut, le Collège se mit à craindre une « chasse aux sorcières » semblable à l'Inquisition espagnole.

Sans un mot, Faustin écoutait encore le petit prêtre. L'étendue de ses connaissances semblait infinie.

— Le Collège décida donc de mettre sur pied une troupe de théurgistes-soldats, le bataillon du Chien d'Or. Ses membres apprendraient à maîtriser, en plus des arcanes, le maniement du sabre, l'équitation et le tir. Le Chien d'Or contribua à renforcer considérablement les défenses de Québec et, parmi eux, se trouvait un talentueux sorcier métis, Jean-Pierre Lavallée.

— Oui, intervint Faustin, je me souviens que François m'avait lu un compte rendu maçonnique où il est dit que Lavallée avait assuré du beau temps pendant l'érection des fortifications et que le soleil brillait sur la ville alors que la pluie tombait non loin.

— En effet. C'est ainsi que Lavallée attira l'attention d'Hohenstaufen. En secret, l'Étranger initia Lavallée à la goétie, ce qui lui permit de déclencher des épidémies à bord des navires de Phips. Il récidiva, vingt ans plus tard, face aux navires de Walker, avant de décéder quelques années plus tard. Quant au bataillon du Chien d'Or, il perdura jusqu'à la chute de la Nouvelle-France, en 1759. Officiellement, le Chien d'Or fut alors dissous ; mais en réalité, ses derniers membres se replièrent non loin d'ici, à l'Islet. Un théurgiste puissant qui occupait la charge d'aumônier

au sein du Chien d'Or fit construire une chapelle où le bataillon attendit l'ordre de l'abbé Briand, alors maître du Collège, de revenir à la charge contre l'envahisseur.

Le père Masse resta songeur un instant, puis il revint à ses explications.

— Mais l'ordre n'arriva jamais. Briand usa plutôt de stratégie politique, signa un traité secret avec le gouverneur Murray et réussit à accorder sa survivance au Collège. Les théurgistes quittèrent l'île d'Orléans pour le Mont à l'Oiseau. Quant aux sorciers-soldats du Chien d'Or, nul n'entendit plus parler d'eux. Le bataillon n'existe plus désormais, mais ses connaissances sont toujours là.

— Elles pourraient nous aider à affronter l'Étranger, non? Le Stigma Diaboli souhaite prendre Québec; s'il y a des enchantements qui permettent de protéger la ville d'une telle invasion, ou du moins d'y faire face… Possédez-vous une copie du Grimoire du Chien d'Or?

— Malheureusement, non. Mais si tu prends le temps d'aller fouiller les ruines de la chapelle de l'Aumônier, tu en trouveras peut-être une copie, qui sait?

Le père Masse réfléchit un moment, puis ajouta:

— Ce serait peut-être une façon d'affronter Hohenstaufen, considérant l'impossibilité de lancer le contre-sortilège. Si vous allez au village de l'île, par-delà la pinède de la *man'ido*, vous trouverez assurément un batelier pour vous mener à l'Islet. Vous devriez pouvoir vous renseigner sur place quant à l'emplacement exact de la chapelle. Je ne puis que vous inciter à y faire un détour.

Faustin consulta du regard ses compagnons, qui hochèrent silencieusement la tête.

— Je m'y rendrai, père Masse, décréta-t-il. Merci beaucoup.

— Et ensuite, iras-tu voir cette Dame Blanche?

Ce fut au tour de Faustin de rester songeur.

— Je crois bien. Si Gamache y a jadis amené un chef patriote, c'est sûrement parce qu'il est possible de discuter avec elle. Nadjaw prétendait qu'elle pourrait m'aider. Nous passerons fouiller la chapelle de l'Aumônier, puis nous irons à la chute Montmorency.

— Si vous voulez vous rendre à l'Islet aujourd'hui, il vous faut partir sans tarder.

Hochant la tête, Faustin ramassa son sac à dos, passa son sabre à sa ceinture et la courroie de son fusil à son épaule. Quand lui et ses compagnons furent prêts à partir, le père Masse s'avança solennellement vers lui. Il lui ouvrit la main et posa son anneau dans la paume de Faustin.

— Lartigue, dernier maître de notre Ordre, m'avait choisi comme successeur. Lui mort, on peut me considérer comme le maître du Collège, bien que cela ne signifie plus grand-chose.

Le père Masse referma les doigts de Faustin sur le bijou.

— Si tu parviens à sauver ton ami et à bannir Lavallée, tu lui offriras mon anneau. Il lui faudra probablement le porter à l'auriculaire ou comme pendentif, mais peu importe. Dis-lui que le maître de l'Ordre Théurgique lui confère le rang d'Arcaniste d'Albert le Grand et le désigne comme son digne successeur.

Faustin hocha silencieusement la tête en signe d'assentiment.

— Et si tu ne parviens pas à ramener l'apprenti de ton oncle, conclut le prêtre, il t'appartiendra de choisir quelqu'un méritant de le porter… ou d'ensevelir symboliquement l'anneau où bon te semblera.

— Je m'en chargerai, père Masse. Merci pour tout.

— Revenez me voir avant de vous en prendre à Hohenstaufen. D'ici là, j'aurai peut-être fait quelques découvertes qui pourraient vous aider.

Après avoir lui aussi remercié le père Masse, Baptiste entreprit de passer la porte de l'abri-épave, puis, Ti-Jean bien en selle sur son épaule, il se mit en route vers le village de l'Isle-aux-Grues, enjoignant d'un geste à Faustin et à Shaor'i de le suivre.

CHAPITRE 31

L'Islet

Le batelier de l'Isle-aux-Grues, un solide gaillard du nom de Lévesque, n'avait accepté qu'à contrecœur de conduire Faustin et ses compagnons à l'unique quai de l'Islet, une plateforme constituée de troncs pour la plupart pourris auxquels il n'avait attaché l'amarre que pour la forme.

Faustin avait dû débourser une forte somme pour qu'il accepte d'attendre leur retour.

— Quand vous y s'rez allés une fois, les avait-il mis en garde, ça s'ra assez pour vous autres. C'te monde-là, c'est trop loin du monde pour être du monde comme tout l'monde.

Baptiste avait haussé les épaules et donné une tape rassurante au batelier, lui remémorant le salaire promis : pour soixante-quinze cents par jour, le passeur avait juré de patienter. Fusil chargé à ses pieds.

◆

La vieille seigneurie de l'Islet-Saint-Jean avait été fondée au XVIIe siècle. Confinée dans les repaires d'une campagne peu fréquentée, elle n'avait guère prospéré, mais s'était repliée dans une sorte d'isolement

qui l'avait presque totalement coupée du reste de la rive sud.

Le seigneur des lieux ne se préoccupait guère de ses paysans – en fait, il n'habitait même pas ses propres terres. Au changement de Régime, le manoir seigneurial avait été abandonné; de cette maison en pierres des champs qui n'avait de manoir que le nom, il ne restait que les murs de la cave, à demi mangés par les ronces, et les vestiges d'une cheminée depuis longtemps effondrée.

L'industrie ne s'y était guère implantée; les ruines d'un moulin étaient la seule trace de modernité dans ce hameau désolé. Les maisons, très éloignées les unes des autres, montraient toutes le même état de délabrement. Les champs n'étaient qu'à demi entretenus et les plants de pomme de terre poussaient tant bien que mal à travers les fardoches. En y regardant de plus près, on pouvait constater que la plupart de ces maisons étaient abandonnées.

Quand les compagnons aperçurent enfin une habitante de l'Islet, ils s'en approchèrent. La femme maigrelette, au teint jaunâtre, était de ces personnes de la trentaine qui avaient déjà toute leur vie derrière elles. Vêtue de hardes minables – Faustin avait vu des poches de jute plus élégantes –, elle allait pieds nus sur la berge avec un seau rouillé qu'elle emplissait lentement d'huîtres, d'écrevisses, de crabes et de petits poissons abandonnés par le retrait de la marée. Autour d'elle, grues et goélands faisaient repas de la même pitance.

Elle cessa sa besogne quand Faustin la héla, passa une main brune de vase dans sa chevelure huileuse pour écarter les mèches de son visage et afficha un rictus édenté qui pouvait passer autant pour un sourire que pour une grimace.

— Excusez-moi, ma bonne dame…

— Qué qu'y'a? répondit la femme en le fixant de ses yeux chassieux.

— Je cherche la chapelle de l'Aumônier et…

La femme cracha une chique de tabac et lui tourna le dos pour retourner à sa cueillette. Réprimant un soupir agacé, Faustin plongea la main dans sa bourse et lui tendit deux cents dans sa paume ouverte.

— Je cherche la chapelle de l'Aumônier, répéta-t-il.

La femme se moucha du coude, regarda à gauche et à droite, puis ramassa les pièces qu'elle empocha furtivement.

— La dernière qu'a été là, a l'est virée folle. L'curé Panet l'a guérie. Allez pas là.

— Et ce curé Panet, où puis-je le rencontrer? demanda Faustin en essuyant sur son pantalon sa main que la femme avait effleurée. Je ne vois d'ici aucun clocher d'église.

— Y'a crevé v'là six ans, l'Panet.

— Et cette femme que le curé a guérie?

— Est folle.

— Mais vous venez de me dire que le curé…

— Guéri son âme, pas sa tête…

Me voilà bien avancé… songea Faustin en insistant:

— Mais la chapelle, vous savez où elle se trouve?

— Z'allez virer fous. Tous fous.

— C'est un risque que je suis prêt à courir, commenta Faustin en présentant de nouvelles pièces que la femme fit de nouveau disparaître en un clin d'œil.

— C'est vot'trouble, dans l'fond.

— Précisément.

La femme tourna le regard en direction du sud-ouest:

— J'vas pas pointer, manière qu'on pourrait m'voir faire. Par là-bas, dit-elle en levant le menton, y a un

rocher à pic. Allez tout drette, pis cherchez l'vieux puits. Arrivé là, vous s'rez pas loin.

Puis l'habitante se mit en quête de nouveaux crustacés, signifiant par là que la conversation était terminée.

— Grand merci, marmonna Faustin pour la forme avant d'aller rejoindre ses compagnons.

Faute de meilleures indications, ils suivirent un sentier serpentant plus ou moins dans la direction montrée par la femme. À travers les champs mal entretenus, ils croisèrent quelques habitants, occupés à faucher une maigre récolte de blé.

Les paysans de l'Islet avaient tous un air de famille, chose fréquente dans les villages trop isolés. La plupart portaient les stigmates de leur pauvreté : silhouettes émaciées et noueuses, petite taille, visages prématurément parcheminés et chevelure tirant sur le gris jaunâtre dès qu'était passée la vingtaine. Les habitants observaient silencieusement Faustin et ses compagnons traverser l'unique rang de terre battue du lieu-dit, l'air de marmonner des imprécations entre leurs dents gâtées. Afin de ne pas attirer inutilement la méfiance, Baptiste enjoignit à Ti-Jean de se cacher dans sa poche et se laissa guider par Shaor'i.

Malgré beaucoup d'efforts et de nombreuses pièces de monnaie offertes, les compagnons n'obtinrent pas de meilleures informations sur l'histoire contée par la femme de la berge. La fille d'un habitant que personne ne nommait était devenue folle après être allée dans la chapelle – pour voler des objets saints et les faire fondre, avait précisé quelqu'un. On avait retrouvé la malheureuse hurlant et vociférant comme une damnée sur un rocher non loin de la berge. L'ancien curé de la paroisse avait sauvé son âme à défaut de la guérir de sa folie, puis il avait été emporté par le choléra en 43 plus ou moins, car la plupart des habitants ne savaient

même pas en quelle année ils étaient. Il n'y avait pas eu de nouveau prêtre à l'Islet depuis. Quant à la pauvre folle, elle vivait ailleurs dans sa famille, mais personne ne semblait savoir où était ce « ailleurs ».

Néanmoins, tous les paysans n'eurent pas les mêmes scrupules que la femme de la berge en ce qui avait trait à la localisation exacte de la chapelle. L'un d'eux se proposa même pour les y guider, moyennant ce qu'il appelait du « temps spécial » en lorgnant les jambes fuselées de Shaor'i. Évitant une altercation avec l'Indienne, qui avait déjà les mains sur le pommeau de ses armes, Baptiste décréta que des indications claires suffiraient et fit signe à Faustin de payer l'homme de quelques piécettes.

Quand ils eurent finalement un itinéraire précis en tête, l'après-midi était bien entamé.

◆

C'était une campagne désolée dont le terrain s'élevait peu à peu alors que les compagnons s'éloignaient de la rive.

D'après ce qu'on leur avait expliqué, ils auraient à marcher cinq ou six lieues.

— Vous trouvez pas ça dépareillé, une chapelle si loin du village ? demanda Baptiste alors qu'ils cheminaient depuis déjà un bon moment.

— C'était supposé être un lieu dédié aux arcanes militaires, répondit Faustin. Je suppose qu'ils voulaient garder les paysans loin ; ceux qui souhaitaient prier n'avaient qu'à aller à l'église de l'Islet.

— Alors pourquoi pas une place encore plus éloignée, comme le Collège ?

— Va savoir. Peut-être était-ce un lieu stratégique contre les États ?

Le bûcheron se tut un instant, puis reprit :

— Pis vous en pensez quoi, de c't'histoire de femme virée folle ?

— Je suppose qu'elle était déjà fragile et qu'elle a dû voir quelque chose qu'elle n'a pas pu assumer. Comme lorsque le meunier Crête a vu son engagé se changer en loup pour affronter Shaor'i, lors du dernier réveillon de Noël.

— Je ne savais pas qu'il en était devenu fou, marmonna Shaor'i. Remarque que je ne suis pas restée longtemps après l'affrontement. C'était quel genre d'homme, ce meunier ?

— Un mécréant, un menteur, un bagarreur et un ivrogne… qui trichait aux dames, en plus.

— Pas une grosse perte, alors, fit la jeune femme en haussant les épaules.

— Reste que ce doit être ce qui est arrivé à cette fille de l'Islet. Elle a dû être témoin d'une manifestation d'esprit, d'une transformation ou de l'activation d'un sortilège de protection.

— Ou p'tête juste qu'était déjà folle pis qu'elle s'isolait dans la chapelle de temps en temps.

— Peut-être, concéda Faustin. Ce sont des choses qui arrivent parfois. Les populaces des petits villages ont tendance à réarranger les historiettes locales.

Les terres devenaient de plus en plus vallonneuses alors qu'ils s'éloignaient du village. En cette fin d'après-midi, l'humidité était tombée, ce qui laissait présager un automne pluvieux. La lande s'était couverte d'un léger brouillard qui réduisait la portée de la visibilité. Par trois fois, ils croisèrent d'énormes rochers qu'ils prirent, de loin, pour la chapelle de l'Aumônier.

Le soleil avait amorcé sa descente quand ils parvinrent finalement à destination. Le brouillard avait failli leur faire manquer la chapelle tant son emplacement

était discret. Située contre un monticule rocheux en forme de coude, elle aurait passé inaperçue n'eût été de son clocher. Un petit lac lui faisait face, touchant le coude de pierre à l'une de ses extrémités, de sorte que seule une langue de terre d'une cinquantaine de verges permettait d'accéder à l'endroit.

Le vent, un peu frais, chassa les lambeaux de brume et révéla la forme de la chapelle. C'était un bâtiment sinistre en pierres des champs dont le clocher semblait poignarder les cieux vespéraux. Le soleil couchant baignait le flanc ouest de l'église d'une vive lueur écarlate et l'ombre du bâtiment, grandissant sur la campagne déserte, évoquait un mauvais présage.

Jetant un œil méfiant sur la clé de voûte qui surplombait la porte gothique, Baptiste marmonna :

— Ça va s'effondrer d'ici dix ou vingt ans, c'te place-là.

L'œil d'habitant de Faustin confirma l'opinion du bûcheron. Le mortier qui retenait les pierres était craquelé de partout, et de larges interstices apparaissaient ici et là.

Ils poussèrent la porte, faisant du même coup couler du plafond des ruisselets de poussière crayeuse. La nef de la chapelle n'avait pas accueilli de visiteurs depuis longtemps. La plupart des bancs de l'église manquaient, peut-être volés afin de servir de bois de chauffage.

Seuls les vitraux, stupéfiants de réalisme, étaient en bon état ; Faustin les aurait sans hésiter qualifiés de chefs-d'œuvre si ce n'avait été de la morbidité des scènes reproduites. Ayant été élevé par un curé, il reconnut les représentations de sainte Agnès de Rome, sainte Olive de Palerme et sainte Eugénie de Rome. Chacune de ces femmes était montrée lors de sa mort sur le bûcher, le rouge des flammes étant la couleur dominante de chaque vitrail ; ainsi, la lumière filtrant par les vitres prenait une teinte sanguine qui donnait

à la nef un inquiétant aspect, comme si les lieux avaient été cernés par un incendie.

Tout au fond, on pouvait voir dans le chœur que le tabernacle avait été forcé. Juste derrière le maître-autel se trouvait un vitrail colossal montrant Jeanne d'Arc, elle aussi livrée au bûcher. Le visage de la Pucelle était d'une incontestable beauté, l'air extatique. En lettres dorées, on avait recopié les mots qu'elle avait jadis prononcés : *Sur l'amour ou haine que Dieu a pour les Anglais, je ne sais point, mais je sais bien qu'ils seront tous boutés hors de France, excepté ceux qui y périront.*

Derrière le chœur, le déambulatoire menait à une porte que Faustin croyait donner sur la sacristie. Lorsqu'il en tourna la poignée, il eut la surprise de voir qu'elle s'ouvrait sur un long tunnel de pierre dont les parois avaient été polies pour obtenir des murs lisses.

— On doit être rendus dans la p'tite montagne, commenta Baptiste.

Faustin opina du chef sans cesser d'observer. Des gravures de bois montrant, à la manière d'un chemin de croix, les épisodes marquant de la vie de la Pucelle d'Orléans, étaient accrochées de chaque côté de la galerie.

— Qui est cette femme ? demanda Shaor'i alors que les compagnons examinaient un panneau à la lueur du fanal.

— Jeanne d'Arc. Une vierge soldate qui, inspirée par Dieu, combattit l'envahisseur anglais en France, au XVe siècle.

Perplexe, l'Indienne répliqua :

— Mais c'est le même dieu que celui des Anglais, non ?

— Tout à fait.

— Alors pourquoi ce dieu aurait-il exigé que meurent des Anglais ?

— Va savoir… Reste que l'histoire de la Pucelle d'Orléans devait plaire à ces gens, chargés de protéger la Nouvelle-France des Anglais.

— Et elle est morte au combat, cette pucelle ?

— Non. On l'a brûlée vive pour sorcellerie.

Shaor'i soupira et ne prêta plus attention aux gravures.

La galerie menait à une lourde porte de chêne à double battant au-dessus de laquelle était gravé un bas-relief montrant un chien endormi. Juste en dessous était écrit un quatrain :

Je suis un chien dormeur
En dorman j'attise ma fureur
Un tems viendra qui nest pas encor
Où je m'eveilleray en semant la mort

Baptiste insista pour ouvrir et entrer le premier, hache au poing. La porte donnait toutefois sur une pièce où trônait une massive table à huit côtés, chacun des sièges ayant un dossier gravé d'un chien. Les deux murs latéraux portaient des étagères où ce qui avait jadis été des livres était à présent réduit à l'état de poussière. Seules restaient les couvertures de cuir, mangées par le temps, et sur lesquelles les titres étaient depuis longtemps devenus illisibles.

— Merde, pesta Faustin en toussant sous le nuage qu'il avait levé en fouillant les reliquats. Ces grimoires ne serviront plus à rien.

— L'livre du Chien d'Or est p'tête ailleurs, proposa Baptiste. Ton oncle mettait pas tous ses livres aux mêmes places.

Un escalier menait à une cave et le bûcheron le descendit le premier, puis fit signe aux autres de le suivre.

La cave consistait en quelques geôles dont les grilles de fer forgé avaient depuis longtemps été attaquées par la rouille. Au fond du couloir, ils trouvèrent quelques paires de menottes, un boulet et un pilori, mais rien n'indiquant qu'ils touchaient au but.

Néanmoins, lorsqu'ils firent demi-tour pour remonter, une sensation s'accrocha subitement à l'esprit de Faustin, comme du chardon à une pièce d'étoffe. Intrigué, le jeune homme s'arrêta devant une cellule et sentit un bref effleurement mental. Fixant le squelette qui gisait dans la geôle, il avança d'un pas et murmura :

— Cet homme… ce prisonnier-là… je le connais.

Shaor'i le dévisagea avant de commenter :

— Ces gens sont morts il y a presque un siècle. Comment peux-tu…

— Je connais cet homme, s'entêta Faustin. Je l'ai déjà rencontré – ou presque. C'est…

Fronçant les sourcils, il fouilla sa mémoire, puis une image se révéla à lui avec limpidité.

— … Walpole.

— Qui ?

— Walpole. J'ignore son prénom. En fait, je ne l'ai jamais vu personnellement, mais son souvenir est de ceux que ma mère m'a transmis. C'était l'un des hommes qui devait juger en secret de son sort avant qu'elle ne passe devant la cour martiale. Des trois hommes présents, Walpole était celui qui la craignait le plus. C'est lui qui a insisté pour qu'elle reçoive un châtiment effroyable. La Siffleuse prétendait qu'il s'agissait d'un émissaire de l'Église anglicane chargé de traquer les sorciers et que ses idées n'auraient pas dissoné avec celles de Torquemada… ou de Cotton Mather, je suppose.

Curieux, Faustin s'approcha encore du prisonnier trépassé.

— Je me demande comment il a abouti ici…

— Les sorciers du Chien d'Or l'ont jugé à leur tour, de toute évidence.

Les sens spirites de Faustin furent soudainement frappés avec une incroyable brutalité, déflagration mentale pareille à un coup de tonnerre.

S'élançant pour retenir le jeune homme dont les genoux venaient de se dérober, Baptiste s'inquiéta :

— Faustin ? T'es correct ?

— Là-haut…

Pour Faustin, la présence d'esprits frappeurs se manifestait avec violence. Juste au-dessus de lui, là où devait se trouver le chœur de l'église, le jeune homme sentait une entité impérieuse qui manifestait son influence par-delà la tombe.

Alors qu'il tentait d'expliquer à ses compagnons ce qu'il percevait, une voix caverneuse émergea du plafond.

— *Facti sunt hostes eius in capite inimici illius locupletati…*

— Apparence que quelqu'un donne une messe, commenta Baptiste. Ç'a pas d'bon sens !

— *… sunt quia Dominus locutus est super eam propter…*

— Qu'est-ce qu'il raconte ? chuchota Shaor'i.

— Qu'est-ce que j'en sais ? répondit Faustin. C'est du latin. J'ai l'air d'un prêtre, peut-être ?

Les compagnons se ruèrent vers l'escalier, qu'ils gravirent avant de s'élancer à travers le couloir rocheux.

Ils se pétrifièrent de stupeur en découvrant la scène qui se déroulait devant l'autel de la chapelle de l'Aumônier.

Ils étaient six. Six êtres vaporeux, parfaitement visibles tout en semblant dépourvus de substance.

Cinq d'entre eux portaient le tricorne et le long manteau qu'arboraient les fusiliers français pendant

la guerre de Sept Ans. À genoux, fusil en main, ils recevaient une bénédiction de la part d'un prêtre vêtu d'une riche chasuble.

Et, bien qu'il continuât de réciter les Écritures, le prêtre n'avait pas de tête. Son corps brumeux s'arrêtait aux épaules, là où la partie de cou restante suffisait à peine à retenir l'étole qui la drapait.

— ... *multitudinem iniquitatum eius parvuli eius ducti sunt captivi ante faciem tribulantis...*

Les cinq fusiliers se levèrent en remarquant les intrus. Les silhouettes de fumée épaulèrent aussitôt leurs mousquets.

— Nous sommes à la recherche d'un livre, expliqua Faustin. Nous ne souhaitons pas troubler votre éternel repos. Nous voulons seulement...

Il n'y eut aucun bruit de déflagration, mais des traits vaporeux fusèrent des canons. Shaor'i fut la seule à avoir l'instinct de se jeter au sol. Baptiste grogna, atteint à la cuisse, et Faustin poussa un cri quand le rai éthéré lui traversa le coude gauche.

Il n'y avait ni plaie ni effusion de sang, mais la douleur le mordit comme s'il avait été transpercé d'une pique de métal glacé. Son fusil lui glissa des mains et, quand il comprit que sa main gauche ne répondait plus, il dégaina son sabre, juste à temps pour parer le coup de baïonnette du soldat spectral qui venait de le charger.

Le soldat jeta aussi son arme et sortit son propre sabre. Lame d'acier et lame éthérée se heurtèrent sans bruit, bien que Faustin pût sentir toute la force de son adversaire dans la poigne qu'il avait sur son arme. Sans attendre, le fusilier fantôme partit en septime d'un bond avant, ce qui força le jeune homme à reculer.

Faustin luttait pour rester calme, car le soldat spectral s'avérait un fin escrimeur. De peine et de misère, il

restait sur la défensive et parait les coups sans parvenir à en porter. D'aucune façon il ne pouvait interpréter les réactions physiques de ce corps vaporeux ; quant à son silence, c'était un silence de mort, celui de l'absence totale et du vide absolu, un silence que la *saokata* ne pouvait utiliser à son avantage.

Aux prises avec deux adversaires, Baptiste avait reculé vers l'un des murs, s'assurant ainsi de ne pas être pris à revers et limitant la marge de manœuvre des deux spectres. Par de grands moulinets de sa hache, il parvenait à les garder à distance.

De son côté, Shaor'i combattait en tirant avantage de sa grande mobilité. La hauteur de la nef lui permettait de faire des sauts d'une incroyable hauteur, ce qui forçait ses adversaires à la poursuivre continuellement.

Sans relâche, Faustin parait les assauts de son adversaire. Le soldat spectral, spécialement redoutable, obligeait sans cesse le jeune homme à se cantonner dans l'esquive. Le fil de l'arme immatérielle, l'effleurant à la cuisse, lui causa une douleur aiguë qu'il ravala tant bien que mal en priant pour que l'un de ses amis vienne lui prêter main-forte.

Or le bûcheron ne semblait guère en meilleure posture. Les deux soldats s'acharnaient contre le colosse et, s'ils ne parvenaient pas à l'atteindre sans risquer d'être fauchés par l'énorme hache à deux tranchants, ils obligeaient Baptiste à un effort constant. L'homme fort commençait à montrer des signes d'épuisement, son visage rouge ruisselant de sueur, tandis que ses ennemis bénéficiaient d'un corps éternel, immunisé contre la fatigue.

L'Indienne semblait en meilleure posture. Tournoyant et sautant, Shaor'i parvenait à empêcher ses adversaires de l'attaquer de front. En désespoir de cause,

les soldats défunts tentèrent de la prendre simulta-
nément de face et de revers.

Satisfaite, la jeune femme eut un sourire carnassier.
Écartant les bras en croix, elle projeta chacun de ses
couteaux vers l'un des fusiliers qui l'assaillait. Les
deux spectres se dissipèrent avec le bruit d'un soupir.

Mais elle n'eut guère le temps de se réjouir de sa
ruse.

Le prêtre sans tête prononça quelques mots arcaniques ; un pentacle s'illumina sur l'autel et deux silhouettes vaporeuses se matérialisèrent derrière lui.

Les fusiliers dissipés venaient de réapparaître.

Plongeant pour ramasser l'une de ses lames, la
jeune femme esquiva *in extremis* le sabre du soldat qui
s'était jeté sur elle, sans parvenir toutefois à éviter le
tir du second fusilier, qui l'atteignit dans le bas du dos.
Se recroquevillant sur le plancher, l'Indienne poussa
un râle alors que le spectre lui faisant face saisissait à
deux mains la poignée de son sabre, lame pointée
vers le bas, bien décidé à transpercer la jeune femme.

Ayant vu la scène, Faustin, aux prises avec son
propre spectre, estima qu'il n'aurait guère la possibilité de rejoindre l'Indienne à temps pour la défendre.
Il évoqua mentalement le diagramme d'un sort qu'il
connaissait et qu'il savait être utilisé par l'Étranger.
Lorsque l'image du pentacle se dessina dans son esprit,
il incanta :

— *Ashek saen-irstean al-ibnar !*

Son fusil quitta le sol et partit comme une flèche en
direction du fantôme qui menaçait Shaor'i. Projetée à
toute vitesse, l'arme transperça le fusilier en le pénétrant
de sa baïonnette.

Le spectre se dissipa de nouveau et l'Indienne se
leva derechef, ayant déjà ramassé le fusil qu'elle tenait
comme une lance.

Cette fois, Faustin garda ses sens spirites en alerte et sentit l'esprit du prêtre sans tête s'arrimer à celui du fusilier, prêt à lui rendre une fois de plus son incarnation éthérée.

« *Non…* » émit Faustin à l'intention du prêtre fantôme, bien décidé à l'empêcher d'agir.

Les deux consciences s'entrechoquèrent violemment et, de surprise, le jeune homme échappa son sabre et tomba à genoux. Le prêtre était d'une puissance qui outrepassait de loin ce qu'il avait rencontré jusque-là, et l'esprit de Faustin s'engourdit sous l'impact mental, secoué par d'intenses décharges psychiques.

Le fusilier devant lui fendit l'air de sa lame, bien décidé à le tuer; il fut dissipé par l'un des couteaux de Shaor'i, lancé à travers la pièce.

Mais Faustin le remarqua à peine. Les poings serrés, le jeune homme s'opposait au prêtre. Luttant pour raffermir son emprise, il livra une sorte de bras de fer mental. Chaque seconde qui passait, ses dons s'affirmèrent avec plus d'acuité et lentement, très lentement, il fut en mesure de rivaliser avec le prêtre sans tête.

L'Indienne, découvrant que les fusiliers ne réapparaissaient plus, courut dans la nef en tenant le fusil de Faustin et empala l'un des adversaires de Baptiste. Le bûcheron, pouvant se retourner contre un seul ennemi, ne fut pas long à avoir raison de celui-ci.

Seuls subsistaient le fusilier resté derrière l'autel et le prêtre auquel Faustin livrait un invisible combat. Le jeune homme continuait de sentir qu'il gagnait peu à peu de l'ascendant sur le prêtre et ce dernier, percevant la même chose, tenta le tout pour le tout en incantant pour ramener ses hommes.

— *Ashek dar-nìran, ashek sader…*

Il n'eut pas le temps de terminer. L'infime instant où il dut diviser sa force mentale entre le lancement

du sortilège et sa lutte contre Faustin lui fut fatal. Le jeune homme sentit qu'une limite était atteinte, puis dépassée, et que, désormais, c'était lui qui dominait le prêtre.

— *RETIRE-TOI !* hurla Faustin tout en émettant l'ordre mentalement.

Des fissures lumineuses fendillèrent le corps spectral du prêtre sans tête. Le fantôme se mit à rayonner d'une lueur de plus en plus vive, puis implosa.

Du spectre du prêtre, ou de celui du fusilier qui restait, il n'y avait désormais plus aucune trace.

À bout de souffle, Baptiste s'allongea dos au plancher, les bras en croix. Sa respiration étant laborieuse, Shaor'i se pencha au-dessus de lui. Par quelques mots entrecoupés de sifflements, le colosse insista sur le fait que « ça allait aller ». Après l'avoir prestement examiné et avoir jugé que le repos était la meilleure chose pour lui, l'Indienne vint s'asseoir à côté de Faustin, yeux fixés vers l'autel devant lequel s'était tenu le prêtre spectral, deux minutes auparavant.

— *Awan !* murmura-t-elle, ébranlée. Qu'étaient… ces morts… capables de blesser les vivants ?

— Je ne sais pas, Shaor'i. Je l'ignore. J'ai vu des esprits frappeurs tenter de tuer des vivants en projetant des objets, mais jamais encore une chose comme celle-là…

Repensant au combat, le jeune homme reprit :

— Ils avaient l'air si… humains, ces corps de brume…

— Matshi Skouéou sera encore plus… réelle, lui rappela-t-elle. Tu es certain de vouloir te mesurer à la Dame Blanche ?

Faustin réfléchit un moment, se retournant pour s'assurer que Baptiste allait toujours bien. Le colosse avait retrouvé son souffle et s'était levé pour inspecter les lieux, son fidèle Ti-Jean à l'épaule.

— Oui, décréta finalement Faustin. J'irai voir la Dame Blanche. Mais pas sans le Calice des Moires.

— Alors nous irons le chercher, promit l'Indienne.

Faustin hocha la tête avec reconnaissance alors que les rejoignait Baptiste qui tenait un épais volume à la couverture métallique.

— C'était à terre, expliqua le bûcheron, drette ousque l'prêtre était.

Le jeune homme inspecta la couverture d'or massif. Un chien rongeant un os y était gravé, ainsi que des mots latins, *Dulce et decorum est pro patria mori*. Il n'avait jamais appris cette langue, mais il connaissait ce vers d'Horace : « Il est doux et beau de mourir pour la patrie. » Son oncle le lui avait appris alors qu'il était enfant et que, partout, on ne parlait que de la révolte des Patriotes.

Sur le revers de la couverture était gravé un autre quatrain, similaire à celui qu'ils avaient vu peu avant :

Je suis un chien qui sommeille
Gardien de pouvoir sanspareil
Un tems sera qui nest pas hui
Où je montreray qui je suis.

Faustin feuilleta rapidement l'ouvrage, puis le bûcheron demanda, les poings sur les hanches et l'air décidé :

— Bon. T'as ton grimoire. Faque on va où, à c't'heure ?

— À Québec, répondit le jeune homme en refermant le volume. J'ai de nouveau rendez-vous au manoir Sewell.

LIVRE IX

L'ARMÉE DU CRÉPUSCULE

En vain le soir, du haut de la montagne,
J'appelle un nom : tout est silencieux.
Guerriers, levez-vous : couvrez cette campagne,
Ombres de mes aïeux !

François-Xavier Garneau,
Le Dernier Huron

CHAPITRE 32

En Haute-Ville

Ils avaient tous dormi sur le pont de la goélette, à l'Islet. Le batelier Lévesque n'en avait guère été ravi et avait insisté pour partir dès les premiers signes de la marée montante, une heure avant les premières lueurs de l'aube. L'après-midi était entamé quand on accosta à Québec, au quai Saint-André.

Sitôt descendu, Faustin faillit tourner de l'œil tant les miasmes infects le serrèrent à la gorge.

Le quai Saint-André accueillait les halles de poissons et les pêcheurs montraient des prises rares, allant des homards des Maritimes jusqu'aux morues de Gaspésie en passant par la chair de dauphin ou de béluga de Kamouraska. Les stocks, prétendument pêchés le matin même dans le fleuve, empestaient tant que Faustin sentit que son dîner menaçait de remonter. Le soleil de plomb n'aidait en rien, chauffant le sol gluant jonché d'entrailles et des têtes de poissons autour desquelles grouillaient des nuées de mouches. Nombreux étaient les clients qui fouillaient les étals avec un mouchoir plaqué sur le nez; ainsi l'odorat de renard de Faustin, à ce moment une malédiction plus qu'un atout, força le jeune homme à fuir le quai à grandes enjambées, sans même remercier le marin. Shaor'i

s'esquiva d'une manière similaire et Faustin se dit qu'elle les suivrait sûrement en volant, comme chaque fois qu'ils se trouvaient dans un espace urbain.

Avec soulagement, le jeune homme trouva de l'air plus pur là où s'étendaient les étalages des vendeurs d'étoffes et de lainages. Néanmoins, la marée humaine ne permettait pas le moindre calme.

Six mois auparavant, Faustin avait découvert Québec et avait été pétrifié par la quantité incroyable de gens qu'il y avait vue. Or, il constatait qu'il existait pire encore : pendant les marchés d'été, la capitale devenait si surpeuplée qu'il était presque impossible d'avancer dans les rues. Le brouhaha des réclames de marchands, des disputes entre clients et vendeurs ou des conversations des badauds était si assourdissant que les passants criaient plus qu'ils ne discutaient.

— Correct, garçon ? lança la voix de Baptiste derrière lui.

Le bûcheron, ayant demandé à un matelot de le guider, venait de rejoindre Faustin. Celui-ci se morigéna. Il oubliait sans cesse que Baptiste devait jouer les aveugles quand ils étaient en public. Une fois le marin parti, le jeune homme s'expliqua.

— C'était l'odeur, répondit-il en projetant sa voix.

— De quoi ?

— L'odeur, cria Faustin en se pinçant le nez.

Le bûcheron sembla comprendre davantage le geste que les mots et tenta d'avancer. Sur son épaule, Ti-Jean démontrait des signes de nervosité manifeste, poussant de petits cris et s'agitant d'une telle manière que Baptiste dut poser la main sur l'épaule de Faustin pour garder une démarche sûre.

Fort heureusement pour l'aveugle, la foule obligeait à des déplacements lents : non seulement des gens

avaient-ils stationné leurs charrettes n'importe comment, les laissant parfois au beau milieu du chemin, mais les curieux bloquaient la circulation devant les nombreux amuseurs qui exhibaient leurs numéros dans l'espoir de soutirer quelques cents aux spectateurs les plus argentés. Refoulant son agacement, Faustin s'arrêta un instant pour contempler les acrobaties d'un saltimbanque métis qui, tout en roulant un tonneau sous ses pieds, jonglait avec des torches allumées. Le rythme des passants devint plus hâtif non loin d'un violoneux qui arrachait des accords douteux à un crincrin misérable, puis la foule reprit son allure traînarde devant un numéro de chien savant qui parvenait à faire bonne figure face à son rival, un ours si apprivoisé qu'il semblait d'une timidité comparable à celle d'une jouvencelle se faisant conter fleurette.

Des câbles qu'on avait tendus entre quatre poteaux délimitaient l'espace de combat dans lequel les plus courageux des badauds pouvaient affronter un homme massif répondant au surnom du « Démon de la Gatineau ». Ayant repéré la carrure de Baptiste à travers la foule, l'agent du fier-à-bras héla le bûcheron qui, avec un haussement d'épaules nonchalant, se contenta de tourner vers lui son visage aux orbites vides et de poursuivre son chemin.

La foule était si dense qu'il leur fallut près d'une heure pour parcourir le tiers d'un mille et aboutir sur la place Royale, où l'on réservait l'espace aux bouchers et aux veneurs. Quartiers de viandes et volailles toujours emplumées chauffaient au soleil, pendus aux étals. Les maraîchers étaient tout proches ; fier de sa marchandise hâtive, un vendeur portant l'accent du fond de la Beauce proposait pommes, poires et prunes aux clients qui n'avaient pas la patience d'attendre encore deux semaines pour mordre dans un fruit frais.

L'espace le plus calme et le moins achalandé était celui des marchands de semences qui vendaient par pleins lots, notant les commandes sur papier. Shaor'i émergea d'une ruelle où elle avait discrètement repris forme humaine et rejoignit les deux hommes.

— J'ai repéré l'endroit indiqué par ton grimoire. Ce n'est pas loin d'ici.

En naviguant vers Québec, Faustin avait pris le temps d'étudier le Grimoire du Chien d'Or. Outre un impressionnant inventaire de sortilèges destinés à un usage militaire, il y avait trouvé la description exhaustive des secrets architecturaux de la Haute-Ville.

L'un de ces secrets – l'ancienne salle de réunion du Cercle du Chien d'Or – lui permettrait de pénétrer chez les Sewell sans attirer l'attention.

Du moins l'espérait-il.

— Le bâtiment a été reconverti en un lieu où l'on reçoit des lettres, précisa la jeune femme.

— Un bureau de poste ? s'étonna Faustin. C'est un peu étrange, considérant que ce fut jadis un haut-lieu arcanique.

Shaor'i allait répondre quand ils furent interrompus par une singulière visite : se faufilant à travers la marée humaine, un bambin de cinq ou six ans qui avait échappé à la surveillance de sa mère dépassa Faustin en courant. Il alla se planter devant Shaor'i et, avec cet air sérieux d'une personne certaine de la justesse de ses déductions, il la désigna du doigt en déclarant :

— Toi, t'es une Sauvagesse, hein ?

L'Indienne ne fit que hausser un sourcil vaguement méprisant et répondre :

— Seuls les Blancs me nomment ainsi. Je suis une *Migma'q*.

— Nah, coupa l'enfant en croisant les bras, sûr de lui. T'es une Sauvagesse.

Poussant un soupir ennuyé, la jeune femme détourna le regard pour ignorer le garçon. Obstiné, celui-ci insista :

— Si t'es une Sauvagesse, c'est que t'es là pour apporter un bébé, hein ?

Faustin dut simuler une quinte de toux pour s'empêcher de pouffer devant la mine de totale incompréhension de Shaor'i. Aussi jugea-t-il bon d'intervenir :

— Désolé, mon garçon. Elle n'est pas là pour apporter un bébé…

— Pas juste, bouda l'enfant en leur tournant le dos. J'voulais un p'tit frère…

Alors que le garçon s'éloignait, Shaor'i marmonna :

— C'est quoi, cette histoire-là ?

— Les mères, pour ne pas expliquer le mode de conception des bébés à leurs enfants, affirment que ce sont les… Sauvages… qui les apportent.

Shaor'i digéra l'information quelques secondes avant de répliquer :

— Ça n'a aucun sens. Et nous, où les prendrait-on, ces bébés ?

— Les enfants ne se questionnent pas jusque-là, d'habitude…

— N'empêche. Ne vaudrait-il pas mieux leur dire la vérité ?

— À leur âge ? s'outra Faustin en rougissant violemment. Ce serait terriblement inconvenant !

Haussant les épaules, Shaor'i s'éloigna avec un claquement de langue agacé. Faustin soupira de soulagement. Non seulement il était inconvenant d'aborder pareil sujet avec les enfants, mais ce l'était tout autant avec une femme…

— Assez farfiné, coupa le bûcheron. On va s'trouver un coin tranquille pour passer l'restant d'la journée, pis on ira voir c'te bureau d'poste quand y fera noir.

Faustin laissa Baptiste poser une main sur son épaule et les compagnons marchèrent vers des ruelles peu fréquentées. La clameur s'éloigna, mais il ne fallut pas longtemps à Faustin pour regretter les marchés.

Dans ces étroits passages, il sentait sur le pavé l'odeur des pots de chambre vidés du haut des lucarnes. Des dessous d'escaliers montaient les miasmes émanant des flaques de vomissures et d'urine. Les arrière-cours puaient le crottin et les colombages avaient un remugle écœurant de moisissure. Partout dans l'air, l'odorat de Faustin percevait les effluves des gens malpropres qui vivaient dans la cité, mélange de sueur et de crasse.

Je ne m'y habituerai jamais, songea Faustin en allumant sa pipe, timide tentative pour masquer la puanteur. À ses côtés, Shaor'i pâlissait sans mot dire. *Si les harfangs ont un aussi bon odorat que leur vision,* pensa-t-il avec compassion, *elle est vraiment à plaindre.*

Baptiste sembla remarquer leur malaise car il décréta :

— On va r'monter jusqu'aux Plaines. On s'ra dans un grand espace, on s'trouvera bin un coin.

Faustin et Shaor'i acquiescèrent d'un *oui* parfaitement synchrone.

◆

Ils avaient passé le reste de la journée à discuter des plus récents événements et de ce qu'ils prévoyaient faire. Faustin avait acheté à un marchand ambulant du pain et des pommes et le groupe avait soupé frugalement en attendant que s'installe la noirceur. Peu à peu, le soleil s'en était allé et les ténèbres étaient tombées sur Québec. Alors le groupe décida de se remettre en route.

Il n'y avait pas de lune, cette nuit-là. Néanmoins, les rues de la Haute-Ville n'étaient pas plongées dans l'obscurité pour autant. Les réverbères au gaz, tout récemment installés, donnaient l'impression que chaque intersection était gardée par une sentinelle portant un fanal.

Cette section de la ville était occupée par les riches boutiques anglaises. S'il y avait des tavernes, elles avaient une clientèle irréprochable et, comme c'était en semaine et passé minuit, la plupart des habitués avaient regagné leurs pénates. Les rues du quartier environnant le château Haldimand étaient aussi silencieuses que des tombeaux.

Faustin et ses compagnons longeaient les murs, en essayant de se montrer aussi discrets que possible. Après avoir gravi les escaliers de la côte de la Montagne, ils arrivèrent à une vieille maison de pierre de taille immense, dont les deux rangées de fenêtres droites étaient surmontées de lucarnes. Sur le fronton de son porche à colonnade était inséré un bas-relief montrant un chien couché rongeant un os, fort similaire à celui qu'ils avaient vu dans la chandelle de l'Islet. En lettres d'or était gravée une autre inscription en vieux français :

Je suis un chien qui ronge l'os
En le rongeant je prends mon repos
Un tems viendra qui nest pas venu
Que je morderay qui maura mordu

L'ouïe et l'odorat à l'affût, Faustin s'assura que personne n'approchait dans un sens ou dans l'autre. Ayant scruté chaque fenêtre des environs avec sa vue de harfang, Shaor'i ajouta :

— Il n'y a personne se tenant à une fenêtre donnant sur la rue.

Avec un hochement de tête, Faustin s'approcha de la porte, essaya la poignée et découvrit sans surprise que la porte était verrouillée.

— C'est à Ti-Jean de jouer, chuchota-t-il.

Baptiste opina et s'adossa au mur, laissant le petit singe albinos s'élancer le long de la paroi. Il lui fallut quelques secondes à peine pour atteindre le toit, d'où il testa chacune des lucarnes.

— Au pire, murmura Baptiste, y pourra s'essayer par la cheminée, y aura pas de feu à c'temps-ci de l'année. Ah, pas besoin !

Renversant la tête vers l'arrière, Faustin vit le lutin se faufiler par l'une des fenêtres et s'infiltrer à l'intérieur du bâtiment. D'après ce qu'avait raconté le père Masse, cet endroit avait jadis été le lieu de réunion de quelques arcanistes français alliés à Talon et à Frontenac, parmi lesquels se trouvait, bien entendu, Jean-Pierre Lavallée. Avant de devenir un sorcier honni, Lavallée avait super-visé la construction des fortifications de Québec. C'était donc dans ce bâtiment que le Cercle du Chien d'Or avait délibéré de la protection de la cité et cela, depuis la fondation du cercle par le théurgiste-guérisseur Roussel en 1688.

Étrange, songea Faustin, *que ce soit à présent un bureau de poste qui se trouve en ces lieux. Comme quoi le temps efface la mémoire des peuples.*

— Ti-Jean est arrivé, annonça Baptiste. Sauf que…

— Quoi ?

— Le verrou est compliqué pour lui. On va d'voir l'faire ensemble.

Toujours adossé au mur, Baptiste tendit les bras devant lui et, par de lents mouvements, mima la ma-nière de déverrouiller une porte géante. À l'intérieur, comprit Faustin, le *mah oumet* devait ressentir par le lien qu'il partageait avec le colosse les gestes qu'il lui

fallait exécuter. *À moins que Baptiste n'ait carrément pris les commandes de son corps*, songea le jeune homme en observant l'étrange pantomime.

Un cliquetis attira l'attention de Faustin et celui-ci entrouvrit délicatement la porte. Le lutin jaillit de l'intérieur en sautillant et se jucha sur son épaule habituelle. Après avoir vérifié une fois de plus l'absence de témoins, Faustin franchit rapidement le seuil, suivi de l'Indienne et du bûcheron.

L'intérieur était tout ce qu'il y avait de plus banal : un comptoir derrière lequel se trouvaient de petites cases de bois où lettres et colis étaient rangés. Près de la fenêtre trônait un bureau d'écrivain public et, contre un mur, un guéridon portait quelques exemplaires des journaux *Le Canadien* et *The Morning Chronicle*.

Sans tarder, les compagnons se mirent en quête d'une trappe que Shaor'i repéra derrière le comptoir. Elle l'ouvrit, dégaina un couteau, qu'elle serra entre ses dents, et sauta dans la cave.

— C'est libre ! lança-t-elle d'en bas.

Faustin descendit l'échelle à son tour, puis Baptiste et Ti-Jean. Le bûcheron gratta une allumette, et ils découvrirent une pièce où s'entassaient les caisses de courrier non réclamé, les sacs de charbon et les réserves de papeterie. Avisant un bougeoir, Baptiste alluma la chandelle et la passa à Faustin qui la posa sur une caisse, s'éclairant pour consulter le Grimoire du Chien d'Or.

À la page que Faustin avait marquée était indiquée la présence sur le mur ouest de la cave d'une pierre qui différait des autres, noire et volcanique. Faustin la repéra sans mal, s'y rendit et y posa la main.

— *Ast adhe-mann, ist korezan, nirerth zader dìr len'edör !* lut-il à haute voix dans le grimoire.

Sous la pression qu'il exerça, la main de Faustin s'enfonça doucement dans la pierre, comme si cette

dernière était liquide. *Comme pour les catacombes de l'église Saint-Laurent*, se souvint le jeune homme – ce qui était logique, se dit-il, étant donné que Lavallée avait supervisé la construction de cette église.

Ramassant le bougeoir, Faustin fit trois pas en avant et passa à travers le mur de pierre dont la structure était momentanément altérée par les arcanes. Il aboutit dans une seconde cave, beaucoup plus vaste. Comme dans la chapelle de l'Islet s'y trouvait une table octogonale couverte de poussière et entourée de huit sièges, chacun portant sur son dossier une gravure représentant le chien rongeant l'os. Sur les murs étaient affichées des cartes immenses montrant Québec telle que la ville était avant le changement de Régime.

Personne n'a dû entrer ici après la Conquête, pensa Faustin.

Il marcha jusqu'à l'un des murs où étaient gravés de petits rectangles dans un grand cercle de pierre. Chaque rectangle portait un numéro et, en tournant la page du Grimoire du Chien d'Or, Faustin repéra la reproduction de cette figure et un index où chaque rectangle chiffré était associé à un endroit, comme *17-Poudrière* ou *21-Vivres et boissons*.

— Il faut tracer un diagramme de téléportation spécialement modifié au sein de ce cercle gravé et l'enchantement imprégné dans la pierre nous permettra de nous déplacer avec plus de précision et sur une plus grande distance qu'une téléportation normale, expliqua Faustin. Le cercle représente la Haute-Ville et chaque rectangle correspond à une chambre souterraine ou à un tunnel – il semble que le cap Diamant soit un vrai gruyère. Cette chambre, par exemple, se situe tout juste sous le Séminaire.

— Laquelle mène sous le manoir Sewell? demanda Shaor'i.

— Le manoir n'était pas construit à l'époque, aucune n'y mène donc. Mais le livre dit que la porte Saint-Jean est juste ici, et le tunnel qui passe sous les fortifications est représenté par ce long rectangle étroit.

— Donc le tunnel passe sous le manoir ?

— Exactement. Sauf que ce n'est plus un tunnel : on l'a muré en petites caves peu avant le changement de Régime. L'une d'elles constitue à présent le sous-sol du manoir.

— Et comment savoir si on apparaîtra dans la bonne cave ?

— Ça se calcule au moment de tracer le diagramme, répondit Faustin. Les indications du Grimoire du Chien d'Or sont suffisantes : en donnant un angle de 77 degrés 22 minutes à l'apothème central, on apparaît hors des murs, juste à la fin du tunnel. Avec un angle de 76 degrés 6 minutes, on apparaît au début du tunnel, sous un magasin. Donc, en me servant de ces données, je peux déduire l'angle qui conduira à l'endroit voulu.

— J'aurais été à l'aise si ton frère l'avait fait, mais venant de toi... tu es certain d'y parvenir ? demanda l'Indienne avec méfiance.

— C'est un calcul assez élémentaire.

— Pis si tu t'trompes, intervint soudainement le bûcheron, pis qu'on arrive en dehors du tunnel, on est pris dans'roche ?

— Non. L'espace est déjà occupé alors le sort échoue.

— Déjà ça...

Ma parole, la confiance règne, songea Faustin en tirant une chaise pour effectuer ses calculs. *Après tout, c'est une simple règle de trois.*

Cela ne l'empêcha pas de la recalculer six fois pour être certain d'arriver toujours au même résultat. Il fit de même quand il mesura son pentacle au rapporteur d'angle puis, aussi satisfait de son résultat qu'il pouvait

l'être, il plaça ses compagnons devant le cercle gravé et lut l'incantation du Grimoire du Chien d'Or.

— *Derkan izan azif, issus ni-khira, eth silukar-an sahsìr eth serener !*

◆

L'Indienne remarqua dès leur apparition la présence d'une jeune soubrette. À la lueur de la chandelle portée par la domestique, Faustin vit la jeune fille ouvrir la bouche pour hurler puis s'effondrer sur le sol, frappée au front par le pommeau d'un couteau.

— Elle n'aura qu'une vilaine bosse, dit Shaor'i pour rassurer les deux hommes.

— On est au bon endroit, murmura Faustin alors que la jeune femme installait sa victime sur un tas de poches vides. Je me souviens de cette servante.

— Oui-da, répondit Baptiste. On va pouvoir s'informer à c'te fille-là quand elle va s'réveiller et… P'tite ?

— Mmm ?

— Tu la bardasseras pas trop, correct ? Elle a rien à s'reprocher, la pauvre.

— Faustin la sonde mentalement ou on la questionne ? demanda Shaor'i.

— On la questionne, répondit le jeune homme. Si je suis interrompu pendant le sort – disons, par une autre soubrette –, je risque de la tuer.

Shaor'i hocha la tête puis gravit silencieusement l'escalier pour aller verrouiller la porte de la cave. Quand elle revint, elle bâillonna d'une main la servante inerte, ferma les yeux et laissa agir sa magie.

La jeune domestique émergea de l'inconscience et, réalisant qu'on la retenait, elle ouvrit de grands yeux horrifiés avant d'émettre un cri étouffé à travers la main de l'Indienne.

D'un ton qui ne laissait présager rien de bon, Shaor'i lui dit à voix basse :

— Tu vas être gentille, hein ?

Épouvantée, la servante hocha vigoureusement la tête.

— Si je libère ta bouche, tu ne vas pas te mettre à hurler, n'est-ce pas ? Tu m'as l'air d'une fille brillante, donc tu sais que je réglerais ton cas avant qu'arrive le moindre secours.

Des larmes plein les yeux, la soubrette hocha la tête de nouveau.

Shaor'i écarta doucement la main, son regard planté dans celui de la jeune femme.

— Alors dis-moi : Sewell est-il ici ?

La domestique entrouvrit les lèvres et, ses pleurs l'empêchant d'articuler, elle se contenta de faire oui de la tête.

— Si je te parle des membres du Stigma Diaboli, vois-tu de qui je parle ?

Signe de dénégation.

— Si je te parle d'un étranger vêtu de noir, à la prestance surnaturelle…

Cette fois, la soubrette articula un faible *oui*.

— Est-il ici ?

— Non.

— Il y a des gens dans son entourage, comme le marchand Ferrier. Tu vois à quel type de personne je fais référence ?

— Oui.

— Lesquels sont ici ?

— Juste… messire… Légaré, hoqueta la fille.

— Où se trouve-t-il ?

— À… la… bibliothèque.

— Où ça ?

— Au troisième.

— Qui d'autre est ici, à part les domestiques ?

— Seulement... monsieur... Sewell. Il dort.

— Et si je te parle d'un calice en argent, gravé de squelettes qui dansent, ça t'évoque quelque chose ?

La soubrette réfléchit un instant avant de secouer la tête. Shaor'i leva les yeux sur Faustin et Baptiste qui, n'ayant rien à demander de plus, se contentèrent de hausser les épaules. L'Indienne pinça alors la domestique quelque part entre l'épaule et le cou.

La soubrette s'évanouit de nouveau et Shaor'i lui posa les mains sur les tempes.

— Voilà, conclut-elle. Elle aura tout oublié. Cela dit, c'est Légaré qu'il faudra questionner. Reste maintenant à se faufiler subtilement dans le manoir et à ne réveiller personne, déclara Shaor'i.

— L'gros des domestiques doivent dormir, lança Baptiste.

— Je vais y aller sous forme de renard, proposa Faustin. Je serai silencieux et je pourrai facilement me cacher si quelqu'un passe. De toute façon, je suis déjà venu au manoir, alors je connais un peu les lieux.

— J'aime pas trop l'idée de t'laisser y aller tout seul, argumenta le bûcheron. J'aimerais mieux qu'tu prennes Ti-Jean avec toé pour que j'sache si jamais t'es mal pris. Quand t'auras flairé Légaré, la P'tite pis moé on ira te rejoindre.

— Excellente idée, approuva Shaor'i.

Ne trouvant rien à répliquer, Faustin ferma les yeux et laissa son corps se remodeler. Sitôt qu'il posa ses pattes de renard sur le sol, le lutin quitta l'épaule du colosse et grimpa sur le dos de Faustin. Le renard gravit l'escalier, laissa Shaor'i lui ouvrir la porte et se faufila hors de la cave.

◆

L'escalier menait aux cuisines. Sitôt qu'il le put, Faustin se précipita sous la crédence et écouta. Ses oreilles ne perçurent pas le moindre bruit et les vibrisses ne sentirent pas le moindre mouvement. Ti-Jean descendit de son dos, courut à quatre pattes jusqu'à une desserte, effectua un bref tour et indiqua d'un geste éloquent que la voie était libre.

Faustin marcha jusqu'à la porte restée entrouverte. Ti-Jean à nouveau sur son dos, il passa dans l'autre pièce et la reconnut sans mal : c'était la grande salle à manger où s'était tenu le banquet du Stigma Diaboli, six mois auparavant. Faustin trottina discrètement sous la table, huma profondément l'air puis fut alerté par une vibration régulière dans le sol qu'il perçut par ses coussinets. Planqué sous une chaise, il vit passer des souliers élimés et l'ourlet d'une robe noire : une autre servante. Immobile, Faustin l'entendit marcher jusqu'à la cuisine, lancer un discret *Cordélia ?* puis revenir sur ses pas en maugréant.

Elle cherche notre soubrette, comprit Faustin. *Autant me hâter.*

Quand il sentit que la domestique était partie, Faustin marcha jusqu'à une nouvelle porte. Il reprit forme humaine le temps de l'entrouvrir, puis redevint renard et poursuivit sa recherche.

L'escalier menant aux étages se trouvait dans le hall. Faustin posa les pattes antérieures sur la première marche et leva le museau vers le plafond. Ses vibrisses lui indiquant que l'escalier était libre, il s'élança vers l'étage supérieur, silencieux comme une ombre avec son lutin sur le dos.

Au troisième plancher, il fut dérangé par un étrange relent de brûlé. Avec prudence, il marcha vers la pièce d'où émergeait l'odeur et aboutit dans la bibliothèque.

C'était une vaste pièce dont chaque mur portait des étagères en bois d'ébène qui montaient jusqu'au

plafond. Des échelles permettaient d'accéder aux rayons les plus élevés. L'endroit était richement meublé de fauteuils de maroquin posés sur des tapis ottomans.

Toutefois, l'attention de Faustin fut aussitôt attirée par le corps inerte de Joseph Légaré gisant dans un voltaire. Le jeune homme fit descendre Ti-Jean et redevint humain. L'artiste-devin, dont le visage était barbouillé d'une écume mêlée de sang, avait manifestement vieilli de plusieurs années depuis la dernière fois que Faustin l'avait vu, trois mois auparavant.

Instinctivement, Faustin posa les doigts sur la gorge du goétiste et vérifia son pouls. Le cœur battait faiblement, Légaré était toujours vivant. L'une de ses mains était tachée de poudre noire et les restes d'un bâton de fusain étaient abandonnés sur le sol, non loin de deux larges feuilles à dessin.

Se penchant pour les ramasser, le jeune homme avisa le Calice des Moires juste à côté du siège. L'intérieur était souillé de sang brûlé. Faustin tendit la main pour récupérer l'artefact, mais il la retira aussitôt en étouffant un cri de douleur : le Calice était chaud comme un fer à repasser.

Faustin se releva et jeta un coup d'œil interdit au devin. *Ne va pas me faire croire que tu as tenté ça…* songea-t-il, frappé de stupeur. Ça n'avait aucun sens : Légaré avait certes des visions prémonitoires, mais il n'était pas un spirite, faute de quoi l'Étranger n'aurait pas réincarné la Voyante des Trois-Rivières. Et si une spirite aussi talentueuse que la Siffleuse avait jugé l'artefact trop puissant pour elle… C'est en faisant de nouveau le tour de la bibliothèque du regard que Faustin aperçut le livre posé sur le récamier tout près de Légaré. Un marque-page y était inséré.

Son ouïe lui assurant qu'aucun domestique n'était dans les parages (après tout, Légaré devait avoir exigé

de n'être dérangé sous aucun prétexte avant de tenter son expérience), Faustin s'empara de l'ouvrage.

Il était titré *Faits et chroniques de la maison Rioux de Trois-Pistoles*. Faustin l'ouvrit et prit le temps de lire la page marquée :

> *Adoncques le père Ambroise Rouillard se rendit à Trois-Pistoles pour quérir le Calice à la famille Rioux qui en était gardienne depuis des générations, il s'informa des pouvoirs réels dudit artefact. Le seigneur Rioux n'avait que faible connaissance de l'art de la* nekuia, *mais il se trouvait en sa famille un don pour la voyance temporelle qui s'exerçait de fort singulière façon, c'est-à-dire que la connaissance des temps à venir se produisait non pas par visions, mais par l'expression artistique.*
>
> *L'un des neveux du seigneur, chez qui le don était le plus vivace, fut prié de décrire le phénomène : en temps normal, il était pris d'une furieuse envie de peindre et s'exécutait dans une sorte d'état second. Ce n'était que lorsque s'achevait cet état que l'artiste pouvait contempler son œuvre et découvrir les temps à venir. Or, si le devin n'avait aucun contrôle sur le propos de sa vision, le Calice, correctement utilisé, permettait d'orienter le sujet.*
>
> *Il prit envie au seigneur Rioux d'en faire démonstration et ledit neveu s'exécuta sous l'œil étonné du bon père qui avait proposé que l'on prédise son propre avenir. La curiosité passa à l'effroi quand l'artiste peignit le corps d'un noyé flottant sur une rivière tumultueuse. Ébranlé, le père se jura de revenir chez lui à cheval. Or, quelques jours plus tard, on le somma de revenir d'urgence et il n'eut d'autre choix que de se faire conduire en canot.*

*C'est ainsi que dans les environs de la Pointe-
à-la-Cive, le canot, on ne sait par quel accident,
chavira : le père et un des hommes qui conduisaient l'embarcation se noyèrent.*

Voilà qui explique tout, conclut Faustin. Ou bien
la maison Rioux disposait d'un don identique à celui de
Légaré, ou bien – ce qui était probable, étant donné la
singularité du don –, Légaré était un descendant de
cette famille.

Le jeune homme tourna aussitôt son regard vers la
première des esquisses… et il se pétrifia d'horreur en
contemplant la scène brossée à grands traits : il s'agissait des remparts de Québec, que gravissaient des
dizaines de silhouettes dont la posture évoquait des
jacks mistigris. D'autres silhouettes, celles-là à posture plus normale, fuyaient l'invasion.

La prise de Québec par l'Étranger, comprit Faustin
en déglutissant avec peine.

Avec appréhension, il jeta son dévolu sur le second dessin, puis haussa les sourcils, stupéfait.

Mais… c'est moi ?

L'image montrait l'angle d'une pièce dont l'un des
murs était couvert de rayons délabrés et l'autre, d'un
diagramme arcanique. Sur le sol couraient des tiges
végétales, comme dans un camp depuis longtemps
abandonné.

Un personnage se trouvant dans ce coin de pièce
tenait une feuille de papier entre ses mains.

Traits froncés, Faustin approcha son regard de
l'étrange portrait.

Le visage n'était qu'ébauché, et ce n'était certes pas
à sa coiffure paysanne, pareille à celle de la plupart
des hommes de son village, pas plus qu'à sa chemise
aux carreaux suggérés par quelques traits perpendicu-

laires qu'on aurait pu le reconnaître. Mais le pantalon du personnage était percé au genou, tout comme celui de Faustin, et le fusil muni d'une baïonnette qu'il portait au dos, et le sabre qui pendait à sa ceinture l'identifiaient sans risque d'erreur.

*Quoique le sabre pende à droite plutôt qu'à gauche…
à moins que ce trait, de l'autre côté, ne soit une seconde
lame ?*

Et cet endroit ? C'est où ?

C'est… quand ?

À ses pieds, il sentit Ti-Jean tirer sur son pantalon : Baptiste lui signifiait probablement de se dépêcher.

Faustin fourra les deux esquisses dans sa poche puis se pencha prudemment pour effleurer le Calice du bout des doigts : il était encore chaud, comme s'il eut été empli de thé brûlant, mais Faustin put le saisir en enroulant sa main dans son mouchoir. En s'en emparant, il remarqua que le tapis avait joliment roussi là où était tombé le Calice des Moires – voilà qui expliquait l'odeur qui l'avait attiré ici.

Il était temps de quitter discrètement la bibliothèque. Tout en descendant l'escalier, il émit quelques mots à l'Indienne :

« *Rendez-vous dans le hall. Baptiste a vu le chemin par les yeux de Ti-Jean.* »

Au bas de l'escalier, Faustin dressa les oreilles et s'assura que personne n'approchait. Sûrement appelé par Baptiste, Ti-Jean courut vers les cuisines. Il revint cinq minutes plus tard, accompagné du bûcheron et de l'Indienne.

Sans plus attendre, Faustin retrouva son apparence humaine, ramassa la clé pendue à un crochet, déverrouilla la porte et laissa sortir ses compagnons.

— C'est toi, Cordélia ? lança une voix irritée de l'autre bout du hall.

Sans répondre, Faustin sortit à son tour, en refermant la porte derrière lui. Dans l'obscurité, les compagnons s'empressèrent de s'éloigner du manoir. Ils passèrent la porte Saint-Jean et ce n'est qu'au bout d'un bon mille qu'ils furent certains que leur larcin n'avait été remarqué par personne.

La grande ville avait fait place à un quartier plus pauvre, qui lui-même cédait peu à peu aux champs formant la périphérie de Québec.

— On va rejoindre le sentier aux Cèdres jusqu'à la colline du Trappeur. Y aura mon camp, vous vous souvenez ? J'sais point dans quel état y s'trouve, mais on pourra finir la nuit là.

En silence, Faustin opina du chef. Alors qu'ils poursuivaient leur chemin, il se demanda combien de temps ils avaient avant que le Stigma Diaboli ne se lance à leur poursuite.

◆

C'était une vaste église de maçonnerie, beaucoup plus imposante que la plupart des églises de village. Au sommet de la voûte trônait un énorme lustre, qui n'était probablement allumé qu'une fois l'an, à la messe de minuit. Les vitraux du transept laissaient filtrer une lumière multicolore qui inondait le maître-autel devant lequel un prêtre en soutane était agenouillé.

Faustin se tenait dans le narthex. Ayant reconnu la silhouette, il traversa lentement le chœur. Ces épaules carrées, ces cheveux blond paille, cette haute taille qui le rendait encore grand même s'il était à genoux…

François.

Le vicaire acheva de se signer, se leva et se retourna. Ayant parcouru la moitié de la distance qui le séparait de son frère, Faustin s'arrêta, incrédule.

C'était le François d'avant les feux de l'île d'Orléans, celui d'avant la vieillesse prématurée, l'émaciation et les pentacles scarifiés. Le François aux yeux bleus rieurs, aux traits exempts de tourments.

— *Eh oui, je prie,* dit-il en écartant les bras comme un coupable pris en faute.

Il eut un petit rire franc, et ce rire remua d'heureux souvenirs chez Faustin.

— *J'en suis réduit à ça,* reprit le vicaire. *C'est le seul espoir qu'il me reste.*

François quitta l'autel pour marcher jusqu'à Faustin. Il le dépassait d'une tête et Faustin comprit que son propre corps était celui d'avant le vieillissement des Forges, ce corps de seize ans qui avait trop longtemps été le sien.

— *Tu m'as manqué, p'tit frère.*

— *Tu m'as manqué aussi, François.*

— *Te rappelles-tu, quand nous étions jeunes – j'avais dix-sept ans et toi quatorze –, nous nous étions cachés dans les fardoches près de la mare aux crapets pour espionner la grande Ardélia qui se baignait. Nous ne l'avons jamais dit à personne.*

Faustin dévisagea son ami.

— *Je te remémore ça,* expliqua le vicaire, *pour te prouver que je suis moi-même, et que ce n'est pas Lavallée qui te contacte traîtreusement.*

— *Mais…*

— *Je suis aux Forges, Faustin. Cette salope de Siffleuse m'a contrôlé mentalement et, depuis quelques jours, je régénère le corps de son maître. Or, pendant ce temps-là, je suis celui qui gouverne mon enveloppe charnelle et je reprends des forces mentales. Depuis hier, mon ancêtre est affaibli par la tempête qu'il a déchaînée contre toi ; pour la première fois depuis longtemps, c'est moi qui suis aux commandes de mon*

corps. D'où l'usage de ce sortilège de rêve messager. Suis-moi.

François se dirigea vers l'escalier étroit menant au clocher. Il passa le premier et enjoignit à Faustin de le suivre. Alors qu'il grimpait, Faustin vit la lumière diminuer, comme si la nuit était tombée d'un seul coup. Le vicaire le regarda d'en haut et dit :

— J'ai su ce que tu as tenté aux Forges pour me sauver, Faustin. Merci.

— Je...

Un coup de tonnerre ébranla le clocher. Le vent se mit à souffler et, au-dessus de sa tête, Faustin entendit la cloche qui commençait à se balancer.

Lorsque le vicaire et lui purent se tenir à côté d'elle, François montra la lande du doigt. Sous un ciel obscur d'où menaçait d'éclater une tempête, Faustin contempla avec horreur des centaines de silhouettes amaigries.

Des non-morts. Pourtant, leur posture était plus droite, plus humaine que celle qu'adoptaient généralement les jacks mistigris.

— Ce sont des bakaak, expliqua François. Tu te souviendras de ce mot ? Tu dois le répéter à Shaor'i.

— Bakaak, répéta Faustin.

Un éclair déchira le ciel, les arbres se mirent à ployer sous le vent et Faustin reconnut l'endroit.

— C'est l'église de Saint-Laurent, n'est-ce pas ?

— Oui. Cachée dans les forêts de l'île, l'armée de l'Étranger attend son heure. C'est elle qui...

Le visage de François s'assombrit.

— C'est cette armée qui a détruit notre village, c'est ça ? compléta Faustin à sa place.

Le vicaire hocha la tête.

— Il ne me reste plus beaucoup de temps, Faustin. Je dois savoir : le brasier de Notre-Dame des Tempérances, c'était toi ?

— Oui.

— *Et le vol du Calice, qui vient tout juste de nous être annoncé ?*

— *Moi aussi.*

— *Alors tout dépend de toi, à présent. Tu disposes de l'outil et de la puissance qu'il te faut pour contrer l'Étranger. Mon ancêtre le sait et il te craint. Il y a des moments où je suis suffisamment « présent » lorsqu'il discute avec son maître pour entendre ce qu'il dit. Écoute-moi : il te faudra l'assistance d'une défunte nommée Matshi Skouéou. Elle est près de la chute Mont...*

— *...morency ? Tu veux parler de la Dame Blanche ?*

— *Précisément. Elle saura...*

Soudain, François tomba à genoux en se prenant la tête à deux mains. L'église trembla subitement, secouée par un séisme qui fissura la terre.

— *Lavallée revient, Faustin !*

Le vicaire le dévisagea et hurla :

— *Fuis, p'tit frère, FUIS !*

Faustin s'éveilla en sursaut. Il lui fallut plusieurs secondes avant de se souvenir de l'endroit où il se trouvait : un camp de bois rond, sobrement meublé, la porte remplacée par une couverture tendue en rideau.

Le pied-à-terre de Baptiste, non loin de la ville de Québec. Faustin et ses compagnons s'y étaient installés après avoir quitté la vieille ville.

Le jeune homme se leva de sa paillasse. Baptiste dormait profondément sur son lit de camp, Ti-Jean roulé en boule sur son ventre. Couchée sur le plancher, Shaor'i avait les yeux ouverts.

— Raconte-moi ta vision, chuchota-t-elle en s'asseyant en tailleur.

Faustin hocha la tête, tira un tabouret et narra son cauchemar. À la mention du mot *bakaak*, les traits de Shaor'i se figèrent.

— Les *bakaak* sont des wendigos créés pour la guerre. Ils sont doués d'intelligence, capables de fabriquer et d'utiliser des armes… ils emploient la langue des Anciens et disposent d'une agilité bien supérieure aux non-morts plus communs.

— Alors l'Étranger aurait élaboré des *bakaak* à partir des malades de Grosse-Île ?

— C'est un rituel ancestral… je ne peux pas croire que Nadjaw l'aurait adapté en version goétique si elle s'est refusée à suivre l'Étranger après qu'il eut libéré Kabir Kouba… Mais si vraiment nous interprétons justement ton message onirique, ça signifie que l'Étranger dispose à présent d'une armée de soldats efficaces et immortels.

Faustin inspira profondément, puis sortit de sa poche les esquisses de Légaré. Shaor'i inspecta celle qui représentait la prise de Québec par des non-morts.

— Des *bakaak*, oui. On ne pourrait coordonner un assaut aussi précis avec de simples wendigos. Et l'autre feuille, qu'est-ce que c'est ?

Faustin déplia la scène le représentant dans une pièce inconnue. Shaor'i haussa un sourcil.

— Je croyais qu'il peignait des désastres, comme l'incendie du Parlement ou celui du faubourg Saint-Jean ?

— Oui. Mais pas seulement ça. J'y ai repensé pendant que nous marchions jusqu'ici. Ce n'est pas la première fois que je vois des esquisses de Légaré qui prédisent nos déplacements. Aux Forges, l'Étranger m'avait fait porter dans un atelier où travaillait Légaré. J'y avais vu une esquisse de nous, avec François, non loin des ruines du Collège. C'est sûrement grâce à cette vision que le Stigma Diaboli avait pu nous tendre une embuscade.

— Des embuscades, il y en a eu plusieurs depuis que toute cette histoire a commencé…

— Justement. Et pendant que j'y songe de nouveau, dans cet atelier, il y avait aussi une peinture à l'huile inachevée montrant une goélette sur le point de sombrer.

— La *Rosamund*?

— Pas sûr, mais...

Shaor'i observa de nouveau l'ébauche au fusain.

— Il nous faudra être vigilants. Si un jour nous reconnaissons cet endroit, cela voudra dire que le Stigma saura que nous y sommes – du moins que Légaré le sait.

— Mais l'esquisse du Collège, l'huile de la *Rosamund*, les tableaux des grands incendies... est-ce que ça ne prouve pas que la prise de Québec est inévitable ?

— Rien n'est encore fait, et le futur n'est pas encore. La Dame Blanche te guidera.

— Tu as sûrement raison. Nadjaw et François m'enjoignent de quérir son aide, et le père Masse aussi allait dans ce sens.

— En effet, acquiesça l'Indienne. Ça me semble la meilleure chose à faire.

Jugeant la conversation close, Shaor'i referma les yeux et reprit sa méditation.

Quant à Faustin, il ne retrouva guère le sommeil.

CHAPITRE 33

Les secrets de la Dame Blanche

Il y avait, quand on s'engageait dans le sentier menant au village situé au pied de la chute Montmorency, une agréable odeur de sciure de bois qui plut aussitôt à Faustin. Toutefois, l'effet s'atténuait rapidement à mesure qu'on approchait des installations du petit bourg d'exploitation : le vacarme des moulins à scie le prit bientôt à la tête et, se remémorant son séjour aux Forges du Saint-Maurice, Faustin songea une fois de plus qu'il n'était pas fait pour la vie en milieu industriel.

Orgueil de la seigneurie de Beauport, dans ce village-ci trônait comme aux Forges un grand manoir, manifestement la résidence de la famille propriétaire – des Anglais nommés Patterson, selon les dires de Baptiste.

À petite distance de la somptueuse demeure cascadait la chute, immense et imposante, haute de plus de quatre-vingt-dix verges, à ce qu'on racontait. Émerveillé, Faustin contempla longtemps les milliers de gallons d'eau qui tombaient à un rythme stupéfiant, la puissance du débit assurant le fonctionnement de deux moulins, l'un de quatre-vingt-une scies, l'autre de quarante-trois, expliqua un ouvrier hélé par le bûcheron. L'employé, un homme aux manières joviales, passa

une dizaine de minutes à expliquer comment fonctionnaient les installations avant de se plaindre de la baisse de demande pour le bois équarri. Finalement, il salua les compagnons du bout des doigts, se hâtant de regagner son ouvrage.

Alors que le groupe se dirigeait vers l'auberge indiquée par l'ouvrier, Faustin sourit en songeant que l'ambiance ici était bien différente de l'oppressante atmosphère des Forges. Près des empilements de bois, des ouvriers à la barbe broussailleuse les regardaient passer ; si leurs yeux étaient éteints par la fatigue du labeur, ils arboraient tout de même une ombre de sourire, l'air accueillant. La présence de la Dame Blanche, toute terrible la décrivait-on, ne devait pas être ressentie comme un joug écrasant.

Ils étaient partis très tard du pied-à-terre de Baptiste, ayant longuement discuté des rêves par lesquels François s'était manifesté à Faustin. Si la présence de *bakaak* plutôt que de simples wendigos avait grandement inquiété Shaor'i, le colosse avait avoué n'avoir aucune connaissance au sujet de cette engeance, ni par expérience ni par ouï-dire.

Ils avaient ensuite marché une bonne partie de la journée et l'heure du souper approchait. L'estomac de Faustin se contracta quand une bonne odeur de légumes mijotés accueillit le groupe.

Il n'y avait aucun autre client à l'auberge, ce qui ne manqua pas d'étonner Faustin. Il s'en fit expliquer la cause quand il déclara qu'ils souhaitaient manger :

— Faudra patienter, répondit la serveuse, ou endurer qu'les patates soyent encore dures.

— Z'êtes entre deux *shifts*, ajouta l'aubergiste en guise d'explication.

— Pas d'problème avec vos patates, lança Baptiste. Autant manger tranquille de suite que plus tard, tassés comme des vaches en pacage.

La serveuse, une solide jeune femme du nom d'Alphonsine, posa la main sur le bras du bûcheron aveugle pour le guider vers une table avant de lui tirer obligeamment le siège. Elle fronça les sourcils à la vue de Ti-Jean mais ne passa aucun commentaire.

Sitôt qu'il prit place à son tour, Faustin sentit le vertige le gagner.

Sa vue se brouilla.

L'auberge et ses compagnons avaient cessé d'exister.

Une voix de femme hurla dans son esprit.

« *Craignez l'Autre, fils de l'Immortel.* »

Alors il l'aperçut juste devant lui : une dame recroquevillée, toute vêtue de blanc, l'air d'une bête traquée.

« *Repartez !* » reprit la voix.

Puis tout disparut : brouillard, dame et voix.

La serveuse venait de poser devant chacun d'eux une portion généreuse de ragoût. Sans pudeur, Shaor'i triait avec écœurement les morceaux de patate de ceux de lard, posant ces derniers dans l'écuelle de Baptiste. Le bûcheron mangeait déjà avec appétit, passant de temps en temps un bout de viande à Ti-Jean.

— J'ai dit : du pain ?

Se tournant vers la serveuse, Faustin hocha machinalement la tête.

— T'es correct, garçon ? lança Baptiste quand la femme fut repartie.

La porte s'ouvrit avec fracas, ce qui empêcha Faustin de répondre.

L'ouvrier qui venait d'entrer, après avoir aperçu les compagnons, demanda à l'aubergiste de s'approcher. Il s'entretint avec lui à mi-voix et Faustin, encore trop ébranlé par sa vision, ne fut pas assez attentif pour comprendre la discussion malgré son ouïe acérée.

Quand l'ouvrier fut reparti, l'aubergiste lança à sa serveuse :

— Finis d'servir les clients, Phonsine, pis après t'iras dire au monde du village de rentrer leurs enfants : Joseph vient de m'avertir que le voile d'la Dame est visible à soir.

La jeune femme blêmit. Elle revint vers les compagnons, posa le beurrier en réprimant un tremblement puis retira son tablier et essuya ses mains avant de l'accrocher à un clou.

À peine fut-elle sortie que Baptiste demanda à l'aubergiste :

— C'est quoi, c't'histoire de voile ?

— Si vous étiez point aveugle, mon pauvre m'sieur, j'pourrais vous montrer qu'autour du bassin, y a une espèce de brume épaisse qui commence à s'lever. C'est comme un filet d'fumée de cheminée qui rampe à partir d'la petite chute pis qui vient faire le tour du bassin. Ça va rester toute la nuit, pis après on l'verra pus pendant des mois.

— Permettez ? demanda Faustin en se levant. Je voudrais voir.

— Finissez vot'assiette avant, j'ai dit que ça s'rait là toute la nuit.

— C'te Dame, commenta Baptiste, c'est quek' chose…

L'aubergiste fixa le colosse et fronça les sourcils.

— Z'en avez entendu jaser ?

— Pour sûr ! Une Dame en blanc qu'attire les enfants dans l'bassin pour les noyer…

— C'est pas différent icitte qu'ailleurs, répondit l'aubergiste au bûcheron. En Beauce, y z'ont un problème avec les loups qu'attaquent le bétail. Au Port-Neuf, faut pas s'bâtir trop proche du fleuve, rapport aux inondations. À Québec, c'est des voleurs aux trois

coins d'rue. Nous autres, on a la Dame. À chaque place ses menaces, comme on dit.

— Mais quand même, un revenant qui s'en prend aux enfants !

— Ça dépend. Si elle a sa robe de mariée, quelqu'un dans l'coin va avoir une faveur. Mais si elle a des glaïeuls dans les cheveux…

L'homme s'approcha d'une fenêtre et contempla l'horizon un instant avant de reprendre :

— Mais même si elle a ses glaïeuls, y s'passera rien tant que les parents tiennent leurs enfants dans leur maison. On fait avec. Personne a vraiment envie de partir d'icitte : la paye est bonne, l'Anglais traite bin ses ouvriers, les *shifts* font juste dix heures, l'village est plein d'agréments. La Dame, on s'habitue. Pareil que pour les loups : faut surveiller ses marmots, c'est toute. De toute manière, les curés y croient point. Qu'est-ce que vous voulez qu'on fasse ?

En effet, admit Faustin. Que pouvaient-ils faire d'autre ? S'ils parvenaient vraiment à empêcher les enfants d'être tués, l'essentiel était accompli.

Après avoir terminé son repas, Faustin se rendit à la fenêtre. Naissant d'une petite cascade, on pouvait voir une volute de brouillard serpenter doucement en direction du bassin.

— Nous prendrons une chambre, déclara-t-il. S'il vous en reste.

— Pour sûr. J'ai celle à deux lits, pour dix cennes la nuite.

Le jeune homme trouva le prix élevé, mais plongea tout de même la main dans sa bourse.

— Voici cinq pièces de deux cents.

— C'est que… de coutume, j'demande une cenne de plus quand y a un chien, rapport qui pourrait y avoir des dommages.

Faustin haussa un sourcil.

— Nous n'avons pas de chien, que je sache !

— C'te bête sur l'épaule d'votre ami, c'est pas un chien, mais…

De mauvais gré, Faustin extirpa un sou de plus.

— En vous remerciant, dit-il en tournant le dos au tenancier.

◆

Faustin, qui avait escompté partager un lit avec Baptiste, se trouva fort embêté quand il découvrit la chambre.

Les lits étaient si étroits que le bûcheron tiendrait tout juste sur l'un d'eux. Virant à l'écarlate, il se tourna vers Shaor'i, qui le foudroya du regard, puis il tourna les yeux vers le plancher sans mot dire.

— Je dormirai en harfang, perchée sur la patère, déclara l'Indienne.

Soulagé, Faustin posa son paqueton sur l'un des lits avant de s'asseoir sur le bord. Puis il raconta la vision qu'il avait eue durant le repas.

Baptiste fut le premier à parler.

— J'suis contre c't'idée-là depuis l'début. La Dame aux Glaïeuls, c't'une folle pis une tueuse. Souvenez-vous de c'que l'aubergiste a conté.

— François m'a incité par rêve à quérir l'aide de cette Dame. Et je dispose du Calice des Moires.

— P'tite, dis quek chose…

Shaor'i soupira.

— Je n'aime pas ça non plus. Mais nous n'avons pas vraiment le choix. De toute façon, tous nous poussent à aller dans cette direction : le vicaire, Nadjaw, le père Masse…

— Je serai prudent, promit Faustin. Si ça ne se déroule pas comme prévu, je la bannirai comme le prêtre sans tête. Avec le Calice, j'y parviendrai sans mal.

— C'est toi qui vois, répondit le bûcheron en soupirant.

Sans rien ajouter, il s'allongea sur son lit.

◆

Il était passé minuit quand Faustin sortit pour marcher vers la volute de brume que l'aubergiste avait nommée « le voile de la Dame ».

Il avait confusément conscience des bruits nocturnes autour de lui : les beuglements des bœufs à char, le son de la grande chute, le lointain clapotement des roues des moulins, le grondement des machines encore actives… Néanmoins, il n'y avait absolument personne aux environs de la petite cascade.

Shaor'i et lui avaient convenu qu'il s'agissait probablement du meilleur endroit pour tenter la *nekuia*. Le livre de Pierre Le Loyer proposait également cette approche, arguant qu'une manifestation spectrale était toujours la voie d'or entre le monde mortel et l'outremonde.

Lorsqu'il atteignit le « voile », Faustin s'installa sur une pierre plate et y traça le diagramme spirite. Il posa le Calice tout au centre, s'entailla la main, laissa couler quelques gouttes dans l'artefact en invoquant la formule :

Ad-esra !
Sakim seran sanem,
Id lameb ibn ganersta-ishek lamir !
Nazad isk ! Nasad isk !
Ektelioch !

Comme attirée par l'incantation, la volute de brume rampa vers Faustin et remonta vers le Calice, à la manière d'un filet d'eau coulant d'aval en amont.

Le voile de la Dame se mêla à la vapeur qui montait de l'artefact.

Puis la souffrance se mit à vriller la tête de Faustin. Il sentit sa force mentale éclater comme du cristal fracassé contre un mur de pierre. Des tremblements le secouèrent. Du Calice s'éleva une épaisse fumée et, dans l'esprit de Faustin, les pensées se bousculèrent sans pouvoir s'organiser en un tout cohérent.

La brume se mit à tourbillonner sans cesser de s'épaissir, engloutissant le jeune homme dans un linceul de brouillard.

Douleur !

Faustin ouvrit la bouche pour hurler. Cette fois, il n'éprouvait pas la sensation d'un fil qui se dévidait de sa nuque – c'étaient des barbelés qu'on lui arrachait de toute l'échine.

La brume s'épaissit encore, devint un écran opaque.

Le diagramme brillait tant qu'il devenait aveuglant. Une flamme jaillit soudain du Calice et monta de plusieurs pieds, devenant une véritable colonne de feu.

Douleur, douleur !

L'esprit de Faustin fut emporté par la tourmente, sa force spirite balayée comme un tas de poussière sur lequel on souffle.

Alors il perçut la puissance de l'entité qu'il invoquait : une présence impérieuse, aussi inébranlable qu'incontrôlable.

Et c'était à cela qu'il avait voulu imposer son ascendant !

On ne pouvait dominer cette entité, pas plus qu'on ne pouvait maîtriser les flots de l'océan.

Un ricanement explosa dans son esprit, un rire de femme dans lequel se mêlaient mépris et amusement, puis une phrase s'imposa à sa psyché :

« *Alors, prends-tu conscience de ta folie ?* »

Faustin sentit son corps soulevé du sol et commencer à tournoyer dans les airs. Puis il chuta et percuta durement la terre. Il se recroquevilla en criant sous les lancinations mentales. Il s'entendit supplier, implorer grâce. Misérablement, il tenta de rassembler ses forces spirites pour couper le lien, fétu de paille dressé contre la violence d'un typhon. La voix hurla encore :

« *Pauvre présomptueux, je vais… – Non! Laisse-moi au moins lui parler !* »

Alors tout cessa subitement.

La brume se dissipa, ne laissant qu'une forme blanche et vaporeuse. Le diagramme cessa de briller, le feu disparut du Calice des Moires, qui roula sur le côté. Le cyclone psychique s'éteignit et Faustin put à nouveau penser de façon cohérente.

Tandis que la douleur commençait à devenir supportable, il entrevit la silhouette d'une femme à la noire chevelure, au teint mat, saisissante de beauté dans sa robe couleur de nacre. Parvenant à se dresser à quatre pattes pour cracher le sang qu'il avait dans la bouche, Faustin sentit une onde bienfaisante apaiser son corps et son esprit.

— Tu n'aurais pas dû faire ça, murmura la femme d'une voix à la fois moqueuse et sensuelle. Tu l'as mise dans une effroyable colère.

— Qui ? lâcha Faustin entre deux quintes de toux.

— L'autre moi. Si je ne l'avais pas suppliée, elle te tuait deux fois.

Sans comprendre, le jeune homme leva les yeux vers l'apparition.

— Elle aurait brisé ton corps et réduit ton esprit à l'état de lambeaux flottants dans l'outremonde. Tu n'aurais jamais dû tenter de t'imposer à elle.

S'agenouillant aux côtés de Faustin, la Dame Blanche susurra à son oreille en l'effleurant de ses lèvres :

— Demain soir, je reviendrai pour te convier en mon castel. Mais elle sera là aussi. Tu devras en tenir compte.

La femme posa quelque chose aux pieds de Faustin puis se releva. Elle perdit son éclat, sembla se fondre dans la nuit avant de disparaître complètement. Alors le jeune homme baissa les yeux sur le présent laissé par la Dame.

Une fleur de glaïeul.

◆

Quand Shaor'i avait fini par le retrouver, il était étendu sur le dos dans le ruisseau, inconscient. Une fleur de glaïeul entre les mains, il avait le teint si pâle et la peau si froide qu'elle l'avait cru mort. Elle avait eu peur pour lui – Faustin l'avait lu sur ses traits en s'éveillant – et cela, elle ne le lui pardonnait pas.

C'était pour cette raison qu'elle refusait désormais de le laisser sortir de leur chambre d'auberge.

Cela et… le fait qu'on avait découvert une fillette d'environ trois ans, noyée dans le bassin qui s'étendait au pied de la chute. Elle était nuitamment sortie de sa chambre à l'insu de ses parents : la mère avait poussé un cri d'horreur en découvrant le lit vide au matin. On avait dû tirer le petit corps ballotté par les remous à l'aide d'une cantouque.

Du moins, c'est ce que les clients de l'auberge avaient raconté.

Au début, on avait hésité à mettre le décès sur le dos de la Dame aux Glaïeuls : en général, la gardienne de la chute Montmorency ramenait les corps sur la berge. Néanmoins, si les fleurs avaient été emportées

par les flots, la tige des glaïeuls était restée coincée dans les vêtements de la fillette.

À croire que la Dame avait été dérangée avant de parachever son œuvre macabre.

De la fenêtre de sa chambre, Faustin avait observé le fossoyeur emporter la dépouille roulée dans son linceul. Il frissonna. Matshi Skouéou était terrifiante, tant par son obsession meurtrière que par son effroyable puissance mentale. Et elle l'avait convoqué à son castel.

Un rendez-vous auquel Shaor'i refusait qu'il se rende.

Sitôt qu'il leur avait narré sa rencontre, l'Indienne avait ramassé le Calice resté à l'abandon sur la berge et avait refusé de le lui redonner. Puis elle lui avait ordonné de monter à sa chambre, l'y avait suivi et ne l'avait plus quitté.

Il avait eu beau argumenter, lui rappeler qu'elle devait le laisser agir comme bon lui semblait – comme elle l'avait fait après avoir fui les Forges, quand il avait tenté de secourir François –, elle n'eut aucune autre réponse qu'un coup de poing au ventre et des menaces en micmac quand il eut dépassé les limites de sa patience.

Appelé en renfort, tant par le jeune homme que par l'Indienne, Baptiste avait refusé de donner son avis. Son opinion, Faustin et Shaor'i le savaient autant l'un que l'autre, aurait tranché la question. Pourtant le colosse était descendu à la grande salle de l'auberge et n'était pas revenu.

Assise en tailleur, le dos appuyé contre la porte, la guerrière méditait. Quant à Faustin, il avait laissé s'écouler les heures, en ruminant ses pensées et ses craintes. Après tout, une entité aussi terrible que la Dame aux Glaïeuls allait-elle ignorer impunément le refus de se présenter à l'une de ses convocations ?

Qu'elle vienne donc te chercher, avait craché l'Indienne quand Faustin lui avait lancé cet argument.

Ils avaient décidé de rester jusqu'à ce que Baptiste apprenne tous les détails de la mort de la fillette – peut-être certaines informations seraient-elles utiles. Par la suite, ils repartiraient vers l'Isle-aux-Grues et étudieraient avec le père Masse les possibilités qu'offrait le Grimoire du Chien d'Or.

La journée s'était écoulée avec monotonie, Faustin ayant partagé son temps entre sculpter un morceau de bois pour lui donner la forme approximative d'un canard, fumer pipe sur pipe et jouer des parties de dames contre lui-même. Shaor'i n'avait quitté sa posture de méditation qu'une fois pour exécuter une série d'exercices dans le vide, sorte de mélange entre une lente chorégraphie et la pantomime d'un combat au ralenti. Faustin l'avait distraitement observée toute l'heure durant puis, lorsqu'elle s'était rassise en tailleur sans lui adresser le moindre mot, il avait haussé les épaules et s'était allongé sur le lit en bâillant.

Des frissons le gagnèrent bientôt et, quand il se leva pour aller clore les volets, il constata que le soleil achevait sa descente. Le ciel tournait de l'orangé au sombre.

C'est alors qu'il sentit sur ses chevilles un contact froid, comme s'il avait été pieds nus dans un ruisseau. Il baissa les yeux et s'étonna de voir que le plancher était masqué par une sorte de brume blanchâtre, couvrant les six premiers pouces du sol.

— Tu as vu ça, Shaor'i? demanda Faustin, inquiet.

L'Indienne ne broncha pas le moins du monde et le jeune homme traversa la pièce en trois enjambées, secouant l'épaule de son amie.

— Shaor'i? Shaor'i!

L'Indienne n'esquissa pas le moindre mouvement. Faustin la trouva froide au toucher. L'observant avec attention, il se rendit compte qu'elle ne respirait même pas. Il recula d'un pas, trembla encore plus en constatant que le brouillard atteignait maintenant ses genoux, puis il fit un tour sur lui-même et s'arrêta, pétrifié d'horreur.

C'était *son* corps qui était allongé là, sur le lit, exactement dans la posture où il s'était installé quelques minutes auparavant. Effrayé, Faustin se contempla lui-même pendant une interminable seconde, puis un mouvement attira son regard dans un coin de la pièce.

Une femme s'y dressait, toute vêtue de blanc. Elle était nimbée d'un éclat pâle et tremblant comme celui d'un cierge. Sans mot dire, elle tendit la main vers Faustin et, d'un geste, lui enjoignit d'approcher.

Son regard ne cessant de passer de la Dame à son corps gisant sur le lit, le jeune homme sentit la panique le gagner. Il voulut crier, sentit qu'une force l'en empêchait, puis perçut que cette même force le contraignait à avancer vers la femme.

Malgré lui, Faustin fit quelques pas, les yeux fixés sur l'entité. Une couronne de glaïeuls blancs mettait en valeur la noirceur de sa chevelure qui cascadait sur ses épaules. Ses yeux sombres avaient un éclat surnaturel.

— Je suis venue te chercher ainsi que m'en a défiée la dernière représentante de mon ordre, le Cercle des Sept Danseurs, énonça froidement la Dame aux Glaïeuls, drapée dans une altière prestance.

Faustin voulut répondre, mais s'en trouva incapable.

— Tu parleras bien assez tôt, murmura la Dame. Il me tarde de connaître ton histoire.

Le jeune homme éprouva la même sensation que s'il avait trop bu. Les contours de la pièce devinrent

flous et, par bribes visuelles, il comprit que la Dame et lui étaient sortis de l'auberge et marchaient désormais vers la chute.

◆

D'une voix atone, Faustin poursuivait son récit :

— C'est alors qu'il y a eu un grand hurlement. Une créature immense a jailli du cercueil de fer forgé, une sorte de primate de plus de neuf pieds que Shaor'i a nommé « *mestabeok* ». Nous l'avons combattu dans l'église engloutie sous le domaine Poulin, puis François s'est servi de son sceptre pour nous faire quitter les lieux par un tunnel. Une fois de retour aux Forges, les ouvriers étaient rassemblés devant Ferrier qui affirmait en être devenu le propriétaire légitime...

La Dame marchait à son bras, le visage dépourvu de toute expression. Tout autour, le décor était voilé d'une brume épaisse qui empêchait de voir les lieux avec précision. Ils avaient quitté le village ouvrier de Montmorency, de cela Faustin était certain, ou du moins ils s'en étaient assez éloignés pour ne plus entendre la machinerie.

Alors qu'il racontait ce qu'avait été sa vie depuis le décès de son oncle, Faustin éprouvait une frayeur innommable. Si rien ne le menaçait directement, les mots quittaient ses lèvres sans qu'il eût la moindre possibilité de retenir le flot de ses paroles.

Pendant que sa bouche égrenait les péripéties, ses yeux parcouraient l'horizon à la recherche de repères. Mais dès que son regard tentait de s'accrocher à un point, celui-ci se couvrait de brouillard avant que Faustin n'ait pu reconnaître le moindre détail.

Il ne sut jamais combien de temps il marcha ainsi, guidé par la Dame qui se tenait toujours à ses côtés,

jusqu'à ce qu'elle lui indique l'entrée d'une caverne dans laquelle ils pénétrèrent tous les deux.

La galerie était immense, sorte de gueule rocheuse hérissée de dents stalagmitiques. Une rivière y coulait et Faustin eut un vague souvenir de la caverne des *mah oumet*.

Toujours impassible, la Dame le guida plus profondément dans les entrailles de la terre. Un courant d'air, sifflant à travers les interstices, évoquait le ricanement d'un démon ou de quelque chose d'encore plus ancien, un de ces esprits à la fois moqueur et maléfique des époques sauvages, une entité comme celles que Shaor'i avait déjà nommées *kek-oua-gou*, *ouésoume* ou d'autres encore plus terrifiantes. Faustin avait jadis relégué ces histoires au rang de simples contes, mais entendre la voix d'une *man'ido* sur l'Isle-aux-Grues avait tout changé.

Comment différencier une simple histoire d'une vérité déguisée ? Après tout, six mois auparavant, il avait entretenu les mêmes réflexions au sujet des loups-garous.

Le flot de ses propres paroles s'était enfin tu et Faustin avait retrouvé la maîtrise de ses mots. Quoi qu'il advienne désormais, la Dame savait absolument tout de lui.

— Nous y sommes, déclara-t-elle en indiquant des marches taillées dans la pierre menant à une salle.

Docilement, Faustin gravit les degrés pour aboutir dans un lieu à l'apparence surréelle. Il avança en rejetant la tête vers l'arrière, souffle coupé devant la magnificence de l'endroit.

C'était une salle voûtée aux croisées d'ogives soutenues par d'énormes piliers de pierre. Les murs étaient savamment gravés de bas-reliefs montrant des oiseaux en plein vol ou de motifs végétaux évoquant le lierre.

Le sol était pavé de marbre d'une blancheur immaculée où tombait la lumière provenant d'une délicate rosace dont le centre représentait une fleur de glaïeul. L'éclairage était complété par les flammes des cierges que portait chacun des chandeliers d'argent faisant face à chaque pilier.

Faustin secoua la tête. Pareil castel souterrain ne pouvait exister. Ses sens devaient être altérés et il voyait ce que la Dame voulait bien lui montrer.

— Sois le bienvenu, Charles Ier alias Faustin Lamare, héritier de la maison Hohenstaufen et fils de l'Ensorceleuse de Pointe-Lévy. Ne vient pas en ces lieux qui veut ; il s'agit d'un privilège extraordinaire que je t'offre avec le consentement de l'Autre qui est en moi.

Matshi Skouéou écarta les bras en croix et éclata d'un rire qui n'avait rien de sain. Quelque chose toucha Faustin à l'épaule et, levant les yeux, il vit qu'un éclat rocheux s'était détaché du plafond qui avait commencé à se fendiller.

— Tu es le bienvenu, engeance de la Corriveau, mais peut-être aurais-tu préféré ne pas l'être… J'ai également donné mon consentement à ta présence, mais la partie de moi qui t'a accompagné ici ne s'est jamais doutée de ce que je comptais faire…

Au-dessus de sa tête, Faustin entendit la pierre se fendre et d'autres pierres se détachèrent de la voûte. La Dame aux Glaïeuls poussa alors un hurlement assourdissant et, d'un seul coup, toutes les flammes des cierges s'éteignirent.

Plongé dans l'obscurité, Faustin était assourdi par l'écho du cri qui se réverbérait sur les parois. Il n'osait esquisser le moindre geste quand l'aura lumineuse de la Dame Blanche se manifesta d'un seul coup, révélant que la femme n'était qu'à quelques pouces de lui.

— Au revoir, fils d'Hohenstaufen, ricana-t-elle en poussant vivement Faustin vers l'arrière.

Le jeune homme perdit pied.

Sentit le sol se dérober sous lui.

Tenta, sans y parvenir, de retenir son hurlement lorsqu'il chuta dans le vide.

◆

Obscurité, ténèbres.

Une noirceur si opaque, si impénétrable qu'il ne voit aucune différence en levant ou en baissant les paupières.

Dans son dos, une paroi irrégulière, froide comme la mort, une sorte de puits naturel.

Faustin attend.

De l'attente naît la crainte : rien de plus terrifiant que ces secondes qui s'égrènent pour devenir minutes ou heures sans qu'il ne sache quand – ou même si – la Dame le fera sortir.

Il croit avoir somnolé mais n'en est pas certain – peut-être s'est-il juste égaré dans ses pensées.

À tout le moins, il n'a pas faim. Il ne peut donc pas être là depuis si longtemps.

Silence.

Faustin remue les pieds dans le seul but d'entendre un son.

L'angoisse qui le tenaille lui donne envie de fumer – aussitôt il se souvient des allumettes qu'il a dans sa poche.

Flamme fugitive, ersatz de réconfort ; rien à contempler à part la paroi rocheuse.

Et soudain, quand l'allumette est consumée et que la prison de pierre replonge dans le noir, une première note musicale monte, claire et magnifique.

Quelque part au-dessus de lui, la Dame chante et sa voix est si triste que la gorge de Faustin se serre.

Il m'adorait, il m'appelait son ange
Et pauvre enfant je ne rêvais qu'à lui
Ô jours d'ivresse, ô bonheur sans mélange!
Ah! pour jamais nos doux rêves ont fui…

Sans un mot, Faustin écoute. Doucement, une lueur monte de l'ouverture. Les parois rocheuses, entrevues dans la lueur de l'allumette, se muent en murs de maçonnerie, transformant le puits naturel en oubliette. Tiré vers le haut par une force invisible, Faustin émerge de sa prison pour retrouver le castel de Matshi Skouéou et ses piliers de marbre.

La Dame Blanche, assise sur un banc de pierre, fredonne les dernières notes de sa complainte. Quand elle a terminé, elle tourne vers Faustin des yeux brillant d'une infinie tristesse.

— J'ai connu cet homme qui a pris possession du corps de ton ami, Faustin. Lavallée… chef de l'Ordre du Chien d'Or, bras droit de l'Immortel… maître de Louis de Beauport, mon doux Louis… approche, Faustin.

À pas prudents, Faustin se rapproche de la Dame, qui lui indique un autre banc de pierre finement ouvragé. S'y assoyant, Faustin ne peut s'empêcher de se demander à quoi peut ressembler ce meuble dans la réalité – une large pierre plate?

— Lavallée… poursuit la Dame. Les Danseurs qui sont venus après moi lui ont donné le nom d'Atontarori, la Tempête-qui-agite-les-Eaux. Il avait une compréhension et un talent exceptionnels pour maîtriser les éléments.

— Oui, acquiesce Faustin. J'en ai été témoin sur le fleuve.

— Il était métis, mais son cœur était davantage celui d'un Blanc. Sa forme animale, le cheval, le démontrait. Ce fut le seul Danseur à assumer l'apparence d'un animal qui n'était pas libre et sauvage. Capturé par les jésuites, qui ont voulu le brûler pour sorcellerie, il a été sauvé par l'intendant Talon. Par la suite, il a accepté le baptême, a reçu un nom chrétien, Jean-Pierre Lavallée, et été régulièrement invité aux assemblées du Conseil souverain. Il a bientôt intégré les rangs du Cercle du Chien d'Or, où il a usé de son contrôle sur les éléments pour faire pleuvoir en période de sécheresse ou favoriser la construction des fortifications. Bien sûr, il ne pouvait qu'attirer l'attention de l'Immortel.

Le regard de la Dame Blanche se perd dans les délicats dessins des bas-reliefs. Ses grands yeux sombres prennent un air triste et elle baisse la voix pour poursuivre.

— Ces lieux ont connu tant de conflits... C'est du sang que cette montagne devrait cracher en chute et non pas de l'eau. Ce n'est guère loin d'ici qu'il y a un siècle et demi, l'Anglais Phips a fait débarquer son armée d'invasion. Les Britanniques étaient très supérieurs en nombre et Québec allait tomber sans l'ombre d'un doute. Lavallée s'était attaché à cette cité. Le Cercle du Chien d'Or se donnait sans compter, et le comte de Frontenac avait tant confiance en la puissance de Lavallée que lorsqu'un émissaire l'a invité à se rendre, il lui a répondu : « La seule réponse que je donnerai à votre général viendra de la bouche de mes canons et du feu de mes mousquets. »

Faustin sourit, ne pouvant qu'admirer le courage de Frontenac.

— Le combat a été vicieux, reprend la Dame, et l'Ordre du Chien d'Or est parvenu à repousser l'ennemi.

Mais durant la bataille, l'Immortel avait donné à Lavallée la façon de marier son ascendant sur les tempêtes avec les diagrammes de la goétie. Alors que les
Britanniques battaient en retraite, Lavallée a suscité
une série d'orages qui a coulé trois navires, puis il a
déclenché par magie noire une épidémie de variole
sur les vaisseaux restants. Les Anglais n'avaient perdu
que trente hommes durant la bataille, mais les interventions de Lavallée leur en ont fait perdre un millier
de plus.

Le jeune homme n'ose prononcer le moindre son.
L'instabilité de l'équilibre mental de la Dame est si
grande que la moindre parole peut avoir des conséquences imprévisibles. Hochant la tête, il incite son
interlocutrice à poursuivre.

— Il existe chez les Danseurs un important tabou,
celui de déclencher les épidémies et les maladies in-
fectieuses. Notre peuple n'en a que trop souffert. Pour
avoir semé la variole chez les Britanniques, Lavallée
a été renié, ce qui a donné encore plus d'ascendant à
l'Immortel pour l'attirer vers la goétie. Sept années
plus tard, Lavallée achevait sur l'île d'Orléans la
construction de l'église qui est alors devenue le haut
lieu de l'Ordre du Stigma Diaboli. Pour l'assister,
Lavallée avait reçu un sceptre lui permettant de drainer
la vie d'autrui plutôt que sa propre longévité.

La Dame détache une fleur de glaïeul de ses cheveux, en hume le parfum en souriant, puis se tourne
vers le jeune homme.

— Qui t'a envoyé ici, Faustin ?

— C'est Nadjaw… l'ancienne Exécutrice des Danseurs… elle m'a dit que je trouverais grâce à vous
une façon de vaincre l'armée levée par l'Étranger.

La Dame Blanche se lève doucement et lui tourne
le dos.

— C'est donc une armée que tu es venu quérir…

— Une armée ? hoquette Faustin, incrédule.

— Certes… cette femme, cette Nadjaw… c'est l'épouse de Gamache, l'ancien Patriote ?

— Oui, c'est bien d'elle qu'il s'agit.

— Nous nous sommes rencontrées il y a une décennie… Elle avait escorté jusqu'ici Chevalier de Lorimier, afin que je lui offre un présent tout particulier… mais de Lorimier craignait les arcanes – séquelle de la chrétienté, tout ce qui est surnaturel est soit miraculeux, soit démoniaque, et je sais que je n'évoque pas très exactement l'image qu'on se figure d'une sainte…

Le visage de la Dame est secoué de tics, puis elle murmure :

— Elle sait ce que Lavallée a obligé mon Louis à commettre… Louis…

Se rassoyant sur son banc, Matshi Skouéou se met à se balancer d'avant en arrière en ânonnant :

— Louis… Louis… mon Louis… mon Louis…

Puis elle s'arrête subitement et se tourne vers Faustin en disant :

— Le dernier exploit de Lavallée a été la destruction de l'escadre de Walker, tu le sais ? C'était en 1711.

Faustin se contente de hocher la tête, sentant que l'équilibre mental de la Dame est en ce moment spécialement fragile.

— Il a usé du sceptre à l'arrivée de Walker cette année-là, reprend-elle. L'amiral venait pour s'emparer de Québec et avait plus de huit cents hommes à son bord. Il s'était engouffré dans le golfe du Saint-Laurent, certain de sa victoire, si certain qu'il avait laissé monter à bord sa promise afin de briller de gloire devant elle… sa belle… son aimée… sa mie… sa fiancée…

La Dame se balance de nouveau de l'avant vers l'arrière en marmonnant d'autres petits noms d'amoureux, puis elle cesse et poursuit :

— Lavallée se trouvait sur la berge de l'île aux Œufs. Il était au sommet de sa puissance et portait le Bâton. Son contrôle des éléments était encore meilleur que lorsque ses orages avaient coulé les navires de Phips. Le brouillard est tombé en quelques secondes, le navire s'est fracassé contre les récifs, les flots glacés du golfe ont englouti hommes et biens... et la fiancée de Walker...

Faustin hoche encore la tête. Il connaît cette histoire, mais ne l'a jamais entendue de cette façon. Il attend la suite, mais la Dame fixe le vide, les yeux inexpressifs, marmottant des paroles incompréhensibles avant de dire à voix haute :

— Et il a perdu... pour toujours... à jamais... sa belle... sa promise... son cœur... comme j'ai perdu Louis... Louis... mon Louis... LOUIS !

D'un bond, la Dame se dresse et pointe le doigt vers Faustin. Une douleur atrocement aiguë déchire le cœur du jeune homme.

— TOI ! hurle la Dame aux Glaïeuls en serrant le poing, accroissant les douleurs de Faustin. Tu crois que tu vas lui ramener sa belle ? TU OSES SONGER À LA TIRER DE L'OUTREMONDE ?

Gémissant en se tenant la poitrine à deux mains, Faustin ne parvient qu'à secouer la tête. Chaque battement lui cause une effroyable souffrance, qui le fait choir sur le sol.

— Personne ne ramènera jamais mon Louis... et personne ne ramènera qui que ce soit, tu m'entends ? PERSONNE ! Tu vas payer de ta vie cette odieuse prétention...

Le champ de vision de Faustin commence à s'étrécir et ses membres deviennent gourds. Aussi, n'entend-il la chansonnette d'enfant que lorsqu'elle est bien entamée :

Il y a longtemps que je t'aime
Jamais je ne t'oublierai…

Malgré sa vue qui se brouille, Faustin remarque la petite silhouette blanchâtre, haute de trois pieds.

— Mère… s'il vous plaît… lance la frêle apparition.

— Dégage ! hurle Matshi Skouéou en relâchant néanmoins l'emprise qu'elle exerce sur Faustin.

Sans hésiter, la fillette détale prestement. Matshi Skouéou marche vers Faustin, qui cherche toujours son souffle.

— Debout ! ordonne-t-elle.

Le jeune homme parvient avec peine à se dresser à quatre pattes. Il lui faut une bonne minute pour obtempérer alors que la Dame continue de s'approcher.

— Une armée, c'est donc ce que tu veux… dit-elle en ricanant. Et tu te crois l'étoffe d'un chef de guerre ?

— J'ignorais qu'il était question d'armée ! se défend Faustin en articulant avec peine à travers ses halètements. Je suis venu parce que Nadjaw…

— Oh, mais j'en ai une, une armée pour toi, fils de Hohenstaufen… J'en ai une, et toute une, une armée toute particulière…

Comme une danseuse, la Dame Blanche se met à virevolter autour de Faustin. Regard absent, vague sourire aux lèvres, elle susurre quelques mots chaque fois que ses yeux rencontrent ceux du jeune homme.

— Ils sont des centaines, Faustin… plus de huit cents soldats morts la rage au cœur, engloutis par les flots du Golfe à la suite de l'intervention de Lavallée… ils hantent les abords de la Pointe-aux-Anglais, nommée en souvenir d'eux…

Le jeune homme tente de suivre les délires de la Dame. *Une armée ?* Jamais il ne lui est venu une telle idée à l'esprit. *La Pointe-aux-Anglais ? Le Golfe ?*

Cela se situe à, quoi, cinq cents milles? Un millier de milles? Comment aurait-il pu…

— … ce sont des spectres dévorés par la soif de vengeance, poursuit la morte. Des hommes qui étaient destinés à combattre sur un champ de bataille, non pas à mourir inutilement pour errer… appelés d'entre les morts, ils s'éveilleront… un spirite de ta trempe pourra leur donner un corps tangible, comme pour les fusiliers de l'Islet… des corps sculptés par les arcanes, capables de blesser et de tuer les non-morts qui constituent l'armée de l'Immortel…

Se jetant subitement sur le sol, Matshi Skouéou éclate d'un grand rire saccadé.

— Ils ne te suivront pas, pauvre fou… ils sont des centaines, ne m'as-tu guère entendue? Aucun spirite, pas même moi, pas même Sev'hannär de l'Ancien Peuple, ne peut tenir en laisse autant de trépassés…

Reculant d'un pas, Faustin demande:

— Mais alors, pourquoi…

De sa voix plus douce, la Dame reprend:

— Ils ne te suivront pas tous, certes… Mais ils suivront l'amiral, de cela tu peux être certain… MAIS L'AMIRAL NE TE SUIVRA PAS!

Rejetant la tête vers l'arrière, elle pousse un hurlement strident.

Faustin recule davantage, effrayé. Doit-il fuir? Dans quelle direction? Il dévisage la Dame, qui se recroqueville maintenant sur le sol en gémissant.

— Il me manque, gémit-elle, mon âme est déchirée par son absence…

Des larmes plein les yeux, elle regarde Faustin et murmure:

— Ce sera pareil pour lui… l'amiral ne te suivra pas… mais il se pliera à tout ce que tu voudras pour retrouver sa fiancée…

Secouée de spasmes, la Dame se laboure le visage de ses ongles en poussant des cris qui, au bout d'un long moment, finissent par s'éteindre. Alors la femme se relève dignement malgré les filets carmin qui ruissellent sur son visage, et elle plante son regard dans celui de Faustin. Elle franchit en deux enjambées l'espace qui les sépare, pose les mains sur ses épaules et prononce près de son oreille :

— Alicia Routh… la fiancée de Walker… Elle a fui les terres de la perfide Albion pour épouser l'amiral en secret, elle a voyagé sur l'un des navires de l'escadre. Noyée comme les centaines de soldats qui hantent le golfe. Asservis cette jouvencelle, Faustin Lamare, et l'amiral Walker te suivra, tant pour la retrouver que pour se venger du sorcier responsable de son échec…

— … et ses soldats aussi me suivront, comprend Faustin.

— Tu auras une emprise sur une armée capable d'anéantir celle de ton géniteur, complète la Dame Blanche.

— Mais… il y a une sacrée distance d'ici à l'île aux Œufs…

— Il y a non loin d'ici un diagramme qui peut t'amener là-bas d'une seule formule… et Walker se chargera du retour.

Faustin fixe la Dame. Est-ce là un autre lambeau de démence issu des méandres de sa folie ? Se peut-il qu'il parvienne à imposer sa volonté à des centaines de soldats rendus tangibles comme les fusiliers de l'Islet ?

— Ne reste maintenant qu'à te protéger de l'Immortel lui-même, déclare la spirite défunte. Marche avec moi, fils de Hohenstaufen…

Sans mot dire, Faustin lui emboîte le pas.

◆

Ils quittèrent la grande salle et passèrent par une sorte de couloir immense que la défunte appela en marmonnant « triforium ». La voûte, d'une hauteur impensable, était ornée d'une délicate mosaïque aux motifs floraux que Faustin ne distinguait qu'imparfaitement tant elle était élevée. Le sol, couvert de plaques de marbre blanc et noir posées en damier, résonnait sous leurs pas alors qu'ils traversaient ce lieu d'abondante lumière. Les fenêtres étaient si grandes qu'elles faisaient presque disparaître les murs : les piliers fasciculés formaient un squelette de pierre, le reste étant en verre. Les vitraux représentaient eux aussi des éléments végétaux, surtout des arbres, si bien que les piliers entourés de multiples colonnettes et les arbres de verre aux perspectives savantes se succédaient pour donner l'impression d'une forêt.

Ils arrivèrent à un espace semblable à un chœur d'église, au-dessus duquel une rosace jetait un faisceau de lumière sur ce que Faustin crut d'abord être un autel. Il se détrompa quand Matshi Skouéou l'incita à s'approcher et qu'il découvrit une sorte de coffre de pierre sans couvercle dans lequel reposait un sabre délicatement ciselé, à la garde couverte d'une coquille d'or massif.

La Dame Blanche désigna l'arme d'un geste lent.

— Voici Lys Blanc, dit le Fléau d'Albion, le sabre qui fut forgé à la demande de l'intendant Talon pour le comte de Frontenac. Le dernier à l'avoir porté fut le général Montcalm ; après sa défaite, le sabre me fut rapporté par Ariane Lavallée, fille du sorcier Lavallée. L'enchantement de cette arme est puissant et empêche les arcanes de fonctionner à la manière d'une lueur polaire.

— Vous voulez parler d'une marionnette magnétique ? demanda Faustin en repensant à cette sorte

d'aurore boréale qui avait failli les happer, ses compagnons et lui, alors qu'ils revenaient du Mont à l'Oiseau en chasse-galerie.

— Précisément. Le sortilège qui imprègne cette lame assure une protection presque impénétrable. Une vingtaine de prêtres catholiques et de soldats du Chien d'Or ont participé à sa création. Elle fut créée pour que l'envahisseur anglais soit tenu en échec. Lys Blanc est passé de général en général jusqu'à ce que Montcalm soit défait sur les Plaines et que la Nouvelle-France soit perdue; si on me l'a apportée, c'est qu'on a jugé que mon immortalité ferait de moi la gardienne la plus apte à conserver le Fléau d'Albion jusqu'à ce que vienne l'Élu capable d'unir les hommes sous une même bannière pour reconquérir la colonie perdue.

Faustin ne souffla pas un mot, les yeux rivés sur le sabre qui avait été manié par tant de grands hommes. Sur la lame était gravés des mots latins, *Gladius legis custos*, et il s'interrogea brièvement sur leur signification. La Dame ajouta :

— Pareille arme te protégerait de la sorcellerie de l'Immortel et de ses sbires, sans compter des sortilèges de Lavallée.

Matshi Skouéou se tut. Faustin resta interdit un moment, sans savoir quelle attitude adopter puis, quand il comprit que la Dame ne ferait rien avant qu'il eût réagi, il inclina la tête et avança respectueusement les mains vers le sabre nommé Lys Blanc.

Pareille à une paroi de verre, une force arcanique bloqua son geste.

La Dame éclata d'un ricanement méprisant.

— Sérieusement, misérable bedeau de village, tu te croyais digne d'être l'Élu ? Toi, un neveu de curé, tu pensais bouter l'envahisseur anglais hors des terres canadiennes ?

Le ricanement gagna en ampleur et Faustin serra les dents, fâché d'avoir été joué et de se voir tourné en ridicule. La Dame se mit à rire avec démence, le son gagnant rapidement les aigus, alors qu'elle couinait à travers son hilarité :

— Toi, l'Élu ? Héritier de Talon, de Frontenac et de Montcalm ? Porteur de l'arme que Chevalier de Lorimier a refusée ? Toi, le premier à brandir le Fléau d'Albion depuis la bataille des Plaines ?

Matshi Skouéou rit quelques secondes de plus, puis stoppa subitement.

— Les Plaines… murmura-t-elle, toute gaîté ayant quitté son visage.

L'obscurité s'abattit soudain autour de Faustin, les magnifiques vitraux ayant tout à coup disparu. Du peu qu'il pouvait en distinguer, le couloir n'était plus qu'un tortueux tunnel rocheux.

Ses yeux s'habituant rapidement à la nouvelle situation, il aperçut le halo de la Dame, seule lueur présente alors qu'elle continuait d'ânonner :

— Les Plaines, les Plaines… les Plaines…

Craignant une nouvelle crise, Faustin recula instinctivement d'un pas.

— Les Plaines… Louis… non… Louis…

Rejetant la tête vers l'arrière, la Dame hurla :

— *Louis !*

Matshi Skouéou serra le poing et Faustin sentit à nouveau une effroyable douleur dans sa poitrine.

Il s'effondra.

Puis tout cessa quand jaillit une comptine enfantine, les paroles pourtant connues résonnant d'une façon fort insolite en ces lieux :

Nous n'irons plus au bois,
Les lauriers sont coupés,

La belle que voilà
Ira les ramasser.
Entrez dans la danse,
Voyez, comme on danse…

Matshi Skouéou se laissa tomber à genoux, éclatant en sanglots. Pétrifié, Faustin vit émerger du tunnel la frêle silhouette blanche, haute d'à peine trois pieds, puis une seconde, puis une troisième… Bientôt, une procession de petits enfants défilait, les plus âgés ne dépassant pas six ans, chacun portant dans ses mains une gerbe de glaïeuls blancs.

La stupéfaction de Faustin passa à l'ébahissement quand son odorat de renard lui révéla que les enfants étaient dépourvus de l'odeur propre aux humains. *Des effigies*, comprit-il alors que la quinzaine d'enfants formaient un cercle autour de la Dame Blanche, qui n'avait toujours pas cessé de sangloter. Ils émirent une espèce de chuintement qui sembla apaiser la Dame. Revinrent alors dans la mémoire de Faustin les propos de Baptiste : « *Elle s'est mise à attirer des enfants qui jouaient sur l'bord de la berge dans les flots pour les noyer…* »

« *Elle dépose toujours des glaïeuls sur le corps du noyé, après avoir ramené le cadavre sur la grève* », avait ajouté Shaor'i.

Elle a tué ces enfants, réalisa Faustin, horrifié. *Elle les a tués… pour s'en entourer.*

— Mes enfants… murmura Matshi Skouéou, le visage soudainement serein. Mes enfants…

— Cessez de vous en faire pour votre aimé, Mère, murmura une fillette d'environ cinq ans portant un bébé dans ses bras.

— Il s'est servi de vous, ajouta le bébé, rendu terrifiant par sa voix trop mature.

— Mais grâce à l'intervention de l'Aimé, vous nous avez et nous vous avons, conclut un garçonnet.

— Mes enfants… mes enfants… mes enfants… ne cessait de chuchoter la Dame en distribuant caresses et baisers sur les défuntes petites têtes blondes.

Si les sens et la raison de Faustin lui enjoignaient de fuir, il ne parvenait pas à esquisser le moindre geste. Un coin de son esprit encore apte à réfléchir se demandait comment ces enfants avaient pu adopter une telle forme par-delà la mort. *Que cette spirite ait été à cheval entre l'outremonde et la terre des mortels est une chose,* se disait-il, *mais comment ces enfants sont-ils devenus comme elle…*

… ou comme les fusiliers de l'Islet?

— Cela vous intrigue, spirite? demanda une fillette d'environ trois ans.

— … de… quoi? bredouilla Faustin.

— Notre état. Ne croyez pas que nous ne savons pas interpréter votre regard.

— Venez avec moi, spirite, reprit la fillette en lui tournant le dos pour s'enfoncer dans le tunnel d'où elle était sortie.

— Tu peux la suivre, doux Faustin, susurra lentement la Dame Blanche, extatique.

◆

La galerie souterraine était étroite et humide. L'obscurité qui y régnait était si dense que même les yeux de Faustin, rendus plus perçants par sa nature animale, avaient peine à y voir. De larges stalagmites montaient vers la voûte rocheuse couverte de limon alors que sur le sol couraient des araignées aux longues pattes graciles.

Suivant le spectre de la fillette, Faustin avança avec peine jusqu'à ce que, subitement, la lumière envahît

l'espace, l'éblouissant momentanément. Quand les taches s'estompèrent de son champ de vision, Faustin constata que le tunnel s'était transformé en un riche couloir, les stalagmites devenues piliers, le sol rocheux un pavé de marbre et les parois de roc des murs de maçonneries percés de vitraux.

— Mère s'est enfin apaisée, murmura la fillette en guise d'explication. Ça tombe bien, nous arrivons.

L'enfant précéda Faustin dans une pièce guère plus grande qu'une chambre d'habitant. L'endroit, dépourvu de fenêtres, n'avait pour seul ameublement qu'une table de travail en granit sur laquelle se trouvait un chandelier à cinq branches aux côtés d'une pile de feuilles de papier.

Détaillant la pièce des yeux, Faustin remarqua un diagramme sur le sol.

— Un cercle d'arcanes ? s'étonna-t-il. Mais la Dame…

— … Mère…

— … ta mère est… était… une médianiste ?

— Une Danseuse, oui.

— Mais alors, d'où vient ce cercle ?

— De son Aimé, capitaine de l'armée sous Montcalm, éminent membre du Cercle du Chien d'Or.

Louis.

— Mère n'a jamais voulu nous raconter leur première rencontre. De Matshi, il l'avait rebaptisée Mathilde – et Mère, folle d'amour pour lui, avait accepté ce changement même si cela bafouait ses origines. Elle lui cacha son état d'immortelle, espérant passer auprès de lui des jours heureux, des jours de bonheur tels qu'elle n'avait pu en vivre alors qu'elle était de chair et de sang.

Faustin frissonna. Si un spectre avait le formidable pouvoir de passer pour un mortel, c'était sûrement la Dame aux Glaïeuls.

— Mais l'Aimé savait déjà pour l'état de Mère, quoiqu'il le cachait bien. Il avait effectué de nombreuses recherches sur cette fameuse Dame Blanche. L'Aimé avait un plan pour protéger la cité fortifiée : des fusiliers immortels, dirigés par un prêtre théurgiste rendu lui aussi éternel…

— Les revenants de l'Islet !

— Mère a lu en vous que vous les aviez combattus. C'est pour cela, et seulement pour cela, qu'elle a accepté de vous aider – autrement elle vous aurait réduit à néant lors de votre pathétique tentative de convocation. Ignorez-vous l'effort de contrôle sur elle-même qu'elle doit assumer à chaque instant pour éviter que sa nature meurtrière ne prenne le dessus et ne la pousse à vous détruire ?

— Je suppose que…

— Non, vous n'en savez rien. Cela ne vous a même pas effleuré l'esprit. Bref…

La fillette se hissa sur la table, s'assoyant sur le rebord pour laisser ses jambes se balancer.

— L'Aimé l'a séduite pour se servir d'elle, poursuivit-elle. Pour l'étudier, comprendre l'état de Mère et le transposer en un diagramme propre à la magie des Blancs. Et lorsqu'il a réussi… il a cessé de se manifester. Il a amené ici une poignée de volontaires, en a fait d'immortels soldats… puis n'est jamais revenu.

Le balancement des jambes cessa et l'enfant fixa Faustin droit dans les yeux, ses iris sombres évoquant deux insondables puits noirs.

— Au début, Mère le crut mort. La bataille des Plaines venait d'avoir lieu. Mais l'Aimé n'avait pas péri en combattant l'envahisseur anglais, Ariane Lavallée le lui confirma lorsqu'elle vint confier Lys Blanc à sa garde. L'Aimé était tout simplement parti pour l'Islet afin de poursuivre ses recherches. Quand Mère comprit

de quelle manière elle avait été dupée, elle se jeta du haut de la chute.

Interloqué, Faustin releva :

— Mais elle était déjà morte, non ? Comment pouvait-elle espérer se suicider ?

Esquissant un pâle sourire, la fillette expliqua :

— Elle s'était convaincue que cela était possible tant grande était sa souffrance. L'envie d'y mettre fin était trop impérieuse. Bien sûr, son corps ne s'est pas abîmé sur les rochers, mais son esprit s'est définitivement brisé. Et alors…

Rivant les yeux sur le diagramme, l'enfant termina :

— Pour ne plus jamais souffrir de l'abandon, pour ne plus jamais perdre l'objet de son affection, elle décida de se servir du diagramme pour devenir… Mère. Et nous tous, ramenés d'entre les morts, serons éternellement ses enfants.

Faustin déglutit, ne sachant quoi répondre. L'enfant défunt ajouta :

— Vous passerez la nuit ici, spirite. Vous étudierez ce diagramme, le mesurerez, le recopierez. Vous le tracerez cent fois, mille fois, à la craie, à l'encre, au charbon, tant et tant que son architecture deviendra aussi naturelle pour vous que respirer. C'est grâce à ce pentacle que vous donnerez corps aux soldats de Walker. Le sort ne s'active qu'en présence de l'esprit d'un défunt n'ayant pas déjà un corps comme le mien.

Sans proférer un son, Faustin hocha la tête. La fillette sauta au sol, fit quelques pas pour s'éloigner, puis s'immobilisa. Sans se retourner, elle dit :

— Répétez après moi, spirite : *Ashek dar-nìran, ashek sader, ibn lamed dahir ibn kalimar.*

— *Ashek dar-nìran, ashek sader, ibn lamed dahir ibn kalimar.*

— Telle est la formule élaborée par l'Aimé. Redites-la, faites en sorte que sa prononciation vous vienne

aussi naturellement que celle de votre prénom. Lorsque l'escadre sera à portée de main, vous ne pourrez risquer la moindre hésitation.

— Entendu, répondit Faustin. *Ashek dar-nìran, ashek sader, ibn lamed dahir ibn kalimar.*

— Bonne nuit, spirite, lui souhaita le spectre-enfant en quittant la pièce.

◆

Et Faustin obéit.

Il mémorisa la mesure de chaque rayon, de chaque angle, de chaque trait.

Il recopia tant et tant le diagramme que ses doigts en vinrent à se replier comme ceux d'un arthritique alors que son poignet élançait.

Et de nombreuses heures plus tard – dix, vingt, cent ? –, la fillette l'ayant escorté dans la pièce revint le chercher.

De nouveau, ils traversèrent le couloir dont l'apparence était l'œuvre de l'esprit puissant et tourmenté de Matshi Skouéou, la mortelle ayant vécu parmi les défunts avant de devenir une défunte vivant parmi les mortels.

Le spectre-enfant indiqua un riche escalier de marbre blanc que Faustin fut invité à gravir. Tout au sommet se trouvait une ouverture menant à un balcon.

La lumière du soleil réchauffa le visage de Faustin. Il était au sommet de la falaise, la chute Montmorency cascadant à une dizaine de verges de là.

Le port altier, la Dame Blanche contemplait le soleil levant. Elle se tourna vers eux à leur arrivée et dit simplement, en souriant à son enfant :

— Va.

La petite s'inclina et repartit vers l'intérieur. La Dame Blanche porta alors son attention sur Faustin :

— Vers l'ouest, à quelques lieues d'ici, se trouvent les ruines du château Bigot, que certains nomment Ermitage de Beaumanoir. L'intendant Bigot y hébergeait le sorcier Lavallée quand celui-ci devait séjourner aux abords de la capitale. Dans la cave se trouve un pentacle de téléportation gravé dans la pierre, sculpté afin que Lavallée puisse se rendre à l'embouchure du fleuve au moindre signal d'invasion, c'est-à-dire à l'île aux Œufs – c'est en l'utilisant que le sorcier de l'île d'Orléans est parvenu à détruire les vaisseaux de Walker.

La Dame accentua soudain le poids de son regard.

— Je vois dans ton esprit un souvenir qui n'est pas le tien et qui l'est en même temps, celui d'une téléportation exécutée pour fuir une femme qui s'est avérée être ta mère. Tu connais d'ores et déjà la formule qui te permettra d'activer le pentacle du château Bigot. Une fois là-bas, tu n'auras qu'à asservir Alicia Routh, la fiancée de l'amiral… et ensuite à donner corps à l'escadre.

— Et comment vais-je revenir ?

— Je te l'ai déjà expliqué : l'amiral s'en chargera. Comme moi, son cœur est lacéré par un insupportable chagrin.

Un bruit derrière lui détourna soudain l'attention de Faustin. La fillette était de retour, portant le sabre de Frontenac.

— Mère a décidé de vous confier le Fléau d'Albion, annonça-t-elle en tendant la lame posée sur ses deux paumes.

Le visage de Faustin exprima sa surprise la plus totale, mais il n'eut pas le temps de former sa question que la réponse fusait déjà :

— Non, vous n'êtes pas l'Élu, ajouta la fillette. L'attente d'un nouveau chef de guerre destiné à chasser l'envahisseur anglais est vaine : les temps ont changé, cette terre est devenue la leur autant que la vôtre.

— Il y a douze ans, enchaîna la Dame Blanche, si Chevalier de Lorimier avait accepté mon invitation, qui sait… mais désormais, le destin de ces terres est scellé : elles seront partagées. C'est pourquoi j'ai brisé l'entrave. Ce n'est plus la perfide Albion que doivent craindre les habitants de la cité fortifiée, ce sont les troupes de l'Immortel. À genoux, Faustin.

Sans un mot, le jeune homme s'exécuta. Matshi Skouéou se saisit de la lame et s'approcha.

— Charles Ier, alias Faustin Lamare, héritier de la maison Hohenstaufen et fils de l'Ensorceleuse de Pointe-Lévy, je te confie Lys Blanc, dit le Fléau d'Albion, sabre de Louis de Buade, chevalier de Frontenac. Puisse-t-il te permettre de pourfendre l'envahisseur qui menace ces terres et te protéger des sombres enchantements de l'ennemi.

D'une habile flexion du poignet, la Dame Blanche entailla l'épaule droite de Faustin, qui tressaillit légèrement. Sentant que c'était ce qu'on attendait de lui, il tendit les mains ouvertes et sentit le poids de l'arme sur ses paumes lorsque la Dame l'y déposa. Alors il se releva, passa le sabre de Frontenac à sa ceinture, du côté opposé à celui où pendait déjà l'arme des Sewell.

Il murmurait des remerciements quand une sorte de vertige le saisit alors qu'une brume épaisse envahissait les lieux. Il battit des paupières, sentant une sorte de torpeur l'engourdir, puis il tomba, ou crut tomber…

◆

… il ouvrit les yeux.

Réalisa qu'il était couché et se redressa.

Shaor'i était devant lui, en position de méditation, se tenant devant la porte de leur chambre d'auberge.

Désorienté, Faustin marmonna :

— … que… qu'est-ce que…

L'Indienne se releva et marcha vers lui.

— Tout va bien, Faustin ? Tu t'étais assoupi et…

La jeune femme s'interrompit, stupéfaite.

Au pied du lit de Faustin était posé Lys Blanc.

CHAPITRE 34

Le domaine Bigot

De l'avis de Baptiste, le chemin qu'avait indiqué la Dame pour passer de la chute Montmorency aux ruines du château Bigot n'était pas le plus simple. Il y avait des routes et des rangs pour cela, affirmait-il, et mieux aurait valu louer une charrette ou embaucher un habitant pour parcourir ces quatre ou cinq lieues.

Néanmoins, Faustin avait décidé de prendre la route indiquée et cela, pour deux raisons. Premièrement, il craignait la puissance de Matshi Skouéou et ne souhaitait pas la mettre en colère en ignorant ses conseils d'une façon aussi éhontée. Mais plus encore, il était persuadé que la partie compatissante de l'esprit de la défunte avait ses propres raisons de leur imposer ce chemin.

Les compagnons bataillaient donc à travers les ronces et les chardons, se fiant à la hache de Baptiste lorsque les buissons étaient trop épais. Quant à l'Indienne, elle ne s'ouvrit pas des causes de sa nervosité, mais gardait en permanence les mains sur la garde de ses couteaux, nerfs tendus comme une corde d'arc.

Ils avaient vite découvert que la forêt cachait des ruines, dissimulées sous la mousse et les fougères. Çà et là, on apercevait encore des amoncellements de

pierres de maçonnerie. Un pan de muraille, branlant comme une rangée de dents gâtées, semblait prêt à s'effondrer au prochain coup de vent.

Lentement, alors qu'ils contournaient les épais taillis d'aubépines aux pointes acérées, ils commencèrent à remarquer quelques pièces d'artilleries abandonnées : un canon dévoré par la rouille, quelques fusils dont il ne restait que le canon métallique, deux boulets si usés par le temps que Faustin les prit d'abord pour des roches. Alors qu'il escaladait prudemment les éboulis d'une sorte de maisonnette, il aperçut au loin une espèce de gros bâtiment carré, au toit en pyramide tronquée. Les murs étaient percés d'étroites meurtrières et les vestiges d'une palissade pourrissaient à quelques pas de la construction.

Faustin identifia aussitôt la structure. Quand il était encore enfant, il y avait à Pointe-Lévy les ruines d'une installation similaire que son oncle nommait un « blockhaus ». C'était un petit bâtiment défensif érigé lors du changement de Régime, sorte d'avant-poste et d'entrepôt. Celui de Pointe-Lévy avait été de bois et, le temps l'ayant rendu dangereusement instable, il avait été démoli au cours de l'été 1835.

Ce blockhaus-ci était de pierre, probablement construit à partir des ruines d'un bâtiment plus ancien. Il semblait tout aussi délabré que l'ancien fortin de la Pointe.

Arrivés sur les lieux, ils virent que la porte était tombée depuis des lustres. Shaor'i scruta l'intérieur de ses yeux dorés.

— Il n'y a rien là-dedans à part des carcasses d'animaux morts.

Faustin s'avança pour inspirer profondément.

— Une ourse noire y a passé l'hiver dernier.

— Elle s'tient encore dans l'coin ? demanda le bûcheron.

— Je n'en ai pas l'impression.

Ils poursuivirent leur chemin, en suivant toujours à la lettre la route indiquée par Matshi Skouéou. Plus loin, ils découvrirent une petite tour hexagonale à l'architecture gothique, haute d'une quinzaine de pieds. Des signes de détérioration avancée lui donnaient un aspect sinistre. Tout au sommet, on pouvait voir un court canon sur la partie du toit qui ne s'était pas effondrée.

Baptiste jeta la tête vers l'arrière pour contempler la ruine et commenta :

— C'te tour-là, par exemple, c'est point militaire. J'me rappelle que ton oncle pis moé, dans notre jeune temps, on avait eu affaire avec un sorcier à la tour de Trafalgar, sur l'mont Royal. Ces tours-là, c'est une manière de monument pour les morts célèbres. On tire des coups du canon sur le toit à la date d'anniversaire du mort.

— Il y a une plaque de bronze juste ici, remarqua Shaor'i en désignant le pied de la tour.

> *In memoriam of*
> *General James Wolfe*
> *Deceased on*
> *September the 13th*
> *1759, Anno Domini*
> *Requiescat in pace*

Après avoir traduit la plaque pour ses compagnons, Faustin ajouta :

— Je croyais que le corps du chef des envahisseurs avait été renvoyé en Angleterre dans un tonneau de rhum...

— C'est juste à sa mémoire, rappela Baptiste. Le corps est pas censé être là pis...

La phrase du colosse s'acheva par un gargouillis étranglé. Alors que Ti-Jean hurlait frénétiquement,

Faustin vit Baptiste poser les mains sur son abdomen ensanglanté. De son ventre émergeait la hampe d'une flèche, profondément enfoncée.

L'ouïe acérée de Faustin perçut un sifflement et son corps lui commanda de plonger au sol ; il évita de justesse un second projectile. Shaor'i accourut vers le colosse qui s'effondrait dans l'herbe, et elle aussi évita du même coup la flèche qui lui était destinée.

Un non-mort se jeta du haut de la tour en poussant un grand cri, arc au poing.

Prestement, Faustin épaula son fusil et tira, faisant éclater le crâne de la créature d'une balle d'argent. Deux autres non-morts jaillirent des fourrés, armés de lances à pointe de pierre.

— Des *bakaak* ! cria Shaor'i en arrachant la flèche du ventre du colosse.

Baptiste émit un grognement et serra les poings, puis l'Indienne apposa ses mains pour guérir la blessure.

Faustin dégaina le Fléau d'Albion, prêt à protéger ses amis. Alors que les non-morts n'étaient plus qu'à quelques verges, il banda sa volonté, arrima son esprit à celui de Shaor'i et suscita cette transe martiale grâce à laquelle elle l'avait formé au combat.

Instinctivement, il frappa du tranchant, coupant la colonne du premier *bakaak* au niveau du bassin. Alors que le non-mort s'effondrait, Faustin fit un demi-tour vers la gauche, évitant la lance que l'autre monstre avait projetée, puis fonça vers l'avant pour décapiter son ennemi.

— *Kwiark ! Ej'nesth !* hurla une voix rauque alors que jaillissaient de nouveaux guerriers non-morts, armés d'arcs et d'épieux.

Avec soulagement, Faustin vit Shaor'i le rejoindre. Elle courut à la rencontre d'un premier *bakaak* qui la chargeait, épieu pointé vers l'avant. L'Indienne sauta

puis atterrit en posant les pieds sur l'épieu du non-mort pour ensuite bondir au-dessus de la créature. Elle poignarda le *bakaak* qui se tenait derrière le premier, profita que celui-ci se retournait pour empoigner son épieu et l'enfoncer dans un troisième non-mort, puis lui arracha l'arme des mains pour la projeter en travers du crâne d'un quatrième adversaire. Elle se retourna en enfonçant sa lame dans le cœur du tout premier *bakaak*, puis lança ses couteaux contre deux nouveaux venus. Dégainant la hachette d'Otjiera, elle frappa à la tempe la dernière créature, qui s'effondra sur le sol.

— *Gwerden nerok! Kwiark!* cria de nouveau la voix sépulcrale qui semblait commander la troupe.

D'autres *bakaak* surgirent d'entre les arbres, ceux-là armés d'arcs. Shaor'i exécuta une roulade sur le sol, ramassa l'arc et le carquois d'un des non-morts déjà abattu puis encocha une flèche. Elle tira un premier monstre, tapi dans le feuillage d'un arbre, et ce n'est que lorsque le cadavre chuta que Faustin remarqua la créature embusquée.

Shaor'i décochait flèche sur flèche, faisant pleuvoir la mort sur les *bakaak* à mesure qu'ils sortaient des fourrés. Ce n'est qu'une fois à court de munitions qu'elle bondit pour récupérer ses couteaux.

L'ennemi riposta en décochant de nouveaux traits. Shaor'i et Faustin s'empressèrent de se mettre à couvert, entraînant Baptiste et Ti-Jean avec eux dans la tour Wolfe.

Les *bakaak* décidèrent alors de charger. Épieux et couteaux au poing, ils foncèrent en hurlant.

Shaor'i et Faustin sortirent à leur rencontre. Si l'Indienne se jeta aussitôt dans la mêlée en tourbillonnant dans un ballet mortel, Faustin préféra l'observer un instant, comme s'il hésitait.

Ils sont si nombreux que je serai vite submergé, songeait-il, à *moins que…*

Le lien entre Shaor'i et lui était toujours présent.

Telle une araignée au bout de son fil, l'esprit de Faustin remonta le lien mental et rejoignit la source psychique de la transe martiale.

D'une pensée brève, il obtint ce qu'il souhaitait.

Tout en gardant le Fléau d'Albion dans sa main droite, Faustin dégaina le sabre Sewell de sa main gauche. Ainsi armé, il se rua sur l'ennemi. Il décapita un premier *bakaak* de sa lame droite, tourna sur lui-même en frappant au ventre deux ennemis en même temps, para d'une épée l'épieu d'un non-mort en lui tranchant le bras de l'autre, puis abattit sa lame droite sur le cou de l'adversaire en empalant de la gauche le *bakaak* qui le prenait par le flanc.

Il n'eut toutefois pas le loisir de s'émerveiller long-temps de ses prouesses. Une autre vague d'ennemis émergeait des taillis.

Un rugissement jaillit derrière Faustin. Avant qu'il n'ait pu se retourner, il vit le *bakaak* lui faisant face être percuté par quelque chose et s'effondrer sur le sol, poitrine défoncée.

Jetant un œil par-derrière, Faustin vit Baptiste se pencher pour empoigner un nouveau boulet qui traînait sur le sol et, de son bras herculéen, le projeter comme eut fait un canon bien servi. Le projectile franchit plus de vingt verges avant de fracasser le crâne d'un nouveau non-mort. Faustin repartit à l'attaque et, bientôt, en compagnie de Shaor'i, qui avait trouvé de nouvelles flèches, ils vinrent à bout des derniers *bakaak*.

Lorsqu'ils furent certains qu'aucun autre ennemi n'allait surgir, les compagnons retournèrent dans la tour pour reprendre leur souffle.

— C'était quoi, demanda Baptiste, ces jacks mis-tigris qu'ont des armes pis… qui parlent ?

— Les *bakaak* ne sont pas de simples machines à tuer comme les wendigos. Ils gardent une bonne partie de leur esprit. Le rituel ancestral leur infuse même le savoir de la langue des Anciens et le maniement de leurs armes.

— Qui peut avoir transmis ce savoir à l'Étranger? demanda Faustin. Nadjaw?

— Non. Même elle n'aurait pas fait ça. Je songe à un être plus fourbe: Ikès le Jongleur.

— Je me souviens, répondit le jeune homme, que sa dépouille reposait dans les catacombes sous l'église Saint-Laurent.

— C'est pour ça que je pense à lui.

— Il a vécu il y a plus d'un siècle, non?

— L'Étranger lui aura soutiré ce secret il y a cent ans.

Shaor'i s'avança vers Baptiste et inspecta de nouveau sa blessure au ventre.

— Vieil ours entêté, marmonna-t-elle, je t'avais dit de ne pas te mêler du combat…

Le bûcheron se racla la gorge, gêné, et l'Indienne apposa les mains pour le soigner encore une fois.

— Et tâche de rester tranquille pour une heure, de grâce. Quant à toi, Faustin… depuis quand es-tu ambidextre?

Pris au dépourvu, le jeune homme bafouilla en répondant:

— J'ai… puisé… ça en toi.

— Ce n'est pas censé être possible, murmura Shaor'i.

« *Pourtant j'arrive aussi à te parler mentalement*, émit-il, *et cela non plus n'est pas censé être possible.* »

— *Awan!* Arrête! Je déteste ça…

— Je ne m'en servirai qu'en cas d'absolue nécessité, promit le jeune homme.

— Tu aurais intérêt, gronda Shaor'i en le foudroyant du regard.

Faustin jeta un regard à l'extérieur de la tour. Le calme perdurait.

— Continuons notre route. Si d'autres *bakaak* ont été envoyés à notre poursuite, nous serons moins faciles à repérer en restant en mouvement.

◆

Il ne fallut pas longtemps pour que les bois se muent en une épaisse forêt. Tout autour, les arbres mettaient mal à l'aise Shaor'i, car ils avaient atteint des hauteurs stupéfiantes. Incapable de définir la source de son malaise, l'Indienne affirmait que « quelque chose » semblait affecter l'endroit. Faustin dut admettre qu'il ressentait une sorte de « présence », quoiqu'il ne s'agissait ni d'un esprit frappeur, ni d'un spectre incarné comme la Dame Blanche ou les soldats de la chapelle. S'il avait eu à la définir, il aurait rapproché cette sensation de la présence de la *man'ido*, sur l'Isle-aux-Grues.

Soudain, Shaor'i s'immobilisa, pointant le doigt vers le sol.

La terre était couverte de milliers de papillons aux ailes orange veinées et bordées de noir. *Des monarques…* songea Faustin en se souvenant du nom qu'utilisait son oncle pour les désigner. Les papillons couvraient la terre en un vaste tapis de petits corps. Comment pouvaient-ils être tous morts au même endroit ?

Percevant son interrogation muette, Shaor'i répondit :

— Ils se sont rejoints ici pour migrer vers le sud. C'est la saison : ils se regroupent toujours en essaims la nuit et prennent leur envol le jour.

— Ceux-ci ne partiront pas…

— Ça arrive quand un froid imprévu les surprend. Sauf que la nuit dernière a été bien assez chaude.

— Comme si on avait drainé leur vie d'un coup, commenta Faustin en repensant au mode de survie de l'Étranger ou au bâton de Lavallée.

— Les choses sont étranges, ici. Comme ces aulnes, qui ne ressemblent pas à ceux qu'on voit ailleurs.

Faustin fronça les sourcils et examina les arbres de plus proche.

Enfant, Madeleine l'envoyait avec François pour cueillir les chatons de ces arbres qu'elle séchait et utilisait à la place du poivre. Leur bois se travaillait spécialement bien pour les ouvrages décoratifs et Faustin en avait très souvent sculpté.

— Je n'ai jamais vu d'aulne dépasser les douze verges, dit-il en reversant la tête pour contempler les cimes. Ceux-là doivent bien atteindre cent pieds…

— Regarde les feuilles, coupa l'Indienne. Il n'y a pas de doute possible.

— Une forêt altérée ? Comme celle qui pousse au-dessus de la tombe de l'Étranger ?

— Non. Un esprit puissant est à l'œuvre ici, mais ces arbres n'en sont pas négativement affectés.

Contournant le cimetière des monarques, le groupe poursuivit sa route. Ils traversèrent quelques minutes plus tard un terrain désolé, où le sol était couvert de ces espèces de pissenlits orangés que Madeleine appelait des *épervières*. Les fleurs étaient si nombreuses qu'elles donnaient l'impression que le sol était grêlé par la vérole.

Puis un nouveau détail monopolisa leur attention.

Ce qu'ils avaient d'abord pris pour une pierre moussue était une statue mariale depuis longtemps tombée de son socle. À demi recouverte de terre et de feuilles mortes, la Vierge avait été forgée dans le fer que la rouille avait partiellement gangrené. Le visage de la Très-Sainte, à qui l'on avait donné une expression bienveillante, était désormais plus effrayant qu'autre

chose, la moitié rousse de son visage évoquant une sorcière à demi brûlée par le bûcher.

— On doit approcher du château Bigot, commenta Faustin. On n'installe pas une statue au beau milieu de nulle part.

Baptiste opina du chef et, d'un signe discret, désigna Shaor'i. La jeune femme avançait lentement, croisant les bras comme si elle avait froid, son teint mat ayant étrangement pâli.

— Ça va, P'tite ?

— Ça ira. Je n'aime pas cette forêt, c'est tout. Cette... présence me rend nerveuse.

Pourtant, je ne la sens pas si envahissante, songea Faustin en s'abstenant toutefois de commenter.

Un bruit de clapotis ne tarda pas à se faire entendre. Ils virent bientôt un ruisseau dont l'eau, presque opaque, tirait sur le rouge. Baptiste affirma qu'elle devait passer à travers un gisement de fer, ce dont il avait déjà été témoin en travaillant aux mines. Pour prouver ses dires, il en sortit un galet, lequel était devenu orangé tant il était taché de rouille.

Non loin, le ruisseau était enjambé par un petit pont briqueté en forme d'anse de panier. La structure couleur sang-de-bœuf supportait une rampe de fer forgé, oxydé comme le reste des objets ferreux du domaine. Deux canons de petit calibre – six livres, d'après Baptiste – avaient été placés à chaque extrémité du ponceau.

Faustin remarqua que les aulnes étaient un peu différents de l'autre côté du pont : leur tronc, complètement enserré par du lierre, laissait à peine voir l'écorce à travers l'épais feuillage.

Shaor'i pesta en s'en rendant compte.

— Damné lierre ! Ce n'est pas une plante d'ici. Ce sont les Blancs qui l'ont amené. Par esthétisme ! Mais le lierre prolifère et envahit tout.

— Si c'est une plante ornementale, commenta Faustin, nous sommes sur la bonne route.

— Sûrement... il y a une tristesse qui plane, ici... chuchota l'Indienne, si bas que seule l'ouïe acérée de Faustin l'entendit.

En effet, admit le jeune homme en son for intérieur. L'espèce de présence que les sens spirites de Faustin percevaient se manifestait avec plus d'acuité, projetant une sorte de mélancolie sur les lieux.

Tout à ses pensées, il faillit trébucher. Les tiges ligneuses du lierre ne se contentaient pas de grimper aux arbres pour les enserrer; elles rampaient sur le sol comme des filins tendus pour piéger l'intrus.

Une odeur rance mit soudainement les sens de Faustin en alerte et il se dirigea aussitôt vers l'un des arbres.

Un corps pendait à la branche d'un aulne géant.

C'était une jeune femme de seize printemps tout au plus, une tige de lierre nouée autour de la gorge. Malgré son bonnet, sa robe et son tablier d'habitante, elle avait du sang indien, comme le révélaient sa chevelure aile-de-corbeau et son teint mat.

La jeune pendue ne devait pas être morte depuis plus de quelques jours. La brise lui imprimait un lent mouvement de balancier.

— Pauvre fille, déplora Baptiste avec affliction. C'est effrayant d'en venir là aussi jeune.

— Comme c'est horrible, murmura Faustin. On dirait que c'est l'arbre qui l'a étranglée et... là !

Au pied d'un autre arbre gisaient des ossements couverts de mousse. Non loin, une autre forme attira l'attention du bûcheron et de Faustin.

— Bon sang de bois, qu'est-ce que...

À voir les vestiges des vêtements, cette dépouille-là était aussi celle d'une femme indienne. Ce qui restait

de chair, à demi momifiée sur le squelette, avait une teinte grisâtre sur laquelle contrastaient les dernières touffes de cheveux noirs du cadavre. Une odeur de charogne imprégnait l'air.

— Elle aussi s'est pendue avec une tige de lierre, observa Faustin.

— Pis celle-là avec, on dirait, enchérit le colosse en désignant un autre arbre du doigt.

Un autre corps en état de décomposition avancée y était suspendu. Faustin marcha vers cette nouvelle dépouille. Le corps portait une ceinture en cuir ornée de billes d'os et de perles de coquillages. Le jeune homme approcha la main pour observer l'objet de plus près et étouffa un cri de surprise quand le cadavre chuta à son contact.

— Pardon... murmura-t-il, mal à l'aise, en retenant le réflexe de se signer.

— Qu'est-ce qui s'est passé, garçon ? demanda Baptiste.

— La ceinture de cette femme a les mêmes ornements que celle de Shaor'i et... où est Shaor'i ?

Constatant l'absence de la jeune femme, le bûcheron se mit à scruter les environs.

— Où c'est qu'elle... *P'tite ! Non !*

Se retournant au cri de Baptiste, Faustin eut tout juste le temps de repérer la jeune femme debout sur la branche d'un aulne géant, passant un bout de lierre autour de sa gorge.

— *Shaor'i !* hurla-t-il à son tour.

Un éclair blanc fusa à toute vitesse sur le sol forestier. Courant à quatre pattes, Ti-Jean traversa en quelques secondes la distance qui le séparait de l'aulne où se trouvait l'Indienne.

Shaor'i enserrait le lierre à son cou et adressait un pâle sourire à ses compagnons.

Ti-Jean fit un saut de plusieurs pieds, atteignit le tronc de l'arbre et y grimpa avec l'agilité d'un écureuil.

L'Indienne ferma les yeux et se laissa basculer vers l'arrière.

Le lutin fonça le long de la branche et bondit à la ceinture de la femme.

Droite comme un arbre, Shaor'i tomba.

Du couteau qu'il avait saisi, Ti-Jean trancha la tige de lierre.

La jeune femme acheva sa chute dans les bras tendus de Faustin.

— *Na tujiw nemi'g gitpu gnegg musigisg'tug alaqsing aq gesigawtoqsit. Teluet « Majulgwali ni'n »*... dit l'Indienne alors que Faustin l'allongeait au sol.

— Elle dit qu'elle a entendu un aigle l'appeler pis dire d'la suivre, traduisit Baptiste en caressant le *mah oumet* qui l'avait rejoint.

L'Indienne marmonna quelques mots incompréhensibles puis s'endormit.

— Qu'est-ce qui lui arrive ? demanda Faustin.

— J'sais pas. Comme tu disais, y a une présence icitte. Inquiète-toé pas : je la perdrai pus d'vue, à c't'heure.

— C'est terrible ! Elle a tenté de se tuer !

— Comme c'tes pauvres filles...

— Il y a quelque chose qui les pousse à se pendre... cette présence...

Au moment même où il percevait le sifflement, les instincts de Faustin le poussèrent à se jeter au sol. Une flèche se planta dans un aulne après avoir traversé l'espace qu'occupait sa tête une seconde auparavant. Se précipitant auprès de l'Indienne inconsciente, Baptiste cria :

— Ton paqueton, garçon !

Faustin s'empressa de lancer son havresac au bûcheron, qui s'en servit, avec le sien, pour recouvrir le corps de Shaor'i et ainsi la protéger des projectiles.

Les flèches fusèrent et Faustin se mit à l'abri derrière un arbre. Des *bakaak* fonçaient vers eux, arc en main. Sans hésiter, Faustin tira un premier coup de fusil qui envoya un ennemi au sol, puis il ramassa un galet, y traça un diagramme et le lança comme pour faire un ricochet. La pierre parcourut une bonne distance, puis se posa à mi-chemin entre lui et les non-morts.

Tout en rechargeant son arme, le jeune homme incanta. Des flammes jaillirent, mettant le feu aux jambes d'une autre créature.

De nouveau, Faustin épaula.

Son tir élimina un troisième *bakaak*.

Un quatrième monstre s'effondra, ayant reçu à la tête la hachette d'Otjiera que venait de projeter Baptiste.

Désormais trop proches pour tirer, les non-morts laissèrent tomber leurs arcs et dégainèrent des couteaux de silex.

Faustin quitta l'abri de son arbre, ses deux sabres au clair, décapitant un *bakaak* de la lame droite et traversant le torse d'un autre ennemi avec la lame gauche. Son ouïe détecta encore la charge d'un monstre – Faustin lui transperça le cœur sans même regarder, puis son odorat capta un changement indiquant l'arrivée d'un non-mort derrière lui.

En une série d'éclairs mentaux, ses instincts lui dictaient ses actes : *derrière* – Faustin se retournait, parant un épieu en plaçant ses sabres en croix – *à terre* – il s'accroupissait prestement – *cibler les tendons* – ses lames sifflaient, coupant les tendons d'Achille du non-mort et le faisant s'effondrer – *sauter* – il exécutait un bond de plus de deux verges…

Déstabilisé par l'impensable hauteur de son saut, Faustin perdit l'équilibre pour retomber durement sur le sol en roulant dans l'herbe.

Baptiste arriva à la charge, hache au poing, sauvant *in extremis* son compagnon de l'assaut d'un *bakaak*. Le jeune homme se releva, se plaça dos à dos avec le bûcheron pour que chacun protège les arrières de l'autre, puis fendit le crâne d'un non-mort qui fonçait vers lui.

Par de grands moulinets, Baptiste fauchait les créatures de sa hache. Faustin en faisait autant, frappant d'estoc et de taille, chacune de ses mains agissant indépendamment. Il ne restait que trois *bakaak* lorsqu'ils entendirent une voix sépulcrale hurler :

— *Gestanerdiak danerken.*

Les *bakaak* quittèrent la mêlée pour reculer de plusieurs pas, puis un autre non-mort émergea de la forêt.

Le nouveau venu était armé d'une hache de silex à long manche ornée de longues plumes. Par des gestes, il commanda aux autres *bakaak* d'adopter une posture défensive autour de lui. Il s'apprêtait à attaquer quand il tomba soudain à genoux. Shaor'i surgit derrière lui pour retirer ses lames profondément enfoncées dans son dos.

Écartant les bras en croix, elle lança de nouveaux ses couteaux et élimina deux autres non-morts.

Un tir de Faustin acheva le dernier.

Sans même jeter un œil aux *bakaak* qui gisaient, l'Indienne enjamba les corps pour rejoindre ses compagnons.

— *Mesgei'.* Je suis désolée. Je vous ai de nouveau fait défaut.

— Bin voyons, P'tite… on y passe tous. Y a eu moé qu'a reçu une flèche pas plus tard que tantôt, pis…

Mais la jeune femme ne l'écoutait pas.

— *Welálin*, Ti-Jean, ajouta-t-elle en se tournant vers le lutin, juché comme à son habitude sur l'épaule du bûcheron.

Le *mah oumet* émit quelques clics dans son langage.

Faustin soupira. Trop sévère avec elle-même, l'Indienne s'en voulait d'avoir cédé à la présence surnaturelle. Il avait déjà vu François dans cet état avant que Lavallée ne prenne emprise sur son corps.

— Shaor'i, il s'est passé quelque chose quand j'ai combattu, tout à l'heure... C'était si étrange. Je ne pensais plus. Ou, plutôt, on aurait dit que mon bras pensait pour mon bras, que ma jambe pensait pour ma jambe, et que mon corps réagissait avant que mon esprit ne comprenne pourquoi il agissait.

— C'est ta nature animale qui a pris le dessus, répondit Shaor'i d'un ton las. Tes instincts ont dicté ta conduite plus que ta raison.

— Mais j'ai réussi un saut... inhumain...

— ... au moins six pieds d'haut... enchérit Baptiste.

— Rien d'anormal, je saute beaucoup plus haut que ça.

— Ça ne vaut pas ! Tu as les os creux avec une musculature de guerrière. Je t'ai déjà portée, tu dois peser cinquante livres tout au plus – moins que ça depuis que tu as rapetissé lors du combat contre Gamache. Alors que moi...

— Du calme, Faustin. Deux verges, ce n'est pas une performance impossible pour un humain bien entraîné. On peut même faire mieux avec un bon élan. Mais les détentes musculaires que tu as exécutées sous forme de renard ont servi d'apprentissage à ton cerveau humain, qui sait désormais commander tes muscles avec plus d'efficacité... Peu à peu, tu te transformes, Faustin. Ta nature de renard se mêle à ta nature humaine.

Malgré lui, Faustin contempla la chevelure blanche de l'Indienne. Lui aussi commençait à changer, il s'en rendait bien compte. De plus en plus, il se fiait à son odorat, à son ouïe ou aux vibrations dans le sol. Sa vision nocturne s'était aiguisée, et il réagissait plus promptement lorsqu'il se sentait menacé... sans compter que se transformer en renard lui était devenu aussi anodin que de changer de vêtements.

Qu'arriverait-il à son corps? Il songea à Misaël, prisonnier de son corps de loup, et frissonna.

Sitôt que tout sera terminé, je cesserai de me métamorphoser, à moins d'une question de vie ou de mort, se promit-il.

— Faustin! cria soudainement Baptiste en lui faisant de grands signes.

Le jeune homme accourut et découvrit le colosse blanc comme un linge, qui fixait l'arbre où avait été pendue l'une des filles.

— Qu'est-ce qu'il y a?

— J'ai voulu donner un coup de hache pour couper c'te tige de lierre afin de coucher c'te pauvre fille au sol, t'sais, pour lui r'donner sa dignité. Mais j'ai cogné fort pis entamé aussi l'écorce de l'aulne.

— Et alors?

— L'arbre... il saigne.

Les yeux exorbités, Faustin se rapprocha de l'écorce meurtrie et recula aussitôt.

L'arbre saignait bel et bien.

Son bois avait tourné à l'écarlate et de fines gouttelettes carmin suintaient de la plaie.

— *Awan*... murmura Shaor'i, qui s'était rapprochée à son tour. Je déteste ça. Partons d'ici.

Pressant le pas, les compagnons poursuivirent leur chemin, un sentiment d'appréhension grandissant de plus en plus en eux.

◆

C'est à quelques pas de là que s'élevaient les restes de Beaumanoir, dit l'Ermitage ou le château Bigot.

Faustin ne fut guère impressionné par les vestiges de ce qui avait été un pavillon de chasse certes somptueux, mais bien humble en comparaison du domaine Poulin. De fait, le château Bigot se résumait désormais à un amas de ruines, des murs crénelés où courait le lierre et une tour partiellement détruite. L'endroit était à demi à ciel ouvert, la toiture s'étant effondrée ici et là au fil des années.

— *Awan, gisna gil mentoin!* pesta Shaor'i, de nouveau très pâle. Je ne pourrai pas avancer plus loin. La présence se manifeste avec trop de force dans ces ruines. Je risque de céder de nouveau.

— Soit, décida Faustin. Reste avec Baptiste. Il veillera à te retenir si l'entité parvient encore à te posséder. J'irai fouiller les ruines et je te contacterai en esprit si j'ai besoin d'aide.

— Ça me va, murmura l'Indienne.

Faustin, passant par l'une des portes, dérangea des oiseaux qui nichaient dans ce qui avait jadis été un hall. Lys Blanc en main, il s'avança à travers les débris de toutes sortes. Attentif, il scruta une à une l'intérieur des pièces, dépourvues de mobilier, usant de son acuité visuelle de renard pour percer les ténèbres. Le lierre, qui avait envahi l'espace, couvrait par endroits le sol d'un immense tapis végétal. Il put poursuivre ainsi son exploration du rez-de-chaussée avant de s'engager dans l'escalier aux marches branlantes qui menait à l'étage.

Ce dernier était d'une seule pièce, dont le centre s'était partiellement effondré en même temps que le

toit. Sur l'un des murs était accrochée une rangée d'armoiries. Les deux blasons du centre étaient de taille très supérieure aux autres. L'un d'eux, d'azur à trois lys d'or, était associé à « Sa Majesté le Roi Louis XV » – Faustin en avait vu une représentation dans le Grimoire du Chien d'Or. L'autre grand blason, présenté comme égal à celui du roi, montrait trois lions rampants, de couleur sable sur champ d'or. Le père Masse les avait décrites durant la longue conversation à l'Isle-aux-Grues : il s'agissait là des armes de la maison Hohenstaufen.

Mes armes, se surprit à penser Faustin.

Il regarda rapidement les autres blasons, plus petits, qui se succédaient sur le mur – il n'en reconnaissait aucun –, puis il redescendit. Il lui fallait trouver l'entrée de la cave.

La verdure couvrant le sol nuisait beaucoup à sa recherche, mais il repéra, dans une grande salle où gisaient les vestiges d'un âtre, une trappe qu'il dut ouvrir en se servant d'un vieux tisonnier comme levier. Une échelle menait à une petite chambre froide aux tonneaux encore intacts, lesquels ne revêtaient que peu d'intérêt. Par contre, Faustin constata sans peine que, sous le niveau du sol, la présence gagnait en force.

Il remonta et reprit sa recherche en déplaçant le lierre à l'aide du tisonnier. Il trouva finalement l'ouverture menant à la cave dans une pièce minuscule, qu'il avait d'abord prise pour un grand placard. Faustin s'engagea avec précaution dans l'escalier de pierre dont les degrés disjoints menaçaient de le faire chuter.

Il aboutit dans un couloir souterrain froid et très humide, au point que la chemise de Faustin devint moite en quelques minutes. Le long des murs, un vaste réseau racinaire couvrait les pierres. On aurait dit une multitude de petites ficelles qui, étrangement,

semblaient toutes émerger de la direction dans laquelle Faustin s'engageait.

Le couloir s'avéra long et sinueux. À plusieurs reprises, Faustin faillit s'empêtrer dans l'amas de racines. Il aboutit néanmoins dans une pièce qui ne pouvait être qu'une cache arcanique – il avait déjà entendu François dire qu'on en avait construit plusieurs durant la guerre de Sept Ans.

La cache mesurait environ six verges de côté. L'un des murs avait jadis été couvert de livres; il n'en restait, sur les rayons de bois vermoulu, que les couvertures de cuir mangées par la moisissure. Sur un autre se trouvait une grande plaque noircie où était gravé le diagramme de téléportation. Faustin avait trop souvent eu pour corvée de polir l'argenterie du presbytère pour ne pas reconnaître là de l'argent oxydé, une constatation qui le rassura: François lui avait déjà dit que ce métal était un excellent conducteur d'électricité et que l'incantation se servait un peu du corps humain comme d'une pile de Volta.

Pris d'une illumination soudaine, Faustin fouilla dans sa poche et en extirpa une feuille de papier à dessin froissée. Ébahi, il contempla le dessin que Légaré avait fait de lui, lors de sa transe au manoir Sewell. Tout y était: la bibliothèque délabrée, le pentacle gravé, les deux sabres à sa ceinture… jusqu'à lui-même qui tenait précisément entre ces mains le dessin du devin.

Ça veut dire qu'ils savent que je suis ici!

Des bruits de pas confirmèrent ses pensées.

— On m'avait bien avertie que je te croiserais ici, mon fils.

Sourire moqueur aux lèvres, la Corriveau lui faisait face, dans un corps âgé d'environ seize ans. Faustin s'empressa de reprendre Lys Blanc en main.

— Ou devrais-je dire mon père? ajouta-t-elle en s'esclaffant.

Malgré lui, Faustin détailla cette jeune femme qui aurait dû être sa fille si l'esprit de sa mère n'y avait pas été implanté magiquement. Elle ressemblait beaucoup à Rose Latulipe : même chevelure, mêmes courbes avantageuses, même minois charmeur…

Sauf qu'elle a mes yeux, songea Faustin. *Et peut-être mon nez, aussi. Celui de Rose est plus retroussé. Quant à sa ligne de mâchoire…*

Sans attendre de réponse, la Corriveau lui tourna le dos. Elle s'agenouilla pour empoigner une masse de racines qu'elle arracha d'un coup sec. Après avoir répété son geste à trois ou quatre reprises, Faustin comprit qu'elle mettait à jour les restes d'un cercueil de bois pourri, dont elle retira les vestiges du couvercle.

Une jeune femme indienne reposait en dessous, son corps aussi frais que si elle venait de s'endormir. C'était de son corps que se répandait la terrible vague de nostalgie qui avait manqué ravir la vie de Shaor'i.

— Voici Caroline de Saint-Castin, petite-fille d'un chef abénaquis, expliqua la Corriveau. Une Danseuse de haut calibre, et une grande Exécutrice. Son clan l'avait envoyée ici pour qu'elle assassine l'Étranger… Pauvre idiote.

En scrutant la femme inerte, Faustin remarqua les deux couteaux *saokata* posés en croix sur son abdomen. Mais l'Ensorceleuse poursuivait :

— C'est l'une des premières tâches que l'Étranger m'avait confiée. Il avait conclu un pacte avec une certaine Angélique des Meloises, qui souhaitait se débarrasser d'une Danseuse que l'intendant avait accueillie entre les murs de Beaumanoir. Je me souviens parfaitement de cette Angélique : une femme magnifique à la resplendissante chevelure dorée. Un esprit de vipère dans un corps d'ange. Quelle goétiste elle aurait été si elle avait possédé l'outrevision ! L'Étranger le regrettait amèrement. Mon corps d'origine avait

l'âge qu'a celui-ci, mais ce n'est pas sous cette apparence qu'Angélique me vit. Elle avait entendu des histoires d'une vieille sorcière à Saint-Vallier, la veuve Bellemare, et c'est en altérant magiquement mes traits que je me fis passer pour elle – et lui fournis la fiole d'*aqua tofana* qui lui a permis d'éliminer Caroline de Saint-Castin.

— Mais cette tristesse qui émane d'elle… elle n'est pas morte. Enfin, pas vraiment.

— Une expérience de Louis de Beauport… Il s'intéressait à la survivance de l'âme et cherchait une façon de créer des gardiens immortels pour la ville de Québec. En fait, il souhaitait adapter en goétie le rituel indien pour engendrer un manitou, les esprits-gardiens de…

— Je sais ce qu'est une *man'ido*, coupa Faustin. Et j'en déduis que ce Louis a échoué.

— Lamentablement. Caroline de Saint-Castin est devenue quelque chose de terriblement anormal, une grave erreur qui n'aurait pas dû exister. Pour survivre, son corps draine l'essence vitale des femmes indiennes, un peu comme l'Étranger draine les spectres et les feux follets.

— C'est elle qui force les femmes à se pendre au lierre.

— En vérité, elle leur permet de ressentir son chagrin, de partager ses rêves et ses visions. Puis ces femmes se livrent à elle de bon gré.

— Mais c'est affreux…

La Corriveau tiqua.

— Ça n'arrivera plus, si ça peut te rassurer. L'Étranger m'a envoyée terminer ma tâche. Caroline de Saint-Castin va enfin trépasser et la forêt d'aulnes mourra lentement.

— C'est à cause d'elle qu'ils sont anormaux, ces arbres ?

— Non. Mais c'est grâce à elle qu'ils survivent. Ils viennent de la côte ouest ; des plants ont été offerts à l'intendant Bigot par les représentants d'une grande compagnie de commerce, je ne sais plus laquelle... des aulnes plus grands, plus robustes. Leur charbon donne une meilleure qualité à la poudre à canon, avait-on dit à Bigot – c'est pourquoi il en avait fait une vaste plantation.

— Et... le sang...

Un ricanement résonna dans la pièce souterraine.

— Ce bois vire au rouge quand il est coupé, c'est une propriété naturelle. Quant à la sève, elle est rouge à cause des eaux fuligineuses. Les aulnes rouges ne sont pas supposés vivre ici, mais Caroline les aimait. Quant au lierre... même Nadjaw n'y comprenait rien. Ça restera un mystère.

De son vêtement, la mère de Faustin extirpa une flasque de métal. Elle dévissa le bouchon pour en verser le contenu dans la bouche de la femme inerte. Faustin la regardait agir, impuissant.

— Vin au cyanure. Beaucoup plus efficace que l'*aqua tofana*. C'est déjà fini, ajouta Marie-Josephte Corriveau après quelques secondes.

Au moment où elle prononçait ces mots, Faustin sentit la présence s'engourdir puis s'éteindre, une touche ténue de reconnaissance teintant sa disparition.

— Voilà, conclut l'Ensorceleuse. L'Étranger pourra maintenant disposer de ces ruines comme avant-poste lorsqu'il se lancera à l'assaut de Québec. Ce qui me ramène à ma première question, mon cher enfant : qu'es-tu venu manigancer ici ?

Ce n'est plus ma mère, se remémora Faustin. La douce et sensible femme qu'il avait rencontrée chez les Sewell ou qui l'avait défendu contre l'Étranger, six mois auparavant, était pour ainsi dire morte, sa

personnalité altérée par son maître. Cette jouvencelle, c'était la fillette qui avait transformé le Collège d'Albert le Grand en ruines fumantes, tuant le père Bélanger du même coup, la petite furie du manoir Poulin qui avait jeté contre eux un essaim de diablotins.

Et pourtant. Ce regard doux, cette délicatesse, ces regrets dans la voix…

Non. Le souvenir de la Siffleuse lui revint. Il ne serait pas ainsi manipulé deux fois.

— Je suis venu, mentit Faustin, à la recherche du Grimoire du Chien d'Or. C'était jadis l'un des lieux de réunion du Cercle.

La Corriveau le contempla un instant, un pli amusé au coin des lèvres.

— Alors les craintes de Lavallée sont fondées? Tu cherches vraiment à défendre Québec des troupes de l'Étranger?

Elle pourrait me tuer sur-le-champ si elle sentait que je puis compromettre les plans de son maître.

— Non, mère. Je ne souhaite qu'assurer ma propre protection. Ce que l'Étranger a fait de mon village…

La voix de Faustin se brisa et cela n'avait rien de feint.

— Tu aurais dû laisser l'Étranger mener à bien ses projets aux Vieilles Forges sans t'en mêler, murmura la Corriveau.

Elle avait dans la voix ce qui ressemblait à de la compassion. Eût-elle été une mauvaise arcaniste qu'il aurait tenté de pénétrer son esprit pour défaire les scellés mentaux imposés par l'Étranger et ramener sa réelle personnalité.

— Peu m'importait alors les visées de l'Étranger, rétorqua Faustin. La seule chose que je souhaitais, à l'époque, était de vous libérer de son emprise.

Et cela non plus, se dit Faustin, *n'avait rien de feint.*

— J'étais loin de me douter, poursuivit-il, que votre personnalité avait été à ce point altérée par mon géniteur.

— Ainsi vont les choses. Nous ne sommes que des pantins entre ses mains.

— Il ne me traquera pas, a-t-il dit. Je ne m'opposerai pas à lui. Je prendrai un navire vers les vieux pays, la France ou l'Angleterre...

— Et tu prétends que tu as affronté l'Étranger pour me libérer, moi, mais que tu n'en feras pas autant pour ce prêtre que tu vois comme ton frère?

— François n'existe plus, articula péniblement Faustin. Pas plus que vous. Des pantins, comme vous le dites. Je n'ai plus ni famille ni foyer. Je ne souhaite que partir. M'en empêcherez-vous?

La Corriveau soutint son regard un long moment. Tout amusement avait quitté ses traits. Se pouvait-il qu'elle...

Non, se morigéna de nouveau Faustin. *Pense aux mensonges de la Siffleuse.*

— As-tu trouvé ce livre que tu étais venu chercher? demanda l'Ensorceleuse de Pointe-Lévy.

Sans un mot, Faustin extirpa le Grimoire du Chien d'Or de son sac et le montra à sa mère. La Corriveau eut un pâle sourire.

— Dans ce cas... adieu, fils.

La mère de Faustin lui tourna le dos et marcha lentement vers la sortie.

Dans l'esprit du jeune homme s'éveilla une tourmente de pensées contradictoires. L'une d'elles domina les autres: libérer sa mère. Même si pour cela, il devait...

— Je vous aime, mère.

La Corriveau s'arrêta net.

Faustin inspira.

— J'aurais voulu que les choses se passent autrement, ajouta-t-il.

La femme se mit à ricaner avec mépris.

Sans se soucier des larmes qui coulaient sur ses joues, Faustin rengaina ses sabres et épaula son fusil. Le cliquetis du chien fit se retourner à demi la Corriveau.

— *Salima khaleb ibn sarëna-ir*, incanta-t-elle.

À la ceinture de Faustin, le Fléau d'Albion vibra avec intensité.

Une expression de totale stupéfaction se peignit sur les traits de l'Ensorceleuse.

— Comment résistes-tu ? cria-t-elle. *Saër-nisan denerys kalmera !*

Le sabre de Frontenac vibra encore.

Faustin posa le doigt sur la détente. *Libère-la !* s'ordonna-t-il.

Les incantations de la Corriveau se succédaient, mais Lys Blanc vibrait chaque fois et dissipait l'énergie arcanique.

— Je suis désolé, mère, continua le jeune homme en sanglotant.

Mais tire ! se répéta-t-il. *Tire et libère-la !*

Des hurlements de rage mêlés de terreur jaillirent de l'Ensorceleuse.

— Espèce de monstre ! vociféra-t-elle. Comment parviens-tu à…

Tire ! Fais-le pour elle !

— Adieu, mère, murmura Faustin en pressant la détente.

Avant que ne retentisse le coup de feu, elle eut le temps d'incanter une dernière fois, comme le confirmèrent les vibrations du sabre.

Néanmoins, le jeune homme n'y prêta guère attention. Ses yeux suivirent la gerbe écarlate qui avait soudainement jailli de la gorge de sa mère.

Pantin privé de ses ficelles, la Corriveau s'effondra sur les dalles du château Bigot.

Faustin laissa tomber son arme.

Fit deux pas.

S'agenouilla.

Posant sur ses cuisses la tête morte de celle qui avait été à la fois sa mère et sa fille, il laissa couler ses larmes.

S'efforça de ne pas hurler.

N'y parvint pas.

Et sut que désormais il aurait envie de hurler toute sa vie.

◆

Il caressait toujours les cheveux de sa mère quand Baptiste et Shaor'i le trouvèrent. Longtemps, les compagnons de Faustin restèrent silencieux d'un silence trop commun, celui qu'on adopte lorsqu'il n'y a rien à dire.

Puis le jeune homme reposa la tête de sa mère sur le sol. Enfin, il se retourna :

— Finissons-en, parvint-il à articuler. Bientôt s'achèvera la vie de Frédéric II de Hohenstaufen. Je le jure.

Sans un regard pour ses compagnons, il se dirigea vers la plaque d'argent noirci, y posa la main.

— Faustin, attends ! eut-il vaguement conscience d'entendre crier Shaor'i.

— *Izan azif, issus khira, eth silukar-an sahsìr…* fut sa réponse.

CHAPITRE 35

L'éveil de l'escadre

À ce qu'ils lui avaient raconté, ils l'avaient trouvé sur le sable ferrugineux du rivage. Au début, ils le croyaient noyé et s'étaient mis en tête de le dépouiller de ses possessions – un mort n'avait guère besoin de ces choses et la vie était rude sur ces îles isolées. Puis ils s'étaient demandé d'où venait ce corps : ils n'avaient pourtant vu passer ni navire ni frêle esquif. C'est à ce moment qu'il avait exhalé une espèce de râle et qu'ils avaient compris qu'il était toujours vivant.

D'autres l'auraient jugé assez mort pour l'achever sans regrets – pas eux, ils le lui répétèrent plusieurs fois. Eux, ils étaient de bons chrétiens. Les vivants, ils les laissaient vivre. Quant aux noyés, ils ne les abandonnaient pas sur la grève. Ils les conduisaient au cimetière (ils prononçaient *cémiquière*) de la Pointe-aux-Anglais et s'ils les allégeaient de leurs possessions, valait mieux que ce soit eux que le diacre Rheault, s'il voyait ce qu'ils voulaient dire.

Mais non, Faustin ne voyait pas – pas en ce moment, alors que son esprit tentait de rassembler ses idées en un tout cohérent. Allongé sur une paillasse crasseuse dans ce qui semblait être une bicoque de pêcheur, il peinait pour s'asseoir, attiré par l'odeur de poisson cuit

qui flottait tout autour, un supplice pour son estomac qu'il découvrait affamé.

Une maigre femme en haillons, dont la bouche empestait les dents gâtées et le jus d'oignons, l'aida à se redresser, ses mèches crasseuses tombant comme des queues de rat sur le visage de Faustin. Celui qui devait être son époux lui tendit une écuelle de bois dans laquelle flottaient des bouts de chair blanche et floconneuse dans une eau épaissie à la farine de sarrasin. L'idée d'un repas donna au jeune homme de violentes crampes au ventre. Ses bras se mirent à trembler et il lui fallut une bonne minute pour se maîtriser.

Sa main trémulait quand il prit la cuillère et il fit deux tentatives infructueuses pour porter la nourriture à sa bouche. Lorsqu'il se rendit compte qu'il tremblait trop, il s'essaya à boire à même le bol, non sans renverser sur ses cuisses une partie du liquide chaud qui essayait de passer pour un bouillon. Résigné, il accepta que la poigne solide de la vieille femme l'aide à stabiliser l'écuelle.

Après avoir tout avalé, il remercia d'un hochement de tête et se laissa retomber sur sa paillasse. Recroquevillé, il tremblait de froid malgré le feu qui brûlait au centre de la cabane. Son esprit, se refusant au sommeil, cherchait une explication à son état. Manger lui avait cependant éclairci les pensées et, maintenant, il s'inquiétait de cette faiblesse aussi soudaine qu'inattendue.

Il avait lu, plus d'une fois, les explications scientifiques que le Grimoire du Chien d'Or donnait sur le processus de téléportation, au point d'en connaître certains extraits par cœur et de pouvoir se les remémorer avec une limpide précision. Quelque part après l'explication du rôle que jouait la mesure du cosinus

dans l'évaluation de la distance et de l'importance de la mettre en corrélation avec le rapport de pi déterminant l'altitude, il était question de *ces lignes qu'il est possible de tracer afin de générer par la vibration d'une incantation choisie une courbure insolite dans l'espace, offrant aux points éloignés la possibilité de s'effleurer à travers ledit continuum spatial, permettant à un groupe de particules primordiales de sortir et de retrouver aussitôt notre sphère dimensionnelle en point autre sans altérer son organisation d'origine...*

Faustin n'y comprenait que le minimum. Sa connaissance en arcanisme se limitait aux mathématiques de base, à la géométrie et au gros bon sens du « *si je fais ceci, il se produira cela* ». La physique spéculative, les notions de molécules et d'*atomos*, tout cela le dépassait.

Or, ce même bon sens venait d'en prendre un coup. *Lorsque je prononce cette formule devant ce diagramme, je me téléporte*, voilà ce qu'il comprenait du processus. Alors pourquoi cet état vaseux ? Pourquoi l'incantation avait-elle à ce point drainé ses forces ?

Il y avait la notion d'éloignement, peut-être. François avait déjà dit que la téléportation ne marchait bien qu'à courte distance. Dépassée la limite des cinquante verges, ou cent si l'on était un spécialiste, le sort perdait sa précision.

Faustin avait déjà expérimenté une téléportation à plus longue distance. De la cache secrète du manoir Poulin, il s'était téléporté à la Grande Maison des Vieilles Forges. Un transfert de, quoi, une demi-lieue tout au plus ? S'il avait été ébranlé à l'arrivée à la Grande Maison, physiquement et psychiquement, il avait mis cela sur le compte de la Siffleuse qui lui avait arraché l'emprise qu'il avait sur Plaçoa, mais... et s'il s'était agi du contraire ? Si, connaissant les effets collatéraux

d'une téléportation longue, la Siffleuse avait profité de sa faiblesse passagère pour lui saper son lien avec Plaçoa ? Après tout, lorsqu'il s'était opposé à elle pendant la *nekuia* pour contacter son oncle, elle n'avait guère été de taille face à lui.

Tout cela se tenait. La présente téléportation s'était effectuée sur une distance de plus de cent vingt lieues. Peut-être son corps et son esprit l'avaient-ils difficilement supportée. Pourquoi ? Cela ne lui importait pas. *Si j'exécute une téléportation longue, je subis un contrecoup physique et mental.* Il ne lui fallait rien de plus. François aurait voulu des chiffres, des équations, des explications scientifiques. Mais pas Faustin.

Satisfait d'avoir trouvé une explication qui le rassurait, il put enfin se permettre de dormir, sombrant dans un sommeil de plomb qui le coupa du monde extérieur.

◆

Ce fut le bruit d'un coup de feu qui l'éveilla. Se redressant sur sa couche, il regarda autour de lui, main posée sur la garde d'un de ses sabres. La vieille femme le surveillait d'un air attentif.

La porte de la cabane s'ouvrit sur l'homme du foyer qui tenait par les pattes un oiseau noir de très grande taille, d'une envergure d'au moins cinq pieds avec un corps qui en faisait quatre. La femme sortit rejoindre son homme à l'extérieur et se saisit de la prise, de toute évidence pour le plumer.

L'homme entra, posa son arme contre un mur et Faustin reconnut son fusil monté d'une baïonnette. Son hôte écarta les mains dans un geste d'excuse.

— C'est dur, han, de c'temps. Là, j'avions pris vot' feu, mesure qu'on va être trois à grailler, han ?

Faustin mit un instant pour décoder les propos du pêcheur. Ce n'était pas la première fois qu'il entendait un accent régional : les coureurs des bois et les ouvrageux prenaient des expressions des Hauts, Shaor'i avait son français soutenu qu'elle tenait d'Otjiera, et il se souvenait aussi de l'épique dispute qu'il avait eue avec le beau-frère de Madeleine, originaire de Montréal, sur la juste prononciation de *baleine*.

— Aucun problème, mon brave, le rassura Faustin. Et merci de m'avoir recueilli.

— Pas d'un trouble. Z'avions point la parlure des abords.

— Je suis de Pointe-Lévy.

— Han ?

— En face de Québec.

— Han-han. Plus qu'un jet d'pisse.

Le pêcheur fit craquer ses jointures et tira la bûche qui servait de siège.

Faustin détailla son hôte : un homme au teint brûlé par le soleil, aux cheveux poivre et sel, maigre comme un trop long carême. Ses vêtements semblaient goudronnés tant ils étaient crasseux.

— Lemay, se présenta l'homme en tendant une main noire de saleté.

— Lamare, répondit Faustin en la serrant.

Un sourire fourbe fendit la face mal rasée de Lemay.

— L'île aux Œufs, ça faisions pas qu'un mille de long, deux cents verges de large.

— Euh… d'accord, dit Faustin, incertain de l'attitude à adopter.

— Icitte, pas qu'un qu'avions vu d'bâteau dans les abords, hier. Pis si t'étions largué de plus loin, han… moé-là, un presque noyé que sa poudre à feu reste sèche, j'trouvions ça bin adonné.

Le sourire de Lemay devint encore plus grand.

— Anticosti, c'point trop loin. On entendions de plein jaser, d'la Baie.

— J'ai bien du mal à vous suivre, monsieur Lemay…

— L'sorcier d'Anticosti, Gamache. Tu r'viens d'aller l'voir, han ? T'es sorcier, itou ?

Merde, songea Faustin. *S'il vient à l'idée de cet homme de se débarrasser de moi, je devrai me résigner à…*

— T'inquiétions point, le rassura le pêcheur. J'savions déjà: ma criature t'avions vu arriver de même, pchitt !

Il claqua des doigts pour appuyer ses propos.

— On étions là pour toé, pis tu vas t'souviendre de nous autres, han ?

— Quoi ?

— Les sorciers, ça avions manière de r'mercier son monde, han ?

La femme de Lemay rentra à cet instant, son énorme oiseau plumé, vidé et étêté. Elle l'avait transpercé d'une tige de fer qu'elle plaça au-dessus de l'âtre, simple amas de pierres rendues noires par la suie.

L'homme ajouta en murmurant:

— Moé, han, que l'or venions du Charlot ou des saints, y sert à payer les mêmes affaires.

— Espérance que l'cormoran serions d'vos aisances, lança la femme sans détourner les yeux du feu.

Faustin se contenta de hocher la tête.

— Je vais… me recoucher, prétexta-t-il pour s'offrir le luxe de réfléchir.

— Pas d'un trouble.

Retenant un soupir, Faustin ferma les yeux, essayant d'oublier le pêcheur qui ne le quittait pas des yeux. Simulant le sommeil, il réfléchit. Il avait effectivement une bourse épaisse, lourde de l'argent qu'il avait ramassé chez le notaire Lanigan, six mois auparavant.

Parmi les sous, les cents et les piastres espagnoles, il avait bien quelques louis d'or, mais ceux-ci, bien que de grande valeur, ne satisferaient pas un vieux couple bercé par les contes de coffres de boucaniers débordant de pièces que les légendaires sorciers-pirates étaient censés posséder. Certes, le couple ne représentait pas une grande menace et le peu d'arcanes qu'il maîtrisait suffirait à les effrayer. Néanmoins, l'incantation pour laquelle il était venu ne tolérerait aucun dérangement de la part de curieux ou, pire, de pêcheurs avides d'allumer un bûcher. Reste qu'il n'allait tout de même pas ligoter ces gens, ni les menacer...

Il profita d'un moment d'inattention pour fouiller sa bourse, trouva six demi-louis et un louis. Une fortune que son sens de l'économie paysan répugnait à laisser partir. Mais le plus vite il serait débarrassé de ces gêneurs, le mieux ce serait. Soudain, il sourit en se rappelant une histoire du conteur Jos Violon.

— Monsieur Lemay, lança-t-il subitement, combien êtes-vous sur cette île ?

— À c'te soir, quatre : ma criature pis moé-cite, Renault pis la sienne.

— Approchez-moi ce seau.

Lemay se leva pour aller ramasser un vieux seau rouillé qu'il posa au pied de la couche de Faustin.

Celui-ci sortit trois demi-louis d'or de sa poche.

— Voici trois pièces d'or. L'une pour vous, tout de suite. L'autre pour le nommé Renault.

— Pis la troisième ? demanda le pêcheur avec un air rapace.

— Je vous dois la vie. Ce soir, j'appellerai sa majesté Lucifer et lui demanderai d'emplir ce seau de pièces comme celle-ci.

Faustin jeta le dernier demi-louis dans le contenant rouillé et reprit, en fixant Lemay dans les yeux :

— Le Diable s'emparera de toute âme qui sera sur l'île au moment de sa visite. Et je ne veux pas être dérangé en discutant avec mon maître. Votre épouse, vous-même et le couple Renault devrez quitter l'île pour la nuit vers la Pointe-aux-Anglais, où la présence du diacre éloignera le Malin. Vous utiliserez la pièce pour convaincre votre voisin. Et demain à l'aube, si je n'ai pas été dérangé, votre seau débordera d'or. Cela vous convient-il?

La face barbue du pêcheur s'éclaira. Il y avait dans les yeux avides de Lemay une lueur de cupidité comme Faustin en avait rarement vu.

— Correct, han. J'allions faire comme pareil que vous disez.

Poussant un soupir de soulagement, Faustin serra la main du pêcheur et se leva pour aller souper de la pitance que touillait la femme de Lemay.

◆

Fugitive comme un feu follet, la lueur du fanal accroché à la proue de la barque voltigeait au-dessus des flots, montant et descendant au gré des vagues, pour finir par se perdre dans la brume naissante qui couvrait peu à peu le mince bras fluvial séparant la Pointe-aux-Anglais de l'île aux Œufs. Louvoyant entre les traîtres écueils, le frêle esquif se distançait de l'île, où Faustin était maintenant seul, assis sur une souche et la tête entre les mains.

Au fur et à mesure qu'il s'était remis de sa téléportation, il avait perçu une fureur qui, d'heure en heure, avait augmenté d'intensité.

Cette île minuscule, langue de terre désolée et hérissée de brisants, semblait pulser sous les lamentations des esprits n'ayant point trouvé le repos.

Il ne s'agissait pas d'une impression comme celle qu'il avait éprouvée à Notre-Dame des Tempérances, où dominait la terreur, ni comme celle de Grosse-Île, où les dix mille morts souffraient encore du désespoir qui les avait saisis avant qu'ils succombent aux maladies.

Bien au contraire.

Ici, parmi les nombreux écueils sur lesquels la mer déferlait, rage et haine étaient seules reines.

Cela se sentait sur les pierres coupantes, affûtées comme des lames, mais aussi sur les sables rendus rougeâtres par la présence de minerai ferreux et dans les reliquats des embarcations des pêcheurs imprudents.

Colère.

Le jeune homme se leva pour marcher à travers les buissons de chiendent.

Fureur.

Les vagues mentales s'abattaient sur ses sens spirites comme les vagues se brisaient sur les écueils. Des volutes résiduelles donnaient l'impression de s'accrocher à lui, semblables à des linceuls immatériels destinés à ces soldats noyés plus d'un siècle auparavant.

Même si l'île était petite, il lui fallut une bonne heure pour atteindre les récifs où avaient sombré les navires de l'escadre de Walker. À cet endroit, le rivage devenait plus rocheux. Faustin avisa une immense pierre plate, pareille à une dalle géante, rendue lisse par le flux et le reflux du golfe. S'y agenouillant, il déposa sa lanterne, le Grimoire du Chien d'Or et le Calice des Moires.

Cette pierre sera la surface parfaite pour y tracer les diagrammes, songea Faustin avant de frissonner sous une idée subite : le sorcier Lavallée s'était-il dit la même chose, lorsqu'il était venu pour engloutir dans les eaux glaciales les navires anglais et leur équipage ?

Secouant la tête, le jeune homme chassa cette idée pour se concentrer sur le sortilège appris de la Dame

Blanche, puis il s'appliqua à recopier le diagramme à l'aide de sa craie.

Mais qu'est-ce que je m'apprête à tenter?

Il s'arrêta, pris de doute. Le souvenir des soldats de l'Islet lui revint en tête. Quelle force s'apprêtait-il à déclencher? En donnant une tangibilité à des centaines de spectres qui attisaient leur courroux depuis treize décennies, ne risquait-il pas de déclencher une calamité pire que celle qu'avait engendrée l'Étranger? Et s'il advenait que ces défunts échappent à son contrôle ou refusent carrément de s'y soumettre? Qu'il s'agisse d'une armée de jacks mistigris ou de revenants, le résultat serait le même: les simples mortels ne pourraient l'affronter.

La Dame Blanche est cent fois plus puissante que moi. Si cela tourne mal, Shaor'i ira quérir son aide, pensa Faustin pour se rassurer. Mais comment prévoir ce que ferait cette Dame à demi folle?

Comme le mien, son cœur est lacéré par un insupportable chagrin, avait confié la Dame. Elle semblait convaincue que la promesse d'une éternité auprès de sa promise suffirait à convaincre Walker…

Ai-je un autre choix? finit par se dire Faustin.

Ayant complété le diagramme, il prit le temps de le remesurer deux fois, puis il traça le pentacle de *nekuia* au centre duquel il posa le Calice des Moires.

Et maintenant… venez à moi, miss Alicia Routh.

De son couteau, le jeune homme s'entailla la main, se redressa et incanta:

Ad-esra!
Sakim seran sanem,
Id lameb ibn ganersta-ishek lamir!
Nazad isk! Nasad isk!
Ektelioch!

La tourmente mentale s'empara aussitôt de son esprit. Comme si une tempête d'âmes venait de pénétrer en lui, porteuses d'une rage sans nom. Comme si des centaines de spectres se ruaient sur lui.

Faustin hurla ou crut hurler.

Fut démembré ou persuadé de l'être.

Réduit à néant ou convaincu de ne plus exister.

L'océan mental se déchaînait alors que les âmes s'entremêlaient, s'entrechoquaient, chacune criant la virulence de son inimitié pour un trépas dépourvu de sens, chacune souhaitant abattre son courroux sur l'impudent mortel qui osait troubler son sommeil.

Ils étaient dix, cent, presque mille.

Ils traversaient l'esprit de Faustin comme autant de lames acérées, froides comme la mort, glacées comme les flots qui étaient leur tombeau.

Des hommes rendus fous par le ressentiment, le désir de vindicte, la soif de vengeance.

À genoux sur le sol, la tête entre les mains, Faustin émit une sorte de cri psychique : « JE VOUS L'APPORTE ! »

La tempête mentale, changeant très subtilement, se déchaîna soudain autour de lui plutôt qu'à travers lui. Faustin en profita pour crier tant mentalement que de vive voix :

— SOLDATS DE L'ESCADRE ! JE VOUS APPORTE VENGEANCE !

Faustin repéra alors la petite brindille de peur et de chagrin perdue parmi les âmes enragées.

Alicia Routh.

Sans perdre un instant, il arrima sa conscience à la sienne, perçut aussitôt cet esprit empreint de douceur et de mélancolie, une femme délicate trop vite arrachée à la terre des mortels.

« What… who… »

« *Je me nomme Faustin, miss Routh. Je suis venu quérir votre aide.* »

Tout autour, la tempête s'amenuisa sans pour autant s'éteindre. Ils attendaient. Tous autant qu'ils étaient, les trépassés de l'escadre attendaient la suite des choses.

« Les flots sont si froids, milord. »

« Je n'en doute guère, miss Routh. »

« Pourquoi m'avoir éveillée ? Comment ? Ai-je dormi ? »

« Oui… on peut dire ça… »

Un oisillon. Alicia Routh était une petite chose fragile et innocente.

« Je suis venu quérir la présence de votre fiancé, miss Routh. »

« Hovenden ? Mais… »

La puissance de l'assaut frappa Faustin de plein fouet, si durement qu'il s'effondra sur le sol et faillit échapper son emprise sur Alicia Routh.

Lion rugissant, l'amiral Hovenden Walker se tenait devant Faustin, courroucé de voir troublé l'éternel repos de sa fiancée.

Un moment, le jeune homme fut décontenancé. Ce n'était pas l'extraordinaire chef de guerre qu'il s'était imaginé, au port altier plein de prestance, au caractère forgé dans les flammes du combat, un homme de fer à la poigne puissante. L'homme qui venait de se manifester par-delà la mort était un être hésitant et instable, à la personnalité pleine de doute… bien que fou d'un amour inconditionnel et protecteur, prêt à tout pour défendre sa fiancée.

Un être infiniment plus dangereux qu'un officier à l'âme d'acier.

Tout près, l'armée des âmes haineuses n'attendait que le signal de son officier pour donner libre cours à sa rage.

« Amiral Walker… commença Faustin en se relevant, *je suis venu offrir à votre promise le repos éternel, et à vos hommes la vengeance qu'ils méritent. »*

Ces mots déstabilisèrent Walker.

Faustin raffermit son emprise sur miss Routh au moment où l'amiral disait :

« *Je vous écoute, sorcier. Souhaitez-vous nous offrir une nouvelle chance de prendre la colonie de Nouvelle-France ?* »

« *Québec est tombée il y a presque cent ans, amiral. La Nouvelle-France a été conquise et la colonie est devenue anglaise.* »

L'équivalent psychique d'un cri de joie retentit parmi les soldats défunts et Faustin serra les dents d'amertume – l'heure n'était guère au patriotisme.

« *Quelle vengeance nous offrez-vous alors, sorcier ?* reprit Walker, radouci par la déclaration. *Qu'attendez-vous de moi et de mes hommes, qui mérite que vous troubliez la quiétude de ma douce fiancée ?* »

Retrouvant davantage de contenance à chaque instant, Faustin déclara solennellement :

« *Le sorcier responsable de votre naufrage, celui qui a invoqué le brouillard, est revenu d'entre les morts.* »

Un cri unique, émis par les huit cents âmes réunies, ébranla les sens spirites de Faustin comme un séisme.

« *Lavallée !* »

« *Oui. Jean-Pierre Lavallée foule à nouveau la terre des mortels, et il s'est joint à une armée qui veut arracher Québec à la couronne britannique.* »

Un second séisme spirituel secoua Faustin.

« *Amiral Walker, entendez-moi : je donnerai corps à vos hommes par-delà la mort*, reprit-il rapidement. *Portez-moi jusqu'à l'île d'Orléans et combattez à mes côtés contre les troupes de Lavallée. J'offrirai à votre armée une seconde chance, comme nul soldat n'en eut jamais, mais j'apaiserai d'abord, pour vous prouver ma bonne foi, les tourments de votre promise en la libérant de l'entrave qui la lie aux flots glacés du golfe.* »

Sans attendre un instant, Faustin obligea l'âme asservie d'Alicia Routh à s'approcher du diagramme.

— *Ashek dar-nìran, ashek sader, ibn lamed dahir ibn kalimar,* déclama-t-il.

À l'outrevision, le pentacle s'embrasa d'une vive lueur d'argent qui crépita comme un énorme brasier. Alicia Routh, forcée de le traverser, apparut aux yeux de Faustin.

Elle avait le même genre de corps que celui de la Dame aux Glaïeuls, vaporeux et pourtant tangible. C'était une femme très jeune, de quinze ans tout au plus, aux longs cheveux roux tirant sur le vermillon. Son minois, fort délicat, portait des éphélides discrètes sur les joues. Ses grands yeux larmoyants, d'un vert pailleté d'or, s'agrandirent alors qu'elle regardait tout autour d'elle.

Faustin raffermit son emprise et cria à vive voix :

— Alors Walker ? Me suivrez-vous ? Permettrez-vous à vos hommes de trouver une fin honorable, combattrez-vous avec moi le démon responsable de votre éternel tourment ?

Une décharge d'énergie draina un peu des forces vives de Faustin et une nouvelle silhouette se matérialisa pour se jeter dans les bras d'Alicia Routh. L'homme, petit et émacié, portait le manteau long des officiers anglais et, sous son tricorne, la perruque blanche du siècle précédent.

Après de longues embrassades, Walker se tourna vers Faustin, et c'est avec un regard d'acier qu'il déclara :

— Mes hommes sont dorénavant à votre service, sorcier.

Une nouvelle décharge d'énergie ébranla Faustin. Puis une seconde, une troisième, une dixième, une cinquantième…

Un à un, les soldats de Walker traversaient le pentacle arcanique pour prendre corps sur les rivages de l'île aux Œufs.

Faustin s'effondra sur le sol tant le phénomène lui soutirait d'énergie vitale. Il sentait l'impact du sortilège répété des centaines de fois lui labourer les entrailles. Son cœur s'affola bientôt, sa respiration devint sifflante. Les années qu'il avait en surplus fondirent à vue d'œil. Non seulement le contrecoup le faisait vieillir, mais il commença à entamer ses nouvelles années en réserve.

À travers le brouillard qui s'épaississait, Faustin vit une nappe de brume se densifier, se sculpter et prendre la forme d'un imposant trois-mâts.

Quand le dernier soldat se fut incarné, il put enfin se relever, mais il n'eut qu'un bref instant pour jeter un œil à ses mains, désormais celles d'un homme mûr.

Devant lui mouillait un bâtiment de guerre très semblable à une corvette, constitué de la même matière vaporeuse que les corps des soldats de Walker, des fusiliers du Chien d'Or ou des marsouins de Rivière-Ouelle.

L'un des soldats spectraux portant une caisse claire se mit à frapper un rythme répétitif, deux coups lents, trois coups vifs. En suivant la cadence, les fantômes des soldats montèrent à bord en rangs exemplaires. Au-dessus d'eux, les voiles s'étaient gonflées. Le long des haubans de hune crépitaient de petites étincelles couleur d'améthyste rappelant des feux follets. Elles s'animèrent progressivement et leur éclat culmina en atteignant les extrémités des mâts du navire, auréolant d'une lueur violacée le navire de brume.

Derrière lui, Faustin entendit la voix de l'amiral Walker, resté auprès d'Alicia Routh.

— Mes hommes ont suscité le feu de Saint-Elme. Le navire est paré à faire voile. Mettrons-nous tout de suite le cap vers Québec ?

Ébahi par le tableau grandiose qui se dévoilait à lui, Faustin mit un instant à répondre.

— Nous accosterons d'abord à l'Isle-aux-Grues, finit-il par déclarer. Je vous indiquerai les lieux quand nous approcherons.

Le spectre de Walker hocha la tête, puis invita d'un geste Faustin à gravir la rampe menant au pont. Intimant à miss Routh de le suivre, le jeune homme se rendit au vaisseau.

Posant le pied sur le plan incliné, Faustin constata qu'il s'enfonçait légèrement dans la matière brumeuse composant le trois-mâts avant de sentir une résistance. Comme dans un rêve, il monta la rampe, prit place à la proue, Alicia Routh à ses côtés, tout comme l'amiral. Une sorte de torpeur se saisit de lui, semblable à celle qu'il avait ressentie en chevauchant un marsouin de Rivière-Ouelle, mais cette fois-ci il resta pleinement conscient.

Les feux de Saint-Elme crépitèrent, nimbant la totalité du navire de leur luisance violâtre, la rampe s'estompa dans le brouillard et le trois-mâts s'élança sur les flots, glissant dans le silence le plus complet… et sans produire la moindre ride sur l'eau.

◆

Le temps devint une chose très relative pour Faustin.

Il n'aurait pu dire depuis combien de temps il faisait voile sur les eaux du fleuve. Peut-être depuis une heure, peut-être depuis un jour. Peut-être aussi avait-il rejoint l'équipage de l'escadre dans ses immortels tourments et naviguait-il depuis des siècles.

Autour de lui, les soldats spectraux gardaient la même immobilité que celle qu'ils avaient adoptée à leur embarquement. Alicia Routh se tenait au bras de l'amiral

et le couple semblait destiné à demeurer figé jusqu'à la fin des temps. Un épais brouillard enveloppait le navire de sorte que personne, de la rive, n'aurait pu ne serait-ce que les entrevoir.

« *Vous vous êtes égaré, Spirite* », fit une voix dans la tête de Faustin.

« *Plaçoa ?* »

« *Vous êtes perdu dans l'éternité. Aucun mortel ne peut rester ainsi dans l'outremonde sans être guidé. Soyez heureux que je vous aie perçu à temps.* »

Des formes fuselées se mirent à bondir à bâbord comme à tribord du navire : les marsouins de Rivière-Ouelle venaient de les rejoindre et semblaient les escorter.

« *Où sommes-nous, Plaçoa ?* »

« *À une époque proche de celle où vous vous êtes égaré. Moins d'un jour s'est écoulé.* »

Faustin en fut soulagé, mais redemanda :

« *Je pensais au sens géographique du terme.* »

« *Là où vous voguez, il n'y a pas de géographie, Spirite.* »

Autour de lui, Faustin voyait pourtant les soldats spectraux s'agiter, tirer des cordages, carguer une voile.

« *Je ne comprends pas ce que…* »

« *Quelle est votre destination ?* » le coupa Plaçoa.

« *L'Isle-aux-Grues, comme la dernière fois.* »

« *Mes frères vont vous y amener, tout en maintenant votre assise dans le temps des mortels. Et n'oubliez pas de me contacter lorsque vous remonterez sur ce navire, Spirite. Vous n'avez pas l'expérience pour le gouverner sans aide.* »

Les marsouins formèrent un cercle autour du navire et, quelques minutes plus tard, celui-ci décéléra et s'arrêta. Une volute de brume se densifia pour former une rampe de débarquement. Faustin s'y engagea et il

eut la surprise de voir devant lui ses amis rassemblés sur la berge de l'Isle-aux-Grues.

Si tous semblaient aussi abasourdis que lui, ce n'était pas en raison du vaisseau spectral, à peine visible dans son écrin de brume. Après un instant d'hésitation, ce fut le père Masse qui s'adressa le premier à Faustin :

— Mon pauvre garçon, l'épreuve a été bien éprouvante pour toi.

— Batêche, Faustin, t'as l'air d'avoir fin quarantaine, enchérit Baptiste.

Ces propos n'ébranlèrent pas Faustin ; il avait déjà fait le point sur ce que lui avait coûté sa téléportation. Il déclara :

— Mes amis, j'ai ramené l'armée proposée par la Dame. Je porte le Fléau d'Albion et le Grimoire du Chien d'Or. Puisse le règne de l'Étranger s'achever !

Il regarda pensivement les mines atterrées de ses amis avant d'ajouter :

— Le reste m'importe peu.

— Nous aussi, dit alors Shaor'i, nous avons rassemblé nos forces.

Sur la plage de rochers moussus, une vingtaine de *maymaygwashi* armés d'épieux inclinèrent la tête.

— Ce sont les derniers guerriers de leur peuple, expliqua-t-elle. Ils sont là pour exterminer Kabir Kouba.

Faustin eut un mouvement de recul.

— S'ils sont les derniers, ils n'ont rien à faire ici. Qu'ils retournent auprès des leurs afin d'assurer la pérennité de leur race !

Baptiste et Shaor'i s'entreregardèrent.

— Tu peux laisser c'te navire-là sans surveillance, garçon ?

— Je crois…

— Parce qu'il faut qu'tu viennes avec nous.

Bandant sa volonté, Faustin força la fiancée de l'amiral à descendre sur la berge.

— Voici miss Alicia Routh, présenta-t-il en se tournant vers la jeune femme défunte. Miss Routh, poursuivit-il, je vous interdis de quitter cette plage, est-ce bien compris?

La fille répondit d'un hochement de tête accompagné d'une parfaite révérence. Faustin se tourna alors vers le vaisseau spectral et lança:

— Quant à vous, capitaine Walker, je vous interdis de quitter le navire. Même chose pour vos hommes!

Un bruit inquiétant monta du vaisseau, mais Faustin, n'en tenant pas compte, reporta son attention sur ses compagnons.

— L'amiral ne s'en ira pas sans elle, expliqua-t-il.

Les compagnons restèrent silencieux un moment, puis Shaor'i dit:

— C'est toi le spirite. Maintenant vous m'accompagnez, toi et Baptiste.

Jetant un regard au père Masse, qui l'encouragea d'un geste à accepter l'offre de l'Indienne, Faustin emboîta le pas de ses amis.

◆

Ils suivaient un sentier serpentant à travers les arbres de la pinède. Shaor'i avançait d'un bon pas, comme si elle cherchait à garder une certaine distance entre elle et ceux qui la suivaient. Ce qui n'empêchait pas Faustin d'exprimer ses pensées à l'Indienne:

— Il faut que tu leur parles, Shaor'i. En te servant des *komkwejwika'sikl*, explique-leur qu'ils doivent repartir chez eux, au lac Supérieur. Tu as affirmé que leur nombre déclinait, ils ne peuvent tout de même pas affronter Kabir Kouba!

La jeune femme resta muette. Faustin insista :

— Shaor'i… nous sommes capables de l'affronter nous-mêmes ! À bord du trois-mâts de Walker, le monstre ne pourra rien contre nous. Nous le détruirons à l'aide d'un enchantement…

L'Indienne n'ouvrait toujours pas la bouche et Faustin échappa un grognement de frustration.

— J'te comprends, garçon, avoua Baptiste en lui posant la main sur l'épaule.

— Tu vois ? Même Baptiste pense…

— Hola ! Prends l'temps d'm'écouter, Faustin. C'est vrai, pas plus tard qu'hier, j'voulais que Ti-Jean s'en aille. Qui soit pas exposé à c'te combat-là. Y a des enchantements, m'avait dit la P'tite, qui pouvaient me permettre de retrouver ma vision le temps d'une bataille. J'avais dit à Ti-Jean qu'sa place, c'tait avec les lutins du grand tunnel, dans la vallée du Saint-Maurice ousqu'on est déjà allés. Sa race s'éteint, c'est comme qui dirait son devoir de s'trouver une blonde. Pis fallait aller porter la poudre des os des membres de sa tribu, pour saupoudrer les bébés, comme la P'tite nous l'avait déjà expliqué.

Faustin hocha la tête. La réflexion qu'exprimait son ami suivait exactement sa propre ligne de pensée. Pourtant, Ti-Jean était toujours sur l'épaule de Baptiste.

— C'est surtout ça qui a décidé Ti-Jean, poursuivait le colosse, le saupoudrage des bébés. Y'est parti avec deux sirènes – j'veux dire des *maymaygwashi*.

Devant eux, Shaor'i s'était arrêtée sur un petit promontoire rocheux et les attendait. L'affleurement de granit était plutôt escarpé et Faustin dut prendre son temps pour monter pendant que le bûcheron continuait son récit :

— Pis Ti-Jean, y'a rencontré les lutins du grand tunnel. Y leur a parlé de c'qui s'était passé, d'la

transformation de sa tribu à lui, les lutins des cavernes des Hauts. Y'a parlé aux mâles qui dirigent les chasses, aux femelles sages-femmes pis, surtout, à l'Aîné, celui qui décide des choses importantes...

D'entre les fougères surgit un *mah oumet* un peu plus grand et massif que les autres, portant sur son dos un lutin plus petit. Ce dernier, très âgé à en juger par ses traits, avait un pelage ayant pris une teinte ivoirine sur le devant alors que son dos arborait une fourrure gris argenté. Posé sur le sol avec grand égard par son porteur, le vieux *mah oumet* s'inclina devant Faustin.

Le jeune homme esquissa un signe de tête respectueux, comme s'il se trouvait devant un curé. Alors qu'il commençait à entrevoir ce à quoi Baptiste le préparait, Faustin arrivait au sommet du promontoire et ce qu'il aperçut au loin le pétrifia de stupeur.

Ils étaient des centaines.

Des centaines de singes albinos couvraient le sol de la grande clairière, les branches des arbres avoisinants et les rochers les plus massifs. Babillant dans leur langue à clics, ils s'affairaient à fouiller le sol pour trouver des cailloux qu'ils taillaient.

Qu'ils affûtaient.

Faustin avait déjà vu un lutin procéder à ce travail et comprenait sans mal ce que cela signifiait : dans cette clairière, les *mah oumet* se fabriquaient des armes.

Baptiste le rejoignit.

— Y sont venus, Faustin. Tous les lutins du grand tunnel. Y sont là pour se battre avec nous autres, pour venger la mort de la tribu à Ti-Jean.

Horrifié, Faustin sentit ses jambes se dérober sous lui. Il s'agrippa à un jeune tronc pour éviter de tomber et bafouilla :

— Il faut... qu'ils repartent... ils ne peuvent pas...

Shaor'i se tourna vers lui, les yeux humides.

— Ils ne le feront pas. De toute façon, il est trop tard. Ils ont mis fin à leur Chant.

D'un geste de la tête, Faustin manifesta son incompréhension.

— Te souviens-tu, reprit-elle, lorsque nous sommes passés par leur tunnel, de ce ronronnement très grave, lent et rythmique, qui se réverbérait sur la voûte?

— Oui, bien sûr. Tu prétendais qu'ils chantaient leur mythe créateur.

— Depuis des générations, ils se relayaient pour le perpétuer sans relâche. S'ils ont cessé le Chant, ça signifie qu'ils ne peuvent plus retourner là-bas. Il leur faudra trouver une autre demeure.

— Quoi? Mais...

— Ce sont leurs croyances, Faustin. Tu n'as pas à les juger.

— Là n'est pas la question! cria le jeune homme. Ils ne peuvent pas se battre avec nous! Ils vont tous mourir...

Baptiste l'interrompit.

— Y vont déjà toute mourir, Faustin. De suite ou plus tard, quelle différence ça fait? C'est ça qu'y ont pensé, après avoir écouté Ti-Jean.

Outré par les propos de Baptiste, Faustin recula lentement. Malgré lui, il croisa le regard de l'Aîné des *mah oumet*, deux yeux rougeâtres à la fois résolus et brillant de larmes.

Quelque chose se brisa en Faustin.

Adoptant sa forme de renard, il détala en vitesse.

◆

Le renard courait à travers les arbres, les champs et les fourrés. Il avait traversé la pinède, le village et

ses terres. Il courait à présent sur les battures situées à l'extrémité orientale de l'île.

Encore une fois, la voix de la *man'ido* se manifesta dans sa tête.

« *Tsintnn't arwn, geskn'htr…* »

Exaspéré, Faustin reprit forme humaine et se redressa pour crier :

— Allez-vous me laisser tranquille ? Je ne comprends rien à ce que vous me dites !

À peine perçut-il le changement dans l'air qu'une main lui attrapa le bras. Sans se retourner, il comprit que Shaor'i l'avait suivi en vol et retrouvé.

— Que signifie cette fuite ? gronda-t-elle dans son dos.

Irrité, Faustin tenta de se dégager de la poigne de la guerrière et, s'en voyant incapable, fit volte-face pour lancer :

— Que signifie leur arrivée, tu veux dire ! Qu'est-ce qu'ils espèrent de moi, maudit calvaire ?

— Tu parles des *mah oumet* ?

— De qui d'autre ?

— Ils n'espèrent rien du tout, voyons, répondit l'Indienne, les traits chargés d'incompréhension.

— Je ne peux pas les sauver, bon sang ! Même s'ils m'aident à affronter l'Étranger, je ne pourrai rien tenter pour eux en retour…

— Crois-moi, ils le savent…

— Alors pourquoi sont-ils venus ?

La jeune femme recula comme s'il l'avait frappée. Stupéfaite, elle le dévisagea et murmura doucement :

— Mais… parce qu'ils croient en toi…

— Je viens de dire que je ne peux pas !

— … et pour que tu donnes un sens à leur disparition.

Ahuri, Faustin ne parvint qu'à bafouiller.

— Quoi ?

La gifle fusa si vite qu'il ne put l'esquiver, pas plus que le coup de pied qui le frappa au plexus et l'envoya au sol pendant qu'il cherchait son air.

— Tu n'es qu'un pauvre imbécile ! cria l'Indienne. Tu ne vois pas que, sans toi, il ne leur reste plus qu'à attendre passivement l'extinction de leur espèce, au fur et à mesure que les grands pins seront abattus, sachant qu'il est déjà trop tard pour eux, que même en migrant ils ne seront plus jamais assez nombreux ?...

Mâchoire serrée pour empêcher son menton de trembler, la jeune femme tenta de retenir ses larmes.

— Mais grâce à toi, reprit-elle, leur disparition aura un sens, une raison d'être... Et c'est pareil pour les *maymaygwashi* dont la race se meurt aussi, victime des fusils des pelletiers qui les confondent avec des loutres...

Doucement, Faustin se releva en restant à prudente distance de l'Indienne qui avait commencé à sangloter tout en parlant.

— Comme ces soldats défunts que tu as ramenés... Grâce à toi, ils ne seront pas morts en vain, stupidement coulés au fond des eaux sans même livrer bataille, mais pour être ressuscités le temps d'un combat infiniment plus important que la conquête d'une cité !

Ses sanglots devinrent plus bruyants, ses paroles plus hachées.

— Et tous ces gens de ton village... et Otjiera... ils ne seront plus morts pour rien...

Faustin fit deux pas en avant.

— ... et même la disparition des arcanes... tu donnes un sens à ça en t'opposant à l'Étranger...

Shaor'i renifla, s'avança elle aussi.

— ... et même à ma vie, couina-t-elle faiblement. À quoi veux-tu que je serve, maintenant qu'Otjiera n'est plus, que les Danseurs n'existent plus ? Ne vois-tu pas que tu donnes un sens au sacrifice que je suis prête à accepter ?

Elle ne cherchait plus à retenir ses pleurs et Faustin, tout près d'elle, ne se retint pas pour la serrer dans ses bras. Il pressa doucement la jeune femme contre sa poitrine, laissant le chagrin se déverser, puis s'apaiser.

Quand il fut certain que les larmes ne coulaient plus, il demanda :

— Et toi, Shaor'i, donnerais-tu un sens à ma vie ?

L'Indienne s'écarta silencieusement de Faustin. Il reprit :

— Quand tout ça sera terminé, Shaor'i... si nous nous en sortons tous les deux indemnes... pas tout de suite, mais quelques mois plus tard, disons en hiver...

Méfiante, la jeune femme lui jeta un regard oblique. Faustin inspira profondément.

— Cet hiver, disons quelques semaines après le jour de l'An... ferais-tu une promenade sous la neige avec moi, dans les rues de Québec ?

Le silence tomba comme une pierre dans l'eau. Sans émettre le moindre son, Shaor'i planta ses yeux dorés dans ceux de Faustin.

— Tu veux dire... une promenade... dans le sens où je marcherais à ton bras, c'est ça ?

— Tu ne serais pas obligée de me tenir le bras... répondit Faustin en tournant les yeux vers le sol.

— Tu ne réalises pas ce que tu...

— Au contraire.

La jeune femme soupira. Ses yeux fixes se voilèrent d'une infinie tristesse.

— Mon ami... je ne pourrai jamais te porter *ce genre* d'intérêt. Jamais.

— Je sais, répondit Faustin avec un sourire. Ce n'est pas à ça que je pense. Mais quand tout sera terminé et que je serai seul à me souvenir des arcanes, prisonnier d'une longévité qui m'empêchera de m'établir dans un village sans attirer l'attention... que je devrai mener une vie nomade... à ce moment-là, la solitude me pèsera bien

lourdement. Et toi, où iras-tu ? Chez ces Indiens qui ne parlent plus leur langue, qui ont oublié leurs coutumes ?

Comme Shaor'i ne répondait pas, il laissa son regard se perdre dans les eaux du fleuve.

— Je ne pense pas à fonder un foyer. Je ne veux pas d'enfants qui hériteront de ma longévité et… moi non plus, je ne peux pas te porter *ce genre* d'intérêt. Pas après tout ce que nous avons vécu ensemble.

Faustin effleura la main de son amie et, comme elle ne se dérobait pas au contact, il la prit doucement dans la sienne.

— Quand tout sera terminé, nous vivrons dans un monde où nous n'aurons plus notre place. Nous serons des vestiges vivants d'une époque révolue et…

— N'ajoute rien, mon ami, le coupa Shaor'i, de nouvelles larmes coulant sur ses joues. J'ai compris.

La jeune femme serra un peu plus fort la main de Faustin, avant de déclarer :

— C'est d'accord. L'hiver prochain, sous la neige, je marcherai à ton bras.

Sans la moindre pudeur, Shaor'i se blottit de nouveau contre Faustin qui, laissant aller une larme, posa un chaste baiser sur la pâle chevelure.

Avant de refermer ses bras sur sa petite sœur.

◆

À la demande de Shaor'i, il avait accepté de tenir un conseil de guerre.

Ses compagnons n'avaient pas chômé pendant son absence. L'Indienne avait même couru le risque d'effectuer un vol de reconnaissance au-dessus de l'île d'Orléans.

Ainsi, dans l'abri-épave, Faustin écoutait le rapport de l'Indienne à la lueur pâlotte d'un fanal, en compagnie de Baptiste, de Ti-Jean et du père Masse.

— En vol, l'île d'Orléans ressemble à peu près à ça, expliquait-elle en se servant d'un bout de fusain prêté par le père Masse pour illustrer ses propos. L'église de Saint-Laurent est environ ici. Il y a une pente abrupte ici et la forêt commence là.

Alors qu'elle dessinait, Faustin se remémorait son passage sur l'île, six mois auparavant. Ce qu'exposait l'Indienne était conforme à son souvenir. Elle continua en esquissant, sur une autre feuille de papier, un plan à plus petite échelle où l'on voyait bien la forme de l'église.

— Il y a des *mestabeok* ici... et ici... expliqua-t-elle en traçant de petits X devant les portes de l'église. J'en ai compté sept, mais j'ignore s'il y en a davantage.

— Je ne pense pas, intervint Faustin. Dans les souterrains, je n'ai vu que huit sarcophages de stase temporelle aux proportions des *mestabeok* et nous en avons déjà tué un dans la chapelle ensevelie.

— Donc, ils sont sept. Ils doivent former la garde rapprochée de l'Étranger. En affronter un seul a déjà été difficile, alors j'imagine mal comment faire face à cette troupe de géants.

— Nous avons les soldats de Walker pour ça, commenta Faustin.

— Pis les lutins, ajouta Baptiste.

— De combien d'hommes disposes-tu, Faustin ? demanda le père Masse.

— Plus ou moins huit cents.

Baptiste laissa échapper un sifflement.

— Pas si vite, coupa Shaor'i. Les *bakaak* sont plus de deux mille.

Le silence tomba sur le conseil de guerre pendant un long moment, jusqu'à ce que demande le père Masse :

— Comment Hohenstaufen parvient-il à tenir la population aussi éloignée de l'église ? Ça n'a aucun

sens! Ce devrait être le bâtiment le plus achalandé de la paroisse, mis à part son magasin général.

— Il y a un cercle de répulsion, expliqua Shaor'i, que l'on peut voir à l'outrevision. Le même qu'il y avait aux Vieilles Forges. Les gens n'ont pas envie d'y aller et les chevaux s'y refusent. Ce ne peut qu'être temporaire, bien sûr…

— … jusqu'à ce qu'il amène ses troupes aux ruines du château Bigot, supposa Faustin.

— Ce qu'il ne pouvait faire tant que Caroline de Saint-Castin gardait les lieux, précisa Masse.

— Le gros des *bakaak* a été levé il y a quelques jours, à Grosse-Île. C'était un lundi. Ils n'auront pas le choix de les faire traverser avant dimanche, alors que tous les paroissiens risquent de remarquer que quelque chose ne va pas avec leur église.

— Pis on est quel jour, déjà? demanda Baptiste.

— S'il est passé minuit, nous sommes vendredi.

Un autre silence tomba avant que Shaor'i reprenne:

— Le mieux serait d'arriver par la rive sud de l'île. L'église de Saint-Laurent sera toute proche. Les *mah oumet* n'accepteront pas de monter sur le navire fantôme et c'est pourquoi, avant ton arrivée et sous le conseil du père Masse, nous avons loué au batelier la goélette que nous avons utilisée l'autre jour.

— En fait, y préférait ça à nous mener dans une autre place pas catholique, s'amusa Baptiste.

— Et nous la piloterons comment? demanda Faustin.

— Il y a un enchantement pour ça, affirma le père Masse, et je m'en souviens très bien. C'est toi qui devras le lancer, mais par la suite je pourrai m'occuper de la navigation, ce qui ne m'occasionnera que des contrecoups minimes.

— En chemin, continua la jeune femme, nous devrons peut-être de nouveau faire face aux tempêtes magiques de Lavallée ou à Kabir Kouba.

— Pour ça, les *maymaygwashi* sont là, décréta le père Masse.

— Soit. Une fois à terre, il nous faudra éliminer les *bakaak,* qui sont deux fois plus nombreux que nous, remonter une longue pente abrupte sous les assauts des *mestabeok* et, une fois sur place, affronter l'Étranger.

— S'il est là, commenta Faustin.

— Il y est, confirma Shaor'i. Du moins, il y était lorsque j'ai survolé la zone.

— Il nous faudra ensuite disposer du temps nécessaire pour incanter le contre-sort de longévité, ajouta le prêtre. Il va sans dire que je ne l'ai jamais testé et que je suis trop vieux pour en assumer le contrecoup. Même mon sacrifice serait vain, car il empêcherait le sort d'être parachevé.

— Je devrai donc l'apprendre? s'inquiéta Faustin.

— Si nous avions une année pour te former en véritable arcaniste, peut-être. Mais à ce que tu m'as décrit de tes performances, même toutes les années de crédit héritées de Hohenstaufen ne suffiraient peut-être pas à assumer l'impact d'un sort d'une telle puissance si l'incantation est bâclée.

— Mais dans ce cas…

— Mon plan consiste à utiliser le bâton du Fort pour puiser à même ta source.

Faustin dévisagea le vieux prêtre.

— Vous plaisantez? Pas que je refuse, mais le sceptre est en possession de Lavallée.

— Alors nous le lui arracherons.

Se prenant la tête entre les mains, le jeune homme s'abstint de commenter, mais son attitude en disait long.

— Et en passant, continua le père Masse, j'éviterais de laisser l'amiral Walker prendre la moindre initiative: c'est l'un des pires commandants et stratèges de l'Histoire. Tu voyageras donc sur le navire fantôme afin de lui dicter ses moindres mouvements.

— Moi ?

— Tu ne peux pas être pire que Walker, crois-moi...
avant de se lancer contre Québec, il avait négligé les
problèmes de logistique, n'avait pas déniché de main-
d'œuvre, n'avait pas fait le plein de munitions... et je
ne te parle même pas de ses échecs dans les Antilles,
des années auparavant !

— Ça ira, père Masse... le moins j'en saurai...

— Et autre chose : il faudra que tu ordonnes à tes
spectres de nettoyer le champ de bataille après ta victoire – tu imagines la réaction des paroissiens s'ils
découvraient, juste avant la messe de dimanche, des
milliers de cadavres de *bakaak* ?

Faustin soupira. Cela semblait tout simplement perdu
d'avance.

Et pourtant...

... *ne peux-tu voir qu'il a peur de toi ?* avait dit
Shaor'i.

— D'autres questions ? demanda l'Indienne.

Des tonnes, se retint de répondre Faustin, jugeant
que ce serait en vain. Il secoua plutôt la tête, résuma
le plan de bataille dans ses propres mots, puis trouva
un prétexte pour s'isoler dans la pièce de l'abri-épave
que lui avait prêtée le père Masse.

*Dans quelques heures, nous serons peut-être tous
morts*, pensa-t-il en refermant la porte.

◆

Afin d'être certain d'avoir assez de lumière, il avait
allumé une grosse poignée de chandelles – à un tel
point que, mêlée à la moiteur de la fin d'été, la chaleur
des flammes faisait perler la sueur sur son front.

Isolé dans la petite pièce, Faustin avait ouvert l'un
de ses manuels arcaniques avant de se saisir, résolu,

d'un petit couteau. Malgré lui, il grognait de douleur à chaque nouvelle incision.

Merde, comment François parvenait-il à endurer ça ? Le couteau pénétra sa chair et compléta l'apothème. Posant la lame, Faustin vérifia l'angle à l'aide de son rapporteur.

Une voix brisa le silence :

— Tu peux m'expliquer ce que tu fais, jeune homme ? demanda le père Masse, furtivement entré dans la pièce.

— Merci d'avoir attendu que je pose la lame.

Masse tira à lui une caisse de bois et s'en servit comme siège.

— Question de bon sens. Et alors, que signifient ces mutilations ?

Le jeune homme se tourna vers le prêtre pour expliquer :

— À l'origine, c'est une idée de ma mère durant les feux de l'île d'Orléans : scarifier un diagramme dans sa chair pour éviter que l'Étranger ne puisse l'effacer.

— Draconien mais astucieux, je l'avoue.

— François avait récupéré l'idée pour avoir nombre de diagrammes déjà tracés.

— … et dans la situation actuelle, ça t'a semblé…

— … une précaution nécessaire.

Hochant la tête d'une manière qui ne semblait ni approuver ni réprouver la méthode, le père Masse se leva, fit quelques pas et posa le regard sur le damier que Faustin avait installé non loin.

— Tu m'avais pourtant semblé un habile joueur de dames, l'autre soir.

— Je me plais à croire que je le suis, marmonna le jeune homme en épongeant le sang qui coulait de son bras.

— Deux rangées de rouges à chaque extrémité du damier, et toutes les noires au centre… Je ne crois pas que cette configuration soit possible.

Faustin inspecta son avant-bras d'un œil critique, serra les dents en creusant une ultime incision, puis se tourna vers le petit prêtre pour expliquer :

— C'est pourtant notre plan de bataille. Peu importe de quelle façon je retourne la chose dans ma tête, ça me semble la seule solution : nous attaquerons sur deux fronts.

— Et sur quel front te battras-tu, Faustin ?

— Les deux, répondit le jeune homme avec un sourire en coin.

— Il faudra en discuter avec tes amis…

Au-dehors, le ciel gronda. Le père Masse grimaça de douleur en faisant craquer ses jointures.

— Il pleuvra demain. Ça se sent dans l'air autant que dans mes rhumatismes. Allez, mon garçon. Termine ce que tu as commencé. J'ai des choses à régler pour demain, moi aussi.

Emportant l'une des chandelles avec lui, le prêtre quitta la pièce, laissant Faustin vérifier une fois de plus si le pentacle qu'il avait gravé dans sa chair était irréprochable.

◆

Lorsqu'il avait expliqué son idée à Shaor'i et à Baptiste, ses amis l'avaient longuement dévisagé. Si attaquer l'église de Saint-Laurent sur deux fronts ne semblait pas une si mauvaise stratégie – l'Indienne précisa que l'histoire orale des Micmacs gardait souvenir de nombreuses batailles gagnées de cette manière –, il fallut à Faustin un bon moment pour expliquer de quelle façon il comptait être présent sur ces deux fronts successivement.

Shaor'i avait objecté de nombreux contre-arguments mais Faustin, persuadé qu'il entrevoyait la meilleure méthode possible, réussit à convaincre la jeune femme.

Ainsi, il parvint à exiger d'être laissé seul sur la goélette qu'ils avaient louée. Le navire mouillait près de l'abri-épave et Faustin, portant avec lui le Grimoire du Chien d'Or et le livre de Le Loyer, monta à bord pour s'occuper des ultimes préparatifs.

S'assurant d'abord que le père Masse pourrait piloter le navire, Faustin utilisa le ciseau à bois prêté par le prêtre pour reproduire les diagrammes de navigation sur la proue, la poupe et le mât. Il ensorcela également la coque afin de la rendre plus résistante aux chocs – le souvenir des assauts de Kabir Kouba était encore vivace.

Ces sortilèges implantés, il s'isola dans la cabine où il entreprit de sculpter des pentacles beaucoup plus complexes dont il vérifia les mesures à de nombreuses reprises. Quand il fut certain de l'exactitude de chaque angle, il s'allongea et incanta.

La sombre cabine s'illumina d'une vive lueur émanant des diagrammes.

Faustin s'autorisa un sourire de satisfaction.

Bien qu'il ne fût qu'un arcaniste novice, tout semblait fonctionner tel qu'il l'avait escompté.

◆

Lorsqu'il ressortit de la cabine, près de trois heures plus tard, ce fut pour découvrir que son armée était prête.

Les *maymaygwashi* avaient décoré leurs épieux de plumes de grues. Assis en rond sur la grève avec le père Masse, ils avaient posé un bout de bois sur le sol pour figurer Kabir Kouba et tracé dans le sable les trajectoires qu'il conviendrait de prendre à la nage selon telle ou telle situation.

Walker et ses soldats spectraux étaient toujours à bord de leur navire fantôme, et seule sa promise, Alicia Routh, était visible sur la plage. Debout sur un rocher, elle

contemplait le soleil qui achevait de se coucher. Dans quelques heures, quoi qu'il arrive, elle rejoindrait pour l'éternité son amoureux.

Et puis il y avait les *mah oumet*. À sa grande surprise, les paisibles lutins du grand tunnel s'étaient mués en une légion de redoutables guerriers, ayant chassé les lucioles des environs pour se barioler de leur fluide luminescent à la manière de peintures de guerre.

Restée avec les *mah oumet*, Shaor'i s'était elle aussi préparée pour la bataille. Crâne rasé à l'exception d'une longue queue-de-cheval blanche où elle avait piqué des plumes de grue, son visage était paré de peintures guerrières noires : de petits points sur son front évoquant les taches d'un harfang et des traits horizontaux sous ses yeux. Son dos portait un carquois et un arc ramassé sur un *bakaak*. Chacune de ses cuisses était ceinte d'une lanière de cuir retenant les étuis de couteaux supplémentaires – ceux de Nadjaw, lui révéla-t-elle, qu'elle avait juré de n'utiliser que pour affronter l'Étranger, et ceux de Caroline de Saint-Castin, qu'elle avait récupérés dans les ruines du château Bigot. Quant à la hachette d'Otjiera, elle la gardait coincée entre son dos et sa ceinture.

Elle avait choisi de se départir de ses bottes et ses pieds-serres étaient visibles, trois longs orteils à l'avant et un autre au lieu du talon. À la place des ongles, elle avait désormais de longues griffes noires, vicieusement recourbées.

— Nous sommes prêts, Faustin, déclara-t-elle sans ambages.

— Donc je le suis, répondit le jeune homme. Si des puissances favorables nous écoutent, puissent-elles veiller sur nous.

« *D'ettng, gesznay* », fit dans son esprit la voix de la *man'ido*.

— Allons-y, Baptiste, lança alors Shaor'i au bûcheron.

Sur l'épaule du colosse, Ti-Jean émit un cri modulé, qui fut relayé par l'Aîné des *mah oumet*. D'un même mouvement, les lutins se dirigèrent vers la goélette, vite suivis des *maymaygwashi*.

Baptiste s'arrêta devant Faustin pour lui donner l'accolade, puis le père Masse lui tapa l'épaule. Shaor'i plongea son regard de rapace dans les yeux de Faustin et prit ses mains dans les siennes.

— Bonne chance, mon frère, murmura-t-elle.

— Bonne chance, ma sœur, répondit Faustin sur le même ton.

Puis elle se détourna pour sauter lestement à bord de la goélette.

Faustin se tourna vers le rocher où se tenait toujours Alicia. Il l'invita à regagner le navire avec lui.

— Amiral Walker, nous montons à bord, cria-t-il.

La rampe brumeuse se forma aussitôt et le couple s'y engagea. Quand Faustin passa à côté de l'amiral, venu accueillir sa belle, il inclina la tête tout en disant :

— Il est temps d'appareiller, amiral.

Sans bruit, le navire éthéré quitta l'Isle-aux-Grues. La navigation était si silencieuse que Faustin put entendre Baptiste entonner un chant à bord de la goélette qui s'éloignait elle aussi de l'île.

Ce sol a produit des héros
Il est peuplé de braves,
Il n'est sur terre aucun drapeau
Pour nous tenir esclave.

Il ne put comprendre la suite, même avec son ouïe de renard. La distance entre le navire de ses amis et le sien croissait trop rapidement.

Malgré le brouillard qui enveloppait tout, Faustin resta à la proue, bien décidé à ne pas quitter son poste tant qu'il ne verrait pas apparaître la pointe de l'île d'Orléans.

CHAPITRE 36

À *l'assaut de l'île d'Orléans*

Avec le vent, le fin crachin tombant du ciel se mêlait aux gerbes d'eau glacée des vagues du fleuve. Autour de lui, l'équipage rappelé du trépas s'acquittait de ses fonctions, parlant de force du vent, de nœuds et de milles nautiques. Au-devant, les marsouins de Rivière-Ouelle guidaient le navire.

L'impatience des soldats aurait été palpable pour quiconque eût osé monter à bord du vaisseau fantôme. Pour les sens spirites de Faustin, la fébrilité créait une sorte d'électricité dans l'air qui le plongeait dans un état de vigilance alerte.

La hâte de *son* armée.

De *ses* hommes.

Faustin sentait que, peu importait l'issue de cette bataille, il s'accomplirait ce soir-là *quelque chose* qui avait pris naissance en même temps que lui, lorsque l'imprévisible s'était produit – à savoir que le fils de la Corriveau, plutôt que de croître normalement afin que l'Étranger dispose d'un réceptacle dans lequel transférer son esprit, avait été « reconnu » par les enchantements du maître du Stigma Diaboli et avait hérité de sa stupéfiante longévité.

Une impondérable erreur de calcul qui se nommait dorénavant Faustin Lamare.

Et quoi qu'il puisse arriver quand son armée déferlerait sur les berges de l'île d'Orléans, Faustin savait que cette erreur serait fatale aux plans de l'Étranger… ou qu'elle serait gommée par l'immortel sorcier.

Debout à la proue du navire, les mains sur le pommeau de ses sabres, Faustin observait la distance s'amenuiser entre l'île d'Orléans et les troupes de l'amiral Walker.

— *Sir !*

Faustin se retourna. Walker, approchant d'un air décidé, désigna une langue de terre à l'horizon.

— Notre objectif est visible. Nous longerons bientôt la rive sud de l'île, et, en prévision du débarquement imminent, qui aura lieu à une demi-lieue des escarpements, je suggère de positionner les premiers fusiliers.

— Faites, acquiesça Faustin.

Du second plancher montèrent une centaine de soldats, tous armés de longs fusils du siècle précédent. Se plaçant en trois lignes sur le flanc droit du navire, ils chargèrent puis se mirent en position, première ligne à genou, seconde debout en joue, troisième au garde-à-vous.

Après avoir observé la mise en place de ses hommes, Faustin riva de nouveau son regard vers l'avant.

Tu n'as que trop retardé ta mort, Frédéric Hohenstaufen, songea-t-il. *Dans quelques heures, tu rejoindras l'outremonde.*

Bientôt, ils avaient dépassé le village de Saint-Jean et Faustin commençait à deviner les contours sinistres de l'église de Saint-Laurent quand une soudaine déflagration le fit sursauter. Il eut le temps de voir un boulet de canon s'écraser dans les flots du fleuve, à quelques verges du navire fantôme.

Ça n'a pas de sens ! songea-t-il, pris de panique, avant de beugler :

— Amiral Walker !

Au moment où le spectre apparaissait à ses côtés, deux autres tirs détonèrent, leurs boulets chutant dangereusement près de la proue.

— Walker ! vociféra Faustin. Vous disiez que le navire serait camouflé par le brouillard...

Une salve de tirs successifs retentit. D'autres boulets tombèrent en sifflant, l'un d'entre eux atteignant le centre du pont, où il passa sans dommage, comme s'il ne s'y trouvait que de la vapeur.

— J'ignore comment ils sont au courant que nous approchons, *sir*. La seule chose que je sais, c'est qu'ils ne peuvent nous atteindre par les moyens propres aux simples mortels.

Au loin, Faustin put voir les nuages de fumée soulevés par les canons ramenés des Forges.

— *Sir*, reprit l'amiral, je suggère une approche rapide de la berge.

Faustin hocha la tête et l'amiral lança ses ordres. L'équipage s'activa dans les mâtures et, malgré l'impassibilité du vent, le navire fantôme prit soudain de la vitesse. La rive se rapprochant à vue d'œil, il put distinguer des formes qui s'agitaient sur les rochers.

— Ce sont ces hommes non-morts dont vous nous avez parlé, confirma Walker qui scrutait la berge avec sa longue-vue.

De nouveaux tirs interrompirent l'amiral. Plusieurs boulets traversèrent le navire spectral pour s'écraser dans l'eau.

Mais pourquoi s'obstinent-ils à nous tirer dessus s'ils savent que c'est sans effet ? se demanda Faustin.

Il ne fut pas long à comprendre quand il aperçut la dizaine de boulets qui fusaient dans leur direction sans qu'aucune détonation ne les annonce.

Par deux fois déjà, Faustin avait vu des boulets voler ainsi : aux Forges, sous les assauts de Lavallée qui

venait tout juste de se réincarner, et sur la *Rosamund*, que le sorcier avait fait échouer sur Grosse-Île.

Trois de ces boulets enchantés passèrent à travers la coque brumeuse et, soudainement, le navire fantôme se mit à donner dangereusement de la gîte.

— LAVALLÉE ! hurla Walker en frappant le bastingage du poing.

— Les canons tiraient pour tester la distance ! s'exclama Faustin. Nous allons couler !

— Nous avons encore le temps d'arriver ! Smith, tribord toute ! Carter, faites descendre la grand-voile ! Dodgson, ordonnez le…

Subitement, le crachin qui durait depuis la matinée cessa et, surgissant de nulle part, un épais brouillard tomba sur le fleuve, réduisant la visibilité à néant.

— Lavallée, *fucking bastard* ! jura l'amiral. Je ne me laisserai pas reprendre à cette…

D'un seul coup, une vingtaine de soldats s'effondrèrent, la gorge percée d'une flèche dont la pointe portait les traces d'un enchantement ténu. Leurs effigies s'estompèrent puis disparurent sans bruit.

— Les *bakaak* nous tirent dessus ! cria Faustin.

— Ripostez ! ordonna aussitôt Walker. Feu à volonté !

Les spectres des deux premières lignes tirèrent à l'aveuglette, puis ceux d'en avant passèrent en dernière ligne et les tirs se succédèrent. L'épaisseur de la brume empêchait de savoir si les assauts faisaient mouche, mais de nouvelles flèches atteignaient toujours les soldats de Walker.

— Tous les soldats sur le pont ! ordonna Walker alors qu'il n'en restait guère de la première vague.

D'autres spectres montèrent aussitôt des entrailles du vaisseau, puis un choc terrible ébranla tout le navire.

Le trois-mâts venait de s'échouer sur les rives de l'île d'Orléans.

Des hurlements sauvages retentirent et la brume se dissipa soudain. Les *bakaak* fonçaient par centaines sur l'épave.

Aussitôt, les premières rangées de spectres se ruèrent au bastingage.

— Feu ! cria Walker, et cent vingt fusils tirèrent à l'unisson, faisant choir les *bakaak* par dizaines.

Pressés par leurs supérieurs, les soldats de Walker se déployèrent sur la grève, couverts par les tirs nourris de ceux des leurs qui étaient positionnés sur le pont. Faustin débarqua avec eux, son fusil chargé d'une balle d'argent.

À cent verges de là, dévalant la pente escarpée qui les séparait de l'église de Saint-Laurent, des non-morts portant épieux, arcs et couteaux de pierre accouraient par centaines.

À la vue de cette horde, Faustin sentit son cœur se serrer. Jusque-là, il n'avait vu que des jacks qui avaient été, jadis, des hommes adultes. La légion de l'Étranger comptait maintenant dans ses rangs tout ce que le docteur Douglas avait pu obtenir parmi les malades de Grosse-Île : les femmes formaient presque la moitié des troupes, et des jouvenceaux se détachaient parfois du lot.

Les soldats spectraux s'empressèrent d'adopter leur position.

— Feu ! ordonna-t-on de nouveau, et cette fois ce fut l'entièreté de l'escadre qui tira.

D'autres *bakaak* tombèrent, vite piétinés par leurs semblables qui chargeaient. Les archers non-morts tirèrent à leur tour, et de nombreux hommes de Walker se dissipèrent.

Les tirs des mousquets devinrent de moins en moins synchrones, puis les *bakaak* ne furent plus qu'à quelques verges.

Puis qu'à quelques pieds.

Les soldats spectraux se levèrent et dégainèrent leurs sabres d'un même mouvement.

Faustin les imita.

Des épieux furent lancés, d'autres spectres se dissipèrent.

Puis les armées s'entrechoquèrent.

Sabres éthérés et armes de silex se croisèrent, causant des pertes de chaque côté. Militaires spectraux et soldats non-morts s'affrontèrent avec acharnement. Lorsque le premier *bakaak* l'approcha, Faustin laissa tomber ses lames, épaula son fusil et tira. Puis il reprit ses sabres, juste à temps pour frapper au cœur un second ennemi qui venait de pénétrer les rangs. Un sifflement attira l'attention de son ouïe acérée et, écoutant son instinct, il fendit l'air de son sabre gauche, fracassant au vol une flèche qui l'aurait atteint en plein cœur.

Des clairons sonnèrent et les soldats spectraux se divisèrent en plus petites sections. Certains reculèrent pour être en meilleure position pour tirer, d'autres continuaient d'affronter la horde.

Bondissant comme des singes fous, des archers *bakaak* gravirent un affleurement et, parvenus à son sommet, se redressèrent pour décocher traits sur traits. Plusieurs soldats spectraux se dissipèrent.

— Première troupe, chargez ! ordonna Walker en tranchant de son sabre la gorge d'un non-mort.

Un porte-clairon sonna un trille. Formant un carré serré, six rangs de six soldats foncèrent vers les archers. Avant même d'avoir parcouru la moitié du chemin, les deux premiers rangs s'évaporèrent sous la pluie de flèches.

— À couvert ! cria Faustin en courant pour les rattraper.

Obéissant aussitôt, la vingtaine de spectres restants s'accroupirent contre un large roc. Les flèches

ricochèrent sans les atteindre et Faustin parvint à les rejoindre en zigzaguant de rocher en rocher.

Ailleurs sur la plage, la bataille était tout aussi meurtrière. Au sol, les hommes de Walker semblaient avoir l'avantage, car ils étaient mieux entraînés ; mais au tir, les *bakaak,* plus rapides, épaulaient deux ou trois fois avant que les soldats puissent faire feu à leur tour.

Un autre trille retentit et un nouveau carré de soldats chargea les archers de l'affleurement.

Mais combien Walker va-t-il massacrer de soldats avant de comprendre que ce n'est pas la bonne stratégie? pesta Faustin quand la nouvelle troupe fut sublimée sous les projectiles.

Nouveau trille de clairon, troisième troupe.

— Imbécile ! jura Faustin.

Du coup, il tenta de se figurer la situation comme une partie de dames ou d'échecs et songea que le contexte se prêtait à un gambit. Il ordonna aux soldats restés à couvert :

— L'attention des *bakaak* est tournée vers cette nouvelle troupe. Allons les surprendre par le flanc droit.

Hochant la tête, les spectres attendirent son signal. Quand la nouvelle troupe fut à portée d'arc de l'ennemi, ils se faufilèrent pour contourner les tireurs non-morts.

— Tirez ! ordonna Faustin.

Attaqués par le flanc, les archers *bakaak* tombèrent par dizaines. Les soldats de Faustin eurent le temps de gravir l'affleurement avant d'être repérés. Ils dégainèrent leur sabre. Sans autre arme que leur arc, les tireurs non-morts durent les affronter à mains nues et furent rapidement écrasés.

Maintenant qu'ils se trouvaient dans un emplacement avantageux, Faustin ordonna à ses soldats de tirer à volonté. Il fallut plusieurs minutes pour que Walker remarque qu'ils avaient pris l'affleurement.

Relativement en sécurité, Faustin put se permettre de scruter la scène.

Les *bakaak* ne parvenaient pas à profiter de leur avantage numérique : comme l'avait suggéré le père Masse à l'amiral, les troupes de Walker s'étaient déployées entre deux collines, avec les eaux du fleuve derrière eux.

Aux yeux de Faustin, le moment était opportun pour essayer d'amener la situation à leur plein avantage. Certes, il n'avait jamais tenté ce qu'il s'apprêtait à faire, mais quelques lectures du père Masse suggéraient que la chose était possible.

Après avoir ordonné à quelques spectres d'assurer sa protection, Faustin fit le vide dans son esprit et projeta sa volonté en direction du navire fantôme. Ses sens spirites palpèrent une sorte d'énergie semblable à une âme sans en être tout à fait une. Les lueurs violacées du trois-mâts se mirent à crépiter et, alors que Faustin bandait sa volonté, toute la mâture s'auréola d'une lueur d'améthyste révélant l'énergie qui assurait la structure du navire, ce que les militaires spectraux appelaient « le feu de Saint-Elme ».

Faustin n'entendait presque plus les bruits de la bataille. Toute son attention était rivée sur le feu de Saint-Elme. Comme il ne s'agissait pas d'un esprit à proprement parler, il ne pouvait lui ordonner de lui obéir, mais, en resserrant sa concentration, il perçut qu'il pouvait le modeler à sa guise.

Il fixa son esprit sur le concept d'une nappe de brouillard et, lentement, la forme du trois-mâts devint floue.

Peu à peu, le navire disparut, ne laissant en place et lieu qu'une épaisse mare de brume.

Pour s'aider à visualiser l'effet qu'il désirait, Faustin tendit la main vers le brouillard et mima un déplacement vers la plage où se déroulait l'affrontement.

La nappe de brume, s'avançant selon le vouloir de Faustin, engloutit soldats spectraux et *bakaak*. Les spectres, n'ayant pas besoin d'yeux pour voir, ne furent guère incommodés par ce brouillard, contrairement aux *bakaak*.

Aveuglés, les non-morts archers furent contraints de tirer au hasard pendant que ceux qui luttaient au corps-à-corps s'empressèrent de battre en retraite. En quelques minutes à peine, la majorité des *bakaak* avait été contrainte de se regrouper afin de se mettre à couvert.

Un sourire aux lèvres, Faustin passa à la seconde phase du plan.

Il en appela à la force arcanique qui l'habitait.

Brûlez...

... le torrent de flammes jaillirait suffisamment en arrière pour n'atteindre que des *bakaak* et aucun spectre. Une satisfaction carnassière s'empara de lui : au moins la moitié des *bakaak* y passerait...

...Brûlez...

Des souvenirs revinrent en rafale dans l'esprit de Faustin : les malades dupés à Grosse-Île, les ouvriers terrifiés des Forges, les *mah oumet* changés en diablotins...

...BRÛLEZ...

... la destruction de Notre-Dame des Tempérances, la mort de son oncle et celle de Madeleine...

...BRÛLEZ !

La puissance accumulée atteignit son point culminant, mais aucun diagramme n'apparut dans l'esprit de Faustin.

Alors l'énergie suscitée implosa dans le corps du jeune homme. Faustin hurla alors qu'une intense froidure lui déchirait l'intérieur et qu'il sentait un terrible contrecoup le drainer.

La brume spectrale s'évapora d'un coup.

Il tomba à plat ventre sur le sol rocheux.

Une flèche l'atteignit à la cuisse, mais il ne la sentit pas.

Il se dressa avec difficulté et n'eut que vaguement conscience du *bakaak* qui chargeait pour le prendre à revers.

Ce fut le choc de l'impact, plus que la douleur, qui surprit Faustin.

Incrédule, il contempla la pointe de la lance qui avait jailli de son sternum, lui perçant le cœur.

Pas… si… tôt… eut-il le temps de songer tandis qu'il s'effondrait et que sa vue se voilait.

Il n'avait déjà plus conscience en touchant de nouveau le sol.

◆

Il se redressa d'un coup sur la couchette de la cabine.

Les pentacles qu'il avait gravés sur les murs cessèrent de luire.

À ses côtés, silencieux et rongé par l'inquiétude, le fantôme de la belle Alicia Routh le contemplait. Le visage de la demoiselle au port altier ne trahissait aucune expression.

Derechef, Faustin se leva pour se ruer sur le pont.

Le crachin tombait encore du côté nord de l'île d'Orléans. Rassemblés sur le pont de la goélette, des centaines de *mah oumet* attendaient, couteau de pierre en main, que le bateau du père Masse accoste sur la rive.

Ils s'écartèrent du passage de Faustin quand celui-ci se dirigea vers la proue, là où se tenaient Baptiste, Ti-Jean, Shaor'i et le père Masse. Les quatre se retournèrent à son arrivée.

— Ton effigie est déjà dissipée ? lança le père Masse en le voyant surgir.

— L'Étranger savait que nous arrivions, cria Faustin par-dessus le bruit du vent. Les *bakaak* étaient déjà en position et Lavallée avait levé les défenses. Le navire de brouillard a été touché par des boulets ensorcelés… mais nous avons eu le temps d'accoster, ajouta-t-il devant l'air catastrophé de ses compagnons.

Soulagés, ils le dévisagèrent, attendant la suite.

— Spectres et *bakaak* se battent sur la rive sud. Le déploiement des troupes a été difficile, mais je crois que nous prenions l'avantage du terrain au moment où mon effigie a été dissipée. Toute l'attention de l'Étranger devrait être tournée vers le combat opposant son armée à la nôtre, désormais…

— … à moins qu'il ne sache déjà que nous l'attaquons sur deux fronts, compléta le père Masse.

— Grâce aux pouvoirs de Légaré, c'est possible, admit Faustin. Tout dépend de la façon dont il s'est remis de son expérience avec le Calice.

— Ne perdons pas une minute alors.

Fermant les yeux, le petit prêtre murmura une brève formule. Bien qu'ils fussent à contrevent, les voiles de la goélette se gonflèrent et le bateau fonça en direction de l'île, qui ne se trouvait plus qu'à une lieue.

— Père Masse… reprit Faustin. J'ai tenté, comme prévu, de faire appel aux diagrammes gravés dans la voûte où repose l'Étranger. L'énergie a culminé, le pentacle ne s'est pas manifesté mentalement et la puissance a implosé.

Accroché au bastingage, le vieux prêtre dévisagea Faustin, son front barré d'un pli soucieux.

— Alors ça veut dire qu'Hohenstaufen est parvenu à régénérer son corps et que celui-ci ne repose plus sous la Fontaine du Diable. Qu'il a recouvré la totalité de ses pouvoirs et qu'il n'utilise plus que le lien arcanique le rattachant aux pentacles qui absorbent les feux follets pour le sustenter.

Un choc puissant ébranla le navire, suivi d'un terrible grincement. L'espace d'un moment, Faustin songea à un écueil, puis il vit le corps titanesque et écailleux de la créature qui, après avoir buté contre la coque, s'enfonçait dessous. L'embarcation se souleva alors que le monstre passait et retomba sur les flots en tanguant.

Tout autour, les *mah oumet* hurlaient de peur. De l'épaule de Baptiste, Ti-Jean cria dans son langage un ordre transmis par le bûcheron et les singes blancs se réfugièrent dans la mâture.

Le monstre marin émergea. Son corps immense décrivait déjà un large arc de cercle pour charger de nouveau la goélette. Le second impact soulevait la poupe au moment où Faustin projeta sa volonté vers l'esprit du dernier maître du monstre marin.

« *Plaçoa, la bête est là* », déclara-t-il sans ambages.

« *Je sais,* répondit l'esprit. *Mes frères vous rejoignent.* »

De la cale surgirent au même moment les *maymaygwashi*. Épieux en main, ils se placèrent côte à côte le long de la rampe avant de commencer à émettre une sorte de ronronnement, d'abord à l'unisson, puis chacun à un intervalle différent.

L'onde sonore qui en résulta créa une telle résonance que Faustin ressentit un vague vertige. Les *komkwejwika'sikl* tracés sur le bastingage par le peuple des rivières se mirent à luire avec intensité et tous ceux qui assistaient à l'événement durent rétrécir les yeux pour éviter d'être aveuglés.

L'air se condensa, ce qui créa une brume épaisse, puis la température chuta d'un coup.

Avec un craquement assourdissant, une partie de l'eau du fleuve, en se solidifiant, emprisonna la quasi-totalité de Kabir Kouba dans un écrin de glace. Seule la partie supérieure de son dos émergeait de la gangue.

Baptiste et le père Masse tirèrent trois coups successifs. Touchée chaque fois, la bête bandait ses muscles après chaque coup, tentant de remuer et de fendre le glacier, qui s'évaporait déjà dans l'air estival.

Sans perdre un instant, Faustin sortit de sa poche une petite boîte de bois et la tendit à Shaor'i qui, ayant assumé sa forme de harfang, prit aussitôt son envol en tenant l'objet dans ses serres.

En trois battements d'ailes, elle fut au-dessus du monstre et laissa tomber la boîte près de sa tête.

— *Ashek akkad baath ahmed dazan il-bekr !* incanta Faustin.

De la lumière jaillit du pentacle gravé sur le fond de la boîte ; celle-ci s'enflamma, faisant détoner la poudre à fusil qu'elle contenait.

L'explosion abîma sérieusement la carapace de la créature, mais l'esturgeon titanesque réussit néanmoins à se libérer de sa prison de glace quelques secondes plus tard.

Deux autres coups de feu retentirent, et les charges pénétrèrent au milieu des plaies noircies. La bête se tordit de douleur.

Les *maymaygwashi* se jetèrent alors par-dessus bord, épieu au poing. Chacun ressortit des flots monté sur un marsouin, la main gauche agrippée à l'aileron du cétacé fantôme, la droite brandissant l'épieu. Les groupes à bâbord et à tribord convergèrent vers l'avant du navire, là où l'énorme corps cuirassé préparait une nouvelle charge.

Portés par leurs montures, les premiers *maymaygwashi* foncèrent sur la bête, la vélocité des marsouins décuplant la force des épieux à la pointe acérée. L'esturgeon géant fit volte-face lorsqu'une arme pénétra sa cuirasse à la base de la queue. La créature s'agita, combative, et secoua les flots d'une façon telle que les

autres marsouins durent décrire un large arc de cercle pour éviter la chute de leur cavalier. Deux *maymayg-washi* parvinrent cependant à se positionner, et leur charge permit de déchirer encore plus la peau du monstre.

La bête se mit à tournoyer sur elle-même en soulevant d'énormes vagues qui s'abattirent tant sur ses attaquants que sur le pont de la goélette, où les petits *mah oumet* qui avaient grimpés évitèrent de justesse d'être emportés. Kabir Kouba frappa ensuite de la queue, assommant l'un des *maymaygwashi* qui coula vers une mort certaine, puis se jeta gueule ouverte sur un second assaillant, qui fut broyé par l'énorme mâchoire.

Les remous provoqués par la bataille faisaient tanguer le navire avec violence. Sur le pont, Faustin, Baptiste et le père Masse peinaient pour rester sur leurs pieds. Avec grande difficulté, les trois hommes, qui avaient épaulé de nouveau leurs armes, tirèrent à l'unisson, visant toujours la zone la plus abîmée du monstre.

À voir la réaction frénétique de ce dernier, la charge d'au moins l'un d'eux pénétra jusqu'à un endroit névralgique.

L'un des *maymaygwashi* émit un long sifflement, auquel Baptiste réagit aussitôt. Le colosse lança en l'air une corde que Shaor'i attrapa au vol dans ses serres. Filant comme une flèche, le harfang se rendit jusqu'à un proche récif et, redevenu humain, s'empressa d'y ancrer solidement la corde.

L'Indienne reprit le sifflement quand elle eut terminé.

À ce signal, Faustin incanta de nouveau :

— *Ashek saen-irstean al-ibnar !*

Un harpon fusa de la goélette, en faisant siffler dans l'air la corde auquel il était attaché. Il alla se ficher

profondément dans la chair de l'esturgeon géant, qui bondit hors de l'eau sous la puissance de la douleur et obligea les passagers à se cramponner pour éviter de choir lorsque les vagues provoquées par sa retombée secouèrent le navire.

Lié au récif, Kabir Kouba tournoyait sur lui-même, cherchant à briser la gênante entrave. Les *maymaygwashi* en profitèrent pour charger une nouvelle fois et enfoncer leurs épieux aussi profondément qu'ils le purent, ce qui coûta de nouvelles vies tant la bête demeurait vigoureuse.

Et elle s'agita tant qu'elle réussit à rompre son amarre. Libéré, Kabir Kouba s'empressa de plonger dans les profondeurs du fleuve. Sans hésiter, les guerriers du peuple des rivières le suivirent en eaux creuses.

En surface, la houle se calma, ne laissant rien entrevoir du combat qui se poursuivait sous les flots. Se précipitant à la poupe, Faustin extirpa de son sac le Grimoire du Chien d'Or qu'il feuilleta vivement, cherchant en vain un sort qui pourrait assister le peuple des rivières.

— Bonne chance, murmura Faustin, les yeux rivés sur les eaux tumultueuses où il ne distinguait déjà plus les *maymaygwashi*.

— C'est leur bataille, décréta le père Masse. Ils se sont préparés pour ça depuis qu'ils savent que la bête est réveillée. Notre combat à nous aura lieu sur la terre ferme.

À cent verges de là se trouvaient les rives du village de Saint-Pierre, que seule une lieue de forêt séparait de l'église de Saint-Laurent, de l'autre côté de l'île.

— On arrive ! lança Baptiste, agrippé à la proue.

◆

Les berges étaient désertes, aussi personne ne vit la goélette s'approcher du rivage.

Personne ne vit non plus les centaines de petits singes blancs, au pelage couvert de bariolures lumineuses, descendre des mâts et des cordages, couteau de pierre à la main. Sitôt sur la terre ferme, la légion de petits êtres s'élança pour gravir le tronc des grands arbres.

Afin de garder la mainmise sur l'armée spectrale qui se battait sur l'autre rive, Faustin s'assura mentalement que le fantôme d'Alicia Routh ne quitterait pas la cabine de la goélette.

Après avoir psalmodié une courte prière dans sa langue, Shaor'i se tourna vers Faustin. Elle fixa le jeune homme dans les yeux, l'air résolu, puis elle murmura tout simplement:

— Je ne reculerai pas.

Aussitôt, elle adopta sa forme de harfang et s'envola afin d'ouvrir le chemin. Baptiste proposa au père Masse, trop âgé pour courir, de le porter. Le loup Misaël fit de même, en laissant s'agripper à son pelage une demi-douzaine de lutins; puis Faustin adopta sa forme de renard et se coucha au sol, en s'offrant comme monture à l'Aîné des *mah oumet*.

Celui qui assumait l'autorité au sein de la dernière tribu du petit peuple des cavernes s'installa dignement. Bien droit sur le dos du renard, le vieux *mah oumet* hocha la tête en direction d'un bosquet d'arbres.

Les lutins, s'élançant de branche en branche, firent route vers la rive sud où se poursuivait la bataille. Encouragé par Ti-Jean, Baptiste s'empressa de les suivre, imité par Faustin.

Au pas de course, ils parcoururent le sentier. Partout autour, on pouvait voir les petits êtres blancs sauter d'un arbre à l'autre, avec pour seule preuve de leur

passage le bruissement des feuilles dans les chênes et les érables.

On dirait le son d'une brise, songea Faustin en galopant. *Ou plutôt, celui d'un vent chargé de colère.*

Ils ne furent pas longs à déboucher sur un champ fraîchement labouré, au bout duquel se dressait la pente portant l'église de Saint-Laurent.

Sur son dos, Faustin sentit remuer l'Aîné et l'entendit donner des ordres dans sa langue à clics.

La nuée de *mah oumet* quitta le refuge des branchages et, formant un essaim dense, s'élança vers la colline de l'église. Faustin partit d'un grand sprint, car il souhaitait offrir à l'Aîné la position de tête afin qu'il puisse mieux coordonner les actes des siens.

Quand la pente ne fut plus qu'à quelques verges, Faustin bondit sur un rocher et scruta les abords de l'église. Il laissa descendre l'Aîné pour s'asseoir le temps de retrouver son souffle, langue pendante.

Les *mestabeok* n'avaient toujours pas remarqué leur présence. On pouvait toutefois, même d'aussi loin, apercevoir leurs silhouettes titanesques. L'Aîné des lutins prit quelques secondes pour contempler la scène, des larmes coulant de ses petits yeux rouges.

Sans difficulté, Faustin comprenait les pensées qui habitaient le lutin.

Ils y étaient. Ce serait leur fin.

La dernière marche des *mah oumet*.

Serrant les poings avec résolution, l'Aîné remonta sur le dos de Faustin et leva le bras vers le ciel en lançant un long appel.

Des centaines de voix lui répondirent.

Tout en se ruant sur l'ennemi, les *mah oumet* exigeaient vengeance.

Comme une marée vivante, l'essaim de lutins déferla sur les terres de l'église de Saint-Laurent.

Au-dessus d'eux, le cri strident d'un rapace leur fit écho.

La distance s'amenuisait à vue d'œil.

Les bruits de l'armée spectrale affrontant l'armée non-morte furent bientôt audibles.

L'église se dressait comme un austère castel. De seconde en seconde, son clocher semblait croître à l'horizon.

Bientôt, la légion de lutins ne fut plus qu'à cent verges.

Devant les portes, sept hommes-singes géants se retournèrent vers eux, de grands troncs en main.

Plus que cinquante verges.

L'armée des lutins hurla sa colère.

Les *mestabeok* beuglèrent leur réponse en se martelant la poitrine.

Vingt verges.

Les géants foncèrent à leur rencontre.

Les yeux baignés de larmes, les *mah oumet* levèrent leurs couteaux de pierre.

En une seule vague blanche, les derniers survivants de la race des *mah oumet* se jetèrent à l'assaut des êtres géants. À travers les cris et les plaintes, les lutins se servaient de leurs lames de pierre pour grimper plus haut, toujours plus haut, afin d'atteindre les parties les plus vulnérables des *mestabeok* : gorge, yeux, tempes…

Beuglant de douleur, les géants moulinèrent l'espace de leur gourdin, avant de les laisser tomber au sol pour tenter des deux mains d'arracher de leur torse ces insectes gênants qu'ils écrasaient et piétinaient ensuite.

Un nouveau cri de rapace résonna et Shaor'i tomba du ciel, lames au poing, pour atterrir sur les épaules d'un géant où elle planta les griffes de ses pieds-serres. Le monstre, agitant les bras au-dessus de sa tête, força l'Indienne à se déplacer. La jeune femme

se laissa retomber en glissant une lame le long du dos du *mestabeok*.

D'un même mouvement, dix ou douze *mah oumet* bondirent du sol pour poignarder la plaie béante, fouailler les chairs et mettre l'épine dorsale à nu. Shaor'i empoigna la hachette d'Otjiera et la projeta contre la colonne vertébrale dépouillée de sa peau.

Le monstre s'effondra, secoué de spasmes.

Puis des flèches se mirent à pleuvoir, transperçant plusieurs lutins.

Incrédule, Faustin scruta le champ sud et découvrit ce qu'il craignait : l'armée des *bakaak* s'était divisée en deux moitiés, l'une continuant d'affronter les soldats spectraux, plus bas vers la rive, l'autre remontant la pente vers les *mah oumet* massés devant l'église.

« *Walker !* » émit Faustin en bandant sa volonté. « *Envoyez maintenant vos troupes nous prêter main-forte devant l'église !* »

« *Nous tiendrons bientôt la plage, Sir ! Laissez-nous encore une demi-heure !* »

Horrifié, Faustin vit les lutins bondir sur les non-morts et choir aussitôt, paralysés par le contact gelé des créatures. Presque machinalement, les *bakaak* transperçaient les petits corps de leurs épieux avant de poursuivre leur avancée.

« *Au Diable la prise de la plage, Walker !* » tempêta-t-il mentalement. « *Envoyez vos troupes sur-le-champ ou je fais le serment de contraindre votre fiancée à passer l'éternité dans les flots glacés d'où je l'ai tirée !* »

Walker ne répondit pas, mais des notes de clairon retentirent au loin et les sens spirites de Faustin perçurent l'approche des soldats spectraux alors que les *mah oumet* continuaient de tomber sous les coups des *bakaak*.

Sans hésiter, Faustin adopta sa forme de renard et se mit à courir de long en large sur le champ de bataille,

cherchant désespérément l'odeur musquée propre à l'Aîné des *mah oumet*. Il repéra le vieux lutin, contraint par quelques-uns de ses semblables de rester en retrait. Le chef du petit peuple semblait avoir compris la situation et, sans hésiter, il sauta sur le dos de Faustin, accompagné de deux lutins de bonne carrure.

Faustin, s'élançant avec une formidable poussée, traversa comme une flèche le champ de bataille. Il atteignit la ligne d'assaut où un nouveau groupe de *mah oumet* s'apprêtait à attaquer les *bakaak*. L'Aîné lança plusieurs fois le même long cri, ordonnant aux lutins d'annuler l'offensive. Obéissant sur-le-champ, les singes blancs firent demi-tour et retournèrent affronter les *mestabeok* restants.

Satisfait de voir les lutins se jeter face à un ennemi duquel ils pouvaient venir à bout, Faustin scruta l'horizon et poussa un soupir de soulagement en voyant que des soldats fantômes approchaient au pas de course et que les *bakaak* s'en retournaient les affronter.

Un jappement impérieux détourna son attention. Portant six *mah oumet* sur son dos, le loup Misaël indiquait du museau un *mestabeok* qui s'apprêtait à abattre son gourdin sur Faustin.

D'un geste preste, Faustin réussit à éviter le coup mais, ne pouvant reculer, il dut se résoudre à passer à l'assaut.

Se faufilant entre les combattants, Misaël chargea lui aussi le monstre, profitant que sa cible s'était penchée pour lui bondir à la gorge et planter ses crocs dans le cou massif.

Faustin contourna le géant, s'élança pour lui grimper sur le dos, courut le long de son échine et enfonça ses dents dans sa nuque.

Quittant leurs montures, les lutins se jetèrent sur les parties vulnérables de la tête.

Le monstre tournoya sur lui-même en hurlant, puis chuta.

N'ayant plus de *mah oumet* sur le dos, Faustin reprit forme humaine afin de poursuivre l'attaque contre les autres adversaires quand il entendit les cris terrifiés de plusieurs *mah oumet*, auxquels se joignit le long hurlement de Misaël.

Le *mestabeok* qu'ils avaient terrassé venait de laisser tomber de son poing un petit corps désarticulé sur le sol.

Le corps de l'Aîné.

L'émotion paralysa Faustin pendant plusieurs secondes. L'Aîné était mort ! C'est un autre grondement enflant derrière lui qui le ramena à la réalité : un autre géant fonçait sur lui, mais Baptiste, arme au poing, le chargeait comme un cheval lancé au galop. Il décrivait un large moulinet avec sa hache, prêt à l'abattre dans le genou du *mestabeok* quand le monstre remarqua l'assaut.

La hache rencontra l'énorme gourdin et s'y incrusta profondément.

Un sourire mauvais sur son faciès bestial, le géant souleva sa massue, arracha la hache et la projeta à plusieurs verges de là.

Sans se laisser intimider, le bûcheron saisit l'énorme cuisse du *mestabeok* de ses deux bras et tira de toutes ses forces.

Déséquilibré, le géant tituba.

Baptiste raffermit sa prise en tirant de plus belle, évitant de justesse le gourdin qui s'abattit à deux pieds de lui. Gardant la cuisse du monstre emprisonnée dans l'étreinte de son bras droit, le bûcheron agrippa du gauche le poignet du géant, puis pivota sur lui-même en grognant sous l'effort.

Avec un bruit sourd, le *mestabeok* s'effondra au sol et disparut aussitôt sous une marée de fourrure blanche.

Alors qu'il se ruait pour leur prêter main-forte, Faustin projeta sa psyché pour appeler Shaor'i en renfort; or son esprit ne parvint pas à s'accrocher et le contact qu'il maintenait avec la jeune femme vacilla.

Inquiet, il la chercha du regard et la repéra alors qu'elle se ruait à leur rencontre.

Elle avait encore changé.

Elle était encore plus petite qu'auparavant. Peut-être moins de quatre pieds.

Et ses yeux étaient beaucoup trop grands.

Qu'est-ce que… ça ne peut pas être…

Faustin fronça les sourcils en voyant l'Indienne reprendre sa forme animale.

— saut arrière —

Le gourdin du *mestabeok* le plus proche s'écrasa juste à l'endroit où, une seconde auparavant, s'était tenu Faustin avant que ses instincts ne le poussent à bondir.

Près de Faustin, le harfang gagna en altitude, fit un piqué, planta ses serres dans la gorge du géant. Le *mestabeok,* se frappant pour se débarrasser de l'oiseau, l'effleura au passage.

Shaor'i reprit forme humaine en tombant au sol.

Elle avait encore changé et semblait porter des dizaines d'ornements blancs – Faustin ne fut pas long à comprendre qu'il s'agissait de plumes sortant de sa chair en divers endroits.

Elle se battait en se servant de ses pieds qui étaient désormais de vraies serres couvertes d'écailles jaunâtres.

Le *mestabeok* qu'elle affrontait leva son gourdin pour l'écraser.

Faustin se remémora les derniers mots qu'elle lui avait dits : *Je ne reculerai pas*.

« *Shaor'i, arrête!* » émit Faustin, en vain tant le lien mental était ténu.

Le tronc du géant balaya l'air.

L'Indienne sauta.

— Shaor'i, NON ! hurla Faustin avec la force du désespoir.

Elle adopta sa forme de harfang.

Dans l'esprit de Faustin, le lien se brisa avec l'équivalent mental d'un claquement de fouet.

Griffes au clair, le harfang déchiqueta le visage du géant en lui crevant les yeux. Le *mestabeok* tourna sur lui-même, désorienté. Ayant vu la manœuvre, Baptiste, qui avait récupéré sa hache, l'abattit dans le genou du monstre qui s'effondra par terre. Le harfang plongea vers le géant, replanta ses serres dans sa gorge et lui ouvrit les veines de son bec acéré.

Impuissant, Faustin contemplait la scène. Tous ses sens spirites lui confirmèrent ses craintes : son amie venait de passer de l'autre côté, et elle n'en reviendrait plus.

Prisonnière à jamais de sa forme animale.

Le harfang décrivit un large arc de cercle et piqua de nouveau sur un géant, lui labourant le torse de ses griffes avant de s'envoler, puis elle recommença.

— Faustin ! lança une voix derrière lui.

— Père Masse ! cria-t-il en se retournant. Shaor'i s'est dépassée !

Le regard du vieux prêtre se voila, puis il déclara :

— Les *mah oumet* ne tiendront plus longtemps sans elle et l'Aîné, et les *bakaak* les anéantiront. Fonce ! Entre dans l'église et mets fin à cette démence !

— Mais, Shaor'i est…

— Tu ne peux plus rien pour elle ! Fais ce que je te dis, que son sacrifice, que leur sacrifice à tous ne soit pas vain !

Faustin jeta un dernier coup d'œil tout autour de lui. Baptiste ruisselait de sueur et respirait avec bruit.

Les corps désarticulés des lutins s'amoncelaient sur le sol. Le harfang s'élevait et plongeait, encore et encore.

« *Adieu, ma sœur* », tenta de lui transmettre Faustin.

Le contact échoua.

Ravalant ses larmes, il courut vers l'église, enfonça l'une des petites portes d'un coup d'épaule et se précipita à l'intérieur.

◆

Au-dehors, la bataille se poursuivait, mais les bruits de la mêlée étaient étouffés par l'épaisseur des murs de pierre.

S'il n'était jamais entré dans l'église de Saint-Laurent, il l'avait visitée en rêve par trois fois. C'était une vaste église de maçonnerie, beaucoup plus imposante que la plupart des églises de village. Malgré le temps gris, les vitraux du transept laissaient filtrer une lumière multicolore qui inondait le maître-autel. Au sommet de la voûte trônait un énorme lustre, qui n'était probablement allumé qu'une fois l'an, à la messe de minuit.

Tout était identique à ses visions.

Y compris la présence apparente de François, agenouillé devant l'autel.

Faustin cessa d'avancer. La tonalité de l'âme qui habitait ce corps n'était pas celle de l'homme qu'il avait toujours considéré comme son frère.

Jean-Pierre Lavallée, dit le Sorcier du Fort, se leva après avoir parachevé un diagramme. Lentement, il se retourna vers Faustin, qui sursauta.

Le visage était celui d'un vieillard. La peau était parcheminée, les yeux éteints, les cheveux blonds avaient tourné à l'ivoire jauni.

— Toi… gronda la voix rauque du vieil homme qui avait été, six mois auparavant, un vicaire de vingt-cinq ans.

— Libérez mon frère, ordonna Faustin, les sabres brandis.

— Toi… répéta Lavallée sans prêter attention à l'injonction. Vois ce que tu m'as obligé à faire subir à ce corps !

Faustin se tint coi, fixant le sorcier dans les yeux.

— Tu as libéré Plaçoa et j'ai été forcé de contrôler ce monstre de Kabir Kouba… en vain ! Des années drainées, alors que cette folle de Siffleuse y avait laissé des mois pour asservir ce fantôme… et tout ça pour rien ! Ces maudites créatures l'ont anéanti !

Les maymaygwashi *ont réussi,* comprit Faustin avec soulagement.

— Et voilà que tu débarques avec ces singes afin de trucider les derniers représentants de la glorieuse race des géants !

— Sans compter votre armée de *bakaak,* déclara Faustin. D'ailleurs, l'amiral Walker sera bientôt là et il brûle de se venger de vos enchantements…

— J'aurais dû te tuer à mon premier réveil, dans la chapelle engloutie sous les Forges ! vociféra Lavallée.

— L'Étranger me jugeait encore utile, à l'époque.

— Et vois les conséquences…

— N'est-il pas malavisé de juger ainsi les décisions de votre maître ? provoqua le jeune homme.

— *Ad iskan saïr soleima ibn adur, sikg salim darennar, vaden estera !*

Le diagramme au bras de celui qui avait été François se mit à briller à travers son vêtement.

Le sabre de Frontenac vibra.

— La Barrière de Saint-Damien, commenta Faustin. Astucieux : vous auriez coupé mon lien avec l'armée spectrale et…

— Comment peux-tu… ? grogna Lavallée. *Ashek akkad baath ahmed dazan il-bekr !*

Un globe de feu jaillit en direction de Faustin, qui leva Lys Blanc.

L'arme vibra de nouveau.

Les flammes se dissipèrent quelques pouces avant de l'atteindre.

— Si tu me crois au bout de mes ressources... tempêta Lavallée.

De ses longues manches, le sorcier fit jaillir deux couteaux de pierre qu'il empoigna avec force.

Des lames *saokata*.

Lavallée était métis, se souvint Faustin au moment où le sorcier fonçait sur lui avec un hurlement sauvage.

Les lames de silex soulevèrent des gerbes d'étincelles en rencontrant celles d'acier. Faustin esquiva, pivota sur lui-même, para de justesse le coup dirigé vers sa gorge sans pouvoir éviter celui qui lui entailla la cuisse.

Écoutant ses instincts, Faustin se mit hors de portée d'un leste bond en arrière. Il atterrit plusieurs pieds plus loin, où il s'accroupit à temps pour éviter les deux lames lancées dans sa direction.

Bon sang, c'est un guerrier redoutable... mais le voilà désarmé...

Un sabre en défense, l'autre pointé vers l'avant, Faustin fonça sur le sorcier du Fort.

Lavallée bondit à son tour hors de portée, tout en incantant :

— *Ashek saen-irstean al-ibnar !*

De nouveau immobile, Faustin vit les couteaux de pierre fuser d'eux-mêmes à travers la nef pour retrouver les mains du sorcier, qui se rua sur Faustin en hurlant.

Silex et acier s'entrechoquèrent. La force de l'impact força Faustin à reculer, ce qui lui permit tout juste de parer le coup visant son cœur. Il pivota un instant trop tard, et la lame destinée à lui ouvrir la gorge lui entailla l'épaule.

Grimaçant de douleur, il se mit à virevolter sur lui-même à la manière de Shaor'i, profitant de la longueur de ses lames pour forcer Lavallée à reculer… mais le sorcier adopta plutôt sa forme chevaline.

L'étalon noir se cabra et Faustin dut plonger pour éviter d'être terrassé par un violent coup de sabots. Il roula sur le sol et, afin de ne pas être mortellement piétiné, adopta sa forme de renard, se faufila entre les pattes du cheval et lui mordit vicieusement au passage le tendon d'une cheville arrière. Hennissant de douleur, le cheval dans une ruade heurta le renard, qui alla bouler contre un mur.

Sonné, Faustin reprit forme humaine, juste à temps pour placer ses sabres en croix et se protéger des deux couteaux du sorcier.

Il rompit, bondit vers l'avant en pointant.

Sa lame laissa une estafilade sur le bras de son ennemi.

Si Lavallée était un guerrier beaucoup plus expérimenté, Faustin bénéficiait d'un corps plus jeune. Il avait également pour lui le silence *saokata*, lequel attira son attention sur l'assurance de Lavallée, une assurance anormale qui n'était pas celle d'un guerrier sûr de sa supériorité – non, c'était une assurance pleine d'imprudence, pleine de risques inutiles. Et c'est en écoutant le silence que masquaient les cris de Lavallée que Faustin comprit.

Le sorcier était persuadé que Faustin l'épargnerait afin de ramener son frère. De cette certitude naissait sa témérité.

Quand Lavallée frappa de nouveau, Faustin fut convaincu d'avoir vu juste : un combattant craignant la mort n'exposait jamais ainsi son cœur.

Enhardi par cette découverte, Faustin joua le jeu et fit une fausse attaque en direction de la gorge.

Lavallée ne leva même pas de lame pour parer.

Alors le jeune homme, décrivant de larges moulinets, concentra ses assauts sur les flancs et les membres, assauts que Lavallée parait sans peine en répliquant vers les parties les plus vulnérables de Faustin.

Ce dernier esquiva une nouvelle fois, frappa vers l'épaule d'une main, vit son attaque contrée, et feinta de l'autre main vers la jambe.

Dupé, Lavallée abaissa son arme.

Alors Faustin leva Lys Blanc et l'enfonça dans la gorge du sorcier.

Les yeux exorbités par la surprise, Lavallée cracha, tenta d'incanter alors que le sang s'écoulait par sa bouche et son cou.

Horrifié, Faustin retira son arme.

Il venait de tuer Lavallée… et François.

L'heure n'était toutefois pas au chagrin.

Il savait que ce dénouement était probable et il s'y était préparé.

Pendant que Lavallée s'étranglait dans ses propres fluides, Faustin arrima son esprit au sien. Il put sentir toute la puissance, la rage et la volonté du Sorcier du Fort. Naviguant à travers les méandres mentaux, il chercha une trace, si infime soit-elle, de l'âme de François, cherchant des souvenirs précieux.

Une image du presbytère s'imposa à Faustin.

Il s'y fixa. Puis incanta.

— *Ashek dar-nìran, ashek sader, ibn lamed dahir ibn kalimar!*

Le pentacle qu'il s'était scarifié la veille sur l'avant-bras brilla avec intensité. L'âme de François se manifesta avec plus d'acuité et Faustin put effleurer d'autres souvenirs, des traits de personnalité, des tournures de pensées, des connaissances diverses…

Puis le corps vaporeux se constitua.

Et le spectre du vicaire François Gauthier revint d'entre les morts.

— P'tit renard… murmura-t-il en observant ses mains translucides.

— Heureux de te revoir, grand frère, murmura Faustin avec émotion.

— Faustin, s'empressa de dire François, l'Étranger n'est pas loin… en fait, il devrait…

Il fut interrompu par le bruit de mains applaudissant avec sarcasme.

Juste à côté de l'autel, l'Étranger observait les deux frères.

— Touchantes retrouvailles, commenta-t-il ironiquement.

Sabres aux poings, Faustin se retourna vers son père. Celui-ci n'avait plus rien de l'homme à la ténébreuse beauté patricienne qu'il avait toujours eue sous forme d'effigie. Fortement appuyé sur le bâton du Fort, l'Étranger avait le crâne chauve, le visage couvert de cicatrices et la peau brunie de larges taches. Il avançait péniblement, son corps presque entièrement caché par un long manteau noir qui lui arrivait aux mollets. Il le portait détaché, à la manière des officiers militaires, et Faustin pouvait distinguer que les vêtements dessous, chemise et pantalon sombres, étaient très amples.

Dressant la tête, Faustin déclara :

— Je suis venu mettre un terme à votre folie, Hohenstaufen.

L'Étranger haussa un sourcil et laissa échapper un ricanement.

— Ainsi tu sais… J'en déduis que tu as trouvé le père Masse avant moi.

— Me voici, *Imperator*, clama une voix derrière Faustin.

Le jeune homme se retourna. Le père Masse venait de franchir l'une des petites portes de l'église et se tenait dignement dans le narthex.

— C'est un plaisir de vous rencontrer enfin après avoir ainsi étudié votre vie, Empereur Hohenstaufen.

Du chœur, l'Étranger inclina la tête.

— C'est également un plaisir, ajouta le vieux prêtre, d'y mettre fin.

Dessiné sur la porte qu'il venait de franchir, un pentacle se mit à luire alors que le père Masse commençait à incanter :

— *Ad sëresnar ! Ibn salima, desan salima, ist anestdìr kenderas…*

L'Étranger soupira avec lassitude.

Serra négligemment le poing.

— *… estàn nahir kir sederz samir. Id est, kir est…*

Le reste de la formule mourut dans la gorge du père Masse en même temps que Faustin entendit le craquement sinistre des os du vieillard qui se brisaient.

De l'extérieur résonna un long hurlement poussé par le loup Misaël. Le prêtre s'effondra sur le sol, succombant aux innombrables fractures.

— Monstre ! hurla Faustin.

— Tu croyais peut-être que j'allais bêtement le laisser me tuer ? rétorqua l'Étranger. Que je suis trop naïf pour déduire ce qu'un arcaniste de sa trempe a pu élaborer à l'aide de l'*Opus æternum* de Bacon ? Déjà que ma *Reconquista* est pour le moment ajournée… Bellement joué, mon fils. Il me faudra reprendre du début et reporter mes projets à plus tard, peut-être dans cent autres années… mais peu me chaut. Le siècle prochain ne gardera aucun souvenir des arcanes avec lesquels on a pu me tenir tête, et je ne risquerai pas d'être contrarié par les vestiges d'un ordre théurgiste dépassé. Tout n'est qu'une question de temps, et le temps n'a pas d'emprise sur moi.

S'appuyant sur sa canne, l'Étranger avança de quelques pas en passant derrière l'autel.

— Je recommencerai, Charles. Autant de fois qu'il le faudra. Les arcanes furent mon plus grand accomplissement et je refuse de les voir disparaître. Mon cheptel est en place et si bien implanté que même sans mon influence, les habitants des Forges se reproduisent entre eux et préservent l'outrevision. Le savoir arcanique est à l'abri dans des bibliothèques inattaquables. Je devrai me passer des *mestabeok*, mais les *bakaak* peuvent être engendrés aussi souvent que je le désire… il me suffira de déclencher d'autres épidémies.

Déclencher des épidémies ? songea Faustin, épouvanté. Certes, il savait que Lavallée avait été banni de sa tribu indienne pour ce crime, mais…

— En effet, poursuivit l'Étranger. Le choléra de Québec, l'an dernier, est mon œuvre. Et pourquoi crois-tu que j'ai posté Gamache à l'île d'Anticosti ?

— Pour infecter les navires des immigrants irlandais ! comprit Faustin.

— Précisément. Ta pathétique insurrection n'est qu'un contretemps. Tout est planifié à la perfection. Ma seule erreur aura été ta conception… mais je compte bien y remédier.

L'Étranger tendit impérieusement la main vers Faustin.

Dans celle du jeune homme, Lys Blanc vibra avec tant d'intensité qu'il dut lâcher le sabre des Sewell pour tenir celui de Frontenac à deux mains.

Entre l'amusement et la contrariété, l'Étranger esquissa un demi-sourire.

— Et c'est le Fléau d'Albion que tu portes ! Impressionnant… Cette vieille folle de Matshi Skouéou a été assez démente pour te confondre avec l'Élu espéré par Montcalm.

— Elle sait que je ne suis pas l'Élu, répliqua Faustin.

— Et moi, je connais le fonctionnement de cet enchantement. J'en ai supervisé la conception. J'en connais donc les failles.

Balayant l'air de son sceptre, l'Étranger souleva l'un des énormes bancs d'église et le projeta vers la nef. L'immense siège fusa droit sur Faustin, qui brandit le Fléau d'Albion pour se protéger.

Le banc percuta Faustin en plein dans les jambes. Le jeune homme tomba sur le sol en gémissant de douleur, le tibia droit fracturé.

— Que... comment... couina-t-il en s'efforçant de supporter la souffrance.

— Le sabre te protège contre les effets magiques. Ce banc ne l'était pas, seule la force l'ayant projeté l'était. La loi de la gravité s'est chargée du reste.

Faisant flotter un autre banc alors que Faustin rampait péniblement, l'Étranger dit tout doucement :

— Adieu, fils.

Le second banc fila à toute vitesse.

— *Kesh-indira al-mestareün ibn lamedir sadn karesh!* cria le spectre de François, et le siège se fracassa en milliers d'éclats contre une invisible barrière.

Là où il s'était tenu quelques instants auparavant, un pentacle tracé à la hâte achevait de luire.

Protecteur, le vicaire se dressait maintenant devant Faustin.

Cette fois, l'Étranger éclata de rire.

— Fort bien, vicaire Gauthier. Nous verrons combien de temps vous pourrez maintenir cette barrière sans vous consumer vous-même. Vous le sentez déjà, n'est-ce pas ? Votre âme est certes immortelle, mais votre effigie ne l'est que si vous n'en drainez pas la substance... sinon pourquoi aurais-je eu besoin, tout ce temps, d'aspirer l'énergie des feux follets ?

Pointant le sceptre vers eux, l'Étranger fit s'élever trois autres sièges qui allèrent s'écraser contre la bar-

rière magique. Jetant un regard paniqué à François, Faustin remarqua que l'effigie vacillait à chaque impact.

Avec un cri de rage, l'Étranger écarta les bras en croix. Six bancs d'église volèrent en milliers d'éclats acérés qui fusèrent comme des carreaux d'arbalète.

Le spectre de François leva la main et fronça les sourcils.

La salve de projectiles percuta le mur magique et les éclats tombèrent avec bruit, mais l'effigie du vicaire avait pâli de nouveau.

L'Étranger esquissa un autre mouvement de la main.

De l'autel, ce fut au tour du livre des Saintes Écritures d'aller heurter la paroi invisible, puis une vasque d'huile qui éclata au même endroit, imbibant les pages de combustible…

— Vous tenez bon, Gauthier ! tonna l'Étranger. Votre mentor peut être fier de vous…

De la lumière se mit à jaillir du plafond et, levant la tête, Faustin vit que les chandelles de l'énorme lustre venaient de s'allumer d'un coup.

— … et il vous le dira quand vous le rejoindrez !

Le candélabre se détacha de la voûte pour s'écraser au sol, boutant le feu au livre saint. Les flammes se répandirent dans les éclats de bois et les autres débris. Si le feu ne pouvait traverser la barrière, il exerçait une pression continue sur le mur magique et exigeait du vicaire un effort soutenu.

Dès que François flanche, c'en est fini de moi, songea Faustin.

Enragé de ne pouvoir rien faire, il se morigéna : pourquoi n'avait-il pas demandé au père Masse de lui enseigner le contre-sort de longévité ?

Puis un déclic s'effectua dans sa tête.

Il sortit sa craie, traça sur le sol le diagramme de Le Loyer.

Jetant un dernier coup d'œil à François, dont le corps éthéré semblait devenir plus ténu chaque seconde, il incanta.

— *Ad-est kareza, sürdanresh-zonrik aniir, margesht al-fontir.*

Puis ouvrant toutes grandes les portes de son esprit, il émit :

« *Venez à moi, père Masse !* »

Aussitôt, la sensation familière d'hameçon se fichant dans sa nuque se manifesta avec une acuité toute particulière.

« *Faustin !* » répondit l'esprit défunt du père Masse.

« *Père Masse, votre diagramme est intact ! Il me faut la formule, maintenant !* »

« *Le contrecoup sera encore plus grand vu ton inexpérience, mon garçon.* »

Ce fut cette fois l'autel de pierre qui s'écrasa contre la barrière invisible et le corps de François devint si diaphane que Faustin crut un instant que le vicaire avait été dissipé.

« *Ai-je le choix ? Allez-y !* »

« *Quoi qu'il arrive, surtout n'arrête pas. Tu serais oblitéré sur-le-champ.* »

« *Entendu.* »

« *Répète après moi :* Ad danestera, sider kadera, linen lamed ibn suliman… »

— *Ad danestera, sider kadera, linen lamed ibn suliman…* énonça Faustin à haute voix.

« *… dishna fiera ka el-cipher, materos kahd-tizel shaz sedah kirsiten…* »

— *… dishna fiera ka el-cipher, materos kahd-tizel shaz sedah kirsiten…*

Le pentacle sur la porte se mit à luire.

Du chœur d'où il bombardait Faustin, l'Étranger le remarqua, tout comme il dut entendre la formule.

Il fit un geste vague de la main et la lueur s'éteignit. Se retournant, Faustin vit que le diagramme venait d'être effacé.

« *Ne t'arrête pas !* ordonna Masse. …da el shiza kahisten eda naster tihitern shad… »

— … *da el shiza kahisten eda naster tihitern shad…* prononça Faustin en obéissant au spectre du père Masse.

« … mazer ibn sachem dozish ibn salima… »

Contre toute attente, Faustin sentit que l'énergie du sortilège continuait de s'accumuler. Comment était-ce possible ?…

Le visage de l'Étranger fut secoué de tics.

Il leva son sceptre.

Derrière lui, Faustin entendit craquer la balustrade du jubé.

— … *mazer ibn sachem dozish ibn salima…*

« … nazer saderan, ibn salima. »

Il remarqua alors la lueur qui sourdait des vêtements du père Masse.

Il s'est scarifié lui aussi ! comprit Faustin en achevant la formule :

— … *nazer saderan, ibn salima !*

L'énergie s'écoula de Faustin et déferla en direction de l'Étranger. Le corps du père Masse se mit à briller de façon intense avant de se sublimer d'un coup.

Faustin sentit ses forces l'abandonner. À quatre pattes sur le sol, il vit ses bras et ses mains vieillir, leur peau se parcheminer et se couvrir de taches brunes. Le froid se mit à l'engourdir, puis tout s'arrêta.

— *NON !* hurla l'Étranger, son corps tremblant sous le formidable impact arcanique.

Alors l'Immortel Seigneur du Stigma Diaboli leva les bras et se transforma. Le faucon qui avait été l'Étranger prit son envol, bien décidé à fuir l'église de Saint-Laurent.

Le vitrail de la rosace éclata au même moment en mille fragments, fracassé par le piqué du harfang qui venait de le traverser. Le faucon modifia sa trajectoire brusquement, mais pas assez.

Le hibou d'albâtre le laboura de ses serres et le faucon tomba sur le sol, reprenant forme humaine.

Les marques des serres lui labouraient le ventre. À quatre pattes, l'Étranger se vidait de ses fluides vitaux.

Faustin se leva à grand-peine. Son dos l'élançait, ses jambes paraissaient lestées de plomb. Péniblement, il boita jusqu'aux côtés de l'Étranger et arriva juste à temps pour le voir parachever un pentacle qu'il avait tracé de son sang.

Les doigts raidis par l'arthrite, Faustin parvint à empoigner fermement le Fléau d'Albion.

Dans un râle, l'Étranger commença à prononcer sa formule, et le pentacle se mit à luire.

Faustin dut tenir l'arme à deux mains pour être certain d'avoir assez de force lorsqu'il l'abattit sur la nuque de l'Étranger.

La tête roula sur le sol, détachée des épaules par le sabre de Frontenac.

Après six cent cinquante ans, le règne de Frédéric II de Hohenstaufen venait de se terminer.

— Faustin ! Tu dois sortir !

Faustin se tourna vers le vicaire. Des pierres se détachaient une à une de la voûte.

À ses pieds, le pentacle de sang de l'Étranger n'émettait plus aucune lumière.

La tour du clocher commença à trembler alors que le jubé finissait de s'écrouler, véritable averse de fragments de pierre et de mortier.

Faustin s'élança pour fuir mais s'effondra, ses muscles ne lui obéissant plus aussi bien. Ses articulations étaient raides, ses membres faibles.

Le clocher vacilla et des pans de mur se détachèrent. Dans un épouvantable vacarme, les trois énormes cloches de l'église de Saint-Laurent s'écrasèrent sur le parvis.

La grande porte s'ouvrit quelques secondes plus tard avec violence. Guidé par le harfang des neiges, Baptiste arrivait en courant, Ti-Jean sur son épaule.

D'énormes blocs dégringolaient maintenant de la voûte du bâtiment.

À peine Faustin eut-il le temps de ramasser le sceptre de l'Étranger que le bûcheron l'avait pris sur son dos et l'entraînait à l'extérieur, alors que le clocher s'écroulait pour de bon en fracassant le toit.

Je suis allé revoir cette tombe ignorée ;
Et seul, quand j'ai voulu retrouver le chemin,
Quelqu'un était debout, en défendant l'entrée :
C'était l'Oubli, pensif, et le front dans la main.

Eudore Évanturel
La Tombe ignorée, 1878

POINT D'ORGUE

Le vieux mendiant

La première fois qu'on entendit parler du vieux mendiant « Jeteux-de-sorts », ce fut en 1853, à propos de l'incendie d'un manoir. On avait vu le vieillard, disait-on, tendre la main vers la demeure du shérif Sewell et proférer des incantations sataniques. Le manoir, à ce que les journaux rapportèrent, fut la proie des flammes à la suite d'un feu ayant démarré dans la bibliothèque. On aurait pu parler d'une chandelle oubliée et du brasier se répandant dans les rayonnages de papier, mais l'histoire accusant le quêteux était plus intéressante.

Ce n'est donc pas sans raison qu'on lui attribua, deux ans plus tard, la série d'incendies de Pointe-Lévy et cela, dès le premier brasier qui dévora partiellement la demeure de l'ancien notaire Lanigan. On s'insurgea encore davantage lorsque le vieux presbytère du regretté père Masse fut à son tour la proie des flammes et, tout au long de l'été, on injuria le moindre mendiant qui osait se présenter à la Pointe.

Toutefois, c'est un peu plus tard cette année-là que l'opinion des bonnes gens changea du tout au tout au sujet de ce mendiant. On l'avait vu, à l'île d'Orléans, offrir son aide pour la démolition de l'église de Saint-Laurent – le tremblement de terre de 1849

*l'avait endommagée et il fallait bien se résoudre, six
ans plus tard, à déconstruire pour ensuite reconstruire.
On s'étonna que le vieillard démontre autant de vigueur
et de vaillance à l'ouvrage. Les travaux sur cette église
semblaient lui tenir à cœur – dès lors, pouvait-on
vraiment douter de sa bonne âme ? Un déshérité du
monde, n'ayant pas le moindre sou en poche, se mettant
ainsi au service de l'Église… il ne pouvait tout de même
pas être un fou incendiaire !*

*Après tout, on racontait n'importe quoi au sujet
du pauvre miséreux : qu'il voyageait avec un immense
hibou blanc, que les flammes naissaient toutes seules
dans les bâtiments qu'il fixait après qu'il eut marmonné quelques imprécations, qu'il savait lire et
écrire – et pourquoi pas parler anglais, tant qu'à y être ?
Allons donc ! Pourquoi un mendiant irait-il, par
exemple, mettre le feu à une partie de la galerie d'art
du député Légaré ? Quant à ceux qui poussaient l'au-
dace jusqu'à le rendre responsable de la mort de ce
dernier, la même année… Tant qu'à montrer un tel
intérêt pour la fabulation, peut-être auraient-ils dû
accueillir le quêteux pour un soir et écouter les histoires qu'il racontait avec tant de talent. Certes, ce
n'était pas un Jos Violon, mais ce dernier se faisait
désormais rare à mesure que l'âge le rattrapait.*

*Jeteux-de-sorts – c'était malgré tout devenu son
sobriquet, car il n'avait jamais révélé son nom à quiconque – offrait à ceux qui lui donnaient gîte et couvert une panoplie de contes fantastiques, comme celui
de la jeune fille enlevée par le Diable et sauvée par
un vaillant curé alerté par une vision divine ; celui du
canot volant qu'utilisèrent huit bûcherons pour aller voir
leurs promises grâce à un pacte passé avec le Démon ;
celui des lutins, ces hommes miniatures qui montaient
les chevaux à la nuit tombée ; ou encore, celui de la
sorcière Corriveau qui, sous forme d'un squelette revenu*

d'entre les morts, forçait les passants à la porter dans sa cage jusqu'au sabbat de l'île d'Orléans.

Il connaissait aussi des chansons, de belles complaintes de chantier qu'il prétendait avoir appris du draveur Baptiste Lachapelle – ce qui était de toute évidence un mensonge, mais on le lui pardonnait bien : après tout, était-il quelqu'un à Pointe-Lévy qui n'affirmait pas avoir déjà entendu chanter le fameux Lachapelle, au moins une fois ?

Incorrigible nomade, Jeteux-de-sorts allait et venait au gré des saisons et des voyages qu'on lui offrait de bon cœur : où qu'allât le charretier ou le marin, le vieux mendiant était prêt à s'y rendre, portant avec lui ses récits pleins de fi-follets, de fantômes, de bêtes à grand'queue et de loups-garous – autant d'histoires de grand-mères, de contes à faire peur et de fariboles qui égayaient les longues soirées de ceux qui avaient l'amabilité de le recevoir.

On le vit pour la dernière fois en 1885, lors d'une mémorable veillée de contes. Certains dirent qu'il était parti pour les Trois-Rivières – après tout, il y avait passé beaucoup de temps quand les Vieilles Forges avaient définitivement fermé en 83 – et d'autres affirmèrent qu'un curé lui avait offert un gîte permanent. Mais la plupart des gens s'entendaient pour croire que le temps avait finalement eu raison du bon vieux Jeteux-de-sorts. Après tout, personne n'est éternel. Son mode de vie n'était pas le plus doux pour un homme de son âge et plusieurs se souvenaient que la première fois qu'on l'avait vu, plus de trente ans auparavant, il semblait déjà très vieux. On raconte aussi qu'un richard fit chanter une messe pour l'âme du mendiant le soir même où le monument des Tempérances de Pointe-Lévy fut démonté – comme quoi il n'y a pas que Jeteux-de-sorts qui savait raconter des fadaises.

ÉPILOGUE

24 décembre 1888

Le souffle du vent força Faustin à réajuster son manteau. Bonnet enfoncé jusqu'aux yeux, il avançait en luttant contre la neige qui s'était amoncelée le long de la rue. Le froid nocturne, de mordant, allait devenir intolérable ; aussi lui tardait-il d'arriver à destination.

Si son ouïe n'était plus ce qu'elle avait déjà été, il capta quand même le tintement des grelots d'une *sleigh* qui approchait dans la tempête naissante. Aussi rapidement que son corps perclus de rhumatismes et d'arthrite le lui permettait, Faustin se dissimula entre deux énormes épinettes aux rameaux couverts de neige.

Le traîneau passa sans que son conducteur ne remarque sa présence.

Un vieillard esseulé dans la nuit alors que tous réveillonnaient bien au chaud, voilà qui n'aurait pas manqué d'attirer l'attention.

Car c'était la nuit de Noël, pour le peu qu'il s'en souciait.

Sortant une vieille courroie de cuir, il l'enroula autour de son avant-bras et enfonça ses deux doigts dans sa bouche pour siffler. Un cri de rapace lui répondit et le harfang des neiges ne tarda pas à se poser sur son bras.

L'oiseau accepta une caresse sur le ventre.

— Il aura fallu plusieurs années, murmura Faustin, mais tu m'offres finalement cette promenade à mon bras.

Le harfang laissa aller un sifflement.

— C'est la dernière fois que nous venons ici, Shaor'i. Je ne fais qu'apporter la hache de Baptiste et régler ce dont je t'ai parlé hier. Ensuite, je ne reviendrai plus, c'est promis : je sais que tu as horreur de ça.

Alors qu'il regagnait la route, harfang au bras, il usa de sa main libre pour réajuster la hache qu'il portait au dos.

Il lui avait fallu longtemps pour la retrouver et il lui tardait de s'en débarrasser.

Après la bataille de l'église de Saint-Laurent, Baptiste n'avait plus jamais été le même. Il s'éveillait dans la nuit, en proie à d'effroyables cauchemars, amalgames de souvenirs et de scenarii rêvés. De jour, le moindre bruit sec le faisait se dresser à l'affût, poings serrés, paré au combat. Des médecins à qui Faustin avait parlé lui avaient dit que certains soldats revenus de la guerre contre les États avaient présenté des symptômes similaires ; lui-même se souvenait du cas de Poutré, l'ancien Patriote, devenu fou après la perte d'un ami.

Les choses avaient empiré à la mort de Ti-Jean, moins d'un an après la bataille. Le lutin avait été profondément affecté de voir les siens mourir par centaines, une première fois mués en non-morts, une seconde fois au champ d'honneur. Il avait partagé les cauchemars de Baptiste, ou peut-être le bûcheron partageait-il ceux du lutin. Peut-être aussi que les deux amis, en plus de leurs propres tourments, avaient partagé ceux de l'autre.

Quoi qu'il en eût été, Ti-Jean avait cessé de se nourrir puis s'était éteint. De nouveau muré dans

l'obscurité de sa cécité, le colosse était devenu un homme taciturne et apathique. Comme il ne pouvait emmener Baptiste avec lui dans ses pérégrinations, Faustin s'était mis en frais de retrouver la demi-sœur du bûcheron, dont l'homme fort lui avait un jour parlé. La bonne dame l'accueillit et celui qui avait été l'homme fort de Pointe-Lévy, maître-draveur et héros des Hauts, finit ses jours chez elle, alors que se succédaient cauchemars, réminiscences et brève lucidité muette. Il ne fallut que quelques mois pour qu'il aille rejoindre Ti-Jean dans la tombe.

Quant à sa hache, la demi-sœur l'avait vendue avant le retour de Faustin. S'en étaient suivis six mois de recherches vaines, l'acheteur ayant quitté Pointe-Lévy pour le Nord-Ouest. Faustin avait alors promis une forte somme à la famille de l'acheteur s'ils parvenaient à retrouver l'objet.

Un miracle qu'ils s'en soient souvenus autant d'années plus tard en recevant la hache en héritage. Mais ne dit-on pas que, lorsqu'une forte somme est en jeu, les souvenirs deviennent plus vivaces ? Ainsi Faustin avait-il retrouvé la hache qu'avait jadis enchantée son oncle.

Un objet qu'il valait mieux ne pas laisser en circulation en ces temps nouveaux où la magie n'existait, disait-on, que dans les contes de grands-mères.

Le harfang hulula et Faustin vit qu'il avait dépassé sa destination – il avait de plus en plus tendance à s'égarer dans ses pensées. Revenant sur ses pas, il parvint à la vieille chapelle. Le bâtiment était petit et, ce soir, il paraissait destiné à disparaître sous la neige.

C'est donc avec beaucoup d'effort que Faustin le contourna pour se rendre à la façade arrière. Inquiet, il tendit l'oreille et huma ; presque en vain, car son

ouïe et son odorat étaient partiellement bloqués par la force du vent.

Il semblait n'y avoir personne dans les environs : les célébrations de Noël auraient sûrement lieu dans la grande église, plus loin.

Quoique avec cette récente histoire de statue, qui sait ? songea Faustin.

Le harfang le poussa de sa tête, comme pour lui enjoindre de continuer. Inspirant profondément, il murmura une formule arcanique, ce qu'il n'avait pas fait depuis fort longtemps.

— *Ast adhe-mann, ist korezan, nirerth zader dìr len'edör !*

Vérifiant une dernière fois qu'aucun passant ne les observait, Faustin traversa le mur arrière de la chapelle comme si c'était de la brume.

L'homme et l'oiseau pénétrèrent dans la pièce secrète dissimulée entre la façade et la sacristie : un espace d'une verge de large sur trois de long, caché entre deux murs d'épaisse maçonnerie, et qui donnait sur un escalier de pierre en colimaçon.

Le harfang quitta le bras de Faustin le temps qu'il sorte une chandelle de la poche de son manteau. Ses mains d'arthritique peinèrent à gratter l'allumette et c'est avec beaucoup d'effort qu'il suscita une flamme.

Cierge dans la main, Shaor'i à son bras, il descendit l'escalier. À mesure que se succédaient les degrés poussiéreux, Faustin sentait que sa résolution menaçait de s'effriter. Il longea ensuite un couloir menant à une cave dérobée.

Il ne devrait pas flancher.

Pas cette fois.

La flamme de la chandelle illumina l'endroit, qui avait la moitié de la taille de la nef située juste au-dessus. Les deux murs latéraux étaient couverts de rayon-

nages. Sur le mur du fond se trouvait une sorte de râtelier.

D'un geste ayant l'assurance de l'habitude, le harfang alla se percher sur un portemanteau. Faustin installa le cierge dans un chandelier, posa son paqueton et la hache, se débarrassa de son manteau.

Puis il prit l'arme de Baptiste et marcha vers le râtelier où se trouvaient déjà Lys Blanc, le sabre des Sewell, le sceptre du Fort, la hachette d'Otjiera, deux couteaux *saokata* et de menus objets magiques : quatre fers à cheval, une baguette de tremble, une herminette, la baïonnette de Faustin, un miroir et le pendentif de Lord Seaton.

Faustin ajouta la hache de Baptiste et, après une brève hésitation, sortit de sa poche le Calice des Moires pour l'y placer également.

Avec un soupir, il revint à son paqueton, en tira un épais traité de Matthew Walpole, *Of Sorcerers, Seers, Witches and Warlocks in Nouvelle-France*. Sur les rayonnages, il alla déposer l'ouvrage qui rejoignait ainsi tout ce qui restait de littérature arcanique au Nouveau Monde.

Faustin avait beaucoup trié et purgé. Dans le cas de plusieurs bibliothèques, comme chez les Sewell, mieux avait valu tout brûler pour éviter les risques. Par la suite, il avait arpenté la province, rapportant des ouvrages de l'abri-épave du père Masse et de l'ancienne demeure du notaire Lanigan... Quant à Gamache, il avait livré tous les ouvrages de son fort sur l'île d'Anticosti sans opposer la moindre résistance.

Tout ce qu'il avait décidé de préserver était là. Sorts de guérison en grande partie, divination et spiritisme dans une moindre proportion, ouvrages de portance et de téléportation, métamorphose... Rien, absolument rien n'avait été préservé de la magie martiale, sauf le Grimoire de l'Ordre du Chien d'Or.

Deux ouvrages plus récents attirèrent son attention. Il ne fut guère étonné en découvrant leurs titres : *Recherches sur des hybrides végétaux* de Gregor Mendel et *Sur l'origine des espèces au moyen de la sélection naturelle* de Charles Darwin.

Il soupira de nouveau et lança :

— C'est inutile, François. À présent que les Forges sont fermées, les ouvriers vont s'exiler un peu partout et se marier dans d'autres paroisses. Le sang de l'outrevision va se diluer.

N'obtenant pas de réponse, il insista :

— Je perçois ta présence, François. N'essaie pas de me la cacher.

Le spectre du vicaire Gauthier apparut à ses côtés.

— Ça faisait longtemps, Faustin.

— Trois ans, je crois. Je ne pensais pas revenir…

— Mais tu es venu pour moi, n'est-ce pas ?

Faustin détourna le regard.

— Pourquoi me forces-tu à ça, François ? Déjà que ton *miraculeux* pont de glace a permis aux habitants de transporter leurs pierres d'une rive à l'autre, histoire de construire leur fameuse seconde église et de sauver cette chapelle du même coup… Depuis, les pèlerins viennent chaque année plus nombreux. Au cours de la dernière décennie, les offrandes se sont multipliées. Au grand séminaire, on ne parle que de ça. Et voilà qu'une statue de la Vierge ouvre les yeux…

Le vicaire tiqua.

— Et toi, bien sûr, tu préférerais que tout ça passe pour de la superstition… Ne crois pas que j'ignore l'histoire du mendiant Jeteux-de-sorts.

Faustin eut un sourire sans joie.

— J'ai beaucoup narré ce que je savais du monde de jadis sous forme de contes. Il y a un homme qui m'a proposé d'en écrire quelques-uns, un ancien prisonnier. C'était un beau projet, l'histoire de Rose est

dans son recueil – dans cette version, mon oncle arrive à temps pour la sauver. Moyennant une coquette somme, j'ai même réussi à convaincre l'imprimeur d'antidater l'année de publication. D'autres lettrés vont imiter cet homme, je suppose : je vais suivre ça de près.

— Tu as tout prévu, à ce que je vois, marmonna François avec de l'amertume dans la voix.

— Je n'avais pas prévu que tu te manifesterais encore par tes sortilèges à des gens d'une génération qui relègue la magie au rang de superstition. J'aurais cru que tu comprendrais l'importance de mettre fin à ce que Hohenstaufen a engendré il y a sept cents ans.

Sans bruit, François marcha jusqu'au râtelier, où il prit le temps de contempler chaque objet. Rêveusement, il glissa un doigt sur le bâton de son ancêtre.

— Nous avons encore la possibilité de fonder un nouvel ordre, Faustin. Les plus jeunes enfants du village des Forges portent encore le sang de l'outrevision. Les recueils arcaniques les plus pertinents sont rassemblés ici. En secret, nous pourrions…

Faustin ferma les yeux un instant. Certes, il y avait songé. Chaque jour, l'anneau qu'il gardait dans sa poche, jadis transmis par le père Masse, lui ramenait ces réflexions. « Tu lui offriras mon anneau », avait dit le vieux prêtre en parlant de François. « Dis-lui que le maître de l'Ordre Théurgique le désigne comme son digne successeur. »

Toutefois, Faustin ne l'avait jamais donné au vicaire. Mais c'était encore envisageable. François était, pour ainsi dire, éternel. La possibilité de former de nouveaux apprentis en sélectionnant les potentiels les plus prometteurs… un ordre secret, qui finirait par développer des pouvoirs immenses, dans un monde qui n'aurait aucune connaissance de l'existence des arcanes…

… et un jour, l'inévitable se produirait.

— Non, décréta Faustin, catégorique. Le temps des arcanes est révolu.

Le ton de François devint accusateur.

— Tu crains de te retrouver avec un autre Étranger sur les bras, c'est ça?

Faustin courba l'échine. Il se sentait très las, tout d'un coup.

Ou très vieux.

— Oui, avoua-t-il. C'est précisément ce que je crains.

Ce fut au tour du vicaire d'afficher une expression de lassitude.

— Pourquoi préserver tout ça, alors? Tous ces livres, ces artefacts…

— Au cas où une nouvelle menace viendrait à planer. Mon corps est âgé, mais il lui reste encore un dernier soixante-six ans de crédit à entamer. C'est bien assez pour que trépasse quiconque garderait un vague souvenir des arcanes.

— Et ensuite, c'en sera fini.

Le vicaire tourna le dos aux artefacts et retourna vers la bibliothèque. Il se saisit des ouvrages de Mendel et de Darwin pour les tendre à Faustin.

— Prends-les. Puis fais ce que tu as à faire. C'est pour ça que tu es venu, non?

— J'espérais pouvoir te raisonner, mon frère.

Le spectre le dévisagea.

— Sans les arcanes, quelle existence veux-tu que j'aie? Je ne peux pas me mêler à la populace. Le peu que je connais de l'évolution du monde extérieur, je l'apprends lorsque je me permets de déambuler la nuit, profitant de l'obscurité qui masque la translucidité de mon corps, hantant les rues comme un…

Le vicaire se tut.

— … comme un fantôme? compléta Faustin.

François serra le poing.

— Tu peux purger les dernières bibliothèques de leurs grimoires. Tu peux réduire tout ce que nous avons vécu à de simples contes de grand-mère. Mais tu ne feras pas de moi une vulgaire créature de légende. Si le temps des arcanes est passé, le mien aussi.

Faustin eut peine à soutenir le regard de celui qu'il avait toujours vu comme son frère aîné. C'est pour cette décision qu'il était venu, il le savait ; cependant, maintenant qu'il se trouvait en face d'elle, sa volonté vacillait.

François lui posa une main affectueuse sur l'épaule.

— Fais-le. Tu m'as offert quarante ans de plus pour habiter – ou hanter – ce monde.

— Si seulement tu voulais…

— Non. Finissons-en.

Avec la même douceur qu'il utilisait, enfant, lorsqu'il aidait Faustin à revêtir ses vêtements d'hiver, François releva le bras de la chemise de son jeune frère. Il dénuda ainsi le pentacle qu'il y avait scarifié, longtemps auparavant.

La gorge de Faustin se noua et il secoua la tête.

— Je ne peux pas, grand frère.

François esquissa un sourire.

— Je m'en doutais. Et c'est pour ça que j'ai étudié. *Ashek dar-nìran, ashek sader, ibn…*

Horrifié, Faustin murmura :

— Non…

— *…lamed dahir ibn kalimar…*

— NON !

Le diagramme s'illumina sur le bras de Faustin alors qu'il tentait vainement d'empêcher l'énergie arcanique de se manifester.

Le corps fantomatique se fit plus ténu.

— Au revoir, p'tit renard. Je présenterai tes salutations à ton oncle.

Le spectre se dissipa, puis sa présence ne fut plus perceptible.

— Adieu, grand frère, murmura Faustin.

Qui laissa couler ses larmes, les premières depuis la bataille de l'église Saint-Laurent.

◆

Longtemps, il resta à écouter le silence.

Puis, quand beaucoup de temps fut passé, il sortit de sa poche l'anneau de platine du père Masse.

Les vieux genoux de Faustin craquèrent quand il s'accroupit pour creuser le plancher de terre et y ensevelir le bijou.

Alors, sans souffler un mot, il remit son manteau, ramassa son paqueton. Le harfang vint se poser sur son bras. Faustin reprit la chandelle et remonta l'escalier.

Quand il passa de nouveau à travers le mur, le vent hivernal souffla la flamme de la chandelle. Avec un bruissement d'ailes, le hibou blanc s'envola. Sans se retourner, Faustin s'éloigna de la chapelle, serrant son manteau contre lui pour se protéger du vent et de la neige.

Au-dessus de sa tête, il entendit crier le harfang et sut que c'était la dernière fois qu'il le verrait.

Étrangement, il n'éprouvait plus ni chagrin ni regret.

Seulement une tranquille certitude : désormais, la nuit pourrait tomber sur les arcanes.

FIN

Saint-Barnabé-Nord, 12 octobre 2010
Trois-Rivières, 17 mai 2015

Notes de l'auteur

Dans le temps passé c'est à peine si vous auriez pu rencontrer une seule personne de nos endroits qui n'eût délivré son loup-garou et conversé deux ou trois fois au moins avec les morts. Aujourd'hui plus rien ; mais aussi les temps sont bien changés...

Hubert LaRue
Les Soirées canadiennes

Comme pour les livres précédents, tout l'aspect fantastique du dernier tome se base sur un maximum de sources historiques ou folkloriques.

La description du *skwahdem* provient du livre *Le Saguenay légendaire* de Marius Barbeau, dans lequel il dit : « Un autre animal fabuleux était le skwahdem, espèce de salamandre [...] beuglant comme un taureau. » On fait aussi vaguement référence à cette créature dans la légende du sorcier Belleau, disant de lui qu'« il se mit à beugler comme le skwahdem ». Pour donner vie au skwahdem, je me suis basé sur le ménopome, salamandre géante d'Amérique du Nord dite « salamandre-alligator » qui peut atteindre plus de soixante-quinze centimètres (des ossements nous révèlent des spécimens dépassant cent vingt

centimètres ayant vécu avant que la pollution n'altère l'alcalinité des eaux). On ne la rencontre plus désormais qu'entre New York et le Mississippi, alors qu'elle était jadis beaucoup plus répandue.

On trouve effectivement de nombreux rochers aux angles réguliers en Mauricie, allant du fameux Rocher de Grand'Mère jusqu'aux pierres droites du parc national mauricien. L'idée d'en rassembler plusieurs dans l'anse de Yamachiche me vient du conte « Le Fantôme de La Roche » relaté dans *En bâtissant des églises*... de Joseph-Philippe Héroux, où il est notamment fait mention d'un ancien autel autochtone constitué d'un bloc de granit parfaitement cubique et d'un fantôme qui y serait enchaîné. Si, de nos jours, il ne reste qu'une petite section du marais (la réserve du marais Saint-Eugène), il fut une époque où ces terres humides étaient très vastes ; elles furent asséchées pour favoriser l'agriculture.

Bien que la ville de Portneuf ait été fondée en 1861, la seigneurie du Port-Neuf date de 1636. Intimement lié au Chemin du Roy par lequel était acheminé l'approvisionnement nécessaire, le Port-Neuf était une étape mineure pour la diligence et les navires. L'auberge du *Silver Star* est une invention, mais les *bodhran*, ces tambours du Port-Neuf, sont réels et furent probablement amenés par les immigrants irlandais.

Kabir Kouba est une créature qui amalgame la plupart des mythes de monstres lacustres du Québec – lesquels sont fort nombreux. Il est vrai que Samuel de Champlain mentionne une créature titanesque qui, selon toute vraisemblance, aurait été un spécimen de lépisostée osseux. Néanmoins, les Iroquois parlaient d'un grand serpent marin portant des cornes bien avant l'arrivée des Blancs et Philippe Aubert de Gaspé le cite dans l'un de ses contes. L'assimiler à un esturgeon particulièrement vieux (et donc de taille démesurée) est l'une des hypothèses les plus crédibles pour expliquer les légendes de monstres lacustres, d'ailleurs défendue par Louis-Philippe Roy pendant plus de vingt-cinq ans.

George Mellis Douglas, médecin et surintendant de Grosse-Île, a réellement existé et fut, à partir du 2 mars 1849, le seigneur de l'île au Ruau, où il érigea un domaine aristocratique victorien. Bien vite, les autorités suspecteront de nombreuses irrégularités dans sa gestion à Grosse-Île et le docteur Douglas mettra fin à ses jours, ruiné et harcelé par les hommes de loi. On a prétendu que des défunts de Grosse-Île revenaient d'entre les morts par magie noire : cette légende est probablement due à l'ensevelissement trop hâtif de cholériques encore vivants qui, parfois, parvenaient à trouver la force de se frayer un chemin vers la surface.

La légende des *marsouins fantômes de Rivière-Ouelle* fut rapportée en 1931 par Edward C. Woodley dans son recueil *Legends of French Canada*. Elle fut reprise par Claude Aubry dans *Le Violon magique et autres légendes du Canada Français* en 1968.

Les *man'ido*, plus connues dans la version francisée (ou anglicisée) de « manitou », étaient dans les mythes originels des esprits protecteurs de la nature. Le concept de *man'ido* a beaucoup évolué au contact des Blancs, qui les fusionnèrent en une seule entité nommée Manitou, pour ensuite forcer les autochtones à l'assimiler au Diable. La rare *floerkée* existe réellement et ne se retrouve, au Québec, que sur quelques îles du Saint-Laurent. Elle sacrifie effectivement sa longévité pour produire des graines. Quant à la forêt de la Pointe-aux-Pins, elle est toujours intacte et constitue aujourd'hui une réserve naturelle protégée.

Le père *Michel Masse* est un personnage historique. Né en 1764, ordonné en 1788, il fut le curé de Pointe-Lévy de 1794 à 1831. Réputé pour son érudition, il fut impliqué en 1799 dans une étrange histoire de possession qui l'opposa à une soi-disant magicienne venue de Saint-Jean-Port-Joli. Décédé en 1845, on l'a longtemps cru encore vivant quoique « caché ». Je l'ai associé au mythe du *petit bonhomme sans tête*, évoqué par Auguste Béchard dans son *Histoire de l'Île-aux-Grues et des îles*

voisines. Son compagnon, le loup *Misaël Longneau*, est tiré du conte « Le Loup-garou » de Pamphile Le May.

On trouve plusieurs légendes traitant du *spectre d'un prêtre sans tête*. La plus connue est celle rapportée en 1889 par F. A. Baillargé dans *Coups de crayon*, situant ce prêtre à l'île Dupas ; néanmoins, des versions antérieures mentionnent d'autres lieux. Ainsi, en 1877 dans *Souvenirs et légendes*, Pierre-Joseph-Olivier Chauveau place cette histoire dans la paroisse de l'Islet. La présence de fusiliers fantômes ayant refusé de se rendre face à l'envahisseur anglais est rapportée par Alphonse Leclerc dans *Le Saint-Laurent historique, légendaire et topographique*, et par Louis Fréchette dans *La Légende d'un peuple*. L'histoire de la possédée de l'Islet et du curé Panet se trouve dans l'opuscule *La Légende du rocher Panet*, écrit par T. S. Jemnat en 1905.

Construite en 1688 comme demeure privée, la maison portant le bas-relief du *Chien d'Or* devint une boutique dans les années 1730. Elle a été revendue autour de 1786 pour devenir une auberge comprenant une salle de réunion des Francs-Maçons, le *Freemasons' Hall*. Benjamin Sulte affirme qu'auparavant « l'endroit servait de lieu de réunion à une autre fraternité, dissoute après la Conquête ». La maison fut transformée en bureau de poste en 1846 et démolie en 1871 ; toutefois, on prit soin de préserver la pierre du Chien d'Or et de l'installer au-dessus du péristyle d'entrée d'un nouvel édifice. Elle fut d'ailleurs restaurée et redorée en 2015.

Le personnage de *Matshi Skouéou* est une fusion de trois légendes. Il est question d'une première Dame Blanche dans le tome III des *Relations des jésuites*, en date du 8 juillet 1665. Celle-ci aurait nourri des enfants affamés. Une seconde Dame Blanche, fiancée d'un jeune soldat de Beauport, est citée en 1928 par Pierre-Georges Roy dans *L'Île d'Orléans*. Quant à la Dame aux Glaïeuls, elle provient de la légende *La Jongleuse* rapportée par l'abbé Casgrain. Peu à peu, on trouvera des légendes à propos de dames blanches partout en Amérique du Nord et le

mythe a évolué vers des versions modernes, comme celle de l'auto-stoppeuse fantôme. Pour ce qui est de la présence des enfants-spectres habillés de blanc, Philippe Aubert de Gaspé en fait mention dans *Les Anciens Canadiens*. Cette légende se répandra et se modernisera elle aussi, devenant la célèbre fillette vêtue de blanc du cinéma, comme dans le film américain *The Ring*. Le réseau de galeries souterraines où j'ai placé le castel de la Dame est, en vérité, la grotte de Boischâtel.

Les *bakaak* (ou *pakàk* selon le *Lexique de la langue algonquine* publié en 1886 par Jean André Cuoq) sont des guerriers-squelettes des mythes algonquins dont on trouve une trace dans de nombreux contes amérindiens. De nos jours, on rencontre davantage l'orthographe anglicisée *baykok*.

La légende des *arbres qui saignent* est présente dans la culture orale, et plusieurs conteurs en font mention – toutefois aucun auteur du XIXe siècle ne semble avoir couché sur papier cette macabre légende. Je l'ai retrouvée dans quelques archives audio; la version d'Elzéar Caron affirme qu'un arbre qui se met à saigner quand on le coupe révèle qu'une personne s'est jadis pendue à l'une de ses branches. On trouve dans les archives d'un certain A.F. de l'Université Laval la mention d'un conteur narrant l'histoire d'un arbre étrangleur se vengeant du bûcheron l'ayant fait saigner. En 1991, Nicole Guilbault cita une autre version dans laquelle un arbre se serait mis à saigner pour punir un blasphémateur. Pour mes propres arbres qui saignent, j'ai tenté de concilier toutes ces versions en restant aussi plausible que possible. L'arbre que j'ai employé, l'aulne rouge (*alnus rubra*) est plus grand et massif que notre aulne québécois, l'aulne vert (*alnus viridis*). L'aulne rouge possède vraiment un bois qui devient carmin une fois entaillé et on ne le trouve normalement que sur la côte ouest.

Pour ce qui est du *château Bigot*, aussi nommé l'Hermitage ou Beaumanoir, on rasa définitivement ses derniers vestiges en 1908. C'est dans le roman *Le Chien d'Or*

de William Kirby qu'on trouve la plus riche évocation
de ce manoir, de même qu'une magnifique description
de *Caroline de Saint-Castin*. Dans le même roman, on
croise la Corriveau dépeinte sous les traits d'une vieille
femme – anachronisme de l'auteur, car en 1748 (année
pendant laquelle se déroule l'histoire), Marie-Josephte
Corriveau (née en 1733) n'a que quinze ans. J'ai tenté
de réconcilier l'erreur de Kirby avec la vérité historique
en dotant Marie-Josephte d'un sortilège altérant son
apparence. Néanmoins, comme le roman de Kirby se
passe alors que le château était en bon état, j'ai dû chercher des descriptions des ruines qui en restaient un siècle
plus tard. Je me suis donc basé sur une gravure publiée
dans *L'Opinion publique* du 26 avril 1877, sur la description qu'en fait Amédée Papineau dans sa nouvelle
« Caroline », alors qu'il affirme avoir réellement visité ces
ruines, et sur celle de Joseph Marmette dans *L'Intendant
Bigot*.

Tel que je l'ai spécifié dans le tome 1, la principale
description de *Jean-Pierre Lavallée* nous vient de l'article
« The Folk Lore of Lower Canada » publié par Edward
Farrer en 1882 dans *Atlantic Monthly*. Jusqu'à présent, il
s'agit de la seule référence écrite que j'ai pu retrouver.
La culture orale semble se souvenir beaucoup mieux de
Lavallée, et plusieurs conteurs aiment à narrer ses exploits
allégués. J'ai décidé de fusionner le personnage avec le
chamane Atontarori, à qui deux conteurs wendats attri-
buent des exploits forts similaires : se transformer en
cheval, influencer le climat et repousser l'envahisseur
anglais (on parle chez eux de Phips plutôt que de Walker).
Comme Lavallée, Atontarori est métis (l'un des conteurs
le prétend fils du chef Kondiaronk et d'une sorcière
française arrivée clandestinement sur le navire des Filles
du Roy). Les deux sorciers sont si semblables qu'il est
difficile de ne pas voir deux versions d'une même légende.

L'amiral Phips fit voile vers Québec en 1690 et fut
repoussé par Frontenac et Couture lors d'un cuisant échec
militaire, qui sera suivi d'épidémies à bord des navires

et de graves dommages à la suite d'intempéries. Il fut réellement mêlé à l'hystérie qui entourait l'affaire des sorcières de Salem.

Si le naufrage de l'île aux Œufs est réel, l'*amiral Walker* n'a pas péri avec son escadre. On le prétend toutefois dans plusieurs contes, et la légende de l'escadre fantôme est citée par de nombreux auteurs. L'une des plus belles évocations de cette légende est « L'Amiral du brouillard » de Faucher de Saint-Maurice ; ce même auteur rapporte les fiançailles de Walker avec une certaine miss Routh, ce qui semble n'être qu'une fiction romantique.

Frédéric II de Hohenstaufen, né le 26 décembre 1194 et mort le 13 décembre 1250, a régné sur le Saint-Empire romain germanique. D'une érudition stupéfiante, il parlait au moins six langues. Durant son règne, il accueillit à sa cour des sages du monde entier ; il portait un vif intérêt aux mathématiques et devint un ami du célèbre scientifique Fibonacci. Féru de divination et de magie, Hohenstaufen fit aussi venir à sa cour l'alchimiste et astronome Michael Scot, et il ne prit bientôt plus une seule décision sans consulter ce devin mathématicien. Se livrant à des expériences scientifiques sur des êtres vivants, Hohenstaufen entra en contact avec le théologien musulman Ibn Sabin et s'interrogea sur l'immortalité. Cela lui valut des conflits permanents avec la papauté et il se vit excommunié par deux fois, le pape Grégoire IX voyant en lui l'incarnation de l'Antéchrist. Dernier empereur de la dynastie des Hohenstaufen, on le surnomma *Stupor Mundi* (la « merveille du monde ») – il inspira même Machiavel pour la rédaction du *Prince*. Sa réputation était telle qu'on attendit son retour après sa mort : on racontait que l'Empereur dormait d'un sommeil magique dans les profondeurs d'une caverne sous l'Etna.

On trouve de nombreuses légendes à propos d'un *vieux mendiant jeteur de sorts* et cela, dans toutes les régions du Québec. En faire la liste occuperait plusieurs pages. En réalité, il s'agit du personnage le plus répandu de

notre folklore après le Diable. « Une étrange poursuite » d'Adèle Lacerte et « La Maison hantée » de Louis Fréchette sont deux belles évocations de ce personnage.

En 1853, le manoir des Sewell fut effectivement incendié et n'en subsista que la façade. Il est également vrai qu'il y eut une vague d'incendies à Pointe-Lévy en 1855 et qu'on démolit l'église de Saint-Laurent de l'île d'Orléans la même année pour en construire une autre. Le monument des Tempérances a réellement existé, situé sur le territoire de l'actuelle ville de Lévis sur un promontoire entre les rues Vaudreuil et Saint-Joseph. Il fut démonté en 1885.

Une paroisse doit réellement la construction de son église à un miraculeux pont de glace et on y aurait vu, dix ans plus tard, une statue mariale ouvrir les yeux. C'est dans cette paroisse que j'ai situé les derniers vestiges des arcanes.

◆

À la suite de la publication de *La Voyante des Trois-Rivières*, des lecteurs m'ont demandé plus de détails sur la philosophie *saokata*. J'en traiterai brièvement ici. *Saokata* est un terme nébuleux, très rare dans la culture écrite et aux définitions parfois contradictoires. Dans les *Relations des jésuites*, le terme désigne un oniromancien huron (wendat) : « ... *les Hurons croyent qu'il y a de certaines personnes plus esclairées que le commun [...] qu'ils appellent Saokata* ». Les publications de la société Champlain affirment, en 1951, que « saokata » ne désigne pas le devin mais bien l'art du rêve conscient et des danses guerrières. Des couteaux dits « de danse saokata » m'ont été montrés par Pierre Grandmont, un ethnologue d'ascendance wendate. Dans *Divination and Healing : Potent Vision*, Michael Winkelman affirme que le Saokata était un guérisseur iroquois posant le diagnostic grâce au contact avec un aide-esprit. La thèse doctorale en anthropologie de G. Levasseur lie au terme « saokata » l'art de laisser

entrer un esprit animal (oki) dans son corps. Ainsi, de ces sources viennent la technique de combat à deux couteaux de Shaor'i, qui ressemble à une danse guerrière, ses méditations, ses dons de guérison et, bien sûr, sa transformation animale.

◆

C'est toute une aventure qui se termine ici, et je ne parle pas des péripéties de Faustin. Ma saga à moi a débuté en octobre 2010, alors que Nathalie, mon ex-conjointe, m'a botté l'arrière-train pour que je me décide enfin à rédiger *Le Crépuscule des Arcanes*. Il aura ensuite fallu qu'elle et mon petit frère redoublent d'efforts pour que je me décide à poster le manuscrit aux éditions Alire, en mars 2011. J'ai reçu ma réponse plus d'un an après. Je me souviens sans mal du message que monsieur Pettigrew avait laissé sur mon répondeur et de mes jambes qui m'avaient lâché à ce moment-là.

On ne soupçonne pas ce que représente la publication pour une personne qui a rêvé toute sa vie d'être auteur. À travers la rédaction de ma trilogie, un peu à l'image de Faustin, je me suis découvert moi-même. J'ai trouvé en moi des capacités que je ne croyais pas avoir, pas seulement en écriture, mais surtout pour ce que le métier d'auteur amène en périphérie de la publication : parler devant des groupes, rencontrer de nouvelles personnes, aborder des idoles de jeunesse, participer à des événements, oser aller au-devant des gens. Le moi-même d'aujourd'hui est bien différent de celui qui avait amorcé l'écriture du *Crépuscule des Arcanes* et j'ai énormément grandi à travers cette aventure.

On ne remercie jamais assez les gens qui le méritent et c'est pour cela que j'exprimerai, encore une fois, ma gratitude à mon éditeur Jean Pettigrew, qui a accepté de donner sa chance à cet obscur inconnu sorti de nulle part. Par ricochet, ma plus sincère reconnaissance va à Francine Pelletier, qui a lu ledit manuscrit avant de le

référer à son éditeur et qui a accepté de s'essayer à la direction littéraire pour m'accompagner tout au long du voyage... sans cesser, au passage, de m'aider à m'épanouir au quotidien.

Comme toute bonne histoire, cette aventure s'est terminée par une fin merveilleuse. Alors que j'achevais les derniers chapitres de ce troisième roman, une amie très proche est devenue ma nouvelle compagne. Ma chère Sonya, merci pour l'extraordinaire complicité que nous en sommes venus à partager.

Finalement, même si cela paraît un peu étrange, je te dis merci à toi, Faustin. Pendant plus de quatre ans, j'ai pensé à toi presque chaque jour. Tu étais là pour me changer les idées au cours de ma séparation, pendant que des amis combattaient des maladies graves, après le décès de ma grand-mère et celui de mon oncle Joël. Sans toi, vieux frère, je ne sais pas ce que j'aurais fait. À présent, ton histoire est terminée. La mienne doit continuer : j'ai d'autres univers à créer, d'autres personnages à faire vivre, d'autres histoires à raconter. Malgré tout, tu vas beaucoup me manquer...

... mais je pense bien qu'on se reverra, un de ces jours.

Donc, *à la revoyure !*

S.C.

CHAPTER ONE

LETTY SPENCER HUNCHED her shoulders against the frosty February night as she pushed out of the Brooklyn diner, door swinging behind her. Her body was exhausted after her double shift, but not half as weary as her heart.

It had not been a good day.

Shivering in her threadbare coat, Letty lowered her head against the biting wind on the dark street. Snow flurries brushed against her exposed skin.

"Letitia." The voice was low and husky behind her. Letty's back snapped straight.

No one called her Letitia anymore, not even her father. Letitia Spencer had been the pampered heiress of Fairholme. Letty was just another New York waitress struggling to make ends meet for her family.

And that voice sounded like...

He sounded like...

Gripping her purse strap tight, she slowly turned around. *And lost her breath.*

Darius Kyrillos stood against a glossy black sports car parked on the street. Dark-haired and dark-eyed, he was devastatingly handsome and powerful in his well-cut suit and black wool coat, standing beneath the softly falling snowflakes illuminated by a streetlight.

For a moment, Letty struggled to make sense of what her eyes were telling her. Darius? Here?

"Did you see this?" her father had said excitedly that morning, spreading the newspaper across their tiny kitchen counter. "Darius Kyrillos sold his company for twenty billion dollars!" He looked up, his eyes unfocused with painkillers, his recently broken arm awkward in a sling. "You should call him, Letty. Make him love you again."

After ten years, her father had said Darius's name out loud. He'd broken the unspoken rule. She'd fled, mumbling that she'd be late for work.

But it had affected her all day, making her clumsily drop trays and forget orders. She'd even dumped a plate of eggs and bacon on a customer. It was a miracle she hadn't been fired.

No, Letty thought, unable to breathe. This was the miracle. Right now.

Darius.

She took a step toward him on the sidewalk, her eyes wide.

"Darius?" she whispered. "Is it really you?"

He came forward like a dark angel. She could see his breath beneath the streetlight like white smoke in the icy night. He stopped, towering over her. The light frosted his dark hair, leaving his face in shadow. She half expected him to disappear if she tried to touch him. So she didn't.

Then he touched her.

Reaching out, he stroked a dark tendril that had escaped her ponytail, twisted it around his finger. "You're surprised?"

At the sound of that low, husky voice, lightly accented from his early childhood in Greece, a deep shiver sent a rush of prickles over her skin. And she knew he wasn't a dream.

Her heart pounded. Darius. The man she'd tried not to crave for the last decade. The man she'd dreamed about against her will, night after night. Here. Now. She choked out a sob. "What are you doing here?"

His dark eyes ran over her hungrily. "I couldn't resist."

As he moved his head, the streetlight illuminated his face. He hadn't changed at all, Letty thought in wonder. The same years that had nearly destroyed her hadn't touched him. He was the same man she remembered, the one she'd once loved with all her innocent heart, back when she'd been a headstrong eighteen-year-old, caught up in a forbidden love affair. Before she'd sacrificed her own happiness to save his.

His hand moved down to her shoulder. Feeling his warmth through her thin coat, she wanted to cry, to ask him what had taken so long. She'd almost given up hope.

Then she saw his gaze linger on her old coat, with its broken zipper, and her diner uniform, a white dress that had been bleached so many times it was starting to fray. Usually, she also wore unfashionable nylons to keep her legs warm while she was on her feet all day in white orthopedic shoes. But today, her last pair had been unwearable with too many rips, so her legs were bare.

Following his gaze, she blushed. "I'm not really dressed for going out…"

"Your clothes don't matter." There was a strange undercurrent in his voice. "Let's go."

"Go? Where?"

He took her hand in his own, palm to palm, and she suddenly didn't feel the snowflakes or cold. Waves of electricity scattered helter-skelter across her body, across her skin, from her scalp to her toes.

"My penthouse. In Midtown." He looked down at her. "Will you come?"

"Yes," she breathed.

His sensual lips curved oddly before he led her to his shiny, low-slung sports car and opened the passenger door.

As Letty climbed in, she took a deep breath, inhaling the scent of rich leather. This car likely cost more than she'd earned the past decade waiting tables. She moved her hand along the fine calfskin, the color of pale cream. She'd forgotten leather could be so soft.

Climbing in beside her, Darius started the engine. The car roared away from the curb, humming through the night, leaving her neighborhood to travel through the gentrified areas of Park Slope and Brooklyn Heights before finally crossing the Manhattan Bridge into the New York borough that most catered to tourists and the wealthy: Manhattan.

All the while, Letty was intensely aware of him beside her. Her gaze fell upon his hand and thick wrist, laced with dark hair, as he changed gears.

"So." His voice was ironic. "Your father is out of prison."

Biting her lip, she looked at him hesitantly beneath her lashes. "A few days ago."

Darius glanced back at her old coat and fraying uniform. "And now you're ready to change your life."

Was that a question or a suggestion? Did he mean that *he* wanted to change it? Had he actually learned the truth about why she'd betrayed him ten years ago?

"I've learned the hard way," she said in a low voice, "that life changes, whether you're ready or not."

His hands tightened as he turned back to the steering wheel. "True."

Letty's eyes lingered on his profile, from the dark slash of eyebrows to his aquiline nose and full, sensual mouth. She still felt like she was dreaming. *Darius Kyrillos.* After all these years, he'd found her at the diner and was whisking her off to his penthouse. The only man she'd ever truly loved...

"Why did you come for me?" she whispered. "Why today, after all these years?"

His dark gaze was veiled. "Your message."

She hadn't sent any message. "What message?"

"Fine," he murmured, baring his teeth in a smile. "Have it your way."

Message? Letty felt a skitter of dark suspicion. Her father had wanted her to contact Darius. For the last few days, since he'd broken his arm in mysterious circumstances he wouldn't explain, he'd been home on painkillers, sitting next to her ancient computer with nothing to do.

Could her father have sent Darius a message, pretending to be her?

She glanced at Darius, then decided she didn't care. If her father had interfered, all she could be was grateful, if this was the result.

Her father must have revealed her real reasons for betraying Darius ten years ago. She couldn't imagine he would even be talking to her now otherwise.

But how to know for sure?

Biting her lip, she said awkwardly, "I read about you in the paper this morning. That you sold. Your company, I mean."

"Ah." His jaw set as he turned away. "Right."

His voice was cold. No wonder, Letty thought. She sounded like an idiot. She tried to steady herself. "Congratulations."

"Thank you. It cost ten years of my life."

Ten years. Those two simple words hung between them in silence, like a small raft on an ocean of regret.

Their car entered Manhattan, with all its wealth and savagery. A place she'd avoided since her father's trial and sentencing almost a decade before.

Her heartbeat fluttered in her throat as she looked down at her chapped hands, folded tightly in her lap. "I've thought of you a lot, wondering how you were. Hoping you were well. Hoping you were happy."

Stopping at a red light, Darius abruptly looked at her.

"It was good of you to think of me," he drawled in a low voice, once again with that strange undercurrent. In the cold night of the city, headlights of passing cars moved shadows across the hard lines of his face.

The light changed to green. It was just past ten o'clock,

and the traffic was starting to lessen. Heading north on First Avenue, they passed the United Nations plaza. The buildings had started climbing higher against the sky as they approached Midtown. Turning off Forty-Ninth onto the gracious width of Park Avenue, they approached a newly built glass-and-steel skyscraper on the south side of Central Park.

As he pulled his car into the porte cochere, she was craning her neck back in astonishment. "You live here?"

"I have the top two floors," he said casually, in the way someone might say, *I have tickets to the ballet.*

His door opened, and he handed the keys to a smiling valet who greeted him respectfully by name. Coming around, Darius opened Letty's door. He held out his hand.

She stared at it nervously, then put her hand in his.

He wrapped it tightly in his own. She felt the warmth and roughness of his palm against hers.

He had to know, she thought desperately. He had to. Otherwise, why would he have sought her out? Why wouldn't he still hate her?

He led her through the awe-inspiring lobby, with its minimalist furniture and twenty-foot ceilings.

"Good evening, Mr. Kyrillos," the man at the desk said. "Cold weather we're having. Hope you're staying warm!"

Darius held Letty's hand tightly. She felt like she might catch flame as he drew her across the elegant, cavernous lobby. "I am. Thank you, Perry."

He waved his key fob in front of the elevator's wall panel and pressed the seventieth floor.

His hand gripped hers as the elevator traveled up. She felt the warmth of his body next to hers, just inches away, towering over her. She bit her lip, unable to look at him. She just stared at the electronic numbers displaying the floors as the elevator rose higher and higher. *Sixty-eight, sixty-nine, seventy...*

The bell dinged as the door slid open.

"After you," Darius said.

Glancing at him nervously, she stepped out directly into a dark, high-ceilinged penthouse. He followed her, as the elevator door closed silently behind them.

The rubber soles of her white shoes squeaked against the marble floor as she walked through the foyer beneath the modern crystal chandelier above. She flinched at the noise, embarrassed.

But his handsome face held no expression as he removed his long black overcoat. He didn't turn on any lights. He never looked away from her.

With a gulp, she turned away.

Gripping her purse strap, she walked forward into the shadowy main room. It was two stories high, with sparse, angular furniture in black and gray, and floor-to-ceiling windows twisted around the penthouse in every direction.

Looking from right to left, she could see the dark vista of Central Park, the high-rise buildings to the Hudson River, and the lights of New Jersey beyond it, and to the south, the skyscrapers of Midtown, including the Empire State Building, all the way to the Financial District and the gleaming One World Trade Center.

The sparkling nighttime view provided the only light in the penthouse, aside from a single blue gas fire that flickered in the stark fireplace.

"Incredible," Letty breathed, going up to the windows. Without thinking, she leaned forward, putting her overheated forehead against the cool glass, looking down at Park Avenue far below. The cars and yellow cabs looked tiny, like ants. She felt almost dizzy from being so high off the earth, up in the clouds. It was a little terrifying. "Beautiful."

His reply was husky behind her. "*You* are beautiful, Letitia."

Turning, she looked at him in the soft blue glow of firelight. Then, as she looked more closely...

Her lips parted with an intake of breath.

She'd thought Darius hadn't changed?

He'd changed completely.

At thirty-four, he was no longer a slender youth, but a powerful man. His shoulders had broadened to match his tall height, his body filling out with hard muscle. His dark hair had once been wavy and tousled, like a poet's, but was now cut short, as severe as his chiseled jawline.

Everything about Darius was tightly controlled now, from the cut of his expensive clothes—a black shirt with the top button undone, black trousers, black leather shoes—to his powerful stance. His mouth had once been expressive and tender and kind. Now his lips had a hard twist of arrogance, even cruelty.

He towered over her like a king, in his penthouse with all of New York City at his feet.

At her expression, his jaw tightened. "Letitia…"

"Letty." She managed a smile. "No one calls me Letitia anymore."

"I have never been able to forget you," he continued in a low voice. "Or that summer we were together…"

That summer. A small noise came from the back of her throat as unwanted memories filled her mind. Dancing in the meadow. Kissing the night after her debutante ball. Escaping the prying eyes of servants in Fairholme's enormous garage, steaming up the windows of her father's vintage car collection for weeks on end. She'd been ready to surrender everything.

Darius was the one who'd wanted to wait for marriage to consummate their love.

"Not until you're my wife," he'd whispered as they strained for each other, barely clothed, panting with need in the backseat of a vintage limousine. "Not until you're mine forever."

Forever never came. Their romance had been illicit, forbidden. She was barely eighteen, his boss's daughter; he was six years older, the chauffeur's son.

After a hot summer of innocent passion, her father had been infuriated when he'd discovered their romance. He'd ordered Darius off the estate. For one awful week he and Letty had been apart. Then Darius had called her.

"Let's elope," he'd said. "I'll get a day job to support us. We'll get a studio apartment in the city. Anything as long as we're together."

She'd feared it would hurt his dream of making his fortune, but she couldn't resist. They both knew there was no chance of a real wedding, not when her father would try to stop the marriage. So they'd planned to elope to Niagara Falls.

But on the night his car waited outside the Fairholme gate, Letty never showed up.

She hadn't returned any of his increasingly frantic phone calls. The next day, she'd even convinced her father to fire Eugenios Kyrillos, Darius's father, who'd been their chauffeur for twenty years.

Even then, Darius had refused to accept their breakup. He'd kept calling, until she'd sent him a single cold message.

I was only using you to get another man's attention. He's rich and can give me the life of luxury I deserve. We're engaged now. Did you really think that someone like me would ever live in a studio apartment with someone like you?

That had done the trick.

But it had been a lie. There had been no other man. At the ripe old age of twenty-eight, Letty was still a virgin.

All these years, she'd promised herself that Darius would never know the truth. He could never know how she'd sacrificed herself, so he'd be able to follow his dreams without guilt or fear. Even if it meant he hated her.

But Darius must have finally found out the truth. It was the only explanation for him seeking her out.

"So you know why I betrayed you ten years ago?" she said in a small voice, unable to meet his eyes. "You forgive me?"

"It doesn't matter," he said roughly. "You're here now."

Her heart pounded as she saw the dark hunger in his eyes.

She looked down at the coffee stain on her uniform, the smear of ketchup near the cheerful name tag still on her left breast: LETTY! She whispered, "You can't still...want me?"

"You're wrong." He pulled her handbag off her shoulder. It felt unspeakably erotic. He pulled off her coat, dropping it to the marble floor. "I wanted you then." Cupping her face with both hands, he whispered, "I want you now."

Electricity ran up and down her body. Involuntarily, she licked her lips.

His gaze fell to her mouth.

Tangling his hands in her hair, he pulled out her ponytail, and her long dark hair tumbled down her shoulders. He stroked down her cheek, tilting back her head.

He was so much taller. He towered over her in every way.

She felt crazy butterflies, like she'd gone back in time and was eighteen again. Being with him now, all the anguish and grief and weariness of the last ten years seemed to disappear like a bad dream.

"I've missed you for so long," she choked out. "You're all I've dreamed about..."

He pressed a finger to her lips. At the contact, fire flashed from her mouth and down to her breasts. Sparks crackled between them in the shadowy penthouse, as she breathed in his woodsy, musky scent. Tension coiled low and deep in her belly.

Pulling her body tight against his own, he lowered his mouth to hers.

His kiss was hot and demanding. The stubble on his rough jawline scratched her delicate skin as he gripped her hard against him. She kissed him back with desperate need.

A low growl came from the back of his throat, and he pushed her back against the wall. His hands ran down her body to rip apart the front buttons of her white dress. She gasped as her naked skin was exposed, along with her plain white bra and panties.

"Take this off," he whispered, and he pulled her white dress off her body, dropping it to the floor. Kneeling in front of her, he pulled off her white shoes, one by one. She was nearly naked, standing in front of the floor-to-ceiling windows that revealed the whole city.

Rising to his full height, he kissed her. His mouth plundered hers, searing her to the core. She realized her hands were unbuttoning his black shirt to feel the warmth of his skin, the hard muscles of his body. She stroked his chest, dusted with dark hair, and trembled. He felt like steel wrapped in satin, hard and soft.

She desperately wanted to feel him against her, all of him. She wanted to be lost in him—

As he kissed her, his hands roamed over her shoulders, her hips, her breasts. Her fingers twisted in his hair. She felt dizzy with longing as he pressed her against the wall, kissing her with savage desire, nipping at her lips until they bruised.

He kissed down her throat, reaching beneath the white cotton fabric of her bra to cup her bare breasts. She felt his rough warm hands against her naked skin, and her taut nipples ached, until with a low curse he reached around and unhooked the clasp of her bra.

She heard his intake of breath as it fell to the floor. She now wore only panties, while he was still fully dressed, with his black shirt unbuttoned to reveal his bare chest. As he lowered his head, taking her exposed breasts fully in his hands, her head fell back, hair tumbling down, as she gripped his bare, muscular shoulders.

She gasped as she felt the wet heat of his mouth envelop a taut nipple. Lightning shot down her body as he suckled her in his stark, shadowy penthouse, with its spectacular view of nighttime New York at their feet. She moaned softly.

Abruptly, he pulled away. She opened her eyes, feeling dizzy. Her lips parted to ask a question, but before she could remember it, he lifted her into his arms.

She didn't try to resist as he carried her through the great room into an enormous bedroom in the opposite corner. That, too, had windows on both sides, twenty feet high. She could see all of Midtown, from the Chrysler Building to the Empire State, a forest of skyscrapers between two dark rivers with their bright, moving barges.

Manhattan sparkled coldly in the dark night as Darius spread her across his bed, his expression half shadowed. He undid his cuffs and dropped his shirt to the floor.

For the first time, Letty saw the full strength of his hard-muscled torso and powerful arms. His shoulders were broad, narrowing to tight, hard abs. Removing his belt, he kicked off his shoes. Wearing just low-slung black tailored trousers, he climbed onto the bed.

Lowering his head, he kissed her against the pillows, his lips hard and rough. She felt his desire for her; she felt his heavy weight over her. Darius wanted her... He cared...

Something broke, deep inside her heart.

All this time, Letty had thought their love had ended forever. But nothing had changed, she thought in wonder, tangling her hands in his dark hair. *Nothing.* They were the same two people, still young and in love...

He slowly kissed his way down her body, his hands

stroking her. She quivered, helpless beneath his touch. He dropped kisses here and there as he traversed the softness of her belly to the top edge of her white cotton panties. Drawing up, he looked down at her.

"You're mine, Letty," he whispered. "At last."

Then his heavy, hard body crushed hers deliciously, sensually. Her fingertips moved down the warm skin of his back, feeling his muscle, his spine. He moved his hips against hers, and she felt how huge and hard he was for her. Desire coiled low and deep in her belly.

He slid her white cotton panties down her thighs, down her legs. Like a whisper, they were gone.

Pushing her legs apart, he knelt at the foot of the bed. She held her breath, squeezing her eyes shut in the shadowy bedroom as he kissed the tender hollow of each foot. He moved up her calves, his fingertips caressing her skin as he lifted each knee for a slow kiss in the hollow beneath. She shivered as she felt the warmth of his breath on her thighs.

His hands moved beneath her, cupping her backside. Her thighs melted beneath his breath, hips trembling.

Finally, with agonizing slowness, he lowered his head between her legs.

Moving his hands, he kissed her inner thighs, one then the other. She felt his breath against the most intimate part of her and tried to squirm away, but he held her firmly.

Spreading her wide, he took a long, deep taste. The pleasure was intense. She choked out a gasp.

Holding her hips down against the bed, he forced her to accept the pleasure, working her with his tongue, twirling against her aching nub for long exquisite moments, then lapping her with the full width of his tongue.

She forgot to breathe, held by ruthless pleasure like a butterfly pinned to a wall. Her hips lifted involuntarily off the bed as she soared, and she gripped the white bedspread so she didn't fly up into the sky.

Waves of pleasure crashed against radiating joy. She'd never stopped loving him. And now he'd forgiven her. He wanted her. He loved her, too…

Twisting and gasping beneath his mouth, she exploded with a cry of pure happiness that seemed to last forever.

Instantly lifting his body, he pushed her arms above her head, gripping her wrists against the pillow, and positioned his hips between her legs. As she was still soaring between ecstasy and joy, he ruthlessly impaled her.

She felt him push all the way inside her, the entire enormous length of him going deep, to the heart. Her eyes flew open in shock and pain.

His back straightened at the moment he tore through the barrier that he clearly had not expected. Feeling her flinch, he looked down at her in shock.

"You were—a virgin?" he panted.

She nodded, closing her eyes and twisting her head away so he couldn't see the threatening tears. She didn't want to mar the beauty of their night, but the pain cut deep.

He held himself still inside her.

"You can't be," he said hoarsely. "How, after all these years?"

Letty looked up at him, her throat aching. And she said the only thing she could say. The words that she'd repressed for ten years, but that had never stopped burning inside her.

"Because I love you, Darius," she whispered.

CHAPTER TWO

DARIUS STARED DOWN at her. Letitia Spencer, a virgin?

Impossible. Not in a million years.

But her words shocked him even more.

"What do you mean, *you love me*?" he choked out.

Her dark eyelashes trembled against her pale skin. Then those big, beautiful hazel eyes shone up at him from the shadows of the bed as she whispered, "I never stopped loving you."

Looking down at her beautiful heart-shaped face, Darius was overwhelmed by emotion. Not the good kind, either.

He felt the cold burn of slow-rising rage.

Once, he'd loved Letty Spencer so much he'd thought he'd die without her. She'd been his angel. His goddess. He'd put her on such a pedestal, he'd even insisted they wait to make love. He'd wanted to marry her.

The memory made him writhe with shame.

How far she'd fallen. Today, she'd sent him a message—her first direct communication with him since she'd dumped him so coldly ten years before—offering him her body. For money.

All afternoon, Darius had tried to ignore her message, to laugh it off. He'd gotten over Letty years ago. He wasn't interested in paying a hundred thousand dollars to have her in his bed tonight. He didn't pay for sex. Women fought for his attention now. Supermodels fell into his bed for the price of a phone call.

But the part of him that still couldn't completely forget the past relished the idea of seeing her one last time.

Only this time, she'd be the one begging. He'd be the one to reject her.

As he'd signed the contracts that afternoon to formally sell his company, built on a mobile messaging app with five hundred million users worldwide, to a massive tech conglomerate for the price of twenty billion dollars, he'd barely listened to his lawyers droning on. Holding 90 percent of equity in the company made him the beneficiary of an eighteen-billion-dollar fortune, minus taxes.

But instead of rejoicing in the triumphant payoff of ten years of relentless work, he'd been picturing Letitia, the woman who'd once betrayed him. Imagining her trying to seduce him with an exotic dance of the seven veils. Picturing her wearing nothing but a black negligee. Begging him to take her to bed, so she could perform Olympic-level sexual feats for his pleasure.

After the papers were signed, he practically ran out of the office, away from all the congratulations and celebrations. All he could think about was Letty and her offer.

He'd spent hours trying to talk himself out of it. Then, gritting his teeth, he'd driven to the Brooklyn diner when the message said she'd be getting off work.

He didn't intend to actually sleep with her, he told himself. He'd only wanted to make her feel as small and ashamed as he'd once felt. To see her humiliated. To see her beg to give him pleasure.

Then he'd planned to tell her he no longer found her attractive, and toss the money in her face. He'd watch her take it and slink away in shame. And for the rest of his life he'd know that he'd won.

What did he care about a hundred thousand dollars? It was nothing. It would be worth it to see her abject humiliation. After her savagely calculated betrayal, he craved vengeance far more than sex.

Or so he'd thought.

But so far nothing had gone according to plan. Seeing her outside the diner, he'd been shocked at her appearance.

She didn't look like a gold digger. She looked as if she were trying to be invisible, with no makeup, wearing that ridiculous white diner uniform.

But even then, he'd been drawn to her. She managed to be so damn sexy, so sweetly feminine and warm, that any man would want to help her, to take care of her. *To possess her.*

Bringing her back to the penthouse to enjoy his vengeance, Darius had allowed himself a single kiss.

Big mistake.

As he'd felt the soft curves of her body press against his, all his plans for vengeance were forgotten against the ruthless clamor of his body. For ten years, he'd desired this woman; and now she was half-naked in his arms, willing to surrender everything.

Suddenly, it all came down to two simple facts.

She'd sold herself.

He'd bought her.

So why not take her? Why not enjoy her sensual body as a way to finally excise her memory, once and for all?

She'd lied her way through the evening, pretending it was a romantic date, instead of a commercial transaction. He'd almost been surprised.

Until now.

Naked beneath him, Letty looked up, her eyes luminous in that lovely face he'd never been able to forget.

"Say something," she said anxiously.

Darius set his jaw. After her heartless betrayal, followed by ten years of silence, she'd just told him out of the blue she loved him. What could he say in response? Go to hell?

Letitia Spencer. So beautiful. So treacherous. So poisonous.

But now, at last, he understood her goal. She wasn't just playing for a hundred thousand dollars tonight. No. Tonight was just the sample that was supposed to leave him wanting more.

Because he'd seen her face as she left that diner. She was tired. Tired of working. Tired of being poor. Perhaps her father, newly free from prison, had been the one to suggest how to easily change her life—by becoming Darius's wife.

She must have seen his company's sale trumpeted in the newspaper today and decided it was time she made a play for his billions. He almost couldn't blame her. She'd been holding on to her virginity all these years—why not cash in?

She loved him.

Cold, sardonic anger pulsed through him.

She thought he'd learned nothing all these years. She actually thought, if she told him she loved him, he would still swoon at her feet. That he was still the lovesick idiot of long ago.

If Darius had despised her before, it was nothing compared to how he felt about her now.

And yet, he still desired her. Holding himself motionless inside her hot, tight sheath, he was still so hard, he was close to exploding.

That fact enraged him even more.

He wanted to make her pay. Not just for this last insult, but for everything that had gone before. Suddenly, causing her one night of humiliation wasn't nearly enough.

Darius wanted *vengeance.*

He wanted to raise her up, give her hope, then bring it crashing down as she'd once done. Fantastical plans coursed through his skull. He wanted to marry her, fill her with his child. He wanted to make her love him, then coldly spurn her. He wanted to take everything, and leave her penniless and alone.

That wouldn't be revenge. It would be *justice.*

"Darius?" A shadow of worry had crossed her face as she looked up at him, naked on the bed.

Lowering his head, he kissed her almost tenderly. She trembled in his arms, her plump breasts crushed against his naked chest, her amazing hips spread wide for him. Seeing her stretched out on his bed, with the play of shadows and light on the sexy curves of her tantalizing breasts, stretched the limits of his self-control.

"I'm sorry I hurt you, *agape mou*," he said in a low voice. Lie. His lips brushed the sensitive flesh of her cheek. As lightly as a butterfly setting down, he kissed the two tears that had overflowed her lashes. "But the pain won't last." Another lie. He would make sure it lasted the rest of her life. He smiled grimly. "Just wait."

She looked up at him, the picture of wide-eyed innocence. Then sighed, relaxing in surrender.

The kiss he gave her then was anything but tender. It was demanding, rough, fierce. He had experience, and she did not. He knew how to lure her. How to master her.

Unless—she could be feigning her desire?

No, he thought coldly. He would make sure she did not. That would be one insult he'd not allow her to pay. He would make sure every bit of her pleasure was real.

He stroked her soft body, taking his time, caressing her, until, slowly, she started kissing him back.

She wrapped her arms around his shoulders, pulling his weight back down on her. He shifted his hips, testing her ability to accept him, still rock hard and huge inside her. She whimpered, then exhaled, swaying her hips.

He moved expertly, drawing back slowly, then pushing inside her a second time. She gripped his shoulders, closing her eyes. He suckled a nipple, watching her face carefully. It wasn't until he saw the glow of ecstasy return to her face, and felt her muscles start to tighten around him, that he knew he'd succeeded. Triumph filled him as he began to ride her.

Filling her so deeply, this woman he'd desired for almost a third of his life, he felt light-headed. His body started to shake with pleasure so intense that it was almost like pain. They were so intertwined it was hard to know where one ended and the other began.

Pleasure and pain.

Hatred and desire.

As he thrust into her, sweat covered his body with the effort of keeping control. Her breasts swayed as he thrust inside her, all the way to the hilt. Gasping, she put her hands against the headboard, bracing against the force of his thrust. Her breathing became shallow as her body twisted beneath him with building need.

Her eyes were closed, her head tilted back, as she panted for breath. She moved her hands to his shoulders. He barely noticed her fingernails digging into his skin. He was lost in the sensation of possessing her, filling her, owning her, the glory of her flesh, the sweetness of her skin.

He felt simultaneously lost and found. Every corner of his soul that had ever felt hollow was miraculously filled. His body was pure light.

From a distance, he heard a low ragged shout and realized the sound was coming from his own mouth, releasing emotion he'd kept locked up for a decade. Her voice joined his as she cried out her own joy and grief and pain.

His body spasmed with a final, violent thrust and he poured himself into her, collapsing over her on the bed, their bodies slick with sweat, fused together.

It was much later when he opened his eyes and discovered Letty was sleeping in his arms. He stared down at her in wonder.

He wondered how he'd ever been satisfied by those pallid, skinny supermodels who had filled his bed till now.

Those affairs had been insipid, hollow, dull compared to this fire. Tasting her, feeling her shake, hearing her cry of pleasure had pushed him to the limit.

It's hatred, he realized.

Hatred had made him utterly lose self-control in a way he'd never done before, in a way he'd never imagined possible. As he'd taken possession of her body, after ten years of frustrated desire, he'd slaked his ache in a dark, twisted fantasy of vengeance.

It had been the single best sexual experience of his life.

But as he pulled away from her, he sucked in his breath.

The condom had broken.

He'd worn one, of course. No matter how he might fantasize about revenge, no matter how much he hated her, the last thing he would want was to actually get her pregnant and drag an innocent child into this.

Now he stared down, unable to believe his own eyes. How could the condom have broken?

Had he been too rough, forgetting everything in his need to possess her, to relieve the savage, unrequited desire of ten years?

He'd wanted to brand her forever with the deepest mark of his possession. Had he actually wanted to fill her with his child?

A curse filled his heart.

Unraveling himself from her, he pulled away, rising naked from the bed.

He walked to the window and looked down at the bright skyscrapers of this dark city. His throat was tight as he pressed his hand against the cold glass. Catching his own reflection in the window, he was startled by the cold rage in his eyes.

Disaster. He hadn't done anything like he'd planned. He'd actually slept with Letty. And now…it might be so much worse. His hand tightened against the window. He looked back, and his jaw tightened.

Her fault, he thought. All hers.

"Are you up?" Letty murmured. "Come back to bed."

She was beneath the blankets now, looking sleepy and adorable with her dark hair tumbling over his pillows. She'd covered herself with the comforter. As if he hadn't seen everything, touched everything, tasted everything already.

His body hardened against his will, already desiring her again. He'd just had her, and he already wanted more. He wanted to take her on the bed. Against the wall. Against the window. Again and again. He stared at her in bewildered fury. Truly she was poison.

But did he really imagine after everything that had gone wrong tonight, the gold digger couldn't achieve her ultimate goal—marriage and total command, not just of his fortune, but of his body and soul?

He clawed a hand through his hair.

"Darius, what's wrong?"

He repeated flatly, "You love me?"

"It's true," she whispered.

He took a step toward the bed.

"What is it, Letty?" he said in a low voice. "Did you plan all along to renegotiate the deal? One night isn't enough, is that it? You don't want to be a rental, but a permanent sale?"

She frowned. "What are you talking about?"

Darius's jaw felt so tight it ached. Grabbing gray sweatpants from a sleek built-in drawer, he pulled them up over his naked body. He forced his shoulders to relax, forced himself to face her. When he spoke, his voice was like ice.

"You don't love me. You don't even know what the word means. When I think of how I once adored you, it sickens me. Especially now—now we both know what you really are."

Her forehead creased. "What are you talking about?"

"This night. This whole night. Don't pretend you don't know."

"I don't!"

"Don't play the outraged innocent. You sold your virginity to me for the price of a hundred thousand dollars."

For a moment, his hard words echoed in the shadowy bedroom. The two of them stared at each other in silence.

"What are you talking about?"

"Your email," he said impatiently. "Claiming you needed to pay off some mobster who'd broken your father's arm and threatened to break his whole body if he didn't come up with a hundred thousand dollars within the week." He tilted his head curiously. "Is it true? Or just a convenient excuse?"

Her eyes were wide. "My father's broken arm..." She seemed to shudder as she pulled the blankets up higher against her neck. "I never sent any message."

His lips curved sardonically. "So who did?"

Letty's cheeks were bright red. "I..." Running her hand over her eyes, she said, "So that's why you came for me? You were buying a night in bed?"

"What did you think?"

"I thought..." She faltered. "I thought you'd forgiven me for what I did..."

He snorted. "Ten years ago? You did me a favor. I've been better off without you. Your other fiancé must have realized that fast, since he didn't bother to stick around, either." His jaw set. "What I'll never forgive is what you and your father did to my dad. He died an early death because of you. Lost his job, his life savings. He lost everything, had a heart attack and died." He bared his teeth in a shark-like smile. "Because of you."

"Darius, it's not what you think," she blurted out. "I..."

"Oh, is this the part where you come up with an explanation that makes you look like an innocent saint?" he drawled. "Go on, Letty. Tell me how your betrayal was actually a favor. Explain how you destroyed my family at great personal sacrifice, because you loved me so much." His voice dripped contempt. "Tell me all about your *love*."

She opened her mouth.

Then snapped it closed.

Darius's lip twisted coldly. "That's what I thought."

She blinked fast, her beautiful eyes anguished. She took a deep breath and spoke one small word. "Please…"

But mercy had been burned from his soul. He shrugged. "I thought it would be amusing to see you again. I didn't actually intend to sleep with you, but you were so willing, I finally thought, why not?" He sighed as if bored. "But though I paid for the whole night, I find I've already lost interest." Leaning forward, he confided, "And just as one entrepreneur to another, you sold yourself too cheaply. You could have bartered for a higher price with your virginity. Just a suggestion as you go forward with your new career. What is it called now? Paid mistress? Professional girlfriend?"

"How can you be so cruel?" She shook her head. "When you came to the diner tonight, I saw the same boy I loved…"

"Really?" He tilted his head, quirking a dark eyebrow. "Oh. Right. Since you'd kept your virginity in reserve all these years, you thought if you tossed in a little romance, I'd fall for you like a stone, just like I did back then. 'I love you, Darius. I never stopped loving you,'" he mimicked mockingly.

"Stop!" she cried, covering her ears with her hands. "Please stop!"

Some of her blanket had slipped where she sat on his bed, revealing a curvy breast. He could see the faint pink tip of her nipple, and he could still taste the sweetness of her, still remember how it had felt to be deep inside her.

His breath came hard. Sleeping with her hadn't satiated his desire. To the contrary. He only wanted her more.

The fact she still had such power over him was infuriating.

Turning sharply, he went to his desk. He pulled a cashier's check from a leather binder. Returning to the bed, he tossed it toward her.

"There. I believe this concludes our business."

Letty's lovely face looked dazed as she picked up the cashier's check from the bed. She looked at it.

"If you have another client tonight, don't let me keep you," he drawled.

She briefly closed her eyes and whispered, "You're a monster."

"*I'm* a monster." He barked a low, cruel laugh. "Me?"

Turning away, she rose naked from the bed. He waited, wondering for a split second if she'd toss the check in his face and prove him wrong. If she did…

But she didn't. She just picked up her panties from the floor and walked to the door. He sneered at himself for being naive enough to even imagine the possibility she'd give up her hard-earned money for the sake of honor, or even pride!

She left the bedroom, going out into the great room of the penthouse. He followed, watching as she collected her bra and shoes, then scooped her white dress from the floor. Putting it on after slipping on her panties, she buttoned the dress quickly, leaving gaps where he'd ripped off buttons in his haste to get it off her. She wouldn't meet his eyes.

Darius wanted to force her to look at him. He wanted her humiliated. He wanted her heartbroken. His pride demanded something he couldn't name. *More.*

She stuffed her bra in her handbag and put her bare feet into her shoes and turned to go.

"It's just a shame the condom broke," he said.

She froze. "What?"

"The condom. Of course I was wearing one. But it broke.

So if you wind up pregnant, let me know, won't you?" He gave a hard smile. "We will negotiate a good price."

He was rewarded. She finally turned and looked at him, aghast.

"You'd pay me? For a baby?"

He said coldly, "Why not, when I paid you for the act that created it?" His expression hardened. "I will never marry you, Letty. So your attempt at gold digging ends with that check in your bag. If by some unfortunate chance you become pregnant, selling me our baby would be your only option."

"You're crazy!"

"And you disgust me." He came closer to her, his eyes cold. "I would never allow any child of mine to be raised by you and that criminal you call a father. I would hire a hundred lawyers first," he said softly, "and drive you both into the sea."

For a moment, Letty looked at him, wide-eyed. Then she turned away with a stumble, but not before he saw the sheen of tears in her eyes. She'd become quite the little actress, he thought.

"Please take me home," she whispered.

"Take you home?" Darius gave a sardonic laugh. "You're an employee, not a guest. A temporary employee whose time is now done." His lip curled. "Find your own way home."

CHAPTER THREE

LETTY SHIVERED IN the darkest, coldest hours of the night as she walked to the Lexington Avenue subway station and got on the express train. It was past one in the morning, and she held her bag tightly in the mostly empty compartment, feeling vulnerable and alone.

Arriving at her stop in Brooklyn, she came numbly down the stairs from the elevated station and walked the blocks to her apartment. The streets were dark, the shops all closed. The February—no, it was March now; it was past midnight—wind was icy against her cheeks still raw with tears.

She'd thought it was a miracle when she saw Darius again. She'd thought he'd found out the truth of how she'd sacrificed herself, and he'd come back for her.

Telling him she loved him had felt so right. She'd honestly thought he might tell her the same thing.

How could she have been so wrong?

You disgust me.

She could still hear the contempt in his voice. Wiping her eyes hard, she shivered, trembling as she trudged toward her four-story apartment building.

While many of the nearby buildings were nice, well kept, with flower boxes, hers was an eyesore, with a rickety fire escape clinging to a crumbling brick facade. But the place was cheap, and the landlord had asked no personal questions, which was what she cared about. Plugging in a security code, Letty pushed open the door.

Inside, the temperature felt colder. Two of the foyer's lights were burned out, leaving only a single bare lightbulb to illuminate the mailboxes and the old delivery menus littering the corners of the cracked tile floor.

Even in the middle of the night, noises echoed against the concrete stairwell, a Doppler tangle of tenants yelling, dogs barking, a baby crying. A sour smell came up from beneath the metal stairs as she wearily climbed three flights. She felt wretched, body and soul, torn between her body's sweet ache from their lovemaking and her heart's incandescent grief.

The fourth floor had worn, stained carpet and a bare lightbulb hanging from the ceiling. Going past the doors of her neighbors—some of whom she'd never met even after three years—she reached into her handbag, found her keys and unlocked the dead bolt. The door creaked as she pushed it open.

"Letty! You're back!" Her father looked up eagerly from his easy chair. He'd waited up for her, wrapped in both a robe and a blanket over his flannel pajamas, since the thermostat didn't work properly. Turning off the television, he looked up hopefully. "Well?"

As the door swung shut behind her, Letty stared at him in disbelief. Her handbag dropped to the floor.

"How could you?" she choked out.

"How could I get you and Darius back together so easily?" Her father beamed at her. "All I needed was a good excuse!"

Her voice caught on a sob. "Are you kidding?"

Howard frowned. "Are you and Darius not back together?"

"Of course we're not! How could you send him a message, pretending to be me? Offering me for the night!"

"I was trying to help," he said falteringly. "You've loved him for so long but refused to contact him. Or he you. I thought…"

"What? That if you forced us together, we'd immediately fall back into each other's arms?"

"Well, yes."

As she stared at him, still trembling from the roller coaster of emotion of that night, anger rushed through her.

"You didn't do it for me!" Reaching into her bag, she grabbed the cashier's check and shoved it at him. "You did it for this!"

Her father's hands shook as he grasped the cashier's check. Seeing the amount, his eyes filled with visible relief. "Thank God."

"How could you?" She wanted to shake her father and scream at him for what he'd done. "How could you sell me?"

"*Sell* you?" Her father looked up incredulously. "I didn't sell you!" Struggling to untangle himself from his blanket, he rose from his chair and sat beside her on the sofa. "I figured the two of you would talk and soon realize how you'd been set up. I thought you'd both have a good laugh, and it would be easier for you each to get over your pride. Maybe he'd send money, maybe he wouldn't." His voice cracked. "But either way, you'd be together again. The two of you love each other."

"You did it for love." Letty's eyes narrowed skeptically. "So the fact that you read about Darius's billion-dollar deal this morning had nothing to do with it."

He winced at her sarcasm, then looked down at the floor. His voice trembled a little as he said, "I guess I thought there was no harm in also trying to solve a problem of my own with a...dissatisfied customer."

Glaring at him, Letty opened her mouth to say the cruel words he deserved to hear. Words she'd never be able to take back. Words neither one of them would ever be able to forget. Words that would take her anguish and rage, wrap them up into a tight ball and launch them at her father like a grenade.

Then she looked at him, old and forlorn, sitting beside

her on the sagging sofa. The man she'd once admired and still absolutely loved.

His hair had become white and wispy, barely covering his spotted scalp. His face, once so hearty and handsome, was gaunt with deep wrinkles on his cheeks. He'd shrunk, become thin and bowed. His robe was too big on him now. His near decade in prison had aged him thirty years.

Howard Spencer, a middle-class kid from Oklahoma, had come to New York and built a fortune with only his charm and a good head for numbers. He'd fallen in love with Constance Langford, the only daughter of an old aristocratic family on Long Island. The Langfords had little money left beyond the Fairholme estate, which was in hock up to the eyeballs. But Howard Spencer, delirious with happiness at their marriage, had assured Constance she'd never worry about money again.

He'd kept his promise. While his wife had been alive, he'd been careful and smart and lucky with his investment fund. It was only after his wife's sudden death that he'd become reckless, taking bigger and bigger financial risks, until his once respected hedge fund became a hollowed-out Ponzi scheme, and suddenly eight billion dollars were gone.

The months of Howard's arrest and trial had been awful for Letty, and worrying about him in prison had been even worse. But now, as she looked at the old man he'd somehow become, was the worst of all.

As she looked at his slumped shoulders, his heartbroken eyes—at his broken arm, still hanging uselessly in the cast—she felt her anger evaporate, leaving in its place only grief and despair. Her mouth snapped shut.

Slumping forward, she covered her face with her hands.

The memory of Darius's words floated back to her. *You needed to pay off some mobster who'd broken your father's arm and threatened to break his whole body if he didn't come up with a hundred thousand dollars within the week.*

Chilled, she looked up. "Why didn't you tell me someone broke your arm, Dad? Why did you let me think it was an accident?"

Howard looked down at the floor guiltily. "I didn't want you to worry."

"Worry?" she cried.

His wan cheeks turned pink. "A father's supposed to take care of his daughter, not the other way around."

"So it's true? Some thug broke your arm and threatened you if you didn't pay him back his money?"

"I knew I could handle it." He tried to smile. "And I have. Once I sign over this check, everything will be fine."

"How do you know you won't have more thugs demanding money, once it's known you actually paid someone back?"

Her father looked shocked. "No. Most of the people who invested in my fund were good, civilized people. Not violent!"

Letty ground her teeth. For a man who'd been in a minimum-security federal prison for nine years, he could be surprisingly naive.

"You should have told me."

"Why? What would you have done except worry? Or worse—try to talk to the man yourself and put yourself in danger?" He set his jaw. "Like I said, I didn't know if Darius would actually send the money. But I knew, either way, you would be safe because you'd be with him." He shook his head, trying to smile. "I really thought you and Darius would take one look at each other and be happy again."

Letty sagged back against the sofa cushions. Her father'd really thought he was doing her a favor. That he was reuniting her with a lost love. That he was protecting her, saving her.

She whispered bleakly, "Darius thought I was a gold digger."

Howard looked indignant. "Of course he didn't! Once you told him you hadn't sent the message…"

"He didn't believe me."

"Then…then…he must have believed you were just a good daughter looking out for your father. Darius has so much money now, you can't tell me he'll miss such a small amount. Not after everything you did for *him*!"

"Stop," she choked out. Just remembering how Darius had looked at her when he handed her the cashier's check was enough to make her want to die. But after he'd told her about the threat against her father's life, what choice had she had?

Her father looked bewildered. "Didn't you tell him what happened ten years ago? Why you never ran away with him?"

She flinched as she remembered Darius's acid words. *Go on, Letty. Tell me how your betrayal was actually a favor. Explain how you destroyed my family at great personal sacrifice, because you loved me so much.*

"No," she whispered, "and I never will. Darius doesn't love me. He hates me more than ever."

Howard's wrinkled face looked mournful. "Oh, sweetheart."

"But now I hate him, too." She looked up. "That's the one good thing that happened tonight. *Now I hate him, too.*"

Her father looked anguished. "That was never what I wanted!"

"It's good." Wiping her eyes, she tried to smile. "I've wasted too many years dreaming of him. Missing him. I'm done."

She was.

The Darius Kyrillos she'd loved no longer existed. She saw that now. She'd tried to give him everything, and he'd seduced her with a cold heart. Her love for Darius was burned out of her forever. Her only hope was to try to forget.

But four weeks later, she found out how impossible that would be. She'd never be able to forget Darius Kyrillos now.

She was pregnant with his baby.

She'd taken the pregnancy test, sure it would be negative. When it was positive, she was shocked. But shock soon became a happy daze as Letty imagined a sweet fat baby in her arms, to cuddle and adore.

Then she told her father.

"I'm going to be a grandfather?" Howard was enraptured at the news. "That's wonderful! And when you tell Darius—"

That caused the first chill of fear. Because Letty suddenly recalled this baby wouldn't just be hers, but Darius's.

He hated her.

He'd threatened to take her baby from her.

Letty shook her head violently. "I can never tell him about the baby!"

"Of course you will." Her father patted her on the shoulder. "I know you're angry at him. He must have hurt you very badly. But that's all in the past! A man has a right to know he's going to be a father."

"Why?" She turned to him numbly. "So he can try to take the baby away because he hates me so much?"

"Take the baby?" Her father laughed. "Once Darius finds out you're pregnant, he'll forget his anger and remember how much he loves you. You'll see. The baby will bring you together."

She shook her head. "You're living in a dream world. He told me..."

"What?"

Letty turned away, hearing the echo of that coldly malevolent voice. *I would never allow any child of mine to be raised by you and that criminal you call a father.*

"We need to start saving money," she whispered. "Now."

"Why? Once you're married, money will never be a worry for you again." Howard looked ecstatic. "You and my grandchild will always be cared for."

Letty knew her father couldn't believe Darius wanted to hurt her. But she knew he did.

I would hire a hundred lawyers first and drive you both into the sea.

They had to leave this city as soon as possible.

Under the terms of her father's probation, Howard was required to remain in the state of New York. So they'd go north, move to some little town upstate where no one knew them, where she could find a new job.

There was just one problem. Moving required money. First and last month's rent, a security deposit and transport for Letty, Howard and all their belongings. Money they didn't have. They were barely keeping their heads above water as it was.

Over the next few months, Letty's fears were proved true. No matter how hard she worked, she couldn't save money. Howard was always hungry or needed something urgently. Money disappeared. There were also the added expenses of medical co-payments for Letty's doctor visits, and physical therapy for her father's arm.

There was some good fortune. After Howard had paid off the mobster, no other angry former investors had threatened him, demanding repayment.

But there, their luck ended. Just when Letty was desperate for overtime pay, all the other waitstaff suddenly seemed to want it, too. But warmer summer weather meant fewer customers at the diner craving the fried eggs and chicken fried steak that were the diner's specialties. Her work hours became less, not more.

Each morning when she left for work, her father pretended to look through job listings in the paper, looking shifty-eyed and pale. Pregnancy exhausted her. Each night when she got home from work, almost falling asleep where she stood, she cooked dinner for them both. She'd do the dishes and go to bed. Then the whole day would start again.

Every day, she anxiously counted the savings she kept in her old chipped cookie jar on the kitchen counter. And every day, she looked at the calendar and felt more afraid.

By late August, amid the sticky heat of New York City, Letty was growing frantic. She could no longer hide her baby bump, not even with her father's oversize shirts. Everyone at the diner knew she was pregnant, including her friend and coworker Belle Langtry, who kept teasing her about it.

"Who's the father?" Belle demanded. "Is it Prince Charming? I swear I saw you leave here once with a dark-haired man in a sports car."

No. It wasn't Prince Charming, Letty thought numbly. Her baby's father was no prince, but a selfish, coldhearted beast who wanted to steal her child away.

Finally, as her yearlong lease on the apartment ended, she knew she couldn't wait any longer. She gave two weeks' notice at the diner. She still hadn't saved enough money, but time had run out.

On the first of September, Letty splashed cold water on her face in the darkness before dawn, then looked at her drawn face in the mirror.

Today was the day.

They couldn't rent a truck to move their belongings. No money for that. Instead, they'd just take what would fit in two suitcases on the bus.

They'd have to leave behind all the final memories from Fairholme. From her childhood. From her mother.

The thought made her throat ache.

But Letty was six months pregnant now. Her heart pounded as she put her hand protectively over her baby bump. She knew from the ultrasound at the doctor's office that she was expecting a boy. How had time fled so quickly? In less than three months, by late November, she'd be cuddling her sweet baby in her arms.

Or else she'd be weeping as the baby's coldhearted father took him away from her forever. She still remembered Darius's cold, dark eyes, heard the flat echo of his voice.

If by some unfortunate chance you become pregnant, selling me our baby would be your only option.

She was suddenly terrified she'd waited too long to leave New York.

Going into the tiny kitchen, she tried to keep her voice cheerful as she said, "Dad, I'm going to pick up my last paycheck, then buy bus tickets."

"I still don't understand why Rochester," he said with a scowl.

She sighed. "I told you. My friend Belle knows someone who knows someone who might be able to get me a job there. Everyone says it's nice. I need you to start packing."

"I have other plans today." His voice was peevish.

"Dad, our lease is up in two days. I know it's not fun, but whatever you don't pack, I'm going to have to call the junk dealer to take." Her throat ached. Maybe all their leftover stuff *was* junk, but it was all they had left. Of Fairholme. Of her mother. Her voice tightened. "Look, I know it won't be easy."

Sitting at the peeling Formica table where he was doing the crossword, Howard glared at her with irritation. "You just need to tell that man of yours you're pregnant."

They'd been having this argument for months. She gritted her teeth. "I can't. I told you."

"Poppycock. A man should be given the opportunity to take care of his own child. And you know, Letty," he added gruffly, "I won't always be here to look after you."

Howard—look after her? When was the last time that

had been true, instead of the other way around? She looked at her father, then sighed. "Why don't you believe me?"

"I knew Darius as a boy." Fiddling with his untouched coffee mug, he looked at her seriously. "If you'd just help him see past his anger, he's got a good heart—"

"I'm not gambling on his *good heart*," she said bitterly. "Not after the way he treated me."

Her father looked thoughtful. "I could just call him…"

"No!" Letty shouted. Her eyes blazed. "If you ever go behind my back like that again, I will never talk to you for the rest of my life. Do you understand? *Never.*"

"Okay, okay," he grumbled. "But he's your baby's father. You should just marry him and be happy."

That left her speechless for a minute.

"Just be packed by the time I return," she said finally, and she went out into the gray, rainy September morning. She picked up her last check at the diner—for a pitiful amount, but every dollar would help—and said farewell to her fellow waitress Belle, who'd moved to New York from Texas the previous Christmas.

"Anytime you need anything, you call me, you hear?" Belle hugged her fiercely. "No matter where you are, Rochester or Rome, remember I'm only a phone call away!"

Letty didn't make friends easily, so it was hard to say goodbye to the only real friend she'd made since she'd left Fairholme. The thought of going to yet another new apartment in a new town where she didn't know anyone, in hopes of starting a job that might not even exist, filled her with dread. She tried to smile.

"You too, Belle," she managed. Then, wiping her eyes, she said goodbye to everyone else at the diner and went back out into the rain to deposit her check at the bank and get two one-way bus tickets to Rochester.

When Letty got back home, her hair and clothes were damp with rain. Her father wasn't at the apartment, and his suitcases were empty. All their belongings were still untouched, exactly where she'd left them.

She'd just sort through everything herself, she thought wearily. Once she'd figured out how many boxes they'd have to leave behind, she'd call the junk dealer.

Of the eight billion dollars her father's investment fund had lost, three billion had since been recovered. But the authorities had been careful not to leave him with anything of value. Their possessions had been picked over long ago by the Feds and bankruptcy court.

What was left was all crammed into this tiny apartment. The broken flute her mother had played at Juilliard. The ceramic animals Constance had painted for her daughter as gifts, starting with her first birthday. The leather-bound classic books from her grandfather's collection, water-damaged, so worthless. Except to them. Her great-grandfather's old ship in a bottle. Her grandma Spencer's homemade Christmas ornaments. All would have to be left.

We'll get through it, Letty told herself fiercely. They could still be happy. She'd raise her baby with love, in a snug cottage overlooking a garden of flowers. Her son would have a happy childhood, just as Letty had.

He wouldn't be raised in some stark gray penthouse without a mother, without love...

Letty started digging through the first pile of clutter. She planned to stay up the whole night scrubbing down the apartment, in hopes their landlord might actually give back her security deposit.

Hearing a hard knock at the door, she rose to her feet, overwhelmed with relief. Her father had come back to help. He must have forgotten his key again. Sorting through their possessions would be so much easier with two of them—

Opening the door, she gasped.

Darius stood in her doorway, dressed in a black button-down shirt with well-cut jeans that showed the rugged lines of his powerful body. It was barely noon, but his jaw was dark with five-o'clock shadow.

For a moment, even hating and fearing him as she did, Letty was dazzled by that ruthless masculine beauty.

"Letty," he greeted her coldly. Then his eyes dropped to her baby bump.

With an intake of breath, Letty tried to shut the door in his face.

He blocked her with his powerful shoulder and pushed his way into her apartment.

CHAPTER FOUR

SIX MONTHS AGO Darius had wanted vengeance.

He'd gotten it. He'd ruthlessly taken Letitia Spencer's virginity, then tossed her out into a cold winter's night. He'd seduced her, insulted her. He'd thrown the money in her face, made her feel cheap.

It had been delicious.

But since then, to his dismay, he'd discovered the price of that vengeance.

In Darius's childhood, back on the Greek island where he was born, his grandmother had often told him that vengeance hurt the person who committed it worse than the one who endured it. When the kids at school mocked his illegitimate birth, sneering at his mother's abandonment—*Even your own* mitéra *didn't want you*—his grandmother had told him to ignore them, to take the high road.

He'd tried, but the boys' taunts had only grown worse until he was finally forced to punch them. They'd all been bloodied in the fight, but especially Darius, since it had been one against four.

"So you see I'm right," his grandmother had said gravely, bandaging him afterward. "You were hurt worse."

In Darius's own opinion, that vengeance had been not only justified, but strategic. The boys at school had never taunted him again.

But this time, his grandmother had been proved right. Because Darius's vengeance against Letty had hurt him more than he'd ever imagined.

Instead of quenching the flame, that night together had only built his desire for her into a blazing fire.

He wanted her. Every night for the last six months, he'd

half expected Letty to contact him. Once her prideful anger had faded, surely she would want him back—if not for his body, then obviously for his money.

But she never had. And when he'd remembered the haunted look on her beautiful heart-shaped face the night she'd told him she loved him, the night he'd taken her virginity and tossed her ruthlessly into the dark, he'd had moments when he'd wondered if he might have been wrong.

But how could he be wrong? The evidence spoke for itself.

Still, in the months since their night together, his continual raw desire for her had made him edgy. He'd intended to remain as his company's CEO for a year, guiding his team in the transition after the sale. Instead, he'd gotten into an argument with the head of the conglomerate and left within weeks. Darius could no longer endure working for someone else, but he'd signed a noncompete clause, so couldn't start a new business in the same field.

Bereft of the twenty-hour workdays that had been the entirety of his life for a decade, he hadn't known how to fill his hours. He tried spending some of his fortune. He'd bought a race car, then ten cars, then a race track. He'd bought four planes, all with interiors done in different colors. No. Next he'd tried extreme sports: skydiving, heli-skiing. Yawn.

Worst of all, he'd been surrounded by beautiful women, all keen to get his attention. And he hadn't wanted a single one of them.

He'd been *bored*. Worse. He'd felt frustrated and angry. Because even with the endless freedom of time and money, he couldn't have what he really wanted.

Letty.

Now, seeing her in the flesh, so beautiful—so *pregnant*—he hated himself for ever taking his vengeance. No matter how richly she'd deserved it, look where that thrill of hatred and lust had led.

Pregnant. With his baby.

Even wearing an oversize white T-shirt and baggy jeans, Letty was somehow more sensual, more delectable, than any stick-thin model in a skintight cocktail dress. Letty's pregnancy curves were lush. Her skin glowed. Her breasts had grown enormous. With effort, he forced his gaze down to her belly.

"So it's true," he said in a low voice. "You're pregnant."

She looked frozen. Then she squared her shoulders, tossing her dark ponytail in a futile gesture of bravado. "So?"

"Is the baby mine?"

"Yours?" Her eyes shot sparks of fire, even though she had dark shadows beneath, as if she hadn't been sleeping well. "What makes you think the baby's yours? Maybe I slept with ten men since our night. Maybe I slept with a hundred—"

The thought of her sleeping with other men made Darius sick. "You're lying."

"How do you know?"

"Because your father told me."

The fight went out of her. She went pale. "My...my father?"

"He wanted me to pay for the information, but when I refused, he told me everything. For free."

"Maybe he was lying," she said weakly. She looked as if she might faint.

"Sit down," Darius ordered. "I'll get you a glass of water. Then we'll talk."

She sank into the old pullout sofa, her cheeks pale. It wasn't hard for him to find the kitchen. The apartment was pathetically small—just a postage-stamp-sized living room, surrounded by an even smaller bedroom, bathroom and kitchen.

He looked around him, amazed that the onetime heiress of Fairholme, born into a forty-room mansion, was now living with her father in an apartment the same size as the room her mother had once used to arrange flowers off the solarium.

Old boxes and mementos were packed everywhere. The leftovers of her family's former life—items that obviously weren't valuable enough to be sold, but too precious to be thrown away—were clustered around the old television and piled tightly along the walls. A pillow and folded blanket sat beside the pullout sofa.

Darius walked across the worn carpet to the peeling linoleum of the telephone-booth-sized kitchen. Dust motes floated in the weak gray sunlight. The barred window overlooked an air shaft that faced other apartments, just a few feet away. With the bars across the window, it felt like prison.

It's better than they deserve, he told himself firmly. And it was still nicer than his childhood home in Heraklios. At least this place had electricity, running water. At least this place had a parent.

Darius's own parents had both left him, in different ways, two days after he was born. His unemployed father had discovered his newborn son crying in a basket by his door, left out in the rain by his former lover, a wealthy, spoiled heiress who'd abandoned the child she'd never wanted.

Fired from his job, Eugenios Kyrillos found himself unable to get another. No other rich Greek fathers, it seemed, wanted to risk their daughters' virtue to a chauffeur who didn't know his place. Desperate to find work, he'd departed for America, leaving his baby son to be raised by his grandmother in the desolate house by the sea.

The first time Darius had spoken to his father in person had been at his grandmother's funeral, when he was eleven.

Then his father had taken him from Greece, away from everything and everyone he'd ever known, and brought him to America.

Fairholme had seemed like an exotic palace, where everyone spoke a language he couldn't understand. His father had seemed just as strange, the emotionally distant chauffeur of this grand American king—Howard Spencer.

And look what the Spencers had come to now.

Darius had long ago torn down his grandmother's shack in Heraklios and built a palatial villa. He had a penthouse in Manhattan, a ski chalet in Switzerland, his private race track outside London. His personal fortune was greater than anything Howard Spencer ever dreamed of.

And the Spencers were now living in this tiny, threadbare apartment.

But instead of feeling a sense of triumph, Darius felt strangely unsettled as he walked through her dreary kitchen and poured a glass of water from the tap. Returning to the equally depressing living room, he handed Letty the glass, then looked at the folded blankets and pillow on the floor.

"Who sleeps on the sofa?"

Letty's cheeks turned pink as she looked down at the sagging cushions. "I do."

"You pay all the rent, and your father gets the bedroom?"

"He hasn't been sleeping well. I just want him to be comfortable."

Darius looked at her incredulously. "And you're pregnant."

"What do you care?" she said bitterly. "You're just here to take my baby away."

Well. True. His eyes fell on the empty suitcases. "Where were you planning to go?"

"Anywhere you couldn't find us."

Darius stared down at her grimly. After his conversation with Howard Spencer, he'd had his investigator check up on Letty and found she'd only recently left her job as a waitress. She was still broke. None of the other employees remembered seeing any men around her, except one waitress, Belle, who had described Darius himself.

It seemed that, contrary to all previous assumptions, Letty wasn't a gold digger. Not with other men.

Not even with Darius.

In that, he'd misjudged her. After the way Letty had crushed him so devastatingly ten years ago, informing him that she was leaving him for a richer man, he'd believed Letty was a fortune hunter to the core.

It made sense. His own mother had abandoned him as a two-day-old newborn for the exact same reason. To Calla, Darius had been the embarrassing result of a one-night liaison with her wealthy family's chauffeur. She'd been determined to marry as befitted her station. She'd cared only about money and the social position that went with it.

But Letty wasn't the same. At least not anymore.

Darius abruptly sat down on the sofa beside her. "Why didn't you come to me when you found out you were pregnant? You had to know I would give you everything you needed and more."

"Give? I knew you'd only take!" she said incredulously. "You threatened me!"

He ground his teeth. "We could have come to some arrangement."

"You threatened to buy my baby, and if I tried to refuse, you would take the baby from me and—what were your words?—drive me into the sea?"

Darius didn't like to be reminded of what he'd said six months ago. He'd rationalized his cruelty on the grounds of justice. But now…strictly speaking, he might have sounded a little less than civil, if not outright crazy. Irritated, he glared at her. "Drink your water."

"Why? What did you put into it?" She sniffed the glass.

"Some drug to make me pass out so you can kidnap me to a Park Avenue dungeon?"

He snorted a laugh in spite of himself. "The water came from your tap. Drink it or not. I just thought you looked pale."

She stared at him for a moment, then took a tentative sip.

He looked around the tiny apartment. "Why are you living here?"

"Sadly, the presidential suite at the St. Regis was already booked."

"I mean it, Letty. Why did you stay in New York all these years? You could have just left. Moved west where no one would know you or care about what your father did."

She blinked fast. "I couldn't abandon him. I love him."

The man was a liar and a cheat, so of course Letty loved him. And she'd intended to raise their baby with him in the house, the man Darius blamed for his own father's death. He ground his teeth. "Are you even taking care of yourself? Do you have a doctor?"

"Of course," she said, stung. "How can you ask me that?"

"Because you've been working on your feet all day, until recently. And living in a place like this." He gestured angrily around the threadbare, cluttered apartment. "It never occurred to you I'd want better for our child?"

She glared at him. "*I* wanted better! I wanted my baby's father to be a good man I could trust and love. Instead, I got you, Darius, the worst man on earth!"

"You didn't think so ten years ago."

He immediately wished he could take the words back, because they insinuated that he still cared. Which he didn't.

"Oh, you're actually willing to talk about ten years ago? Fine. Let's talk about it." She briefly closed her eyes. "The reason I never showed up the night we were supposed to elope was because I was protecting you."

His lip curled scornfully. "*Protecting* me."

"Yes." Her expression was cool. "The day we were going to elope, my father told me his investment fund was a fraud. It had stopped making money years before, but he'd continued making payouts to old investors by taking money from new ones. The Feds were already on his tail. I knew what was going to happen." She lifted her luminous gaze. "I couldn't let you get dragged into it. Not with all your big dreams. You'd just started your tech company..." She took a deep breath and whispered, "I couldn't let my father's crime ruin your life, too."

For a moment, Darius's heart twisted as he looked at her beautiful face, her heartbreaking hazel eyes. Then he remembered that he no longer had any heart vulnerable enough to break.

"You're lying. You left me for another man. A rich man who could—how did you express it?—*give you the life of luxury you deserved.*" He snorted. "Though obviously he wasn't much good. He must have dumped you the moment your father was arrested."

"He couldn't dump me." She gave a low laugh. "He never existed."

"What?"

"It was the only way I knew you'd let me go." She lifted her chin and added with deliberate lightness, "I knew your weakness, even then."

"Weakness?" he growled.

"You always said a man could be measured by his money. I knew you wouldn't accept my just breaking up with you without explanation. So I gave you one. I told you I wanted someone richer. I knew you'd believe that."

He stared at her. "It's not true."

"I've always been a terrible liar." She looked sad. "But you still believed it. And immediately stopped calling me."

Darius's cheeks burned as he remembered how he'd felt that day. She was right.

He had loved her beyond reason, had been determined to fight for her at any cost. Until she'd told him she didn't want him because he was poor. He'd believed it instantly. Because money made the man. No money, no man.

His throat felt tight as he looked at her, struggling not to believe she was telling the truth when every fiber of him believed her.

"And my father?" he said hoarsely. "Were you protecting him, too—getting him fired?"

"It's true. I did have him fired. I told Dad I couldn't bear to look at Eugenios because he reminded me of you. I did it because I was afraid my dad might ask him to invest his life savings in the bankrupt investment fund. My dad still believed he could fix everything then. I knew your father would give him his savings. He was loyal to the core."

"Yes, he was," he bit out. His father had always made his employer his top priority, even over his own son.

Darius couldn't remember when his father had ever put his son first, over his job. He hadn't attended Darius's school events, not even his high school graduation. Being eternally at Howard Spencer's beck and call, keeping the ten luxury cars all gleaming and ready, had been Eugenios's total focus in life.

Oh, his father had fed and clothed him and given him a place to live in the two-bedroom apartment over the Fairholme garage that went with his job. But emotionally, they were oceans apart. The two men never talked.

Until that one awful day Darius told his father what he really thought of him...

But that memory was so white-hot with pain, he pushed it from his mind with all the force of a ball thrown from the earth to the moon.

Letty sighed beside him on the sofa. "I was trying to get

your father away from Fairholme before he lost everything. But it was too late. He'd already invested his life savings years before. My dad had accepted it for his fund, even though it was such a small amount," she said in a small voice. "As a favor."

A small amount? His father's life savings! The arrogance of them! Darius's dark eyebrows lowered in fury.

"Howard Spencer is a liar and cheat," he said harshly. "He destroyed people's lives."

"I know," she whispered, looking down. She bit her full, rosy lower lip. "He never meant to."

"He deserves to suffer."

She looked up. "He has suffered. During his arrest and trial, I tried so hard to be strong for him. When he was in prison, I was there every visiting day. I cheered him up. Encouraged him. And all the time, I felt so scared. So alone." She gave him a watery smile. "Sometimes the only thing I had to cling to was you."

"Me?"

"At least I hadn't dragged you down with me," she whispered. "At least you were able to follow your dreams."

Darius stared at her in shock.

Then he narrowed his eyes. She was trying to take credit for his accomplishments. To claim that if not for her sacrifice, he never would have made his fortune. She thought so little of him. Ice chilled his heart.

"And you expect me to be grateful?"

She looked startled. "I—"

"When you found out about your father's crime," he said tightly, "you should have come to me. I was your future husband. Instead, you lied to me. You cut me out of your life. Rather than asking for my help, you apparently believed I was so incompetent and useless, you felt you had to sacrifice yourself to save me."

"No," she gasped, "you've got it all wrong…"

"You never respected me." He forced his voice to remain calm when his shoulders were tight with repressed fury. "Not my intelligence, my judgment or my strength."

"Respected you?" she choked out. "*I loved you.* But I knew what was about to happen. I couldn't let you drown with us. You had nothing—"

"You're right," he said coldly. "I had nothing. No money. No influence. You knew I couldn't pay for lawyers or speak to politicians on your behalf. So you decided I was useless."

"No." She looked pale. "I just meant you had nothing to do with it—"

"You were my fiancée. I had *everything* to do with it. I would have tried to protect you, to comfort you. But you never gave me the chance. Because you believed I would fail."

Her voice sounded strangled. "Darius—"

He held up his hand sharply. "But now I have made my fortune. Everything has changed. And yet you still intended to disappear and keep my child secret from me for the rest of your life." A new, chilling thought occurred to him. "What story did you intend to tell the baby, Letty?"

"I don't know," she whispered.

"What were you going to raise my child to believe? That he or she had no father? That I hadn't wanted him?" An old childhood grief he'd thought long buried suddenly shook the ground beneath his feet, like an earthquake threatening to swallow him whole. "That I'd purposefully abandoned him?"

"I don't know!" Letty cried. "But you said you'd take the baby from me. I had no choice but to run!"

Darius stared at the woman he'd known for most of his life. He'd loved her for such a short, sweet time. He'd hated her far longer.

He himself had been abandoned by everyone who should

have loved him as a child. His whole young life he'd never felt like he really belonged anywhere.

And then there was Letty.

He'd loved her so wildly, so truly, so recklessly. She had finally destroyed what was left of his heart. That had been Darius's final lesson.

He was determined that his child would never learn such a lesson.

Darius's jaw tightened. His child would be surrounded by love from the beginning. His son or daughter would have a solid place in the world and never doubt their worth.

The blindfold of rage and hurt pride lifted from his eyes. He looked at Letty, and suddenly everything became crystal clear. Calm settled over him like rain.

Their child needed both of them.

For the last decade, he'd tried to forget about the Letty he'd once known. About her character. About her kind heart.

He saw now that in Letty's mind, her hurtful lies a decade before hadn't shown disrespect, but love. She really had been trying to protect him. As she still was trying to protect her father.

As she was trying now, in her own misguided way, to protect their child.

Letty hadn't betrayed him. She'd loved him, as recently as February, the night they'd conceived their child. Yes, she'd shown bad judgment ten years ago, lying to him, hiding the truth about her father. She'd continued to show bad judgment today, planning to run away with his child. A chill went down his spine to think of what might have happened if her father hadn't called him today.

But it wasn't entirely her fault. Her love blinded her. It made her weak. And after the cold way he'd treated her, and his threats to take the child, he couldn't blame her for being afraid.

It didn't make her a monster. It wasn't enough of a reason to brutally separate her from their child. Not after he himself had known what it was to have no mother. No father. No real place in the world.

Their baby would have both parents and a secure, settled home.

Darius knew he had to rebuild Letty's trust in him. He had to find a way to strengthen her occasionally faulty judgment with his own. If Darius was wiser, it was because he never allowed love to blind him. He always focused on the bottom line. So what was it here?

The answer was simple.

He had to make Letty his wife.

It was the only way to properly secure their child's future. It would guarantee the stability of two parents and a permanent home.

And also, his body suddenly whispered, marrying Letty would permanently secure her in his bed.

The thought electrified him. That settled it.

"I misjudged you," he said.

Letty glared at him. "Yes!"

"I treated you badly."

"You think?"

"So let me make up for it now." Leaning toward her on the sofa, Darius said, "I want you to marry me, Letty."

Her jaw dropped. "Marry you!"

"I've realized now I blamed everything on you. It wasn't your fault..."

"No."

"It was your father's," he finished grimly. "He's ruined your life. I won't let him ruin our child's."

Her eyes were wide as she put her hands over her large belly. "You're crazy. My father loves the baby, just as he loves me!"

"And what about the next time some thug decides to attack him? What if that man decides to hurt your father's family instead?"

Letty's expression became troubled. Swallowing, she whispered, "That wouldn't happen..."

"No. It won't. Because you and the baby will be miles away from Howard Spencer and safe with me." He rose abruptly to his feet. "You will have to sign a prenuptial agreement..."

"I won't, because I'm not going to marry you."

She wasn't joking or playing coy. She actually sounded serious.

Darius stared down at her in confusion. So many women were dying to marry him, he'd assumed that Letty—jobless, penniless, faced with threats on all sides—would be thrilled at the thought of being his bride. "Of course you want to marry me."

"Marry someone I hate? Who hates me back? No, thanks."

He couldn't believe she was trying to fight him when it was the only practical solution. He gritted his teeth. It was that idea of *love*, once again interfering with all common sense!

"Have you thought this through?" Folding his arms, he regarded her coolly. "I could take you to court. Have you declared an unfit mother, selfishly placing our child at risk."

Letty rose to her feet in turn, matching him toe-to-toe, though he was bigger by a foot in height and at least sixty pounds of muscle. She narrowed her eyes. "You could *try*."

In spite of himself, he almost smiled. Another thing he'd forgotten about her character. She fought harder for others than she ever did for herself.

"You really think you can handle a custody battle? You think there are waves of lawyers out there, willing to support Howard Spencer's daughter pro bono, when all they'd get for their trouble is a lot of bad PR?"

Her cheeks flushed, even as she lifted her chin defiantly. "We'll see, won't we?"

But beneath her bravado, her expression was soft and sad. Her long dark ponytail gleamed in waves down her back, and his eyes strayed to the roundness of her belly and full breasts, voluptuous beyond belief. In this moment, Darius thought she looked like everything desirable in a woman—the perfect image of what any man would dream of in a wife.

He suddenly imagined how she might look in court. Whatever her father's sins, if she did find a good attorney, she could be packaged and sold to the presiding judge as the poor, innocent, poverty-stricken waitress threatened by the cold, power-hungry billionaire. No matter how many legal sharks he hired, Darius wasn't guaranteed to win. There was some small possibility he might lose.

He abruptly changed tack.

"Does our baby deserve to have parents at war? Living in here—" he motioned to the peeling wallpaper, the cracked ceiling "—instead of my penthouse? Does he deserve to grow up in poverty without the protection of his father's name? Without my love?"

Letty looked stricken. "Our baby could still have your love."

"He deserves everything I can provide. Are you really so selfish as to make our child suffer for the sake of your own angry pride?"

He saw emotions struggle on her face. She really was a terrible liar. He knew he was very close to getting what he wanted—her total surrender.

"We could make our marriage work," he murmured. "Our son or daughter would be our priority, always."

"Son," she said unwillingly.

He looked at her sharply.

She took a deep breath, then slowly smiled. "We're having a boy."

"A boy!" The nebulous idea of a baby suddenly solidified in Darius's mind. He could imagine his son smiling, playing soccer, laughing, hugging him. And the fact that she'd revealed that detail proved how close she was to agreeing to his proposal. His resolve solidified. Stepping closer, he said softly, "Marry me, Letty."

Looking uncertain, she bit her lip. "It would be a disaster. Not just for me. For you. Don't you know how much people hate me?"

"Not once you're with me," he said confidently.

"You don't understand how bad it is…"

"I'm sure you're exaggerating." He'd all but won. Now that his unborn child was secure, he was already jumping ahead to the thought of enjoying Letty's surrender in full, imagining her naked and writhing with desire in his arms. He wanted to take her back to the penthouse immediately. Then he remembered. "I am hosting a charity event tonight. The Fall Ball."

She looked impressed in spite of herself. "You're hosting that this year?"

"We can announce our engagement to all of New York."

"It's a mistake!"

"Let me worry about that."

"Okay, but…"

"But what?"

A shadow crossed her face. "But I don't love you anymore."

He felt a strange emotion, deep down inside. He crushed it down before he could identify what it was.

"I do not need your love. I can assure you that you'll never have mine. Love is for children. I just need your compliance." When she still hesitated, he took a deliberate step back. "Or I can walk out that door and go straight to my lawyer."

Letty looked wistful in the gray light from the small window. She sighed sadly. "Have it your way."

"You'll marry me?"

She nodded.

He felt a surge of smug masculine triumph. "Good choice."

Pulling her roughly into his arms, he did what he'd yearned to do for six months and kissed her.

From the moment he felt her lips against his and tasted her sweetness—her mouth, her tongue—he was lost, and at the same time, found. Her lips parted, and as she melted against him, he savored her surrender. His body and long-dead soul roared back to life.

Letty wrenched away. "But first, you'll take me to your charity ball tonight. And see firsthand what it would be like to actually have me as your wife."

"Good—"

"Just remember." She gave him a crooked smile. "You asked for it."

CHAPTER FIVE

LETTY ALMOST DIDN'T leave a note for her father. Her anger at his betrayal was too high. But in the end she didn't want him to worry, so she scribbled a note and left it on the counter.

Out with Darius, and I'm never talking to you again.

Darius had taken one look at her closet and told her he was taking her shopping for the ball. She'd tried to protest, but he'd retorted, "There's no point in announcing our engagement if you turn up at the ball dressed in rags. No one would believe it."

"Fine," she said sulkily. "Waste your money on a ball gown. See if I care."

But she had the sudden disconcerting feeling that her life was no longer her own.

As she climbed into his sports car, her stomach growled with hunger. But she vowed she wasn't going to say a word about it. It was bad enough he was buying her a dress. She wasn't going to ask him for food, like a beggar!

But as Darius climbed into the driver's seat beside her, all her senses went on high alert. Having him so close did strange things to her insides. As he drove through the busy traffic, she glanced at him out of the corner of her eye. His dark hair wasn't even mussed, and his powerful body was relaxed in the leather seat. He looked so much calmer than she felt.

But why wouldn't he be relaxed?

He'd won.

She'd lost.

Simple as that.

Or so Darius thought. Letty clasped her hands together in her lap as she looked out the window. Once he actually saw what life would be like for him with her at his side, he wouldn't be able to get rid of her fast enough. Maybe she and her father could still be on that bus to Rochester tomorrow.

Darius didn't yet see that her family's scandal wasn't something he could master or control. That was why he'd been so angry that she'd protected him ten years ago with her silence. He still somehow thought, if he'd known the truth back then, he could have prevented disaster.

She looked up through the window, seeing flashes of blue sky between the skyscrapers like a strobe light. Darius would get a dose of reality today. He'd discover how toxic the Spencer name was, even now. It had been even worse at the time of her father's arrest and trial, when reporters and angry, tomato-throwing hecklers had camped outside her father's pied-à-terre on Central Park West!

Let Darius get just a glimpse of what he would have been up against if she'd actually followed her heart and married him ten years ago instead of setting him free. He didn't appreciate the way she'd tried to protect him? Fine. Still staring out the window, she wiped her eyes hard. Let him just see.

The rain had stopped. The sky was blue and bright on the first of September. As they drove through Manhattan, puddle-dotted sidewalks were full of gawking tourists, standing still like islands as a current of New Yorkers rushed past them, coming up from the subway, hurrying back to work after lunch.

When their car stopped at a red light, Letty glanced at a fancy chauffeured town car stopped beside them. In the backseat, she saw a man speaking angrily into his phone and staring at a computer tablet, totally wrapped in his own bubble. Rich people lived in a separate world. Letty hadn't fully realized that.

Not until she'd fallen out of it.

After her father's confession that awful night long ago, after she'd tried her best to protect Darius and his father by getting them away from the manor, she'd begged Howard to go to the police and throw himself on their mercy.

He'd loved her, so a few months later he'd done it.

The police and Feds had descended on him like the hardcase criminal they believed him to be. Within six months, he was in prison on a nine-year sentence.

Letty had tried to remain in one of the exclusive small towns on Long Island near Fairholme. But it proved impossible. Too many people recognized her and didn't hesitate to yell or even—more than once—physically take the few dollars in her wallet, saying her father owed them. Manhattan had been even worse, and anyway was way out of her price range. So she'd moved to a working-class neighborhood in Brooklyn where she could be anonymous. No one bothered her. Mostly, people were kind.

But without money or family or friends, Letty had learned the hard way what it meant to struggle and always have too much month at the end of her paycheck.

No one likes self-pity. Help someone else, baby. Letty could almost hear the whisper of her mother's voice, so kind, so warm, so loving. Almost see her mother's eyes glowing with love. *The best way to feel better when you're sad is to help someone who's hurting more.*

Good advice.

Taking a deep breath, Letty turned to Darius in the sports car. "So tell me about your charity, the one benefiting from the Fall Ball tonight."

Driving, he glanced at her out of the corner of his eye. "It provides college scholarships for foster kids."

"Nice," she said, surprised. "But I never pegged you as the society-ball-hosting type."

He shrugged. "I have the time. Might as well use it."

"You could just waste your days dating beautiful women and spending your obscene amounts of money."

He pulled his car to a curb where a valet waited. "That's exactly what I plan to do today."

"You're going on a date?" Then she saw his look and realized he meant her. She blushed. "Oh."

The door opened, and Letty stepped out onto Fifth Avenue, which was lined with exclusive designer shops from famous international brands to quirky boutiques less well-known but every bit as expensive. The last time she'd shopped on this street she'd been a pampered seventeen-year-old looking for a white dress for the graduation ceremony at her private school, Miss Parker's. She hadn't fit into society, even then. She'd been too bookish, too tenderhearted, too socially awkward.

But now Letty was actually scared. She glanced at the people coming out of an exclusive department store, almost expecting one of them to tell her to get lost, that she no longer belonged here.

"Which shop first?" Darius asked, his dark eyes smiling.

"I changed my mind," she muttered. "I don't want to go."

The smile disappeared. "Too late for that."

"Darius…"

Ignoring her protests, he grabbed her hand. Letty tried not to notice the sizzle of electricity from their touching palms as he pulled her into a famous luxury store.

As soon as they passed the doorman into the store's foyer, a salesgirl came up to them, offering a tray of champagne. "Monsieur?"

He took a glass. "Thank you."

Noting Letty's pregnant belly, the salesgirl didn't offer

champagne. "And for madame? Some sparkling water, perhaps, some juice of *pamplemousse*?"

"No, thanks," Letty said, pulling away from Darius. Ducking her head, she pretended to look through the nearest dress racks, sparsely and expensively filled with garments that seemed to be designed for a size zero.

"We require assistance," he said.

"Sir?"

He turned to an elegant white-haired woman, apparently the manager, dressed in an expensive-looking tweed suit. "I need a ball gown for my fiancée."

Fiancée. The word made Letty shiver. But it was true, in a way. She'd agreed to his marriage proposal.

It's not a real engagement, she told herself firmly. She glanced down at her bare left hand. There was no ring. No ring meant it wasn't real. Anyway, the engagement would be over before the end of the night.

"Couture or ready-to-wear, Mr. Kyrillos?" The white-haired woman somehow already knew who he was.

"It's for tonight."

"We can, of course, do any last-minute alterations that madame may require. If you'll please come this way?"

They were led to a private area with a white leather sofa and a three-way mirror, as a succession of salesgirls, under the sharp-eyed direction of the manager, brought in clothes.

"She'll try on everything," Darius said, standing in front of the sofa as his cell phone rang. Lifting it from his pocket, he told Letty, "Come out when you have something to show me."

As salesgirls filled her arms with gowns and gently pushed her toward the changing room, she hesitated. "What do you want to see?"

Looking her body over slowly, Darius gave her a heavy-lidded sensual smile. "Everything."

Beneath his hot gaze, somehow, he made her feel like

a goddess of sex—even at six months pregnant, in her old T-shirt and jeans!

Darius sat down calmly on the white leather sofa, talking into his phone and sipping champagne. She turned away with a sigh to try on gowns for a ball that she was dreading.

Maybe it wouldn't be all bad, she tried to tell herself. She couldn't remember the last time she'd had new clothes. Everything in her closet was either from high school or purchased from the bargain bin at the thrift store. It might be fun to get a dress that was not only pretty, but actually fit.

Then she saw the price tag of the first gown.

Darius looked up expectantly when she came out of the dressing room. His expression changed to a scowl. "Why are you still in your old clothes?"

"The price of these gowns is ridiculous! We can go to the local thrift shop and find a barely used prom dress..."

"Letty."

"I mean it. It's foolish for you to throw money away when you might never see me again after tonight."

"Now you're talking nonsense." He tilted his head, looking her over critically. "Are you not feeling well? Are you hungry? Thirsty? Tired?"

She wasn't going to say a word about being hungry. Wild horses couldn't drag it out of her!

Her stomach growled again.

"Um. I might have missed breakfast."

It wasn't her fault! The baby made her say it!

He looked mad. "You should have told me." He grabbed a glass of sparkling mineral water from a salesgirl. "Here," he said gravely, pushing it into her hand. "Start with that. Breakfast or lunch?"

The cool water tasted delicious, and did make her feel slightly better. "Breakfast?"

Turning to one of the hovering assistants, he ordered, "Have a large breakfast sent down from your café."

"Oh, sir." The salesgirl looked sorrowful. "I'm afraid that's impossible…"

"Of course it's possible for Mr. Kyrillos," the white-haired manager snapped, turning to them with a bright smile. "A pregnant woman must never go hungry. What would madame like?"

"Everything," Darius said. "Send down a tray or two. We'll be here a while. We need a ball gown, but also a great deal more. Shoes, accessories, maternity clothes. Price is no object. We may be here for hours."

"Yes, sir," the woman replied happily, clapping her hands at her assistants, who rushed to obey.

"Darius, you don't need to make a fuss!"

"You're wrong. I can see all too well that I need to be in charge. Because you've always been better at taking care of others than yourself." He drew Letty gently to the white sofa. "Here. Sit down. Take a breath."

"But I left all those dresses in the changing room—"

"They will wait. Relax. You do not have to shop hungry. Breakfast is on its way."

The white leather cushion shifted beneath them, tipping her toward him on the sofa. The edge of her thigh brushed against his. She jumped away with an intake of breath, looking up at him with big eyes.

"I'm not your responsibility."

"You are now." Reaching out, he tucked a long tendril of her dark hair back behind her ear and said softly, "And taking care of you will be my pleasure."

His…pleasure?

A sudden terrifying thought occurred to her.

"Darius," she said haltingly, unable to meet his eyes. "You surely can't think…"

"Think what?"

Taking her courage in her hands, she looked into his dark wicked eyes. However charming he might seem at the moment, she couldn't forget the heartless man he'd revealed himself to be. She couldn't let herself confuse him with the boy she'd once loved. No matter how much Darius's dark eyes, his smile, his kindness might seem the same. *He was nothing like the man she'd loved.*

"You can't think…" She took a deep breath. "That our marriage would be real."

"Of course it will be real. Legal in any court."

"I mean…" She licked her lips, hating him for making her spell it out. "It would just be a marriage of convenience, nothing more. For our baby. We wouldn't… You and I, we would never…"

"You will sleep in my bed, Letty." His dark eyes burned through her. "Naked. Every single night."

His sensual voice swirled around her body like a hot wind, making her toes curl.

She had to resist. She had no intention of sleeping with him again, no matter how seductive he might be. She'd been a virgin till twenty-eight, waiting for love. That love was gone.

"I loved you the night we conceived our baby. Everything has changed. Unlike you, I can't have sex with a cold heart," she said in a low voice. "No love, no sex."

He wrapped her hand in his larger one. She felt his palm against hers, and a shiver ricocheted through Letty's body, deep, to blood and bone. He leaned forward.

"We'll see," he whispered.

CHAPTER SIX

LETTY WAS SAVED when the salesgirls interrupted them with trays of pastries and fruit and juices, followed closely behind by yet more racks of clothes for her to consider.

A proper breakfast tray soon followed with maple bacon pancakes drizzled in maple syrup, hash brown potatoes and hot fried sausages. Thus fortified, Letty spent another hour trying on all the clothes she liked in that luxury store. Then they moved to a designer boutique. Then an exclusive department store.

By the end of the afternoon, Darius had bought her so many bags of clothes, he'd had to call his bodyguard and driver down to Fifth Avenue to carry everything back to the penthouse.

He took her to a world-famous jewelry store where they were ushered to an exclusive, private floor. She tried to protest, for about the thirtieth time. "You really don't need to keep spending more money on me!"

Darius held up a twenty-carat diamond necklace with a critical eye. "You're going to be my wife. Of course you need clothes."

"Those are diamonds."

He grinned. "Hard, sparkling clothes."

She harrumphed. "You're wasting your money."

"So let me waste it. What do you care?" Lifting his eyebrow, he said mildly, "I seem to recall your saying you hate me. So why not make me suffer?"

Why not indeed? Put that way, it didn't sound so unreasonable. "You do have it coming."

Setting the necklace down, he looked at her with a heavily lidded gaze.

"And I intend to take it." Turning back to the jeweler, he nodded toward the diamond necklace. "Starting with that."

But though Darius insisted on buying her an entire wardrobe of fancy clothes, he was never satisfied by any of the ball gowns she tried on. Truth be told, even Letty thought most of them hideous. A hoop skirt on a baby bump? She looked like a cartoon hippo.

In spite of Letty's misgivings, the afternoon flew by in an irresistible whirlwind of small pleasures. Her new wardrobe wasn't comprised of minimalist black and gray clothes as he had originally suggested, currently popular with chic society women, nor were they the plain, sensible, washing-machine-ready clothes she'd worn for the last ten years. No.

Darius had watched her carefully as she'd tried on each outfit, and he seemed to notice the colors that made her face light up with joy. Bright, vivid jewel tones—emerald green, cerulean blue, fuchsia, ruby red—in impractical sensual fabrics like silk.

"We'll take it," he would say immediately.

Letty felt guilty revealing her own pleasure, but she couldn't help herself. For so long, survival had been her only goal. She couldn't remember the last time that her happiness had mattered to anyone, least of all her.

But Darius treated her as if her happiness was actually the main goal.

Because I carry his baby inside me, she told herself, as she changed her clothes yet again in a private dressing room.

But his hot dark gaze had told her it was more than that. He didn't just want custody over their baby.

He wanted to possess Letty, too.

You will sleep in my bed. Naked. Every single night.

She shivered, then tried on yet another formal gown, this one made of a slinky knit fabric in a delicious shade of hot pink, her favorite color.

The dress fell softly over her body. Reaching back, she couldn't quite zip it all the way. She looked at herself in the mirror.

The long stretchy gown fit perfectly over her pregnant body, curving over her full breasts and huge belly. She liked it, but weren't pregnant women supposed to wear tent dresses?

"I want to see," Darius's voice commanded outside the dressing room. She took a deep breath, then came out, her cheeks hot.

"What do you think?" she said timidly.

His expression said everything. He walked slowly around her, looking up and down her body in a way that made her shiver inside.

"That," he said softly, "is the dress."

She bit her lip. "I'm afraid it's too formfitting..."

"It's perfect."

"I couldn't zip it all the way up..."

Drawing close, he wrapped his arms around her. She felt his arms brush against her body as he pulled on the zipper. His eyes never left hers as he towered over her, so close. He made her breathless.

A hint of a smile lifted the edges of his cruel, sensual mouth. He cupped her cheek, then stroked down her throat. "The necklace will be perfect here. Against your skin."

Looking down, she realized how low cut the gown was. Her cheeks went redder. "I shouldn't wear this."

"Why?"

"It's too revealing. Everyone will stare."

"They will stare regardless."

"Because I'm the daughter of a criminal."

"Because you're an incredibly beautiful woman."

At his soft words, Letty's throat suddenly hurt. "You don't realize how much they hate me." Her eyes stung as she pushed away. "When they see me...it'll be like dropping raw meat in a shark tank. And the more they notice me, the more they'll rip me apart." She took a deep breath, tried to smile. "I sound like I'm complaining. I'm not. I can handle it. I'm used to it. But…"

"But what?"

She looked down at the floor.

"Letty?"

She said in a small voice, "I don't want them to say rude things about you at your own party. And they will if I'm your date."

Reaching out, he lifted her chin. "I can take care of myself, *agape mou*," he said in a low voice. "When will you learn that?"

His dark gaze fell to her mouth, and Letty's whole body tightened as, for a moment, she wondered if he was going to kiss her, right there in the luxurious store. For a wild moment, it didn't seem like such a bad idea.

He turned to the nearest salesgirl. "We'll take this dress. Wrap it up. We need shoes to match."

Letty tried on ten pairs before she found stiletto heels that made her gasp at their outrageous beauty.

"Those," Darius said, looking at Letty's face.

"No, I couldn't possibly. They're too impractical. I'll never wear them again!" She looked doubtfully at her feet, wobbling in the high heels. "I'm not even sure I can wear them now."

But even as she protested, she couldn't look away from the beautiful shoes, which were encrusted with glittery pink crystals and had a red sole.

"We'll take them," he told the salesgirl firmly.

Though they pinched Letty's toes and made her wobble ever so slightly, she was filled with joy as she sat down and handed the precious pink crystal stilettos to the salesgirl. She couldn't remember the last time she'd had anything so outrageous, just because of their beauty. And their cost! She was trying not to think about owning shoes worth three months' rent. And when would she ever wear them again? Working as a waitress? Going to the grocery store?

It was wicked, letting him buy her these shoes. Letting him buy her so many things, when after tonight, he'd likely never want to see her again.

She would just leave everything behind, she decided. Most of the clothes could be returned, unworn, with tags. She'd have nothing to feel guilty about when he tossed her out of his life. Nothing!

"Now—" Darius's gaze lingered on her lips, then dropped lower "—lingerie."

Letty made a sound like a squeak. "Forget it!"

"Ah. You intend to wear nothing beneath your gown tonight? I approve."

Her cheeks burned. "Of course I'm going to wear something!"

"Then you need undergarments." He nodded toward three hovering salesgirls. "Get us a selection of lingerie that would suit the gown."

They departed in a rush to obey.

"I hope you don't expect me to try *those* on for you," Letty said sulkily.

"No?" He looked at her lazily. "Maybe later."

Her blush deepened.

Right here, in the exclusive department store, with strangers everywhere, Darius was looking at Letty as if he wanted nothing more than to drag her into a changing room and roughly make love to her. Possibly while she was wearing nothing but those pink crystal stilettos. Not a bad idea...

She blinked, realizing she'd been licking her lips. She put her hand unsteadily to her head. What was happening? Was she losing all her morals over a pair of beautiful shoes and for the body of a dangerously beautiful man?

Except Darius wasn't just beautiful. He was also the only man she'd ever slept with. The only man she'd ever been in love with. She was even now carrying his child deep inside her. He wanted her in his bed. He wanted to marry her. All of those things together were likely to distract any woman.

And with every moment, she felt herself being drawn into his world. Remembering what it was like when money was no object. To be without worry or care.

To be cherished.

It had been a long time since she'd felt that way. She'd been a lonely teenager, far happier spending her time with the estate staff, pets or books instead of other debutantes. At fourteen, she'd fallen hopelessly for Darius, the chauffeur's son, six years older and totally out of her league. Funny now to recall that she'd actually imagined herself to be unhappy then.

She'd discovered soon after what unhappiness really meant, when her beloved mother, the heart of their home, had suddenly fallen ill. She'd wasted away and died within months.

Her father had been gutted. A few years later, he'd gone to prison. Letty had tried to be tough. She'd tried to be strong. She'd hadn't let herself think. Hadn't let herself feel.

But now...

For the first time in years she realized how it felt to be truly looked after. To be cared for. As the salesgirls wrapped up a thousand dollars' worth of silky lingerie, she tried to tell herself it was just an illusion. Exactly like Cinderella. After midnight tonight it would all disappear.

Darius signed the credit card receipt, smiling at her out of the corner of his eye. "Is there anything else you desire?"

Letty looked at him, her heart in her throat. Then she just shook her head.

"It's growing late." He took her hand. "We have one more place to go."

The bodyguard had already left in Darius's sports car filled with bags. As his driver walked ahead, weighed down by yet more bags, toward the waiting town car, Darius never let go of her hand. His dark eyes glowed down at her as the sun slipped down between the skyscrapers, toward a horizon she couldn't see.

Maybe it was the pregnancy hormones, but as they climbed into the back of the elegant car, emotion squeezed her heart as she looked at him. All day, Darius had been beside her, ready to push through any crowds, to make sure that she got—in his opinion—proper attention. When she was thirsty, when she was hungry, when she was tired, he seemed to know even before she did, and like a miracle, whatever she desired would instantly appear.

It was as if she were no longer alone. Someone else was looking out for her. Someone tough and strong. Someone who made her feel safe.

Safe?

She shook herself hard. Darius was dangerous. Selfish. Arrogant and cold.

He frowned at her in the backseat. "Are you crying?"

She wiped her tears. "Nope."

"Letty."

"I'm sorry. I just..." She faltered. "You've been so kind."

"Buying you clothes?" he said incredulously. He gave a low laugh. "Is that all it takes?"

It was more than the clothes, far more, but she couldn't explain. She said miserably, "I shouldn't go with you to the ball tonight."

His mouth turned down grimly. "You're going."

"Don't you understand? It'll only cause you trouble."

"Stop trying to protect me," he said evenly. "I mean it."

"But—"

"It's not your job to protect me. It's my job to protect you now. And our baby. Never again insult me by insinuating

I am incapable of it." At her expression, he said more gently, "Don't you understand, Letty? I will watch over you. I'll make sure no one ever hurts you again. You'll always be taken care of now. You're safe."

She was suddenly shaking as the town car drove down the street. How she wished it were true! How she wished she could believe in him, as she had so long ago.

The car door opened. Looking up in surprise at Darius's driver, who was holding it open, Letty looked back at Darius. He gave her a cheeky grin.

"I'm just dropping you off. This is the best day spa in the city. Collins is bringing your gown and everything else you'll need for the ball tonight. I'll collect you here at eight."

"A day spa? Why?"

"You deserve some pampering. Enjoy yourself." He leaned forward in the car's backseat. She felt his warmth and breathed in his scent as he brushed back her hair and whispered in her ear, "I'll be back for you soon."

As he drew back, her heart beat rapidly, and she felt prickles of sensation and desire course through her body, down her spine and over her skin.

And all he'd done was whisper in her ear!

Oh, this was bad.

Her legs were shaky as she stepped out of the car and was whisked into the gorgeously bright day spa with its tall windows, green plants and kitschy pink furniture. A team of specialists, including massage therapists, beauty therapists, stylists and more, surrounded her, moaning about Letty's cuticles, her tense shoulders, her dry skin...

Hours passed in a flash. Her nails were done and her muscles rubbed and her skin freshened until dewy. Hairstylists and makeup artists came next, and once they were done, it was nearly eight.

Letty put on the new silk bra and panties, the perfectly

fitting pink gown and sparkly stiletto heels. She looked at herself in the mirror.

Her long, freshly shaped dark hair was now glossy and shiny and bouncy from the hairstylist's efforts. Red lipstick made her look glamorous, and her eyes were emphasized with dark liner and even a few false eyelashes for drama. Her full breasts, pushed up by the bra, were laid out like a platter in the knit pink dress, her hips thrust forward by the stilettos, her voluptuous belly the star.

She was dazzled by her own image. She barely recognized herself.

"Wait until Mr. Kyrillos sees you," the proprietress of the spa said with a broad smile. "Our finest creation!" There was a whisper, then a gasp. "He's here!"

Nervously, Letty came down into the foyer. She wondered if he would think she looked silly. She couldn't bear it if her appearance embarrassed him, on top of everything else.

But as Darius came into the foyer, she saw his face. And she knew he approved. Deeply.

"You look incredible," he whispered. "So beautiful."

She gave him a shy smile. "You don't look so bad yourself."

The truth was, she couldn't take her eyes off him. His hard jaw was freshly shaved, and his dark eyes wickedly bright. He looked impossibly handsome, tall and broad-shouldered in his sophisticated black tuxedo, which was obviously tailored. No tuxedo off the rack could have fit his muscled body so perfectly.

Wordlessly, Darius held out his arm.

Wrapping her hand around his hard, thick bicep, she shivered, remembering how six months ago, she'd felt his naked, powerful body over hers. Inside hers. She nearly stumbled at the memory.

He stopped.

"Sorry, I'm still getting the hang of my shoes," she lied. She couldn't explain that it wasn't the stilettos that had made her stumble, but the memory of that hot February night they'd conceived their baby.

A night that would never happen again, she thought wistfully. After tonight, he'd run away from her so fast that there would be flames left on the ground, like in a cartoon.

This time, a limousine waited for them. Collins, the driver, wore his formal uniform with a peaked cap as he held open her passenger door.

"Where is the ball this year?" she asked Darius.

"The Corlandt," he said, naming a venue that was nearly as famous as the Met or Frick or Whitney.

She gulped. It was even worse than she'd thought. As the limo took them uptown, she felt sick with dread. She looked out the window, frantically trying to build ice around her heart and get herself back into a place where she was too well armored to feel any attack.

But her newly scrubbed skin felt far too thin now. Wearing this beautiful dress, and being with Darius, she felt vulnerable. She felt visible. She felt raw.

Even though she no longer loved him, she still didn't want him hurt because of her. She tried to tell herself it would be for his own good, so he'd realize they had no future. But she couldn't bear the thought of what was about to happen.

All too soon, the limo arrived. Looking out at the crowds and red carpet and paparazzi, Letty couldn't breathe. Collins got out and opened their door.

Darius went first. There was a low roar from the crowds, watching from behind the cordons of the red carpet, at seeing Darius Kyrillos, the host of the evening and currently New York's most famous billionaire bachelor, get out of the limo, gorgeous in his tuxedo. As cameras flashed in the darkening twilight, he gave a brusque wave.

Looking at the photographers, Letty felt so weak she wasn't sure she could get out of the limo.

Turning back, Darius held out his hand to where she sat quivering in the backseat. He lifted a challenging eyebrow.

Shaking, Letty put her hand in his.

As she exited the limo, a low murmur started amid the photographers and press waiting outside the red carpet as someone recognized Letty.

Then it spread.

There was a gasp of recognition traveling among the photographers and crowd like a rumble of thunder rolling across the ground. The camera flashes went crazy as journalists and celebrity bloggers started screaming at her.

"Letitia Spencer!"

"Where have you been for the last ten years?"

"How does it feel now that your father's out of prison?"

"Do you feel guilty for your father's victims as you're coming to a ball in diamonds?"

"Are you two together?"

"Mr. Kyrillos, with all the city at your feet, why would you date a jailbird's daughter?"

Darius responded only with a glower as he arrogantly walked past them, Letty gripping his hand tightly. He led her past the reporters and inside the magnificent beaux-arts-style granite building. Only after she'd walked up the steps and past the imposing columns through the oversize door, and he'd shut it behind them, did she exhale. Immediately, he pulled her close. Letty closed her eyes, still shaking as she breathed in his strength, his warmth, his comfort.

"It's over," he said softly as he finally drew back, tucking back a dark tendril of her hair behind her ear. "That wasn't so bad, was it?"

"You think it's over?" She gave him a trembling smile. "It's only just begun."

Darius's expression darkened, but they were interrupted

as a famous white-haired society matron covered in jewels entered the foyer behind them. Her face brightened when she saw Darius. She immediately left her much younger date to come forward and give him air-kisses.

"Darius, how lovely to see you! Thank you again for hosting this important event." She simpered. "Though I think there will be many broken hearts when they see you brought a date—"

But as the matron turned to Letty, her smile froze. Her expression changed to shock, then outrage.

"Hello, Mrs. Alexander," Letty said bashfully. "I don't know if you remember, but I used to go to school with your daughter, Poppy. We were both debutantes at the—"

"Stop." The woman's eyes blazed. "Don't you dare speak to me." Looking back at Darius, she hissed, "Do you know who this girl is? What she's done?"

He looked at her coldly. "Of course I know who Letty is. We've been friends since childhood. And as for what she's done—I think you have her confused with her father."

The woman turned to Letty with narrowed eyes. "You have some nerve coming here. Your father stole money from nearly every person attending tonight." She looked at Darius incredulously. "And you are insane to bring her. Take my advice. Send Letitia Spencer straight out the door. Or you might find that you suddenly have no guests, and your charity will suffer. For what? So you can get that little tart in your bed?" She looked pointedly at Letty's belly. "Or perhaps you did that already?"

Letty's cheeks went hot. She suddenly felt like a tart, too, wearing this low-cut, formfitting pink dress that showed off every curve. Beneath the society matron's scrutiny, even her beautiful sparkly shoes lost their gleam, and suddenly just pinched her feet.

"It's only out of respect for those poor foster children that I'm not leaving here right now." The woman glared between them, then flounced away in her jewels and fluttering silk sleeves.

Letty was left paralyzed from the ambush.

"Don't listen to her," Darius said, putting his hand on her shoulder. "She's a witch."

"I don't blame her for being mad," Letty said in a low voice. "Her family lost a lot of money. Tens of millions."

"It obviously hasn't cut into her jewelry and plastic-surgery budget. Forget her. Let's go in."

Wrapping her arm securely over his, he marched her into the ballroom as cheerfully as a revolutionary leading a French aristocrat to the guillotine.

But it was no good. The rest of the evening was just as Letty had feared. As lovely and magical as the afternoon had been, the ball sucked the joy out of everything.

Darius insisted on keeping her by his side as he greeted his society guests, each of whom had paid thousands of dollars to attend this ball, ostensibly for the benefit of college scholarships for foster kids but mostly just to have a good excuse to party with friends and show off new couture.

Letty felt their hostile stares, though with Darius beside her, none were as brave or foolhardy as Mrs. Alexander. None of them said anything to her face. Instead, the cream of New York society just stared at her in bewildered horror, as if she had a contagious and fatal disease, then looked at Darius as if they were waiting for him to reveal the punch line of whatever joke had inspired him to bring a pariah like Letitia Spencer to the Fall Ball when he could have had any beauty in the city for the asking.

She heard whispers and felt their hard stares as she and Darius passed through the crowds in the ballroom. When he briefly left her to get drinks, she felt vulnerable, alone. She kept her eyes focused on the floor, trying to be quiet and invisible, as if facing wild animals. If they didn't notice her, they might not tear her to shreds with their teeth and claws.

It didn't work.

Within moments, three former debutantes blocked her like bouncers at a bar.

"Well, well, well." A skinny young woman in a designer gown gave her a hard-edged smile. "Letitia Spencer. This is a surprise. Isn't it, Caroline?"

"A big surprise."

Letty vaguely recognized the two women from her school, where they'd been a year older. They were looking at her now with the cold expressions of mob enforcers. She could suddenly imagine how her father must have felt right before that thug had broken his arm.

But the third woman stood a slight distance from the first two. It was Poppy Alexander. She and Letty had once been study partners, sophomore year. Poppy just stood there, looking pale and uneasy.

"Excuse me." Letty backed away. "I don't want any trouble."

"You don't want trouble?" The first woman's lip twisted scornfully. "How very amusing."

"Amusing," Caroline echoed with a sneer.

"You shouldn't be here."

"You're a disgrace to society."

"If you had any decency, you'd disappear or die."

Poppy stood silently beside her friends, looking faintly sick, as if she wished she were a million miles away. Letty sympathized with that feeling.

The first woman continued with a sneer, "You might think you're safe on Darius Kyrillos's arm, but…"

"Ah, there you are, Letty," Darius said smoothly, coming up behind them. "I brought your drink." Turning to the other women, he gave a charming smile. "Ah. Augusta. Caroline. And Poppy Alexander. How lovely to see you."

"Hello, Darius," they cooed with weak smiles, then departed, the first two with a final venomous glance at Letty, Poppy hanging her head, looking guilty and ashamed.

Emotions Letty knew well.

"Everything all right?" Darius murmured after they left.

She exhaled, blinking fast. "Fine. Just fine."

The night only got worse. It was past ten when the formal dinner was finally served, and Letty felt half-starved as she sat down beside Darius at the prestigious head table. But as she felt the glares from the four other couples at the table, she could barely eat a bite of salad or the lobster with white truffle cream. At any moment, she half expected one of the hedge fund millionaires or society wives might smash a three-hundred-dollar champagne bottle against the table and attack her with it.

That might have been preferable to the waves of unspoken hatred overtaking her like a blast of heat from all sides. During the unendurably long meal, Darius tried several times to start conversations with the others at the table. Each time, he succeeded. Until he tried to include her. Then the conversation instantly died.

Finally, Letty could stand it no longer.

"Excuse me," she breathed, rising from her seat. "I have to—"

She couldn't finish her sentence. Turning, she rushed past all the other tables and out of the ballroom. Going down the long hall, she found a ladies' bathroom, where she was violently sick. Going to the sink, she washed out her mouth. She looked at herself wanly in the mirror. She felt like she'd rather die than go back into that ballroom and see Darius trying to stick up for her.

Better for her to just leave quietly. Better for both of them.

After lingering as long as she could in the cool quiet of

the empty, marble bathroom, with the old-fashioned elegance of a more genteel era, she went out into the hallway.

She found Darius waiting for her, smolderingly handsome in his tuxedo, leaning against the wall with his arms folded and his jaw tight.

"Are you all right?"

He was angry. She could hear it in his voice. She stopped, barely holding back her tears. "Have you seen enough?" she choked out. "You're surely not enough of an idiot to marry me."

He came closer in the empty hallway, with its plush carpets and gold light fixtures. She tensed, waiting for him to tell her he'd obviously made a mistake, bringing her to his ball, and that there was no way he would marry her now or in fact ever wanted to see her again. She waited for him to give her what she'd wanted and set her free.

Except in this moment the thought didn't make her as happy as it once did.

He narrowed his eyes. "I didn't realize how bad it was for you."

She'd successfully fought back tears all night. But she could do it no longer. Not now, when the illusion of having a protector—even for a night—was coming to an end.

Letty took a deep breath, trying to ignore the lump in her throat, wiping her eyes before he'd see the tears. She tried to smile. "But now you know. So tomorrow I'll go to Rochester with my father. You can continue to be rich and famous and popular here. You can visit our baby anytime you want..." Something in his eyes made her voice trail off uncertainly. "If you even want to see our baby anymore," she whispered.

His eyes suddenly blazed with cold fury. "No."

"What?"

He gripped her arm. "I said no."

She tried to pull away, but couldn't. "What are you doing?"

"What I should have done the moment we arrived here."

He pulled her grimly down the hall, back toward the ballroom.

"No," she choked out, struggling. "Please. I can't go back in there. Don't make me..."

Darius was merciless. He dragged her back into the enormous ballroom, with its high ceiling and crystal chandeliers. He gripped her wrist as she limped behind him in the tight stiletto shoes and pink dress, going past all the big round tables, where a thousand people were now drinking after-dinner brandies and coffees and the men, at least, were eating desserts. Letty felt each ten-person table fall silent as they went by. She felt everyone's judgment. Their blame. Their hatred.

Ruthlessly, Darius pulled her through the ballroom, leaving people silent in their wake. As he walked past their own table, he grabbed his glass of champagne. Crossing the small dance floor, he dragged her up the stairs to the stage, where, still holding her wrist, he took the microphone at the podium. He cleared his throat.

Letty's knees were trembling with fear. She wished she'd never come here—wished she'd never taken a single risk—would have given twenty years of her life to be back at her tiny apartment, snug on the sofa with a blanket over her head!

"Good evening," Darius said into the microphone. His husky, commanding voice rang over the ballroom. A spotlight fell on him. "For those of you I haven't yet met personally, I'm Darius Kyrillos. Thank you for coming to my party, the event kicking off the New York fall social season, and thank you for supporting scholarships for kids in need. It's because of you that many deserving youngsters will be able to go to college or learn a trade."

A smattering of applause ensued; much less enthusiastic than it would have been if Letty hadn't been standing with him on stage. She was ruining everything, she thought unhappily. Even for those kids who needed help. She hated herself. Almost as much as she hated him.

Darius deliberately turned away from the microphone to give her a searching glance, and her stomach fell to the floor. *Here it comes*, she thought. *He's going to announce that he brought me here as a joke and have me thrown me out.* She was social poison, so he really had no choice but to distance himself. This was exactly what she'd expected.

She just hadn't expected it to hurt so much when it happened.

Darius's lips twisted. He turned back to the microphone. "Most of you know this beautiful woman on stage with me. Miss Letitia Spencer." There was a low hiss across the ballroom, a rumble of muffled booing. He responded with a charming smile. "Since we're all friends, I wanted you to be the first to know...I just asked her to marry me."

Letty's eyes went wide. What? Why would he say that? Was he insane?

"And she has accepted," he finished calmly. "So I want you all to be the first to wish us joy."

This time, the gasp came from Letty. Forget insane. Was he suicidal?

The low hisses and boos changed to ugly muttering across the ballroom, angry, obscene words that made Letty squirm. Instinctively, she covered her belly with her arms to protect her unborn baby from the cruel words.

But Darius's smile only widened as he put his large hand over hers, on her belly.

"We're expecting a baby, too. All of this has left me so overwhelmed with joy, I want to share it with all of you. Now. Some of you might know of her father's troubles..."

A white-haired man, unable to contain himself any longer, sprang up from his table. "Howard Spencer defrauded my company of millions of dollars!" he cried, shaking his fist. "We were only repaid a fraction of what we lost!"

A low buzz of rage hummed around him.

"Letty's father is a criminal," Darius agreed. "He abused your trust, and I know over half of what he stole is still unaccounted for. But *Letty* did nothing wrong. Her only crime was loving a father who didn't deserve it. That's why I've decided, in my future bride's honor, to make amends."

Suddenly, it was dead quiet across the tables.

Darius held his champagne glass high. "I will personally pay back every penny her father stole."

A collective gasp ripped through the ballroom.

The white-haired man staggered back. "But that's... *five billion dollars!*"

"So it is," Darius said mildly. He looked over the crowd. "So if your family is still owed money by Howard Spencer, I personally guarantee repayment. All in honor of my beautiful...innocent...unfairly hounded...bride." Turning back toward Letty on stage, he held up his champagne glass and said into the microphone, "To Letitia Spencer!"

As photographers rushed forward, Letty felt faint. Camera flashes lit up everywhere. There was a rumble of noise, of shouts and gasps and chairs hastily pushed aside as a thousand people scrambled to their feet and lifted their champagne glasses into the air.

"Letitia Spencer!" they cried joyfully.

CHAPTER SEVEN

IT WASN'T EVERY day a man spent five billion dollars on a whim.

Darius hadn't intended to do it. He'd had a different surprise in mind for Letty tonight: a black velvet box hidden in the pocket of his tuxedo jacket, which he'd planned to spring on her as soon as the evening was over and all her overblown fears had proved unfounded.

Instead, he'd realized how much she'd endured over the last ten years. Alone. While he'd been happily free to live an anonymous life and make his fortune.

Standing in the hallway, when he'd seen her come out of the bathroom looking shattered and as pale as a ghost, he'd finally realized the toll it had taken on her. And if this was how people treated Letty now, how much worse had it been ten years ago, when their rage had been white-hot?

He'd been forced to ask himself: If Letty had actually shown up the night they were going to run away together and told him about her father's confession, what would have happened?

Darius would have of course insisted she marry him anyway. After all, what did her father's stupid investment fund have to do with their love?

But as her husband, he would have been at her side throughout the scandal and media circus of a trial. He might not have received the critical early loan that enabled him to build his software, to hire employees, to lease his first office space. He would have been too tainted by association as Howard Spencer's son-in-law.

If Letty hadn't set him free, he might have been unemployable, unable to easily provide for his wife or children.

He might be living in that tiny Brooklyn apartment, too, struggling with the loss of his dreams. Struggling to provide for his family. Struggling not to feel like a failure as a man.

It was Letty's sacrifice ten years ago that had made his current success possible.

While he'd been triumphantly building his billion-dollar company, she'd lived in poverty, suffering endless humiliations for a crime that wasn't even hers. And she'd kept her sacrifice a secret, so he'd never once had to feel guilty about deserting her.

Even now, she continued to protect him. She'd warned him what would happen if he brought her as his date. And now he'd finally seen how the members of the so-called upper class had treated her all this time. He'd watched Letty bear their insults without complaint. And he'd realized her stigma was so bad that, in spite of his arrogant earlier assumption, his presence alone wasn't enough to shelter her.

He knew how it felt to be treated badly.

He'd once been the poorest child in his village, mocked as an unloved bastard. He was now the most beloved, feared man of Heraklios. He did pretty well in Manhattan, too. And London. And Paris and Rome, Sydney and Tokyo.

Money could buy everything from houses to souls.

Money made the man.

It astonished him that not everyone realized this. Some people seemed to think love was the most important thing. They were either fools, Darius thought grimly, or gluttons for punishment. He'd learned his own lesson well. The sick truth was that love only led to pain.

Love was a pale facsimile of money. Love begged.

Money demanded.

So when Darius had seen how badly New York society had treated Letty for all these years—these people who didn't have a fraction of her kindness or her loyalty or her heart—ice had seized his soul.

Especially when he'd realized that he'd treated her even worse. After a decade of ignoring her, he'd taken revenge for her so-called sins through cold seduction, insults and threats.

His jaw tightened. He would pay that debt.

Darius didn't love her. The part of his heart that had once craved love had been burned away. Love wasn't something he ever wanted to feel for anyone.

But there were other qualities Darius did believe in.

Honor.

Loyalty.

Protecting his woman.

So he'd settled the matter, once and for all.

Now Letty would be the most popular girl in the city. Every person who'd once treated her shabbily would be begging for an invitation to their wedding. Begging to be her friend.

At the moment of Darius's triumph, as he toasted her on stage, he turned to face Letty at the podium. Rough, raw desire surged through his body as he looked at her—his woman now, *his*—lush and pregnant and obscenely beautiful in that pink gown, which slid over her breasts and belly like a caress.

She stood unsteadily in those ridiculous stiletto heels, beneath the blinding spotlight, as a thousand people applauded from the darkness. People who had treated her like garbage just minutes before started chanting her name. Camera flashes lit up the darkness as reporters shouted questions.

"Miss Spencer, what's it like to be loved to the tune of five billion dollars?"

"When's the wedding?"

"When's your baby due?"

"How does it feel to suddenly be the most popular girl in New York?"

Letty looked at Darius with the expression of a terrified deer, and he realized she wasn't enjoying this as much as he was.

Turning back to the microphone with a smile, Darius answered for her. "The wedding will be soon. No plans yet. Our baby will be born soon, too." He looked past the reporters to the well-heeled crowd. "That's all. Thank you for your support! Enjoy your night. And since you're now all so much richer, don't forget to be generous to the scholarship fund—it's for the kids." Setting his empty champagne glass on the podium, he glanced at the full orchestra. "Let's start the music!"

"Kick off the dancing, Darius!" someone shouted from the back.

"Yes, the first dance to you and Letty!" someone else cried.

Darius led her down the steps from the stage, and as they reached the dance floor, the music started, a slow, romantic song he'd purposefully requested from the orchestra earlier because he knew Letty would remember it from that long-ago summer.

He was right. She stopped when she heard it, eyes wide.

Darius looked down at her with a crooked half smile. "What do you say? Will you dance with me, Letty?"

She looked around at all the people who had treated her with such contempt for the last ten years, now beaming at her as if they were best friends.

"Why are they acting as if they like me?" she said softly, for his ears alone.

"People love to talk about character and loyalty and love. They mean money." He allowed himself a grim smile. "Now the money's been paid, so they can love you again."

Letty's head snapped back to look at him. Her big hazel

eyes, fringed with dark lashes, were wide, as if he were a superhero who'd flown down from the sky. "Why did you do it, Darius? Why pay five billion dollars for a debt that isn't yours?"

The music swirled around them like a whirlwind. "Do you remember our old waltz?"

Her forehead creased. "Of course…" She looked back at the people yelling encouragement for them to dance. She bit her lip. "But not in front of everyone…"

"Now." Darius pulled her against his tuxedo-clad body. "Dance with me."

Letty's long dark hair was falling softly around her beautiful face to her shoulders, nestling against the diamonds sparkling around her neck. He'd already wanted her, but as he felt her body in his arms, and the crush of her belly and swollen breasts against his chest, he wanted her even more.

Just like that long-ago summer…

"Come on, Letty," he said in a low voice. "Let's show them all we don't give a damn."

He moved commandingly onto the dance floor, leading her in the first steps of the waltz he'd helped her practice for her debutante ball long ago, the spring of her senior year. They'd practiced the waltz over and over in the sunlit spring flower meadow on the Fairholme estate, overlooking the sparkling bay, as music sang from her phone.

They'd started out as friends and ended as something else entirely.

When she'd left for her debutante ball in Manhattan that May, looking beautiful beyond belief in her white dress, Darius spent the whole evening prowling the meadow in a rage, hating the Harvard boy who was her date.

He'd been shocked when Letty came back early, whispering, "I didn't want to dance with anyone but you…"

Darius had taken one look at Letty's joyous, upturned face surrounded by spring flowers, and then he, the chauffeur's son, had done the unthinkable: he'd wrapped her in his powerful arms and kissed her...

Now, as he swirled her around in that waltz, it was like going back in time. The audience standing on the edge of the dance floor clapped their approval. In this moment, in this place, Darius and Letty were the king and queen of the city, the pinnacle of all his youthful dreams.

But he barely noticed the crowds. There was only Letty. He was back in that meadow, a young man so sure of his own heart, so naively enthusiastic about his future, dancing with the beautiful princess he'd dreamed about, the one he could never deserve. And, oh, how he'd craved her to his very core...

Now, Darius pulled her more indecently close to his hard, aching body than any waltz allowed. She lifted her luminous gaze to his, visibly holding her breath. The electricity between them suddenly sizzled with heat.

He stopped dancing. Louder than the music, he heard the rush of his blood in his ears, the pounding of his own heart.

He needed her in his bed.

Now.

The music abruptly ended, and the ballroom exploded in applause echoing from the high ceiling. Without a word, Darius led her from the dance floor. He pulled her through the crowds, which parted for them like magic. Compliments and cheers followed them. Everywhere, people were apologizing to Letty for how badly they'd treated her. He recognized Poppy Alexander.

"I'm so sorry, Letty," the girl blurted out. "I was afraid to be your friend. I knew it wasn't your fault, what happened, but I was a coward..."

"That's all right, Poppy," Letty replied gently. She looked around at everyone else. "I don't blame anyone."

Darius thought about the dragon Poppy had for a mother, and he couldn't blame her for being scared. Until he thought of how bad Letty's life had been for the last decade, and he didn't think any of them deserved another minute of Letty's time.

He swept Letty away without looking back. He didn't care about anyone or anything right now, except getting her into his bed.

Darius pulled his phone from his tuxedo jacket pocket. By the time they exited the stately beaux-arts building, his limo was waiting at the curb. Collins leaped out and opened the passenger door.

The second they were in the backseat, and the door closed behind them, Darius pulled Letty roughly into his arms and kissed her.

Her lips were sweet as sin. She trembled, her curves melting against him. His whole body was hard with need. He had to have her.

"Sir?" said Collins from the driver's seat.

"Home," he said hoarsely. "As fast as you can."

Then he pressed the button that raised the barrier between front and back seats. Just those few seconds were agony. But he was not willing to share Letty with anyone. He'd shared her enough.

She belonged to him now. To him alone.

Once they had privacy in the backseat, he kissed her passionately as the limo moved through the sparkling streets of the lit-up city at midnight. But all he could see was her sensual beauty. All he could feel was the soft brush of her long dark hair, and her warm skin like silk beneath his hands. He pushed her back against the leather seat, devouring her soft lips, kissing her neck, running his hands over her full breasts overflowing the tight pink bodice of her dress.

He kissed her savagely, biting and sucking her lower lip. A gasp of need came from her throat as she returned his kiss with matching fire, gripping his shoulders through his tuxedo jacket. He kissed slowly down her neck as her head fell back, her eyes closed, her expression one of ecstasy.

When he saw that, it was all he could do not to take her, right here in the back of the limo. He was unconsciously reaching for his fly when he realized they'd stopped.

Resurfacing from his haze of desire, he saw the limo was parked beneath the porte cochere in front of his building. Just in time, too. He glanced at Letty, stretched back against the smooth calfskin leather seat. Her big hazel eyes were smoky with passion, her dark hair mussed, her pink dress disheveled. Another moment and he would have yanked up her dress and roughly pushed inside her.

That wasn't how he wanted this night to be, fast and brutish in the back of a limo. No. After the disaster of their first night together, when he'd taken her virginity then insulted her and tossed her out of the penthouse into the snow, he wanted this night to be perfect.

He would finally treat Letitia Spencer, the forbidden princess of his youth, as she deserved to be treated.

He would enjoy her as he deserved to enjoy her.

Thoroughly.

Reaching over, he smoothed the fabric of Letty's bodice modestly back over her breasts just as the passenger door opened behind him.

Taking her hand, he led her out of the limo and into the elegant lobby, where the doorman greeted him. "Good evening, sir."

"Good evening, Jones." Such civilized words. Wearing a tuxedo, Darius knew he must appear civilized on the outside. On the inside, he felt anything but.

Gripping Letty's hand, he desperately kept himself in check. Neither of them looked at each other as they went through the high-ceilinged lobby, past the front desk to the elevator. Civilized.

But as soon as the door closed behind them, they were

in each other's arms. He pushed her against the wall, kissing her hungrily, desperately.

She breathed against his skin, "I still can't believe you're doing this."

"Kissing you?"

"Giving five billion dollars away. Why did you do it?"

"Don't you know?" he growled, his lips against hers. "Can't you guess?"

Panting, she shook her head. "You hate my father…"

Darius's lip curled as he drew back. "I didn't do it for him."

"For your friends?"

"Those aren't my friends."

"For the other victims, then. All those hardworking people with pensions. Firemen. Nurses…"

"I'm not that noble."

The elevator door opened. The floor-to-ceiling windows flooded the penthouse with moonlight. Taking her hand, he led her inside. He could hear the tap of her stiletto heels against the marble.

She stopped, staring up at him.

"Then why?" she whispered.

"I couldn't stand to see you treated badly," Darius said huskily, "when all you've done is give your love and loyalty to someone who doesn't deserve it."

She bit her lip. "I know my father isn't perfect—"

"Perfect?" His jaw tightened. "He's a criminal—" He cut himself off, then said, "You're under my protection now."

She looked troubled. "Your protection—or your rule?"

"It is the same. I protect what is mine."

"Our baby."

His eyes met hers. "And you."

Letty stared at him, her eyes wide, as if she had no idea how to react. As if she had forgotten what it was like to have anyone properly look after her.

He wondered how long it had been since anyone had tried to take care of her, rather than the other way around. He suspected Letty always sacrificed herself to take care of others—especially that father of hers—while her own heart bled.

"But I'm not yours," she said quietly. "Not truly. We got pregnant by accident. I didn't think you were serious about marriage."

"I am."

"That commitment is serious, Darius. It means...forever."

"I know," he said.

She swallowed, searching his gaze. "I was sure after tonight you'd never want to see me again."

Taking her hand, he lifted it slowly to his lips. She seemed to hold her breath, watching as he kissed the back of her hand, breathing against her skin. Straightening, he held her hand tightly in his own. "I want to see you tomorrow, and every other tomorrow for the rest of our lives."

"Darius..."

"You will marry me, Letty," he said in a low voice. "You know it, and I know it. In your heart, you were always meant to be mine."

Marry him? For real?

How could she?

Even if Darius no longer hated her, he certainly didn't love her. And she was starting to fear she could love him again. Perhaps all too easily.

What hope could they have of happiness?

He'd never love her back. All he wished to do was possess her. He offered sex and money, and in return, he'd expect sex and total devotion. For her, those things went together. He wouldn't have just her body, but her soul.

So why was she still so tempted?

She shivered, caught between fear and desire.

"Are you cold?" he asked huskily, his eyes dark.

"No, I...I..." Hugging her baby bump, she gasped, "I need some fresh air."

He smiled. "Come with me."

Still holding her hand, he led her through the moon-bathed penthouse, and she thought dimly how she was getting in the habit of following where he led. But with his hand enveloping hers so protectively, she didn't want to do anything else.

She still couldn't believe what he'd done, announcing their engagement, defending her in front of all those people—and then telling the world he intended to pay billions of dollars of his own money to repay what her father had stolen.

She'd been dazed. Then she'd danced with him, the same routine he'd helped her learn so long ago, and she'd been back in that spring meadow, practicing the waltz not for the pimply-faced Harvard boy, who was the nephew of her father's lawyer, but for Darius, always for him, only for him. As they'd danced in the ballroom, she'd felt time melt away.

Darius was right. She was his. From the very beginning, Darius Kyrillos had been the only man she'd ever wanted. The only man she'd ever loved.

I don't love him anymore, she told herself desperately. She wouldn't let him buy her!

Darius led her up an elaborate staircase, then pushed open a glass door that led out onto a private rooftop garden.

Letty gasped at the beauty of the ivy-covered pergola decorated with fairy lights near a lit lap pool gleaming bright blue in the warm September night.

Above them, distant stars sparkled like diamonds across a dark velvety sky. Past the glass walls of the terrace, the night skyline of Manhattan glittered.

She kept her distance from the edge, afraid to go too

close. But Darius went right to it. He leaned against the short glass wall, totally unfazed and unafraid of plummeting seventy floors to his death. He looked out at the city.

Letty crept closer, her heart pounding. "This terrace is amazing."

"All the flowers remind me of home," he said simply. She wondered if he meant Greece or Fairholme, but didn't have the nerve to ask. She slowly turned her head, marveling at the lavish beauty of a rooftop garden that treated all of Manhattan as nothing but a backdrop.

"You're king of the mountain now," she said softly. "Looking down on a valley of skyscrapers."

Turning to her, he came forward. Then he abruptly fell to one knee in front of her astonished eyes.

Reaching into his tuxedo jacket pocket, he pulled out a small black velvet box.

"Rule it with me, Letty," he said quietly. "As my wife."

Shivering, she put her hand on her heart. "I already said..."

"You said yes when you thought I'd back out. This is a real proposal. I expect a real answer." He held up the black velvet box. "Letty Spencer, will you do me the honor of marrying me?"

He opened the lid. Inside the black velvet box was an enormous pear-shaped diamond set in platinum. It was the hugest, most outrageous ring she'd ever seen.

But that wasn't what made her lose her breath.

It was Darius's face. His dark, yearning eyes. As he looked at her in the moonlight, she saw the man who'd just bruised her with the intensity of his kisses. Who'd just defied all of Manhattan and paid five billion dollars for her. The man whose child she carried.

In his eyes, she saw the shadow of the younger man she'd once loved, strong and kind, with such a good heart. The one who'd loved her so fervently. *They were the same.*

Letty's heart skipped a beat.

It's an illusion, she told herself desperately. *He's not the same.* But as she reached out and brushed her fingers against the diamond engagement ring, it sparkled like the stars. Like the lights of this powerful city.

Like the smolder in Darius's dark eyes.

"It would destroy us," she said shakily, but what she really meant was *it would destroy me.*

Darius slowly rose in front of her, until his tall, powerful body towered over hers. Waves of blue light from the pool reflected against him as the warm wind moved across the water. Putting his hand on her cheek, he lowered his head.

"Say yes," he whispered. "Say you'll be mine."

His kiss was tender at first. She felt the rough warmth of his lips, the gentle hold of his arms.

Then his grip tightened. His embrace became hungry, filled with need. Spirals of heat twisted through her body, and she gripped his shoulders. Until he pulled away.

"Say it," he demanded.

"Yes," she choked out.

A flash of triumph crossed his starkly handsome face. "You will?"

She nodded, tears in her eyes.

"There will be no going back," he warned.

"I know." She tried to ignore the thrill that crept into her heart. Excitement? Terror?

Right or wrong, disaster or not, there was nothing to be done. What he'd said was true. She'd always been his. In many ways, this decision had been made for her long ago.

He slid the diamond ring over the third finger of her left hand. It fit perfectly. She looked down at it, sparkling in the moonlight. "How did you know my ring size?"

"It's the same ring."

She frowned. "What?"

"It's the same I bought for you ten years ago." His voice was low. "I had it set with a different stone."

The thought that he'd kept their original ring all these years made her heart ache. Whatever he might say, didn't that mean he might still care for her, at least a little?

Could love, once lost, ever be regained?

Looking at him with tears in her eyes, she breathed, "Darius…"

"You're mine now, Letty," he whispered, kissing her forehead, her eyelids, her cheeks. "You belong to me. Forever."

Then he kissed her lips as if those, too, were his possession.

Sparks of pleasure went up and down Letty's body, coiling low and deep inside her, and she felt his hands running down her bare arms, her sides, cupping her breasts over the pink dress.

She fell back against the ivy-covered stone wall. Above them, fairy lights swayed gently in the warm wind, the skyscrapers of Manhattan illuminating the moonlit sky.

Letty's eyes closed as he kissed his way down her throat. She felt breathless, like she was lost in a dream.

He kissed over the diamond necklace to her bare clavicle and the valley between her full breasts, half revealed above the low-cut bodice of her gown.

Picking her up, he carried her past the sweeping ivy into a half-enclosed room protected on two sides by walls, with a rustic chandelier hanging over a long table. Two leather sofas were arranged around a fireplace and well-stocked bar.

He flicked a switch, and the gas fire lit up. She saw Darius's face clearly in the flickering firelight as they faced each other silently. The soft wind blew against her hair, her skin.

Slowly, Darius removed his tuxedo jacket and dropped it to the flagstone floor. Coming closer, he unzipped her pink dress. She felt the brush of his fingertips, then the warm night air against her bare skin as her gown dropped to the floor beside his jacket. She stepped out of the fabric, wearing only the diamonds, a lace bra, panties and the wicked pink crystal stiletto heels.

He stepped back, looking at her.

"Incredible," he breathed in deep masculine appreciation, and she realized that, just as he'd promised, he was seeing her in the lingerie. She scowled.

"Do you always get what you want?" she said accusingly.

"I do," he said, caressing her cheek. "And now, so will you."

She licked her lips and felt a thrill of delight as his expression changed to raw desire. Reaching up, she saucily loosened his tuxedo tie, before tugging on it, drawing him closer for a kiss.

It was the first time she'd ever made the first move, and he growled fierce approval. Holding her tight, he kissed her back hungrily.

His hands caressed her naked skin, her arms, her shoulders, the small of her back. And suddenly she couldn't remove his clothes fast enough. His tie, cuff links, shirt. They all dropped to the floor.

His tanned body, laced with dark hair, looked like sculpted marble in the flickering firelight, all hard muscles and taut belly. She brushed her hand lightly against his chest. His skin felt like silk over steel. Biting her lip, she lifted her eyes to his.

"If I'm yours, Darius," she whispered, standing in front of him in the half-enclosed room, "you're mine."

Brushing back long dark tendrils of her hair, he pulled her roughly into his arms. His hard-muscled chest moved against her full, aching breasts and pregnant belly. The soft wind whispered against her bare skin as he unhooked her silk lace bra, and her breasts sprang free. He looked down at her body and gave a quick breath.

Pressing her breasts together, he cupped their weight in his hands before he lowered his head to suckle one pink, full nipple, then the other.

Shuddering with pleasure, she closed her eyes.

His hands stroked gently, reverently, down her body to her naked belly to her hips, still covered with the tiny silk panties.

Running his hand down her legs, he knelt before her and pulled off one stiletto, then the other, as she balanced against him, her hands gripping his shoulders. She remained standing—barely—as he caressed upward from her manicured toes, to the tender hollows of her knees, and higher still. She swallowed, holding her breath as he stroked up her thighs.

She closed her eyes, heart pounding as he pulled her panties down her legs. She couldn't move fast enough. He impatiently ripped them off in his powerful hands, tossing the flimsy silk aside.

"Those were expensive—" she protested.

He looked up, and the edges of his cruel, sensual mouth curved upward. "They served their purpose."

An icy fear suddenly crept through her heart as Letty wondered if she, too, might someday have served her purpose. If he might someday rip her apart, then discard her.

Then all her rational thought fled as, still on his knees, he gripped her hips and moved between her legs.

She felt the warmth of his breath on the most sensitive, intimate part of her body, as she stood naked with the warm night breeze swirling against her skin, as one of New York's most famous billionaires knelt before her in the firelight, beneath the ivy walls of a rooftop garden.

Holding her tight, he lowered his mouth between her thighs and tasted her with a soft moan. He licked her as if she were a melting ice cream cone in his favorite flavor, creamy and sweet. As she gasped, his rhythm intensified, until he worked her with his tongue, sliding sensuously against her. Pleasure exploded through her body almost immediately, and he gripped her hips, keeping her firmly against his mouth as her body twisted with the sudden intensity of pleasure that left her knees weak and sent spasms all over her body.

She was still dizzy in the heights of pleasure as he rose to his feet and drew her toward the sofa. He lay down first, stretching out naked against the black leather, hard and ready for her. She took a step, then hesitated, biting her lip.

"What is it?"

She tried not to look at how huge he was, his hard shaft jutting arrogantly from his body. She blushed, feeling shy. "Um, what do I do?"

He gave a low, lazy laugh, then pulled her over him.

"I'll show you," he said huskily.

He spread her across him on the sofa, her thighs over his hips, his arousal pressing low against her pregnant belly. He reached up, cupping her cheek. As he drew her down for a kiss, her long dark hair fell like a veil against his skin.

The kiss was tender at first. She relaxed into it with a sigh, her body curving over his as his hands roamed gently over her back, her arms, her belly, her breasts. Then his kiss deepened, turning urgent and fierce. Placing his hands on her hips, he lifted her up, positioning himself beneath her.

He slowly lowered her down on him, filling her, inch by delicious inch, in tantalizing slow motion.

She gasped as she felt him inside her, going deep, then deeper still. Her whole body started to tighten, more savagely than it had before.

Lifting her hips, he lowered her again, showing her the rhythm, until her body started to move of its own accord.

Closing her eyes with fervent intensity, she rode him, slowly at first, then faster. The pleasure built and built...

Her lips parted in a silent cry as joy burst like fireworks shaking through her body. She heard his low gasp as he, too, exploded, pouring inside her.

She collapsed, falling softly against him on the black leather sofa.

For long moments, he held her tenderly, as if her weight were nothing. Their bodies were still fused, slick with sweat, as he leaned up to kiss her. He felt so solid and strong beneath her. Like a foundation that could never be shaken.

She shivered in his arms. In the half-enclosed outdoor room, the September night was growing cool. But that wasn't the reason.

The idea of being Darius's wife had seemed like a recipe for disaster, if not outright doom. And so it would be, if she were tempted into giving him her heart, while in return, he gave her only money.

Letty looked down at the heavy diamond ring, now shining dully on her left hand.

If only Darius could again be the young man she remembered, with the kind nature and forgiving heart. She would willingly give him everything. Not just her body, not just her name, but her heart.

CHAPTER EIGHT

HE WAS A GENIUS, Darius thought as he woke in his bed the next morning with sunlight flooding in through the windows. He looked down at Letty sleeping beside him and smiled. A damn genius. Best five billion dollars ever spent.

And he would spend the rest of his life being thrilled, if it continued paying off like it did last night. The sex had been spectacular. And even more. Something had changed in the way Letty looked at him. He loved the mixture of gratitude and shy hope he saw in her eyes.

He kissed Letty's temple tenderly. She yawned, stretching like a cat.

"What time is it?" she murmured, her eyes still closed.

"Late," he said, amused. "Almost noon."

Her eyes flew open. "Oh, no! I'm late for—" Then she seemed to remember how much had changed in the last twenty-four hours, and that being late for work was no longer an issue. "Oh. Right." She bit her lip, blushing and looking so adorable that he was tempted to keep her in bed another hour.

It was incredible how much he still wanted her, when they'd made love *four times* last night—on the rooftop terrace, here in bed, and in the shower when they decided to wash off. Only to promptly get all sweaty again when they returned to bed.

Letty was meant to be his, Darius marveled. He'd never felt so sexually satisfied in his life.

And yet already he wanted more. How was it possible?

He smiled down at her. "Hungry?"

"Starving," she admitted. "And thirsty."

"I can solve that." Rising from the bed, he got a white

terry cloth robe and handed her one, too. "Come out to the kitchen."

She gave a sudden scowl, and even that was adorable. "You didn't tell me you had staff staying at the penthouse. What if they heard us last night? What if they—"

"There are no live-in staff. I have a housekeeper who comes in four times a week, that's it."

She blinked in confusion. "Then who's going to cook?"

"I'm not totally useless."

She looked at him with unflattering shock in her eyes. "You can't cook, Darius."

"No?" His smile widened to a grin. "Come see."

She ate her words shortly afterward, sitting in the brightly lit kitchen at the counter, as he served her an omelet to order with tomatoes, bacon and five kinds of cheese, along with orange juice over ice. When she took the first bite of the omelet, her eyes went wide.

"Good, huh?" he said smugly, sitting beside her with his own enormous omelet of ham and cheese, drenched in salsa. Being a sexual hero all night definitely had built his appetite.

And hers, as well. If he felt like a hero, Letty was a sex *goddess*, he thought. Even now, he felt aware of her, just sitting companionably beside her at the counter with its dazzling view of the city through floor-to-ceiling windows. But he wasn't looking at the view. He was watching her.

"Delicious," she moaned softly as she gobbled it down, bite after bite. "We should serve omelets at our wedding."

He gave a low laugh. "I appreciate the compliment, but I don't see myself whipping up omelets for a thousand."

She froze. "A thousand? *Guests?*"

Gulping black coffee, he shrugged. "Our wedding will be the social event of the year, as you deserve. All of New York society will come and grovel at your feet."

She didn't look thrilled. She took another bite of omelet. "That's not what I want."

"No?" he said lazily, tucking back a tendril of her dark hair. His eyes traced the creamy skin of her neck, down to the smooth temptation of her clavicle and swell of her breasts above the luxurious white cotton robe. He glanced down to her belt, tied loosely between her breasts and pregnant belly. He had the sudden impulse to sweep all the dishes to the floor, tug open her robe and lean her back naked against the counter.

"A wedding should be a happy occasion." She shook her head. "Those society people aren't my friends. They never really were. Why would I invite them?"

"To rub your new status in their faces? I thought you'd glory in your return to status as the queen of it all."

"Me?" Letty snorted. "I was never queen of anything. As a teenager I never knew the right clothes to wear or understood how to play the society game. I was a total nerd."

He frowned. "I never saw you that way. I just assumed…"

"That I was a spoiled princess?" She gave him a funny smile. "I *was* spoiled, though not the way you mean. I always knew I was loved." Her face was wistful. "My parents loved each other and they loved me."

Revenge wasn't Letty's style, Darius realized. She never showed off or tried to make others feel bad. Even when she was younger, she'd always been most comfortable reading the dusty leather-bound books in Fairholme's oak-paneled library, baking cakes with the cook in the kitchen or playing with the gardener's kittens in the yard. Letty never wanted to be the center of attention. She was always more worried about other people's feelings than her own.

In this respect, Darius thought, the two of them were very different.

"And I had a real home," she whispered.

Memories of that beautiful gray stone manor on the edge of the sea, surrounded by roses, came to his mind. He said gruffly, "You still miss Fairholme after all this time?"

She gave him a sad smile. "I know it's gone for good. But I still dream about it. My mother was born there. Four generations of my family."

"What happened to it?"

She looked down at her plate. "A tech billionaire bought it at a cut-rate price. I heard he changed everything, added zebra-print shag carpeting and neon lights, and turned the nursery into his own private disco. Of course that was his right. But he wouldn't let me take a picture of my great-grandmother's fresco before he destroyed it with his sand-blaster."

A low growl came from Darius's throat. He remembered the nursery fresco, a charming monstrosity picturing a sad-eyed little goose girl leading ducks and geese through what looked like a Bavarian village. Not his cup of tea, but it was part of the house's history. "I'm sorry."

She looked up with a bright, fake smile. "It's fine. Of course it couldn't last. Good things never do."

"Neither do bad things," he said quietly. "Nothing lasts, good or bad."

"I guess you're right." She wrapped her arms around her pregnant belly. "But I don't want a big society wedding, Darius. I think I'd just like you and me, and our closest family and friends. I don't need ten bridesmaids. I just want one."

"An old friend?"

She smiled. "A new one. Belle Langtry. A waitress at the diner. How about you? Who would you choose as your best man?"

"Ángel Velazquez."

"Ángel?"

"It's a nickname. His real first name is Santiago, but he

hates it, because he was named after a man who refused to recognize him as his son."

"How awful!"

Darius shrugged. "I call him by his last name. Velazquez hates weddings. He recently had to be the best man for a friend of ours, Kassius Black. He complained for months. All that tender love gave him a headache, he said."

Letty was looking at him in dismay. "And you want him at our wedding?"

"He needs a little torture. When you meet him you'll see what I mean. Completely arrogant, always sure he's right."

"Hard to imagine," she said drily.

"So Velazquez. And my extended family."

Her eyes brightened. "Your family?"

"My great-aunt, Theia Ioanna, who lives in Athens. Assorted uncles, aunts and cousins, and the rest of my village on Heraklios, the island I'm from."

"Could we bring them all over from Greece? And of course we'll have my father..."

Darius stiffened. "No."

"No?" She frowned. "We could get married on Heraklios, if they can't travel. I've always wanted to visit the Greek islands..."

"I mean your father. He's not invited."

"Of course he's invited. He's my father. He'll walk me down the aisle. I know you don't like him, but he's my only family."

"Letty, I thought you understood." His jaw was taut, his voice low and cold. "I don't want you, or our baby, within ten feet of that man ever again."

"What?"

"It's not negotiable." Swiveling to face her at the counter, Darius gripped her shoulder. "I will pay back everything he stole. But this is the price." His dark eyes narrowed.

"You will cut your father completely and permanently out of our lives."

She drew back. "But he's my father. I love him—"

"He lost the right to your loyalty long ago. Do you think I want a con artist, a thief, around my wife…my child…my home?" He looked at her in tightly controlled fury. "No."

"He never meant to hurt anyone," she tried. "He always hoped the stock market would turn and he'd be able to pay everyone back. He just lost his way after my mom died. And he hasn't been well since he got out of prison. If you just knew what he's been through…"

"Excuses on top of excuses! You expect me to feel sympathy?" he said incredulously. "Because he was sick? Because he lost his wife? Because of him, you and I were separated. Because of him, my own father never had the chance to grow old! After he'd worked for him with utter devotion for almost twenty-five years. And that's how your father repaid him!"

"Darius, please."

"You expect me to allow that man to walk you down the aisle? To hold my firstborn child in his arms? No." He set his jaw. "He's a monster. He has no conscience, no soul."

"You don't know him like I do…"

Remembering her weakness where her father was concerned, her senseless loyalty at any cost, Darius abruptly changed tack. "If you truly love him, you will do as I ask. It will benefit him, as well."

"How can you say that?"

"Once I've paid all his debts, he'll never need to be afraid of someone breaking his arm again. He'll be treated better by his probation officers. By potential employers."

"He can't work. No one would hire him. He would starve in the street."

Revulsion churned in Darius's belly, but he forced himself to say, "I will make sure that does not happen. He can remain in your Brooklyn apartment and his rent will be paid. He will always have food and any other necessities he might require. But he must face the consequences of what he's done. He's taken enough from you, Letty. Your future is with me."

Pushing away the breakfast plates, he stood up from the kitchen counter and went to her handbag on the entryway table. Pulling out her phone, he held it out to her.

"Call him," he said quietly. "See what he tells you to do."

Sitting at the counter in her white robe, Letty stared at the phone with big, stricken eyes, as if it were poison. She snatched it up, and with an intake of breath, dialed and held it up to her ear.

"Hi, Dad." She paused, then said unhappily, "Yes. I'm sorry. I don't blame you for worrying. I should have... Ooh? You saw that?" She looked up and said to Darius, "Your announcement about repaying the five billion is already all over the news. Our engagement, too. Dad is thrilled."

"Of course," he said acidly.

"What?" She turned her focus back to her father. "Oh, yes," she whispered, looking up at Darius with troubled eyes. "We're very happy." She bit her lip. "But, Dad, there's this one thing. It's a big thing. A big horrible thing—" her voice broke a little "—and I hardly know how to say it..." She took a deep breath. "I won't be able to see you anymore. Or let you see the baby."

Darius watched her face as she listened to her father's response. Her expression was miserable.

He blocked all mercy from his soul. He was being cruel to be kind. Saving her from her own weak, loving heart.

"No," she whispered into the phone. "I won't abandon you. It's not..."

She paused again, and her expression changed, became numb with grief. Finally, she choked out in a voice almost too soft to hear, "Okay, Dad. All right. I love you, too. So much. Goodbye."

Tears were streaming down her face. Wiping them away, she handed Darius the phone. "He wants to talk to you."

He stared down at the phone in dismay. He hadn't expected that. He picked it up and put it to his ear.

"What do you want?" he said coldly.

"Darius Kyrillos." He recognized Howard Spencer's voice. Though the voice had aged and grown shaky, he could almost hear the older man's smile. "I remember when you were a little boy, just come to Fairholme. You barely spoke English but even then, you were a great kid."

Unwanted memories went through him of when he'd first come to Fairholme with a father who was a stranger to him, a lonely eleven-year-old boy, bereaved by his grandmother's death. He'd felt bewildered by America and homesick for Greece. Back then Howard Spencer had seemed grand and as foreign as a king.

But he'd welcomed the bereft boy warmly. He'd even asked his five-year-old daughter to look after him. In spite of their six-year age difference, Letty, with her caring and friendly heart, had swiftly become his friend, sharing her toys and showing him the fields and beach. While her father had given Darius Christmas presents and told him firmly he could do anything he wanted in life.

In an indirect way, Howard Spencer had even helped start his software company. As a teenager, Darius had been fascinated by computers. He'd taught himself to tinker and code, and soon found himself responsible for every tech device, security feature and bit of wireless connectivity at Fairholme. It was Howard Spencer who'd hired him as the estate's first technical specialist and allowed him to continue to live there. He'd even paid for Darius to study computer science at the local community college...

Darius felt a twist in his gut. Like...guilt? No. He rushed

to justify his actions. All right, so Spencer had encouraged him and paid for his schooling. Using stolen money from his Ponzi scheme!

"Yes, a good kid," Howard continued gruffly. "But stubborn, with all that stiff-necked Greek pride. Always had to do everything yourself. Letty was the only one you really let help you with anything. And even then, you always thought you had to be in charge. You never recognized her strength."

"Your point?" Darius said coldly.

He heard the other man take a deep breath.

"Take good care of my daughter," he said quietly. "Both Letty and my grandchild. I know you will. That's the only reason I'm letting them go."

The line abruptly cut off.

"What did he say?" Letty's miserable face came into view.

"He said..." Darius stared down in amazement at the phone in his hand.

He ground his teeth. Damn the old man. Taking the high road. He must be playing the long game. Trusting that Letty would wear him down after their wedding and make him relent. Make him forgive.

But Darius would never forgive. He'd die before he let that man worm his way back into their lives.

"Tell me what he said," Letty pleaded.

He turned to her with an ironic smile. "He gave our marriage his blessing."

Her shoulders slumped.

"That's what he said to me, too," she whispered.

So his theory was correct. Clever bastard, he thought grudgingly. He really knew how to pull his daughter's heartstrings.

But Howard Spencer had finally met someone he couldn't manipulate. The old man would end his days alone, in that tiny run-down apartment, with no one to love him. Just as he deserved.

While they—they would live happily ever after.

Darius looked at Letty tenderly.

After their marriage, after she was legally his forever, she would come to despise her father as Darius did. At the very least, she would forget and let him go.

She would love only Darius, be loyal only to him.

He wouldn't love her back, of course. The childish illusion that love could be anything but pain had been burned out of him permanently. But love was still magic to Letty, and he realized now it was the only way to bind her and make her happy in their marriage. For the sake of their children, he had to make her love him.

This was just the beginning.

"You did the right thing," Darius murmured. Pulling her into his arms, he kissed the top of her head, relishing the feel of her body against his, the crush of her full breasts and her belly rounded with his child. "You'll never regret it."

"I regret it already."

Leaning forward, he kissed the tears off her cheeks. He kissed her forehead, then her eyelids. He felt her shudder and pulled her fully into his arms. He whispered, "Let me comfort you."

He lowered his mouth to hers, gripping her smaller body to his own, and kissed her passionately. A sigh came from her throat as she wrapped her arms around him. He opened the belt of her robe and ran his hands down her naked body. Then with a large sweep of his arm, he knocked all the dishes to the floor with a noisy clatter.

Lifting his future bride up onto the countertop, Darius did what he'd wanted to do for the last hour. He made love to her until she wept. Tears of joy, he told himself. Just tears of joy.

* * *

Letty had never been the sort of girl to dream about weddings. At least not since she was eighteen, when her one attempt at elopement had ended so badly.

But she'd vaguely thought, if she ever did get married, she'd have a simple wedding dress, a cake, a bouquet. And her father would give her away.

This wedding had none of that.

Two days after Darius's proposal, they got married in what felt like the worst wedding ever.

Her own fault, Letty thought numbly, as she stood in front of a judge, mumbling vows to honor and cherish. She had no one to blame but herself.

Well, and Darius.

After her phone call with her father, Letty had been too heartsick to care about planning a wedding ceremony. Even Darius ruthlessly taking possession of her body on the kitchen counter hadn't cheered her up. Her heart felt empty and sad.

Darius had tried to tempt her with outrageous ideas for a destination wedding. "If you don't want a big society wedding, there's no reason to wait. The sky's the limit! Do you want a beach wedding in Hawaii? A winter wedding in South America? If you want, I'll rent out the Sydney Opera House. Just say the word!"

She'd looked at him miserably. "What I want is for my father to be there. Without love, what difference does the wedding make?"

The temperature in the room had dropped thirty degrees. "Fine," he said coldly. "If that's how you feel, we might as well just get married at City Hall."

"Fine," she'd said in the same tone.

So they'd gone to the Office of the City Clerk near Chinatown this afternoon, where they'd now been killing time for three hours, surrounded by happy couples all waiting for their turn.

Letty felt exhausted to the bone. She hadn't slept at all the night before. Neither she nor Darius had even bothered to dress up for the ceremony. She wore a simple blouse and maternity pants. Darius wore a dark shirt, dark jeans and a dark glower.

Nor had it helped that the two friends they'd brought to be their witnesses had hated each other on sight. The constant childish bickering between Belle Langtry and Santiago Velazquez, who'd introduced himself as Ángel, had been the final nail in the coffin of Worst Wedding Ever.

It could have been so different, Letty thought sadly. If her father had been there, if she and Darius had been in love, nothing else would have mattered.

But there was no love anywhere on this wedding day.

As she and Darius had sat waiting, listening to their best man and maid of honor squabble, she couldn't stop tears from falling. Darius's glower only made them fall faster.

Their number was the very last to be called in the late afternoon. The four of them had gone up to the desk. As the officiant swiftly and matter-of-factly spoke the words that would bind her to Darius forever, Letty couldn't stop thinking about how she was betraying her father. The man who'd taught her to roller-skate down Fairholme's long marble hallways, who'd taught her chess on rainy days. The man who'd told her again and again how much he loved her.

"I screwed everything up," Howard had told her sadly when he got out of prison. "But I swear I'll make it up to you, Letty. I'll get you back the life you lost…"

He'd never once criticized her for getting pregnant out of wedlock. He'd just been delighted about a future grandchild. Even when she'd phoned him before the wedding, and told him she was marrying Darius, she'd felt his joy.

Though it had been abruptly cut off when she'd tearfully told him the rest of the deal.

Then he'd said quietly, "Do it, sweetheart. Marry him. It's what you've always wanted. Knowing you're happy, I'll be at peace."

Now, as she watched Darius speak his marriage vows, Letty's heart twisted. She blinked as she heard the officiant solemnly finish, "...I now pronounce you man and wife."

The whole ceremony had taken three minutes.

She dimly heard Belle clapping and hooting wildly as Darius leaned forward to kiss her. Some instinct made her turn away and offer him only her cheek.

His glower turned radioactive.

After signing the marriage certificate, their small party of four trundled out of the City Clerk's Office to discover the cold gray September skies pouring rain.

"Such a beautiful ceremony. I'm so happy for you," Belle sighed, obviously caught up in some romantic image that had nothing to do with reality. "You make a perfect couple."

"You're living in a fairy tale," Santiago Velazquez muttered. "They can obviously barely stand each other."

Belle whirled on him irritably. "Just once, could you keep your bad attitude to yourself?" Her voice was shrill. "I'm sick of hearing it!"

He shrugged, glancing at Darius. "You got married because she's pregnant, right?"

"Velazquez, don't make me punch you on my wedding day."

"See?" Belle crowed. "Even *Darius* can't stand you."

The Spaniard looked superior. "Just because I'm the only one who is willing to speak the truth..."

"The truth is that marriage is about love and commitment and a whole bunch of sophisticated emotions you obviously can't handle. So keep your opinions to yourself.

You might think you're being all deep, but talking like that at a wedding is just plain tacky!"

The Spaniard's eyes narrowed and for a moment Letty was afraid that the constant bickering between them was about to boil over into something truly unpleasant. But to her relief, the man abruptly gave a stiff nod.

"You are right."

Belle stared at him wide-eyed, then tossed her hair, huffing with a flare of her nostrils. "Course I'm right. I'm always right."

Letty exhaled as they seemed to drop the matter.

"Except for when you're wrong," came his sardonic response, "which is every other time but now, since you're obviously living in some ridiculous romantic dream world."

Belle glared at him, then whirled on Letty with a beaming smile. "Are you having a good wedding day, sweetie? Because that's what I care about. Because I'm not rude like some people. We learn manners in Texas."

"I have a ranch in Texas," the Spaniard rejoined. "And I learned an expression that I believe applies to you, Miss Langtry."

"The meek shall inherit the earth?"

He gave her a sensual half smile. "All hat, no cattle."

Belle gave an outraged intake of breath. Then she said sweetly, "That's a lot of big talk for a man with a girl's name."

He looked irritated. "You're saying it wrong. An-hel. And it is a man's name. In every Spanish-speaking country…"

"Aaain-jel, Aaain-jel!" she taunted, using the pronunciation that involved harps and wings. She blinked. "Oh, look, the limo's here."

Letty almost cried in relief.

"Finally," Darius muttered. The limo had barely slowed down at the curb before he opened the back door for his bride. Letty jumped in, eager to escape.

"Where are we going?" Belle said, starting to follow, the Spaniard coming up behind her. Darius blocked them from the limo.

"Thank you so much. Both of you. But I'm afraid Letty and I must leave immediately for Greece."

Belle frowned. "I thought you weren't leaving until tomorrow. We were going to take you out for dinner..."

"Unfortunately, we must get on the plane immediately. My family is waiting to meet my new bride."

"Oh," Belle said, crestfallen. "In that case... Of course I understand." Leaning into the back of the limo, she hugged Letty. "Have a wonderful honeymoon! You deserve every bit of your happiness!"

Belle was right, Letty reflected numbly as the limo pulled away from her friend still beaming and waving on the sidewalk. She'd get all the happiness she deserved after abandoning her father to marry Darius: none.

Letty stared out at the gray rain. Darius sat beside her silently for the hour and a half it took to drive through the evening rush-hour traffic to the small airport outside the city. As they boarded his private jet, he continued to ignore her.

Fine. Letty didn't care. She felt exhausted and miserable. Walking to the separate bedroom in the back of the jet, she shut the door behind her. Climbing into bed, she pulled the blanket up to her forehead, struggling to hold back tears. She closed her eyes.

And woke up in a different world.

Letty sat up with an intake of breath.

She was no longer on the jet. She found herself in a big, bright bedroom, empty except for a king-size wrought-iron bed.

Brilliant sunlight came through the open windows, leaving warm patterns against the white walls and red tiled floor. She heard laughter outside and conversation in an exotic language and the sweet singing of birds.

She looked down at the soft blanket and cotton sheets. Where was she? And—her lips parted in a gasp. She was wearing only her bra and panties! Someone had undressed her while she was asleep! The thought horrified her.

How had she gotten into this bed?

The flight across the Atlantic had been lonely and dark. She remembered crying herself to sleep on the plane. After her sleepless night before their wedding, she'd slept deeply.

She dimly remembered Darius carrying her, the warmth of his chest, the comforting rumble of his voice.

"So you're awake."

Looking up with an intake of breath, Letty saw her husband now standing in the open doorway, dressed more casually than she'd ever seen him, in a snug black T-shirt and long cargo shorts. Sunlight lit him from behind, leaving his expression in shadow.

"Where are we?"

"The island of Heraklios. My villa."

"I barely remember arriving."

"You were exhausted. Overwhelmed from the happiness of marrying me," he said sardonically.

"What time is it?"

"Here? Almost two in the afternoon." He motioned to a nearby door. "There's an en suite bathroom if you'd like a shower." He indicated a large walk-in closet. "Your clothes have already been unpacked."

"Are you the one who took off my clothes?"

"Just so you'd sleep more comfortably."

She bit her lip as she looked down at the bed. "Um. And did you…did we…uh, share this bed?"

His shoulders tensed. "If you're asking if I took advantage of you in your sleep, the answer is no."

She took a deep breath. "I didn't mean…"

"Get dressed and come out on the terrace when you're ready. My family is here to meet you."

Letty stared at the empty doorway in dismay, then slowly rose out of bed. Her body felt stiff from sleeping so long.

Going into the elegant marble bathroom, she took a hot shower, which refreshed her. Wrapping herself in a towel, she wiped the steam off the mirror. Her face looked pale and sad.

A fine thing, she thought. When she was about to meet his family. They'd take one look at Letty's face and assume, as Santiago Velazquez had, that she and Darius had gotten married only because of her pregnancy. Why else would someone as handsome and powerful as Darius Kyrillos ever choose a penniless, ordinary-looking woman like her?

He was taking a risk even bringing her to meet them. She could embarrass him, treat them disrespectfully. She could even explain how he'd blackmailed her into marriage.

Letty looked at her eyes in the mirror. She didn't want to hurt Darius. She just wanted him to forgive her dad.

Maybe she could start by treating his family with the same respect she wanted for her father.

Letty dressed quickly and carefully, blow-drying her long dark hair and brushing it till it shone. She put on lipstick, and chose a pretty new sundress and sandals from the closet. Her knees shook as she went down the hallway. A maid directed her toward the terrace.

With a deep breath, she went outside into the sunshine.

Bright pink bougainvillea climbed the whitewashed walls of the Greek villa, above a wide terrace overlooking the mountainous slopes of the island jutting out of the Ionian Sea.

Against the blue horizon, she saw the shaded forest green of a distant island. The whole world seemed bright with color: blue and white buildings, sea and sky, pink flowers, brown earth and green olive, fig and pomegranate trees.

She felt the warm sun against her skin, and pleasure

seeped through her body. Then she saw the group of people sitting at a long wooden table.

Darius rose abruptly from the table. Silence fell as the others followed his gaze.

Wordlessly, he came over to her. His dark eyes glowed as he lowered his head to kiss her cheek. Turning back to the others, he said in English, "This is Letty. My wife."

An elderly woman got up from the table. Standing on her tiptoes, she squinted, carefully looking Letty over from her blushing face to her pregnant belly. Then she smiled. Reaching up, she patted Letty on the cheek and said something in Greek that she didn't understand.

"My great-aunt says you look happy now," Darius translated. "Like a beautiful bride."

"How sweet... Did she see me before?" Letty asked.

"When I brought you in. She said you looked like death warmed over."

She stared at him in horror, then narrowed her eyes accusingly. "She never said that."

He gave a sudden grin. "She says our island has obviously revived you, all our sun and sea air. Plus, clearly—" he quirked a dark eyebrow "—marriage to me."

The elderly woman said something quickly behind him. He glanced back with an indulgent smile. *"Nai, Theia Ioanna."*

"What did she say?"

Darius turned back to Letty. "She said marriage to you seems to agree with me, as well." Looking down at her, he hesitated. "Our wedding was..."

"Horrible."

"Not good," he agreed. His dark eyes caressed her face, and he leaned forward to whisper, "But something tells me our honeymoon will make up for it."

Letty felt his breath against her hair, the brush of his lips against her earlobe, and electricity pulsed through her at the untold delights promised by a honeymoon in the Greek villa. In that enormous bed.

She tried not to think about that as he introduced her to the other people around the table, aunts and uncles and innumerable cousins. She smiled shyly, wishing she could speak Greek as one Kyrillos family member after another hugged her, their faces alight with welcome and approval.

One of the younger women grabbed her arm, motioning for her to take the best seat at the table. On learning she was hungry, other relatives dished her out a lunch from the tempting dishes on the table. Tangy olives, salad with cucumbers, tomatoes and feta, vine leaves stuffed with rice, grilled meats on skewers, fresh seafood and finally the lightest, flakiest honey pastries imaginable. After sleeping so long, and having no appetite yesterday, Letty was ravenous and gobbled it all up as fast as she could get it.

The women around her exclaimed approvingly in Greek. Darius sat beside her, smiling, his dark eyes glowing beneath the warm Greek sun.

"They like how you eat," he told her.

She laughed in spite of herself. In this moment, beneath the pink flowers and warm Greek sun, with the blue sea beyond, she felt suddenly, strangely happy. Finally, she pushed her chair away from the table, shaking her head as his relatives offered yet more plates. "No, thank you." She turned anxiously to Darius. "How do I say that?"

"Óchi, efharisto."

"Óchi, efharisto," she repeated to them warmly.

One by one, his family members hugged her, speaking rapidly, patting her belly, then hugging Darius before they hurried into the villa.

"Your family is wonderful."

"Thank you." He lifted a dark eyebrow. "By the way, some of them speak English quite well. They're just hoping if you don't realize that, you'll be inspired to learn Greek."

She laughed, then looked around the terrace at the flowers and sea view. "I'm feeling very inspired, believe me."

"They already love you. Because you're my wife." He put his arm along the back of her chair. "Not only that, you're the first woman I've ever brought home to meet them."

Her eyes went wide. "Really?"

He grinned, shaking his head. "For years, they read about my scandalous love life and despaired of me ever settling down with a nice girl." He sipped strong black coffee from a tiny cup. "Great-aunt Ioanna is delirious with joy to see me not only sensibly married, but also expecting a child. And she remembers you."

Letty's smile fell. "She does?"

"Yes."

"Does she blame me for—?"

"No," he cut her off. "She remembers you only as the girl that I loved and lost long ago. In her mind, that means our marriage is fate. *Moíra.* She believes our love was meant to stand the test of time."

Letty blinked fast. *Our love was meant to stand the test of time.*

Leaning forward, he took her hand. "You are part of the family. You are a Kyrillos now."

It was true, she realized. She had a new last name. When she updated her passport, she'd no longer be Letitia Spencer, the daughter of the famous white-collar criminal, but Letitia Kyrillos, the wife of a self-made billionaire. Just by marrying, she'd become an entirely different person. What a strange thought.

But maybe this new woman, Letitia Kyrillos, would know how to be happy. Maybe their marriage, which had been so bleak at the start, could someday be full of joy, as her own parents' marriage had been.

She just had to change Darius's mind about her father. It wouldn't be hard.

Like making it snow in July.

One of Darius's female cousins came back out of the villa and pulled on his arm, talking rapidly in Greek, even as she smiled apologetically at Letty.

"They need to move the big table," he explained. "To get the terrace ready for the party tonight."

"What party?"

"They wouldn't let us come all this way without making a big fuss." He grinned. "There's a party tonight to welcome you as my bride. Only family and friends from the village have been invited…"

"Good," she said, relieved.

"Which, naturally, means the entire island will be here, and a few people from neighboring islands, as well."

Her heart sank to her sandals at the thought of all those people judging her, possibly finding her unworthy of being Darius's bride. She whispered, "What if they don't like me?"

Reaching out, Darius lifted her chin. "Of course they will," he said softly. "They will because I do."

As the hot Greek sun caressed her skin in the flower-dappled terrace, the dark promise in his gaze made her shiver.

As his relatives bustled back out on the terrace, with maids following them, they started clearing dishes, wiping the table and sweeping the terrace.

Letty looked around anxiously. "Ask them how I can help."

He snorted. "If you think they'll allow either of us to lift a finger, you're out of your mind."

"We can't just sit here, while they do all the work!"

"Watch this." Pushing his chair back, Darius rose from

the table and said casually in English, "Hey, Athina, hand me that broom."

"Forget it, Darius," his cousin replied indignantly in the same language, yanking the broom out of his reach. "You sent my sons to college!"

"You gave me a job when I needed work," a man added in heavily accented English, as he lifted fairy lights to dangle from the terrace's leafy trellis. "We're doing this. Don't think you're getting out of it!"

They all gave a low buzz of agreement.

Looking at Letty, Darius shrugged. She sighed, seeing she was outmatched. His great-aunt was now, in fact, shooing them away with a stream of steady Greek, a mischievous smile on her kindly, wizened face.

Letty drew closer to him. "So what should we do with ourselves?"

Darius's eyes darkened as he said huskily, "We *are* on our honeymoon..."

She shivered at his closeness and at the tempting thought of going back to the bedroom. But she was distracted by the sweep of the brooms and the loud cries of the relatives and house staff bustling back and forth across the villa as they cleaned and set up for the party, all the while watching Darius and Letty out of the corners of their eyes with frank interest and indulgent smiles.

"I couldn't," Letty whispered, blushing beneath all the stares. "If we stay, I'll feel like we should help cook and clean."

"Then let's not stay." He took her hand. "Let me show you the island."

He drew her out of the enormous, luxurious villa, past the gate and out onto unpaved road. Looking around, she saw the rural rolling hills were covered with olive and pomegranate trees, dotted with small whitewashed houses beneath the sun. But there was one thing she didn't see.

"Where are all the cars? The paved roads?"

"We don't have cars. Heraklios is too small and mountainous, and there are only a few hundred residents. There are a few cobblestoned streets by the waterfront, but they're too winding and tight for any car."

"So how do you get around?"

"Donkey."

She almost tripped on her own feet. She looked at him incredulously. "You're joking."

He grinned. "I managed to put in a helicopter pad, and also a landing strip, at great expense, and it isn't even usable if the wind is too strong. Here we transport most things by sea." As they walked closer to an actual village clinging to a rocky cliff, he pointed to a small building on a hill. "That was my school."

"It looks like one room."

"It is. After primary school, kids have to take a ferry to a bigger school the next island over." As they continued walking, he pointed to a small *taverna*. "That's where I tasted my first sip of *retsina*." His nose wrinkled. "I spit it out. I still don't like it."

"And you call yourself a Greek," she teased. His eyebrow quirked at her challenge.

"I'd take you in and let you taste it, except—" he looked more closely at the closed door "—it looks like old Mr. Papadakis is already up at the villa. Probably setting up drinks."

"The whole town's closing—just for our wedding reception?"

"It's a small island. I don't think you realize how much pull I have around here."

Letty slowed when she saw a ruined, lonely-looking villa at the top of the hill, above the village. "What's that?"

His lips tightened, curled up at the edges. "That was my mother's house."

"Oh," she breathed. She knew his mother had abandoned him at birth. He'd never talked much about her, not even when they were young. "No one lives there anymore?"

"My mother left the island right after I was born, her parents soon after. It seems they couldn't stand the shame of my existence," he added lightly.

She flinched, her heart aching. "Oh, Darius."

"My mother moved to Paris. She died in a car crash when I was around four." He shrugged. "I heard her parents died a few years ago. I can't remember where or how."

"I'm so sorry."

"Why? I didn't love them. I don't mourn them."

"But your mother. Your grandparents..."

"Calla Halkias died in a limousine, married to an aristocrat." His voice was cold as he looked back to the ghostly ruin on the hill. "Just as I'm sure she would have wanted. The prestigious life her parents expected for her."

A lump rose in her throat as she thought of Darius as a child on this island, looking up at the imposing villa of the people who'd tossed him out like garbage. She didn't know what to say, so she held his hand tightly. "Did you ever forgive them?"

"For what?"

"They were your family, and they abandoned you."

His lips pressed down. "My mother gave birth to me. I'm glad about that. But I wouldn't call them *family*. From everything I've heard, they were a total disaster. Like..." He hesitated. But she knew.

"Like my family?" she said quietly.

He paused. "Your mother was a great lady. She was always kind. To everyone."

"Yes," she said over the lump in her throat.

"My *yiayiá* raised me. Our house didn't have electricity or plumbing, but I always knew she loved me. When I finally made my fortune, I had the old shack razed and built a villa in its place. The biggest villa this island has ever seen." Looking up at the ruin, he gave a grim smile. "When I was young, the Halkias family was the most powerful here. Now I am."

She noticed he'd never said if he forgave them. She bit her lip. "But, Darius…"

"It's in the past. I want to live in the present. And shape the future." Taking both her hands in his own, Darius looked down at her seriously on the dusty road beneath the hot Greek sun. "Promise me, Letty. You'll always do what's best for our family."

"I promise," she said, meaning it with all her heart.

Lowering his head, he whispered, "And I promise the same."

He softly kissed her, as if sealing the vow. Drawing back, he searched her gaze. Then he pulled her back into his arms and kissed her in another way entirely.

Feeling the heat of his lips against hers, the rough scrape of the bristles on his chin, she clung to him, lost in her own desire. He was her husband now. *Her husband.*

He finally pulled away. "Come with me."

He led her to the end of the dusty road, through the winding cobblestones of the small village of whitewashed houses. On the other side, they went through a scrub brush thicket of olive trees. She held his hand tightly as the branches scraped her arms, and they went down a sharp rocky hill. Then suddenly, they were in a hidden cove on a deserted white sand beach.

Letty's eyes went wide in amazement. The popular beaches of the Hamptons and even around Fairholme would have been packed on a gloriously warm September day. But this beach was empty. "Where is everyone?"

"I told you. They're at the villa, getting ready for the party."

"But—" she gestured helplessly "—there must be tourists, at least?"

He shook his head. "We don't have a hotel. The tourists are at the resorts up in Corfu. So we all know each other here. Everyone is a friend or relative, or at least a friend of a relative. It's a community. One big family."

No wonder this island felt like a world out of time. She felt her heart twist. Turning away, she looked around at the hidden cove with the white sand beach against the blue Ionian Sea and tried to smile. "It's wonderful."

"You're missing Fairholme," he said quietly.

She looked down at the white sand. "It's been ten years. It's stupid. Any psychiatrist would tell me it's time to let it go."

"I miss it, too." He grinned. "Do you remember the beach at Fairholme? Nothing but rocks."

"Yes, and the flower meadow where you taught me to dance."

"What about the pond where I tried to catch frogs and you always wanted to give them names and take them home—?"

Suddenly their words were tumbling over each other.

"The brilliant color of the trees in autumn—"

"Roller-skating down the hallways—"

"The secret passageway behind the library where you'd always hide when you were upset—"

"Your mother's rose garden," Darius said with a sudden laugh, "where she caught me that time I tried a cigarette. My first and last time—"

"And how Mrs. Pollifax scolded us whenever we tracked mud into her freshly cleaned kitchen." Letty grinned. "But she always gave us milk and cookies after we'd made it right. Though it took a while. You weren't very good at mopping."

"We always turned it into a game."

The two of them smiled at each other on the deserted beach.

Letty's smile slipped away. "But we'll never see Fairholme again."

Darius stared at her for a long moment, then abruptly started taking off his shoes. "The sea should be warm."

She lifted her eyebrows. "What are you doing?"

"I'm getting in." He leaned over to unbuckle her sandals. "And you're coming with me."

Barefoot, they went splashing out into the sea. Letty delighted in the feel of the water caressing her feet, then her calves and finally knees. She was tempted to go deeper into the water, to float her pregnant body in the seductive waves that would make her feel light as air. She took a few more steps, until the sea lapped the hem of her white sundress.

Splashing behind her, Darius suddenly pulled her into his arms.

As the waves swirled around them, he kissed her, and there was no one to see but the birds soaring across the sky. For hours, or maybe just minutes, they kissed in the hidden cove, between the bright blue sea and sky, beneath the hot Greek sun. He ran his hands over her bare shoulders, over her thin cotton sundress, as the salty sea spray clung to their skin and hair.

Waves swirled around them, sucking the sand beneath their toes, as the tide started to come in. The waves crashed higher, moving up against their thighs.

Finally pulling away, Darius looked down at her intently. She felt his dark gaze sear her body. Sear her heart.

"Letty, the house we grew up in might be gone," he whispered. "But we still have each other."

The lowering afternoon sun shone around the edges of his dark hair, making Darius shimmer like the dream he was to her.

And it was then Letty knew the worst had happened.

The doom and disaster. And it had happened more swiftly than she'd ever expected.

She loved him.

All of him.

The man he'd been.

The man he was.

The man he could be.

Since the February night they'd conceived their child, Letty had tried to convince herself that he'd changed irrevocably. That she hated him. That he'd lost her love forever.

It had all been a lie.

Even in her greatest pain, she'd never stopped loving him. How could she? He was the love of her life.

Glancing back at the lowering sun, Darius sighed. "Can't be late for our own party. We'd better get back to the villa." He glanced down at his shorts, now splattered with sand and seawater. "We might have to clean up a little."

"Yes," she said in a small voice.

"We'll finish this later," he said huskily, kissing her bare shoulder. He whispered, "I can hardly wait to make love to you, Mrs. Kyrillos."

As they splashed their way to the beach, and made their way up the shore, Letty stumbled.

He caught her, then frowned, looking at her closely. "Did you hurt yourself?"

"No," she said, hiding the ache in her throat, struggling to hold back tears. It wasn't totally a lie. She wasn't hurt.

But she knew she soon would be.

One day married, and her heart was already lost.

CHAPTER NINE

DARIUS NEARLY GASPED when he first saw Letty at the party that night. When she came out onto the terrace, she looked so beautiful she seemed to float through the twilight.

She wore a simple white maxi dress, which fit perfectly over her full breasts and baby bump. The soft fabric showed off the creamy blush of her skin and bright hazel of her eyes. Bright pink flowers hung in her long dark hair.

As the red sun was setting into the sea below the cliffs, three hundred people on the terrace burst into spontaneous applause amid a cacophony of approving Greek.

Darius's heart was in his throat as he looked at her. He was dazzled. He thought she'd put Aphrodite, freshly risen from the sea, completely to shame.

And the fact that he'd even have such a ridiculously poetic thought stunned him.

As she came closer, he cleared his throat awkwardly. "You look nice."

"Thank you," she said, smiling shyly.

He did not touch her. He was almost afraid to. She was simply too desirable, and after their hours of kissing on the beach, he did not know how much more temptation his self-control could take. They'd been married for over twenty-four hours, but had not yet made love.

The party was torture. It lasted for hours, testing his resolve. If it had been any other situation, he would have told everyone to go to hell and taken his bride straight to bed.

But this was his family. His village. He couldn't be rude to them or reject the warm welcome they gave his bride.

His whole body ached to possess her. He could think of nothing else. It was causing him physical pain. He was just glad he was wearing a long, loosely tailored jacket and loose trousers so the whole village could not discuss with amused approval his obvious desire for his bride.

The party was over the top, as only village affairs could be, with music, drinking and dancing. A feast had been lovingly prepared by his family and all the rest of the village. So many people rushed to Letty and started talking excitedly in Greek that she'd announced she planned to start taking Greek lessons as soon as possible. Some of his cousins immediately started cheering, and when Darius translated her words for his elderly great-aunt, Theia Ioanna actually stood on tiptoe to kiss Letty on both cheeks. His family loved her.

Of course they did. Letty Kyrillos was the perfect bride. She would be the perfect wife and mother. Now he'd gotten her away from her father, there would be no bad influences in her life.

Darius would be the only one to claim her loyalty. And the expression in Letty's eyes as she looked at him now—a mix of longing, hero worship and fear—did strange things to his insides. It made him feel oddly vulnerable, reminding him of the insecure, lovesick youth he'd once been for her.

No. He just desired her, he told himself firmly. He was appreciative that she was comporting herself as a proper Greek wife, with kindness and respect to his family. And he hoped—expected—that she would soon love him. It would make all their lives easier.

Darius did not intend to love her in return. He would never leave himself that vulnerable again. As the protector of their family, as a husband, as a father, as a man, it was his duty to be strong.

Letty's heart was her weakness. It would not be his.

His great-aunt went to bed at midnight, and the rest of the older generation soon after, but with the ouzo flowing and loud music and enthusiastic dancing, his cousins and many of the younger villagers remained well into the wee hours. It wasn't until the ouzo was gone and the musicians were falling asleep over their instruments that the last guests finally took the hint and departed, after many congratulations and kisses for the newly married couple.

Darius and Letty were finally alone on the terrace, surrounded by streamers and empty champagne glasses.

She looked at him, her eyes huge in the moonlight, the pink flowers wilting in her dark lustrous hair.

Without a word, he took her hand.

Leading her to their bedroom suite at the farthest end of the south wing, he closed the door behind them and opened the windows and sliding glass door to the balcony. The wind blew from the sea, twisting the translucent white curtains, illuminated by moonlight.

Turning back to her, he lifted her long dark hair from the nape of her neck and slowly unzipped her dress. In the hush of the night, it felt like an act that was almost holy.

Her dress dropped to the floor. She turned to him, her eyes luminous in the silvery light. Reaching up, she pulled off his jacket. She unbuttoned his shirt. He felt the soft brush of her hands against his chest and caught them in his own. She looked up at him questioningly.

A strange feeling was building in his heart. *Desire*, he reminded himself fiercely. *I desire her.* He kissed her hands—first one, then the other.

The wind blew against her hair, causing pink flower petals to float softly to the floor like a benediction. Without a word, he pulled her to the enormous bed.

This time, as they made love, there were no words beyond the language of touch. There was only pleasure and delight.

He'd thought he'd known ecstasy the night they'd made love over and over in his Manhattan penthouse.

But this was something else. It felt different.

Why? Because they were married now, and she was permanently his? Because she knew him better than anyone on earth? Because she'd truly joined his family?

Whatever the reason, as he made love to her on this, their first true wedding night, it felt sacred.

It felt like...

Happiness.

After they'd both joined and shattered like a supernova in each other's arms, Darius held her as she slept. As he stared at the ceiling, her words on the beach floated back into his mind.

We'll never see Fairholme again.

Her voice had been quietly despairing. As if she'd accepted bleak loss as her due.

Darius scowled. He didn't accept that.

He suddenly wanted to give Letty back everything she'd lost. And more.

Careful not to wake her, he rose from the bed in the gray light of dawn. Going out onto the balcony, with its view of the wild gray sea, he made a quiet phone call to his long-suffering executive assistant in New York. Mildred Harrison had worked for him for seven years, so she didn't even sound surprised that he'd be rude enough to call her so late.

"Pity you left New York right when you're the city's hero," she said drily. "Your picture is on the cover of the *Daily Post.* Apparently you're some kind of Robin Hood figure now, robbing from your own fortune to pay back Howard Spencer's victims."

"Glad I'm not there, then. We'll be back in two weeks, by which time I expect the papers will all be insulting me again. Anything else?"

"That Brooklyn apartment building has been purchased as you requested. Your father-in-law—"

"Never call him that again," Darius said tersely.

She cleared her throat. "Um, Mr. Spencer has been advised that he will be allowed to remain in the apartment for as long as he wishes, free of charge."

"Good," he said, already bored with the subject.

She paused. "There's something else you should know."

"Well?"

"The investigator following him says Spencer has been visiting an oncologist. Apparently he's sick. Maybe dying."

Darius's eyes widened. Then he gave a snort. "It's a trick."

"Mr. Green didn't think so. He managed to get his hands on the medical records. It seems legit."

"Spencer must have paid the doctor off."

"Maybe." Mildred sounded doubtful. "But if it were my father, I'd still want to know."

Yes, Darius thought. He looked back at the shadowy form of Letty sleeping in his bed. She would want to know. But there was no way he was telling her. Not when the old man was probably just trying once again to cause trouble between them.

At worst, Spencer probably had a cold and thought he could use it to get out of his well-deserved punishment. Darius was not going to let it happen.

"I won't have my wife bothered," he said shortly. "Spencer must have known he was being followed."

"As you say, Mr. Kyrillos."

He set his jaw. "I called you for another reason. I want to buy my wife a wedding gift."

"Beyond the billions you're already putting in trust for her father's victims? We've had a whole team of accountants coming through here, by the way, working with the Feds to determine accurate payments, including those for third-party clients. We're not really staffed for this..."

"You'll sort it out. And at the end, I'll send you and your husband to Miami for a week of well-deserved rest."

"Rome," she said firmly. "For three."

He grinned. Mildred knew what she was worth. He respected that.

"Three," he agreed. "But I need you to do something first. I want to buy a home."

"Your penthouse is too small?"

"I have a special place in mind. Find out what it would cost."

He explained, and she gave a low whistle. "All right, boss. I'll call you soon as I know. What's your ceiling?"

"Whatever it takes."

After he hung up the phone, Darius went back to the king-size bed he shared with his pregnant bride. Joining her under the blankets, he wrapped his arm around her as she slept. He heard the birds singing as, outside the window, the sun started to rise.

Holding Letty in his arms, he suddenly saw the reward for everything he'd done right in his life. He had Letty. He'd have the rest. Home. Children. Joy. All the things he'd stopped dreaming about long ago. He would have it all.

And nothing, especially not her criminal of a father, would come between them.

As their private jet began its descent through the clouds toward New York City, Letty felt a mixed sense of relief and regret.

She was glad to be returning closer to her father. Darius had assured her that Howard was fine and living rent-free in their old apartment with a stipend to supply his needs. "Your father is spending his days playing chess with friends down at the park," he'd told her irritably. She could only assume Darius had someone watching him, but she didn't even mind because she was glad to know he was all right. It felt so wrong never to see him, never to call him.

But at least now she'd know her dad was only a quick

drive away, if needed. And soon she hoped he'd be back in their lives for good.

The heart attack that had caused the death of Darius's father was a tragic accident. But surely he couldn't hate her dad forever? She loved Darius too much to believe that. Soon they would all be a family again.

And family was all Letty cared about. As she'd promised her husband in Greece, she would always put her family above everything else.

She already felt wistful for the tiny Greek island where she'd been immediately accepted into Darius's extended family. Their honeymoon had been the happiest two weeks of her life. She'd loved everything about Heraklios. The village. The beach. The vivid colors and bright sun. The villa. The people. Her eyes met Darius's across the airplane cabin.

The man.

He was sitting in a white swivel chair and had spent much of the flight typing on his laptop, with some idea he'd had for a new business venture. But as his gaze caught hers, she felt every bit of his attention. She always felt it to her toes when he looked at her.

Lifting a dark eyebrow, he teased, "We could still turn the plane around."

"I loved our visit," she said wistfully, then glanced out the window. "But it'll be nice to be back home." She paused, biting her lip. She knew she shouldn't ask, but she couldn't help it. "Now we're back in the city, maybe you could talk to my dad. Then you'd see his side…"

"Forget it," he said flatly.

"He never meant to hurt anyone, he—"

Darius closed his laptop with a thud. "Stop."

"Forgiveness frees the soul. You never know—" her voice sounded desperate even to her own ears "—*you* might have to ask someone for forgiveness one day!"

He snorted. "I don't intend to commit any crimes, so I think I'm safe."

"Darius—"

"No."

Disappointment filled her heart. Clenching her hands, she told herself she'd just have to be patient. She forced herself to take a deep breath and change the subject. "I loved spending time with your family. Maybe your great-aunt could come visit us in New York."

His expression relaxed and he smiled. "Theia Ioanna hates planes. She thinks of them as newfangled machines, a dangerous fad. She's waiting for everyone to come to their senses. But after our baby's born we could go back to Heraklios."

"I'd like that." Outside the window, the plane was descending through clouds that looked like white cotton candy. "In the meantime, I'm going to start learning Greek." She looked at him coyly beneath her lashes. "You'd like to teach me your native tongue, wouldn't you?"

His eyes darkened with interest. He started to rise from his seat, but as the plane broke beneath the clouds, the pilot announced over the intercom that they should buckle their seat belts for landing. Letty smiled.

Then she looked through the porthole window. "That's not Teterboro."

Now he was the one to smile. "No."

Staring down, she suddenly recognized the airport. Long ago, her family had landed here every time they went on a trip. She looked up with a frown. "Long Island? Is there a problem?"

"Wait and see."

After the plane landed at the small airport, the two of them came down the steps. A town car waited on the tarmac, and his driver and bodyguard swiftly loaded their suitcases from the plane.

"But why are we here?" she asked Darius helplessly in the backseat of the car a few minutes later as it pulled away from the airport.

"You'll see."

"You're really vexing."

His dark eyebrows lifted. "Vexing?" he teased, then moved closer as he whispered, "Is that what I am?"

Then he kissed her senseless in the backseat, until she was forced to agree rather unsteadily that he did have one or two good qualities, as well.

But she tensed when the limo turned onto the coastal road that she'd once known very, very well. Her suspicions were confirmed as they drove down the same country lane that she knew led to the massive 1920s beachfront estate that had once been her home. She turned on Darius angrily.

"Why would you bring us here?" she choked out. "Just to torture me? You can't see the house from the road." She felt a sudden ache in her throat as she looked out toward the gray-blue bay that led to the Atlantic. "The gate is guarded. That tech billionaire is serious about privacy. So if you're hoping to get a peek of the house, it won't happen."

"You tried?"

"A month after it was sold at auction. As I told you, I just wanted a picture of my great-grandmother's fresco. His guard did everything but set the dogs on me."

"That won't be a problem today."

Letty pointed at the road ahead. "See? I told you—"

Then her eyes went wide.

The gate was wide open. Their limo drove right past the empty guardhouse, up the wide driveway to the glorious windswept oceanfront manor that had been built by Letty's great-great-grandfather, a steel baron named Edwin Langford.

Fairholme.

Letty's breath caught in her throat as she leaned out the

car window, and her eyes were dazzled as she saw, for the first time in ten years, her beloved home.

Tears swelled in her eyes as she looked up at the gray stone mansion with its turrets and leaded glass windows soaring against the sky. Looking back at her husband, she breathed, "What have you done?"

He was smiling. "I've given you what you want most."

The limo had barely stopped before she flung open her car door and raced eagerly into the house. Pushing aside the stately front door—unlocked!—she hurled herself into the foyer where she'd played as a child.

"Dad?" she cried out. "Dad, where are you?"

Letty ran from room to room, calling his name, overwhelmed with happiness that somehow, while pretending he was never going to forgive her father, Darius had seen the desperate desire of her heart.

I've given you what you want most.

"Dad!" she cried, moving from one elegant, empty room to the next. Memories followed her with every step.

There she had played pirates with her father.

There she had slipped down the marble floor in socks as the two of them competed to see who could slide farthest and make her mother laugh loudest.

There she'd played with the gardener's kittens.

There she'd played hide-and-seek with Darius when they were kids…

There—every Saturday in summer—she'd tucked roses into the priceless Ming dynasty vase to make her mother smile.

But where was her dad? Where?

As Letty finished going through the main entrance rooms, she ran up the sweeping staircase toward the second floor. She stopped halfway up the stairs, realizing she was hearing only the echo of her own voice.

Her dad wasn't there.

Letty's shoulders sagged with savage disappointment. Turning back down the stairs, she saw Darius standing in the front doorway, watching her. The happy, smug expression had disappeared from his handsome face.

He said tightly, "Why do you think I would invite your father here?"

"You said—you said," she faltered, biting her lip, "you were giving me what I wanted most."

"This house." His expression now could only be described as grimly outraged. "Your childhood home. I arranged to buy it for you. It wasn't easy. I had to pay the man a fortune to leave before we arrived. But I wanted you to have all your dreams. Everything you'd lost."

Everything she'd lost...

Gripping the banister for support, Letty sagged to sit on a stair. Heartbreaking grief was thundering through her, worse than if she'd never gotten her hopes up at all.

She struggled to hide it. She knew she was being churlish. Her mother would be ashamed of her. Here Darius had given her the stars and she was crying for the sun.

She should be overjoyed.

Fairholme.

Letty took a deep breath, looking up at the high painted ceilings, at the oak-paneled walls. *Home.* She was really here. Darius had given her back the home that had raised generations of Langfords, her mother's family.

What an amazing gift.

Wiping her eyes, Letty looked at Darius and tried to smile.

His handsome face was mutinous.

She couldn't blame him. He'd gone to a lot of trouble and expense to give her this incredible surprise, and she'd been completely ungrateful.

Rising unsteadily to her feet, she walked down the stairs to the foyer where he stood with a scowl, his arms folded.

"Thank you," she whispered. "I love your wonderful gift."

He looked distinctly grumpy. "It didn't look like it."

Feeling ashamed at her bad manners, she wrapped her arms around his neck and kissed him.

"I love it," she said softly. "It's a miracle to be here."

Looking mollified, he accepted her embrace. "I've also hired Mrs. Pollifax to come back as our housekeeper."

"You have!"

He smiled, clearly pleased by her reaction. "Along with as many of the original staff who were available. Giving them a big raise, naturally. I've also established a bank account in your name."

"Whatever for?"

Darius gave her a sudden grin. "You obviously haven't seen the stripper pole the last owner put up in the library. I knew you'd want to oversee the remodeling personally. Perhaps the fresco can be repaired? I've instructed the bank to give you unlimited funds. Use the money however you please."

"For the house?"

"Yes."

"The baby?"

"Of course. And you, Letty. Anything you want, jewelry, cars, furniture. You don't have to ask me. Buy anything you desire."

Biting her lip, she blurted out, "Could I send some money to my father?"

She knew immediately it was a mistake.

His expression turned icy. "I weary of your constantly bringing up this topic. We have an agreement."

"I know, but—"

"Your father already has far more than he deserves."

"If I could only just see him, so I could know he's all right…"

"He's fine."

Letty searched his gaze, hoping for reassurance. "He's fine? You know for sure?"

He paused. Then he finally said, "Yes."

He wouldn't meet her eyes.

"I miss him," she whispered. She took a deep breath, reminding herself of everything she had to be grateful for. Taking Darius's hand, she pressed it to her cheek and looked up at him with gratitude. "But what you've done for me today, buying Fairholme back... I'll never forget."

For a long moment, the two of them stood together in the foyer, with sunlight pouring in through the open door. She breathed in scents she'd craved so long, the tangy salt of the ocean, the honeyed sweetness of her mother's rose garden. The salt and sweetness of a lifetime of memories.

"Thank you," she whispered. "For bringing me home."

He cupped her cheek. "You're worth it, Letty," he said huskily. "For you, I would pay any price."

Lowering his head, he kissed her, claiming her lips as he'd already claimed her body and soul. Words lifted unbidden to her throat. Words she hadn't tried to say since that horrible night in February. Words straight from her heart.

"I love you, Darius," she said softly.

He gave her an oddly shy smile. "You do?"

Smiling back through her tears, she nodded. Her blood was rushing through her ears, pounding through her veins, as she waited for what he'd say next.

Without a word, he kissed her.

As she stood in the Fairholme foyer, her heavily pregnant belly pressed between them as her husband kissed her so tenderly, miracles seemed to be spinning around her like a whirlwind.

They were married now. Expecting a baby. He'd paid off her father's debts. He'd just brought her home. She loved him.

And someday, he would love her.

Letty was suddenly sure. They'd already had so many miracles. Why not more?

Darius would soon forgive her father and let him back into their family. He was too good a man not to forgive, especially when it meant so much to her. It was the only thing he hadn't given her. That, and those three little words.

It was the same thing, she realized. When he forgave her father, that was how she would know that he truly loved her.

When he finally pulled away from their embrace, she looked up, still a little dazzled. "Is there really a stripper pole in the library?"

Darius gave a low laugh. "Come with me."

Taking her hand, he drew her down the long marble hallway to the oak-paneled library. When she saw the gleaming stripper pole set in the brand-new white shag carpeting, she burst into horrified snorts of laughter.

"I told you," he said.

"I'll get it removed. Don't worry. I'll make this house just like it was," Letty said. "Just like we remember."

"All those memories." He pulled her against his chest, his dark eyes intense as he whispered huskily, "But as I remember, there's one thing we've never done in this house."

And as her husband pulled her against him in a hot, fierce embrace, Letty knew all her deepest dreams were about to come true.

CHAPTER TEN

HOME. LETTY LOOKED around with satisfaction. Was there any sweeter word?

The remodel was finished just in time, too. The former owner's monstrous decor had been removed—the shag carpeting, the stripper pole, the "ironic" brass fixtures and all the rest of it—and everything at Fairholme had been returned to its former glory.

The sitting room felt cozy, especially compared to the cold November weather outside. A fire crackled in the fireplace. Polished oak floors gleamed beneath priceless Turkish rugs. The sofas and chairs were plush and comfortable, the lamps sturdy and practical. Family photos now decorated the walls.

Letty snuggled back against the sofa. Her husband was sitting at the other end, tapping away on his laptop, but periodically he would rub her feet, so she made sure they were strategically available. Earlier, they'd had a delicious hearty meal of lamb stew and homemade bread, her favorite meal from childhood, prepared by Mrs. Pollifax.

The housekeeper had just left, saying that she needed to go visit a friend at a Brooklyn hospital. She'd had a strange expression when she said it, causing Letty to reply with a sympathetic murmur, "Please take all the time you need for your friend."

"I just might," the housekeeper had replied tartly, "since his own family can't be bothered to go see him."

"Poor man," Letty had sighed, feeling sorry for him. She couldn't imagine what kind of family wouldn't visit a sick man in the hospital.

That reminded her of how much she missed her father

after more than two months of not seeing him or talking to him. Darius still refused to forgive him. But surely, after their baby was born, his heart would be so full, he would have a new capacity to forgive? To love.

Letty looked at her husband hopefully. With the departure of Mrs. Pollifax, and the rest of the staff in their outlying cottages on the estate, the two of them were now completely alone in the house. The room felt snug and warm with her afghan blanket, the crackling fire and Darius's closeness as outside the cold November wind blew, rattling the leaded glass windows.

She was getting close to her due date, and happier than she'd ever imagined.

The nursery was ready. She'd been overjoyed to discover that her great-grandmother's precious fresco hadn't been completely destroyed. A well-known art restorer had managed to bring a good portion of it back to life. The ducks and geese were far fewer in number, and the Bavarian village mostly gone, but the little goose girl no longer looked so sad. It was a joy to see it again, and though Darius pretended to mock it and roll his eyes as he called it "art," she knew he was happy for her.

The nursery was the most beautiful room in the house, in Letty's opinion, the place where she'd slept as a baby, as had her mother and her grandfather before. It was now freshly painted and decorated, with a crib and rocking chair and brand-new toys. All they needed was the baby.

"Soon," she whispered aloud, rubbing her enormous belly. "Very soon."

"Talking to the baby again?" Darius teased.

Holding up a tattered copy of a beloved children's book, she responded archly, "I'm just going to read him this story."

His dark eyebrows lifted. "Again?"

"The pregnancy book said..."

"Oh, have you read a pregnancy book?"

Letty's lips quirked. Her constant consultation of pregnancy books and blogs was a running joke between them. But as a first-time mother and an only child, she had little experience with children and was anxious to do it right.

"It's been scientifically proven," she informed him now, "that a baby can hear, and therefore obviously listen to stories, from the womb."

He rolled his eyes, then put his large hand tenderly on her belly. "Don't worry, kid," he said in a whisper. "I have something to read you that I know you'll find way more interesting than the bunny story."

"Oh, you do, do you?" she said, amused.

"Absolutely." Turning back to his laptop, he clicked a few buttons and then started reading aloud, with mock seriousness, the latest business news from overseas.

Now she was the one to roll her eyes. But she found Darius's low, deep voice soothing, even when he was describing boring tech developments. Sipping orange spice herbal tea, she nibbled on the sugar cookies she'd made earlier that afternoon. She'd been eating so much lately she felt nearly as big as a house herself.

But Darius didn't seem to mind. Her cheeks grew hot as she recalled how he'd made love to her all over the house. Even the bathrooms—those with showers, at least. Almost forty rooms.

"We have to make this house ours," he'd growled, and she'd loved it.

Now as she felt his gentle hand resting on her belly, she grew drowsy listening to his low voice reading news stories to their baby and punctuating them with exclamations when he felt the baby kick.

"Letty," Darius said in a low voice, "are you awake?"

"Barely." She yawned. "I was just going to head up to bed. Why?"

He was quiet for a long moment, then said quietly, "Never mind. It'll wait. Good night, *agape mou.*"

The next morning, she kissed Darius goodbye as he left for lower Manhattan, as was his usual schedule Monday through Thursday. He'd set up an office for a new business he was excited about, to create software that would teach math and coding skills. Each day, Darius hired more employees, paying for their salaries out of his own pocket. There hadn't been any profits. "And there might never be any," he'd confessed sheepishly. But he wanted to make a difference in the world.

She'd never been so proud of him. He had a new spark in his eyes as he left Fairholme for his ninety-minute commute to the office.

Letty went up to the nursery, her favorite room, to fold all the cute tiny baby clothes one more time and make sure everything was ready. She'd had a dull ache in her lower back all morning. She went down to the kitchen, intending to ask Mrs. Pollifax if she knew of any natural remedy for back pain.

Instead she found the housekeeper crying.

"What's wrong?" Letty cried, going up to her in the enormous, gleaming kitchen. "What's happened?"

"My friend." The woman wiped her eyes with the edge of her apron. "He's dying."

"I'm so sorry," Letty whispered.

Mrs. Pollifax's eyes looked at her accusingly. "You should be. Since it's your own father."

Letty stared at her in shock. For a long minute, she couldn't even make sense of the words.

"I'm sorry—I can't be silent any longer," the housekeeper said. "Whatever caused you to be estranged from him, you're wrong to let him die alone. You'll regret it the rest of your life!"

"My father...?" Letty said slowly. "Is dying?"

Mrs. Pollifax's expression changed. "You didn't know?"

Shocked, she shook her head. "There must...must be some mistake. My father's not sick. He's fine. He's living without a care in the world...going to the park every day to play chess..."

"Oh, my dear." Coming closer, the housekeeper gently put her hand on Letty's shoulder. "I'm sorry. I judged you wrongly. I thought you knew. He collapsed a few weeks ago and has been in the hospital ever since. When I visited him yesterday, he didn't look well. He might have only weeks left. Days."

A loud rushing sound went through Letty's ears.

"No," she said numbly. "It has to be a mistake."

"I'm so sorry."

"You're wrong." Shaking off the housekeeper's hand, Letty reached for her phone. She dialed Darius's number first. When it went to voice mail, she hung up.

She took a deep breath. Her hands shook as she deliberately broke her vow to her husband for the first time. Her father had always hated cell phones, disparaging them as "tracking devices," so she called him at their old apartment number.

That, too, went to voice mail. But it was no longer Letty's voice on the phone greeting. Her father had replaced it with his own. For the first time in two months, she heard his recorded voice, and it sounded different. Fragile. Weak.

Terror rushed through her.

Her body was shaking as she looked up at Mrs. Pollifax. "Which hospital?"

The housekeeper told her. "But you're in no fit state to drive. I'll have Collins bring around the car. Shall I come with you?"

Letty shook her head numbly.

The older woman bit her lip, looking sad. "He's in room 302."

The drive to Brooklyn seemed to take forever. When they finally arrived at the large, modern hospital, Letty's body shook as she raced inside.

She didn't stop at reception, just hurried to the elevator, holding her heavy, aching belly. On the third floor, she followed the signs toward room 302.

Her steps slowed when she saw a man sitting in the waiting area. He looked up and saw her, too. She frowned. She recognized him from somewhere...

But she didn't stop, just headed straight for her father's room.

"Miss!" a nurse called anxiously as she passed the third-floor reception desk, barreling toward the corner room. "Please wait just a moment."

"It's all right," Letty said. "I'm his daughter." She pushed open the door. "Dad. Dad! I'm—"

But the room was empty.

Letty stared around in shock. Was she in the wrong room? Had she misunderstood?

Was he—oh, God—surely he couldn't be...?

"I'm sorry," a woman said behind her.

"You should be!" her father's gruff voice retorted.

With a sob, Letty whirled around.

In the doorway her living, breathing father was sitting in a wheelchair, glaring back at the dark-haired nurse struggling to push him through the doorway.

"You practically ran me into a wall. Where'd you learn how to drive?"

Letty burst into noisy tears. Her father turned his head and saw her, and his gaunt, pale features lit up with joy.

"Letty. You came."

Throwing her arms around his thin frame in the wheelchair, she choked out, "Of course I came. As soon as I heard you were sick. Then when I didn't see you in the bed, I thought..."

"Oh, you thought I was dead? No!" Glancing back at the nurse, he added drily, "Not for *some* people's lack of trying."

"Hmph." The nurse sniffed. "That's the last time I agree to help you win a wheelchair race, Howard."

"Win! We didn't win anything! Margery crushed us by a full ten seconds, in spite of her extra pounds. After all my big talk, too—I'll never live this down," he complained.

Letty drew back with astonishment. "Wheelchair race?"

"Admittedly not one of my best ideas, especially with Nurse Crashy here."

"Hey!"

"But it's what passes for fun here in the hospice wing. Either that or depress myself with cable news."

"It's totally against hospital protocol. I can't believe you talked me into it. Ask someone else to risk their job next time," the nurse said.

He gave her his old charming grin. "The race was a good thing. It lifted the spirits of everyone on the wing."

Looking slightly mollified, she sighed. "I guess I'd better go try convince my boss of that." She left the room.

Her father turned back to Letty. "But why are you crying? You really thought I was dead?"

She tried to smile. "You're crying, too, Dad."

"Am I?" Her father touched his face. He gave her a watery smile. "I'm just glad to see you, I guess. I was starting to wonder if you'd ever come."

"I came the instant I heard," she whispered, feeling awful and guilty.

Howard gave a satisfied nod. "I knew he'd eventually tell you."

"Who?"

"Darius. Sure, I promised I'd never contact you. But there was nothing in our deal that said I couldn't contact *him*. I left him a message four weeks ago, when I woke up in the hospital. I'd collapsed in the street, so an ambulance brought me here."

Four weeks? Letty was numb with shock. Darius had known for a *month* that her father was in the hospital, just an hour away from Fairholme?

Her father stroked his wispy chin. "Though I'm pretty sure he knew even before that. He's had me followed since the day you ran off with him. The guy must have noticed me going to my doctor's office three times a week."

She sucked in her breath, covering her mouth. Not just one month, but two? Darius had known her father was sick, dying, but he'd purposefully kept it from her?

Your father is spending his days playing chess with friends down at the park.

A lie!

Last night, when she and Darius had been cuddled by the fire, dreaming about their child, even then, her husband had been lying to her. While Letty had been eating cookies and drinking tea, her father had been spending yet another night in this hospital. Alone. Without a single word of love from his only daughter.

A cold sweat broke out on her skin. She trembled as if to fight someone or flee. But there was no escaping the horrible truth.

Darius had lied to her.

The man she'd loved since childhood. The center of all her romantic dreams and longings. He'd known her father was dying, and he'd lied.

How could Darius have been so callous? So selfish, heartless and cruel?

The answer was obvious.

He didn't love her.

He never would.

A gasp of anguish and rage came from the back of her throat.

"He never gave you the message, did he?" her father said, watching her. When she shook her head, he sighed. "How did you know I was here?"

"Mrs. Pollifax."

"I see." He looked sad. Then his eyes fell to her belly and he brightened as he changed the subject. "You're so big! You're just a week or two from your due date, aren't you?"

"Yes."

"I've almost made it." His voice was smug. "The doctors said I was a goner, but I told them I wasn't going anyplace yet."

Letty's body was still shaking with grief and fury. In the gray light of the hospital room, she turned toward the window. Outside, she saw November rain falling on the East River, and beyond it she could see the skyscrapers of Manhattan. Where Darius was right now.

Howard said dreamily behind her, "I was determined to see my grandbaby before I died."

She whirled back to her father. "Stop talking about dying!"

His gaunt face sagged. "I'm sorry, Letty. I really am."

"Isn't there any hope?" Her voice cracked. "An operation? A—a second opinion?"

Her father's eyes were kind. He shook his head. "I knew I was dying before I left prison."

She staggered back. "Why didn't you tell me?"

He rubbed his watery eyes. "I should have, I guess. But I didn't want you to worry and take all the stress on yourself like you always do. I wanted, for once, to take care of you. I wanted to repair the harm I did so long ago and get you back where you deserved to be. Married to your true love."

True love, Letty thought bitterly. Her stomach churned every time she thought of Darius lying to her all this time. The unfeeling bastard.

"It was my only goal," her father said. "To make sure

you'd be looked after and loved after I was gone. Now you and Darius are married, expecting a baby." He grinned with his old verve and said proudly, "Getting my arm broken by that thug was the best thing that ever happened to me, since it helped me bring you back together. I can die at peace. A happy man."

"Darius never told me you were sick," she choked out, her throat aching with pain. "I'll never forgive him."

Her father's expression changed. "Don't blame Darius. After all my self-made disasters, it just shows his good sense. Shows me he'll protect you better than I ever did." He looked up from the wheelchair. "Thank you, Letty."

She felt like the worst daughter in the world. "For what?"

"For always believing in me," he said softly, "even when you had no reason to. For loving me through everything."

She looked at her dying father through her tears. Then looked around the hospital room at the plain bed, the tile floor, the antiseptic feel, the ugly medical equipment. She couldn't bear to think of him spending his last days here, whiling away his hours with wheelchair races.

Her eyes narrowed. "Do you really need to be in the hospital?"

Howard shrugged. "I could have gone to full hospice. Other than pain meds, there's not much the doctors can do for me."

Her belly tightened with a contraction that felt like nothing compared to the agony of her heart. She lifted her chin. "Then you're coming home with me."

Howard looked at her in disbelief. "Back to that apartment? No, thanks. At least the hospital isn't cold all the time and someone brings me meals..."

"Not the apartment. I'm taking you to Fairholme."

His eyes looked dazzled.

"Fairholme?" he breathed. She saw the joy in his

wrinkled face. Then he blinked, looking troubled. "But Darius—"

"I'll handle him." Wrapping her arms around her father's thin shoulders, she kissed the wispy top of his head. Her father's last days would be happy ones, she vowed. He would die in the home that he'd adored, where he'd once lived with his beloved wife and raised his child, surrounded by comfort and love.

Letty would take care of him as he'd once taken care of her.

And, she thought grimly, she'd also take care of Darius.

She'd loved her husband with all her heart. Now she saw that all the sacrifices she'd made, all of her trust, had been for nothing. For an illusion. Darius didn't love her. He would never love her.

It was his final betrayal. And for this, she would never forgive him.

Darius walked into his office near Battery Park with a smile on his face and a spring in his step. He was late but had an excellent reason. He'd stopped at his favorite jeweler's on Fifth Avenue to buy a push present for his wife.

He'd read about push presents in a parenthood article. It was a gift that men gave the mothers of their children after labor and delivery, in celebration and appreciation of all their hours of pain and hard work. Since Letty's due date was so close, Darius had known he had no time to lose. He'd found the perfect gift—exquisite emerald earrings, surrounded by diamonds, set in gold, almost as beautiful as her hazel eyes. They'd even once belonged to a queen of France. With Letty's love of history, he knew she'd get a kick out of that, and he could hardly wait to give them to her. And even more amazing: when he did, their son would be real at last, and in their arms.

Darius realized he was whistling the same hokey lullaby that his wife had sung in the shower that morning to their unborn baby.

He loved Letty's voice.

He loved their home.

And he loved that he'd been able to blow off half a morning of work in order to get her a gift. It was supposedly one of the perks of being a boss, but at his last company, he'd been too grimly driven to do anything but grind out work. So he could build his fortune. So he could be worth something.

But even after he'd succeeded, even when he'd finally been rich beyond imagination, he'd been unhappy. He realized that now. He'd spent ten years doing nothing but work, and when he'd sold his company he'd felt lost. Money hadn't fulfilled him quite as much as he'd thought it would.

But now, everything had changed. Both in his work and his life.

He was building a new company. A free website would teach software coding, math and science skills, so others could have the opportunities he'd had, to get good jobs or perhaps even start their own tech companies someday.

His goal wasn't to build a fortune. He already had more than he could spend in a lifetime. When he'd paid out billions of dollars to Howard Spencer's victims, he hadn't even missed it.

Letty was teaching him—reminding him?—how a good life was lived.

Throughout their marriage, as Fairholme had every day become more beautiful, so had his pregnant wife. She was huge now, and she glowed. Every day she told him how much she loved him. He could feel it, her love for him, warming him like a fire in winter.

There was only one flaw.

One secret he was keeping.

And he knew it might ruin everything.

Darius's steps slowed as he crossed through the open office with the exposed brick walls.

Letty's father was dying. And Darius didn't know how to tell her.

He hadn't wanted to believe it was true at first. For weeks, he'd insisted it was all an elaborate con. "Call me when he's dead," he'd told his investigator half-seriously.

Then he'd gotten a message from Howard Spencer himself, saying he was in the hospital. Even then, for a few days, Darius had told himself it was a lie. Until his investigator had combed through the hospital records and confirmed it was true. Darius had no choice but to face it.

Now he had to tell Letty.

But how? How could he explain to her all his weeks of silence, when he'd known her father was dying in a Brooklyn hospital?

Darius still believed he'd done the right thing. He and Letty had made a deal at the start of their marriage: no contact with her father. There hadn't been any fine print or "get out of jail free" card if the man decided to die. All Darius had done was uphold their deal. He had nothing to feel guilty about. He hadn't just paid Spencer's debts, but also his living expenses and even his medical bills. He'd practically acted like a saint.

Somehow, he didn't think Letty would see it that way.

Darius dreaded her reaction. He'd halfheartedly started to tell her last night, but stopped, telling himself he didn't want to risk raising her blood pressure when she was so close to delivery. He didn't want to risk her health, or the baby's.

After the baby's born, he promised himself firmly. Once he knew both mother and baby were safe and sound.

She would be angry at first, he knew. But after she'd had some time to think it over, she'd realize that he'd only been trying to protect her. And it was in her nature to forgive. She had no choice. She loved him.

Feeling calmer, he walked past his executive assistant's desk toward his private office. "Good morning, Mildred."

Lifting her eyebrows, she greeted him with "Your wife is on the line."

"My wife?" A smile lifted unbidden to his face, as it always did when he thought of Letty.

"She said you weren't answering your cell."

Instinctively, Darius put his hand to his trouser pocket. It was empty. He must have left it in the car.

"Mrs. Kyrillos sounds pretty stressed." His executive assistant, usually stern and no-nonsense, gave him a rare smile. "She said it's urgent."

Letty never called him at work. His smile changed to a dazed grin. There could be only one reason she'd call now, so close to her due date!

"I'll take it in my office," he said joyfully and rushed inside, shutting the door behind him. He snatched up the phone. "Letty? Is it the baby? Are you in labor?"

His wife's voice sounded strangely flat. "No."

"Mildred said it was urgent—"

"It is urgent. I'm leaving you. I'm filing for divorce."

For a long moment he just gripped the phone, that foolish grin still on his face, as he tried to comprehend her words. Then the smile fell away.

"What are you talking about? Is this some kind of joke?"

"No."

He took a deep breath. "I've read about pregnancy hormones…"

Anger suddenly swelled from the other end of the line.

"Pregnancy hormones? *Pregnancy hormones?* I'm divorcing you because you lied to me. You've been lying for months! My father is dying and you never told me!"

Darius's heart was suddenly in his throat.

"How did you find out?" he whispered.

"Mrs. Pollifax couldn't understand how I could be such a heartless daughter to just let my father die alone. Don't worry. I've let her know that the heartless one is you."

He looked up, past his desk to the window overlooking the southern tip of Manhattan, and the Atlantic beyond it. Outside, rain fell in the gray November morning.

He licked his lips and tried, "Letty, I don't blame you for being upset—"

"Upset? No. I'm not upset." She paused. "I'm happy."

That was so obviously not true he had no idea how to react. "If you'll just give me a chance to explain."

"You already explained to me, long ago, that you wouldn't love me. That love was for children. You told me. I just didn't listen," she said softly. "Now I really, truly get it. And I want you out of my life for good."

"No—"

"I've brought my father to Fairholme."

Gripping the phone, he nearly staggered back. "Howard Spencer—in my house?"

"Yes." Her voice was ice-cold. "I'm not leaving him in the hospital, surrounded by strangers. He's going to spend his last days surrounded by love, in the home where he was married to my mother."

"It's not just your decision. I bought that house and…" He stopped himself, realizing how pompous he sounded. But it was too late.

"Right." Her voice was a sneer. "Because money makes the man. You think you can buy your way through life. That's what you do, isn't it? Buy things. You bought my virginity, and ever since, you've kept buying me. With marriage. With money. You didn't realize it was never your money I wanted." Her voice suddenly broke to a whisper. "It was you, Darius. My dream of you. The amazing boy you were." She took a breath. "The man I actually thought you still were, deep down inside."

"I'm still that man," he said tightly. "I was going to tell you. I just didn't want you upset…"

"Upset by my father dying!"

Darius flinched at the derision in her voice. "Perhaps I made a bad decision, but I was trying to look after you."

"And you assumed I would forgive you."

He felt shaken. "Forgiveness is what you do."

She gave a hard laugh. "How convenient for you. Only the idiots who love you have to forgive. But since you never love anyone, you never have to worry about that. You're free to hurt whomever you please."

She didn't sound like his wife at all, the kindhearted woman who greeted him every day with kisses, who gave so much of herself and asked for very little in return.

Except for him to forgive her father, Darius realized. That was the one thing she'd actually asked for. And the one thing he'd refused, again and again.

He, who was never afraid of anything, felt the first stirrings of real fear. "If you'll just listen to me—"

"I've had suitcases boxed up for you. Collins is taking them to your penthouse in Midtown. Don't worry. I won't stay here forever. You can have Fairholme back after…" Her voice was suddenly unsteady. "After. I don't want anything from you in our divorce. The baby and I will be leaving New York."

"You can't be serious."

"Poppy Alexander lives in Los Angeles now. She offered me a job a while back. I told her no. Now I'm going to say yes."

"No."

"Try and stop me. Just try." He could hear the ragged gasp of her breath. "You called my dad a monster. You're the real monster, Darius. Because you know what it was like to have your father die alone. That was the reason for all your vengeance and rage, wasn't it? That was the big reason you wouldn't let me see my dad. Well, you know what? My dad nearly died alone, too. Because of you."

The pang of fear became sharper, piercing down his spine. He licked his lips. "Letty—"

"Stay away from us," she said in a low voice. "I never want to see you again. Better that our son has no father at all than a heartless one like you."

The line went dead. He stared down at the phone in his hand.

Numb with shock, Darius raised his head. He looked blankly around his office, still decorated with his wife's sweet touches. A photo of them on their Greek honeymoon. A sonogram picture of their baby. He stared in bewilderment at the bright blue jeweler's bag on his desk. The push present for his wife, the emerald earrings once owned by a queen that he'd bought to express his appreciation and joy.

Above him, he could hear the rain falling heavily against the roof. Loud. Like a child's rattle.

And felt totally alone.

He'd known this would happen. Known if he ever lowered his guard and let himself care, he would get kicked in the teeth. Teeth? He felt like his guts had just been ripped out. For a second, he felt only that physical pain, like the flash of lightning before thunder.

Then the emotional impact reached his heart, and he had to lean one hand on his desk to keep his balance. The pain he felt then was almost more than he could bear.

Standing in his office, in the place he'd been happily whistling a lullaby just moments before, anguish and rage rushed through him. Throwing out his arm, he savagely knocked the jewelry bag to the ground.

Suddenly, he could almost understand why Howard Spencer had turned criminal when he'd lost his wife. Because Darius suddenly wanted to set fire to everything in his life, to burn it all down.

Slowly, as if he'd gained fifty years, he walked out of his office.

"Everything all right, sir?" Mildred Harrison said serenely from her desk. "Are you headed to the hospital for Mrs. Kyrillos?"

Mrs. Kyrillos. He almost laughed at the name. She'd never been his wife, not really. How could she, when she'd seen through him from the start?

You always said a man could be measured by his money.

He looked slowly around the bustling office loft, with its exposed brick walls, its high ceilings, the open spaces full of employees busily working on computers or taking their breaks at the foosball table. He said softly, "No."

His executive assistant frowned. "Sir?"

"I don't want it anymore." Darius looked at her. "Take the company. You can have it. I'm done."

And he left without looking back.

He spent the afternoon in one of Manhattan's old dive bars, trying to get drunk. He could have called Santiago Velazquez or Kassius Black, but they weren't exactly the kind of friends who shared confidences and feelings. Darius had only really done that with Letty. He told himself Scotch would keep him company now.

It didn't.

Finally he gave up. He was alone. He would always be alone. Time to accept it.

Dropped off by the taxi, Darius came home late that night to his dark penthouse. All the bright lights of Manhattan sparkled through the floor-to-ceiling windows. He saw nothing but darkness and shadows.

And three expensive suitcases left in his foyer. Suitcases Letty had packed for him when she'd taken his measure, found him completely lacking and tossed him out of their family home.

You think you can buy your way through life. That's what you do, isn't it? Buy things.

Slowly, Darius looked around the stark, impersonal penthouse at the sparse, expensive furniture. Everything was black and white. He'd bought this place two years ago, as a trophy to show how far he'd come from the poverty-stricken village boy he'd once been. A trophy to prove to himself that Letitia Spencer had made a fatal error the day she'd decided he wasn't good enough to marry.

This penthouse was not his home.

His home was Fairholme.

Darius closed his eyes, thinking of the windswept ocean-front manor with its wide windows over the Great South Bay and the Atlantic beyond. The roses, fields and beach. The sun-drenched meadow where he'd taught Letty to dance. Where he'd first learned to love.

Letty.

He opened his eyes with a slow intake of breath.

Letty was his home.

Even during their brief marriage, he'd experienced happiness he'd never known before. The comfort and love of having a wife who put him first, who waited for him every night, who kissed him with such passion. Who slept warm and willing beside him every night in bed.

More than that. She'd reminded him who he'd once been.

You didn't realize it was never your money I wanted. It was you, Darius. My dream of you. The amazing boy you were. The man I actually thought you still were, deep down inside.

Numbly, he looked out the two-story-high windows that overlooked the twinkling lights of the city.

Letty was always determined to protect those she loved.

Now she was trying to protect their child from him. Just as he'd once tried to protect Letty from her father.

You called my dad a monster. You're the real monster.

He leaned his forehead against the cold window glass.

Howard Spencer had been a good man once. He'd been a good employer to Darius's father and kind to everyone, including the scared eleven-year-old boy newly arrived from Greece. Then he'd changed after he'd lost his beloved wife.

What was Darius's excuse?

He took a deep breath, looking out bleakly into the night. Why had he been so determined to wreak vengeance on her father? So determined that he hadn't even cared how badly it might hurt Letty as collateral damage?

He should have told her the truth from the start.

He should have taken her in his arms. He should have fallen to his knees. He should have told her he was sorry, and that he'd do whatever it took to make it right.

Why hadn't he?

What the hell was wrong with him?

Darius had convinced himself he was justified for his actions, because he blamed Howard Spencer for his father's early, unhappy death.

Letty was right. He was a liar. And he'd lied to himself worst of all.

The truth was, deep in his heart, there had always been only one person Darius truly blamed for his father's death, and it had been too painful for him to face till now.

Himself.

He closed his eyes as a memory that he'd pushed away for over a decade pummeled him. But today, he could no longer resist the waves of guilt and shame as he remembered.

Eugenios had called Darius in the middle of the day.

"I've lost everything, son." His Greek father, usually so distant and gruff, had sounded lost, bewildered. "I just got a certified letter. It says all my life savings—everything I invested with Mr. Spencer—it's all gone."

Darius had been busy working in his first rented office, a windowless Manhattan basement. He'd only gotten three hours of sleep the night before. It was the first time the two men had talked in months, since Letty had dumped him and caused Eugenios to be fired and tossed from Fairholme. Just hearing his voice that day had reminded Darius of everything he was trying so hard to forget. A lifetime of resentment had exploded.

"I guess that pays you back for all your loyalty to Spencer, huh, Dad? All those years when you put him first, even over your own family."

Darius had been so young, so self-righteous. It made him feel sick now to remember it.

"That was my job." His father's voice had trembled. "I wanted to make sure I never lost a job again. Never felt again like I did that awful day we found you on the doorstep..."

The awful day they found him? Darius's hurt and anger blocked out the rest of his father's words as Eugenios continued feebly, "I had no money. No job. I couldn't let my family starve. You don't know what that does to a man, to have nothing..."

It was the most his father had ever spoken to him. And Darius's cold reply had haunted him ever since.

"So you had nothing then, huh, Dad? Well, guess what? You have nothing now. You ignored me my whole childhood for nothing. You have nothing. You *are* nothing."

He'd hung up the phone.

An hour later, his father had quietly died of a heart attack in his Queens apartment, sinking to his kitchen floor, where he was found later by a neighbor.

Darius's hands tightened to fists against the window.

His father had never been demonstrative. In Darius's

childhood, there had been no hugs and very little praise. Even the attention of criticism was rare.

But Darius and his grandmother hadn't starved. Eugenios had provided for them. He'd taught his work ethic by example. He'd worked hard, trying to give his son a better life.

And after all his years of stoically supporting them, after he'd lost his job and money, Darius had scorned him.

Remembering it now, he felt agonizing shame.

He hadn't wanted to remember the last words he'd spoken to his proud Greek father. So instead he'd sought vengeance on Howard Spencer, carefully blaming him alone.

Darius had thought if he never loved anyone, he'd never feel pain; and if he was rich, he'd be happy.

Look at me now, he thought bitterly, surveying the elegant penthouse. Surrounded by money. And never more alone.

He missed Letty.

Craved her desperately.

He loved her.

Darius looked up in shock.

He'd never stopped loving her.

All these years, he'd tried to pretend he didn't. Tried to control her, to possess her, to pretend he didn't care. He'd hidden his love away like a coward, afraid of the pain and shame of possible loss, while Letty let her love shine for all the world to see.

He'd thought Letty weak? He took a shuddering breath. She was the strongest person he knew. She'd offered him loyalty, kindness, self-sacrifice. She'd offered him every bit of her heart and soul. And in return, he'd offered her money.

Darius clawed back his hair. She was right. He'd tried to buy her. But money didn't make the man.

Love did.

Darius loved her. He was completely, wildly in love with

Letty. He wanted to be her husband. To live with her. To raise their baby. To be happy. To be home.

His eyes narrowed.

But how? How could he show her he had more to offer? How could he convince her to forgive him?

Forgiveness. His lips twisted with the bitter irony. The very thing he'd refused to give her all these months, he would now be begging for...

But for her, he'd do anything. He set his jaw. With the same total focus he'd built his empire, he would win back his wife.

Over the next month, he tried everything.

He respected her demand that he stay away from her, even after his friend Velazquez sent him a link to a birth announcement, and he saw his son had been safely born, weighing seven pounds and fourteen ounces. Both mother and baby were doing well.

Darius had jumped up, overwhelmed with the need to go see them in the hospital, to hold them in his arms.

But he knew bursting into her room against her express wishes would have only made things worse, not better. So he restrained himself, though it took all his self-control. He cleaned out a flower shop and sent all the flowers and toys and gifts to her maternity suite at the hospital. Anonymously.

Then he'd waited hopefully.

He'd found out later that she'd immediately forwarded all the flowers, toys and gifts straight to the sick children's ward.

Well played, he'd thought with a sigh. But he wasn't done. He'd contacted Mildred and she'd sent him via courier the jewelry bag he'd left in his office. He'd sent it to Fairholme, again anonymously.

A few days later he received a thank-you card from Mrs. Pollifax, stating that the earrings had been sold and the money donated to the housekeeper's favorite charity, an animal shelter on Long Island.

He'd ground his teeth, but doggedly kept trying. Over the next week, he sent gifts addressed to Letty. He sent a card congratulating her on the baby. On Thanksgiving, he even had ten pies from her favorite bakery delivered to her at Fairholme.

Pies she immediately forwarded to a homeless shelter.

As the rain of November changed to the snows of December, Darius's confidence started to wane. Once, in a moment of weakness, he drove by Fairholme late at night, past the closed gate.

But she was right. He couldn't even see the house.

After the pie incident, Darius gave up sending gifts. When she continued to refuse his calls, he stopped those, too. He kept writing heartfelt letters, and for a few weeks, he was hopeful, until they were all returned at once, unopened.

His baby son was now four weeks old. The thought made him sick with grief. Darius hadn't seen him. Hadn't held him. He didn't even know his name.

His wife wanted to divorce him. His son didn't have a father. Darius felt like a failure.

In the past, he would have taken his sense of grief and powerlessness and hired the most vicious, shark-infested law firm in Manhattan to punish her, to file for full custody.

But he didn't want that.

He wanted her.

He wanted his family back.

Finally, as Christmas approached, he knew he was out of ideas. He had only one card left to play. But when he went to see his lawyer, the man's jaw dropped.

"If you do this, Mr. Kyrillos, in my opinion you're a fool."

He was right. Darius was a fool. Because this was his last desperate hope.

But was he brave enough to actually go through with it? Could he jump off that cliff, and take a gamble that would either win him back the woman he loved, or cost him literally everything?

The afternoon of Christmas Eve Darius got the package from his lawyer. He was holding it in his hands, pacing his penthouse apartment like a trapped animal when his phone rang. Lifting it from his pocket, he saw the number from Fairholme.

His heart started thudding frantically. He snatched it up so fast he almost dropped it before he placed it against his ear. "Letty?"

But it wasn't his wife. Instead, the voice on the line belonged to the last person he'd ever imagined would call him.

CHAPTER ELEVEN

"It's your very first Christmas," Letty crooned to her tiny baby, walking him through Fairholme's great hall. She was already dressed for Christmas Eve dinner in a long scarlet velvet dress and soft kid leather bootees. She'd dressed her newborn son in an adorable little Santa outfit.

She'd asked Mrs. Pollifax to make all her father's holiday favorites, ham, plum pudding, potatoes, in hopes of tempting him to eat more than his usual scant bites. They'd even brought the dining table into the great hall, beside the big stone fireplace, so they could have dinner beneath the enormous Christmas tree.

Letty wanted this Christmas to be perfect. Because she knew it would be her father's last. The doctor had said yesterday that Howard's body was failing rapidly. It would likely be only days now.

Her heart twisted with grief. Her only comfort was that she'd tried her best to make his last few weeks special.

A lump rose in Letty's throat as she looked up at the two-story-high tree, decorated with sparkling lights and a mix of ornaments, old and new. Some of them Letty had treasured since childhood. And now they were back here, where they belonged. Funny to think she had Darius to thank for that. If he hadn't found her in Brooklyn and stopped her from taking that desperate bus ride out of the city, the ornaments would have been long lost to a junk dealer or the landfill.

Without him, she wouldn't be here now. Her father couldn't have come to Fairholme for his last Christmas, nor would her baby be here for his first one. It was because of Darius.

She missed him. No matter how much she denied it. No matter how she tried not to.

Every time some thoughtful gift had arrived at the house, she'd pictured how her father had looked in the hospital, so pale and alone. She'd remembered how Darius had taken her love for granted, and selfishly lied. She'd told herself she was done loving someone who could never love her back.

But as the gifts tapered off, and the phone calls stopped, and the letters stopped arriving in the mail, she hadn't felt triumphant. At all.

"I hate him," she said aloud. "I never want to see him again." She wasn't sure she sounded convincing, even to her own ears. So turning to her son, she held out one of the homemade ornaments. "Look!"

"Gah," the baby replied, waving his little hands unsteadily.

"You're so smart!" She let him feel the soft fabric of the dove against his cheek, then put it back on the tree before he tried to eat it. "Your grandma Constance made that," she said softly. "I just wish she could have met you."

Her six-week-old baby smiled back, Letty would swear he did, even though her father continued to rather annoyingly claim it was only gas. Letty knew her own baby, didn't she?

Even though Darius didn't.

The thought caused an unpleasant jolt. She'd thought she was doing the right thing to exclude him. She couldn't allow such a heartless man near her baby. Even if he *was* the father.

But Darius hadn't even laid eyes on their baby, or held him, or heard the sweet gurgle of his voice or his angry cry when he wasn't fed fast enough. Darius had already missed so much. Six weeks of sleepless nights, of exhaustion and confusion.

But also six weeks of getting to know this brand-new little person. From the moment her son had been placed in her arms at the hospital, Letty had felt her heart expand in a way she'd never known before.

Darius didn't know that feeling. He didn't know his son at all. Because of her actions.

Two weeks ago, her baby had been irritable and sleepless at midnight, so she'd wrapped him in a warm blanket and put him in the stroller to walk him up and down the long driveway, behind the gate. Then she'd seen a dark sports car driving slowly by.

Darius! She'd practically run to the gate, panting as she pushed the stroller ahead of her. But by the time she reached the gate, the car was long gone. For long moments she stared through the bars of the gate, looking bleakly down the dark, empty road, hearing only the waves crashing down on the shore. And she'd realized for the first time how empty the house felt without him, even with her father and her baby and all the household staff. She missed him.

No. I don't, she told herself desperately. And if she hadn't filed for divorce yet or hired an attorney, that was only because she just hadn't had the time. Taking care of a newborn, caring for her father and decorating for Christmas would be enough to keep anyone busy, wouldn't it?

Letty's lips twisted downward. She'd said things that would never be forgiven. She'd made her choice clear. She'd used his every olive branch as a stick to stab him with.

That car probably hadn't even been his. He'd probably moved on entirely, and if she ever heard from him again, it would be only via his lawyer, demanding custody. She stiffened at the thought.

Carrying her baby up to the nursery, she fed him, rocking him for nearly an hour in the glider until he slept and she was nearly asleep herself. She smiled down at his sweet little face. His cheeks were already growing chubby. Tucking him gently in his crib for his late afternoon nap, she turned on the baby monitor and crept out of the darkened nursery.

She closed the door softly behind her. Light from the leaded glass windows reflected against the glossy hardwood floors and oak paneling of the second-floor hallway, resting with a soft haze on an old framed family photo on the wall. She looked at her own chubby face when she'd been just a toddler with two parents beaming behind her.

Trying to ignore the ache in her throat, Letty started to turn toward the stairs. Then she heard low male voices coming from down the hall.

Her father's bedroom was the nicest and biggest, the room he'd once shared with her mother, with a view of the sea. He rarely got up from his bed anymore, except when Letty managed to cajole him into his wheelchair and take him down in the elevator for a stroll around the winter garden, or to sit in a comfortable spot near the fire, beneath the Christmas tree, as the baby lay nearby.

But the male voice Letty heard talking to her father didn't sound like Paul, his nurse. Who was it? Frowning, she drew closer.

"Yes," she heard her father say, his voice a little slurred. "Always a good kid."

"I can't believe you're saying that, after everything."

Hearing the visitor's voice, low and clear, Letty's knees went weak outside her father's door. What was Darius doing here? How had he gotten into Fairholme?

"You weren't so bad. Just prickly, like your father. Eugenios was the best employee I ever had. We used to talk about you. He loved you."

"He had a funny way of showing it." Her husband's voice wasn't bitter, just matter-of-fact.

Howard gave a laugh that ended in a wheeze. "In our generation, fathers showed love differently."

"Yet Letty always knew you loved her."

"I didn't grow up with your father's fears." Howard paused. "From the age of fifteen, he was your grandmother's sole support. When you came along, he lost any chance of a job in Greece."

"I know."

"His greatest fear was of not providing for you." Coughing a laugh, Howard added, "Maybe if I'd been a little more careful about that myself, I wouldn't have left my daughter destitute while I spent years in prison. It's only because of you that we're back home now. That's why I called. I'm grateful."

Darius's voice was suddenly urgent. "Then convince Letty to stay."

"Stay? Where would she go?"

"She says as soon as you're dead, she's leaving New York."

Howard gave a low laugh. "That sounds like her. Foolish as her old man. Can't see the love right in front of her eyes, has to flee her own happiness because she's afraid. Actually, now that I think about it, she sounds like you."

Letty's heart was pounding as she leaned against the oak-paneled wall beside the open door, holding absolutely still as she listened intently.

Silence. Then Darius said in a voice so low she almost couldn't hear, "I'm sorry I blamed you for my father's death all these years. The truth is, the person I really hated was myself. I said something terrible to my dad right before he died. I'll never forgive myself."

"Whatever it was," Howard said simply, "your father forgave you long ago. He knew you loved him. Just as he loved you. He was proud of you, Darius. And seeing that you were brave enough to come here today, I am, too."

Her father was proud of the man who'd treated her so

badly, who'd lied to her? Letty sucked in her breath with an astonished little squeak.

There was a pause.

"Letty," her father said drily, "I know you're there. Come in."

Her heart was in her throat. She wanted to flee but knew she'd only look foolish and cowardly. Lifting her chin, she went into her father's room.

His bedroom was full of light from the bay window. Her father was stretched out beneath the blankets, propped up by pillows, his nightstand covered with pill bottles. His gaunt face smiled up at her weakly, his eyes glowing with love.

Then, with a deep breath, Letty looked at the man standing beside the bed.

Tall and broad-shouldered and alive, Darius seemed to radiate power. For a moment, her eyes devoured his image. He was dressed simply in a dark shirt, dark jeans. His hands lifted, then fell to his sides as he looked at her, as if he had to physically restrain himself from touching her. But his dark eyes seared her. Their heartbreak and yearning cut her to the bone.

Her body reacted involuntarily, stumbling back as her heart pounded with emotion. Fury. Regret. Longing...

"What are you doing here?" she whispered.

"He's here to meet his son," her father said.

She whirled on her father, feeling betrayed. "Dad!"

"And I want him to stay for Christmas Eve dinner," he continued calmly.

She stared at him in shock. "No!"

Her father gave her a weakened version of his old charming smile. "Surely you wouldn't refuse your dying father his last Christmas wish?"

No. Of course she couldn't. She ground her teeth. "He kept me from you for two months!"

Her father stared her down. "Only a little longer than you've kept him from his son."

"I would like to meet him," Darius said quietly. "But if you don't want me around after that, I won't stay."

Trembling, she tossed her head defiantly. "Did he tell you the baby's name?"

"No."

"It's Howard." She lifted her chin, folding her arms. "Howard Eugenios Spencer."

To her shock, Darius didn't scowl or bluster. He didn't even flinch. He just looked at her with that same strange glow of longing in his eyes.

"That's not the name I would have chosen." Triumph surged through her as she waited for him to be sarcastic and show his true colors in front of her father. Instead, he just said quietly, "His last name should be Kyrillos."

Darius was upset only about the surname? Not about the fact that she'd named their precious baby son after her father—his hated enemy?

"Aren't you furious?" she said, dropping her arms in bewilderment.

His lips curved as he looked down at her father, then slowly shook his head. "Not as much as I used to be."

Darius came toward her. It took all Letty's willpower not to step back from him as he towered over her. It wasn't him she was afraid of, but herself. Her whole body was trembling with her own longing. Her need. She missed him.

But she couldn't. She'd made her choice! She wouldn't be married to a man who didn't love her!

"Please let me see my son," he said humbly. He bowed his head, as if waiting for her verdict.

"Let him," her father said.

Looking between the two men, she knew she was outnumbered. She snapped, "Fine."

Turning on her heel, she walked out. She didn't look

back to see if Darius was following her. Her hands were trembling.

All these weeks when she'd pushed him away, she'd pictured him as angry, arrogant, heartless. It was why she hadn't been tempted to open his letters—why would she, when she knew he'd only be yelling at her?

She'd never once imagined Darius looking at her the way he did now, with such heartbreaking need. But it wasn't just desire. He had an expression in his eyes that she hadn't seen since—

No! She wasn't going to let her own longing talk her into seeing things in his eyes that weren't there, things that didn't exist.

Pressing a finger to her lips, she quietly pushed open the nursery door and crept into the shadowy room, motioning for him to follow. Darius came in behind her.

Then, as they both stood over the crib, Letty made the mistake of looking at her husband when he saw their son for the very first time.

Darius's dark eyes turned fierce, almost bewildered with love when he looked at their sleeping baby. Tenderly, he reached out in the semidarkness and stroked his dark downy head as he slept.

"My son," he whispered. "My sweet boy."

A lump rose in her throat so huge it almost choked her. And she suddenly knew that Darius wasn't the only one who'd been heartless.

What had she done?

Blinded by furious grief at his lie about her father, Letty had actually kept Darius from his own firstborn son. *For six weeks.*

Anguish and regret rushed through her in a torrent of pain. Even if Darius could never love her, she had no doubt that he loved their baby. Especially as she watched him now, gently stroking their baby's small back through his

Santa onesie as the sleeping child gave a soft snuffle in the shadowy room.

She'd had no right to steal his child away.

"I'm sorry," she choked out. He looked up.

"You're sorry?"

Unable to speak for misery, she nodded.

Reaching out in the shadowy nursery, beneath the hazy colors of the goose girl fresco, Darius put his hand gently on Letty's shoulder, and she shuddered beneath his touch.

"Letty...there's something you should know."

Their eyes locked, and she saw something in his black eyes that made the world tremble beneath her feet.

Panic rushed through her heart. Seeing Darius make peace with her father, seeing him look so lovingly at their baby, had cracked open her soul and everything she hadn't wanted to feel had rushed in.

She'd painted him so badly in her mind. She'd called him a monster. And yes, he never should have lied about her father.

But when she'd said horrible things and threatened to take his child permanently away, he hadn't hired some awful lawyer to fight her. He'd done what she asked, and stayed away. Obviously at great emotional cost.

Now, she saw his sensual lips part, heard his hoarse intake of breath and knew whatever he was about to say would change her life forever. He was going to tell her he was done with her. She'd won. He'd given up. Now he wanted to talk like reasonable adults about sharing custody of their son.

She'd destroyed their marriage with her anger and pride. She'd told herself she'd rather be alone than married to a man who didn't love her. Now she suddenly couldn't bear to hear him speak the words that would end it...

"No," she choked out.

Turning, she fled the nursery. She ran down the hall, down the stairs, her heart pounding, gasping for breath.

She heard him coming down after her. "Letty!"

She didn't stop. Pushing off the stairs, she ran outside, into the snow.

Her mother's rose garden was barren in winter, nothing but thorny vines and dead leaves covered in a blanket of white. Letty's soft black boots stumbled forward, her long red dress dragging behind, scarlet against the snow.

But he swiftly caught her, roughly pushing her wrists against the outside wall of the greenhouse with its flash of exotic greenery behind the steamy glass. She struggled, but he wouldn't let go.

She felt his heat. His power. She felt the strength of her own longing for this man, whom she continued to love in the face of despair.

"Let me go," she cried.

"Forgive me," Darius choked out. He lowered his head against hers. She heard the heavy gasp of his breath. "You were right, Letty. About everything. I'm so sorry."

Her lips parted. She looked up at him in shock.

"*You're* sorry?" she whispered. "I kept you from our baby."

"You were right to kick me out of your life." He cupped her face in both his hands. "I blamed you and your father for so much. I blamed everyone but the person really at fault. Myself."

"Darius—"

"No." He held up his hand. "Let me say this. I don't know if I'll get another chance."

All around them in the silent white garden, soft snow began to fall from the lowering gray clouds. Letty's heart was suddenly in her throat. Now he was going to tell her that they were better off apart...

"You're right, Letty," he said in a low voice. "I did try

to buy you. I thought money was all I had to offer anyone. I thought I could selfishly claim your love, while being cowardly enough to protect my own heart. But I failed." He gave a low laugh. "The truth is, I failed long ago."

His dark eyes had a suspicious gleam. Surely Darius Kyrillos, the ruthless Greek billionaire, couldn't have tears in his eyes? No. It must be the cold winter wind, whipping against his skin.

"I loved you, Letty. It terrified me. My whole life, all I've ever known of love is loss. Losing you all those years ago almost destroyed me. I never wanted to feel like that again. So I buried my soul in ice. Then when I saw you again, when I first took you to my bed, everything changed. Against my will, the ice cracked. But even then I was afraid." Taking a deep breath, he lifted his eyes to hers. "I'm not afraid anymore."

"You're not?" she whispered, her heart falling.

With a little smile, he shook his head. He took her hand in his larger one. "Now I know the truth is that love never ends. Not real love. The love your father has for you and my father had for me. The love your parents had for each other." His hand tightened over hers as he said softly, "And even if you divorce me, Letty, even if you never want to see me again after tonight, I can still love you. And it won't bring me pain, but joy, because of everything you've brought to my life. You saved me. Made me feel again. Taught me to love again. Gave me a son." Stroking her cheek, he whispered, "No matter what happens, I will always be grateful. And love you."

His hand was warm over hers. With him so close, she didn't even feel the snow. Trembling, she whispered, "Darius…what are you saying?"

His jaw tightened. "If you still want to divorce me, you won't need a lawyer." He reached into his shirt pocket, where a single page was folded in quarters. "Here."

Opening the paper, she looked down at it numbly. She tried to read it, but the words jumbled together. "What's this?"

"Everything," he said quietly. "Fairholme. The jets. My stocks, bonds, bank accounts. It's all been transferred to your name. Everything I possess."

She gasped, then shook her head. "But you know money doesn't mean anything to me!"

"Yes, I know that." He looked at her. "But you know what it means to me."

Letty's eyes went wide.

Because she did know what Darius's fortune meant to him. It meant ten years of twenty-hour workdays and sleeping in basements. It meant working till he collapsed, day after day, with no time to relax or see friends. No time to even *have* friends. It meant borrowing money that he knew he'd have to pay back, even if his business failed. It meant taking terrifying risks and praying they would somehow pay off.

Those dreams had been fulfilled. Through work and will and luck, a poverty-stricken boy whose mother had abandoned him as a baby had built a multibillion-dollar empire.

This was what she now held in her hand.

"But I'm not just offering you my fortune, Letty," he said quietly. "I'm offering everything. My whole life. Everything I've been. Everything I am." Lifting her hand, he pressed it against his rough cheek and whispered, "I offer you my heart."

Letty realized she was crying.

"I love you, Letitia Spencer Kyrillos," he said hoarsely. "I know I've lost your love, your trust. But I'll do everything I can to regain your devotion. Even if it takes me a hundred years, I'll never…"

"Stop." Violently, she pushed the paper against his chest. When he wouldn't take it, it fell to the snow.

"Letty," he choked out, his dark eyes filled with misery.

"I don't want it." She lifted her hand to his scratchy cheek, rough and unshaven. Reaching her other arm around his shoulders, she whispered, "I just want you, Darius."

The joy that lit up his dark eyes was brighter than the sun.

"I don't deserve you."

"I'm not exactly perfect myself."

He immediately began protesting that she was, in fact, perfect in every way.

"It doesn't matter." Smiling, she reached up on her toes to kiss him, whispering, "We can just love each other, flaws and all."

Holding her tight, he kissed her passionately against the greenhouse, with the hot wet jungle behind the glass, as they embraced in the snow-swept bare garden. They kissed each other in a private vow that would endure all the future days of sunshine and snow, good times and bad, all the laughter and anger and pleasure and forgiveness until death.

Their love was meant to be. It was fate. *Moíra.*

They clung to each other until he broke apart with a guilty laugh.

"Ah, Letty, I'll never be perfect, that's for sure," Darius murmured, smiling down at her through his tears. "But there's one thing you should know..." Cupping her cheek, lightly drawing away the cold wet tendrils of her hair that had stuck to her skin, he whispered, "For you, I intend to spend the rest of my life trying."

Spring came early to Fairholme.

Darius had a bounce in his step as he came into the house that afternoon with a bouquet of flowers. He'd had to work on a Saturday because it was crunch time developing the new website. But he was hoping the flowers would make her forgive the fact that he'd missed their new Saturday morning family tradition of waffles and bacon.

Darius had started that tradition himself, in the weeks he'd taken to focus only on Letty and their beloved son, whom they'd nicknamed Howie. After that, encouraged by Letty, he'd sheepishly called Mildred and apologized, then asked if there was any way she could try to reassemble his team at the office.

"The office is still in fine fettle," she'd replied crisply. "I've been running everything just as you requested. I knew whatever you were going through you'd soon come to your senses. I haven't worked for you all these years for nothing."

He choked out a laugh, then said with real gratitude, "What would I do without you?"

"You'll find out next summer," she'd said firmly, "when you send my husband and me on a four-week first-class cruise through Asia. It's already booked."

Darius grinned to himself, remembering. He was grateful to Mildred. Grateful to all the people around him, his employees and most of all his family, who saw through all his flaws but were somehow willing to put up with him anyway.

Money didn't make the man. He knew that now. What made a man was what he did with his life. With his time. With his heart.

His father-in-law had died in January, surrounded by family, with a smile on his drawn face. Right before he died, his eyes suddenly glowed with joy as he breathed, "Oh. There you are…"

"He saw my mother before he died," Letty told Darius afterward, her beautiful face sparkling with tears. "How can I even be sad, when I know they're together?"

Darius wasn't so sure, but who was he to say? Love could work miracles. He was living proof of that.

Now he looked around his home with deep contentment. The oak floors gleamed and fresh-cut flowers from the greenhouse filled all the vases.

Fairholme was about to be invaded by more of the Kyrillos family. He'd sent his private plane to Heraklios, and tomorrow, Theia Ioanna, along with a few cousins, would arrive for a monthlong visit. His great-aunt's desire to meet her great-great-nephew had finally overcome her fear of flying.

He relished the thought of having his extended family here. Heaven knew Fairholme had plenty of room.

Love was everywhere. Love was everything. His son was only five months old, but he'd already collected toys from all the people who loved him around the globe. His wife did that, he thought. With her great heart, she brought everyone together with her kindness and loyalty. She was the center of Darius's world.

"Letty!" he called, holding the flowers tightly.

"She's outside, Mr. Kyrillos," the housekeeper called from the kitchen. "The weather's so fine, she and the baby went for a picnic in the meadow."

Dropping his computer bag, he went outside, past the garden, where even though the air was cool beneath the sunshine, tulips and daffodils were starting to bloom. He walked the path through the softly waving grass until he reached the meadow where he'd first taught his wife to dance. Where she'd first taught him to dream.

He stopped.

The sky was a vivid blue, the meadow the rich gold-green of spring, and in the distance, he could see the ocean. He saw Letty's beautiful face, alight with joy, as she sang their five-month-old baby a song in Greek, swinging him gently in her arms as he giggled and shrieked with happiness. Behind them on the hillside, a blanket was covered with a picnic basket, teething toys and that well-worn book about the bunny rabbit. But now, as always, Letty was dancing. Letty was singing.

Letty was love.

Darius stared at them, and for a moment the image caught at his heart, as he wondered what he'd ever done to deserve such happiness.

Then, quickening his steps, he raced to join them.

* * * * *

*If you enjoyed this story, take a look at
Jennie Lucas's other great reads!*
BABY OF HIS REVENGE
A RING FOR VINCENZO'S HEIR
Available now!

Also look out for more
ONE NIGHT WITH CONSEQUENCES *stories*
A CHILD CLAIMED BY GOLD
by Rachael Thomas
THE GUARDIAN'S VIRGIN WARD
by Caitlin Crews
CLAIMING HIS CHRISTMAS CONSEQUENCE
by Michelle Smart
Available now!

'So we're still, technically speaking, man and wife,' Xanthe clarified.

'You had better be kidding me!'

'I've come all the way from London this morning to get you to sign the newly issued papers so we can fix this nightmare as fast as is humanly possible. So, no, I'm not kidding.'

She flicked through the document until she got to the signature page, which she had already signed, frustrated when her fingers wouldn't stop trembling. She could smell him—the scent that was uniquely Dane's—clean and male and far too enticing.

She drew back. Too late. She'd already ingested a lungful, detecting expensive cedarwood soap now, instead of the supermarket brand he had once used.

'Once you've signed here.' She pointed to the signature line. 'Our problem will be solved and I can guarantee never to darken your door again.'

She whipped a gold pen out of the briefcase, stabbed the button at the top and thrust it towards him like a dagger.

USA TODAY bestselling author **Heidi Rice** lives in London, England. She is married with two teenage sons—which gives her rather too much of an insight into the male psyche—and also works as a film journalist. She adores her job, which involves getting swept up in a world of high emotions, sensual excitement, funny, feisty women, sexy, tortured men and glamorous locations where laundry doesn't exist. Once she turns off her computer she often does chores—usually involving laundry!

Books by Heidi Rice

Beach Bar Baby
Maid of Dishonour
One Night, So Pregnant!
Unfinished Business with the Duke
Public Affair, Secretly Expecting
Hot-Shot Tycoon, Indecent Proposal
Pleasure, Pregnancy and a Proposition

Visit the Author Profile page at
millsandboon.co.uk for more titles.

VOWS THEY CAN'T ESCAPE

BY
HEIDI RICE

First Published in Great Britain 2017
By Mills & Boon, an imprint of HarperCollins*Publishers*
1 London Bridge Street, London, SE1 9GF

© 2017 Heidi Rice

ISBN: 978-0-263-92510-4

VOWS THEY CAN'T ESCAPE

With thanks to my cousin Susan,
who suggested I write a romance with a female CEO
as the heroine, my best writing mate Abby Green,
who kept telling me to write a classic Modern,
my best mate Catri, who plotted this with me on the train
back from Kilkenny Shakespeare Festival, and to
Sarah Hornby of the Royal Thames Yacht Club,
who explained why having my hero and heroine
spend a night below decks while sailing a yacht together
round the Caribbean probably wasn't a good idea!

CHAPTER ONE

XANTHE CARMICHAEL STRODE into the gleaming steel-and-glass lobby of the twenty-six-storey office block housing Redmond Design Studios on Manhattan's West Side, satisfied that the machine-gun taps of her heels against the polished stone flooring said exactly what she wanted them to say.

Watch out, boys, woman scorned on the warpath.

Ten years after Dane Redmond had abandoned her in a seedy motel room on the outskirts of Boston, she was ready to bring the final curtain crashing down on their brief and catastrophic liaison.

So the flush that had leaked into her cheeks despite the building's overefficient air conditioning and the bottomless pit opening up in her stomach could take a hike.

After a six-hour flight from Heathrow, spent power-napping in the soulless comfort of Business Class, and two days and nights figuring out how she was going to deal with the unexploded bomb the head of her legal team, Bill Spencer, had dropped at her feet on Wednesday afternoon, she was ready for any eventuality.

Whatever Dane Redmond had once meant to her seventeen-year-old self, the potentially disastrous situation Bill had uncovered wasn't personal any more—it was business. And *nothing* got in the way of her business.

Carmichael's, the two-hundred-year-old shipping company which had been in her family for four generations, was the only thing that mattered to her now. And she would do anything to protect it and her new position as the majority shareholder and CEO.

'Hi, I'm Ms Sanders, from London, England,' she said to the immaculately dressed woman at reception, giving the false name she'd instructed her PA to use when setting up this meeting. However confident she felt, she was not about to give a bare-knuckle fighter like Dane a heads-up. 'I have an appointment with Mr Redmond to discuss a commission.'

The woman sent her a smile as immaculate as her appearance. 'It's great to meet you, Ms Sanders.' She tapped the screen in front of her and picked up the phone. 'If you'd like to take a seat, Mr Redmond's assistant, Mel Mathews, will be down in a few minutes to escort you to the eighteenth floor.'

Xanthe's heartbeat thudded against her collarbone as she recrossed the lobby under the life-size model of a huge wing sail catamaran suspended from the ceiling. A polished brass plaque announced that the boat had won Redmond Design a prestigious sailing trophy twice in a row.

She resisted the urge to chew off the lipstick she'd applied in the cab ride from JFK.

Bill's bombshell would have been less problematic if Dane had still been the boy her father had so easily dismissed as 'a trailer trash wharf rat with no class and fewer prospects,' but she refused to be cowed by Dane's phenomenal success over the last decade.

She was here to show him who he was dealing with.

But, as she took in the ostentatious design of Dane's new headquarters in New York's uber-hip Meatpacking District, the awe-inspiring view of the Hudson River from the lobby's third-floor aspect and that beast of a boat, she had to concede the meteoric rise of his business and his position as one of the world's premier sailing boat designers didn't surprise her.

He'd always been smart and ambitious—a natural-born sailor more at home on water than dry land—which was exactly why her father's estate manager had hired him that summer in Martha's Vineyard to run routine maintenance on the small fleet of two yachts and a pocket cruiser her father kept at their holiday home.

Running routine maintenance on Charles Carmichael's impressionable, naive daughter had been done on his own time.

No one had ever been able to fault Dane's work ethic.

Xanthe's thigh muscles trembled at the disturbingly vivid memory of blunt fingers trailing across sensitive skin, but she didn't break stride.

All that energy and purpose had drawn her to him like a heat-seeking missile. That and the superpower they'd discovered together—his unique ability to lick her to a scream-your-lungs-out orgasm in sixty seconds or less.

She propped her briefcase on a coffee table and sank into one of the leather chairs lining the lobby.

Whoa, Xan. Do not think about the superpower.

Crossing her legs, she squeezed her knees together, determined to halt the conflagration currently converging on the hotspot between her thighs. Even Dane's superpower would never be enough to compensate for the pain he'd caused.

She hid the unsettling thought behind a tight smile as a thirtysomething woman headed in her direction across the ocean of polished stone. Grabbing the briefcase containing the documents she had flown three thousand miles to deliver, Xanthe stood up, glad when her thighs remained virtually quiver-free.

Dane Redmond's not the only badass in town. Not any more.

* * *

Xanthe was feeling less like a badass and more like a sacrificial lamb five minutes later, as the PA led her through a sea of hip and industrious young marketing people working on art boards and computers on the eighteenth floor. Even her machine-gun heel taps had been muffled by the industrial carpeting.

The adrenaline which had been pumping through her veins for forty-eight hours and keeping her upright slowed to a crawl as they approached the glass-walled corner office and the man within, silhouetted against the New Jersey shoreline. The jolt of recognition turned the bottomless pit in her stomach into a yawning chasm.

Broad shoulders and slim hips were elegantly attired in steel-grey trousers and a white shirt. But his imposing height, the muscle bulk revealed by the shirt's rolled-up sleeves, the dark buzz cut hugging the dome of his skull, and the tattoo that covered his left arm down to his elbow did nothing to disguise the wolf in expensively tailored clothing.

Sweat gathered between Xanthe's breasts and the powder-blue silk suit and peach camisole ensemble she'd chosen twelve hours ago in London, because it covered all the bases from confident to kick-ass, rubbed against her skin like sandpaper.

The internet hadn't done Dane Redmond justice. Because the memory of the few snatched images she'd found yesterday while preparing for this meeting was comprehensively failing to stop a boulder the size of an asteroid forming in her throat.

She forced one foot in front of the other as the PA tapped on the office door and led her into the wolf's den.

Brutally blue eyes locked on Xanthe's face.

A flicker of stunned disbelief softened his rugged features before his jaw went rigid, making the shallow dent in his chin twitch. The searing look had the thundering beat of Xanthe's heart dropping into that yawning chasm.

Had she actually kidded herself that age and money and success would have refined Dane—tamed him, even—or at the very least made him a lot less intense and intimidating? Because she'd been dead wrong. Either that or she'd just been struck by lightning.

'This is Ms Sanders from—'

'Leave us, Mel.' Dane interrupted the PA's introduction. 'And shut the door.'

The husky command had Xanthe's heartbeat galloping into her throat to party with the asteroid, reminding her of all the commands he'd once issued to her in the same he-who-shall-be-obeyed tone. And the humiliating speed with which she'd obeyed them.

'Relax, I won't hurt you. I swear.'

'Hold on tight. This is gonna be the ride of your life.'

'I take care of my own, Xan. That's non-negotiable.'

The door closed behind the dutiful PA with a hushed click.

Xanthe gripped the handle on her briefcase with enough force to crack a nail and lifted her chin, channelling the smouldering remains of her inner badass that had survived the lightning strike.

'Hello, Dane,' she said, glad when her voice remained relatively steady.

She would *not* be derailed by a physical reaction which was ten years out of date and nothing more than an inconvenient throwback to her youth. It would pass. Eventually.

'Hello, *Ms Sanders*.'

His thinly veiled contempt at her deception had outrage joining the riot of other emotions she was busy trying to suppress.

'If you've come to buy a boat, you're all out of luck.'

The searing gaze wandered down to her toes, the inso-

lent appraisal as infuriating as the fuses that flared to life
in every pulse point en route.

'I don't do business with spoilt little rich chicks.'

His gaze rose back to her face, having laid waste to
her composure.

'Especially ones I was once dumb enough to marry.'

CHAPTER TWO

Xanthe Carmichael.

Dane Redmond had just taken a sucker punch to the gut. And it was taking every ounce of his legendary control not to show it.

The girl who had haunted his dreams a lifetime ago—particularly all his wet dreams—and then become a star player in his nightmares. And now she had the balls to stand in his office—the place he'd built from the ground up after she'd kicked him to the kerb—as if she had a right to invade his life a second time.

She'd changed some from the girl he remembered—all trussed-up now in a snooty suit, looking chic and classy in those ice-pick heels. But there was enough of that girl left to force him to put his libido on lockdown.

She still had those wide, feline eyes. Their sultry slant hinting at the banked fires beneath, the translucent blue-green the vivid colour of the sea over the Barrier Reef. She had the same peaches-and-cream complexion, with the sprinkle of girlish freckles over her nose she hadn't quite managed to hide under a smooth mask of make-up. And that riot of red-gold hair, ruthlessly styled now in an updo, but for a few strands that had escaped to cling to her neck and draw his gaze to the coy hint of cleavage beneath her suit.

The flush high on her cheekbones and the glitter in her eyes made her look like a fairy queen who had swallowed a cockroach. But he knew she was worse than any siren sent to lure men to their destruction, with that stunning body and that butter-wouldn't-melt expression—and about as much freaking integrity as a sea serpent.

He curled his twitching fingers into his palms and braced his fists against the desk. Because part of him wanted to throw her over his knee and spank her until her butt was as red as her hair, and another part of him longed to throw her over his shoulder and take her somewhere dark and private, so he could rip off that damn suit and find the responsive girl beneath who had once begged him for release.

And each one of those impulses was as screwed-up as the other. Because she meant nothing to him now. Not a damn thing. And he'd sworn ten years ago, when he'd been lying on the road outside her father's vacation home in the Vineyard, with three busted ribs, more bruises than even his old man had given him on a bad day, his stomach hollow with grief and tight with anger and humiliation, that no woman would ever make such a jackass of him again.

'I'm here because we have a problem…' She hesitated, her lip trembling ever so slightly.

She was nervous. She ought to be.

'Which I'm here to solve.'

'How could *we* possibly have a problem?' he said, his voice deceptively mild. 'When *we* haven't seen each other in over a decade and I never wanted to see you again?'

She stiffened, the flush spreading down her neck to highlight the lush valley of her breasts.

'The feeling's mutual,' she said. The snotty tone was a surprise.

He buried his fists into his pants pockets. The last thin thread controlling his temper about to snap.

Where the heck did she get off, being pissed with him? *He'd* been the injured party in their two-second marriage. She'd flaunted herself, come on to him, had him panting after her like a dog that whole summer—hooked him like a prize tuna by promising to love, honour and obey him, no matter what. Then she'd run back to daddy at the first sign of trouble. Not that he'd been dumb enough to really believe those breathless promises. He'd learned when he was still a kid that love was just an empty sentiment. But he *had* been dumb enough to trust her.

And now she had the gall to turn up at *his* place, under a false name, expecting him to be polite and pretend what she'd done was okay.

Whatever her problem was, he wanted no part of it. But he'd let her play out this little drama before he slapped her down and kicked her the hell out of his life. For good this time.

Lifting her briefcase onto the table, Xanthe ignored the hostility radiating from the man in front of her. She flipped the locks, whipped out the divorce papers and slapped them on the desk.

Dane Redmond's caveman act was nothing new, but she was wise to it now. He'd been exactly the same as a nineteen-year-old. Taciturn and bossy and supremely arrogant. Once upon a time she'd found that wildly attractive—because once upon a time she'd believed that lurking beneath the caveman was a boy who'd needed the love she could lavish on him.

That had been her first mistake. Followed by too many others.

The vulnerable boy had never existed. And the caveman had never wanted what she had to offer.

Good thing, then, that this wasn't about him any more—it was about *her*. And what *she* wanted. Which was exactly what she was going to get.

Because no man bullied her now. Not her father, not the board of directors at Carmichael's and certainly not some overly ripped boat designer who thought he could boss her around just because she'd once been bewitched by his larger-than-average penis.

'The problem is...' She threw the papers onto the desk, cursing the tremor in her fingers at that sudden recollection of Dane fully aroused.

Do not think about him naked.

'My father's solicitor, Augustus Greaves, failed to file the paperwork for our divorce ten years ago.'

She delivered the news in a rush, to disguise any hint of culpability. It was not her fault Greaves had been an alcoholic.

'So we're still, technically speaking, man and wife.'

CHAPTER THREE

'YOU HAD BETTER be freaking kidding me!'

Dane looked so shocked Xanthe would have smiled if she hadn't been shaking quite so hard. That had certainly wiped the self-righteous glare off his face.

'I've come all the way from London to get you to sign these newly issued papers, so we can fix this nightmare as fast as is humanly possible. So, no, I'm not kidding.'

She flicked through the document until she got to the signature page, which she had already signed, frustrated because her fingers wouldn't stop trembling. She could smell him—that scent that was uniquely his, clean and male, and far too enticing.

She drew back. Too late. She'd already ingested a lungful, detecting expensive cedarwood soap instead of the supermarket brand he had once used.

'Once you've signed here—' she pointed to the signature line '—*our* problem will be solved and I can guarantee never to darken your door again.'

She whipped a gold pen out of the briefcase, stabbed the button at the top and thrust it towards him like a dagger.

He lifted his hands out of his pockets but didn't pick up the gauntlet.

'Like I'd be dumb enough to sign anything *you* put in front of me without checking it first...'

She ruthlessly controlled the snap of temper at his statement. And the wave of panic.

Stay calm. Be persuasive. Don't freak out.

She breathed in through her nose and out through her mouth, employing the technique she'd perfected during the last five years of handling Carmichael's board. As long as Dane never found out about the original terms of her father's will, nothing in the paperwork she'd handed him would clue him in to the *real* reason she'd come all this way. And why would he, when her father's will hadn't come into force until five years after Dane had abandoned her?

Unfortunately the memory of that day in her father's office, with her stomach cramping in shock and loss and disbelief as the executor recited the terms of the will, was not helping with her anxiety attack.

'Your father had hoped you would marry one of the candidates he suggested. His first preference was to leave forty-five per cent of Carmichael's stock to you and the controlling share to your spouse as the new CEO. As no such marriage was contracted at the time of his death, he has put the controlling share in trust, to be administered by the board until you complete a five-year probationary period as Carmichael's executive owner. If, after that period, they deem you a credible CEO, they can vote to allocate a further six per cent of the shares to you. If not, they can elect another CEO and leave the shares in trust.'

That deadline had passed a week ago. The board—no doubt against all her father's expectations—had voted in her favour. And then Bill had discovered his bombshell—that she had still technically been married to Dane at the time of her father's death and he could, therefore, sue for the controlling share in the company.

It might almost have been funny—that her father's lack of trust in her abilities might end up gifting 55 per cent of his company to a man he had despised—if it hadn't been more evidence that her father had never trusted her with Carmichael's.

She pushed the dispiriting thought to one side, and the echo of grief that came with it, as Dane punched a number into his smartphone.

Her father might have been old-fashioned and hopelessly traditional—an aristocratic Englishman who believed that no man who hadn't gone to Eton and Oxford could ever be a suitable husband for her—but he had loved her and had wanted the best for her. Once she got Dane to sign on the dotted line, thus eliminating any possible threat this paperwork error could present to her father's company—*her* company—she would finally have proved her commitment to Carmichael's was absolute.

'Jack? I've got something I want you to check out.' Dane beckoned to someone behind Xanthe as he spoke into the phone. The superefficient PA popped back into the office as if by magic. 'Mel is gonna send it over by messenger.'

He handed the document to his PA, then scribbled something on a pad and passed that to her, too. The PA trotted out.

'Make sure you check every line,' he continued, still talking to whomever was on the other end of the phone. He gave a strained chuckle. 'Not exactly—it's *supposed* to be divorce papers.'

The judgmental once-over he gave Xanthe had her temper rising up her torso.

'I'll explain the why and the how another time,' he said. 'Just make sure there are no surprises—like a hidden claim for ten years' back-alimony.'

He clicked off the phone and shoved it into his pocket.

She was actually speechless. For about two seconds.

'Are you finished?' Indignation burned, the breathing technique history.

She'd come all this way, spent several sleepless nights preparing for this meeting while being constantly tormented by painful memories from that summer, not to mention having to deal with his scent and the inappropriate heat that would not die. And through it all she'd remained determined to keep this process dignified, despite the appalling way he had treated her. And he'd shot it all to hell in less than five minutes.

The arrogant ass.

'Don't play the innocent with me,' he continued, the self-righteous glare returning. 'Because I know just what you're capable—'

'You son of a...' She gasped for breath, outrage consuming her. 'I'm not *allowed* to play the innocent? When you took my virginity, carried on seducing me all summer, got me pregnant, insisted I marry you and then dumped me three months later?'

He'd never told her he loved her—never even tried to see her point of view during their one and only argument. But, worse than that, he hadn't been there when she had needed him the most. Her stomach churned, the in-flight meal she'd picked at on the plane threatening to gag her as misery warred with fury, bringing the memories flooding back—memories which were too painful to forget even though she'd tried.

The pungent smell of mould and cheap disinfectant in the motel bathroom, the hazy sight of the cracked linoleum through the blur of tears, the pain hacking her in two as she prayed for him to pick up his phone.

Dane's face went completely blank, before a red stain of fury lanced across the tanned cheekbones. '*I* dumped *you*? Are you *nuts*?' he yelled at top volume.

'You walked out and left me in that motel room and you didn't answer my calls.' She matched him decibel for decibel. She wasn't that besotted girl any more, too timid and delusional to stand up and fight her corner. 'What *else* would you call it?'

'I was two hundred miles out at sea, crewing on a bluefin tuna boat—that's what I'd call it. I didn't get your calls because there isn't a heck of a lot of network coverage in the middle of the North Atlantic. And when I got back a week later I found out you'd hightailed it back to daddy because of one damn disagreement.'

The revelation of where he'd been while she'd been losing their baby gave her pause—but only for a moment. He could have rung her to tell her about the job *before* he'd boarded the boat, but in his typical don't-ask-don't-tell fashion he hadn't. And what about the frantic message she'd left him while she'd waited for her father to arrive and take her to the emergency room? And later, when she'd come round from the fever dreams back in her bedroom on her father's estate?

She'd asked the staff to contact Dane, to tell him about the baby, her heart breaking into a thousand pieces, but he'd never even responded to the news. Except to send through the signed divorce papers weeks later.

She could have forgiven him for not caring about *her*. Their marriage had been the definition of a shotgun wedding, the midnight elopement a crazy adventure hyped up on teenage hormones, testosterone-fuelled bravado and the mad panic caused by an unplanned pregnancy. But it was his failure to care about the three-month-old life which had died inside her, his failure to even be willing to mourn its passing, that she couldn't forgive.

It had tortured her for months. How many lies he'd told about being there for her, respecting her decision to have the baby. How he'd even gone through with their farce of a marriage, while all the time planning to dump her at the first opportunity.

It had made no sense to her for so long—until she'd finally figured it out. Why he'd always deflected conversations about the future, about the baby. Why he'd never once returned her declarations of love even while stoking the sexual heat between them to fever pitch. Why he'd stormed out that morning after her innocent suggestion that she look for a job, too, because she knew he was struggling to pay their motel bill.

He'd gotten bored with the marriage, with the responsibility. And sex had been the only thing binding them together. He'd never wanted her or the baby. His offer of marriage had been a knee-jerk reaction he'd soon regretted. And once she'd lost the baby he'd had the perfect excuse he'd been looking for to discard her.

That truth had devastated her at the time. Brought her to her knees. How could she have been so wrong about him? About *them*? But it had been a turning point, too. Because she'd survived the loss, repaired her shattered heart, and made herself into the woman she was now—someone who didn't rely on others to make herself whole.

Thanks to Dane's carelessness, his neglect, she'd shut off her stupid, fragile, easily duped heart and found a new purpose—devoting herself to the company that was her legacy. She'd begged her father for a lowly internship position that autumn, when they'd returned to London, and begun working her backside off to learn everything she needed to know about Europe's top maritime logistics brand.

At first it had been a distraction, a means of avoiding the great big empty space inside her. But eventually she'd stopped simply going through the motions and actually found something to care about again. She'd aced her MBA, learnt French and Spanish while working in Carmichael's subsidiary offices in Calais and Cadiz, and even managed to persuade her father to give her a job at the company's head office in Whitehall before he'd died—all the while fending off his attempts to find her a 'suitable' husband.

She'd earned the position she had now through hard

work and dedication and toughened up enough to take charge of her life. So there was no way on earth she was going to back down from this fight and let Dane Redmond lay some ludicrous guilt trip on her when *he* was the one who had crushed her and every one of her hopes and dreams. Maybe they had been foolish hopes and stupid pipe dreams, but the callous way he'd done it had been unnecessarily cruel.

'You promised to be there for me,' she shot back, her fury going some way to mask the hollow pain in her stomach. The same pain she'd sworn never to feel again. 'You swore you would protect me and support me. But when I needed you the most you weren't there.'

'What the hell did you need *me* there for?' he spat the words out, the brittle light in the icy blue eyes shocking her into silence.

The fight slammed out of her lungs on a gasp of breath.

Because in that moment all she could see was his rage.

The hollow pain became sharp and jagged, tearing through the last of her resistance until all that was left was the horrifying uncertainty that had crippled her as a teenager.

Why was he so angry with her? When all she'd ever done was try to love him?

'I wanted you to be there for me when I lost our baby,' she whispered, her voice sounding as if it were coming from another dimension.

'You wanted me to hold your hand while you aborted my kid?'

'What?' His sarcasm, the sneered disbelief sliced through her, and the jagged pain exploded into something huge.

'You think I don't *know* you got rid of it?'

The accusation in his voice, the contempt, suddenly made a terrible kind of sense.

'But I—' She tried to squeeze the words past the asteroid in her throat.

He cut her off. 'I hitched a ride straight to the Vineyard once I got back on shore. We'd had that fight and you'd left some garbled message on my cell. When I got to your old man's place he told me there was no baby any more, showed me the divorce papers you'd signed and then had me kicked out. And that's when I figured out the truth. Daddy's little princess had decided that my kid was an inconvenience she didn't need.'

She didn't see hatred any more, just a seething resentment, but she couldn't process any of it. His words buzzed round in her brain like mutant bees which refused to land. *Had* she signed the divorce papers first? She couldn't remember doing that. All she could remember was begging to see Dane, and her father showing her Dane's signature on the documents. And how the sight of his name scrawled in black ink had killed the last tiny remnant of hope still lurking inside her.

'I know the pregnancy was a mistake. Hell, the whole damn marriage was insane,' Dane continued, his tone caustic with disgust. 'And if you'd told me that's what you'd decided to do I would have tried to understand. But you didn't have the guts to own it, did you? You didn't even have the guts to tell me that's what you'd done? So don't turn up here and pretend you were some innocent kid, seduced by the big bad wolf. Because we both know that's garbage. There was only *one* innocent party in the whole screwed-up mess of our marriage and it wasn't either one of us.'

She could barely hear him, those mutant killer bees had become a swarm. Her legs began to shake, and the jagged pain in her stomach joined the thudding cacophony in her skull. She locked her knees, wrapped her arms around her midriff and swallowed convulsively, trying to prevent the silent screams from vomiting out of her mouth.

How could you not know how much our baby meant to me?

'What's wrong?' Dane demanded, the contempt turning to reluctant concern.

She tried to force her shattered thoughts into some semblance of order. But the machete embedded in her head was about to split her skull in two. And she couldn't form the words.

'Damn it, Red, you look as if you're about to pass out.'

Firm hands clamped on her upper arms and became the only thing keeping her upright as her knees buckled.

The old nickname and the shock of his touch had a blast of memory assaulting her senses—hurtling her back in time to those stolen days on the water in Buzzards Bay: the hot sea air, the shrieks of the cormorants, the scent of salt mixed with the funky aroma of sweat and sex, the devastating joy as his calloused fingers brought her body to vibrant life.

I didn't have an abortion.

She tried to force the denial free from the stranglehold in her throat, but nothing came out.

I had a miscarriage.

She heard him curse, felt firm fingers digging into her biceps as the cacophony in her head became deafening. And she stepped over the edge to let herself fall.

CHAPTER FOUR

WHAT THE—?

Dane leapt forward as Xanthe's eyes rolled back, scooping her dead weight into his arms before she could crash to earth.

'Is Ms Sanders sick?' Mel appeared, her face blank with shock.

'Her name's Carmichael.'
Or, technically speaking, Redmond.

He barged past his PA, cradling Xanthe against his chest. 'Call Dr Epstein and tell him to meet me in the penthouse.'

'What—what shall I say happened?' Mel stammered, nowhere near as steady as usual.

He knew how she felt. His palms were sweating, his pulse racing fast enough to win the Kentucky Derby.

Xanthe let out a low moan. He tightened his grip, something hot and fluid hitting him as his fingertips brushed her breast.

'I don't know what happened,' he replied. 'Just tell Epstein to get up there.'

He threw the words over his shoulder as he strode through the office, past his sponsorship and marketing team, every one of whom was staring at him as if he'd just told them the company had declared bankruptcy.

Had they heard him shouting at Red like a madman? Letting the fury he'd buried years ago spew out of his mouth?

Where had that come from?

He'd lost it—and he *never* lost it. Not since the day on her father's estate when he'd gone berserk, determined to see Xanthe no matter what her father said.

Of course he hadn't told her that part of the story. The part where he'd made an ass of himself.

The pulse already pounding in his temple began to throb like a wound. He'd been dog-tired and frantic with worry when he'd arrived at Carmichael's vacation home, his pride in tatters, his gut clenching at the thought Xanthe had run out on him.

All that had made him easy prey for the man who hadn't considered him fit to kiss the hem of his precious daughter's bathrobe, let alone marry her. He could still see Charles Carmichael's smug expression, hear that superior I'm-better-than-you tone as the guy told him their baby was gone and that his daughter had made the sensible decision to cut all ties with the piece of trailer trash she should never have married.

The injustice of it all, the sense of loss, the futile anger had opened up a great big black hole inside him that had been waiting to drag him under ever since he was a little boy. So he'd exploded with rage—and got his butt thoroughly kicked by Carmichael's goons for his trouble.

Obviously some of that rage was still lurking in his subconscious. Or he wouldn't have freaked out again. Over something that meant nothing now.

He'd been captivated by Xanthe that summer. By her cute accent, the sexy, subtle curves rocking the bikini-shorts-and-T-shirt combos she'd lived in, her quick, curious mind and most of all the artless flirting that had grown hotter and hotter until they'd made short work of those bikini shorts.

The obvious crush she'd had on him had flattered him, had made him feel like somebody when everyone else treated him like a nobody. But their connection had never been about anything other than hot sex—souped up to fever pitch by teenage lust. He knew he'd been nuts to think it could ever be more, especially once she'd run back to Daddy when she'd discovered what it was *really* like to live on a waterman's pay.

Xanthe stirred, her fragrant hair brushing his chin.

'Settle down. I've got you.' A wave of protectiveness washed over him. He didn't plan to examine it too closely. She'd been his responsibility once. She wasn't his responsibility any more. Whatever the paperwork said.

This was old news. It didn't make a damn bit of difference now. Obviously the shock of seeing her again had worked stuff loose which had been hanging about without his knowledge.

'Where are you taking me?'

The groggy question brought him back to the problem nestled in his arms.

He elbowed the call button on the elevator, grateful when the doors zipped open and they could get out of range of their audience. Stepping inside, he nudged the button marked Penthouse Only.

'My place. Top floor.'

'What happened?'

He glanced down to find her eyes glazed, her face still pale as a ghost. She looked sweet and innocent and scared—the way she had once before.

'It's positive. I'm going to have a baby. What are we going to do?'

He concentrated on the panel above his head, shoving the flashback where it belonged—in the file marked Ancient History.

'You tell me.' He kept his voice casual. 'One minute we were yelling at each other and the next you were hitting the deck.'

'I must have fainted,' she said, as if she wasn't sure. She shifted, colour flooding back into her cheeks. 'You can put me down now. I'm fine.'

He should do what she asked, because having her soft curves snug against his chest and that sultry scent filling his nostrils wasn't doing much for his equilibrium, but his heartbeat was still going for gold in Kentucky.

His grip tightened.

'Uh-huh?' He raised a sceptical eyebrow. 'You make a habit of swooning like a heroine in a trashy novel?'

Her chin took on a mutinous tilt, but she didn't reply.

Finally, score one to Redmond.

The elevator arrived at his penthouse and the doors opened onto the panoramic view of the downtown skyline.

At any other time the sight would have brought with it a satisfying ego-boost. The designer furniture, the modern steel and glass structure and the expertly planted roof terrace, its lap pool sparkling in the fading sunlight, was a million miles away from the squalid dump he'd grown up in. He'd worked himself raw in the last couple of years, and spent a huge chunk of investment capital, to complete the journey.

But he wasn't feeling too proud of himself at the moment. He'd lost his temper downstairs, but worse than that, he'd let his emotions get the upper hand.

'Stop crying like a girl and get me another beer, or you'll be even sorrier than you are already, you little pissant.'

His old man had been a mean drunk, whom he'd grown to despise, but one thing the hard bastard had taught him was that letting your emotions show only made you weak.

Xanthe had completed his education by teaching him another valuable lesson—that mixing sex with sentiment was never a good idea.

Somehow both those lessons had deserted him downstairs.

He deposited her on the leather couch in the centre of the living space and stepped back, aware of the persistent ache in his crotch.

She got busy fussing with her hair, not meeting his eyes. Her staggered breathing made her breasts swell against the lacy top. The persistent ache spiked.

Terrific.

'Thank you,' she said. 'But you didn't have to carry me all the way up here.'

She looked around the space, still not meeting his eyes.

He stifled the disappointment when she didn't comment on the apartment. He wasn't looking for her approval. Certainly didn't need it.

'The company doc's coming up to check you out,' he said.

That got her attention. Her gaze flashed to his—equal parts aggravation and embarrassment.

'That's not necessary. It's just a bit of jet lag.'

Jet lag didn't make all the colour drain out of your face, or give your eyes that haunted, hunted look. And it sure as hell didn't make you drop like a stone in the middle of an argument.

'Tell that to Dr Epstein.'

She was getting checked out by a professional whether she liked it or not. She might not be his responsibility any more, but this was his place and his rules.

The elevator bell dinged on cue.

He crossed the apartment to greet the doctor, his racing heartbeat finally reaching the finish line and heading into a victory lap when he heard Xanthe's annoyed huff of breath behind him.

Better to deal with a pissed Xanthe than one who fainted dead away right before his eyes.

CHAPTER FIVE

'WHAT I'M PRESCRIBING is a balanced meal and a solid ten hours' sleep, in that order.'

The good Dr Epstein sent Xanthe a grave look which made her feel as if she were four years old again, being chastised by Nanny Foster for refusing to go down for her nap.

'Your blood pressure is elevated and the fact you haven't eaten or slept well in several days is no doubt the cause of this episode. Stress is a great leveller, Ms Carmichael,' he added.

As if she didn't know that, with the source of her stress standing two feet away, eavesdropping.

This was *so* not what she needed right now. For Dane to know that she hadn't had a good night's sleep or managed to eat a full meal since Wednesday morning. Thanks to the good doctor's interrogation she might as well be wearing a sign with Weak and Feeble Woman emblazoned across it.

She'd never fainted before in her life. Well, not since—

She cut off the thought.

Do not go back there. Not again.

Rehashing those dark days had already cost her far too much ground. Swooning 'like a heroine in a trashy novel,' as Dane had so eloquently put it, had done the rest. The only good thing to come out of her dying swan act was the fact that it had happened before she'd had the chance to blurt out the truth about her miscarriage.

After coming round in Dane's arms, her cheek nestled

against his rock-solid shoulder and her heart thundering in her chest, the inevitable blast of heat had been followed by a much needed blast of rational thought.

She was here to finish things with Dane—not kick-start loads of angst from the past. Absolutely nothing would be achieved by correcting Dane's assumption now, other than to cast her yet again in the role of the sad, insecure little girl who needed a man to protect her.

Maybe that had been true then. Her father's high-handed decision to prevent her from seeing Dane had robbed them both of the chance to end their relationship amicably. And then her father had mucked things up completely by hiring his useless old school chum Augustus Greaves to handle the admin on the divorce.

But her father was dead now. And with hindsight she could see that in his own misguided, paternalistic way he had probably believed he was acting in her best interests. And the truth was the end result, however agonising it had been to go through at the time, *had* been in her best interests.

Who was to say she wouldn't have gone back to Dane? Been delusional enough to carry on trying to make a go of a marriage that had been a mistake from the start?

Nothing would be gained by telling Dane the truth now, ten years too late. Except to give him another golden opportunity to demonstrate his me-Tarzan-you-Jane routine.

She'd found his dominance and overprotectiveness romantic that summer. Believing it proved how much he loved her. When all it had really proved was that Dane, like her father, had never seen her as an equal.

The fact that she'd felt safe and cherished and turned on by the ease with which he'd held her a moment ago was just her girly hormones talking. And those little snitches didn't need any more excuses to join the party.

Much better that Dane respected her based on a misconception, even if it made him hate her, than that she encourage his pity with the truth. Because his pity had left her confidence and her self-esteem in the toilet ten years ago—and led to a series of stupid decisions that had nearly destroyed her.

She was a pragmatist now—a shrewd, focused career woman. One melodramatic swoon brought on by starvation and exhaustion and stress didn't change that. Thank goodness she wasn't enough of a ninny to be looking for love to complete her life any more. Because it was complete enough already.

Maybe there was a tiny tug of regret at the thought of that young man who had come to her father's estate looking for her, only to be turned away. But the fact that he'd come to the worst possible conclusion proved he'd never truly understood her. How could he *ever* have believed she would abort their child?

'I appreciate your advice, Doctor,' she replied, as the man packed the last of his paraphernalia into his bag. 'I'll make sure I grab something to eat at the airport and get some sleep on the plane.'

No doubt she'd sleep like the dead, given the emotional upheaval she'd just endured.

She glanced at her watch and stood up, steadying herself against the sofa when a feeling of weightlessness made her head spin.

'You're flying back tonight?' The doctor frowned at her again, as if she'd just thrown a tantrum.

'Yes, at seven,' she replied. She only had an hour before boarding closed on her flight to Heathrow. 'So I should get going.'

The elderly man's grave expression became decidedly condescending. 'I wouldn't advise catching a transatlantic flight tonight. You need to give yourself some time to recover. You've just had a full-blown anxiety attack.'

'A...*what*?' she yelped, far too aware of Dane's over-bearing presence in her peripheral vision as he listened to every word. 'It wasn't an anxiety attack. It was just a bit of light-headedness.'

'Mr Redmond said you became very emotional, then collapsed, and that you were out for over a minute. That's more than light-headedness.'

'Right...well, thanks for your opinion, Doctor.' As if she cared what 'Mr Redmond' had to say on the subject.

'You're welcome, Ms Carmichael.'

She hung back as Dane showed Dr Epstein out, silently fuming at the subtle put-down. And the fact Dane had witnessed it. And the even bigger problem that she was going to have to wait now until the doctor had taken the lift down before she could leave herself. Which would mean spending torturous minutes alone with Dane while trying to avoid the parade of circus elephants crammed into his palatial penthouse apartment with them.

She didn't want to talk about their past, her so-called anxiety attack, or any of the other ten-ton pachyderms that might be up for discussion.

However nonchalant she'd tried to be with Dr Epstein, she *didn't* feel 100 per cent. She was shattered. The last few days *had* been stressful—more stressful than she'd wanted to admit. And the revelations that had come during their argument downstairs hadn't exactly reduced her stress levels.

And, while she was playing Truth or Dare with herself, she might as well also admit that being in Dane's office had been unsettling enough.

Being alone with him in his apartment was worse.

She shrugged into the jacket she'd taken off while Dr Epstein took her blood pressure. Time to make a digni-fied and speedy exit.

'Where's my briefcase?' she asked, her voice more high-pitched than she would have liked, as Dane walked back towards her.

'My office.'

He leaned against the steel banister of a staircase leading to a mezzanine level and crossed his arms over that wide chest. His stance looked relaxed. She wasn't fooled.

'I couldn't scoop it up,' he continued, his silent censure doing nothing for the pulse punching her throat, 'because I had my hands full scooping up *you*.'

'I'll get it on my way out,' she said, deliberately ignoring the sarcasm while marching towards the elevator.

He unfolded his arms and stepped into her path. 'That's not what the doctor ordered.'

'He's not *my* doctor,' she announced, distracted by the pectoral muscles outlined by creased white cotton. 'And I don't take orders.'

His sensual lips flattened into a stubborn line and his jaw hardened, drawing her attention back to the dent in his chin.

She bit into her tongue, assaulted by the sudden urge to lick that masculine dip.

What the heck?

She tried to sidestep him. He stepped with her, forcing her to butt into the wall o' pecs. Awareness shot up her spine as she took a hasty step back.

'Get out of my way.'

'Red, chill out.'

She caught a glimpse of concern, her pulse spiking uncomfortably at his casual use of the old nickname.

'I will not chill out. I have a flight to catch.' She sounded shrill, but she was starting to feel light-headed again. If she did another smackdown in front of him the last of her dignity would be in shreds.

'You're shaking.'

'I'm *not* shaking.'

Of course she was shaking. He was standing too close, crowding her, engulfing her in that subtly sexy scent. Even though he wasn't touching her she could feel him every-where—in her tender breasts, her ragged breathing and in the hotspot between her thighs which was about to spon-taneously combust. Basically, her body had reverted to its default position whenever Dane Redmond was within a ten-mile radius.

'Unless you've got a chopper handy, you've already missed your flight,' he observed, doing that sounding rea-sonable thing again, which made her sound hysterical. 'Midtown traffic is a bitch at this time of day. No way are you going to make it to JFK in under an hour.'

'Then I'll wait at the airport for another flight.'

'Why not hang out here and catch a flight out tomor-row like Epstein suggested?'

With him? In his apartment? Alone? Was he bonkers?

'No, thank you.'

She tried to shift round him again. A restraining hand cupped her elbow and electricity zapped up her arm.

She yanked free, the banked heat in his cool blue gaze almost as disturbing as what he said next.

'How about I apologise?'

'What for?'

Was he serious? Dane had been the original never-give-in-never-surrender guy back in the day. She'd never seen him back down or apologise for anything.

'For yelling at you in my office. About stuff that doesn't matter any more.'

It was the last thing she had expected. But as she searched his expression she could see he meant it.

It was an olive branch. She wanted to snatch it and run straight for the moral high ground. But the tug of regret in the pit of her stomach chose that precise moment to give a sharp yank.

'You don't have to apologise for speaking your mind. But, if you insist, I should apologise, too,' she continued. 'You're right. I should have consulted you about…about the abortion.'

The lie tasted sour—a betrayal of the tiny life she'd once yearned to hold in her arms. But this was the only way to finally release them both from all those foolish dreams.

'Hell, Red. You don't have to apologise for that.'

He scrubbed his hands over his scalp, the frustrated gesture bringing an old memory to the surface of running her hands over the soft bristles while they lay together on the deck of the pocket cruiser, her body pleasantly numb with afterglow from the first time they'd made love.

She pressed tingling palms against the fabric of her skirt, trying to erase the picture in her head, but the unguarded memory continued to play out—one agonising sensation at a time. Goosebumps pebbling her arms from the warm breeze off the ocean…the base of her thumb stinging from the affectionate nip as he bit into the tender flesh.

'You sure you're okay? I didn't hurt you? You're so small and delicate…'

'I get why you did it,' Dane continued, as the erotic memory played havoc with her senses. 'You weren't ready to be a mom, and I would have been a disaster as a dad.'

He was telling her he agreed with her. Case comprehensively closed. But what should have been a victory only made the sour taste in her mouth turn to mud.

She *had* been ready to be a mother. How could he have doubted that? Didn't he *know* how much she had wanted their baby? And why would he think he'd make a terrible father? Was this something to do with all his scars, the childhood and the family he had never been willing to talk about?

Good grief, get real. You are not *still invested in that fairytale.*

The idiotic notion that she could rescue him by helping him to overcome stuff he refused to talk about had been the domain of that romantic teenage girl. That fairytale was part of her past. A past she'd just lied through her teeth to put behind her. This had to be the jet lag talking again, because it was not like her to lose her grip on reality twice in one day.

'I'd really like to settle this amicably,' she said at last, determined to accept his olive branch.

'We can do that—but you need to stay put tonight. You took a couple of years off my life downstairs, and you still look as if a strong breeze could blow you over.'

That searing gaze drifted to the top of her hair, which probably looked as if a chinchilla had been nesting in it. Awareness shimmered, the sharp tug in her abdomen ever more insistent.

'I feel responsible for that,' he said, the gentle tone at odds with the bunched muscle jumping in his jaw.

'I told you. I'm okay.' She couldn't stay. Couldn't risk becoming that poor, pathetic girl again, who needed his strength because she had none of her own. 'And, more importantly, I'm not your responsibility.'

'Think again,' he said, trampling over her resistance, the muscle in his jaw now dancing a jig. 'Because until I sign those papers you're still my lawfully wedded wife.'

It was an insane thing to say. But much more insane was the stutter in her pulse, the fluttering sensation deep in her abdomen at the conviction in his voice.

'Don't be ridiculous, Dane. We are not *actually* married and we haven't been for over ten years. What we're talking about is an admin error that you wouldn't even know about if I hadn't come to see you today.'

'About that...' He hooked a tendril of hair behind her

ear. 'Why *did* you come all the way to Manhattan when you could have gotten your attorney to handle it?'

It was a pertinent question—and one she didn't have a coherent answer for.

The rough pad of his fingertip trailed down her neck and into the hollow of her throat, sending sensation rioting across her collarbone and plunging into her breasts.

She should tell him to back off. She needed to leave. But something deeper and much more primal kept her immobile.

'You know what I think?' he said, his voice hoarse.

She shook her head. But she did know, and she really didn't want to.

'I think you missed me.'

'Don't be silly. I haven't thought of you in years,' she said, but the denial came out on a breathless whisper, convincing no one.

His lips lifted on one side, the don't-give-a-damn half-smile was an invitation to sin she'd never been able to resist.

'You don't remember how good it used to be between us?' he mocked, finding the punching pulse at the base of her throat. 'Because I do.'

His thumb rubbed back and forth across her collarbone, the nonchalant caress incinerating the lacy fabric of her camisole.

'No,' she said, but they both knew that was the biggest lie of all.

A wad of something hard and immovable jammed her throat as his thumb drifted down to circle her nipple, the possessive, unapologetic touch electrifying even through the layers of silk and lace.

The peak engorged in a rush, poking against the fabric and announcing how big a whopper she'd told.

She needed to tell him to stop. He had no right to touch

her like this any more. But the words refused to form as her back stretched, thrusting the rigid tip into his palm.

He dipped his head as his thumb traced the edge of her bra cup, rough calluses rasping sensitive skin as it slid beneath the lace. His lips nudged the corner of her mouth, so close she could smell coffee and peppermint.

'You were always a terrible liar, Red.'

She couldn't breathe. Couldn't think. Certainly couldn't speak.

So objecting was an impossibility when he eased the cup down to expose one tight nipple and blew on the sensitive flesh.

'Oh, God.'

Her lungs seized and her thigh muscles dissolved as he licked the tender peak, then nipped at the tip. She bucked, the shock of sensation bringing her hip into contact with the impressive ridge in his trousers. She rubbed against it like a cat, desperate to find relief from the exquisite agony.

He swore under his breath, then clasped her head and slanted his lips across hers. She opened for him instinctively and let his tongue plunder her mouth, driving the kiss into dark, torturous territory.

Her fingers curled into his shirt to drag him closer, absorbing his tantalising strength as the slab of muscle crushed her naked breast.

Her sex became heavy and painfully tender. Slick with longing. The melting sensation a throwback to her youth— when all he'd had to do was look at her to make her ready for him.

How can I still need him this much?

Her mind blurred, sinking into the glorious sex-fogged oblivion she'd denied herself for so long. *Too long.* Her tongue tangled with his, giving him the answer they both craved.

He kissed the way she remembered. With masterful

thrusts and parries joined by teasing nips and licks as he devoured her mouth, no quarter given.

The day-old beard abraded her chin. Large hands brushed her thighs, bunching the skirt around her waist until he had a good firm grip on her backside.

Excitement pumped through her veins like a powerful narcotic, burning away everything but the sight, the sound, the scent of him.

He boosted her up—taking charge, taking control, the way she had always adored.

'Put your legs round my waist.'

She obeyed the husky command without question, clinging to his strong shoulders. Her heartbeat kicked her ribs and pummelled her sex as their tongues duelled, hot and wet and frantic.

Her back hit the wall with a thud and the thick ridge in his trousers ground against her panties, the friction exquisite against her yearning clitoris.

Holding her up with one arm, he tore at her underwear. The sound of ripping satin echoed off the room's hard surfaces, stunning her until he found her with his thumb. She moaned into his mouth, the perfect touch charging through her system like lightning.

His answering groan rumbled against her ear, harsh with need. 'Still so wet for me, Red?'

Blunt fingers brushed expertly over the heart of her, then circled the swollen nub, teasing, coaxing, demanding a response. Everything inside her drove down to that one tight spot, desperate to feel the touch which would drive her over. The coil tightened like a vice and propelled her mindlessly towards the peak.

'Please…' The single word came out on a tortured sob.

Dane was the only man who knew exactly what she needed and always had.

Suddenly he withdrew his fingers, sliding them through

the wet folds to rest on her hip. Leaving her teetering on the edge of ecstasy.

She panted. Squirmed. Denied the touch she needed. The touch she had to have.

'Don't stop.'

He buried his face against her neck, the harsh pants of his breathing as tortured as her own. 'Have to,' he grunted.

'Why?'

Her dazed mind reeled, her flesh clenching painfully on emptiness. Desire clawed at her insides like a ravenous beast as he left her balanced brutally on the sharp edge between pleasure and pain.

'No *way* am I taking you without a condom.'

As the sex fog finally released its stranglehold on her brain the comment registered and horrifying reality smacked into her with the force and fury of an eighteen-wheeler. The nuclear blush mushroomed up to her hairline.

Did you actually just beg him to make love to you? Without protection?

If only there was such a thing as death by mortification.

This was now officially *the* most humiliating moment of her life. The trashy novel swoon had merely been a dress rehearsal.

She scooped her breast back into her bra, its reddened nipple mocking her.

She had to get away from here. Sod the divorce papers. She'd deal with them later. Right now saving herself and her sanity was more important than saving Carmichael's.

CHAPTER SIX

DANE BREATHED IN the sultry scent of Xanthe's arousal, still holding on to her butt as if she were the only solid object in the middle of a tornado.

How could it be exactly the same between them? The heat, the hunger, the insanity?

He felt as if he'd just been in a war. And he was fairly sure it was a war he hadn't won.

What were you thinking, hitting on her like that?

He'd been mad. Mad that he'd shouted at her, mad that she'd collapsed in front of him, and madder still that he cared enough about her to be sorry. But most of all he'd been mad that he could still want her so much, despite everything.

The come-on had been a ploy to intimidate her, to make her fold and do as she was told. But she hadn't. She'd met his demands with demands of her own. And suddenly they'd been racing to the point of no return like a couple of sex-mad teenagers—as if the last ten years had never happened.

'Dane, put me down. You're crushing me.'

The furious whisper brought him crashing the rest of the way back to reality.

He drew in an agonising breath of her scent. Light floral perfume and subtle sin. And lifted his head to survey the full extent of the damage.

Her hair had tumbled down, sticking in damp strands to the line of her throat. A smudge of mascara added to the bluish tinge under her eyes, the reddened skin on her chin and cheek suggesting she was going to have some serious beard-burn in the morning.

He should have shaved. Then again, he should have done a lot of things.

She looked shell-shocked.

He had the weird urge to laugh. At least he wasn't the only one.

She pushed against his chest, struggling to get out of his arms in earnest.

'Stop staring at me like that. I have to leave.'

He let her go and watched her scramble away, trying to be grateful that he'd at least managed to stop himself from leaping off the deep end this time. The painful erection made sure he didn't feel nearly as great about that last-minute bout of sanity as he should.

She swept her hair back and bent to slip on the heels which must have fallen off at some point during their sex apocalypse, making it impossible for him not to notice how the slim skirt highlighted the generous contours of her butt. He tore his gaze away.

Haven't you tortured yourself enough already?

She pressed a hand to her forehead, glancing round— still struggling to calm down, to take stock and figure out what the heck had just happened was his guess.

Good luck with that.

'I should go.' She smoothed her clothing with unsteady hands and brushed a wayward curl behind her ear. It sprang straight back.

He planted his hands in his pants pockets and resisted the urge to hook it back round her ear a second time. Because look how that had ended the first time.

She was right. She should go. Before the urge to follow through on what they'd just started got the better of them.

Hitting on her had been a dumb move. What exactly had

he been trying to prove? That she still wanted him? That he was the one in charge? Or just that he was the biggest dumbass on the planet?

Because, whatever way you looked at it, that dumb move had stirred up stuff neither one of them was ready to deal with. Yet.

'You think?' he sneered, because their sex apocalypse wasn't just on *him*.

She'd made the decision to sneak back into his life and poke at something that had died a long time ago. And when he'd made that first dumb move, instead of telling him no she'd gone off like a rocket—giving him a taste of the girl he remembered which he wasn't going to be able to forget any time soon.

She glared at him, picking up on his pissy tone.

Yeah, that's right, sweetheart. I'm the guy you decided wasn't good enough for you. The guy you still can't get enough of.

'Don't you dare try to put this insanity on *me*,' she said. 'I didn't start it. And, anyway, we finished it before things got totally out of hand. So it's not important.'

Hell, yeah, it is. If I say it is.

'*We* didn't finish it,' he pointed out, because scoring a direct hit seemed vitally important. '*I* did.'

The flush scorched her skin and she blew out a staggered breath. 'So what? I got a little carried away in the heat of the moment. That's all.'

'A *little*?' Talk about an understatement.

Her lips set in a mulish line, the blush still beaming on those beard-scorched cheeks.

'It was a mistake, okay? Brought on by stress and fatigue and...' She paused, her gaze darting pretty much everywhere but his face. 'And sexual deprivation.'

'Sexual deprivation?' He scoffed. 'How do you figure *that*?'

She was going to have to spell that one out for him.

'I've been extremely busy for the past five years. Obviously I needed to blow off some steam.'

He should have been insulted. And a part of him was. But a much larger part of him wanted to know if she'd really just told him she'd been celibate for five years.

'Exactly how long has it been since you got to "blow off some steam"?'

Her eyes narrowed. 'That's none of your business.'

'That long, huh?' he mocked, enjoying the spark of temper—and the news that he'd been her first in a while—probably way too much.

He'd never sparred with her when she was a girl. Because she'd always been too cute and too fragile. It would have been like kicking a puppy. He'd always had to be so careful, mindful of how delicate she was. Back then he'd been terrified he'd break her, that his rough, low-class hands would be too demanding for all that delicate, petal-soft skin. So he'd strived hard to be gentle even when it had cost him.

But she'd given as good as she'd gotten a minute ago. And damn if that didn't turn him on even more.

The flush now mottled the skin of her cleavage, and suddenly he was remembering gliding his tongue across her nipple, her soft sob of encouragement as he captured the hard bud between his teeth.

His blood surged south. And he got mad all over again.

She'd been so far out of his reach that summer. But somehow she'd hooked him into her drama, her reality, made him want to stand up to her daddy, to fight her demons, to brand her as his and follow some cock-eyed dream. When she'd told him she was pregnant he'd been horrified at first, but much worse had been the driving need that had opened up inside him—the fierce desire to claim her and their child.

She'd convinced him she wanted to keep his baby. And that was all it had taken to finally tip him over into an alternative reality where he'd kidded himself they could make it work. That she really wanted to make it work. With him. A British heiress and a nobody from Roxbury. *As if.*

He'd spent years afterwards dealing with her betrayal, determined that no one would ever have the power to screw him over like that again—even after he'd finally figured out that she'd probably just been playing him all along so she could stick it to her overbearing daddy.

The thought that he could still want her so much infuriated the hell out of him. But he'd just behaved like a wild man, making it tough to deny.

He'd ripped off her panties, damn it. When was the last time he'd done something like *that*? Been so desperate to get to a woman he'd torn off her underwear? Hadn't even taken the time or trouble to undress her properly, to kiss her and caress her?

He might not be a master of small talk, but he had some moves. Moves women generally appreciated and which he'd worked at acquiring over the last ten years.

Until Xanthe had strolled back into his life and managed to rip away all those layers of class and sophistication and bring back that rough, raw, reckless, screwed-up kid. The kid he'd always hated.

She made a dash for the elevators.

'Hey, wait up!' He chased her down, grabbed her wrist.

She swung round, her eyes bright with fury and panic. 'Don't touch me. I'm not staying.'

He lifted his hand away. 'I get that. But I want to know where you're going.' He scrambled for a plausible reason. 'So I can get the papers delivered tomorrow.'

In person.

'You'll sign them?'

She sounded so surprised and so relieved he wondered if there was more to those papers than she was letting on. Because she *had* to know there was no way on earth he would want to contest their divorce—no matter how hot they still were for each other.

Focus, dumbass.

He shook off the suspicion. His objective right now was to make sure she didn't hightail it all the way back to London before he was finished with her.

This wasn't over. Not by a long shot. But he'd learned the hard way that it was better to retreat and work out a strategy rather than risk riding roughshod straight into an ambush.

Her old man and his goons had taught him that on the night he'd come to collect his wife—believing he had rights and obligations only to discover that promises meant nothing if you were rich and privileged and already over the piece of trash you'd married.

The anger surged back, fresh and vivid, but he was ready for it now, in a way he hadn't been earlier.

So had he been kidding himself that he was over what she'd done? That didn't have to be bad. As long as he dealt with it once and for all.

'Sure, I'll sign them,' he replied.

Once I'm good and ready.

She'd stirred up this hornets' nest, so he wasn't going to be the only one who got stung.

'Thank you,' she said, and the stunned pleasure in her voice crucified him a little. 'I'm glad we finally got the chance to end this properly. I didn't have—' She stopped abruptly, cutting off the thought, her cheeks heating.

'You didn't have what?'

What had she been about to say? Because whatever it was she looked stricken that she'd almost let it slip.

'Nothing.'

Yeah, right. Then why was her guilty flush bright enough to signal incoming aircraft?

'I hope we can part as friends,' she said, thrusting her hand out like a peace offering, the long slim fingers visibly shaking.

Friends, my butt.

They weren't friends. Or their marriage would not have ended the way it had. Friends were honest with each other. Friends were people you could trust. And when had he ever been able to trust *her*?

But still he clasped her hand, and squeezed gently to stem the tremor.

She let go first, tugging free to press the elevator button. She stepped into the car when it arrived, her eyes downcast. But as she turned to hit the lobby button their gazes met.

The muscle under his heart clenched.

'Goodbye, Dane.'

He nodded as the doors slid shut. Then he pulled out his mobile and dialled his PA.

'Mel? Ms Carmichael—' he paused '—I mean Ms Sanders, whose real name is Carmichael, is going to be stopping by any second to collect her briefcase. I want you to book her a suite at The Standard for the night and bill it to me. Then arrange a car to take her there.'

The place was classy, and only a few blocks away on the High Line. He wanted to know exactly where she was.

He didn't want any more nasty surprises. From here on in this was his game and his rules. And he was playing to win.

'Okay,' Mel said, sounding confused but, like the excellent assistant she was, not questioning his authority. Unlike his soon-to-be ex-wife. 'Is there anything else?'

'Yeah, if she kicks up a fuss…' He wouldn't put it past the new, improved kick-ass Xanthe to do the one thing guaranteed to screw up his plans. 'Tell her taking care of her accommodation is the least I could do...' He paused, the lie that would ensure Xanthe accepted his offer tasting bittersweet. 'For a *friend*.'

CHAPTER SEVEN

THAT EVENING XANTHE stood in front of the bathroom mirror in the corner suite her ex-husband had booked for her as a final gesture of 'friendship,' still trying to feel good about the outcome of their forced trip down memory lane that afternoon.

Tomorrow morning she would have the signed divorce papers in her hand, all threats to Carmichael's would be gone, and she and Dane could both get back to their lives as if Augustus Greaves and his shoddy workmanship had never happened.

Mission accomplished.

The only problem was she didn't feel good about what had happened in Dane's office and later in his apartment. She felt edgy and tense and vaguely guilty—thoughts and emotions still colliding in her brain three hours later, like a troop of toddlers on a sugar rush.

She smoothed aloe vera moisturiser over the red skin on her face which, fresh from a long hot bath loaded with the hotel's luxury bath salts, beamed like a stop light. If only she'd seen that warning before she'd let Dane devour her, because stubble rash was the least of her worries.

The memory of his rough, frantic handling sent an unwelcome shiver of awareness through her exhausted body. Firm, sensual lips subjugating hers, that marauding tongue plunging deep and obliterating all rational thought, solid pecs rippling beneath her grasping fingers, his teeth biting into her bottom lip and sending need arrowing down to her core…

She gripped the sink, her thighs turning to mush. *Again*.

She shivered, even though the bathroom's central air was set at the perfect ambient temperature. She needed to sleep. And forget about this afternoon's events.

But sleep continued to elude her.

She'd had some success in distracting herself for the first hour after Dane's driver had deposited her at the striking modernist hotel on Manhattan's High Line Park by doing what she did best—formulating an extensive to-do list and then doing it to death.

The first order of business had been to book herself on the evening flight to Heathrow tomorrow and bump herself up to first class. After today's 'episode' a lie-flat seat was going to be a necessity.

With her flight booked, she'd messed around for another thirty minutes selecting designer jeans, a fashionable T-shirt, fresh underwear and a pair of flats online from a nearby boutique and getting a guarantee that it would be express-delivered by tomorrow morning at 10 a.m. No matter how washed out she felt, at least she wouldn't have to *look* washed out, wearing her creased silk suit on the flight home.

Unfortunately while actioning her to-do list she'd got a second wind that she didn't seem able to shake—even after soaking for twenty minutes in the suite's enormous bathtub.

She just wanted to turn her brain off now and get comatose. But she couldn't. Maybe it was the jet lag kicking in? It was close to dawn now in the UK—the time she usually woke up to get ready for work and have her morning caffeine hit while sitting on the balcony of her luxury flat by the River Thames, allowing herself five minutes to enjoy the sun rising over Tower Bridge.

Her body clock had obviously decided that habit wasn't going to change, no matter what time zone she was in. Or how shattered she felt.

Unfortunately, being unable to sleep had given her far too much time to dissect all the things that had gone wrong this afternoon. Her fainting fit, the shocking revelation that Dane had assumed she'd aborted their child, but most of all her ludicrous reaction to Dane's come-on.

And she'd come to one irrefutable conclusion. When she got back to London she needed to look at options to get back in the dating game—because all work and no sex had clearly turned her into an unexploded bomb. She hadn't had a date in three years, no actual intimate contact in at least four, and she hadn't gone all the way since...

Xanthe watched the frown puckering her brow in the mirror deepen into a crevice.

Since the last time she'd made love to Dane.

No wonder she'd lost it with him. Her physical reaction to him had nothing to do with their past—or any lingering feelings—and everything to do with her failure to find another man with the same orgasm-on-demand capabilities as her ex-husband.

Since Dane, she'd always taken care of her own orgasms. At first she had put it down to some kind of perverse physical loyalty to the man who had abandoned her. Whenever another man touched her, her body had insisted on comparing him to Dane. Her failure to get aroused hadn't bothered her too much—in fact she'd begun to think it was a boon. After all, she never wanted to be a slave to her sex drive again—so in thrall to a guy's sexual prowess that she confused lust with love.

But apparently her sex drive was still a slave to *Dane's* sexual prowess.

Don't go there. It doesn't mean anything.

Dane wasn't unique. He didn't have some special mojo

that made her more susceptible, more in tune to his touch than to any other guy's. She just hadn't found the right guy yet—the right 'other guy' to hit all her happy buttons—because she hadn't been looking.

She'd got so used to taking care of her own business the loss hadn't become apparent until she'd walked into Dane's office this afternoon and had some kind of sexual breakdown. Triggered by Dane, who—in his usual in-your-face style—had decided to demonstrate exactly what she had been missing.

Of course she'd responded to Dane with all the restraint of a firecracker meeting a naked flame. She'd been running on stress and adrenaline for three days, and working herself to the bone for a great deal longer.

Dane had always known how to trip her switch, how to touch and caress and take her in ways that gave her no choice but to respond. And that obviously hadn't changed. But only because she'd been holding herself hostage for ten years…not exploring the possibilities.

After the trauma of their marriage, she had convinced herself in the last ten years that an active and fulfilled sex-life wasn't important. But clearly it *was* important—to her sense of self and her sense of well-being.

When she got back to the UK she was going to remedy that. Why not check out a few dating websites?

She shuddered involuntarily.

But until then she needed to get rid of all the sexual energy pumping around her system and stopping her from dropping into the exhausted sleep she so desperately needed.

She touched her fingertip to the tender skin on her chin, then trailed the nail down, inadvertently following the path Dane had taken three hours ago. Parting her robe, she sucked in a breath as the cool satin brushed over the tender skin of her nipple. Hooking the lapel round her breast to expose herself, she circled the ripe areola, still supremely sensitive from Dane's attentions. Her nipple rose in ruched splendour, the air cool against heated flesh. The gush of response between her thighs settled low in her abdomen, warm and fluid and heavy. She pinched the nipple, remembering the sharp nip of his teeth, and the coil of need tightened into a knot.

Untying the robe's belt, she let it fall open, revealing the neatly trimmed curls at the apex of her thighs, and spotted a small bruise on her hip. She ran her finger over the mark, remembering the feel of Dane's fingers digging into her skin as he boosted her into his arms.

'Wrap your legs round my waist.'

She cupped her aching sex, pressing the heel of her palm hard against her pelvic bone.

But as she closed her eyes all she could see was Dane's eyes staring back at her, the iridescent blue of the irises almost invisible round the lust-blown pupils, the hot look demanding she come…but only for him.

She parted the wet folds, but as she ran the pad of her finger over the tight bundle of nerves all she could feel were the urgent flicks and caresses of thick, blunt, calloused fingers.

'Always so damn wet for me, Red.'

His low, husky voice reverberated through her as she rubbed her clitoris in urgent, helpless strokes. She knew the right touch, the perfect touch to take her over quickly and efficiently. But this time the memory of Dane's fingers, firm and sure, mocked her battle for release, teasing and tempting her, taking her higher, and higher.

She panted. Not quite there yet. Never. Quite. There.

'Please, please…'

She slammed her palm down on the vanity unit and opened her eyes to see a mad woman staring back at her— hot, bothered and still hopelessly frustrated.

Every nerve-ending pulsated, desperate for release. A release that remained resolutely out of reach. Tantalising her senses…torturing her already-battered brain. A release she was very much afraid only Dane could give her.

The bastard.

Damn her ex-husband. Had he ruined her now for herself? As well as for every other man? How was that fair? Or proportionate?

She tied the robe with shaking hands, covering her nakedness. The flushed skin was screaming in protest, too sensitive now even for the silky feel of satin. She washed her hands and swallowed round the fireball in her throat, which was equal parts mortification and arousal. Cursing Dane and his clever, commanding caresses with every staggered breath.

She walked back into the bedroom of the suite and crossed to the phone. She would call down and ask for some sleeping pills. She hated taking any kind of medication, hated having her senses dulled, but if she didn't do something soon the toddlers in her head were liable to explode right out of her ears.

Whatever black magic Dane had worked on her sex-starved body this afternoon would be undone by a decent ten hours' sleep, and tomorrow evening she would be winging her way back across the Atlantic, the signed papers snug in her briefcase.

She was never going to see him again. Or feel his knowing fingers. Or watch his sexy I'm-gonna-make-you-come-like-an-express-train smile. And that was exactly how she wanted it. She was her own woman now. Or she would be again, once she was out of his line of fire.

A sharp rap at the door had her hesitating as she lifted the handset.

It took her tired mind a moment to process the interruption, but then she remembered. Her clothes. In typically efficient New York City style, the boutique had delivered them ahead of schedule.

Dropping the phone she crossed the room and flung open the door without bothering to check the peephole.

All the blood drained out of her head and raced down to pound in her already pouting clitoris. And the toddlers in her head began mainlining cocaine.

'Dane, what are you doing here?'

And why do you have to look so incredible?

Her ex stood on the threshold in worn jeans and a long-sleeved blue T-shirt covered by a chequered shirt. The buzz cut shone black in the light from the hallway, complementing the dark frown on his handsome face. Wisps of chest hair revealed by the T-shirt's V-neck announced his overwhelming masculinity. Not that it needed any more of an introduction.

With his broad shoulders blocking the doorway, his imposing height towering over her own five feet six inches in her bare feet and his blue eyes glittering with intent, he looked even more capable of leaping tall buildings in a single bound in casual clothing than he had in his captain of industry outfit.

'We need to talk.'

Flattening a large hand against the door, he pushed it open and strolled past her into the room before she could object.

'We've already talked,' she said, her voice as unsteady as her heartbeat as she gripped the lapels of the flimsy robe, drawing them over her throat in a vain attempt to hide at least some of the marks left by his kisses.

She squeezed her traitorous nipples under folded forearms to alleviate the sudden rush of blood which had them standing out against the satin-like torpedoes ready to launch.

Good grief, she was as good as naked, while he was

fully dressed. No wonder her heartbeat was punching her pulse points with the force of a heavyweight champ.

He turned, his size even more intimidating than usual as he stepped close. *Too close.* She took a step back, not caring if it made her look weak. Right now she *felt* weak. Too weak to resist her physical reaction to him. And that would be bad for a number of reasons. None of which she could recall, because her brain was packed full of cotton wool and rampaging toddlers tripping on cocaine.

'You shouldn't be here,' she said, wanting to mean it.

'What didn't you have?'

The terse question had the toddlers hitting a brick wall while the endorphin rush detonated into a thousand fragments of shrapnel.

'Excuse me?'

'You said, "I didn't have," and then you stopped. What were you about to say?'

'I have no idea.'

'You're lying.' Dane could see it in her eyes. The translucent blue-green was alive with anxiety as her teeth trapped her bottom lip.

Unfortunately he could also see she was naked under her robe. And his body was already riding roughshod over all sensible thought.

Blood charged into his groin, but he kept his gaze steady on hers. He'd spent the last three hours trying to convince himself that seeing her again would be nuts. Why not just sign the divorce papers, have Mel deliver them tomorrow and put an end to this whole fiasco?

But that one half-sentence, that one phrase that she'd left hanging kept coming back to torment him. That and the brutal heat that he had begun to realise had never died.

'I didn't have...'

Eventually he'd been unable to stand it any more. So

he'd walked the three blocks to the hotel. There was something she wasn't telling him. And that something was something he needed to know.

Maybe they meant nothing to each other now. But they had once, and not all his feelings had faded the way they should have. Which might explain why his libido hadn't got the memo.

He still wanted her, and it was driving him crazy.

The light perfume of her scent, the sight of her hair curling in damp strands to her shoulders, the moist patches making the wet satin cling to her collarbone, the trembling fingers closing the robe while he imagined all the treasures that lay beneath...

Damn it, Redmond. Concentrate. You're not here to jump her. You're here to get the truth.

He'd convinced himself that she'd got rid of their kid because she'd *had* to, because it had been the only way she could be shot of him, and he'd never questioned it, but in the last three hours he'd begun picking apart the evidence—and not one bit of it made any sense.

He'd always known Xanthe didn't love him, because no one *really* loved anyone else. But when had she ever given him any indication that she didn't want to keep their baby? Never. Not once. She had been the one who had insisted she wanted to have it when the stick had turned blue. She had been the one to say yes instantly when he'd suggested marriage. She had been the one who had kept on smiling every morning as she'd puked her guts up in the motel bathroom while he was left feeling tense and scared. And she'd been the one who had never stopped talking about the tiny life inside her. So much so, that she'd made him believe in it, too.

How could that girl have given up on their baby because of one dumb argument?

'I'm not lying,' she said. 'And you need to leave.'

The quiver of distress in her voice made a mockery of the spark of defiance in her eyes. He could see the war she was waging to stay strong and immune. Her back was ram-rod-straight, and her chin stuck out as if she were waiting for him to take a shot at it.

Frustration tangled with lust.

Gripping her upper arms, he tugged her towards him. Her muscles tensed under his palms, the thin layer of smooth satin over warm skin sending sex messages to his brain he did not need.

'Tell me the truth, Red. What really happened to our baby? You owe me that much.'

A shudder ran through her and she looked away—but not before he spotted the flare of anguish.

'Please don't do this. None of it matters any more.'

'It does to me,' he said, and the feelings inside him—feelings he'd thought he'd conquered years ago—raced out of hiding to sucker-punch him all over again.

Hurt, loss, sadness, but most of all that futile festering rage.

Except this time the rage wasn't directed at Xanthe but at himself. Why hadn't he fought harder to see her? Why hadn't he made more of an effort to get past her father and his goons and find out what had really happened?

She kept her head down, but a lone tear trickled down the side of her face. Pain stabbed into his gut—a dull echo of the pain when Carmichael's goons had dragged him off the estate and beaten him until he'd been unable to fight back.

'Look at me, Xan.'

She gave a loud sniff and shook her head.

Cradling her cheek, he brushed the tear away with his thumb and raised her face to his. Her eyes widened, shadowed with hopelessness and grief, glittering with unshed tears.

And suddenly he knew. The truth he should have figured out ten years ago. The truth that would have been obvious to him then if he'd been less of a screwed-up, insecure kid and more of a man.

He swore softly and folded his arms around her, trying to absorb the pain.

'You didn't have an abortion, did you?'

He said the words against her hair, breathing in the clean scent of lemon verbena, anchoring her fragile frame against his much stronger one.

His emotions tangled into a gut-wrenching mix of anger and pain and guilt. How could he have got things so wrong? And what did he do with the information now?

She stood rigid in his arms, refusing to soften, refusing to take the comfort he offered. The comfort her old man had denied them both.

He swallowed down the ache in his throat. 'That sucks, Red.'

She drew in a deep, fortifying breath, her whole body starting to shake like a leaf in a hurricane. He tightened his arms, feeling helpless and inadequate but knowing, this once, that he was not going to take the easy road. She wasn't that girl any more—sweet and sunny and stupidly in love with a guy who had never existed—and up until two seconds ago he would have thought he was glad of it. But now he wasn't so sure.

His throat burned as she trembled in his arms and he mourned the loss of that bright, optimistic girl who had always believed the best of him when he had been unable to believe it himself.

CHAPTER EIGHT

'I'M SO SORRY, *Mrs Redmond. There's no heartbeat and we need to operate to stop the bleeding.'*

The storm of emotion raged inside her, the sobs she'd repressed for so long choking her as her mind dragged her back to that darkest of dark days. Lying on the hospital gurney, the white-suited doctor looking down at her with pity in his warm brown eyes…

Dane's hand stroked her hair. His heartbeat felt strong and steady through worn cotton, his chest solid, immovable, offering her the strength she'd needed then and been so cruelly denied. Tearing pain racked her body as she remembered how alone, how useless, how helpless she'd felt that day. And the horror that had followed.

She gulped for air, her arms yearning to cling to his strength as tears she couldn't afford to shed made her throat close.

Be strong. Don't cry. Don't you dare break.

He kissed her hair, murmuring reassurances, apologies that she'd needed so badly then but refused to need now. Then his hips butted hers and she felt the potent outline of him, semihard against her belly.

Arousal surged in her shattered body, thick and sure and so simple. Reaction shuddered down to her core.

Flattening her hands against the tense muscles of his belly, she pushed out of his arms and looked up to find him watching her, his expression grim with regret and yet tight with arousal. Reaching up, she ran her palms over his hair, the way she'd wanted to do as soon as she'd walked into his office.

Absorbing the delicious tingle of the short bristles against her skin, she framed his face and dragged his mouth down to hers. 'You're ten years too late, Dane. There's only one thing I want now.'

Or only one thing she could still allow herself to take.

His eyes flared and her body rejoiced. This was the one thing they had always been good at. She didn't want his pity, his regret, his sympathy—all she wanted was to feel that glorious heat pounding into her and making her forget about the pain.

His mouth captured hers, his tongue plunging deep, demanding entry. She opened for him, the heady thrill obliterating the treacherous memories.

Large hands ran up her sides under the robe, rough calluses against soft skin bringing her body to shimmering life. He crushed her against him, banding strong arms around her back, forcing her soft curves to yield to his strength. She draped her arms over his shoulders as he picked her up, carried her to the king-sized bed and dropped her into the centre. Parting the thin satin with impatient hands, he swept his burning gaze over her naked skin, the dark rapture in his eyes making her feel like a sacrifice already burning at the stake.

She reached for his belt, desperate to wrap her fingers round his thick length and make him melt, too. But he gripped her wrists and pinned her hands to the mattress above her head, leaving her naked and exposed while he was still fully clothed.

'Not yet,' he growled, the barely leashed demand in his gruff voice exciting in its intensity. 'Let me touch you first. Or this is gonna last about two seconds.'

She stopped struggling against his hold, the terse admission more gratifying than a thousand declarations of undying devotion. Lying boneless, she let her own hunger overwhelm her, frantic to feel the rush of release that would make her forget everything but this day, this hour, this moment.

It was madness, but it was divine madness—the perfect end to a disastrous day. She was sick of thinking about consequences, about her own troubled emotions and the implications of everything that had happened ten years ago. She was sick of thinking, full stop. And, however else Dane had failed her—as a husband, as a friend—he had never failed her as a lover.

Still holding her wrists, he bent to kiss her lips, his mouth firm and demanding, before trailing kisses down her neck, across her collarbone. She rose off the bed, his groan a potent aphrodisiac as he licked at one pouting nipple.

A soft sob escaped her as he ran his tongue around the areola and then suckled the hard bud, making it swell against his lips into a bullet of need. She moaned, low and deep, as he bit into the tender flesh. Hunger arrowed down to her core. Sharp and sure and unstoppable. And then he transferred his attentions to the other breast.

She panted, writhing under the sensual torture. 'Please, I need you...'

'I know what you need, baby,' he growled. 'Open your eyes.'

She did as he demanded, to find his striking blue gaze locked on hers. Bracketing her wrists in one restraining hand, he watched her as he found her wet and wanting. She lifted her hips, pushing into the unbearably light caress as the moisture released.

She couldn't think, couldn't feel, her skin burned as his playful strokes had the pleasure swelling and then retreating, tempting and then denying.

'Dane...' His name came out on a broken cry. 'Stop messing about.'

He barked out a harsh laugh, the fierce arousal in his face sending her senses into overdrive. 'You want me to use my superpower?'

'You know I do. You...'

Her angry words dissolved in a loud moan as he released her wrists to part her legs. Holding her open with his thumbs, he blew across the heated flesh. She bucked off the bed. The tiny contact unbearable.

She watched, transfixed, shaking with desire as his dark head bent and his tongue began to explore her slick folds. A thin, desperate cry tore from her throat as blunt fingers entered her, first one, then two, stretching her, torturing that hotspot deep inside only he knew would throw her over the edge.

She screamed, her fingers digging into his hair, urging him on as he set his mouth on her at last, suckling the swollen nub. She hurtled into glorious oblivion, exquisite rapture slamming into her as her senses exploded into a thousand shards of glittering light.

Dane lifted himself up, the lingering taste of her sweet and succulent, the need for release unbearable. She stared at him, her eyes wide, the sea-green dazed and wary, her body flushed with pleasure, her skin luminous.

Damn, but she was the most beautiful woman he'd ever seen. Even more beautiful than before. She'd lost that openness, that faith in him that had always scared the hell out of him, and now she had a million secrets of her own, but he could still zap her with his superpower.

The old joke made him smile—but the smile turned to a grimace as the insistent throbbing in his groin tipped from torment into torture.

If he didn't get inside her in the next two seconds he was liable to embarrass himself.

Dane located the condoms in the front pocket of his

jeans and grappled with his belt and shoved his pants down. He ripped open a foil packet and rolled on the protection. Grasping her hips, he lifted her up, then paused.

'Tell me you want this.'

Tell me you want me.

The pathetic plea echoed in his head and made him tense. This was about sex and chemistry, pure and simple. Raw, rough, elemental. He didn't need her approval. He just needed to be inside her.

'You know I do,' she said, bold and defiant.

He stopped thinking and plunged deep, burying himself to the hilt, then groaned, struggling to give her time to adjust before he began to move.

'You okay? You're so tight…' His mind reeled, remembering it had been a while for her. Five years at least. His heady sense of victory at the thought was almost as insane as the delirious wish to be able to take her without a condom.

Draping her arms over his shoulders, she lifted herself up to angle her hips and take him deeper. 'Just move.'

'Yes, ma'am,' he said, laughing.

She was his. She had always been his in the only way that really meant anything.

He drew out, thrust back, feeling her clench around him. The heat in his abdomen built into an inferno as he established a ruthless rhythm, determined to drive her over again before he found his own release.

He clung on to control, an explosive orgasm licking at the base of his spine as her soft sobs became hoarse cries and she reached the point of no return. Her muscles clamped tight, massaging his length as she hit her peak. He thrust once, twice, and collapsed on top of her, his brutal release violent in its intensity as his seed exploded into the sweet, shuddering clasp of her body.

CHAPTER NINE

'WELL, THAT WAS...' Xanthe struggled to breathe while being crushed into the mattress, the floaty, fluffy sensation fading fast to be replaced with all the aches and pains of not one but two mind-blowing orgasms.

Her brain knotted with the stupidity of what they'd just done.

He shifted, lifting his weight from her, and the sensual smile on his too-handsome face was both arrogant and strangely endearing.

'Awesome,' he supplied.

'Actually, I was going to say insane.'

He grunted out a strained laugh and rolled off her. Xanthe watched him sitting on the edge of the bed with his back to her as he bent to untie his boots and then kick his pants off the rest of the way.

'More like inevitable.' He took off his shirt and balled it up to drop it next to his jeans. 'Since we've both been primed for it since this afternoon,' he added, his voice muffled as he pulled his T-shirt over his head and dumped it on the pile of clothing.

Her throat clogged at the sight of his broad back, deeply tanned but for the whiter strip of skin on his backside and the now faded scars that stood out in criss-crossing stripes across his ribs. An echo of sympathy and sorrow and curiosity about those marks hit her unawares. She forced the feelings down, disturbed by the direction of her thoughts.

Dane's secrets were his own and always had been, and they were no concern of hers.

He stood up and strolled across the room, gloriously naked, his languid stride both arrogant and unashamed. Xanthe became transfixed by the bunch and flex of the gluteal muscles in his tight, beautifully sculpted butt cheeks. Her body hummed back to life—like one of those relighting candles people put on a birthday cake as a joke, with a flame that keeps flaring no matter how hard you try to blow it out.

She slipped under the sheets, far too aware of her own nakedness now. She'd always thought those candles were really annoying.

'What do you think you're doing?' she ventured, trying to sound stern.

He glanced back over one broad shoulder as he opened the bathroom door. 'Grabbing a shower.'

She hauled the sheet to her neckline to cover any hint of vulnerability. 'I don't remember inviting you to stay.'

He leaned against the door, thankfully shielding at least some of his more impressive assets and sent her a stern look that she suspected was much more effective than her own.

'I'm having a shower and then we're going to get to that talk.'

'I don't want to talk.' She ignored the raised eyebrow. 'All I want to do is sleep,' she protested.

And try to forget about the fact that Dane's position as her go-to guy for earth-shattering orgasms had not diminished in the least.

'Preferably alone,' she added for good measure.

Now that stallion had bolted out of the stable. Twice. She did not need a repeat performance.

'And you can,' he said. 'Once we're finished talking.'

'But...'

The door slammed behind him.

'I don't want you here,' she finished lamely as the power shower was switched on behind the closed door.

Oh, for—she swore, using a word that would have had Nanny Foster reaching for the soap.

The man was incorrigible. Domineering and dictatorial and completely contrary. Surely there could be nothing left to say about what had happened ten years ago? He'd figured out the truth, they'd jumped each other, had multi-orgasmic make-up sex…end of story.

If she were at full strength she would pick up the phone right now and call hotel security to have him thrown out. Even if it *would* be somewhat problematic explaining why they should be kicking out the man whose credit card details were on the room.

Unfortunately, though, she wasn't at full strength. She dragged her weary body out of the bed. If nothing else, the make-up sex had killed her second wind stone dead. She could happily sleep for a month now.

So she'd just have to go for damage limitation.

Grabbing a bunch of cushions off the sofa, she jammed them into the middle of the bed in case he got any ideas about joining her once he'd finished his shower.

And just in case *she* got any ideas…

She whisked his discarded T-shirt off the floor as the only nightwear option on offer—the hotel's satin robe had been about as useful as a negligee in a rugby scrum—and put it on to establish a second line of defence. The shirt hung down to mid-thigh, the sleeves covering her hands, and looked less enticing than a potato sack. Perfect.

Not so perfectly, it smelled of him—that far too enticing combination of washing powder and man.

She hauled herself back into the bed, trying not to notice the sexy scent as she prepared to stay awake for a few minutes more in order to give Dane his marching orders.

Curling into a tight ball with her back to the wall of cushions, she watched the winking lights across the Hudson
River through the hotel's floor-to-ceiling glass walls, and
stared at the corner suite's awe-inspiring view of the Jersey shoreline.

The buzz of awareness subsided into a relaxing hum
and the tender spot between her thighs became pleasantly
numb. She inhaled his scent, lulled by the sound of running water from the shower.

The thundering beat of her heart slowed as her mind
began to drift. Her eyelids drooped as she floated into
dreams of hot, hazy days on the water and muscular arms
holding her close and promising to keep her safe.

For ever.

Dane sat in his shorts and concentrated on finishing off
the last few bites of the burger and fries he'd ordered from
room service, mindful of the soft snores still coming from
the pile of bedclothes a few feet away.

What was he still doing here?

Xanthe had been dead to the world ever since he'd come
out of the bathroom. He'd thought at first she might be faking sleep to avoid the conversation they still needed to have
about why she'd lied to him in his apartment. Letting him
believe she had terminated the pregnancy. Why the heck
hadn't she just told him about the miscarriage then, instead
of waiting for him to figure it out on his own?

But after ten minutes of watching her sleep, her slim
body curled in the bed like a child and barely moving, he'd
conceded that not only wasn't she faking it, but she wasn't
likely to stir until morning.

Given that, he had no business hanging around. They
weren't a couple. And he didn't much like hanging around
after sex even when the woman he'd just had sex with was
a casual date, let alone his almost-ex-wife.

But once he'd begun to get dressed he'd been unable to locate his T-shirt. After hunting for a good ten minutes, he'd finally spotted a blue cuff peeking out from under the bedclothes. A quick inspection under the covers had been enough to locate the missing shirt—and trigger a series of unwanted memories.

Xanthe in her wet swimsuit on the deck of the pocket cruiser, pulling on his old high school sweatshirt to ward off the chill after a make-out session in the water. Him grabbing one of his work shirts to throw over her as she raced ahead of him into the motel bathroom, her belly rebelling in pregnancy. And a boatload of other equally vivid memories—some mercilessly erotic, others painfully poignant.

That old feeling of protectiveness had struck him hard in the chest—and stopped him from walking out.

He'd messed up ten years ago. She was right. He hadn't been there when she needed him. But there was nothing he could do about that now. Except apologise, and she hadn't wanted his apology.

He knew a damn distraction technique when he saw one, and that was what she'd done—used sex and chemistry as a means of keeping conversation at a minimum.

He'd been mad about that once he'd figured it out in the shower, but he'd calmed down enough now to see the irony. After all, mind-blowing sex had always been *his* go-to distraction technique when they were kids together and she'd asked him probing questions about the humiliating scars on his back.

Dumping the last of the burger on the plate, he covered the remains of the meal with the silver hood and wheeled the room service trolley into the hall.

Uneasiness settled over him as he returned to the suite. He needed to leave. She could keep the undershirt. He had a hundred others just like it. He didn't even know what he was still doing here.

But as he approached the bed to grab his work shirt off the floor and finish getting dressed a muffled sob rose from the lump of bedclothes, followed by a whimper of distress.

Edging the cover down, he looked at her face devoid of make-up, fresh and innocent, like the girl he remembered. But then her brow puckered, her lips drew tight, and her hand curled into a tight fist on the pillow beside her head. Rapid movement under her eyelids suggested she was having some kind of nightmare as she stifled another sob.

His heart punched his ribcage and got wedged in his throat. He needed to go. But instead of heading for the door he crouched beside the bed and rested his palm on her hair. He brushed the wild curling mass back from her forehead, instinct overriding common sense.

'Shh, Red, everything's okay. Go back to sleep.'

She shook off his hand, her breathing accelerating as the nightmare gripped her. 'Please pick up the phone Dane… *Please.*'

The hoarse, terrified whimpers tore at his conscience, guilt striking him unawares. Awake, she'd been strong and resilient. But asleep was another matter.

He couldn't walk away. Not yet.

Tugging on his jeans and leaving the top button undone, he whipped back the sheets to discover a row of cushions from the couch laid out down the middle of the bed. A rueful smile tugged at his mouth.

What was the great wall of throw pillows supposed to keep in check? His libido or hers?

Digging the makeshift barrier out of the bed, he slung the cushions back on the couch. Climbing in behind her, he gathered her shaking body into his arms until her back lay snug against his chest, her bottom nestled into his crotch.

He ignored the aching pain as blood pounded into his lap, grateful for the confining denim while waiting for her laboured breathing to even out—the renewed rush of heat not nearly as disturbing as the rush of tenderness.

Holding her wrist, he laid his arm across her body, careful not to touch any part of her that would make the torment worse. But the memory of spooning with her like this, after they'd made love that final time ten years ago, came flooding back to fill the void. Except that time his hands had caressed the compact bump of her belly, his head spinning with amazement and terror at what the future would hold.

Tortured thoughts of what she'd endured without him rose to the surface.

Eventually she stilled, the rigid line of her body softening against his.

Obviously, some remnant of the misguided kid he'd once been still remained. Because a part of him wanted to stay and hold her through the night, in case she had any more nightmares. But he couldn't go back and erase what he'd done, and she wouldn't want him here when she woke up in the morning.

So he'd just stay for a short while—until he was sure she was okay. Then he'd leave and get Mel to send over the divorce papers in the morning. So she'd lied about the miscarriage? Did he really want to know why? Delving into her reasons now wouldn't serve anyone's purpose.

But as he listened to the comforting murmur of her breathing his body relaxed against hers and all his sound decisions drifted out into the night, shooting across the Hudson River, heading up towards the Vineyard and back into fitful dreams.

CHAPTER TEN

SOMETHING HEAVY BECKONED Xanthe out of sleep. Deep, drugging, wonderful sleep that made her feel secure and happy.

Her eyelids fluttered open and her gaze focused on a hand. A large tanned hand with a tattoo of a ship's anchor on the thumb was holding hers down on the pillow, right in front of her face. The hand looked male. Very male. And very familiar.

She blinked, struggling to bring her mind into focus, and realised that a male arm, attached to the male hand, lay across her shoulders. She drew in a deep breath, the scent of clean sheets and clean man reminding her of the good dreams that had danced through her consciousness before waking. She shifted, aware of the long, muscular body wrapped around hers, and his deep breathing made the hair on the back of her neck prickle.

Dane.

Thin strands of sunlight shone through the slatted blinds, illuminating the hotel room's luxurious furnishings as the events of the evening before crowded in and her abdomen warmed, weighed down by the hot brick in her stomach.

She stole a moment to absorb the comfort of being cocooned in a man's arms for the first time in... She frowned. For the first time in a decade.

Dane had always gravitated towards her in his sleep. She'd always woken up in his arms during the brief weeks of their marriage. It was one of the things she'd missed the most. And this time she didn't have the stirrings of morning sickness to cut through her contentment.

She had a vague recollection of nightmares chasing her, and then his arms and his voice lulling her back to sleep.

Holding her breath, she shifted under his arm and inched her hand out from under the much larger one covering it.

The rumble of protest against her hair froze her in place.

Long fingers squeezed hers, before his thumb inched down her arm, sliding the sleeve of the T-shirt down to the elbow—the T-shirt that was supposed to be protecting her from the thoughts making her belly melt.

'You playing possum?' A gruff voice behind her head asked.

'I'm trying to.' She sighed, annoyed and at the same time stupidly aroused.

She could feel the solid bulge against her bottom, the unyielding wall of his chest that was sending delicious shivers of reaction up her spine.

'Mmm...' he mumbled, sounding half-asleep as his hand lifted and then settled on her thigh.

His calloused caress had goosebumps tingling to life as he trailed his hand under the hem of the T-shirt and rubbed across her hip.

Awareness settled between her legs and she rolled abruptly onto her back to halt his exploration.

His hand rested on her belly as he rose up on one elbow to peer down at her. His short hair was flattened on one side, and the stubble on his chin highlighted that perfect masculine dimple. Amusement and desire glinted in the impossible blue. Her breath squeezed under her diaphragm.

He'd always looked so gorgeous in the morning—all rumpled and sexy and usually a little surly. He'd never been much of a morning person, unlike her. But he didn't look surly now. He looked relaxed and devastatingly sexy.

'I didn't plan to stay the night,' he said, by way of explanation. 'But seeing as I'm here…'

His hand edged down, that marauding thumb brushing the top of her sex. Her belly trembled in anticipation.

'This isn't a good idea,' she murmured, trying to convince herself to push his hand away.

Pressing his face to her neck, he nuzzled kisses along her jaw. 'Nope.'

The tremor of awareness drew her the rest of the way out of sleep and into sharp, aching need. He cupped her, slid his fingers through her slick folds, locating the knot of desire with pinpoint accuracy.

She gasped and rolled towards him, letting him lift the soft cotton shirt over her head and throw it away. He captured one aching nipple with his lips as his fingers continued to work their magic.

Memories assailed her of waking up just like this, with his hands and tongue and teeth beckoning her out of sleep and into ecstasy. She pushed back the rush of memory, the sapping tide of romanticism, until all that was left was the hot, hard demand of sexual need.

She desired Dane—she always had. But that was all it had ever been.

Reaching out, she cradled the bulge confined behind a layer of denim. 'Why are you wearing your jeans in bed?'

'Stop asking dumb questions,' he grumbled. 'And help me out of them.'

She didn't need any more encouragement. This was wrong, and they both knew it, but it didn't seem to matter any more. In a few short hours they will have declared the end of their marriage. And she wanted him here, now, more than she'd ever wanted any man. Just once more.

She released the button fly with difficulty, to find him long and hard beneath stretchy boxers.

'Take them off,' she demanded, pleased to hear the power, the assurance in her voice.

She was taking control. He couldn't walk all over her any more. And here was the proof.

But as he threw the covers back and divested himself of the last of his clothes she found herself feeling strangely vulnerable as he climbed over her, caging her in.

'Tell me exactly what you want, Red. I want to make you come so hard you scream.'

The words excited her beyond bearing. And terrified her, too. Reminding her of the boy who had once taken her to places no other man ever had.

She'd never been coy about sex, but she'd never been bold either—except with him.

Folding her hand around his huge length, she flicked her thumb across the tip, trying to regain control. Regain the power. Adrenaline rushed through her as his thick erection jerked against her palm.

His mouth took hers as his fingers delved into her hair and he angled her head to devour her. The scrape of his beard ignited tender skin...her tongue tangled with his.

He reached across her to grab a condom from the bedside table.

She took it from him. 'Let me.'

'Go ahead,' he said, relinquishing control.

The fire in his eyes was full of approval, and a desire that burned her to the core. No other man had ever desired her the way he had.

She fumbled with the foil packet, her skin flushing at his strained laugh.

He chuckled. 'You need more practice.'

She slipped the condom on, aware that she had never done this for another man. Determined not to let him know it. He wasn't special, He was just…filling a need. A need that she had neglected for far too long.

Her thoughts scattered, centring on his thumb as he began to stroke her again. Stroking her into a frenzy. One long finger entered her and she flinched slightly. Evidence of their rough coupling the night before was still present, still there.

'Hey…' He cupped her cheek, forcing her to meet his eyes. 'Are you too sore for this?'

His concerned expression had her heartbeat kicking her ribs. Bringing with it a myriad of unwanted memories. His rough hand holding her hair, rubbing her back as she threw up in the motel toilet. Those lazy mornings when the nausea hadn't hit and he'd taken her slowly, patiently, watching her every response, gauging her every need and meeting it.

'I'm fine,' she said, precisely because she wasn't.

Don't be kind. Please don't be kind. I can't stand it.

'Uh-huh.' He didn't look convinced. Holding her, he rolled, flipping onto his back until she was poised above him, her knees on either side of his hips.

'How about *you* take charge this time?' he said, and she felt her heart expand in her chest.

But then his thumb located that pulsing nub and every thought flew out of her head bar none. *She had never been in charge of her hunger for him.*

He coaxed the orgasm forth as she sank down on his huge shaft.

'That's it, Red. Take every inch.'

He held her hips, lifting her as she parted round the thick length, almost unable to bear the feeling of fullness, of stretching, but unable to stop herself from sinking down again to take more, to take him right to the hilt.

His harsh grunts matched her moans as she rode him, increasing the tempo. A stunning orgasm was racing towards her. Her mind reeled as his gaze locked on hers, encouraging, demanding, forcing her over that perilous edge as he gave her one last perfect touch.

She sobbed, throwing her head back, her body shattering as she came hard and fast. She heard him shout out moments later, his penis pulsing out his release as his fingers dug into her thighs.

She fell on top of him, her forehead hitting his collarbone with a solid *thunk* as her heart squeezed tight.

She closed her eyes, her staggered breathing matching the pounding beat of her heart as his large hands settled on her back and stroked up to her nape. Blunt fingers massaged her scalp.

He laughed, the sound low and deep and self-satisfied. Warning bells went off, but they sounded faint and unimportant, drowned out by the glorious wave of afterglow.

'How about…before we finalise our divorce…' his deep voice rumbled against her ear '…we treat ourselves to a honeymoon?'

She lifted herself off him with an effort. 'What are you talking about?'

'I've got a week's vacation coming.' He brushed his fingers down her arms, setting off a trail of goose pimples and reigniting those damn birthday candles. 'I was supposed to be heading to Bermuda this afternoon, for a sailing trip to Nassau. I could postpone it for a couple of days.'

For a split second her endorphin-clouded mind actually considered it. Being with him—escaping from the endless stress and responsibilities of her job, from all the pain and regret of their past. But then her heart jumped in her chest and reality crashed in on her.

This was *Dane*. The man who had always been able to separate sex from intimacy in a way she never had. Or at least not with him.

She didn't hate him any more. And he still had the ability to seduce her and turn her into a puddle of lust with a single touch, a single look. She couldn't risk being alone with him for another hour, let alone for another night.

'I don't think so,' she said.

She climbed off him and bent to retrieve his discarded T-shirt, suddenly desperate for clothing. But his hand clamped on her wrist. His face was devoid of the lazy amusement of a moment ago.

'Why not?'

He looked genuinely irritated by her refusal, which told her all she needed to know.

'Because I have a company to run. I'm CEO of Carmichael's now—I can't afford to take time off,' she finished, giving him the face-saving answer.

She couldn't tell him the real reason—that she didn't want to risk spending time alone with him. He'd think she was nuts. Maybe she *was* nuts.

She was stronger, wiser and older now, with a healthy cynicism that should protect her from remaking the catastrophic mistakes of her youth. But the new knowledge that Dane had only abandoned her because he'd thought she'd abandoned *him* left a tiny sliver of opportunity for those old destructive feelings to take hold of her emotions again—especially coupled with more mind-altering sex.

She didn't want to be that idiot girl again, and if anyone could sway her back into the path of destruction it was a juggernaut like Dane. And the worst of it was *he* would remain unscathed. The way he always had before. For him, sex was always just sex—and that hadn't changed, or he would never have suggested another night of no-holds-barred sex after the tumult of the last twenty-four hours.

But why wouldn't he when *he* didn't have to worry about stirring up old feelings because he had never loved her the way she'd loved him? He'd only suggested marriage because of the guilt and responsibility he'd felt over her pregnancy—and, however her father had interfered in their break-up, it was obvious their marriage had been doomed to failure.

Deep down, she would always be a romantic—an easy target for a man like Dane who didn't have a single soft or sensitive or romantic bone in his body.

He'd never let her in. Had never let his guard down during the whole three months they'd lived in that motel.

He finally let go of her wrist and she scooted to the edge of the bed to put on the T-shirt, feeling awkward and insecure, reminded too much of that romantic child.

'So you're running daddy's company now?'

She dragged the T-shirt over her head. 'It's not his company any more. It's mine.'

Or it would be as soon as she had Dane's signature on those divorce documents and the controlling 6 per cent of the shares could be released to her.

She swallowed down a prickle of guilt at her deception. Dane had no claim on Carmichael's—it was simply a paperwork error. A paperwork error that, once corrected, he need never know about.

'He hated my guts when we were kids...'

The non sequitur sounded casual, but she could hear the bite in his voice and knew it was anything but.

What did he expect her to say? That her father had been a snob and had decreed Dane unsuitable? How could she defend Dane without compromising herself and her decision to take on Carmichael's after her father's death? The company had meant everything to her father and she understood that now—because it meant everything to *her*. And if a small voice in her head was trying to deny that and assert that there was more to life than running a successful business, it was merely an echo of that foolish girl who had believed that love was enough.

'He didn't hate you,' she said. 'I'm sure he just thought he was doing what was best for me.'

Even as she said the words they sounded hollow to her, but she refused to condemn her father. He had loved her in his own way—while Dane never had.

'Did it ever occur to you that if I'd been able to see you that day, things might have turned out differently?' He raised a knee and the casually draped sheet dipped to his waistline.

His expression was infuriatingly unreadable. As always.

'I don't see how.' She hesitated, trying to force thick words out past the frog in her throat. 'And it worked out okay for both of us, so I have no regrets.'

She turned away from the bed, desperate not to be having this conversation. It would expose her. She didn't want him to know how hard it had been for her. How much losing him and their baby had hurt her at the time. And how much else it had eventually cost her.

But he reached over and snagged her wrist again. 'That's bullshit. And you want to know how I *know* it's bullshit?'

'Not particularly,' she said, far too aware of the way his thumb was stroking her pulse, hoping he couldn't feel it hammering in her wrist like the wings of a trapped hummingbird.

'Last night you had a nightmare about losing the baby,' he said. 'That's why I stayed. That's why I was here when you woke up. Maybe if I had been able to do that ten years ago, I wouldn't still need to do it now.'

Her pulse pummelled her eardrums. She wanted to ask him how he knew she'd been having a nightmare about the miscarriage. But she definitely didn't want to know how she'd given herself away in her sleep. She felt vulnerable enough already.

'You didn't need to stay. I would have been fine. I've had them before and...'

She realised her mistake when his expression hardened.

'How many times have you had them before?'

Too many.

'Not often,' she lied.

'That bastard.' His fury wasn't directed at her, but still she felt the force of his anger.

'It's okay. Really. I've come to terms with what happened.'

'Don't lie, Red.'

He hooked his thumb round her ear, brushing her hair back and framing her face. The gesture was gentle, and full of concern. Making her heart pulse painfully.

'You can lean on me—you know that, right?'

'I don't need to lean on you,' she said, denying the foolish urge to rest her head into the consoling palm and take the comfort he offered.

'What are you so scared of?' he said, cutting through the defences she'd spent ten years putting in place.

'I'm not scared.' How could he know that when he had never really known *her*? 'Why would I be?'

'I don't know—you tell me,' he said tightly. 'Why did you let me go on believing you had an abortion yesterday?'

She stiffened and pulled away from him. How could he still read her so easily?

'Why would I bother to correct you? I didn't think it mattered any more. It was so long ago.'

'Of course it matters. I deserve to know what really happened. Especially if you're still having nightmares because—'

'Why, Dane?' she interrupted. 'Why do you deserve to know? When you never wanted our baby the way I did?'

He tensed and something flashed over his face—something that might almost have been hurt. But it was gone so quickly she was sure she had misinterpreted it. Dane had never wanted the baby—that much she knew for sure.

'If you had, you would have demanded to see me,' she said, cutting off the painful thought. 'Instead of assuming I'd had an abortion.'

'I *did* demand to see you.' Temper flashed in his eyes. 'Your father had his goons throw me out.'

'He...*what?*' The breath left her lungs in a painful rush. Anguish squeezed her chest. 'Did they hurt you?'

She could still remember those men. They'd terrified her, even though her father had always insisted they were there to protect her.

His eyes narrowed, and the annoyed expression was one she recognised. If there was one thing Dane had always despised, it was anything remotely resembling pity.

'I handled myself,' he said.

She didn't believe him. At nineteen he'd been tough and muscular, and as tall as he was now, but he'd also been a lot skinnier, a lot less solid—still partly a boy for all his hard knocks. Four of those men against one of him would have done some serious damage.

She noticed the crescent-shaped scar cutting across his left eyebrow and knew it hadn't been there before—she'd once known every one of the scars on his body. The scars he would never talk about.

She pointed at the thin white mark bisecting his brow. 'Where did you get that scar?'

He shifted, avoiding her touch. She dropped her hand, aware of the heavy weight in her belly.

'I don't remember.'

He sounded unconcerned. But that guarded expression told a different story. He did remember—he just wasn't prepared to discuss it.

The hollow pain blossomed. Why was she pressing the point? Maybe because he'd held her last night, through her nightmare...making her feel weak and needy. And then made love to her this morning with such unerring skill, coaxing the exact response he'd wanted out of her.

He'd held all the power in their relationship and it was now brutally obvious he held it still.

'My father had no right to treat you that way,' she said. 'If you tell me what injuries you suffered I'll have my legal team work out suitable compensation.'

Paying him off suddenly seemed like the perfect solution. The only way to get herself free and clear of him and the emotions he stirred in her. Her only chance of acquiring the distance she'd surrendered so easily ever since walking into his office yesterday.

'Don't play the princess with me. I don't want your money. I never did. And I sure as hell don't need it any more.'

'It's a simple matter of compen—'

'You didn't do anything wrong,' he said, slicing through her objection. '*He* did. If anyone owes me an apology, it's him.'

'Well, he's been dead for five years. So you're not likely to get one.'

'I don't want an apology from a dead guy—what I want is for you to acknowledge what he did to us was wrong. Why is that so damn hard for you?'

She threw her hands up in the air. 'Fine. I agree what he did was wrong. Is that enough for you?'

'No. I want you to stay here with me.'

'What has that got to do with anything?'

'He split us up before we were ready. We've got a chance now to take some time to say goodbye to each other properly.'

His gaze flicked down her frame, and the inevitable flare of heat she felt in response made it doubly clear exactly what their goodbye was supposed to entail.

'We're both grown-ups now and we deserve to finish this thing right. Why can't you see that?'

Because I'm scared I might still care about you. Too much.

'I've told you—it's just bad timing.'

'Don't give me that. If you're running the company you can make time for this. But you won't. And I want to know why.'

'I won't because I don't *want* to spend time with you,' she shouted back, determined to mean it. 'If your ego can't accept that, that's your problem—not mine. We're over— we've been over for ten years.'

'Yet I can still make you come so hard you scream. And you haven't let another guy do that to you for five years. Five years is a heck of a long time.'

The blush flushed through her to the roots of her hair. His eyes went razor-sharp.

'What the...? Has it been *longer* than five years?'

How could he know that?

'I didn't say that.' She scrambled to deny it. Knowing she couldn't lie because he would read her like a book and know the truth instantly.

Dane had always been able to use her need for him against her. He'd never treated her like a wife when they were married. Had never been capable of opening up to her and sharing anything of himself with her. And she'd been so pathetically grateful for any sign that he cared about her at all, she'd found that romantic.

She knew the truth now, though—that his possessiveness, his protectiveness, hadn't been a sign of his love. It had simply been a sign of his need to claim ownership. If he ever found out that she'd never shared her bed with any other man but him, she'd be handing him a loaded gun.

'You don't have to say it,' he said. 'It's written all over your face.'

'Oh, shut up!' She stormed off, determined to lock herself in the bathroom before he discovered the humiliating truth and shot down the last remaining shreds of her composure.

His laugh followed her all the way into the shower cubicle.

Who knew Xanthe could be so cute when she was mad?

Dane let out a strained chuckle as she slammed the bathroom door behind her, then rubbed the heel of his palm over the ache in the centre of his chest. The choking feeling returned.

It shouldn't really matter to him that his wife hadn't slept with that many other guys, but somehow it did. It also shouldn't matter to him that she didn't want to hang out at the hotel for another night.

He wasn't a possessive guy, or a particularly protective one. But with Xanthe it had always been different. Because he'd been her first. And she'd once been pregnant with his child.

And seeing her have that nightmare, knowing it wasn't the only one she'd had, had affected him somehow. Made him feel guilty for not being there when she'd needed him, even though his head was telling him it wasn't his fault.

She'd been stressed and exhausted when she'd arrived in his office yesterday. Enough to face-plant right in front of him. And in that moment she had reminded him of the girl she'd been—the girl he'd felt so in tune with because of the way she'd been bullied by her father. That girl had always been trying to please a guy who would never be pleased. And now it looked as if she was still doing it.

That had to be why she'd worked herself into the ground to take on her old man's company. She'd never had any interest in it back then. He didn't doubt she was good at her job—she'd always been smart and conscientious, and it seemed she'd added a new layer of ball-buster to the mix since then. But if she enjoyed it so much why didn't she have a life outside it?

He knew how easy it was to lose sight of your personal life, your personal well-being when you were building a business. He'd done the same in the last few years. Hell, he'd only managed a couple of short-term hook-ups since they'd split. But his company had been his dream right from when he was a little kid and he'd hung around down by the marina to avoid his father's belt.

And he was a lot tougher than Xanthe would ever be. Because he'd been born into a place where you hit the ground running or you just hit it—hard.

He knew how to take care of number one. He always had. Because no one else had wanted the job. Xanthe had always been way too open, way too eager to please. And it bugged him that she was still trying to please a dead man.

He didn't like seeing that hollow, haunted look lurking behind the tough girl facade. And she was still his wife until those papers were signed.

After getting dressed, he picked up his cell phone and keyed in his attorney's number. He'd promised to sign the damn papers, but who said he had to sign them straight away?

'Jack, hi,' he said, when his attorney answered on the second ring. 'About those papers I sent over yesterday...'

'I had a look at them last night,' Jack replied, cutting straight to the chase as usual. 'I was just about to call you about them.'

'Right. I've agreed to sign them, but I—'

'As your legal counsel, I'd have to advise against you doing that,' Jack interrupted him.

'Why?' he asked, his gut tensing the way it had when he was a kid and he'd been bracing himself for a blow from his old man's belt. 'They're just a formality, aren't they?'

'Exactly,' Jack replied. 'You guys haven't lived together for over ten years, and two to five years separation is the upper limit for most jurisdictions when it comes to contesting a divorce.'

'Then what's the deal with telling me not to sign the papers?'

Jack cleared his throat and shifted into lecture mode. 'Truth is, your wife doesn't require your signature on *anything* to get a divorce. She could have just filed these papers in London as soon as she found out about the failure to file the original documents and I would have gotten a heads-up from her legal representative. That's what got me digging a little deeper—I got to wondering why she'd come all the way to Manhattan to deliver them in person and that's when I found something curious buried in the small print.'

'What?' Dane asked, the hairs on his neck standing to attention.

The fact that Xanthe hadn't needed to bring the documents over in person had already occurred to him. That she hadn't needed to bring them at all seemed even more significant. But the anxiety jumping in his stomach wasn't making him feel good about that any more.

'There's a codicil stating that neither one of you will make a claim on any property acquired after the original papers should have been filed.'

'Then I guess I can quit worrying about her trying to claim back-alimony.' He huffed out a breath. He was not as pleased with the implication that Xanthe had made a point of not wanting any part of his success as he ought to be.

'Sure, but here's the thing—it goes on to state all the assets that can't be claimed on. Why would she need to itemise those in writing? She'd have a hell of a legal battle trying to claim any of your property on the basis of a separation made years before your company even began trading. But that's when I got to thinking. What if it wasn't *your* property she was trying to protect but her own?'

'I don't get it. I couldn't make any claim on her property.'

Did she think he *wanted* her property? Her old man had once accused him of being a gold-digger. Of getting his daughter pregnant and marrying her to get his hands on Carmichael's money. Had she believed the old bastard? Was that why she'd let him go on believing she'd had an abortion? To punish him for something he hadn't done?

Anger and injured pride collided in his gut, but it did nothing to disguise the hurt.

'Turns out you're wrong about that,' Jack continued. 'You've got grounds to make a claim on her company. I just got off the phone with a colleague in the UK who checked out the terms of her father's will. A will that was written years before she even met you. One thing's for sure—it answers the question of why she came all the way over to Manhattan to get you to sign her divorce papers.'

As Dane listened to Jack lecturing him about the legalities and the terms of Charles Carmichael's will his stomach cramped and fury at the sickening injustice of it all started to choke him. The same futile fury he'd felt after the beating he'd taken all those years ago because he'd wanted to see his wife, to know what had happened to his child.

Each word Jack uttered felt like another blow he couldn't defend himself against. Suddenly he was furious with Xanthe as well as her old man. For making him feel like that again. Worthless and desperate, yearning for something he couldn't have.

She'd planned to play him all along by coming here. How much of what had happened in the last day had even been real? She'd said she didn't want to spend any more time with him. And now he knew why—because once those papers were signed she'd have the guarantee she needed that he couldn't touch her father's precious company.

She'd lied. Because she'd decided he didn't deserve the truth. She'd even accused him of not caring about their baby. And then…

He thought about her whimpers of need, those hot cries as she came apart in his arms. She hadn't just lied to him, she'd used his hunger for her against him. Turned him back into that feral kid begging for scraps from a woman who didn't want him. Then she'd slapped him down and offered to pay him off when he'd had the audacity to ask for one more night.

He signed off with Jack, then sat down and waited for her to come out of the bathroom. The bitterness of her betrayal tasted sour on his tongue.

The good news was he had more leverage now than he could ever have dreamt of. And he was damn well going to use it. To show her that *no one* kicked him around— not any more.

CHAPTER ELEVEN

It took Xanthe twenty minutes to realise she could not hide in the bathroom for the rest of her natural life.

She'd faced a hostile board for five years and her father's stern disapproval for a great deal longer. She could deal with one hot as hell boat designer.

But even so she jumped when a knock sounded on the door.

'You still in there or have you disappeared down the drain?'

The caustic tone was almost as galling as the flush that worked its way up her torso at the low rumble of his voice.

'I'll be out in a minute.'

'A package got delivered for you.'

Her clothes.

Hallelujah.

She reached for the bolt on the door, then paused.

'Could you leave it there?'

With the hotel's satin robe somewhere on the floor of the suite and his T-shirt neatly folded to give back to him on the vanity unit, all she had to cover her nakedness was a towel.

'Why don't you order us some breakfast?' she added, trying to sound unconcerned. Because clearly he was not going to do the decent thing and just leave her in peace.

'You want the package—you're gonna have to come out and get it.'

Blast the man.

Grasping the towel tight over her breasts, she flicked back the bolt and opened the door. She shoved the T-shirt at him, far too aware of his spectacular abs peeping out from behind his unbuttoned shirt.

He took it, but lifted the package out of reach when she tried to grab it. 'Not so fast.'

'Give me the package,' she demanded, using her best don't-mess-with-me voice—the one that had always worked so well in board meetings but seemed to be having no impact at all on the man in front of her. 'It has my clothes in it. If you still want to talk we can talk, but I refuse to discuss anything with you naked.'

Because look how well that had turned out the last time she'd done it.

He kept the package aloft. 'If I give you this, I want a promise that you'll come out of there.'

She frowned at him, noticing the bite in his tone. Something was off. Something was *way* off—the muscle in his jaw was working overtime to keep that impassive look on his face.

'What's wrong?'

'Not a thing,' he said, his jaw as hard as granite. 'Except that you've been sulking for a good half hour.'

She hadn't been sulking. She'd been considering her options—very carefully. But she was finished with being a coward now. Better to face him and get whatever he had to discuss over with. Because standing in a towel with that big male body inches away was not helping.

She reached out for the package. 'Deal.'

He slapped it into her palm.

Whipping back into the bathroom, she locked the door and leaned against it. Something was most definitely wrong. Where had the wry amusement gone? That searing look he'd given her had been as hard as it was hot.

Blowing out a breath, she got her new clothes out of the

packaging. Sitting in the bathroom wouldn't solve anything. It was time to face the music and wrap this up once and for all.

Five minutes later she walked back into the suite, feeling a lot more steady with the new jeans and T-shirt and fresh underwear on. He'd donned his T-shirt and discarded the overshirt, but even covered, his pecs looked impressive as they flexed against the soft cotton while he levered himself off the couch.

She noticed the divorce papers on the coffee table in front of him. He must have had them couriered over. Relief was mixed with a strange emptiness at the thought that he'd already signed them. Which was, of course, ridiculous.

'Sorry to keep you waiting,' she said, polite and distant, even though her body was already humming with awareness. Clearly that would never change.

'Really?'

He still sounded surly. Maybe she should have come out a bit sooner.

She didn't dignify the question with an answer. Crossing the room to the coffee pot on the sideboard, she poured herself a cup to buy some time. Even after half an hour of prepping she didn't know what to say to him.

The tense silence stretched between them as she took a quick gulp of the hot liquid and winced. 'I see you still like your coffee strong enough to Tarmac a road,' she commented.

The unbidden memory made her fingers tremble. She turned to find him watching her.

'I don't know what you want from me, Dane. I've said I'm sorry for what my father did, for what happened. Obviously our break-up...' She paused, clarified. 'The way our break-up happened was regrettable. But I want to end this amicably. I can't stay in New York any longer.'

Because, however tempting it would be to indulge herself, let her body dictate her next move, she never wanted to be a slave to her libido again.

'That's why you came here? To end this amicably?'

It was a leading question. And, while it hadn't been the reason she'd boarded the plane yesterday morning at Heathrow, she felt an odd tightening in her chest at the thought of what they'd shared the day before and through the night. Stupid as it was, her heart skipped a beat.

Had she been kidding herself all along? Despite the implications for Carmichael's, she could have done this whole process by proxy. It would have been simpler...more efficient. But as soon as Bill had mentioned Dane's name to her she'd been bound and determined to do it in person. And she suspected her reasons were much more complex than the ones she'd admitted to herself.

How much had her coming here *really* had to do with the threat to Carmichael's? And how much to do with that grief-stricken girl who had mourned the loss of him as much as she had mourned the loss of their baby?

He had been the catalyst—the one who'd shown her she was more, *could* be more than her father had ever given her credit for. And, despite the shocks to her system in the last hours, she would always be grateful to have discovered that he hadn't abandoned her the way her father had wanted her to believe.

Placing the coffee mug back on the counter, she faced him fully. 'Honestly? I think I needed to see you again. And, as difficult as this has been—I'm sure for both of us—I'm glad I did.'

'Yeah?'

'Yes.' Why did he still sound so annoyed?

'Nice speech. I guess that's my cue to sign these?' He scooped the divorce papers up from the table. 'And then get out of your way?'

'I suppose…' she said, feeling oddly ambivalent about the papers, her pulse beginning to hammer at her collarbone.

He didn't just sound surly now. He sounded furious. And he wasn't making much of an effort to hide it.

'Tough, because that's not gonna happen.' He ripped the papers in two, then in two again, the tearing sound echoing around the room. Then he flung the pieces at her feet.

'Why did you do that?' She bent to pick them up, her heart hammering so hard now she thought it might burst.

Grasping her arm, he hauled her upright. 'Because I'm not as dumb as you think I am. I know what your phoney divorce papers are really for. To stop me claiming the fifty-five per cent of your old man's company he left to *your husband* in his will.'

'But…' Her knees dissolved. The blow was made all the more devastating by the look of total disgust on his face.

'You didn't come here to end a damn thing *amicably*. You came here to play me.'

'That's not true.'

But even as she said it she could feel the guilt starting to strangle her. Because when she'd come here that was exactly what she'd intended to do.

'Well, it is partially true. But that was before I found out…'

'You think you can lie and cheat and say and do whatever the hell you want to get your way? Just like your old man? Well, you're gonna have to think again. Because *no one* screws with me any more.'

There were a million things she could say in her defence. A million things she wanted to say. But her throat closed, trapping the denial inside her. She felt herself shutting down in the face of his anger. Wanting to crawl away and make herself small and invisible. The way she had whenever her father had shouted at her, had bullied and

belittled her, had derided her for being too soft, too sentimental, too much of a *girl*.

'I've got to hand it to you...the seduction was a nice
touch.'

Heat seared her to the core as his gaze raked over her,
as hot as it was derisive.

'You've certainly learned how to use that fit body to
your advantage.'

The contemptuous comment felt like a smack in the
face. Releasing the anger which had lain dormant for far
too long.

'How dare you imply...?'

Hauling herself out of his arms, she slapped him hard
across the face, determined to erase that smug smile.

His head snapped back on impact. And fire blazed in
her palm.

But her anger faded as quickly as it had come, the vol-
canic lava turning to ash as he lifted a hand to his cheek
to cover the red stain spreading across the tanned skin.
His eyes sparked with contempt, and his powerful body
rippled with barely controlled fury.

Shock reverberated through her.

He manipulated his jaw, then licked his lip, gathering the
tiny spot of blood at the corner of his mouth. The nonchalant way in which he had accepted the blow made her feel
nauseous. How many other times had he been hit before?

'So daddy's little princess finally learned how to fight
back,' he said, the fury in his tone tempered by an odd
note of regret.

The shock disappeared, to be replaced with weariness and a terrible yearning to turn back the clock. What
were they doing to each other? She couldn't hate him any
more—it hurt too much to go there again.

But how could he have such contempt for her? Know
so little about who she'd been then and who she was now?

'Dane, I can explain. This isn't what it looks like.'

Except it was in some ways.

She reached for him, needing to soothe the blotchy mark she'd caused. He jerked away and brushed past her, heading for the door.

'It's *exactly* what it looks like.'

He opened the door, and part of her heart tore inside her chest. He was walking away from her again—the way he had once before. But she couldn't find the words to stop him, all her protests lodged inside her.

He paused at the door, fury still blazing in the ice-blue eyes. 'I never wanted your old man's money—or his crummy company. Which just makes it all the sweeter now that I can take a piece of it if I want to. Just for the hell of it. Don't contact me again.'

Xanthe collapsed onto the couch as the door slammed, her mind reeling and her whole body shaking.

She wrapped her arms around her midriff, taking in the unmade bed, the torn pieces of document on the carpet, the unfinished mug of black coffee. A gaping wound opened up in her stomach and threw her back in time to that dingy motel room in Boston. Lost and alone and terrified.

Tears squeezed past her eyelids as she sniffed back the choking sob that wanted to come out of her mouth.

If Dane followed through with his threat she might very well lose everything she'd worked so hard for in the last ten years. Even the *threat* of legal action would be enough to destroy her position as CEO. If the board ever found out she'd mismanaged this situation so catastrophically they would surely withdraw their support.

But far worse than the possibility of losing her job was that look of contempt as he'd accused her of being daddy's little princess.

Was that really what he'd thought of her all those years ago? That she was some spoilt little rich girl? Was that why he'd never trusted her with his secrets? Was that what he thought of her now, despite all she'd achieved?

And why did it sting so much to know he'd always thought so little of her?

She stood up and thrust shaky fingers through her hair, scrubbing away the tears on her cheeks.

No. Not again. She was not going to fold in on herself. Or let his low opinion of her matter.

Ten years ago stuff had happened that had been beyond their control. Her father's interference... The miscarriage... But there had been so much more they could have controlled but hadn't. And anyway the past was over now. Dane Redmond didn't mean anything to her any more.

Maybe she should have told him about the will as soon as she had discovered he hadn't abandoned her. She could see now that hadn't played well when he'd figured it out. But *he* was the one who had assumed she'd had an abortion, who had never trusted in her love, and *he* was the one who was threatening to take her company away from her. Why? Because she'd had the audacity to protect herself?

This was all about his bull-headed macho pride. Dane, in his own way, was as stubborn and unyielding as her father.

Well, she wasn't that timid, fragile, easily seduced child any more. And she was *not* going to sit around and let him crucify her and ruin everything she'd worked for.

She had the guts to stand up to him now. He was in for a shock if he thought this 'princess' wasn't tough enough to get him to sign the damn divorce papers and eliminate any threat to her company—even if she had to scour Manhattan to find him.

Four hours later, after a frantic trip to his offices and a fruitless interrogation of his tight-lipped PA, she discovered it wasn't going to be that easy.

Sitting in the first-class departure lounge at JFK, en

route to St George, Bermuda, she felt a knot of anxiety start to strangle her as she contemplated how she was going to stay strong and resolute and indomitable if she was forced to confront her taciturn and intractable ex-husband on a yacht in the middle of the Atlantic...

CHAPTER TWELVE

'THERE, ON THE HORIZON—that has to be it.' Xanthe pointed at the yacht ahead of them and got a nod from the pilot boat operator she'd hired that afternoon at the Royal Naval Dockyard on Ireland Island, Bermuda. She pushed back the hair that had escaped her chignon and started to frizz in the island's heat.

The punch of adrenaline and purpose had dwindled considerably since her moment of truth at the hotel the day before—now the snarl of nerves was turning her stomach into a nest of vipers. The boat sped up, skipping over the swell. She held fast to the safety rail. The sea water sprinkling her face was nowhere near as refreshing as she needed it to be.

At least her madcap chase to find Dane and confront him was finally at an end, after a two-hour flight from JFK, a sleepless night at an airport hotel in St George, scouring the internet for possible places he might have harboured his boat, and then a three-hour taxi journey criss-crossing Bermuda as she checked out every possible option.

She'd arrived at the Royal Naval Dockyard on the opposite tip of the island, the very last place on her list, at midday, with her panic starting to eat a hole in her stomach. The discovery that Dane had been there and just left had brought with it anxiety as well as relief at the thought of confronting him.

She gripped the rail until her knuckles whitened as the pilot boat pulled closer to the bobbing yacht.

At least her frantic transatlantic call to London at four that morning had confirmed Dane had yet to start any legal proceedings against her. So there was still time—if she could talk sense into him.

The gleam of steel stanchions and polished teak made the sleek vessel look magnificent as the blue-green of the water reflected off the fibreglass hull.

Her heart stuttered as she read the name painted in swirling letters on the side.

The Sea Witch.

The teasing nickname whispered across her consciousness.

'I'm under a spell...you've bewitched me, Red...you're like a damn sea witch.'

The muscles of her abdomen knotted as she tried to erase the memory of his finger circling her navel as he'd smiled one of his rare smiles while they'd lain on the beach at Vineyard Sound together, a lifetime ago, and he'd murmured the most—and probably the only—romantic thing he'd ever said to her.

Beads of sweat popped out on her upper lip as she spotted Dane near the bow, busy readying the boat's rigging. She'd caught him just in time. His head jerked round as the pilot boat's rubber bumpers butted the yacht's hull and the boat's captain shouted to announce their arrival.

She shook off the foolish memories and slung her briefcase over her shoulder. She had a short window of opportunity. She needed to get on board before Dane could object or the pilot boat's captain would realise the story she'd spun him about being a guest who had missed the sailing was complete fiction.

Grabbing hold of the yacht's safety line, she clambered

into the cockpit. She quickly unclasped her life jacket and flung it back to the pilot boat.

'I can take it from here—thank you so much!' she shouted down to the captain.

The man glanced at Dane, who had finished with the rigging and was bearing down on her from the other end of the boat. 'You sure, ma'am?'

Not at all.

'Positive,' she said, flinching when Dane's voice boomed behind her.

'What the *hell* are you doing here?'

She ignored the shout and kept her attention on the pilot boat's captain. 'I'll be in touch in approximately twenty minutes. And I'll double your fee if you leave us now.'

Dane didn't want her on board, which meant he would have to listen to reason. It wasn't much of a bargaining chip, but it was the only one she had.

'Okay, ma'am.' The pilot boat captain tipped his hat as his nervous gaze flicked to Dane and back. 'If you say so.'

The boat's engine roared to life. The captain had peeled the nimble vessel away from the yacht, obviously keen to avoid unnecessary confrontation, and was headed towards the marina when Dane reached her.

'Where is he going?'

She turned to face him. 'He's returning to the harbour and will come to pick me up once I give him the signal.'

Her rioting heartbeat slammed into her throat.

He looked furious, his face rigid with temper.

'Is this some kind of joke? Get off my boat.'

'No.' She locked her knees, forcing her chin up. 'Not until you sign the divorce papers.' She dumped the briefcase at his feet. 'I have a new set in there to replace the ones which fell victim to your temper tantrum at the hotel.'

His scowl darkened at the patronising comment, and

the punch of adrenaline she'd felt after he'd stormed out on her returned full force. Bolstering her courage.

That's right, you don't have the tiniest notion who you're dealing with now.

The slap of the sea against the hull and the cry of a nearby seabird pierced the silence as the seconds ticked by—seeming to morph into hours—and the rigid fury rippling through him threatened to ignite. With his tall, muscular body towering over her, and the dark stubble covering his rigid jaw he looked more disreputable than a pirate and a lot more volatile.

She forced herself to resist flinching under the contemptuous appraisal as his gaze scoured her skin. Okay, maybe she'd underestimated the extent of his anger. But showing him any weakness would be the height of folly, because Dane would exploit it. The way he had exploited it once before. When she'd been young and naive and completely besotted with him.

His T-shirt was moulded to the wall of pecs in the breeze, the pushed-up sleeves revealing his tattoo, which bulged as he crossed his arms over his broad chest and stared her down. The sweet spot between Xanthe's thighs hummed, the unwanted arousal tangling with the punch of adrenaline to make anxiety scream under her breastbone like a crouching tiger waiting to pounce.

'What makes you think I won't haul you overboard?'

The ice-blue of his eyes made her brutally aware that this was no idle threat.

'Go ahead and try it.' She braced herself, prepared for the worse, bunching her hands into fists by her side. After the last twenty-four hours spent chasing him across the Atlantic she wasn't going to give up without a fight.

And, if the worst came to the worst, she could survive the two-mile swim back to the marina…

If she absolutely had to.

* * *

What the ever-loving—?

Dane cut off the profanity in his head, desire already pooling in his groin like liquid nitrogen.

To say he was shocked to see Xanthe was an understatement of epic proportions. Maybe not as stunned as when she'd shown up in Manhattan to inform him they were still married. But close.

She was the only woman, apart from his mother, who had ever managed to hurt him. And while he knew she couldn't hurt him any more, because he was wise to her, he hadn't planned to test the theory. Especially on the vacation he had been looking forward to for months. Hell, *years*.

This was supposed to be a chance for him to get some much needed R & R. To enjoy the simplicity of being out on the water with nothing to worry about but keeping his course steady and the wind in his sails.

But as she stood in front of him, her lush hair dancing around her head in a mass of fire and those feline eyes glittering with defiance, he couldn't deny the leap of adrenaline.

When was the last time a woman had challenged him or excited him this much? Xanthe was the only one who had ever come close. But the girl he'd married was a shadow of the woman she was now.

They'd always been sexually compatible. But that firecracker temper of hers was something he'd only ever seen small glimpses of ten years ago—on those rare occasions when she'd stood up to him.

Unfolding his arms, he cracked the rigid line of his shoulders in a shrug and headed back towards the bow.

Big deal—she had more guts than he'd expected. He'd see how far that got her once she discovered he wasn't going to play ball.

Ducking under the mainsail, he set about untying the line he'd secured to the anchor chain and then pressed the button to activate the yacht's windlass.

'What are you doing?'

The high-pitched squeak of distress from over his shoulder told him she'd followed him.

'Weighing anchor,' he said, stating the obvious as he lifted the anchor the rest of the way into the boat, then marched back past her. 'You've got two minutes to call your guy before we head for open water.'

She scrambled after him. 'I'm not getting off this boat until you agree to sign those papers.'

He swung round and she bumped into his chest. She stumbled back to land on the bench seat of the cockpit, her cheeks flushed with a captivating mix of shock and awareness.

Arousal powered through his system on the heels of adrenaline.

'I'm not signing a damn thing.'

Taking the wheel, he adjusted the position of the boat until the breeze began to fill the mainsail.

'It's a four-day trip to the Bahamas, which is where I'm headed. With nowhere to stop en route. You want to be stuck on a boat with me for four days, that's up to you. Either that or you can swim back to the marina.'

He cast a look over his shoulder, as if assessing the distance.

'You're a strong swimmer. You should be able to make it by sunset.'

The mulish expression on her face was so priceless he almost laughed—until he remembered why she was there. To protect the company of a man who had treated him like dirt.

She glared back at him. 'I'm not budging until you sign those papers. If you think I'm scared of spending four days on a yacht with you, you're very much mistaken.'

The renewed pulse of reaction in his crotch at this ball-busting comment forced him to admire her fighting spirit. And admit that the fierce temper suited her.

Unfortunately for her, though, she'd chosen the wrong balls to bust.

The mainsail stretched tight and the boat lurched forward.

She gripped the rail, and the flash of panic that crossed her face was some compensation for the fiery heat tying his guts in knots as the yacht picked up speed.

'Yeah, well, maybe you should be,' he said, realising he wasn't nearly as mad about the prospect as he had been when she'd climbed aboard the yacht.

She'd chosen to gatecrash his solo sailing holiday and put them both into a pressure cooker situation that might very quickly get out of control. But if it did, why the hell should *he* care?

Doing the wild thing with Xanthe had never been a hardship. And seeing the unwanted arousal in her eyes now had taken some of his madness away, because it proved one incontrovertible fact. What had happened between them in that hotel room had been as spontaneous and un-stoppable for her as it had been for him.

He wasn't going to sign her phoney papers because that would be the same as admitting she'd been right not to trust him with the truth back in Manhattan. That her father had been right not to trust him all those years ago, too.

Charles Carmichael had accused him of being a gold-digger, of being after the Carmichael money, and his daughter must believe it too or she wouldn't have tried to trick him into signing those papers.

He was a rich man now—he could probably buy and sell her precious Carmichael's twenty times over—but even as a wild-eyed kid, starved of so many things, he'd never asked for a cent from her *or* her old man.

Xanthe had been his once—she'd insisted she loved him. But even so a part of her had stayed loyal to her old man or she would have asked questions when her father had told her lies about him. She would have tried to contact him after the miscarriage. She wouldn't have let him go on believing she'd had an abortion up to two days ago. And she sure as hell wouldn't need any guarantee that he wasn't going to rip her off for 55 per cent of a company he had never wanted any part of.

If she wanted to spend the next four days pretending she was immune to him, immune to the attraction between them, so be it.

They'd see who broke first.

Because it sure as hell wasn't going to be him.

Exhaustion and nerves clogged Xanthe's throat as the boat bounced over the swell. She bit down on her anxiety as she watched the land retreat into the distance. She'd come all this way to reason with him—and argue some sense into him. And she'd do it. Even if she had to smack him over the head with a stanchion.

'I apologise for not telling you about my father's will.' She ground out the words, which tasted bitter on her tongue. Her ability to sound contrite and subservient, which was probably what he expected, had been lost somewhere over the Atlantic Ocean. 'I should have been straight with you once I knew you hadn't abandoned me ten years ago, the way my father led me to believe.'

He'd put his sunglasses on, and his face was an impassive mask as he concentrated on steering the boat—making it impossible for her to tell if her speech was having any impact.

The strong, silent treatment, which she had been treated

to so many times in the past, only infuriated her more, while also making greasy slugs of self-doubt glide over her stomach lining.

She breathed deeply, filling her lungs with the sea air. Stupid how she'd never realised until now how easily he had undermined her confidence by simply refusing to communicate.

She dug her teeth into her bottom lip.

Not any more.

She wasn't that giddy girl, desperate for any sign of affection. And she wasn't getting off his precious boat until she had what she'd come for: namely, his signature on the replacement documents she had stuffed in her briefcase so she could end their marriage and any threat of legal action.

She glanced past him, back towards the mainland. Her pulse skipped a beat as she realised the pilot boat had disappeared from view and that Ireland Island was nothing more than a haze on the horizon dotted by the occasional giant cruise ship.

She pulled in a staggered breath, let it out slowly. The plan had been to get Dane's signature on the divorce documents—not to end up getting stuck on a yacht with him for four days.

She'd expected him to be uncooperative. What she *hadn't* expected was for him to call her bluff. Somewhere in the back of her mind she'd convinced herself that once she got in his face he'd be only too willing to end this charade.

But as the spark of sexual awareness arched between them, and the hotspot between her thighs began to throb in earnest, she realised she'd chronically underestimated exactly how much of an arrogant ass he could be.

The one thing she absolutely could *not* do was let him know how much erotic power he still wielded.

'You don't want me here, and I don't want to be here.

So why don't we just end this farce and then we never have to see each other again?'

His gaze finally lowered to hers. The dark lenses of his sunglasses revealed nothing, but at least he seemed to be paying her some attention at last.

Progress. Or so she thought until he spoke.

'I don't take orders, Princess.'

The searing look was meant to be insulting, with the cruel nickname adding to her distress. Her anxiety spiked.

'Fine. You refuse to meet me even halfway...' She scooped the briefcase off the bench seat in the cockpit. 'I guess you're stuck with me.'

She headed below decks.

It wasn't a retreat, she told herself staunchly, simply a chance to refuel and regroup.

The cool air in the cabin's main living space felt glorious on her heated skin as she took a moment to catch her breath and calm her accelerated heartbeat.

But her belly dropped to her toes and then cinched into tight, greasy knots as her eyes adjusted to the low lighting and she took in the space they would be sharing for the next four days.

The yacht had looked huge from the outside, but Dane had obviously designed it with speed in mind. While the salon was luxuriously furnished in the best fabrics and fittings, and boasted a couch, a table, shelves crammed with books and maps, a chart table and a well-appointed galley equipped with state-of-the-art appliances, it was a great deal snugger than she had anticipated.

The man was six foot three, with shoulders a mile wide, for goodness' sake. How on earth was she going to fit in a space this compact with him without bumping up against that rock solid body every time the boat hit a wave?

And then she noticed the door at the end of the space,

open a crack onto the owner's cabin, where a huge mahogany carved bed took up most of the available space, its royal blue coverlet tucked into the frame with military precision.

A hot brick of panic swelled in her throat, not to mention other more sensitive parts of her anatomy. She swallowed it down.

Dane wouldn't be spending much time below decks, she reasoned. No solo sailor could afford to spend more than twenty minutes at a time away from the helm if they were going to keep a lookout for approaching vessels or other maritime dangers. And she had no plans to offer to share the load with him, given she was effectively here against her will—not to mention her better judgement.

Dumping her briefcase, she crossed into the galley and flung open the fridge to find it stocked—probably by his staff—with everything she could possibly need to have a five-star yachting vacation at his expense.

He'd accused her of being a princess, so it would serve him right if she played the role to the hilt.

It didn't matter if the living space was compact. It had all the creature comforts she needed to while away her hours on board in style until he saw reason. With Dane occupied on deck, she could use this as her sanctuary.

After finding a beautifully appointed spare berth, with its own bathroom, she cleaned up and stowed her briefcase. Returning to the galley, she cracked open one of the bottles of champagne she'd found in the fridge, poured herself a generous glass and made herself a meal fit for a queen—or even a princess—from the array of cordon bleu food.

But as she picked at her meal her heartbeat refused to level off completely.

How exactly was she going to dictate terms to a man who had always refused to follow any rules but his own?

A man she couldn't get within ten feet of without feeling as if she were about to explode?

Dane held fast to the wheel and scanned the water, blissfully empty and free of traffic now they'd left Ireland Island and the pocket cruisers and day trippers behind. He wheeled to starboard. The sail slapped against the mast, then drew tight as the boat harnessed the wind's power. He tipped his head back as *The Sea Witch* gathered speed. Elation swelled as the dying sun burned his face and the salt spray peppered his skin.

Next stop the Bahamas.

What had he been thinking, waiting so long to get back on the water?

But then his gaze dropped to the door to the cabin, which had been firmly shut ever since Xanthe had stormed off a couple of hours ago.

He imagined her sulking down there, and wondered if she planned to hide away for the rest of the trip.

The boat punched a wave and the jolt shimmered through his bones.

His heartbeat sped up. Her little disappearing act confirmed what he already knew—that he wasn't the only one who'd felt the snap and crackle of that insane sexual chemistry sparking between them when she'd arrived. The fact he was the only one prepared to admit it gave him the upper hand.

He sliced the boat across the swell and felt the hull lurch into the air.

She'd made a major miscalculation if she thought they would be able to avoid it on a fifty-five-foot boat, even if she planned to hide below decks for the duration.

Switching on the autopilot as the sun finally disappeared below the horizon, he ventured below—to find the salon empty and the door to the spare berth firmly shut.

But he could detect that subtle scent of spring flowers that had enveloped him two nights ago, when he'd been wrapped around her in sleep.

He rubbed his chin, feeling two days' worth of scruff. He imagined her fingernails scraping over his jaw. What was that saying about opposites attracting?

They were certainly opposites—him a 'wharf rat' who had made good and her the princess ballsy enough to run a multinational company, even if she *was* only doing it to please her old man. But the attraction was still there, and stronger than ever.

He wasn't going to push anything because he didn't have to. She would come to him—the way she had before. And then they'd see exactly who needed who.

He grabbed a beer from the fridge, a blanket from his cabin and the alarm clock he kept on hand to wake him up during the night while he was on watch. But as he headed back up on deck, ready to bed down in the cockpit, he spotted an artfully arranged plate of fancy deli items sitting on the galley counter covered in sandwich wrap. Next to it was an open bottle of fizz, with a note attached to it.

For Dane, from his EX-wife.
Don't worry, the princess hasn't poisoned it...yet!

He coughed out a gruff chuckle. 'You little witch.'

But then the memory of the meals she'd always had waiting for him in their motel room when he'd got back from another day of searching for work slammed into him. And the rueful smile on his lips died. Suddenly all he could see was those brilliant blue-green eyes of hers, bright with excitement about the pregnancy. All he could hear was her lively chatter flowing over him as he watched her hands stroke the smooth bump of her stomach and shovelled up the food she'd made for him in silence. Too scared to tell her the truth.

Heat flared in his groin, contradicting the guilt twisting in his gut as the crushing feeling of inadequacy pressed down on him.

That agonising fear felt real again—the fear of going another day without finding a job, the terror that had consumed him at the thought that he couldn't pay their motel bill, let alone meet the cost of Xanthe's medical care when the baby arrived.

Putting the beer back in the fridge, he chugged down a gulp of the expensive champagne and let the fruity bubbles dissolve the ball of remembered agony lodged in his throat.

Get a grip, Redmond.

That boy was long gone. He didn't have anything to prove any more. Not to Xanthe, not to himself, not to anyone. He'd made a staggering success of his life. Had worked like a dog to get to college and ace his qualification as a maritime architect, then developed an award-winning patent that with a clever investment strategy had turned a viable business into a multimillion-dollar marine empire—not to mention acing the America's Cup twice with his designs.

He had more than enough money now to waste on bottles of pricey fizz that he rarely drank. Getting hung up on the past now was redundant.

She'd thought she loved him once and, like the sad little bastard he'd been then, he'd sucked up every ounce of her affection—all those tender touches, the adoring looks, all her sweet, stupid talk about love and feelings.

But he wasn't that sad little bastard any more. He knew exactly what he wanted and needed now. And love didn't even hit the top ten.

He sat on deck, wolfing down the food she'd made for

him and watching the phosphorescent glow of the algae shine off the water in the boat's wake while a very different kind of hunger gnawed at his gut.

He didn't need Xanthe's love any more, but her body was another matter—because, whether she liked it or not, they both knew that had always and *would* always belong to him.

CHAPTER THIRTEEN

XANTHE STEADIED HERSELF by slapping a hand on the table the following morning and glared at the hatch as the boat's hull rocked to one side. How fast was he driving this thing? It felt as if they were flying.

Luckily she'd already found her sea legs which, to her surprise and no small amount of dismay, were just where she'd left them the last time she'd been sailing—ten years ago. With Dane.

The boat lurched again, but her stomach stayed firmly in place.

Don't get mad. That had been her mistake yesterday. She needed to save herself for the big battles—like getting him to sign the divorce papers. Provoking him was counterproductive.

After a night of interrupted sleep, her body humming with awareness while she listened to him moving about in the salon on his short trips below deck, she knew just how counterproductive.

Given the meteoric rise in the temperature during their argument yesterday, she needed to be careful. Knowing Dane, and his pragmatic attitude to sex, he wouldn't exert too much effort to keep the temperature down, even if it threatened to blaze out of control. So it would be up to her to do that for both of them.

Xanthe poured herself a mug of the strong coffee she'd found brewing on the stove and added cream and sugar, adjusting to the sway of the boat like a pro.

While she wasn't keen to see Dane, she couldn't stay down here indefinitely. Early-morning sunlight glowed through the windows that ran down the side of the boat. Each time the hull heeled to starboard she could see the horizon stretching out before them.

Her pulse jumped and skittered, reminding her of the days they'd spent on the water before, and how much she'd enjoyed that sense of freedom and exhilaration. Of course back then she'd believed Dane would keep her safe. That he cared about her even if he couldn't articulate it.

She knew better now.

Good thing she didn't need a man to keep her safe any longer.

She dumped the last of the coffee into the sink and tied her hair back in a knot.

She wasn't scared of Dane, or her reaction to him, so it was way past time she stopped hiding below deck.

Even so, her heart gave a definite lurch—to match the heel of the boat—when she climbed out of the cabin and spotted Dane standing at the wheel. On the water, with his long legs braced against the swell, his big capable hands steering the boat with relaxed confidence and his gaze focused on the horizon, he looked even more dominant and, yes—damn it—sexy. Her pulse jumped, then sank into her abdomen, heading back to exactly where she did not need it to be.

She shut the door to the cabin with a frustrated snap. His gaze dropped to hers. Her face heated at the thorough inspection.

'You finished sulking yet, Princess?' His deep voice carried over the flap of canvas and the rush of wind.

Her temper spiked at the sardonic tone. 'I wasn't sulking,' she said. 'I was having some coffee and now I plan to do some sunbathing.'

After a night lying awake in her cabin and listening

to him crewing the boat alone, she had planned to offer to help out this morning. She needed to get him to sign those papers, and she'd never been averse to good honest work, but his surly attitude and that 'princess' comment had fired up her indignation again.

She'd be damned if she'd let his snarky comments and his low opinion of her and her motives get to her.

Ignoring him, she faced into the wind, letting it whip at her hair and sting her cheeks. The sea was empty as far as the eye could see, the bright, cloudless blue of the sky reflecting off the brilliant turquoise water. She licked her lips, tasted salt and sun…and contemplated making herself a mimosa later.

Gosh, she'd missed this. Despite having the fellow traveller from hell on board, maybe this trip wouldn't be a complete nightmare. But as she reached to swing herself up onto the main deck, a bulky life jacket smacked onto the floor of the cockpit in front of her.

'No sunbathing, princess, until you put that on and clip yourself to the safety line.'

She swung round. 'I'm not going to fall off. I'm not an amateur.'

'How long since you've been on a boat?'

'Not that long,' she lied.

She didn't want him to know she hadn't been sailing since they'd parted. He might think her enforced abstinence had something to do with him.

'Uh-huh? How long is "not that long"? Less than ten years?'

She sent him her best death stare. But the hotspots on her cheeks were a dead giveaway.

'Yeah, I thought so,' he said, doing his infuriating mind reading thing again. 'Now, put on the PFD or get below.'

'No. There's barely a ripple on the water. I don't need to wear one.' He was just doing this out of some warped desire to show her who was boss. 'If it gets at all choppy I'll put it on straight away,' she added. 'I'm not an idiot. I have no desire to end up floating around in the middle of the Atlantic.'

Especially as she wasn't convinced he'd bother to pick her up. But she refused to be bullied into doing something completely unnecessary just so *he* could feel superior.

Instead of answering her, he clicked a few switches on the wheel's autopilot and headed towards her.

She pressed against the hatch to avoid coming into contact with that immovable chest again as he reached past her for the jacket. She got a lungful of his scent. The clean smell was now tinged with the fresh hint of sea air.

Hooking the jacket with his index finger, he dangled it in front of her face.

'Put it on. Now.'

Her jaw tightened. 'No, I will not. *You're* not wearing one.'

'This isn't a negotiation. Do as you're told.'

Temper swept through her at his dictatorial tone.

'Stop behaving like a caveman.' She planted her feet, all her good intentions to rise above his goading flying off into the wild blue Caribbean yonder.

Once upon a time she would have been only too willing to do anything he said, because his certainty, his dominance had been so seductive. Not any more.

The backs of her knees bumped against the seat of the cockpit as he loomed over her. Traitorous heat blossomed between her legs as she got another lungful of his exquisite scent. Fresh and salty and far too enticing.

'The hard way it is, then,' he announced, flinging the jacket down.

Realising his intention, she tried to dodge round him— but he simply ducked down and hiked her over his shoulder.

She yelped. Dangling upside down, eyeballing tight

male buns in form-fitting shorts, as she rode his shoulder blade.

Finally getting over her shock enough to fight back, she punched his broad back with her fists as he ducked under the boom and hefted her towards the hatch.

'Put me down this instant!'

He banded an arm across her legs to stop her kicking. 'Keep it up, princess, and I'm tossing you overboard.'

She stopped struggling, not entirely sure he wouldn't carry out his threat, and deeply disturbed by the shocking reaction to his easy strength and the delicious scent of soap and man and sea.

Damn him and his intoxicating pheromones.

He swung her round to take the steps. 'Mind your head.'

When he finally dumped her in the salon she scrambled back, her cheeks aflame with outrage.

The tight smile did nothing to disguise the muscle jumping in his jaw and the flush of colour hitting tanned cheeks. She wasn't the only one far too affected by their wrestling match.

'Are you completely finished treating me like a two-year-old?'

She absorbed the spike of adrenaline when his nostrils flared.

'You don't want to be treated like a toddler?' His voice rose to match hers. 'Then don't act like one. You want to go on deck, you wear the jacket.'

'Being stronger and bigger than me does *not* make you right,' she said, her voice gratifyingly steely...or steely enough, despite the riot of sensations running through her. 'Until you give me a valid reason I'm not wearing it. You'll just have to keep carrying me down here.' Even if having his hands on her again was going to increase the torment. 'Let's see how long it takes for that to get *really* old.'

She stood her ground, refusing to be cowed. This stand-off was symptomatic of everything that had been wrong with their relationship the first time around. She'd given in too easily to every demand, had never stuck up for herself. Never made him explain himself about anything—which was exactly how they'd ended up being so easily separated by her father's lies and half-truths.

Dane had threatened her company and refused to listen to reason, all to teach her a lesson about honesty and integrity—well, she had a few lessons to teach *him*. About respect and self-determination and the fine art of communication.

She wasn't a doormat any more. She was his equal.

'If you want me to wear it, you're going to have to explain to me why I need to when you don't. And then *I'll* decide if I'm going to put it on.'

He cursed under his breath and ran his hand over his hair, frustration emanating from him.

Just as she was about to congratulate herself for calling him on his Neanderthal behaviour, he replied.

'We're sailing against the prevailing winds, which means the swell can be unpredictable. I know when to brace because I can see what's coming. Without a jacket on you could go under before I could get to you.'

'But…that's…' She opened her mouth, then closed it again. 'Why didn't you just say that to start with?' she finally managed, past the obstruction in her throat.

He looked away, that muscle still working overtime in his jaw.

And the melting sensation in her chest, the sharp stab of vulnerability, gave way to temper and dismay. Why had it always been so hard for him to give her even the smallest sign that he cared? It was a question that had haunted her throughout their relationship ten years ago. It was upsetting to realise it haunted her still.

'You know why.'

His eyes met hers, the hot gaze dipping to brand the glimpse of cleavage above the scooped neck of her T-shirt. Heat rushed through her torso, darting down to make her sex ache.

He cupped her cheek, his thumb skimming over her bottom lip, the light in his eyes now feral and hungry. 'Because when I'm with you not a lot of thinking goes on.'

'Don't…' She jerked away from his touch, desperate to dispel the sensual fog. But it was too late. His compelling scent was engulfing her, saturating her senses and sending pheromones firing through her bloodstream.

Her breathing became ragged, her chest painfully tight, as arousal surged through her system.

'Quit pretending you don't want it, too,' he said as he watched her, the lust-blown pupils darkening the bright blue of his irises to black.

'I…I don't.' She cleared her throat, disgusted when her voice broke on the lie. 'We're not doing this again. That's not why I'm here.'

If they made love she was scared it would mean more than it should. To her, at least. And she couldn't risk that.

'Then stay out of my way,' he said. 'Or I'm going to test that theory.'

He walked away, heading back on deck.

'I'm not staying below decks for three days!' she shouted after him, gathering the courage that had been in such short supply ten years ago.

So what if she still wanted him? She couldn't let him control the terms of this negotiation. If she didn't speak out now she'd be no better than the girl she'd been then, ready to accept the meagre scraps he'd been willing to throw her way.

'I came here to save my company,' she added as he mounted the steps, still ignoring her. 'If you think I'm going to sit meekly by while you attempt to steal fifty-five per cent of it, you can forget it.'

His head jerked round, the scowl on his face going from annoyed to furious in a heartbeat, but underneath it she could see the shadow of hurt.

'I didn't want a cent from your old man when I was dead broke. Why the hell would I want a part of his company *now*?' he said as he headed back towards her.

She'd struck a nerve—a nerve she hadn't even realised was still there.

'Then why did you threaten to sue for a share of it?' she fired back, determined not to care about his hurt pride.

She had nothing to feel ashamed of. *She* wasn't the one who had stormed out of their hotel room claiming he was going to sue her just for the hell of it.

'I never said I was going to sue for anything,' he added. 'You made that assumption all on your own.'

'You mean…' Her mouth dropped open. Was he saying she'd come all this way and got stuck on a yacht with him for no reason? 'You mean you're *not* planning to take legal action?'

'What do you think?'

The concession should have been a relief, but it wasn't, the prickle of shame becoming a definite yank. She'd always known how touchy he was about her father's money, but how could she have forgotten exactly how important it had always been to him never to take anything he hadn't earned?

'Then why wouldn't you sign the divorce papers?' she asked, trying to stay focused and absolve her guilt.

How could she have known that his insecurities about money ran so deep when he'd never once confided in her about where they came from? If he'd simply signed the papers in Manhattan, instead of going ballistic, she never

would have made the assumption that he intended to sue
for the shares in the first place.

'And why won't you sign them now?'

'Your *phoney* divorce papers, you mean?'

'They're not phoney. They're just a guarantee that—'

'Forget it.'

He cut off her explanation, the scowl on his face disappearing to be replaced with something else—something
that made no sense. He didn't care about her, he never really had, so what was there to regret?

'I'm not signing any papers that state I can't claim those
shares if I want to.'

'But that's just being contrary. Why wouldn't you sign
them if you don't want the shares?' she blurted out.

'I don't know,' he said, his tone mocking and thick with
resentment. 'Why don't you try figuring it out?'

She didn't have to figure it out, though. Because it suddenly all became painfully obvious.

He expected her to *trust* him. In a way he'd never
trusted her.

The searing irony made her want to shout her frustration at him, but she bit her lip to stop the brutal accusation
coming out of her mouth.

Because it would make her sound pathetic. And it might
lead to her having to ask herself again the heartbreaking
question that had once nearly destroyed her.

Why had he never been able to believe her when she'd
told him she loved him?

She refused to butt her head against that brick wall
again—the brick wall he had always kept around his emotions—especially as it was far too late to matter now.

But then he touched her hair, letting a single tendril
curl round his forefinger. The gentleness of the gesture
made her heart contract in her chest, and the combination
of pain and longing horrified her.

He gave a tug, making the punch of her pulse accelerate. And the yearning to have his mouth on hers became almost more than she could bear.

'Dane, stop,' she said, but the demand sounded like a plea.

She placed her palms on his waist, brutally torn as she absorbed the ripple of sensation when his abdominal muscles tensed under her hands.

'Don't push me, Red,' he murmured, his lips so close she could almost taste them. 'Or I'm gonna make you prove exactly how much you don't want me.'

For tantalising seconds she stood with desire and longing threatening to tear her apart. She should push him away. Why couldn't she?

But then he took the choice away from her.

Cursing softly, he let her go.

She watched him leave, feeling dazed and shaky. She'd fallen under Dane's sensual spell once before and it had come close to destroying her...because he'd always refused to let her in.

But until this moment she'd had no idea exactly how much danger she was in of falling under it again. Or that all those tangled needs and desires to understand him, to know the reasons why he couldn't love her or trust her, had never truly died.

Dane yanked the sail line harder than was strictly necessary and tied it off, his heart pumping hard enough to blow a gasket.

He reprogrammed the autopilot. The maritime weather report had said they were in for a quiet day of smooth sailing.

Smooth sailing, my butt.

Not likely with Xanthe on board.

He'd wanted to bring the princess down a peg or two

when she'd shown up on deck looking slim and beautiful and superior. He sure as hell wasn't going to let her sunbathe in front of him while he took the wheel like a lackey. Or that's how it had started. But the truth was he'd wanted her to wear the PFD, had decided to insist upon it, because he'd been unable to control the dumb urge to make sure she was safe.

And as soon as he'd had her in his arms again, yelling and punching as he carted her below deck, the desire to have her again had all but overwhelmed him too... Then he'd lost it entirely when she'd made that crack about him wanting a piece of her precious company.

He hated that feeling—hated knowing she could still get to him. Knowing that there was something about Xanthe that could slip under his guard and make him care about her opinion when it shouldn't matter to him any more.

Resentment sat like a lead weight in his stomach.

From now on there was going to be no more sparring and no more conversations about their past. He wasn't going to get hung up on why she hadn't been sailing for ten years, even though she'd once been addicted to the rush. Or waste one more iota of his time getting mad about the fact she didn't trust him.

Their marriage was over—had been over for a long time—and it wasn't as if he wanted to resurrect it.

Arousal pulsed in his crotch, adding to his aggravation.

He usually averaged five hours' sleep a night when he was sailing solo, despite the need to wake up every twenty minutes and check the watch. Last night he hadn't managed more than two. Because he'd spent hours watching the stars wink in the darkness, thinking about all the stuff that might have been, while waiting for the night air to cool the heat powering through his body.

The only connection between them now was sexual, pure and simple—an animal attraction that had never died.

Complicating that by sifting through all the baggage that had gone before would be a mistake.

So keeping Xanthe at arm's length for a little while made sense—until he knew for sure that he could control all those wayward emotions she seemed able to provoke without even trying.

He doubted they'd be able to keep their hands off each other for the three days they had left together on the boat—but he could handle the heat until she got one thing straight.

Sex was the only thing he had to offer.

CHAPTER FOURTEEN

'DANE, IS EVERYTHING OKAY?' Xanthe yelled above the whistling wind as she clambered on deck and clipped her safety harness to an anchor point.

The yacht mounted another five-foot wave as water washed over the bow and the rain lashed her face.

Their argument over the life jacket yesterday seemed like a distant memory now.

'Get below, damn it, and stay there!' he shouted back, wrestling with the wheel to avoid a breaking wave—which brought with it the danger of capsizing.

The squall had hit with less than an hour's warning that morning. Dane had woken her up from a fitful sleep to issue some curt instructions about how to prepare the belowdecks, given her a quick drill on the emergency procedures if they had to use the life raft, insisted she take some seasickness pills and then ordered her to stay below.

After yesterday's argument and the evening that had followed—with the tension between them stretching tight as they both avoided each other as best they could—the rough weather and their clearly defined roles this morning had actually come as a relief.

So she'd obeyed his terse commands without question, even while smarting at his obvious determination not to give her anything remotely strenuous to do. When it came to skippering the boat, he was in charge. It would be foolish to dispute that, or distract him, when all his attention needed to be on keeping them afloat.

Correcting his 'princess' assumptions could wait until they got through this.

But as the hours had rolled by and the storm had got progressively worse she'd become increasingly concerned and frustrated by his dogged refusal to let her help. Thunder and lightning had been added to the hazards aboard as the squall had moved from a force-four to something closer to a force-eight by the afternoon, but through it all Dane had continued to insist she stay below.

Rather than have a full-blown argument, which would only make things more treacherous with the visibility at almost zero, she'd kept busy manning the bilge pump, rigging safety lines in the cabin and locking down the chart table when the contents had threatened to spill out. All the while trying to stay calm and focused and zone out the heaving noise outside.

They'd come through the worst of it an hour ago. The torrential rain was still flattening the seas, but the winds were dying down at least a little bit. But two seconds ago she'd heard a solid crash and she'd rushed up on deck, no longer prepared to follow orders.

Relief washed through her to see Dane standing at the wheel, the storm sails intact. But her relief quickly retreated.

His face was drawn, his clothing soaked, his usually graceful movements jerky and uncoordinated. He looked completely shattered. She cursed herself for waiting so long to finally confront him about his stubborn refusal to allow her on deck.

He'd been helming the yacht for over five hours and hadn't slept for more than twenty minutes at a time since they'd left Bermuda two days ago because he'd been keeping watch solo.

Maybe it had been ten years ago, but she'd once been a competent yachtswoman because she'd learnt from a master. She should take the helm. There weren't as many breakers to negotiate now, visibility was lifting and a quick survey of the horizon showed clear skies off the bow only a few miles ahead.

'Dane, for goodness' sake. Let me take over. You need some sleep.'

'Get back below, damn it!'

He swung the wheel to starboard and the boat heeled. But as she grabbed the safety line she saw a trickle of blood mixed with the rain running down his face, seeping from a gash at his hairline.

Horror gripped her insides, and her frustration was consumed by panic. 'Dane, you're bleeding!'

He scrubbed a forearm across his forehead. 'I'm okay.'

Hauling herself up to the stern, she covered his much larger hand with hers, shocked by the freezing skin as he clung to the wheel.

'This is insane,' she said, desperate now to make him see reason. 'I can *do* this. You have to let me do this.'

An involuntary shudder went through him, and she realised exactly how close he was to collapsing when he turned towards her, his blue eyes bloodshot and foggy with fatigue. Good grief, had he given himself a concussion?

'It's too rough still,' he said, the words thick with exhaustion. 'It's not safe for you up here.'

'It's a lot calmer than it was,' she said, registering the weary determination in his voice. However stupidly macho he was being by refusing to admit weakness, his determination to stay at the helm was born out of a desire to protect her.

'At least go below and clean the cut,' she said, clamping down on all the treacherous memories flooding back to make her heart ache.

The mornings when he'd held her head as she threw up her breakfast in the motel bathroom...the intractable look on his face when he'd demanded she marry him after the stick had gone blue…and the crippling thought of him battered and bruised by her father's bodyguards when he'd come back to get her…

Her gaze drifted over his brow to the scar that he'd refused to explain. She shook off the melancholy thoughts as blood seeped from the fresh injury on his forehead. She couldn't think about any of that now. He had a head injury. She had to get him to let go—at least for a little while.

'Seriously, I can handle this!' she shouted above the gusting wind, her voice firm and steady despite the memory bombarding her of another argument—the one they'd had the morning he'd left her…

She'd let him have the last word then, because she hadn't had the courage to insist she was capable of handling at least some of the burden of their finances. She'd been so angry about his attitude that morning, at his blank refusal to let her get a job.

But maybe it was finally time to acknowledge the truth of what had happened that day. *Of course* he'd had no faith in her abilities—because she'd had no faith in them herself. And he hadn't left her. He'd gone to find a job so he could support her.

He hadn't been able to rely on her because she *had* been weak and feeble, beaten down by her father's bullying. And her one show of strength—the decision to run off and marry Dane and have the baby growing inside her—had really been nothing more than a transference of power from one man to another.

Dane had made all the decisions simply because she'd been too scared, too unsure to make them herself. That Dane might have been equally scared, equally terrified, had never even occurred to her. But what if he had been? And what if he'd kept his feelings hidden simply to stop himself from scaring her?

'I'm not a princess any more, Dane!' she shouted, just in case he was still confusing her with that girl. She didn't want to argue with him, but she had to make him believe she could handle this. 'I'm a lot tougher than I look now,' she added.

Because I've had to be.

She cut off the thought. She could never tell him all the reasons why she'd been forced to toughen up because that would only stir up more of the guilt and recriminations from their past. Until she'd found herself alone in that motel bathroom she'd let him take all the strain. But she didn't need to do that any more.

'Please let me do this.'

She braced herself for an argument, keeping an eye on the sea, but to her astonishment, instead of arguing further, he grasped her arm and dragged her in front of him.

His big body bolstered hers and she felt the familiar zing of sexual awareness, complicated by a rush of emotion when his cold palms covered her hands on the wheel.

Tears stung her eyes and she blinked them away.

'You sure you can hold her?' he said, and the exhilaration in her chest combined with a lingering sense of loss for that complicated, taciturn boy who had taught her to sail a lifetime ago. And whom she had once loved without question.

She nodded.

He stood behind her, shielding her from the beating rain. She melted into him for a moment and the punch of adrenaline hit her square in the solar plexus, taking her breath away as she felt the boat's power beneath her feet.

When she'd been that frightened, insecure girl, scared of her father's wrath, always looking for his approval, Dane had given her this—the freedom and space to become her own woman. And she'd screwed it up by falling for him hook, line and sinker.

If this time with him taught her one thing, let it be that she would never do that again. Never look for love when what she really needed was strength.

'Go below! I've got this!' she shouted over her shoulder, trying to concentrate on the job at hand and not let all the what-ifs charging through her head destroy the simple companionship of this moment.

'I won't be long,' he said, and the husky words sprinted up her spine.

Giving her fingers a reassuring squeeze, he took a deep breath and stepped away, leaving her alone at the helm. He pointed towards the horizon.

'Head towards the clear blue. And avoid the breakers.'

She concentrated on the break in the storm line, scanning the sea for the next wave. 'Will do. Take as long as you need.'

Widening her stance, she let her limbs absorb the heel of the boat as it rode over the swell. The rain was finally starting to trail off. Arousal leapt, combining with the deep well of emotion, as she watched him unclip himself from the safety line and saw his shoulders fill the entryway before he disappeared below.

The boat rolled to the side and Dane's heart went with it, kicking against his ribs like a bucking bronco as he staggered into the salon, his head hurting like a son of a bitch, but his heart hurting more.

He shook his hands and the shivering racked his body as he stripped off the life jacket and the wet clothing with clumsy fingers and headed back to his cabin.

He didn't want to leave Xanthe alone up there too long. She'd always been a natural sailor, and he'd sensed a new toughness and tenacity in her now, a greater resilience than when they were kids together. But even so she was his responsibility while she was on the boat, and he didn't want to screw it up. *Again.*

He winced as shame engulfed him. He'd already put her at risk, sailing them both straight into a force-eight because he'd been too damn busy thinking about the hot, wet clasp of her body and trying to decipher all the conflicting emotions she could still stir in him, instead of paying the necessary attention to the weather report, the cloud formation and the sudden dip in air pressure.

They'd been lucky that it hadn't been a whole lot worse.

But he knew when he was beaten. He had to sleep—get a good solid thirty minutes before he could relieve her at the helm. Gripping the safety line she'd rigged, he made his way to the head, dug out a piece of gauze to dab the cut on his forehead, then staggered naked into the cabin.

Thirty minutes—that was all he needed—then he'd be able to take over again.

His eyes closed, and his brain shut off the minute his head connected with the pillow.

He woke with a start what felt like moments later, to find the cabin dark and the boat steady. The events of the day—the last few days—came back in a rush.

Xanthe.

He jerked upright and pain lanced through the cut on his forehead where he'd headbutted the boom. He cursed. How long had he been out? He'd forgotten to set an alarm before crashing into his berth. He looked up to see clear night through the skylight. Then noticed the blanket lying across his lap.

The blanket that hadn't been there when he'd fallen headlong into the bunk what had to be *hours* ago.

Emotion gripped as he pulled the blanket off.

Was she still on deck? Doing his job for him?

Ignoring the dull pain in his head, he pulled on some

trunks and a light sweater. Heading through the salon, he noticed the debris left by the storm had been cleared away and the film of water that had leaked in through the hatch onto the floor had been mopped up. His wet clothes hung on the safety line, brittle with salt but nearly dry.

The night breeze lifted the hairs on his arms as he climbed onto the deck. The helm was empty, the autopilot was on, the storm sails were furled and the standard rigging was engaged as the boat coasted on a shallow swell.

Xanthe lay curled up in the cockpit, out cold, her PFD still anchored to the safety line, her fist clutching the alarm clock.

His heart hammered hard enough to hurt his bruised ribs.

He cast his gaze out to sea, where the red light of a Caribbean dawn hung on the horizon, and struggled to breathe past the emotion making his chest ache.

She'd seen them through the last of the storm, then kept watch all night while he slept. How could someone who looked so delicate, so fragile, be so strong underneath? And what the hell did he do with all the feelings weakening his knees now? Feelings he'd thought he had conquered a decade ago?

Desire, possessiveness, and a bone-deep longing.

He'd convinced himself a long time ago that Xanthe had never really belonged to him. That what he'd felt for her once had all been a dumb dream driven by endorphins and recklessness and desperation. He didn't want to be that needy kid again. So why did this feel like more than just the desire to bury himself deep inside her?

He crouched down on his haunches, forcing the traitorous feelings back.

He was still tired—and more than a little horny after three days at sea with the one woman he had never been able to resist. It had been an emotional couple of days.

And the storm had been a sucker punch neither of them had needed.

He pressed his hand to her cheek, pushing the wild hair, damp with sea water, off her brow. She stirred, and the bronco in his chest gave his ribs another hefty kick.

'Hmm...?' Her eyes fluttered open, the sea green dazed with sleep. 'Dane?' she murmured, licking her lips.

The blood flowed into his groin and he welcomed it. Sex had always been the easy part of the equation.

'Hey, sleepyhead,' he said, affection and admiration swelling in his chest.

This wasn't a big deal. She'd done a spectacular job and he owed her—that was all. Unclipping her harness, he lifted her easily in his arms.

'Let's get you below. I can take over now.' The way he should have done approximately twelve hours ago.

He realised how groggy she was when she didn't protest as he carried her down the steps into the salon and headed to his own cabin.

He wanted her in his bed while he took charge of the boat. By his calculation they'd reach the Bahamas around twilight. They'd have to anchor offshore, and dock first thing tomorrow morning, but he intended to keep his hands off her for the rest of the trip. Even if it killed him.

Then he'd sign her divorce papers.

And let her go.

Before this situation got any more out of hand.

Sitting her on the bed, he crouched down to undo her jacket. She didn't resist his attentions, docile as a child as he pulled it off and chucked it on the floor. Her T-shirt was stuck to her skin, the hard tips of her nipples clear through the clinging fabric.

He gritted his teeth, ignoring the pounding in his groin. The desire to warm those cold nubs with his tongue almost overwhelming.

'How's your head?' she murmured sleepily.

He glanced up to find her watching him, her gaze unfocused, dark with arousal.

'Good,' he said, his voice strained.

She needed to get out of her wet clothes, grab a hot shower. But if he did it for her he didn't know how the heck he'd be able to keep his sanity and not take advantage of her.

'Have you got it from here?'

He tugged the clock out of his back pocket. Fifteen minutes before he had to check the watch.

'I should head back on deck,' he said, hoping she couldn't see the erection starting to strangle in his shorts. Or hear the battle being waged inside him to hold her and tend to her and claim her again...

Because he knew if that happened he might never be able to let her go.

Sleep fogged Xanthe's brain, as her mind floated on a wave of exhaustion. He looked glorious, standing before her in the half-light—the epitome of all the erotic dreams which had chased her through too many nights of disturbed sleep. Strong and unyielding... The raw, rugged beauty of his tanned skin, his muscular shoulders, the dark heat in his pure blue eyes, blazed a trail down to tighten her nipples into aching points.

She shivered, awareness shuddering through her.

She heard a strained curse, then the bed dipped and her T-shirt was dragged over her head. The damp shorts and underwear followed. Her limbs were lethargic, her skin tingling as calloused fingers rasped over sensitive flesh with exquisite tenderness, beckoning her further into the erotic dream and making her throat close.

'Red, you're freezing...let's warm you up.'

She found herself back in strong arms, her body weightless. But she didn't feel cold. She felt blissfully warm and languid, with hunger flaring all over her tired body as she stood on shaky legs.

Hot jets of water rained down on her head as strong fingers massaged her scalp. She breathed in the scented steam—cedarwood and lemon—her body alive with sensation as a fluffy towel cocooned her in warmth, making her feel clean and fresh, the vigorous rubbing igniting more of that ravishing heat.

Back on the bed, she looked into that rugged face watching her in the darkness, its expression tight with a longing that matched her own.

Struggling up onto her elbows, she traced a finger through the hair on his chest, naked now, down the happy trail through the rigid muscles of his abdomen to his belly button.

She heard him suck in a staggered breath, and the sound was both warning and provocation. Emotion washed through her as she stroked the heavy ridge in his pants and felt the huge erection thicken against her fingertips.

A hand gripped her wrist and gently pulled her away. 'Red, you're killing me,' he murmured, his low voice raw with agony.

She lifted her head, saw the harsh need that pierced her abdomen reflected in Dane's deep blue eyes. Drifting in a sensual haze, she let the uncensored swell of emotion fill up all the places in her heart that had been empty for so long.

'Stay with me.'

The words came out on a husk of breath, almost unrecognisable. Was that *her* voice? So sure, so uninhibited, so determined?

'I need you.'

A tiny whisper in her head told her it was wrong to ask, wrong to need him this much. But this was just a dream, a dream from long ago, and nothing mattered now but satisfying the yearning which had begun to cut off her air supply and stab into her abdomen like a knife.

'There's never been anyone else,' she said. 'Only you. Don't make me beg.'

Moisture stung her eyes—tears of pain and sadness for all those dreams that had been forced to die inside her, along with the life they'd once made together. If she could just feel that glorious oblivion once more all would be well.

Only he could fix this.

'Shh… Shh, Red…' Rough palms framed her face, swiping away the salty tears seeping from her eyes. 'I've got this. Lie down and I'll give you what you need.'

She flopped back on the bed, then bowed up, racked with pleasure as his tongue circled her nipples, firm lips tugging at the tender tips. Desire arrowed down. Sharp and brutal. Obliterating every emotion but want.

Moisture flooded between her thighs as blunt fingers found the swollen folds of her sex. Her breath sawed out, her lungs squeezing tight as the agony of loss was swept away by the fierce tide of ecstasy.

She bucked, cried out, as those sure, seeking lips trailed across her ribs, delved into her belly button, then found the swollen bundle of nerves at last. Sensation shot through her, drawing tight, clutching at her heart and firing through her nerve-endings, making everything disappear but the agonising need to feel him filling her again.

Large fingers pressed inside her and her clitoris burned and pulsed under the sensual torment. The wave of ecstasy crested, throwing her into the hot, dark oblivion she sought. She screamed his name, the cry of joy dying on her lips as she tasted her own pleasure in a hard, fleeting kiss.

'Now, go to sleep.'

She registered the gruff command, making her feel safe and cherished.

His hand cradled her face and she pressed into his palm, the gentle touch making new tears spill over her lids as she closed her eyes. A blanket fell over her and she snuggled into a ball, drifting on an enervating wave of afterglow.

And then she dived into a deep, dreamless sleep.

CHAPTER FIFTEEN

'Is that Nassau?' Xanthe called out to Dane, hoping the flush on her face wasn't as bright as the lights she could see across the bay, which had to be the commercial and cultural capital of the Bahamas.

A kaleidoscope of red and orange hues painted the sky where the sun dipped beneath a silhouette of palm trees and colourful waterfront shacks on the nearby beach.

She'd slept the whole day away. Her body felt limber and alive, well-rested and rejuvenated... Unfortunately that wasn't doing anything for her peace of mind as snatches of conversation from the hour before dawn, when Dane had come to relieve her on deck after her shattering stint at the helm, made her heart pummel her chest and her face burn with the heat of a thousand suns.

Had she actually begged him to give her an orgasm?

Yup, she was pretty sure she had.

And had she blurted out that he'd been the only man she'd ever slept with?

Way to go, Xanthe.

How exactly did she come back from that with any dignity? Especially as she could still feel the phantom stroke of his tongue on her clitoris?

He stopped what he was doing with the rigging and strolled across the deck towards her.

The fluid gait, sure-footed and purposeful and naturally predatory, put all her senses on high alert and turned the tingle in her clitoris to a definite hum.

'Yeah, the marina is on Paradise Island,' he said as he approached, his deep voice reverberating through her sternum. 'But we're anchored here till morning. It's too dangerous to try docking after sunset.'

The blush became radioactive as he studied her face.

'You slept okay?'

'Yes… Thank you.' Like the dead, for twelve solid hours.

The memory of him washing her hair, rubbing her naked skin with a towel and then blasting away all her other aches and pains made her heart jam her larynx.

'You're welcome.' His lips kicked up on one side, the sensual curve making the pit of her stomach sink into the toes of her deck shoes. 'Thanks for taking such good care of *The Sea Witch*,' he murmured.

Her knees trembled, her heart swelling painfully in her throat at the thought of how carefully he'd taken care of *her*.

Who was she kidding? This wasn't just about sex—not any more. Or at least not for her. The fear she thought she'd ridden into the dust kicked back up under her breastbone. She was falling for him again. And she didn't seem to be able to stop herself.

His gaze glided over the blush now setting fire to her cheeks.

'Is there a problem?' he asked.

She cleared her throat.

Backing down had never been the answer with Dane— she of all people ought to know that by now. Being coy or embarrassed now would be suicidal.

He'd left her feeling fragile and vulnerable and scared. Which almost certainly hadn't been his intention, because having her love him had never been part of Dane's agenda. She had to turn this around, make it clear that sex was the only thing they still shared… Or he'd know exactly how much last night had meant to her.

'Actually there is, and it has to do with your extremely altruistic use of your superpower,' she said, cutting straight to the chase.

His eyebrows hiked up his forehead.

'And how is that a problem?' he asked, but it wasn't really a question. The bite of sarcasm was unmistakable.

She'd annoyed him. This was good.

'Not a problem, exactly,' she said—as if she could dispute that, when he'd turned her into a quivering mess who had screamed his name out at top volume. 'But I would have been fine without it. I didn't need a pity orgasm.'

'A... A pity *what*?' Dane choked on the words as the tension in his gut gripped the base of his spine and turned his insides into a throbbing knot of need. 'What the *hell* are you talking about?'

'I didn't need you to take pity on me. When I said I wanted to make love to you, I planned to hold up my end of the bargain.'

'How?'

Anger surged through him. He'd been on a knife-edge all damn day, his emotions in turmoil, his hunger for her driving him nuts—but not nearly as much as his yearning to ask her to stay with him. Which was even more nuts. They'd grown up, gone their separate ways. They had nothing in common now—nothing that should make him want her this much. And now she was accusing him of... What?

He didn't even know what she was talking about. He'd given her the one thing he was capable of giving her without sinking them both any further into the mire. And she'd just told him she hadn't wanted that either.

'You were exhausted—barely awake,' he ground out. 'Because you'd been up all night doing *my* damn job for me.' Blood was pulsing into his crotch, making it hard for him to regulate his temper. Or his voice, which had risen to a shout they could probably hear back in Manhattan. 'You needed to sleep.'

Her cheeks flushed. 'So you decided to help me with that? Well, thanks a bunch. Next time I have insomnia I'll be sure to order up Dane's pity orgasm remedy.'

'You ungrateful little witch.'

Fury overwhelmed him. He'd wanted nothing more than to feel her come apart in his arms, make her moan and beg and say his name and *only* his name. But she'd been tired and emotional. And then she'd struck him right through the heart with that statement about him being the only one.

It had taken him a moment to figure out what she was telling him. But when he'd got it—when he'd realised he was the only guy she'd ever slept with—it had felt like watching his boat shoot across the finishing line of the America's Cup and being knifed in the gut all at the same time.

The burst of pride and pleasure and possessiveness had combined with the terror of wanting to hold on to her too much—throwing him all the way back to the grinding fear of his childhood. So he'd held back. He'd given her what she needed without taking what he wanted for himself.

And now she was telling him what he'd given her wasn't enough.

'Ungrateful?' She seared him with a look that could have cut through lead. 'Don't you get it? I don't *want* to be grateful. I'm not a charity case. I want to be your equal. In bed as well as out of it.'

He grabbed her arms, dragged her close. 'You want to participate this time? I don't have a problem with that.'

She thrust her hands into his hair, digging her fingers into the short strands to haul his mouth to within a whisper of hers. The desire sparking in her eyes turned the mossy green to emerald fire.

'Good, because neither do I,' she said, then planted her lips on his.

The kiss went from wild to insane in a heartbeat. The need that had been churning in his gut all day surged out of control as he boosted her into his arms.

He couldn't keep her, but he could sure as hell ensure she never forgot him.

Rough stubble abraded Xanthe's palms as her whole body sang the 'Hallelujah Chorus.' Her breasts flattened against his chest and their mouths duelled in a wild, uncontrollable battle for supremacy.

His tongue thrust deep, dominant and demanding, parrying with hers as wildfire burned through her system. She hooked her legs round his waist, clinging on as he staggered down to the cabin with her wrapped around him like a limpet.

Barging through the door, he flung her onto the bed. She lurched onto her knees, watching as he kicked off his trunks. The thick erection bounced free, hard and long and ready for her.

Everything inside her melted. All the anger and agony and the terrifying vulnerability was flushed away on a wave of longing so intense she thought she might pass out.

This was all they had ever been able to have. She had to remember that.

He grabbed the front of her T-shirt and hauled her up, ripping the thin cotton down the middle. His lips crushed hers, his tongue claiming her mouth again in a soul-numbing kiss. Drawing back, he helped her struggle out of the rest of her clothing, his groans matched by the pants of her breathing.

At last they were naked, the feel of his skin warm and firm, tempered by the steely strength beneath. Muscles rippled with tension beneath her stroking palms. He cupped her sex, his fingers finding the heart of her with unerring accuracy. She bucked off the bed, his touch too much for her tender flesh. He circled with his thumb, knowing just how to caress her, to draw out her pleasure to breaking point. His lips clamped to a nipple and drew it deep into his mouth.

Sensations collided, then crashed through her. She sobbed as the blistering climax hit—hard and fast and not enough.

'I need you inside me,' she sobbed, desperate to forget about the aching emptiness that had tormented her for so long.

He rose up, grasped her hips, positioned himself to plunge deep. But as he pressed at her entrance he froze suddenly. Then dropped his forehead to hers and swore loudly. 'I don't have any protection. This wasn't supposed to happen.'

His dark gaze met hers, and her brutal arousal was reflected in those blindingly blue eyes. She blurted out the truth. 'It's okay. As long as we're both clean. I won't get pregnant.'

'You're on the pill?'

The gruff assumption reached inside her and ripped open the gaping wound she'd spent years denying even existed. She slammed down on the wrenching pain. And on the urge to tell him the terrible truth of how much she'd lost by loving him.

Don't tell him. You can't.

'Yes,' she lied.

He kissed her, his groan of relief echoing in her sternum, feeding her own need back to her. Then he angled her hips and thrust deep.

Her body arched, and the sensation of fullness was overwhelming as she struggled to adjust to the thick intrusion.

He began to move, driving into her in a devastating rhythm that dug at that spot inside only he had ever touched.

'Let go, Red. I want to see you come again. Just for me.'

The possessive tone, the desperation in his demand felt too real, too frightening. She'd given him everything once. She couldn't afford to give it all to him again.

'I can't.'

'Yes, you can.' He found her clitoris with his thumb. Swollen and aching.

The perfect touch drove her back towards the peak with staggering speed. Her whole body clamped down, euphoria driving through the fear. His eyes met hers, the intensity in their blue depths reaching out and touching her heart.

She gripped broad shoulders, the muscles tensed beneath her fingertips as she tried to shield herself against the intense wave of emotion. But it rose up anyway, shaking her to the core as her body soared past that last barrier to plunge into the abyss.

He shouted out, the sound muffled against her neck, as he emptied his seed into her womb.

She came to moments later, his body heavy on hers. The bright, beautiful wave of afterglow receded, to be replaced by the shattering feeling of an emotion she hadn't wanted to feel.

Lifting up on his elbows, he brushed the hair back from her brow. The shuttered look in his eyes made her shudder with reaction. The feeling of him still intimately linked to her was too much.

'Are you okay?' he said.

The wariness in his expression made her heart feel heavy. How could he protect himself so easily when she'd never been able to protect herself in return?

One rough palm caressed her cheek and she turned

away from it, feeling the sting of tears behind her eyelids
at this glimpse of tenderness.

This was just sex for him. That was all it had ever been.

'Never better.' She pressed her palms against his chest,
suddenly feeling trapped. And fragile. 'I need to clean up.'

He rolled off her without complaint. But as she tried to
scramble off the bed firm fingers caught her wrist, holding her in place. 'Xan, don't.'

She glanced over her shoulder. 'Don't what?'

'Don't run off.'

He tugged her back towards him and slung an arm
around her shoulder, and—weak and feeble woman that
she was—she let him draw her under his arm until her
head was nestled against his chest, her palm resting over
his heart, which was still beating double time with hers.

His thumb caressed her cheek, and the rumble of his
voice in her ear drew her in deeper. 'Why has there never
been anyone else?'

She considered denying it. If he'd sounded smug or
arrogant she probably would have, but all he sounded was
guarded.

'I wish I hadn't told you that.' She sighed. 'It was a weak
moment. Can't you forget it?'

'Nope,' he murmured into her hair.

It occurred to her that he probably didn't want *this* burden any more than he'd wanted any of the others she'd
thrust upon him.

'If it's any consolation,' he said, his fingers threading
through her hair as his deep voice rumbled against her ear,
'there hasn't been anyone important for me either.'

Her heartbeat hitched into an uneven rhythm. Ten years
ago that admission would have had her bursting with happiness. She would have taken it as a sign. A sign that she
meant something to him. Something beyond the obvious.
But she wasn't that optimistic any more. Or as much of

a pushover. And she couldn't risk letting herself believe again. Because it had already cost her far too much.

'I guess we've both been pretty busy…' She tried to smile, but the crooked tilt of her lips felt weak and forced.

'I guess,' he said.

The husky agreement let them both off the hook. Until he spoke again.

'That scar—low under your belly button. How did you get it?'

She stilled, unable to talk, struggling to stop her eyes filling with unshed tears.

'Was it the baby?'

The hint of hesitation in his voice made her heart pound even harder, emotion closing her throat.

She nodded.

His arm tightened.

She needed to talk about this. To tell him all the things she'd been robbed of the chance to tell him then.

Perhaps this was why it had always felt as if there was more between them? She clung to the thought. So much of their past remained unresolved. Maybe if she took this opportunity to remedy that they could go their separate ways without so many regrets?

All she had to do was get enough breath into her lungs to actually speak.

Dane's heart thudded against his collarbone. He could feel the tension in her body, her silent struggle to draw a full breath. He'd known it had been bad for her. He hadn't meant to bring all that agony back. But the question had slipped out, his desire to know as desperate as his desire to comfort her. And for once his anger at her father was nowhere near as huge as his anger with himself.

Whatever the old bastard had done after the fact, Dane

was the one who'd stormed out of that motel room and hadn't contacted her for days.

So when all was said and done it was down to him that he hadn't been there when she'd needed him. However much he had tried to put the blame on her old man.

'Can you talk about it?' he asked, the husk of his voice barely audible.

She nodded again and cleared her throat. The raw sound scraped over his temper and dug into the guilt beneath. When her voice finally came it wasn't loud, but it was steady.

'I have a scar because they had to operate. I was bleeding heavily and they...'

She hesitated for a moment, and the slight hitch in her breathing was like a knife straight into his heart.

'They couldn't get a heartbeat.'

Hell.

He settled his hand on her head, tugged her closer. The urge to lend her his strength impossible to deny, however useless it might be now.

'I'm so damn sorry, Red. I should never have insisted on marrying you and taking you to that damn motel. It was a dive. You would have been okay if you'd stayed on daddy's estate...'

She pulled out of his arms, her eyes fierce and full of raw feeling as she silenced him with a finger across his lips.

'Stop it!'

Her voice sounded choked. And he could see the sheen of tears in her eyes, crucifying him even more.

'That's not true. It would have happened regardless. And I wanted to be with *you*.'

He captured her finger, his heart battering his ribs so hard now he was astonished that it didn't jump right out of his chest.

'He was right about me, though,' he said.

'What was he right about?' She seemed puzzled—as if she really didn't get it.

'He called me a wharf rat. And that's exactly what I was.'

He pushed the words out, and tried to feel relieved that he'd finally told her the truth. The one thing he'd been so desperate to keep from her all those years ago.

'I grew up in a trailer park that was one step away from being the town dump. My old man was a drunk who got his kicks from beating the crap out of me, so I hung around the marina to get away from him until I got big enough to hit back.'

Even if the squalid truth about who he really was and where he'd come from could never undo all the stuff he'd done wrong, at least it would go some way to show her how truly sorry he was—for all the pain he'd caused.

'If that doesn't make me a wharf rat, I don't know what does.'

Xanthe clutched the sheet covering her breasts, which were heaving now as if she'd just run a marathon. Her mind reeled from Dane's statement. So it *was* his father who had caused those terrible scars on his back. She'd always suspected as much. Sympathy twisted in her stomach—not just for that boy, but for the look in Dane's eyes now that told her he actually *believed* what he was saying.

How could she have got it so wrong? She had believed his silence about himself and his past had been the result of arrogance and pride and indifference, when what it had really been was defensiveness.

'I'm sorry your father hurt you like that.'

And what did she do with the evidence that it still hurt her so much to know he'd been abused?

'Don't feel sorry for that little bastard,' he said. 'He didn't deserve it.'

Of course he did. But how could she tell him that without giving away the truth—that a part of her had never stopped loving that boy.

'My father called you a wharf rat because he was an unconscionable snob, Dane. It had nothing to do with you.' That much at least she could tell him.

'He loved you, Xan, and he wanted to protect you. There's nothing wrong with that,' he said with a weary resignation. 'If I could have…' His gaze strayed to her belly and the thin white scar left behind by the surgeon's incision. 'I would have protected our baby the same way.'

The admission cut through her, and emotions that were already far too close to the surface threatened to spill over.

God, how could she have accused him of not caring about their child when it was obvious now that he might have cared too much? Enough to blame himself for the things that her father—both their fathers—had done.

She bit down on the feelings threatening to choke her.

'That's where you're wrong. He didn't love me. He thought of me as his property.'

How come she had never acknowledged that until now? All those years she'd worked her backside off to please her father, to get his approval, never once questioning what he had ever done to deserve it.

'I was an investment. The daughter who was going to marry a man of *his* choosing who would take over Carmichael's when he was gone. My falling in love…having a child by a man he disapproved of and who refused to bow down to the mighty Charles Carmichael…they were the real reasons he hated you.'

Dane cupped her cheek, the cool touch making her heart ache even more.

'I guess we both got a raw deal when the good Lord gave out daddies.'

She let out a half laugh, and the tears that had refused to fall for so long threatened to cascade over her lids.

She settled back into his arms, so he wouldn't see them. 'The baby was a little boy,' she said, determined to concentrate on their past and not on their future, because they didn't have one.

'For real?'

She heard awe as well as sadness in his tone.

'I thought you should know.'

Their baby, after all, was the only thing that had brought them together. Surely this chance to say goodbye to him properly would finally allow them to part.

'I'm glad you told me,' he murmured, his fingers linking with hers, his thumb rubbing over her wrist where her pulse hammered.

She hiccupped, her breath hurting again, the tears flowing freely down her cheeks now.

'Hell, Red, don't cry,' he said, kissing the top of her head and gathering her close. 'It's all over now.'

She splayed her fingers over the solid mass of his pectoral muscles, feeling exhausted and hollowed out. Because she knew it *wasn't* over. Not for her. And she was becoming increasingly terrified that it never had been.

CHAPTER SIXTEEN

XANTHE WOKE THE following morning feeling tired and confused.

Dane had woken her twice in the night. The skill and urgency of his lovemaking had been impossible to resist. He'd caught her unawares, that clever thumb stroking her to climax while she was still drifting on dreams... She stretched, feeling the aches and pains caused by the energy of their lovemaking.

Last night's revelations had been painful for them both, but getting that glimpse of the boy she'd once known and finally knowing more of what had haunted him felt important.

The boat swayed and she heard a bump. Glancing out of the window, she could see the masts of another boat. They had arrived at the marina on Paradise Island.

Getting out of bed, she slung on capri pants and one of Dane's T-shirts and poured herself a cup of coffee from the pot Dane had already brewed. As she loaded it up with cream and sugar she tried to deal with all the confusing emotions spiralling through her system.

She was in trouble. Big trouble. That much was obvious. And it wasn't just a result of last night's confidences, the hot sex, or even the tumultuous day spent battling the elements together. This problem went right back to her decision a week ago to bring Dane those divorce papers in person.

Every single decision she'd made since had proved

one thing. However smart and focused and rational and sensible she thought she'd become in the last ten years, and however determined never to let any man have control over her life, one man always had. And she'd been in denial about it.

But she wasn't that fanciful girl any more—that girl who had loved too easily and without discrimination. She was a grown woman who knew the score. She had to bring that maturity to bear now.

She poured the dregs of her barely touched coffee down the sink.

Taking a deep but unsteady breath, she headed up on deck. Dane stood on the dock, tall and indomitable and relaxed, talking to a younger man in board shorts and a bill cap. Her heart jolted as it had so often in the past, but this time she didn't try to deny the profound effect he had on her.

He'd shaved, revealing the delicious dent in his chin which she could remember licking last night.

She shook off the erotic thought.

Not helping.

Dane spotted her standing on the deck and broke off his conversation. His hot gaze skimmed down her body as he walked towards her.

'Morning,' he said.

'Hi.'

She stood her ground as he climbed onto the boat, the heat in his eyes sending her senses reeling.

'I should head home today,' she said, as casually as she could, and held her breath, waiting for any flicker of acknowledgement that what had happened last night was a big deal. 'I thought I'd check out the flights from Nassau.'

She silently cursed the way her heart clenched at his patient perusal.

'Why don't you stay for one more night?' he said at

last. 'I've got a suite booked at the Paradise Resort before I head back to Manhattan tomorrow.'

She sank her hands into the back pockets of her capri pants to stop them trembling and control the sweet hit of adrenaline kicking under her breastbone. What was making her so giddy? It was hardly a declaration of undying love.

'Why would you want to do that?' she asked, determined to accept the casual invitation in the spirit it was offered.

He gave her a long look, and for a terrible moment she thought he could see what she was trying so hard to hide— the panic, the longing, and all those foolish dreams which had failed to die.

But then his lips lifted in a sensual smile and heat fired down to her core. 'Because we've both been through hell in the last couple of days and I figure we've earned a reward.'

He touched a knuckle to her cheek, skimmed it down to touch the throbbing pulse in her neck. The snap and crackle of sexual awareness went haywire.

'I could show you the town,' he added. 'Nassau's a cool city.'

'But I don't have anything to wear,' she said, still trying to weigh her options.

This wasn't a big deal. After the enforced intimacy of the boat, the intensity of emotion brought on by the storm, not to mention the lack of sleep and the stresses and strains of what had happened so long ago still hanging between them, why shouldn't he suggest one more night of fun? After all, they'd had precious little fun in their acquaintance. She had to take this at face value. Not read more into it than was actually there.

'You're not going to need much,' he said, his smile loaded with sensual promise. 'I was kidding about showing you around. We probably won't get out of the suite.'

She laughed, the wicked look in his eyes going some way to relieve the tension. 'What happens to *The Sea Witch* once you've gone back to Manhattan?' She glanced back at the boat, feeling a little melancholy at the thought of leaving it.

He nodded towards the young man still standing on the dock. 'Joe's my delivery skipper—he'll take it back to Boston.'

His hand cupped the back of her neck, sending sensation zinging all over her body.

'Now, quit stalling—do we have a deal or don't we?'

She swallowed heavily, her heart thudding against her throat. She could say no. She probably *should* say no. But having his gaze searching her face, his expression tense as he waited for her answer... She knew she didn't want to say no.

The man was intoxicating...like a dangerously addictive drug. She needed to be careful—conscious of all the emotions that had tripped her up in the past—but she was a stronger, wiser woman now, not a seventeen-year-old girl. And while she was riding the high had there ever been anything more exhilarating?

He tugged her into his arms, his lips inches from hers, the fire in his eyes incendiary. 'Say yes, Red. You know you want to.'

'Yes,' she whispered.

His lips covered hers and she let the leap of arousal mask the idiotic burst of optimism telling her that this might be more than she'd hoped it could be.

'Slow down, Dane. I'm stuffed. I don't want to burst the seams on this dress.'

Xanthe tried to sound stern as Dane clasped her hand and led her past the quaint, brightly coloured storefronts of Nassau's downtown area. The colonnades and verandas announced the island city's colonial heritage, while SUVs vied for space on the tourist-choked streets with horse-drawn carriages.

After four days on the yacht, the four-course meal in the luxurious surroundings of a Michelin-starred restaurant had been sensational, but the truth was she'd barely managed to swallow a bite. The potent hunger in his eyes every time he looked at her had turned her insides to mush.

She'd been riding a wave of endorphins since their bargain on the boat—but was determined not to let his invitation get the better of her. Then something had shifted when he had appeared in their enormous suite at the resort on Paradise Island looking breathtakingly handsome in a dark evening suit and told her he was taking her out on a date.

After all the sex they'd shared the suggestion shouldn't have seemed so sweet. So intimate. So overwhelming. But somehow it had.

'And you bursting out of your dress is supposed to be a problem?'

His eyes dipped to the hem of the designer dress she'd picked from the array of garments he'd had sent up to their suite. The incendiary gaze seared the skin of her thighs, already warmed by the Caribbean night.

'It *is* on a public street,' she shot back, struggling to quell the erratic beat of her heart.

The evening had been a revelation in some ways—Dane had played the gentleman with remarkable ease—but it had been only more disturbing in others.

Because getting a glimpse into his life now, and seeing the level of luxury he could afford, had only made her more aware of how far he'd come. He'd always been tenacious and determined, but she couldn't help her fierce wave of pride at the thought of how hard he'd worked to leave that boy behind and escape the miserable poverty of his childhood.

She shouldn't have been surprised by the exclusiveness of the five-star resort hotel on Paradise Island, or by the lavish bungalow that looked out onto a private white sand beach and the sleek black power boat he'd piloted to take them into Nassau—especially after seeing the penthouse apartment Dane owned in Manhattan—but, like Nassau itself, which was a heady mix of old world elegance, new world commerce and Caribbean laissez-faire, Dane seemed like a complex contradiction.

His animal magnetism was not dimmed in the slightest by this new layer of wealth and sophistication. Even in an elegant tuxedo, the raw, rugged masculinity of the man still shone through. The tailored jacket stretched tight over wide shoulders now, as he led her back towards the dock where the speedboat was moored.

'I've always thought clothes are overrated,' he teased, helping her into the boat. 'Especially on you.'

He shrugged off the jacket and dumped it in the back of the boat, then tugged off the tie, too, and stuffed it into the pocket of his suit trousers.

'I don't care how damn fancy that restaurant is,' he said, and the vehemence in his tone was surprising. 'Nothing's worth getting trussed-up like a chicken for.'

'You didn't like the food?' she asked.

'The food was great—but it was way too stuffy in there.'

He smiled at her, and the glint of white against his swarthy skin was a potent reminder of the boy. Wicked and reckless and hungry—for so much.

But was he hungry for *her*? In anything other than the most basic way?

He switched on the engine and the boat roared to life, kicking at the soft swell as he directed the boat away from the dock and into the water.

She glanced back at the fading lights of Bay Street, the wind pulling tendrils of hair out of her chignon as Dane handled the powerful boat with ease. And tried not to let the question torture her.

She mustn't get ahead of herself—read too much into this night.

She was concentrating so hard on getting everything into perspective that she didn't register that they weren't returning to the resort until the boat slowed as it approached a beach on the opposite side of the bay. A cluster of fairy lights and the bass beat of music covered by the lilting rumble of laughter and conversation announced a bar in the distance.

Dane released the throttle and let the boat drift into a small wooden dock lit by torches. Jumping out, he secured the line.

'Where are we?' she asked accepting his outstretched hand as he hauled her off the boat.

'An old hang-out of mine,' he said as she stepped onto the worn uneven boards.

He tugged her into his arms. Awareness sizzled through her system, but alongside it was the brutal tug of something more. Something that made her feel young and carefree and cherished—something she had been certain she would never feel again.

'I'm taking you dancing,' he said.

'You…? Really…?' Her breath choked off in her throat, and the panicked leap of her heart was almost as scary as the thundering beat of her pulse.

Was this another coincidence? Like the name of the boat? Surely it had to be.

But the wonder of the only other time they'd been dancing echoed in her heart regardless. The dark shapes of the cars in the car park…the strains of a country and Western band coming from the bar where they'd been refused entry when they'd spotted Dane's fake ID… Dane's strong arms directing her movements as he'd shown her the intricate steps and counter-steps of a Texas line dance and they'd laughed together every time she stepped on his toes.

And the giddy rush of adoration as they eventually settled into a slow dance on the cracked asphalt.

She'd been so hopelessly in love with him then.

She tried to thrust the memory aside as he led her down the dock, and ignored the swoop of her heart as he swung her into his arms to cross the sand.

She let out a laugh, though, desperate to live in the moment. Was this fate, testing her resolve?

Surely it was just the Caribbean evening, the promise of dancing the night away with such a forceful, stimulating man again and all the hot sex that lay in their immediate future that was making her as giddy as a teenager.

Dane's thoughts and feelings were still an enigma. And *her* thoughts and feelings had matured. She mustn't invest too much until she knew more.

She clung on to her resolve as he held her close in the moonlight, igniting her senses as they bumped and ground together to the sound of the vintage reggae band.

But as he guided the boat back towards Paradise Island her heart battered her ribcage, and excitement burst inside her like a firework when he murmured, 'I hope that made up for our wedding night.'

So he had remembered that treasured memory of dancing in the parking lot, too.

As they entered the suite he banded an arm round her waist and hauled her into his body.

'That's got to be the longest evening of my life.'

Breathing in the scent of salt and cedarwood soap which clung to him like a potent aphrodisiac, she spread her hands over his six-pack, felt his abs tense as arousal slammed into her system. The way it always did.

Everything seemed so right this time, so perfect.

'I know,' she said.

His nose touched hers. 'I want to be inside you.'

The heat in his gaze burned away the last of her fears as her fingertips brushed the thick arousal already tenting the fabric of his trousers.

'I know.'

Gripping her fingers, he headed towards the bedroom, hauling her behind him.

And she let her heart soar.

Dane didn't question the frantic need driving him to claim her, possess her. Because he couldn't. Not any more.

The sight of her in the designer dress, its sleek material sliding over slender curves, watching the sultry knowledge in her mermaid's eyes, had been driving him wild all evening. And the last vestiges of the civilised, sensible guy he'd become had been blown to smithereens—the way they had been every day, one crucial piece at a time, ever since she'd marched into his office a week ago.

This hunger wasn't just lust. He knew that—had known it for days, if he was honest with himself. And for that reason he should just let her go. But he couldn't.

Because she was his—any way he could get her. And the desire to mark her as his, keep her near him, had become overwhelming.

He'd insisted on taking her out to dinner, then tortured them both with a slow dance at the Soca Shack to prove that he could hold it together. That this didn't have to mean more than it should. But he'd felt as if he were holding a moonbeam in his arms as she moved against him—so bright, so beautiful, and still so far out of reach—and it had finally tipped him right over the edge of sanity.

He slammed open the first door he came to—the bathroom suite. Swinging her round, he pressed her up against the tiles, filled his hands with those lush breasts. He sucked her through the shimmering silk of her gown, groaning against the damp fabric when he found her braless.

She bucked against him, her response instant and oh-so-gratifying when he tugged the straps off her shoulders, freeing her full breasts.

He kicked off his shoes and pushed down his pants, his gaze fixed on the ripe peaks of her breasts, reddened from his mouth.

She found his erection, but he dragged her hand away.

'Lose the dress,' he said as he tore off his shirt, and the gruff demand in his voice made the light of challenge spark in her eyes.

'I don't take orders,' she said, sounding indignant, but he could see the hot light of her lust. She understood this game as much as he did—even if it didn't feel like a game any more.

'Lose the dress or it gets ripped off.'

'Oh, for...'

She shimmied out of the clinging silk to reveal the lacy panties he adored. Palming her bottom, he lifted her onto the vanity unit, shoving her toiletries off the countertop. The bag crashed to the floor, scattering her stuff across the tiles.

Need careered through his system along with pain and possession—the same damn combination that had tortured him a lifetime ago.

She placed trembling palms on his chest. 'Dane, slow down.'

'In a minute,' he said, the need to have her, to claim her, powering through him like a freight train.

He ripped the delicate panties. And plunged his fingers into the hot, wet heart of her at last.

She sobbed, gasped and grasped his biceps. He stroked the slick flesh, knowing just how and where to touch her to send her spiralling into a stunning orgasm. He watched

her go over, and the powerful emotion coiling inside him—
part fear, part euphoria—made his erection throb harder
against her thigh.

'You ready for me?' he demanded, barely able to speak
as need tormented him.

She nodded, dazed. He sank into her to the hilt, the euphoria bursting inside him as she clasped him tight.

Yes. If this was the only way he could have her, the
only way he could make her his, he was going to show
her that this was one thing no other man would ever be
able to give her.

She clung to his arms as he thrust hard and dug deep,
her muscles milking him as she started to crest again. The
hunger gripped him, as painful as it was exquisite. He
shouted out as she sobbed her release into his neck. And
his seed burst into the hot, wet grip of her body.

The wish that they could create another baby and then
she'd *have* to be his was savage and insane. Just the way
it had been all those years ago.

Reality returned as he came down, tasting the salty
sweat on her neck, and the first jabs of shame and panic
assaulted him. Hell, he'd taken her like an animal. He
should have held back. He didn't want her to know how
much he needed her.

He eased out of her. Felt her flinch.

'Did I hurt you?'

She was trembling. 'No, I'm fine.'

The words pulsed in his skull. Mocking him and making him ache at the same time. He forced an easy smile
to his lips and turned on the hot jets of the shower. Steam
rose as he checked the temperature.

'Let's get cleaned up.'

He dragged her under the spray with him. But as he
washed her hair, feeling the strands like wet silk through

his fingers, that need consumed him all over again. To hold her, to have her, to make her stay.

And the visceral fear that had lurked inside him for so long roared into life and chilled him to the bone.

'Is everything okay?'

Xanthe watched Dane leave the shower cubicle and grab a towel, feeling his sudden withdrawal like a physical blow.

He wrapped the towel round his hips. 'Sure,' he said, but he didn't turn towards her as he bent to pick up the toiletries scattered over the floor.

The joy that had been so fresh and new and exciting a moment ago, when he'd taken her with such hunger and purpose, faded. She turned off the shower and pulled one of the fluffy bath sheets off the vanity unit to wrap around herself, suddenly feeling exposed and so needy.

Had she completely misjudged everything? All the signals she'd thought he'd been sending her this evening that there might be more? That his feelings matched her own?

'I'll do it.' She stepped towards him to help pick up her toiletries, but he shrugged off her outstretched hand.

'I made the mess. I'll clean it up.' He placed the bag on the vanity unit, dumping the last of its scattered contents inside.

The strangely impersonal tone sent a shudder through her. She wrapped the towel tighter. Then lifted another towel to dry her hair.

'Where are the birth control pills?'

The clattering beat of her heart jumped into an uneasy rhythm at the flat question. 'Sorry?'

'Your pills? You said you were on the pill,' he prompted. 'I don't see them here.'

He'd checked her toiletries for contraceptive pills? Agony twisted in the pit of her stomach. Slicing through the last of the joy.

'I'm not on the pill.'

His brows arrowed down in a confused frown. 'So what type of birth control are you using?'

She could see the accusation in his eyes, hear the brittle demand in his voice, and all the blurred edges came together to create a shocking and utterly terrifying truth.

She'd been wrong—so wrong—all over again.

'I'm not using any,' she said.

'What the hell—?'

He looked so shocked she felt the hole in the pit of her stomach ripped open—until it was the same gaping wound that had crippled her once before.

He marched towards her and gripped her arm. 'What kind of game are you playing? Are you *nuts*? I could have gotten you pregnant again.'

She tugged her arm free, the accusation in his face cutting into her insides. How stupid she had been to keep this a secret. When it was the thing that had grounded her for so long. Stopped all those stupid romantic dreams from destroying her.

'I'm not going to get accidentally pregnant. Because I can't.'

She walked past him, suddenly desperate to get away from him. She needed to have some clothes on and to get out of here.

'Wait—what are you saying?' He followed her out of the bathroom and dragged her round to face him.

She thrust her forearms against him. 'Let me go. I want to leave.'

She tried to wrestle free, but he wouldn't let go.

'You need to tell me what you mean.'

She could feel the storm welling inside her, tearing at her insides the way it had for so many years while she'd struggled to come to terms with the truth. But she didn't want to break in front of him. She had to be in control, to be measured, not let him see how much this had devastated her when she told him the details—or he would know she'd fallen for him again. And the one thing she could not bear was his pity.

'I told you—I can't get pregnant.'

'Why can't you?'

The probing question was too much.

'What gives you the right to ask me that?'

'Hell, Red, just tell me why you can't have another child. I want to know.'

The storm churned in her stomach, more violent than the one they'd survived together, and tears were stinging her eyes.

'Because I'm barren. Because I waited too long in that motel room to call my father. I was sure that you would come for me. I was haemorrhaging. There was an infection. Understand?'

She headed towards the lounge, frantic now.

'I need to leave. I should have left yesterday.'

This time she held back the tears with an iron will. Pity, responsibility, sex—those were the only things Dane had ever had to give. She could see that so clearly now.

'Why didn't you tell me?' His voice sounded strained.

'Because it happened and now it's over,' she said.

She got dressed while he watched. Grateful when he didn't approach her. She was stronger now. She could get through this. She wasn't the bright, naive girl she'd once been—someone who'd come close to being destroyed by her past. She could never let him have that power over her again.

Shoving the few meagre items she had brought with her into her briefcase, she turned to look at him.

He stood in the doorway, the towel hooked around his waist, his expression frozen and unreadable.

'You know what's really idiotic?' she said. 'For a moment there I thought we could make this work. That some-how we could overcome all the mistakes from our past, all the things we did wrong, and make it right.'

'What?'

He looked so stunned she hesitated—but only for a mo-ment. This was a ludicrous pipe dream. It always had been and always would be.

'It was a stupid idea,' she said. 'Like before.'

She wanted to be angry with him, so she could fill the great gaping hole in the pit of her stomach. But she couldn't. Because all she could feel was an agonising sense of loss.

'Damn it, Red. I'm sorry. I didn't mean to hurt you.'

He approached her and lifted his hand, but she stiffened and stepped back.

'Can't you see that just makes it even more painful?' she said.

He let his hand drop. His expression wasn't frozen any more. She could see confusion, regret, maybe even sad-ness, but she steeled herself against the traitorous wobble in her heart that made her want to believe they still had a chance.

She pulled the papers out of the briefcase. The papers she'd come all this way to make him sign in order to end their marriage, without ever realising that what she had really wanted to do was mend it.

'You expected me to trust you, Dane. And you got angry when I didn't. But despite all the confusion with these—' she lifted the papers and dropped them on the coffee table '—the truth is I do trust you. And I think I always did. Be-cause I never stopped loving you. That's why it's so ironic that you were never able to trust me.'

His jaw flexed. His gaze was bleak. But he didn't try to stop her again as she walked out the door.

She felt herself crumpling. The pain was too much. But

she held her body ramrod-straight, her spine stiff, until she climbed into a cab to take her to the airport.

She collapsed onto the seat, wrenching sobs shuddering through her body.

'You all right, ma'am?' the cab driver called through the grille.

'Yes, it's okay. I'm okay,' she murmured as she scrubbed away the tears with her fist and tried to make herself believe it.

She *would* be okay. Eventually. The way she had been before. Dane was a part of her past. A painful, poignant part of her past. She'd just forgotten that for a few days.

He'd never been a bad man. He had simply never been able to love her. Not the way she needed to be loved.

Once she was back in the UK—back where she belonged, doing what she loved—everything would be okay again.

But as they headed to the dock, and the boat to Nassau, even the promise of a fifteen-hour workday and her luxury apartment overlooking the Thames couldn't ease the lonely longing in her battered heart—for something that had only ever been real in her foolish romantic imagination.

CHAPTER SEVENTEEN

'Bill says they're ready to sign off on the Calhoun deal. He's checked through the contracts and everything looks good.'

'Right. Thanks, Angela,' Xanthe murmured as she studied the small pleasure boat making its way up the Thames.

July sunlight sparkled off the muddy water, reminding her of...

'Is everything okay, Miss Carmichael?'

Xanthe swung round, detaching her gaze from the view out of the window of her office in Whitehall to find her PA studying her with a concerned frown on her face. The same concerned frown Xanthe had seen too often in the last two weeks. Ever since she'd returned from the Bahamas.

Get your head back in the game.

'Yes, of course.' She walked back to her desk, struggling to pull herself out of her latest daydream.

Everything *wasn't* okay. She wasn't sleeping, she'd barely eaten a full meal in two weeks, and she felt tired and listless and hollow inside.

Maybe it was just overwork. After the... She paused to think of an adequate word... After the *difficult* trip to the Caribbean, she'd thrown herself back into work as soon as she'd returned. She'd wanted to be busy, to feel useful, to feel as if her life had purpose, direction—all those things she'd lacked so long ago when she'd allowed herself to fall into love with Dane Redmond the first time.

But work wasn't the panacea it had once been.

She missed him—not just his body and all the wonderful things he could do to hers, but his energy, his charisma, the dogged will, even the arrogance that she'd once persuaded herself she hated. Even their arguments held a strange sort of nostalgia that made no sense.

Their trip had only been five days in total. Her life, her outlook on life, couldn't change in five days. This was just another emotional blip that she would get over the way she'd got over all the others.

But why couldn't she stop thinking about him? About the feeling of having his arms around her as she wept for their baby? The force field of raw charisma that had energised everything about their encounter and made everything since her return seem dull and lifeless in comparison?

And that look on his face when she'd told him of her foolish hopes… He'd looked astonished.

Every night since her return she'd lain awake trying to analyse that expression. Had there been disbelief there? Disdain? Or had there been hope?

Angela slipped a pile of paperwork onto the desk blotter. Then pointed at the signature field on the back page. 'You just need to sign here and here, and I'll get it back to Contracts.'

Xanthe picked up the gold pen she used to sign all her deals. Then hesitated, her mind foggy with fatigue and confusion. 'Remind me again—what's the Calhoun deal?'

She heard Angela's intake of breath.

When her PA finally spoke, her voice was heavy with concern. 'It's the deal you've been working on for three months…to invest in a new terminal in Belfast.'

Xanthe wrote her signature, the black ink swimming before her eyes, the tears threatening anew.

Good Lord, why couldn't she stop going over the same ground, reanalysing everything Dane had said and done? Trying to find an excuse to contact him again?

This was pathetic. *She* was pathetic.

The intercom on her desk buzzed. She clicked it on as Angela gathered up the documents and began putting them back into the file. 'Yes, Clare?' she said, addressing the new intern Angela had been training all week.

'There's a gentleman here to see you, Miss Carmichael. He says he has some papers for you. He's very insistent. Can I send him in?'

'Tell him to leave them outside.' She clicked off the intercom. 'Could you handle it, whatever it is, Angela? I think I'm going home.'

'Of course, Miss Carmichael.'

But as Angela opened the door Xanthe's head shot up at the low voice she could hear outside her office, arguing with the intern. Her mind blurred along with her vision at the sight of Dane striding into her office.

'Excuse me, sir, you can't come in here. Miss Car—'

'The hell I can't.'

He walked past Angela, who was trying and failing to guard the doorway.

'We need to talk, Red.'

Xanthe stood up, locking her knees when her legs refused to cooperate. A surge of heat twisted with a leap of joy, making her body feel weightless. She buried it deep. Shock and confusion overwhelmed her when he marched to the desk, his muscular body rippling with tension beneath a light grey designer suit and crisp white shirt.

'What are you doing here?'

Hadn't she made it clear she never wanted to see him again? Couldn't he respect at least *one* of her wishes? She couldn't say goodbye all over again—it wasn't fair.

Pulling a bunch of papers from the inside pocket of his suit, he slapped them down on the desk. 'I've come to tell you I'm not signing these.'

'Shall I call Security?' Angela asked, her face going red.

If only it could be that simple.

'That's okay, Angela.'

'I'm her husband,' Dane growled at the same time.

Angela's face grew redder. 'Excuse me...?'

'I'll handle this,' Xanthe reiterated. Somehow she *would* find the strength to kick him out of her life again. 'Please leave and shut the door.'

The door closed behind her PA as heat she didn't want to feel rushed all over her body and her heart clutched tight in her chest. She glanced down at the crumpled papers. Their divorce papers. The ones she'd tried to make him sign to protect her company.

'If you've quite finished bullying my staff, maybe you'd like to explain to me why you found it necessary to come barging in here to tell me something I already know.'

She'd had new papers drawn up as soon as she'd returned. Papers without the codicil.

'Dissolving our marriage is merely a formality now,' she said, trying to keep the panic out of her voice. She couldn't argue about this now—not when she was still so close to breaking point. 'In case your lawyer hasn't told you, I've filed new papers,' she added. Maybe this was simply a misunderstanding. 'There's nothing in them you should find objectionable. I trust you not to sue for the shares. You've got what you wanted.'

'I know about the new papers. I'm not signing those either.'

'But... Why not?' Was he trying to torture her now? Prolong her agony? What had she done to deserve this punishment?

'Because I don't want to,' he said, but he didn't look belligerent or annoyed any more. His features had softened. 'Because you matter to me.'

'No, I don't—not really,' she said, suddenly feeling desperately weary. And sad.

Did he think she wanted his pity? Maybe he was trying to tell her he cared about her. But it was far too little and way too late.

'Don't tell me how I feel, Red.'

'Then please don't call me Red.'

The sweet nickname sliced through all her defences, reminding her of how little she'd once been willing to settle for. And how she'd nearly persuaded herself to do so again.

He walked round the desk, crowding into her space. She stiffened and tried to step back, but got caught between the chair and the desk when his finger reached out to touch a curl of hair.

'I came here to ask you to forgive me,' he said. 'For being such a monumental jerk about pretty much everything.'

She drew her head back, her heart shattering, the panic rising into her throat. 'I can't do this again. You have to leave.'

Dane looked at Xanthe's face. Her valiant expression was a mask of determination, but the stark evidence of the pain he'd caused was clear in the shadows under her eyes that perfectly applied make-up failed to disguise. And he felt like the worst kind of coward.

He'd spent the last fortnight battling his own fear. Had come all this way finally to confront it. He had to risk everything now. Tell her the truth. The whole truth.

'I don't want to dissolve our marriage. I never did.'

It was the hardest thing he had ever had to say. Harder even than the pleas he'd made as an eight-year-old in that broken-down trailer.

'I love you. I think I always have.'

She stilled, the pants of her breathing punctuating the silence. The sunlight glowed on the red-gold curls of her hair. But then the quick burst of euphoria that he'd finally had the guts to tell her what he should have told her a decade ago died.

'I don't believe you,' she murmured. She looked wary and confused. But not happy. 'If you had ever loved me,' she said, her voice fragile but firm, 'you would be able to trust me. And you never have.'

He felt a tiny sliver of hope enter his chest, and he who had never been an optimist, nor a romantic, never been one to explain or justify or even to address his feelings knew he had one slim chance. And no matter what happened he wasn't going to blow it.

'I do trust you. I just didn't know it.'

'Don't talk in riddles. You didn't trust me over the miscarriage—you thought I'd had an abortion. And you didn't trust me not to get pregnant again. For God's sake, you even searched my toiletries.'

'I know. But that was down to me and stuff that happened long before I met you. I can see that now.'

'*What* stuff that happened?'

Oh, hell.

He might have guessed Xanthe wouldn't take his word for it.

He stood back, not sure he could explain himself with any clarity but knowing he would have to if they were going to stand any chance at all.

'You asked me once a very long time ago what happened to my mother.'

'You said she died when you were a child—like mine.'

He shook his head. How many other lies had he told to protect himself?

'She didn't die. She left.'

'What? When?'

Xanthe stared blankly at Dane as he ducked his head and braced his hands against the desk. She felt exhausted, hollowed out, her heart already broken into a thousand tiny fragments. He'd said he loved her. But how could she believe him?

'When I was a kid.' He sighed, the deep breath making his chest expand. 'Eight or maybe nine.'

'I don't understand what that has to do with us.'

He raked his fingers over his hair, finally meeting her eyes. The torment in them shocked her into silence.

'I didn't either. I thought I'd gotten over it. I missed her so much, and then I got angry with her. But most of all I convinced myself I'd forgotten her.'

'But you hadn't?'

He nodded, glanced out of the window.

Part of her didn't expect him to explain. Part of her wasn't even sure she wanted him to. But she felt the tiny fragments of her heart gather together as his Adam's apple bobbed and he began to talk.

'He hit her, too, when he was wasted. I remember she used to get me to hide. One night I hid for what felt like hours. I could hear him shouting, her crying. The sound of...'

He swallowed again, and she could see the trauma cross his face. A trauma he'd never let her see until now.

'She was pregnant. He slapped her a couple of times and went out again. To get drunker, I guess. When I came out she was packing her stuff. Her lip was bleeding. I was terrified. I begged her to take me with her. She said she couldn't, that she had to protect the baby. That I was big enough now to look out for myself until she could come back for me.'

His knuckles turned white where he held the edge of the desk.

'But she never did come back for me.'

Was this why he had always found it so hard to trust her? To trust anyone? Because the one person who should have stayed with him, who had promised to protect him, had abandoned him?

'Dane, I'm so sorry.'

Xanthe felt her heart break all over again for that boy who had been forced to grow up far too fast. But as much as she wanted to comfort him, to help him, she knew she couldn't go back and make things better now.

'Don't be sorry. It was a long time ago. And in some ways it made me stronger. Once I'd survived that, I knew I could survive anything.'

'I understand now why it was so hard for you to ever show weakness.'

And she *did* understand. He'd had to survive for so long and from such a young age with no one. His self-sufficiency was the only thing that had saved him. Why would he ever want to give that up?

'But I can't be with someone who doesn't need me the way I need them. It was like that with my dad. And it was the same way with us. I waited too long to call him that day because I didn't want to betray you.'

Her voice caught in her throat, but she pushed the words out. She had to stand up for herself. For who she had become. She couldn't be that naive, impressionable girl again. Not for anyone.

'I love you, Dane. I probably always will. You excite me and challenge me and make me feel more alive than I've ever felt with any other person. But I can't be with you, make a life with you, if we can't be equal. And we never will be if you always have to hold a part of yourself back.'

But as she opened her mouth to tell him to leave he took her wrists, first one, then the other, and drew her against him. He touched his forehead to hers, his lips close to hers, his voice barely a whisper. Tension vibrated through his body as he spoke.

'Please give me another chance. I loved that girl because

she was sweet and sexy and funny, but also so fragile. I thought I could protect her the way I could never protect my mom. And I love knowing that some of that cute, bright, clever kid is still there.'

He pressed his hand to her cheek, cradled her face, and the tenderness in his eyes pushed another tear over her lid.

'But don't you see, Dane? I can't be that girl any more. You walked all over me and I let you.'

He wiped the lone tear away with his thumb. 'Shh, let me finish, Red.'

The lopsided smile and the old nickname touched that tender place in her heart that still ached for him and always would.

'What I was going to say was, as much as I loved that girl, I love the woman she's become so much more.'

She pulled back, scared to let herself sink into him again. 'Don't say that if it isn't true.'

'You think I told you about my mom to make you feel sorry for me?'

She shook her head, because she knew he would never do that—he had far too much bullheaded pride. 'No, of course not. But…'

He touched his thumb to her lips. 'I told you because I want you to know why it's taken me so damn long to figure out the obvious. The truth is I was scared witless, Red. Of needing you too much. The way I'd once needed her. But do you know what was the first thing I felt when you walked into my office and told me we were still married?'

'Horror?'

He laughed, but there wasn't much humour in it. 'Yeah, maybe a little bit. But what I felt the most…' His lips tipped up in a wary smile. 'Was longing.'

'That was just the sex talking.'

His hands sank down to her neck. 'Yeah, I wanted to believe that. We both did. But we both know that's a crock.'

She ducked her head, but he lifted her chin.

'I love that you're your own woman now. That you're still tender and sweet and sexy, but also tough and smart enough to stand up to me, to never let me get away with anything. We're likely to drive each other nuts some of the time. I'm not always going to be able to come clean about stuff. Because I'm a guy, and that's the way I work. But I don't want to sign those papers. I want to give our marriage another chance. A *real* chance this time.'

'But I live in London and you live in New York. And we—'

'Can work anything out if we set our minds to it,' he finished for her. 'If we're willing to try.'

It was a huge ask with a simple answer. Because she'd never stopped loving him either.

'Except... I can't have children naturally. But I want very much to be a mother.'

'Then we'll check out our options. There's IVF, adoption—tons of stuff we can look at.'

'You'd be willing to do all that for me?' His instant commitment stunned her a little.

'Not just for you—for me, too. I want to see you be a mother. I always did. I was just too dumb to say so because I was terrified I wouldn't make the grade as a father.'

She sent him a watery smile, stupidly happy with this new evidence of exactly how equal they were. While she'd been busy nursing her own foolish insecurities she'd managed to miss completely the fact that he had some spectacularly stupid ones, too.

'Hmm, about that...maybe we should look at the evidence?' she teased.

'Do we have to?' he replied, looking adorably uncomfortable.

'Well, you're certainly bossy enough to make a good

father.' Her smile spread when he winced. 'And protective enough, and tough enough, and playful enough, too.'

She pressed herself against him, reached up to circle her arms round his neck, tug the hair at his nape until his mouth bent to hers.

'I guess we'll just have to work on the rest.'

'Is that a yes?' He grinned, because he had to be able to see the answer shining in her eyes through her tears. Her happy—no, her *ecstatic* tears. 'You're willing to give this another go?'

'I am if you are.'

His arms banded round her back to lift her off the floor. 'Does that mean we get to have lots of make-up sex?' he asked.

His hot gaze was setting off all the usual fires, but this time they were so much more intense. Because this time she knew they would never need to be doused.

'We're in my office, in the middle of the day. That would be really inappropriate.'

His grin became more than a little wicked as he boosted her into his arms. 'Screw *appropriate*.'

EPILOGUE

'YOU GRAB THAT ONE... I've got this one.'

Xanthe laughed, scooping up her three-year-old son, Lucas, before he could head for the pool while she watched her husband dive after their one-year-old daughter who, typically, had crawled off in the opposite direction.

Rosie wiggled and chortled as her favourite person in all the world hefted her under his arm like a sack of potatoes—very precious potatoes—into the beach house that stood on a ridge overlooking the ocean.

After facing their third round of IVF, almost two years ago now, she and Dane had embarked on the slow, arduous route to adoption. The discovery a few months later that Xanthe was pregnant, in the same week they'd been given the news that they'd been matched with a little boy in desperate need of a new home, had been like having all their Christmases come at once, while being totally terrifying at the same time.

They would be new parents with *two* children. But could they give Lucas the attention he needed after a tough start in life while also handling a newborn?

Xanthe could still remember the long discussions they'd had late into the night about what to do. But once they'd met Lucas the decision had been taken out of their hands. Because they'd both fallen in love with the impish little boy instantly. As quickly as they'd later fallen in love with his sister, on the day she was born.

'Mommy, I want to do more swimming,' Lucas demanded.

'It's dinnertime, honey,' Xanthe soothed as her son squirmed. 'No more swimming today.'

'Yes, Mommy—*yes*, more swimming!' he cried out, his compact body full of enough energy to power a jumping bean convention—which was usually a sign he was about to hit the wall, hard.

'Hey, I'll trade you.' Pressing a kiss to Rosie's nose, Dane passed her to Xanthe. 'You give the diaper diva her supper and I'll take the toddler terminator for his bath.'

Dane nimbly hoisted their son above his head.

'Come on, Buster, let's go mess up the bathroom.'

'Daddy, can we race the boats?'

'You bet. But this time I get to win.'

'No, Daddy, I *always* win.'

Lucas chuckled—the deep belly chuckle that Xanthe adored—as Dane bounced him on his hip up the stairs of the palatial holiday home they'd bought in the Vineyard, and were considering turning into their permanent base.

Dane had already moved his design team to Cape Cod, and was thinking of relocating the marketing and sponsorship team from the New York office, too. His business was so successful now that clients were prepared to come to him.

Xanthe allowed her gaze to drift down Dane's naked back, where the old scars were barely visible thanks to his summer tan, until it snagged on the bunch and flex of his buttocks beneath the damp broad shorts as he mounted the stairs with their son. The inevitable tug of love and longing settled low in her abdomen as her men disappeared from view.

Extracurricular activities would have to wait until their children were safely tucked up in bed.

Rosie yawned, nestling her head against Xanthe's shoulder, and sucked her thumb, her big blue eyes blinking owlishly. She cupped her daughter's cheek. The flushed baby-soft skin smelled of sun cream and salt and that delicious baby scent that never failed to make Xanthe's heart expand.

'Okay, Miss Diaper Diva, let's see if we can get some food into you before you fall asleep.'

After a day on the beach, trying to keep up with her daddy and her big brother while they built a sand yacht, her daughter had already hit that wall.

Ella, their housekeeper, arrived from the kitchen, as the aroma of the chicken pot pie she'd prepared for the children's evening meal made Xanthe's stomach growl.

'Would you like me to feed her while you take a shower?'

'No, we're good.' Xanthe smiled.

In their late fifties, and with their own children now grown, Ella and her husband John had been an absolute godsend when she'd gone back to work—taking care of all the household chores and doing occasional childcare duties while she and Dane concentrated on bringing up two boisterous children and running two multinational companies with commitments in most corners of the globe.

'Why don't you take the rest of the evening off? I've got it from here,' Xanthe added. 'That pie smells delicious, by the way.'

'Then I'll get going—if you're sure?' Ella beamed as Xanthe nodded. 'I made a spare pie for you and Dane, if you want it tonight. If not just shove it in the freezer.'

'Wonderful, Ella. And thanks again,' she said.

The housekeeper gave Rosie a quick cuddle and then bade them both goodbye before heading to the house she and her husband shared in the grounds.

As Xanthe settled her daughter in the highchair she watched the July sunlight glitter off the infinity pool and heard wild whooping from upstairs. Apparently Dane and their son were flooding the children's bathroom again during their boat race.

The sunlight beamed through the house's floor-to-ceiling windows, making Rosie's blonde hair into a halo around her head. Xanthe's heart expanded a little more as she fed her daughter. To think she'd once believed that her life was just the way she wanted it to be. She'd had her work, her company, and she'd persuaded herself that love didn't matter. That it was too dangerous to risk her heart a second time.

Her life was a lot more chaotic now, and not nearly as settled thanks to her many and varied commitments. They had a house on the river in London, and Dane's penthouse in New York, as well as this estate in the Vineyard, but as both she and Dane had demanding jobs and enjoyed travel they rarely spent more than six months a year in any of them.

As a result, their children had already climbed the Sugarloaf Mountain, been on a yacht trip to the Seychelles and slept through the New Year's Eve fireworks over Sydney Harbour Bridge. Eventually she and Dane would have to pick one base and stick to it, which was exactly why Dane was restructuring his business and why she'd appointed an acting CEO at Carmichael's in London, giving herself more flexibility while overseeing the business as a whole.

But with Dane's nomadic spirit, her own wanderlust, and their children still young enough to thrive on the adventure, they'd found a way to make their jet-set lifestyle work for now.

By risking her heart a second time she had created a home and a family and a life she adored, and discovered in the process that love was the *only* thing that really mattered.

Rosie spat out a mouthful of food, looking mutinous as she stuffed her thumb into her mouth.

Xanthe grinned. 'Right, madam, time to hand you over to your daddy.' She hauled her daughter out of the high-chair and perched her on her hip. 'He can read you a bedtime story while I feed your brother, and then rescue the bathroom.'

And once all that was done, when both her babies were in bed, she had *other* plans for her husband for later in the evening.

She smiled. Love mattered, and family mattered, but sometimes lust was pretty important, too.

'How do you feel about taking the munchkins to Montserrat next month?'

'Hmm...?' Xanthe eased back against her husband's chest as his words whispered into her hair and his hands settled on her belly.

The sun had started to drift towards the horizon, sending shards of light shimmering across the ocean and giving the surface of the pool a ruddy glow. She felt gloriously languid, standing on the deck. The children were finally out for the count, and Ella's second chicken pot pie had been devoured and savoured over a quiet glass of chardonnay.

The adult promise of the evening beckoned as warm calloused fingertips edged beneath the waistband of her shorts.

'Montserrat? Next month?' he murmured, nipping at her earlobe. 'I've got to test a new design. Figured we could rent a house...bring Ella and John along to help out with the kids while we're working. We might even get some solo sailing time.'

She shifted and turned in his arms, until her hands were resting on his shoulders and she could see the dusk reflected in his crystal blue eyes.

'Sounds good to me,' she said. 'As long as we have a

decent internet connection I can handle what I need to on the Shanghai development.'

She pressed her palms to the rough stubble on his cheeks and sent him a sultry grin which made his expression darken with hunger.

'But right now all I want to handle is *you*.'

His lips quirked, his challenging smile both promise and provocation. 'You think you can *handle* me, huh?'

Large hands sank beneath her shorts to cup her bare bottom and drag her against the solid ridge forming in his chinos.

Arousal shot to her core, staggering and instantaneous. 'Absolutely,' she dared.

'We'll just see about that,' he dared back, as he boosted her into his arms.

She laughed as he carried her into the house, then took the steps two at a time to get to their bedroom suite. But after he'd laid her on the bed, stripped off her clothes and his, his gaze locked on hers and her heart jolted—she could see all the love she felt for him reflected in his eyes.

'You're a witch.' He trailed his thumb down her sternum to circle one pouting nipple. 'A sea witch.'

She groaned as he cupped her naked breasts.

'But you're *my* damn sea witch.'

She bucked off the bed as he teased the tender peak with his teeth.

'Perhaps you should use your superpower to make sure I never forget it,' she said breathlessly.

'Damn straight,' he growled, before demonstrating to her, in no uncertain terms, just how thoroughly she belonged to him, while she gave herself up to the passionate onslaught and handled everything he had to offer just fine.

* * * * *

MILLS & BOON®

MODERN™

POWER, PASSION AND IRRESISTIBLE TEMPTATION

A sneak peek at next month's titles…

In stores from 9th February 2017:

- **Secrets of a Billionaire's Mistress** – Sharon Kendrick *and* **The Sicilian's Defiant Virgin** – Susan Stephens
- **Claimed for the De Carrillo Twins** – Abby Green *and* **The Temporary Mrs Marchetti** – Melanie Milburne
- **The Innocent's Secret Baby** – Carol Marinelli *and* **Pursued by the Desert Prince** – Dani Collins
- **A Debt Paid in the Marriage Bed** – Jennifer Hayward *and* **The Forgotten Gallo Bride** – Natalie Anderson

MILLS & BOON®

EXCLUSIVE EXTRACT

Raul Di Savo desires more than Lydia Hayward's
body—his seduction will stop his rival buying her!
Raul's expert touch awakens Lydia to irresistible
pleasure, but his game of revenge forces
Lydia to leave… until an unexpected
consequence binds them forever!

Read on for a sneak preview of
THE INNOCENT'S SECRET BABY

Somehow Lydia was back against the wall with Raul's
hands either side of her head.

She put her hands up to his chest and felt him solid
beneath her palms and she just felt him there a moment
and then looked up to his eyes.

His mouth moved in close and as it did she stared
right into his eyes.

She could feel heat hover between their mouths in a
slow tease before they first met.

Then they met.

And all that had been missing was suddenly there.

Yet, the gentle pressure his mouth exerted, though
blissful, caused a mire of sensations until the gentleness
of his kiss was no longer enough.

A slight inhale, a hitch in her breath and her lips
parted, just a little, and he slipped his tongue in.

The moan she made went straight to his groin.

At first taste she was his and he knew it for her hands

moved to the back of his head and he kissed her as hard back as her fingers demanded.

More so even.

His tongue was wicked and her fingers tightened in his thick hair and she could feel the wall cold and hard against her shoulders.

It was the middle of Rome just after six and even down a side street there was no real hiding from the crowds.

Lydia didn't care.

He slid one arm around her waist to move her body away from the wall and closer into his, so that her head could fall backwards.

If there was a bed, she would be on it.

If there was a room they would close the door.

Yet there wasn't and so he halted them, but only their lips.

Their bodies were heated and close and he looked her right in the eye. His mouth was wet from hers and his hair a little messed from her fingers.

Don't miss
THE INNOCENT'S SECRET BABY,
By Carol Marinelli

Available March 2017
www.millsandboon.co.uk

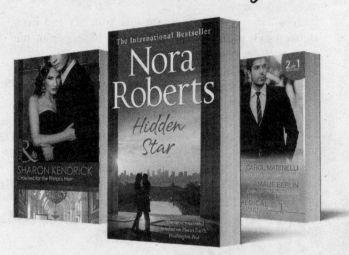